KU-997-243

REFERENCE ROOM
LOCATION

Biography

AUTHOR

DICTIONARY
OF BUSINESS
BIOGRAPHY

HOUSE OF COMMONS LIBRARY

TO BE
DISPOSED
BY
AUTHORITY

Dictionary of Business Biography

Editorial Advisory Board

Professor Leslie Hannah (chairman) (London School of Economics)
Professor T C Barker (London School of Economics)
Professor S G Checkland (Glasgow)
Professor D C Coleman (Cambridge)
Professor H C Edey (London School of Economics)
Professor Sir Douglas Hague (Oxford)
Professor A R Hall (Imperial College)
Professor D G MacRae (London School of Economics)
Professor P Mathias (Oxford)
Professor L S Pressnell (Kent)
Dr W J Reader (London School of Economics)
Professor B C Roberts (London School of Economics)
Professor Z A Silberston (Imperial College)
Professor C Wilson (Cambridge)
Professor B S Yamey (London School of Economics)

Editorial Staff

Dr David J Jeremy (editor)
Dr Christine Shaw (deputy editor)
Dr Geoffrey Tweedale (researcher)
Margaret Kiely (researcher)
Helena Peake (secretary)

Dictionary of Business Biography

A Biographical Dictionary of Business Leaders
Active in Britain in the Period 1860–1980

edited by

David J Jeremy

Research Fellow, Business History Unit
London School of Economics and Political Science

deputy editor

Christine Shaw

Research Officer, Business History Unit
London School of Economics and Political Science

Volume 3
H-L

London
Butterworths
1985

England	Butterworth & Co (Publishers) Ltd, 88 Kingsway, LONDON WC2B 6AB
Australia	Butterworth Pty Ltd, SYDNEY, MELBOURNE, BRISBANE, ADELAIDE, and PERTH
Canada	Butterworth & Co (Canada) Ltd, TORONTO
	Butterworth & Co (Western Canada) Ltd, VANCOUVER
New Zealand	Butterworths of New Zealand Ltd, WELLINGTON
Singapore	Butterworth & Co (Asia) Pte Ltd, SINGAPORE
South Africa	Butterworth Publishers (Pty) Ltd, DURBAN
USA	Mason Publishing Co, ST PAUL, Minnesota
	Butterworth Legal Publishers, SEATTLE, Washington; BOSTON, Massachusetts; and AUSTIN, Texas
	D & S Publishers, CLEARWATER, Florida

© London School of Economics and Political Science 1985

All rights reserved. No part of this publication may be reproduced or transmitted in any form or by any means, including photocopying and recording, without the written permission of the copyright holder, application for which should be addressed to the publisher. Such written permission must also be obtained before any part of this publication is stored in a retrieval system of any nature.

This book is sold subject to the Standard Conditions of Sale of Net Books and may not be re-sold in the UK below the net price fixed by Butterworths for the book in our current catalogue.

ISBN *for the complete set of volumes:*   0 406 27340 5
      for this volume: 0 406 27343 X

HOUSE OF COMMONS
LIBRARY
CATALOGUED

Typeset by Whitefriars Composertype Ltd, Chichester
Printed by The Whitefriars Press Ltd, Tonbridge

Introduction and Acknowledgements

Volume III of the *Dictionary of Business Biography* adds 231 biographies of entrepreneurs active in Britain (excluding Scotland which is covered by a parallel project at the University of Glasgow) since 1860 to the 460 biographies in Volumes 1 and 2. The purpose of the *Dictionary* and the principles upon which individuals have been selected have been indicated in Volume 1. Suffice it to say here that our aim is to cover the whole gamut of business from mining and manufacturing to public utilities, construction, distribution and financial and miscellaneous services. Academics, civil servants, trade unionists and agriculturalists have been excluded where their involvement in the business world was incidental to their central career. Those still active in business have also been excluded.

The acknowledgements in Volume 2 cover succeeding volumes but inevitably the preparation of additional volumes produces further obligations. The whole project, as was stated in Volume 1, owes its existence to the support of the Economic and Social Research Council; we are pleased to acknowledge its continued support until the completion of the *DBB*, with the despatch of the text of Volume 5 (S–Z) to the publishers, in July 1985. The editor is likewise most grateful to the contributors who have so willingly supported the project. Their names and affiliations are given below. Indispensable for the editor's work of assessing entries covering such a wide range of business activity has been the generous co-operation of referees, mostly economic historians in academic departments.

Of the learned institutions which have provided support to the *DBB*'s editorial functions, special mention must be made of the British Library of Political and Economic Science at the LSE, situated conveniently, it so happens, in the same buildings as the *DBB*'s offices. Without its unparalleled collection of works on the social sciences (its set of *Parliamentary Papers*, its trade journals, its sets of the *Times*, the *Economist* and other financial periodicals, its academic monographs, its basic reference works and its inter-library loan service) the editorial function of strengthening and checking *DBB* entries would have been scarcely possible. Needless to say, we are greatly indebted to the Librarian, Mr D A Clarke, and his staff, especially all those on the loan counter. In the same breath we must also record our gratitude to Dr Angela Raspin, in charge of Manuscripts and Rare Books within the BLPES, whose custody includes the Edwards Seminar papers and the Tariff Commission papers. Where the BLPES has, on rare occasions, been lacking, we have of course gone to the British Library, whose resources have also commanded our admiration and gratitude. The BL's incomparable Newspaper Library at Colindale has been an important asset to the *DBB* project.

Within the editorial team high levels of commitment and co-operation on everyone's part have allowed us to meet the tight deadlines and budgets faced by the *DBB* project. The enormous burden of word processing has been borne by Miss Kiely and Mrs Peake. Their stamina and good humour have been essential. Mrs Peake has maintained the *DBB* office's secretarial functions and Miss Kiely has taken over the work of collecting birth and marriage certificates. The editors and Dr Tweedale have also re-written sections of some entries to bring factual information in line with that provided by the generality of biographies. Francis Goodall, who is contributing voluntary work to the *DBB*, has done most of the bibliographic research for this volume; we are particularly grateful to him for this assistance.

The editor has read and commented on every entry, normally imposing the usual *DBB* format; Dr Shaw has been responsible for the final editing of many of the H and L entries. Proofing has been shared between the editor, deputy editor and Dr Tweedale but we are very grateful to Mr Michael Robbins for also reading the I–L galleys — he has spared us a number of errors.

The illustrations, assembled by Miss Kiely, are designed to act as 'triggers' to the imagination, showing portraits of some of the entrepreneurs and a selection of their workplaces, products and the like. We are grateful to all those who have helped by providing illustrations and again, for any unwitting invasions of copyright (which we have tried to avoid or rectify), we apologise.

Once more I would like to underscore my gratitude to everyone who has supported the *DBB* project in any way, emphasising that none, besides the editors, is responsible for the editorial faults that remain.

David J Jeremy

Contents

List of Contributors to Volume 3

(affiliations at the time of writing)

H W Abbey	Assistant Managing Director, William Hill Organisation Ltd.
Margaret Ackrill	Visitor, Business History Unit, London School of Economics and Political Science.
Alison Adburgham	Wadebridge, Cornwall.
D G C Allan	Curator-Librarian, Royal Society of Arts, London.
Donald Anderson	Director, Quaker House Colliery Co Ltd, Ashton-in-Makerfield, Lancashire.
John Armstrong	Senior Lecturer, Department of Business and Management, Ealing College, London.
M M Armstrong	Sutton, Surrey.
T Atkins	Senior Information Officer, Information Department, Lloyds plc.
Colin Baber	Lecturer, Department of Economics, University College, Cardiff.
Philip S Bagwell	Professor Emeritus in History, the Polytechnic of Central London.
Geoffrey Battison	Consultant Editor, *Gas World*, Benn Gas Group.
G T Bloomfield	Professor and Chairman of the Department of Geography, University of Guelph, Ontario.
Michael Bonavia	formerly Academic Visitor, Economic History Department, London School of Economics and Political Science.
John Booker	Archivist, Lloyds Bank plc, London.
Jonathan S Boswell	Senior Lecturer, The City University Business School, London.
Brian Bowers	Deputy Keeper, Department of Electrical Engineering and Communications, Science Museum, London.
Gordon Boyce	formerly Research Student, London School of Economics and Political Science.
Emily Boyle	Lecturer, School of Marketing and Business Policy, Ulster Polytechnic.
Trevor Boyns	Lecturer, Department of Economics, University College, Cardiff.

Richard Brewer	Child Health Research Unit, University of Bristol.
Lord Briggs of Lewes	Provost, Worcester College, Oxford.
John H Y Briggs	Senior Lecturer, Department of History, University of Keele.
J P Bristow	Aldeburgh, Surrey.
David Brooke	Lecturer, Department of Humanities, University of Bath.
Helen Brooks	formerly Senior Woman Tutor, Garnett College, Roehampton Lane, London.
Peter W Brooks	Regional Executive, Aircraft Group, British Aerospace PLC.
David Burgess-Wise	Co-ordinator of Car Product Information, Public Affairs, Ford of Europe.
W A Campbell	Lecturer, Department of Inorganic Chemistry, University of Newcastle upon Tyne.
Youssef Cassis	Department of History, University of Geneva, Switzerland.
Philippe Chalmin	Maitre-Assistant, Chaire de Géographie Industrielle et Commerciale, Conservatoire National des Arts et Métiers, Paris, France.
Geoffrey Channon	Principal Lecturer, Department of Humanities, Bristol Polytechnic.
J F Clarke	Principal Lecturer, Department of Geography and Environmental Studies, Newcastle upon Tyne Polytechnic.
Helen Clay	formerly Research Student, Department of Economics, University of Salford.
Esmond J Cleary	Senior Lecturer, Department of Economics, University College of Swansea.
Hugh Cockerell	Visiting Professor in Business Studies, City University Business School.
D C Coleman	Emeritus Professor of Economic History, Pembroke College, Cambridge.
D A Collier	Course Tutor, Department of Economic History, Mid-Warwickshire College of Further Education.
E J Connell	Lecturer, Extra Mural Department, University of Leeds.
E W Cooney	Reader in Economic and Social History, Department of Economics, University of York.

T A B Corley	Senior Lecturer, Department of Economics, University of Reading.
Robin S Craig	Senior Lecturer in Economic History, Department of History, University College, London.
Jenny Davenport	Kensington, London.
R P T Davenport-Hines	Research Officer, Business History Unit, London School of Economics and Political Science.
Rhys David	*Financial Times,* London.
Alun C Davies	Senior Lecturer, Department of Economic History, The Queen's University, Belfast.
P N Davies	Senior Lecturer and Head of the Department of Economic History, University of Liverpool.
Laurie Dennett	Company Archivist, Standard Telephones & Cables plc.
Stephanie Diaper	ESRC Research Fellow in Business History, School of Management, University of Bath.
C G Down	Lecturer, Department of Mineral Resources Engineering, Imperial College of Science and Technology.
J B F Earle	Kyle, Ross-shire.
John R Etor	Lecturer in Computing, College of Further Education, Plymouth.
David Fanning	Lecturer, Department of Business Administration and Accountancy, University of Wales Institute of Science and Technology.
R W Ferrier	Company Historian, BP, Britannic House, London.
S Martin Gaskell	Assistant Rector, Liverpool Polytechnic.
Frank Geary	Lecturer, Department of Economics, New University of Ulster.
Francis Goodall	Researcher, *Dictionary of Business Biography,* Business History Unit, London School of Economics and Political Science.
John Goodchild	Principal Local Studies Officer and Archivist, Wakefield M D Libraries.
Margaret Gowing	Professor, Department of Modern History, University of Oxford.
Edwin Green	Archivist, Midland Bank plc.
Robert Greenhill	Senior Lecturer, School of Business Studies, City of London Polytechnic.

James Greig	Professor Emeritus, King's College, University of London.
C P Griffin	Senior Lecturer, Department of History and Geography, Trent Polytechnic.
L F Haber	Reader, Department of Economics, University of Surrey.
A A Hall	NCB History Project.
Kerry Hamilton	Research Assistant, School of Economic and Social Studies, University of East Anglia.
Leslie Hannah	Professor of Business History and Director, Business History Unit, London School of Economics and Political Science.
Jerry Harris	formerly Archivist, Shaw Savill & Albion Co Ltd, London.
J R Harris	Professor, Department of Economic and Social History, University of Birmingham.
Ian Harrison	Wilmslow, Cheshire.
Charles E Harvey	Senior Lecturer, Department of Humanities, Bristol Polytechnic.
R J Hercock	formerly with Ilford Ltd.
John Hibbs	Director of Transport Studies, Department of Business and Management Studies, City of Birmingham Polytechnic.
Robin Higham	Professor, Department of History, Kansas State University.
Graeme M Holmes	Senior Lecturer, Department of Economics and Banking, University of Wales Institute of Science and Technology.
A C Howe	Lecturer, Department of International History, London School of Economics and Political Science.
Kenneth Hudson	Bath.
John A Iredale	Lecturer, Project Planning Centre for Developing Countries, University of Bradford.
A G Jamieson	Channel Isles Research Fellow, Department of History, University College, London.
D T Jenkins	Lecturer, Department of Economics and Related Studies, University of York.
David J Jeremy	Research Fellow, Business History Unit, London School of Economics.

Walford Johnson	Lecturer, Department of Economics, The New University of Ulster, Coleraine.
Edgar Jones	Group Historian, GKN plc.
Geoffrey Jones	Lecturer, Economic History Department, London School of Economics and Political Science.
Ralph Kaner	Director, Rowntree Mackintosh, York.
Shirley Keeble	formerly Research Student, Business History Unit, London School of Economics and Political Science.
*David Kenning	late Chairman and Managing Director, Kenning Motor Group Ltd, Chesterfield.
John King	London.
Joan Lane	Lecturer, Centre for the Study of Social History, University of Warwick.
Rachel Lawrence	Southwold, Suffolk.
Stephen Lawrence	Conference Officer, University College of Wales, Aberystwyth.
Anthony A Letts	Chairman, Charles Letts & Co Ltd, London.
Ian Lloyd MP	Economic Adviser, Kayzer Irvine Ltd, London.
Roger Lloyd-Jones	Senior Lecturer, Department of History, Sheffield City Polytechnic.
Bryan Little	Bristol.
Jonathan M Liebenau	Research Officer, Business History Unit, London School of Economics and Political Science.
Sheila Marriner	Reader, Department of Economic History, University of Liverpool.
Sir Peter Masefield	formerly Chairman of British European Airways and of the London Transport Executive.
John J Mason	Lecturer, Department of Economics and Economic History, Manchester Polytechnic.
Ranald C Michie	Lecturer, Department of Economic History, University of Durham.
A L Minkes	Emeritus Professor, University of Birmingham.
D E Moggridge	Professor, Department of Economics, University of Toronto, Canada.

Charles More	Senior Lecturer, Department of Humanities, College of St Paul and St Mary, Cheltenham.
J E Morpurgo	Professor Emeritus, University of Leeds.
George Muirhead	Postgraduate student, University of Newcastle upon Tyne.
Christopher Murphy	Bromley, Kent.
T R Nevett	Principal Lecturer, School of Business Policy and Marketing, Polytechnic of the South Bank, London.
*Harold Nockolds	late Deputy Chairman of IPC Transport Press.
Derek Oddy	Professor and Head of the Department of History, Faculty of Social Sciences and Business Studies, Polytechnic of Central London.
Richard Overy	Lecturer, Department of History, Kings College, London.
Henry Parris	Wokingham, Berkshire.
D C Phillips	Archivist, Institute of Agricultural History and Museum of English Rural Life, University of Reading.
J Gordon Read	Keeper of Archives, Merseyside County Museums, Liverpool.
W J Reader	Texaco Visiting Fellow, Business History Unit, London School of Economics and Political Science.
Hew Reid	Director of Studies, Department of Furniture Technology, Buckinghamshire College of Higher Education.
Jack Reynolds	Honorary Visiting Lecturer, Department of Social Sciences, University of Bradford.
D G Rhys	Senior Lecturer, Department of Economics, University College, Cardiff.
David J Richardson	Headmaster, Laxton School, Oundle.
*Kenneth Richardson	late of the Department of Politics and History, Coventry (Lanchester) Polytechnic.
Margaret Richardson	Chichester.
W G Rimmer	Professor and Head of the Department of Economic History, University of New South Wales, Australia.
David E Roberts	Senior Lecturer, Department of Economics and Public Administration, Trent Polytechnic.

Richard Roberts	Lecturer, Department of History, University of Sussex.
Mary B Rose	Lecturer, Department of Economics, University of Lancaster.
Catherine M Ross	Keeper, Clifton Park Museum, Rotherham MBC.
D J Rowe	Lecturer, Department of Economics, University of Newcastle upon Tyne.
Alan J Scarth	Assistant Keeper, Merseyside Maritime Museum.
Cecil Martin Sharp	Cheltenham, Gloucester.
Christine Shaw	Research Officer, Business History Unit, London School of Economics and Political Science.
Colin Simmons	Lecturer, Department of Economics, University of Salford.
Judy Slinn	London.
P Eynon Smart	formerly with The Institute of Bankers, London.
Julie G Stark	London.
Richard Storey	Archivist, Modern Records Centre, University of Warwick Library.
J O Stubbs	Associate Professor, Department of History, University of Waterloo, Ontario, Canada.
Jennifer Tann	Reader, Management Centre, University of Aston.
Carole Taylor	Research Student, Humanities Doctoral Programme, Syracuse University, USA.
Robert Thorne	Historian, Historic Buildings Division, Greater London Council.
Richard Trainor	Lecturer, Department of Economic History, University of Glasgow.
J Malcolm Trickett	Senior Lecturer in Yarn Manufacture, Department of Textiles, Bradford and Ilkley Community College.
D Gordon Tucker	Emeritus Professor, Department of Economic and Social History, University of Birmingham.
Geoffrey Tweedale	Researcher, Business History Unit, London School of Economics and Political Science.
Kathleen M Wain	London.
David H E Wainwright	Economic and Social Research Council, London.

Philip Wallis   formerly Director, Longmans, Green & Co.

David Welch   Senior Lecturer, Department of Social Science and Business Studies, Polytechnic of Central London.

Oliver M Westall   Lecturer, Department of Economics, University of Lancaster.

L J Williams   Senior Lecturer, Department of Economic and Social History and Sociology, University College of Wales, Aberystwyth.

Charles Wilson   Emeritus Professor of Modern History, Jesus College, Cambridge.

Hugh Woolhouse   Research Officer, Centre for Business Strategy, London Business School.

Maurice Zinkin   London.

*Now (January 1985) deceased.

Notes to Readers

1 Biographies are in the alphabetical sequence of subjects' family names. In the case of *hyphenated* surnames the first name in the compound family name determines the sequence.

2 In entry headings the title 'Lord' has been confined to barons, holders of the lowest degree in the British peerage; holders of degrees above baron have been given their exact peerage title, 'Viscount', 'Duke' etc. Peers are all listed in the alphabetical sequence of *family* names, not titles.

3 Place names are normally used according to the contemporary usage pertaining to the particular entry.

4 County boundaries are usually those prevailing before the reorganisation of local government in 1975.

5 For a note on British currency usage, see abbreviations (below), under £.

6 Foreign words have not been italicised.

7 The place of publication in bibliographical references is London, unless otherwise stated.

8 In the case of books running to several editions, bibliographical information is provided for the first or major edition.

9 Cross references to entries in the *Dictionary of National Biography, Who's Who of British Members of Parliament* and *Who Was Who* are regularly provided in the lists of sources but in many cases contributors have relied on ampler or more recently discovered sources.

10 On probate: the biography of any *DBB* subject dying in England or Wales includes the gross valuation of his/her estate where this has been recorded in the probate calendars at Somerset House, London, under a civil system commenced in January 1858. These figures should however be used with great caution, bearing in mind the following caveats:

(a) Before 1898 probate was required in respect of personalty only ie only 'moveables' like personal effects, stocks and shares and bank credits but also leaseholds.

(b) From 1898 onwards (following the Land Transfer Act of 1897) the probate valuation included realty, or immovable property like land and houses.

(c) Valuations of both personalty and realty always included unsettled property ie property in the absolute possession of the testator and not preserved in any way for future generations by some legal act of settlement.

(d) Settled land (ie that tied up by acts of settlement) was included in the probate calendar figures from 1 January 1926 under the Settled Land Act of 1925.

(e) Inter vivos gifts were not included in probate.

(f) Gross probate valuations of estates are those made before the deduction of funeral expenses and debts due on the estate.

(g) Prior to 1881 the value of an estate was given in round figures eg not exceeding £450,000 or £500,000 etc.

(h) The figures given in these entries are taken from the calendars at Somerset House and therefore miss any Scottish, Irish or foreign probates, unless these are specifically identified.

For further historical notes on this complex subject see Josiah Wedgwood, *The Economics of Inheritance* (Harmondsworth, Middlesex: Penguin Books Ltd, 1939 ed); Colin D Harbury and D M W N Hitchens, *Inheritance and Wealth Inequality in Britain* (George Allen & Unwin, 1979); William D Rubinstein, *Men of Property. The Very Wealthy in Britain Since the Industrial Revolution* (Croom Helm, 1981).

11 Subjects' writings. These do not include unpublished works. Where these are known they are cited as an unpublished source. Subjects' writings have been checked against holdings recorded in the British Library and National Union catalogues as well as those of the BLPES.

12 Company reports have been regarded as an unpublished source.

13 Patents have been classed as writings.

Abbreviations

AA	Automobile Association *or* anti-aircraft
AC	Alternating current
& Co	and Company
ADC	aide-de-camp
AEG	Allgemeine Elektrizitäts Gesellschaft
AEI	Associated Electrical Industries
AFC	Air Force Cross
AG	Aktiengesellschaft (joint-stock company)
AGM	Annual General Meeting
AIOC	Anglo-Iranian Oil Co
am	ante meridiem (before noon)
APCM	Associated Portland Cement Manufacturers
APOC	Anglo Persian Oil Co
ARP	air-raid precautions
ASE	Amalgamated Society of Engineers
Aslef	Associated Society of Locomotive Engineers and Firemen
ATA	Air Transport Auxiliary
ATV	Associated Television
b	born
BA	Bachelor of Arts *or* British Airways
BASF	Badische Anilin-und-Soda Fabrik
BAT	British American Tobacco Co *or* British Automobile Traction Co Ltd
Bateman	John Bateman, *Great Landowners of Great Britain* (Harrison, 1879).
BBC	British Broadcasting Association

BBFT	British Bank for Foreign Trade
BC & CC	British Cocoa & Chocolate Co
BCe	Birth certificate from General Register Office, St Catherines House, London WC1B 6JP
BCe (Scots)	Scottish birth certificate from The Registrar General, New Register House, Edinburgh EH1 3YT
BDA	Bradford Dyers' Association
BDC	British Dyestuffs Corporation
BEA	British European Airways *or* British Electricity Authority
BEF	British Expeditionary Force
BET	British Electric Traction Co
bhp	brake horsepower
BICC	British Insulated Callender's Cables
BIDC	Bankers' Industrial Development Corporation
BISF	British Iron and Steel Federation
BL	British Library, Great Russell Street, London WC1B 3DG
BLPES	British Library of Political and Economic Science, London School of Economics, Portugal Street, London WC2A 2HD
BMC	British Motor Corporation *or* British Metal Corporation
BMH	British Motor Holdings
BMMO	Birmingham & Midland Motor Omnibus Co Ltd
BMPM	Bowater's Mersey Paper Mills Ltd
BOAC	British Overseas Airways Corporation
Boase	Frederic Boase, *Modern English Biography, Containing Memoirs of Persons Who Have Died since 1850* (6 vols, Truro: Netherton & Worth, 1892-1921).
BP	British Petroleum
BPC	British Printing Corporation

BPCM	British Portland Cement Manufacturers
Bros	Brothers (used in company titles)
BS	Bachelor of Surgery (Britain) *or* Bachelor of Science (USA) *or* Bristol-Siddeley
BSA	Birmingham Small Arms
BSc	Bachelor of Science (Britain)
BSC	British Steel Corporation
BST	British Stockbrokers' Trust Ltd
Bt	Baronet
BT	Board of Trade
BTC	British Transport Commission *or* British Trade Corporation
Burke's Landed Gentry	(Burke's Peerage Ltd. Various editions since 1836; edition identified by date).
Burke's Peerage and Baronetage	(Burke's Peerage [Genealogical Books] Ltd. Various editions since 1826; edition identified by date).
BVC	British Vacuum Cleaner
ca	circa
CB	Companion of the Bath
CBE	Commander of the Order of the British Empire
CBI	Confederation of British Industry
CEGB	Central Electricity Generating Board
ch	chapter
CIE	Companion of the Order of the Indian Empire
Cif	cost, insurance, freight
C-in-C	Commander-in-Chief
CIWL	Compagnie Internationale des Wagons-Lits
CME	Chief Mechanical Engineer

CMG	Companion of the Order of St Michael and St George
CND	Campaign for Nuclear Disarmament
Co	Company
Col	Colonel
comp	compiled, compiler
Complete Peerage	George Edward Cokayne, *The Complete Peerage of England, Scotland, Ireland, Great Britain and the United Kingdom, Extant Extinct or Dormant* (13 vols, St Catherine Press, 1910-59).
CPA	Calico Printers' Association
C Reg	Companies Registration Office file(s); microfiche versions of the files have been obtained from Companies Registration Office, 55 City Road, London EC1Y 1BB.
C Reg(w)	Notes made from company files subsequently despatched to the PRO and there subjected to a random destruction rate of 80–90 per cent.
CRO	County Record Office
Crockfords	*Crockfords Clerical Directory* (various editions, 1858 to present).
cwt	hundredweight (112 pounds, avoirdupois)
d	died
d (following a monetary figure)	pence [See note under £ at the end of this list]
DAB	*Dictionary of American Biography* edited by Allen Johnson and Dumas Malone (22 vols, New York: Charles Scribner's Sons, 1928-1944). The abbreviation also covers supplements to the *DAB*.
DBB	*Dictionary of Business Biography*
DCe	Death certificate from General Register Office, St Catherines House, London WC2B 6JP
DCL	Doctor of Civil Law *or* Distillers Co Ltd
DCM	Distinguished Conduct Medal
DCO	Dominion, Colonial and Overseas (Barclays Bank DCO)
DD	*Directory of Directors* (annual, East Grinstead: Thomas Skinner Directories, 1880-1983).

Debrett	*Debrett's Peerage, Baronetage, Knightage and Companionage with Her Majesty's Royal Warrant Holders* (Kingston upon Thames, Kelly's Directories. Numerous editions since 1803).
DH	de Havilland
DL	Deputy-Lieutenant
DLB	*Dictionary of Labour Biography* edited by Joyce M Bellamy and John Saville (6 vols, Macmillan, 1972-82, in progress).
DLitt	Doctor of Letters
DNB	*Dictionary of National Biography* edited by Leslie Stephen and Sidney Lee (63 vols, Oxford University Press, 1885-1933). The abbreviation also covers supplements to the *DNB*.
DOT	Department of Overseas Trade
DoT	Department of Trade
DSc	Doctor of Science
DSC	Distinguished Service Cross
DSIR	Department of Scientific and Industrial Research
DWB	*Dictionary of Welsh Biography down to 1940* edited by Sir John Edward Lloyd and R T Jenkins (London: The Honourable Society of Cymmrodorion, 1959).
EAC	Employers' Advisory Council
ECC	English China Clays
ECSC	European Coal and Steel Community
Edwards seminar paper.	Almost 450 papers, chiefly by businessmen and women presented in Professor Ronald S Edwards' Seminar at the LSE, 1946-1973, on 'Problems in Industrial Administration' (in BLPES Manuscripts). A number of these papers were published in *Business Enterprise* (Macmillan, 1959), *Studies in Business Organisation* (Macmillan, 1961) and *Business Growth* (Macmillan, 1966) edited by R S Edwards and H Townsend.
EE	English Electric
EEC	European Economic Community
EEF	Engineering Employers' Federation

EFTA	European Free Trade Association
Elliott research notes.	The biographical research notes on British MPs (mostly of the twentieth century) compiled by the late Anthony Elliott and kindly loaned to the *DBB* project by his widow Mrs Thea Elliott.
EMGAS	East Midlands Gas Board
EMI	Electric & Musical Industries
Erickson workcards.	Biographical workcards prepared by Professor Charlotte Erickson on steel and hosiery leaders, for her book *British Industrialists. Steel and Hosiery, 1850-1950* (Cambridge: Cambridge University Press for the National Institute of Economic and Social Research, 1959) and kindly loaned by her to the *DBB* project.
ESC	English Steel Corporation
ETU	Electrical Trades Union
F	Fahrenheit (temperature)
FBI	Federation of British Industries
FCS	Fellow of the Chemical Society (now FRCS)
FCSDA	Fine Cotton Spinners' & Doublers' Association
fl	floreat (flourished)
FO	Foreign Office
fob	free on board
Foster, *Alumni Oxonienses.*	Joseph Foster, *Alumni Oxonienses, The Members of the University of Oxford 1715-1886* (4 vols, Oxford: James Parker & Co, 1891).
FRS	Fellow of the Royal Society
GB	Great Britain (England, Wales and Scotland)
GBE	Knight *or* Dame Grand Cross of the Order of the British Empire
GCVO	Knight *or* Dame Grand Cross of the Royal Victorian Order
GDP	Gross Domestic Product
GEC	General Electric Co
GER	Great Eastern Railway

GHQ	General Headquarters
GKN	Guest, Keen & Nettlefolds
GL	Glaxo Laboratories
GLC	Greater London Council
GmbH	Gesellschaft mit beschränkter Haftung (private limited liability company)
GNP	Gross National Product
GRA	Greyhound Racing Association Ltd
GWR	Great Western Railway
HC	House of Commons
HLRO	House of Lords Record Office
HM	His/Her Majesty/Majesty's
HMS	His/Her Majesty's Ship
HMV	His Master's Voice
Hon	Honourable
HP	Handley Page
hp	horsepower
HT	High Tension
HTS	Hilton Transport Services
IAL	Imperial Airways Ltd
IBA	Independent Broadcasting Authority
ibid	ibidem (the same source as the one previously quoted)
ICAEW	Institute of Chartered Accountants in England and Wales
ICE	Institution of Civil Engineers
ICI	Imperial Chemical Industries
IEE	Institution of Electrical Engineers

IG	Interessengemeinschaft (combine)
IME	Institution of Mechanical Engineers
Inc	Incorporated
JISI	*Journal of the Iron and Steel Institute*
JP	Justice of the Peace
Jr	Junior
KBE	Knight Commander of the Order of the British Empire
KCB	Knight Commander of the Order of the Bath
KCIE	Knight Commander of the Order of the Indian Empire
KCMG	Knight Commander of the Order of St Michael and St George
KCVO	Knight Commander of the Royal Victorian Order
KG	Knight of the Order of the Garter
KLM	Koninklijke Luchtvaart Maatschappij NV (Royal Dutch Air Lines)
KT	Knight of the Order of the Thistle
kV	kilovolt
kW	kilowatt
£	£: see end of list
lb	pound(s), weight
LBC	Left Book Club *or* London Bicycle Co
LCC	London County Council
LCD	London, Chatham & Dover Railway
Lieut Col	Lieutenant Colonel
LLB	Bachelor of Laws
LLD	Doctor of Laws
LMS	London, Midland & Scottish Railway *or* London Missionary Society
LNER	London & North Eastern Railway

LNWR	London & North Western Railway
LSE	London School of Economics and Political Science
Ltd	Limited
MA	Master of Arts
MAP	Ministry of Aircraft Production
MBE	Member of the Order of the British Empire
MC	Military Cross
MCe	Marriage certificate from General Register Office, St Catherine's House, London WC2B 6JP
MCe (Scots)	Scottish marriage certificate from The Registrar General, New Register House, Edinburgh EH1 3YT
MCe (Irish)	Irish marriage certificate from The Registrar General, Oxford House, 49/55 Chichester Street, Belfast BT1 4HL (Northern Ireland), or The Registrar General, Custom House, Dublin 1 (Southern Ireland)
MCWF Co	Metropolitan Carriage, Wagon & Finance Co
MD	Doctor of Medicine
mk or MK	Mark
MM	Military Medal
MMS	Methodist Missionary Society
MP	Member of Parliament
MSc	Master of Science
MSS	Manuscripts
MVO	Member of the Royal Victorian Order
MW	megawatt(s)
NAAFI	Navy, Army, and Air Force Institutes
NATO	North Atlantic Treaty Organisation
NCB	National Coal Board
NCO	non-commissioned officer

nd	no date
NEDC	National Economic Development Council
NER	North-Eastern Railway
NHS	National Health Service
NLR	North London Railway
np	no place
NPA	Newspaper Proprietors' Association
NRA	National Register of Archives, Quality House, Quality Court, London WC2A 1HP
NSPCC	National Society for the Prevention of Cruelty to Children
NV	naamloze vennootschap (limited company)
OBE	Officer of the Order of the British Empire
OB St John	British Order of the Hospital of St John of Jerusalem
ODI	Overseas Development Institute
OPEC	Organisation of Petroleum Exporting Countries
OTC	Officers' Training Corps
P&O	Peninsular & Oriental Steamship Co
PA	Press Association
passim	here and there
PATA	Proprietary Articles Trade Association
PC	Privy Councillor
PD	*Parliamentary Debates* (Hansard)
PEP	Political and Economic Planning, now the Policy Studies Institute, London
PFR	Prototype Fast Reactor
pH	measure of hydrogen in concentration (indicating level of acidity)
PhD	Doctor of Philosophy

PLA	Port of London Authority
PLC (*or* plc)	public limited company
pm	post meridiem (afternoon)
PP	*Parliamentary Papers*
pp	privately printed or published
PrC	Probate Calendar in Principal Registry of the Family Division, Somerset House, Strand, London WC2R 1LP
PRO	Public Record Office, Chancery Lane, London WC2A 1LR, or Ruskin Avenue, Kew, Richmond, Surrey TW9 4DU
psi	pounds per square inch
Pty	Proprietary (private limited company in Australia and South Africa)
PVC	polyvinyl chloride
qqv	quae vide (which see; cross reference to several other entries)
qv	quod vide (which see; cross reference to another entry)
RA	Royal Artillery *or* Royal Academician
RAC	Royal Automobile Club
R&D	research and development
RAeS	Royal Aeronautical Society
RAF	Royal Air Force
RAFVR	Royal Air Force Volunteer Reserve
RAOC	Royal Army Ordnance Corps
RASC	Royal Army Service Corps
RC	Royal Commission
RCA	Radio Corporation of America
RE	Royal Engineers
REA	Royal Exchange Assurance
REME	Royal Electrical and Mechanical Engineers

rep	reprinted
RFC	Royal Flying Corps
RIBA	Royal Institute of British Architects
Rly	Railway
RM	Royal Marines
RN	Royal Navy
RNAS	Royal Naval Air Service
RNR	Royal Naval Reserve
RNVR	Royal Naval Volunteer Reserve
RO	Record Office
RPM	resale price maintenance
RSA	Royal Society of Arts
Rt Hon	Right Honourable
RTZ	Rio Tinto-Zinc Corporation
RUSI	Royal United Services Institute
s (following a monetary figure)	shillings [see note under £ at the end of this list]
SA	Société Anonyme (limited liability company)
SC	Select Committee
Scots DBB	*Scottish Dictionary of Business Biography*, Department of Economic History, Glasgow University
SE&CR	South Eastern & Chatham Railway
SHAEF	Supreme Headquarters, Allied Expeditionary Forces
Singer, *History of Technology.*	Charles Singer, E J Holmyard, A R Hall and Trevor Williams (eds), *A History of Technology* (7 vols, Oxford: Clarendon Press, 1954-78).
SMT	Securities Management Trust
SOAS	School of Oriental and African Studies, London University
SR	Southern Railway

Sr	Senior
SSRC Elites data.	Biographical workcards from SSRC project on 'The Economic Worth of Elites in British Society since 1880' conducted by Professor H J Perkin of Lancaster University, and kindly loaned by him to the *DBB* project.
STOL	Short take-off and landing
sv	sub verbo (under the heading cited)
TA	Territorial Army
TD	Territorial Decoration
TDG	Transport Development Group
Times *Prospectuses.*	*Prospectuses of Public Companies Including the Number of Bonds Drawn and Cancelled. Reprinted from the Advertisement Columns of the Times* (biannual, Times Publishing Co Ltd, 1891-1964).
TNPG	The Nuclear Power Group
TT	Tourist Trophy
TUC	Trades Union Congress
TV	television
TWA	Trans World Airlines
UAC	United Africa Company
UCL	University College, London
UDC	Urban District Council
UERL	Underground Electric Railway Co of London
UK	United Kingdom (England, Wales, Scotland and Northern Ireland)
USA	United States of America
USAF	United States Air Force
V	volt(s)
VCH	*Victoria History of the Counties of England*
Venn, *Alumni Cantabrigienses*	John Venn and J A Venn, *Alumni Cantabrigienses. A Biographical List of All Known Students, Graduates and Holders of Office at the University*

	of Cambridge, from the Earliest Times to 1900 Part II *1752 to 1900* (6 vols, Cambridge: Cambridge University Press, 1946-54)
V/STOL	vertical or short take-off and landing
VTOL	vertical take-off and landing
Will	Will of subject (unless otherwise stated) in Principal Registry of the Family Division, Somerset House, London WC2R 1LP
WPM	Wallpaper Manufacturers
WW	*Who's Who* (annual, Adam & Charles Black, 1849-1983).
WWMP	Michael Stenton and Stephen Lees, *Who's Who of British Members of Parliament. A Biographical Dictionary of the House of Commons* (4 vols, Hassocks, Sussex: Harvester Press, 1976-81).
WWW	*Who Was Who, 1897-1980* (8 vols, Adam & Charles Black, 1920-81).
WWW Theatre	*Who Was Who in the Theatre, 1912-1976* (Detroit: Gale Research Co, 1978)
YMCA	Young Men's Christian Association
£	Pound (monetary). In all entries, for dates before 15 February 1971 (when Britain switched to a decimal currency) the pound quoted is the old one, ie divided into 20 shillings each of 12 pence. Monetary sums under this old system are expressed as follows: £2 12s 6d. The decimal system abandoned shillings and divided the pound into 100 pence. The conversion rate for shillings is therefore one (old) shilling of 12 pence to five decimal pence.

H

HACKING, Sir John

(1888-1969)

Electrical engineer

Sir John Hacking (courtesy of the Electricity Council).

John Hacking was born at Crawshaw Booth, Lancashire, on 16 December 1888, the only son of William Edward Hacking, an engineer, and Martha née Birtwistle. He was educated at Burnley Grammar School and Leeds Technical Institute. His first job was with the Newcastle upon Tyne Electricity Supply Co, which he joined in 1908 when it was already established as one of the largest and most successful electric utilities in Britain. The enterprise had been largely planned and developed by Charles Merz (qv), and in 1913 Hacking was offered a job by the Merz & McLellan consulting engineering partnership. Over the following two decades, as well as working in their Newcastle and London offices, he spent many years abroad on major consulting projects on the electrification of Argentine and Indian railways and on electrical projects in South Africa.

Returning to work in the Newcastle office from Bombay in 1933, he was offered a post as deputy chief engineer by the Central Electricity Board, which had engaged the consultancy firm to help complete the Grid system for national interconnection and transmission. Hacking played an important part in the Grid's operational development, which became a vital source of flexibility in wartime electricity supplies. He became chief engineer of the CEB in 1944 and, when his chairman felt slighted and turned down the number two position in the newly-nationalised electricity supply industry, he became deputy chairman of the British Electricity Authority in 1948. The traditional knighthood followed in 1949.

Hacking would have liked to continue within the new organisation as an independent head of generation and transmission pursuing the policies of the old CEB with wider powers of control, but his two colleagues at the top of the British Electricity Authority, Citrine (qv) and Self (qv), who had no experience of the industry, insisted on a functional division of responsibilities. Under this he was in addition responsible for technical and engineering matters on the distribution and consumer sides, while

Self had overlapping responsibility for administrative matters on the generation side. The system never worked well, and the centralised bureaucracy they jointly created did not significantly improve the slow completion times on the power station construction programme which aggravated the severe post-war electricity shortages. In an attempt to overcome the backlog, Hacking mistakenly supported conservative policies, feeling they would be implemented rapidly. He initially failed to realise the potential of a higher voltage 275 kV Grid, and when he belatedly recognised that the generating sets being installed in new power stations were too small and thermally inefficient, he only embarked on a more advanced programme with hesitancy. Citrine, as chairman, generally supported Self rather than Hacking, and when all their contracts came up for renewal in 1952, Hacking threatened to resign if the minister renewed Citrine's. The minister did do so, and Hacking retired in 1953, leaving his successor, Josiah Eccles (qv), to make the fundamental engineering changes required. Although he was much liked for his modesty and quiet competence, Hacking had too often failed to live up to the fundamental strategic challenges of the top engineering job in the state electricity industry.

He married Janet Stewart of Newcastle upon Tyne in 1917; they had one son and one daughter. He was president of the Institution of Electrical Engineers in 1951-52 (and was made an honorary member in 1962) and of various other electrical organisations including the prestigious dining club, the Battiwallah's Society (of which he was president in 1952-53). His sporting activity changed from the cricket of his youth to more relaxed rounds of golf in his mature years. After retirement from the British Electricity Authority he worked again for some years as a consultant with Merz & McLellan. He died on 29 September 1969 leaving £15,146 gross.

LESLIE HANNAH

Writings:

(with J R Beard) 'Transmission and distribution: a review of progress' in *Journal of the Institution of Electrical Engineers* 69 (1931).

(with J D Peattie) 'The British Grid System in Wartime' *ibid* 94 part 2 (1947), and *Proceedings of the Institution of Electrical Engineers* 96, part 2 (1949).

'Presidential Address' *Proceedings of the Fifth British Electrical Power Convention, 1953, Torquay* (Northampton: Lea & Co Ltd, 1953).

'The Electricity Supply Industry of Great Britain' *Journal of the South African Institution of Electrical Engineers* 1954.

A fuller file of his writings is available at the Intelligence Section of the Electricity Council.

Sources:

Unpublished

Electricity Council, 30 Millbank, London, CEB Archives (available); British Electricity Authority Archives (not available to scholars until 1993).

PrC.

Published

DNB.

Leslie Hannah, *Electricity before Nationalisation: A Study of the Development of the Electricity Supply Industry in Britain to 1948* (Macmillan, 1979).

—, *Engineers, Managers and Politicians: The First Fifteen Years of the Nationalised Electricity Supply in Britain* (Macmillan, 1982).

WWW.

HADFIELD, John

(1893-1980)

Managing director of limestone quarrying companies

John Hadfield was born in Sheffield on 3 August 1893, the son of John William Hadfield, a master asphalter, and Florence née Hilldred. In 1869 his grandfather had founded John Hadfield & Sons Ltd, which developed into a small civil engineering enterprise. Hadfield was educated at Sheffield Central School and Sheffield University, gaining an MSc in chemistry in 1915. He was then attached to the British War Mission in America for work on explosives. He joined the family firm of paving contractors in 1918, becoming managing director; his brother and two cousins were also directors.

In conjunction with their contracting business, Hadfields worked limestone quarries. They opened up Hope quarry in Derbyshire in 1907, and in 1934 acquired by tender the lease of the large Caldon Low quarry in Staffordshire from the LMS railway. However as a result of a reduction in road expenditure in Great Britain of over 20 per cent between 1930 and 1934, the Derbyshire (and North Staffordshire) limestone industry suffered badly.

John Hadfield's response to these difficulties was to bring together other Derbyshire limestone businesses with his own in 1935. In that year the combined profits of the five businesses were little more than £40,000. The new company, Derbyshire Stone Ltd, had an initial share capital of £426,000; the parties to the merger also had to find £60,000 working capital. John Hadfield was appointed managing director. In 1945 he became chairman as well as managing director. When he retired in 1966,

HADFIELD John

Derbyshire Stone Ltd, the merged company, had an annual profit of £2.6 million. Hadfield held the chief executive position throughout. Shortly after his retirement, the company merged with Tarmac Ltd.

Hadfield was very quick to perceive trends and develop his business accordingly. He made numerous small acquisitions, sometimes to eliminate competition, or to stabilise prices. He gathered round him an excellent staff and paid attention to their views; his relations with them were cordial, though he was regarded as somewhat niggardly in payment of salaries. His consideration for his workpeople was exemplary; he led the industry in pension and life insurance schemes and in safety measures. He was always in the forefront of co-operation in industry. In 1956 he was chosen as chairman of the Committee of Roadstone Producers, who organised the defence of the industry's restrictive practices. Similarly, when his family company acquired an interest in Ragusa Asphalt Ltd, of which he became chairman, he promoted the important asphalt merger in 1957, known familiarly as Amasco.

His weakness was perhaps a lack of appreciation of the importance of technical 'know-how' in entering unfamiliar fields. Derbyshire Stone's involvements in deep lead-mining in Derbyshire, in the East African groundnuts scheme and in Baird & Tatlock, the chemical industry's suppliers, were not successes.

Hadfield was very interested in art, and had a good collection of nineteenth century landscapes and Dutch interiors. In 1924 he married Laura Mary, an elementary school mistress, daughter of Rev Willie Barrett, a Primitive Methodist minister. They had two children. John Hadfield died in Sheffield on 10 October 1980, leaving an estate proved at £165,770.

J B F EARLE

Sources:

Unpublished

BCe.

MCe.

PrC.

Published

J B F Earle, *A Century of Road Materials* (Oxford: Basil Blackwell, 1971).

—, *Black Top* (Oxford: Basil Blackwell, 1974).

Sheffield Telegraph 12 Oct 1980.

Times *Prospectuses* 99 (1946).

HADFIELD, Sir Robert Abbott

(1858-1940)

Steel manufacturer

Robert Abbott Hadfield was born at Attercliffe, near Sheffield on 28 November 1858, the only son of Robert Hadfield and Marianne née Abbott. At the time of Robert Abbott's birth, his father was a vestry clerk; later he entered the steel trade, and pioneered the manufacture of steel castings and projectiles at the Hecla Works of Hadfield's Steel Foundry Co, Sheffield, from 1872. His mother came from an Oxfordshire family of shire-horse breeders. John Brown (qv) was a second cousin on his father's side.

Robert Abbott attended the Collegiate School in Sheffield, and was taught chemistry by William Baker, whose lectures seem to have attracted him. A brief apprenticeship in the nearby firm of Jonas & Colver, experiments with a steel melting furnace in the basement of his father's house, and instruction by leading chemical analyst A H Allen, completed his education. From the age of twenty-four he had to take over the administration of the firm owing to his father's ill-health, and on the death of the elder Hadfield in 1888 the concern was formed into a limited company, the young metallurgist becoming the chairman and managing director.

It was as a metallurgist that Hadfield achieved his most striking success. Inspired by a visit to America in 1882 and French discoveries concerning the properties of ferro-manganese, he embarked on the study of special steel alloys. In September 1882, in the laboratory belonging to his father's firm, he began his investigations of the effects of progressive additions of manganese to carbon steel. Hadfield's finding that additions of 12 to 13 per cent of manganese produced an alloy with entirely novel properties, especially resistance to wear, was the revolutionary discovery which is commonly regarded as inaugurating the age of alloy steels. The new steel was patented in 1883.

Further researches led to the introduction of silicon steel, which possessed valuable electrical properties, and also what Hadfield claimed to be the innovatory study of chromium steel (stainless steel). Eventually, Hadfield's researches resulted in more than 200 papers and addresses. He also published two classic accounts of the development of metallurgy: *Metallurgy and Its Influence On Modern Progess* (1925) and *Faraday and His Metallurgical Researches* (1931).

It was some time before the talents of the chairman were reflected in the trading performance of the company. The exploitation of the manganese patents depended upon many years of costly experimentation, and development was further delayed by the conservatism of consumers. It was to be fifteen years before there were any significant sales of manganese steel. Once the early problems were overcome, however, the enormous

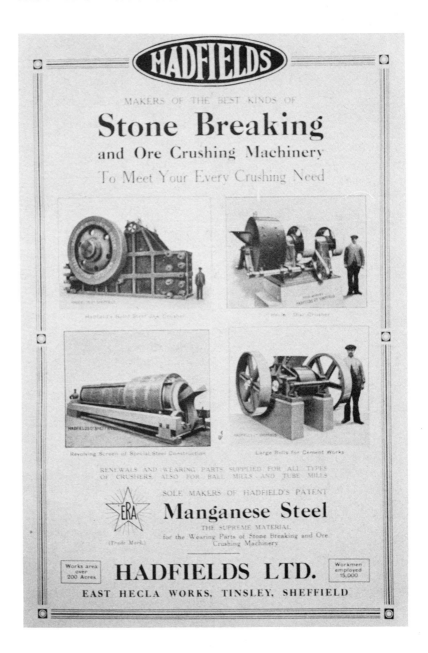

Hadfield advertisement (courtesy of Dr G Tweedale).

demand from Government and the railways brought a rapid expansion of Hadfields around the turn of the century: between 1894 and 1914 total authorised capital grew from £135,750 to £700,000, and the workforce from 530 to 5,980. Extensions became necessary, and in August 1897 the construction of the East Hecla Works at Tinsley, Sheffield, commenced. Hadfield's expertise with projectile manufacture and the suitability of manganese steel for war material gave an enormous boost to the company in the war years: between 1914 and 1918 Hadfields' output and labour force doubled and the period was marked by extremely high profits. Post-war recession, plant obsolescence, labour troubles, and the erosion of the firm's lead in special steel technology, meant it was never again as profitable or productive during Hadfield's lifetime. Nevertheless, Hadfields continued to prosper in the inter-war years and at its chairman's death, with some 6,000 workers, a steel melting capacity of some 3,500 tons a week, and an annual turnover approaching £5 million, it was still one of the largest steel foundries in the world.

Throughout his life Hadfield, with a tremendous capacity for sustained work, exercised a close personal control over the firm. Though inside the foundry he was happy to rely on technical advisers such as John and Sam Mallaband, not until 1905, when he appointed Alex M Jack as managing director, did he delegate authority in any other sphere. There was little attempt to begin manufacturing abroad, despite the fact that Hadfield's patents were taken up extensively in other countries by firms such as Schneider and Westinghouse, and he himself supervised the introduction of manganese steel into America at the Taylor Works, New Jersey. Even in the 1920s and 1930s, when the burden of running the firm was taken up by the triumverate of Major A B H Clarke, P B Brown and W B Pickering, Hadfield was almost always present at board meetings and a constant stream of telegrams and telephone calls from his homes in London and the South of France kept him informed of company affairs.

Hadfield's painstaking attention to detail and methodical scientific approach were reflected in his attitude to business. Labour was to be economised by systematic organisation. He held liberal views on labour questions, and was one of the first employers to introduce the eight-hour day, in 1891. He later collaborated with Rev H Gibbins in the publication of *The Shorter Working Day*.

Hadfield made numerous visits abroad (between 1892 and 1914 he made 11 visits to the USA) and his circle of friends became particularly wide. This led him to take the lead in movements to establish an Empire Development Board, and to form a central institution for all engineering societies. He furthered the application of science to industry in his native city by benefactions to Sheffield University and the foundation in 1938 of the Sir Robert Hadfield Metallurgical Laboratories. These endowments were a practical expression of his belief in the importance of continual research. For these and other services he was given the freedom of the City of Sheffield on 6 June 1939.

Hadfield received many other honours throughout the world. In 1908 he was knighted, and in 1917 he was made a baronet. President of both the Faraday Society and the Iron and Steel Institute, he was elected an FRS in 1909, and in 1925 he was made an Officer of the Légion d'Honneur; he was the Master Cutler of Hallamshire in 1899, and in 1917 he received the freedom of the City of London. Numerous honorary degrees and awards, such as the Elliot-Cresson and John Fritz gold medals, also came his way. He was elected an honorary member of no less than 27 scientific and technical societies at home and abroad.

As a staunch Liberal, he was repeatedly invited to stand for Parliament, but his scientific and business activities engaged all his time. In fact, work was his chief hobby. On the few occasions when he could relax he sought recreation in golf and motoring. He also played tennis and was fond of fishing.

On 19 September 1894, at St Peter's Church, Philadelphia, he married Frances Belt née Wickersham, a daughter of Colonel S M Wickersham, an engineer whose brother was Attorney-General under the Taft Administration. Soon after the outbreak of war in 1914 Sir Robert and Lady Hadfield founded a hospital at Wimereux. Lady Hadfield's wartime services were recognised by the award of a CBE in 1918. Sir Robert and Lady Hadfield had no children.

Sir Robert died at Kenry House, Kingston Hill, Surrey, on 30 September 1940. He left a personal estate, after settlements, of £218,276 gross, with numerous bequests to scientific and research bodies.

Autocratic, with a reputation as a hard task-master, at once modest about his own achievements and fully conscious of his own special position in the world of metallurgy, Hadfield successfully combined his scientific and business careers. His standing as a metallurgist is well established; a final assessment of his career as a businessman awaits a closer scrutiny of the manuscripts extant from the East Hecla Works, Sheffield.

GEOFFREY TWEEDALE

Writings:

'Manganese Steel. I Manganese in Its Application to Metallurgy. II Some Newly Discovered Properties of Iron and Manganese' *Proceedings of the Institution of Civil Engineers* 93 (1888).

'On Manganese Steel' *Journal of the Iron and Steel Institute* 1888.

'On Alloys of Iron and Silicon' *ibid* 1889.

'Aluminium Steel' *ibid* 1890.

(with Henry de Beltgens Gibbins) *A Shorter Working Day* (Methuen, 1892).

'Alloys of Iron and Chromium' *Journal of the Iron and Steel Institute* 1892.

The Work and Position of the Metallurgical Chemist, also References to Sheffield and Its Place in Metallurgy (C Griffin & Co, 1921).

Metallurgy and Its Influence on Modern Progress with a Survey of Education and Research (Chapman & Hall, 1925).

Faraday and His Metallurgical Researches. With Special Reference to Their Bearing on the Development of Alloy Steels (Chapman & Hall, 1931).

Empire Development and Proposals for the Establishment of an Empire Development Board (Chapman & Hall, 1935).

A full listing is held in *DBB* office files.

Sources:

Unpublished

Sheffield City Library, Archives Division, diaries of Sir Robert Hadfield, 1875-78, microfilm no A 70; personal papers, patents, agreements, and correspondence relating to Hadfield's Ltd; reports of AGMs, 'A Record of 50 Years Progress (1888-1938)'; S A Main, 'The Hadfields of Sheffield: Pioneers in Steel' (nd); A W McKears, 'The First Hundred Years. Hadfields of Sheffield' (nd). Hadfields Ltd (1919-40); Annual General Meetings.

BCe.

MCe.

PrC.

Published

DNB.

Hadfield's Steel Foundry Company Ltd (Sheffield: Hadfields, 1905).

'Hadfield's Steel Foundry' *Engineering* 8, 22 Feb 1895.

A Short Description of Hadfields Ltd: Its History, Plant and Manufactures (Sheffield: Hadfields, 1938).

Visit of His Majesty the King to the East Hecla Works of Hadfields Ltd (Sheffield: Hadfields, 1915).

WWW.

HAIN, Sir Edward

(1851-1917)

Shipowner

Edward Hain was born at St Ives, Cornwall, on 26 December 1851, the son of Edward Hain, of a family of seamen and shipowners, and Grace née Paynter. After education at a private school, Edward Jr at first found employment in the Cornish banking firm of Bolitho, which had given financial support to the Hain fleet of relatively small but efficient wooden sailing vessels which traded coastwise and deep-sea, particularly to Mediterranean ports. Following a short period in the office of a London merchant, Edward returned to St Ives in 1878 and announced his intention of investing in the iron screw steamers which were by this time ousting the older sailing vessels from their dominance in oceanic commerce. In pursuit of this aim he promoted his first venture in steam shipping when he placed an order for an iron screw steamer of 1,730 deadweight tons, costing £18,000. This vessel was named *Trewidden* after the Bolitho estate near Penzance (all subsequent Hain steamers were given characteristically

The steamship Trelissick 3077 tons deadweight, was a typical Hain vessel. Completed in 1909, she came from the shipyard of John Readhead & Sons Ltd, South Shields, and cost £34,288 to build (courtesy of Tyne & Wear County Council Museum Service).

Cornish names with the suffix *Tre*, and were registered in the port of St Ives). Each sixty-fourth share in *Trewidden* cost subscribers £281 5s and investors were drawn from a wide spectrum locally, including several farmers and spinsters, a bank manager, a mine agent, a licensed victualler, a ship chandler, a fisherman, a draper and an ironmonger. The vessel was ordered from the shipyard of John Readhead & Co of South Shields in 1878, and began an association between a shipowner and shipbuilder which is unique in the annals of the merchant marine. Between 1878 and 1965 Readheads built no fewer than 87 vessels for the Hain Steamship Co.

The success of Edward Hain's enterprise may be judged by the speed with which the fleet expanded: by mid-1885, Readheads had built 12 steamers for Hain of an aggregate tonnage of over 18,000 tons gross, representing an investment of nearly £244,000. In January 1884, Edward Hain registered his first vessel under the Companies Acts as a single-ship firm in substitution for the older '64th' system of ownership, with the formation of the Trevider Steamship Co Ltd, having a capital of £24,000. By 1890, the fleet comprised 19 steamers, with an insured value of £364,000 and Hain decided to arrange self-insurance for this impressive fleet. In 1901, with 22 steamers, the enterprise was reorganised under one joint-stock, limited liability company with a capital of £500,000 in £10 shares. The book value of the ships stood at £720,019 in June 1906, with new vessels valued at £111,465 contracted for, and by August 1913 the fleet numbered 36 vessels with orders placed for five further ships valued at £275,000. Between 1878 and 1917, a period of thirty-nine years, 74 steamers had been acquired at a cost of £2,620,000.

The firm had soon outgrown its St Ives offices, and a partnership was entered into with Richard A Foster of Cardiff in 1881 which gave access to a port which was a vital ingredient in its success, since Hain steamers regularly resorted to Cardiff for export cargoes of coal and many Hain vessels were drydocked and surveyed there preparatory to their outward voyages. Access to the Cardiff Coal Exchange was of great importance in securing favourable freights. Similar considerations led to the establishment of a London office in 1887, when Robert Sawle Read of St Ives took charge of chartering operations there and became the third partner in the enterprise. When the company was reorganised in 1901, the directors of the Hain Steamship Co Ltd were Edward Hain himself, R A Foster, and R S Read, representing the Cardiff and London offices of what had become an exceedingly prosperous and well-conducted business.

Edward Hain was a mayor of St Ives on six occasions. He was a Cornwall county councillor for fifteen years and was made a JP in 1889. A Liberal Unionist in politics, he was MP for St Ives, 1900-6, and High Sheriff of Cornwall in 1912. He was knighted in 1910, the year in which his great services to the shipping industry were recognised when he became president of the Chamber of Shipping of the United Kingdom. He was appointed to the Government Advisory Shipping Committee in 1916 and was thus a contributor to the important and influential Report of the Departmental Committee appointed by the Board of Trade to consider the position of the shipping and shipbuilding industries after the war. This was published after his death, in 1918.

Edward Hain married in 1882 Catherine Seward, second daughter of James Hughes, an accountant at Cardiff. They had two children, a daughter who died tragically young, and a son who was killed in action at Gallipoli in 1915 at the age of twenty-eight, virtually in sight of the seaway which had been traversed by countless Hain steamers on their way to load cargoes of Black Sea grain, the predominant homeward freight for Hain shipping.

Hain died soon afterwards, on 20 September 1917 at the age of sixty-five, leaving an estate proved at £628,677 gross. His entire fleet was purchased by Lord Inchcape (qv) of the P&O Co, which paid £80 for each share. However, Inchcape wisely kept the Hain fleet under its previously-established management and the ships retained their Hain colours, the funnel being black with a distinctive large white 'H'. This distinctive mark of the origin of the firm was retained by P&O until the 1970s.

ROBIN S CRAIG

Sources:

Unpublished

BCe.

MCe.

PrC.

Published

Sir George P Christopher, *Roots and Branches* (Liverpool, ca 1950).

Fairplay Annual Summary of British Shipping Finance.

Percy Harley, *My Life in Shipping 1881-1938* (pp, ca 1938).

WWMP.

WWW.

HALFORD, Frank Bernard

(1894-1955)

Aero engine designer and consultant

Frank Bernard Halford was born in Nottingham on 7 March 1894, the son of Harry Baker Halford, an estate agent and one-time Sheriff of Nottingham, and of his wife, Ethel née Grundy. Halford went to Felsted School and then, briefly, to Nottingham University to study engineering. He did not relish university life and at the age of eighteen, in 1912, he left university to learn to fly with the British & Colonial Aeroplane Co's 'Bristol' School at Brooklands, where he gained Royal Aero Club Certificate No 639. On 2 October 1913 he graduated to become a flying instructor at Bristol's Brooklands School and then, in 1914, left to pursue his engineering bent as an aero-engine examiner, at £2 10s for a forty-eight hour week, in the newly-formed Aeronautical Inspection Directorate (AID) of the War Office under Captain Bagnall-Wild, chief inspector of engines.

At the outbreak of war in 1914, Halford joined the Royal Flying Corps as a foreman-artificer sergeant and went to France. In January 1915, he was commissioned as a second lieutenant and posted back to England to work, initially, as assistant inspector of engines at the Royal Aircraft Factory at Farnborough. Shortly afterwards he was sent to the Arrol Johnston Car Co in Scotland to work with C T Pullinger on development of the German Austro-Daimler 120 hp, six-cylinder in-line, water-cooled engine, then being built by Beardmore. His experience in France of the Hispano-Suiza engines stood him in good stead, especially in the use of cast aluminium, monobloc cylinders with steel liners, then unknown in England.

Halford and Pullinger set to work to increase the power of the Austro-Daimler engine by increasing the bore to a cylinder capacity of 20 litres and to an output of more than 200 bhp. In due course, Sir William Beardmore & Co of Dalmuir was selected to build the developed engine as the 230 hp 'BHP', the initials standing for 'Beardmore-Halford-Pullinger'.

In 1916 Halford was introduced by Hereward de Havilland to his brother, Geoffrey (qv) who was building the DH4 bomber prototype at the Aircraft Manufacturing Co's works at Hendon. As a result, the prototype BHP engine was installed in the prototype DH4 and flown for the first time in August 1916 by Geoffrey de Havilland himself. Subsequently, the BHP engine was further developed by the Siddeley-Deasy Motor Co as the 246 BHP Siddeley Puma engine, of which some thousands were built to power the Airco's DH9 bombers. Through their collaboration at the time, Halford and de Havilland formed a close friendship which was to have fruitful future results.

Halford followed up the BHP engine with the BHP Siddeley Atlantic, a 500 hp engine made up of two BHP cylinder blocks on a common crankcase; it was flown in the DH15 biplane as a development of the DH9. The Atlantic was built by the Galloway Engine Co which had completed 25 engines by the time of the Armistice. Halford went on to design a successor, the Siddeley Pacific (a double Puma), which was in production for the bombing of Berlin but was stopped by the ending of the war.

During 1918, Halford also worked with H R Ricardo (later Sir Harry) on the development of the first super-charged aero-engine — the RHA (Ricardo-Halford-Armstrongs), an upright V-12. Modified, at Halford's suggestion, to run inverted (a solution which he used to good effect later), the Ricardo-Halford 'Inverted Supercharger' engine was successfully flown in a DH4 at Farnborough but its development was abandoned at the Armistice.

By the end of the war in 1918, Frank (now Major) Halford was assistant to Colonel Alan E L Chorlton, head of engine production (excluding Rolls Royce) at the Air Ministry. In 1919 Major Halford joined the staff of Harry Ricardo's 'Engine Patents Ltd' of Pall Mall, London and, on behalf of Ricardo's consulting engineering group, spent two-and-a-half years in the United States on the negotiation of engine licence agreements for both aircraft and tanks. This work greatly widened his experience of manufacturing procedures and of business generally. When he returned to England and to Ricardos, Halford helped in the development of the four-valve Triumph-Ricardo motor-cycle on which, in 1922, Halford himself set up a 500 cc record at Brooklands at almost 70 miles in an hour and a 'flying mile' at 87.89 mph.

With his experience in the USA and at Ricardos on consulting work, in 1923 the twenty-eight-year-old Frank Halford made the bold decision to set up on his own as a consulting engineer in North Kensington with one assistant, John L P Brodie (later to become engineering director of the de Havilland Engine Co). The first year of the new consultancy was spent in developing for the Aston Martin Co a 1.5 litre, six-cylinder, short-stroke engine with an aluminium block, designed to operate at up to 6,000 rpm. With it he successfully raced for Lionel Martin at Brooklands, starting in 1923 with the Aston Martin 'Razor Blade' car with a streamlined body built by the de Havilland Aircraft Co.

From 1924 to 1927 Halford acted as consultant to Frederick Handley Page's (qv) Aircraft Disposal Co at Croydon Aerodrome. Using war-surplus components to produce new, low-price engines Halford designed first, the 120 hp Airdisco eight-cylinder Vee engine, and then the Cirrus 4.5 litre, 60 hp four-cylinder upright in-line engine. The latter made possible the success of Geoffrey de Havilland's 'Cirrus Moth' light aeroplane, first flown in February 1925.

Major George P Bulman, Director of Engine Development at the Air Ministry, wrote of Frank Halford in this period:

> Of dynamic enterprise, warm in heart, extraordinarily magnetic, gay in adventure with the panache of a d'Artagnan and an echo of the Robin Hood of his beloved Nottingham, Frank Halford had no engineering training at all and none of the academic qualifications normally expected. He was the essential creative artist, anxious always to get on with the next project and, later, a little too apt to leave to his devoted staff the drudgery and the sweat of carrying his latest-but-one-design into production. He had an immense

and dynamic charm with his mind over busy with engines. {Journal of the Royal Aeronautical Society 63 (1959) 205}

On 29 October 1926 Frank Halford, with John Brodie and W H Arscott, began design for de Havillands of the first of the classic series of Gipsy engines for which Frank Halford became especially renowned. The first Gipsy was in the form of a refined Cirrus, because the war-surplus parts from which he had built these earlier engines had begun to be exhausted. Built at Stag Lane, the first experimental DH Gipsy I prototype engine was flown for the first time in the DH71 Tiger Moth racing monoplane in August 1927, in which it established world records in its class. In that same year, 1927, Halford opened a new office in Windsor House, Victoria Street, Westminster, where he was joined by Eric Moult on 27 November. By then the Gipsy I was going into production and this 5.25 litre four-cylinder upright, aircooled engine, derated to 100 hp from the 135 hp of the prototype — and weighing only three lbs per hp and so well in advance of the Cirrus — first flew in production form in the DH60G Gipsy Moth on 28 June 1928: an aircraft which achieved 100 mph on 100 hp. Between 1930 and 1937, a series of Gipsy engines was built, culminating in the 12 cylinder, 525 hp, 18.4 litre, supercharged Gipsy Twelve (or Gipsy King) — an inverted Vee aircooled engine for the de Havilland DH 91 Albatross: essentially two Gipsy VI engines on a common crankcase.

From 1928, Halford had further exploited his design independence by embarking upon an innovative series of new aircooled engines for D Napier & Sons of Acton. The first was the 165 hp Napier-Halford Javelin of 1933. It was followed by the 395 hp Napier Rapier, 16-cylinder, 8.33 litre, aircooled 'H' engine, and then in 1935 the 1,000 hp Napier Dagger, 24-cylinder, 16.8 litre, aircooled engine of H-type which was ordered in quantity by the Air Ministry for the Handley Page Hereford twin-engined night bomber and for the Hawker Hector army co-operation aircraft.

In 1935, in the middle of this work, Halford accepted for the first time — and 'rather uneasily' {Wilson and Reader (1958) 149} — an appointment to the board of D Napier & Sons while still maintaining his independent consultancy at new offices in Golden Square, London, and his close association with the de Havilland Co as its chief engine designer.

Halford's agreement of 1928 with the Napier Co was that de Havilland would have manufacturing rights for Halford-designed engines of 6.6 to 11.8 litres capacity. Above that size he would be free to develop engines for Napiers. With the expansion of the Royal Air Force and the appearance of the Napier-Halford Dagger engine, a substantial Air Ministry order was given for 90 engines at £3,800 each and this development work led to the very ambitious 36.65 litre, 2,400 hp Napier Sabre, liquid-cooled 24-cylinder, horizontal 'H' sleeve-valve engine. The Sabre was eventually built in quantity for the Hawker Typhoon single-seat fighter, whose first flight with the Sabre was on 24 February 1940. Halford's experience of sleeve valves was, however, limited and after some catastrophic failures of the Sabre engine in the air, he had to turn to his friend, Roy Fedden (qv) of Bristols to seek guidance on how to overcome the problems. In due course, the 3,055 hp Sabre VII produced better than one hp for each pound of dry weight.

Parallel with this development work on the Napier high-power piston engines, in January 1941 Halford began discussions with the Air Ministry and the de Havilland Engine Co on the possibilities of a Whittle-type, gas turbine engine which he learned about through his membership of the Royal Aeronautical Society's Advisory Committee to the Minister of Aircraft Production from 1941 to 1946. Work began on the Halford H1 jet engine in April 1941, and the first prototype engine made its first run on 13 April 1942, having been completed from first drawing in 248 days under wartime pressures. The new engine, named the DH Goblin, was flown for the first time in a Gloster Meteor on 5 March 1943, and then became the first jet engine to be installed in a classic, single-engine, single-seat fighter for squadron service with the Royal Air Force, the DH100 Vampire. The Goblin Mark I, of 2,700 lb static thrust (a simple single-stage, centrifugal flow, jet engine) gave the Vampire a maximum speed of 540 mph and was first flown by Geoffrey de Havilland Jr on 20 September 1943. The Goblin, of which more than 300 were built, was followed by the 4,450 lb static thrust DH Ghost 50 mk 1 engine, of 4,450 lb thrust, which first flew on 27 July 1949 in the DH106 Comet, the world's first jet transport aeroplane.

Halford finally abandoned his independent status on 1 February 1944 to become chairman of the newly-formed de Havilland Engine Co with John Brodie as general manager and Eric Moult as chief engineer, the team which had worked together since 1927. In the same year, Halford accepted a directorship of the de Havilland Aircraft Co.

He continued to supervise the development of the Gipsy range of engines and to produce what was at the time the world's most powerful jet engine, the DH Gyron of 15,000 lb static thrust, which ran for the first time on 5 January 1953, and flew in the Short Sperrin four-engine test-bed bomber on 7 July 1955. Sadly, Frank Halford did not live to see this flight.

Frank Halford will be remembered in aviation history chiefly for his series of de Havilland Gipsy engines (which remained in every day service for more than sixty years) at the lower power end of the spectrum; for his high power, but unreliable, Napier Sabre engine of the 1940s; for his early jet engines; and for his independence as an 'own account' businessman. In 1948 he was made CBE and in 1951-52 he was president of the Royal Aeronautical Society.

Frank Halford at the age of forty-five, married in 1939, Marjorie Moore, formerly Myers, daughter of Alfred James Puttick, an auctioneer; they had one daughter. Halford died of cancer of the throat on 16 April 1955, at the age of sixty-one, at his home, Monk Barns, Sandy Lane, Northwood, Middlesex. He left £153,866 gross.

ROBIN HIGHAM *and* SIR PETER MASEFIELD

Sources:

Unpublished

BCe.

MCe.

HALFORD Frank Bernard

PrC.

Personal knowledge.

Published

The Aeroplane 22 Apr 1955.

F R Banks, *I Kept No Diaries* (Air Life, 1983).

Flight 22 Apr 1955.

A J Jackson, *D H Aircraft since 1909* (Putnam, 1978).

Journal of the Royal Aeronautical Society 63 (1959), 70 (Jan 1966).

C Martin Sharpe, *D H — a History of de Havilland* (Air Line, 1982).

Charles Wilson and William J Reader, *Men and Machines: D Napier and Sons 1808–1958* (Weidenfeld & Nicolson, 1958).

WWW.

Everard A Hambro, portrait by Sir John Lavery ca 1915 (courtesy of Hambro Bank Archives).

HAMBRO, Sir Everard Alexander

(1842-1925)

Merchant banker

Everard Alexander Hambro was born in Willesden, London on 11 April 1842, the youngest of four children and the only one not to have been born in Denmark. His mother, Caroline, was the daughter of a London merchant called Theofilus Gostenhofer. His father, Carl Joachim Hambro, was a third-generation banker from Copenhagen who visited England in the early 1830s and then in 1839 established a London branch. Despite the family's Jewish background, Carl Joachim had been fostered out as a young child to a Christian family and subsequently had been baptised. Christianity played an important role in Everard's childhood and it was significant that in later life his business associates were to be found among the Barings and Morgans not the Rothschilds and Cohens.

Everard studied at Trinity College, Cambridge, before joining C J Hambro & Son in 1864. By then the Danish bank had been sold and all assets were concentrated in London where after a difficult beginning Carl Joachim had eventually prospered. When Carl Joachim died in 1877, Everard rather than his two older brothers inherited all his father's banking assets, giving him 75 per cent of the bank's capital, which then stood at £650,000. His two brothers never held any significant stake in the bank and the remainder lay in the hands of his two partners, Edward Rawlings and Robert Heriot. At this time, C J Hambro & Son was just one-third the size of Baring Bros, the oldest and one of the most respected merchant banks in London. In the prosperous decade which followed, however, Everard transformed the size and status of C J Hambro & Son, as an accepting and an issuing house. His income from the bank grew from £52,000 in 1878 to an annual average of £150,000 in the mid- to late-1880s, and through re-investment he was able by 1 January 1890 to raise his own capital to £1 million and to increase that of the bank to £1.3 million.

Nothing better illustrates his determination to succeed than his agreeing to issue the £29 million Italian currency loan in 1881. He was aware that the Paris Rothschilds had already refused the loan due to the likelihood of unfavourable conditions on the Paris Bourse, then regarded as the traditional market for Italian securities. £29 million was far beyond all his previous dealings and so he formed a strong syndicate, including Baring Bros in London, Banque d'Escompte in Paris and two Italian banks. With the proceeds he had to arrange the purchase of gold and silver for the Italian Government on a sensitive market without forcing up the price. The press debated the question daily and many argued it could not be done.

To cope with the overwhelming size of the loan he split it in two parts and the first issue was entirely successful. The second half, however, was plagued by a number of factors which together almost ruined the whole operation. Three times the Paris Rothschilds tried to break into the syndicate. Each time, Everard resolutely refused their assistance despite the withdrawal of the Banque d'Escompte, a direct result of the Rothschilds' manoeuvrings. It took him nearly three years to bring the issue to its conclusion. Profits of £335,000 were not great but in the circumstances Everard felt proud enough to publish the results in the press. Even the bullion aspect had been completed without shaking the market.

In 1879 Everard was elected to the Court of the Bank of England where he served for forty-five years. He was very outspoken and during the 1890s his relations with the senior members, those who had passed the Governor's chair, became particularly strained on the question of internal reform. Henry Gibbs (qv), outstanding among past Governors, described him as 'being antagonistic unlike anything he had known in his forty-one years at the Bank.' {Bank of England Archives} Everard never held the year-long tenancy of Governor but in 1910, two years after becoming KCVO, tradition was broken and Sir Everard was admitted to the Committee of Treasury, which up to this time had been reserved only for past Governors. From then onwards, Sir Everard was fully involved at the centre of the Bank's affairs and during the war years he gave invaluable help on exchange rate matters.

Sir Everard had always treasured his traditional links with Denmark and the rest of Scandinavia. When the relatively new and successful British Bank of Northern Commerce Ltd (BBNC) approached him in 1920 with a proposal to amalgamate the two banks, he welcomed the idea. The BBNC was backed by some powerful Scandinavian bankers eager to get a stronger foothold in London, and whose support would be invaluable in the future.

Thus Hambros Bank of Northern Commerce Ltd was formed in October 1920 with capital and reserves of just over £5 million and Sir Everard as its chairman; within ten months it was officially known as Hambros Bank Ltd. Sir Everard remained chairman until his death in 1925, aged eighty-three, holding on to the reins until the very last when his eldest son Sir Eric Hambro finally succeeded him.

Sir Everard married first in 1866 Gertrude Mary Stuart (1848-1905), who bore him three sons and a daughter, and second in 1911, Ebba Whyte (1887-1961). In 1873 he established the Hambro Orphanage for Girls at Roehampton which he supported for thirty-six years.

His main interests were golf, shooting, gardening and a herd of pedigree Guernseys.

Sir Everard Hambro died on 20 February 1925, leaving £2,323,711 gross.

KATHLEEN M WAIN

Sources:

Unpublished

Bank of England Archives.

BCe.

MCe.

PrC.

Published

Bo Bramson and Kathleen Wain, *The Hambros 1779-1979* (Michael Joseph, 1979).
WWW.

HAMILTON, Lord Claud John

(1843-1925)

Railway company chairman

Lord Claud John Hamilton was born at Harrow in Middlesex on 20 February 1843, the second son of James, the First Duke of Abercorn, sometime Lord Lieutenant of Ireland, and Lady Louisa Russell, the second daughter of John, the Sixth Duke of Bedford. He was educated at Harrow. In 1862 he joined the Grenadier Guards, retiring from the regiment in 1867, and then became colonel of the 5th Battalion, Royal Inniskilling Fusiliers, a position he retained until 1892 when he became their honorary colonel. His experience of military service had a lasting effect on his character, and on his approach to labour relations in his business life. During the 1860s he also began a long career in Parliament, sitting as Conservative MP for Londonderry, 1864-68, unsuccessfully contesting Brecon in April 1869, and later that year being elected for King's Lynn.

In 1872, on the recommendation of Lord Salisbury, the retiring chairman, Hamilton was appointed a member of the board of directors of the Great Eastern Railway, and was promoted to vice-chairman only two years later. For the next twenty years he worked in close accord with the company's chairman, Charles Henry Parkes. When Parkes retired in 1893 Hamilton succeeded to the chair, staying in command until the GER was absorbed into the London & North Eastern Railway in 1923. Thus his period of service on the board was only ten years short of the company's sixty-one year history.

The Great Eastern was never a very prosperous concern since most of the territory it served was agricultural and sparsely populated. When Hamilton joined the board in the early 1870s its fortunes were at a low ebb, its ordinary shares being quoted at 40. In the next forty years his principal contributions to the improvement of the company's profitability were the development of the Continental traffic; the opening up of the coal trade with the Derbyshire and South Yorkshire coalfields; and the expansion of the hotel, restaurant and restaurant car services. The opening of Parkeston Quay in 1882 and the growth of the traffic from Harwich helped to boost the company's receipts from its Continental business from £131,765 in 1881 to £268,718 in 1897. The inauguration of the Great Northern and Great Eastern joint line from March to Doncaster in 1882 resulted in the GER obtaining an important share in the coal traffic to London, and the acquisition of running powers over the lines of the North Eastern Railway between Doncaster and York ten years later led to a further expansion of both metropolitan and Continental traffic. As chairman of the Hotels Committee of the company for forty-eight years Hamilton substituted direct employment for sub-contracting of catering labour, and thereby improved the quality of the services provided. All these measures helped to enhance the value of the company's ordinary shares which reached par for the first time in 1896.

In the Edwardian era Hamilton was best known for his intransigence in labour relations. He treated the members of the GER staff in the same way as he had earlier treated the soldiers in the regiments he commanded. He combined a paternalistic concern for their welfare with a refusal to accept any form of collective bargaining. Wherever he travelled on the company's network he made it a practice to shake hands with the stationmaster and other railwaymen at every stop along the line. He had an intense dislike of the Amalgamated Society of Railway Servants and told the members of the Royal Commission on the Railway Conciliation Scheme in 1911 that had it not been for the action of its members 'they would have been a fairly happy and contented family on the Great Eastern' {PP (1912-13) Cd 6014, q 10,010}. He deplored the early settlement of the national railway strike of 1911, confessing shortly afterwards, 'I would have fought out that strike' {*ibid* q 10,237}. His advice to the Government on the run-up to the railway strike of 1919 was 'Take off the velvet gloves' {*Times* 8 Feb 1919}.

His antipathy to government interference with the running of the railways was second only to his stubborn resistance to unionisation. From his vantage point as a long-serving member of the Railway Companies Association, an organisation which he chaired, 1906-8, he led the resistance to Ritchie's Railways (Prevention of Accidents) Bill in 1899-1900. He secured postponement of its enactment until a Royal Commission had examined the problems involved: but he failed in his attempt to stage last ditch opposition in the House of Lords and the Bill became law in 1900.

Lord Claud Hamilton had a long, but not very distinguished, parliamentary career. After representing Londonderry, 1865-68, he sat for King's Lynn, 1869-80, Liverpool, 1880-88, and South Kensington, 1910-18. He spoke in defence of railway company interests and on Irish land questions.

His business interests, apart from the Great Eastern Railway, included directorships on the East London and the Sheffield & District railway companies, the Hadfield Steel Foundry Co, the Employers' Liability Assurance Corporation, the Guyaquil & Quito Co and the London & South Western Bank. He was chairman of Egyptian Hotels Ltd. In 1887-1907 he was chairman of the Railway Clearing House.

His approach to business was authoritarian and paternalistic. He was slow to come to a point of view but thereafter most reluctant to abandon or modify it. His business associates, therefore, made a practice of briefing him thoroughly before a board meeting lest he become entrenched in an untenable position.

In his early manhood he supported Sir Wilfred Lawson's temperance campaigns through the United Kingdom Alliance. On 19 May 1870 he addressed a large meeting at the St James's Hall in London advocating a 'Permissive Prohibitory Liquor Bill' that is, a scheme for 'local option'.

He was an enthusiastic sportsman, particularly enjoying fishing and shooting. Fond of music, he prided himself on his artistic taste, and personally supervised the decoration of the Great Eastern Hotel.

In 1873 he married Carolina, daughter of Edward Chandos Pole and Lady Anna Chandos Pole. There were one son and one daughter of the marriage. Hamilton died on 26 January 1925, leaving unsettled property to the value of £110,613 gross.

PHILIP S BAGWELL

Writings:

Report on the Conference on the Rosenthal Case, by the Bishop of Rochester, Lord Claud John Hamilton etc (Longmans, Green, Reader & Dyer, 1866).

The Permissive Prohibitory Liquor Bill (Manchester: United Kingdom Alliance, 1870).

PP, RC on Railway Conciliation Scheme of 1907 (1912-13) Cd 6014.

Sources:

Unpublished

PRO, RAIL 227 Great Eastern Railway Board Minutes.

BCe.

MCe.

PrC.

Published

DNB.

Times 8 Feb 1919, 27 Jan 1925.

WWMP.

WWW.

HAMMOND, Robert

(1850-1915)

Consulting electrical engineer

Robert Hammond was born at Waltham Cross, Hertfordshire, on 19 January 1850, the son of Robert Hammond, a brewer and Ann née Weston. He was educated at Nunhead Grammar School. He worked first as a clerk with a London cloth merchant, then became involved in the iron ore trade. After a brief period in partnership as Hammond, Kyle & Co, he established Hammond & Co, iron and iron ore merchants of London, Middlesbrough and Bilbao, who appeared in trade directories from 1880 to 1887.

Hammond's attention was drawn to electric lighting when he saw Jablochkoff candle arc lights illuminating the Victoria Embankment, London, in December 1878, and in 1880 he equipped iron works in Middlesbrough with arc lighting. In November 1881 Hammond lent equipment to illustrate a lecture on electric lighting at the Cleveland Institution of Engineers. In his contribution to the discussion Hammond referred to several iron works he had lit in the area, and put forward the possibility of establishing a 'centre' in Cleveland where electricity might be generated to light a number of premises.

By 1881 Hammond had a house in Highgate, London, lit throughout by electric incandescent lamps; he gave parties to advertise the new lighting system. The same year he installed electric street lighting for Chesterfield (Derbyshire) Town Council, and formed the House to House Electric Lighting Co. The only engineer on the board of the House to House Co was A P Trotter, who did not like Hammond, finding him rather high-handed and overbearing. Hammond's company was one of the those with a concession to sell electric lighting equipment made by the Brush Co, an American firm, and in the electric lighting boom of 1882 it was the Brush concessionaire that came closest to success. It moved from selling and installing Brush arc lighting plant in factories to installing arc lighting in the streets of several towns including Brighton, Hastings and Eastbourne. In 1882 Hammond's company made a profit of £8,000 (probably by sub-selling its concession in some areas) but in 1883 there was a net loss of £30,000 and in 1885 the company went into liquidation.

Being dissatisfied with the education offered to prospective electrical engineers in the early 1880s, he founded the Hammond Electrical Engineering College in London, subsequently renamed Faraday House, which ran until 1967.

Hammond gave many lectures on electricity and electric lighting, and published in 1884 *Electric Light in Our Homes*, a detailed account of the state of electric lighting at that time. He was closely associated with the pioneer electricity system at Brighton, and many other public supply undertakings. After 1893 he gave up contracting to concentrate on consulting work, and was much in demand as an expert witness in parliamentary proceedings under the Electric Lighting Acts. He founded the journal *Lighting* in 1891, intended not just as a trade paper but also to educate the public into wanting electric light. Hammond joined the Institution of Electrical Engineers in 1888, served on its council from 1899, and became honorary treasurer in 1902.

He died on 5 August 1915 leaving £7,828 gross.

BRIAN BOWERS

Writings:

Electric Light in Our Homes (Frederick Warne & Co, 1884).

Sources:

Unpublished

BCe.

MCe.

A P Trotter, 'Reminiscences', copy in Institution of Electrical Engineers, archives.

Published

Ian C R Byatt, *The British Electrical Industry, 1875-1914. The Economic Returns to a New Technology* (Oxford: Clarendon Press, 1979).

The Electrician 6 Aug 1915.

Journal of the Institution of Electrical Engineers 43 (1915).

F W Lipscomb, *The Wise Men of the Wires* (Hutchinson, 1973).

'Pioneers of the Electrical Age: XX Robert Hammond' *Incorporated Municipal Electrical Association Journal* May-June 1938.

Proceedings of the Cleveland Institution of Electrical Engineers 43 (1915).

HAMPDEN, 1st Viscount Hampden
see BRAND, Henry Bouverie William

HANBURY-WILLIAMS, Sir John Coldbrook

(1892-1965)

Textile manufacturer

John Coldbrook Hanbury-Williams was born in Henley-on-Thames on 28 May 1892, the son of Major-General Sir John Hanbury-Williams, GCVO, KCB, CMG, who became Marshal of the Diplomatic Corps, and Annie Emily, elder daughter of Emil Reiss of the merchant firm of Reiss Brothers. After attending Wellington College, he worked for his maternal grandfather's firm who were London- and Manchester-based traders to the East. During the First World War he served with the Hussars, returning thereafter to his firm and travelling on their behalf in China and Japan. In 1926 he joined Courtaulds Ltd, became concerned with the yarn export trade and was appointed a director in 1930 at the notably young age of thirty-eight, making him by far the youngest member of the board. He remained there for thirty-two years, becoming deputy chairman in 1943 and chairman, in succession to Samuel Courtauld (qv), in 1946. He had meanwhile also been made a director of the Bank of England in 1936; he served on its Court until 1963.

As a director of Courtaulds in the 1930s his primary responsibility was for the company's foreign affairs, which meant at that time its export trade in rayon, its overseas subsidiaries, and its complex relations with its European rivals. Courtaulds had already in 1927 taken a large investment in the Italian rayon concern, Snia Viscosa, and Hanbury-Williams joined its board. He participated in numerous discussions with continental European producers in connection with various efforts to arrange price-stabilising and market-sharing agreements. For carrying out these functions in international commercial diplomacy, Hanbury-Williams was apparently well-equipped. He greatly enjoyed foreign travel; he was skilful in the deployment of urbane phrases and assiduous in the writing of polite letters. Courteous, dignified, formal and handsome, he had presence. As the *Times* obituary put it, he 'retained something of the air of the cavalry officer that perhaps he always remained at heart' {*Times* 11 Aug 1963}. In the later 1930s he was one of an inner circle of the Courtaulds board with whom Samuel Courtauld shared his concern at the company's weaknesses in organisation and its loss of technical leadership in man-made fibres. ICI had acquired from Du Pont the British rights for the manufacture of the revolutionary new fibre, nylon, and Hanbury-Williams was instrumental in securing agreement with Lord McGowan (qv) of ICI for the setting up in 1940 of a joint company, British Nylon Spinners, for the exploitation of these rights. In 1941 Hanbury-Williams took part in the unsuccessful negotiations in the USA to prevent the sale of Courtaulds' subsidiary, American Viscose Corporation, as a part of the price of American lend-lease. Like Samuel Courtauld, he remained deeply indignant at the enforced sale.

Consequently, when he took over as chairman in October 1946 one of his main aims was to restore to Courtaulds what he saw as the company's lost prestige in the international business world. Under his aegis Courtaulds recommenced production in the USA, started production in Australia, went into forestry and wood-pulp manufacture in South Africa, and continued their involvements in continental Europe. What he did not bring was any new ideas — about management or sales, improved productivity, higher profits or technical advance. He remained ignorant of, or indifferent to, new production techniques or new trends in industrial organisation. For these he relied on others. In 1937 he had shown an awareness of the company's managerial deficiencies; yet in 1952 he was still seeking to preserve what he described as the 'Gentlemen's Club atmosphere in the Board Room' {Coleman (1980) 24} which he saw as being part of the goodwill of the company. Increasingly it was the younger men on the board, notably Alan Wilson and Frank Kearton (qqv), who were providing initiatives towards expansion and change. By the later 1950s, with the absorption of British Celanese and investments in paint, chemicals, packaging and other diversified interests, Courtaulds was becoming too big and complex for Hanbury-Williams to understand and control. The overseas investments which he cherished had not yet produced worthwhile returns; falling profits from 1955 to 1959 left him dispirited. His powers were failing, but he clung to office and could be capriciously autocratic. His use of a divide-and-rule technique in exercising power was not conducive to harmony; divisions and friction within the board were exacerbated. In the summer of 1961 his retirement was announced: it was to take effect from July 1962 when he would be seventy years of age. Wilson was elected chairman-designate.

Meanwhile, however, there burst upon Courtaulds the most dramatic event of Hanbury-Williams's period of chairmanship, a take-over bid by ICI. In the summer of 1960 the chairman of ICI, Sir Paul Chambers (qv), suggested to Hanbury-Williams the possibility of a merger between the two companies. Ensuing discussions in the Courtaulds board revealed that Hanbury-Williams, unhappy about gloomy profit forecasts, liked the idea but a majority of his fellow directors did not. Although Chambers was informed of this by Hanbury-Williams he again broached the subject in October of the following year. As Hanbury-Williams was then about to depart for South Africa to visit company plants there, he handed the matter over to his deputy and chairman-designate, Alan Wilson, who continued discussions with Chambers. Hanbury-Williams returned at the end of December, by which time ICI's bid for Courtaulds had been made public. In the ensuing battle, which ended in March 1962 with effective defeat for ICI, Hanbury-Williams played no significant part. To those younger members of the board who were active in beating off the challenge he had come not merely to represent an outdated view of business behaviour but also to seem defeatist, to have lost confidence in the company of which he was still nominally head.

He was in many ways an unlikely boss of a large manufacturing company in the mid-twentieth century. His skills were those of a diplomat; his business attitudes more akin to those of a banker than an industrialist. He liked large reserves and conservative finance; he had no taste whatever for the bold or the risky in entrepreneurial adventures.

In the 1940s Hanbury-Williams undertook a number of tasks for the Government. He served at the Ministry of Economic Warfare in 1942; in 1945 he led a trade mission to Egypt; in 1948 he was appointed a government consultant on the ordering of civil aircraft, chairing a committee appointed by the Prime Minister; and from 1947 to 1953 he was a member of a committee discussing ways of reducing the costs of ligitation. In 1954 he was invited by the Duke of Edinburgh onto the Council of the Duke's Study Conference; Hanbury-Williams became honorary treasurer and later a trustee of the Study Conference fund. He was a vice-president of the National Council for Social Service, and in 1959-60, president of the International Association for the Protection of Industrial Property.

He apparently relished Court appointments and formal roles: as well as being Sheriff of the County of London in 1943 and 1958 and one of HM Lieutenants for the City of London from 1936, he was also a gentleman usher to George V, Edward VIII, and George VI and an extra gentleman usher to George VI and Elizabeth II. Hanbury-Williams was knighted in 1950 and was made CVO in 1956.

In 1928 he married Princess Zenaida Cantacuzene, daughter of the

Russian Prince Michael Cantacuzene; they had one son and two daughters. He died on 10 August 1965, leaving an estate proved at £101,441.

D C COLEMAN

Writings:

Report of the British Goodwill Trade Mission to Egypt, November-December 1945 (HMSO, 1946) (chairman).

Sources:

Unpublished

PrC.

Published

Burke's Landed Gentry.

Donald C Coleman, *Courtaulds. An Economic and Social History* (3 vols, Oxford: Clarendon Press, 1969–80) 2 and 3.

DNB.

Times 11 Aug 1965.

WWW.

HANDYSIDE, Andrew

(1806-1887)

Iron founder and constructional engineer

Andrew Handyside was born in Edinburgh in 1806. Nothing is known of his early career until 1848 when he took over the Britannia Ironworks in Duke Street, Derby, which had been founded thirty years earlier by Weatherhead & Glover. This was primarily an iron foundry famous for the production of ornamental ironwork known as 'Derby Castings', but under Handyside it began to make iron products of every kind, from machinery such as colliery winding engines and pumps to major engineering structures. A promotional book, *Works in Iron* (1868),

An Iron Kiosk manufactured by Andrew Handyside & Co displayed at South Kensington before being shipped out to Bombay, taken from the Builder *December 1866 (courtesy of Robert Thorne).*

described the firm's full range of capabilities, citing examples such as the 125-foot-span roof of the Agricultural Hall in Islington, the Royal Horticultural Society's conservatory at South Kensington and numerous railway bridges at home and abroad. For export, Handysides were ready to supply a 'Colonial Bridge' which could be put together without any rivetting or a prefabricated bungalow delivered complete with wallpaper, doors and windows. The firm's specialised knowledge of such structures enabled it to offer clients, especially railway companies, an integrated service of design, manufacture and construction with significant savings in time and cost.

Many of the firm's special commissions were designed by noted architects but for most purposes its own staff made the necessary designs and calculations. Ewing Matheson, author of two subsequent editions of *Works in Iron*, is one staff member whose name is known: R M Ordish, engineer of the Albert Bridge at Chelsea and the roof of St Enoch's Station, Glasgow, was closely associated with the firm even if not on its payroll. Handyside's constructional expertise was well illustrated in 1907 when Henry Royce, discussing the erection of the first Rolls-Royce works in Derby, wrote that by employing the company 'it would be quite unnecessary to employ an architect to prepare drawings, or to supervise the erection of the buildings, as Messrs Handyside are engaged, and have for some years been engaged, in erecting buildings of a similar nature' {Nixon (1969) 171}.

The firm was incorporated in 1873 as Andrew Handyside & Co with a nominal capital of £120,000. The workforce was then about 360 but by the end of the century had reached 1,000. Handyside was a strict disciplinarian, though concerned for the personal well-being of his workforce. He tried to stamp out the custom of Saint Monday, but he was unsuccessful in 1852 in preventing his men observing their supposed right to attend a public execution.

Handyside played a modest part in Derby public life. He was a town councillor, 1855-58, and was a director of the Derby Waterworks and the Derby & Derbyshire Banking Co. He died on 9 June 1887, leaving his Polish-born wife but no children. His personal estate was valued at £6,622. As the commission to build the Rolls-Royce works suggests, his company continued to flourish but from a height of activity in 1907, when it employed more men than ever, it plunged into liquidation in 1910.

ROBERT THORNE

Sources:

Unpublished

PRO, J13: 00314 of 1910.

PrC.

Published

Derby Daily Express 9 July 1908.

Derby Mercury 15 June 1887.

Derbyshire Advertiser 7 Apr 1961.

The Engineer 29 July 1904.

Andrew Handyside & Co, *Works in Iron* (E & F N Spon, 1868).

Gilbert Herbert, *Pioneers of Prefabrication* (Baltimore: Johns Hopkins Press, 1978).

Malcolm Higgs, 'The Exported Iron Buildings of Andrew Handyside and Co of Derby' *Journal of the Society of Architectural Historians* 29 (May 1970).

Ewing Matheson, *Works in Iron. Bridge and Roof Structures* (E & F N Spon, 1873).

Frank Nixon, *Industrial Archaeology of Derbyshire* (Newton Abbot: David & Charles, 1969).

Henry Harben (courtesy of Professor Hugh Cockerell).

HARBEN, Sir Henry

(1823-1911)

Life assurance manager

Henry Harben was born in Bloomsbury, London, on 24 August 1823, the eldest son of Henry Harben, a wholesaler in the City of London, and his wife Sarah, daughter of Benjamin Andrade. He was a first cousin of Joseph Chamberlain (qv). He was educated privately, and after a few years working in his uncle's stores, became articled to a surveyor. In 1849 he published a ready reckoner, *The Weight Calculator*, which went into several editions.

In the same year he insured his life with a newly-formed insurance company, the Prudential Mutual Insurance Investment & Loan Association (renamed in 1867 the Prudential Assurance Co Ltd). In 1852 he was one of two candidates selected for interview for the post of secretary to the association. The other candidate did not appear and Harben accepted the post but withdrew when it was represented to him that the other candidate was better placed to influence the provision of capital which the association needed. Instead he was appointed accountant, becoming secretary in 1856 when the association's annual premium income was £4,500 and its paid-up capital £5,396.

In 1854 the Prudential had started to transact industrial life assurance; at first, it was in competition with the Safety Life Assurance Co of which Bright and Cobden were directors, but that company collapsed. Industrial assurance involved the appointment of agents (salesmen-collectors) who obtained small life assurances by door-to-door solicitation and collected the premiums weekly or monthly. From 1858 Harben devoted three days a week to travelling for the purpose of appointing district superintendents and agents and addressing meetings in factories and schoolrooms. One who knew him wrote:

> A personal interview with him was an inspiration which would revive energy, create enthusiasm and ensure loyalty ... His large magnetic eyes commanded every audience and his strong yet melodious voice kept every man in the hall in rapt attention. {Plaisted (1917) 69}

He proved to have a remarkable faculty for selecting men and the Prudential slowly began to make headway against its competitors, the local burial clubs and collecting friendly societies whose agents were, he once said, 'without harshness the veriest scum of England' {*ibid* 25}.

In 1859 a chance meeting on Harben's travels led to an approach from the British Industry Life Assurance Co, a Liverpool industrial assurance company, which the Prudential took over with its staff of salesmen. Recognising Harben's part in the acquisition, the Prudential directors gave him a gold watch and offered him the choice of a debenture payable in two years, a free whole life policy for £1,000, or an endowment policy payable at age fifty. Typically Harben said he would take a whole life policy for £500 only and offered to relinquish £100 of salary owing to him, since the company was experiencing difficulty in financing its expansion. On another occasion he accepted shares in lieu of salary due. In 1863 he brought his son into the office for two years training without pay or position.

The progress of the Prudential's industrial assurance business is shown by the growth of annual premium income from £3,709 in 1856, £18,447 in 1861, £114,729 in 1866, £309,888 in 1871, to £907,444 in 1876. After the early years, expansion was self-financing.

In the 1860s the company attempted to transact sickness and fire insurance but was unsuccessful and soon withdrew. Instead it concentrated on industrial assurance and did not begin to transact ordinary life assurance on a significant scale until 1877 after Harben had left the secretaryship for the board.

Harben became an 'official associate' of the Institute of Actuaries in 1861 and a fellow in 1864. In 1870 he was appointed actuary as well as secretary to the Prudential. In 1871, the year after he became a fellow of the Institute, he addressed that body on industrial assurance. He identified the requirements for success as a more than ordinarily careful selection for outdoor work, the exercise of the most constant supervision, the closest attention to detail and above all 'a most stringent attention to the method and regularity observed at the chief office' {Harben, 20 Apr 1871}. His prescription was based on personal experience.

The business required a large clerical staff to administer it. In 1872, thanks to Harben's initiative, the Prudential became the first insurance company to employ women clerks. Growth in the head office staff was such that the Holborn Bars building, opened in 1879, had to be extended in 1898 to accommodate 2,000.

Harben's management style was that of a benevolent autocrat. To a shareholder who complained of apparent idleness in the office he said, 'I fully admit that our clerks do read the papers and chatter ... I am not prepared as manager of this company to be a nigger-driver' {Barnard (1948) 24}. In 1864 fines for lateness at the office were instituted but the money was devoted to forming a cricket club for the staff (Harben was a cricket enthusiast). In 1874 football was forbidden as it could cause staff absence through injury. The ban remained in force until after Harben's death in 1911.

Harben placed great stress on systematic contact between employers and staff, for which the Prudential has provided ever since. In 1879, for example, when 450 superintendents came to London for the company's annual dinner, each man was allowed a ten-minute interview with Harben, then resident director.

In 1872-73 Harben began to transfer his activities from day-to-day management to board membership. Under him two actuaries were appointed in 1872 and two general managers in 1873. In 1874 he relinquished the secretaryship and became resident director. He was deputy chairman from 1878 to 1905, when at the age of eighty-two he became chairman. In 1907 he was made president. His only son Henry Andrade Harben, a director of the Prudential from 1879, succeeded his father as chairman but died before him in 1910.

Harben was an innovator. In 1864 his company formed an estate department and a statistical department. In 1866 medical examinations for all purposes were discontinued. In 1871 the Prudential published its mortality experience with observations by Harben.

Harben became the recognised authority on sound industrial assurance. He gave evidence to the Royal Commission on Friendly Societies (1871-74). His organisation of the Prudential was the model for the (unconnected) Prudential Insurance Co of America (1875) which became the largest life assurance company in the USA. His work for the Prudential was well summarised by Sydney Webb, who said 'The history of the Prudential is a record of steady endeavour in many directions to reform the conduct of industrial assurance business ... colossal and long continued expansion secured by a prudent and skilful and extremely economical administration [is] remarkable for its continuity' {*New Statesman* Special Supplement 13 Mar 1915}.

It was Harben's achievement to lay a lasting foundation for the enterprise that by 1887 held three-quarters of the companies' share of industrial assurance, with 7 million policies in force and a premium income of £3 million. The Prudential became and has remained the largest life assurance company in Britain. By the time he died it had 20 million policies in force and its investments exceeded £60 million.

For much of his life Harben was a teetotaller and non-smoker. Outside his business he had many public activities in his later years. Living for nearly fifty years in Hampstead he represented Hampstead on the Metropolitan Board of Works from 1881, and from 1889 to 1894 on the London County Council. He became Hampstead's first mayor in 1900. He paid for a wing of the Hampstead General Hospital and gave £5,000 towards building the Central Public Library.

Among other benefactions he gave large sums to the Carpenters' Company for educational work, endowed lectures and a gold medal for the Institute of Public Health, and spent over £50,000 on a convalescent home for working men at Rustington, Sussex.

Harben acquired a landed estate at Warnham, Sussex where he built the village hall and club, and a fine cricket ground. He was a DL for Sussex and was High Sheriff of the county in 1898. He was knighted in 1897. A Conservative, he unsuccessfully contested Norwich in 1880 and Cardiff in 1885.

In 1846 Harben married Ann (d 1883), daughter of James Such; they had one son, Henry Andrade. In 1890 he re-married, to Mary Jane, daughter of Thomas Bullman Cole; they had at least one daughter. He died on 2 December 1911, leaving an estate proved at £393,929 gross.

H COCKERELL

Writings:

The Weight Calculator, Being a Series of Tables ... Exhibiting the Exact Value of Any Weight from 1 Lb to 15 Tons ... from 1 Penny to 168 Shillings per Cwt. (1849).

History of Industrial Assurance — abstract of a paper read at the Institute of Actuaries, 20 Apr 1871.

Mortality Experience of the Prudential Assurance Company ... for the Years 1867, 1868, 1869, 1870, with Observations by Henry Harben (C & E Layton, 1871).

PP, RC on Friendly and Benefit Building Societies, 3rd Report (1873) C 842.

The Discount Guide; Comprising Several Series of Tables for the Use of Merchants, Manufacturers ... (C Lockwood & Co, 1877).

Sources:

Unpublished

MCe.

PrC.

Published

R W Barnard, *A Century of Service — The Story of the Prudential, 1848-1948* (Prudential Assurance Co, 1948).

DNB.

Insurance Record 8 Dec 1911.

H Plaisted, *The Prudential Past and Present* (C & E Layton, 1917).

Post Magazine 9 Dec 1911.

Times 4 Dec 1911.

Cornelius Walford, *The Insurance Cyclopaedia* (6 vols, C & E Layton, 1871-80) 6.

Sydney Webb, 'Industrial Assurance' *New Statesman* Special Supplement 13 Mar 1915.

Sir Arnold Wilson and Hermann Levy, *Industrial Assurance: An Historical and Critical Study* (Oxford: Oxford University Press, 1937).

WWW.

HARDING, Sir Robert Palmer

(1821-1893)

Accountant

Robert Palmer Harding was born in 1821, the son of Robert Harding (d 1862), an auctioneer, appraiser and house agent. Reportedly he began his

Sir Robert Palmer Harding (1821–1893) by Sir Edgar Boehm (courtesy of Ernst & Whinney).

business career running a fashionable West-End hatters. When this got into financial difficulties and his books were produced in court, Harding was complimented on his record keeping and the official suggested that he might enter accountancy. He followed this advice and set up on his own in July 1847. Forming a partnership with Edmund Pullein (d 1866) in August 1848, the two practised in the City at 16 Gresham Street by 1850. They prospered and in November 1857 Frederick Whinney (qv) was admitted as a partner; in December 1858 a fourth, James Boatwright Gibbons, joined the partnership, its style changing in January 1859 to Harding, Pullein, Whinney & Gibbons. The death of Gibbons in 1872 resulted in the name becoming Harding, Whinney & Co with R P Harding remaining as the senior partner until 1883 when he retired from the firm.

During the mid-Victorian period insolvencies contributed the principal share of an accountant's fees, and Harding was successful because he became one of the City's acknowledged experts in liquidations and bankruptcy work. Among the concerns he liquidated were: the Marylebone Bank (from 1853), Royal British Bank (1856), Athenaeum Life Assurance Society (1856), Mexican & South American Co (1857), National Alliance Assurance (1859), Mitre General Life (1860) and National Assurance (Bank of Deposit), Professional Life, Life Assurance Treasury, and English and Irish Church Assurance (all in 1861). During 1858 93 per cent of his firm's fee income was earned from insolvencies, a percentage that only declined to 72 per cent in 1880 and 66 per cent in 1884. In 1866 the Select Committee on the Limited Liability Acts revealed that of the 259 companies then in liquidation 61 were being handled by Harding, Whinney & Co and that this represented £20.3 million of the £92.1 million involved. It was significant, therefore, that Harding in conjunction with William Turquand (qv) should have been appointed to wind up the affairs of Overend, Gurney & Co, which crashed with spectacular repercussions on 11 May 1866, known in financial circles as 'Black Friday'. Such was the scale of the collapse that the insolvency work continued for twenty-eight years and in total Harding's firm earned £43,205 in fees. His contribution may, in part, be measured by Harding, Whinney & Co's growing fee income; it rose from £221 in 1848 (August-December) to £12,470 in 1883, having reached £32,268 in 1866, the year of the Overend, Gurney failure.

Harding's expertise did not lie primarily in the field of auditing. Like other leading City accountants of the day, his audit practice was limited and made only a minor contribution to the firm's fee income even in 1884 (19.8 per cent). Nevertheless, in view of its future importance the value of this work should not be ignored. Harding himself was auditor of the Central Argentine Railway and living near to his close friend Octavious V Morgan in Queen's Gate, Kensington, he secured Morgan Bros, the Battersea iron founders, as clients. Other audits attracted during the period of Harding's senior partnership included the International Financial Society (1863), Law Union Life Insurance Co (1863) and the Union Bank of Australia (1880).

Before the promulgation of a code of professional conduct, accountants generally performed a variety of tasks. Harding & Pullein were described in the *Post Office Directory* for 1850 as arbitrators; others doubled as auctioneers, agents and appraisers. Indeed, Harding continued to act as a house agent (his father's occupation) throughout the 1860s and early 1870s

A Victorian accountant's office, re-created for the English Institute's Centenary Exhibition in 1980, which features a number of account books from the firm that Sir Robert Palmer Harding founded in August 1848 (courtesy of Ernst & Whinney).

in the Norwood, Beulah Hill and Peckham areas. Doubtless the large fees to be earned from insolvency (and the introduction of the English Institute's rules in 1880) meant that this work was both inadvisable and comparatively unprofitable.

Much debate surrounded the question whether liquidations should be performed by officials or by members of the profession and there was discussion over their remuneration. A commission system operated after the passage of the 1869 Bankruptcy Act when trustees in bankruptcy were appointed directly by the courts. In 1883 Joseph Chamberlain (qv), the President of the Board of Trade, decided to set up a Bankruptcy Department and create a network of 67 Official Receivers to superintend the work. Because of his 'large experience in the administration of estates' {*The Accountant* 6 Oct 1883} and possibly because in 1864 he had been a commissioner called to inquire into the Bankruptcy Acts and in 1877 gave evidence to the Select Committee on the 1862 and 1867 Companies Acts, R P Harding was asked to serve as Chief Official Receiver. Having completed his year of office as president of the English Institute of Chartered Accountants, he had, in fact, been about to retire from the senior partnership of Harding, Whinney & Co and had to be persuaded by Chamberlain to postpone a life of comparative leisure. His salary was £2,000 per annum (without a pension) and although appointed for five years this term was extended for a further eighteen months. Acceptance of the post in October 1883 resulted in his resignation from the Institute's council and he also gave up his membership. On retiring from the post in 1890 Harding received a knighthood and became the first chartered accountant to gain such an honour.

Harding, like Turquand, played a major role in the campaign to win recognition for accountants as a respected profession. He was among the 37 who signed the draft rules of the Institute of Accountants in London (a predecessor body of the English Institute of Chartered Accountants) and sat on the first council of twelve during its foundation year, 1870. The deputation (consisting of Turquand, the president, S L Price and Harding) that gave evidence in 1877 before Disraeli's Select Committee on the 1862 and 1867 Companies Acts, by participating in the Parliamentary process, did much to pave the way for official approval. Eventually in May 1880 a petition for a charter of incorporation was granted. Because John Ball had died in 1879, Harding had been elected vice-president of the Institute and he and Turquand actually received the charter. Harding in due course became second president of the Institute of Chartered Accountants in England and Wales, 1882-83. Together with Whinney, Turquand, Kemp and Arthur Cooper (qv), he was delegated to negotiate with the Board of Trade on any matters that might affect the profession.

An obituary stated that 'Sir Robert was a conspicuously able man, although unlike his partner [Frederick Whinney], not showing to great advantage in public. But his powers of organisation and control were superb; but this will be apparent from the long list of large concerns he was engaged in.' {*Accountant* 30 Dec 1893} Harding, in common with his colleagues on the first council of the Institute, was a man of entrepreneurial vision and energies. First, he had to establish his own firm as a profitable business in its own right, then devise means to cope with changing accounting problems, and finally join in the campaign to raise his calling to the level of a profession, whilst in later life Harding put his accumulated knowledge to the test as a senior civil servant. Harding & Pullein eventually became Whinney, Smith & Whinney, a practice which, through internal growth and merger, was to be included among the 'Big Eight' as Ernst & Whinney.

He married in 1845 Marion Martha Ryle, the daughter of Joseph Ryle, and they had eight children (Ann, Edith, Arthur, Kate, Cornelia, Stanley, Alice and Mabel) who variously married into the Morgan (of Morgan Crucible), Peto (the builders) and Chapman (the publishers) families.

When Harding died on 22 December 1893 he left £54,530 gross.

EDGAR JONES

Writings:

PP, HC 1877 (365) VIII, SC on Companies Acts, 1862 and 1867.

Sources:

Unpublished

PrC.

Published

The Accountant IX, No 461 (6 Oct 1883), XVI, No 787 (4 Jan 1890), XIX, No 995 (30 Dec 1893).

The History of the Institute of Chartered Accountants in England and Wales 1870-1965 (Heinemann, 1966).

Edgar Jones, *Accountancy and the British Economy 1840-1890, the Evolution of Ernst & Whinney* (Batsford, 1981).

Robert H Parker (ed), *British Accountants, a Biographical Sourcebook* (New York: Arno Press, 1980).

PP 1867 (329) X, SC on Limited Liability Acts.

HARLAND, Sir Edward James

(1831-1895)

Shipbuilder

Edward James Harland was born in May 1831 in Scarborough, the sixth child of a family of eight. His father, William Harland, a native of Rosedale, North Yorkshire, had studied medicine at Edinburgh

Sir Edward Harland (courtesy of Harland & Wolff Ltd).

University, and practised in Scarborough almost until his death in 1866. Dr Harland, three times mayor and a JP for the borough, had a great interest in mechanical matters: he patented a steam-carriage for running on roads in 1827, and was a friend of George Stephenson. Edward Harland's mother was the daughter of Gawan Pierson, a landed proprietor of Goathland, near Rosedale. She shared her husband's mechanical interests, and under her direction the nursery became a miniature workshop with the children making their own toys. Harland in his later years remarked that he had been brought up in a house of 'industry and mechanism' {Harland (1884) 290-91}.

Harland was educated at Sunderland Grammar School until the age of twelve, when he was sent to the Edinburgh Academy. After two years, however, he returned to Scarborough following the death of his mother. At school Harland was fond of drawing and geometry, but preferred to spend his time (including schooltime) watching and assisting the men in the town's various workshops, and in the yards of the wooden-shipbuilding firm of William & Robert Tindall. (William, who lived in London, was associated with Lloyds.) While at the Edinburgh Academy Harland received a classical training, but this was supplemented by valuable instruction in mathematics and mechanics from his eldest brother William, who was then a medical student at the University.

Although his father would have preferred him to be a barrister, Harland decided to become an engineer. Through George Stephenson, Harland's father arranged for him to serve a five-year apprenticeship at the engineering works of Robert Stephenson & Co in Newcastle upon Tyne, where he started on his fifteenth birthday. He spent the first four years in the various workshops, and the final year in the drawing office. On completion of his apprenticeship in May 1851 Harland became a journeyman, but as business was slack he decided to leave the firm. After spending two months visiting the Great Exhibition in London, he proceeded to Glasgow with a letter of introduction to the engine-building firm of J & G Thomson. This letter was furnished by James Bibby of the Liverpool shipping firm of J Bibby, Sons & Co, at the instigation of Harland's friend Gustav Christian Schwabe, a large shareholder in the Bibby line and the uncle of Harland's future partner, Gustav Wilhelm Wolff (qv). When Thomsons decided to start building their own vessels they made increasing use of Harland, and he was promoted to head draughtsman. In 1853, on the recommendation of Messrs Stephenson, Harland was appointed manager by Thomas Toward, a shipbuilder at St Peter's-on-the-Tyne. Toward left Harland in charge of the works but as there did not appear to be much prospect of developing the business, Harland moved to the Belfast shipyard of Robert Hickson & Co in late December 1854.

Hickson, who owned the Eliza Street Ironworks in Belfast, had started to build iron sailing ships in the previous year. His yard comprised a 1.84 acre site on the Queen's Island, which he leased from the Belfast Harbour Commissioners, who had formed the Island at the end of the 1840s when making a cut to straighten the River Lagan. (It ceased to be an island when the bed of the old river was filled up.) Harland found wages there to be above what he regarded as the normal rate. His decision to reduce wages while raising the quality of the work provoked a strike, to which Harland responded by enlisting fresh labour from the Clyde and Newcastle. After three years as manager he decided to start his own shipbuilding firm, and made enquiries at various places, including Garston and Birkenhead. When Hickson, who had no practical knowledge of shipbuilding, heard of Harland's plans, he offered to sell him the yard, as he had no desire to continue the business without him. The purchase was completed, at a price of £5,000, with the assistance of G C Schwabe whose nephew, G W Wolff, had been Harland's private assistant for a few months. The precise nature of the transaction between Harland and Schwabe is not known, but it is possible that Schwabe lent £5,000 to Harland on condition that he took his nephew into business as a partner. Harland and Wolff were acting as partners from the date of Hickson's handover to Harland on 1 November 1858, even though the actual partnership agreement was not signed until 11 April 1861.

Schwabe was also instrumental in gaining customers for the new partnership in its early years. From the beginning he persuaded the Bibby partners to place substantial orders, and then in 1869 he suggested to Thomas Henry Ismay (qv), the owner of the White Star Line, that if Ismay built a fleet of iron ships for the Atlantic service and entrusted its construction to Harland & Wolff, then he would provide finance. Harland and Wolff both became individual shareholders in Ismay's newly incorporated Oceanic Steam Navigation Co, which operated the White Star Line.

The orders by the Bibby and White Star Lines were each responsible for initiating revolutionary changes in ship design. Harland was the first shipbuilder to perceive that an iron ship need not be kept to the lines that were most suitable for wooden vessels. The ships built for Bibby were made much longer than usual in relation to their breadth, so giving them increased carrying capacity without any loss of speed. To compensate for this extra length the upper deck was made entirely of iron, the hull becoming like a box girder, far stronger than the more orthodox designs. Carrying capacity was increased further by making the bottoms of the ships flatter and the bilges squarer (the 'Belfast bottom'), while the manoeuvrability of these longer vessels was improved by making their stems almost vertical. Although these new ships were expected by some critics to break their backs in rough weather, and were named by them 'Bibby coffins', in fact they proved robust, and Harland & Wolff gained additional work lengthening vessels built by other firms. The *Oceanic*, launched for the White Star Line in 1870, was in design the first of the modern ocean liners. A major novelty with this vessel was the placing of the first-class accommodation amidships, where the motion of the ship was felt least, away from the traditional location at the stern. In addition the first-class saloon area was made more spacious by extending it to the full width of the vessel. These changes were quickly adopted by other companies.

The period from 1860 to 1913 was one in which there was a growing international traffic of people and commodities, and a significant upward trend in the world demand for shipping services. With the development of the iron, and then the steel, steamship, UK shipping companies came to dominate this growing international commerce; at the same time the UK became the leading shipbuilding country in the world. As Harland &

Wolff was able to compete effectively with other UK yards, it received increasing numbers of orders from various shipping firms. For the period from 1859 until Harland's death in 1895, White Star was the chief customer, purchasing nearly 20 per cent of total output in terms of gross tonnage launched, while the Bibby Line bought 7 per cent. (In 1859-69, however, Bibby purchased just over 50 per cent of Harland & Wolff's total production.) Other shipping lines, which purchased between 3 and 7 per cent of output, included F Leyland & Co, the Elder Dempster Group (including the African Steamship Co), the Asiatic Steamship Co, T & J Brocklebank, the Union Steamship Co, the Pacific Steam Navigation Co, and the British Shipowners Co. Admiralty orders totalled only 0.5 per cent. Contrary to general belief, Harland & Wolff did not specialise in passenger liners, although it does seem to have specialised in larger-sized vessels. Nor were fluctuations in its output evened out by large liner companies, such as White Star, placing orders mainly in years of depression or cyclical downswing.

In the first two decades of production Harland & Wolff's steamers were fitted with engines supplied from England and Scotland, but in 1880 the firm established its own engine works and boiler shops, and started to make all its own machinery. This development necessitated an extension of the works, which increased from 9.5 acres in 1874 to 40 acres in 1880. The land was still leased from the Belfast Harbour Commissioners who, with Harland as their chairman, co-operated fully in the development of the shipyard, particularly in the building of graving docks to accommodate the growing size of vessels.

By this time, however, Harland was withdrawing from active involvement in the firm, and direction passed increasingly to William James Pirrie (qv), who had been made a partner in the business, together with Walter H Wilson, in 1874. Both men had served apprenticeships under Harland. In 1885 the firm was incorporated in Dublin as the Queen's Island Shipbuilding & Engineering Co Ltd, with an issued share capital of £297,500. Three years later the company reverted to the name of Harland & Wolff. By the time of Harland's death in 1895 the firm's paid-up capital had increased to £446,000, of which Harland held a third. Apart from three token shares held by wives, the rest was divided among the other partners.

The output of the firm, in terms of gross tonnage launched, reached a peak of 15,925 tons in 1874 and it did not surpass this figure until the early 1880s. In each of the four years 1891-94 output was well over 60,000 gross tons, which was the greatest output of any single shipbuilding firm in the UK, and represented over 6 per cent of total UK output for these years. Harland & Wolff's performance contributed substantially to Belfast becoming the fastest-growing shipbuilding region in the UK in the late nineteenth century. By the mid-1890s the yard, which then covered 80 acres, employed nearly 8,000 men. The average wage of these men was below that paid to shipyard workers in other major regions, as it had been from 1871 and probably earlier, but the differential was narrowing. It would seem that labour inputs were the main source of the firm's growth and this would accord with the traditional hypothesis that a major cause of Belfast's shipbuilding development was the availability of cheap labour, particularly in the case of less-skilled men. (The wage differential between skilled and unskilled labour was much higher in Belfast than in Great Britain.)

By the time of his death Harland had long ceased to have any active involvement in the firm that bore his name. He had already started to reduce these commitments after the extension of the partnership in 1874. The following year he became chairman of the Belfast Harbour Commissioners, having already served three years as a commissioner, and he retained this office until retiring from the board in 1887. Harland became alderman for the St Anne's Ward of Belfast Council in 1884, and he was elected mayor in 1885 and again in 1886. During his first year of office a baronetcy was conferred upon him. Sir Edward Harland was appointed High Sheriff for County Down in 1887. He became a member of the Westminster Parliament in August 1889, when he was returned unopposed as Conservative MP for the North Belfast constituency. He held the seat until his death six years later. As an MP Harland opposed Gladstone's second Home Rule Bill in 1893.

Harland was a Unitarian and a member of the First Congregation in Rosemary Street, Belfast. In 1860 he married Rosa Matilda, daughter of Thomas Wann of Vermont, Belfast. There were no children. He died on 24 December 1895, leaving an estate proved at £67,438 gross (in England) and at £226,638 gross (in Ireland).

W JOHNSON *and* F GEARY

Writings:

'Shipbuilding in Belfast — Its Origins and Progress' in Samuel Smiles, *Men of Invention and Industry* (John Murray, 1884).

PP, RC on Belfast Riots (1887) C 4925-1.

Sources:

Unpublished

Harland & Wolff Ltd, Queen's Island, Belfast, archives.

PrC.

D Rebbeck, 'The History of Iron Shipbuilding on the Queen's Island up to July 1874' (Queen's University, Belfast PhD, 1950).

F Geary and W Johnson, 'Growth and Fluctuations in Belfast Shipbuilding Output, 1859-1913' Paper for the Annual Conference of the Economic and Social History Society of Ireland, Sept 1981.

Published

Roy Anderson, *White Star* (Prescot: T Stephenson & Sons, 1964).

Belfast Evening Telegraph 24 Dec 1895.

The Belfast News-Letter 25, 28 Dec 1895.

W E Coe, *The Engineering Industry of the North of Ireland* (Newton Abbot: David & Charles, 1969).

Laurence Dunn, *Famous Liners of the Past: Belfast Built* (Adlard Coles, 1964).

Basil Greenhill and Ann Giffard, *Travelling by Sea in the Nineteenth Century: Interior Design in Victorian Passenger Ships* (Adam & Charles Black, 1972).

Herbert Jefferson, *Viscount Pirrie of Belfast* (Belfast: Wm Mullan & Son, 1948). 1948).

The Northern Whig 25 Dec 1895.

C H Oldham, 'The History of Belfast Shipbuilding' *Proceedings of the Statistical and Social Inquiry Society of Ireland* 1911.

Wilton J Oldham, *The Ismay Line: The White Star Line, and the Ismay Family Story* (Liverpool: *Journal of Commerce*, 1961).

David J Owen, *A Short History of the Port of Belfast* (Belfast: Mayne, Boyd & Son, Ltd, 1917).

—, *History of Belfast* (Belfast: W & G Baird, 1921).

J Gordon Peirson, *Great Ship Builders or The Rise of Harland and Wolff* (Arthur H Stockwell, 1935).

Sidney Pollard and Paul Robertson, *The British Shipbuilding Industry, 1870-1914* (Cambridge, Massachusetts: Harvard University Press, 1979).

A Wilson, 'The Shipbuilding Industry in Belfast' *Proceedings of the Belfast Natural History and Philosophical Society* 1915.

WWMP.

HARMAN, Alfred Hugh

(1841-1913)

Photographic equipment manufacturer

Alfred Hugh Harman was born in 1841, the son of Thomas Harman, a bootmaker. Nothing is known of his early life until in 1860 he married Amelia Ann Taylor, the daughter of a greengrocer, John Taylor. They had seven children.

By 1863 Harman was in partnership with a Frenchman called Dage in a photographic printing business in Peckham. He set up on his own in the following year, and in 1868 moved to larger premises in Peckham High Street and opened a studio in Surbiton, Surrey. He advertised a wide

HARMAN Alfred Hugh

A H Harman (courtesy of Mr R J Hercock).

range of photographic services including printing and enlarging by the bromide, carbon or collodion processes and enlargements hand-coloured in water or oil colours.

In 1879 he decided to manufacture the newly-invented photographic dry plates. To this end, he sold his photographic business and, with his second wife, Nina Octavia Helvetia née du Gué, moved to the small village of Ilford in Essex. There he rented a large house in Cranbrook Road, where with the help of two men and three boys, and at busy times of his wife and his housekeeper, he made the emulsion and coated it on glass plates. Daily he drove to London in a pony and trap to deliver the previous day's production to his agents, Marion & Co of Soho Square. He called his firm the Britannia Works.

This business prospered and within a short time he rented a cottage for 10s a week on the Clyde Estate near Ilford Broadway, where plates were coated with emulsion made in Cranbrook Road. Shortly afterwards he bought houses in Grove Terrace nearby and thereafter emulsion was made in the cottage and coated, packed and stored in the Grove Terrace houses. To meet the increasing demand for his products a special factory was built on the site in 1883.

In 1885 he quarrelled with Marion & Co and ended their agreement. At the same time he changed the name of his products from 'Britannia' to 'Ilford', halved his prices and changed the firm's name from Britannia Works to the Britannia Works Co.

In 1891 he formed a private limited company with a capital of £120,000. The firm was by now producing a range of plates and photographic papers and machine coating had replaced hand coating. He introduced a profit-sharing scheme for his employees and paid them better than average rates for the times.

As his health failed Harman decided to retire and in 1893 engaged Edward Ball Knobel (qv), who was distantly related to his second wife, as a scientific expert and managing director. The following year Harman retired to Grayswood Place, a large house standing in its own grounds near Haslemere in Surrey. However, he did not entirely relinquish control of the company.

In 1895 he had the Britannia Institute built at his own expense and presented it to the firm. The object of the Institute was to provide hot breakfasts and lunches for his workmen (they worked from 6.0 am to 6.0 pm) and for their recreation, entertainment and education.

Between 1892 and 1897 profits increased from £31,000 to £47,000 a year. In 1892, £24,000 was distributed to shareholders and in 1897, £33,000. As Harman was the major shareholder, most of the profits went to him (98 per cent in 1892, 80 per cent in 1897). Over these six years he received about £150,000.

In 1898 he sold the business for £380,000, of which he received 80 per cent. He refused a directorship in the new company and ceased to have an active interest in it although he was still consulted on various matters from time to time.

Harman took an interest in local affairs in Haslemere and in 1898 he financed and endowed a new church and vicarage at Grayswood. The church was consecrated in 1902. Sadly, the first person to be buried in the churchyard was his wife, Nina.

Harman died on 25 May 1913, leaving £333,739 gross. Most of his net estate of £266,000 was left to various charities.

R J HERCOCK

Sources:

Unpublished

MCe.

PrC.

Published

R J Hercock and G A Jones, *Silver by the Ton. The History of Ilford Limited, 1879-1979* (McGraw-Hill, 1979).

HARMOOD-BANNER, Sir John Sutherland

(1847-1927)

Accountant and steel manufacturer

John Sutherland Harmood-Banner (taken from E Gaskell Lancashire Leaders. Social and Political *Queenhithe Printing and Publishing Co Ltd).*

John Sutherland Harmood-Banner was born at Dingle Mount, Liverpool on 8 September 1847, the second son of Harmood Walcot Banner (1814-78), of Harrington Chambers, Liverpool and Pool Bank, New Ferry, Wirral, Cheshire, and Margaret née Sutherland. His paternal grandfather was a founder of the Liverpool Stock Exchange; his father was a Liverpool accountant who left under £160,000, and was sometime chairman of the Liverpool & Harrington Water Co and Liverpool & Harrington Gas Co. He was educated at Radley in 1856-64, and entered his father's accountancy firm in 1865, becoming a partner in 1870. His elder brother Harmood Banner was a coffee planter in Ceylon, where he died in 1868. In 1875 he married Elizabeth (1850-1903), daughter and co-heiress of Thomas Knowles (1824-83), of Darnhall, Winsford, Conservative MP for Wigan from 1874. They had four sons and two daughters. His father-in-law, who was mayor of Wigan in 1864 and 1865, was a cotton spinner and bleacher and colliery owner in Lancashire who left £194,977 (naming Harmood-Banner as an executor); he also chaired Pearson & Knowles, a Warrington company formed in 1874 by the amalgamation of several coal and iron works. Harmood-Banner's marriage proved important in shaping his later

43

career, as he joined the board of Pearson & Knowles and became deputy chairman after his father-in-law's death.

Harmood-Banner's business interests outside accountancy were mostly based in Liverpool in the 1880s and 1890s, when he lived at Puddington Hall in Cheshire. He joined the board of the Liverpool Reversionary Co and remained there until his death, long after the company's acquisition by Eagle Star Insurance. He was also a director of the Liverpool Electric Supply Co, and in 1888 joined other Liverpool businessmen in forming the Taquah & Abosso Gold Mining Co which held a fifty-year lease on mining properties at Wassaw on the Gold Coast. The mine's gold production in 1889-93 was worth a total of £49,137, but its accounts were in deficit of £29,196 and its debentures were in arrears by 1894. Harmood-Banner in 1889 also became a director of the newly-formed Spes Bona Mining Co with properties in Transvaal, and acted as chairman of the reconstructed company in 1891-94. Though gold worth £26,011 was extracted from the Spes Bona mines in the first four months of 1894, owing to heavy capital expenditure, profit of only £745 was yielded and the company was suspended until fresh capital could be raised. Its properties were subsequently transferred to a company registered in South Africa. Around 1896 Harmood-Banner became a trustee of the Anglo-Chilian Nitrate & Railway Co which held many of its interests at Antofagasta.

His father had been a city councillor in Liverpool, and in 1895 Harmood-Banner became councillor for its Exchange Ward. He served as chairman of the council's finance committee, and used his financial expertise in negotiating corporation loans. He was a JP and DL for Cheshire, of which he was High Sheriff in 1902, and was president of the Association of Municipal Corporations in 1907. After serving as Lord Mayor of Liverpool in 1912, he was made an alderman in 1914. At a by-election in 1905 Harmood-Banner was elected Unionist MP for Everton. Like other Lancashire Unionists such as Birch Crisp (qv), he described himself as a 'Tory Democrat', but from then until his retirement from parliament in 1924 he also presented himself as a 'Reformation candidate who denounced ritualism, an endowed Catholic university for Ireland and a revised King's declaration' {Waller (1981) 211}. A strong supporter of Ulster Protestants, his political success in Liverpool was based on sectarian bigotry. In the House of Commons he was highly influential as a member of sub-committees on commercial subjects and was recognised as a spokesman of Lancashire business opinion. He was listed by the *Brewers Almanack* as a political friend of the licensed trade which was as typical of Liverpool Tory politics as his strident Orange position. This later led to him holding several directorships in the liquor business, and in 1915 he was a member of the Cabinet Committee on the financial aspects of liquor trade restrictions. As representative of Pearson & Knowles, he was a founding member of the Executive Council of the Federation of British Industries in 1916, but Harmood-Banner was not always malleable to the wishes of the Birmingham manufacturers who dominated the FBI in its early years. They clashed, for example, over the Education Bill of 1918.

He was a member of the Government committee on a luxuries tax in 1918, of the Royal Commission on income tax in 1919 and a member of the Railway Rates Tribunal in 1921-22. He was knighted in 1913 and created a baronet in 1924.

Having served as deputy chairman of Pearson & Knowles for some two decades, he was its chairman in 1912-20, and also chaired its subsidiary the Moss Hall Coal Co and was first chairman of the Partington Steel Co. Pearson & Knowles bought in 1906-7 the wire firm of Rylands, with which it had long shared a chairman and which under the style of Rylands Bros continued as the wire department of Pearson & Knowles. It was subsequently decided that the group should be able to supply Rylands with semi-manufactured steel for its wire rod, hoop and strip from its own facilities, and in 1910 the Partington Steel Co was promoted with capital of £700,000. A site of 90 acres was acquired at Irlam near Warrington on the banks of the Manchester Ship Canal, and three blast-furnaces were erected, together with by-product coke ovens, open-hearth furnaces and rolling mills to produce 3,000 tons weekly of billets, rails, joists and sections. Full production began in 1913. The development of Partington was the largest single investment project in the Edwardian steel industry.

The group was enormously expanded during the First World War. Partington alone built three new blast furnaces in 1914-18, and the Pearson & Knowles group almost doubled its steel milling capacity, duplicated its wire rod mill, increased fourfold its output of barbed wire and added 152 new coke ovens. The expansion was hectic and strenuous: after the war the conjunction of surplus capacity and heavy interest charges considerably embarrassed the group. Before the full extent of these difficulties was evident, control of Pearson & Knowles, together with its subsidiaries, was sold in 1920 to Armstrong, Whitworth. Harmood-Banner thereupon left Pearson & Knowles' board, and it was left to Sir Peter Rylands (qv) to fight the mismanagement and misuse of resources by Armstrong's chairman, Sir Glynn West (qv).

As an accountant Harmood-Banner was involved in the reconstruction of several companies in financial difficulties. After the interest on the debentures of the Burton on Trent brewers, Samuel Allsopp & Son, fell into arrears in 1911, he acted in the capital reduction of 1912-13. In 1916 the refreshment contractors of Spiers & Ponds, who owned Bailey's Hotel and the South Kensington Hotel, went into liquidation after failing to pay debenture and debenture stock interest and continued under Court supervision until 1918, when a reorganisation scheme was agreed. New management and directors were appointed under Harmood-Banner's chairmanship.

Harmood-Banner, who condemned the Licensing Bill of 1908 as 'gross and abominable robbery' {Waller (1981) 236}, was subsequently chairman of the Liverpool brewers and spirit merchants, Robert Cain & Sons. He was a parliamentary advocate of a Land Values Bill, and was chairman in 1922-26 of Peter Walker Ltd, a property company based at Warrington and Burton on Trent. Another property company which he chaired was Canadian City & Town Properties formed in 1910.

In his latter years Harmood-Banner was deputy chairman of British Insulated & Helsby Cables. He was also a director of its subsidiary Midlands Electric Corporation, which held concessions in Staffordshire and Worcestershire, of the Electric Supply Co of Victoria owning light, power and tram rights at Ballarat and Bendigo, of La Plata Electric Tramways, of Automatic Telephone Manufacturing Co and of Telegraph

Manufacturing (Colonial) Ltd. His associates on all these boards included Alexander Roger (qv).

Other directorships were given to him by fellow Conservative backbenchers, such as Davison Dalziel (qv) of the Pullman Car Co, and Major Sir Richard Barnett (1863-1930) of the Oilfields Finance Corporation. In addition to joining the board of these two companies, he was chairman of Black Sea Amalgamated Oilfields which was part of the Anglo-Maikop group, and of Kuban Black Sea Oilfields which held leases at Suvorov-Tcherkess from 1911 but lost control after the Russian Revolution.

Harmood-Banner became chairman in 1921 of the grandiosely-named Imperial & Finance Corporation, and a director in 1921 of a foreign banking firm in London run by Nevile Foster. He also chaired the General Investors & Trustees Co formed in 1907. He was president of the Institute of Chartered Accountants in 1904-5, and long-serving auditor of the Bank of Liverpool and the Lancashire & Yorkshire Railway.

After the death of his first wife, he married secondly, in 1908, Henrietta Sella Linford (1878-1954). He relinquished most of his engagements because of ill-health around 1924-25, and died on 24 February 1927 at Ingmire Hall, Sedbergh. He left £449,279 gross.

R P T DAVENPORT-HINES

Writings:

letter on administration of Hulton colliery accident relief fund *Times* 23 Oct 1913.

letter on British investments in Brazil *ibid* 6 July 1914.

Sources:

Unpublished

HLRO, Lloyd George papers C/23/2/11-13.

PRO, Cab 37/127/14.

University of Warwick, Modern Records Centre, papers of Federation of British Industries.

BCe.

PrC.

Published

James C Carr and Walter Taplin, *History of the British Steel Industry* (Oxford: Blackwell, 1962).

Avner Offer, *Property and Politics 1870-1914* (Cambridge: Cambridge University Press, 1981).

Times 25 Feb 1927.

Philip J Waller, *Democracy and Sectarianism* (Liverpool: Liverpool University Press, 1981).

WWMP.

WWW.

*Alfred Harmsworth, Lord Northcliff
(from Mrs Stuart Menzies,* Modern
Men of Mark, *Herbert Jenkins Ltd,
1921).*

HARMSWORTH, Alfred Charles William

Viscount Northcliffe

(1865-1922)

Newspaper and periodicals proprietor

Alfred Charles William Harmsworth was born at Chapelizod, near Dublin, on 15 July 1865, the eldest of fourteen children (three of whom died in infancy) of Alfred Harmsworth (1837-1889), a former schoolteacher then reading for the Bar, and Geraldine Mary (1838-1925), daughter of William Maffett, a prosperous Dublin land agent. The Harmsworths were Hampshire labourers and smallholders, though in later years the family liked to hint at some infusion of noble, perhaps even royal, blood in the early nineteenth century. The reality of the Harmsworths' family life during Alfred's childhood was much less romantic: Alfred Sr qualified for the Bar in 1869, two years after they had settled in London, but was never a success. A charming, popular but weak man, with a taste for drink which became increasingly dominant in his life, he was much less of an influence on Alfred than was Geraldine. She adjusted to her hard life of unaccustomed comparative poverty and constant child-bearing by developing into a strong, undemonstrative but dependable woman with strict moral standards. She was always the most important person in his life. His love for her was obsessive (even she found his devotion embarrassing): her opinion meant more to him than that of anybody else; hardly a day went by without his sending a letter or a telegram to her, often signed 'Your Firstborn'.

Alfred, a good-looking, self-confident child, attended a private school near his home before he was sent to Stamford Grammar School in Lincolnshire as a boarder. After two years he returned to London to attend Henley House, a day school in St John's Wood. He showed no particular academic gifts; he was bad at arithmetic, better at spelling and composition. While at Henley House, he edited a school magazine — its first issue included a feature, 'Answers to Correspondents' — and contributed a few pieces to the *Hampstead & Highgate Express*. He left school at the age of sixteen, determined to be a journalist. His initial attempts as a freelance journalist met with no great success, but following a bout of pneumonia, the outcome of one of the strenuous long-distance bicycle rides that Harmsworth enjoyed at this time, he answered an advertisement in the *Times* and was engaged as a companion by a son of Lord Lilford for a Continental tour in the summer of 1882. The trip also provided a welcome opportunity to escape parental disapproval, incurred by his seduction of the parlour-maid, Louisa Smith. She returned home to Essex where her baby, christened Alfred Benjamin, was born on 5 November 1882.

When he returned to England, his mother refused to let him stay in the house. Alfred moved into lodgings, writing stories and articles for magazines such as *Weekly Budget, Young Folks' Tales* and *Youth,* and sometimes earning about £3 a week. He was, briefly, editor of *Youth,* and then in 1886 was offered the editorship of a Coventry paper, *Bicycling News,* by William Iliffe (qv). Harmsworth soon enlivened the paper and improved the circulation, and continued to contribute to other periodicals, including *Tit-Bits,* the creation of George Newnes (qv). Alfred wanted to produce his own general interest magazine, and asked Iliffe for backing for a popular weekly, on the lines of *Tit-Bits,* to be called *Answers to Correspondents.* Iliffe refused, but Alfred found a backer (though not for *Answers*) in William Carr, the fiancé of a childhood friend of Geraldine Harmsworth, who had come from Dublin with £1,500 to invest on behalf of his future wife. Carr and Harmsworth moved into lodgings together in Kilburn in 1887 and took a room in a publishing office in Paternoster Square. Their first publications were a series of booklets called *A Thousand Ways to Earn a Living,* published in collaboration with Newnes and a magazine, *The Private Schoolmaster.* The business did not flourish, but Harmsworth cherished his scheme for a popular weekly, and, while still earning most of his income from freelance journalism, was married in April 1888 to Mary (Molly) Milner, the daughter of a failing sugar merchant. The bridegroom and the best man both had a dummy copy of *Answers to Correspondents* sticking out of their pockets. With the promise of printing credit from Iliffes, and financial backing from Captain Alexander Beaumont and his wife, who had been introduced to Carr & Co by one of their editors, the first number of *Answers to Correspondents* came out in June 1888.

Answers to Correspondents, a mine of useless information filched from other magazines, newspapers, popular encyclopaedias and the like, was not an immediate success. By the end of the first year, circulation was 48,000 and a gross profit of £1,097 had been earned. It was competitions that firmly established *Answers* (as it was known to the public long before the formal adoption of the shorter title in 1893) as a major popular weekly, above all one in late 1889 in which readers had to guess how much gold and silver coin would be in the Bank of England on a certain afternoon; the prize was £1 a week for life. Just before the competition was launched, in October 1889, new offices at 108 Fleet Street were taken. In May 1890 *Comic Cuts,* a weekly aimed at young readers, with the slogan 'Amusing Without Being Vulgar', was launched, and soon achieved a steady sale of 300,000 copies. Within two years it had become more profitable than *Answers. Illustrated Chips* (soon simply known as *Chips*), essentially another *Comic Cuts* with line drawings, followed in July 1890. This was the first indication of one of the strategies on which the success of the Harmsworth publications would be built: to bring out journals that would compete with their own publications, leaving less room in the field for rivals. In 1892 the joint sales of the Harmsworth publications reached one million a week. A year later, when *Home Sweet Home* had been added to the list, joint sales reached nearly 1.5 million. A public limited company, Answers Ltd, was set up in June 1893, with a share capital of £275,000. 125,000 7 per cent £1 preference shares and 50,000 of the 150,000 £1 ordinary shares were offered to the public. New Harmsworth publications, including a number of weekly adventure stories for boys, were being launched every few months.

Alfred provided the flair as journalist and editor; the financial sense was largely supplied by his brother Harold (qv). Other brothers were brought in too, Cecil, Leicester and later Hildebrand and St John. But Alfred remained firmly in charge, and directed his brothers' private lives almost as dictatorially as he directed their part in his business. Only Harold was really a match for him.

In 1894 the Harmsworths moved into newspapers. Alfred had already made enquiries about purchasing a suburban daily, when he was approached by two journalists, Louis Tracy and Kennedy Jones, with an offer to negotiate the purchase of an ailing Conservative London evening newspaper, the *Evening News*. It was bought for £25,000, including plant and premises. The content and presentation of the news were livened up, the finances monitored more carefully, and politics gave way to crime as the staple of the news pages. Under the new management the *Evening News* soon became modestly profitable, and earned its purchase price within three years. As soon as it was well secured, Alfred began to consider publishing a daily newspaper. These plans came to fruition in 1896 with the launch of the *Daily Mail*. At the time, Alfred Harmsworth said that it cost £100,000 to set up the *Daily Mail* (later claims he made for this expense ranged from £15,000 to £500,000). It was aimed at a mass readership, and used the latest in typography and journalistic style to attract the newly literate classes who had learned to read but not to think. But Alfred was determined to have well-written copy, with a great deal of foreign news, gathered by the speediest means of telephone and wire. Advertising was to be kept in its place, and the newspaper printed in clear type on good paper. To protect the paper from Harold's cost-cutting, he was not put in charge of the management. Alfred kept control of the paper by retaining 51 per cent; Harold had 24 per cent. The remainder was divided amongst Leicester, Cecil, Hildebrand and Kennedy Jones. The *Daily Mail* was an immediate success, with the first issue selling nearly 400,000. Its reputation was firmly established with its reporting of the Boer War; on some days during the war the circulation exceeded a million, the largest in the world.

In 1898 a private company was formed to take over the *Daily Mail*, with a capital of £200,000. Alfred was appointed chairman, with 'literary and political control of any papers issued by the company during his life' {Pound and Harmsworth (1959) 239}. He took 95,000 shares, Harold 48,000. By 1899 the *Evening News* was making £50,000 a year; its shares had risen in value from 3d to £3. Answers Ltd, with 19 periodicals, was paying dividends of 30 per cent (its main rivals in this field, the firms of

Newnes and C A Pearson (qv) were paying 10 and 15 per cent respectively). Part-works of rather greater literary and educational worth than the magazines had been successfully added to the Harmsworth list. In 1901 the periodicals and part-works were brought together under the Amalgamated Press, with Alfred as chairman.

During the Boer War special trains had been hired to dispatch the *Daily Mail* throughout the country; other newspapers swiftly followed the example. The *Daily Mail* countered by establishing an office and printing plant in Manchester to issue a duplicate Northern edition; once again, its competitors were forced to follow suit. Permanent headquarters in Manchester were opened in 1902; in 1905, offices were opened in Paris for the *Continental Daily Mail*. By then, other newspapers had been added to Harmsworth's group. The ailing *Weekly Dispatch* was acquired from Newnes in 1903. Of greater significance was the launch in that year of the *Daily Mirror*. Alfred Harmsworth had been the first to provide a 'women's page' in a daily newspaper, inspired by the fact that Harold was able to charge top rates for advertisements on the magazine page of the *Daily Mail*, which had a direct appeal to women readers. In the *Daily Mirror* he aimed to produce a paper written and edited by women, for women. It was not a success; within three months it had become 'A Paper for Men and Women'. It was not until it became 'An Illustrated Paper for Men and Women' that the losses (which totalled about £100,000) were finally stemmed. An illustrated paper was no novelty; the *Daily Graphic* had been quietly successful for fifteen years. Nor was the standard of reproduction of the illustrations very high (it was the first time that half-tone pictures were printed on rotary presses). But persistence paid off, though Harmsworth, once the initial battle had been won, lost interest in the paper, disliking its increasingly strident and populist tone. His affection for the paper grew no stronger when its circulation overtook that of the *Daily Mail* (which was not to reach again the levels it had attained in the Boer War until the First World War). In 1914, the *Mirror's* circulation reached 1.2 million, but Alfred Harmsworth was not interested, and sold his share in the paper cheaply to Harold early that year.

Shares in the Harmsworth newspapers were offered to the public in April 1905, when Associated Newspapers Ltd was incorporated with a share capital of £1.6 million. 500,000 5 per cent £1 cumulative preference shares, and 600,000 £1 ordinary shares were offered to the public; it was announced that up to £100,000 of the £200,000 cash capital provided by the issue would be used towards the purchase of 'a large tract of Timber land with extensive water power — the object being to safeguard the supply of paper for the production of the Company's papers and associated journals in the event of a rise in the price of that commodity', the beginning of the Grand Falls project in Newfoundland {*Times Prospectuses* 29 (1905) 99}. This was the first opportunity for the general public to invest in newspapers and the issue was heavily over-subscribed. Alfred Harmsworth's success was recognised by a barony conferred at Edward VII's suggestion in Balfour's Resignation Honours List of December 1905; he had already received a baronetcy eighteen months before. He took the title of Lord Northcliffe.

Northcliffe was now thinking of trying his hand with quality newspapers. He acquired the *Sunday Observer* in May 1905, but gave the distinguished editor he appointed in 1908, J L Garvin, considerable autonomy before he sold the paper in 1911 to Waldorf Astor. But it was his purchase of the *Times* in 1908 that tested whether his exceptional talents as a popular journalist could affect the fortunes of a quality newspaper. He had already tried to buy the *Times* in 1898, 1900 and again in 1902. In late 1907 he heard that the main proprietors of the *Times*, the Walter family, were desperately seeking fresh finance for the paper, which was entrammelled by its own traditions, and whose circulation had declined to an unremunerative 38,000. The Walters had already made arrangements with a group of financiers headed by Sir Arthur Pearson, but the manager of the paper, Moberley Bell, who had not been informed of these arrangements, recoiled from the scheme when he finally was informed. He preferred Northcliffe, and after elaborately secret negotiations, with Northcliffe staying in France much of the time to still speculation, won the senior member of the Walter family round to his scheme, though concealing the identity of the prospective purchaser. The sale went through for £320,000. By the end of 1908 it was widely known that Northcliffe was the new proprietor, a revelation that induced a state of shock in those, particularly among the staff of the paper, who cherished a sense of the unique history and dignity of the august *Times*. Northcliffe in turn was appalled at the financial mismanagement, the incoherent accounting, the stubborn conservatism of journalists who insisted on writing their copy by hand. But he too had a sense of the importance of the *Times*, and though he brought in new men and new features, insisted on a more attractive 'make-up' and more alert news-gathering, the essential spirit of the paper emerged unscathed from its trial by constant barrage of memoranda, suggestions and demands from its unlikely proprietor. The circulation improved, particularly in the early years of the war (reaching a peak of 318,000 at the outbreak), but for all Northcliffe's attempts to find the right price for the paper (making seven changes in the cover price between 1913 and 1922) that might tempt new readers while providing sufficient revenue from sales, the circulation began to decline again. The financial state of the paper was increasingly unsatisfactory in Northcliffe's last years as proprietor.

Northcliffe did not participate, even as a non-executive director, in running any company outside his own business; even his investments were in unadventurous securities, recommended by Harold. The great pulp- and paper-producing complex built up at Grand Falls, Newfoundland, and the Imperial Paper Mills in Kent, founded in 1910, were primarily his brother Harold's responsibility, not his. Nonetheless, Northcliffe was very proud of the scale of the investment and activities in Newfoundland.

Northcliffe was fundamentally a journalist, not a businessman. He told his brother Leicester, 'The only capacity I have as a man of business is to find men of business and leave them alone, which I do' {Pound and Harmsworth (1959) 823}. Whether his editors and managers, on whom he rained complaints, suggestions, reminders and orders to the end of his life, would have agreed that he left them alone is open to doubt; his nephew Cecil King (qv) said Northcliffe was effectively managing director as well as editor-in-chief of all his publications, and that the disorder in the *Daily Mail* after his death revealed the incapacity of those who were nominally in charge. It was in journalism that he contributed those innovations of style, format and approach to news and to the readers, that transformed the popular newspaper and magazine market. Often he adopted or adapted ideas current in the press in Britain and the USA, but he had an uncanny (though not infallible) instinct for what news and information would interest the mass readership, and how it should be presented to appeal to them most. It has often been pointed out that he was not a profound or creative thinker: his mind was shallow and restless, quick to seize on some fact or theory with intense interest and attention, but quick to pass on to the next new obsession. But his responsiveness to new ideas had its good side, too. He was excited by the latest inventions, and quick to perceive the impact on daily life that motor cars, aeroplanes, and the telephone might have. The prizes he offered, like the *Daily Mail* prize of £10,000 for the first transatlantic aeroplane flight, were more than publicity stunts for the *Daily Mail*: they were intended to draw the attention of the public, and the politicians, to the implications of technological development. Not that he did not have his share of silly publicity-seeking stunts, which he took with disquieting seriousness, like the campaign to popularise a *Daily Mail* hat: it was as though he had to try his strength occasionally to see that he could still reach his public. In one instance his persistence, in a campaign against the 'soap trust' of William Lever (qv), cost him over £200,000 in legal damages. (He tried to set it all off against profits, but in the end paid most of it himself.)

Northcliffe transformed newspapers not only for their readers, but also for the journalists who worked on them. From the very first, Northcliffe believed in paying journalists well — even in the very early days of *Answers* he paid contributors three times the going rate. His printers, too, had generous wages. It has been argued that he paid his staff too well, forcing his competitors to pay more than they could really afford for their staff, and raising the expectations of Fleet Street journalists and printers to levels that could, and still can, make it difficult to run a newspaper economically. The huge sales of his publications brought advertisers flocking to them, willing to pay high prices for space. But this heralded increasing dependence of newspapers on advertising revenue, a development Northcliffe much disliked. Throughout his career, he made repeated demands that advertisers should be kept in their place; only months before his death, he sent a series of complaints to the *Daily Mail* saying 'For twenty-five years I have been emphasising: "do not let the advertisements rule the paper"' {Pound and Harmsworth (1959) 847}.

Northcliffe also transformed the public image of the newspaper proprietor. With Northcliffe, the newspaper proprietor became a public figure of the first importance. He himself was never a political figure in the conventional sense. After declining the nomination for Folkestone in 1894, he agreed to stand as Conservative Unionist candidate for Portsmouth in the general election of 1895. He worked hard canvassing his constituency, but he was no public speaker, and was hardly suited to the round of committees and public meetings that would have been his lot if he had serious political ambitions. In the event, he came third of four candidates, declined the safe Conservative seat of Brixton when it was offered to him in December 1895, and never tried for the Commons again. After his election defeat, he had remarked: 'my place is in the House of Lords where they don't fight elections' {*ibid*, 186}. But after he became a peer in 1905 he made little impact in the House of Lords. He did not cultivate the acquaintance of politicians as his brother Harold did, and did not much enjoy the social life by which his wife set such store. According to Beaverbrook (qv), Northcliffe believed that a newspaper proprietor should have no friends, and he suffered much from his wife's friends asking him for favours. But the power he had — or rather, was believed to have — over public opinion made politicians keep a close watch on what the Northcliffe press was saying. During the First World War, half the daily newspapers sold in London were Northcliffe publications. Beaverbrook considered that Northcliffe's 'power was so considerable that it was of the utmost importance in all matters of public interest to secure his assistance or at any rate his neutrality' {Beaverbrook (1956) xxii}. But Beaverbrook was himself, of course, a newspaper proprietor, and newspaper proprietors, particularly following Northcliffe, are perhaps inclined to exaggerate the real impact of their views on political matters on the public mind, a delusion which is fostered by politicians, hypersensitive about their public image and standing, attributing too much importance to what newspapers say about them. Newspapers and their proprietors are at their most influential when they articulate opinions or moods widespread among the public. Northcliffe's campaigns against the military and political ambitions of Germany before the war, for more and better shells for the British army in France, and his attacks on the Coalition Governments of Asquith and Lloyd George had impact because they expressed public opinion, not because they created it. Northcliffe had a rare nose for news and for developments just over the horizon; that is not the same as the power to bring events about, though Northcliffe and those who feared him increasingly spoke as though it was.

Northcliffe's skills as a publicist were harnessed to the Government by Lloyd George, first by appointing him as Director of the British War Mission to the United States, a position he held from June to November 1917. Imperialist though he was, Northcliffe had great admiration and respect for many aspects of American life, and was more effective in this role than might have been expected by those who had seen in his appointment only an attempt by Lloyd George to get him out of the way. On his return to England Northcliffe was made a viscount in recognition of his services. Lloyd George sounded him out about the possibility of his becoming Secretary of State at the newly-created Air Ministry; Northcliffe chose to treat this as a definite offer of the job and to refuse it publicly, by publishing a letter in the *Times* setting out his reasons for doing so. He was forgiven this breach of etiquette, and was offered, and accepted the post of director of propaganda in enemy countries in February 1918. This appointment drove the German press, which had already attacked him as the devil incarnate, to new heights of hostility against him. But Northcliffe's relations with Lloyd George were permanently soured when he was not offered the position of influence at the Versailles Peace Conference which he coveted, and to which his exaggerated sense of his own importance made him feel he was entitled.

Northcliffe's income was enormous. By 1900 it was £150,000 a year, his net capital worth being estimated as £900,000 in 1901-2, including a valuation at cost of his shareholdings in his own companies. In 1900 he took a twenty-one year lease of a superb Tudor house, Sutton Place, in

Surrey, which his wife used for some of her more ambitious entertaining, but which never replaced Elmwood, a much less grand house near Broadstairs bought in 1890, in his affections. Later, his income rose to about £200,000 a year, though wartime taxation helped to reduce this to about £100,000 (after tax) in 1918. From this income he made generous allowances to members of his family, especially his mother and sisters, as well as numerous small pensions and annuities to those who had worked for him, or had somehow come to his attention, or their families. It was in such personal gifts and those subscriptions and donations which it was almost impossible for a rich man of public prominence to avoid making, rather than in any individual large endowments, that Northcliffe's contributions to charity were made.

Apart from Harold, the Harmsworth brothers who joined Alfred in his business all left the family firm sooner or later to pursue their own careers and interests. Cecil (1869-1948), educated at Trinity College, Dublin, in the 1890s worked as a writer and editor on *Comic Cuts*, *Answers* and the *Harmsworth Magazine*. In 1900, with his brother Hildebrand (1872-1929), he established the *New Liberal Review*. An understated, gentlemanly, discreet figure, considered by his siblings to lack push, Cecil made a quietly successful career for himself in politics, becoming Liberal MP for Droitwich, 1906-10, and for Luton, 1911-22. He was appointed Under-Secretary at the Home Office in 1915, joined Lloyd George's private staff, 1917-19, and then served as Under Secretary at the Foreign Office, 1919-22, retiring from politics in October 1922. He was given a barony in 1939.

Hildebrand worked on the circulation staff of *Answers*, travelling the country in the first years of the magazine; then, when the family fortunes improved, he was sent to Oxford University. In 1890 he was given a 10 per cent share in *Comic Cuts* and *Chips*. Like Cecil, he was defeated in the 1900 election when he stood as a Liberal. He left the Amalgamated Press in 1905, having sold some of his Harmsworth shares to Alfred. He kept the rest, and by shrewd investment gradually accumulated a fortune of about £1.5 million. He lost £80,000 in 1908-11, though, as proprietor of the London evening newspaper *The Globe*. In his later years he farmed in Sussex before retiring to a private hotel in Brighton, where he lived a secluded, empty life. A practical joker, who liked making silly wagers, he did not take the more self-important members of the family seriously enough for their liking. He was made a baronet in 1922, at the request of Harold, then Lord Rothermere, because Rothermere liked his eldest son, and not for love of Hildebrand.

Leicester (1870-1937) first worked as a clerk in the Inland Revenue, then joined the circulation staff of *Answers*. He edited *Forget-me-Not*, which was started in 1891, and played an important part in getting *Home Chat*, another Harmsworth women's magazine, through its initial difficulties. He bought *Golf* in 1898 for £1,350. In 1900 he narrowly won the Caithness seat in the general election, and sat for this constituency as a Liberal until 1922, when he was defeated after a thoroughly undistinguished political career. He left the Amalgamated Press in 1906, partly because of ill-health, partly because of disagreement with Harold. He sold his Harmsworth shares to invest in the company manufacturing Darracq motor cars (making £100,000 in the first year from this investment), and then made a fortune in the flotation of oil companies. He was made a baronet in 1918.

In 1920 he bought a major provincial paper, *The Western Morning News*, and also acquired the *Western Times* and the *Field*. A gloomy, serious-minded man, he was a collector, with good taste in silver, pictures and books.

St John (1876-1933), educated at Oxford University, joined the board of the Amalgamated Press in 1898. Alfred destined him for a post on the *Continental Daily Mail*, and St John was sent to France in 1902 to perfect his French. While there he found a spring of sparkling water near Nimes, owned by a doctor named Perrier. He bought the spring in 1903, selling his family shares to do so. An excellent sportsman, St John was crippled in a motor accident in 1906, and spent the rest of his life in a wheelchair. The Perrier business was his main interest in life, but it was never quite the financial success St John believed it could be, and it was kept going with help from Northcliffe. The two remaining brothers, Vyvyan and Charles, did not join the business, and lived quietly in the country, Vyvyan from choice, Charles, who was mentally subnormal, because his family preferred to keep him in luxurious seclusion. The withdrawal of his younger brothers from the firm saddened Northcliffe; in later years he would say he did not believe in employing relatives.

By the end of the war, Northcliffe's mental health was giving concern to those around him. He had always been something of a hypochondriac, frequently issuing bulletins on the state of his health to his family and staff, chronicling every sore throat or fluctuation in his weight in his letters and private diaries. His temper had always been uncertain too: great charm and courtesy alternated with brutality and vindictiveness. Now he became more than ever unpredictable, more than ever obsessed by the size of the organisation he had created and by the mission in life he felt this organisation gave him to admonish and influence the politicians he had never really liked, or understood. He went on a world tour in 1921, but when he returned in 1922, though he continued to badger his staff with complaints, suggestions and queries, his physical and mental health still gave cause for concern. By late June his family had him under restraint; at times he was violent; much of the time he was under sedation. He died on 14 August 1922 at his home in Carlton Gardens, leaving an estate proved at £5,248,973. After his death, his shares in Associated Newspapers were sold to his brother Rothermere, in the *Times* to J J Astor, and in the Amalgamated Press to William and James Berry (qqv).

It seems ironic, given the fortunes he made for his family, or that he had helped them to make, and the proliferation of Harmsworth peers and baronets, that Northcliffe himself had no heir to his title. He and his wife had no children, but apart from his son by Louisa Jane Smith (Alfred, who became a journalist) he had three children by the most important of his many mistresses, Kathleen Wrohan. Northcliffe had made several wills, including a couple during the last months of his life; these latter were far more favourable to his widow than earlier ones had been (though she had always been generously provided for) at the expense of other members of the family. The last wills were of doubtful validity, but in order to avoid a scandal, the family came to a compromise arrangement with Lady Northcliffe — and largely cut her thereafter.

CHRISTINE SHAW

HARMSWORTH Alfred Charles William

Writings:

As a journalist, particularly in the earlier years of his career Northcliffe wrote many articles. He also contributed an article 'Price of Newspapers' to the *Encyclopaedia Britannica* (11th ed, 1911).

Sources

Unpublished

British Museum, Northcliffe MSS (other Northcliffe papers are in the possession of his family).

The Times, London, archives.

MCe.

PrC.

Published

Lord Beaverbrook, *Men and Power, 1917-1918* (Hutchinson, 1956).

DNB.

Paul Ferris, *The House of Northcliffe: The Harmsworths of Fleet Street* (Weidenfeld & Nicolson, 1971).

Cecil King, *Strictly Personal: Some Memoirs of Cecil H King* (Weidenfeld & Nicolson, 1969).

Alan J Lee, *The Origins of the Popular Press in England, 1855-1914* (Croom Helm, 1976).

Stanley Morison, *The History of The Times* (4 vols, *The Times*, 1935-52) 3.

Reginald Pound and Geoffrey Harmsworth, *Northcliffe* (Cassell, 1959).

A P Ryan, *Lord Northcliffe* (Collins, 1953).

Sir Campbell Stuart, *Opportunity Knocks Once* (Collins, 1952).

Times *Prospectuses* 5 (1893), 29 (1905).

WWW.

This bibliography represents only a fraction of the literature on Northcliffe; only the books found most directly useful in describing his business career have been mentioned here.

Harold Harmsworth, aged thirty (taken from R Pound and G Harmsworth Northcliffe *Cassell, 1959).*

HARMSWORTH, Harold Sidney

1st Viscount Rothermere of Hemsted

(1868-1940)

Newspaper and periodicals proprietor and paper manufacturer

Harold Sidney Harmsworth was born in St John's Wood, London, on 26 April 1868, the third child and second son of the fourteen children of Alfred Harmsworth and Geraldine Mary née Maffett. He was educated at Henley House, a private school near his home (the same school that his elder brother Alfred, later Lord Northcliffe (qv), attended) and at Marylebone Philological School. There he was 'particularly good at arithmetic' {Pound and Harmsworth (1959) 64}, but showed no aptitude for any other subjects. A shy, cautious, stolid child, he was overshadowed by his attractive elder brother; he did not enjoy the school holidays. On leaving school he became a clerk with the Board of Trade at Tower Hill. In 1889, reluctantly, under pressure from his family, he left his post to become company secretary and business manager of Answers Co Ltd on its founding by Alfred Harmsworth.

Harold remained the 'business manager' of most of his brother's enterprises for the rest of Alfred's life. Harold Harmsworth's forte was financial control; his obsession, economy. The early Harmsworth publications were printed on poor-quality paper, often coloured to disguise just how bad it was, because of Harold's penny-pinching. Printing was another area in which Harold was allowed to drive hard bargains. Harold did not delude himself as to the quality of the paper and printing he was providing. In 1892 he advised Alfred against using small type in *Answers*, saying it was 'almost unreadable. Our bad paper and cheap printing will not stand much in the way of small type' {Ferris (1971) 45}. He was not allowed to reduce Alfred's generous fees to contributors, though he frequently complained about them. Harold was usually a pessimist about any new journal, and would, if given half a chance, 'knife' any publication that he felt was not paying its way. He waited until his brother was away, preferably abroad, before indulging in some of his more stringent cost-cutting. Thus Northcliffe's absence in Canada in 1909 seemed to him 'a first class opportunity of overhauling the entire expenditure side' of the book publishing branch of the Amalgamated Press, and so he issued instructions to 'get in, and cut everything down' {Pound and Harmsworth (1959) 386}.

Since the Harmsworth publishing business was built on popular mass circulation magazines and newspapers, and unit costs needed to be kept under strict control, Harold's compulsive economising served a very useful purpose. But it could be taken too far for Alfred's liking, and probably too far for the ultimate health of the publications. Alfred kept the business management of the *Daily Mail* out of Harold's hands. Alfred claimed to be offering 'A Penny Newspaper for a Halfpenny'; if Harold had been let loose on it, their brother Leicester once said, they might have ended up with a farthing newspaper for a halfpenny. Harold was offended, but still got a 24 per cent share in the paper to console him. He was excluded from the *Times*, too, when Northcliffe bought it in 1908. Northcliffe's talents as a journalist and editor created the circulations that Harold used as incentives to advertisers, and to secure higher rates for advertising space in their publications. But Northcliffe had to fight throughout his life to stop Harold squeezing the space for editorial copy to fit in yet more lucrative advertising.

Harold was given the major share of responsibility for the Harmsworths' only major venture outside publishing proper. In 1905 the Amalgamated Press (the Harmsworth periodical company, incorporated in 1901) and Associated Newspapers (formed to run the *Mail*, the *Evening News* and the *Weekly Dispatch* in April 1905) acquired 3,100 square miles of timber in Newfoundland, after Harold became anxious about the future prospects of newsprint supply for their publications. They set up the Anglo-Newfoundland Co based at Grand Falls, to build the mills, the transport facilities, and the housing for the workers that were needed to exploit this timber. By 1912, 2,400 tons of paper and 2,000 tons of pulp were being sent to the UK from Grand Falls every three weeks, although the Harmsworth publications demanded such a wide variety of paper and so much of it, that this could not provide all they needed. Furthermore, when Grand Falls was first selected as the base, it was not yet technically possible to transmit the hydro-electric power needed to operate the mill, so it had to be built at the waterfall, 20 miles from tidal water. Two years later, the technical problem had been solved; but the mill had already been built, and was thus fixed in the wrong place. In 1910 a paper mill, Imperial Paper Mills, was set up in England at Gravesend to supply more paper; much of the pulp came from Grand Falls. By 1912 it was producing 300 tons a week. It was planned to manufacture 2,000 tons a week, but this expansion was prevented by the war.

Northcliffe was always ready to acknowledge the importance of his brother's contribution to the success of the Harmsworth periodical and newspaper publishing business. Reflecting on his life in 1917, he described Harold as 'mainly responsible for the Newfoundland adventure ... the business side of the Amalgamated Press, the business foundation and success of the "Evening News" and "Daily Mail"' {Pound and Harmsworth (1959) 535}.

As well as his considerable share in the family business, Harold developed separate interests of his own. In 1895 before the launch of the *Daily Mail*, the Harmsworths had bought the *Glasgow Mail and Record* for about £7,000, most of which was supplied by Harold. Racing tips, wired from London, helped the paper to prosper. Later, Harold acquired full ownership of the paper; with the help of the *Daily Mail's* news service, the *Daily Record* became the most widely circulated daily paper in Scotland. He sold it in 1924 for over £1 million. Before 1910 (the year he was made a baronet), Harold sold his *Daily Mail* shares to develop his other financial interests. It may have been at this stage that he began to invest heavily in the USA; his nephew, Cecil King (qv) was told that his principal interests were in Canadian and American public utilities. In 1914 he bought Northcliffe's shares in the *Daily Mirror*, in which Northcliffe had lost interest. Harold was not troubled, as Northcliffe had been, by the vulgarity of the paper, which by that time had a circulation of 1.2 million, even more than Northcliffe's beloved *Daily Mail* (in 1917 the *Daily Mirror* had the largest circulation in the world). Harold was in newspapers to make money; to Alfred (by then of course a very rich man) money meant less than the quality of his newspapers. In 1915, Harold founded the *Sunday Pictorial*, a Sunday illustrated newspaper, which he rushed out to forestall Sir Edward Hulton's (qv) *Sunday Herald*. It was alleged that Rothermere had heard of Hulton's plans through trade associations. If so, Rothermere's bad faith was unfairly rewarded: the *Sunday Pictorial* was a success from the start, and by 1926 had built up a circulation of 2.2 million.

Harold was more interested than Northcliffe in political intrigue, and the cultivation of political associates and contacts. Harold's intervention was one factor which persuaded Northcliffe to play down the Marconi affair in his newspapers in 1912-13. Unlike Northcliffe, he was at that time nominally a Liberal. It was the Liberal Party which gave him his barony in 1914, following his help in attempts to minimise publicity for the Marconi scandal; he took the title Rothermere of Hemsted.

In 1916 Lloyd George appointed him to be Director-General of the Royal Army Clothing Department; in his work there, Northcliffe claimed, Rothermere 'saved the country millions, in addition to eradicating a vast amount of corruption' {Pound and Harmsworth (1959) 525}. He was appointed the first Air Minister in November 1917, with the difficult task of amalgamating the Royal Flying Corps, which had grown up under the Army, and the Royal Naval Air Service. Neither unit wanted the merger to take place, and Rothermere, who lacked any tact or talent for personal relations, was not the man to deal with the problem. The death of his eldest son, Vyvyan, who died in February 1918 from wounds received at Cambrai, was a crippling blow, coming as it did after the death in battle of his second son, Vere, in November 1916. Rothermere's resignation from the Air Ministry in April 1918, after he had driven General Trenchard, the chief of the new air staff, to resign a month before, was greeted, literally, with cheers by the staff. Yet he got his reward, a viscountcy, in 1919.

After the war Rothermere began to expand his interests in paper and pulp. First, in January 1919 he laid plans to develop Grand Falls on a large scale, demanding a salary of £5,000 tax free; Northcliffe, who considered him to be 'the only person who properly understands Newfoundland' {Reader (1981) 28}, agreed to the expansion, but paid him £7,500 (taxable). A few months later he bought a large interest in a mill at Greenhithe from the Wallpaper Manufacturers. He and his associate, a man called Becker, whom Rothermere described as 'the biggest pulp man in this country' {*ibid*} paid considerably less than the cost of erecting the mill, which had been £600,000. Rothermere converted the mill to newsprint, changed its name to Empire Mills, and offered Northcliffe 100,000 £1 7 per cent preference shares in the enterprise for the Amalgamated Press. Northcliffe, after a little persuasion, agreed. In 1920 the executors of Albert E Reed (qv) offered Rothermere shares in the Reed paper business, Albert E Reed Ltd. Rothermere bought 52 per cent of the ordinary shares, only to find that this did not give him control, because the preference shares had voting rights. Rothermere tried to dispose of the shares, but failed, leaving his newspaper with a substantial minority interest in Reeds which was only made a controlling interest by Cecil King in the 1950s.

Northcliffe's death in August 1922 brought important changes in Rothermere's career. A month after his brother's death he bought 400,000 deferred shares in Associated Newspapers at £4 each from the administrator of Northcliffe's estate, thus acquiring a controlling interest in the *Daily Mail*. He also bid for the *Times*, but it is not clear whether he genuinely wanted to acquire it, or was merely trying to push the price up for the benefit of his family (the *Times* was in fact sold to J J Astor). Rothermere formed a company called the Daily Mail Trust in 1923, and raised capital by selling £8 million of debentures on the market (he asked the public for £8 million; they offered £100 million). He used the proceeds to acquire the Hulton group of newspapers from Beaverbrook (qv), who had bought them only days before. He paid Beaverbrook the price Beaverbrook had paid to Hulton, £6 million, while Beaverbrook kept the *Evening Standard* as commission. However, the following year Rothermere sold the Hulton provincial interests to the Berry brothers (qv), and in 1925 sold them the *Daily Sketch* as well; he is said to have made a profit of £1.8 million on these transactions with the Berrys.

Even before these dealings with the Hulton papers, Rothermere and Beaverbrook had made a rather curious exchange of shares in each other's newspapers. Rothermere approached Beaverbrook in November 1922, asking 'how would you like me to purchase an interest in your newspapers' {Taylor (1972) 213}. Beaverbrook replied that he would be pleased to work in co-operation with Rothermere. Together they bought out the minority shareholders in Beaverbrook's *Daily Express*, and the Daily Mail Trust bought 49 per cent of Beaverbrook's holding in London Express Newspapers, for £200,000 cash and 80,000 Daily Mail Trust shares. When Beaverbrook kept the *Evening Standard* during the Hulton deal, the Daily Mail Trust took 49 per cent of the *Standard* in exchange for 40,000 DMT shares. This financial interlocking did not prevent ferocious competition between the *Daily Mail* and the *Daily Express*, nor did it prevent Beaverbrook from ploughing back profits from the *Express* to build the paper up, while receiving substantial dividends from the Daily Mail Trust. Rothermere grew increasingly dissatisfied with this situation, particularly as the *Express* was bidding fair to replace the *Mail* as the largest selling newspaper in the country (the *Mail* had recovered its lead over the *Mirror*). In 1927 he demanded that Beaverbrook sell his newspaper interest to him, offering £2.5 million, on condition that Beaverbrook should not begin any other newspaper enterprise. When Beaverbrook refused this condition, Rothermere's offer fell to £1 million; Beaverbrook retorted by offering £1 million for the Daily Mail Trust's 49 per cent share in Express Newspapers. Negotiations were broken off after this exchange of fire. In the end, Beaverbrook sold his DMT shares on the open market in 1928-29, at a time when he was disposing of many of his investments in ordinary shares.

This did not end the financial co-operation of the two men. The Daily Mail Trust retained its shares in Express Newspapers, and perhaps even as Beaverbrook was disposing of the last of his DMT shares, he and Rothermere were both acquiring substantial interests in Bowater's Mersey Paper Mills Ltd. Rothermere already had a controlling interest in W V

Bowater & Sons Ltd, paper merchants, since the *Daily Mirror* had bought 90,000 of the 150,000 ordinary shares in 1927. When Bowaters set up Bowater's Mersey Paper Mills Ltd to build and run newsprint mills at Ellesmere Port, the whole of the ordinary capital was taken up by W V Bowater & Sons Ltd, Rothermere's newspaper companies and Beaverbrook's newspaper companies, holding roughly £100,000, £100,000 and £200,000 respectively. W V Bowater (effectively Rothermere) appointed half the board of the new company, including the chairman and managing director, Eric Bowater (qv), London Express Newspapers (effectively Beaverbrook) the other half. The arrangement did not work well, particularly as the Express directors on the BMPM did not trust Eric Bowater, who was also chairman of W V Bowater and Bowater's Paper Mills, 'to be impartial in judging between the claims of the various companies of which he was chairman' {Reader (1981) 75}, suspecting that BMPM would come off worst. Beaverbrook's prime interest in this investment was to secure a reliable source of paper supplies; Rothermere, who had other substantial paper interests, seems to have been concerned principally with any financial advantages he could secure.

In March 1930, Associated Newspapers offered the £400,000 ordinary share capital of Empire Mills to W V Bowater for £208,302. Bowaters, rather unwisely, agreed, but soon after the transaction was completed, were notified that the *Daily Mail* contract, which they had been promised would continue unchanged for at least a year, was to be reduced, and would cease entirely after September. This loss of their major customer at Empire Mills made life extremely difficult for Bowaters, but fortunately for them in September 1931 Associated Newspapers offered to buy the Empire Mills shares back for the same price. Rothermere's motives in this transaction are not known: the likely explanation is that one or more of his companies needed cash badly. The Anglo-Canadian Pulp and Paper Mills Ltd, which Rothermere had set up in 1926 to develop the Manicouagan timber limits on the north shore of the St Lawrence, was in difficulties; the Manicouagan limits proved unworkable, and other sources of timber had to be found in a hurry to feed the mill. Anglo-Canadian was a subsidiary of Daily Mirror Newspapers, which considered selling the *Daily Mirror*'s holding in Bowaters to the Canada Power & Paper Corporation in the summer of 1930 (presumably Rothermere knew of this scheme) though in the end decided against it. However, in 1932 when Daily Mirror Newspapers was in urgent need of cash to meet the liabilities of Anglo-Canadian, Rothermere's newspaper companies sold 120,000 shares in W V Bowater & Sons, thus relinquishing control of the Bowater group, and 100,000 shares in BMPM, making Bowater an equal partner with Beaverbrook in BMPM. Beaverbrook was outraged by Rothermere's sale of these shares; but after much blustering, he finally sold his shares in BMPM to Bowater too. It is probably no coincidence that Beaverbrook, in the following months, bought out the 80,000 shares which the Daily Mail Trust still held in Express Newspapers, for about £550,000. In February 1933 he approached the Trust asking for an option on the *Evening Standard* shares which the Trust held. The Trust wanted a firm offer of £324,405. Beaverbrook offered only £282,030; the Trust refused this, but was evidently short of cash. Beaverbrook waited, and in May 1933 purchased the *Evening Standard* shares for £275,483.

Whatever his contribution to the success of the Harmsworth newspapers in Northcliffe's day, as a sole newspaper proprietor Rothermere was not a success. Northcliffe's judgement that Harold must be kept away from the financial management of the *Daily Mail* if it was to achieve the quality Alfred planned for it had been sound. Northcliffe had run the paper with such tight personal control until the end of his life that there was no management structure. Rothermere never went to the *Daily Mail* offices, and hardly knew his own staff. He cut the paper's expenses, and let advertising encroach upon editorial space. Profits rose, circulation reached a peak of 1,954,635 in 1929, but gradually the standard of the paper fell, and in 1933 the *Express* replaced it as the largest selling daily paper (the *Mail* averaged 1,772,188 in that year; the *Express* 1,829,708). Under Rothermere, the *Daily Mirror* also suffered from its proprietor's neglect, and lost impetus. By the early 1930s the circulation was declining by 70,000 a year, and fell below 800,000 in 1933. Rothermere formally relinquished control in 1931, and slowly disposed of his shareholding over the next several years; he used his newspapers to boost the shares of the *Daily Mirror*, although he believed that it was sure to cease publication, so that he could obtain a better price. In the event, the *Mirror* was revived after he had given up control, his nephew Cecil King playing a considerable part in this revival.

Rothermere had made an unsuccessful attempt to found a chain of provincial papers in the later 1920s. He is said to have been irked by statements in the American press, following the purchase of the *Daily Telegraph* by the Berry brothers, that they were now the largest newspaper proprietors in Britain. Rothermere, who was travelling in the USA, cabled instructions to London to announce he would start evening newspapers in some of the towns where the Berrys owned newspapers, in Manchester, Sheffield, Cardiff, Bristol and Newcastle. Northcliffe Newspapers Ltd (a title that seems to reveal hurt Harmsworth pride) was launched in 1928, £3 million in guaranteed debentures was raised, and ordinary capital of £2,333,334 was also issued over the next few years. Rothermere founded some papers and bought others, but enjoyed little success with them. Northcliffe Newspapers went into liquidation in 1932. It was an expensive failure.

Apart from making money, Rothermere's chief interest in his newspapers was as a platform for his political views. It was not until after the war that he began to use his papers in this way. His first campaign, against 'Squandermania', with repetitive diatribes against high taxation and government spending appearing under Rothermere's name, was an echo of Northcliffe's campaign for reduced public spending in his last years. Rothermere became president of an Anti-Waste League, which sponsored parliamentary candidates; one or two of them were elected in 1921. Politics were not Rothermere's forte: his views were inconsistent, extreme, at times plain silly. The most consistent note of his political opinions was a liking for authoritarian figures and remedies, in domestic and foreign politics. He suggested to Lloyd George in 1927 'you should make a move from your present standpoint and travel the road — the road almost invariably pursued by all great democrats — towards a very modified political dictatorship' {Ferris (1971) 289}. He offered his support to Baldwin at the election of 1928, but only on certain conditions, which included knowing the names of the next Conservative Cabinet in advance. Baldwin's refusal to satisfy him brought Rothermere, together with Beaverbrook, into attempting to stage a takeover of the Conservatives. Rothermere's papers scouted Beaverbrook as a successor to Baldwin; Beaverbrook acclaimed Rothermere as 'the great master of popular opinion' and 'the greatest trustee of public opinion that we have seen in the history of journalism' {Cudlipp (1980) 157-58}. Rothermere endorsed Beaverbrook's United Empire Party. Baldwin, despite his genuine political difficulties, survived their attacks and repudiated their efforts to influence the fortunes of the Conservative party, employing a famous phrase (written for him by his cousin Rudyard Kipling) 'What the proprietorship of these papers is aiming at is power, and power without responsibility — the prerogative of the harlot throughout the ages' {Cudlipp (1980) 274}. In the 1930s Rothermere supported Oswald Mosley, until the *Daily Mail's* advertisers finally became restless at his support for fascism.

Rothermere's attempts to influence European politics were farcical. Under the influence of Princess Hohenlohe-Waldenburg, in 1927 he took up the cause of the injustice done to Hungary in the determination of her post-war boundaries by the Treaty of Trianon. The Hungarians took him to their hearts (something no-one else ever did); he was even offered the Crown of Hungary, though he had the sense to refuse it. His campaign boomed on for over a year, and still echoed in his newspapers throughout the 1930s. He admired Mussolini, and for many years spoke of Hitler as the strong man Germany needed. Even in 1939 he argued there was a better side to Hitler, that Britain did not understand the reason for the brutality in Germany was the threat from Communists. He visited Germany several times, and met Hitler and other Nazi leaders; he and Hitler exchanged letters, pictures and presents. (In 1939 he justified the adulatory language used in his letters to Hitler by saying 'I used the language that he was accustomed to hear from those about him' {Rothermere (1939) 29}.) This mission to explain Nazi Germany to Britain went, paradoxically, with a campaign for rearmament, with especial stress on the need for Britain to strengthen her airforce. With the exception of this campaign, Rothermere's political crusades could be said to have done more than any other actions by newspaper proprietors in this century, to have given the concentration of press power in the hands of private individuals a bad name.

Rothermere had never been a happy man, but became increasingly pessimistic and gloomy as he grew older. His marriage in 1893 to Lilian, daughter of George Wade Share, a city hardware merchant, was not a success. Pretty and gay, she was ill-suited to be the wife of a man who called his secretary in to talk business the morning after his wedding. After bearing three sons, she refused to have any more children, much to the grief of her husband, who wanted a large family. She was unfaithful to him, and left him before the First World War to make her home in France. The death of two of his sons during the war affected him deeply. After that, he lived largely to make money, as much money as possible. He wanted to be the richest man in the country, but told Cecil King that he thought 'that he never got further than No. 3'. {King (1969) 76} He did become very wealthy, deriving a huge income from investments, as well as from his businesses. His personal secretary estimated that by 1926 his holdings were worth £26 million. However, even this consolation failed him, for he lost heavily in the Wall Street slump of 1929; according to Cecil King he lost 40 million dollars in a month. He lived much of the time in hotels, but had a knack of making himself uncomfortable wherever he lived. He was lavish with gifts to his relatives, and to girls procured to spend the night with him.

He also gave large sums away for charitable purposes. His donations to universities included the endowment of a chair at Oxford and two at Cambridge. He gave many pictures to municipal galleries (he had little taste of his own, but relied on advice, often bad advice). He gave £40,000 to the Middle Temple, and in 1926 bought the site of the Bethlehem Hospital in South London for £155,000 and turned it into a park and playground in memory of his mother, who had died the previous year.

Rothermere formally retired from active control of the *Daily Mail* in 1937. In May 1940, Beaverbrook, in his capacity of Minister of Aircraft Production, asked Rothermere to visit the United States. He became ill in North America, and was sent to Bermuda to rest. He died there on 26 November 1940; just before he became unconscious he said 'There is nothing I can do to help my country now' {Ferris (1971) 300}. His estate in the United Kingdom was proved at £281,000; after death duties, there was not enough to pay the legacies, although there may well have been money that was still invested abroad, or had been disposed of in trusts and settlements.

CHRISTINE SHAW

Writings:

Solvency or Downfall? Squandermania and Its Story (Longmans & Co, 1921).

My Campaign for Hungary (Eyre & Spottiswoode, 1939).

My Fight to Rearm Britain (Eyre & Spottiswoode, 1939).

Warnings and Predictions (Eyre & Spottiswoode, 1939).

Sources:

Unpublished

British Museum, Northcliffe MSS.

House of Lords RO, Beaverbrook MSS.

BCe.

MCe.

PrC.

Published

Lord Beaverbrook, *Men and Power 1917-1918* (Hutchinson, 1956).

Viscount Camrose, *British Newspapers and their Controllers* (Cassell & Co, 1947).

Hugh Cudlipp, *The Prerogative of the Harlot: Press Barons and Power* (Bodley Head, 1980).

DNB.

Paul Ferris, *The House of Northcliffe: The Harmsworths of Fleet Street* (Weidenfeld & Nicolson, 1971).

Hamilton Fyfe, *Press Parade: Behind the Scenes of the Newspaper Racket and the Millionaires' Attempt at Dictatorship* (Watts & Co, 1936).

Franklin Reid Gannon, *The British Press and Germany 1936-1939* (Oxford: Clarendon Press, 1971).

Harold Hobson, Philip Knightley and Leonard Russell, *The Pearl of Days: An Intimate Memoir of the Sunday Times 1822-1972* (Hamish Hamilton, 1972).

Cecil King, *Strictly Personal: Some Memoirs of Cecil H King* (Weidenfeld & Nicolson, 1969).

Reginald Pound and Geoffrey Harmsworth, *Northcliffe* (Cassell, 1959).

PP, RC on Press (1947-48) Cmd 7318, 7448, 7500.

W J Reader, *Bowater: A History* (Cambridge: Cambridge University Press, 1981).

Sir Campbell Stuart, *Opportunity Knocks Once* (Collins, 1952).

Times *Prospectuses* 66 (1923).

Alan J P Taylor, *Beaverbrook* (Hamish Hamilton, 1972).

WWW.

HARRIMAN, Sir George William

(1908-1973)

Motor vehicle manufacturer

George William Harriman was born in Coventry on 3 March 1908, the son of George Harriman, a motor machinist and May Victoria née Cooper. At the age of fifteen he began an apprenticeship at the Hotchkiss works in the town, where his father was a general foreman.

Shortly afterwards, the Hotchkiss factory was bought by William Morris (qv) for use as the engine plant of the rapidly expanding Morris Motors. Under the direction of Frank Woollard (qv), this factory became a

Sir George Harriman (taken from G Turner The Leyland Papers *Eyre & Spottiswoode, 1971).*

centre of the British adoption of American production technology. Here, in addition to learning the details of production engineering, Harriman made the acquaintance of Leonard Lord (qv), then in the drawing office at the Coventry engine works. Much of Harriman's subsequent career was as a protégé of Lord. During the 1930s Harriman was actively involved in the modernisation of the Cowley assembly plant where material conveyors and a moving assembly line were finally installed in 1934. By 1938 he was appointed assistant works manager at the new Courthouse Green engine works in Coventry.

Two years later Harriman followed Lord to the Austin works at Longbridge, Birmingham, where he became machine shop superintendent responsible for engine production. In addition to his duties at Longbridge he worked closely with Lord, who had been appointed as government controller of Boulton & Paul Ltd, to expedite production of Defiant night fighters. For this work Harriman was awarded an OBE in 1943. In the following year he became production manager at Austins.

In 1945 George Harriman became general works manager and was also appointed a director of the company. He was an active member of the planning group which transformed Austin into a dynamic company of increasing significance in world markets. The Longbridge manufacturing base was enlarged and modernised. By the introduction of automatic transfer machines for engine production, the firm made some major advances in productivity with no increase in factory floor space and only small additions to the labour force. A large innovatory assembly building was opened at Longbridge in 1951. Harriman accompanied Lord (then chairman of the Austin Motor Co) to the United States in 1948 where he developed some appreciation of the significance and difficulties of the export drive. The new post-war designs, especially the A40 Devon car, were marketed world-wide and in 1948 about 63 per cent of the company's 85,400 vehicles were exported. Many of the vehicles were shipped as knocked-down components and were assembled by local distributors. Harriman's role in the company was recognised by his appointment as deputy managing director in 1950 and deputy chairman in 1952.

With the formation of the British Motor Corporation in February 1952 Harriman's responsibilities vastly increased. The merged interests of Austin and Morris had created a company with an initial capitalisation of £14 million and an annual output of 200,000 units. The company was the largest motor manufacturer in Europe and ranked fourth in the world after the big three US corporations. With assembly plants in Australia and distribution centres elsewhere the new company was a multinational enterprise. Size and complexity brought many problems. Austin was essentially a single-plant firm with a large integrated production centre at Longbridge. Morris was a multi-plant enterprise with several British assembly plants and many separate component-manufacturing factories. Integration and rationalisation of plants and products was a major activity in which Harriman was involved in the 1950s. It was a difficult task, since the Austin and Morris companies had long been rivals and there was, according to most commentators, a legacy of bitterness and conflict of personalities lasting for a decade after the merger.

BMC not only had to rationalise but to grow, and to develop new ranges of vehicles. Longbridge and some other plants were extended and in 1953

Fisher & Ludlow, a large Birmingham car body supplier and appliance manufacturer, was acquired. By the late 1950s, however, regional planning policies in Oxford and the West Midlands forced BMC to expand beyond its traditional, though dispersed, production areas. New factories were built in Llanelly, South Wales for pressings, in Liverpool for appliances and in Bathgate, Scotland for trucks and tractors. This required a massive investment programme completed in 1963 at a cost of nearly £50 million. Productive capacity was increased from 750,000 to one million vehicles, and about 11,000 new jobs were created in peripheral areas. This government-induced regional dispersion was not a success; it expanded capacity in distant areas at a time when the post-war growth of the industry had ended. By 1963 BMC had an authorised capital of £51 million and was producing nearly 700,000 cars, about 63 per cent of total national output. At this time the company with its innovative designs, notably the Mini and the 1100/1300 range, was at the highest point in its development.

Harriman became deputy chairman and joint managing director of BMC in 1956. Five years later, in 1961, he was appointed chairman and managing director in succession to Sir Leonard Lord. Harriman's appointment as chief executive came at a difficult time. The British motor industry had completed its main phase of post-war expansion, there was a sudden and severe collapse of the US export market in 1960, and internal problems of labour relations were beginning to undermine the ability of companies to make reliable vehicles to a regular production schedule. BMC had been overtaken in the late 1950s by Volkswagen as the largest European motor manufacturer, and after 1960 was to be surpassed in size by Fiat. Within Britain there were new challenges from the dynamic Leyland Motor Corporation, which had acquired Standard-Triumph in 1960, as well as from the expanding US-controlled firms. As the world motor industry became more mature the problem of economies of scale grew more pressing. If VW (1960 production 866,000 cars and vans) represented one extreme of efficiency with a small model range, BMC (1960 production 541,000 cars, vans and trucks) tended to represent the other extreme. Economies of scale were lost with low-volume models, and profitability was low. In 1961 it was estimated that the company was making before tax profits of only £6.50 per car. Model development in a more competitive world became more costly and risky. The 1800 series, for example, was a commercial failure.

In the 1960s the motor industry tended to become more volatile, especially in labour relations and in sales, which would swing violently, upsetting company marketing forecasts and financial planning. National economic policies of 'stop and go' contributed to some of the sales fluctuations. Mergers were regarded at the time as one solution to the problems of world scale and as an attempt to balance sales between different market sectors. In 1965 BMC merged with Pressed Steel, the last of the large independent body suppliers. This acquisition triggered off a further series of corporate readjustments. A surprise move by Jaguar to join with BMC in the following year resulted in the formation of British Motor Holdings Ltd. Harriman became chairman of this new holding company. At the time of the merger, BMH was the fourteenth largest industrial corporation outside the USA. It had assets of £210 million; 114,000 employees (8,000 in Australia and South Africa); 32 factories worldwide; 5,800 BMC dealers and 9,000 in the Jaguar group. It had a production capacity of about 1.1 million vehicles and an extensive range of models and brand names. The Jaguar merger brought additional names such as Daimler, Guy and Coventry Climax fork-lift trucks.

Before any significant rationalisation of BMH had begun Harriman and Sir Donald Stokes (qv) of the Leyland Motor Corporation were having exploratory talks about a possible merger of the two remaining British-owned companies. (The Wilson Government was then encouraging the formation of very large companies through the Industrial Reorganisation Corporation.) When BMC/BMH had to report a loss of £15 million in 1967, Harriman and his company had a weaker position in the bargaining which produced the new giant merger. Leyland men dominated the new corporation and while Harriman became the first chairman of British Leyland in 1968, he was effectively ousted by the more dominant Stokes in the following year. Harriman became honorary president in 1969 and had a very limited role in the direction of the company until his final retirement in March 1973.

Most of Harriman's working life was spent as a company executive. His wider contribution to the British motor industry was, however, recognised by the Society of Motor Manufacturers and Traders which he served as president, 1967-69. From 1971 he headed a new firm of international management consultants, Harriman, Green & Associates, with offices in London, Paris, Switzerland and New York, advising companies within the EEC on ways to improve efficiency and profitability.

As a key figure in the post-war British motor industry, George Harriman was essentially a production man, at his best grappling with the problems of engineering, factory layout and vehicle output. He never forgot that teamwork was an essential feature of the assembly line system of the industry. He was well-liked by fellow executives and workers on the shop floor. In spite of adversity he was unfailingly cheerful and enthusiastic. As a leading figure in BMC he sustained the business through some difficult post-merger problems and contributed to the technical successes of the Mini and the 1100 series. He was much less successful as a business strategist, failing to merge effectively and completely the Austin and Morris interests and factories. Both companies retained separate boards of directors and books until 1966. The development of an efficient, well-integrated company was clearly needed in the early 1960s when the cumulative and largely negative effects of government policies were beginning to show. Harriman may well have given more priority to production planning than to the bigger strategic issues facing BMC and the industry as a whole. The financial management of BMC was never wholly successful and Harriman, along with many others, was surprised at the rapid collapse of BMC/BMH in 1966-67, a situation which led to the loss of influence in the British Leyland merger a year later. The complex empire for which Harriman had worked for many years did not survive for very long under different management.

Harriman was awarded the CBE in 1951, and was knighted in 1965 for services to exports.

George Harriman was always a keen sportsman. In the early 1930s he was a leading rugby player and captained both the Coventry and

Warwickshire County XVs. In 1933 he played for England v The Rest. He found relaxation in his later years in golf and trout fishing. For many years he lived in Solihull and latterly in the nearby village of Knowle. Harriman was very reticent about his private life; all that is recorded is that he was survived by a widow and one daughter.

Sir George Harriman died on 29 May 1973 leaving £42,109 gross.

G T BLOOMFIELD

Sources:

Unpublished

BCe.

PrC.

Published

G T Bloomfield, 'The Changing Spatial Organisation of Multinational Corporations in the World Automotive Industry' in F E Ian Hamilton and G J R Linge (eds), *Spatial Analysis, Industry and the Industrial Environment* (2 vols, Chichester: Wiley, 1979-81) 2.

Coventry Evening Telegraph 30 May 1973.

Keith Cowling et al, *Mergers and Economic Performance* (Cambridge: Cambridge University Press, 1980).

John H Dunning and Clifford J Thomas, *British Industry: Change and Development in the Twentieth Century* (Hutchinson, 1961).

Times 30 May 1973.

Graham Turner, *The Leyland Papers* (Eyre & Spottiswood, 1971).

Peter Wilsher, 'Big Man in Small Cars' *The Sunday Times* 22 Dec 1963.

WWW.

G J Harris (courtesy of Rowntree Mackintosh Ltd).

HARRIS, George James

(1895-1958)

Chocolate manufacturer

George James Harris was born at Largs, Ayrshire, Scotland, on 8 August 1895, the son of Charles Harris and his wife Agnes. Charles Harris was an engineer — as were others of his family — who eventually became chief engineer of Tate & Lyle, sugar refiners, in Liverpool: it was with some disappointment that George Harris's family watched his career develop outside engineering.

George Harris was educated at Ayr Academy, from which he went directly into the Royal Flying Corps as a pilot in 1914. After being shot down in flames, he transferred to the King's Liverpool Regiment, reaching the rank of major at the age of twenty-three. His record was a most distinguished one: he was on active service throughout the whole war, fought on the Somme and at Passchendaele, was mentioned in dispatches and won the MC at Delville Wood, and a bar to his MC during the last German advance. He was described by those who knew him as entirely without fear, with the power to inspire fearlessness in those who were with him. On demobilisation, he held the rank of acting colonel.

When the war ended Harris entered the London School of Economics to study mathematics 'to get his mind working again' {Oral, Mrs Friede Harris}. He left before finishing the degree course to take up articles with the firm of accountants Deloitte & Co, qualifying in two years as a chartered accountant.

On 23 February 1923 he married Friede Rowntree, daughter of Frank Rowntree, the cousin of Benjamin Seebohm Rowntree (qv) who in that year succeeded his father, Joseph Rowntree (qv), as chairman of Rowntree & Co in York. Friede Rowntree and George Harris had met at the LSE, where Friede Rowntree was reading social science.

Rowntree & Co was a family firm engaged in the manufacture of cocoa, and chocolate and sugar confectionery. As Friede Rowntree's husband, George Harris was by custom entitled to an appointment in the firm, and he joined it in 1923 as secretary of the Research Groups, which were concerned with such subjects as engineering, time study, and the chemical department.

In 1925 he moved to the sales side of the organisation, and until 1930 held appointments away from York. He spent one year in the USA, primarily investigating the possibility of making a business there out of a fruit-flavoured product, 'Chu-Frus', a possibility which was rejected. He eventually became London sales manager, a post he left in January 1931 to become marketing manager for chocolate products. He was appointed to this position by F G Fryer, who had just relinquished his role as director in charge of the engineering, chemical and research departments to turn his much-needed experience and abilities to the fields of marketing and distribution.

Rowntree & Co's turnover in 1931 was £2,671,462: like many other companies, it was in the grip of the recession; the factory was working only three days a week and recovery, and at times even survival, seemed difficult and often in doubt. It was George Harris who more than anyone fought for, inspired and led the company's resurgence.

The engine of his success was his attitude to what should be offered for sale and how it should be sold. The company's product range was, at that time, elaborate and undistinguished in both quality and concept, in a confectionery industry dominated by Cadbury. By 1939, it contained by contrast a group of unique products of individual excellence and design, each nationally known by its own brand name, and poised to challenge for market leadership. In that year turnover reached £6,672,124.

Possibly just as important as the invention and development of these products, from Black Magic in 1933, through Kit Kat, Aero, Dairy Box, to Smarties in 1938, were the criteria and techniques by which they were chosen. Harris was an assiduous student of successful enterprise in consumer goods. Forrest Mars recalled that 'for example, he came to see me at Slough without an introduction. He wanted to sell me chocolate, but he was also very interested in the techniques I had used to build a business from scratch based on one product'; Harris also 'had a close relationship with Mr Marks [Simon Marks] of Marks & Spencer ... and Sainsbury ... who were very successful. Again he was interested in how they were able to take the largest share of the market'. {F E Mars to R A Kaner, 18 Jan 1983} Close observation of what contributed to others' success, and intelligent and rational analysis were as important as creativity; and just as crucial, objective, quantitative evaluation of what was then created, followed.

Harris directed attention to the consumers' judgement of products, and insisted on testing ideas about what would increase the consumer's liking for something, by using statistically-based consumer research. When what is now Kit Kat (fingers of wafer sandwich moulded in milk chocolate) was being developed, his brief for product development was to make a wafer that would achieve a statistically significant preference over the acknowledged best wafer on the market, made then by Huntley & Palmer. The original advertising for his first major brand, the chocolate assortment Black Magic, made much of the large-scale use of consumer research in its design.

His collaborator in the application of statistical techniques to consumer research was Nigel Balchin, of the National Institute of Industrial Psychology, an organisation that had owed its survival from infancy in the 1920s to Seebohm Rowntree's support. Balchin, though never a full-time employee of Rowntree & Co, was its consultant on marketing and advertising for many years.

Harris's emphasis on consumer research in product development was paralleled by his use of advertising as the means of direct communication with consumers. Together with Ray Smith of the J Walter Thompson Co he established in Rowntrees a habit of sophisticated, single-minded use of advertising that is still valid.

In addition to these external collaborators, Harris assembled in the

Press advertisement 27 Feb 1937 for Black Magic (courtesy of Rowntree Mackintosh Ltd).

company an able and committed team. He was a hard taskmaster, persistent in his pursuit of his objectives, never willing to accept second-best; but as in his wartime commands, he drove himself even harder than he drove others, securing not only their respect but also their often passionate loyalty. With their help he had, by 1939, succeeded in so strengthening the Rowntree business by the establishment of its range of major brands that his almost obsessive desire to end Cadbury's dominance of the market could be regarded as fulfilled, though these products would not make their full impact on Rowntree's performance for some years after the Second World War. Though he saw the Cadbury business as his competitor in the market (which probably made easier the close personal relationship he established with Forrest Mars) there was no personal animosity in his attitude. Similarly, in his dealings with his own staff, though he could be verbally brutal in castigating lapses from the high standards of accuracy that he set for them as for himself, he bore no lasting grudges.

Not surprisingly, this marketing-led success of the company, coupled with George Harris's personal qualities of leadership and his wide-ranging experience, resulted in his taking an increasingly wider role in Rowntree's affairs. On his return to York in 1931 he had become a member of the York board, which ran the main section of the business; in 1933 he joined the Rowntree & Co board; in 1938 he became chairman of the York board, and in 1941 company chairman on the retirement of Seebohm Rowntree.

The Second World War imposed new demands on Harris's energies. In 1941 he was elected president of the UK industry organisation, the Cocoa, Chocolate and Confectionery Alliance, a position he held until 1946, and chairman of the Cocoa and Chocolate (War-Time) Association, which he remained until 1947. In these capacities he played the leading part in defending the industry's proper interests in the context of wartime restrictions and shortages, arguing strenuously and formidably on the whole industry's behalf, and earning respect for his integrity in this from everyone involved. As chairman of the Reconstruction committee, he did much to rebuild the Alliance's organisation to meet the post-war problems of the industry. Harris also initiated the formation of a Food Front which resulted in the setting up of the Food Industries Council.

The unsparing way he spent his own mental and physical resources in the interests first of his company, and then of his industry, took their toll. In 1946 he visited the USA, once again looking for what had enabled others to succeed, but he was taken ill, while staying with Forrest Mars; though he soon recovered, in 1947 he suffered another serious illness, which compelled him to cease work for a while. He returned to Rowntrees, accepting that because of impaired health he should shed some of his responsibilities, but in 1952 on his doctor's advice retired finally. He died on 11 September 1958 at his home, Bossall Hall, near York, survived by his wife and three daughters. He left £10,421 gross.

R A KANER

HARRIS George James

Sources:

Unpublished

BCe (Scots).

MCe.

PrC.

Personal Interviews with Mrs F R Harris (widow); C E Pratt (formerly chairman, Mars Ltd); A Norton (formerly deputy chairman, Rowntree Mackintosh PLC); A R Clifford (formerly director, Rowntree Mackintosh PLC); S E Patrick (formerly marketing manager, Rowntree & Co Ltd); N Walker (formerly product development manager, Rowntree & Co Ltd).

Letter from F E Mars to R A Kaner 18 Jan 1983.

Published

Cocoa Works Magazine (Rowntree & Co Ltd) Easter 1952, Autumn 1958.

Times 19 Sept, 20 Oct 1958.

Yorkshire Evening Press 21 Jan 1952.

Sir Cyril Harrison, portrait by Desmond Groves (courtesy of Mr I W Harrison).

HARRISON, Sir Cyril Ernest

(1901-1980)

Textile manufacturer

Cyril Harrison was born at Sileby, near Leicester on 14 December 1901, the eldest son of Alfred John Harrison and Edith née Perry. His father was manager of the Sileby Gas Works and later moved to Great Harwood, Lancashire when appointed general manager of the Accrington District Gas & Water Board in 1917. Cyril was educated at Padiham Wesleyan School and later won a scholarship to Burnley Grammar School.

In 1917 his father was responsible for the installation of a gas heating system at the large mansion of a local textile manufacturer, Herbert Noble. In appreciation of this work Herbert Noble took Cyril, at the age of sixteen, as an office boy at Perseverance Mill, Padiham, with the promise of managerial responsibility once he had learned the business. However, when Noble's two sons left Rossall School, Cyril was dismissed to make way for them. This was a major blow to Cyril's ambitions but he was determined to learn the business. He went for a period to a local weaver in Great Harwood to gain practical experience of weaving. Shortly after this, Noble's representative on the Manchester Cotton Exchange, a Mr Bentley, saw that his own position might not be too safe with the sons' arrival in the business and decided to set himself up as a dealer on the Exchange. He approached Cyril's father to see whether Cyril would join him to learn fabric marketing. Cyril joined Bentley, but after a period saw that his future would be limited.

In 1928 he decided to go into partnership with a friend, Ralph Harling, and they formed C E Harrison & Co in Bloom Street, Manchester to merchant loom-state cotton fabric. At that time sales of fabric from the numerous small cotton weaving companies went through the large merchant community in Manchester. During these years he also studied secretarial practice and qualified as a fellow of the Chartered Institute of Secretaries.

In 1939 English Sewing Cotton Co Ltd of Manchester, one of the two largest sewing thread manufacturers in the UK, was actively looking for management talent and in particular for someone to manage their yarn sales division (Sir Richard Arkwright & Co). A Burnley man, Sir Harold Parkinson, who later became High Sheriff of Lancashire, had been impressed by Cyril's activities in the Burnley Chamber of Commerce and recommended him to ESC. As a result Cyril was offered the post, which he accepted after arranging a mutually acceptable agreement with his partner. In 1940 Harrison was seconded by ESC to the Cotton Control Board which was set up that year by the Government to allocate wartime supplies of raw materials and to direct production of the cotton industry to areas of national need.

In 1948 Harrison was appointed managing director of ESC, vice-chairman in 1952, and then chairman in 1963. He initiated a sustained period of expansion that was to build ESC into one of the giants of the textile industry. ESC was primarily a sewing thread and yarn producer, one of its products being the well-known 'Sylko' domestic cotton thread. It also owned the American Thread Co, one of the largest thread companies in the USA. The first expansion under Harrison came in 1951 with the purchase of the Rose Manufacturing Co (Ramsbottom) Ltd, a weaving firm in the Rossendale valley, followed by Hollins Mill Co of Manchester, who were large merchant converters. One major acquisition was that of Tootal, Broadhurst Lee Co Ltd in July 1963. This was one of the results of attempts by Courtaulds and ICI to transform the industry from a chaotic collection of firms with outdated machinery and merchanting practices into a few strong and market-orientated companies. Harrison skilfully avoided too close an association with either ICI or Courtaulds by persuading them both to invest £6 million, in equal proportions, in ESC, thus creating a situation which enhanced the prospect for the continuing financial independence of ESC unless the two large companies acted jointly, an unlikely eventuality at that time. Tootals was acquired for £1,066,687 ordinary stock and £3,897,411 cash. Another major acquisition in the last year of Harrison's chairmanship, 1968, was that of the Calico Printers Association Ltd for £21,182,323 in shares and stock and £474,375 cash. Following the acquisition of Calico Printers, ESC was renamed English Calico Ltd. These acquisitions, and capitalisation of reserves in

1954, 1960 and 1964 had greatly increased ESC's share and loan capital. In 1948, ESC had an issued capital of £3 million; £1 million 3.5 per cent first mortgage debenture stock was issued in November of that year. In 1968, following the acquisition of Calico Printers, English Calico had an issued share capital of £39,911,471 and £17,598,024 of debentures and loan stock.

Emrys Roberts, who joined the new group from Tootal and was its secretary, 1963-68, wrote after Harrison's death in March 1980, 'The nucleus of the new structure was the joining together of English Sewing Cotton Co Ltd and Tootal Ltd. I saw it from the Tootal side and worked closely with Sir Cyril in the five years from 1963 to 1968, never ceasing to admire his clear sense of purpose and strong direction in difficult days'. {*Times* 24 Mar 1980}

Throughout his business career, Harrison believed strongly in the dignity of the working man and gave a great deal of thought to labour relations. He instituted a company pension scheme for the manual workers and built up an excellent relationship with the unions; he particularly valued a friendship with Joseph King, leader of the cotton spinners' union. His belief in leading by example created a strong sense of unity within the company and although he was a very positive leader his employees at all levels knew that they would receive a fair hearing and treatment.

During this difficult time for the industry, Harrison, who became vice-chairman of ESC in 1952 and chairman in 1963, devoted increasing time to outside public activities. From 1957 to 1959 he was chairman of the North West Regional Council of the Federation of British Industries and was president of the Manchester Chamber of Commerce, 1958-60. His appointment as president of the Federation of British Industries, 1961-63, was a compliment to his outstanding ability and the way he had maintained the commercial health of ESC at a particularly difficult time for the industry. As president of the FBI he was tireless in his criticism of the amateurish, fragmented nature of British employers' bodies and particularly castigated what he saw as a lack of awareness in industry of the necessity to think of commercial functions and labour relations together. He also felt strongly that decisions to close factories might not have been taken so easily if chief executives lived closer to their factories and workers, not 200 miles away in London. Following his term as president of the FBI, he remained on the Grand Council of the newly-formed CBI and became a member of the first National Economic Development Council. He was knighted for his services to industry in 1963.

He was president of the Cotton, Silk and Man-Made Fibres Research Association (The Shirley Institute). In recognition of his services to the textile industry he was elected a Companion of Honour of the Textile Institute in 1961. In 1965 he joined the British National Export Council and served as a member until 1972.

From 1965 to 1972 he was joint deputy chairman of William & Glynn's Bank, and joined the board of the Royal Bank of Scotland in 1966. He found the banking world an interesting contrast to the problems of a rapidly contracting textile industry. He was a member of the North West Electricity Board. Harrison became a member of the Court of Governors of Manchester University in 1968 and was made an honorary MA of the

University in 1961. He served on the Council of the Manchester Business School, 1967-73.

His appointment in 1959 as chairman of the Christie Hospital and Holt Radium Institute, whose work on cancer treatment and research was world-famous, kindled an interest in the National Health Service which became increasingly absorbing. In 1966 he began an eight-year term as chairman of the Governors of the United Manchester Hospitals, the Manchester teaching hospitals with close links to Manchester University School of Medicine. In 1970 he was invited to become High Sheriff of Lancashire but due to the serious illness of Lady Harrison, who died in 1971, he felt unable to accept this honour.

Throughout his life Sir Cyril was a committed member of the Congregational Church (later United Reformed Church). After his appointment to ESC he moved to Wilmslow, Cheshire and became a church deacon of Wilmslow Congregational Church in 1940, later becoming church secretary, 1942-58. During 1960 to 1961 he was chairman of the deacons and church meetings, becoming an elected life deacon in 1963. He was also vice-chairman of St Ann's Hospice in Cheadle, a charitable foundation for the terminally ill.

In 1927 he married Ethel Wood, daughter of Edward Wood, FCA, JP, a prominent chartered accountant and qualified steam engineer in Burnley. They had two sons. Sir Cyril Harrison died suddenly in March 1980 at the age of seventy-eight. His way of life had always been modest and his will was proved at £53,000 gross.

IAN HARRISON

Sources:

Unpublished

BCe.

PrC.

Personal knowledge.

Published

Times 18, 24 Mar 1980.

WWW.

Robert Harrison (from G C H Whitelock's official history of the Barber, Walker Co ca 1955, printed for private circulation).

HARRISON, Robert

(1824-1891)

Coalmines manager

Robert Harrison was born in Eastwood, Nottinghamshire in 1824, the son of John Harrison, a mining engineer. After some private schooling, he was trained, from an early age, in the profession of mining engineer by his father, and his uncle, Robert. He spent the whole of his working life in the employ of the Barber, Walker Co — a partnership of capitalists-cum-mining engineers established in 1787. He succeeded his uncle as 'over-looker' of the mines in 1852 and was appointed to a newly-created post of general manager two years later; a position which he held until his death in 1891. Harrison was a prominent member of a new class of professional mining engineers who were transforming the East Midland coalmining industry in the third quarter of the nineteenth century, and his 'great activity ... in remodelling our old arrangements ... [and] the development of new collieries' {Martin (1872) 109} was recognised by his election to the North of England Institute of Mining Engineers in 1861 and his honorary membership of the Chesterfield and Derbyshire Institute of Mining, Civil and Mechanical Engineers.

In the early 1850s the firm worked seven relatively small collieries mining the best seam of coal — the top hard — at depths of between 80 and 100 yards but were 'in a low, even delapidated state' {Barber, Walker archives, general manager's annual report, 1888} when Harrison was appointed. The owners of the third generation enterprise had eschewed technical education and lived rather in the style of leisured gentlemen. Consequently they starved their collieries of capital because of disputes with lessors and of uncertainties about their potential. Harrison was the expert appointed to remedy the situation and he advocated a vigorous investment programme aimed initially at remodelling existing collieries and, in the longer run, at replacing them, when their coal reserves were exhausted, by a series of new 'super' collieries. This policy resulted in the fixed capital of the firm growing from £49,235 in 1856 to £80,371 in 1865, £187,601 in 1873 and £350,000 in 1888. Between 1861 and 1878, four new collieries, working several seams of coal at depths of between 200 and 300 yards, were opened and an existing one completely re-equipped. All embodied the most modern, proven technology such as ventilation fans, underground mechanical haulage, shafts with conductors and multiple cages and a modern pair of horizontal winding engines which made them both efficient and safe units of production. Harrison also introduced the first coal-cutting machine, a compressed air-powered Winstanley, into the East Midlands mining industry in 1879 and the collieries were pioneers in the use of various coal-cutters thereafter.

Harrison also took an uncommonly keen interest in coal utilisation and other commercial aspects of the industry and gave evidence before the

The Watnall Colliery, Nottinghamshire, ca 1890 (from G C H Whitlock's official history of the Barber, Walker Co ca 1955, *printed for private circulation).*

Royal Commission of 1881 on these matters. He was an enthusiast for transportation by rail rather than by canal and turnpike as hitherto, and a system of efficient screening at the collieries combined with competitive pricing and the purchase of a large Nottingham retail outlet enabled the firm to make great strides in the domestic hearth market from the 1870s in particular. Investment, production and marketing were so successfully matched that annual average sales increased from 150,000 tons in the mid-1850s to 256,000 in 1860-63, 680,000 in 1865-78 and 1,003,048 tons in 1891-93, and ensured that the firm always made a profit in slump and boom alike. A 6 per cent return on capital was regarded as 'very disappointing' and gross profits were about £900,000 between 1856 and 1888.

The recruitment and welfare of the labour force was another aspect of the industry in which Harrison took a personal interest. The firm not unjustifiably prided itself on both the quantity and the quality of its colliery housing built from the 1860s onwards, and the low accident rate and favourable working conditions in the collieries. The firm also contributed to the building and running of schools, chapels and miners' institutes in the Eastwood area and supported 'respectable' leisure activities amongst its workforce such as gardening, cricket and brass bands.

His son and nephew maintained the Harrison tradition and were both trained by Robert in the firm's collieries. Robert William Harrison, Jr, became manager of the first 'Super' mine, High Park, while John Robert Harrison became manager of Brinsley colliery and eventually agent for the whole Eastwood colliery group when the firm's activities expanded into other coalfields in the early twentieth century. Both men were elected to the Chesterfield and Derbyshire Institute in 1872.

Robert Harrison married Catherine Argile. He died on 11 September 1891, leaving an estate proved at £12,473 gross.

C P GRIFFIN

Writings:

PP, RC on Accidents in Coal Mines (1881) C 3036.

Sources:

Unpublished

Barber, Walker Co, Lamb Close, Eastwood, Nottingham, archives, particularly the general manager's annual reports to the partners 1854-91.

PRO, Census Ennumerators' Returns, Eastwood, Ho 167/2125 (1851).

PrC.

Published

Alan R Griffin, *Mining in the East Midlands 1550-1947* (Cass, 1971).

C P Griffin, 'Robert Harrison and the Barber Walker Company: A Study in Colliery Management 1850-1890' *Transactions of the Thoroton Society* 82 (1978).

R F Martin, 'On Coal Cutting Machinery' *Transactions of the Chesterfield and Derbyshire Institute of Mining, Civil and Mechanical Engineers* 2 (1873-74).

W Weston, 'On the Winning and Working of High Park Colliery, Notts' *ibid*.

G C H Whitelock, *250 Years in Coal. The History of Barber, Walker and Company Limited 1680-1946* (Derby: pp, 1955).

Thomas Harrison (taken from Francis E Hyde Shipping Enterprise 1830–1939. Harrisons of Liverpool *Liverpool: Liverpool University Press, 1967).*

HARRISON, Thomas and HARRISON, James

(1815-1888)   (1821-1891)

Shipowners

Thomas Harrison, born in 1815 and James Harrison, born in 1821, were among four of the five sons of a substantial Lancashire farmer, James Harrison of Garstang, who went to serve apprenticeships to Liverpool shipbrokers or general brokers. Thomas and James were apprenticed to Samuel Brown & Co. The Browns had a connection with the Williamson family of Scarborough, small shipowners and masters, whose principal trade was that of bringing brandy from the Charente and taking out coal, largely for the distillers. This French connection had been strengthened when the Richard Williamsons, father and son, were captured in the Napoleonic Wars and the son married in France. By 1820 they were partly trading from Liverpool, using the Brown agency, and in the mid-1820s the firm was holding shares in the Williamson vessels. Richard Williamson Jr settled at Tonnay-Charente and by 1836 the Harrison brothers were investing in vessels with him, having shares in four small ships by 1842.

Thomas Harrison became a partner of the Browns in 1841 and the firm was renamed Brown Harrison. Outside the staple trade, their vessels made voyages to European ports and, under Richard Pierre Williamson, to Brazil, to the Crimea for war charter, and even to China. The Cobden-Chevalier treaty of 1860, favourable to brandy imports and guaranteeing the French cheap coal, encouraged the Harrisons and Williamsons to enter steamers in the brandy trade, beginning with the little *Cognac* in 1860, swiftly followed by two others; by then the Harrison brothers were major owners. An attempt to use the steamers to break into the London brandy trade was met with opposition from the long-established General Steam Navigation Co, closely associated with firms like Hennessy and Martell. Eventually the Harrisons agreed to cease to ship to London, in return for a free hand in Liverpool, Glasgow and Irish ports. Their steamers and sailing vessels, now underemployed, temporarily tried to develop the Spanish trade and cast about for other regular trades. The shipbroking firm had become T & J Harrison by 1853, and John William Hughes (qv), originally the firm's bookkeeper, began to take increasing shares in his seniors' ships, followed by his brother Thomas. In 1866 the Harrisons began to put ships in to the New Orleans cotton trade and within a few years they sent out Alfred Le Blanc to set up a branch office there, followed by the appointment of William Parr & Co for Galveston. In this trade tough negotiation with American railroads supplying the cotton ports was a main feature. The shipowning business was formed in the Charente Steamship Co in 1871, with Thomas and James Harrison as principal shareholders and their brothers, E H Harrison and John Harrison, and R P Williamson, minor ones. In the same year John died and J W Hughes bought his share.

HARRISON Thomas and HARRISON James

James Harrison (taken from F E Hyde Shipping Enterprise and Management 1830–1939. Harrisons of Liverpool *Liverpool: Liverpool University Press, 1967).*

As early as the 1840s Thomas and James Harrison had a separate interest in a vessel in the India trade and by the early 1860s contemplated a more permanent participation. By 1863 a ship with what was to become the typical 'vocational' line name, *Botanist*, reached Madras, and soon six sailing vessels were in the trade with about 12 calls a year at Indian ports, chiefly Calcutta. With the opening of the Suez Canal, however, with whose administration members of the firm were later associated, Harrisons began to put steamships on the Calcutta route, and move towards a regular line, 50 calls being made at Indian and Far Eastern ports in 1870, 90 in 1871. By the end of the decade voyage profits were around £2,000 to £4,000. An Indian coolie trade to Caribbean ports was carried on between 1870 and 1880 as a final employment for the last sailing vessels; the coolie trade was carried on unusually humane lines, while the ships began to open up the New York trade as a means of obtaining homewards cargoes to Liverpool. Simultaneously trades developed based on Central America and the Caribbean and reaching out to South American Pacific ports, Mexico and Brazil, the initial trade to Colon beginning in 1875, to Belize in the late 1870s, to Vera Cruz in 1876. Harrisons expanded the last till they carried half of Anglo-Mexican trade. A limited earlier Brazil trade was extended and made a regular line by 1864; from 1866 at least one ship a month served this trade.

The Harrisons were early accepters of the idea of shipping conferences, and entered the first, the Calcutta Conference, in 1875. Their notable place in the trade allowed them to send a ship to Calcutta every twelve days. The later development of the line, for instance the important entry into the South Africa trade, falls outside this survey, for James Harrison had retired from active management in 1880 and Thomas's health began to fail. This may have led to a relatively early move to limited liability by Liverpool standards, the Charente Steam-Ship Co of 1884, which had a paid-up capital of £500,000. Ownership of ships, previously separate for each vessel, was now consolidated, but the Harrisons, the Hugheses and the Williamsons still dominated. The fleet now consisted of 22 ships of 40,000 gross tons, a tonnage which was to be trebled before the end of the century.

Thomas and James Harrison were not notable for technical innovation in shipping: they had built up great skill as shipbrokers and agents and proved remarkable masters of the commercial aspect, with a willingness to experiment with new trades and press their development when the currents of international trade flowed towards new regions. They shifted from sail to steam once the economic advantage was significant and from 1860 carefully evaluated each new trade before serious commitment. They showed early interest in the Suez route, accepted conference working readily, and established the firm's long-continued system of buying ships only out of ploughed-back capital. They showed loyalty in keeping the Williamsons in the firm after the brandy trade ceased to be the main operation; and they recognised and advanced talent in their employees the Hughes brothers, a family which was to make an increasing entrepreneurial contribution.

Thomas Harrison had six sons by his wife, Sarah. He died on 22 April 1888, leaving an estate proved at £271,512. James Harrison had two sons and three daughters; he died on 7 January 1891 leaving an estate proved at £66,738.

J R HARRIS

Sources:

Unpublished

PrC.

Published

Francis E Hyde, J R Harris and A M Bourn, *Shipping Enterprise and Management 1830-1939. Harrisons of Liverpool* (Liverpool: Liverpool University Press, 1967).

HARRISON, Thomas Elliot

(1808-1888)

Railway engineer

T E Harrison (from Proceedings of the Institution of Civil Engineers *vol 94, part 4, 1887-8).*

Thomas Elliot Harrison was born in Fulham, London, on 4 April 1808. Shortly after Thomas's birth his father William, an official at Somerset House, moved to Sunderland in order to establish a ship-building firm. After being educated at Houghton-le-Spring Grammar School, Thomas became a pupil of William and Edward Chapman, civil engineers of Newcastle. His apprenticeship with this partnership included experience of dock building for the coal trade. In 1829 Harrison briefly left the North to pursue his career in London but, following a discouraging meeting with Thomas Telford during which the great engineer attempted to dissuade him from continuing in the profession of civil engineering, he spent a year learning accountancy and bookkeeping, which later proved to be a most valuable acquisition. In this period too he met and struck up a friendship with Robert Stephenson who employed him in surveying on the section of the proposed London & Birmingham Railway between Wolverton and Rugby.

In 1832 Harrison became resident engineer under Robert Stephenson, as chief engineer, for the Stanhope & Tyne Railway, which ran over extraordinarily difficult terrain for railway building, and two years later became engineer for the Durham Junction line. The construction of the latter included the erection of the celebrated Victoria Bridge over the River Wear which was designed by Harrison. During the years 1842-49, he played a leading role through his position as resident engineer for both the Newcastle & Darlington Junction and Newcastle & Berwick companies in the completion of the rail network between Darlington and the Border, and in 1849 became chief engineer and general manager of the York, Newcastle & Berwick Railway, an amalgamation of the principal English East Coast lines north of York. As Robert Stephenson, who was nominally in charge of construction, publicly admitted, the burden of responsibility for the building of the line from Newcastle to Berwick, including the High Level Bridge, Newcastle, and the Royal Border Bridge, Berwick, had fallen almost entirely on Harrison. Having survived the fall of George Hudson with his reputation untarnished, Harrison was soon heavily involved in drawing up plans for the more efficient working of the York, Newcastle & Berwick system and devising financial schemes to cover depreciation in permanent way, locomotives and rolling stock. He was also concerned from 1852 in the negotiations with the York & North Midland and Leeds Northern companies which led two years later to the incorporation of the North Eastern Railway. This at the time of its formation possessed a greater mileage of line than did any other British railway. Harrison later claimed to have been the first to appreciate that only an amalgamation of the three companies and not, as was originally proposed, simply a traffic agreement would permanently end the competition then taking place with the Leeds Northern.

In his position as engineer-in-chief, Harrison during the following thirty years fostered the expansion of the North Eastern not only through the construction of new lines — amongst which the York to Doncaster, via Selby, the direct route between Doncaster and Hull, via Goole, the Team Valley and Alnwick to Coldstream were outstanding — but also by contribution to the negotiations and parliamentary enquiries preceding the amalgamations with the Newcastle & Carlisle (1862) and Stockton & Darlington (1863) companies. These amalgamations gave the North Eastern a territorial monopoly of unprecedented size. Amongst other activities, Harrison produced the plans and estimates for York Station (completed 1877) and built docks at Hartlepool, Middlesbrough and on the Tyne.

Careful and methodical preparation and caution characterised his work, and claims concerning his role as an innovator in the use of hydraulic power may, with the exception of its application for shunting in goods yards, exaggerate the importance of his contributions in this field. The hydraulically-operated lock gates for Tyne Dock, Jarrow, differed little from those already installed at Victoria Dock, London, and the significance of the swing bridge over the Ouse at Goole on the line between Hull and Doncaster lay less in the use of hydraulics than in the weight of this structure and the decision to locate its primary source of power, a steam engine, in the centre pier. His instinctive approach to innovation is exemplified by his cautious attitude to the use of steel for rails. He regarded steel as being often too brittle and until at least 1874 preferred to use iron hardened by T W Dodds's patent process.

Nevertheless, shortly before his death, the North Eastern had 1,700 miles of track laid with steel rails as compared with only 650 miles in iron, and by then he confessed that he had underestimated the durability of steel.

On the national railway scene, Harrison sat on the Royal Commission on Railway Accidents, 1874-77, and, as part of the report of that body, submitted a paper which gave only qualified approval to the introduction of the block system and expressed that oft-voiced but by then clearly mistaken opinion that this system would reduce the vigilance and sense of responsibility of drivers. The block system should, he stated, be confined to stations and junctions. In contrast to his conservative attitude in this matter, Harrison welcomed a contemporaneous development in the field of railway safety, the continuous brake, and after prolonged trials recommended the introduction of the Westinghouse air compression brake on the North Eastern on the grounds that it provided more power than did its chief rival, the vacuum type. Harrison was also appointed to the Royal Commission on Water Supply, 1867-69, and he gave evidence to the Royal Commission on Railways, 1865-67. In addition, his reputation for integrity and expertise in accountancy and with statistical information meant that he was much in demand as an arbitrator in disputes between railway companies, and the London & South Western secured his services as its consulting engineer.

Harrison became president of the Institution of Civil Engineers in 1873 and in his presidential address opposed the establishment of rigid rules for the training of engineers but urged all entrants to the profession to learn bookkeeping. The Institution of Mechanical Engineers elected him a member in 1858.

'Honest Tom' Harrison died in his home at Whitburn, near Sunderland on 20 March 1888. He had been at work on the day of his death and was still chief engineer of the North Eastern, although his influence had diminished in the field of traffic management and in the 1880s was largely confined to that of civil engineering.

Harrison married twice, first to a Miss White of Whitburn, near Sunderland and on the second occasion to Sophia Jane Collinson, daughter of Rev Collinson, the Rector of West Boldon, and left two sons and five daughters. His estate was valued at £133,748 gross. Richard Hodgson, his brother-in-law, frequently worked with him on railway and dock schemes and was also his partner in a lucrative private practice based in Westminster. Throughout his life Harrison showed no ambition for a career in politics or for personal honours of any sort.

DAVID BROOKE

Writings:

Paper on Tyne Docks at South Shields; and the Mode Adopted for Shipping Coals *Proceedings of the Institution of Civil Engineers* 18 (1858-59).

Comments on the Use of Steel for Rails *Proceedings of the Institution of Civil Engineers* 20 (1860-61), 25 (1865-66), 42 (1874-75).

HARRISON Thomas Elliot

PP, RC on Railways (1867) 3844-I.

Presidential address *Proceedings of the Institution of Civil Engineers* 37 (1873-74).

PP, RC on Railway Accidents (1877) C 1637-I.

The index to the *Proceedings of the Institution of Civil Engineers* Vols I-LVIII, pp 208-11, covering Harrison's years of membership from 1834, lists his papers and contributions at meetings.

Sources:

Unpublished

PRO, RAIL 165/1: Durham Junction Railway, Directors' Minutes, 1834-44; RAIL 772/2,3: Newcastle & Darlington Junction Railway, Committee of Management and Directors' Minutes, 1842-47; RAIL 772/4,6: Newcastle & Berwick Railway, Directors' Minutes, 1845-47; RAIL 506/2: Newcastle & Berwick Railway, Statement on the Merits of the Proposed Railway Newcastle-Berwick (1845?); RAIL 772/24: York, Newcastle & Berwick Railway, Report to the Committee of Investigation on the Maintenance of Permanent Way, 20 July 1849; RAIL 772/25: York, Newcastle & Berwick Railway, Report on the Requirements for a Dock at South Shields, 14 Apr 1851; RAIL 527/284: North Eastern Railway, Report on an Equalising Fund for the Renewal of Permanent Way, 1 Nov 1855; RAIL 527/12-17: North Eastern Railway, Directors' Minutes, 1865-88; RAIL 527/332: North Eastern Railway, Memorandum on Steel Rails, 2 Feb 1886.

PrC.

Published

DNB.

Engineer 55 (1888).

Engineering 45 (1888).

Kenneth Hoole, *A Regional History of the Railways of Great Britain* vol 4 *The North East* (Newton Abbot: David & Charles, 1965).

John Marshall, *A Biographical Dictionary of Railway Engineers* (Newton Abbot: David & Charles, 1978).

Newcastle Weekly Chronicle 24 Mar 1888.

Proceedings of the Institution of Civil Engineers 94 (1887-88).

Proceedings of the Institution of Mechanical Engineers 1878, 1888.

William W Tomlinson, *The North Eastern Railway, Its Rise and Development* (Newton Abbot: David & Charles, 1967).

Yorkshire Gazette 24 Mar 1888.

WWW.

W E Harrison (courtesy of Mr John Briggs).

HARRISON, William Edward

(1875-1937)

Colliery owner

William Edward Harrison was born at Leamington Spa on 14 August 1875, the son of William Bealey Harrison and his wife Georgina Charlotte née Bancroft. The Harrisons, principal landowners in the area of Wall to the west of Lichfield, moved from agriculture by way of limestone-working to coal-mining and iron manufacture, though through three generations the farming interest remained active. Teesdale's Map of Staffordshire of 1834 shows Harrison's Collieries at Brownhills, where the first William Harrison (d 1877), of Norton Hall, Cannock, was one of the first to stop an issue of free beer to his miners, giving them a supplement in wages in lieu. Alongside J R McLean, he pioneered new developments in the Pelsall outcrop in the 1840s and 1850s and bequeathed to his son, William Bealey Harrison (1838-1912), who had been educated at Rugby, the playing of a similar role in the 1870s. By this time the Harrison enterprises had moved north-west from the Grove at Brownhills to Great Wyrley. William B Harrison was a leader in the expansion and the modernisation of the Cannock and Rugeley Coalfield: what had been an industry limited to extracting coal from shallow workings for an essentially local market with very limited local finance was transformed into a capital-intensive, deep-mining, expansive-market field. Harrison seized the opportunity offered by the incapacity of the South Staffordshire field to supply the local Black Country iron industry as the local coal measures became exhausted. Quick to see the strategic importance of securing railway links to ensure the full exploitation of the mid-Staffordshire deposits, he was elected both chairman of the Cannock Chase Colliery Owners' Association and president of the Mining Association of Great Britain.

William E Harrison was educated at Eton and Oriel College, Oxford. After graduating he worked three months underground and three months on the surface at the Cannock and Rugeley Colliery at Hednesford, to familiarise himself with all the miner's tasks, taking his snappings with the men in the dimly lighted stalls. It was this intimate knowledge of actual conditions that stood him in good stead in dealing with the disputes in the industry in 1921 and 1926. As principal of some of the most important coal-mining enterprises in the area, he became chairman of the Cannock Chase Coal Owners' Association from his father's retirement in 1908, and also sat on the Central Committee of the Mining Association of Great Britain. By the early twentieth century William Harrison Ltd were working in the Cannock region as well as at Brownhills and Wyrley, having purchased pits cheaply as a result of the earlier depression in the industry; for example in 1896 the Cannock & Rugeley Colliery Co took over the Wimblebury Pit. Another example was mid-Cannock, which had been sunk in 1873 but closed within a few years until reopened by W

Harrison Ltd in 1913, with coal drawing commencing the following year. In that year, one of his other companies built 100 terrace houses at Rawnsley for their workers.

Harrison's company chairmanships included the William Harrison Colliery Co Ltd, the Cannock & Rugeley Colliery, and later the Cannock Associated Collieries when the family companies amalgamated with the Littleton Collieries and the Conduit Collieries. In 1937 Cannock Associated Collieries had an authorised capital of £2,591,380. He was also chairman of John Russell & Co (iron and tube manufacturers) and James Russell (tube manufacturers) of Wednesbury and Walsall until these firms were taken over by Stewarts & Lloyds in 1929.

Harrison received the OBE for his service with the Royal Engineers in the First World War, having been twice mentioned in dispatches. After the armistice, his demobilisation was specially hastened at the request of the Coal Controller, although he continued his military interest as colonel in the territorials.

William E Harrison, JP, DL and High Sheriff of Staffordshire, was chairman of the County Council from 1927 until his death, having been first elected to the Council in 1913, and having previously served as the chairman of both Finance and General Purpose Committees.

The family residence moved from Hagley Hall near Rugeley, where William Bealey Harrison is reported to have employed out-of-work miners in the 1870s to develop the caves and water gardens, to Aldershawe, at Wall, and finally to Wychnor Park near Burton. Colonel William E Harrison married Edith, daughter of H W Gardner of Armitage, in 1907 and had two sons and one daughter. He died on 23 March 1937, leaving £1,392,037 gross.

JOHN H Y BRIGGS

Sources:

Unpublished

Staffordshire CRO, NCB archives and Coal Mining reports.

BCe.

Published

Frederick W Hackwood, 'The Development of the Cannock Chase Coalfield' *The Chronicles of Cannock Chase* (Lichfield, 1903).

Mining Year Book 1937

C M Peel, 'History of Coal Mining on Cannock Chase' *Transactions of the Institute of Mining Engineers* 110.

George Rickwood and William Gaskell, *Staffordshire Leaders: Social and Political* (Alexander, 1907).

Sentinel Year Book of the Potteries and North Staffordshire (Hanley: Staffordshire Sentinel Newspapers, 1928).

Staffordshire Advertiser 23 Mar 1937.

VCH Staffordshire 2, 5.

Who's Who in Staffordshire (Worcester, 1934).

HARTLEY, Sir Harold Brewer

(1878-1972)

Transport executive

Harold Brewer Hartley was born in Pimlico, London on 3 September 1878, the only son of Harold T Hartley, a mineral water manufacturer and partner in the publishing firm of Emmott, Hartley & Co and Kate née Brewer. His mother died when he was six and Harold was brought up by his stepmother.

Hartley was educated at Dulwich College. His subsequent career as a scientist was essentially academic and he had a long association with Balliol College, Oxford where he read chemistry, obtaining a first in natural science in 1901, although he was actually elected to a fellowship at the College before taking his degree. He was successively tutorial fellow (1901-31), senior research fellow (1931-41) and honorary fellow at Balliol. His earlier scientific researches were largely in crystallography, but he then developed an interest in the problems of the physical chemistry of electrolytic solutions which were to form the subject of his main contribution to scientific research. At the same time, he started to develop an interest in chemical engineering and the chemical industry both in this country and in Germany, which perhaps laid the foundations for his later career.

In 1914, following the outbreak of war, Hartley, who had been a member of the Oxford University OTC, applied for a commission in the army. His application for the Royal Engineers was rejected on the grounds that his qualifications were 'inadequate' and until 1915 he commanded a company in the 7th Battalion, the Leicestershire Regiment. Following the use of poison gas by the Germans at the second Battle of Ypres, his qualifications were remembered and he was appointed chemical adviser to the Third Army. He was successively assistant director of Gas Services in France and controller of the Chemical Warfare Department of the Ministry of Munitions. He rose to the rank of brigadier general and in 1919 was created CBE.

After demobilisation he returned to his fellowship at Balliol and resumed his scientific research, concentrating in the ensuing decade on the conductivity of electrolytes. His first direct involvement with industry occurred in 1923 when he became a director of the Gas, Light & Coke Co (remaining on the board until 1945). In 1926 Hartley was elected FRS. His activities widened in these years and government committees, directorships and universities made increasing inroads on his time. In 1928 he was knighted.

It was not until 1930 that Hartley made his entry at the age of fifty-two into the business world as one of the vice-presidents of the London, Midland & Scottish Railway. This was a result of an approach by Sir Josiah Stamp (qv), chairman of the railway, who was struggling with the internecine war still being waged between the men from the LNWR and Midland Railway. Hartley was not at all enamoured of the prospect and it took all Stamp's powers of persuasion to win him over. At first the tough hard-liners at Euston were upset, but it was not long before they realised that a great intellect with powers of analysis and decision had come among them. He was subsequently instrumental in establishing a scientific research department in the railway.

In 1934 the railways decided to utilise their parliamentary air powers and provide air services. The LMSR was one of the major forces in this decision and it was decided to operate a service between London and Belfast and Glasgow. The motive of the railways was to check the competition that might develop from the small number of internal airlines that had sprung up in 1933, the lesson of their experience with road transport having been learnt in part.

Since the LMSR was the main sponsor of air services by the jointly-owned Railway Air Services Ltd, it was not surprising that the chairman of the airline should be provided by that railway. Having carried out some studies on railway shipping services, Hartley was not surprised that Stamp sent for him. Stamp told Hartley that he wanted him to help develop air transport in Britain, although nothing could be further from the truth since Stamp always had a profound fear of flying and had no wish to see air transport add to the problems of railway traffic.

Hartley served as chairman of Railway Air Services Ltd from its beginning in 1934 until 1946 when its services were taken over by the new public corporation British European Airways. Throughout these years he took a close interest in the airline's development. (His journey on the inaugural Glasgow-Belfast-London service on 20 August 1934 was not without event when, as the small aircraft encountered a down current of air, his head pierced the fabric roof). Hartley did not, however, share the philosophy of Stamp and the senior railway officers who were unable to accept that other forms of transport might be more efficient than the railways, although air transport certainly showed no signs of becoming efficient and economical within the British Isles in that period. On occasions, Hartley became irritated when he had to spend a great deal of time with arguments which Stamp had initiated with a government minister for allegedly supporting the Irish government in not allowing the railway airline to operate to Dublin; but Hartley did not appear to try to change the conventional wisdom of the railways, especially as the commercial policy of the railway airline was usually dictated by the individual sponsoring railway.

Throughout his period with the railways until the war, Hartley contributed to other fields. In 1932 he became chairman of the Fuel Research Board of the Department of Scientific and Industrial Research and later adviser to the Mines Department. In the former position, he foresaw that, in the event of hostilities in Europe, aviation spirit would be needed in vast quantities and he began to think and plan accordingly. It was not surprising, therefore, that Hartley was made chairman in 1939 of the government factory for the production of 100-octane fuel. As adviser to the Ministry of Fuel and Power, he became a national advocate of fuel economy. He also served as chairman from 1941 of the committee that estimated the production and consumption of oil by the Axis powers and advised on the choice of the targets for bombing, and as chairman of the Fido Scientific Committee (Fido was a means of dispensing fog on RAF runways).

Hartley continued his chairmanship of Railway Air Services in the war, as well as chairing the Associated Airways Joint Committee which supervised, on behalf of the Air Ministry, the other internal airlines of which the railways had earlier gained control. Most of the internal air services were suspended during the war, but in the latter part of the conflict, Hartley became involved in negotiations with Government and others about railway aspirations to develop and thereby control the post-war growth of civil aviation. He also helped during the war to turn over the LMS railway workshops to aircraft and tanks.

Hartley certainly did not share the oligopolistic philosophy of many of his railway colleagues, although he was painfully aware of the economics of air transport — all the pre-war internal air services had been operated without profit. It was, therefore, not very surprising when the Government asked him to be chairman of British European Airways which by 1946, following the change of Government the previous year, was no longer to be controlled by the railways, but by the state. During the first months of BEA's formation, decisions were taken under his chairmanship which were crucial in determining subsequent achievements of the state-owned airline. Hartley did not stay long at BEA and in 1947 was promoted at the age of sixty-nine to the chairmanship of the larger state-owned British Overseas Airways Corporation which had been formed in 1940 out of Imperial Airways and British Airways Ltd. By this time he was a semi-cripple suffering from acute arthritis, but he refused to accept immobility and made a point of travelling the whole network using the airline's scheduled services in contrast to his predecessor who had a special aircraft. If there was a problem to be solved, Hartley would get colleagues around him and a meeting would often extend well into the evening until a decision was reached. By setting up committees and sub-committees he encouraged middle rank executives to take a lead in discussions. He saw BOAC through two difficult years before the delivery of its first new aircraft after the war. This involved him in a fight with the Treasury which was opposed to the purchase of more readily-available and suitable American aircraft.

Upon leaving BOAC in 1949 he became the first chairman of the Electricity Supply Research Council, serving until 1952. In 1950 he was chairman of the fourth World Power Conference in London, having served as chairman of the British National Committee and International

Executive Council of the World Power Conference, 1935-50. At the London Conference he was elected president of the World Power Conference, serving until 1956. In 1950 he also served as president of the British Association for the Advancement of Science. He was president of the Institution of Chemical Engineers, 1951-52 and 1954-55, and president of the Society of Instrument Technology, 1957-61.

In the 1950s Hartley was a keen advocate of coal and deplored the conversion of power stations to oil. He served as chairman of the Energy Commission of the Organisation for European Economic Co-operation, 1955-56, and prepared a paper for the OEEC which he submitted to the then Minister of Power, Aubrey Jones. The theme of the paper was the maximisation of the use of coal in Europe generally. Though he was urging this policy at a time of acute coal shortage in Britain and just before coal was to become increasingly uncompetitive against oil, the report was well received by the Minister who asked his officials to formulate an energy policy; however, they avoided such action during the remainder of the Minister's period of office.

In the mid-1950s Hartley became a friend of the Duke of Edinburgh, as a consequence of his service on the Council of the Duke of Edinburgh's Study Conference on Human Problems of Industrial Communities, 1954-56. In the post-war years Hartley also pursued his interest in the history of science, frequently contributing articles to journals and editing others; he was first chairman of the joint committee of the Royal Society and Historical Manuscripts Commission.

In 1954 Hartley became a consultant to a civil engineering firm, Costain-John Brown which subsequently became Constructors John Brown Ltd after Costain opted out. He retired from this position in 1961 but was a consultant to the CEGB until his death.

In 1906 he married Gertrude (d 1971) eldest daughter of A L Smith, a fellow (and later Master) of Balliol College. They had a son, Christopher, later Air Marshal Sir Christopher Hartley, and a daughter. Sir Harold Hartley died on 9 September 1972, a week after his ninety-fourth birthday party at which, although bed-ridden, he had received and chatted with nearly 100 guests. His estate was proved at £48,406 gross.

JOHN KING

Writings:

Various papers on chemistry and industrial research.

Great Britain in the Twentieth Century — a Political, Social and Economic Contract with the Victorian Age (print of a lecture given in Brussels, 1938).

Science and Industry — the Pattern of the Future? (Southampton: University of Southampton, 1954).

(ed) *The Royal Society, Its Origins and Founders* (Royal Society, 1960).

Balliol Men (Oxford: Basil Blackwell, 1963).

Notes and Records of the Royal Society (editor for 18 years).

The Contribution of the British Economy (Oxford University Press, 1965).

Humphry Davy (Thomas Nelson & Sons, 1966).

Sources:

Unpublished

BCe.

PrC.

Interviews with Sir Harold Hartley by contributor, 26 June, 7 Aug 1972.

Information supplied by Sir Christopher Hartley and Rt Hon Aubrey Jones, 1982.

Published

BEA News 14 Sept 1972.

Times 11, 13, 14, 19 Sept 1972.

WWW.

HARTLEY, James

(1811-1886)

Glass manufacturer

James Hartley was born in Dumbarton on 13 March 1811, the son of John Hartley, manager of the local glassworks. The family moved to Bristol and then to Smethwick, Birmingham, where John Hartley, a talented manufacturer, became managing partner in the Birmingham crown glass firm of Chance & Hartley. James Hartley served a practical apprenticeship as a glass maker and on his father's death ca 1832 became a junior partner in the firm. Whilst at Chances, Hartley made several valuable contributions to the firm. He introduced notable economies into the firm's production of crown glass, firstly by using sulphate of soda instead of kelp or carbonate of soda in the batch, and secondly by reducing the wasteage of glass in the centre bullion; a process which James and his brother John patented in 1834.

More importantly, Hartley played a central part in the firm's successful launch, in 1832, of a new and improved process for producing flat glass. This process — the cylinder or sheet process — was well established on the

Continent and Hartley acquired his understanding of it at a French factory to which he had been sent in the early 1830s by William Chance. Hartley's familiarity with the cylinder process was a significant advantage in his subsequent career — sheet glass would not fully supplant the traditional crown glass until the repeal of the glass duties in 1845. However, flat glass manufacturers who had prepared themselves for repeal by establishing sheet glass departments during the 1830s proved far better able to seize the opportunities of the post-repeal market than those manufacturers who had clung to crown glass alone. Hartley's own proficiency with cylinder glass is reflected in a patent he took out in 1838. In 1836 James and John Hartley left Birmingham to commence business on their own at the Wear Glass Works near Sunderland; John Hartley quit the firm in the early 1840s to pursue a successful career in the Staffordshire iron trade. The glass works experienced a rapid growth and by the 1840s consisted of five glass houses producing both crown and sheet glass. This growth was checked by the upheaval created by the repeal of the glass duties in 1845. The sudden fall in prices and sudden increase in the number of producers created a temporary but severe depression in the North-East flat glass industry. Hartley was forced to discharge a portion of his workforce and until 1849 he himself took on additional employment as the manager of the Birmingham Plate Glass Works.

It was whilst at Birmingham that he developed the process which he patented in 1847 and which adapted the traditional method of casting plate glass to the manufacture of a new type of glass — rolled plate glass. The manufacture of rolled plate was a major factor in Hartley's success during the 1850s and 1860s. Besides being a lucrative product in itself it also strengthened Hartley's position in relation to his two rivals in the flat glass trade, the firms of Chance Brothers and Pilkingtons. Although rolled plate took some time to establish itself in the market, by the early 1850s it was clear that its low price and lightness in weight made it uniquely suited to take advantage of the new trend for light framed glass and iron structures. It was a sufficiently attractive product to persuade Pilkingtons and Chances to obtain licences for its manufacture in 1854 and to cause them to object strongly when Hartley proposed to extend licences to other manufacturers. It was subsequently agreed that no further rolled plate licences should be granted without the joint consent of all three firms. This agreement reinforced the alliance between the three leading flat glass firms. They had already come to dominate the manufacturers' association and they consolidated their position of power during the late 1850s by jointly buying up smaller flat glass firms in order to close them down; by the 1860s the three firms were said to be producing three-quarters of the country's total production of window glass. This was a particularly profitable period for Hartley whose works, by the 1860s, consisted of ten furnaces employing a workforce of 600-700.

During his later life Hartley devoted much of his energies to the public life of Sunderland. He served as Mayor in 1851 and 1862, was president of Sunderland Infirmary and in 1853, after having renounced the Wesleyan Methodism in which he had been brought up, became a staunch Churchman and a generous donor to the churches of Sunderland. He was a borough JP (from 1861) and a county JP (from 1867), a DL for Durham, and also a member of the Sunderland School Board and the Sunderland

Board of Guardians. In 1865 he was elected to parliament as a Conservative but retired at the dissolution of 1868.

Hartley retired from active management of the Wear Glass Works in December 1869. He was replaced as managing director by his second son John who, unfortunately, possessed none of his father's practical or business talents. During the 1870s and 1880s the firm's failure to introduce low cost manufacturing processes such as the continuous tank resulted in its rapid decline, and a year-long strike in 1891-92 followed by a disastrous fire pushed the already weakened firm beyond the point of recovery. A joint stock company was hastily formed to rescue the works but it failed and the works was demolished in 1896.

Hartley's main commercial interest apart from glass was the railway, of which he had always been an enthusiastic advocate. He was a director of the North Eastern Railway and promoted a railway bridge across the Wear in 1879 in order to expand Sunderland's transport facilities. He was also an active member of the River Wear Commission which took over the South Dock and rebuilt the iron road bridge at the Wear.

He married Annie Blenkinsop of Felling in 1837. She and their two sons and three daughters survived James Hartley when he died on 24 May 1886, leaving a gross personal estate of £147,623.

CATHERINE ROSS

Writings:

British Patents:

1834 (6702)

1838 (7886)

1847 (11891).

Sources:

Unpublished

PrC.

Published

William G Armstrong (ed), *The Industrial Resources of the Tyne, Wear and Tees* (1864).

Theodore C Barker, *The Glassmakers. Pilkington: The Rise of an International Company 1826-1976* (Weidenfeld & Nicolson, 1977).

W Brockle, *Sunderland Notables* (Sunderland, 1894).

Newcastle Daily Journal 25 May 1886.

Sunderland Daily Echo 24, 27 May 1886.

Sunderland and Durham County Herald 10 Oct 1862.

Sunderland Times 6 Nov 1866.

WWMP.

William Pickles Hartley (taken from W H Beable, Romance of Great Businesses*).*

HARTLEY, Sir William Pickles

(1846-1922)

Jam and marmalade manufacturer

William Pickles Hartley was born at Colne, Lancashire, on 23 February 1846, the only child to survive infancy of John Hartley (1824-92), a whitesmith, and Margaret née Pickles (1824-70). William attended the local British and Foreign School Society school until he was thirteen and then spent one year at Colne Grammar School. Prevented by lack of local openings from becoming a chemist (his first ambition), he helped his mother in her grocery shop and successfully urged his parents to take on a larger business on Colne's main street. At the age of sixteen he took charge of this shop and added drysaltery to grocery. Slowly he moved into wholesaling, by building up a trade in grocers' sundries in the villages and towns round Colne: hard work, usually starting at 5.0 am and involving walks of 20 miles or more a day.

At the age of twenty he married Martha O'Connor Horsfield, youngest of the 13 children of Henry and Ann Horsfield, grocers of Colne. In his business career her caution and coolness tempered his enthusiasm, while her understanding of the retail trade provided informed counsel and criticism. They had eight daughters, one of whom died in infancy, and a son who died soon after his father.

Hartley became a jam manufacturer by accident: after a local grocer failed to honour a contract to supply him with jam, he decided to make his own. With an established reputation for quality groceries, Hartley followed his market when he turned to jam-making, and throughout the rest of his career pursued high quality both in the fruit he used and the methods he employed to process it. The rapid growth of his jam-making sidelines eventually led Hartley, much against the advice of family and friends, to leave Colne and his grocery shop and build a factory at Pine Grove, Bootle, close to Liverpool and his supplies of imported fruit, like oranges for marmalade. The factory opened in 1874 but the risk nearly ruined him, for he poured all his capital into fixed assets (valued at £4,000 in 1881) and had to borrow working capital on terms which for seven years took three-quarters of his profits. These rose from £300-400 in 1877-78 to well over £2,000 in 1881-82 and, with a good summer, shot up to £18,000 in 1884. The Bootle factory had to be extended twice before 1885, when William Hartley & Sons Ltd was incorporated with a nominal capital of £100,000. This apparently paved the way for a move to Aintree, where there was more room for expansion. In the year of Hartley's death, the ten-acre plant at Aintree was producing 600 tons of jam a week. Hartley's business at Aintree soon became prosperous for in 1889-90 he, with John Bunting (qv), a fellow Primitive Methodist, promoted three turnover cotton spinning companies during the Oldham boom.

Until the late 1890s Hartley's markets were almost entirely restricted to the North of England and the Midlands. Growing demand for his jams led him southwards and in 1901 he opened a London factory at Tower Bridge Road, Southwark, capable of making 400 tons of jam a week. On the occasion of the opening Hartley announced with some pride that his works made preserves and marmalade directly from fresh fruit and lump sugar and no other ingredient whatever, while rival manufacturers relied on salicylic acid as a preservative. In 1920 Wm P Hartley (London & Aintree) Ltd was registered as a private company to take over the assets (valued at £1,004,270) of the earlier Hartley companies, for which £1 million was paid. In this new company Sir William, now the governing director, owned all the issued £1 ordinary shares (749,900) and 10,000 of the 250,000 preference shares. Soon after he sold to the new company 57,128 shares which he personally held in 19 other companies (18 of them cotton mill companies) for £81,121 15s; as it turned out this was a well-timed sale for cotton mill shares declined steeply, like the industry, in the 1920s.

Hartley became a benevolent paternalist impelled by an overriding sense of stewardship which arose from his Christian convictions. Replying to a critic in 1906, he publicly asserted that his wage rates for females were 20 to 40 per cent higher than those of his competitors; that his Aintree employees had access to a doctor's services without charge; that rentals in his model village ranged between 3s 6d and 4s 6d per week, inclusive of rates, taxes and water; that a thousand or more women came back to Aintree every fruit season to work in his factory; and that he practised profit-sharing. Certainly associates of Gertrude Tuckwell, then with the Industrial Law Committee, testified to the improved working conditions at Aintree, and his model village (built in 1888) ranked with Port Sunlight and Bourneville in the 1890s. In his factories he demonstrated concern for his female employees by providing gentle work slopes and labour-saving equipment.

He introduced profit-sharing at Aintree in 1889, after reading about French schemes. In his scheme, Hartley distributed profits (in proportions to total profits rising over the decades) according to the individual employee's work record rather than his wage level. The arrangement imposed considerable demands on Hartley who insisted, even as late as 1921, on reviewing each employee's case annually himself. By 1919 he was assessing, with the aid of his departmental heads, the claims of about 800 persons; at the time of his death Hartley had distributed, in all, £145,000 of profits to his employees, though in a difficult year like 1920-21 profit sharing was suspended and employees were paid a (presumably lower) bonus.

He gave at least twice as much to charity. Among the Primitive Methodists, whose working class origins militated against the emergence of wealthy benefactors, Hartley became a notable philanthropist and leading layman. Never a local preacher (as his father and most other active laymen in his denomination were) because he played the chapel harmonium instead, he found a new vocation as patron and statesman of Primitive Methodism. To mention only his outstanding contributions: he organised a Chapel Aid Association in 1886-89 to mobilise loans for church building; for three decades, starting in 1890, he served as general treasurer of the Primitive Methodist Missionary Society (and rigorously criticised mission station farming from a commercial viewpoint); he endowed a ministerial training college at Manchester and was responsible for recruiting to it, from Oxford, Arthur Samuel Peake, later to become an internationally-regarded Biblical scholar; and, on his own initiative, he purchased Holborn Town Hall, London, enlarged and refurbished it and then sold it back at two-thirds of the cost price to the Primitive Methodist Church for its national headquarters and publishing house. His services were recognised in his election as vice-president of the Primitive Methodist Conference in 1892 and then as president in 1909. In later life he promoted Methodist reunion.

Each January Hartley, as a spiritual discipline, set aside part of his income for philanthropic purposes, starting in 1877 when he gave a tenth of his weekly salary of £5 and a tenth of £380, his share of the year's profits. The greater one's income, he believed, the greater the proportion that should be given away, and during his career he increased his own donations from a tenth to a third of his gross income. Sometimes he bore the whole cost of a philanthropic enterprise, more commonly he gave a percentage to encourage others to do likewise. His friend and biographer, A S Peake, recorded nearly £300,000 given away, of which £230,000 went to charities serving the whole community, like the Aintree Institute, the Colne Cottage Hospital, Colne Hospital, the Liverpool Maternity Hospital, Homes for the Aged at Colne, and departments of the universities of Liverpool and Manchester. It could be argued however that Hartley ought to have directed more charity towards relieving the pauper masses of Liverpool and less towards his home town.

While he was emotionally very attached to the town of his birth, Hartley was publicly active in the wider sphere of South Lancashire, being appointed JP for the county in 1893 and serving on the Walton School Board. A Liberal, he sat on the Liverpool City Council, 1895-98, became a passive resister against the 1902 Education Act, approved of old age pensions and free trade (though his faith in this weakened after the First World War) and distrusted socialism. He was knighted in 1908. A life-long teetotaller, Hartley generously supported temperance education and became a vice-president of the British Temperance League and in this cause gave the diocese of Liverpool £500 when the brewers tried to pressure the bishops against the Licensing Bill of 1908.

Sir William Hartley died on 25 October 1922, leaving £1,086,444 gross.

DAVID J JEREMY

Writings:

The Use of Wealth (National Council of the Evangelical Free Churches, nd).

Sources:

Unpublished

Cadbury-Schweppes archives, Dollis Hill, London, Wm P Hartley (London & Aintree) Ltd, board minute book 9 Jan 1920 - 15 May 1942.

SOAS, Methodist Missionary Society Archives, Primitive Methodist Missionary Society, Hartley file 1913-18.

Private MS, Sir William P Hartley, notebook of income and charitable gifts, 1877-1883 (xerox copy in possession of Peter Fearon of Leicester University).

C Reg: William Hartley & Sons Ltd (20,755). William Hartley Ltd (39,710).

BCe.

MCe.

PrC; Will.

Information from Dr Douglas A Farnie.

Geoffrey E Milburn, 'Big Business and Denominational Developments in Methodism during the Late Nineteenth and Early Twentieth Centuries' (unpublished paper prepared for a seminar on Christianity and Business held in the Business History Unit, LSE, 26 March 1982).

Published

Henry William Beable, *Romance of Great Businesses* (2 vols, Heath Cranton, 1926) I.

British Monthly June 1902.

Walter L Creese, *The Search for Environment. The Garden City: Before and After* (New Haven: Yale University Press, 1966).

Manchester Evening News 7 Feb 1923.

Arthur S Peake, *The Life of Sir William Hartley* (Hodder & Stoughton, 1926).

The Primitive Methodist Aldersgate Magazine 1893, 1920, 1921.

Times 26 Oct 1922.

WWW.

HARWOOD, Harold Marsh

(1874-1959)

Textile company chairman, playwright and theatre manager

Harold Marsh Harwood was born in Eccles in Lancashire, on 29 March 1874, the son of George Harwood, Liberal MP for Bolton and Alice née Marsh. The family was engaged in the Bolton cotton industry, running the firm of Richard Harwood & Sons, founded by Harold's grandfather in 1854. Harold was educated at Marlborough and Trinity College, Cambridge, and had hoped on graduation to enter the family firm, but George Harwood had other ambitions for his son. Following his father's instructions Harwood went to St Thomas's Hospital in London, where he qualified as a doctor, and became house physician. After a short period at St Thomas's, Harwood set up his own practice in the City of London at Throgmorton Avenue. In this period Harwood was beginning to show that strong interest in the theatre which was to dominate his middle career, and despite the demands of a growing practice he wrote two plays, neither of which was produced. In 1900 George Harwood's ambition for his son underwent a reversal and Harold was called back to Bolton to begin his career in the family firm, which had been incorporated as a private limited company in 1898.

Harold's father required assistance as the firm's business activities were growing rapidly, enjoying the Edwardian export boom. Harwoods exported to Asia, then becoming an increasingly important outlet, and to France, Italy, Spain and Russia, finding expanding markets for their fine yarns. Harold appeared eager to join the cotton trade, showing no reluctance to leave medicine or metropolitan life, but work as an active businessman proved rather strenuous and after two years with the firm his health broke and he left for one year's rest. He returned in 1903 and remained with the firm until the outbreak of the war, taking full management responsibility on his father's death in 1912. The firm at that time operated 140,000 spindles in three mills, two of which were of very recent origin, having been erected in 1905 and 1907. Richard Harwood was among the top 20 of Bolton's 87 spinning firms and Harold's managerial responsibilities were heavy. Nevertheless, this did not curtail his other main interest. In 1908 he was instrumental in founding the Bolton Amateur Dramatic Society and he continued to nurture his ambition of becoming a recognised playwright. He wrote and produced two plays in the period immediately before the war.

Up to 1914 Harwood was a businessman first and a playwright second, but the First World War led him temporarily to abandon both for his original profession of medicine. At the start of hostilities Harwood joined the RAMC, with which he served in France and Egypt, reaching the rank of captain. Like many young men of his class the war led to a radical change in direction. (Both his grandfather and father had also made significant shifts in direction in their own careers and the young Harwood was thus continuing a family tradition.) During the inter-war years, although he maintained a loose connection with the cotton trade, he devoted his working life to establishing a professional career in the theatre. In this he was encouraged by his wife Fryniwyd Tennyson Jesse, herself a successful writer, whom he married in 1918. In pursuing this ambition he achieved considerable success, writing and producing numerous plays, involving himself in theatre management, and for a short period in the early 1930s going to Hollywood as a script writer. His plays generally were light comedies and he avoided any detailed treatment of politics or business. The one exception was to be his most critically-acclaimed play, *The Grain of Mustard Seed*, which firmly established Harwood as a West End playwright. This play, written and produced in 1920, was an attempt to explore party politics from the point of view of the individual in conflict with the party. Harwood believed that politics was too much dominated by party hierarchy and the individual who attempted to make a stand against the party machine would be subordinated to the need to maintain power. The play expressed Harwood's commitment to liberal individualism, which had run deep in his family's politics and which later was to inform his business philosophy and lead him to attack state intervention bitterly in the 1940s. He also showed a talent for production and theatre management, being closely associated with the Ambassador Theatre where he frequently produced his own and other writers' plays. Harwood was essentially a period writer, a skilful and practical craftsman but not an original dramatist. In broad terms his attitude towards playwriting reflected his business approach to the theatre. A concentration on light comedy provided a higher probability of commercial success than experimentation with original drama. In that he became a commercially successful playwright, Harwood satisfied his own objectives.

The outbreak of a European war was once again to lead to a change in the direction of Harwood's career. In 1940 he returned full time to the business world, becoming the chairman of the Fine Cotton Spinners' & Doublers' Association Ltd (the company's name was changed to Fine Spinners & Doublers Ltd in 1946). He had become an ordinary director in 1920 following Fine Spinners' purchase of R Harwood & Sons in October 1917 for £420,000 (£100,000 cash, the rest in shares at 2s 9d per £1 share). His activities in the theatre kept his involvement to a minimum and it was not until the late 1930s that he took a more active role. He returned to active membership of the board in 1938, became vice-chairman in April 1940 and just five months later, in September 1940, became chairman on the death of the incumbent.

When he was appointed, it was expected that Harwood would be little more than a figure-head, taking little part in the day-to-day running of the company. But the exigencies of war changed the conception of Harwood's role. In March 1941 the Association's managing director A M G Debenham stated

> when the chairman was appointed ... it was not contemplated that he would be a working chairman in the sense that he now is, but owing to altered conditions the chairman has put in a lot of work both here and at home and is also doing this without the assistance of a vice chairman. {Fine Spinners Minute Books, Board of Directors, 16 Mar 1941}

In view of Harwood's more demanding role, the board approved an increase in his remuneration from £2,500 to £4,000 a year. Throughout the war years Harwood worked closely with Debenham. Among the most pressing problems they faced were the implementation of the company's programme of plant rationalisation, the question of raw material and labour supplies, and negotiations concerning the level of excess profits tax and government compensation for closed plant. These activities brought Harwood into direct contact with the elaborate system of state controls constructed during the hostilities and largely taken over by the post-war Labour Government. It was in his opposition to state intervention that Harwood's business philosophy was clearly revealed.

Harwood utilised his position as chairman of a major company to attack the prevailing official opinion concerning the relationship between the state and business, and stoutly defended private enterprise and the profit motive. From the outset Harwood focused attention on the question of profit controls. He warned shareholders as early as 1942 that profits would be substantially reduced for a period of years due to the imposition of state controls. He returned to this theme in 1944, when he attacked as 'a delusion' the notion that firms could shelter permanently behind price controls and that a minimum price could be held which gave a steady profit whatever the demand for the product or the level of efficiency of the firm. Harwood was particularly critical of the 1944 government White Paper on Employment. He detected within it implicit support for an 'ominous slogan [which is] going the rounds ... "Production for use, not for profit"' {*Economist* 17 June 1944}. Harwood maintained that while in wartime the needs and interests of the nation are well defined, in normal times the interests of the state do not offer such clear definitions. At the end of hostilities, he argued, business would be faced with two key problems. On the one hand, a large volume of savings had been built up among the public at large, on the other, industry needed capital investment for the reconstruction of plant and equipment. The central economic problem of the immediate post-war years was how savings could be deflected from a rush for consumer goods into the demand for capital investment. Harwood feared that in the prevailing atmosphere of state controls nationalisation might be the preferred solution, though he was quick to point out that the cotton industry had little to fear in this direction. For Harwood, the problem should be left in the hands of the businessman who could raise the capital required for reconstruction from that source which in the past had served him so well, the ordinary shareholder. State controls threatened this group, which Harwood referred to rather theatrically as the 'old paratroopers of industry' {ibid}. They should be encouraged by lifting restraints on dividends and profits. But the 1944 White Paper, Harwood argued, offered no support to the ordinary investor: price controls merely frightened them away. In view of the risks industry was necessarily going to face in the post-war years he was particularly insistent that investors should be allowed a reasonable return on capital outlay.

Harwood set himself up as the champion of the small investor, a defender of the investing community against the growing encroachment of the state. He was, however, sufficiently astute to realise that he was out of step with the times. He admitted to shareholders at the 1944 annual company meeting that:

> I am probably out of date, but, in my opinion, a man who conducts — on whatever scale — an honest and profitable business is serving the state much better than he would by mixing business with vague and often ill-directed philanthropy. {*ibid*}

Harwood's pronouncements, as he anticipated, received little support. Even the *Economist*, which acknowledged the validity of some of his criticisms, referred to his 'negative stance' and argued that his position did 'not add up to a statement of policy' {ibid}. Harwood was not deterred. Throughout the remainder of his period as chairman he returned repeatedly to the need for businessmen to be left in control of their own affairs and to arouse stronger public recognition of the central role of profits in the private enterprise system. These two factors were seen by Harwood as the key to attract back the ordinary investor. In support of Harwood's crusade the Fine Spinners' board agreed in 1945 that '... arrangements be made for a full report of the chairman's speech to be inserted in the Manchester Guardian ...' {Fine Spinners Minute Book, 5 Apr 1945}.

By the late 1940s one can detect a growing confidence in Harwood's pronouncements. A variety of factors was obviously at work here, not least the realities of power as opposed to the vision of victory of the Labour Government, as it faced severe macro-economic constraints in the implementation of its post-war reconstruction programme. In his jubilee speech to the 1948 company meeting Harwood attacked what he termed the apologetic attitude toward profit-making. For Harwood profit creation was a wholly useful activity that had made Britain a great international power, and that eminence could only be regained by a return to the acceptance of profit-making. He told shareholders: 'it is not for those who make profits to apologise but for those who do not' and he called on the business community to attack what he now termed the 'silly slogan of Production for use and not for Profit.' {*Manchester Guardian* 15 June 1948} The shift from 'ominous' to 'silly' in Harwood's reference to this slogan illustrates his belief that opinion was now running in his direction, and he concluded his speech by a rallying call: 'It is high time this issue (the profit motive) was put frankly to the test of public opinion.' {*ibid*}

It is difficult to gauge the extent to which Harwood's crusade influenced other business leaders. He was less constrained in his approach than his fellow industrialists but he did take his critique of controls seriously and by the late 1940s he had the satisfaction of witnessing a concerted attack by industry on government economic policy. The FBI in 1949 attacked the high level of profits tax, and in a memorandum sent to the Chancellor made a number of points that Harwood in his more individual style had been propagating for some years. In particular the FBI argued that the incidence of profit tax fell most heavily on the ordinary shareholder, the very investor whom Harwood insisted should be protected and encouraged {*Economist* 15 Jan 1949}. By 1950 the climate of business opinion was more amenable to Harwood than it had been five years previously.

At the end of Harwood's chairmanship in 1950 Fine Spinners' trading profits stood at £2.9 million compared with £614,761 in 1940 and fixed assets had risen from £6.63 million (1941) to £12.43 million. A capital reorganisation scheme had been introduced, important rationalisation of plant and equipment had been undertaken and the company was a progressive innovator, especially in the field of new products. However, apart from the establishment in 1945 of special committees on research and finance there was little change in the top management structure. The firm moved only gradually towards a centralised system of company organisation. Harwood, in his foreword to the company's jubilee history (1948) stated: 'Of recent years circumstances have increased the desirability of more centralisation but the cause of individual initiative is still jealously watched both by branches and by the central directorate. It is on the proper balance of these two factors that our prosperity ... rests.'

HARWOOD Harold Marsh

{*Jubilee Distaff* 3} Harwood's successor to the chairmanship, W T Winterbottom, clearly thought that the optimum balance had not been struck. His first act as chairman was to introduce a policy of radical organisational change and a thorough overhaul of the top management structure of the company. Harwood's commitment to individualism may well have delayed the move towards greater central control and direction.

Throughout his chairmanship his theatrical activities were restricted, but in 1949 he co-wrote with his wife *A Pin to See the Peepshow*, a play based on an actual murder case and written as a book by his wife in 1934. It was refused a licence for public performance and although there were a number of offers from West End management to put the play on, the Lord Chamberlain refused permission. It was eventually produced on Broadway but it received a mixed reception and had only a short life.

Outside business and the theatre Harwood was a keen yachtsman, a passion he shared with his wife. He sailed ocean-going yachts both in the Mediterranean and along the coast of Africa. Harwood died on 20 April 1959, a year after his wife, and left £34,899 gross.

ROGER LLOYD-JONES

Writings:

Over 30 plays, the main ones being:

The Grain of Mustard Seed (1920), *A Social Convenience* (1921), *The Transit of Venus* (1927), *So Far and No Father* (1929).

Contributions to:

Who's Who in the Theatre (1957);

Paul Jordan-Smith, *For the Love of Books* (New York: Oxford University Press, 1934).

Foreword to *Jubilee Distaff: Fine Spinners and Doublers Ltd 1898-1948* (Manchester: Richard Potts & Partners Ltd, 1948).

Sources:

Unpublished

Bolton Central Library, 'Bolton Spinning Mills' (nd).

Courtaulds, Northern Spinning Division, Manchester, Fine Spinners and Doublers Minute Books: Board of Directors and Executive Directors.

BCe.

MCe.

PrC.

Published

'Pioneers of the Cotton Trade: the Harwood Family', *Bolton Guardian and Journal* 23 June 1933.

Joanna Colenbrander, *A Portrait of Fryn: A Biography of F Tennyson Jesse* (Deutsch, 1984).

Economist 17 June 1944, 15 Jan 1949.

Manchester Guardian 15 June 1948, 21 Apr 1959.

Arnold A Rogow, *The Labour Government and British Industry 1945-51* (Oxford: Basil Blackwell, 1955).

Skinners Cotton Trade Directory (Thomas Skinner & Co, 1923).

Joseph R Vose (ed), *Bolton: Its Trade and Commerce* (Derby: Bemrose Publicity Co Ltd, 1919).

WW Theatre.

WWW.

HASLAM, Sir Alfred Seale

(1844-1927)

Manufacturer of refrigeration equipment

Sir Alfred S Haslam (taken from J T Critchell and J Raymond A History of the Frozen Meat Trade Constable & Co, 1912).

Alfred Seale Haslam was born in Derby on 27 October 1844, the fourth son of William Haslam, a bell hanger, and his wife Ann née Smith. He went to school locally but subsequently received private tuition. Apprenticeship with the Midland Railway Works at Derby prepared him for employment with Sir William Armstrong & Co, hydraulic engineers at Newcastle. In 1868 at the age of twenty-four, he returned to Derby and set up in business on his own account, taking over the forty-year-old Union Foundry with a staff of no more than 20, specialising initially in the production of hydraulic machinery of an improved kind. Alongside that production, he was from the earliest years experimenting with new technologies, addressing himself particularly to the problem of how, mechanically, to preserve the surplus meat of the colonies in the Antipodes for home consumption. It was, however, as the developer and exploiter of other men's discoveries that he made his fortune. That he was not unique in technological expertise simply serves to underline his commercial acumen in being able to exploit a critical period in market development with well-developed reliable technology.

From 1876, the year that his firm became a private company with a nominal capital of £100,000, he was working at this problem, initially employing an ammonia absorption technology in collaboration with the firm of Pontifex & Wood, whom he subsequently took over. The timing of his movement into this activity was crucial. The market for meat from the

The SS Strathleven, *which brought a successful cargo of frozen meat from Melbourne to London in February 1880 (taken from J T Critchell and J Raymond* A History of the Frozen Meat Trade Constable & Co, 1912).

Antipodes was clear: from the mid-1860s both canning and Liebig's meat extract techniques were in use, so that by 1880 16 million pounds of canned meat were being imported by the UK alone. But refrigeration techniques proved difficult to apply to shipping. Until the problems of surface mould had been overcome by better sterilisation techniques at the turn of the century, chilled beef was thought to have a limited maximum life of fifteen to twenty days and to be totally irrelevant to the carriage of lamb and mutton because of the discolouration of the fat. Chilling, then, could be used on the North Atlantic crossing from the USA but was at that time inappropriate to the long haul routes from the Southern continents. Similarly immersion in ice or salt was not successful and ice-chambers proved economically unviable when 25 per cent of the cargo space had to be devoted to the ice itself. Attempts to resolve the problem took place in Australia (Mort and Harrison, 1861-73) and in the late 1870s in France and the UK: Carré and Tellier, using an ammonia technique, brought a part-edible cargo from Buenos Aires to Rouen in 1877 and a wholly successful cargo to Le Havre the following year, whilst Bell and Coleman, using a dry air technique which they had patented in 1877, brought a successful cargo of 40 tons of beef and mutton at 30 degrees Fahrenheit on the *Strathleven* from Melbourne to London, arriving 2 February 1880. It was Bell and Coleman's patents that Haslam took over and from 1880 he

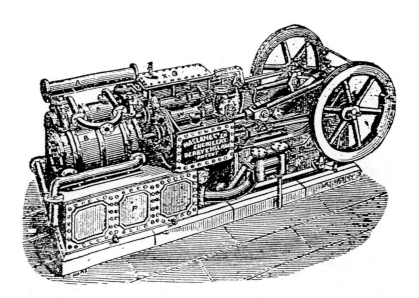

Haslam's Dry Air refrigerator,
taken from Alan Bott, The Sailing
Ships of the New Zealand
Shipping Company, 1873–1900
(Batsford, 1972).

exercised 'what amounted practically to a monopoly of British marine
meat refrigeration for 14 years during the life of the patents concerned'
{Critchell and Raymond (1912) 34}. The first installation of the Haslam
Dry Air Refrigerator was apparently in 1881 on the Orient Steam
Navigation Co's steamship the *Cuzco*, which brought 4,000 carcasses to
the UK at a cost of 2.25d per carcass. However, the slightly later voyage in
the same year of the same company's *Orient*, which brought some 17,000
frozen carcasses to Britain from Australia, received much more publicity.

From then on Haslam's refrigeration machinery and cooling chambers
served to open up European markets for perishable goods, especially fruit
and meat, to the produce of all parts of the world. Maybe the local Derby
author who claimed that as a result of Haslam's invention 'the poorest of
our working classes are now enabled to procure meat at a nominal cost',
and that without loss of 'any of the constituents necessary to the support of
life' {Wette (1892) 13-14}, was too extravagant in his praise but
Haslam'scommercial success was undoubted; ships equipped with his
machines carried the major proportion of the meat imported into the UK
for many years. The principle employed was that of compressing and
intensively cooling the air, thereafter allowing this intensely cold air to
expand and to circulate in insulated chambers, resulting in freezing or
chilling according to the needs of the cargo. The whole idea of refrigerated
foods was not immediately acceptable and met with considerable scorn.
This led Haslam to offer a guarantee, of up to £30,000, that imported
carcasses would not suffer from his process. After this initial hesitation the
response was vast, both in application and acknowledgment, winning
Haslam medals at the Fisheries Exhibition, 1883, the Liverpool
International Exhibition, 1886, and the Havre Exhibition, 1887, amongst
many others. Not only was Haslam's technology almost universally
employed on meat and fruit carriers, but it also became standard
equipment in warehouses and stores, both in this country and all over the

world. The new refrigeration technique was so efficient that it was applied to sailing vessels as well as to steam ships 'putting to the severest imaginable test the practical utility of this system of preservation' {*ibid*, 240}. The New Zealand sailing ship the *Mataura* successfully brought 4,000 carcasses of mutton to London after a voyage of 102 days, with a 70 hp steam engine controlling the refrigeration at an expense of 160 tons of coal: this, however, almost proved the end of Haslam's career in so far as he accidentally became locked in the refrigeration chamber at the time of the fitting-out of the ship with the Haslam machinery, at a cost of £5,000.

After 1893 the American ammonia technology (with which, interestingly, Haslam's earliest experiments had been concerned) became dominant, and electricity after 1900 replaced gas as the power source. Prior to those changes, however, it seems that Haslam attempted to preserve his position in the trade by entering into restrictive agreements with various shipping companies, undertaking not to fit out competing liners in return for a royalty (4.5d per carcass until 1888 and 2.25d per carcass thereafter) on the shipments by the existing companies; this was condemned at the time as 'unwarranted interference with the expansion of the frozen meat trade' {Macdonald (1958) 138}.

Alongside the production of refrigeration plant, for which Haslam constructed a mock-up of a ship's hold in a large building at Derby, Haslam's foundry also undertook general engineering. Employing some 600-700 men in 1898, it manufactured many kinds of boilers and hydraulic apparatus, hoists and mill machinery, the whole enterprise being driven by three steam engines. By the end of the century, when Haslam's refrigeration production also included the ammonia system of compression and absorption technology the units being built were capable of producing 200 tons of ice and refrigerating a cargo of 3,000-4,000 tons of meat or other produce. Refrigeration technology was by then applied beyond the carriage of perishable goods to brewing, milk-condensing and cream manufacture, vinegar-making, oil works, the craft of the coppersmith and of air-conditioning in hospitals overseas. Refrigeration was important in the manufacture of explosives and in rendering them stable in transit. Accordingly, Haslam's machinery was in demand for the proper equipment of warships in the early decades of an increasingly tense and uncertain twentieth century. All this spelt success; a Derby journalist recollected Haslam as a dour old gentleman, prone to grumbling over the fact that he had to pay £300 a week in tax.

Haslam's business career, which also included a directorship of the Derby & Derbyshire Bank, ran alongside a lifetime of public service which received its due recognition: in 1879 he became a town councillor and in 1886 a JP; he was awarded the Freedom of the City of London in 1889: and was made Lord Lieutenant of the County of Derbyshire in 1891, having served as Mayor of Derby in the previous year. In 1890-91 he was much engaged with raising funds to replace the old County Infirmary and it was on the occasion of Queen Victoria's laying the foundation stone of the new hospital that she announced the conferment of a knighthood on Haslam. Converted from being a Liberal to a Fair-Trader (as also from Nonconformity to Anglicanism), Haslam failed to take Derby for the Unionists in 1892, but represented Newcastle-under-Lyme from 1900 to 1906 as a Liberal Unionist and was mayor of the borough, 1901-4. At

Westminster he favoured the reorganisation of the War Office, poor law reform and fiscal reform. His philanthropy was principally concerned with medical charities, the Manchester Unity of Oddfellows, and with church restoration in his native Derby, but also included the presentation of statues of Queen Victoria to London and Newcastle-under-Lyme as well as to Derby. From 1899 his residence was at Breadsall Priory.

Haslam in 1875 married Ann Tatam, daughter of Thomas Tatam, a farmer of Little Eaton: they had five children.

Sir Alfred Haslam died in a London hotel on 13 January 1927, leaving £1,064,394 gross. Eric Haslam, the only one of three sons to survive his father, worked for the family business which subsequently became the Derby Pure Ice & Cold Storage Co Ltd. Of Haslam's two daughters, Edith was a spinster and Hilda was married to a clergyman.

JOHN H Y BRIGGS

Sources:

Unpublished

BCe.

MCe.

PrC.

Published

Alan J Bott, *The Sailing Ships of the New Zealand Shipping Company, 1873-1900* (Batsford, 1972).

John Potter Briscoe, *Nottingham and Derbyshire at the Opening of the Twentieth Century. Contemporary Biographies* (Brighton: W T Pike, 1901).

James T Critchell and Joseph Raymond, *A History of the Frozen Meat Trade* (Constable, 1912).

Derby Illustrated: Its Art, Trade and Commerce (Brighton, ca 1895).

Derby Mercury 14 Jan 1927.

Derbyshire Advertiser 14 Jan 1917.

C Loach, *A History of the New Zealand Refrigeration Company* (Christchurch, New Zealand, 1969).

G R MacDonald, *The Canterbury Frozen Meat Co Ltd, the Past Seventy-five Years* (Christchurch, New Zealand, 1958).

Richard Perren, *The Meat Trade in Britain. 1840-1914* (Routledge & Kegan Paul, 1978).

Proceedings of the Institution of Mechanical Engineers 1898.

E W Wette, *The Oddfellows Companion and Guide to Derby* (Derby: Bemrose, 1892)

WWMP.

WWW.

HATRY, Clarence Charles

(1888-1965)

Company promoter and financier

Clarence Charles Hatry was born at Belsize Park, London, on 16 December 1888, the son of Julius Hatry, a prosperous silk merchant, and his wife Henriette Ellen née Katzenstein. His childhood was lonely and disheartening, despite the presence of three younger brothers. His father was an archetypal Victorian patriarch, austere and severe; his mother was greatly concerned with her position in Hampstead society and gave little time to her children. The young boy was left to fend for himself and he developed a penchant for mechanical gadgets and similar inventions. Between January 1903 and April 1905, he attended St Paul's School in Hammersmith, where he excelled in Latin and drawing; on leaving school, he intended to go to university and then into business. Hatry was wholly unprepared for the commercial life into which he was thrust at the age of eighteen, when he took over the family business on the death of his father. Stricken with rheumatic fever within a few months after taking over, Hatry spent the best part of the next year convalescing. The business did not survive and was placed in liquidation; the young Hatry had given personal guarantees totalling £8,000 and was made bankrupt. It is a measure of the man that he paid off all those liabilities within a period of two years.

In 1909 he married Violet ('Dolly') Marguerite née Ferguson. Two years later, he established himself as an insurance broker, specialising in the negotiation of insurance company loans to reputable individuals and to prospective beneficiaries under wills and settlements. Revealing a considerable flair for inventiveness and negotiation, Hatry went from strength to strength; within a matter of months, he was enjoying a comfortable income. Amalgamation and consolidation were the touchstones of his success. Before lending to individuals, insurance companies required two guarantors of standing; Hatry set up two- or three-man syndicates of borrowers, backed by a pool of commission-receiving guarantors, and cajoled the insurance companies into dealing with these groups.

His business thrived, and in 1914 Hatry was able to secure control of City Equitable Fire Insurance Co Ltd from its German owners. He borrowed £60,000 from a friend and spent some months reorganising the group, before selling it in 1915 to Gerard Lee Bevan (qv) for some £250,000. The experience of buying, restructuring and selling at a profit whetted Hatry's appetite for 'wheeler-dealing' and he took early advantage of the post-war atmosphere of company promotion and acquisition. In 1916 he took over the Commercial Bank of London Ltd (reconstructed in January 1920 and renamed the Commercial Corporation of London Ltd in

April 1921 to reflect a change of emphasis from banking to financing) to act as a 'clearing house' for his acquisitions and company promotions.

His activities in this period were characterised by the apparent economic good sense of most of his proposals; again, the belief in strength through consolidation directed his plans. Most of his corporate creations fared ill in the ensuing economic climate, and several had no other commercial or industrial logic. Amalgamated Industrials Ltd (formed in 1919) brought together interests in cotton spinning, shipbuilding and pig farming; a more attractive operation gathered together several jute manufacturers into Jute Industries Ltd (formed in 1920). Other companies — such as British Glass Industries Ltd (formed in 1919) — saw the loss of most of their capital, and of a large part of Hatry's personal fortune. He sought always to bear the brunt of the failure of his schemes, and, for instance, sank £750,000 or so into the Commercial Corporation of London to try to save it. He was unsuccessful and the bank collapsed in 1923 with an estimated deficiency of nearly £3 million.

In typical fashion, Hatry did not accept defeat willingly or for long. In January 1925, he set up Aylesbury Trust Ltd as a private company to take over his liabilities to earlier creditors and to act as a finance house. By the end of that year, he had negotiated the first of a series of promotional coups. Hatry promoted the Drapery & General Investment Trust Ltd, designed to amalgamate department stores in London and the regions. Capitalised at just under £4 million, the conglomerate was sold to Debenhams at a very substantial profit.

In May 1927, he introduced Austin Friars Trust Ltd, a £300,000 finance house which was to be the linchpin of his later enterprises and the central company in a complicated network of interrelated investment and industrial undertakings. At Hatry's trial, it was argued by Sir Gilbert Garnsey (qv), the group's liquidator, that the whole group had been insolvent from the very start. One of the pervasive characteristics of Hatry's business affairs was the frequency of voluntary liquidations, reconstructions, changes of name and intra-group share dealings — making the whole network extremely difficult to untangle.

Emboldened by success, and welcomed back into the City fold, Hatry launched on an enthusiastic and headlong progress of amalgamations, consolidations and promotions. His developments took two disparate paths: in the one direction, he challenged the old-established money market, wresting from it the lucrative provision of loan funds for Britain's municipal corporations; in the other, he set about reorganising British industry along his favourite lines — merger and consolidation. He maintained also his enjoyment of mechanical innovations, floating Photomaton Parent Corporation Ltd (which operated photographic booths in public places) and Associated Automatic Machine Corporation Ltd in 1928. In industrial terms, his legacy is impressive. Many of his industrial enterprises survived his downfall, albeit in altered form. He merged independent bus companies in and around London, sold them to London General Omnibus Co Ltd and thereby created the forerunner of London Transport. He tackled the major problems of the British steel industry, first by merging two dozen light steel manufacturers into Allied Ironfounders Ltd in 1929, and then by trying to reorganise the heavy steel industry.

As part of that strategy, Hatry sought to take over the United Steel Companies Ltd and United Strip & Bar Mills Ltd; he planned to restructure them as Steel Industries of Great Britain Ltd, and float the new company on the London Stock Exchange. The steel industry at that time was in a very depressed state, seriously disorganised and desperately in need of fresh capital and fresh management. Hatry offered both, but at an enormous cost to his parent company. The net effect of Hatry's offer to buy United Steel was that Austin Friars Trust had to find more than £8 million in cash.

Despite the withdrawal of some of his backers, Hatry managed to borrow or arrange to borrow most of the cash, but there was always a sizeable shortfall. Hatry had made several powerful critics on his way through the City; one was Montagu Norman (qv), Governor of the Bank of England, a staunch advocate of industrial reorganisation but an implacable opponent of Hatry's scheme, which Norman saw as grandiose and industrially and managerially unwise. Norman acted against Hatry's steel proposals in every possible way, even persuading a number of finance houses to withdraw previously-pledged support for the project. Hatry became desperate, faced with the prospect of abandoning a cherished venture and of forgoing a substantial profit. He turned to fraud to acquire the necessary funds.

His venture into the municipal loan business had been spectacularly successful, his aggressive and entrepreneurial practices winning business away from the older, traditional and conservative money brokers. Within a few years of the establishment of Corporation & General Securities Ltd in 1926, the company and its subsidiaries were supplying nine-tenths of the funds raised on the money markets by British local authorities and by several colonial Governments. Faced with the collapse of his steel industry plans, Hatry saw a way to utilise municipal funds held by Corporation & General — he intended to rob Peter to pay for Paul and to reimburse Peter from the profits of selling Paul. The essence of the plan was simple: borrow from banks on the security of forged corporation scrip certificates (for Gloucester, Swindon and Wakefield), which need never be presented for registration and could be redeemed when the steel combine was floated. It is hard to distinguish the author of this plan; many commentators have attributed the blame to John Gialdini, a member of the Hatry group of directors and a shadowy figure who never faced trial, having fled to Italy. Certainly, evidence at the trial supported that view. Hatry had not signed any of the cheques or documents associated with the frauds, and few of the prosecution witnesses even knew him.

Hatry bought United Steel and United Strip & Bar Mills in early 1929, set up Steel Industries of Great Britain Ltd, and immediately faced a swingeing stock market slump. In early autumn 1929, rumours on the Stock Exchange that Hatry's companies were in trouble brought drastic falls in the shares of Hatry's group of companies — especially Photomaton and its subsidiaries.

True to his colours, Hatry determined to support the market by buying shares to keep the prices up, ending up with more than 80 per cent of the issued shares of Photomaton, for instance. The immense cash resources needed proved overwhelming. Hatry and his three remaining directors faced the inevitable and on 19 September 1929 revealed the true situation to Garnsey, who had been conducting an investigation of the Austin Friars group on behalf of its bankers. The following day, Hatry and his three fellow directors visited the Director of Public Prosecutions, Sir Archibald Bodkin, when Hatry made an extraordinarily inaccurate confession, taking virtually all the blame for the entire fraud — a statement which undoubtedly led to the very severe prison sentence he received.

The Hatry group of companies crashed in September 1929 with debts totalling around £14 million; the amounts raised from banks and others on the security of forged and worthless stock and share certificates also ran into millions of pounds. At his trial in January 1930, Mr Justice Avory sentenced Hatry to fourteen years' penal servitude, stating that Hatry stood convicted of 'the most appalling frauds that have ever disfigured the commercial reputation of this country' {*Times* 25 Jan 1930}.

Due to the intercession of influential friends and helped by his consistently co-operative attitude towards those charged with clearing up the Hatry empire's convoluted affairs, Hatry was released from prison in 1939 before his term was up. He went to the Continent to start a new life, but the outbreak of war drove him back to England in 1940. He sought out his friends (principally Lord Jersey), borrowed money from them and bought Hatchards bookshop in London for around £6,000.

He launched his new enterprise with typical resolve and energy, turning substantial losses into substantial profits and following the familiar path of merger, takeover and consolidation. By 1950, the business was making profits of almost £200,000 a year and Hatry was again a wealthy man. His burning belief in consolidation was, once more, to prove his downfall. Anxious to achieve a stable, vertically-integrated structure for his bookselling, printing and publishing empire, Hatry sought to make the machines that stitched the books that his companies printed, published and sold. He bought the rights to one such machine and immediately became embroiled in successive rounds of teething problems, acrimonious litigation, boardroom disputes and substantial losses. Virtually a broken man, Hatry retired to the country.

Though his life afterwards was punctuated by several bouts of serious illness, and a number of coronary thromboses, Hatry steadfastly held to his business strategies. In 1958 he was buying coffee bars in London's West End; in 1962 he was revealed as the man behind a new group of industrial cleaning companies (subsequently sold to the public); in 1963 he surfaced in Scotland, engaged in takeover discussions with a large Scottish industrial group; and in 1965, only weeks before his death, he was negotiating to amalgamate a group of Scottish knitting firms.

Hatry was one of the first, albeit perhaps the least successful, of those modern financiers who recognised the marked benefits and advantages in business combinations. His activities had not only a considerable effect on the industrial and commercial life of the country but also a longlasting impact on the methods of controlling the stock market and the securities industry generally. Coupled with other financial imbroglios of the late 1920s, the Hatry affair was a significant factor in the establishment of future policies for the regulation and supervision of Britain's capital markets.

Hatry died on 10 June 1965 in the Westminster Hospital, London, after another coronary thrombosis. His will was proved at just £828 and probate was granted to his widow; the net value of his estate, however, was nil.

DAVID FANNING

Writings:

Light Out of Darkness (Rich & Cowan, 1936).

Sources:

Unpublished

BCe.

PrC.

Published

The Accountant 28 Sept, 5 Oct 1929, 25 Jan, 1 Feb 1930.

DNB.

Economist 1928, 1929 (passim).

David Fanning, *Financial Means: A Biography of Clarence Hatry* (forthcoming).

R A Haldane, *With Intent to Deceive: Frauds Famous and Infamous* (Edinburgh: Blackwood, 1970).

William Hall, 'The First Great Crash of '29' *Financial Times* 22 Sept 1979.

Cecil Hatry, *The Hatry Case: Eight Current Misconceptions* (Pollock & Co, 1938).

P S Manley, 'Clarence Hatry' *Abacus* 12 (1976).

Michael Pearson, *The Millionaire Mentality* (Secker & Warburg, 1961).

Times Sept 1929-Jan 1930.

Aylmer Vallance, *Very Private Enterprise: An Anatomy of Fraud and High Finance* (Thames & Hudson, 1955).

R G Walker, 'The Hatry Affair' *Abacus* 13 (1977).

Peter Wilsher, 'Hatry: No More Silver Bullets' *Sunday Times* 13 June 1965.

HATTERSLEY, Richard Longden

(1820-1900)

Textile machinery manufacturer

Richard Longden Hattersley was born in Keighley, Yorkshire, on 1 December 1820, the elder of the two sons of George Hattersley and Elizabeth née Mitchell. Both of Hattersley's parents hailed from Keighley: his mother was the daughter of a noted local worsted manufacturer, and his father ran a whitesmith and textile engineering firm that had been established in the town as early as 1789 by his grandfather Richard Hattersley.

It is possible that Hattersley's pre-occupation with fostering the family firm was related to his comparatively narrow and short-lived formal education. He attended two private schools of no great distinction, one in Keighley, the other in nearby Yeadon, and neither of these modest establishments was likely to have opened up wider horizons in his mind. Soon after his fourteenth birthday he was inducted into his father's concern and, as was the prevailing custom, was 'put through' the entire works. This 'apprenticeship' proved to be extremely valuable in that 'Little Dick' — a nickname which, despite (or perhaps because of) its increasingly improbable ring, stuck throughout his life — acquired a close familiarity with all the existing work processes, the technicalities of production and design, and the commercial aspects of the business. The very year that Hattersley entered the firm his father brought out the first powerloom for the worsted trade (although the first batch of machinery was smashed on the way to its Bradford destination, probably by a group of fearful hand-loom weavers). The production of a powerloom was the culmination of a trend which had been under way for some three decades. From the late eighteenth century Hattersleys were steadily moving away from their general engineering origins towards greater specialisation, supplying the expanding textile industry with a range of parts such as rollers, spindles and flyers. Once it became obvious, however, that the Lancashire-based machinists had secured the market for plain single-shuttle looms, George Hattersley decided to concentrate the firm's activities upon the production of weaving equipment for the woollen, and particularly the worsted, end of the market. By the time Richard Hattersley took over sole control of the firm (his father died in 1869, and his brother, Edward, a co-partner from 1861, concentrated upon the cloth weaving mills at Haworth, a subsidiary of the parent organisation), the overall direction of the enterprise had already been determined. It was therefore left to Richard to build upon these solid foundations and to transform the firm (registered as a private limited company in 1888 with a paid-up capital of £90,000) from a relatively small and local concern into a nationally, and later internationally, known and respected one.

The basis of this achievement was twofold. In the first place Hattersley developed a line of looms and accessories (primarily, but not exclusively, geared toward the worsted sector) which enabled purchasing mills both to improve upon existing levels of efficiency and, more significantly, to open out new areas of textile demand. These advances came about partly as a result of his undoubted capacity as an innovator and, somewhat more contentiously, through his skills as an inventor. Almost from the outset of his career Hattersley began tinkering with the machinery, and at the age of twenty-one sought independent advice from a firm of London solicitors about how best to secure inventions. At this early stage he appears to have been interested in the possibility of making specialised looms for canvas, linen, sacking and towelling (which eventually led to the growth of a useful sales outlet), but very quickly he concentrated upon the task of perfecting looms with multiple box motions. The original circular box principle had been worked out in 1843 by Luke Smith but was clumsy and deficient on a number of counts, and in 1858 Hattersley patented his own revolving box loom, which soon became the standard model. This loom permitted a significant increase in working speeds (from 120 to 180 picks per minute), and considerably enlarged the range of colours that could be woven. The loom won the first prize at the prestigious London Exhibition of 1862, and the favourable publicity that followed paved the way for a substantial increase in both the volume of Hattersley's loom output (829 produced in 1861, 2,400 two years later), and the value of its sales (£11,964 to £25,631 over the same period). Not content with this, Hattersley constantly sought to improve his product, and in 1869 had a hand in the invention of the circular skip box (on the rack-and-pinion principle) which allowed greater flexibility in the ordering sequence of coloured threads in the weave. The main credit for this device belonged to an employee, James Hill, an overlooker who eventually fell out with his boss over the royalties (Hill started legal proceedings against the firm in 1891 and the terms of their out-of-court settlement were certainly favourable to the plaintiff). A second major technological breakthrough was the invention and subsequent innovation of the dobby loom in the mid-1860s. The first baulk dobby, which became universally known as the Keighley dobby, was patented by Hattersley and Smith (another of the firm's inventive employees, and of the same calibre as Hill) in September 1865, and perfected two years later. The dobby, a shedding mechanism, was second only to a Jacquard attachment in allowing the production of a highly complex and multi-coloured weave. The potential advantages of this machine were enormous, and the firms which had just begun to manufacture light, fancy fabrics, mainly using the revolving box loom in and around the twin towns of Nelson and Colne, were eager to acquire it. So popular did the dobby become that upon the expiry of the patent rights Hattersley's competitors made a determined effort to manufacture it and exploit its appeal. Many modifications were attempted over the following half-century (not least by Hattersleys themselves), but none could fundamentally alter its performance, and the Keighley dobby retained its reputation. These two crucial mechanical developments were merely the outstandingly successful peaks of Richard Hattersley's experimentation, and his name (usually in conjunction with a member of his design team) appears on several hundred patent applications.

The second bedrock of the firm's growth and prosperity (the surviving profit and loss statements reveal only two years of unprofitability between 1889 and 1903) was the energy and flair of its salesmanship. Hattersley had much to do with the promotion of his firm's products, and the organisation of an increasingly complex web of market outlets. His extant diaries and notebooks reveal an extraordinarily active and indefatigible traveller, at first by pony, and then by rail. Hattersley seems to have made many hundreds of personal visits to mills both at home and abroad, and he devoted much time and effort to promoting exports, an activity which his father had begun but in a limited way. No linguist himself (though most of the catalogues printed in his time were written in French and German as well as English), he spent longish periods in Western Europe, and he later despatched expert staff to more distant areas in Eastern Europe, Asia and the USA. Although the order books await definitive analysis, just after his death over half the firm's sales were to overseas markets (£62,400 out of £114,600, with an additional £12,700 for spares and parts probably equally split between the two), mainly bound for France, Belgium and Italy (the so-called 'tapestry' trade). No opportunity was lost to take part in international exhibitions, and selling agency contracts were concluded for the chief markets in order to maintain the necessary degree of continuity and retain the regular flow of parts. Closer to home, Hattersley was a well-known figure at the Bradford and the Manchester Exchanges, and he was a founder-member of the Keighley Chamber of Commerce. Although there is no record of any particularly novel innovations in Hattersley's marketing policies, it was unusual for a producer of capital goods of that period to take such an informed and assiduous interest in selling. A long time after the quality of the firm's products was established, he continued to stress the need to 'go to the market', rather than simply wait for prospective clients to come to Keighley. This is all the more surprising in view of his technical interests on the one hand, and the pressing calls upon his time of his civic career on the other. All this effort is, imperfectly, reflected in the growth of the firm. Between 1861 and 1900 the annual number of looms produced increased from a little over 800 to slightly over 3,500; total sales expanded from approximately £12,000 to nine times that figure; and by the latter date (there are no reliable returns for the earlier years) some 500 operatives were employed (excluding an equal number working in the Haworth mills, which were under the indirect control of the company).

As an employer, Hattersley may be described as a benevolent despot. He took close personal interest in the well-being of his workers, and deepened and extended the various welfare schemes that his father had pioneered. On one matter, however, he was implacable: he would brook no trade unionism, and branded any disaffected employee as an 'agitator'. His attitude may be surmised from a chiding address he made to a group of workmen towards the end of his life:

> If you will take advice from me I would impress upon you the necessity, the absolute wisdom, in your own interests, of never quarrelling with your employers. Work on as hard as you can, make what you can, put by what you can, and you will make far more money than by being influenced by outside people ... if men will only work there is generally not much difficulty in arranging it with employers ... we are not such oppressors as these agitators would have everybody believe {*Keighley News* 4 Aug 1900}.

Two influences probably underpinned this view of labour: his strong commitment towards Wesleyanism (which included a spell as a Sunday School teacher), and his almost lifelong attachment to the Liberal cause. Following his father's example he was an active member of the local party, but his allegiance was suddenly terminated in 1894 when, as a result of a personal slight associated with the growth of a Socialist grouping in the town, he became a Unionist.

This political affiliation was undoubtedly the crucial motivating force which propelled Hattersley into a second, and no less demanding career, that of civic improver. From 1869, when he joined the Local Board (soon becoming chairman), until 1894, Hattersley held civic office almost without break, and he was elected mayor in 1883. During his long service he applied his business acumen, his characteristic 'no-nonsense' sense of purpose and, not least, an unbounding drive and energy towards a great many local issues. There were few aspects of the town's growth over those years that Hattersley did not directly or indirectly influence. If any one element stands out, it is probably his shrewd steering of the gas supply subcommittee: between 1877 and 1882 he organised the laying-down of a municipal gas works which, unspectacular though it may sound today, provided a much appreciated supply of cheap lighting for the Keighley citizens. Besides this work for the council, he acted as a chief magistrate, was the governor of a number of schools and — probably somewhat altruistically — became involved with the running of the Mechanics' Institute. The combination of these two hectic careers left little time for the pursuit of personal leisure and his outside interests and hobbies were confined to the occasional concert and the billiard table.

Hattersley married a local girl, Ann Smith in 1847; they had seven daughters. The eldest daughter married a Skipton textile manufacturer, Alfred Smith, whom Hattersley groomed for the succession, with excellent results. Hattersley died on 3 August 1900 at his second home in Harrogate. Although there are no precise details of his estate, he left a little over £1 million — which included £245,531 worth of shares (much of it, uncharacteristically, in speculative mining companies) and stocks. His estate was proved at £356,529 gross, but before his death he gave £100,000 each to his daughters.

COLIN SIMMONS *and* HELEN CLAY

Sources:

Unpublished

George Hattersley & Sons Ltd, Keighley, archives, especially: Articles of Copartnership, George Hattersley, Richard L Hattersley and Edwin G Hattersley, 25 Apr 1861; 'George Hattersley & Sons Ltd, 1789 to 1953', typed MS, 5 Jan 1953; R L Hattersley, pocket diary, 1864, diary, 1899 and notebooks, 1846, 1853-54,1855, 1867, 1871-72, 1882; High Court of Justice, Queens Bench Division, *Hill versus Hattersley & Others* 28-29 Oct 1891 (4 vols); Loom Order Book, 5 Apr 1872 to 9 Nov 1900 (17 vols), and Posted Order Books, 1860 to Dec 1905 (6 vols); minute book of the Executors of the late R L Hattersley, Aug 1900-37; Private Ledger Nos

1 and 2, G Hattersley & Sons; Private Ledger R L Hattersley, 1881-86; Register of Shareholders, 1889-1949; Sale Catalogues; A Statement of the Proprietary Shares and Debentures of Public Companies held by the Deceased, R L Hattersley, 1901; 'The Story of Hattersley's', typed MS (1929).

PrC.

Interviews with Ronald Longden Smith (formerly Managing Director, George Hattersley & Sons, and great-grandson).

Published

Bradford Weekly Telegraph 19 Nov 1882.

British Trade Journal 1 Dec 1882.

Douglas A Farnie, 'The Textile Industry: Woven Fabrics' in Singer, *History of Technology* 5.

The Herald 16 Nov 1894.

John Hodgson, *Textile Manufacture, and Other Industries, in Keighley* (Keighley: A Hey, 1879).

Keighley News 4, 18 July 1900, 16 Oct 1937.

J de L Mann, 'The Textile Industry: Machinery for Cotton, Flax, Wool, 1760-1850' in Singer, *History of Technology* 4.

W Wilkinson, 'Power Loom Development' *The Textile Manufacturer* Jubilee Number 1875-1925, Dec 1925.

HAWKSHAW, Sir John

(1811-1891)

Civil engineer

John Hawkshaw was born at Kirkgate, Leeds on 9 April 1811, the son of Henry Hawkshaw, a farmer and publican, and Sarah his wife, daughter of Peter Carrington of Hampsthwaite. John attended Leeds Grammar School but left early to work for Charles Fowler, a turnpike builder. In 1831, he was assistant to Alexander Nimmo, a public works engineer in Ireland. Following Nimmo's death the next year, Hawkshaw went out to Venezuela as manager of the Bolivar Mining Association's copper mines, but was forced by ill-health to return in 1834; he later produced a volume of reminiscences describing his experiences. He worked under Jesse Hartley on the Liverpool Docks and with James Walker on the Leipzig & Dresden Railway. In 1836, he became resident engineer on the Manchester & Bolton Railway, which was completed in 1838. In about 1838, at the request of the Great Western Railway Co, he reported on the advisability of the broad gauge system, which he eventually strenuously opposed. He was appointed chief engineer to the Manchester & Leeds Railway (the nucleus of the Lancashire & Yorkshire Railway) in 1845. Amongst his achievements was the introduction of much steeper gradients than had been used before.

In 1850, Hawkshaw moved to London and set up as a consulting engineer with his son and his old assistant Harrison Hayter, but retained his connection with the L&Y until 1888. For twenty years (1861-81) he was consulting engineer to the South Eastern Railway, for which he built Cannon Street and Charing Cross stations, with the bridges leading to them across the Thames. In 1876, he adapted the elder Brunel's Thames Tunnel for railway use. During the period 1879-84, he collaborated with J Wolfe Barry (qv) on the completion of the Inner Circle, by building the section between Mansion House and Aldgate. Hawkshaw was consulting engineer to the Madras Railway for thirty-one years from 1857, and for a time also to the East Bengal Railway. In addition he worked for railways overseas in Brazil, Jamaica, Mauritius and Russia. Perhaps his greatest achievement was the completion of the Severn Tunnel for the Great Western Railway. Work had already been under way for several years when Hawkshaw took over in 1879. He had to overcome one difficulty after another before finally completing the project in 1886. The final cost was £1.6 million as against the original estimate of £900,000.

Hawkshaw constructed notable bridges at Hull and Londonderry, as well as the Nerbudda Bridge in India, which was nearly a mile long. With W H Barlow, he completed I K Brunel's Clifton Suspension Bridge. In 1863, he visited Egypt at the invitation of the new Viceroy. Work had started on the Suez Canal some years earlier under the previous ruler but following his death there were serious misgivings about the project. Hawkshaw's report dispelled them and work went ahead. When he attended the opening in 1869, de Lesseps introduced him to the engineers as 'the gentleman to whom I owe the canal' {Reid (1890) II, 217}. Hawkshaw was engineer to the Amsterdam Ship Canal which was opened in 1876. Three years later, he was among those invited to the Panama Canal Congress in Paris. Following the death of J M Rendel, he completed Holyhead Harbour which was opened in 1873. Between 1872 and 1886, he was joint engineer with Sir James Brunlees to the original Channel Tunnel Co. Hawkshaw prepared detailed plans and surveys, though later he refused to have anything to do with the Tunnel, believing that it would be a distinct national disadvantage. These were the highlights in Hawkshaw's long, wide-ranging and very successful career. In addition to numerous other projects in the fields already indicated, he was responsible for work in most branches of his profession, including dock building, drainage and flood prevention, the improvement of river navigation, pollution control and sewage schemes.

Hawkshaw held many public appointments. He became a Metropolitan Commissioner of Sewers in 1860 and in the same year, was appointed by the Crown to decide between contending schemes for Dublin's water supply. He was also responsible for a very considerable amount of drainage work in the fen country of England, where, in 1862, he constructed a tidal dam. In 1868 Hawkshaw served on a departmental committee to inquire into the construction of fortifications. When the Government bought up the private telegraph companies in 1868, he was given the task of distributing the purchase money. In 1874 he was sole royal commissioner to inquire into the best means of remedying the pollution of the Clyde. In 1880 he served on a committee of the Board of Trade to investigate the effect of wind pressure on railway structures. He was a fellow of the Royal Society, the Geological Society and the Royal Geographical Society, president of the Institution of Civil Engineers, 1862-64, and of the British Association, 1875, and master of the Masons Company, 1875-76. In 1863 he contested Andover as a Liberal candidate. He was knighted in 1873.

In 1835 he married Ann, daughter of Rev James Jackson, of Green Hammerton, Yorkshire; she died on 29 April 1885, aged seventy-two. Sir John died at his town house, Belgrave Mansions, on 2 June 1891, leaving £220,000 gross.

HENRY PARRIS

Writings:

Reminiscences of South America From Two and a Half Years' Residence in Venezuela (1838).

Die Resultate der Experimente mit Dampfwagen auf der 'Grossen Westlichen' und Anderen Englischen Eisenbahnen; in Auftrag der Directoren, der Ersteren, von den Ingenieuren John Hawkshaw und Nicholas Wood Angestellt (Hamburg: Hoffmann und Campe, 1839).

Some Observations on the Present State of Geological Inquiry as to the Origin of Coal Read before Manchester Geological Society, 25 March 1843 (Manchester: Grant & Co, 1843).

(Descriptions of) the Paddock Viaduct, Lockwood Viaduct, Denby Dale Viaduct, Tithebarn Street Viaduct, Liverpool (1856).

Account of the Cofferdam, the Syphons, and Other Works, Constructed in Consequence of the Failure of the St Germains' Sluice of the Middle Level Drainage (Clowes, 1863).

Rapport ... sur les Travaux du Canal de Suez, Suivi des Observations de M Voisin ... Documents Publiés par M F de Lesseps (Paris, 1863).

Report to the Directors of the Eastern Bengal Railway Company (1870).

Address Delivered before the British Association at Bristol, 1875 (1875).

Melhoramento dos Portos do Brasil: Relatorios de Sir John Hawkshaw (Rio de Janeiro, 1875).

PP, Report ... as to the Purification of the River Clyde. Together with Appendix and Minutes of Evidence (1876) C 1464.

'Introductory Note' to Thomas A Walker, *The Severn Tunnel: Its Construction and Difficulties* (3rd ed, R Bentley & Son, 1891).

Sources:

Published

Boase.

DNB.

Sir Daniel Gooch, *Memoirs and Diary* ed Roger B Wilson (Newton Abbot: David & Charles, 1972).

William Humber (ed), *A Record of the Progress of Modern Engineering* (1863).

Edward T MacDermot, *History of the Great Western Railway* (rev ed by Charles R Clinker, Ian Allan 1964-).

John Marshall, *A Biographical Dictionary of Railway Engineers* (Newton Abbot: David & Charles, 1978).

—, *The Lancashire & Yorkshire Railway* (3 vols, Newton Abbot: David & Charles, 1969-72).

Men of the Time (9th ed, np, 1875; 11th ed, Routledge & Sons, 1884).

Proceedings of the Institution of Civil Engineers 106 (1891).

Proceedings of the Royal Society 50 (1892).

Sir Thomas W Reid, *The Life and Friendships of Richard Monckton Milnes, First Lord Houghton* (2 vols, Cassell & Co, 1890).

Times 3 June 1891.

Thomas A Walker, *The Severn Tunnel: Its Construction and Difficulties ... with an Introductory Note by Sir John Hawkshaw* (3rd ed, R Bentley & Son, 1891).

HAWKSLEY, Thomas

(1807-1893)

Consulting utilities engineer

Thomas Hawksley was born at Arnot Hill, Arnold, Nottingham, on 12 July 1807, the son of John Hawksley, a Nottingham textile manufacturer who was a pioneer of worsted spinning by steam power, and his wife Mary née Whittle. Hawksley received private education under Dr Wood at the old Grammar School in Stoney Street, Nottingham, being a precocious and purposeful pupil. Leaving school at the age of fifteen, Hawksley began serving articles with Edward Staveley, a well-known local architect and surveyor, and also studied the sciences, particularly mathematics, geology, and chemistry. At the age of only twenty-three, he was given the task of designing and constructing a new waterworks for the Trent Waterworks Co. Nottingham's inhabitants at that time were very inefficiently served with water either from rival companies using the Rivers Trent and Leen, or from wells and stand-pumps; many households had to rely on water carriers, who charged a farthing a bucket.

Hawksley sought to provide a simple, but highly efficient and economical system which avoided leaks, provided pure water, and could easily be repaired. He furnished Nottingham with the country's first constant supply of water by means of continuous pressure. A methodical approach rather than inventiveness was the key to his success, although in 1847 he did invent, in collaboration with William George Armstrong (qv), a self-activating valve designed to shut automatically when the velocity of water passing through exceeded a certain limit.

The success of the Trent Waterworks, situated near the *Town Arms Inn* at Trent Bridge, was the launching pad of his career. He became famous throughout Britain as a consultant waterworks engineer and drainage expert. Besides his appointment in 1845 as engineer to the joint companies supplying Nottingham with water, a position he held until municipalisation of the water supply in 1880, there were many places both at home and abroad which used his services. He later claimed to have constructed over 150 waterworks. Particularly long-lasting, were his connections with Liverpool, Sheffield, and Leicester.

In 1846 he recommended the Rivington-Pike plan for Liverpool. This scheme relied on water obtained through gravitation from the Rivington district some 29 miles away, rather than the previously-used wells of the New Red Sandstone, and was completed in 1857. In 1874, a number of plans for supplying additional water from a variety of sources were put forward to cater for rising demand in Liverpool. These were submitted to Hawksley and John F L Bateman (qv) for consideration. Initially Hawksley reported in favour of the scheme utilising the headwaters of the River Wyre but Bateman advised against it. In 1877, the use of Lake Vyrnwy was suggested and supported by George Deacon, the then Borough Engineer, and an Act was obtained in August 1880. Hawksley was appointed engineer-in-chief, but resigned in 1885 following a difference of opinion over costs and responsibilities between himself and Deacon. He also became engineer-in-chief to the Sheffield Water Undertaking, following his report and advice on the disaster of 11 March 1864 when the great earth dam of Dale Dike reservoir burst, causing havoc and 250 deaths. He remained in this post until his death in 1893.

At Leicester, Hawksley planned and became responsible for the construction of reservoirs at Thornton Park and Bradmore Park. Besides being involved with schemes, both gravitational and pumping, in Leeds, York, Derby, Huddersfield, Sunderland, Oxford, and Cambridge, to name but a few, he was also concerned with waterworks in Warsaw, Stockholm, Bridgetown (Barbados), Alton (Germany) and in Austria and Brazil.

Allied to his work on waterworks was his considerable expertise in sewerage and drainage. He was involved with numerous schemes, including the London main drainage scheme in 1857 on which he acted as a consultant.

Hawksley's fame as a water and drainage engineer has overshadowed his contribution to the gas industry, of which he was one of the most eminent of engineers. His first connection with the gas industry was with the Nottingham Gas-Light & Coke Co. Called in to assist them during a troubled period in the late 1830s, he became their engineer, a position he retained until municipalisation in 1874. His skill as an engineer, and as a witness before the Parliamentary Committee on the Nottingham Gas Bills between 1840 and 1842, clearly impressed consultants in both the engineering and legal professions, and his reputation in the gas industry spread rapidly. He was consulted by many local gas undertakings in the UK such as those at Derby, Chesterfield, Newark, Lincoln, Sunderland and Folkestone, and overseas, in India, Denmark and Austria.

Such was his standing in the gas industry that in 1863, whilst he attended the first meeting of the British Association of Gas Managers (forerunner of the Institution of Gas Engineers) as a non-member, he nevertheless came away from the meeting having been unanimously elected as an honorary member and as first president, holding the latter position until 1867.

In 1840 he became a member of the Institution of Civil Engineers. Despite his long membership, election to Council in December 1853, to the vice-presidency in 1863, and presidency in 1871-73, he never directly presented a paper to the Institution. He felt strongly about only presenting work which was worthwhile.

He was also a member of the Institution of Mechanical Engineers, becoming president in 1876-77, and was elected an FRS in 1878. His services abroad were recognised with, for example, decorations from the Emperors of Austria and Brazil, the Swedish Order of the Polar Star, and the Danebrog of Denmark.

Hawksley became a well-known figure at Westminster. In 1852 he was examined on seven different occasions by the Select Committee on the Metropolitan Water Supply. When calling him before Royal Commissions and parliamentary committees as an expert witness, Counsels by the 1870s virtually dispensed with the formality of introducing him. It was known for Select Committees to ask Hawksley to make field tests and then to report back, for his ability to collect data carefully and calculate everything with mathematical precision was much appreciated. He was capable of almost single-handedly steering a bill through parliament. His opening remarks and evidence before the House of Commons Committee on the 1864 Nottingham Gas Bill occupied the best part of two days. So clearly and powerfully did he put the case for the gas company that, after having heard only one of the 23 witnesses against the company, including the town council and lighting commissioners, the committee declared that its mind was more or less made up and that manuscript evidence need no longer be regarded. On this occasion, when asked who had had the audacity to remove lamps from the streets of Nottingham to display as evidence before the committee, Hawksley replied that he had so ordered it — and that was the end of the matter.

As a businessman, Hawksley was evidently highly successful. Following his apprenticeship, he became a partner with Edward Staveley and Robert Jalland. After the departure of Staveley, Hawksley remained with Jalland until 1850 when they went their separate ways. In 1852, Hawksley moved to London where he set himself up in business as a consultant engineer with an office in Great George Street, taking his son Charles into partnership with him in 1866.

Hawksley had a very strong constitution and a tremendous capacity for work. Quite apart from his engineering and business interests, Hawksley found the time to erect a cholera hospital in Nottingham during the epidemic of 1832, and presented a great deal of evidence to the Royal Commission on the Health of Towns in 1844. Later he was appointed Technical Consultant on Water Supply to the Towns Improvement Co which had been formed by Edwin Chadwick in 1844. He was also very actively involved in promoting and carrying through parliament measures for enclosure of the open fields around Nottingham, which enabled the town to expand its building area in the second half of the nineteenth century.

If he had a failing, it was that of taking on more work than he could handle. For example, correspondence and minute-books of the Lincoln gas undertaking during 1845-47 point to delays in his work, and failure to keep appointments. Yet despite the difficulties caused by his elusiveness, the directors were deeply impressed by his professional approach, advice, and ideas for increasing efficiency on the technical side and in accountancy procedures.

Hawksley could be humble yet ruthless, kind and considerate but strict. He would not stand for insubordination from his workforce, nor tolerate rioters. Once during the Chartist riots, a mob bore down on the Nottingham gasworks, intent on plunging the town into darkness. Unperturbed, Hawksley barricaded the entrance, connected some piping to the gas supply, and announced to the would-be attackers the great peril they faced from flame-throwing jets and a mixture of red-hot shot and boiling tar. Needless to say, the rioters withdrew.

Hawksley married twice: firstly to Phillis, daughter of Francis Wright, of the Nottingham banking family, and after her death in 1854, he married in 1855, Eliza, daughter of Joseph Litt, a 'manufacturer' {MCe}, she died a few months before her husband. Two sons and a daughter by his first marriage survived him. He died at his home in Kensington, on 15 September 1893, leaving an estate proved at £104,654 gross.

D E ROBERTS

Writings:

PP, HC 1835 (116) XXIII, RC on Municipal Corporations in England and Wales.

'Atmospherics', *Minutes of the Proceedings of the Institution of Civil Engineers* 4.

PP, HC 1843 (431) XIV, RC on Childrens' Employment.

PP, HC 1844 (572) XVII, RC on Large Towns.

PP, HC 1845 (610) XVIII, RC on Large Towns.

PP, HC 1851 (643) XV, SC on Metropolitan Water Supply.

PP, HC 1852 (395, 395-I, 527) XII, SC on Metropolitan Water Supply.

HAWKSLEY Thomas

PP, HC 1860 (417) XXI, SC on Metropolitan Gas.

PP, HC 1867 (520) XII, SC on Metropolitan Gas.

PP, RC Water Supply (1868-69) C 4169-I.

Presidential Address, *Minutes of the Proceedings of the Institution of Civil Engineers* 33 (9 Jan 1872).

PP, RC Water Supply (1893-94) C 7172-I.

Sources:

Unpublished

EMGAS Museum, Leicester, 468, Report by Hawksley on Derby Gas, and Tender, 1849.

Institution of Civil Engineers, Library: address by Hawksley, 'The New Trent Waterworks, Nottingham' 7 Apr 1840; Tracts 8vo, Vol 105, letter Hawksley to Marquis of Chandos on the General Board of Health; Accident Report by Hawksley on Dale Dike Reservoir, 11 Mar 1864.

House of Lords Record Office, MS evidence before Committee on Nottingham Gas, HC (1841) 9, N, (1849) 1, Group 1, 2, Group 2, (1858) 50, NI, (1864) 54, N4, N5, (1873) 42, N5; HL (1842) 9, (1874) 7.

David E Roberts, 'The Nottingham Gas-Light and Coke Company, 1818-74' (Loughborough MA, 1976).

MCe.

PrC.

Published

G M Binnie, *Early Victorian Water Engineers* (Thomas Telford, 1981).

Boase.

Walter T K Brauholtz, *The Institution of Gas Engineers, The First Hundred Years, 1863-1963* (Institution of Gas Engineers, 1963).

Jonathan D Chambers, *Modern Nottingham in the Making* (Nottingham, 1945).

—, 'Victorian Nottingham' *Transactions of the Thoroton Society* 62 (1959).

Roy A Church, *Economic and Social Change in a Midland Town, Victorian Nottingham, 1815-1900* (Frank Cass & Co, 1966).

DNB.

Duncan Gray, *Nottingham Through 500 Years* (2nd ed, Nottingham: Nottingham Corporation, 1960).

John H Green, *History of the Nottingham Mechanics Institution 1837-87* (Nottingham: Nottingham Mechanics Institution, 1887).

Illustrated London News 30 Sept 1893.

Robert Mellors, *Men of Nottingham and Nottinghamshire* (Nottingham: J & H Bell, 1924).

Minutes of the Proceedings of the Institution of Civil Engineers 20 (1852) 117 (1894).

Nottingham Borough Record 9 (1854), 305 (1883).

Nottingham Review 25 Oct 1844.

David E Roberts, *The Nottingham Gas Undertaking, 1921-1949* (Leicester: EMGAS, 1980).

—, *The Lincoln Gas Undertaking, 1828-1949* (Leicester: EMGAS, 1981).

A Short History of the Water Works (Nottingham: City of Nottingham Water Department, 1930).

Times 14 July 1887, 25 Sept 1893.

Robert G Trease, *Nottingham: A Biography* (Macmillan, 1970).

HAYMAN, Sir Cecil George Graham

(1893-1966)

Chief executive of petro-chemical firm

Sir Graham Hayman, February 1960 (courtesy of British Petroleum Company plc).

Cecil George Graham (known as Graham) Hayman was born in London on 1 April 1893, the son of Charles Henry Hayman, an engineer, and his wife, Clara Annie Cuthbert. Educated in London, he was first employed in the office of a manufacturing chemist for two years and then trained as an articled solicitor. During the First World War he served in the 7th London Regiment, 47th Division. After demobilisation, as a young man with ambition, for a few years he joined F A Hughes Ltd, whose managing director was Charles Ball (qv). It was a firm with extensive merchandising interests and among the first to realise the market potential in this country for thermo-setting resin-based products (eg 'Bakelite') which could be moulded to form, for example, radio sets. This company, later partially acquired by the Distillers Co Ltd (DCL) and completely taken over in 1947, can, in a way, be said to have determined some of the main interests in Hayman's subsequent life. In 1922 he joined Herbert Green & Co, which among other interests had a distillery at Hull which made industrial alcohol from molasses, and of this Hayman became secretary. In 1925, it was with great disappointment to him that the distillery was sold to DCL. For a few years Hayman was not very advantageously employed until he formed a partnership in 1927, Solvent Products, at Dagenham making ethyl alcohol from molasses. This was successful and before long United Molasses Co were interested in the enterprise, but once again DCL intervened in Hayman's life, acquired the business and with its growing involvement in the application of industrial chemicals and solvents, outside its principal interests in whisky and fermentation, offered him a seat on the board in 1936.

This move gave Hayman an opportunity to develop his commercial aspirations and, without the distinction of any Scottish ancestry, or a background in the manufacture and trade of potable spirits, with tremendous application he gradually mastered the details of DCL's widespread interests. After a series of senior managerial positions he became chairman of the Management Committee, the organisational powerhouse of the company, and subsequently chairman of the board, 1958-63, the first non-whisky appointment. In the late 1930s Vyvyan Board, his nephew, Tony Board and Hayman gave a powerful stimulus to the industrial activities of DCL, whilst in the laboratories near Epsom, Herbert Stanley was acquiring a fundamental knowledge of petrochemical constituents and their possible application. Much information was gained about comparable German industrial developments towards the end of the 1930s and there were reciprocal agreements between German companies and those in the United States. Interest in plastics and early polystyrene production was shown when a small company, British Resin Products Ltd, was purchased in 1937.

Much of this work was suspended during the Second World War, though not that on polystyrene, which made a useful contribution to the war effort, but immediately afterwards Hayman embarked on an energetic expansion of the industrial interests of DCL. He was particularly fortunate in his colleagues. He himself knew relatively little chemistry. He was a sensible rather than outstanding administrator, but he possessed a dry and practical ability to work with and get the best out of his staff. He was a good listener, sure of his homework and the commitment of his collaborators, whom he consulted before taking major decisions. Tony Board provided him with indispensable support within DCL, a bridge between the potable and non-potable sides: Eric Stein, eccentric and brilliant, had a flair for investment opportunities in the industrial solvent market; Charles Ball realised the potential appeal of plastics; and Herbert Stanley developed the research which not only successfully underpinned the marketing initiatives but which also resulted in new products. Under Hayman's influence DCL, instead of setting up an international network of plant subsidiaries, made licensing agreements, and manufactured its principal products in bulk, leaving its customers to make up, mould or mix them for direct sales to the public. In this way DCL extended its Continental industrial connections.

His relations with members of industry and his competitors were respectful. He impressed, among many, Sir Norman Kipping (qv), who had preceded him as chairman of the FBI, and Sir Frank Lee of the Treasury. His most fruitful collaboration, however, was with J Jamieson and his colleagues of the Anglo-Iranian Oil Co (AIOC), with whom from 1947 in a series of joint ventures, he created a very close mutual relationship between their respective companies in the field of petrochemicals. He had failed to reach a working understanding with ICI but in co-operation with AIOC he formed the British Hydrocarbon Co on 4 October 1947. This resulted in large petrochemical plants being constructed at Grangemouth in Scotland, Barrow, and Baglan Bay in Wales and extended facilities at Hull, besides installations elsewhere.

These were the boom years of the petrochemical industry and derivatives from crude oil were its principal feedstock. After Hayman's retirement and a reassessment of commercial priorities in the mid-1960s, DCL sold its joint petrochemical interests to BP in 1968.

Hayman's chairmanship of DCL was the crown of a distinguished industrial career to which he gave most of his life, having few interests outside it. By his drive, tenacity, absorption in his work and close association with his colleagues he succeeded in making a leading British whisky company into one of the most dynamic forces in the post-war chemical industry. As a businessman he is remembered for his particular concern for the welfare of the employees of the companies with which he was associated, travelling extensively to see them at work. Wiry, persuasive and resilient, he enjoyed golf, had a sardonic sense of humour, was without affectation, and was happy to describe himself as 'almost a cockney'.

After his retirement from DCL he continued as chairman of British Plaster Board (Holdings) Ltd, 1958-65, and of BTR Industries Ltd, 1952-60. Hayman served as chairman of the Association of British Chemical Manufacturers, 1950-53, and president of the Federation of British Industries, 1955-57. He was knighted in 1954, and made a Commander of the Order of the Dannebrog, 1955 and a Freeman of the City of London, 1957. In 1918 he married Elsie Lilian (d 1950), daughter of Henry Leggett, a house decorator; they had one son, Derek, and a daughter, Gwyneth. Sir Graham Hayman died on 10 March 1966, leaving £80,714 gross.

R W FERRIER

Sources:

Unpublished

BCe.

MCe.

SSRC Elites data.

Sir Norman Kipping, 'Memorial Address' (1966).

Published

DCL Gazette 1966.

WWW.

Sir Charles W Hayward (courtesy of the Hayward Foundation).

HAYWARD, Sir Charles William

(1892-1983)

Industrialist

Charles William Hayward was born in Wolverhampton on 3 September 1892, the son of John Hayward, a locksmith, and his wife, Mary. Both his parents died before his sixth birthday and he was brought up by his grandparents, who paid 6d a week for him to be educated at St John's Church School. After lessons he collected brass castings from a foundry in Skinner Street and took them to his grandfather's lock-making business in Church Lane, while on Sundays he carried finished locks and latches to factors in various parts of the Black Country. At the age of thirteen he was apprenticed to Joseph Evans at the Culwell Foundry (pump manufacturers) as a pattern maker.

Driven by a desire to be his own master, Hayward had saved enough by 1911 to set up as a tool and pattern maker. Employing one assistant, he rented a small workshop at a coal depot in Church Street. The turning point came when Harry Stevens of AJS, the motor-cycle manufacturers, sent him a side-car for repair, the quality of his workmanship earning him a contract to make ten a week. Observing the rising demand for these machines, Hayward channelled profits into expansion, moving to larger premises in Walsall Street, situated between the main line of the Birmingham Canal Navigations and the LNWR, where his factory eventually occupied 150,000 square feet. By 1924, when he was employing over 1,000 workers, C W Hayward & Co were the largest makers of side-cars (and their chassis frames) in Britain, with a weekly output of over 350. He also diversified into the production of light car bodies (75 to 100 a week), which were supplied to Morris and Rootes, whilst accessories included windscreens, hoods, luggage grids and door locks, together with wireless instruments, gramophones and speakers. About 1925-26 he sold the business to AJS but remained as the managing director until his departure for London.

Hayward moved to London in 1928, set upon using his fortune and practical knowledge of engineering to finance new inventions and manufacturing processes. To this end he formed Electric & General Industrial Trusts Ltd, which was instrumental in backing young firms such as Boulton & Paul Aircraft, Lea Francis Cars, Parnall Aircraft, Rotary Hoes, Magnet Joinery and Aeronautical & General Instruments. Having assisted various enterprises, it was not surprising that Hayward eventually re-entered the world of manufacturing. In January 1947 he bought Simmonds Aerocessories Ltd, which in addition became a holding company for further acquisitions. In September 1950 Stenor Ltd, makers of vulcanising equipment for the garage trade, was purchased. Other businesses sold to Simmonds Aerocessories were Whatton & Sons of Wolverhampton, jig and tool makers (1951), Firland Metals and its

C W Hayward & Co's side car and car body factory at Wolverhampton c 1924 (courtesy of the Hayward Foundation).

subsidiaries, the principal ones being the Firth Co, wire drawers of Warrington, and British Lead Mills at Welwyn Garden City (1953), and R E Roberts & Son of Bolton, producers of lead sheet and pipe. In July 1953 Firth Cleveland Ltd was formed to take over the shares of Simmonds Aerocessories and during 1954 the new company acquired a controlling interest in Max Stone Ltd (retailers of electrical goods) and its subsidiary Wolfe & Hollander Ltd (household furnishers), which subsequently became the basis for the group's retail division as Civic Stores. Further acquisitions included Landmaster Ltd, makers of horticultural machinery, and Keeton Sons & Co Ltd (guillotine and metalworking machine tools) both in 1954, with Charles Cooper (Tipton) Ltd, producers of hardened spring steel, being bought in the following year. Eventually Firth Cleveland's holdings grew to such a size that engineering, lead and steel divisions were created. In the 1950s Hayward was the leading member of a group of four who formed the Grand Bahama Port Authority to develop Grand Bahama Island by building a harbour and he subsequently set up the Grand Bahama Development Co and Freeport Commercial & Industrial of which his son later became chairman.

On reaching his eightieth birthday in 1972 and wishing to retire, Sir Charles Hayward (he was knighted in 1974) approached Sir Raymond Brookes (qv), chairman of GKN, to suggest that they might take over his conglomerate. Firth Cleveland's turnover had reached £57.3 million and the acquisition was concluded for £27 million.

Apart from his knighthood, Hayward was awarded a CBE in 1970 (also for services to charity). In 1961 he had put most of his wealth into a trust, the Hayward Foundation, designed to assist charitable organisations but with an emphasis on medical research, improving facilities for the elderly, handicapped and socially disadvantaged. By 1983 grants totalling over £22 million had been made to a wide variety of bodies. Hayward became an honorary fellow of the Institute of Opthalmology in 1967, an honorary FRCS in 1970 and an honorary fellow of Keble College, Oxford in 1973; he became a Knight of St John in 1973 and was awarded an honorary LLD by Birmingham University in 1975.

In 1915 Charles Hayward married Hilda Arnold; they had one child, Jack Arnold (b 1923), who became a director of Firth Cleveland. His first wife died in 1971 and in the following year he married Elsie Darnell George. He died at Jethou, the Channel Islands, on 3 February 1983.

EDGAR JONES

Sources:

Unpublished

Information from the Hayward Foundation, London.

Published

'A Visit of Inspection to Messrs Hayward's Works, Walsall Street, Wolverhampton' *British and Colonial Review* Apr 1924.

Daily Telegraph 5 Feb 1983.

Times 5, 9 Feb 1983.

University of Birmingham Gazette 27 (1975).

WWW.

F T Hearle (courtesy of British Aerospace plc).

HEARLE, Francis Trounson

(1886-1965)

Aircraft manufacturer

Francis Trounson Hearle was born in West End Terrace, Penryn, Cornwall on 12 September 1886, the second child and first son of James Hearle, an agricultural machinery dealer, and Helen née Trounson. He was educated at Trevethan Grammar School, Falmouth, and then apprenticed, at the age of thirteen, to Coxs, marine engineers. He served them for seven years, while attending evening classes. Not wishing to go to sea, he moved to London at the close of 1907, and was employed with the Vanguard Omnibus Co and the London General Omnibus Co at Walthamstow and Dalston. In Walthamstow he came to know Geoffrey de Havilland (qv). He joined de Havilland in March 1909, at 35s a week, to help in building an aeroplane for which de Havilland, also a trained engineer, had been designing a petrol engine of 45 hp.

The wood and fabric flying machine was made by these men in a small workshop in Fulham and then taken, in pieces, in May 1909 to Beacon Hill, south of Newbury. There, it was reassembled in two sheds which Moore Brabazon had erected on Lord Carnarvon's fields. In his first attempts to fly, in December 1909, de Havilland crashed this aeroplane about 30 yards after take-off. He and Hearle took the wreckage back to Fulham, built a much improved aeroplane around the same engine, and returned to Beacon Hill in the summer of 1910. De Havilland successfully flew on 10 September 1910; Hearle was his first passenger.

The two men in December 1910 obtained positions in the government Balloon Factory at Farnborough, de Havilland as aeroplane designer and pilot, Hearle as mechanic. Their aeroplane was acquired for £400, and was developed by de Havilland into the government FE series. Hearle and de Havilland worked together for two years, but when their duties became somewhat separated late in 1912 Hearle, seeking to better himself, moved to the Deperdussin Co in Highgate as works foreman, building their French monocoque monoplane. Deperdussin failed a year later, however, and in October 1913 Hearle joined the Vickers Co at Erith, building the Gunbus.

During the war, in April 1915, Hearle was required to start up a Vickers works at Weybridge, in the old Itala car factory, with an urgent order to build 25 government BE2 biplanes (of de Havilland design) by September. This, with much subcontracting, he accomplished. In January 1917 he was sent to America as the production man on a mission headed by Archie Ford to persuade the Americans, not as yet at war, to put the Vickers Scout into production there. But the Americans were more interested in the DH4; they built it later in large numbers as their standard combat aircraft. Hearle came home and talked things over with de Havilland, who had joined George Holt Thomas (qv) as designer and pilot at the Aircraft

Manufacturing Co on the Edgware Road, and was bringing the DH4 into quantity production and developing other designs. Hearle left Vickers to join his old colleague there in June 1917. He took charge of the experimental department, and thereafter built every de Havilland prototype up to the DH18, which marked the end of the war, the closing of Airco, and the formation on 25 September 1920 of the de Havilland Aircraft Co at Stag Lane, Edgware.

Hearle was one of the five founders of the company, which started in a very small way, with de Havilland as technical director, C C Walker as chief engineer, W E Nixon as secretary, and F E N St Barbe as business manager. Hearle was works manager, was made a director in April 1922, general manager at the end of 1927, and on 15 November 1938 he was appointed managing director.

As general manager from 1928 he played the leading part in the expansion of the business brought about by the success of the Moth, the first practical light aeroplane, which gave rise to a world-wide upsurge in club and private flying. The opportunities for overseas business were vigorously explored, and Hearle encouraged the founding of the de Havilland companies in Australia, Canada, India, South Africa and New Zealand. In this work he had the able support of the sales organisation headed by St Barbe.

Hearle urged a national policy of encouraging British commercial aviation, particularly in the early 1930s, when for reasons of trade, prestige and rearmament, airlines were being ambitiously developed by European and American Governments. He was prominent in the efforts directed through the Society of British Aircraft Constructors to change the British policy of requiring British airlines to 'fly by themselves', that is without subsidy, for that attitude was restricting the industry to produce aircraft that other countries would not purchase. They were turning to American and other builders who offered faster, if less economical, metal monoplanes. Britain was losing business because other countries were looking further ahead.

Following a visit by Hearle to America in 1934, he brought the Hamilton standard propeller into production in Britain. De Havilland produced the major share of all the propellers for the Royal Air Force in the Second World War. Hearle built a large shadow factory near Bolton as a second source of propellers; this commenced production in 1937. The Hatfield aircraft factory adopted metal stressed-skin manufacture with the Flamingo branch liner in 1938. The company preferred not to accept government aid with the launching costs, fearing that it might restrict their freedom in marketing the aircraft. Hearle planned and directed the factory organisation and tooling to introduce metal fabrication, while continuing to develop the specialised carapace construction in wood which was needed concurrently for the larger Albatross liner. This form of construction was later employed throughout the war for the Mosquito, of which some 7,000 were built in England, Canada and Australia.

The direction of de Havilland production through the war up to the peak of exertion in 1944, although a team effort, was mainly the work of Frank Hearle. The labour force grew from 5,000 in 1937 to 38,000; tens of thousands more workers in some 400 subcontractor concerns in Britain worked on de Havilland products. The wartime output included about

12,000 aircraft, 5,500 of them Mosquitoes, the fastest fighter aircraft for over two years. Some 10,000 engines were produced, and 140,000 propellers; in addition, many thousands of aircraft, engines and propellers were repaired.

Hearle handed over day-to-day duties as managing director to W E Nixon in August 1944. He took office again from 1 July 1950 until July 1954 as chairman, and retired from directorships of the group companies from 30 September 1956. His service to the nation was recognised by the award of a CBE in the King's Birthday Honours of 1950.

Throughout his career Hearle eagerly fostered technical training for young people. He started a training scheme as early as 1922, which became in 1928 the de Havilland Aeronautical Technical School, where thousands of engineers were trained. The school had 2,900 apprentices when Hearle retired in 1956.

Aided by his wife, who had actively organised public libraries, he introduced a de Havilland library early in the war which was highly successful and he encouraged literary quality in the *de Havilland Gazette*. He participated in the sporting and social activities of the factories. From the 1930s he promoted the system of consultative meetings to improve understanding, contentment and the sense of responsibility in all ranks. Hearle believed in building a team all of whom, down to the shop floor, could feel that they were part of a joint venture. He had faith in personal enterprise and urged that the company should not look to the Government for orders except as a last resort. He often repeated a saying of de Havilland that unnecessary size in industry was the enemy of success, and size with monopoly the arch-enemy.

Hearle was a well-balanced man, one who would always listen to both sides of a problem. He radiated a benign and open friendliness and humour, combined with the qualities of sound judgement, firmness and discipline. To people in the factories he was above all a lovable gentleman, a happy companion, a man who could not make an enemy. He was universally known with affection as Daddy Hearle.

In 1914, Hearle married Ione, Geoffrey de Havilland's sister, whom he had met at the de Havilland family home at Crux Easton rectory, near Beacon Hill. They had one son, Patrick Prideaux. Ione Hearle died in 1953. Frank Hearle survived Sir Geoffrey de Havilland by only a few weeks, dying on 1 September 1965. He left an estate proved at £43,526 gross.

CECIL MARTIN SHARP

Sources:

Unpublished

BCe.

MCe.

PrC.

Information from Mr Patrick P Hearle.

Published

The de Havilland Gazette 1927-61.

Sir Geoffrey de Havilland, *Sky Fever* (Hamish Hamilton, 1961).

Cecil Martin Sharp, *D H — An Outline of de Havilland History* (Faber & Faber, 1960).

WWW.

HEATH, Cuthbert Eden

(1859-1939)

Insurance underwriter and broker

Cuthbert Heath, portrait by Sir William Orpen (courtesy of C Heath Plc).

Cuthbert Eden Heath was born at Forest Lodge near Southampton on 23 March 1859, the third son of Captain (later Admiral Sir) Leopold George Heath, RN and his wife Mary Emma née March (whose family owned a private bank in Mayfair). Deafness contracted in childhood prevented him following his father (and family tradition) into the Royal Navy and he was sent to school at Brighton College. He left at the age of sixteen to spend two years studying languages in France and Germany and was then found a place with the insurance brokers Henry Head & Co. Elected to membership of Lloyd's in 1880, with the support of a loan of £7,000 from his father, he began underwriting marine risks for a syndicate consisting of himself and two others in the following year. He soon became a distinctive figure, standing six feet two inches tall and always carrying the black box containing his hearing aid.

At this time Lloyd's was almost entirely concerned with the insurance of marine risks and even in that market was being overhauled by company underwriters. Heath's father, as director of the Hand in Hand Fire Office, a non-tariff concern that was excluded from reinsurance facilities with tariff insurance companies, provided a new opportunity by enabling his son to reinsure the company's fire business in 1885. On this foundation, Heath began to write an increasing amount of fire business alongside his marine account.

In the following few years he made two further radical innovations. The first was to offer cover against the loss of profits that a business suffered in the aftermath of a fire, and then, in 1887, he provided burglary insurance. Other ideas followed including 'all risks' policies which covered accidental loss and 'jeweller's block' insurance which protected men in that trade while travelling. Concurrently with this product development, he accumulated richly documented material, including rare maps, to support his underwriting of hurricane and earthquake risks. 'He took large risks but he assessed them carefully, though quickly, and if he considered that insurance of a particular kind was needed for the legitimate business of traders, or for the protection of individuals, he also thought it right to provide the protection' {*Times* 9 Mar 1939}. Yet his underwriting was never solely a matter of statistical assessment. While it is impossible to analyse, there is no doubt that he possessed remarkable intuitive powers of appreciating and quantifying risk. Given this, he always tried to seize, rather than refuse, every opportunity to underwrite.

By 1894 the premium income of Heath's syndicate had nearly reached £100,000, a measure of the new importance of the non-marine market. Other Lloyd's underwriters followed his lead and companies began to copy his policy innovations. Even though utilising the larger syndicate that was becoming more characteristic at Lloyd's, Heath lacked acceptance capacity. He tried to persuade the institution's Committee to take a deposit of the type required from marine underwriters to offer policy-holders security, but it declined the offer, believing that the Lloyd's Act of 1871 did not give it powers to have dealings with non-marine business. Heath's solution was to found the Excess Insurance Co in 1894 with whom part of his syndicate's business was reinsured and whose paid up capital of £5,000 provided the public backing he believed the underwriting required.

From the start Heath engaged in broking as well as underwriting. In 1890 this was formalised by the creation of a partnership, C E Heath & Co, which fed his syndicate with risks and which subsequently became a major independent business. From 1903 it appointed its own agents in overseas markets. The new non-marine underwriting was particularly successful in the United States. Heath played an important role in this. After the 1906 San Francisco earthquake, when all the efforts of local companies were bent towards avoiding their liabilities, he sent a telegram to his local agent, 'Pay all our policy holders in full irrespective of the terms of their policies' {Brown (1980) 95}, thus creating a reputation for Lloyd's policies and his own broking that led to a dramatic growth in business in subsequent years. In 1910 C E Heath & Co was registered as a private company with a capital of £50,000 in which Heath retained a controlling interest until his death. His director's fee from the broking firm was £9,000 per annum in 1910.

Heath had shown in the formation of the Excess Insurance Co an ability to make institutional innovations when these were required to support his business. Further demonstrations of this were provided in the Edwardian years. Starting with a substantial financial scandal in 1902 when an underwriter (Percy G C Burnand) failed after speculating with his syndicate's funds, there was a continuing series of such episodes which shook confidence in the security provided by Lloyd's. Heath persuaded the institution to take a deposit for non-marine business in 1902, but this increasingly seemed inadequate and all Lloyd's business was being adversely affected by the bad publicity. When the *Times* joined the critics in 1908, the Lloyd's Committee turned to Heath for advice. In 1906 he had refused the customary guarantee to a fellow member unless he passed an audit test which Heath devised himself. The Committee accepted his proposals on the form a compulsory general audit might take. When opposition to this developed, Heath circulated a statement of support, signed by leading brokers, which made it difficult for others to object without bringing their reputation into question. In the event, the compulsory audit and a trust fund were adopted. This, along with a second Lloyd's Act in 1913, which incorporated non-marine business properly, provided a new and more solid foundation for Lloyd's business in the twentieth century. The maturity of the business Heath had started was marked by the formation of the Lloyd's Non-Marine Underwriters' Association in 1910.

Throughout this period Heath continued to take Lloyd's into new forms of insurance. He offered insurance against contingencies of all kinds like insurance against smallpox for those who had been vaccinated (1901) and pioneered Workmen's Compensation (following the Employers' Liability Act of 1880) and motor insurance at Lloyd's (1904). Excess of loss cover, a new method of reinsuring companies against loss over an agreed figure, was an innovation of particular technical importance which proved especially popular with American companies after the San Francisco disaster.

While Heath continued to battle with the insurance establishment over such matters as underwriting for the Excess Insurance Co at Lloyd's, he became a leading figure in the business. In 1911 he was elected to the Committee of Lloyd's. His dealings with foreign Governments and businesses gave him influence and sources of information far beyond those of the majority of underwriters. After the outbreak of war, his early prominence in air-raid insurance led to his serving on the government committee which drew up a national scheme for such cover. In 1915 he was appointed a trustee for the Lloyd's Patriotic Fund which supported those suffering from the results of the hostilities. His large country house was converted into a hospital, the running of which he himself funded. He became involved in plans for post-war reconstruction through his involvement in credit insurance. In later years he was seen as an elder statesman of the business, serving on the League of Nations insurance committee in 1929, and presiding over a variety of international insurance conferences.

Yet he remained active, innovatory and combative. While he was not the first to underwrite it, he became an enthusiastic protagonist of credit insurance, in which he was involved from the 1890s. In the closing years of the First World War, government concern that British exporters should be protected against risks associated with overseas trade led to the formation of the Trade Indemnity Co to provide cover against defaulting creditors abroad. The new company established itself by taking over the business that had been underwritten by the Excess Insurance Co and that company's underwriter, H S Spain. Heath, who became its chairman, was enthusiastic that Lloyd's should play an important role in supporting it.

Unfortunately, a financial scandal involving an underwriter (Stanley Harrison) prominent in credit insurance, led the Lloyd's Committee to withdraw its support for such business. Heath plunged into a battle to protect his ability to write it at Lloyd's. Only a compromise was possible. Lloyd's would write credit business as reinsurance, but not directly. As a

LLOYD'S BURGLARY THEFT & FIRE POLICY.

In the name of God, Amen. Whereas

£ 200

E F a Green

has paid .... Premium or Consideration to Us, who have hereunto subscribed our Names to Insure *him* from Loss by Burglary Theft or Robbery with or without violence, or by Fire, of the property herein specified, or any part thereof, from or at the premises herein mentioned, during the period from the

No. *60845*

18th day of *July 1904* to the *17th* day of *July 1905* both inclusive and 15 days' grace for renewal.

Property Insured.

£ *200* on the whole Contents of *14 Alexandra Road South Woodford*

in the occupation of the Assured.

Including risk of damage done by Burglars.

Now know Ye, that we the Insurers do hereby bind Ourselves, each of his own Part, and not One for Another, our Heirs, Executors, and Administrators, to make good to the said *E F a Green* his Executors, Administrators, and Assigns, all such Losses, not exceeding the Sum of *Two hundred pounds* in all as he or they may from time to time sustain by any such Theft or Robbery or Fire as aforesaid during the said period, within Thirty Days, after such Loss is proved, and that in proportion to the several Sums by each of Us subscribed against our respective Names.

£ (one pound) ay

Provided always that there shall be no Claim on this Policy when the whole loss by theft or robbery on any one occasion does not amount to £5; or for loss by theft, robbery, or misappropriation by members of the Assured's household, business staff, or other inmates of the Insured premises.

No claim to attach to this Policy for loss resulting from Insurrection, Riots, Civil Commotion, or Military or Usurped Power.

~~Subject to the Conditions of Average~~ (See Paragraph No. 1 on next page) *ay*

This insurance is subject to the conditions endorsed hereon, but in the event of loss by Fire the £5 Clause and Average Clause do not apply.

IN WITNESS whereof We have subscribed our Names and Sums of Money by us Insured.

Dated in *London*, the *15th* Day of *July* One Thousand Nine Hundred and *four*

£200

EACH C. SIXTH

C. E. Heath
J. S. Follett
F. Heath
G. Heath
A. D. Whitman
S. S. Wreadvery

of Two hundred pounds
Follett & Pryce

Lloyd's burglary theft and fire policy, 1904 (courtesy of C Heath Plc).

result, the Trade Indemnity Co was reconstituted in 1924 with more capital and support from the large tariff companies.

Heath was also involved in attempts to establish aviation insurance. In 1919 he formed with Sir Edward Mountain (qv), of the Eagle Star, the British Aviation Insurance Association. This did not prove successful and was abandoned in 1921, but the idea was resurrected ten years later with the formation of the British Aviation Insurance Co. This, like the Trade Indemnity Co, was supported by the larger tariff companies, together with Heath, and became the main avenue for aviation insurance in Britain.

Finally, Heath facilitated the introduction to the London market of the 'burning cost' system of self-rated reinsurance evolved by the American Guy Carpenter. This eliminated the paperwork and negotiation involved in conventional reinsurance agreements by basing the premium paid for reinsurance directly on a specified number of past years' experience. Heath accepted the proposal for himself and this lead encouraged the Lloyd's market to adopt a form of cover that considerably reduced the cost of reinsurance for all insurers.

Heath gradually withdrew from active daily involvement with the business of his various concerns in the 1920s. Yet he continued to be consulted by those interested in insurance innovation and development from all over the world and retained his mastery of these affairs until shortly before his death. In the same way, though his businesses were now actively managed by able successors, he was perfectly capable of decisive intervention. In 1928 he over-rode the wishes of other directors of his broking house in forcing through a merger with A W Bain & Son, a large firm of provincial insurance brokers founded by Albert Bain (qv). In 1934 he was equally ruthless in containing the alternative views that the Bains had for managing C E Heath & Co and this led to their break with the company in 1936.

Unfortunately it is not possible to provide clear estimates of the size of Heath's businesses. The syndicate and the broking house were privately owned, but not exclusively by him. His biographer suggests that in the 1930s his annual income was in excess of £60,000; on his death he left an estate of £1,052,008 gross.

Insurance has not produced many men who stand out as of especial significance in its history. C E Heath is an exception. No other individual had such a profound effect on the scope of the business, its institutions and its competitive structure in the twentieth century. He made non-marine insurance an integral part of Lloyd's and pioneered the provision of a proper basis for its underwriting, thus bringing that institution into the main stream of insurance, allowing it to develop into a powerful competitor with the companies in many markets. He devised and supported many of the forms of cover and methods of underwriting that allowed British insurers of all kinds to expand their business at home and overseas. These innovations enabled him to build a group of businesses including an underwriting syndicate, a broking house, and related insurance companies, which between them led the market in the very literal sense that many risks were only underwritten when it was clear that Heath was first involved.

This distinguished business career supported a family life of style and opulence. Heath married in 1891 Sarah Caroline Gore Gambier (1859-1944) daughter of Rev Charles Gore Gambier Gambier. They began their married life in Cadogan Mansions, near Sloane Square and here their son Leopold Cuthbert was born in 1894, their daughter, Genesta, in 1899. In 1897 Heath rented a family house from his father at Leith Hill, near Dorking; after his father's death in 1907 he moved into the adjacent Anstie

Grange which the former had built in the 1860s. In their West End homes and in the country his wife presided over an energetic and glittering social round which had few links with Heath's business life. At Anstie Grange 50 servants were employed to assist her. Heath loved walking in the surrounding countryside (he gave 200 acres near Leith Hill to the National Trust in 1929), shooting and hunting as Joint-Master of the Surrey Union. He was a DL of Surrey and the county's High Sheriff in 1925-26; in 1920 he was awarded the OBE; he was also a Knight Grace of the Order of St John of Jerusalem. He found relaxation in water colour painting (and always took his paint box with him on his travels) and in sailing (he was elected a member of the Royal Yacht Squadron in 1910). About 1930 he purchased a small estate at Eze, in the Alpes-Maritimes.

In business so commanding and self-confident, at home and in personal relations of all kinds he was gentle, diffident, reserved, almost shy, perhaps partly because of his deafness. In 1938 he suffered a stroke from which he never recovered properly and died at Anstie Grange on 8 March 1939.

OLIVER M WESTALL

Sources:

Unpublished

C E Heath & Co Ltd, archives: especially directors' minute books for 1909-29 and 1929-37; share ledgers for 1910-28 and 1928-42; and the profit and loss ledger 1925-ca 1942.

BCe.

MCe.

PrC.

Published

Antony Brown, *Cuthbert Heath: Maker of Modern Lloyd's* (Newton Abbot: David & Charles, 1980).

W A Dinsdale, *History of Accident Insurance in Great Britain* (Stone & Cox, 1954).

David E W Gibb, *Lloyd's of London* (Macmillan, 1957).

Times 9, 10 Mar 1939.

WWW.

HEATH II, Robert

(1816-1893)

Coal and iron master

Robert Heath II was born at Sneyd House near Burslem, Staffordshire on 14 August 1816, the son of Robert Heath I (1799-1849) and his wife Jane née Plant. Robert Sr, after apprenticeship at Shelton, and service at Sneyd and Sneyd Green collieries, had become manager at one of William Kinnersley's Clough Hall collieries, at Kidsgrove, in 1825. From him Robert II, after attending Dr Magnus's school at Etruria to the age of fourteen, first learnt the techniques of both mining and iron manufacture. Robert I erected the first modern forges in North Staffordshire at Clough Hall in 1838 and Robert II introduced the hot blast technique when he succeeded his father as Kinnersley's manager in 1849. Within five years he left to enter a partnership with Francis Stanier in the neighbouring area of Silverdale and Knutton for two years, up to Stanier's death in 1856, and thereafter with Stanier's widow until 1860.

By then Heath had already begun an extensive process of colliery and foundry purchases, starting with the Childerplay Colliery in 1857. Acquisition of other workings and the initiation of new collieries built up a group that came to be known as the Biddulph Valley Colliery, which opened its own associated branch railway in 1860, later extended to become a quite considerable railway system. In addition Robert Heath & Son also separately owned the Brownhills Colliery, 1870-1902; the Brown Lees Colliery, 1887-1926; and Bradely Green, 1882-94, as well as other pits in the Norton area.

Much of this production, which increased from 34,000 tons in 1858-59 to more than 170,000 tons in 1863-64, was consumed within the Heath ironworks, but not all the coals mined from the rich range of seams accessible to the Biddulph shafts were appropriate for the manufacture of pig-iron, so some were sold for coking and household consumption. Until almost the end of the century all the coal was got from footrails, or from pits with relatively shallow shafts, none being more than 264 feet in depth. In the 1880s even this enterprise was sufficiently rewarding for Heath to engage in a number of purchases: the Knypersley Hall estate cost him almost £150,000 and alongside this there was the increasing purchase of collieries and furnaces. By 1887, Heath owned or leased a quarter of the whole North Staffordshire coalfield. In 1888, the culminating purchase of Heath's career was the purchase of the Clough Hall estate where he had started his own career forty years earlier. Some of these pits also yielded ironstones, but from early on their contribution was supplemented by other ironstone pits at Packmoor, and from 1857 by a lease taken on ironstone mines at the Grange Colliery in Burslem. This ironstone was calcined on site before being transported by horse and cart (until around 1890 when Heath replaced them with a private railway) to the Biddulph

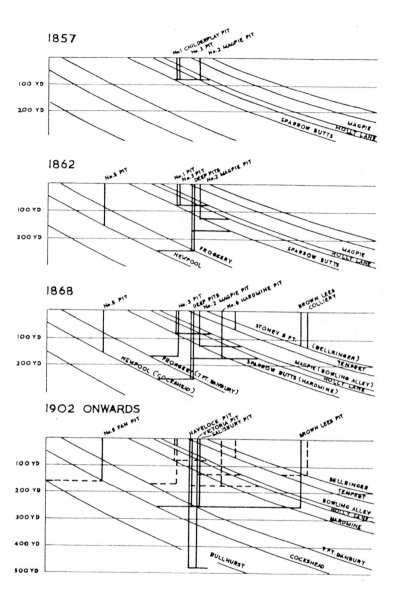

Chart showing development of Biddulph Valley Colliery from 1857 onwards.

Valley Ironworks where his furnaces were in blast by 1860, a further two being added by 1864. Complementary to these were 63 puddling furnaces and 5 rolling mills.

In 1862, the records show a strike of 270 men and boys seeking an extra shilling per ton: Heath offered 6d. An obituary tribute appropriately asserted 'Mr Heath and his miners and ironworkers have not always seen eye to eye': nevertheless it was suggested that they respected his 'bluff and brusque' manner and that this firmness, coupled with their respect, was the secret of his industrial success. {*Staffordshire Sentinel* 9 Oct 1893} To increase the scale of his operation, Heath leased pits at Norton to get at the deeper coals and by 1866 two furnaces were in blast there alongside the necessary puddling furnaces and rolling mills. Heath was not slow to take advantage of the failure of other ironmasters, such as William Bates of Ravensdale, in the depression of the industry in the mid-1860s, purchasing their plant against the hopes of a brighter future. In other words, Heath had built up his enterprise cheaply in the difficult days of the 1860s and stood poised to take advantage of the boom of the early 1870s, unencumbered by long-term contracts.

By 1873 Heath's manufacturing plant comprised 28 coal/ironstone pits (in full work), 8 blast furnaces, 154 puddling/ball furnaces, 9 banks furnaces (erecting), 14 mills and 33 heating furnaces.

Alongside these statistics must be set the fact that the price of finished iron which had been as low as £5 10s per ton advanced in 1872-73 to £14 10s. Developing his industrial empire in such a context, ensured Heath his future. By 1892 Robert Heath & Sons owned the largest ironworks and employed a greater number of men than any other iron-making firm in Staffordshire; starting with the extraction of ironstone, he followed through with the manufacture of pig-iron, wrought iron and the rolling of iron into both bars and plates.

Robert Heath was active in politics on behalf of the Conservative interest from 1841, himself representing the Stoke constituency from 1874 until his defeat in 1880 — a term whch he regarded as the six least happy years of his life. He was temperamentally unsuited to the partisan nature of politics, and further distrusted all progress of what he called an 'unsettling' nature. He, therefore, refused all entreaties to contest subsequent elections. However, his local offices were many: JP, DL, High Sheriff, and County Councillor. He was a staunch Churchman and was generous in his support of local churches and of local charities especially those concerned with mining, health and recreation.

In 1876 Heath owned 3,330 acres in Staffordshire and Cheshire. Until 1873 his residence had been the Brampton Hill House in Newcastle but thereafter the family residence was Biddulph Grange, bought from James Bateman in 1872 and sold by the Heaths for £10,000 in 1922.

Robert Heath married Anne, daughter of James Beech Esq 'of the Staffordshire Potteries' {*WWMP*}. They had four sons, of whom Robert, James and Arthur (qqv) survived their father and developed the family business.

Robert Heath II died on 7 October 1893, leaving £320,045 gross.

JOHN H Y BRIGGS

Sources:

Unpublished

Staffordshire CRO, Robert Heath & Son papers.

PrC.

L Howe, 'The North Staffordshire Coalfield' (Keele MA, 1982).

Published

Percy W L Adams, *Some Notes on Some North Staffordshire Families* (Tunstall, 1930).

Bateman.

Griffiths' Guide to the Iron Trade of Great Britain (1873 ed repr Newton Abbot: David & Chartes, 1967).

Joseph Kennedy, *Biddulph: A Local History* (Keele, 1980).

W H Merritt, 'The North Staffs Coal and Iron District' *Colliery Guardian* 19 Mar 1880.

George Rickword and William Gaskell, *Staffordshire Leaders: Social and Political* (Alexander, 1907).

Staffordshire Advertiser 14 Oct 1893.

Staffordshire Sentinel 9 Oct 1893.

D J Wheelhouse, 'Coalmining in the Biddulph Area up to the End of the Nineteenth Century' *Transactions of the Biddulph Historical Society* No 3 (June 1972).

VCH Staffordshire 2, 8.

WWMP.

Robert Heath III (courtesy of Mr John Briggs).

HEATH III, Robert and HEATH, Sir James
(1851-1932)   (1852-1942)
and HEATH, Arthur H
(1856-1930)

Colliery owners and ironmasters

Robert Heath (qv) had four sons of whom one (William) died in infancy; the others, Robert III, James and Arthur, all entered the family business.

Of the three brothers Robert Heath III, born at Newcastle-under-Lyme on 16 January 1851 devoted most of his energies to the company and was recognised in the local political community. He headed the poll at the first Biddulph Urban District Council election in 1894, and was its chairman in 1894-1912 and 1915-19. Like his father he was appointed High Sheriff for Staffordshire where he served as JP, DL and county councillor. By contrast his younger brothers, James and Arthur followed their father into national politics. In 1875 he married Laura, daughter of Frederick Fielder of Cheshire. Robert Heath III died on 23 February 1932 leaving £36,655.

James Heath was born at Tunstall on 26 January 1852. Educated at

Sir James Heath (courtesy of Mr John Briggs).

Clifton, he was prevented by business concerns from going on to university and from contesting the Newcastle-under-Lyme borough in the 1876 election. The first of his four wives, Euphemia Celina Van der Byl (whom he married in 1881), the daughter of Peter Gerhard Van der Byl, was South African and Heath subsequently developed considerable financial interests in that country. In 1892-1906 he sat for North West Staffordshire as a Unionist and notwithstanding his vociferous opposition to the Eight Hours Day for miners he still contrived to increase his majority in 1895. He declared himself in favour of Chinese indentured labour in South Africa, but in 1906 suffered the fate of so many tariff reformers and lost his seat to his Liberal rival. He was made a baronet in 1904. He made his contribution to industry both in North Staffordshire (as president of the North Staffordshire Mining and Mechanical Institute and of the North Staffordshire Chamber of Commerce) and nationally, serving on the council of the Associated Chambers of Commerce, the British Iron Trade Association and the Colliery Masters' Association. His philanthropic interests were educational and medical: he financed the parish school at Buddulph and served for fifteen years on the Wolstanton School Board. He endowed a convalescent home at Llanfairfechan for his own employees and for others. He was colonel of the Staffordshire yeomanry. Like his father, he sat on the Tunstall Local Boards early in his life, and was also a Guardian of the Wolstanton and Burslem Poor Law Union.

By his first wife James Heath had one son (killed in action in 1914) and a daughter. After his first wife's death Sir James married secondly, in 1924, Ivy Amelia Nitch Smith née Hounsell, a twenty-nine year old divorcée; after divorcing her he married thirdly, in 1927, Sophia Catherine Theresa Mary Pierce Elliott Lynn née Evans, a thirty year old widow; after divorcing her, Sir James, now eighty-three, married Dorothy Mary Hodgson, a thirty-six year old spinster and science graduate. He died on 24 December 1942 leaving £61,514 gross.

Arthur Howard Heath was born at Newcastle-under-Lyme on 29 May 1856 and was educated at Clifton and Brasenose College, Oxford, becoming a considerable cricketer and sharing in the management of Robert Heath & Sons. He married in 1884 Alice, daughter of Rev Herbert Richard Peel of Thornton Hall, Buckinghamshire; they had one son and one daughter. A JP for Staffordshire and colonel of the Staffordshire Yeomanry, he contested Hanley unsuccessfully in the Unionist interest in 1892 and 1895. He was successful in 1900 and sat for Hanley until defeated in 1906; he also sat for the Leek division of Staffordshire between the two elections of 1910. Unlike his brother he became a Balfourite who was opposed to all taxes on food. He was sometime president of the North Staffordshire Royal Infirmary, chairman of the governors of the Newcastle Endowed Schools and president of the North Staffordshire Institute of Mining Engineers. He died on 16 April 1930 leaving £163,284 gross.

This third generation of Heaths saw their father's business enterprise grow to its historic height in the years immediately preceding the First World War with its subsequent collapse in the difficult circumstances of the post-war world. By the late 1890s the exhaustion of the shallower seams of coal necessitated sinking deeper shafts. At the same time the labour force in the larger pits was increased: in 1894 the underground workers at the Magpie, Havelock and Brown Lees pits numbered 533 men; by 1908 the Havelock was in suspension but there were 1,012 men working underground at the other two, the shaft bottoms now being nearly 500 yards deep. Mining and iron manufacturing so prospered that by 1912, the *North Staffordshire Commercial Year Book* was describing Robert Heath & Sons as 'the largest producer of bar iron in the world': the local newspaper more modestly confined the distinction to Europe. In 1899, Robert Heath & Sons employed 6,000 hands and in 1907 the wage bill each week was £11,000. In certain parts of Biddulph — Brown Lees and Black Bull in particular — the company accommodated many of their workers in houses which cost £180-200 to build and which were let at rents from 4s to 4s 6d a week.

Shortly after the First World War, Robert Heath & Sons amalgamated with the Low Moor Co of Bradford; perhaps this was an attempt at securing a broader geographical base in uncertain markets. Certainly by 1923, the Robert Heath part of the enterprise was subsidising the Yorkshire activities of the firm. By 1928 Heath's £1 shares had dropped to 1s and a receiver was called in, with dire consequences for employment in the Biddulph Valley, following as it did upon the failure three years earlier of another Heath enterprise, the Burchenwood Colliery Co Ltd, on which they had expended a million pounds in development and which had not been part of the 1919 amalgamation with Low Moor. Explanations of this sudden demise have to do with the generally depressed state of the nation's economy; an unsuccessful attempt to manufacture mild-steel at Norton; and the lack of entrepreneurial drive amongst the ageing Heaths of the third generation especially after Robert III's death — it is significant that although they retained offices in Staffordshire, both Sir James and Colonel Arthur had their country seats in Warwickshire with town houses in London. They lacked the immediacy of contact with the Biddulph work force which had been so crucial to their father. By this time also the local ironstones were becoming exhausted.

JOHN H Y BRIGGS

Sources:

Unpublished

MCe.

PrC.

L Howe, 'The North Staffordshire Coalfield' (Keele MA, 1982).

Published

Percy W L Adams, *Some Notes on Some North Staffordshire Families* (Tunstall, 1930).

History of the Staffordshire Iron Industry.

Joseph Kennedy, *Biddulph: A Local History* (University of Keele, 1980).

George Rickword and William Gaskell, *Staffordshire Leaders: Social and Political* (Alexander, 1907).

Staffordshire Sentinel 14 Jan 1899, 9 Nov 1904.

D J Wheelhouse, 'Coalmining in the Biddulph Area up to the End of the Nineteenth Century' *Transactions of the Biddulph Historical Society* 3 (1972).

VCH Staffordshire.

WWMP.

WWW.

HEATON, Sir John Frederick

(1880-1949)

Executive of passenger road transport services conglomerate

John Frederick Heaton was born in Bradford, Yorkshire on 18 October 1880, the son of a warehouseman in the woollen trade, and his wife Mary Ellen née Speight. He studied accountancy at Bradford Technical College, and then worked as an accountant for some years before becoming, at the age of twenty-three, a company secretary to the Dewsbury colliery firm of Crawshaw & Warburton. While with them, he continued his studies, and took eighth place in the examinations of the Society of Incorporated Accountants and Auditors.

Heaton's opportunity to show his special abilities came with his appointment in 1915 as accountant to the family business of Thomas Tilling Ltd, 'jobmasters' and bus operators of Peckham, South London. The original Thomas Tilling founded the firm in 1847, and it became one of the largest horse-bus operators in London. When the company went public in 1897, under the direction of his sons, Richard and Edward, and his son-in-law, Walter Wolsey, its issued capital was £400,000. Having survived the problems of motorisation, the business was linked with the London General Omnibus Co, first by a pooling agreement, and then in May 1912 by an agreement to limit its London fleet to 150 buses. The Tilling board thereafter decided to move into provincial operation, starting in April 1914, when they formed the Folkestone District Road Car Co. Walter Wolsey played a large part in the direction of the company for the first few years of Heaton's employment, and was involved with Sidney Garcke (qv) in the merger of Tilling and British Electric Traction interests when the East Kent Road Car Co was formed in 1916. With Garcke, Wolsey initiated the system of area agreements, whereby the country was divided up into the operating territories of those firms large enough to negotiate terms with their neighbours. Thus when Heaton succeeded to power in what had come to be called the 'provincial combine' he inherited its structure of interlocking subsidiaries, owned jointly by Tillings and BET.

In 1916 Heaton was appointed company secretary of Thomas Tilling Ltd. At this stage he was much concerned with the financial aspect of the business, and his knowledge of insurance led him in 1918 to form the Road Transport & General Insurance Co, of which he became managing director. With the expansion of the industry, he formed a subsidiary, Motor Credit Services Ltd, in 1922. But the principal development in his career came in 1921 when he was elected to the Tilling board. Differences had emerged between members of the family as to its future policy but Heaton persuaded them to leave the management to him. He repeated this tactic in the acquisition of numerous firms, convincing their shareholders that he could increase profit levels.

Richard Tilling, who had been responsible for the decision to work with rather than against BET, continued to develop jointly-owned operating subsidiaries, and in 1922 Tillings obtained a substantial interest in British Automobile Traction, the BET subsidiary which was the holding company for its purely bus operating units. In 1928 the complex pattern of holdings was simplified by the formation of Tilling & British Automobile Traction Ltd, a business with which Heaton became closely associated.

He was immediately involved in a major struggle to prevent the railway companies from acquiring control of the provincial bus industry, in a confrontation with Sir Ralph Wedgwood (qv), general manager of the London & North Eastern Railway Co. This turned largely upon bids and counter-bids for the control of United Automobile Services Ltd, then an independent company with bus services in a wide area from Suffolk to the Scottish border. In October 1929 an agreement was signed which gave the railway companies a substantial stake in the industry, but with never more than 49 per cent of the equity of the operating subsidiaries. This preservation of autonomous bus management has always been seen as Heaton's master-stroke: after he convinced the BET board to support him, he was entrusted by both BET and Tillings with the sole conduct of the negotiations.

Richard Tilling died in June 1929, and in 1930 Heaton was elected chairman of the company. Within a year no one on the board bore the Tilling name (although Wolsey continued to serve as a board member until 1950). Heaton was now in sole command of Tillings.

He began to develop a family of subsidiaries in which BET had no share. He picked a team of able engineers and managers, paid them well, and expected loyal and intensive co-operation from them. In 1936 he arranged with BET for the chairmanship of their joint holding company, Tilling & British, to be held by either party in alternate years. In practice, each of the subsidiaries was managed by one or other of the proprietors, and there were tensions built into the situation, which led in 1942 to a major change, when the holding company was wound up, the subsidiaries being redistributed between Tilling and BET organisations. Heaton was far from being a detached financial manipulator, and took a detailed interest in the management of the operating subsidiaries that was in marked contrast with BET practice. He acquired in 19 Crewe House, in the Strand, as group headquarters, a property which reflected the company's status.

During the Second World War Heaton was a member of the Inland Transport War Council, 1941-44, and a member of the Finch Committee set up by the Army Council in 1941. Knighted in 1942, the following year he was appointed unpaid chairman of Short Bros (Rochester & Bedford) Ltd, which position he retained on behalf of the Government until 1945.

The sale of the Thomas Tilling transport interests to the British Transport Commission in 1948 for £24 million has been interpreted as indicating that Heaton favoured state ownership. It would be more true to say that he was inclined to compromise with the Government of the day, regardless of the policy. He was not in fact involved in the negotiations with Sir Cyril Hurcomb (qv) of the BTC. Having seen the distribution to his shareholders of the greater part of the BTC 3 per cent stock (in which payment had been made) Heaton retired as managing director. He was succeeded as head of Tillings by Lionel Fraser (qv).

In a memorial appreciation, Sir John Elliot (qv) recalled that Heaton's reputation for ruthlessness was not undeserved, and mentioned his 'rather abrupt manner and ill-concealed irritation at interruption or procrastination' {*Railway Gazette* 27 May 1949}. But those who knew him personally saw an entirely different side of his character; a sense of humour and a range of kindnesses that were never publicised.

Outside his business he was chairman of Watford and District Peace Memorial Hospital but his main interest, apart from his family, was his Gloucestershire farm, Can Court, Cirencester.

Heaton married twice: in 1908 at St John the Baptist parish church, Kidderminster, to Ethel Irene Roberts, the daughter of a chemist; and in 1927 at Briskley Street Parish Church, Kent, to Mary Stewart Macleod née Thomson, a widow. He had three sons and two daughters, all but one daughter surviving him.

Sir John Frederick Heaton died at his home at Croxley Green, Hertfordshire, of cancer of the prostate, on 27 April 1949, leaving £233,018 gross.

JOHN HIBBS

Sources:

Unpublished

BCe.

MCe.

DCe.

PrC.

Published

W J Crosland-Taylor, 'Pioneers of the Bus Industry, No 8, Sir Frederick Heaton' *Bus and Coach* March 1966.

John Elliot, 'Sir Frederick Heaton — an Appreciation' *Railway Gazette* 27 May 1949.

Charles F Klapper, *Golden Age of Buses* (Routledge & Kegan Paul, 1978).

'Memorial Service for Sir Frederick Heaton' *Railway Gazette* 13 May 1949.

Railway Gazette 6 May 1949.

Times 5 May 1928, 16 July 1929, 28 Mar 1930, 28 Apr, 5 May 1949.

WWW.

HEDLEY, Thomas

(1809-1890)

Soap manufacturer

Thomas Hedley was born at Harnham, Northumberland on 22 April 1809, the son of Anthony Hedley, a sheep farmer whose family had been pastoral farmers for several generations, and his wife Sarah née Armorer. In 1826 Thomas Hedley began his commercial life as a junior clerk with John Greene & Sons, wine merchants and tallow chandlers in Gateshead. After a few years he joined Nichol & Ludlow, shipowners and wharfingers on Newcastle Quayside.

He showed an early interest in figures and finance, and in order to study these he enrolled at the Gateshead Mechanics' Institute. Ten years later he acknowledged his debt to that organisation by joining its management committee.

When John Greene & Sons commenced soap manufacture at Newcastle in 1839, Hedley rejoined the firm as a partner. He managed the soap factory until it passed into his hands in 1861. Thomas was joined in the partnership by his brother Edward Armorer Hedley, and later by his son Armorer Hedley.

Two earlier Tyneside soap manufacturers had made alkali for their own use and had faced harassing litigation, being accused of causing a nuisance; Hedley avoided this hazard by buying his alkali from local producers. He took full and early advantage of the introduction of palm oil as an alternative to tallow. He was evidently an uncomfortable member of the rather unstable trade associations. For example, in 1880 he joined the re-formed Northern Soapmakers' Association whose aim was to agree to prices and prevent underselling, but in 1888 the Association complained that Hedley had reduced his prices without giving adequate notice.

Hedley's financial flair took him into areas far removed from soap. He became chairman of the Newcastle & Gateshead Gas Co, the Solway

Haematite Co of Maryport and the Tyne Steam Shipping Co, and a director of Consett Iron & Steel Co, Clelland's Slipway and the North Eastern Banking Co. On at least one occasion he was able to speak in the Newcastle Town Council on behalf of both buyer and seller.

In 1853 Hedley was elected to Newcastle Town Council to represent the ward in which the factory was situated. His contributions to council debates were mainly financial, often imparting more numerical information than his hearers could immediately grasp. He became chairman of the finance committee. His was not the typical nature of the watchdog who opposes all expenditure on principle. Indeed in 1862 he upbraided the Council for holding down the rates for too long, and so failing to provide funds for necessary improvements. He became Sheriff of Newcastle in 1860-61 and Mayor in 1863-64; he was elected an alderman in 1866. He was made a Newcastle JP in 1864 and became first chairman of Gosforth Local Board of Health when it was formed in 1872. He was a vigorous supporter of the Ragged Schools, and played a leading part in setting up the large mental hospital at Coxlodge to the north of Newcastle. For a time he lived in Coxlodge Hall, a sizeable mansion, until it was burnt down in 1877. Thomas Hedley was a member of the British Association for the Advancement of Science for twenty-seven years.

He married Mary Chicken of Gateshead; they had one son and several daughters. Hedley died on 13 November 1890, leaving £107,103 gross.

After his death the business was continued by his son. In 1897 the company went public and a year later the London office was opened. In 1900 Owen Philipps (later Lord Kylsant (qv)), chairman of Elder Dempster Shipping Co, bought a controlling interest in Hedleys in order to safeguard his oil-carrying trade. Following the collapse of Kylsant's concerns in 1930, the Cincinnati firm of soapmakers Procter & Gamble acquired the Hedley shares, the Thomas Hedley name being preserved until 1962.

W A CAMPBELL

Sources:

Unpublished

PrC.

Published

Newcastle Corporation Reports 1890-91, record of remarkable events during the Mayoralty of Joseph Baxter Ellis, 1-2 (Newcastle upon Tyne: J Dowling).

Newcastle Daily Chronicle 14 Nov 1890.

William J Reader, 'The United Kingdom Soapmakers' Association and the English Soap Trade, 1867-1896' *Business History* I, part 2 (1959).

R Welford, *Men of Mark 'Twixt Tyne and Tweed* (2 vols, Newcastle upon Tyne, 1895).

Alexander Henderson (courtesy of the Faringdon Collection Trust).

HENDERSON, Alexander

1st Lord Faringdon

(1850-1934)

Financier and railway company chairman

Alexander Henderson was born in suburban London on 28 September 1850, the second of the six sons of George Henderson (1819-1889) of Ealing and Eliza, daughter of George Cockshutt of York. His father was a printer's reader and a Greek and Hebrew scholar, who left an estate valued at £2,839. One of his brothers, Sir Brodie Henderson (1869-1936), was a distinguished civil engineer.

After being educated privately, he worked for Deloittes, the leading railway accountants, whose clients included the Great Western Railway. He then joined the stockbroker Thomas Greenwood, who had also been involved in the GWR and specialised in railway finance. Henderson was admitted as a member of the London Stock Exchange in 1873, and as Greenwood's partner specialised in financing big schemes with large long-term growth prospects. By 1889 he had made a fortune and bought the Buscot Park estate in Berkshire.

Henderson became a director in 1894 of the Manchester, Sheffield and Lincolnshire Railway, then crippled by Sir Edward Watkin's wilful improvidence as chairman. He organised an ingenious scheme of financial revival and conceived the device of a rolling-stock trust company which bought equipment for MSL to use on hire-purchase terms. This ingenuity enabled the company to expand from a provincial into a trunk railway, a transformation acknowledged when its name was altered to Great Central in 1897. Henderson became chairman in 1899, as he alone among the directors could raise sufficient money for extensions, and in 1909 was elected chairman of the Railway Companies Association. In 1908-9 he and the chairmen of the Great Northern and Great Eastern Railways, Lord Allerton and Lord Claud Hamilton (qv), made a concerted, but unsuccessful, effort to amalgamate their companies, in which they were supported by Winston Churchill, President of the Board of Trade. When the Great Central disappeared in the re-grouping of 1921-22, Henderson became deputy chairman of the new London & North Eastern Railway in which he remained active until his death.

His other railway participations were in Argentina, Brazil and Uruguay, and he financed ports, telephonic systems and electricity supply schemes throughout South America. In the 1890s he was a trustee of the Central Market in Buenos Aires, and the Pernambuco Tramways were one of his later interests. In an intervention of 1908, he and Lord Rothschild used their great influence in South America to try to curb the naval armaments rivalry between Brazil and Argentina. He was part-proprietor of the Shelton Ironworks in North Staffordshire, having bought Lord Granville's interest at some date before 1891. In 1890-96 he was a director of the Manchester Ship Canal Co and arranged extensive finance, without which the canal could not have been completed. Around the turn of the century he bought control from Eugene Sharrer, a Nyasaland planter, of the Shiré Highlands Railway Co, which in 1908 fulfilled the first stage of its concession to build a line from Port Herald to Blantyre, with an extension to Fort Johnston on Lake Nyasa (a total of 230 miles). Henderson was also a major creditor of the British Central Africa Co until 1912, when his debts were paid by an Anglo-Belgian railway financier, Libert Oury, in return for Henderson's Shiré Highlands company abandoning its proposed line to Quelimane. With Sir Ernest Cassel (qv) he financed that under-nourished sprig of business imperialism, the National Bank of Turkey, in 1909.

He was Liberal Unionist MP for West Staffordshire from a by-election in May 1898 until his defeat in the general election of 1906. In July 1913 he was elected unopposed as Unionist MP for St George's, Hanover Square, which he represented until raised to a barony in January 1916. As a Chamberlainite, he joined W A S Hewins as a founder member of the Tariff Commission (1904), as treasurer of the Tariff Reform League and as a founder of the Unionist Business Committee (1915). The most important of his services to Unionism, for which his baronetcy was a reward in 1902, was as 'launderer' of party funds for investment in London newspapers to ensure their continued partisan loyalty. Bonar Law admitted that 'Everyone connected with newspapers knows that Henderson has acted in these matters for us' {Bonar Law papers 37/5/5, Law to Sir Arthur Steel-Maitland, 18 Dec 1914}. The *Daily Express, Observer, Globe*, and *Pall Mall Gazette* all received subventions through Henderson, and around 1908 he 'tried to lump together the *Standard*, the *Evening Standard*, the *Daily Express* and the *Times* all as one property' {G E Morrison papers, vol 260, f115}. With his fellow railway magnate Davison Dalziel (qv), Henderson acquired the *Standard* and *Evening Standard* in 1910 to serve as protectionist mouthpieces; but by 1914, to Henderson's annoyance, Dalziel had got majority control. He nevertheless remained interested in both newspapers until their sale in 1916. Henderson was also a minority shareholder in the *Daily Express* for a decade after 1912.

Henderson was appointed in October 1915 to the government committee on women substitutes for serving men. In January 1916 he led a government mission to Denmark, Norway and Holland to study the blockade arrangements with the neutral governments, and in the same month he was appointed to Lord Curzon's Shipping Control Committee. Later in 1916-17 he chaired a departmental committee on the re-organisation of British commercial intelligence. He favoured the retention of responsibility of the responsibility by the Board of Trade, but after some acrimony, a majority of the committee (led by Dudley Docker (qv)) recommended a new Trade Intelligence Department under Foreign Office direction. To the fury of the Federation of British Industries and all trade warriors, the Government compromised by establishing in 1917 the Department of Overseas Trade under the joint aegis of the Board of Trade and Foreign Office. As a member of Lord Balfour of Burleigh's committee (1916-17) on commercial and industrial policy after the war, Henderson argued that British exports must greatly expand if the country were not to be bankrupted by post-war surplus capacity; and he submitted a minority report recommending a 10 per cent ad valorem tariff on manufactured imports.

There was a more decisive outcome to the Board of Trade Committee on Financial Facilities for Trade which he chaired in July and August 1916. Having heard evidence of lazy amateurism and complacence among London financial institutions, his committee urged the foundation, under Royal Charter, of an industrial trading bank, capitalised at £10 million, to imitate and supplant German and other foreign banks in export penetration. The new bank, chartered in April 1917 as the British Trade Corporation with Faringdon as its Governor, was, together with the British Stockbrokers Trust (chaired by Lord ffrench (qv)), the chief innovation among financial institutions achieved by the wartime corporatist movement. The list of the first 50 applicants for its capital included the most prominent export-monopolists in Britain (notably leaders of the FBI and directors of Vickers and Armstrong, Whitworth). Although ten joint-stock banks applied for capital in BTC, the London merchant banks resisted it as 'a dangerous and mischievous innovation' and the mercantile community thought it 'the greatest [of] insults' {*PD*, HC, 17 May 1917, cols 1840, 1857}.

In 1919 BTC bought the National Bank of Turkey for £234,119, followed by the Levant Co and the mercantile firm of Whittall, with branches at Salonica and Constantinople. BTC also invested £100,000 in the Portuguese Trade Corporation; formed the Anglo-Brazilian Commercial & Agency Co Ltd jointly with the London & Brazilian Bank; and participated in the Anglo-Belgian oriented Inter-Allied Trade & Banking Corporation, whose very name was redolent of trade war. These and other ventures all sought to entrench British interests in areas where Germans or other political enemies had been strong before 1914. BTC also capitalised at £100,000 a subsidiary to insure exporters' foreign credits, Trade Indemnity Ltd, and made their first capital issue (of £500,000 debentures) for Morgan Crucible Ltd.

Although BTC saw itself as an agent of Empire, and sincerely tried to serve the Government which had chartered it, Whitehall proved disinclined to give preferential treatment, or even use its facilities, in peace-time. Apart from one occasion in 1919 when Lord Curzon insisted that the British group of banks in the Four Power Consortium transacting financial business with China should be enlarged to include BTC, the Foreign Office gave no special support — and even in that case, no Chinese loans eventuated. On the other hand, Faringdon with Docker as his deputy, responded to official pleas for help. Thus in 1919 they agreed to act as adjuncts to the Allied forces in Russia and Turkey by forming the South Russia Banking Agency. This opened branches in anti-Bolshevist towns throughout Transcaucasia, and developed a big trade in manganese ore until the advance of the Red Armies in 1920. A proposal to use BTC to develop capitalism in Kolchak's Siberia was also mooted in 1919; but the Corporation had no place in high policy after 1920, when trade diplomacy was increasingly deprecated.

The enterprises which BTC selected in 1917-19 on strategic criteria proved hopeless commercially. Having paid 2.5 per cent dividend for 1918, and 4 per cent for the two years to 1920, no further payments were made on an issued capital of £1 million. Authorised capital was reduced by £1.5

million to £8.5 million in 1922-23. Fraud involving about £100,000 in BTC's Yugoslav operations preceded its voluntary liquidation in October 1926: its undertakings and assets were acquired by the Anglo-International Bank which had Bank of England backing in Central Eastern European business. BTC's charter, which otherwise expired in 1977, was surrendered, and the Corporation became another forgotten failure of the reconstruction movement of 1916-19. Faringdon was a director of the Anglo-International Bank from 1926.

After the railway strikes of 1919, Henderson was one of the magnates invited to a meeting of the Coalition chief whips which resulted in over £100,000 being collected for propaganda against trade-union militancy. He sat in 1921-22 with Eric Geddes and Guy Granet (qqv) on the Committee on National Expenditure, known to history as the Geddes Axe, which recommended cuts of £86.75 million in government spending. He kept daily contact with the City until 1934, but the deaths of his brother in 1931, and of four of his sons between 1922 and 1933, cut a swath through the succession at Greenwoods: in 1933 the firm amalgamated with stockbrokers Cazenove, Akroyd.

After his purchase of the Buscot Park estate, Henderson became a JP for Berkshire, and served as High Sheriff in 1912. He was a breeder of prize-winning livestock, sometime president of the Shire Horses Society, British Berkshire Society and the Hampshire Downs Sheepbreeders Association. His influence in Berkshire was confirmed when his eldest son was elected Unionist MP for Abingdon in 1910. In 1917 Henderson was made a Companion of Honour; he was Knight of St John of Jerusalem. Henderson was a patron of pre-Raphaelite artists and employed Sir Edward Burne-Jones to decorate Buscot. About 1904 he bought another estate at Glenalmond in Perthshire.

Henderson was treasurer of a fund to promote dispensaries to prevent consumption in London in 1910-19, and a debenture holder of the *Complete Peerage* from 1922. He was baptised into the Church of Scotland, although he addressed the Assembly of the United Free Church in 1913.

In 1874 he married Jane Ellen (1854-1920) daughter of Edward William Davis, 'gentleman' {MCe}, of Ealing; they had six sons and a daughter. Faringdon died at his Piccadilly home on 17 March 1934. He left £1,117,408 gross, whilst his titles descended to his grandson Gavin (1902-77), who became a leading Labour party anti-colonialist, and married a daughter of Lord Kylsant (qv).

R P T DAVENPORT-HINES

Writings:

PP, Committee on Financial Facilities for Trade (1916) Cd 8346 (chairman).

PP, Petition to King George V by Lord Faringdon and others (1917) Cd 8567.

PP, Committee on Commercial and Industrial Policy (1918) Cd 9033, 9034, 9035.

PP, Committee on National Expenditure (1922) Cmd 1581, 1582, 1583.

Sources:

Unpublished

BLPES, Tariff Commission papers.

Bodleian Library, Oxford, Lord Oxford and Asquith papers (vol 29).

Guildhall Library, London, papers of Association of British Chambers of Commerce, MS 14,476/9.

House of Lords RO, Beaverbrook papers; A Bonar Law papers; D Lloyd George papers (F21/4/10).

New South Wales State Library, Sydney, G E Morrison papers.

PRO, Board of Trade and Foreign Office papers; Great Central Railway papers (RAIL 226); Ministry of Transport papers.

Scottish RO, Edinburgh, Sir Arthur Steel-Maitland papers.

Sheffield University Library, papers of W A S Hewins (60/74).

MCe.

PrC.

Published

Anon, 'The Proposals for a British Trade Bank' *Bankers' Magazine* 102 (1916).

Lord Camrose, *British Newspapers and their Controllers* (Cassell & Co, 1947).

Complete Peerage.

P L Cottrell, 'Aspects of Western Equity Investment in the Banking Systems of East Central Europe' in Alice Teichova and P L Cottrell (eds), *International Business and Central Europe 1918-1939* (Leicester: Leicester University Press, 1983).

Richard Davenport-Hines, *Dudley Docker* (Cambridge: Cambridge University Press, 1984).

Documents of British Foreign Policy, 1st ser, 3 (HSMO, 1949), 2nd ser, 8 (HMSO, 1960).

Economist 23 Dec 1916, 8 Sept 1917, 25 Jan, 8 Feb 1919, 14 Feb 1920, 23 Feb 1921, 1 Apr 1922, 14 Apr 1923.

Arthur C Fox-Davies, *Armorial Families* 1 (7th ed, Hurst & Blackett, 1929).

Globe 21 Oct 1916, 17 Feb, 18, 23 May, 20 June, 1 Sept 1917, 16 Aug 1918.

William A S Hewins, *The Apologia of an Imperialist* (2 vols, Constable & Co, 1929).

H J Jennings, 'A British Trade Bank' *Fortnightly Review* 106 (1916).

Journal of British Electrical & Allied Manufacturers Association Oct 1916.

Marian Kent, 'Agent of Empire? The National Bank of Turkey and British Foreign Policy' *Historical Journal* 18 (1975).

Louis W Michael Kettle, *The Allies and the Russian Collapse* (Deutsch, 1981).

—, *Sidney Reilly* (Corgi Books, 1983).

Lord Mersey, *A Picture of Life 1872-1940* (John Murray, 1941).

Sir Francis Oppenheimer, *Stranger within* (Faber & Faber, 1960).

Sir Robert Inglis Palgrave, 'The British Trade Corporation' *Quarterly Review* 229 (1918).

Sir Francis Piggott, 'The Proposed Trade Bank' *Morning Post* 26 Sept 1916.

Alan J P Taylor, *Beaverbrook* (Hamilton, 1972).

Times, 19 Apr-12 May 1898, 3 Apr, 20 June 1906, 3 Aug 1907, 28 Jan, 8 Feb 1908, 11 Jan 1910, 8 Feb, 2, 30 May 1913, 10, 21 Feb, 11 Apr 1914, 3, 15, 21 May 1917, 23 Jan, 1 Feb 1918, 19, 21 Mar 1934.

Leroy Vail, 'The Making of an Imperial Slum: Nyasaland and its Railways 1895-1935' *Journal of African History* 16 (1975).

WWMP.

WWW.

Kenneth Young (ed), *Diaries of Sir Robert Bruce Lockhart* (Macmillan, 1973).

HENMAN, Philip Sydney

(1899-)

Dock and road transport services entrepreneur

Philip Henman (courtesy of P S Henman).

Philip Sydney Henman was born in the Baptist manse at Yalding, Kent, on 21 December 1899, the son of Sydney James Henman, minister at Yalding, and his wife Ellen Gertrude née Brine. Mrs Henman shared her husband's evangelical faith and raised her seven children in an atmosphere of simplicity, piety and discipline as well as deep affection. Philip, the third child, became a committed Christian at the age of fourteen when an evangelist visited his father's congregation at Purley.

Because of his father's moves between seven churches Philip Henman attended several schools, including Caterham School and later Shoreham Grammar School, recalling the latter for its harsh regime of caning but excellent academic results. Here he suffered his first major breakdown in health, an attack of acute rheumatic fever, which thwarted his early ambition to go to college and then into the Christian ministry. Instead he went into the City at the age of seventeen and devoted much of his spare time and his weekends to Sunday School teaching and lay preaching.

Henman joined a firm of Lloyd's insurance brokers, Alexander Howden & Co, through the introduction of an uncle; here he started as an office boy but soon was showing insurance cover on Lloyds. Conscription in

1917 took him into the King's Royal Rifle Corps with which he served in the North of England until 1921 when he was demobilised with the rank of sergeant. The post-war depression prevented Howdens from re-employing him. His next job, posting parcels for a wholesale textile exporter, abruptly ended twelve months later when the firm went bankrupt. Through one of the stricken firm's secretaries, also a Christian, he learned about a new lighterage company which then wanted an accountant. Philip Henman, who had studied some accounting amongst other subjects, got the job.

Thus in summer 1922 Henman found himself as a lighterage manager, operating two barges from the Hay's Wharf office of the newly-registered General Lighterage Co. Colonel Edgar Richard Hatfield DSO founded the firm after the war, with a nominal capital of £10,000, in order to provide a lighterage service for the two vessels of the London & Cologne Shipping Co of which he was a director. In 1929 Philip Henman became managing director of the General Lighterage Co, having bought out Hatfield's original partner with his own resources and loans raised from two friends. The difficulties of the London & Cologne Shipping Co, hindered by navigation problems on the Rhine, lent fresh vigour to Henman's search for new custom. He initiated a programme of expansion in the early 1930s which included the acquisition of wharfage, warehousing, road haulage and other ancillary services, as well as barges and tugs, partly achieved through the purchase of equity capital in other operating companies. Hatfield, now less interested in the business of the General Lighterage Co than in the return on his investment, in 1933 gave Henman the chance to become a substantial owner: he converted his 15,000 £1 ordinary shares into 15,000 6 per cent cumulative preference shares leaving Henman with most of the 40,000 1s ordinary shares.

By 1939 Philip Henman was chairman of the General Lighterage Co; soon after, a carefully accumulated fund enabled him to buy out Hatfield, who resigned from the board in 1942. For Henman's companies the diversion of shipping away from the Port of London during the war was offset by road transport, warehousing and storage contracts including some for the Government, particularly the Ministry of Food.

After 1945 reconstruction brought new opportunities despite the nationalisation of the road haulage industry under the 1947 Transport Act which Henman survived by confining his business to short distance work. In 1950 Philip Henman formed a public holding company, General Lighterage (Holdings) Ltd, to run 16 subsidiaries, mostly operating barges (167) and wharves in the Port of London and haulage services in London, the Home Counties and Birmingham. Together, the subsidiaries offered a 'package' service, from ship to inland customer. The nominal capital of the group was £475,000, its assets £325,000, and its profits before tax over £100,000 (compared to under £40,000 in 1940). But troubled labour relations in the docks and new methods of conveying commodities from ship to shore (such as pipelines and, later, containers) pointed Philip Henman away from lightering and the Port of London, although in 1950 he was still on the way to controlling over 1,200 of the port's 6,700 lighters and other barge fleets in Liverpool and Hull. Everywhere he cut his costs by modernising equipment and adopting labour-saving work methods.

Denationalisation of long distance road services in 1953 gave him the

McKelvie & Co Ltd, a subsidiary of the Transport Development Group, transporting cable to a hydro-electric project in the highlands of Scotland in 1966 (courtest of Transport Development Group).

opportunity to expand greatly his company's road transportation and related storage, exhibition and engineering services. By the time Henman retired in 1969 his group of companies (renamed the Transport Development Group when it became a public company in 1957) operated over 4,500 lorries, compared to 150 in 1950. Henman saw the advantages of road over rail and perceived that scale economies were relatively limited in road transport where short hauls, local services and personal contacts characterised the market. In this situation Henman organised a group structure not unlike that forged by Emile Garcke (qv) in 1896-97 for the BET. He allowed his operating subsidiaries nearly complete independence: to the extent of preserving their own names, liveries and characters; negotiating their own wages and rates; choosing their own equipment; and owning their premises and maintenance facilities. The holding company monitored its subsidiaries through weekly, monthly and half-yearly figures, allowing the stronger ones to grow and trimming or breaking up the weaker ones. Most importantly, Henman ensured that his

Barges owned by the General Lighterage Co, working on the Thames (courtesy of Transport Development Group).

costing system was both efficient and realistic with respect to the major overheads of vehicle maintenance and depreciation.

By 1969 TDG had over 80 operating subsidiaries scattered up and down Britain, three in South Africa and Rhodesia, three in Australia and seven in Europe. Turnover of the whole group stood at £50 million (compared to under £1 million in 1950), net assets at £47 million and profit before tax at £6.3 million. Owners of smaller haulage firms accepted takeover for a variety of reasons, sometimes because of problems in raising finance for expansion, sometimes because owners feared the effects of death duties. Under the umbrella of a non-trading holding company they were guaranteed supplies of capital and managerial talent (attracted to TDG by profit-sharing) while owners who might wish to withdraw from business received shares, and sometimes also cash, in the much less assailable TDG. The holding company, as developed by Henman, functioned as a manager of managers, providing specialist knowledge on administration, finance, insurance, taxation and property. It had the added advantage, from management's viewpoint, of limiting any unions' field of action to an operating company level.

Philip Henman contrived the purchase or creation of 80 trading subsidiaries in less than twenty years largely by strict attention to profitability, both in his selection of companies to acquire and in monitoring their performance once they joined the TDG. By capitalising TDG reserves and profits he created new TDG shares which could be exchanged for those of prospective subsidiaries. One of the largest acquisitions, Beck & Pollitzer (a road haulage, cold storage and exhibition services firm with assets of £2 million), was acquired by the less usual method (for TDG) of a rights issue in which just over 7 million TDG 5s ordinary shares were offered to the market at 18s 6d each (in 1961).

Henman's achievements were built not only on his own entrepreneurial abilities and vision (evident in his paper on London lighterage), and the company structure he framed, but also on the subordinates he chose and inspired. Through them his plans were shaped and forged. In the backbone of Henman's managerial team were William Fraser and, later, James Blair Duncan. Fraser, dismayed by the prospect of the nationalisation of the waterways firm in which he worked, joined Henman in 1947 to pull into shape the East End road haulage and warehousing business of J Spurling Ltd. Like Henman, Fraser was a committed evangelical Christian; when the TDG was formed he, with Henman, became joint managing director. Duncan started with the TDG as company accountant, and eventually followed Fraser who succeeded Henman as TDG chairman.

Philip Henman was also the financial mind behind the Square Grip Reinforcement Co, formed in 1934 when his brother, Frank Espinett Henman, and a few associates set up a production line in Hanger C at Feltham Air Park to make twisted high tensile steel. Frank, a talented engineer and managing director (who built his own motor car in his teens), had little money so Philip Henman, who became chairman of the new company, put up £1,200 and persuaded his friend John W Laing (qv) to do the same. Laing, with a keen eye to business, also promised to purchase high tensile steel for reinforced concrete, but at a price a little below the going rate. On Laing's behalf Andrew Anderson joined the board to watch his investment. With the urgent need for reinforced concrete during the Second World War, Square Grip rapidly expanded. By 1951, when it went public, it had seven subsidiaries (two in Southern Rhodesia), net group assets of £136,000 and pre-tax profits of £63,000. Partly to solve Frank Henman's succession problems, TDG acquired Square Grip (now with a nominal capital of £1.5 million) when it was put on the market in 1968. Frank in his turn served Henman by sitting on the General Lighterage and TDG boards from 1948 onwards, offering counsel and informed technical advice.

Henman met his wife through the Christian activities to which they both devoted a great deal of their time and energy. Jessie Mary née Nairn (1898-1976) was the daughter of the manager of the London branch of the Scottish Provident Life Association. With her fine singing voice she accompanied Henman when he acted as lay pastor to a chapel at Hook near Surbiton, helped him in the Sunday School work, and at the same time gave her husband tremendous support in all his activities. They were married in 1931 and had one daughter, Mary Jessie.

Among the many Christian causes supported by Henman with finance and counsel were the London Bible College (which John Laing and he were instrumental in founding), Inter Varsity Fellowship (of which he became chairman), the British and Foreign Bible Society, the Evangelisation Society and the Africa Inland Mission (whose Home Council he chaired). They were not alone in benefiting from his charitable donations, eventually administered by trusts which he set up: by the end of his career he had become a patron of the Royal College of Surgeons of England and a benefactor of the Royal Society of Medicine.

Professionally Henman's achievements were widely recognised. He became chairman and later vice-president of the council of the London Chamber of Commerce; vice-president of the Institute of Transport; member of the Grand Council of the CBI and chairman of its transport committee; member of three city livery companies, the Paviors, Farmers, and Watermen and Lightermen; honorary doctor of the University of Surrey; High Sheriff of Surrey (1971-72) and DL of Surrey. His massive business burdens (in 1949 he held 29 directorships and when he retired was working a sixteen hour day) and extensive and varied part-time activities took their toll on Henman's health. To relieve the pressures and on a doctor's advice, he took up farming in the late 1930s, forming a company (Coldharbour Farms Ltd) and farming both in Surrey and in Scotland until after he retired.

When pressed, as often he was, to explain his success, Henman stressed, in his soft-spoken manner, those attributes which arose from his Christian convictions and his own business experience: faith in people; flexibility of mind; hard work; fair dealing; enthusiasm; courage; good judgement; liberality; and encouragement of associates. His entrepreneurial approach was summarised on the card which he carried in his wallet during much of his working life:

> It is dangerously easy to be negative. It does not require much vision to see the difficulties in a proposition or in life. Why buy a shop? It may be burned down. Why extend your factory? It may go to the dogs. Why invest your money? The Socialists may get it. So the Negative Mind works away, while

the Positives of the earth go on founding fortunes, carving careers and building Empires.

DAVID J JEREMY

Writings:

'Lighters and Lighterage. With Special Reference to the Port of London' *The Journal of the Institute of Transport* 27 (1956-57).

Missionary Administration (Evangelical Missionary Alliance, 1963).

Sources:

Unpublished

General Lighterage Group of Companies, Annual Report and Accounts (1956).

The Transport Development Group, Annual Report and Accounts (1958, 1968).

C Reg: General Lighterage Co Ltd (183,115). Transport Development Group Ltd (469,605). Square Grip Reinforcement Co Ltd (286,938).

BCe.

MCe.

Interviews with Mr Philip S Henman, 16 Oct, 1 Dec 1980, 19 Feb 1981.

Autobiographical notes of Mr Henman.

Published

Derek Aldcroft, *British Transport since 1914* (Newton Abbot: David & Charles, 1975).

H C, 'Philip Sydney Henman' *Commercial Motor* 4 Dec 1959.

John Darker, 'The Transport Development Group Philosophy' *ibid* 20 June 1969.

—, 'The New World of Road Transport' *ibid* 27 June 1969.

James B Duncan, 'Transport with Profit' *Chartered Institute of Transport Journal* 34 (1972).

Times 19 June 1950.

HENNESSY, Sir Patrick

(1898-1981)

Motor car manufacturer

Patrick Hennessy was born on 18 April 1898 in Middleton, County Cork, Ireland. His father, Patrick Hennessy, a Roman Catholic, was a foreman on an estate; his mother, Mary née Benn, a Protestant, was the daughter of the proprietor of the estate and had been disowned by her family on her marriage. She was a very gifted woman and had great influence on her children. Hennessy was educated at Christ Church School before running away to join, under age, the Royal Inniskilling Fusiliers in 1914. He entered as a private but was later sent to a school for officers and was given a commission. He served in France until he became a German prisoner of war in March 1918. After his release in December 1918, Hennessy took advantage of a government scheme to enable former officers to take university courses. He took an agricultural course at Cork University during which students were required to visit the new Ford tractor plant in Cork to study the machines. Hennessy applied for a job in the foundry at Ford, where he started work in 1920.

It was not the prospect of a career in industry which had initially attracted him. 'I was always keen on rugby, and thought that manual labour in the foundry would help to toughen up my muscles' {Oral, Sir Patrick Hennessy}.

His progress was, nevertheless, steady; from the foundry he went first to the blacksmith's forge, then to the machine shop. After a spell on the assembly line, he was promoted to testing tractors as they came off the assembly line. Eventually, he was given the task of demonstrating tractors to foreign visitors at the farm on the Ford estate, and his ability earned him a transfer to the British plant at Trafford Park, Manchester, to gain greater experience, especially on the sales side.

Soon he became the travelling representative — or 'roadman' in Ford parlance — for the entire Irish territory, returning to Cork as a sales representative in 1923; he then became service manager in 1924. By this time, the collapse of the tractor market in the post-war depression had compelled the Cork plant to switch production to Model T Ford cars, which were assembled for the newly-formed Irish Free State to overcome recently-imposed tariff barriers.

However, in 1928 Henry Ford decided to close down his Dearborn, Michigan, tractor plant and transfer all the production machinery to Cork, which would become the world's largest tractor factory. The changeover gave Hennessy an insight into factory planning and purchasing requirements which would stand him in good stead in the years to come. Shortly before it ceased production, the Dearborn factory had contracted to supply a vast stock of spare parts to service the 25,000 Fordson tractors that were operating in the USSR. Some of the order had been met by

Under the leadership of Sir Patrick Hennessy, Ford introduced a diesel tractor, shown here to Prince Philip.

Dearborn before it closed down; the bulk was expected to be cleared by Cork, and impatient American executives began bombarding the Irish plant with urgent cablegrams.

A production expert was sent over from the USA, but he was incapable of organising the supply of the spare parts for the USSR, a task which was in any case far beyond the capacity of the Cork factory. When he heard that three senior men were on their way over from Dearborn to sort things out, the production expert decided to return to the USA before they arrived; before he left, he handed his job over to Hennessy. Realising that the only way out of the dilemma was to buy in parts from sub-contractors, Hennessy got the services of the Manchester purchasing department, hired a handful of bright young men, and set to work. He found purchase organised on a very casual, ad hoc basis, with many components priced by inspired guesswork, so he changed the buying system so that the price paid by Ford more realistically reflected the manufacturing cost. While he had originally estimated that it would take two years to clear up the Russian order, it was completed inside eighteen months, which gave him great satisfaction.

An American team of efficiency experts was cutting a swathe through employment in the European Ford plants about this time in an attempt to reduce inefficiency and improve sales and profits. During their visit to Cork, they cabled home: 'Hennessy service manager appears most likely candidate for development should visit Detroit January first' {Wilkins and Hill (1964) 157}. And H S Jenkins, who headed Trafford Park during the mid-1920s, singled out Patrick Hennessy as 'a promising young man ... very well informed ... and one that I should say would have very good prospects with the Company.' {ibid}

The successful conclusion of the Russian tractor deal earned Hennessy promotion in 1931 to purchase manager with Ford of Britain, which had just completed a vast new factory beside the Thames at Dagenham in Essex. Producing what were in effect modified versions of Ford's

American models, the new factory faced financial crisis. In the last quarter of 1931, Dagenham sold only five cars, surviving on its truck production. To remedy the situation, approval was given in October 1931 to begin work on a new 8hp small car more suited to the European market. The first prototypes were exhibited in February 1932 and the car, Model Y, went into production at Dagenham in August that year. The divergence in design from American models was an important step in relaxation of the domination of the American parent company. Hennessy's role in this rapid development programme was crucial; despite the company's financial problems, he managed to co-ordinate the supply of all the components and production machinery very quickly. 'No one outside really knew how bad the situation was,' he recalled later. 'We would pay off one supplier, then another, keeping the secret successfully.' {Oral, Sir Patrick Hennessy}

The Model Y proved to be an outstanding success. Selling at £120 — later reduced to £100 — it was the cheapest four-seat saloon car on the British market, and returned Ford's British operations to profit in 1933. By 1934 it had taken a 54 per cent share of the market for cars of 8hp and under. The reduction of Model Y's selling price to £100 in September 1935 to counter growing competition from Morris was again largely due to Hennessy's success in keeping down costs charged by suppliers.

To replace the Model Y and its 10hp sister model, Ford of Britain designed two new small cars intended to be launched in 1937. This ran counter to a directive that all Dagenham cars should be designed in Dearborn, and Hennessy was chosen to take the prototypes to America to 'sell' them to the Ford top management. He was successful, and at the same time established a close friendship with Edsel Ford, Henry Ford's son and the president of Ford Motor Co. He also got to know Henry Ford well, though the relationship here was one of respect rather than friendship: 'He was the only man I ever met who frightened me — he was so unpredictable!' {ibid}

In January 1939, Hennessy was promoted to general manager, one of the triumvirate who ruled Ford of Britain under the chairmanship of Percival (later Lord) Perry (qv). Within a matter of months Hennessy and Perry were approaching the Ministry of Agriculture and Fisheries with a plan to increase tractor output to maintain food supplies in case of war. A reserve of 3,000 machines was created and sold to the Government at a 27.5 per cent discount, to be stored by Ford tractor dealers until a national emergency arose.

When, in early 1940, the Ministry of Aircraft Production was set up under Lord Beaverbrook's (qv) leadership, Hennessy was recommended to take charge of materials supplies. Within a month he had planned increased supplies of aluminium, magnesium and other vital materials that would double production. In August 1940, 782 Spitfires and Hurricanes were produced for the RAF; by September monthly output was up to 1,228, playing a vital role in the Battle of Britain. By now, Hennessy was a member of the Council of the MAP, and in October 1940 he produced an overall plan for future production by the aircraft industry, which was regarded as over-ambitious, but which even in its modified form spurred the aircraft industry on to greater efforts. Hennessy completed his service with the MAP in 1941: he was knighted later that year. Hennessy returned to Dagenham where he remained for the rest of the war. In March 1945, he was made a director of the British company.

With the end of the war, Ford rapidly returned to car production. Hennessy, the youngest of the three men who guided Ford's British operations, was regarded as the company's 'hope of the future'. When Lord Perry retired as chairman in 1948, Sir Patrick Hennessy became managing director of Ford of Britain, and in May 1950 became deputy chairman.

Under his leadership, Ford introduced its first all-new models for almost twenty years, the 1950 Consul and Zephyr. These were the first British Ford cars with overhead valve engines, independent front suspension and integral body/chassis construction. They brought technical and styling prestige to Ford, which for many years had relied solely on low price for its sales.

Another major step forward instigated by Hennessy was the introduction of a Ford-built diesel engine, the cheapest diesel of its class in the world. He had to press hard for the production of this engine, against the initial disapproval of the chairman, Sir Rowland Smith, and the American company. Eventually Sir Rowland backed Hennessy's judgement although he himself was not convinced. Installed in the Fordson tractor in 1951, it was soon specified for almost every tractor built at Dagenham, and greatly improved the model's penetration of export markets.

Ford of Britain was now offering the widest range in its history, and Sir Patrick was closely involved in both styling and engineering. His visits to the design department were so frequent that he became known as 'the chief stylist'. He also insisted on reliability and serviceability.

After several attempts, he managed to engineer the acquisition of Ford's body supplier, Briggs Motor Bodies Ltd, whose plant was adjacent to the Dagenham works, in 1953. He had been particularly anxious to do this, because he foresaw, correctly, the purchase by Chrysler of Briggs in the USA. It was the start of an unprecedented period of expansion which would see Ford's factory area increased by 50 per cent and the company's production capacity doubled. In the late 1950s Ford Dagenham was one of the largest industrial plant complexes in Britain with about 40,000 employees. This expansion programme would culminate in the acquisition of a 329-acre site at Halewood, near Liverpool, where construction of a new plant with a planned annual capacity of 200,000 units began in 1959. When Sir Patrick became chairman of Ford of Britain in April 1956, the company's annual production was 320,742 cars, trucks and tractors, and annual turnover £145 million; four years later, output was up to 546,769 vehicles and turnover was £270 million.

In the late 1950s, Sir Patrick realised that there was a gap in the market between the Anglia/Prefect light cars and the Consul/Zephyr range, and work began on a new model. A 'stop-gap' model, the Classic, appeared in 1961, but it was the Cortina — initiated by Sir Patrick as 'Project Archbishop' — which was destined for long-term production. Developed by a product planning team headed by Terry Beckett (himself a future chairman of Ford of Britain), the Cortina was a full five-seater developed to counter the recently-introduced BMC Mini. It was the start of Ford of Britain's most successful model line, which was to remain in production for over twenty years, though the Cortina of the 1980s had little in common with its ancestor but the name. By 1982, production of the successive marks of Cortina was approaching five million. Other successful model lines begun under Sir Patrick's chairmanship included the Transit van and the D-Series truck, as well as the 105E Anglia car that initiated production at the new Halewood plant in 1963.

He relinquished his executive functions in Ford of Britain in 1963 and retired as chairman of the board in 1968, but remained a consultant to the company until his death in 1981. He also continued as chairman of Henry Ford & Son, the Cork-based Ford company, until 1977 (he had taken this office in 1955). Indeed, he was held in such affection by the Irish Ford company, which regarded him as its father-figure, that when he retired as its chairman, he remained a director, retaining this position until his death. His sixty-one years of service to Ford were a record for any company executive.

During Sir Patrick's years as managing director and chairman, the British company was allowed rather more independence than Ford's French and German subsidiaries. Occasional battles over products and planning, as in the case of the diesel engine produced in the early 1950s, did not mar the essentially good relations between Ford of Britain and the American parent. Hennessy particularly appreciated the advice and encouragement the British company received in the years immediately after the war. In some fields, such as systems of financial control and techniques of management, he followed practices developed in the American company. In labour relations, however, American experience could not be a guide. Before the war neither Ford in Britain nor Ford in America recognised trade unions. The British company made its first trade union agreement in 1944; the Joint Negotiating Committee which was set up under this agreement was chaired by Sir Patrick until he relinquished responsibility as managing director in January 1957. Labour relations were reasonably good until the acquisition of Briggs brought a crop of problems, as Briggs had no formal agreement and very different rates of pay and working conditions. It took three years to resolve these difficulties. Labour relations were perhaps the area in which Sir Patrick was least at home; so high were the standards of dedication and performance he set himself that he found it difficult to understand why every Ford worker could not be as disciplined and loyal.

Sir Patrick undertook few responsibilities outside Ford, except to serve as president of the Society of Motor Manufacturers and Traders, 1965-66, and deputy president, 1967-68.

In 1923 he married Dorothy Margaret (d 1949), daughter of Robert Davis JP of Boardmills, Northern Ireland; they had two sons and a daughter. Sir Patrick died on 13 March 1981, leaving an estate proved at £202,307.

DAVID BURGESS-WISE

Sources:

Unpublished

PrC.

Interview with Sir Patrick Hennessy, 1977.

Sir Patrick Hennessy, 'The Development and Organisation of the Ford Motor Company Limited' (Edwards Seminar paper 159, 30 Nov 1954).

Published

Times 16 Mar 1981.

Mira Wilkins and Frank E Hill, *American Business Abroad: Ford on Six Continents* (Detroit, Michigan: Wayne State University Press, 1964).

WW 1980.

HEPWORTH, Joseph

(1834-1911)

Clothing manufacturer

Joseph Hepworth was born at Lindley, Huddersfield on 12 May 1834, the son of George Hepworth, a shoemaker. 'My grandfathers on both sides were well-to-do men, but my father was a working man and I commenced to earn money when I was ten, as a half-timer' { *Yorkshire Evening Post* 17 Oct 1911}, at Joseph Walker's Plover Mills in Lindley, earning 1s 6d for a thirty-hour week. Two years later he became a full-timer in the woollen mill. At sixteen Hepworth moved to George Walker's Wellington Mill as a teazle setter, and in his spare time studied at the Lindley Mechanics Institute to such effect that by 1853 he became a volunteer teacher. The following year he added temperance work with children to his activities on Sundays.

In 1860 Walkers defaulted and Joseph was without work, but he was so highly regarded in Lindley for his voluntary work that he was appointed assistant overseer at £30 a year. After three years he became a traveller (representative) for a woollen manufacturer, 'for twelve months or more I had a very hard struggle ... packing my samples till nearly midnight and have been up before five to catch my train' {*ibid*}. With a wife (Sarah, whom he married in 1855) and two children to keep he set up as a woollen

The Cutting Room (courtesy of J Hepworth & Son plc).

draper, with his wife's brother, James Rhodes, in Briggate, Leeds, in 1864, having little or no capital, but determined to do his best. His earnings that year were around 15s a week.

In 1865 he set up on his own as a wholesale clothier in Bishopgate Street, Leeds. The clothing industry, that is, the wholesale manufacture of working men's and boys' suits, began in Leeds in the 1850s. It followed the introduction of the sewing machine and, in 1858, the development of the band-knife by Greenwood & Batley. In Leeds the rise of the clothing trade matched the decline of flax-spinning and the influx of Jewish immigrants from the Baltic. John Barran (qv), considered to be the founder of the Leeds trade, opened his first factory in 1856 but Joseph Hepworth's special contribution was to extend from manufacturing into retailing. Hepworth started with 7 sewing machines and 12 'hands'. He was determined to pay decent wages, paying the men £1 a week and women and girls enough to live on; they could make 35s a week on piecework. The business developed slowly but steadily and led to moves to bigger premises so that by 1881 he had a works in Wellington Street, Leeds, employing 500. 'About this time my (eldest) son, Norris, joined me and, tired and disheartened by the constant losses through insolvent tradespeople, we determined to open shops of our own and embark on the retail business' {*ibid*}. Most of his customers left him but Hepworth was persistent and opened more shops so that soon the factory was fully used to supply their shops and a developing export trade to Australia and South Africa. The export trade grew and subsidiary factories were set up in Cape Town and Sydney. In Leeds a new factory, Prospect Works, was built, on Claypit Lane, at a cost of £20,000 in 1891 and Joseph Hepworth & Son became a private company with a capitalisation of £360,000. Norris Hepworth became chairman and Joseph a director with a substantial holding. The Prospect Works was gutted by fire in 1895, the damage being assessed at £60,000 to £80,000; the entire stock of patterns was destroyed. Duplicates were obtained from the overseas subsidiaries and the factory was soon

The Machine Room (courtesy of J Hepworth & Son plc).

rebuilt; at the end of the year there was a profit of £19,333. The business continued to grow. In 1905 there were 143 shops, profits were £33,323 and to celebrate his golden wedding Joseph gave a bonus to all 1,200 employees, based on service with the company. This bonus, 5s per annum up to twenty years, then 10s per annum, amounted to a total of £2,000 — an indication that staff turnover was high, especially amongst young women machinists. The first shop opened was lost in July 1910 when the adjacent Great Northern Hotel caught fire and burned down.

Joseph Hepworth devoted less time to the business after 1891. He was elected to Leeds City Council as a Liberal, for West Hunslet ward, in 1888, and became an alderman in 1892, then a magistrate. The end of a long period of Radical rule deprived him of the mayoralty until he was recalled from retirement in 1906. Although he was described as a useful rather than brilliant councillor he served as chairman of the Free Library Committee and donated paintings to the Art Gallery. His other offices reflected his lifelong interests in education and temperance: Poor Law Guardian, vice-president of the YMCA, treasurer of the Central Leeds Liberal Association, and member of the Free Church Council. He was president of the Leeds Mechanics Institute, a life-governor of the Yorkshire Union of Mechanics Institutes, a life-governor of the Yorkshire College, where he was an active member of the Dyeing and Finishing Department committee, then a governor of Leeds University. Apart from his keen interest in technical education Hepworth was a leading member of the Methodist New Connexion, like many other leading business men in Leeds, and a 'guardian representative'. As president and treasurer of the Leeds Band of Hope from 1869 his views on strong drink were an embarrassment to Leeds Liberal party leaders. When he became Lord Mayor in 1906 he replaced the traditional dinner for the judges with a breakfast and gave £500 to the Education Committee to provide dinners for needy pupils.

To celebrate the formation of the United Methodist Church in 1907 he gave a thousand guineas to their funds; he had previously generously supported their chapels in Torquay, where he spent the winters, and in Harrogate, where he lived in the 'season' from 1900. Joseph Hepworth died on 25 October 1911, leaving an estate proved at £168,218. He was survived by his widow, Sarah, three sons and four daughters.

E J CONNELL

Sources:

Unpublished

Leeds City Archives Department, J Hepworth & Sons, business records.

MCe.

PrC.

Published

British Association Handbook Leeds Meeting 1890.

Harrogate Advertiser 25 Oct 1911.

Ernest P Hennock, *Fit and Proper Persons* (Edward Arnold, 1973).

Industries of Yorkshire part 1 (1888).

Leeds Mercury 18 Oct 1911.

Joan Thomas, *A History of the Leeds Clothing Industry* (Hull: Yorkshire Bulletin of Economic and Social Research, 1955).

VCH Yorkshire 2.

Yorkshire Evening News 17 Oct 1911.

Yorkshire Evening Post 17 Oct 1911.

Yorkshire Post 18 Oct 1911.

HERBERT, Sir Alfred Edward

(1866-1957)

Machine tool manufacturer

Sir Alfred Herbert (taken from C Addison, Politics from Within *vol I).*

Alfred Edward Herbert was born in West Street, Leicester on 5 September 1866, the second son of William Herbert, a 'grazier' {BCe} and builder and his wife Sarah Ann née Thompson. After education at Stoneygate House School in Leicester, he was apprenticed in 1880 to a local firm of crane and hoist builders, Joseph Jessop & Sons.

In 1887, just before his apprenticeship term was complete, at the age of twenty, he went to Coventry as manager of a small engineering firm, Coles & Mathews. He was paid £2 a week by F S Mathews; the firm made and repaired boilers as well as leasing ploughing tackle and steam rollers. A year later Herbert became the firm's owner in partnership with William S Hubbard, who had been his fellow apprentice in Leicester; their fathers provided the young men with £2,000 capital each. About this time Herbert secured the agency for a French patent of great value in manufacturing tubes for the Coventry cycle trade and profits from the tube agency business were ploughed back into machine tool manufacture. The firm, known as Herbert & Hubbard, followed the policy of producing a wide range of specialised tools, at first to suit the cycle trade, later to capture a wider market. In contrast to the much more specialised machine tool manufacturers in the USA, Herbert & Hubbard made drilling and grinding machinery for hub drilling, spoke screwing, rim bending, ball grinding, bracket and hub boring, besides recessing machines and small hand lathes and machinery for ribbon manufacture.

Hubbard left the partnership in 1894 to begin a new business in Leicester and Herbert turned the firm into a limited liability company with an authorised capital of £25,000 divided into 5,000 shares. He quickly saw the importance of holding agencies for foreign, especially American, machine tool products and established offices in many parts of the world. His first foreign branch was in Paris, with later ones at Lille, Lyons and Barcelona. Japanese, Italian and Indian offices followed, while Canada, Belgium and Australia were added over the years. By 1910 Herbert was supporting his Continental sales with a follow-up service, sending out engineers periodically to inspect his machine tools under operating conditions. In the UK the firm had branches in London, Glasgow, Manchester, Birmingham, Leeds, Newcastle upon Tyne, Sheffield and Bristol. Increased output necessitated new premises and in 1899 a foundry was established at Edgwick on the outskirts of Coventry; two years earlier, in 1897, Oscar Harmer (1850-1939) had brought his American machine-tool experience when he joined Herberts. At this period Herberts was one of seven machine tool firms in the city; Webster & Bennett was one of his main competitors. By 1910 Herbert employed 1,500 men and by 1914 a total of 2,000, making the firm the largest in

Britain, with their Number 4 capstan lathe the best-known product. G L Carden, an American who toured European engineering works on behalf of the US Government in 1909-10, reported 'There is no denying that the Herbert machine tools, and in particular the turret lathe of the firm, are strong competitors of the best work turned out from American shops' {Floud (1976) 74}.

During the First World War Herbert was first appointed to take charge of the machine tool department of the War Office; after May 1915 he became Controller of Machine Tools at the new Ministry of Munitions; there he was responsible for organising priority classification for machine tools to be distributed to factories engaged on war-work, for clearing the backlog of machine tools that had collected at the docks and for pressing for the dilution of labour as part of the wartime emergency measures. He was knighted for his services at the Ministry of Munitions in June 1917 and in the same year received the Légion d'Honneur. In February 1918 he was awarded the Order of St Stanislas (second class with star) and in October 1918 the Belgian Order of Leopold. His wartime experiences left him with a permanent concern about British preparedness for war and a deep suspicion of Germany's rearmament plans.

In the inter-war years the firm continued to expand; in 1927 the workforce was 2,500 and a year later the whole organisation moved to a 38-acre site at Edgwick. Later expansion took place at Red Lane, Coventry at Exhall and at Lutterworth in Leicestershire. Herbert was greatly concerned by the late 1930s at the availability of machine tools, labour and German-made supplies in the event of war. He pressed for the greater use of semi-skilled workers, including women, and for night-shifts to increase output; he corresponded regularly with MPs and wrote many letters to the press on productivity, labour dilution and workers' welfare.

In the inter-war years, when the British machine tool industry was generally struggling, with its share of the export market falling from 20 to 10 per cent, Alfred Herbert competed with other manufacturers of world standing and became known as a 'best practice' firm. The firm never joined the Associated British Machine Tool Makers (founded 1916-17), an abstention that reflected Sir Alfred's character and business philosophy. The firm manufactured 65,000 powered machine tools in the Second World War, including innovations such as the combination turret lathe (after the Lutterworth plant was established in 1940) and the chip stream box tool (patented in 1942). After the war Sir Alfred continued to innovate. In 1948 he acquired Sigma Instruments and four years later obtained a patent for tape control systems, followed in 1956 by the introduction of programmed sequence control in his factories, an early instance of industrial computerisation. Although in his eighties, he remained a powerful influence in the firm at all levels, and, alongside his policies of excellence and quality products, he was prepared to take advice on the newest manufacturing techniques and to implement them.

His personal views were forthright, trenchantly expressed, a mixture of progressive and traditional opinions, so that he was a pioneer in matters of industrial safety and welfare provisions for his workers but wished to reduce the school leaving age and increase the hours of the working week. He supported the dilution of labour in the face of union opposition and, while right-wing in his personal outlook, favoured coalition government in the 1950s, 'a time for bickering to give place to statesmanship' {*Coventry Telegraph* 27 May 1957}. He was a strong, paternalistic figure, and expressed his often original views on a wide range of topics regularly in the firm's own journal, in public speeches and in a voluminous correspondence. He wrote with compassion to the families of employees killed or injured in the war or the blitz and frequently aided workers who found themselves in hardship.

Alfred Herbert was appointed chairman of the Machine Tool and Engineering Association in 1912 and became president when it was reformed as the Machine Tool Trades Association in 1919. He held this position until he resigned after a policy disagreement in 1934. He was also president of the Institute of Production Engineers and an honorary life member of the Institution of Mechanical Engineers and a fellow of the Royal Society of Arts. He was made an honorary Freeman of London and, in 1933, of Coventry. He valued apprenticeship as a means of technical training and among his former apprentices who themselves founded important Coventry firms, were (Sir) Harry Harley (Coventry Gauge & Tool, now T I Matrix), Axel Charles Wickman (who set up his own company in 1926) and Harry Weston (Modern Machine Tools). His personal contribution to the firm may be judged from its success during his lifetime and its decline after his death — it was finally put into receivership in 1983.

Alfred Herbert's charitable donations made a very significant contribution to Coventry during the twentieth century. He served as chairman and committee member of the Coventry and Warwickshire Hospital and in 1915 gave £1,000 for a new ward for wounded servicemen there; he subsequently donated a further £10,000. In 1935 he built a range of six almshouses for elderly women in Coventry with an endowment of £8,000 and a further six almshouses two years later endowed with £5,000; these homes were named in memory of his second wife. In her memory also he equipped the Lady Chapel of St Barbara's Church at Earlsdon. In 1939 he presented Town Thorns, a large house in the village of Brinklow, to Coventry Corporation as a camp school for poor city children. He donated £2,500 to the city relief fund after the 1941 air-raids. For fifty years Herbert was president of the Coventry Engineering Society and in 1949 he established a series of five annual lectures covering the arts and culture generally. An active supporter of the Church of England, he chaired a public meeting in 1947 to discuss the rebuilding of Coventry Cathedral and later gave the reconstruction fund a covenant for £25,000. He also launched the industrialists' appeal to augment clergy stipends in the diocese and strongly supported chaplains to youth in industry. However, his largest benefaction to Coventry was of £200,000 for a new city art gallery and museum, named after him, built in 1954-59 in Jordan Well, although the foundations had been laid before the outbreak of war in 1939.

Sir Alfred Herbert married three times; firstly in 1889 to Ellen Adela the daughter of Thomas Ryley of Coventry; they had four daughters. Secondly in 1913 he married Florence (d 1930), widow of Lieutenant Colonel H E E Lucas; thirdly in 1933, Marion (d 1969), widow of Lieutenant Colonel A J Pugh. He lived at Dunley Manor, Whitchurch, Hampshire where he bought an 1,800 acre estate in 1917; he enjoyed fishing and shooting.

Sir Alfred Herbert never retired and was chairman and managing director at the time of his death on 26 May 1957. He left £5,336,051 gross.

JOAN LANE

Writings:

Shots at the Truth (Coventry: A Herbert, 1948).

'Safety in Industry' *Engineer* 1951.

The *AH Review* (monthly publication) usually contained an article or editorial comment by Alfred Herbert.

Sources:

Unpublished

Coventry City RO, Alfred Herbert company records.

Hampshire RO, material relating to Dunley Manor.

Leicestershire RO, parish registers.

Shakespeare Birthplace Trust, Stratford-upon-Avon, personal papers of Sir Alfred Herbert.

Sir Alfred Herbert, 'Machine Chasers' (an MS autobiography listed in Floud (1976) 207).

Interviews with Mr I H Hollick and Colonel C W Clark; information from Mr Ralph Gabriel.

Published

Derek H Aldcroft, 'The Performance of the British Machine-Tool Industry in the Interwar Years' *Business History Review* 40 (1966).

Coventry Telegraph 27 May 1957.

Engineer 203 (1957).

Roderick Floud, *The British Machine Tool Industry, 1850-1914* (Cambridge: Cambridge University Press, 1976).

Joan Lane, *A Register of Business Records of Coventry and Related Areas* (Coventry: Lanchester Polytechnic, 1977).

'Messrs Alfred Herbert, Coventry' *Proceedings of the Institution of Mechanical Engineers* 1927.

Samuel B Saul, 'The Machine Tool Industry in Britain to 1914' *Business History* 10 (1968).

VCH Warwickshire 8.

Times 27 May, 6 June 1957.

WWW.

HERMON, Edward

(1822-1881)

Cotton textiles manufacturer

Edward Hermon was born on 23 March 1822, the son of Richard Hermon, reputedly a 'South Country gentleman of modest rank' {*Fortunes Made in Business* III, 29}, but at the time of Edward's birth a plumber, painter and glazier of King Street, London. Richard Hermon's prosperity in these years of speculative successes in the London building trades enabled him to provide his son with a good education, though no details of his schooling are known. About 1844 or 1845, Edward Hermon entered the London branch of Horrockses, Miller & Co. Thus, unusually among cotton men Hermon, firstly as a salesman and later as principal clerk, gained his knowledge of the textile trades from the merchanting side, in Horrockses' extensive home and foreign trade. Outstanding business prescience and capacity demonstrated in the London office marked Hermon for promotion. Partnership came in 1860 when Thomas Miller, leading partner in the firm, sought a successor, as his sons were uninterested in the business. This stroke of good fortune was the making of Hermon, which his shrewdness, ability and opportunism consolidated. In 1865, on the death of Miller, he became sole controller of the firm, the largest of mid-nineteenth century cotton spinning and manufacturing enterprises. In 1865 it embraced ten factories, 154,334 spindles, 2,775 looms and employed 3,300 operatives.

Apart from occasional visits to the Preston works, Hermon's knowledge of the actual production of cotton was limited, yet he took up the managerial reins with distinctive verve and alacrity. Energy and acumen enabled him to master the details of manufacturing. Active in the search for improvements, he was responsible for the introduction of twilled and plain sheeting, which became a standard 'Horrockses' line. His successor in the London office, Frederick Styles, was taken into partnership in 1866, while the factories were largely run by William Pollard, a manager-turned-partner. Familial continuity was attempted by the introduction of his nephews S O and S A Hermon in 1873. Under Hermon's direction, machinery was to some extent modernised and a new spinning shed was opened in 1875. By 1880 the emphasis was on the physical concentration of the factories, with the closure of the Ribbleton works. The capital value of the firm between 1865 and 1880 was more or less stationary in real terms, although in favourable trading conditions, profits were ample, particularly for Hermon himself. His share of total capital grew rapidly from £2,600 (0.5 per cent) in 1861 to a peak of £538,789 (88.2 per cent) in 1873. Thereafter, it diminished although he continued to take at least half of all profits. Hermon's attitude toward labour was conciliatory: a sympathiser with the operatives' grievances, he readily assented to a joint list of prices in 1865 and resisted wage reductions in 1878, refusing to join his fellow

Interior of yellow mill from a painting of 1864 (taken from Gale Pedrick The Story of Horrockses*).*

employers in a lock-out; to some extent he promoted the comforts of the workforce, earning the repute and popularity of a good paternalist.

Yet even before his retirement in 1880, Hermon had increasingly relished rentier status, using the firm as a milch-cow to support his political aspirations and plutocratic life style. In 1868 he had been elected MP for Preston, and progressively severed his managerial links with the firm without diminishing in any way his receipts from it. In addition to a Scottish shooting-lodge, in the late 1860s he had purchased a 900 acre Oxfordshire estate, where he built an impressive and expensive French Gothic country-house, Wyfold Court, the chef-d'oeuvre of George Somers Clarke. Here he led the life of a country gentleman and housed his extensive collection of modern pictures (sold in 1881 for £37,000). Ruskin would have considered Hermon's collection to lack moral beauty or intellectual interest, yet Hermon was an important patron of artists such as Edwin Long, becoming a figure more familiar to the Royal Academy than to the Manchester Exchange. Preston, however, remained central to Hermon's wealth and politics (although he took no part in the local government of the town). He was a generous benefactor of the town, its clubs, bazaars, bands, schools and many churches, not merely those of his own Anglican faith. Yet if the town benefited, the firm suffered. Little capital was reinvested, machinery was antiquated, the managers incompetent, the partners disgruntled. The rate of profit declined from 12 per cent (1872-77) to 4.8 per cent (1878-80). This was the situation of leaderlessness and stasis from which Frank Hollins (qv) was to rescue Horrockses in the late nineteenth century.

As MP for Preston until his death, Hermon was not a strong 'party' man but a 'liberal-minded' Conservative, a fitting representative for a commercial constituency with strong Tory traditions. In the House of Commons, he was both active and expert on financial and commercial issues, for example, in opposing the East Indian cotton duties of 1879. Interestingly, he was among the first manufacturers to doubt the wisdom of free trade, proclaiming in 1881 the necessity for reciprocity. By and large a friend to the working man, he favoured increased education for the masses (but without compulsion) and the extension of the Factory Acts. He had a keen interest in safety at work, and in 1871 offered prizes for suggestions on the prevention of explosions in mines.

Hermon married well in 1848, to Emily Laetitia, daughter of George Udney, a member of the Bengal Civil Service and of the Indian Supreme Council. His son, George, educated at Oxford and the Bar, became curate of St Neots, Cornwall in 1885. His daughter, Frances Caroline, married in 1877 Robert Hodge, later a Conservative MP, who assumed the name of Hermon-Hodge in 1903 but was to become Lord Wyfold in 1919.

Edward Hermon died on 6 May 1881 leaving £588,000 gross, one of the largest fortunes made in nineteenth century textiles and a notable advance on the £25,000 left by his father in 1849. Yet the visible success of Hermon as a mid-Victorian entrepreneur concealed growing weaknesses in his firm, which by 1880 had ceded leadership in the cotton industry to the Manchester firm of Rylands founded by John Rylands (qv).

A C HOWE

Writings:

PD, 3rd ser 194-209 (1869-81), passim.

Sources:

Unpublished

Lancashire RO, Horrockses' business records.

PRO, Canterbury Wills, PROB 8/242 and PROB 11/2104, f 931.

Westminster City Archives, St James's, Piccadilly, Baptismal Registers, 1819-1828.

PrC.

Published

Sir Charles Brown, *The Origins and Progress of Horrockses* (Preston, 1925).

Fortunes Made in Business (3 vols, Sampson, Low & Co, 1884).

The Hermon Prize Essays: Essays on the Prevention of Explosions and Accidents in Coal Mines (1874).

E Hermon, Catalogue of Modern Pictures (1882).

P Howell, 'Wyfold Court, Oxfordshire' in Howard Colvin and John Harris (eds), *The Country Seat. Studies in the History of the British Country House* (Allen Lane, 1970).

Manchester Guardian 7 May 1881.

Gale Pedrick, *The Story of Horrockses* (Preston: Horrockses, Crewdson & Co Ltd, 1950).

Preston Chronicle 7 May 1881.

Preston Guardian 7, 11 May 1881.

Preston Herald 7 May 1881.

Reading Mercury 14 May 1881.

Times 7 May 1881.

WWMP.

HETHERINGTON, Sir Arthur Ford

(1911-)

Gas industry manager

Arthur Ford Hetherington was born in London on 12 July 1911, the second son of Roger Hetherington and Honoria née Ford. His father was a consulting engineer who became chief engineering inspector of the Ministry of Health, and was knighted in 1945.

Educated at Highgate School, London, and Trinity College, Cambridge, Arthur Hetherington found his first employment with Lebus, the well-known furniture manufacturers, who in 1934 sent him on a business administration course at the London School of Economics. The latter experience proved to be the main benefit in an otherwise unrewarding period and in the following year he applied to the Gas Light & Coke Co for a job as a scientist attached to the service side of the undertaking.

After preliminary training at the Watson House Centre, he became assistant to the company's civil engineer before embarking on a series of progressive posts in the gas service. These included service supervisor at

Finchley Road, service supervisor at Kensington and service manager at Seven Sisters Road in the company's Northern Division.

During the war Hetherington, who was a member of the Royal Naval Volunteer Reserve, served in the Fleet Air Arm, becoming a lieutenant commander (flying) at Scapa Flow. He was awarded the DSC.

Returning to the Gas Light & Coke Co in 1945, he was appointed a joint divisional manager, first of Eastern Division and then of the much more important Central Division. It was while he was divisional manager of the latter that he was appointed commercial manager of the Southern Gas Board in 1955.

By that time the gas industry had been nationalised for six years, yet Arthur Hetherington was the first central officer of that Board; hitherto responsibility for the commercial function had rested with individuals in the various divisions of the area. The event which transformed the Southern Gas Board was the arrival as chairman of C H Leach. It was Arthur Hetherington's good fortune to be appointed deputy chairman under Leach only one year after his move to Southern. Leach's approach to management was dynamic and those who survived the ordeal of working for him became disciples of his philosophy. The Leach advocacy of functionalisation (management organised on the basis of the firm functions, of manufacturing, distributing, marketing and administration) as a tool of management was embraced by Arthur Hetherington. Throughout his three years as chairman of the Southern Gas Board, 1961-64, Arthur Hetherington made no significant changes in the policies which Leach had laid down and which were operating with considerable success; rather, he consolidated those policies while instituting new methods of his own devising.

His appointment as chairman of the East Midlands Gas Board in 1964 enabled him to transfer those methods to a much larger organisation and one which was already a high performer, in no small measure due to its excellent start in life under the chairmanship of Sir Henry Jones (qv), by this time chairman of the Gas Council. At EMGAS Arthur Hetherington made functionalisation work, streamlining the complexity of meetings and recruiting J H Smith (later deputy chairman of the British Gas Corporation) as director of finance to rectify a certain weakness in accounting methods.

Three years later, by which time full-scale conversion to natural gas had started at Burton on Trent, he followed Sir Henry Jones to the Gas Council in London, becoming deputy chairman in succession to Sir Kenneth Hutchison. It was a significant period of expansion with plans afoot to extend the length of the national gas high-pressure transmission system, from little more than 300 miles to 2,500 miles and to treble sales of gas in ten years.

The year 1967 was also an important one in organisational terms. It was then that the independent consultants McKinsey & Co were brought in to report on the organisation and management of the Gas Council. As a result of their recommendations the chairman, Sir Henry Jones, became freed of much administrative work in order to concentrate on matters of policy and future development. Arthur Hetherington as deputy became chief executive with responsibility for all departments and for settling day-to-day issues. It was partly because of this new role for the deputy chairman, partly because of his newness in the post, and also partly because of his natural concern for detail that Arthur Hetherington acquired the reputation of one who was somewhat reluctant to delegate responsibility. In fact his zeal and appetite for work were understandable in the light of the creation of eight new departments — itself another facet of the McKinsey recommendations — the operation of which had to be carefully monitored during their formative period.

In 1972, on the retirement of Sir Henry Jones, Arthur Hetherington became chairman of the Gas Council. Again, this was a particularly important year. The Gas Act of 1972 had sought to recognise both the expansion of the industry and the consequences of its need to search for and distribute natural gas as a single organisational entity. The result of this was the creation in 1973 of a new statutory body, the British Gas Corporation, which stripped the area boards of their autonomy and made them (as gas regions) answerable in most matters to the central body.

It was natural that Arthur Hetherington should become chairman of the Corporation, although he had reservations about the merits of centralisation. While recognising the importance of centralising the supply of gas and unifying such matters as pipeline safety standards, he believed that most activities connected with the customer were best dealt with at local level. Nevertheless it was his task to introduce the sweeping changes embodied in the Bill with a minimum of unrest among the regions. From the former area board chairmen downwards, there was a measure of resentment at the loss of operating freedom, and perhaps one of Arthur Hetherington's greatest contributions to the gas industry lay in the success achieved by his powers of persuasion and reassurance at this difficult period.

Another important factor in his management of gas affairs was his ability to lay the foundations of financial success. This had been demonstrated relatively early in his career but reached its high point in 1974 when he battled with the Government over its interference with gas prices. At the time the Corporation was operating at a £41 million loss, but the situation was reversed in a surprisingly short period of time.

That same year Arthur Hetherington's knighthood was announced in the New Year's Honours List and he received an Hon D Sc (London).

Although a naturally gregarious man, Sir Arthur played little part in societies and institutions, unlike many gas industry worthies. Despite being a fellow of the Institution of Gas Engineers, his involvement was at the minimum level consistent with the requirements of his career. In consequence, he resisted most invitations to present papers.

Following his retirement from the British Gas Corporation in 1976, he was chairman of the British Standards Institute, 1976-79.

In 1937 he married Margaret, daughter of Stephen Lacey, a civil engineer and controller of gas sales in the Gas Light & Coke Co. They had a son and a daughter. His principal hobby continues (1983) to be sailing.

GEOFFREY BATTISON

Sources:

Published

WW 1982.

HEWITT, Sir Joseph

(1865-1923)

Colliery manager

Joseph Hewitt was born in Barnsley on 14 October 1865, the son of Alfred Hewitt, an engine smith, and Margaret, daughter of William Hall. From a local church school he obtained a scholarship to Barnsley Grammar School and subsequently went as a junior clerk to Newman & Bond, one of the most influential firms of solicitors in the town. There he quickly rose to be managing clerk, was articled, and qualified as a solicitor at the age of twenty-six in 1893, remaining with Newman & Bond for some years afterwards.

Hewitt's connection with the firm of Newman & Bond, which itself undertook extensive mineral work, led to what was probably his earliest connection with coalmining administration, when early in 1896 he became a trustee for the newly-established firm of Fountain & Burnley Ltd, which owned the Woolley and North Gawber collieries near Barnsley; in June 1896 he attended the first formal meeting of the directors of that company. In 1899, already established as an able local advocate, he set up his own local practice, but his interests in coalmining continued and grew. By 1922 he was chairman of the Wharncliffe Woodmoor colliery (which had 1,940 employees), and managing director of the Woolley & North Chamber (2,168 employees), Haigh (245), and Darton Main collieries (74), and of the Swallow Hill Colliery, which was apparently not operating in that year.

Hewitt founded his own thin-coal coalmasters' association (distinct from the larger South Yorkshire association), the Barnsley and District Colliery Owners' Association, which existed from 1912 to 1918. Its members employed some 11,000 men in 1912, and more members joined later. Hewitt was also on the central committee of the Mining Association of Great Britain.

Hewitt's non-legal interests were by no means solely confined to the coal industry, and he was a director of the Rylands Glass & Engineering Co Ltd, of the British Association of Glass Bottle Manufacturers Ltd, of J

Tomlinson & Son Ltd and the Barnsley Chronicle Ltd. He was also secretary of the Barnsley Arcade Co Ltd, solicitor to the Barnsley Hide & Skin Co Ltd, and secretary to the Barnsley Theatre Royal Co Ltd. In 1918 he was appointed a Barnsley borough magistrate. As an expert on coalmining his services were utilised by the Government during the First World War as honorary legal adviser to the Coal Controller, and for this work he was knighted in 1919; the reason for his elevation to a baronetcy in 1921 is not quite so clear. Hewitt was much interested in local military affairs from at least 1900, when he was commissioned, and during the First World War he was a prime mover in raising the 'Barnsley Pals'. His own elder son, Captain G A G Hewitt, was killed at Cambrai in 1917. Joseph Hewitt was military representative on the local national service appeal tribunals in the Barnsley area, and acted as commanding officer of the local National Reservists.

In 1891 Hewitt married Margaret Eliza, daughter of George Guest, of Barnsley: she may have been his second wife. They had two sons and four daughters. His recreational interests were tennis and motoring. Hewitt died at his home, Ouslethwaite Hall, Barnsley, on 8 February 1923, at the age of fifty-six, leaving £68,966 gross.

After his death, questionable legal, financial and agency actions on Hewitt's part were brought to light and duly noted in the minute books of the colliery companies with which he was so closely associated, and in a lawsuit. Local recollections of Hewitt are of personal hardness and meanness.

JOHN GOODCHILD

Sources:

Unpublished

City of Wakefield M D archives, Goodchild Loan MSS.

BCe.

Published

Burke's Peerage and Baronetage.

WWW.

Yorkshire Post 9 Feb 1923.

Yorkshire Who's Who 1912.

HEWITT, Thomas Peter

(1848-1933)

Watch manufacturer

Thomas Peter Hewitt was born in Prescot, Lancashire, on 1 December 1848, son of Joseph Hewitt and grandson of George Hewitt, watch-movement makers of Atherton Street, Prescot. His mother was Elizabeth née Moses. In 1863 he became apprenticed to his father, and in 1869 he entered the family firm. He quickly became highly critical of the traditional, inefficient, labour-intensive methods of British watch manufacturing, advocating the adoption of factory production of British watches in order to recapture a domestic market increasingly dominated by Swiss and American timepieces.

In 1882 he purchased the watchmaking business of John Wycherley in Prescot, a firm which had earlier attempted machine production of parts. Over the next few years, with the support of the Earl of Derby, and through the correspondence columns of the *Horological Journal*, he canvassed the idea of reorganising the Prescot watch trade. In December 1888 he became managing director of the Lancashire Watch Co (initially the British Watch Co) which was registered with a working capital of £50,000 (increased to £100,000 in 1895). Some £20,762 of the initial capital was used to buy out a number of older businesses in Prescot. Most was taken in shares: only £5,000 was paid in cash, to some small makers. This strategy ironically contributed to the ultimate downfall of the enterprise, for it absorbed into the company old workers with old tools and old methods, thus perpetuating the very inefficiencies that Hewitt hoped to eradicate.

In January 1888 Hewitt had visited American watch factories, and he brought back some American machine tools. His factory was powered by an 80 hp engine, was steam-heated, and lit by gas jets; it was modelled on the Elgin National Watch Co of Illinois. By 1893 it employed some 1,000 workers, and between 1889 and 1895 it was sufficiently successful to pay 6 per cent annually on both preference and ordinary shares. An annual output of about 60,000 watches before 1893, and 50,000 between 1893 and 1900, declined after the turn of the century. Unable to hold its domestic market or to develop an export market Hewitt's enterprise failed, and by 1910 his company went out of business.

As well as retaining too many old workmen and their methods, the company produced too many models (over 50), some with obsolete designs. Its best-known product was the John Bull watch, 'the cheapest English watch ever produced' selling to the trade at 43s 9d a dozen, and retailing at 5s each. 'The John Bull was a desperate last effort to capture the market for cheap watches, and it was a dismal failure' {Smith (1973) 37}. Hewitt himself was an enthusiastic supporter of Joseph Chamberlain (qv); in 1904 he gave evidence before Chamberlain's Tariff Commission,

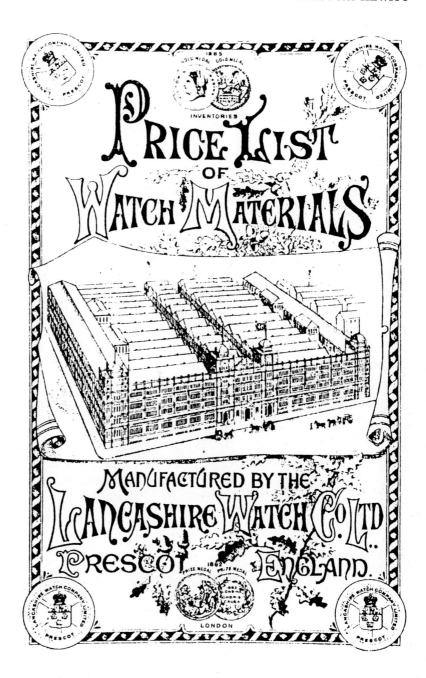

Lancashire Watch Co advertisement (courtesy of Professor Alun C Davies).

presenting the report of the Horological Society. As chairman of the Prescot Watchmakers' Trade Association, in 1903 he published a polemic blaming free trade for the decline of the British horological industry and for his own commercial difficulties, claiming that cheap foreign watches were being dumped on the British market.

After the collapse of the company most of the machinery and equipment was dispersed, although some of it survived in a small concern known as the Prescot Watch Co, later the Prescot Clock & Mechanism Co, which continued in existence until 1969. Hewitt died in 1933.

ALUN C DAVIES

Writings:

English Watchmaking under Free Trade (Liverpool: 1903).

Sources:

Unpublished

BLPES, Tariff Commission papers, TC7 38/2.

BCe.

Published

R A Church, 'Nineteenth-Century Clock Technology in Britain, the United States, and Switzerland' *Economic History Review* 2nd ser, 28 (1975).

Horological Journal 1887-1911.

The Lancashire Watch Company Limited, Prescot, Lancashire: Its Rise and Progress (Prescot: 1893).

D S Landes, 'Watchmaking: A Case Study in Enterprise and Change' *Business History Review* 53 (1979).

Alan Smith, *The Lancashire Watch Company, Prescot, Lancashire, England, 1889-1910* (Fitzwilliam, New Hampshire: Ken Roberts Publishing Co, 1973).

HEWLETT, Alfred

(1830-1918)

Mining engineer, colliery viewer and colliery owner

Alfred Hewlett was born in 1830 at Oxford, the eldest son of Alfred Hewlett, a schoolmaster who was training for the priesthood of the Church of England, and his wife Catherine née Gibson. His father, a strong Calvinist and a powerful personality, became curate of a small chapelry at Astley, ten miles west of Manchester, and later gained a DD. It was at Astley that Alfred was brought up; nothing is known of his education.

At the age of fourteen Alfred was articled to Mr Piggot, the Earl of Bradford's agent and the manager of his collieries near Bolton, Lancashire. After completing his training, he was for a short time manager of Charnock Richard Colliery, near Chorley, belonging to Joseph Darlington; Hewlett married Elizabeth, one of Darlington's daughters. In 1853 he went to the Ince Hall Coal & Cannel Co's very extensive collieries at Ince, near Wigan, to assist his brother-in-law, James Darlington, in their management. There were two disastrous explosions at these collieries in 1853 and 1854, one killing 58 men and the other 89. Shortly after this Hewlett was appointed mine manager to the company, until he succeeded William Peace, the eminent mining agent and manager of the Twenty-fourth Earl of Crawford and Balcarres's collieries near Wigan, on Peace's death in 1860.

During the following five years, Hewlett was one of the principals involved in the discussions and negotiations leading to the merger of four important colliery businesses to form the Wigan Coal & Iron Co, registered in 1865, and capitalised at £2,193,100. The Earl of Crawford's 16 collieries at Haigh, Aspull, Blackrod and Upholland were at that time raising 1,016,000 tons a year, the Kirkless Hall Coal & Iron Co's six pits 1,075,000 tons, the Standish & Shevington Cannel Co's pits 60,000 tons and the Broomfield Colliery 20,000 tons. Hewlett had bought the last for £2,000 in December 1865, but when it was included in the assets of the Wigan Coal & Iron Co it was valued at £20,000 and Hewlett received shares corresponding with that amount. Besides collieries, the Kirkless Hall Coal & Iron Co owned washeries and coke ovens at Kirkless producing 76,000 tons of coke a year, and five blast furnaces each 16 feet in diameter at the base and 45 feet high, complete with hoists and hoist buildings, producing 58,843 tons of pig iron a year. Three hot blast stoves and two large blowing engines served the blast furnaces. When the amalgamation was complete the Wigan Coal & Iron Co was the largest joint stock company in the industry.

Alfred Hewlett was appointed managing director and occupied the position for forty-two years. During this time, he built it up into one of the largest coal and iron concerns in Britain; its ironworks and coke works in 1879 were second only to those of the Barrow Haematite Steel Co.

For the first four years John Lancaster, founder in the 1840s of the Ince Coal & Cannel Co and of the Kirkless Coal & Cannel Co, was chairman of the new company. In 1870 a dispute arose between Lancaster and Hewlett, who was accused by Lancaster of unduly favouring the Earl of Crawford's properties. Lancaster resigned his position and sold his shares in the concern. Most of them were purchased by the Earl, thus giving him the controlling interest. From that time onwards, until nationalisation in 1947, successive Earls of Crawford were chairmen of the company and its enlarged successor, the Wigan Coal Corporation.

Under the direction of Alfred Hewlett, the concern was very successful and paid good dividends in most years. He had very able assistants in his youngest brother William Henry, and in the Percy family who had built and managed the iron and steel works and the large workshops. New collieries were sunk, old ones deepened and improved and the ironworks, coke ovens and associated works expanded. By 1886 there were 10 blast furnaces, five of them 80 feet high and 20 feet in diameter, the five older ones having been increased in height to 65 feet. There were 670 beehive coke ovens. Hewlett replaced many of these between 1902 and 1908 by three batteries of 44 patent by-product ovens of the Semet Solvay type. By 1890, he had also constructed a new steelworks which eventually had five basic open hearth furnaces, producing 1,200 tons of steel a week, in the form of castings and ingots, and two rolling mills. In the early years of the twentieth century, tar macadam- and flag-making plants were established at Kirkless.

The collieries were also greatly expanded. Besides improvements and extensions to older collieries, the 779 yards-deep Alexandra Pit, Wigan, was sunk in 1873, the two Hewlett pits and the Eatock pits were sunk at Westhoughton near Bolton in the 1870s, Gidlow's Hindley Colliery was purchased about the same time, and Victoria Colliery, Standish and Clock Face Collieries, St Helens, were sunk at the turn of the century.

Another major development at that time was the leasing of 60 square miles of the Nottinghamshire coalfield and the sinking of the very important Manton Colliery, now a large unit of the National Coal Board. The last venture of Alfred Hewlett was the sinking of Parsonage Colliery, Leigh, until recent years the deepest pit in Britain at 1,001 yards, with the deepest coal workings in the world at 1,500 yards.

The size of the concern Hewlett managed can be judged by some statistics. As early as 1885 the company owned 20 locomotives, 5,300 railway wagons (many of them built at the Kirkless workshops), 70 canal barges (many of them also built by the company), and there were 11,000 employees at their 32 collieries and ironworks. The company also owned many miles of private railways, and sidings and depots throughout the country, three steamers, a limestone quarry near Carnforth, Lancashire, a haematite mine in Furness and a large interest in the Caucasian Manganese Syndicate in Russia. Hewlett, the manager of this empire, was described as 'the premier authority on mining in the United Kingdom', and 'a commanding figure in the iron and coal trade' {Porteus (1920) 9}. He retired from his position as managing director of the Wigan Coal & Iron Co Ltd in February 1912, but remained on the board until 1916. He was succeeded as managing director by his brother William Henry.

Besides his position with the Wigan Coal & Iron Co, Alfred Hewlett was a partner with his brother, Ebenezer, and his brother-in-law, James Darlington, in the Blainscough Hall & Welch Whittle Collieries at Coppull. He was also chairman of the Cossall Colliery Co Ltd, Ilkeston, Derbyshire and of the Ammanford Colliery in South Wales.

Alfred Hewlett also had other important interests. He was one of the founder members and vice-president of the Lancashire and Cheshire Miners' Permanent Relief Society from 1873, serving as president from 1896 until 1913, when he retired. Under the rules of the Society the owners contributed 10 per cent of the amount subscribed by the members. Hewlett urged that an appeal for contributions should be made to the lessors of minerals, coal merchants and agents, and the many capitalists interested in coal-working. He also pressed for the payment of nurses to care for the injured in their homes. In 1873 there were 10,424 members,

1,304 disablement cases, and £917 6s 3d was paid to surgeons. In 1917, the last year of Hewlett's presidency, there were 57,090 members; 863 widows and 762 children were on the funds, and £7,472 was paid to surgeons, £9,268 to widows and £4,172 to children.

Hewlett was president of the Mining Association of Great Britain, 1873-75, and of the Lancashire and Cheshire Coal Owners Association for many years. He served on various Select Committees and gave evidence to the Select Committee on the Employers' Liability Act in 1886, and to the Royal Commissions on the Depression of Trade, in 1886, and on Mining Royalties, in 1880. For many years Hewlett was vice-president of the Royal Albert Edward Infirmary, Wigan, and chairman of the Wigan Conservative Party; he was made a freeman of the borough in 1901. On succeeding Canon Fergie as chairman of the governing body of the Wigan Mining and Mechanical School, he suggested the building of a new college and eventually raised £50,000 towards its construction; his own contribution included an annual scholarship. However, the Hewletts had their enemies, as was only to be expected — the Wigan Coal & Iron Co was said to have become a refuge for all younger sons and hangers-on of the Hewletts. The *Wigan Comet* in 1893 opined that 'the Hewlett Clan appropriated all the crème de la crème of the Wigan Coal & Iron Concern, leaving nought but the three times skimmed sky blue for the toilers and shareholders' {*Wigan Comet* 2 May 1893}.

Hewlett was a devout churchman and in 1911 was co-donor with his brother-in-law, James Darlington, of the beautiful church of St John the Divine at Coppull, near Wigan. The two had previously jointly provided new schools, with a teacher's house and playground, at Coppull Moor in 1874.

Hewlett lived at The Grange, Coppull, near Wigan, until 1880 when he moved to Haseley Manor, Warwickshire (now Leyland Motors Staff College). He and his wife Elizabeth had two daughters. He died, aged eighty-eight, on 14 September 1918, leaving £286,509 gross.

DONALD ANDERSON

Writings:

PP, HC 1886 (192) VIII, SC on Employers' Liability Act (1880).

PP, RC on Depression of Trade (1886) C 4797.

PP, RC on Mining Royalties (1890) C 6195.

Sources:

Unpublished

John Rylands University Library, Manchester, Crawford MSS.

Lancashire & Cheshire Miners' Permanent Relief Society, Bridgeman Terrace, Wigan, minute books.

Wigan RO, Annual Reports of the Wigan Coal & Iron Co Ltd.

PrC.

Information from Lionel Hewlett, James Peden, Frank D Smith, and Mrs Grandison (née Hewlett).

Published

Raymond Challinor, *The Lancashire and Cheshire Miners* (Newcastle on Tyne: Frank Graham, 1972).

William King, *Bells and Pomegranates* (pp, 1974).

Thomas Cruddas Porteus, *Life of James Darlington* (Chorley: W J Sandeford, 1926).

Wigan Comet 2 May 1893.

Wigan Observer 14 Apr, 22 May 1886, 20 Sept 1890, 11 July 1891, 29 July 1893, 9 Oct 1901.

HEYWORTH, Geoffrey

Lord Heyworth of Oxton

(1894-1974)

Chairman of major multinational commodities, food and detergents processing company

Sir Geoffrey Heyworth. Portrait by Maurice Codner, 1949 (courtesy of Unilever PLC).

Geoffrey Heyworth was born at Oxton, near Birkenhead, on 18 October 1894. His father, Thomas Blackwell Heyworth, was a Liverpool corn merchant. His mother, Florence née Myers, was a woman of character and piety. It was said that she gained the original interview with Lord Leverhulme (qv), and made such an impression on him that he told young Heyworth, 'If you are anything like your mother, you must be good.' So, in 1912, Geoffrey Heyworth, who had just left Dollar Academy in Scotland as dux (captain of the school) got his first job with Lever Brothers Ltd, as a clerk on 15s a week. One of Geoffrey's brothers, Lawrence, was already with the company.

Within a few weeks, Geoffrey was moved to the accounts department and the following year he was sent to Canada. Canada was one of the more profitable Lever enterprises, but it was full of difficulties. Heyworth stayed in Canada until 1924, with a gap of three years, from 1915 to 1918, for war service with the Canadian 48th Highlanders, during which he received a leg wound which troubled him for the rest of his life.

Training under J E Ganong, president of Lever Brothers in Canada, he learned a great deal. The company had severe American competition to face, it was inadequately rationalised, and distances were enormous. It was a good place to learn about American business methods, the location of factories, and the creation of a marketing strategy.

He was allowed a good deal of freedom for one so young, and he exercised his restless curiosity in every direction. He would tell a story of how he tried job enrichment, long before the term was invented, in one of the Canadian factories. But his packing ladies would have none of it. They threatened to go on strike. What he had missed was that the very repetitiveness of their job, which to him seemed so boring, allowed them to chat and day-dream. His reform, without making the job really absorbing, made it sufficiently complicated to require the packer's attention all the time. She could no longer day-dream or chat. So he backed down, but remembered two lessons; one should never judge somebody else's job by what one would feel like if one was doing it oneself; and one should consult before introducing major change.

The same year, he came back to England, once again to Lever Bros, first to exports, then in charge of the sale of soap in the United Kingdom. He introduced Lux toilet soap, already marketed with huge sales in the USA by Francis Countway, into Britain. It was he who perceived the importance of each of the ingredients which went into the original marketing mix. He saw that there was an opening for a mass-market soap of better quality than the cheap soaps, yet of wider appeal and lower cost than the expensive ones. He saw the importance of its being white, the public's favourite colour, and of a noticeable perfume of wide appeal. Above all, at that moment when film stars were just becoming what they were to be for a whole generation, the ordinary woman's ideal of beauty, he understood the value of the film star recommendation, a technique also pioneered in the USA. That recommendation stayed with advertising all over the world for some forty years, even in a country like India where for many years the reputation of film stars was somewhat dubious.

In 1929, he became chairman of Joseph Crosfields of Warrington. Crosfields was, and long remained, technically innovative, far more so than Lever Bros at Port Sunlight, whose technical side until the 1960s tended to look backwards for its image of perfection. Heyworth himself never showed quite as much imagination in ensuring that the company kept ahead technically as he did on the other sides of the business.

In 1931, he was appointed one of three whose task was to reorganise the Lever soap trade in the British market. It was high time. William Lever had justified the prices he paid for the soap companies he bought before the First World War by the economies of rationalisation; but he never did the rationalising. In 1931 there were still 49 manufacturing and 48 selling companies. It took until 1960 to bring them down to one. Factories had to be shut, brands suppressed without too much loss of tonnage, sales forces amalgamated. These were all painful processes, though they were made somewhat easier by the rationing and labour shortage of the Second World War and immediate post-war period. Nor was the operation carried out without loss. Proctor & Gamble in the 1950s possibly took more market share from Lever Bros than they might have done if Levers had been one integrated company before 1960. But without the Soap Executive the losses would almost certainly have been worse.

An advertisement for Lux soap,
1940 (courtesy of Unilever PLC).

From 1941 to 1959 Heyworth was chairman of Unilever Ltd, vice-chairman of Unilever NV and a member of the Special Committee of three which ran both businesses. For much of that time he had Dr Paul Rykens as chairman of Unilever NV, vice-chairman of Unilever Ltd and a colleague on the Special Committee, a man whose vision was equal to his own, and with whom he worked in perfect harmony.

Over these eighteen years, Unilever was transformed. In 1941 much of its top management on the Dutch side still belonged to the old founding families. On the Lever side, most of those at the top, like Heyworth himself, had worked their way up under Lever's enlightened patronage. In 1959, Unilever had already been for several years a pioneer in the recruitment and development of a professional management. In 1941, research and the central staff departments were rudimentary. In 1959, they were among the best in European business, and were rapidly approaching the best in American business.

In 1941, the company in the UK was still paternal in the old Lever way. Sons were found jobs, pensioners were looked after. By 1959, Unilever had established itself as a pioneer in better employee relations. Rates of pay, pension entitlements, hours, were deliberately amongst the best in each industry in which Unilever operated. Styles of management had become less autocratic, more participatory, though in many subsidiaries the process still had a long way to go.

In 1941 Unilever had lost all its Continental businesses. At the end of the war, they were mostly in ruins, especially the great and formerly flourishing German businesses. By 1959, with the exception of Eastern Europe, they had all been restored to much better shape than before the war. Where necessary, factories had been rebuilt or new ones built; subsidiaries, operations and brands had been rationalised. The continent of Europe was again at the heart of the business, with Germany alone contributing perhaps one-quarter of the profits. Indeed, by 1959 the European Community which was to contribute so much to Europe's prosperity had already been formed and nobody had been a more enthusiastic supporter of it than Geoffrey Heyworth, even though in the short run it made it easier for Unilever's American competitors to strengthen themselves in Europe.

The Special Committee had, moreover, seen and seized two growth possibilities for Unilever. The smaller one, never of great importance outside the United Kingdom, was compound animal feeding stuffs. The bigger one, which was in due course to provide Unilever with a business worthy to set beside detergents and margarine, was convenience foods. The development of frozen foods, in a conservative Europe which had few refrigerators in the 1950s and not much money with which to pay for out-of-season vegetables, took years. There were times in the early 1950s when Unilever almost gave up. But the Special Committee's patience held until Europe grew prosperous and frozen foods prospered with it. In that persistence, Heyworth's determination was crucial, though he would reproach himself for a premature entry into Belgium. It took time to discover that, on the continent of Europe, the key frozen vegetable is spinach, not peas.

More difficult was the transformation which Heyworth and his colleagues realised it was necessary to make in their African business. The United Africa Co had long been engaged in importing produce from Africa and exporting manufactures, mainly simple consumer goods, to Africa. In a world where, even in Africa, colonial peoples were beginning to demand a full share in their own economies and the development of their own manufactures, the future of this business was threatened. Earlier than anybody else, Unilever moved to change the nature of what they were doing, to withdraw from areas where Africans could take their place and to use their local knowledge to go into partnership with firms who wanted to manufacture in West Africa or who required extensive after-sales service for such sophisticated products as bulldozers.

Patience was indeed Heyworth's most noticeable characteristic. Those who had the good fortune to listen to him in the late 1940s could watch the flowering of his ideas over the next ten, even twenty years. He realised that, whether the subject was management development, or frozen food, or ice cream in Germany, or the creation of first class personnel and economics and engineering staffs, time was required. He was very persistent in attaining his ends; but he never pushed harder than the machine could stand. He knew that large organisations only absorb ideas slowly, and not too many of them at a time.

He was a great decentraliser. He believed in controlling major capital expenditure (a lesson from the days when money was tight in Unilever) and senior appointments, but otherwise in giving his subordinates the maximum of freedom. He did not demand myriads of reports or endless staff analyses. He did not need them. When he had cross-examined the chairman of a subsidiary for three-quarters of an hour, there was little the chairman knew that Heyworth did not know. When he visited a country for a week — and he was a great believer in going to see — he understood everything he needed to know, from the local politics to whether the factory was overmanned.

He did not confine himself to Unilever business. He was on the London Passenger Transport Board, 1942-47, and then on the board of the Commonwealth Development Finance Co. He was a member of the Company Law Amendment Committee of the Board of Trade (1943), of the Gas Industry Committee (1945), of the Advisory Committee of the DSIR, of the Royal Commission on the Taxation of Profits and Incomes (1951) and of the National Coal Board. He was always willing to give of his knowledge and experience to the state. He was no ideologue. He accepted that there were cases like gas, where nationalisation might be the right answer; but then he wanted the nationalisation to be efficient. He believed that the shareholder was entitled to his returns, but for him the primary purpose of profits was to provide the resources for investment and growth. Unilever in his time always distributed a relatively low proportion of its profits (something like 20 per cent).

His main outside interest, however, was in improving the somewhat weak links between UK industry and the British higher educational system. He was never happier than when talking to dons as a visiting and then an honorary fellow of Nuffield College, Oxford. He was on the governing body of Queen Elizabeth House, Oxford, and he was the prime mover in the creation of the Administrative Staff College, of whose court of governors he became chairman. From 1954 to 1958 he was a member of the University Grants Committee, and from 1963 to 1965 a member of the board of governors of the London School of Hygiene and Tropical Medicine. For him, these were never just honours or a reward for raising money. He used these positions always to contribute his experience to the academic world, and to take from them ideas on organisation or on the future of the economy or whatever it might be, which stimulated him to innovation in Unilever.

Heyworth was knighted in 1948, and created a baron in 1955; in 1947 he was made a Grand Officer of the Dutch Order of Oranje Nassau. After his retirement he was the second chairman of the Council on Productivity, Prices and Incomes, 1960-62, and president of the National Council of Social Service, 1964-70. Only in the last few years of his life did he truly retire. Up to then, discretion had always made him taciturn, but once discretion was no longer necessary, he showed an extraordinary ability to distil the lessons from his vast experience.

Heyworth married in Canada in 1924, Lois Dunlop of Woodstock, Ontario. She was for him exactly the companion he needed, never obtrusive, always relaxing. She soothed away the strain of his work. However busy he was, he always tried to keep the weekend free for her. They had no children. He died on 16 June 1974, leaving an estate proved at £195,574 gross.

MAURICE ZINKIN

Writings:

The Gas Industry. Report of the Committee of Enquiry (HMSO, 1945).

The Organisation of Unilever (1949).

The Place of Margarine in the Economics of Nutrition (1952).

The United Africa Group (Unilever, 1954).

The Control Centre for an International Business (Athlone Press, 1956).

Report of the Committee on Social Studies (HMSO, 1964).

Sources:

Unpublished

BCe.

PrC.

Personal knowledge.

Published

Statist 10 Oct 1959.

Times 17 June 1974.

Charles Wilson, *The History of Unilever* (2 vols, Cassell, 1954).

—, *Unilever, 1945-65* (Cassell, 1968).

WWW.

Lionel Hichens (courtesy of Mrs M H Hichens).

HICHENS, William Lionel

(1874-1940)

Shipbuilder, steelmaker and arms manufacturer

William Lionel Hichens (usually known as Lionel) was born at St Leonards-on-Sea, Sussex, the home of his maternal grandmother, on 1 May 1874, the second and posthumous son of John Ley Hichens, of Lichfield, and Catherine née Bacchus (1843-1924). John Hichens, an army surgeon who died of an ulcer at Isly near Algiers on 2 January 1874, was of Cornish origin and owned some land there; Lionel Hichens felt himself to be a Cornishman and was passionately attached to Cornwall. From an income of £300 a year, his mother saved enough to send him to Winchester (1887-93) and New College, Oxford (1893-97), where he read Greats and rowed in the college eight. He next went to Paris to perfect his French, but finding it impossible to get up before noon there, he moved to Germany to study its language. A schoolmaster at Sherborne in 1898-99, during the 'Black Week' of the Boer War in December 1899, Hichens, with two New College friends, enlisted as a private in the cyclists section of the City Imperial Volunteers, organised by the Inns of Court, and was sent to South Africa; here he served as a despatch rider. On the entry of Lord Roberts into Pretoria in June 1900, he returned to England, but shortly afterwards went to Egypt where his mother was living with his invalid brother John Ley Hichens (1872-1904). There he met Lord Cromer, who appointed him to the Egyptian Ministry of Finance, but after nine months, in 1901, he was recruited by Lord Milner to become town treasurer of Johannesburg.

Hichens thus became a member of Milner's Kindergarten reconstructing the conquered Boer colonies. Almost immediately Johannesburg town council sent him to London where he raised a multi-million-pound municipal loan which, by its stringent provision for a sinking fund, soon became one of the best municipal securities on the British market. He was a thorough success as town treasurer, and after the Peace of Vereeniging (May 1902), Hichens was appointed colonial treasurer of the Transvaal, becoming in addition treasurer of the Inter-Colonial Council of the Transvaal and Orange River Colony. These were difficult posts, with money short, harvests bad, resettlement costly, the Boers bitter and reconstruction elusive. Nevertheless, when he retired from South Africa in 1907, on the granting of internal self-government to the Transvaal and Orange River Colony, he left a substantial financial balance.

He lived for some months with his mother at Falmouth, before visiting India (1907-8) as a member of the Royal Commission on Decentralisation which deliberated over the administrative, and especially financial, relations between the central and provincial governments. In 1908 Lord Milner arranged for his appointment to the board of the Bank of Egypt, but Hichens withdrew at the last moment. 'I could see Lord Milner was forcing me down the throats of the other directors', he explained characteristically, 'and I wasn't going to take it on those terms' {Bodleian, Selborne add 3, Lady Selborne to husband, 24 Sept 1908}. He made this display of integrity despite sorely wanting the directors' fees to finance entering the House of Commons, which was then his ambition. Hichens in 1909 chaired a board of enquiry into the public service of Southern Rhodesia, and during his visit to the country took steps to ensure the preservation of the Zimbabwe ruins.

In August 1910 Hichens was appointed chairman of Cammell Laird, the shipbuilding, steel and armaments company which had been formed in 1903 by the merger of Charles Cammell of Sheffield, Mulliner Wrigley of Coventry and the Laird shipyard at Birkenhead. It had bought half of the capital of the Clyde shipyard of Fairfield in 1905, was a joint owner of the Coventry Ordnance Works, and had an interest from 1909 in the Workington Iron & Steel Co of Cumberland. The group's net profits had risen from £144,000 in 1903 to £273,000 in 1906, but in 1907 it was struck off the list of Admiralty and War Office contractors after irregularities were found in the running of its Grimesthorpe works at Sheffield. The chairman and two managing directors resigned, but the total loss carried forward for 1908 was £169,221 and a net loss of £63,100 was recorded. Unfortunate ore contracts led to further losses. Although the published net profits for 1909 were £48,400, the company was in desperate straits when Hichens took over, paying no ordinary dividends 1908-12, and it was feared that it would have to shut or severely contract. This appointment of a colonial administrator to an armaments board had some parallels to Armstrongs' recruitment of Sir Percy Girouard (qv) in 1912, with the difference that Hichens was a success who soon guided Cammell Laird to prosperity. He told the board frankly at his first interview with them that he knew nothing of armaments or shipbuilding, and their decision to recruit a man in his mid-thirties without previous industrial experience was quixotic. His widow believes that the decisive influence may have been Lord Selborne, a former First Lord of the Admiralty and High Commissioner for South Africa, who with his wife were mentors of Hichens; it is also possible that Lord Milner was involved.

A net profit of £216,100 was recorded in 1910 and of £171,700 for 1913. The company had no liquid assets, and in the period before the war had to live on bank overdrafts because the depressed price of its securities meant that fresh capital could only be raised by debenture issues on expensive terms. Indeed it cost £169,126 and £237,899 to service the company's debentures in 1913 and 1914 alone.

The months immediately before the outbreak of war in 1914 saw Hichens preoccupied with the Irish constitutional crisis, and in June, together with Lionel Curtis and Edward Grigg, he persuaded Austen Chamberlain, Edward Carson and Bonar Law to accept the principle of a federated British Isles. The world war pitchforked Hichens into the centre of the munitions crisis. Together with his friend R H Brand (qv), he was sent by Lloyd George to Canada in the early winter of 1915 to solve the supply bottleneck of the Dominion's Shell Committee. This was a delicate matter, but Hichen's irresistible technique, combining 'conciliation, frankness, courtesy and complete firmness' {*Round Table* 31 (1941) 10}, led to the Committee's supercession by the Imperial Munitions Board of

Canada which placed orders worth £250 million in the next three years. When the Central Council of Associations of Controlled Firms was formed in June 1916, Hichens was selected as chairman, and on behalf of some 2,700 controlled establishments represented the Council in its dealings with the Ministry of Munitions. It was fused with the Federation of British Industries in June 1918, when Hichens was co-opted to the FBI's Committee of Controlled Firms, but he opposed the corporatism of early FBI Presidents such as Dudley Docker or Sir Vincent Caillard (qqv).

Hichens claimed that Cammell Laird 'consistently subordinated questions of profit to the public interest' {PRO Munitions 4/4867} during the war and remonstrated with the Minister of Munitions when one official told the House of Commons Public Accounts Committee that the private armourers had refused to reduce their shell price in 1915 until threatened with an examination of their production costs. In fact, while Hichens had been in Canada, his company had declined to reduce the price of 18-pounder high explosive shell from 20s and had urged that the price should hold for the duration of the war, although within three months the Ministry had obtained a price reduction of 35 per cent. It is nevertheless true that, under Hichens's direction, Cammell Laird was the one big specialist arms company to which no serious charges of war profiteering adhered.

During the war Hichens developed a keen interest in labour relations. As he told a meeting of the Anti-Sweating League (a body seeking a national minimum wage) in 1916, 'mal-distribution of wealth was one of the greatest evils of our time' and he favoured 'the continuance of Excess Profits [Duty] or similar taxation after the War' because it would 'conciliate workers who felt that their employers were getting an undue share of the results of their labour'. 'Mr Hichens thought Trade Unionism was mixed too much with politics at present, though he was in favour of a much stronger Labour representation in Parliament' {SRO, Steel-Maitland papers GD 193/571, Hichens address of 17 July 1916}. He regarded industrial work as a national service which everyone from chairman to the humblest mechanic should give unstintingly to the community. He deprecated personal materialism (he had declined compensation on losing his South African jobs in 1907), and after 1918 urged that the National Debt should be reduced by a capital levy. He was later convinced that the failure to do this had aggravated the industrial depression of the 1920s.

The coming of peace brought grave problems to Cammell Laird. Before the war roughly half of their work was munitions, but having transferred almost all production to war work, the return to civilian lines was hard. While the new shops which had been built during the war could be converted to other uses, much of the machinery used in armament manufacture could not. A more difficult problem, Hichens felt, was to decide what to produce: diversification, he argued, entailed 'enormous risks' {ibid}. Just as Vickers diversified from armaments into rolling-stock and electro-technology, so did Cammell Laird. In 1919 they bought the Midland Railway Carriage & Wagon Co, of Washwood Heath, Birmingham, and the National Ordnance Factory at Nottingham, which they had built and managed for the Government during the war. Subsequently, in 1923, they formed a working alliance with the Leeds

Forge Co, another rolling-stock maker, which had absorbed the Bristol Carriage & Wagon Works in 1920. After the war Cammell Laird relinquished their investment in Fairfield Shipbuilding, and were instrumental in the Coventry and Scotstoun factories of Coventry Ordnance being merged in the English Electric Co in 1919. Hichens also reduced the load of annual debenture interest, which had peaked at £321,372 in 1916 and declined from £303,006 in 1919 to £145,906 in 1922 (he regarded debenture interest as one of the curses of British industry generally). At one stage Lloyds Bank refused an overdraft to Cammell Laird, and Hichens then approached Reginald McKenna (qv) who agreed that the Midland Bank would provide all future requirements.

As part of Hichens's post-war diversification, Cammell Laird developed various interests in Eastern Europe. In 1920 they became interested in an iron mine concession at Ljubja in Bosnia, and in the possibilities of reconstructing and managing the Polish railways. Hichens believed that the British industrial depression would not improve until Britain reconstructed the effective demand of Europe for her goods, and regarded a sound transport system as a prerequisite of economic power. To this end, in 1921, Hichens opened co-operation with the Ostroff works at Ostrow, and attempted to form a syndicate to rebuild, electrify and manage Poland's railway.

His prediction of the 'enormous risks' entailed by Cammell Laird's post-war diversifications was proved right by events. Their steel and shipbuilding interests suffered from the depression of the 1920s; there proved to be a large world productive surplus of rolling-stock; armament orders all but vanished; and English Electric (EE), under P J Pybus (qv), made a succession of strategic and managerial mistakes. Hichens was a personal friend and admirer of Sir Herbert Lawrence (qv) of Vickers, and in 1928 they negotiated the rationalisation of their companies' steel and rolling-stock factories. The steelworks were unified with effect from January 1929 in the English Steel Corporation under joint control, although Hichens declined to become first chairman of the new combine as Lawrence had hoped. Simultaneously the rolling-stock subsidiaries of Vickers and Cammell Laird were merged in the Metropolitan-Cammell Co, and a drastic reduction of their surplus capacity was implemented. Meanwhile EE had undergone a steady decline, and following the nervous collapse of Pybus in 1927, Hichens became chairman. In 1929 EE sustained a loss of £47,000 and approached Lazards to raise £850,000. In the subsequent reorganisation of EE's share capital in 1930, control passed to an American syndicate and Hichens was succeeded as chairman by Sir Holberry Mensforth. 'Mechanisation and economic nationalism, which between them have caused a permanent excess of industrial capacity over effective demand in all the basic industries, are bound to lead to still further rationalisation and the growth of monopolistic organisations', Hichens predicted, adding that in some industries 'healthy competition ... is as doomed as the giraffe and the hippopotamus' {*Times* 25 April 1932}. The management of the Birkenhead shipbuilding yards always held a particular interest for Hichens. Amongst the major armaments contracts secured by Cammell Laird between the wars were those for the battleship *Rodney* (1923-25), the battlecruiser *Prince of Wales*, and the aircraft carrier *Ark Royal* (1933). They also built the luxury liner *Mauretania*.

Hichens was keen to raise the educational level of engineering. Early in his career he recruited to Birkenhead Gerard R L Anderson (1889-1914), an Olympic athlete and fellow of All Souls, who enjoyed a dazzling reputation among his contemporaries at Eton and Oxford. Anderson was killed in the war, and Hichens never again found so brilliant an assistant. Nevertheless he continued to reserve vacancies on the commercial side of the business for university men, and Cammell Laird's research department preferred graduates. The engineering side favoured apprentices aged between sixteen and seventeen working in the shops and drawing-office before taking an engineering course at university. Hichens regretted that the number of public school men who became engineers was so small, and attributed this partly to the absence of scholarships to carry them through their apprenticeship, but chiefly to the timid caution of parents and schoolmasters who felt that engineering held more uncertainty than other careers. He despised much contemporary education for its 'showy superstructure', but deplored pressure 'to commercialise our education — to make it a paying proposition, to make it subservient to the god of wealth, and thus to convert us into a money-making mob' {*Times* 10 Jan 1917}. Hichens was an active chairman of the governors of Birkbeck College, London University, from 1927. Birkbeck specialised in providing graduate and post-graduate evening work to students who earned their living in daytime, and he was largely responsible for raising funds in the 1930s for their Bloomsbury rebuilding programme.

Apart from his main business interests, Hichens was a director of the London & North Western Railway and, after the regrouping of 1921, the London, Midland & Scottish Railway. He was a member of the Industrial Fatigue Board from 1918, of the Ministry of Munitions' Advisory Council on the sale of surplus government property from 1919, the Imperial Shipping Committee in 1920, the Board of Trade Advisory Committee, the Foreign Office Selection Board for the Consular Service after 1923, the government committee on the National Debt in 1924, Lord Colwyn's Committee on Economies in the Fighting Services of 1925, the Royal Commission on Licensing of 1929, and the Royal Commission on Lotteries and Betting of 1932. He was elected to the Athenaeum Club in 1928, was master of the Shipwrights' Company in 1932, sat on the council of the Royal College of Music, and was elected fellow of Winchester College in 1933. He was thereafter a faithful attender at the meetings of the Winchester governing body, and was especially involved in planning the memorial cloister to Wykehamists who were killed during the First World War. Hichens was a generous subscriber to the Oxford University Appeal, the Oxford Preservation Trust and the New College New Library Fund. He was also a Carnegie Trustee.

Following from his membership of the Milner Kindergarten, Hichens was a founder of the Round Table group in Britain. Holding an exaggerated belief in the value of exerting influence on men of position, and recoiling from any direct mass appeal, the group's quarterly journal, *The Round Table*, launched in 1910, was aimed at a limited circle of people already interested in Imperial and foreign affairs. Hichens had deep influence on its contents, although he was sceptical of the real possibility of imperial federation. 'This ironmaster was from the first the pivot on which our work together turned, a steel rod of exquisite temper, revolving firmly and quietly, as an axle fulfilling its purpose should' {*Round Table* 31 (1941) 14}.

Hichens married in 1919, at Chelsea, Mary Hermione (b 1894), third daughter of General Sir Neville Lyttelton (1845-1931), Chief of General Staff 1904-8; they had three sons and three daughters. His wife, who served as a nurse in France during the First World War, was prominent in Oxfordshire affairs, and in 1939 submitted a minority report as a member of the Royal Commission on the Geographical Distribution of the Industrial Population. During the Battle of Britain, Hichens was killed by a bomb which fell on 14 October 1940 on Church House, Westminster, which he himself had been concerned in rebuilding. He left £5,463 gross.

Hichens was a self-confident, steadfast man of exacting standards and unshakeable frankness. He deplored pusillanimity, double-dealing or disloyalty. He was somewhat austere and shy, but he was not a prig, and had great charm and cheeriness. Tall and handsome, he was a powerful public speaker, with a commanding presence and decisive manner. His honesty was inexpugnable, and he was motivated by an idealism rare among armaments manufacturers.

R P T DAVENPORT-HINES

Writings:

letters on price of shells *Times* 16, 24, 28 Oct 1916.

(with R H Tawney, Sir Alfred Zimmern, Tom Jones and J J Mallon) memorandum to Lloyd George on need for a new spirit in government and the conduct of the war, December 1916, printed in R K Middlemas (ed), *Whitehall Diary* (Oxford University Press, 1969) I.

speech on co-operation of labour and capital *Times* Engineering Supplement 25 May 1917.

speech on boy workers' welfare *Times* Educational Supplement 1 Nov 1917.

Some Problems of Modern Industry (Whitehead, Morris, 1918).

PP, Report on Electric Power Supply of the Committee of Chairmen of Ministry of Reconstruction Advisory Council (memorandum of dissent) (1919) Cmd 93.

The New Spirit in Industrial Relations (Nisbet, 1919).

'The Railway Strike and After' *Ways and Means* 11 Oct 1919.

'The Wage Problem in Modern Industry' *Journal of the Royal Society of Arts* 67 (1919).

speech on industrial co-operation *Times* 22 Mar 1919.

letter on import restrictions *ibid* 27 Mar 1919.

speech on coal costs *ibid* 12 July 1919.

speech on Lands Directorate *ibid* 25 Nov 1919.

letter on Lord Londonderry's scheme for district amalgamation of collieries *ibid* 24 May 1921.

statement on retrenchment of national expenditure *ibid* 10 Dec 1921.

letter opposing abolition of Department of Overseas Trade *ibid* 22 Feb 1922.

letter on day continuation schools *ibid* 31 May 1922.

lecture to Industrial League on prices and wages *ibid* 4 Oct 1922.

speech to Church Congress on the Gospel in Business and Politics *ibid* 13 Oct 1922.

letter on proposed Royal Commission on Education *ibid* 17 Oct 1922.

letter on American debt *ibid* 27 Jan 1923.

letter on Austrian loan *ibid* 29 June 1923.

letter on capital levy *ibid* 5 Dec 1923.

letter on industrial peace *ibid* 18 May 1926.

letter on report of Commonwealth Trust *ibid* 6 Mar 1928.

The Task of the Rising Generation Birkbeck College Foundation Oration 1929.

letter on Sidney Gilchrist *Times* 3 Feb 1930.

letter on rationalisation *ibid* 25 Apr 1932.

letter on betting *ibid* 31 Mar 1934.

letter on Ministry of Information *ibid* 7 Oct 1939.

letter on future of Europe *ibid* 17 Aug 1940.

Sources:

Unpublished

Bodleian Library, Oxford, papers of Lionel Curtis, Lord Milner, The Round Table, and Lord and Lady Selborne.

Hopton Hall, Wirksworth, Derbyshire, papers of Philip Lyttelton Gell.

North Aston Hall, Oxfordshire, papers held by Mrs Hermione Hichens.

PRO, Kew, papers of Admiralty, Foreign Office, Ministry of Munitions and War Office.

Scottish Record Office, Edinburgh, papers of Sir Arthur Steel-Maitland.

BCe.

MCe.

PrC.

Information from Mrs Hermione Hichens, H V Hodson.

Published

Paul B Bull, *The Economics of the Kingdom of God* (Allen & Unwin, 1927).

Lionel Curtis, *With Lord Milner in South Africa* (Oxford: Blackwell, 1951).

DNB.

Leslie Hannah, *Electricity before Nationalisation* (Macmillan, 1979).

Janitor (pseudonym of J G Lockhart and Mary Lyttelton [Lady Craik]), *The Feet of the Young Men* (Duckworth, 1928).

John E Kendle, *The Round Table Movement and Imperial Union* (Toronto: University of Toronto Press, 1979).

C More, 'Armaments and Profits: The Case of Fairfield' *Business History* 24 (1982).

Walter Nimocks, *Milner's Young Men* (Hodder & Stoughton, 1970).

Observer 27 Oct 1940.

Round Table 31 (1941).

Times 17 Oct 1940.

WWW.

HICK, John

(1815-1894)

Steam engine manufacturer

John Hick was born at Bolton, Lancashire on 2 July 1815, the son of Benjamin Hick (1790-1842) and his wife Elizabeth née Routledge. He was the eldest in a family of three, having a younger brother, Benjamin Hick Jr, and a sister, Amelia. Having received a good education at a private school near Alderley Edge, Cheshire, and subsequently at Bolton Grammar School, he went into partnership with his father and brother in 1833 to establish the business of Benjamin Hick & Sons, at a six-acre site at Crook Street, Bolton, on which they erected the Soho Ironworks. His younger brother left the partnership after a year to become a partner in a Liverpool firm, and so the concern became Benjamin Hick & Son.

The new firm quickly established a successful business making boilers, stationary steam engines, and mill gearing for local cotton mills, and also railway locomotives and miscellaneous machinery. Between 1834 and 1855 almost 100 locomotives were built at Soho Ironworks, but there was a much larger business in making stationary engines and boilers. During 1833-36 inclusive the firm were engaged in building 56 stationary steam engines, aggregating 2,542 nominal hp or approximately 7,650 indicated hp, and by 1840 had probably built nearly 100 such engines, the majority destined for Lancashire cotton mills, and most supplied with one or more boilers.

*Soho Ironworks, Bolton, of
Benjamin Hick & Son, ca 1840 from
K Hudson, 'Exploring our
Industrial Past' 1975 (courtesy of Mr
D A Collier).*

It is clear that the business quickly expanded and helped to pioneer locomotive building in Lancashire, and John Hick received considerable practical guidance from his father during this period. In particular he was an accomplished draughtsman, and some of his fine engineering drawings have survived. However, Benjamin Hick Sr died in September 1842, leaving John as the sole proprietor of the concern. He continued to develop the business, and by 1844 had extended the Soho Ironworks by designing and building an ingenious octagonal erecting shop. In November 1844 he started a long public career, being elected to the town council on which he served until 1853, and possibly because of this in 1845 he took two brothers into partnership with him, John and William Hargreaves. The title of the firm remained unchanged. John Hick was recognised as an accomplished mechanical engineer, and in 1845 he was also recognised as a civil engineer, when he became a member of the Institution of Civil Engineers. In 1847 he became one of the original members of the Institution of Mechanical Engineers, although he left in 1852, rejoining in 1871.

In 1850 John Hargreaves retired from the business, leaving his brother to continue with John Hick. The firm had a developing export market with Russia by the early 1850s in engines, boilers and mill gearing, their first engine being sent there as early as 1836. Until the 1870s they were the sole supplier of steam engines to Ludwig Knoop (1821-94) of Moscow. It is probable that over 100 engines were built during the period 1841-50, in addition to railway locomotives and some marine engines, while perhaps 130-150 engines were built during 1851-60. It is clear that over 200 stationary engines were built by the firm during 1861-70, aggregating approximately 30,000 indicated hp. In addition there was a sizeable business in boiler-making, and in making various types of small machinery. The firm adopted a progressive approach towards its engine-making business; in 1865 it was the first firm in England to start building the economical Corliss engine, and built nearly 1,000 of them between

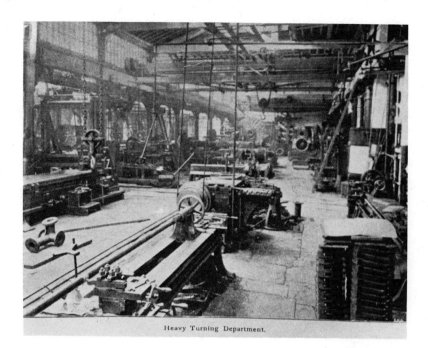

Heavy Turning Department.

Interior of Soho Ironworks, Bolton, ca 1890s, of Hick Hargreaves & Co 'A Descriptive Account of Bolton', Robinson & Co, 1900 (courtesy of Mr D A Collier).

1867 and 1890. It employed 502 in 1852, and became the second largest engineering firm in Bolton, with a workforce of 622 in 1864. In 1863 John Hick became one of the partners in the Bolton Iron & Steel Co (one of the companies floated during the company boom of 1863 in the iron trade), which manufactured iron and steel on a large scale, and supplied the Soho Ironworks with much of its materials.

John Hick continued to take an active part in the management of the firm until 1868, when he was elected Conservative MP for Bolton. Following his election he relinquished his connection with Soho Ironworks, because of government contracts then in the hands of the firm. The firm's title was then changed to Hick, Hargreaves & Co, with William Hargreaves in charge. The firm does not appear to have been adversely affected by this change, with engine output rising to 275 for the period 1871-80, aggregating approximately 60,765 indicated hp.

In parliament, John Hick pursued his interest in engineering matters, particularly the problem of frequent boiler explosions. Upon his proposal a select committee was appointed in May 1870 to investigate the cause of these explosions and means of prevention, on which he served as chairman. Following this investigation, he introduced a bill (which was not passed) in August 1871 to provide for persons injured and property damaged by boiler explosions caused by negligence. In 1874 he served on a select committee to consider the best chain cables and anchors for the navy. He retired from Parliament in 1880.

He was vice-president of the Institution of Mechanical Engineers, 1874-76, and was elected a life honorary member of the Manchester Association of Engineers in 1873. He led an active life in the public affairs of Bolton, being involved in the Mechanics Institute and several local charities. He served as a JP for Bolton for many years and in 1855 was appointed High Constable for the Hundred of Salford, and in 1858 became a JP for Lancashire. He also maintained his engineering interest, becoming a director of the London & North Western Railway in the mid-1870s.

By the time he retired in 1880, Hick had enjoyed two successful careers, his prosperous business career at Soho Ironworks until 1868, enabling him to acquire social status, and begin a second, rewarding career in public life. Soho Ironworks expanded enormously whilst under his management, and by the late 1860s was established as one of the leading firms of engine-makers in Lancashire. It was incorporated as a limited company in 1892 with a capital of £240,000.

Hick married Margaret Bashall, daughter of W Bashall, a spinner of Deane, Bolton in 1846. Following her death in 1872, he married Rebecca Maria, daughter of Edmund Ashworth of Egerton Hall, in 1874. After several months of ill health, John Hick died at his home, Mytton Hall, near Whalley, Lancashire, on 2 February 1894, aged seventy-eight. He left a personal estate valued at £149,707 gross, which was distributed among his relatives and friends, notably his widow and two daughters.

D A COLLIER

Writings:

'Frictional Starting and Disengaging Apparatus for Connecting and Disconnecting the Driving Power with Shafts and Machinery' *Proceedings of the Institution of Mechanical Engineers* 1849.

Experiments on the Friction of the Leather Collars in Hydraulic Presses (The Engineer, 1867).

PP, HC 1870 (370) X, 1871 (298) XII, SC on Steam Boiler Explosions (chairman).

Heavy Rifled Ordnance. Speech in the House of Commons, on Monday June 23 1873 (Bolton: Daily Chronicle Offices, 1873).

Self Help, A Lecture (1884).

Catalogue of the Principal Paintings, Drawings, Books, Bronzes etc, at Mytton Hall, Residence of John Hick (1893).

Sources:

Unpublished

Hick, Hargreaves & Co Ltd, Bolton, engine and company records.

MCe.

PrC.

Published

Bolton Chronicle 3 Feb 1894.

Bolton Journal & Guardian 19 Feb 1894.

'Century of Engineering' *Bolton Journal & Guardian* 10 Nov 1933 (history of Hick Hargreaves & Co).

C P Darcy, *The Encouragement of the Fine Arts in Lancashire 1760-1860* (Manchester: Manchester University Press, 1976).

The Engineer 9 Feb 1894.

Engineering 17 Sept 1875, 9 Feb 1894.

Kenneth Hudson, *Exploring Our Industrial Past* (Teach Yourself Books, 1975).

Manchester Guardian 14 Jan 1852.

John Marshall, *A Biographical Dictionary of Railway Engineers* (Newton Abbot: David & Charles, 1978).

PP, RC on Children's Employment, 3rd Report (1864) 3414-I.

Proceedings of the Institution of Mechanical Engineers Feb 1894.

Proceedings of the Institution of Civil Engineers 1894.

Gerhart Von Schulze-Galvernitz, *Volkswirtschaftliche Studien aus Russland* (Leipzig: Duncker, 1899).

Transactions of the Manchester Association of Engineers 1894.

WWMP.

HICKMAN, Sir Alfred

(1830-1910)

Iron and steel manufacturer and coal master

Sir Alfred Hickman (courtesy of Dudley Art Gallery).

Alfred Hickman was born in Tipton, Staffordshire on 3 July 1830, the son of George Rushbury Hickman (b 1799) and his wife Mary (d 1872), daughter of Benjamin Haden. Both his parents came from business families engaged in the Black Country's iron and coal trades. Like most steelmakers, Alfred Hickman therefore enjoyed a substantial 'head start'. On the other hand, his father — whose estate had a probate value of less than £12,000 — was not among the giants of the district's mid-nineteenth century staple industries. Thus Alfred's family background does not account for his estate of £1 million, his status as 'The Iron King of South Staffordshire' {*Wolverhampton Chronicle* 16 Mar 1910}, or his foundation of one of the area's few successful steel firms.

The details of Hickman's early career are obscure. After Alfred left King Edward VI's School, Birmingham at the age of sixteen he may have worked in an accountant's office in the city. In any case Hickman was soon a partner of the iron merchant J H Pearson. By his twenty-first birthday, however, Alfred had joined his father and his brother, George Haden Hickman, in ironmaking and coalmining at Bilston and Tipton. In 1862, eight years after their father's death, the brothers dissolved their partnership. By 1867 Alfred had acquired the Spring Vale Furnaces in Bilston; during the next fifteen years he enlarged and modernised the plant. In 1881 Hickman could plausibly tell a parliamentary committee that he was the Black Country's 'largest pig-iron maker' {*PP, HC* 1881 (374) XIII, 198}.

Hickman was fortunate in starting his career during a generally prosperous period, which ended in the mid-1870s, in the Staffordshire iron trade. Yet his business skills and relatively modern works also enabled him to prosper during the subsequent crisis in the industry occasioned by depleted raw materials, the advent of steel, and heightened rivalry from districts better suited to foreign competition.

Soon after the basic Bessemer process made local phosphoric ores suitable for steelmaking, Hickman built a steelworks. Organised in 1882 as the Staffordshire Steel & Ingot Iron Co Ltd, the plant was in production by 1884. At the turn of the century Hickman's enterprises had a weekly capacity of 3,000 tons of iron and 1,500 tons of steel. Further expansion followed in both products. Hickman enhanced his competitiveness by securing an economical supply of appropriate raw materials. He supplemented a Bilston mine with collieries near Nuneaton and developed ironstone quarries near Banbury.

At first the steel initiative did not prosper. Although a provisional decision to close the operation was rescinded, no steel dividends were declared until 1893. However, as the Black Country's finishing trades revived, and as the firm's reputation elsewhere grew, Hickman found customers for his heavy steel sections as well as for the portion of his pig iron output that the steelworks did not require. In 1897 confidence in the steel enterprise allowed the financially separate iron and steel operations to be merged into the new firm of Alfred Hickman Ltd. Subsequently the corporation declared regular 10 per cent dividends.

Hickman supplemented judicious expansion, low raw material costs and quick access to West Midland customers with a penchant for innovation. He 'emulated the Germans in the application of science to industry' {*Wolverhampton Journal* Mar 1905}. Lacking formal scientific training, Hickman nonetheless established his own chemical and metallurgical laboratories. The firm boosted profits by exploiting residual products, such as slag sold for fertiliser. Hickman also used a process developed by Tar Macadam (Purnell Hooley's Patent) Syndicate Ltd, which came under Sir Alfred's effective control as Tarmac Ltd in 1905. Moreover, Hickman adopted the latest technology in iron and steel production, developing a two-stage process on a par with advanced Continental experiments, for example.

The business also gained from effective, if by no means especially innovative, management. Endowed with an 'exhaustive manner and great energy' {*Dudley Herald* 3 Jan 1891}, Hickman attended the works daily for decades and remained an active, influential chairman until his death. Sir Alfred's peppery temperament, his zeal for punctuality and his 'almost

*Springvale Furnaces Bilston ca 1910
(courtesy of Dudley Public Libraries).*

startling directness' {*Midland Evening News* 11 Mar 1910} probably had some negative side-effects. Yet Hickman reinforced determination with sophistication. For example, he insisted on separate monthly balance sheets for each department. He was also wise enough to delegate much responsibility. Hickman's eldest surviving son Alfred William (b 1851) played a key role as blast furnace manager until his death in 1902. His brothers Edward (1860-1941) and Victor Emmanuel (1863-1935) subsequently had extra duties. Sir Alfred also relied on William Hutchinson, a veteran of the first British Bessemer plant, who soon became joint managing director. Meanwhile, incorporation brought outside finance and expertise in the form of shareholders and directors such as Percy Gilchrist (qv). Yet the Hickmans retained about three-quarters of the shares and dominated the board of the private company.

The decade following the founder's death was turbulent. The war brought the Hickmans greatly increased profits in return for rapid conversion to military production. Yet, although major expansion was on the drawing board, there were anxieties about outmoded plant and shortages of raw materials. Having sold many of their shares when the firm went public in 1917, the Hickmans accepted a generous takeover bid from Stewarts & Lloyds three years later. The parent firm liquidated Alfred Hickman Ltd in 1925, and in 1932 the Hickman role at Bilston effectively ended. Nevertheless, the family actively pursued large interests in Tarmac Ltd and in their highly profitable Warwickshire collieries until after 1945.

How far had Sir Alfred (who was knighted in 1891 and made a baronet twelve years later) and his descendants diminished their business success by absorption in time-consuming and expensive leisure pursuits? The founder developed 'all the tastes of a country gentleman' {*The County of Stafford* (1897) 24}. Hickman built the elaborate Wightwick Hall in the Staffordshire countryside, where he became one of the best riders in the Albrighton Hunt. Sir Alfred also made regular pilgrimages to Scottish 'shootings'. In addition, Hickman acquired a house in Kensington where he entertained extensively. Yet Sir Alfred did not neglect industry for polite society. He 'combine[d] in an admirable degree the qualities of an industrial king and a country squire and would not be satisfied to relinquish [an] active share in the sphere of either.' {*Birmingham Gazette & Express* 26 Mar 1907} Hickman's landholdings were modest and lay close to Wolverhampton's expanding suburbs, and he merely leased a succession of properties north of the Border for his annual holidays. Hickman's London base assisted his commercially-minded political career, and his home in the Midlands lay within a few miles of the works. Sir Alfred's formidable drive allowed him to cram business as well as hunting and politics into single weeks or even individual days. Nor does the timing and level of dividends suggest that his personal spending was unduly large, though additional reinvestment might have furthered the long-term viability of the Bilston works. Even the next generation, which could not match the founder's energy and dedication, in several cases retained houses close to the urban West Midlands where they remained active participants in the family's business concerns.

Sir Alfred used much of his spare time and resources to exercise significant leadership outside the firm. Hickman devoted comparatively little time to other companies, though he was a director of an iron firm, a chain testing house, a railway and a housing company. Much more significant were his commitments to employers' and other trade organisations. At the national level, Hickman was president of the British Iron Trade Association and a council member both of the Iron and Steel Institute and of the Mining Association of Great Britain. He also sat on Joseph Chamberlain's (qv) Tariff Commission. Yet his principal involvement in trade organisations lay in the Midlands. A leading figure at the Birmingham Iron Exchange, Hickman was a prominent participant in the South Staffordshire and East Worcestershire Ironmasters Association, albeit in an auxiliary capacity to Sir Benjamin Hingley (qv). Hickman's firm withdrew from the association in 1905 after Sir Alfred refused to lower his wages to an agreed level. Yet the firm generally co-operated with fellow producers, notably in a 1911 steel rebate agreement. Furthermore, Hickman won widespread acclaim by heading organisations concerned with threats to the prosperity of the West Midlands: the Wolverhampton Chamber of Commerce, the South Staffordshire Railways and Freighters Association, the Wolverhampton Industrial Development Committee, and a Birmingham group which unsuccessfully attempted to promote a new water route to London.

Hickman's leading role in such ventures owed much to his skill in representing them in national organisations such as the Associated Chambers of Commerce. Sir Alfred also became the Black Country trades' most prominent spokesman in Parliament; as MP for Wolverhampton West 1885-86 and 1892-1906 he proved 'an admirable type of the business representative' {*Birmingham Daily Post* 12 Mar 1910}. Appointed to the Board of Trade's advisory panel on commercial intelligence as well as to select committees, Hickman tirelessly defended Midland industry. Convinced that business there suffered from artificially high transport prices, Sir Alfred campaigned for more effective regulation of railway rates. He even supported nationalisation of the railways. Hickman may have exaggerated the serious local impact of transport costs, but his crusade drew support from other local MPs including his friend the Liberal minister H H Fowler. Confronted by rival interest groups, Hickman failed to obtain across-the-board concessions for the district. Yet he secured significant reductions in canal and railway charges and gained recognition as 'an unrivalled authority on commercial questions' {*Liverpool Courier* 12 Mar 1910}.

Hickman also played a significant part in the civic and political life of the West Midlands. He was a major contributor to projects in the Black Country, especially in Wolverhampton and Bilston, near whose common border his works were located. Sir Alfred was an Anglican, but only a small part of his giving went to the Established Church. Nonconformist chapels also attracted his money, and the bulk of his charity went to secular causes. Hickman subscribed to local organisations ranging from the technical school to the women's hospital. In 1893 he gave Wolverhampton 25 acres which became the core of the town's East Park. An active officer of various local institutions, Sir Alfred made conspicuous appearances at Cup victories as president of Wolverhampton Wanderers Football Club. Thus Hickman identified himself with the civic pride as well as the good works of the district. Additionally, Sir Alfred participated in local government as DL and JP for Staffordshire. Wolverhampton's various local authorities profited from his parliamentary efforts in the form of public loans on easy terms. Sir Alfred also proved useful as a civic celebrity.

'Always a keen politician' {*Birmingham Daily Post* 12 Mar 1910}, Sir Alfred did much to assist the revival of Black Country Conservatism which, in turn, helped to prolong electoral competition there between parties mainly led by the propertied classes. Hickman poured money into Tory newspapers in Wolverhampton as well as into his own campaigns. A council member of the National Union, Hickman also served as a valuable link to the national party. Not the least of his services to local Toryism were his four election victories. These were only partly offset by defeats in 1880, 1886 and 1906, especially as Sir Alfred played a major part in Unionist victories by others in Wolverhampton South in 1898 and 1910.

Many Black Country elections were narrowly decided during these decades, and even in Wolverhampton West most of the electors were working men. In this political environment Hickman capitalised on his employment of about 1,500 men at Bilston. Sir Alfred paid relatively well and negotiated with unions about wages. He enhanced his reputation by keeping his men at work during slumps, experimenting with profit-sharing and providing an elaborate canteen. Thus he was well-equipped, especially as the acknowledged champion of the district's prosperity, to play an electoral role as one of the region's 'industrial celebrities' {*Birmingham Daily Post* 12 Mar 1910}. Despite Hickman's denials, evidence of canvassing by Spring Vale's clerks and foremen suggested coercion as well as persuasion in Sir Alfred's version of 'factory politics'. Yet few of his employees lived in Wolverhampton West, and in the southern division the reception that the baronet and his victorious son T E Hickman (1859-1930) received in January 1910 indicated genuine popularity.

Sir Alfred's electoral success also stemmed from his cautiously progressive approach to social questions. Hickman advocated safeguards for railwaymen, introduced a bill easing working-class home ownership, and proved more flexible than most Black Country employers concerning workmen's compensation statutes. Such attitudes helped dissuade the Wolverhampton Trades Council from opposing Hickman in 1895. In contrast to professional men holding Tory seats in the region, Hickman's perceived self-interest as an employer prevented him from backing measures such as the miners' eight-hour day. Yet the combative Sir Alfred was only narrowly defeated in the landslide of 1906 by a Labour candidate with Liberal support.

Hickman's combination of economic power and substantial popularity, then, gave him considerable influence nationally and, in particular, locally on public as well as business questions. Retaining close ties with the elites of individual Black Country towns, Sir Alfred's wider connections and more expansive lifestyle helped to link these localities to the West Midlands generally and to the Metropolis — an intermediary role symbolised by his becoming a freeman of Wolverhampton on the same day as a local alderman and the Lord Mayor of London. These achievements rested on Hickman's business success which in turn depended on an aggressive, sophisticated entrepreneurship in difficult competitive conditions. One of the first Black Country businessmen to realise the potential of steel, Sir Alfred did help to slow down the region's decline as a manufacturer of basic metals. Although such output was doomed in the long run, steel production did not cease at Bilston until 1979.

Hickman in 1850 married Lucy Owen Smith (c 1829-1914), a native of Staffordshire then living in Portsea with her father, a prosperous civil engineer. They had seven sons and nine daughters; 12 children lived to maturity. Ill for three weeks, Sir Alfred died at at Wightwick Hall on 11 March 1910. The baronetcy passed to his grandson Alfred Edward (1885-1947) and out of the family business.

RICHARD TRAINOR

Writings:

Memorandum on the Improvement of the Canal Communication between Wolverhampton and London submitted ... to the Corporation of Wolverhampton (Wolverhampton: Midland Press, nd).

PP, HC 1881 (374) XIII, SC Charges for the Conveyance of Goods on Railways and Canals.

PP, HC 1890-91 (394) XV, Joint SC Railway Rates and Charges.

PP, HC 1893-94 (395) X, Joint Committee on the Canal Rates.

PP, HC 1893-94 (385, 462) XIV, SC Railway Rates and Charges.

PP, RC Coal Supplies 2nd Report (1904) Cd 1991.

Sources:

Unpublished

British Steel Corporation, East Midlands Regional Records Centre, Irthlingborough, Northamptonshire: Staffordshire Steel and Ingot Iron Co Ltd MS; Alfred Hickman Ltd MS.

History of Parliament Trust, Tavistock Square, London, J C Wedgwood MS.

PRO, Death Duty Register of George Rushbury Hickman (1855), IR 26/2032.

PRO, Staffordshire Steel and Ingot Iron Co Ltd MS; Alfred Hickman Ltd MS, BT31/14714/17246.

PRO, Tar Macadam (Purnell Hooley's Patent) Syndicate Ltd MS, BT31/10334/77739.

Staffordshire RO, South Staffordshire Ironmasters Association MS, D888.

PrC; Will.

Interview with Mr and Mrs W I E Hickman, 20 Sept 1982, and scrapbook and cuttings book in their possession.

Richard H Trainor, 'Authority and Social Structure in an Industrialised Area: a Study of Three Black Country Towns, 1840-1890' (Oxford DPhil, 1981).

R A Wright, 'Liberal Party Organisation and Politics in Birmingham, Coventry and Wolverhampton 1886-1914, with Particular Reference to the Development of Independent Labour Representation (Birmingham PhD, 1978).

Published

George C Allen, *The Industrial Development of Birmingham and the Black Country 1860-1927* (George Allen & Unwin, 1929).

V B Beaumont, *The Wolverhampton Chamber of Commerce 1856-1956* (Wolverhampton: The Chamber, 1956).

Birmingham Daily Post 25, 26, 31 Jan, 1 Feb 1898, 12 Mar 1910.

Birmingham Gazette & Express 26 Mar 1907.

Burke's Landed Gentry 1894.

Burke's Peerage & Baronetage 1908.

Peter J Cain, 'The British Railways Rates Problem 1894-1913' *Business History* 13 (1978).

James C Carr and Walter Taplin, *History of the British Steel Industry* (Oxford: Basil Blackwell, 1962).

The County of Stafford and Many of its Family Records (Exeter: W Pollard, 1897).

Daily Telegraph 12 Mar 1910.

Directory of Directors 1880-1955 passim.

Dudley Herald 3 Jan 1891, 19 Mar 1910.

Charlotte Erickson, *British Industrialists: Steel and Hosiery 1850-1950* (Cambridge: Cambridge University Press, 1959).

Express & Star (Wolverhampton) 29 July 1902, 24 Oct 1930, 3 Jan 1941.

Walter K V Gale, *The Black Country Iron Industry: A Technical History* (The Iron and Steel Institute, 1966).

The Ingot 14 Mar 1910.

Iron and Steel Trades Journal 19 Mar 1910.

The Ironmonger 19 Mar 1910.

George W Jones, *Borough Politics: A Study of the Wolverhampton Town Council, 1888-1964* (Macmillan, 1969).

Journal of the Iron and Steel Institute 48 (1895), 81 (1910).

Patrick Joyce, 'The Factory Politics of Lancashire in the Later Nineteenth Century' *Historical Journal* 18 (1975).

W M Larke, *Brief History of the Bilston Iron & Steel Works* (np, nd).

M LeGuillou, 'The South Staffs Iron and Steel Industry and the Growth of Foreign Competition 1850-1914 (Part II)' *West Midlands Studies* 6 (1973).

—, 'Freight Rates and Their Influence on the Black Country Iron Trade in a Period of Growing Domestic and Foreign Competition' *Journal of Transport History* new ser 3 (1975).

Liverpool Courier 12 Mar 1910.

Midland Evening News (Wolverhampton) 11 Mar 1910.

G R Morton and M LeGuillou, 'Alfred Hickman Ltd, 1866-1932' *West Midlands Studies* 3 (1969).

Norman Mutton, 'Sir Alfred Hickman ... the Man on a Tricycle' *Wolverhampton & West Midlands Magazine* 24 (1975).

PD 3rd and 4th ser, 1885-1905.

George Rickword and William Gaskell, *Staffordshire Leaders Social and Political* (E R Alexander, 1907).

Frederick Scopes, *The Development of Corby Works* (Stewarts & Lloyds Ltd, 1968).

Staffordshire Advertiser 22 Jan, 12, 19 Mar 1910.

Stock Exchange Year Book 1901.

Times 1 Feb 1898, 12 Mar 1910, 13 June 1919.

VCH Staffordshire 2 and 20.

Philip M Williams, 'Public Opinion and the Railway Rates Question in 1886' *English Historical Review* 67 (1952).

Wolverhampton & South Staffordshire Illustrated: Biographical and Commercial Sketches (Robinson & Co, 1898).

Wolverhampton Chronicle 29 June, 6 July 1892, 31 Jan 1906, 5 Jan, 16 Mar 1910.

Wolverhampton Journal Mar 1902, Mar 1905.

WWMP.

WWW.

William Higgs (1824–1883) taken from Higgs & Hill Limited 1898–1948 *(courtesy of Mr E W Cooney).*

HIGGS, William

(1824-1883)

Builder

William Higgs was born at Ferry Street, Lambeth on 8 April 1824, the son of Caleb Higgs and his wife Sarah née Nash. Caleb and his brother Joshua had come to London from the family farm and coopering and wood turning business at Thatcham, Berkshire in the early years of the nineteenth century. Caleb prospered as a dairyman and farmer in South London and Joshua as a builder in Bayswater and later in Mayfair. William was educated at private schools in South London until he was about thirteen and served an apprenticeship with his uncle Joshua before commencing on his own as a builder in 1845, aged twenty-one, with savings of £50. In 1848 he married Letitia Ann née Charlton, daughter of George Charlton. They had three sons and twelve daughters.

Higgs was very successful in business, leaving nearly a quarter of a million pounds. Although even greater wealth was perhaps possible in speculative estate development and housebuilding, he seems to have specialised in contracting and to have undertaken little speculative building. His involvement in a building lease for eight houses in North Kensington in 1848 appears to be exceptional. This probably somewhat reduced the risk of failure in a notably risky industry. His work for Government and local authorities and on social and philanthropic buildings included the Guards Barracks, Chelsea, the Royal Marine Infirmary, Woolwich, post offices, police stations, schools, the Metropolitan Tabernacle, St Thomas's Hospital, the London Orphan Asylum, Watford and the Royal Orphan Asylum, Bagshot. Work of this class required a well-managed, reliable and relatively highly-skilled workforce. Such men could be attracted and retained by a man of whom it was said, 'No employer was more respected, for he was fair, and honourable, in all his dealings, and always had the welfare of his men at heart {Higgs (1933) 142}.

Character may well also have played a part in enabling him to gain use of capital, obviously a major consideration for an entrepreneur who began with £50. Throughout his career he had the patronage of the Duke of Portland, described as a true friend to the young builder, who would from time to time 'pay down a thousand pounds or more *in advance* [original italics], and when reminded that the money was not yet earned, would reply that it did not matter, as he knew he could trust him and it would be something to go on with' {*ibid*, 142}. Another helpful mark of confidence was his admission, in 1850, into the Freedom of the City of London, as a member of the Shipwrights' Company, at the proposal of an uncle, James Nash, a privilege which, it is said, 'benefited him in the work he did in the City' {*ibid*, 146}. Even so, he 'experienced many anxious Saturdays, when wages of workmen had to be met, but having the full confidence of many

HIGGS William

Crown Works in 1918, a drawing by Frank L Emanuel taken from Higgs & Hill Ltd 1898–1948 *(courtesy of Mr E W Cooney).*

real friends, he always managed to tide over the worrying times' {*ibid*, 137}. Among those friends, it may be, was his father-in-law George Charlton, of St John's Wood, London, who, commencing as a boy in a baker's shop, became owner of a very large bakery firm and was able to retire at about forty. He left £40,000. It accords with William Higgs's success to read that 'a love of buying and selling, and getting gain, was undoubtedly a marked feature of his character even from boyhood' {*ibid*, 137}. But this should be taken with his reputation for fair dealing and the observation that jobbery disgusted him.

After nearly thirty years in business, William in 1874 retired as a building contractor. He then handed over to his eldest son, William, still only twenty-two — in a partnership with the older and more experienced brothers, Rowland and Joseph Hill — a firm which was among the leading builders of the metropolis, especially in the work for the Government. Rowland and Joseph Hill came from Islington in North London where they had been in their father's building business. Higgs had come to know the Hill family not through business but through a daughter's friendship with Joseph Hill's wife with whom she had been at school.

Not only was the setting up of this partnership in 1874 the culmination of William Higgs's business career but its records provide insights into the probable scale and nature of his resources, while in business, which are all the more valuable in view of the slightness of such detail for earlier years. After Rowland Hill's withdrawal in 1877 the capital of the two remaining partners was £30,000 equally shared. Since the firm had been paying rent of £740 to William Higgs, Sr, in 1876 it seems that he probably retained ownership of the site and buildings. About half the partners' capital was attributable to plant, machinery and stock, some at building sites and the rest at the Crown Works at Vauxhall in Lambeth (on a four-acre site to which the firm moved from Westminster in 1870). These works were set up by William Higgs Sr and so named because of the numerous government contracts he had obtained. There was £6,854 cash at the bank according to the balance sheet. An inventory made in 1874, when the original partnership was established, showed workshops and stores for all the principal trades of building, some equipped with steam-powered machinery. A 30 hp engine drove machines for cutting and shaping stone and wood and there was also an eight hp portable steam engine. There were nine horses and a variety of vehicles, 25 in all, including stone trucks, timber carriages, carts and vans. The wages bills when considered with contemporary rates of wages and hours of work indicate a force of upwards of 500 men in summer and rather less in winter from the 1870s to the 1890s. Christmas gifts in 1877 show twelve foremen, five clerks and an office boy. From 1877 to 1896 the two partners' joint profit averaged £10,460 a year (but was subject to quite wide fluctuations). From this they drew an average of £9,135 a year, the effect of which was to increase their capital to £56,500. They undertook contracts for many different kinds of public, social and commercial buildings and some private houses, usually working on between half a dozen and a score of sites at a time.

Higgs's emergence into public life in Lambeth in the mid-1850s seems to have been brought about by C H Spurgeon, the eminent Baptist preacher, who recruited him onto the building committee for the great Metropolitan Tabernacle for which he was eventually the contractor. Of Spurgeon as a preacher, Higgs said that he was the only minister who 'keeps bricks and mortar out of my head' during public worship {*ibid*, 139}. Higgs's financial judgement and knowledge of building were at Spurgeon's disposal, particularly (as Spurgeon gratefully acknowledged) in the economical construction of the Tabernacle of which he became a deacon, and in the founding and management of Spurgeon's Children's Homes in Stockwell, of which he was treasurer. Spurgeon's influence may also have led him to serve as a Guardian of the Poor in Lambeth for twenty-one years and to have brought about his support for charity and for chapel building. As his eldest brother, Caleb, remarked to Spurgeon, 'What! has William given you £5 for the work? Well, that shows he's a converted man; for he wouldn't have done it once' {*ibid*, 137}.

William Higgs died on 3 January 1883 at Gwydyr House, his home on Brixton Hill, in South London. The value of his personal estate was proved at £51,372 but his family, in their published history, recorded that he left an estate worth nearly £250,000. His wife outlived him by thirty-nine years, dying in 1922. A century after his death Higgs & Hill were among the leading companies in the UK construction industry.

E W COONEY

Sources:

Unpublished

MCe.

PrC.

Published

The Builder 20 Jan 1883.

E W Cooney, 'The Building Industry' in Roy Church (ed), *The Dynamics of Victorian Business* (George Allen & Unwin, 1980).

'Higgs and Hill, 1874-1974: Our First Hundred Years' *The Crown Journal* (house magazine) 178 (1974).

Higgs & Hill Ltd, *Souvenir of the Fiftieth Anniversary of the Incorporation of the Company of Higgs and Hill Limited 1898-1948* (pp, 1948).

William Miller Higgs, *A History of the Higges or Higgs Family of South Stoke, Oxon and Thatcham, Berks and Their Descendants* (Adelard & Son, 1933).

Francis H W Sheppard (ed), *Survey of London: Northern Kensington* vol 37 (Athlone Press, 1973).

Charles Hadden Spurgeon, *Autobiography* (4 vols, Passmore & Alabaster, 1897-1900).

Sir Charles Higham (courtesy of the History of Advertising Trust).

HIGHAM, Sir Charles Frederick

(1876-1938)

Advertising agent

Charles Frederick Higham was born in Walthamstow on 17 January 1876, the son of Charles Higham, a clerk in the Custom House, and his wife Emily née Trigg. He was educated at St Albans, but it is not known which school he attended there.

When Charles Jr was eleven his father died, and his mother, in reduced circumstances, took her family to the USA. Charles left home two years later, and by his own account was unsuccessful at some 60 jobs during the next seventeen years. Finding himself unemployed in Chicago, he tossed a coin to decide whether to go to London or Hollywood. London won, and he arrived back, penniless, in 1906.

He managed to obtain work as a canvasser for W H Smith & Son, selling advertising space on theatre curtains. Such was his success that within six weeks he had been appointed manager of their advertising agency. By 1909 he had set up his own advertising agency, and proceeded to publicise both the business and himself with such determination that by 1913 *Advertiser's Weekly* could refer to him as 'probably the best known man in advertising today', while Higham for his part described himself as 'the highest-paid business consultant in Europe, and one of the world's leading advertising experts' {*Advertiser's Weekly* 29 Nov 1913}.

With the outbreak of war he put his skills at the disposal of the Government, writing recruitment advertising, serving on the Committee on Recruiting Propaganda, acting as Director of Publicity for the War Savings Committee, helping to organise the Victory Loan Campaign of 1917, and assisting the Army and Navy Canteen Board and the Department of Auxiliary Shipbuilding. In addition he was joint organiser of the War Shrine Movement for Remembrance Day 1917, honorary organiser of the national tribute to Lord Roberts, a member of the Collections Committee of British Red Cross Associations, and a worker for the Star and Garter Fund. In 1920 he was also involved in raising recruits for the Royal Irish Constabulary.

During the 1918 election he was chairman of the Coalition Publicity Committee, and sat as Coalition Unionist MP for South Islington, 1918-22. He was knighted in 1921.

Although in private Higham was a generous and warm-hearted man, he found personal relationships difficult, it being said of him that he knew all about the public but little about people. He also offended many in advertising by his outspoken pronouncements, his assumption of the role of spokesman for the industry, and his flair for self-publicity. Even the speeches he made on truth in advertising, which were widely reported in the national press, were said by his critics to be merely publicity for his agency.

He remained unimpressed by the increasing sophistication of the advertising business. He cared little for qualifications, and publicly attacked the growing use of market research techniques. A natural salesman, he was not an innovator or theorist, but believed simply that the public would buy a product if told something meaningful about it in straightforward terms. He nevertheless remained a leading figure on the advertising scene for nearly thirty years.

Higham was married four times: firstly, in 1911, to Jessie (d 1925), daughter of John Munro of Elgin; secondly, in 1925, to Mrs Eloise Ellis, daughter of J C Rowe of Buffalo, New York; following their divorce in 1930 he married in that year Josephine, daughter of H A Webb of Cheltenham, whom he divorced in 1934; lastly, he married Mrs Ruth Neligan, daughter of Major R Dawes-Smith. He died after a lengthy illness on 24 December 1938, leaving an estate proved at £112,612 gross.

T R NEVETT

Writings:

(ed) *The Optimist* 1910.

(ed) *Higham's Magazine* 1914-22.

Scientific Distribution (Nisbet & Co, 1916).

The Ministry of Information: A Prophecy, Fulfilment and Appeal (Nisbet & Co, 1918).

Looking Forward: Mass Education Through Publicity (Nisbet & Co, 1920).

'The Advertising Agent' in T B Lawrence (ed), *What I Know About Advertising* (Spottiswoode & Co, 1921).

Address at the Civitan Club of New York, February 6, 1923 (New York: Carey Croft, 1923).

Advertising. Its Use and Abuse (Williams & Norgate, 1925).

Value of Colour in Advertisement (Big Six, 1925).

Tittle Tattle, Being Old Saws Resharpened with One or Two New Ones (Iver Heath, 1927).

The Story of Royal Worcester China and Some Notes on a Visit to the Ancient City of Worcester (Rugby, nd).

Sources:

Unpublished

BCe.

PrC.

Conversation with R S Riddell, formerly of C F Higham & Co.

Published

Advertiser's Weekly 29 Nov 1913, 29 Dec 1938.

Advertising World Feb 1939.

T R Nevett, *Advertising in Britain: A History* (Heinemann, 1982).

Times 27 Dec 1938.

World's Press News 5 Jan 1939.

WWMP.

WWW.

HIGHAM, James

(1821-1903)

Building society manager

James Higham was born in London on 11 April 1821. As a young clerk in the City of London he joined a building society and soon became 'convinced that in such societies would be found one of the greatest encouragements to thrift that the world could furnish' {Price (1958) 124}. In 1845 he promoted the Metropolitan Equitable Society and became its secretary. He became secretary of the St Brides and City of London Society in 1846 and of the Eclipse Society two years later. All three were administered from the same office in Old Jewry.

When Higham was first acquainted with building societies they were all terminating societies, that is, they received subscriptions from members until funds provided every shareholder with a home; then the society broke up. The principle worked well enough as long as they were fully mutual with every member a lender and expecting in due course to become a borrower. That principle was under strain when members wished only to be investors; then there was a problem of finding borrowers. Furthermore, once a society had been in existence for a year or so, new members, either as investors or potential borrowers, were difficult to recruit because of the problem of back subscriptions if all members were to be treated equally. The uncertainty of the termination date added to the borrowers' problems. Once societies ceased to be fully mutual, to be successful they needed to recruit many investors at the start, to find many borrowers early and, since accumulated subscriptions would not yet be large, to borrow money from the banks or elsewhere to meet the borrowers' needs.

These problems were brought home to Higham when a society he formed in 1847 was an early failure. He sought to meet them with a number of changes. Firstly, he set a fixed date, rather than a financial objective, for termination when the accumulated funds would be divided. Secondly, he set a fixed interest rate instead of the sale of advances. Investors would get an annual dividend, depending on the progress of the society, in addition to a residual distribution at the terminating date. With these improvements Higham launched his New City Mutual Society in 1852. In 1856 the Second City Mutual was established and in 1860 the Third. The three were successful and terminated after ten years. Despite these successes Higham's next society, the Fourth City Mutual Building & Investment Society was established on the permanent principle. However, since the number of shares in this new society was strictly limited it was at first something of a transitional form. New issues of shares were created from time to time, as in 1869, 1878 and 1883, though these new issues did not immediately rank with the old shares in terms of dividends. By the end of the century the society was a typical permanent society normally accepting new shareholders at any time. The continuing need to attract borrowers led in 1869 to provision for them to share in profits if the return to shareholders reached 8 per cent. In 1873 provision was made to pay 1 per cent commission for introducing borrowers. In 1887 the Fourth City Property Trust was formed to purchase properties taken into possession by the building society.

The Fourth City (which is still extant, as the City of London Society) was successful under Higham's management. Its assets reached £100,000 in 1868 and after ten years passed £150,000. In 1892, after thirty years and before the contraction following the failure of the Liberator Society, it was the tenth largest society, with assets over £600,000. At his death, still in office, in 1903 it was the twelfth largest society with assets of nearly £500,000. Higham was paid partly by a salary and, like most managers of large societies, partly by commission on work done. In 1871 he gave the salary of himself and his four clerks as £600-700 per annum.

While Higham was an able manager his main contribution to building societies was as a London and, later, a national leader. In law, building societies when he joined them were largely governed by the Friendly Societies Acts which were decreasingly appropriate as societies ceased to be fully mutual, rapidly expanded and changed from the terminating to the permanent form. Already in 1849 Higham was proposing to draft a bill to meet the changing situation and joined a loose organisation of London building society secretaries, the Building Societies Institute, which was already concerned with these matters. While no bill resulted and the Institute was defunct by 1852, Higham maintained sufficient contact with other managers to take prompt action when necessary. The Friendly Societies Acts granted exemption from stamp duty and when this privilege was threatened in 1855 Higham formed a London Association which mounted a successful defence. While the main defence effort came from Liverpool and Birmingham where societies were more deeply entrenched, proximity to Westminster gave the London Association a particular importance. Another successful defence was made in 1860, after which the London Association lapsed. In July 1868 the building society exemption from stamp duty was partly ended and Higham felt that the lack of a London Association contributed to that outcome. Consequently, in February 1869 he organised a meeting of London secretaries to start the work of winning back the lost ground. This meeting formed the Building Societies Protection Association which, with Higham as its chairman, grew into a national association, still extant as the Building Societies Association.

The issue of the stamp duty exemptions was soon lost in the much more serious question of the legality of the building society borrowing powers, a matter important to all societies and crucial to terminating societies. These powers were put in jeopardy by a decision in November 1868, in the case of *Laing v Reed*. A series of private members' bills were presented from various quarters to meet the situation but the first result was to refer the whole question of the legal framework for building societies to a Royal Commission. There was a long struggle before the Building Societies Act of 1874 was passed and became the foundation on which societies eventually dominated housing finance. Vigorously led by Higham, the Building Societies Protection Association was the strongest and most continuous force behind the reform movement, successfully resisting determined government efforts to put building societies under the Companies Acts. Throughout the recurrent parliamentary consideration of this matter Higham was on hand to advise his parliamentary supporters when to resist outright and when to accept compromises. He continued as chairman of the Association until 1883 and as a member of the executive committee until his death.

Higham was particularly interested in conveyancing and registration of titles, restrictive covenants in leases and leasehold enfranchisement and used the Association to lobby for change. The Conveyancing and Law of Property Act of 1881 and the Land Transfer Act of 1897 were the result of these activities. The swift passage of the Building Societies Acts of 1875 (correcting a slip regarding registration in the 1874 Act) and 1884 (stopping a loophole for defaulting borrowers opened by a legal decision in March 1884, *Municipal Society v Kent*) are examples of the Association as a sharp and continuous watch dog with strong parliamentary friends. By the time of the Liberator crash in 1892 and the resulting 1894 Act, though Higham was still a member of the Association's executive, leadership had passed to other hands. When he gave evidence to the Select Committee preceding the 1894 Act his performance was unimpressive compared with his comprehensive evidence to the Royal Commission in 1871, but in 1893 he was already seventy-two years old.

As a young man Higham lived in Islington and moved to Walthamstow in the late 1850s. He was active in City affairs as a member of the Candlewick and later the Cheapside Ward Clubs. At Walthamstow he was an active member of the Local Board, sometimes taking the chair. His particular interests were in education, rating valuation, water supply, lighting and highways. 'He was a member of the old Highways Board, had been an overseer and was vice chairman of the first School board. He gradually reduced his parochial duties some 16 years ago (1887). He was somewhat rugged and brusque in his manner but he had a friendly side to his nature and many times assisted widows and orphans not so much with his purse as by obtaining situations for those he deemed worthy of his confidence' {*Walthamstow Guardian* 4 Sept 1903}.

Higham married Mary Allen, daughter of John Goodwin, in 1843 and had four sons (the eldest born in 1845) and a daughter. His second son John joined him at the Fourth City Mutual Society at its formation in 1862, became assistant manager in 1882 and succeeded as manager in 1903 on his father's death. His eldest son James Jr, was the first secretary of the Building Societies Protection Association, a part-time post he held in addition to his employment as bank clerk; he retired through ill-health in 1874 and died in 1877. Higham suffered a further blow in 1883 with the death of his youngest son.

James Higham died of pneumonia at Walthamstow on 28 August 1903, leaving £9,218 gross.

ESMOND J CLEARY

Writings:

PP, RC on Friendly and Benefit Building Societies (1871) C 452.

PP, *HC* 1893-94 (297) IX, SC on Building Societies (No 2) Bill.

Sources:

Unpublished

PrC.

Published

Building Societies Gazette Jan 1869, Aug 1889, Oct 1903.

HIGHAM James

Esmond J Cleary, *The Building Societies Movement* (Elek, 1965).

The National 3, 17 Feb 1849.

Seymour J Price, *Building Societies* (Franey, 1958).

R Rouse, *Building Society Almanack* (1853).

Times 19 Nov 1880.

Walthamstow Chronicle 1877 passim.

Walthamstow Guardian 4 Sept 1903.

Sir Enoch Hill (courtesy of Halifax Building Society).

HILL, Sir Enoch

(1865-1942)

Building society manager

Enoch Hill was born at Ball Haye Green, Leek, in Staffordshire on 10 September 1865, the eldest of the four sons and three daughters of Henry Hill and Elizabeth née Taylor, both of whom were manual workers in the local silk spinning industry. Hill himself found work in that industry as a 'half timer' when eight years old, and full time five years later. The family were very poor and he showed his energy and stamina in taking on a variety of casual tasks that yielded some money. At sixteen he moved to become a farm labourer but soon abandoned that job to become an unindentured printing apprentice. Having acquired some skill, but before his apprenticeship was completed, he took a better-paid post as a journeyman at another printing shop. He continued to supplement his wages by taking extra work, such as selling newspapers.

Hill was a keen and energetic member of the Anglican Church, first as Sunday School pupil, then as teacher and secretary of the Band of Hope and eventually, in 1887, as a licensed lay reader. His capacities and enthusiasm were noticed not only by the vicar but also by a fellow church worker, the local grammar school headmaster. Between them these two men set about making good Hill's educational deficiencies and he responded eagerly. The vicar had a hand printing press which eventually Hill took over, and made the foundation for his own printing shop. It was through church work that he met Esther Haynes. Miss Haynes was an orphan living with an uncle who, though blind, was a successful accountant and was secretary to the Leek United Building Society. While courting Miss Haynes, Hill was useful to her uncle in reading to him and in return received further educational help. When clerical help was needed for the building society (a substantial local one with, at this time, over 1,000 members and assets of £100,000) Hill naturally gave it and by 1886 was taken on as a clerk. Another uncle of Miss Haynes was clerk to the County Court and Hill added process-serving to his sources of income. Having taught himself shorthand he was also local correspondent for the *Staffordshire Advertiser*. In his spare time he worked on the vicar's press, and played cricket and football, and served as a lay reader. From his many activities he added substantially to the £39 a year income he received from the building society.

Hill married Esther Haynes in 1887. Their first child lived only three days, but in 1889 a second son, John Henry, was born. After Hill's marriage, his own home became the base for his expanding printing business. Home, in time, moved to become a small book and stationery shop with the printing machinery upstairs. He added writing to printing with some local guide books and a history of Alstonefield parish. His voluntary work was extended by his co-option, as printing representative, on the Local Education Committee. Challenged as unqualified, not having completed his apprenticeship, he silenced his critics by promptly and successfully sitting City and Guilds examinations in practical and theoretical typography.

In 1895 the many demands he made on himself led to a breakdown in his health and he had to give up his building society clerkship. This break was a brief one. In 1896 the Leek United offered the post of secretary to Hill on condition that he devoted himself substantially to that job. This led to the sale of his shop and the transfer of the printing business to his brothers, who, with his father, were already employed in it. The proceeds of the sale of the shop were used to re-equip the printing operation, which was expanded subsequently by the purchase of the local newspaper, the *Leek Post*. Hill Brothers (Leek) Ltd was formed, in which Hill retained a lifetime interest both as shareholder and director. Hill's local government work increased with his election to the Leek Urban District Council; he served on the finance and gas committees. His increased building society responsibilities led him to become an associate of the Chartered Institute of Secretaries; with the passage of time he became a fellow (1915), council member (1928), treasurer (1933), and president (1935).

Hill was thirty-two when he took charge of the Leek United in 1896. Like most societies it had suffered a loss of public confidence following the Liberator and other building society failures in the early 1890s and its assets had fallen to £50,000. By 1902, when Hill was to leave it, the Leek United had made good the lost ground, doubling its assets to over £100,000.

In 1902 there was a vacancy for the secretary's post with the Halifax Permanent Building Society following the death of Jonas Taylor. Taylor, a founder of that Society in 1852, had run it successfully for fifty years. By 1902 the Halifax Permanent had 50 agencies and branches, and was the fourth largest building society in the country. However, in his later years Taylor was resistant to change both in office management and publicity, and his administration had become somewhat lax. Hill was one of 300 applicants for the post: every member of the Halifax board received a printed statement of his experience and achievements and copies of testimonials. He was appointed secretary in December 1902 at a salary of £600 a year. At that time the Halifax Permanent had assets of £1.4 million. It grew rapidly under Hill's charge, doubling its assets in the first eight years and reaching £5.9 million in 1918. Its share of all building society assets grew from 2.2 per cent to 8.6 per cent over the same period. In 1906 it became the largest society in the country, a place it retained throughout Hill's period of office.

Before the First World War owner-occupiers constituted only a small minority, 10-15 per cent, of all householders. Building society loans were mainly to finance building houses to let. Hill believed in home ownership: as an obituary put it 'Here, there and everywhere he was to be found preaching and interpreting for the mass of the uninitiated those great principles of home ownership in which he had always been a profound believer. His converts became millions. The nation rapidly became home minded under his compelling advocacy' {*Building Societies Gazette* June 1942}. Certainly Hill's beliefs rapidly influenced the mortgage structure of the Halifax Permanent. In 1903 of its total mortgages 15 per cent were for sums of under £500 and 38 per cent for sums over £5,000. Eight years later those proportions were reversed, being respectively 39 per cent and 11 per cent. Hill believed in abolishing entrance fees for owner-occupiers and was prepared to advance 90 per cent on houses valued at under £200. Repayment terms were made flexible to meet borrowers' requirements and mortgages could be redeemed without any penalty.

To attract savers the variety of shares available was increased. By 1915 there were six, with interest rates designed to reflect the low cost of dealing with large accounts and also to attract the small regular saver. In 1903 a penny savings department was opened, planned to attract children among others, that showed a balance of £90,000 by 1913. In 1905 a special reserve fund was opened so that the society's diamond jubilee in 1913 could be celebrated with a 'jubilee bonus' to shareholders, and the prospect of sharing it attracted many new accounts. While not the first to introduce 'home safes', Hill pushed them hard and 10,000 were in use.

When Hill took it over the Halifax was still essentially a local society; while it had 50 branches and agencies, a very large number for that time, these were concentrated in the West Riding and all except one (Darlington) were in Yorkshire. Hill extended the network, both by turning agencies into branches and increasing the number, to 90 by 1915. While Yorkshire still dominated, Lancashire, Durham and Lincolnshire were also included. Given his background in printing, the Halifax's publicity material was soon under review and there was an increasing tide of pamphlets and illustrated leaflets declaring the advantages of home ownership and of thrift. The wider spread of the society in time made the national as well as the local press an appropriate vehicle for advertising. As the arts of publicity developed, Hill was quick to adopt any new form, such as local shows and exhibitions, a members' magazine (1927), cinema advertising and shop windows for branches.

In response to the wish of some investors for facilities for cheques the Halifax Permanent Banking Co was formed in 1909: while a separate legal entity, it operated through the building society's offices and staff. The bank was successful, but with the growth of the building society there were problems of both space and staffing and in 1917 the bank was taken over, on favourable terms to its shareholders, by the Union Bank of Manchester. Hill became chairman of that bank's Yorkshire board, a position he continued with Barclays Bank when it took over the Union Bank. In 1928 he became an advisory director to Barclays head office. From 1904 he was a member of the Yorkshire board of the Alliance Assurance Co and became its chairman in 1924.

The First World War brought substantial problems. Initially there was the possibility of panic withdrawals by investors, and liquid assets were rapidly built up to meet this possibility, though they were not in fact needed. With few new houses being built, the demand for mortgages was not strong and the Halifax, like other societies, invested heavily in government stocks. The disruption of war created major problems for some borrowers and also minor ones for regular investors where there were penalties if obligations were not regularly met. At the beginning of the war the Halifax wrote to all investors and borrowers promising sympathetic treatment if any difficulties should arise. That the society came through the war showing in its returns no loans more than one year in arrears, is fair evidence that the promise was kept and the reputation of the Society was enhanced.

The post-war continuation of the Rent Restriction Acts meant that building of houses to let practically stopped, with a consequent rapid rise in the demand for owner-occupation. The Halifax, with Hill at the height of his powers at fifty-three was well placed to respond. It was already large, with plenty of liquid funds and had a strong commitment to, wide experience of, and a good reputation with, owner-occupiers. In nine years it more than quadrupled its assets, mainly by strongly pursuing existing policies. New branches were rapidly opened and not only in the North; it was becoming a national society. An outlet in Dorset in 1919 was rapidly followed by others in Bournemouth, Plymouth and Worthing. There were in all about 100 additions in ten years. A surprise move was the opening of a London office in Charing Cross in 1924, followed by a City office in Moorgate in 1931 and in 1934 Halifax House in the Strand. The increased standing of building societies made them attractive to larger investors, and with London as the most substantial market for such funds, Hill felt a London base was important. The demand for mortgages was also stronger in the more prosperous South East than in Yorkshire. London societies viewed these moves with some apprehension. By 1937 the Halifax had nearly 100 branch offices and over 200 other agency branches throughout the United Kingdom.

The rapid growth of the Halifax, which had a staff of ten when Hill arrived in 1902, meant an expanded staff — 674 by 1933. A large new head office was opened in Halifax in 1921, but even after extension in 1927 this was soon inadequate and a new headquarters was built, opening in 1931. The expansion of staff meant reorganisation of the management structure, especially in 1924, when, while Hill remained general manager, D W Smith became assistant general manager and a number of other section managers were created. In 1916 Hill had joined the board as managing director, in 1927 he became vice-president and in 1928 president. In 1910 a superannuation scheme had started and a widow's pension fund in 1936. There were annual gatherings of the staff at Halifax, with a dinner at a local hotel. In 1916 a house magazine was started, which served not only as a record of the society's activities but also discussed building society matters. After the war, staff group holidays were started, subsidised by the society, first with tours at home, then cruises and continental tours, in which Hill took part. He was very keen on education and encouraged his staff to gain qualifications, giving grants to those taking examinations. In 1933 of his 674 staff at all grades, 134 were associates or fellows of the Chartered Institute of Secretaries or some other relevant body, and a further 220 were student members of such bodies. Sporting activities were encouraged and there were special grants to those joining the Territorial Forces.

In 1927 the Halifax Permanent began a merger with the Halifax Equitable, which was founded in 1871 and rapidly expanded under J H Mitchell's management after 1897. It was the eleventh largest society in 1911 and second only to the Permanent in 1924. Mitchell was due to retire and Hill's assistant manager, David Smith, was approached. Expecting in due course to succeed Hill, he did not want to move and suggested a merger. Hill was enthusiastic and negotiated the terms of the merger. Under the 1874 Building Societies Act the legal requirements for the merger of two such large societies were formidable, including securing 200,000 signed concurrence forms. The task was completed in 1928 and the Equitable's assets of £14 million added to the Permanent's £33 million gave the new Halifax Building Society 17.5 per cent of all building society assets. When Hill retired as president and general manager in 1938, the new society after its first ten years, in a climate of very intense competition, had assets of £123 million, 16.2 per cent of the building society total. All the difficulties of creating a single organisation were thus achieved with very little loss of momentum.

At the 1911 conference of the National Association of Building Societies Hill made a sharp attack on its Council for its isolation from most societies and failure to make the general public, and especially the government, aware of the role and importance of societies. In 1913 he was elected to that Council and was its chairman, 1921-33. While the Association's views had little influence on immediate post-war reconstruction plans in the housing field, under Hill's vigorous leadership those views did influence the series of Housing Acts in the 1920s. His suggestion of a lump sum subsidy to builders, taken up in the 1923 Act, was particularly important. The Halifax was one of the few societies to give strong support to the effort of the 1933 Act to unite building societies, local authorities and private investors to build small houses for letting. Higher wartime rates of income tax led to questioning of the special arrangements for building societies and there was a series of post-war reviews in which Hill led a successful defence of the building society position. The later years of Hill's chairmanship were dominated by the issue of whether the Association should attempt to control, via a code of practice, the terms on which societies did business. The payment of commission for the introduction of mortgage business was common practice in London societies, but was not done in the North. London societies felt that the Halifax, the first Northern society to open a London office, could scarcely complain. As competition became increasingly fierce in the early 1930s, the support for a code of practice strengthened. There was a feeling that Hill, who was sixty-six in 1930, was not sufficiently committed to such a code and, more important, not vigorous enough in his efforts to attain one. In 1933 'it had in fact been plainly suggested to him that the time had come when he ought to make way for a younger man' {Hobson (1953) 109} and he resigned. He became deputy-chairman and loyally supported the efforts of his successor, Sir Harold Bellman (qv) to achieve an agreed code, which were partially successful. In 1936 Hill became a vice-president of the Association.

On his retirement as managing director of the Halifax in 1938, the Building Societies Association marked the occasion with a presentation to Hill. Over 2,200 people contributed £5,800 to the presentation fund. This was donated to various charitable causes, including £500 for the benevolent fund of the recently-established professional body, the Building Societies Institute and £350 for prizes in its examinations.

In 1913 Hill visited the USA to address the League of Savings and Loan Associations. This visit led to the formation of the International Congress of Building Societies at a meeting in London in 1914. Hill was elected secretary for the second meeting held at Philadelphia in 1915. A third meeting was planned there for 1920 but it was to be 1931 before the Congress met again. Hill was president for the fourth meeting, at London in 1933.

Hill was a lifelong Conservative, for many years president of the Leek Association and from 1930 of the Halifax Association. He was an unsuccessful Conservative candidate at four general elections standing at Leek (1922 and 1923) and Huddersfield (1924 and 1929).

In 1913 he was appointed a magistrate at Halifax and later chaired the Lord Chancellor's Advisory Committee. He was knighted in 1928. A freemason, he joined a Halifax lodge in 1907 and was later a master and also chairman of a Yorkshire freemasons' golf club. His golfing interest was strong; he was captain of the Halifax club and of the Halifax Property Owners and Ratepayers Association, of the Halifax Auto Club and vice-president of the Halifax YMCA. In addition to motoring and golf his recreations were football, cricket, photography and gardening. He travelled widely in Europe, North America and the Eastern Mediterranean. Throughout his years at the Halifax he lived at Willow Hall, a three-hundred-year-old manor house he purchased when he moved to Halifax. He was a member of the Constitutional, City Livery and Halifax clubs.

His son by his first wife, John Henry, qualified as a solicitor and became head of a firm of solicitors with offices in London and Halifax. Following the death of his first wife in 1904, Hill married in 1906 Bertha H B Gee, the daughter of Samuel Gee, a musician and an old Leek friend of Hill.

Sir Enoch Hill died at Halifax on 13 May 1942 leaving an estate of £24,094 gross.

ESMOND J CLEARY

Writings:

A History of the Ancient Parish of Alstonefield (Leek, ca 1890).

Sources:

Unpublished

BCe.

PrC.

Published

Reginald K Bacon, *The Life of Sir Enoch Hill* (Nicholson and Watson, 1934).

Esmond J Cleary, *The Building Society Movement* (Elek, 1965).

Halifax Building Society, *Eighty Years of Home Building* (Halifax, 1937).

Oscar R Hobson, *A Hundred Years of the Halifax* (Batsford, 1953).

WWW.

HILL, John Cathles

(1857-1915)

Builder and brickmaker

John Cathles Hill was born in Hawkhill, Dundee in 1857, the eldest son of Robert and Elizabeth Hill. An older sister had died in infancy and John was followed by two brothers and two sisters. In 1860 the family moved back to the toll cottage at Auchterhouse where Robert succeeded his father and grandfather as tollhouse keeper, a post combined with a wheelwright's and joiner's business.

The boy's upbringing in the village school under a headmaster who was formerly a minister was in the strict Presbyterian and family tradition of his ancestor John Hill, an Elder of the Kirk in 1647. After completing his apprenticeship in his father's trade, he went to Glasgow and attended science and art classes at the Mechanics' Institute.

When barely twenty-one Hill went by boat to London, the most important move of his life, and immediately obtained employment as a craftsman at 9d an hour; within a fortnight he was promoted to foreman. He had a useful contact in his friend and relative George Cathles Porter, who had started a speculative builder's business in Hornsey. In his first nine months Hill saved £50 and began to take on contracts for joinery on his own account, employing as far as possible his own countrymen. When his capital increased to £150, he started building entire houses.

Very soon he discovered the immense scope there was at that time for building enterprise in the development of North London and as the size of his business operations grew, he became a very important figure in the building world ... He was soon building houses by the hundred and held the opinion that it was both sound business and good civic policy to improve the character of the people's dwellings. Instead, therefore, of the long and uninteresting rows of houses which were previously provided ... Mr Hill laid out building estates on broad and generous lines ... wide thoroughfares planted with trees and with frequent open spaces and gardens {*Peterborough Standard* 10 Apr 1915}.

He also built several public houses of some architectural distinction in North London. Nearly all this building was financed by mortgages, which in the end caused cash difficulties and then bankruptcy, but while housing demand was booming enabled Hill's business to expand rapidly.

In 1888, experiencing difficulty with his supplies of bricks, Hill went down to the large brick-producing area of Fletton, a village just outside Peterborough. He purchased bricks for his immediate needs, but decided his future supplies would be guaranteed if he ran his own brickworks; finding Hardy's Works for sale he purchased it for £6,500, and named it, grandiloquently, The London Brick Co. The works consisted of one kiln and two presses on seven acres of clay, and in its first week under new ownership produced 70,000 bricks.

It seems certain that Hill realised the great future of Fletton brickmaking, then in its infancy, with its cheap production costs inherent in a clay with high carbonaceous content. This clay lent itself to a method of manufacture far simpler and cheaper than that of the stock brickmakers around London, who up to this time were the main suppliers of bricks to the metropolis. Even with higher haulage costs to the London market, Hill could still undersell his main competitors, owing to his cheaper manufacturing costs and to bricks which were lighter in weight and thus cheaper to transport.

Soon three other works were opened, and Hill also purchased works at Great Bentley in Essex and at Enfield, Middlesex. At his number 1 works he built the huge 'Napoleon' kiln with 40 chambers each holding 40,000 bricks, producing some 750,000 bricks a week; at that time and for many years after it was the largest kiln in the world. There also in 1902 he introduced a steam excavator to dig the clay, replacing the traditional hand method, and this marked a considerable step forward in the mechanisation of an industry which had always been labour intensive.

Hill took a great interest in all matters affecting the industry and served on various committees and deputations, concerning Home Office regulations, private railway sidings, workers' insurance and much else. In 1890, when brick prices were only 18s 9d per thousand in truck, he urged the necessity for, and planned formation of, the Fletton Brick Masters' Association and in 1910 the Pressed Brick Makers' Association — both Associations endeavouring to bring some co-operation into the trade and prevent the cutthroat competition which threatened to ruin them all.

An enthusiastic supporter of local affairs, Hill was elected to the Huntingdonshire County Council in 1905 and to the London County Council in 1910. In addition he served on numerous local boards and committees. He became known as the maker of modern Fletton.

Hill was a commanding figure in the brick trade in general and in the Institute of Clayworkers in particular, serving as a committee member from the start and as president, 1900, and 1905-7.

Hill was outgoing in nature, and made a great point of welcoming foreign brickmakers to his works; he enjoyed showing them his latest innovations and afterwards treated them with lavish hospitality.

From the early 1890s he began to purchase land in Fletton — about half the parish in total — much for clay but some to aid his speculative building. These purchases were on mortgage, up to some £100,000 in all.

By 1908 a handful of second mortgages had been undertaken by various banks either to help Hill's building activities or to pay interest on previous mortgages. By 1909 almost all these mortgages were transferred to the Eagle Insurance Co, who then conveyed the mortgaged land to the LBC, which had begun to trade as a limited company that year; LBC in turn issued first and second mortgage debentures (some £50,000) to both the insurance company and Hill. By 1912 his finances were in disarray and on 3 May a receiving order was made against him, and a receiver appointed to run the LBC. The statement of affairs showed Hill had liabilities of over £1,202,000 with total assets of about £218,000. He had in all built and acquired or financed building of about 2,397 houses and other buildings in and near London and in the neighbourhood of Peterborough at a total cost of £1,909,845, of which about £1,476,960 was raised on mortgage. He estimated his total expenditure in connection with the Fletton Brick Works at about £120,269, a considerable proportion of which was raised on mortgage. In November 1909 he sold the works to a limited company called LBC Ltd which he had registered in December 1900 with a capital of £1,000 in £1 shares, 994 held by him. He attributed his failure principally to the depreciation in the value of his properties since 1907 and his subsequent inability to sell them or to raise money on them, or to replace loans called in, to depression in the brickmaking trade, and more immediately to pressure by one of his largest mortgagees.

Hill's system of financing through mortgages was inevitably vulnerable to recession and loss of confidence. House building in the 1890s had flourished, to decline sharply in the next decade, while the proposals in Lloyd George's 1909 budget for Land Value Duty (a duty of 20 per cent on the unearned increment of land value whenever land changed hands plus annual duty of a halfpenny in the pound on the capital value of undeveloped land), even though not implemented, shattered the confidence of builders and mortgagees alike. Hill always maintained that this new political threat was the root cause of his troubles.

Despite all this, LBC continued to trade and in February 1915 an application for Hill to be discharged from bankruptcy was made. This was granted but suspended for two years. However, Hill died on 5 April 1915 at Brighton. He was survived by his widow, Matilda née Mose, daughter of William Henry Mose, a grocer, (whom he had married in 1882) and a daughter and two sons. Hill gave his sons the education he would have liked. Both went to Oxford University and both followed in their father's trade. The elder, Robert William (b 1884) established a successful building development and estate agency business in his father's former London office but in his own name (he was killed in Flanders in 1917), while John Edgar (b 1887) became managing director of the Star Brick Co before the outbreak of the First World War which took him, a Territorial Army officer like his brother, away for the duration of the war. On demobilisation he resumed his work as manager. He contributed much to the restructuring of the industry, including in 1923 the amalgamation of LBC and Forders Ltd into its dominant group (changing the name back to London Brick Co Ltd in 1936), of which he was deputy chairman until his death in 1937.

J P BRISTOW

Sources:

Unpublished

MCe.

Information supplied by J E B Hill (grandson of the subject) 1981.

Published

The British Clay Worker Apr 1915.

Mark Girouard, *Victorian Public Houses* (Studio Vista, 1975).

Richard Hillier, *Clay that Burns: A History of the Fletton Brick Industry* (LBC Ltd, 1981).

Peterborough Standard 30 Nov 1912, 10 Apr 1915.

HILL, Philip Ernest

(1873-1944)

Property developer and industrial company chairman

Philip Ernest Hill was born at Torquay on 11 April 1873, the younger son of Philip Hill, cab proprietor, and his wife Mary née Smith, who was originally of Nonconformist stock. The female element in his upbringing was clearly important. The diligent Mary Hill kept a lodging house to supplement her husband's meagre earnings and when she died in 1883, the equally strong-minded daughter Ellen took charge of the family.

In 1886 Philip Ernest became a pupil at Taunton Independent College,

HILL Philip Ernest

Philip Ernest Hill (courtesy of Mrs P Vinnicombe).

later Taunton School, where he received a good commercial education before leaving at the age of sixteen. After a few years as a junior in a Newton Abbot estate agents' office, in 1892 he sought adventure by joining the army on a short service agreement. With impeccable timing — which seldom deserted him throughout his career — he bought himself out two years later, shortly before his cavalry regiment, the 4th Dragoon Guards, was posted to India.

Hill thereupon returned to his former profession, this time in Cardiff. A few years later, he is said to have asked his employers for a partnership, and to have been sacked for his temerity, but in 1897 he was earning enough money to marry, his bride being Katherine Evans, daughter of a Cardiff gentleman. By 1901 he was partner in an estate agents in central Cardiff, but his agreeably settled life was disrupted when his only child, a daughter, died of meningitis at the age of six and the mother shortly afterwards.

He then set his sights on the metropolis: tradition has it that while acting for the Earl of Plymouth, an extensive local landowner, in the sale of some property, he discovered that the London agents were making far more out of the transaction than he was. In London only the best locality would do: in 1912 he established himself as an estate agent and valuer in Albemarle Street, Piccadilly. During the First World War and for several years afterwards, he was also a public works contractor, mainly for the Government, through his contracting firm Hill Richards & Co Ltd.

His breakthrough into the commercial property market came in 1923, when he met for the first time Sir Thomas Beecham Bt (1879-1961). The celebrated conductor's father, Sir Joseph Beecham (qv), who had grown very rich from pill-making, had in 1914 agreed to purchase from the Duke of Bedford, for £2 million, the Covent Garden estate and market in London. The outbreak of the First World War, and the ensuing impossibility of raising private capital, had frustrated the original plan to finance the purchase through a share issue and then sell off the estate in separate plots. Sir Joseph's death in 1916 necessitated his highly complex affairs being handed over to the Court of Chancery. Thanks in part to Hill's sagacity, in 1924 — with the approval of the High Court — all problems to do with the Covent Garden sale were finally settled, and he helped to set up a new company, Beecham Estates & Pills Ltd, of which he became a director.

Since a thriving pill business did not fit in well with an estate company, Hill's next step was very skilfully to separate the two businesses, by buying from Lord Derby some extensive property interests in Liverpool and then assigning them to the estate company in exchange for the pill firm. In 1928 he incorporated the latter as Beechams Pills Ltd and became its first chairman. Having already acquired the ailing cough medicine and ointment makers, the Veno Drug Co (1925) Ltd, he merged Beecham and Veno into what was claimed to be the largest proprietary medicine company in Britain. He then set the pattern for the future giant Beecham Group, pre-eminent as it was to become in pharmaceuticals, food and drink products, and proprietary goods, by three major acquisitions in 1938-39: of Macleans Ltd, J C Eno Ltd, and the County Perfumery Ltd, makers of the hair preparation Brylcreem. The purchase of Macleans brought in H G Lazell (qv), whose initiative in developing research laboratories helped to turn the Beecham organisation into one of the country's foremost science-based corporations.

Meanwhile, Beecham Estates & Pills Ltd was renamed Covent Garden Properties Co Ltd, which in 1933 was joined by a new public company, Second Covent Garden Property Co Ltd; Hill was chairman and managing director of both. His first major flotation of a company on his own behalf had come a few years earlier, in 1927, when he secured control of Taylors Drug Co Ltd and other chemists' chains. That was followed in 1928 with the acquisition of the drug and hardware store Timothy Whites (1928) Ltd. The purchase of Boots Pure Drug Co Ltd (which in fact later took over Timothy Whites and Taylors) was intended to be the culmination of his efforts to rationalise the multiple chemist business. The Boots firm had been sold to American interests by Jesse Boot (qv) in 1920, but after the American purchaser's bankruptcy, the issuing house Philip Hill & Partners Ltd (which Hill had established in 1932) helped to buy it back for resale on the British market. Much against the will of certain Boots top managers, who feared that he was bent on creating a vertically integrated pharmaceutical giant out of Beechams, Timothy Whites, Taylors and Boots, Hill agreed in January 1933 to buy Boots on his own behalf. However, the Treasury refused to authorise the £23 million of foreign exchange outlay involved, and a company with overseas resources, Tobacco Securities Trust (connected with British-American Tobacco Co Ltd), then became the leading purchasers. This was one major failure in his otherwise highly successful career.

His rare financial gifts were by then recognised outside the specifically property world. In 1929 he joined the board of the Eagle Star Insurance Co Ltd (as it later became), and in 1930 the Chancellor of the Exchequer, Philip Snowden, appointed him to a small high-powered committee to investigate the extent and use of government property holdings and recommended possible sales back to the private sector. About the only outside office he held was as vice-president of the Royal Northern Hospital, Holloway, having agreed to finance the construction of a pathology laboratory, known as the Beecham Laboratory, and to contribute to its running expenses.

Hill's other property interests included those to do with the growing leisure industry. Through the Cinema Ground Rents & Properties Ltd he had a large stake in cinemas, and he arranged a deal whereby the film magnate J Arthur Rank (qv) secured an interest in Odeon Theatres Ltd, itself developed by Oscar Deutsch (qv). In 1929 he acquired Olympia (1912) Ltd, which owned the exhibition centre of that name in West Kensington. He also took over the brewers Strong & Co Ltd of Romsey.

The last of his front-ranking corporate flotations occurred in 1935 with the formation of Hawker Siddeley Aircraft Co Ltd. That combined the motor car and aircraft manufacturing interests of Armstrong Siddeley, Armstrong Whitworth and A V Roe (qv), with those of T O M Sopwith (qv) in Hawker Aircraft and Gloster Aircraft. Hill, having organised the public share issue, joined the board as the only financial member of a technically-oriented company. From this combine, assisted by loans from the Air Ministry, was developed the Hurricane aircraft.

Such an enormous amount of labour inevitably took its toll on his private life. A remark attributed to him by Lazell suggesting that the only reward in life was money, almost certainly had a tinge of irony in it. There was no irony in his motto 'Start early and work late': yet he had his own relaxations. Some were not far removed from his work; he enjoyed business entertaining in the company of his cronies, endlessly discussing money matters, and was always good for a game of poker, at which decades of cliff-hanging property deals had made him particularly adept. He read thrillers of the E Phillips Oppenheim and Edgar Wallace type, and was a cinema addict. As to outdoor pursuits, earlier he played golf well and went in for sailing, but in later life he looked what he was: an ex-soldier of the ranks who had boxed in his day but had run to fat. Slightly taller than average, he is believed to have turned the scale at eighteen stones. To his subordinates, he not unexpectedly seemed larger than life and had an aura of power about him. But to employees and business associates alike he behaved fairly if strictly, and was widely respected for his integrity and resolve to make his word his bond.

Lasting marital happiness eluded him until late middle age. In 1917 he married Jessica née Gerrard, an actress formerly married to Eric (later Lord) Fitzwilliam. That marriage, which brought him into the café society of the inter-war period, broke up in 1921 and a year later he married another actress, Vera née Snepp and divorced wife of Henry (later Lord) Graves, a bookmaker. After separating from Vera, in 1930 he met Phyllis Partington, twenty-five years younger than himself, who changed her name to Hill when they began living together. They married in 1934 and lived happily ever after. The hereditary equine connections in his life were revived as she was a noted racehorse owner. There was no issue from any of these marriages. Hill died on 15 August 1944 at Windlesham, Surrey. His will was proved £3,008,327 gross.

Thus ended what was claimed to be one of the most remarkable careers Britain's financial world had ever seen. In a period when radical changes in the structure of British industry were needed, he was instrumental in financing some of the most familiar of the inter-war names: Amami shampoos, Brylcreem, Odeon cinemas, Olympia, and Woolworths. Without his efforts, the later Beecham Group would never have been created, nor probably would the Hurricane aircraft have flown in time to win the Battle of Britain. However, he rarely interfered in the management of the firms which he controlled, even when their results left something to be desired, and it was for his successors to carry out the corporate restructuring necessary to improve overall performance. Rather than a company doctor, therefore, he was a company promoter and financier par excellence.

T A B CORLEY

Sources:

Unpublished

Covent Garden Properties Co Ltd, Beecham Estates and Pills Ltd, Minute Book 1924-28; Beecham Estates and Pills Ltd, Annual Reports 1924-8; Beechams Pills Ltd, Annual Reports 1928-44.

J M Keyworth, 'History of Covent Garden Properties Co Ltd' (Mr Keyworth has generously permitted some information in his history to be used here).

BCe.

DCe.

MCe.

PrC; Will.

Published

Sir Thomas Beecham, *A Mingled Chime* (Hutchinson, 1944).

Stanley Chapman, *Jesse Boot of Boots the Chemists* (Hodder & Stoughton, 1974).

Chemist and Druggist 26 Aug 1944.

T A B Corley, 'From National to Multinational Enterprise: The Beecham Business 1848-1945' University of Reading Discussion Papers in International Investment and Business Studies No 76, Nov 1983.

Economist 26 Aug 1944.

Estates Gazette 19 Aug 1944.

H G Lazell, *From Pills to Penicillin: The Beecham Story* (Heinemann, 1975).

Pharmaceutical Journal 26 Aug 1944.

South Wales Echo and Express 16 Aug 1944.

Times 19 Nov 1927, 16, 17, 18, 19, 22 Aug 1944.

Torbay Times 25 Aug 1944.

HILL, William

(1903-1971)

Bookmaker

William Hill was born in Birmingham on 16 July 1903, the third in the family of eleven children of William Hill, a journeyman coach painter, and his wife, Lavinia née Knight. In his teens, William took up his father's trade for a brief period, and it was while he was working in a factory in Birmingham that he first collected racing bets.

He was not particularly successful in his forays against the bookmakers, so he decided that as the odds were on their side he would join them. He

William Hill presenting the William Hill Gold Cup trophy to Her Majesty the Queen after her horse Charlton had won.

commenced by visiting public houses in the Midlands and collecting bets on a bicycle, but the scope and interest in this sort of operation was limited and he decided to establish himself at the racecourses themselves. However, he was inexperienced in this sort of environment and fell an easy prey to knowledgeable racegoers, and to other bookmakers, and soon lost his initial capital. Undismayed, he acquired another stake and returned, pitching his ambitions on a more modest scale, to establish a reputation and, with it, a moderately successful bookmaking business.

In 1929, at the age of twenty-six, William Hill decided that London was the place to be. He began in London not on the racetrack but at the greyhound stadia which, promoted by Alfred Critchley (qv) and others, were then booming. Eventually he extended his activities to the Northolt Park Racecourse, where he did well enough to own and race a few horses. In 1934, for the convenience of his increasing circle of clients, he opened a credit office in a single room in Jermyn Street, above the premises of a firm of hatters. From this time his business began to expand rapidly and he took the decision to 'go into racing in a big way — make enough money to buy a farm and then retire' {William Hill Organisation, archives, biographical outline}. By 1939 new premises were needed, and were found in Park Lane at the stately former residence of Lord Inchcape (qv). At the same time Hill formed a private company, William Hill (Park Lane) Ltd.

By now William Hill's business included the laying of ante-post odds for major races such as the Lincoln, the Grand National and the classic races. Later in the year he launched fixed odds football coupons; the first week's take for this new departure was £6 18s 5p but the idea rapidly caught on. At the same time he established postal betting, which was illegal in England but permitted in Scotland; to do this he formed a further company, William Hill (Glasgow) Ltd. By 1944/45 both these new companies had outgrown their original premises and the football business had become a separate company, William Hill (Football) Ltd. Fixed odds coupons were now being issued both in London and Glasgow from new premises in Ludgate Circus and Jamaica Street. The hiving off of the football company had relieved pressure at Park Lane but expansion of the original business continued and in 1947 came a further move to offices at Piccadilly Circus.

William Hill was a shrewd judge of form and breeding and would back his own judgement fearlessly. On the grounds that he did not consider their breeding was adequate to stay the Derby course, he fielded against *Big Game* in a wartime substitute Derby and against *Tudor Minstrel* in 1947. In each case the horse had won the 2000 Guineas impressively and he would have lost a fortune had either of them won. However, his success was not based merely upon a sound judgement of horse flesh. He believed that all his customers should receive the most courteous service, no matter how small their bet, and backed this with integrity and the initiative to know what the public wanted and to give it to them in full value. He also acquired two stud and farm estates at which he bred *Nimbus*, the 1949 Derby winner, and conceived a genuine love of horses and a great interest in the breeding of bloodstock.

The business continued to grow and in 1954 William Hill and his colleague Lionel Barber bought 75 per cent of the issued shares of a trust company called Holders Investment Trust, which was quoted on the London Stock Market. Into this shell was sold William Hill (Football) Ltd for £1,050,000 in 1955, to be followed in 1956 by William Hill (Glasgow) Ltd for £1,875,000 and, in 1961, by William Hill (Park Lane) Ltd for £2 million. In 1962 many of the operations of these companies were brought together in Hill House, which had been built for the purpose in Blackfriars Road, London.

William Hill was strongly opposed to the introduction of licensed betting offices, which would enable the man in the street to bet for cash, and when they were legalised in 1962 (the legislation came into effect in 1963) his organisation refrained from entering the field. However, in 1964 a tax of 25 per cent was imposed on fixed odds football betting, a crushing blow which virtually killed this form of betting. A loss of £2.5 million was suffered that year and the outlook was bleak. The firm endeavoured to go into straightforward football pools but this move was not a success. In 1966, by which time it was clear that betting shops were making heavy inroads into the traditional credit business, William Hill decided to buy into the cash betting trade and acquired, over a short period of years, a number of established betting shop companies, including those of Jack Swift, John Hudson, Walter Parkinson and the Hurst Park Syndicate. Despite the difficulties which had been encountered the company weathered the storm and fought back strongly. By the time he retired in 1969 profits were recovering well.

Outside his business William Hill was active with a number of charities. He married his wife, Ivy, in 1923 and they had an only daughter. At his death on 15 October 1971 he left an estate proved at £1,014,803, although the major part of of his assets had been settled in a variety of trusts. A couple of months later the William Hill Organisation Ltd, as the holding company was then known, was taken over by the giant Sears Holdings Ltd, formed by Sir Charles Clore (qv).

H W ABBEY

Sources:

Unpublished

William Hill Organisation Ltd, London, archives.

BCe.

PrC.

Published

Times 16 Oct 1971.

HILLMAN, Edward Henry

(1889-1934)

Transport operator

Edward Henry Hillman was born in Croydon on 19 March 1889, the son of Edward Hillman, a carman, and his wife, Annie née White. He left school at the age of nine to work as a brush maker, joining the army as a drummer boy at the age of twelve. By the end of the First World War he had reached the rank of sergeant major in a cavalry regiment. Hillman left the army with a gratuity, which he used to buy a taxi. Hillman's investment, unlike that of many ex-service men, proved successful, and the taxi was subsequently sold, the proceeds being used to buy a cycle shop in Romford. East London remained his base, and it is said that his entry into the coaching trade followed from his accepting a booking agency for a local firm, and realising, from the commission he obtained, the money that could be made from running his own service.

Obtaining his first vehicles in 1928, Hillman began by operating excursions from a garage and office at 52b Romford Road, Stratford. In December of that year he started, in a very modest way, a regular service from Stratford Broadway to Brentwood. This was both faster and cheaper than the established bus service, and proved an immediate success, giving a frequent service between the intermediate centres of Ilford and Romford.

Early in 1929 Hillman extended six journeys a day to Chelmsford. These became 16 in May, and a further extension to Colchester was made at the end of the year, pushing on to Clacton, Ipswich, Norwich, Southwold and Yarmouth by 1931. A secret of Hillman's success was the provision of short-stage fares over the whole of his routes, the through traffic being catered for by running reliefs non-stop when demand warranted it. By doing this he aroused the opposition of other independent firms as well as that of the London and provincial combines, and defied the conventional wisdom that would separate long and short distance traffics.

Early in 1931 Hillman brought his metropolitan terminal nearer to London when he opened a coach station at 133 Bow Road, opposite the District Line station, but he never attempted to operate from a central point, concentrating always on the eastern suburbs for his trade. After the passage of the Road Traffic Act 1930 he encountered opposition to the grant of road service licences, and he was involved in some rather doubtful business in the takeover of the Aldgate-Upminster service, but the capacity of the man may be judged by his litigation, when he obtained a rule *nisi* to settle the powers of the Minister of Transport under the Act.

The stabilising effect of the Road Traffic Act must have narrowed Hillman's road transport horizons, and no doubt he foresaw the consequence of the London Traffic Act 1933 (which had been before parliament for some three years), and which was to lead to the compulsory acquisition of 65 of his coaches and the transfer of 300 of his staff to the London Passenger Transport Board on 10 January 1934, leaving him 28 coaches for the East Anglian part of his business. (After his death, these services were sold to the Eastern National and Eastern Counties omnibus companies.)

Hillman, however, had in the meantime diversified into air transport (as another busman, W L Thurgood (qv), was to do in late 1933). On 1 April 1932 he opened an air service between Maylands airfield, near Romford, and Clacton, with a three-seater Puss Moth. This was sufficiently successful to encourage him to reinstate it the following year, and in 1933 he added services from Maylands to Paris and to Margate. In 1934, with all-year operation developing, he moved his base to Abridge, to a field sometimes called 'Essex Airport', which was later to be RAF Stapleford Tawney. From here he opened a service to Belfast, later extended to Glasgow, and he was able to obtain a GPO mail contract.

When demand was low, Hillman's Airways offered joyrides, but basically the policy of low fares was extended from the coach business, and passengers on the Clacton services had the opportunity of choice between road and air. The coach fare to Clacton was 12s 6d and the fare by plane £1. When the Paris service started, Imperial Airways and Air France were charging £5 single and £8 10s return: Hillman undercut them with a single fare of £3 15s and £6 return. Despite this, his operating standards were high, both for road and air services, and his airline had only one fatal accident in its history.

Edward Hillman always claimed that he had designed the de Havilland

DH-84 'Dragon' airliner, and there is no doubt that his operating requirements were well met by it. Earlier he had been closely associated with the manufacturers of Gilford coaches, and his home at Hare Street, Gidea Park, was called 'Gilford Lodge'. The coach business was from 1 October 1930 a partnership between Hillman and the R B Syndicate Ltd, which represented the Gilford interests, but this was dissolved in August 1933, when Hillman's Saloon Coaches Ltd was formed, the directors being Hillman himself, his son, also called Edward, and R F Frazer. This company also owned the air side of Hillman's enterprises.

From all accounts, Hillman was a genuine 'rough diamond'. He could be moody and intolerant. But despite the scale of his operations, he remained an 'anti-establishment' figure, and a thorn in the flesh of the 'respectable' operators. His air services were run in the way he had run his coaches, and there is a telling memoir of him, in his shirt-sleeves on the tarmac one Bank Holiday, pushing a mug of tea into the hands of one of his pilots, rejoicing in the heavy traffic and keen to get the aeroplane back in the air. He was not only ready to drive his own coaches, but he also learned to fly, so that he knew what he was asking his staff to do.

Hillman's company went public late in 1934 when Hillman's Airways Ltd was floated with an authorised capital of £150,000; 400,000 5s ordinary shares were offered to investors. Hillman had 19,800 10s shares in the private company, Edward Henry Hillman Ltd, out of the total issued capital of 20,000 shares. 120,000 fully-paid shares of the new company were allocated to the vendors (that is, effectively, Hillman). He was to be managing director of Hillman's Airways at a salary of £1,250 pa, for at least seven years; he was also to be deputy chairman. But he was never able to fulfil the promise of wider low-cost air transport. He died at his home on 31 December 1934, of a heart attack and stroke; he was survived by his wife and son. His estate was £18,217 gross. His interest in the company was acquired by the bankers, d'Erlanger, and subsequently Whitehall Securities Ltd took an interest, merging Hillman's Airways with other firms to form British Airways Ltd, the Government's second 'chosen instrument'. It is ironical that Edward Hillman should have died just as his investment in commercial aviation was becoming profitable, and intriguing to speculate about the impact he might have made upon the 'big battalions' had he lived to bring it to fruition.

JOHN HIBBS

Sources:

Unpublished

BCe.

DCe.

PrC.

Information provided by E A Lainson, J E King and R G Westgate.

Published

P W Brooks, 'A Short History of London's Airports' *Journal of Transport History* 1st ser, 3 (May 1957).

Ronald E G Davies, *A History of the World's Airlines* (Oxford University Press, 1964).

Flight 3 Jan 1935.

Sir Geoffrey de Havilland, *Sky Fever* (Hamish Hamilton, 1961).

Robin D S Higham, 'British Airways Ltd, 1935-40' *Journal of Transport History* 1st ser, 4 (Nov 1959).

—, *Britain's Imperial Air Routes, 1918 to 1939* (G T Foulis & Co, 1960).

W Lambden, *The Manx Transport Systems* (Omnibus Society, 1964).

John Lock and John Creasey, *The Log of a Merchant Airman* (Stanley Paul & Co, 1943).

Omnibus Magazine Feb 1934.

John Pudney, *The Seven Skies: A Study of BOAC and Its Forerunners since 1919* (BOAC, 1959).

D Spurgeon, 'Edward Hillman, Portrait of a Pioneer' *BEA Magazine* May 1952 (see also comments in letters published in issue of June 1952).

Times *Prospectuses* 88 (1934).

HILLMAN, William

(1847/48-1929)

Cycle and car manufacturer

William Hillman was possibly the William Hillman born at Stratford, Essex on 13 December 1848, the son of William Hillman, a shoemaker, and his wife Sarah née Stitchburg. (There were two William Hillmans born in the London area in 1847-48.) Nothing is known about his early life. Like his friend (later business associate) James Starley (qv), he was trained at the engineering works of John Penn & Co, Greenwich. When Starley joined the Coventry Sewing Machine Co at Cheyelesmore, Coventry, Hillman followed him, and both men became involved in the pioneering production of French 'boneshaker' bicycles. Starley, the 'father of the cycle industry', later left the CSM Co and patented the first practical penny farthing bicycle in 1875. This 'Ariel' machine, the first all-metal bicycle, was produced with Hillman's assistance. On the strength of his success, Hillman left Starley's employment in the Coventry Machinist Co and in 1875 founded his own Coventry concern called Auto Machinery — a nut, bearing and cycle company, but also making roller skates and sewing machines.

Hillman demonstrated an abundance of engineering and business skill, but lacked financial resources. Consequently, in order to establish Auto Machinery, he entered into partnership with William Henry Herbert, who had capital from his father, a Leicester builder and farmer. In due course, Herbert's younger brother Alfred (qv) was to establish the UK's largest machine tool company, but in 1875 he was a minor shareholder in Auto Machinery. Hillman's enterprise was so successful that four more plants were opened in Coventry, and in 1896 a new factory was established in Nuremburg, Germany. In that year, George Beverley Cooper of London joined Auto Machinery and with his help the cycle part of the business was hived off from the original nut and bearing enterprise. As a result the New Premier Cycle Co was launched to continue the business of building cycles at the rate of 33,000 per annum with 600 hands. This volume of production had made Auto Machinery and then New Premier, the world's largest manufacturer of cycles. Hillman was a prolific inventor and his numerous patents in the period 1876-83 dealt with all aspects of bicycle design. These enterprises made William Hillman a millionaire and at the turn of the century he moved house from 7 The Quadrant, Coventry to an impressive property in Stoke Aldermoor, Coventry, called Abingdon House.

It appears that Hillman became weary of his two very successful but no longer challenging businesses. In consequence, he decided to establish a car-making company, and in 1905 Hillman began laying plans to build a plant in the grounds of Abingdon House. This time Hillman's venture required him to secure the services of a specialist car designer, for he wanted to build a racing car to enter the Isle of Man Tourist Trophy races. With this objective in view, Hillman enticed the brilliant young French designer, Louis Coatalen (1879-1962) from the Humber company, whose own Stoke factory was only one field away from Hillman's nascent facility. In 1907 the Hillman-Coatalen Car Co was formed. The company and its products established Coatalen's reputation in the UK and his links with Hillman were strengthened when he married one of Hillman's six daughters. However, in 1909 Coatalen was persuaded by the Sunbeam Car Co to join them. Consequently, in that year Coatalen sold out his interest in the Hillman-Coatalen Co to William Hillman. By that date Hillman Car Co was assured of a moderately prosperous future making different models of various sizes and initially concentrating on small keenly-priced cars, indicating that Hillman was among the few British motor manufacturers who 'read the market reasonably accurately in response to Perry and his Model T Ford' {Church (1982) 14}.

The progress of the Hillman car concern was steady, although in producing about 1,500 cars a year in the mid-1920s it was not in the front rank of British car companies such as Morris, Austin, Singer, Ford, Rover, Clyno, or even Humber. In the mid-1920s the last-named embarked upon a major policy of expansion, beginning with the purchase of Commer Cars of Luton in 1926. In 1927 Humber decided to buy

Hillman, their near neighbours in Stoke, Coventry. Although Hillman were not nearly as large a concern as Humber they were reasonably successful in producing family saloons and under the guidance of Hillman's joint managing directors (John Black, later to move to Standard Cars, and Spencer Wilkes (qv), later to move to Rover), Hillman was incorporated into the Humber-Hillman-Commer combine.

William Hillman died at his home, Kerseley Hall, on 4 February 1921, leaving £184,422 gross.

D G RHYS

Sources:

Unpublished

Coventry R O, Lowe Collection.

BCe.

Prc.

Published

Roy Church, 'Markets and Marketing in the British Motor Industry before 1914 with Some French Comparisons' *Journal of Transport History* 3rd ser 3 (1982).

Coventry Herald 11, 12 Feb 1921.

Coventry Standard 11, 12 Feb 1921.

A E Harrison, 'Joint-Stock Company Flotation in the Cycle, Motor-Vehicle and Related Industries, 1882-1914' *Business History* 23 (1981).

Joan Lane (ed), *Register of Business Records of Coventry and Related Areas* (Coventry: Lanchester Polytechnic, 1977).

Motor Cycle and Cycle Trader 12 July 1940.

Samuel B Saul, 'The Motor Industry in Britain to 1914' *Business History* 5 (1962).

HILTON, Ralph

(1923-1981)

Road transport entrepreneur

Ralph Hilton was born in Deptford, London on 8 August 1923, the son of Ralph Hilton, a fruiterer and greengrocer, and his wife Ruby née Williams. He left school at fourteen and became a page boy at the Hotel Rubens. He joined the Army in the Second World War, gaining experience of vehicle servicing. After demobilisation in 1948 he worked in his father's public house. He entered road haulage in Vauxhall in 1954, buying a lorry and driving it part-time whilst continuing to help in the public house, whose licence he took over when his father retired (holding it until 1959). By the late 1950s he was sufficiently successful with his transport business to concentrate exclusively on it, having bought a filling station (with useful facilities for his lorries) in 1956 and developed a fleet of vehicles which reached 16 in 1957 and 49 in 1959. Following the advice of his auditors, he formed a limited liability company, Hilton Transport Services Ltd, in July 1959, but remained sole proprietor, the only other director being his wife, who assisted with the paperwork (a typical situation in road haulage). Mrs Hilton remained a director until 1967, when the board was expanded. The style of direction, however, remained proprietorial until November 1970, as the board does not appear to have functioned in a formal way during this period.

Throughout the 1960s the business continued to grow, mainly by buying similar road haulage undertakings, for their 'A' licences (which entitled the holder to carry goods for hire and reward without restriction), and also in order to acquire premises, vehicles and tax losses. Hilton is described in the *Report* of the Companies Act Investigation as a hard worker with initiative and drive and a 'robust attitude to business affairs' {Hytner and Irvine (1976) para 12}. His willingness to undertake short-term hire contracts also assisted the growth of his business at this time. Many of the subsequent allegations against him remained unproven, but it seems beyond doubt that some at least of Hilton's acquisitions were accompanied by sharp practice, a deal becoming a fait accompli before the terms, differing from those suggested during negotiations, were legally concluded.

During the 1960s, as Hilton Transport Services (HTS) grew by acquisition, the business assumed dimensions greater than Hilton's undoubted abilities could cope with. His flair for transport did not extend to warehousing, to which his interests increasingly turned towards the end of the decade. (A small grocery distribution firm had been acquired as early as 1961.) In this connection there were two crucial developments: the acquisition of six acres of warehousing at Charlton in 1967 and in June 1970 of the nearby Harvey's warehouse, which proved unsuitable for the kind of business Hilton had in mind and expensive to convert.

It is these developments more than any others which led to the flotation of HTS as a public company in November 1970 by the Industrial & Commercial Finance Corporation (ICFC). Two years previously, in October 1968, Shipping Industrial Holdings had considered, but then rejected, the idea of a takeover of HTS, and in August-September 1969 flotation negotiations had gone on with Charterhouse Japhet & Thomasson, but were apparently called off by Hilton.

During the period between mid-1968 and mid-1970 HTS was acquiring larger companies than heretofore, such as the Joy Group with 155 vehicles in January 1969 and Reeves Ltd in December of that year, partly in order to build up a network of provincial depots. Before these two acquisitions, HTS had reached a fleet size of over 400 and an annual turnover in excess of £1 million. This may be compared with industry statistics for 1965 when almost exactly half the 46,000 public hauliers operated a single vehicle, only 3,500 had ten or more vehicles, and of these around 200 operated 50 or more vehicles. The *Report* is critical of the 1970 flotation, considering that HTS had by that time probably passed the optimum size which Ralph Hilton was capable of running and had moved into the field of warehousing where his touch was less sure. Moreover, attention should have been paid to the rumours which already surrounded Hilton and his associates, whatever their truth, and the management structure and finances should have given rise to doubts about the future success of the undertaking as a public company.

The flotation was followed in May 1971 by the acquisition of the J & H Transport Group Ltd, which proved more than the HTS management structure could cope with, and for the year ending July 1971 HTS fell very seriously short of the profit forecasts of its prospectus. The *Report* considers that its management structure virtually collapsed from early autumn 1971. Despite this situation three further haulage companies were acquired in 1971-72 from British Oxygen. This left the company short of cash, and imposed further strain on an already inadequate management, particularly since the companies concerned were not in a healthy trading state. It is not surprising that a takeover bid by Gallaher Ltd in March 1972 was soon dropped when something of the true position of HTS emerged from Gallaher's enquiries.

Peat Marwick Mitchell & Co, the accountants, were called in to investigate HTS in June 1972 and reported in September, pointing to its management problems, critical cash flow and the crucial problem of the Charlton depot. Despite the appointment in June of an independent businessman, James McNaughton, as chief administrator of HTS, its liquidity crisis worsened and Barclays Bank pressed increasingly hard on the subject of the growing overdraft. In March 1973 they called in Cork Gully, specialists in liquidation, to investigate, who urged the reconstitution of the board. In the following month concerted pressure from his fellow directors led Hilton to resign.

However, he still owned 35 per cent of the equity and did not relinquish the reins without several attempts to interfere in HTS affairs. In September he acquired a refrigerating company and William Beadles & Son Ltd, hauliers, both based in the Surrey Docks, and attracted some HTS staff into his employ. At the end of October 1973 he forced the holding of an extraordinary general meeting of HTS in an attempt, backed by the Whitehead Consulting Group, to remove a majority of directors, replacing them by himself and some colleagues. The issue of his 'Programme for Recovery' on 21 January 1974 was followed by his arrest three days later. At his trial in June 1975 he was acquitted of conspiracy but found guilty of falsifying accounts. In the same month a receiver was called in to Roadships Ltd, as HTS had been renamed in August 1974. (At the end of February 1974 ICFC had bought the Hilton family shareholding in HTS.) Hilton went on to develop WBS Transport and South London Inland Clearance Ltd.

Ralph Hilton's son, Ralph John Hilton, was for a time on the staff of HTS and now (1984) heads Hilton Amalgamated Transport Ltd. Hilton was a freemason; his principal hobby was running a power boat, which also provided some publicity for the firm. He died on 28 August 1981 at his home in Chislehurst, leaving £788,397 gross.

RICHARD STOREY

Writings:

'Hilton Transport Services' in Richard Lynn (ed), *The Entrepreneur: Eight Case Studies* (Allen & Unwin, 1974). This gives Hilton's optimistic version of affairs in 1970.

Sources:

Unpublished

BCe.

PrC.

Published

M Cunningham, 'Stuff and No Nonsense from this East Ender' *Motor Transport* 26 Oct 1983.

Samuel L Edwards and Brian T Bayliss, *Operating Costs in Road Freight Transport* (Department of the Environment, 1971).

Benet A Hytner and Ian A N Irvine, *Roadships Limited: Report of an Investigation under Section 165(b) of the Companies Act 1948* (HMSO, 1976).

Roadway Oct 1981.

'The Battle to Drive Ralph Hilton Transport' *Sunday Times* 13 Jan 1974.

Times 12, 16, 20 Nov 1970, 17, 23 Nov 1973, 12, 25, 26 Jan, 1, 28 Feb 1974.

HILTON, Sir Robert Stuart

(1870-1943)

Electrical equipment and steel manufacturer

Robert Stuart Hilton was born in Wigan on 28 December 1870, the son of Thomas Hilton, a cotton spinner and later an agent, and Rosa Elizabeth Hawkins, née Hawthorne. He was educated at Sedbergh School (1884-88) and at Wigan School of Mines, where he was a silver medallist. By 1895 he was a colliery manager at the Wigan Coal & Iron Co then managed by Alfred Hewlett (qv). He was appointed in 1911 as manager of Birmingham Corporation Gas Department, then headed by Sir Hallewell Rogers (qv) and known as one of the most progressive municipal gas departments in England.

In 1914, following the outbreak of war, Hilton was the officer responsible under the Committee on High Explosives for organising, from Birmingham as a centre, the engineering supervision of gas washing in seven areas. When the severity of the munitions crisis had become clear in April 1915, Hilton approached Sir Sothern Holland (who was in charge of High Explosives Supply at the War Office) and Lord Moulton (Director General of Explosives Supplies at the Ministry of Munitions) about forming a Birmingham munitions organisation. On receiving official encouragement, he contacted leading employers and trade unionists in the Birmingham area, and on 19 April 1915 an Executive Committee to organise the munitions output of Birmingham was formed with Dudley Docker (qv) as chairman and Hilton as secretary. Other members of the committee were Sir Gerard Muntz (Muntz Metals), Arthur Keen (qv) (GKN), Sir Harris Spencer (Midland Employers Federation), Sir Hallewell Rogers (BSA), Neville Chamberlain and Arthur Chamberlain (qv). There were also three trade unionists and Sir Ernest Hiley, the town clerk of Birmingham. Hilton, as secretary of the committee (with offices in Birmingham Council House), was responsible for most of the executive and organisational work. Later in 1915 he became a member of the board of management, and executive chief, of the Birmingham and District National Shell Factory. The factory was considerably delayed in reaching production because Hilton and his colleagues were too busy with the Birmingham munitions committee, and for some time controls were weak. A reasonable output was achieved by the factory from 1916, but it never functioned on a large scale: its maximum number of employees was 2,400 (November 1917) and total capital expenditure to March 1918 was only £187,600. For his work Hilton was made an OBE in 1919.

In that year Hilton was appointed managing director of the Metropolitan-Vickers Electrical Co which had recently been reconstructed from the old British Westinghouse Co, and was wholly owned by Vickers. The animating force in Metrovick at this time was Hilton's former chairman on the Birmingham munitions committee, Dudley Docker, and another municipal colleague from the committee, Ernest Hiley, was at the same time recruited as chairman of Metrovick. Metrovick's main works were at Old Trafford near Manchester, but the advent of Hiley and Hilton to the upper echelons of the company marked the ascendancy of Birmingham interests in its direction. In the early days of the new combine there was antagonism between Metrovick officials and the central Vickers sales department, and insufficient integration between the two companies: contrary to the public rhetoric of Docker and Douglas Vickers at the time of Metrovick's acquisition, they simply imposed their own senior management (Hilton, Hiley and others) in place of the old management, without detailed thought about reforms or policies to improve managerial efficiency. Hilton held little, if any, responsibility for these early mistakes, and from the outset his potential was probably limited by the curbs on his autonomy.

At Metrovick Hilton was regarded as taciturn and reticent, a consolidator, who was fair-minded but sometimes aggressive. Many of his Birmingham municipal and industrial associates during 1911-18 had entertained progressive, if paternalistic, social views on labour relations (as expressed for example by the National Alliance of Employers and Employed), and it was doubtless from this source that Hilton brought to Metrovick a sympathy for workers' welfare schemes which was not always appreciated by other colleagues. Together with General Sir Philip Nash (1875-1936), who was chairman of Metrovick from 1922, Hilton managed the business competently, paying '8 per cent dividends on both preference and ordinary shares throughout the whole of the 1920s even though they were not covered by profits in every year' {Jones and Marriott (1970) 63}. Measured against its main competitors, Metrovick did not perform as well as General Electric of Hugo Hirst (qv), but considerably better than English Electric under P J Pybus (qv). Hilton, unlike Hirst but like Pybus, was not his own master, and had to run Metrovick under various constraints arising from the wider financial difficulties and organisational problems of the Vickers group. In February 1927 Hilton retired as managing director of Metrovick, and was promoted deputy-chairman to Nash; but he left the company early in 1928 when Dudley Docker sold control of it to General Electric of America.

In late 1927 Maximilian Mannaberg (qv) engineered a palace coup inside the ailing and crisis-torn United Steel Companies, which led to Hilton being appointed managing director. Helped by the group's new chairman, Walter Benton Jones (qv), and exploiting his own experience of attempting industrial rationalisation at Metrovick, Hilton then led a massive turn round of this large, ramshackle combine between 1928 and 1932. A drastic financial reconstruction was carried through with the help of City institutions; financial controls were tightened; new managers were introduced, particularly on the sales side, often from outside the industry; a loose organisation was considerably centralised with greater head office control of, for example, purchasing, capital spending and sales. Production facilities were rationalised and concentrated but with no large scale divestments, closures or redundancies. By early 1932, although the industry had not yet revived, United Steel had beaten its financial crisis, renewed its management and greatly improved productivity even at low levels of working and with little new capital expenditure.

The Hilton-Benton Jones regime had certain limitations in respect of competitive strategy. United Steel's growth in the 1930s was no more than the industry average. In a series of moves in the important 'Midland Corridor' relating to mergers, iron ore supplies and developments for new outlets, the firm was largely outmanoeuvred by more aggressive and capable competitors, notably Stewarts & Lloyds. However, there were considerable technical advances, for example in the field of electric steelmaking, and internal management techniques were generally outstanding for the industry. Hilton's first phase of efficiency promotion, starting in the late 1920s, included work study and a central research department. To this were successively added systematic evaluation of investment projects, increasingly intricate budgeting-planning systems and, by 1935, a new efficiency promotion phase, this time spearheaded by the firm's accountants. Systematic management recruitment and training schemes, introduced in 1929, were extended. Hilton curbed nepotism, although probably not as much as he would have liked. His organisational policies emphasised not only head office overall control but also participative planning, a multi-divisional system and general managership at branch levels. The resulting efforts to achieve a balance between decentralisation and centralisation, however uneasy and unclear, represented a significant achievement even though Hilton's own innate bias was towards centralisation.

Hilton played a major part in introducing progressive labour policies in United Steel: representative works councils (starting in 1929), sensitivity on redundancy issues (exemplified by policies in West Cumberland), and worker pensions (pioneered in the industry in 1936). He made a key contribution to United Steel's 'co-operative' stance on industry-wide and public policy issues in contradistinction to the 'passivity' or 'separatism' of other firms. Here he was influenced partly by the firm's sectional interests, partly by personal preferences for industrial order, collective solutions and responsiveness to government. Playing a leading part in the industry's counsels, Hilton forcefully advocated industry-wide rationalisation, co-operation and a strong central organisation for iron and steel between 1929 and 1935. He supported tripartite ideas and, despite some disagreements, continued to be a warm supporter of the industry's emergent 'Middle Way' in public co-ordination of private enterprise. His elevation to the British Iron and Steel Federation presidency in 1938 was a natural sequel.

Hilton was not particularly imaginative or diplomatic. His shyness, brusqueness and occasional outright rudeness created enemies, although a measure of ruthlessness was, perhaps, necessary for the rationalising role he eventually played so well. His greatest strengths were those of a policy implementer and field commander rather than in external strategy or entrepreneurship. By the 1930s Hilton had developed a well-rounded view of industrial administration, emphasising measurement and order, corporate loyalty, labour relations and public service. In this an engineering background, the efficiency ethos and disciplinary, perhaps also aesthetic, inclinations played some part, as did his mixed private and public sector experience across diverse industries. Hilton's final achievements in United Steel represented a triumph of professional operating management; and this, together with his role as an arch-reformer at national levels, puts him among the steel industry's outstanding leaders of the inter-war period.

Hilton retired from the general managership of the United Steel Companies in 1939. He was knighted in 1942. In 1899 he married Julia Ethel (1876-1963), daughter of James McBryde; they had one son and one daughter. He died on 10 October 1943, leaving £24,250 gross.

JONATHAN S BOSWELL *and* R P T DAVENPORT-HINES

Sources:

Unpublished

Bank of England, Central Archives Section, Threadneedle Street, London, Securities Management Trust and Bankers' Industrial Development Co papers.

British Steel Corporation North East Regional Records Centre, Middlesbrough, Cleveland, United Steel Companies records, particularly Directors' Minutes, Annual General Meetings, Central and Finance Committee Minutes, Sir Frederick Jones's Correspondence, Chairman's Investigations, Robert Hilton's copy Letter Books, and special files on, for example, 1927-28 reorganisation, iron ore resources, amalgamations, and financial and organisational matters in the 1930s.

British Steel Corporation Midland Regional Records Centre, Irthlingborough, Northamptonshire, National Federation of Iron and Steel Manufacturers' and British Iron and Steel Federation records.

PRO, BT/56/14, 21, 37; BT/55/38; Import Duties Advisory Committee papers, BT/10; MUN 5/149, Birmingham Munitions Committee.

Vickers PLC, Millbank, London SW1, microfilm collection.

Steven Tolliday, 'Industry, Finance and the State: An Analysis of the British Steel Industry in the Inter-War Years' (Cambridge PhD, 1979).

Interview notes of P W S Andrews and E Brunner for their *Capital Development in Steel*, by courtesy of the late Professor E Brunner.

Information from the late P Beynon, H P Forder, D Ward Jones, T S Kilpatrick, R M Peddie, A J Peech, R Scholey, J Y Lancaster (ex-officials of United Steel); Sir M Finniston, S Gray, Mrs R Kydd (née Benton Jones); Mrs Hermione Hichens.

Published

Philip W S Andrews and Elizabeth Brunner, *Capital Development in Steel: A Study of the United Steel Companies Limited* (Oxford: Blackwells, 1952).

Jonathan S Boswell, 'Hope, Inefficiency or Public Duty? The United Steel Companies and West Cumberland, 1918-39' *Business History* 22 (Jan 1980).

—, *Business Policies in the Making, Three Steel Companies Compared* (George Allen & Unwin, 1983).

Duncan L Burn, *The Economic History of Steelmaking 1867-1939* (Cambridge: Cambridge University Press, 1940).

—, *The Steel Industry 1939-59* (Cambridge: Cambridge University Press, 1961).

James C Carr and Walter Taplin, *A History of the British Steel Industry* (Oxford: Basil Blackwell, 1962).

Richard Davenport-Hines, *Dudley Docker* (Cambridge: Cambridge University Press, 1984).

John Dummelow, *1899-1949* (Manchester: Metropolitan-Vickers Electrical Co Ltd, 1949).

History of the Ministry of Munitions (8 vols, HMSO, 1918-22) 2, part II; 7, part IV; 8, part II.

John Jewkes and W Allan Winterbottom, *An Industrial Survey of Cumberland and Furness* (Manchester: Victoria University, 1933).

Robert Jones and Oliver J D Marriott, *Anatomy of a Merger: A History of GEC, AEI and English Electric* (Jonathan Cape, 1970).

W Benton Jones, 'The History and Organisation of the United Steel Companies' in Ronald Edwards and Henry Townsend (eds), *Business Enterprise* (Macmillan, 1958).

Bernard S Keeling and Anthony E Wright, *The Development of the Modern British Steel Industry* (Longmans, 1964).

L Y Lancaster and D R Wattleworth, *The Iron and Steel Industry of West Cumberland, an Historical Survey* (Workington: British Steel Corporation, Teesside Division, 1977).

R M Peddie, *The United Steel Companies* (Sheffield, 1967).

John Vaizey, *The History of British Steel* (Weidenfeld & Nicolson, 1974).

WWW.

HINDLEY, John Scott

Viscount Hyndley

(1883-1963)

Coal distributor and nationalised coal industry chairman

John Scott Hindley was born at Margate, Kent, on 24 October 1883, younger son of Rev William Talbot Hindley (1845-1906), Vicar of Margate (and later of Meads near Eastbourne) and his wife Caroline, daughter of John Scott. His father left £1,375. Hindley was educated in 1899-1901 at Weymouth College, where he was president of the debating society. At an early age he determined to enter business rather than proceed to Oxford which his father believed was too sports-oriented to have utility for business training. On leaving school in October 1901 he was sent as an engineering apprentice to Murton Colliery in County Durham. He did not complete his apprenticeship, and by 1907 had transferred to the commercial side of the industry as a coal exporter.

Hindley soon became junior partner in a firm headed by Colonel Stephenson Clarke (1862-1948) which was in business as coal factors and distributors, wagon and shipowners. He was a cheerful and convivial man, with whom personal relations were a strong point; he enjoyed considerable popularity on the commercial side of the coal industry. Following the outbreak of the First World War, he was chairman of the Newcastle branch of the London Coal Supply Advisory Committee in 1915-17. As a member of the Coal Controller's Export Advisory Committee in 1917-18, he visited the USA and other countries.

Hindley was appointed in 1918 as Commercial Adviser to the Mines Department, a post that he continued to hold (with an interval in 1938-39) until 1942. He was knighted in 1921. The Mines Department was an administrative backwater in Whitehall, a sub-department of the Board of Trade, standing in similar relation to the latter as the Department of Overseas Trade, but holding less prestige and influence. The Mines Department's political chiefs, whether Tories like Colonel George Lane-Fox and Captain Harry Crookshank, or Labour men like Ben Turner, were politicians of at best secondary importance in parliament, and the Department's civil servants were of like calibre. The Department had no outstanding success as an intermediary between the coal industry and Government. Hindley returned to work full-time in the Department during the coal strikes of 1921 and 1926.

Shortly after the war the Stephenson Clarke firm underwent transformation. It was converted from a private partnership into a private company, and Hindley changed from being a partner to a director. Stephenson Clarke & Co owned 85 per cent of the shares in the Maris Export & Trading Co formed in 1920 as coal exporters, shipowners, bunker suppliers and ship agents. Jointly with William Cory & Son Ltd, Stephenson Clarke also owned all the shares in Coal Distributors (South Wales) Ltd, and Hindley was a director of both subsidiaries. After the retirement of Colonel Clarke and the appointment of Sir Stephenson Kent as chairman of the group, Hindley became vice-chairman.

In 1928 Stephenson Clarke was bought by the South Wales mining combine, Powell Duffryn Steam Coal Co (formed 1864), which was then pursuing a policy of buying up bankrupt Welsh collieries so as to be in a strong position when the coal industry revived. Powell Duffryn appointed Stephenson Clarke as sole vendors of their coal, coke and by-products, and to consolidate the whole of the group's distribution services, also transferred their railway wagons to Clarkes. According to Edmund Hann, chairman of Powell Duffryn, 'standing alone, production is quite unable to protect itself': the 1928 merger therefore conceived 'two organisations, one confining itself to efficiency in production, the other to efficiency in marketing' {*Economist* 30 Mar 1929}, with both co-ordinated and controlled by a central committee of Hann and Evan Williams of Powell Duffryn sitting with Kent and Hindley of Clarkes. Stephenson Clarke became a public company in 1933 with issued capital of £1.5 million.

Hindley was a managing director of Powell Duffryn in 1931-46, and in 1938 succeeded Sir Stephenson Kent as chairman of both Stephenson Clarke and of Maris Export & Trading. In 1935 Guest Keen & Nettlefolds merged their Welsh Associated Collieries with Powell Duffryn, and as part of the interchange of directors, Hindley sat on the GKN board for the duration of the Second World War. Apart from coal and coke, Hindley was also responsible for marketing Powell Duffryn's by-products such as Presotim wood preservative, Synthatar and Syntha coal tar products for road dressings, and PhurnoD, a smokeless manufactured fuel for domestic use. Hindley was also chairman of the Harton Coal Co, and a director of Guéret, Llewelyn & Merrett Ltd, River Lighterage Ltd and Cokemart Ltd.

In public life Hindley was Alderman for Tower Ward in the City of London in 1924-30, and was afterwards a Lieutenant for the City of London. He sat in 1924-29 on the government committee on Trade and Industry chaired by Arthur Balfour (qv). Although he was later reticent about his political sympathies, and took no Party Whip in the House of Lords, in the 1920s he was a member of the Carlton and Conservative Clubs, and was created a baronet in 1927 by Baldwin's Government.

In April 1931, at the time that he emerged as an active force in Powell Duffryn's attempts to rationalise Welsh coalmining, he was elected to the Court of the Bank of England. He also received a barony from the Labour Government in January 1931, taking the title of Hyndley. The expectation that Hyndley, as a City dignitary with many financial friends and as a coal distributor with an entrée to many great mineowners, would help Charles Bruce Gardner (qv) in his attempts, under Bank of England auspices, to rationalise Britain's heavy staple industries, led to his election as a director of the Securities Management Trust from January 1932 until April 1946. This expectation was not however justified by events, and his contribution to SMT's limited achievements was modest. He was created GBE in 1939.

In 1942, when the inadequacy of the Mines Department under war conditions compelled the Government to replace it with a Ministry of Fuel and Power, Hyndley was appointed as its first Controller General. He was a sociable and shrewd man, whose forte lay in marketing, and he had neither the detailed administrative sense nor sufficient strategic imagination for the job. There was relief, perhaps on his part too, when he was replaced in late 1943. His removal was made more palatable to him by his appointment to the London committee of the Combined Production and Resources Board, which had liaison responsibilities with the USA. For this work he received the French Légion d'Honneur and in 1947 the American Medal of Freedom with palm leaf.

Hyndley left the Court of the Bank of England, with great reluctance, in May 1945 to become chairman of the newly-established Finance Corporation for Industry. The purpose of this body stemmed from the work done in the 1930s by Charles Bruce Gardner to improve the financial facilities available for industrial investment. Hyndley however had no great impact at FCI before being appointed in 1946 as first chairman of the nationalised coal industry at a salary of £7,500. His attraction to the Labour Government was that he was a man who possessed lifelong experience as an employer in the coal industry, but as a distributor and exporter; he was not tarnished in socialist eyes as a die-hard or obscurantist coalowner. He had also been a favourite since the 1920s of Emanuel Shinwell, Labour's Minister of Fuel in 1945-47. Yet though he set higher standards of fair-dealing with the trade unions, and never let his commercial background interfere with his wish to promote the national interest under a Labour Government, he was not entirely successful as chairman of the National Coal Board. His main strengths were in maintaining good relationships both with politicians and, as far as anyone could have done, within the Board itself. He was faced with an enormous task of putting together a vast organisation and he perhaps lacked the forceful personality and analytical sharpness needed to make a strong impact. According to one friend, 'He was apt to say that his "innards" told him such and such, and those of us who were near him learnt to regard these auguries with respect' {*Times* 14 Jan 1963}.

Although the NCB was not formally established until July 1946, Hyndley and his senior colleagues began work as an organising committee in April of that year. The magnitude of the task of transferring over 800 private companies to public ownership was underestimated by Labour politicians, and Shinwell's insistence that NCB national board members should be full-time heads of its major departments soon proved the source of friction and inefficiency. As it was there were almost no managers in the coal industry with experience of running a nationwide business, and there was little understanding of national organisation. Significantly the only exceptions to this were areas where Hyndley had been involved: 'it was no accident' that NCB's marketing 'was the most efficiently run' of all its national organisation. Moreover Hyndley's own Powell Duffryn, NCB's largest constituent part, although too recent in its growth to have solved the problems of large-scale organisation, was still ahead of most other colliery companies absorbed by NCB {Chester (1975) 556}.

There were other formidable difficulties confronting Hyndley at NCB. He inherited a legacy of poor industrial relations, and an absenteeism rate which had reached 16 per cent in 1946. Hyndley however was 'a human water softener' {Dalton (1960) 66} who enjoyed good relations with the miners' leaders and reduced the traditional ill-feeling in the industry. Productivity had fallen during the war, with output per manshift dropping from 1.16 tons in 1939 to 1.03 tons in 1947. At the same time stocks were appreciably diminished in the post-war period. When NCB began operations in January 1947, it inherited a fuel crisis caused by the insufficiency of output and stocks in 1946, aggravated by transport dislocation during an exceptionally hard winter. Another major difficulty facing the Coal Board was the introduction of the five-day week, which had been virtually promised to the mineworkers by ministers before the nationalisation act was passed, and which the NCB had no option but to introduce, despite many misgivings about its financial consequences. The upshot was that on a saleable output of 184.7 million tons in 1947, NCB made colliery losses of £9.2 million and returned an overall deficit of £23.3 million. Despite the severity of the 1947 fuel crisis, Hyndley and his staff worked throughout the latter half of 1947 to improve manpower and output, and to prevent a repetition of the crisis in 1948.

During 1948 Hyndley began a re-equipment programme intended to raise output and productivity; indeed saleable output per manshift rose from 21.5 cwt in 1947 to 22.3 cwt in 1948 and 24.2 cwt in 1951. Exports and bunker coal supplies had been reduced to 5 million tons in 1947, but the improved conditions of 1948 permitted a resumption of exports, which reached 19 million tons by 1949. Hyndley's colleagues were however disturbed by internal disagreements during 1948. In May Sir Charles Reid (qv), the distinguished mining engineer whose wartime report had given the technical case for compulsory reorganisation of the industry, resigned from the NCB national board in protest at its structure, laid down by Shinwell. Reid felt that Shinwell's scheme of members with fulltime functional duties obscured managerial responsibilities and led to over-centralisation: he particularly clashed with the NCB's labour director, Ebby Edwards, previously general secretary of the National Union of Mineworkers (NUM). A major political controversy ignited, with Conservatives pressing for decentralisation, which socialists and trade unionists opposed because they feared that regional competition would lead to wage reductions.

Partly as a result of the Reid row, in 1949 the new Minister of Fuel, Hugh Gaitskell, with whom Hyndley usually dined every Monday evening, increased the maximum size of the board from nine to 12 and appointed five part-time members (of whom three were businessmen advisers, and two were trade union officials). The surpluses of £1.7 million and £9.5 million secured by NCB in 1948 and 1949 went some way to reducing the deficit of 1947; output per man year rose steadily from 263 tons in 1947 to 293 tons in 1950. Nevertheless, even at national board level, there remained sharp divisions between those such as Sir Eric Young with responsibility for coal production and those such as Ebby Edwards concerned with labour: these divisions were accentuated by Shinwell's rigid functional structure at both national and divisional board levels, and by the predominance of suspicious and embittered former NUM officials in labour and welfare management.

In Hyndley's remaining time at NCB, productivity and output continued to improve, but the national board seemed remote, somewhat directionless and demoralised. The widespread dissatisfaction was reflected by the fact that the none of the board members was reappointed at the expiry of the appointments in 1951, and only one of them wanted to be. Hyndley was succeeded as NCB chairman in July 1951 by Sir Hubert Houldsworth (qv).

Hyndley was Master of the Bakers' Company in 1944 and of the Clothworkers' Company in 1953-54. He was elevated to a viscountcy in 1948, and received an honorary doctorate from Leeds University.

Recruited to Whitehall at the age of thirty-four, when the pressure of war extremities gave many young men chances that would have been unthinkable in peacetime, his successive promotions within British coalmining in the 1940s owed more to his seniority, and his familiarity in official and political circles, than to inherent suitability. As one colleague at NCB concluded, 'Hyndley was a most likeable man, friendly, experienced and broadminded, but lacking in drive', who should have been called 'Lord Kindly' {Citrine (1967) 248}.

Hyndley married in 1909, at Darlington, Vera, elder daughter of James Westoll, of Coniscliffe Hall, County Durham, his first chief at Murton

HINDLEY John Scott

Colliery. They had a son, who died young, and two daughters. He died on 5 January 1963, when his hereditary titles became extinct. He left £241,320 gross.

JENNY DAVENPORT

Sources:

Unpublished

National Coal Board Annual Reports 1946-51.

Information from Dr Edgar Jones, the Bank of England and the National Coal Board.

Published

Sir Norman Chester, *The Nationalisation of British Industry 1945-51* (HMSO, 1975).

Lord Citrine, *Two Careers* (Hutchinson, 1967).

Colliery Yearbook and Coal Trades Directory 1933.

Complete Peerage.

Crockfords.

Edward Hugh J N Dalton, *The Fateful Years* (Muller, 1957).

—, *High Tide and after* (Muller, 1960).

DNB.

Economist 30 Mar 1929.

Charles G Falkner, *The Book of Records of Weymouth College* (Manchester: Johnson, 1923).

Times 7, 9, 10, 14 Jan 1963.

Philip Williams, *Hugh Gaitskell* (Cape, 1979).

— (ed), *Diaries of Hugh Gaitskell 1945-56* (Cape, 1983).

Sir Benjamin Hingley, 1901 by Sir Arthur Stockdate Hope (courtesy of Dudley Art Gallery).

HINGLEY, Sir Benjamin

(1830-1905)

Chain and anchor manufacturer, iron and coal master

Benjamin Hingley was born at Cradley, Worcestershire on 11 September 1830, the third and youngest surviving son of Noah Hingley (1795-1877) and his first wife Sarah (d 1832), daughter of Noah Willett of nearby Kingswinford. He was educated at Halesowen Grammar School.

Noah Hingley was a pioneer in the production of chain cables and anchors in the Black Country — a district far from the sea but endowed with skilled metalworkers and high-quality wrought iron. Inspired by the demands of the port of Liverpool during journeys there on behalf of the family's modest business in small chains and nails, Noah started to produce large chains at Cradley in 1820. Twenty-five years later he opened a larger factory at Netherton, an outlying district of Dudley; by 1848 he was also successfully making anchors there. Noah's desire to ensure regular supplies of suitable raw materials prompted him, from the early 1850s, to raise his own coal and make his own iron. Soon the business, employing about 2,000 men, was a major producer of these staples as well as the dominant force in the district's increasingly important anchor and large chain trades. Having survived the panics of 1857 and 1866, Hingley made huge profits during the boom of the early 1870s.

Benjamin was not content to preside over his father's achievements. By 1890 the son had more than doubled the firm's 1875 valuation. Indeed, after entering the business at the age of fifteen, Benjamin had done much to advance its continuing rapid growth during his father's later years. At first Benjamin concentrated on clerical tasks and on sales expeditions at home and abroad. Nevertheless, he probably played an important part in the firm's iron and coal developments of the 1850s. In any event, after his brother Hezekiah (b 1825) died in 1865, Benjamin rather than his surviving brother Samuel (1829-1901) became effective head of the firm. In a programme of 'continuous expansion' {*Dudley Herald* 20 May 1905}, Benjamin improved the main factory at Netherton, acquired additional ironworks nearby at Old Hill and Harts Hill, sank new collieries and opened iron mines. By the 1890s the business had approximately 3,000 employees and an annual capacity of 40,000 tons of chains and anchors.

This energetic development brought monetary rewards. True, there were awkward periods during the decade-and-a-half of generally poor trade that the Black Country experienced from the mid-1870s. Yet Hingley's relatively sophisticated concerns recovered quickly from these setbacks and participated fully in the subsequent long-term regional revival. From the late 1880s the business also benefited from booming demand for British large-scale chains and anchors. In the typical year of 1896 the profits of N Hingley & Sons — financially separate from the substantial operations at Harts Hill — represented 11.1 per cent of paid-up capital.

Moreover, returns would have been much higher had not persistent improvements been 'mainly constructed out of revenue' {Dudley Library, Hingley MS, Valuations by Alexander Smith, 1890}. These proceeds remained within the family during Benjamin Hingley's lifetime. In 1890 the main business became a limited company. Yet Sir Benjamin (a baronet from 1893) held more than half the shares. The two nephews with whom he worked closely, his eventual successors (Sir) George Benjamin Hingley (b 1850) and Henry Montague Hingley (1854-1908), controlled nearly all the rest. Between 1892 and 1904 dividends averaged 4 per cent.

Installation of appropriate equipment helped to produce this prosperity. Like his father, Benjamin lacked a specialised technical education. Yet Noah had installed the first steam hammer in the Midlands, and Benjamin's blast furnaces incorporated 'the most approved and modern construction' {ibid}, making the firm's Netherton Crown Brand 'among the very best irons made' {Curzon (1883) 51}. By 1914 the chain works used electrical welding. Nevertheless, the firm prized reliable products and highly skilled workmen more than the latest cost-cutting innovations.

The management styles of Noah and Benjamin did much to shape the firm. Although the son had the more polished and sophisticated personality, both were hard-working, forceful and blunt. Each long played a major part in daily operations as well as in general strategy. However, like his father, Benjamin wisely delegated foreign travel and, eventually, routine details of business to the next generation. After Sir George's death in 1918 the family role in the company, already eroded since Sir Benjamin's time, dwindled to insignificance. The firm's chain and anchor trade never regained its pre-1914 preeminence in world markets. Nevertheless, through further diversification within metalworking and repeated amalgamations the firm has survived as the core of Wright Hingley Ltd.

Relatively little of the Hingleys' profits were diverted to conspicuous consumption. In the early 1870s Noah owned only two acres in Cradley where the family's residence, Hatherton Lodge, was situated. Sir Benjamin joined a London club and stayed in the Grand Hotel there but acquired neither a metropolitan home nor a substantial rural property. Sir George, having lived near Halesowen for many years, obtained a more substantial estate in rural Worcestershire but was 'obsessed with business' {Dudley Chronicle 25 Aug 1918} rather than with genteel leisure. Thus, especially during Sir Benjamin's later years, when the daily affairs of the well-established business could be left to reliable family subordinates, the Hingleys retained the resources and time for extensive involvements outside the firm.

Few of these commitments concerned other companies, though Noah held shares in a local railway and a Birmingham bank and Benjamin was director of a local insurance firm as well as chairman of two gas companies in the district. More importantly, as the head of a firm 'affecting the prosperity of a wide area' {Wolverhampton Chronicle 17 May 1905}, and as 'one of the best known men on 'Change in Birmingham' {Birmingham Daily Mail 15 May 1905}, Benjamin played a major part in various employers' organisations. At the national level, he was vice-president of the Iron and Steel Institute and president both of the Mining Association of Great Britain and of the British Iron Trade Association. These honours

Sir Benjamin Hingley —
chainmakers at N Hingley Ltd,
Netherton, ca 1910 (courtesy of
Dudley Public Libraries).

largely resulted from Hingley's most important position — chairman of the South Staffordshire and East Worcestershire Ironmasters Association from 1881 until his death. Hingley frequently served as the trade's official spokesman. Yet he was not a mere mouthpiece: on one occasion Hingley's preference on prices prevailed over those of all the other quality ironmakers.

Aided by experience in his own firm, Sir Benjamin also exerted considerable influence on the Black Country's industrial relations. Noah's provision of employment during slumps, his simple manners, and his elaborate annual treats had made him a generally popular employer. Known as 'Ben' to many workmen, Sir Benjamin provided pensions and became well known for superior working conditions and wages. He also learned to cope with the emerging unions in the local chain, coal and iron trades.

The rise of viable trade unionism, in a district threatened by economic decline, persuaded influential Black Country employers to negotiate with the men's representatives through organisations which presupposed that wages should fluctuate with selling prices. Sir Benjamin became a prominent member of the troubled Coal Trade Wages Board. More significantly, as long-time chairman of the area's ironmasters, Hingley also held the chair of the South Staffordshire Mill and Forge Wages Board (later the Midland Iron and Steel Wages Board). Hingley helped to revive the organisation in 1876 and became a crucial figure in its delicate negotiations thereafter. He defended the board as 'the most satisfactory and only feasible means for peaceably arranging, and with fairness to both sides, the inevitable fluctuations of wages' {*PP* (1892) C 6795-IV, 348}. Although at times both sides refused to accept the organisation's decisions, strikes and lockouts were virtually unknown during Hingley's quarter-century as chairman. Structural forces underpinned this record, and Hingley once caused controversy by attempting to remodel the board's

The Anchor for the Titanic *being carried from Hingley's works, Netherton, 1912 (Dudley Public Libraries).*

'sliding scale' in the employers' favour. Nonetheless, as the union leaders' initiative in presenting the chairman with his portrait suggests, Sir Benjamin's reputation for fairness and his unassuming manner did much to avoid open conflicts.

Hingley was better suited to industrial conciliation than his more aloof colleague Sir Alfred Hickman (qv), but Sir Benjamin was less well-adapted to party politics. The need to choose sides caused him constant difficulties as MP for North Worcestershire from 1885 to 1895. At the outset Hingley — whose father had fought Dudley for the Tories in 1874 — lamely told local Liberals that 'after due consideration he had decided to adhere to Liberal principles' {*Dudley Herald* 6 June 1885}. Benjamin's tolerant Anglicanism contributed to his political dilemma, which was compounded by the Home Rule issue. Having abstained in the crucial division in 1886, Benjamin switched from support to opposition in the subsequent election when another popular manufacturer threatened to challenge him. Hingley's return to the Liberal fold during the subsequent parliament helped him to obtain his title from Gladstone's ensuing Government. Yet Sir Benjamin's retirement at the next election, partly the result of temporary ill health, also reflected increasingly sharp differences of opinion with local Liberal activists. By the turn of the century Hingley's politics were 'somewhat hazy' {*Dudley Chronicle* 25 Aug 1918}. This intermediate position, which suited his role as local industrial statesman, enabled him to be mourned, unusually, by both Liberal and Unionist organisations on his death.

Although neither a frequent nor a particularly able speaker in the Commons, Hingley distinguished himself on commercial questions where partisanship could be set aside. He was a respected member of various committees, notably of an inquiry into Admiralty contracts which enhanced the position of high-class suppliers like his own family firm. Although he supported Hickman's crusade for cheaper transport rates, Hingley never abandoned free trade, a creed which suited his chain, though not his iron, interests. On social issues Sir Benjamin's positions were constrained by his defence of employers' rights. A resolute opponent of the statutory eight-hour day for miners, he condemned the 1897 workmen's compensation bill as a 'revolutionary and communistic' measure {Staffordshire RO, D888/1, 116}. Yet Hingley backed better ventilation in mines, and he fought against abuses by small chainmasters. Such views boosted Hingley's standing with a largely working-class electorate and enabled him to retain some support from organised labour.

Nevertheless, Benjamin's three electoral victories — by overwhelming if declining margins — stemmed as much from his popularity as a major, conciliatory employer as from his limited political progressivism. Public impressions both of father and son were enhanced by the spectacular nature of their products and their widely publicised 'humble' origins. Noah used appeals to workmen's pride, processions by employees, and his position as 'probably the most popular man in the borough' {*Dudley Herald* 9 May 1874} to erode the Liberal majority during his candidature. Benjamin's campaigns, though more subtle, had a similar thrust. As a personable local magnate, Benjamin won 'a great proportion of votes', especially in the area near the family works, which his carpetbagging successor as Liberal candidate lost {*Dudley Herald* 27 July 1895}.

Such popularity was better suited to philanthropy and local government than to partisan politics. Benjamin, like Noah, contributed to Nonconformist as well as Anglican causes. In the secular sphere Benjamin, in particular, was 'connected with an exceedingly large number of institutions and associations' {*Dudley Herald* 20 May 1905}. He served on the committee of Dudley's dispensary, for example, and contributed £500 to Birmingham University. Benjamin, like his father, was an active JP for Staffordshire, Worcestershire and Dudley. In addition, Benjamin was High Sheriff and a DL of Worcestershire as well as a Staffordshire alderman. In municipal government their careers diverged even more. One of Dudley's town fathers, Noah was a Guardian and a controversial member of the School Board as well as a charter councillor, alderman and mayor. Benjamin avoided the disputes of the Poor Law and the Education Acts. In municipal affairs he promoted moderate social reform: while his father had been a rate-cutter, Benjamin backed sanitary schemes and an art gallery. During two terms as mayor the son's principal achievements — smoothing relations with the Second Earl of Dudley and helping to make the town a county borough — reflected the Hingleys' increasing wealth and connections.

Wide-ranging leadership enabled Sir Benjamin, like his father, to command 'an exceptional measure of popularity in his own district' {*Birmingham Gazette & Express* 15 Jan 1908}. Benjamin's lesser partisanship and greater emphasis on public service made him 'loved as well as respected' {*World* 27 Aug 1918}. Thousands of working people attended the funerals of each.

Benjamin Hingley provides a classic instance of a second-generation entrepreneur who significantly expanded the civic involvement as well as the business of a highly successful father. Sir Benjamin differed from most Black Country businessmen in heading a firm which profited directly from the rapid late nineteenth century growth of Britain's ties to the international economy. Yet Hingley was an influential member of the

Black Country's elites, in which his focus on the district complemented the firmer national connections of Sir Alfred Hickman and the more exclusively town-centred work of men like Reuben Farley (qv).

Sir Benjamin Hingley never married. He died at Cradley on 13 May 1905, two days after falling ill at a meeting of the Iron and Steel Institute, and left an estate of £158,696 gross.

RICHARD TRAINOR

Writings:

PP, HC 1881 (374) XIII, SC Charges for the Conveyance of Goods on Railways and Canals.

PP, HC 1889 (165) XIII, SC HL on the Sweating System.

PP, HC 1890-91 (394) XIV, Joint SC Railway Rates and Charges.

PP, RC Labour, Group A (1892) C 6795-IV.

Sources:

Unpublished

Dudley and District Chamber of Commerce, Chamber MS.

Dudley Library, Newspaper Cuttings; N Hingley & Sons Ltd MS.

Staffordshire RO, South Staffordshire Ironmasters Association MS, D888.

C Reg: N Hingley & Sons Ltd (32352).

PrC; Will.

Eric Taylor, 'The Working Class Movement in the Black Country 1863-1914' (Keele PhD, 1974).

Richard H Trainor, 'Authority and Social Structure in an Industrialised Area: A Study of Three Black Country Towns, 1840-1890' (Oxford DPhil, 1981).

Published

George C Allen, *The Industrial Development of Birmingham and the Black Country 1860-1927* (George Allen & Unwin, 1929).

Birmingham Daily Gazette 15 May 1905.

Birmingham Daily Mail 15 May 1905.

Birmingham Dispatch 20 Aug 1918.

Birmingham Gazette & Express 15 Jan 1908.

Birmingham Mail 20 Aug 1918.

E Blocksidge, *Dudley Almanac 1906* (Dudley, the author, 1905).

Burke's Peerage & Baronetage 1900, 1908.

James C Carr and Walter Taplin, *History of the British Steel Industry* (Oxford: Basil Blackwell, 1962).

William D Curzon, *The Manufacturing Industries of Worcestershire* (np, 1883).

Directory of Directors 1880-1940 *passim*.

DNB.

Dudley Chronicle 25, 31 Aug 1918.

Dudley Herald 24 Sept 1870, 9, 16, 23 May 1874, 27 Oct, 3 Nov 1877, 6 June 1885, 15 June, 19 Oct, 9 Nov 1889, 8, 15 Feb, 23 Aug 1890, 28 Feb 1891, 10 June 1893, 6, 13, 27 July 1895, 20, 27 May 1905, 24 Aug 1918.

Express & Star (Wolverhampton) 25 Sept 1962.

Mark H W Fletcher, *Netherton: Edward I to Edward VIII* (Dudley: Dudley Public Libraries, 1969).

Ernest Gaskell, *Worcestershire Leaders Social and Political* (Queenhithe, 1908).

Journal of the Iron and Steel Institute 67 (1905).

Percy Jump, *Historical Notes on Chains and Chain-making* (Stourbridge: Mark & Moody, 1929).

Midland Counties Express (Wolverhampton) 16 May, 13 June 1874.

Norman Mutton, 'The Marked Bar Association: Price Regulation in the Black Country Wrought-Iron Trade' *West Midlands Studies* 9 (1976).

PD, 3rd and 4th ser, 1885-1895.

PP, Owners of Land, 1872-73 (1874) C 1097.

PP, HC 1886 (192) VIII, SC Employers Liability Act Amendment Bill.

PP, Committee on the System of Purchase and Contract in the Navy (1887) C 4987.

PP, HC 1888 (286) XVII, SC Railway and Canal Traffic Bill.

PP, HC 1888 (385) XCI, Report Relating to Nail Makers and Small Chain Makers.

J H Porter, 'Management, Competition and Industrial Relations: the Midlands Manufactured Iron Trade 1873-1914' *Business History* 11 (1969).

Ryland's Iron, Steel, Tin-Plate, Coal, Engineering & Allied Trades Directory 1899.

Stock Exchange Year-Book 1901, 1911.

Stock Exchange Official Year-Book 1935.

Eric Taylor, *The Better Temper: A Commemorative History of the Midland Iron and Steel Wages Board 1876-1976* (Iron and Steel Trades Confederation, 1976).

Times 15 May 1905.

Thomas W Traill, *Chain Cables and Chain* (Crosby & Lockwood, 1885).

VCH Staffordshire 2.

VCH Worcestershire 2.

West Bromwich Weekly News 20 May 1905.

William R Williams, *The Parliamentary History of the County of Worcester* (Hereford, the author, 1897).

Wolverhampton Chronicle 24 Oct 1877, 17 May 1905.

Worcester Advertiser 24 Aug 1918.

World 27 Aug 1918.

WWMP.

WWW.

HINTON, Christopher

Lord Hinton of Bankside

(1901-1983)

Nuclear engineer

Sir Christopher Hinton in front of sphere at Dounreay (courtesy of the United Kingdom Energy Authority).

Christopher Hinton was born at Tisbury, Wiltshire, on 12 May 1901, the son of Frederick Henry Hinton and Kate née Christopher, both of Dorset. His father was master of the tiny boys' school (in 1977 Lord Hinton bought the building for a community centre in memory of his parents). He had an elder sister and younger brother. All four grandparents had been school teachers and his mother a children's nurse. In 1907 his father became head of a much larger school in Chippenham which Hinton attended before going to Chippenham Secondary (later Grammar) School.

Pushed by his over-stern father, he performed precociously at primary school but not conspicuously well at secondary school until his last year. He was devoted to his mother but inherited her reserve which inhibited close friendships. Later, strong mutual affection developed with his father who imparted scholarly interest in history and architecture.

In 1917 Hinton chose as his career engineering; it offered better prospects than any other which the family, supporting his sister at university, could afford. He was first apprenticed without premium to a small firm, Andrew Barclay, of Kilmarnock, but, homesick, he left after a few months. He moved to a premium apprenticeship with the Great Western Railway at Swindon which was one of the best British engineering training schools. He never regretted the initial wearisome repetitive work which inculcated sensitivity to the labour problems of line production. Thereafter he went through every part of the work in the millwrights' shop, the gas engine power house, the tool room, the engine erection shops, the test house, and the drawing office. The tribute of a skilled fitter 'you're the best craft apprentice I've ever had working with me' gave him as much pleasure as his later first class degree.

Hinton took evening classes at Swindon Technical College and studied five hours a day (on top of a fifty-four — later forty-seven — hour week). After distinguished examination results he won in 1923 a three-year scholarship at Trinity College, Cambridge, awarded by the Institution of Mechanical Engineers. These were vintage years of the Cambridge Engineering School with outstanding teachers like Charles Inglis especially and also David Pye and William Farren. Hinton, again stretching himself to the limit, gained a first class degree in the mechanical sciences tripos after two years and spent his third year in research under Inglis. He won university and college awards. At twenty-five, after nine years' training and education, he had acquired a perfect blend of practical and theoretical training, so much so that he was a 'difficult case' to place.

However, Brunner Mond, then one of the three biggest UK chemical firms and soon to become the Alkali Group of the new creation Imperial Chemical Industries (ICI), recruited Hinton. The Cheshire firm was prosperous, with an outstanding research department, but its engineering was fossilised. They quickly recognised Hinton's ability, making him deputy chief engineer at the early age of twenty-seven and chief engineer at twenty-nine. He mastered at first hand and in great detail all areas of the work, including the equipment of laboratories, the provision of instruments, programming, inspection and construction departments, plant operation, design, feasibility studies for big new plants, and the structural problems of the brine fields.

At the time that Hinton became chief engineer, engineers were regarded as second class citizens. He achieved his aim: that the engineering department should have the same status as management and research and play an equal part with them in organising and determining the course of development. When the slump began late in 1930 he was told to sack half his staff: a heart-breaking job which nevertheless enabled him to create an efficient organisation. Moreover, no new work could be put in hand unless it showed a gross return of 33.3 per cent; Hinton found such work in mechanical handling, and fuel economy through the use of high pressure steam. He also standardised stores throughout ICI and greatly advanced welding techniques, where Britain lagged behind Europe.

The engineering department became an extremely efficient and economical organisation with great authority and systems of cost control and programming ahead of their time. Yet although it was usual for chief engineers to be delegate-directors on the 'Group' (ie divisional) board it was nine years before this happened to Hinton. His actions were never determined by popularity.

During rearmament Hinton built chemical plants for war purposes. In 1940 he became a Director of ordnance factory construction at the Ministry of Supply and in 1941 transferred to the explosive filling factories, where such chaos reigned that there was danger of an ammunition shortage scandal similar to that of the First World War. Hinton's system and methods of organisation and programming averted the danger and met swiftly-changing weapon demands smoothly and quickly. In 1943 he became Deputy Director General of the explosive-filling factories. His wartime base was in London away from his family. He shared a flat with two colleagues who had come with him from ICI but when they went north he slept, in the flying bomb period of 1944-45, in the Ministry air raid basement. This, plus exhaustion, led him to the verge of breakdown, a memory which haunted him for the rest of his working life, so that he avoided travelling alone.

Hinton returned only fleetingly to ICI, where there was now no niche for him. Henceforth his work was exclusively in the public sector. When the Government decided, immediately the war ended, to establish urgently a native atomic energy project they hoped ICI, who had been deeply involved in the wartime project, would be a main contractor for the production side. ICI refused, said it should be a government project and suggested that Hinton be asked to take charge. He accepted at the end of 1945 and chose Risley near Warrington as his headquarters. His salary was £2,500 (£500 less than at ICI). He arrived on the virgin site in February 1946 with six of his old ICI and filling factory colleagues, including his London flatmates.

From this tiny nucleus grew the Industrial Group of the British atomic project: the heroic phase of Hinton's career. The Government regarded the production of fissile material as supremely important for the national interest. The reasons were mixed: political status vis á vis the USA; the very probable need for bombs; the future requirements for industrial power; and general research and development. Hinton assumed his task was to produce fissile material, as soon as possible, for bombs. He did not know until twenty-five years later that a decision to make them was not taken until January 1947. The fissile material was to be first plutonium and then, also, uranium 235. This meant a commitment to four very different types of plant: nuclear reactors — an experimental one at Harwell and two plutonium producing reactors at Windscale in Cumberland; a plant at Springfields, near Preston, to produce fuel rods all the way from uranium ore; a chemical plant to separate plutonium and associated fabrication plants at Windscale; a gaseous diffusion plant at Capenhurst, Cheshire to produce uranium 235. Hinton was especially skilled in site selection; he chose the sites and designed the layout himself on a drawing board in his office.

Only one of Hinton's original group had worked in the wartime atomic project. Small groups of British scientists and engineers had indeed done important work on many, though not all, of the processes involved in producing plutonium and U 235 and their knowledge was available. None of them had access to the American large-scale production plants and in 1946 the United States passed the McMahon Act which made illegal the transfer of any such knowledge to Britain. After the war it was the function of Harwell under John Cockcroft to supply Hinton with research information, while ICI also did valuable research for him. These two men, with William Penney, who was in charge of bomb fabrication, worked under Lord Portal (formerly Chief of the Air Staff) as Controller within the Ministry of Supply.

Teamwork was the basis of Hinton's system but he himself played a crucial part in all the phases and plants of the industrial project: programming, site selection, plant design, factory management. His intellect, rapier mind and creativity, allied with the engineering and managerial skills he had acquired in the previous fifteen years, combined to produce a superb performance within the limits of Britain's heavily strained post-war economy, most notably in the face of the shortage of good engineers. In the early years he was ubiquitous — leaning over draughtsmen's shoulders, his thin, tall (six feet six inches) figure striding round construction sites, attending meetings in Harwell or London. He

Dounreay experimental reactor establishment (courtesy of the United Kingdom Energy Authority).

was perhaps most closely involved in the design of one of the most successful plants, for the separation of plutonium. Although financial limits were not tight for so urgent a project, he kept firmly to his interpretation of the art of engineering: finding the cheapest and simplest way of producing the results required. All the plants were built to the programmed time and cost; indeed the cost of the very difficult diffusion plant was £750,000 less than the financial sanction. All of them fulfilled the task set for them, although in 1957 both the Windscale reactors were closed down after one of them caught fire.

The first British bomb was tested in October 1952. Even in the earliest days Hinton had wished to develop nuclear power as well but Risley's military load did not permit this and Harwell pursued power research. There was general agreement on the priority of fast breeder reactors and when Risley had spare capacity in 1952 they became responsible for designing and building an experimental reactor (Dounreay). But thermal reactors were also needed both to produce materials for nuclear weapons and as an immediate step towards nuclear power. Among the many possible types of natural uranium reactors the choice finally fell in 1953 on a Harwell pressurised gas-cooled design, principally because it would best meet big new demands for military plutonium, producing power as a by-product.

This became Calder Hall, always ascribed to Hinton as the first nuclear reactor to feed power into a national grid, and thus giving Britain a world lead when the Queen opened it in 1956. In fact he was less intimately connected with it than with the other plants. But it was the team he had created which built Calder faultlessly to limits of time and cost, and ensured its excellent operating record. When Calder opened, Britain had already, in 1955, announced a first civil nuclear power programme of a modest, manageable size, based on Calder-type reactors initially, but with an open mind about future reactors. These reactors were to be built by consortia of private firms.

Yet this moment of triumph for Hinton soon turned to ashes. In 1954 atomic energy had been transferred from the Ministry of Supply to the quasi-independent Atomic Energy Authority, a reorganisation for which Hinton had little enthusiasm and which, he found, hindered rather than helped him. He was the Authority Member for Engineering and Production. The strain on him greatly increased, especially as he was in great demand as a lecturer — another skill in which he excelled. In 1956, now at the end of his tether, he went on six months' leave, but even this centred round a major, hardworking and triumphant visit to Japan which led to the ordering of a British nuclear reactor. When he returned to England he found to his horror that, in his absence, a new greatly enlarged nuclear power programme had been devised: in 1957 the trebling of the programme was announced.

There had been increasing friction between Hinton and the other members of the Authority on various policy issues, and Hinton feared the effects of the general nuclear euphoria which he could not control. His nervous exhaustion had also made relations with some of his staff increasingly difficult. He had been a demanding master, expecting and therefore getting very high standards. He had given talent every opportunity to rise. He rarely praised people, and could indeed be woundingly scathing, yet morale was very high because everyone knew the organisation and achievement were superb. But Hinton's growing abrasiveness had become harder to bear. His closest friendship had been with Leonard Owen, his deputy and ally in ICI and in the war, and this too was now wrecked. Hinton suspected Owen of disloyalty in the discussions of reorganisation at Risley and the possible move of Hinton to London as a functional board member.

In 1956 the Government had decided to replace the Central Electricity Authority with a Central Electricity Generating Board which would supply electricity in bulk to Area Boards for retailing and in 1957 Hinton accepted the invitation to be its first chairman, at a salary of £10,000. This vast enterprise, with an annual income of £600 million, and annual capital expenditure of £400 million, was nevertheless an anti-climax for Hinton. Indeed he felt that he failed there because as chairman, rather than board member for engineering, he could not succeed in building a strong engineering design and construction department in a board whose success depended on engineering. Hinton believed this weakness led to late commissioning and low availability of plant, and contributed to gross overestimation of demand. The engineering of transmission, however, was excellent. One of Hinton's achievements at the CEGB was to develop its research and he also spent much time on questions of environment and amenity. Meanwhile he asked the right, often quite new, questions about policy, in particular about nuclear power policy — about the size of the nuclear power programme, the type of reactor to be pursued and the choice of consortia to build the reactors. At last, in 1960, he succeeded in reducing the programme to the size he had recommended in 1956. In a famous Axel Johnson lecture in March 1957 he had advocated British concentration on gas-cooled reactors, but he had envisaged that licences might be negotiated with Canadians and Americans if at any stage heavy or light water reactors were found to have the advantage. At the CEGB he investigated the possibilities of these water reactors, and when tenders went out in 1964 for the first of a new, more powerful, generation of reactors (Dungeness B), invitations were for light water, as well as gas-cooled, reactors. The contract for Dungeness B was not placed until after Hinton retired. In 1963 he had been bitterly criticised in the House of Lords and the press for denying a contract for an earlier reactor to the firm which was later awarded the Dungeness B contract.

There were nuclear traumas during this period which, quite wrongly, suggested to some that Hinton had turned against nuclear power. His flexibility and his insistence on basing atomic, like other judgements, on engineering and economic considerations rather than on questions of prestige, were deeply rooted in his mind. Despite his fierce reputation, his weakness at the CEGB was to be insufficiently, rather than excessively, ruthless.

Hinton retired from the CEGB at the end of 1964 with a life peerage, and he himself called his subsequent phase that of 'The Odd Job Man'. The Government immediately asked him to investigate the co-ordination of transport — ten months' work which was pigeonholed. He had already become chairman of the International Executive Committee of the World Energy Conference in 1962, an office that lasted until 1968, and later he again became deeply involved in the Conference. He also became an adviser to the World Bank, which led to fruitful visits to Turkey, Brazil, Taiwan, East Africa and Pakistan, and he studied the prospects of nuclear power in developing countries for the Bank. His wife's illness ended such commitment. In 1966-67 he was president of the Institution of Mechanical Engineers and from 1976 president of both the Council of Engineering Institutions and of the new Fellowship of Engineering, an élite body on Royal Society lines. From 1972 he was active in the House of Lords on Select Committees to consider clauses in private bills, and on Sub-committees scrutinising EEC directives on transport, research, energy and the environment. He served with great distinction as the first Chancellor of the new Bath University, 1966-80.

Lady Hinton died suddenly in 1973 and Hinton's increasing lameness and trouble with his vocal chords — both arising from mishaps on his trips abroad — made his life restricted and lonely. He was unable to walk the countryside, formerly his main recreation. Retirement had not brought some of the employments he would have welcomed. For example, no large engineering firm offered him a directorship. Disappointment was at least mitigated by the increasing and general recognition that he was one of Britain's relatively few truly great engineers. One of his great pleasures arose from his deputy chairmanship, from retirement to his death, of the generating industry's research council. He made frequent visits to the laboratories, always learning, always teaching. The staff loved him and on his birthday in May 1983 held a party for him. He was in splendid form and blew out the 82 candles himself. The following weekend he had a fall which led to his death.

Apart from the Order of Merit in 1976 (a rare honour for an industrialist or engineer), and his peerage in 1964, his most notable honours were a knighthood, 1951, KBE, 1957, FRS, 1954, member of the Imperial Order of the Rising Sun (Japan), 1966. He held honorary fellowships of Trinity College, Cambridge, of all the engineering institutions, and honorary degrees from the universities of Bath, Cambridge, Durham, Edinburgh,

Liverpool, London, Oxford and Southampton. He received the Albert medal (Royal Society of Arts), Melchett medal (Institute of Fuel), Glazebrook medal and prize, Rumford medal (Royal Society), Axel Johnson prize (Royal Swedish Academy of Engineering), Wilhelm Exner medal (Österreichischer Gewerberein), Castner medal (Society of Chemical Industries), and the James Watt International medal (Institution of Mechanical Engineers). He was an honorary member of the American Society of Mechanical Engineers and Foreign Associate of the American Academy of Engineering.

In 1931, in the face of snobbery in the higher reaches of ICI, Hinton married Lillian Boyer, head of the tracing office, the daughter of Thomas Boyer, a powerhouse operator. Their only child Susan (who married the son of Sir Charles Mole, Director-General of the Ministry of Works) was born in 1932. Lord Hinton died on 22 June 1983.

MARGARET GOWING

Writings:

The Future of Nuclear Power (Stockholm: Ingeniörsvetenkapsakademien, 1957).

The ABC of Atomic Energy (BBC, 1958).

Engineers and Engineering (Oxford: Oxford University Press, 1970).

Heavy Current Electricity in the United Kingdom (Oxford: Pergamon, 1979).

Some Speeches of a Chancellor (Bath University Press, 1981).

Hinton's papers, including a copy of his typed memoirs and a collection of his lectures and articles, were bequeathed to the Institution of Mechanical Engineers.

Sources:

Unpublished

BCe.

MCe.

Published

Margaret Gowing, *Independence and Deterrence* 1. *Policy Making* 2. *Policy Execution* (2 vols, Macmillan, 1974).

Leslie Hannah, *Engineers, Managers and Politicians* (Macmillan, 1982).

Times 23, 29 June 1983.

WW 1982.

Sir Hugo Hirst (courtesy of the Electricity Council).

HIRST, Hugo

Lord Hirst

(1863-1943)

Electrical engineering entrepreneur

Hugo Hirst (formerly Hirsch) was born at Altenstadt, near Munich, on 26 November 1863, son of Emanuel Hirsch, a distiller. Around 1870 his family moved to Munich, where he was educated, latterly specialising in chemistry. His earliest memories were of 'the young men who were wounded and belonged to our beaten army' in the Prussian-Bavarian war of 1866, 'swearing and using hateful expressions whenever the name Prussia was mentioned', and in 1880 the effects of 'Prussian militarism and discipline' in his school and his father's factory prompted him to emigrate to London. His uncle, Dr Henry Dick, who had fled from Germany in 1848, was a medical consultant in Wimpole Street, and 'an enthusiast of British institutions, British character and British freedom'. Dick convinced Hirst of 'the ever-narrowing opportunities to individuals remaining in Germany who were provided ... with new blinkers by any arrogant and overbearing Prussian system, killing all individuality and turning everybody into an invisible part of a gigantic machine of State' {BLPES, TC6, 1/15, Hugo Hirst to Edward Hirst, 23 Oct 1915}.

In 1880 Hirst became a clerk in a London shipping office where his knowledge of languages, shorthand and Morse code led to his promotion as amanuensis to the head of the firm, but without extra pay. However, his fellow clerks grew jealous that he was taking work over their heads, and made his life so unhappy that he left to become private secretary to Mr Volckmar, managing director of the Electric Power Storage Co, London, manufacturers of secondary batteries. In 1884 he was dismissed, following a financial crisis and reorganisation of the company, and agreed to go to Australia as salesman for the Manchester Gas Ignition Co. At the last moment, following the Australian land crash, he refused to sail, and instead opened a shop in Queen Victoria Street, London, for the Manchester firm, selling electric bells, medical coils, gas-igniters and similar items. He was paid only a small salary, but with a share in the profits, and had a hard time until 1886 combining the duties of engineer, showman and salesman.

By this time he had appreciated the great waste and expense in electrical engineering entailed by each electrical engineering firm making and installing its own accessories, such as switches, lamp-holders and dynamos. He saw the need for a centralised supplier of such accessories, and in 1886 in association with his fellow Bavarian, Gustav Byng, formerly Binswanger (1855-1910), he began trying to meet this need. He approached pottery-makers to make china-base switches, brass-founders to standardise galleries for lampshades, glassmakers for shades, and other suppliers. The industry was so undeveloped that in some cases he had to invent the accessories required, and he also had to surmount the bitter opposition of established electrical engineers to his scheme of centralised supply. In 1887 Hirst produced the first complete electrical catalogue in Britain, and around this time he and Byng formed the unincorporated General Electric Apparatus Co based in the City of London.

In 1888 Hirst's old employers, the Gas Igniting Co, went bankrupt, and he and Byng bought their small factory in Chapel Street, Manchester, employing 300-400 men to make telephones, electric-bell indicators, cutouts, wood casing and other articles. In the following year they registered the General Electric Co as a private limited liability company, in which the capital of £60,000 was divided equally between the Byng family and a financier called Newgass.

The Edison and Swan lamp patents expired in 1893, and in that year, at Hirst's instigation, GEC opened the Robertson Lamp Works, producing the superior new carbon filament patented by C J Robertson. This was the first British lamp factory outside the Ediswan monopoly. All the glass bulbs for these lamps had to be imported from Germany, and in order to break the high prices charged by the German ring, GEC next bought glassworks at Lemington-on-Tyne to ensure a cheap bulb supply. This glassworks faced great difficulties, including the hostility and restrictive practices of the reactionary Glassblowers' Union, but was an eventual success. Around 1895, in response to German competition, GEC opened the Ileone Works in Birmingham for brasswork and electric light fittings, and later a factory at Salford for making instruments. In 1895-96 Hirst obtained from the Board of Trade a compulsory licence to make the first multi-phase machinery in Britain under the Tesla patents, which enabled electricity to be brought cheaply to rural areas. He believed that their success in this line compelled Westinghouse and General Electric of the USA, and Siemens of Germany, to open British factories. Using the multi-phase system Hirst won his first South African contract, worth £68,000, at this time.

Gustav Byng was an ill and timid man, who almost resented Hirst's energy and enterprise, and GEC's expansion was achieved despite Byng's periodic and fierce rows with Hirst. It was doubtless with knowledge of these tensions that Rathenau and Deutsch of AEG unsuccessfully tried to recruit Hirst in the 1890s as director of AEG responsible for business within the British Empire.

In 1900 GEC was floated as a public company capitalised at £85,000, and 42 acres of land were bought at Witton near Birmingham. Their profits had risen from £16,000 for 1892-94, £20,000 in 1895 to £77,000 (before interest) for the year to March 1900. Hirst originally conceived Witton as a giant works 'covering every phase of electrical production' as in Germany and the USA, but finally concluded 'that under British conditions, where different types of production had become located in certain parts of the country, and specialised skill had become almost hereditary in particular areas, better results could be obtained by a separation of manufacturing facilities' {Whyte (1930) 50}. Instead Witton concentrated on dynamos, motors and switchgear. The expense of developing the factory cut GEC's net profit from £65,000 in 1902 to £52,000 in 1903: in order to improve liquidity, the company transferred

67, QUEEN VICTORIA STREET,

LONDON, E.C.4. *June 26* 19*19*

"TELEGRAMS, "ELECTRICITY":
TELEPHONE Nº 3600 LONDON WALL.

Dear Mr. Hewins

Thanks for your letter. I am just going out of town for a few days. Would next Thursday 1 o'clock Savoy Restaurant suit you? I am looking forward to meeting you again

Sincerely yours

Hugo Hirst

Hewins 74/176

Handwritten letter to Professor Hewins, 17 June 1919 (courtesy of Dr R P T Davenport-Hines).

almost all of its banking business to the Midland Bank in January 1903 in return for overdraft facilities of up to £50,000. This proved a momentous decision in the growth of the company, for Hirst won the complete confidence of S B Murray and Sir Edward Holden (qv) of the Midland, which thereafter treated GEC with generosity and sympathy. Indeed during the First World War Holden told Hirst that GEC must get 'ready after the war to be a strong electrical industry which would feed every other industry in its reconstruction'. GEC therefore spent over £4.5 million on expansion: 'The City & Midland Bank advanced us the money as readily as we could spend it and our engineers had their programme finished before the Armistice' {BLPES, TC6, 1/15, evidence of Hirst to Tariff Commission, Feb 1921}.

Hirst also began the manufacture of lamp carbon at Witton, because he believed that Britain must be self-sufficient in its supply of arc lamps and searchlights, in case of war. He met faint encouragement from the Admiralty, and indifference from the War Office, and lost £70,000 on the carbon works to 1914. It was 'the Cinderella of our enterprise', he wrote, half-ruined by 'the machinations which German competitors engineered ... Interference with workpeople, agitation in the Press that our climate was unsuitable for manufacturing carbons, stoppage of supply of raw material, dumping to Government and Municipal Authorities at prices 50 per cent below those charged for German Government and Municipal Authorities, every trick was tried to ruin these Works' {ibid, Hirst to Edward Hirst 23 Oct 1915}.

In 1905 Hirst visited Budapest to obtain the British patent rights of the Just-Hahnemann tungsten lamp, which were almost immediately menaced by the Welsbach patents in Germany. He reduced the German opposition by threatening to invoke Lloyd George's new Patent Act if they did not manufacture in Britain, and the Osram Lamp Works were erected at Hammersmith in which the Germans, Austrians and GEC each held one-third interest. By 1915 £100,000 had been invested in the Osram works, which then supplied over 60 per cent of British lamps. Before 1914 the foreign interests in Osram insisted that GEC's supply of glass bulbs to Hammersmith should be at prices equal to the dumping prices offered by the Germans; Hirst submitted to this, although it cost GEC up to £4,000 per annum in 1910-14. After the outbreak of war, the Germans were removed from Osram, which was merged with GEC's Robertson and Lemington subsidiaries.

Until the Post Office took over the telephone system in 1912, all telephones were imported from Sweden, Germany and the USA. After nationalisation, GEC built and organised the Peel Conner Works to supply British and colonial telephone equipment. Under Hirst's auspices, the company also developed the ebonite industry, and erected a mica works and a tube works. In 1913 GEC, in conjunction with the Pirelli Co of Milan, opened a cable factory at Southampton on which £250,000 was spent in the following two years. After the outbreak of war, in 1915, GEC bought 10 acres at Coventry to supply magnetos for heavy vehicles and aircraft. Around 1910 Hirst also became a director of the Travancore Minerals Co, established by German interests to mine monasite sand for incandescent gas mantles, and this connection exposed him to wartime criticism by xenophobic journalists.

Hirst testified to the Tariff Commission in 1904, and attributed much of the retardation of the British electrical industry to the lack of 'the security of an assured minimum output' that foreign rivals enjoyed by tariff protection. He complained that 'directly goods get standardised foreign competition sets in'; and to meet dumping by Belgium, Germany and the

USA he advocated 'a real protective tariff for a few years merely to get our house in order and our industry up to the right standing'. Citing the courses of the Spanish-American and Russo-Japanese wars, he urged 'The upholding of every existing industry in this country should form part of our programme for national defence. The country harbouring most industries will be the most resourceful in case of war' {BLPES, TC3, 1/103}. He became a member of the Tariff Commission in 1911, and donated thousands of pounds to its cause. He supplied protectionist arguments and proofs to many parliamentary candidates, lectured and spoke to organisations like the Compatriots Club and the United Empire Club, and sat on the Trades and Industry Committee of the Royal Colonial Institute. He also started in 1914 the *Britannic Review* (edited by the maverick imperialist Richard Jebb), and was spokesman of the British Manufacturers Association, a Birmingham-based protectionist pressure-group formed in 1915. Hirst's Germanophobia was violent and sincere, based on his Bavarian hatred of Prussia, and after his British naturalisation in 1889, he did his utmost to pass as a British gentleman. He dropped Judaism for the Anglican Church, and in 1919 bought the Fox Hill estate near Reading in Berkshire from Sir Rufus Isaacs.

He became an associate of the Institution of Electrical Engineers in 1888, a member in 1898 and an honorary member from 1935. He served on the Institution's Council in 1900-6 and 1911-14, and in 1912 became chairman of its newly-formed Industrial Committee. This did not confine its membership to members of the IEE, but co-opted others to represent the whole of the electrical industry: their attempts in 1913-14 to co-ordinate electrical supply in large cities led to criticism that they were exceeding their remit by entering political work, and the committee was dissolved. Although he was inactive in the Institution after 1914, his generous donation of 1942 was the basis of its Lord Hirst Benevolent Fund.

Hirst became chairman of GEC on Byng's death in 1910, and steered it through its critical period of wartime growth. Net profit rose from £138,000 for 1914-15 to £630,000 for 1920-21, and ambitious expansion and investment were undertaken. Between 75 and 100 per cent of GEC's output in 1914-18 was for the Government at fixed prices, and Hirst wrote that Britain 'should have been in a deplorable and dangerous position' after 1914 but for GEC, 'through our enterprise alone was it possible to produce the bulbs, caps, tungsten wire and every type of lamp from British raw materials by British workers ... It was discovered that special types of most essential lamps had never been made in this country which were sold to the Admiralty as British made by merchants posing as manufacturers, and only by superhuman effort, combined with luck, did we succeed in solving problems at breakneck speed which we have never even had the chance of studying before the war' {SUL, Hewins 76/260, Hirst memorandum of 2 Dec 1920}. Hirst was an active productioneer during the war, and gave powerful and detailed evidence to Sir Charles Parsons' (qv) governmental committee on the position of the electrical trades after the war. 'I have waved over my works the Union Jack all my life', he told them, 'This war means a reconstruction of the world' {PRO BT 55/21/1/4, evidence of 25 Oct 1916}.

In 1919 Hirst launched GEC on an ambitious programme to cover the whole domain of electrical engineering. During the war GEC had been the only British producer of arc lamp carbons for searchlights, and had been a large-scale maker of war equipment such as French telephone sets, French cables, magnetos and wireless valves. Under their peacetime diversification policy, GEC added heavy electrical work to their traditional lines of lamps and supply articles. They bought Frazer & Chalmers, turbine manufacturers, the Express Lift Co, and formed a new mining machinery department. A research and development laboratory was opened by GEC in 1923, and development departments were started in all their factories. By 1925, when GEC's profits first exceeded £1 million, the group was well-established in supplying heavy electrical equipment for power stations, mines and gas stations. This transformation of their sales within half a decade was an outstanding success, for which Hirst was largely responsible. In the later 1920s GEC further diversified, making oil engines designed by their own engineers, and building a sugar beet factory in the Midlands. They were involved in British and foreign railway electrification, did the electrical work for the Cunard-White Star liner *Queen Mary* in 1936, and provided electric lighting systems for aerodromes across Europe, Asia and Africa.

GEC's workforce rose from 14,000 in 1919 to 16,640 in 1921, 17,500 in 1924, 24,000 in 1935 and 40,000 in 1939. Hirst's own imperialism was reflected in GEC's export strategy: 75 per cent of their exports were to the British Empire in 1936. He was also active in repulsing the attempts during 1928-34 of General Electric of America to buy control of British electrical manufacturers such as GEC or Metropolitan-Vickers, although even Hirst's ingenuity was stretched at moments.

After the First World War 'Hirst became increasingly the elder statesman of GEC rather than the day-to-day administrator' and a 'statesman-industrialist in the wider sense' {Jones and Marriott (1970) 86-87}. He was a member of the executive committee of the protectionist manufacturers' pressure-group, the British Commonwealth Union, in 1917-25, and was afterwards treasurer of its successor organisation, the Empire Industries Association. He became president of the Decimal Association in 1927, of the Institute of Fuel in 1932, and at different periods also presided over the Association of Technical Institutions, the British Export Society, the British Electrical Development Society, the Incorporated Society of British Advertisers and the Radio Manufacturers Association. He was president of Reading Football Club, Master of the Glaziers Company in 1928-30, a member of the Tudor Rose League from 1933, and an activist in the Empire Development Union. He was also vice-president of the British Electrical and Allied Manufacturers Association, and a founding committee member of the Empire Economic Union in 1929. At a crucial moment in the contacts between Government and manufacturers over rearmament, he was president of the Federation of British Industries in 1936 and 1937. He was a member of the Cabinet's Trade and Employment Panel in 1923-25, of the Board of Trade's Advisory Council, 1922-25, 1929-32 and 1936-39, of the governmental committee on unemployment insurance of 1925-26, of the committee on co-operative sale of coal in 1926 and of the committee on Industrial Research. In 1927 he was appointed British representative on the grandiosely-named but insignificant sub-committee of Experts on Scientific Property of the League of Nation's Committee on Intellectual

Co-operation. Although he claimed that 'other businessmen laughed at' the activities of Alfred Mond (qv) in labour relations as 'playing politics and trying to attract attention' {SRO, GD 193/25/1/26, memorandum of Sir Arthur Steel-Maitland, 25 Jan 1926}, he participated in the Turner-Mond talks of 1928-29 on industrial understanding. According to one Labour politician, Hirst 'worked like a Trojan to bring Capital and Labour together ... there is no employer of labour so esteemed and respected as the head of the General Electric Co' {Thomas (1937) 247}. To the General Secretary of the TUC Hirst appeared 'extremely shrewd and a great driving force' {Citrine (1964) 251}.

Hirst joined a British economic mission to Australia led by Arthur Duckham (qv) in 1928-29, and in 1927 was appointed to the advisory committee to unravel the financial complexities of Marconi Telegraph Co spun previously by Godfrey Isaacs (qv). However he withdrew from the committee after a short time.

He was created a baronet in 1925 and received a barony in 1934. His qualities at the height of his powers were listed by a contemporary as

A. Very clear cut mind
B. Absolute confidence in himself
C. Controls his own industry absolutely — all others were figureheads and pawns.
D. Immense organising capacity {HLRO, Hannon diary 8 Feb 1921}.

To Leo Amery, Hirst was 'a great public servant' shining with 'absolute sincerity and unaffected simplicity' {*Times* 26 Jan 1943}. An amateur athlete in his youth, he was a pioneer motorist, acquired a racing stable, and practised the scientific farming of Jersey cows on his Berkshire estate. He also played golf and billiards. His salary as chairman of GEC in 1936 amounted to £100,000 gross or £39,590 net. In 1940 he made an interest-free loan to the British Government of £20,000 to aid the war effort. Already in September 1939, 94 per cent of GEC's work was on government contract and the British Government owed GEC £500,000. In November 1939 they borrowed £2 million at 4.5 per cent for five years from Prudential Assurance to cover wartime productive expansion.

Hirst married, in 1892, his cousin, Leontine (1873-1938), daughter of Herman Hirsch, by whom he had one son and two daughters. His son Harold Hugh Hirst (1893-1919) was trained to succeed his father, and worked at the Swiss Bankverein in Zurich for experience in 1914, but died of the effects of illness contracted while fighting as a soldier in the war. Harold's posthumous son was killed in action with the RAF in 1941 aged twenty-one. Hirst's elder daughter Muriel (1894-1969) married in 1919 Sir Leslie Gamage (1887-1972) who was managing director and in 1957-60 chairman of GEC. Hugo Hirst died on 22 January 1943 at Foxhill. He left £498,651 and his titles became extinct.

R P T DAVENPORT-HINES

Writings:

Some Business Aspects of Tariff Reform (Compatriots Club, 1908).

HIRST Hugo

The Manufacturer and the State (GEC, 1910).

letter on commercial training and university men *Times* Engineering Supplement 28 Feb 1912.

The Higher Aspect of Business: A Lecture ... in ... Christ's College, Cambridge ... (Morgan Reeve, 1914).

'The Organisation of Empire Trade' *Britannic Review* 1 (May 1914).

Bank Amalgamations (1918).

'British Industries and Protective Measures: The Position of Electric Lamp Trade' *Empire Review* 34 (Dec 1920).

letter on electrical imports *Times* 14 Mar 1930.

articles on electrical industry *ibid* 21 Sept 1931, 5 Dec 1933.

letters on railway electrification *ibid* 2 Jan, 14 Dec 1933.

letter on imperial markets *ibid* 22 Feb 1935.

letter on Canadian Budget *ibid* 28 Mar 1935.

letter on exports *ibid* 27 Feb 1937.

letter on trade with India *ibid* 30 Sept 1937.

letter on television *ibid* 3 Apr 1939.

Sources:

Unpublished

BLPES, Tariff Commission papers, TC3 1/103, TC6 1/15.

Cambridge University Library, papers of Earl Baldwin of Bewdley.

House of Lords RO, papers of Sir Patrick Hannon.

Midland Bank, Poultry, London, diaries of Sir Edward Holden and S B Murray.

PRO, BT 55/11, 13, 20, 21.

Scottish RO, Edinburgh, papers of Sir Arthur Steel-Maitland.

Sheffield University Library, papers of W A S Hewins.

PrC.

Information from Rachel Lawrence.

Published

Thomas C Bridges and Hubert H Tiltman, *Kings of Commerce* (G G Harrap & Co, 1928).

Gustav Byng, *Protection: The Views of a Manufacturer* (Eyre & Spottiswoode, 1901).

Walter McL Citrine, *Men and Work* (Hutchinson, 1964).

Complete Peerage.

DNB.

T C Elder, *The Coming Crash of Peace* (Simpkin, Marshall, Hamilton Kent, 1916).

Arthur C Fox-Davies, *Armorial Families* (2 vols, Hurst & Blackett, 1929) 1.

Robert Jones and Oliver J D Marriott, *Anatomy of a Merger: A History of GEC, AEI and English Electric* (Jonathan Cape, 1970).

John D B Miller, *Richard Jebb and the Problem of Empire* Institute of Commonwealth Studies paper 3 (Athlone Press, 1956).

James H Thomas, *My Story* (Hutchinson & Co, 1937).

Adam Gowans Whyte, *Forty Years of Electrical Progress* (Benn, 1930).

Adam Gowans Whyte and T C Elder, *The Underwar: Patriotic Policy in British Trade* (Electrical Press, 1914).

WWW.

Lord Hives (courtesy of Rolls-Royce Ltd).

HIVES, Ernest Walter

Lord Hives

(1886-1965)

Aircraft manufacturer

Ernest Walter Hives was born at Reading on 21 April 1886, the son of John Hives, a factory clerk and Mary née Washbourn. He attended the Redlands School in Reading, but by the age of fourteen was driving cars while employed at a local garage. He was working in a bicycle shop when a chance meeting with C S Rolls (qv) in 1903 brought a job with Rolls as a motor repairer. After a spell in the Napier Co, and as racing driver at the newly-opened Brooklands track, he joined the new Rolls-Royce concern in 1908. Soon he was testing cars, and by 1913 was driving in competition on the Continent, and had taken a Silver Ghost to over 101 mph at Brooklands. Henry Royce (qv) liked him because he had a good ear for an engine and an acute diagnostic mind. All his life he drove like a racer, but with a sixth sense for caution.

From 1912 he was involved in the experimental department of the justifiably renowned Rolls-Royce engines, both aero and auto. As a result, in the First World War he was retained in the valuable aero-engine department's experimental shop, had a hand in the inception of the Eagle (1914-15) and was much involved in its intensive development from 225 to 360 hp. By the end of the war he was head of the experimental department, and continued in this role, responsible for both car (chassis) and aero-engine work, in the era of racing aero-engines, which culminated in the special 'R' for the Schneider Cup Trophy Supermarine S6B of 1931

Rolls-Royce logo (courtesy of Rolls-Royce Ltd).

with its 2,500 hp. By that time Hives had become executive officer of the Derby works while A G Elliot worked with Sir Henry Royce at West Wittering, Sussex, until the latter's death in 1933. Elliot then became chief engineer and in October 1936 Hives became general works manager, concentrating on production; he was appointed a director in April 1937. This was a most critical time when the Kestrel, a solid or monoblock engine was in the process of becoming the highly successful liquid-cooled Merlin. The latter, of which 150,000 were eventually produced, was the mainstay of the rearmament and Second World War programmes. Yet in 1921 Rolls-Royce had almost decided to leave the aero-engine business. Even at the time of Royce's death there seemed little sense in continuing the Air Ministry's cost-plus-10-per cent development contracts though Royce was in favour of them. Soon after his death, the drive to rearm began. First came the Hurricane and the Spitfire built around the in-line liquid-cooled engine developed from the Schneider Cup experience, and the twin and then four-engined heavy bombers. The result was a growing demand for the firm's products and, therefore, an increasing demand for Hives's dual talents as trouble-shooter and production manager.

Hives, efficient and far-sighted as ever, had pressed the development of the Merlin so that it had largely been rid of bugs by the time the new aircraft needed it. His specialities were discovering the faults in new equipment, and in picking good young men and teaming them with an older, less academically-trained, man to form a design and development team which combined advanced theory with sound engineering practice and experience. At the same time 'the Boss' or 'Hs' or 'Uncle Ernie' as he was known, had developed a nice knack for getting other members of his staff to work together, especially as he knew most of them personally.

As aero-engine production was obviously going to be of very great importance in the coming war, Hives set out to have Merlins produced in a number of shadow factories. These were built by the Government and then leased to Rolls-Royce on the same or more favourable terms as the airframe industry was getting. Hives made sure that the RR works in Glasgow got off to a good start by being careful to propitiate the unions there, an objective which his natural charm, knowledge of people and ability to do manual mechanical work enabled him to carry off. When the war came he supervised the addition of the Ford Motor Co in the UK to the Merlin manufacturing group, and went to the USA and negotiated the manufacture of Merlin engines by Packard. When the Minister of Supply, Lord Beaverbrook (qv), asked him to take Rolls-Royce into tank-engine production Hives, thinking the firm had enough to do with producing aero-engines, replied that he would want a credit of £1 million and 'no interference' {*Times* 26 Apr 1965}. His bluff was called and he got both. During the war he also served on Roy Fedden's (qv) Advisory Committee to the Minister of Aircraft Production, but found it difficult to attend meetings.

The company had begun to explore jet-engine work before the war and in 1942 the Welland was begun for the early Gloster Meteors. The Whittle designs were also taken in hand, but later discarded when the experimental department concluded that the axial flow jet was the sounder solution. After the war Hives had the courage, as managing director from 1946, to decide at one point in the development of the Avon engine to

Rolls-Royce Merlin engine (courtesy of Rolls-Royce Ltd).

scrap it and begin again. Although the British Government, which held the Whittle patents, in 1943 gave them to General Electric in the United States, Rolls-Royce under Hives as managing director and then, from October 1950 as chairman, pushed ahead in the development of both the pure jet and of the Dart turboprop engines. Soon after he retired in 1957, the company was producing 65 per cent of the free world's gas turbine engines for commercial use.

In 1943 Hives had been created a Companion of Honour. He was raised to the peerage in 1950. The universities of Nottingham and London awarded him honorary DSc degrees, while Cambridge University gave him an LLD. At one time chairman of the National Council on Technological Awards, he was also chairman of the Industrial Development Board for Malta, 1957-60.

His private life was comfortable. He married Gertrude Ethel, daughter of John Warwick, a clerk, in 1913 and she bore him four sons and three daughters; she died in 1961. For recreation he played snooker and golf, went fishing, and largely stayed close to his home, Derby. Lord Hives died at the National Hospital for Nervous Diseases in London on 24 April 1965 at the age of seventy-one, leaving an estate proved at £111,934 gross.

ROBIN HIGHAM

Sources:

Unpublished

BCe.

MCe.

HIVES Ernest Walter

PrC.

Published

F R (Rod) Banks, *I Kept No Diary* (Shrewsbury: Airlife, 1978).

Centenary Journal: Royal Aeronautical Society, 1866-1966 (Royal Aeronautical Society, 1966).

DNB.

R W Harker, *Rolls-Royce from the Wings, 1925-1971: Military Aviation* (Oxford: Oxford Illustrated Press, 1976).

S D Heron, *The Development of Aviation Fuels* (Boston: Graduate School of Business Administration, Harvard University, 1950).

Ian Lloyd, *Rolls-Royce. The Years of Endeavour* (Macmillan, 1978).

—, *Rolls-Royce. The Growth of a Firm* (Macmillan, 1978).

—, *Rolls-Royce. The Merlin at War* (Macmillan, 1978).

Robert Schlaifer, *The Development of Aircraft Engines* (Boston: Graduate School of Business Administration, Harvard University, 1950).

Herschel Smith, *Aircraft Piston Engines* (New York: McGraw-Hill, 1981).

Times 26 Apr 1965.

WWW.

Sir Julian Hodge (courtesy of Mr Colin Baber).

HODGE, Sir Julian Stephen Alfred

(1904-)

Banker

Julian Stephen Alfred Hodge was born in Camberwell, London on 15 October 1904, the second of seven children of Alfred Hodge, a plumber, and his wife Jane née Simcocks. The family moved to South Wales in 1909 and Hodge grew up at Pontllanfraith in Monmouthshire. They were Roman Catholics and Hodge's religion, and his mother, profoundly influenced his life. Despite his London origins, and the difficulties of being a Roman Catholic in a predominantly Nonconformist community, Hodge developed a strong sense of Welsh identity.

Hodge attended the Pontllanfraith Council school and, encouraged by his mother, read many of the English classics by the time he was thirteen.

Alfred Hodge suffered from ill-health, originating from service in the Boer War, and Julian and his elder brother Donald had to help support the family. When Julian was eighteen, his father returned to London to find work, leaving Julian a surrogate father for four children. His father's plight, and the poverty that the family faced from time to time stimulated his determination and ambition to succeed in life.

Hodge's first permanent job, just after the First World War, was as a clerk with the Great Western Railway at Pontllanfraith station, earning 30s a week. He became interested in accountancy, enrolled as a student member in the Corporation of Accountants in 1925 and then embarked upon a five-year programme of correspondence courses, studying in the evenings and on occasional courses at Cardiff Technical College. In 1930 he became a Certified Accountant. Finding little demand for his services in and around Pontllanfraith, he used his now free evenings to sell life assurance from door-to-door. In his first year he made £85 and by 1934 had amassed £430 in his GWR savings account. Selling life assurance gave him a reputation amongst small shopkeepers and the like who needed his accounting skills. By the mid-1930s he had developed a thriving life-assurance business and a modest accounting practice, as well as continuing to hold down his full-time job with the Great Western Railway. But this success was almost ruined by speculations which Hodge then undertook on the Stock Exchange. Despite understanding little of the movements in stocks and shares in quoted companies, he decided to concentrate on rubber companies, and quickly amassed debts of £1,000. The help of friends and of Lloyds Bank enabled him to pay off his debts. Later in the 1930s he formed a number of companies which brought together several cinema interests in South Wales and the West Country, including those of Jackson Withers of Abertillery. The company controlled 48 cinemas by the mid-1950s and remained a valued part of Hodge's interests until the early 1970s.

The Second World War created a decisive watershed in Hodge's career. He took on the supposedly part-time post of internal auditor to Currans, the Cardiff munitions company, but the amount of work snowballed, so that in 1941 he resigned his post as an accountant with the GWR. With his own practice, and the work for Currans, Julian became a full-time accountant. After the war his industrial and financial enterprises burgeoned. In April 1945 he formed Hodge & Co (Insurance) Ltd, and in October 1946 the Gwent & West of England Enterprises Ltd, an industrial holding company itself largely owned by Hodge & Co (Insurance) Ltd. Gwent began with the acquisition of garages, but the decisive step came in 1948 when Hodge brought Anglo-Auto Finance Ltd, an ailing Newport hire-purchase company which in time became the cornerstone of the Hodge empire. By the 1950s Hodge was involved in selling old and new cars, in hire-purchase and insurance as well as the operation of a chain of cinemas. In October 1962 he also moved into car production when he acquired an 86 per cent stake in Reliant Motors. By 1967/68 Anglo-Auto was the sixth largest hire-purchase company in Britain.

During the 1950s Julian Hodge acquired a name in South Wales for a tight but paternal managerial style possibly learnt, though at a distance, from Sir Felix Pole (qv) of the GWR, and for probing and imaginative accountancy methods. He achieved the wider recognition that he desired

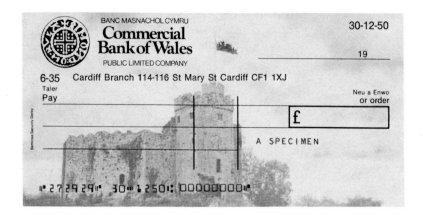

BANC MASNACHOL CYMRU
Commercial
Bank of Wales
PUBLIC LIMITED COMPANY

30-12-50

19

6-35   Cardiff Branch 114-116 St Mary St Cardiff CF1 1XJ

Taler
Pay

Neu a Enwo
or order

£

A SPECIMEN

⑈272929⑈ 30⑈1250⑈ 00000000⑈

Specimen cheque of the Commercial Bank of Wales (courtesy of Mr Colin Baber).

in 1956 when he formed the Investors' Protection Facilities Ltd. The aim of this company was to provide a safeguard for the small investors in companies which were the subject of takeover bids where the asking price was manifestly too low. Armed with carefully-researched information, Julian and his closest aides would distribute circulars to the shareholders presenting the facts and attend shareholders' meetings on their behalf to question the managements concerned. Although making a loss and effectively closing its books in 1959, the company is reputed to have gained well over £20 million for thousands of shareholders by forcing up the offer bids. Small shareholders who benefited saw Hodge as a hero, but his activities made him many enemies in the City of London, and the antagonisms thus created took many years to abate. Although Hodge's activities in general were at times shrouded in controversy, this did not seem to have a significant retarding influence upon the commercial momentum which he continued to build up.

In the 1960s, Hodge's various companies went public. When Gwent was floated in 1961 the 2s shares, after a meteoric rise, settled at 36s, thereby valuing the Hodge family holding of 3,187,531 shares at over £4.5 million. In 1963, the Hodge Group, the old insurance company under a new name, was floated. That year Hodge moved into unit trusts: his Welsh Dragon Trust, one of the first unit trusts to be set up outside London, was especially successful. However, with the market quickly becoming saturated, he sold out this part of his business to Vehicle & General Insurance for a paper profit of £1.4 million in March 1970. By 1973 there were 150 companies in the Hodge empire, but his personal control became diluted as the decade proceeded. The Hodge Group was sold to Standard Chartered Bank in late 1973 for £55 million, the group's assets being valued at £157 million. Julian Hodge joined the main board of Standard Chartered and remained chairman of the Hodge Group until his retirement in 1978. Soon afterwards, the group lost its identity, subsequently becoming known as Chartered Trust, and its fortunes declined.

Much of Hodge's attention in the 1970s was devoted to the Commercial Bank of Wales. He had always been concerned by the lack of financial institutions within Wales, and believed the English, on whom the Welsh largely had to rely for finance for economic development, to have little knowledge of, or interest in, Wales. In the late 1960s Hodge sat on a financial panel to enquire into the availability of public and private investment funds in Wales, which concluded that there was indeed a shortage of risk capital which hindered economic growth in the Principality. The Commercial Bank of Wales was incorporated on 9 February 1971 in an attempt to fill this gap: to provide help, advice and finance to indigenous Welsh industry. Some argued that there was no need for such an institution in Wales: nonetheless, within six years the Bank was earning annual profits in excess of £1 million, there was an almost tenfold increase in deposits and current accounts between 1973 and 1980, from £4.4 million to £42.4 million, and a fourfold increase in its loans and overdrafts in the same period from £7.6 million to £31.3 million.

Julian Hodge has often stated that he did not set out to make money; nevertheless, he has been very successful at it. Whilst not being miserly, he was always careful with money, deploring ostentatious wealth. Although his decisions were based, of course, on thorough knowledge of the intricacies of the financial world, in large part they were guided by instinct. He consistently set out to rehabilitate a wide variety of previously unsuccessful concerns, ensuring that they retained their individual identities.

Julian Hodge married Moira Thomas, a secretary, the daughter of John Thomas, a colliery winder, in 1951; they have two sons and a daughter. Hard work may partly explain the lateness of his marriage; another factor was his concern to support his mother, to whom he was devoted, who died in 1946. In memory of her, Hodge set up in 1962 the Jane Hodge Foundation with a gift of £2.5 million to help fund medical research, various social and welfare programmes and the advancement of education and religion. The Foundation now (1984) has funds in excess of £30 million and has helped charities throughout the world.

For his services to Wales Hodge was awarded a knighthood in 1970, and in 1971 an honorary LLD from the University of Wales for the Jane Hodge Foundation's activities in the academic field. These included the endowment of a number of chairs, particularly to the University of Wales Institute of Science and Technology, where he was treasurer, 1968-76, vice-president, 1976-80 and president since 1981. He was a member of the Welsh Economic Council, 1965-68, and of the Welsh Council, 1968-79. Sir Julian Hodge was made a commander of the Order of St John of Jerusalem in 1972, a knight of the same order in 1977, and a knight of the order of St Gregory in 1978. As yet, however, Sir Julian's last dream has still not been achieved, the building of a new Roman Catholic Cathedral in the Castle Grounds at Cardiff, although the Pope blessed the foundation stone when he visited Wales in June 1982.

COLIN BABER *and* TREVOR BOYNS

Writings:

Paradox of Financial Preservation (1959).

Sources:

Published

The Commercial Bank of Wales: A Banking Enterprise (nd).

A Short History of Gwent, and the Hodge Group (1963).

Timothy O'Sullivan, *Julian Hodge. A Biography* (Routledge & Kegan Paul, 1981).

WW 1982.

Edward Holden — portrait by W W Ouless, 1909 (courtesy of the Midland Bank PLC).

HOLDEN, Sir Edward Hopkinson

(1848-1919)

Clearing banker

Edward Hopkinson Holden was born at the *Bull's Head*, Tottington, Lancashire, on 11 May 1848, the son of Henry Holden, a calico bleacher and later a beerseller, and his wife Anne née Hopkinson. He grew up in the neighbouring village of Summerseat, where he was educated at the Wesleyan Elementary School. After leaving school he was employed as a clerk in local shops and warehouses. In 1866 an introduction from a fellow member of the Summerseat Wesleyan Chapel secured him an apprenticeship at the Bolton branch of the Manchester & County Bank. His salary was £30, rising to £50 in the third year, and after seven years he was promoted to a clerkship at the Manchester head office. Although for the next seven years there was little change in his banking duties, he began a demanding programme of self-education. He regularly attended evening classes at Owen's College, where he was an exhibitioner in political economy; he also persuaded a solicitor to give him tuition in law. Later in his career he always expected bank staff to educate themselves in the same way.

Neither his work as a banker nor his studies gave Holden any obvious advantage in the Manchester & County Bank, and by 1880 he ranked as only the fifth of 12 cashiers. In 1881, however, having answered an advertisement in the *Economist*, he was appointed accountant of the Birmingham & Midland Bank at a salary of £300. Asked by the interviewing committee about his ambitions, Holden is reputed to have replied 'I want to be the manager of a big bank' {*Financial News* 24 July 1919}.

At that time the Midland was by no means 'a big bank'. Established in 1836, it had remained a small Birmingham enterprise with only a handful of branches. By the 1880s the bank's directors faced the choice of either rapidly expanding its capital and its business base or succumbing to the increasingly frequent mergers within the banking industry. After the appointment as chairman in 1881 of John Dent Goodman (partner in Scholefield Goodman, hardware exporters, and chairman of Birmingham Small Arms since 1861) they chose expansion, accepting plans for opening new branches throughout the West Midlands.

As accountant, Holden had his first taste of management and policy decisions. This was clearly where his real skills lay, and the contrast with his slow progress as a bank clerk was telling. In 1883, after he had applied for the sub-managership of the Bristol & West of England Bank, the Midland's directors retained him by promoting him to secretary of the bank at a salary of £500. His duties included the appraisal of premises and the selection of staff for new branches (throughout his career he continued to be meticulous, even obsessive, about the quality of branch buildings and personnel). Nevertheless, new capital and new business were much more rapidly available through the acquisition of other local banks. With J A Christie, the bank's sub-manager, Holden supervised the amalgamation of the Union Bank of Birmingham in 1883. The purchase added £400,000 to the Midland's deposits, and Christie and Holden were awarded bonuses of £100 for their handling of the negotiations. Further amalgamations were negotiated with the Coventry Union Bank and the Leamington Priors & Warwickshire Bank (both in 1889) and the Derby Commercial Bank, the Exchange & Discount Bank, and the Leeds & County Bank (in 1890). These acquisitions introduced over £2 million in deposits, raising the Midland's total deposits to £5.6 million and the total number of branches to 45 in 1890.

Holden's reward was promotion to the sub-managership in 1887 (at a salary of £600), quickly followed by appointments as general manager in 1890 and joint general manager (with Christie) at a salary of £2,000 in 1891. The Midland's entry to London further strengthened his position. He undertook all the negotiations which led to the purchase of the Central Bank of London and the old Smithfield bank of Lacy, Hartland & Woodbridge in 1891. The Central Bank, in addition to approximately £1.5 million in deposits, gave the Midland a seat in the London Clearing House, allowing the transfer of the Midland's headquarters to London.

The enlarged bank (renamed London & Midland Bank in 1891) still lacked the national coverage of some other London-based banks such as the National Provincial Bank and the London & County Bank. Christie and Holden, apparently after only the briefest consultation with their directors, went in search of further amalgamations outside the bank's traditional territories. The Manchester Joint Stock Bank was taken over in 1892, followed by the Bank of Westmorland in 1893 and the Preston Banking Co in 1894. These three acquisitions brought another £2.6 million of deposits. Not all amalgamation negotiations were successful, and in these cases Christie and Holden responded by opening new branches to compete with banks who refused their terms. This pattern was repeated throughout the period of Holden's ascendancy. Each burst of growth was stimulated by a further amalgamation, usually with a joint

*Cartoon sketch of Edward Holden
(courtesy of the Midland Bank PLC).*

stock bank with strong industrial links in the Midlands and North; this preference governed the bank's performance for more than half a century. When amalgamation negotiations broke down or when there were gaps in the network (as in the South and West) Holden opened purpose-built branches as soon as possible, in order to keep the balance between the lending and borrowing regions of the branch system.

In Holden's subsequent career there were three recognisable phases in the growth of his reputation: in the 1890s he was the most fervent exponent of the banking amalgamations; as managing director between 1898 and 1908 he flourished in the roles of innovator and administrator; and as chairman between 1908 and 1919 he emerged more obviously as a leader of the banking community as a whole.

In 1895 the Midland's directors voted him 2,000 guineas for his 'conspicuous ability in conducting and completing the recent amalgamations' {Midland Bank Archives, board minutes, 19 Feb 1895}. Two years later Christie retired, leaving Holden as sole general manager at a salary of £2,500. Holden continued the programme of amalgamating joint-stock country banks at an even greater pace: the Carlisle City & District Bank, the Channel Islands Bank, the Huddersfield Banking Co, the North Western Bank, the Oldham Joint Stock Bank and the City of Birmingham Bank introduced another £7.5 million in deposits between 1896 and 1899. In all these deals, mostly concluded in railway hotels up and down the country, Holden was unceremonious in negotiations. He had a keen eye for bad and doubtful debts and was merciless in his treatment of bankers whose knowledge of their own balance sheets was hazy.

By 1898 amalgamation and branch extension had given the Midland total deposits of over £32 million and 250 branches in England and Wales, making it the fourth largest clearing bank in the UK. By far the most valuable new component was the City Bank, acquired in 1898. Holden had been keen to capture this prize for some years; the City Bank had £9 million in deposits, prestigious headquarters in Threadneedle Street and a relatively large reserve fund of £500,000. This acquisition was handled by Holden alone and it was probably the most risky of his negotiations. For the first and last time he was opposed by a group of the bank's own directors and shareholders. He overcame the protest by trimming the price paid for the City Bank, and thereafter his authority within the Midland was unchallenged. He was promoted to become managing director with a salary of £5,000 and a special bonus of £10,000.

Holden centralised most of the bank's business and administration at the new headquarters in Threadneedle Street. Lending decisions and accounting methods were concentrated under the control of three general managers in London, each responsible for a geographical 'division' of the country. In practice they rarely visited their divisions; major customers and branch managers were normally interviewed in London. Holden also insisted upon uniformity in all the bank's accounting and record-keeping systems, with the result that the office traditions of the constituent banks quickly disappeared.

At first it was not clear whether Holden saw centralization as the best strategy for a clearing bank or whether it was simply a means of retaining close personal control. His diaries give the impression that most decisions were transmitted through his office. With the style and language of a martinet, he dealt with tiny details of staff discipline or the design of bank furniture, as well as with the larger questions of amalgamations or troublesome accounts.

Obsessed as Holden was with the bank's affairs and anxious as he was to promote the image of his own authority, after 1898 he was increasingly ready to delegate his duties. Three joint general managers had been appointed when Holden became managing director in 1898. Samuel Murray and J M Madders had been associated with Holden at Birmingham in the 1880s; the third, D G H Pollock, was from the City Bank. The appointments gave much greater breadth to the Midland's senior management, and in each case the general managers carried punishing responsibilities for administration and the control of lending in their divisions. Murray had already taken a large share of the amalgamation work, and in all the mergers negotiated after 1898 he was expected to complete each settlement after Holden had carried out the initial bargaining.

The strength of the bank's senior management after 1898 released Holden for special projects, including the initiation of a further wave of amalgamations: the Leicestershire Banking Co (1900), the Sheffield Union Bank and the Yorkshire Banking Co (both in 1901), the Nottingham Joint Stock Bank (1905) and the North & South Wales Bank (1908). Each of these new amalgamations brought in large numbers of additional branches: the North & South Wales Bank, for example, had over 100 branches in Wales and the North West. The five amalgamations contributed 240 branches and nearly £23 million in deposits, lifting the Midland's deposits to £70 million by 1909.

Holden's confidence in his general managers also allowed him to take a wider view of the bank's future. He systematically increased the number of reciprocal 'correspondent' links with overseas banks. In 1904 Holden made the first of a series of lengthy visits to North America, which extended the bank's correspondent network and persuaded Holden that the Midland should take a more international role. From that date the Midland was much more heavily involved in loans and new issues for foreign Governments and major international companies. He even considered opening branches in New York and Chicago, although this plan was dropped because of the restrictive American banking laws. The main result of his visit was his decision that the bank should offer foreign exchange services. Much of this business had been captured from the home-based merchant banks by foreign banks in London. Holden established a Foreign Exchange Department in 1905, staffed by experienced dealers recruited from the foreign banks in London. The new department soon built up a large business, particularly in exchange payments on behalf of American banks. The innovation was not welcomed in the City, where there was criticism of the Midland's 'unorthodox behaviour' but Holden was unrepentant and the other major banks soon followed his lead. Holden admired the scale and style of US and Canadian business organisations, and his straightforwardness gave him popularity and influence in the American financial community. Bristling with ideas based on his American tour, Holden threw himself into the task of modernising the Midland's office systems. A much larger internal telephone network was installed, office machinery more widely used and printing and stationery standardised. American practice probably also influenced a change in his attitude to the bank's staff. The emphasis began to shift away from stern discipline towards incentives and training schemes. For example, he devised a voluntary examination on the new Companies Act 1907 and organised special classes in modern languages. Both schemes were heavily oversubscribed. He also tried to persuade British universities to offer courses in international finance, on the grounds that American banks were recruiting from American and German universities.

Holden's accession to the chairmanship in 1908 placed him in a more public role. He remained managing director, with a salary of £6,000 and a special bonus of £15,000. Many of his executive duties were delegated to the joint general managers. Most of his diary appointments were either with exceptionally important customers such as Lord Pirrie, Lord Cowdray and Gordon Selfridge (qqv) or in connection with public or general financial duties. He campaigned for reform of the Institute of Bankers (of which he had been a vice-president since 1906), believing that its educational work should be geared towards the teaching of special skills, particularly languages. He also urged the Institute to become more democratic, both by giving votes to all members and by offering a greater range of activities to members in provincial centres. The campaign was successful. Language courses were established, votes were given to the ordinary members, and the Institute's system of 'local centres' was launched in 1913.

Holden used his annual chairman's speech as a platform for his views on financial policy. He argued that the clearing banks should keep their own gold reserves rather than deposit them with the Bank of England; he urged the creation of a gold-based war-chest as early as 1909; and he advocated a British parallel to the USA's Federal Reserve system. It was probably the broad sweep of these arguments, backed by Holden's strong Liberal pedigree, that persuaded H H Asquith to recommend him for the Chancellorship of the Exchequer in 1910. The recommendation was withdrawn when Lloyd George threatened to resign if Holden were appointed. Nevertheless (and despite Holden's decision to leave the Commons in 1910), the episode marked the beginning of a much closer involvement with the Asquith Government.

In 1911 Holden mobilised the support of the banks for the rescue of the Yorkshire Penny Bank, a large savings bank which had been hit hard by the depreciation of securities. The Government was kept closely informed of the reconstruction scheme, and in 1916, when the Yorkshire Penny Bank was again threatened by the fall in investment prices, Holden persuaded the Treasury to join the banks in guaranteeing the Penny Bank's reserves. A crisis was averted and the Penny Bank was eventually released from the guarantees in 1922.

These activities, and his long-standing anxiety over the power and resources of German banking, gave Holden an influential role during the First World War. With Revelstoke, Rothschild and Schuster (qqv), he recommended to Lloyd George the declaration of the moratorium on lending at the outbreak of war, and he was credited with the idea of issuing currency notes. Then in September 1915 he joined Lord Reading in the special commission to New York which negotiated the stabilisation of exchange rates. The commission won the Americans' confidence and raised the Anglo-French loan of £100 million, for which the American Government agreed to waive collateral. He continued to advise successive Chancellors on the management of the war loans although by 1917, after the fall of Asquith, he had 'no faith whatever in the Premier or in the Chancellor. They mean mischief to the Bankers' {Midland Bank Archives 150/4, Holden to E F Sheppard, 12 Jan 1917}.

Holden's public duties took up an increasing amount of his time during the war years. Yet his energy was undiminished, as he proved to an American reporter in 1919:

> I used to go to bed at 10 and get up at 5 and managed to put in a pretty good day's work. Now I leave the bank at 4.30 get two hours' sleep before dinner and after dinner my two reading secretaries bring me all the points that they have gathered for me during the day. My working secretary also comes to me and my four general managers sit at the table and we thrash things out ... I usually retire at 11, sleep until 8, and am in the bank again at 10 am {*Wall Street Journal* 29 Apr 1919}.

In his last two years he added to this routine the task of training Reginald McKenna (qv) to take over the chairmanship of the bank. Holden had been impressed by McKenna's work as Chancellor of the Exchequer during the negotiations over the Anglo-French loan and the Yorkshire Penny Bank in 1915-16, and he had been quick to recruit him to the Midland's board after the fall of the Asquith Government.

Although Holden was not so closely concerned with banking decisions during the later stages of his chairmanship of the Midland, his contribution to the bank's growth was as great as ever. His style of leadership was obviously influential, especially the way in which he selected his managers and motivated them to compete for business. If there was one area where he refused to delegate responsibility, it was in planning new amalgamations. He continued to select targets and conduct preliminary negotiations. Between 1908 and 1918 he engineered the acquisition of the Bradford Banking Co (1910), the Sheffield & Hallamshire Co and the Lincoln & Lindsey Banking Co (1913), the Metropolitan Bank (1914) and the London Joint Stock Bank (1918). Both the Metropolitan and the London were large banks in their own right, with deposits of £12 million and £58 million respectively, and the two amalgamations helped to raise Midland's total deposits from £94 million in 1913 to £349 million at the end of 1918. These totals and a network of 1,300 branches promoted the Midland to being the largest bank in the world. In addition in 1917 the Belfast Banking Co had become a wholly-owned subsidiary, and at the time of Holden's death in 1919 a similar agreement was being negotiated with the Clydesdale Bank in Scotland. In both cases Holden envisaged separate management for the Irish and Scottish subsidiaries (in contrast to amalgamated companies, which were put into liquidation), foreshadowing the 'group' concept favoured by the modern clearing banks.

Holden's use of amalgamations to obtain rapid growth was the strongest single thread in his career. Towards the end of his life, he attempted to explain why he had pinned so much faith on very large banking units. The proposed merger with the London Joint Stock Bank had been opposed in the press and in parliament when it was announced at the beginning of 1918. In response the Government appointed a Treasury Committee on Bank Amalgamations (the Colwyn Committee) and the Midland's negotiations with the London were suspended. The Committee, which produced its report in May 1918, was hostile to the most recent wave of mergers, largely on the grounds that a 'money trust' would be created; competition would be reduced and the interests of private depositors and traders would be threatened. Holden replied that the Committee had neglected the international dimensions of banking. In war or in peace, the British banks needed to match the capitalisation and deposits base of their German and American rivals. Otherwise, London would lose its role as the centre of international banking deposits, because foreign banks preferred to have accounts with the largest banks. He also rejected the Committee's charge that the amalgamations were squeezing out private customers and shareholders. In the Midland's experience, the balance had altered in favour of small deposits, small loans and small shareholdings during the amalgamations. He was convinced that the enlarged banks offered customers easier access to branch banks, the use of foreign bank connections, and a more secure base for the expansion of credit. In the event the Government did not accept the Committee's proposal to legislate against further amalgamations. Instead the clearing banks agreed not to carry out further amalgamations without Treasury consent, and the Midland's merger with the London was duly completed in July 1918.

Holden did not hold any outside directorships and he had few interests outside the bank. He was a Liberal and a passionate advocate of free trade, and he was also a member of the Fabian Society and the Cobden Club. Adopted as the Liberal parliamentary candidate for Heywood, Manchester, he was narrowly beaten in the 1900 general election (he refused to campaign, as his opponent was serving with the army in South Africa). He won the seat at the 1906 general election, but when he entered the Commons he felt that a high-profile political career would open the bank to criticism from customers and shareholders: 'my course was to say nothing' {Midland Bank Archives, 150/1, Holden to J S Pollitt, 28 Jan 1909}. His attendance at the Commons was infrequent and he did not seek re-election in 1910.

Elsewhere his activities were dominated by the bank and its interests. The membership of Holden Lodge, the freemasons' lodge which he established in 1902, was restricted to the bank's directors and staff. The bank even influenced his choice of recreation. He was an enthusiastic cyclist until he was well past his fiftieth birthday but, when his Elswick bicycle made way for a Lanchester car in about 1903, the main purpose of his touring expeditions was the search for new branch premises.

Holden married Annie Cassie, daughter of William Cassie, 'gentleman' {MCe}, of Aberdeen in 1877. Their family home was The Grange, at Thorpe, Chertsey, where Holden was a churchwarden. His wife died in 1905, leaving two sons, Cassie (a solicitor and later a director of the Midland) and Norman (a stockbroker), and a daughter, Nellie. Holden was created a baronet in 1909, and he twice declined a peerage. In later life he suffered from diabetes and gout but heart trouble was the immediate cause of his death on 23 July 1919. His will was sworn at £100,000 gross and his bequests included an endowment fund for education in the principles and practice of international banking. His trustees were empowered to withhold benefits from any successor to the baronetcy who had not entered a profession, trade or business. Earlier benefactions had included schemes for assisting wounded servicemen from Lancashire and Warwickshire in 1917 and the foundation of an employment bureau for NCOs and soldiers in 1918.

EDWIN GREEN

Writings:

The Depreciation of Securities in Relation to Gold Lecture to Liverpool & District Bankers' Institute (pp, 1907).

'Mr E H Holden's Tour' *Ramsbottom Observer* 30 Sept 1909.

letter proposing formation of a 'land bank' *Times* 28 Feb 1911.

Sir Edward Holden's Statement to the Institute of Bankers (pp, 1912).

The Foreign Exchanges and British Credit in Time of War (Toronto: J Mackay, 1916).

Sources:

Unpublished

Midland Bank Archives, Poultry, London: board minutes, 1881-1919; diaries of Holden and S B Murray, 1896-1916; letters of Holden, 1900-9; 'Mr Holden's report on his visit to America', 1904; letters of Holden to E F Sheppard, 1915-17; 'Sir Edward Holden's evidence before the Bank Amalgamations Committee', 1914; 'Sir Edward Holden's statement to the Standing Committee on Bank Amalgamations', 12 June 1918.

PRO: T170/57, minutes of meeting between Chancellor of Exchequer, cabinet members and bank representatives, 6 Aug 1914; T185/1, Holden's evidence to Committee on Currency and Foreign Exchange, 8 April 1918.

MCe.

PrC.

Information from Miss H E Bowker (relative of the Holden family).

Published

Bankers' Magazine Sept 1919.

Wilfred F Crick and John E Wadsworth, *A Hundred Years of Joint Stock Banking* (Hodder & Stoughton, 1936).

Daily Express 24 July 1919.

Daily Telegraph 24 July 1919.

Economist 26 July 1919.

Faces and Places 15 July 1904.

Financial News 24 July 1919.

Financial Times 24 July 1919.

Financier 24 July 1919.

Charles A E Goodhart, *The Business of Banking, 1891-1914* (Weidenfeld & Nicolson, 1972).

Edwin Green, *Debtors to their Profession. A History of the Institute of Bankers 1879-1979* (Methuen, 1979).

Midland Bank Review Sept 1919.

Morning Post 24 July 1919.

Times 24 July 1919.

Toronto News 24 Sept 1904.

Wall Street Journal 29 Apr, 29 July 1919.

WWMP.

WWW.

Isaac Holden — portrait (courtesy of Dr J Iredale).

HOLDEN, Sir Isaac

(1807-1897)

Worsted manufacturer

Isaac Holden was born in the village of Hurlet, between Paisley and Glasgow, on 7 May 1807, the seventh of nine children of Isaac Halden (sic), a headsman (chargehand) in the local coal-mine, and his wife Mary née Forrest; both parents had strong Wesleyan connections. Isaac's education was erratic, partially due to his ill-health as a child. He started at a Cottage School in 1812 where he remained until 1817, when the family moved a few miles to Kilbarchen, where he attended grammar school for a few months. But times were bad, and he obtained a job as a draw-boy to two hand weavers, although he also attended night school. Alternation between full or part-time education and employment continued for many years.

In January 1828 Isaac Holden moved to Leeds, as a mathematics master. His stay was short owing to incompatibility of religious views, and he moved to a post at Slaithwaite. Later he moved to the Castle Street Academy at Reading as classics master for the salary of £20 per annum. Whilst there he also taught at the Mechanics Institute.

At Castle Street Academy Holden delivered a series of lectures on chemistry. In the course of these he demonstrated the possibility of obtaining instantaneous fire by means of a wood splint dipped in a mixture of chemicals and subjected to abrasion. He modified the standard demonstration by adding sulphur to the mixture to maintain the flame; the result was an improved form of match. It was suggested that a patent should be taken, but this Holden failed to do. Ill-health drove Isaac Holden back to Scotland in June 1830 to set up a school of his own in Glasgow, but before it was opened he received an offer from Townend Bros of Cullingworth, near Bingley, Yorkshire, of the post of book-keeper with the firm at £100 per annum for three years. Townend Bros was a concern of some importance in the developing worsted industry. The book-keeping which took Holden to Cullingworth did not confine him to the office for very long. Soon after his arrival he was taken for a tour of the works and to see handcombing; thereafter the technicalities of the machinery lured him from his desk, and the possibility of mechanising the combing process was an immediate challenge to him. His occupation appears to have changed gradually to that of manager.

In 1834 he visited the Paris Exhibition on behalf of the firm. During the next ten years his employment at Townend Bros was to be punctuated with applications for improving his position, and when the reaction to these suggestions was unsatisfactory, he considered the possibility of starting his own business. Under pressure from his wife, Marion née Love (whom he married in 1832), to 'get a concern of our own' {Leeds

University, Holden papers, Mrs Marion Holden to Isaac Holden, 17 June 1845}, he took this step in the summer of 1846.

The timing of his own venture was unfortunate for it coincided with a period of serious industrial unrest and a decline in trade. The business lasted barely two years and, in the midst of Holden's struggle to establish it, his wife died after an apparently long and progressive illness, leaving him with four children. In addition to spinning genappe yarns, Holden's mill in Bradford was weaving Paisley Shawl 'middles', and contained a hired machine comb. Unpleasant letters arrived from Bradford Bank in the months prior to closure but, although he suffered financial loss involving several thousand pounds, he secured an alliance with Samuel Cunliffe Lister (qv) which eventually led to the foundation of the family fortune.

While he was employed at Townends, Holden had already decided that the way to proceed with his combing inventions was somehow to remove the blockage formed by Donisthorpe's patents. He achieved this by an agreement with Lister, who had acquired an interest in Donisthorpe's inventions. In 1847 a joint patent was taken by Lister and Holden. It was of the 'umbrella' type and covered 'carding, preparing and spinning wool and fibrous substances for Heald and Genappe yarns' {British Patent 1847 (11,896)}. The patentees agreed that Lister should provide capital in exchange for exclusive rights to the combing aspects of the patent, whilst Holden would have the benefit of the spinning aspects; in the carding part they were to have a joint interest.

Holden and Lister then formed a partnership with the intention of mounting a combing concern to exploit the anticipated improvements in machine combing. It was further decided that the firm of Lister & Holden should be based in France. The relations between the two partners alternated between spells of close co-operation and states of extreme antipathy. The undercurrents of disagreement and distrust erupted frequently during the ten years of the partnership and years later, in the 1870s, re-emerged as a bitter confrontation which was to last to the grave. Besides differing politically, they quarrelled bitterly and publicly over who was responsible for the invention of the Square Motion Comb.

The partnership began in 1848. That January Holden was setting up equipment in a rented mill at St Denis, a small town immediately to the north of Paris. Distant from the centre of the French worsted industry, the mill proved to be far from ideal and was eventually closed in 1860. In 1852 the partners built further establishments at Croix (near Roubaix) and Reims. These two mills were managed by Jonathan Holden (Reims) and Isaac Holden Crothers (Croix), both nephews of Isaac.

The partnership came to an end in 1858 when Lister withdrew and Holden bought his share for £74,000. Under Holden's ownership the factories continued to develop until Holden became the largest machine wool comber in France, processing some 20 per cent of the total combed wool consumed by the French worsted spinning industry, a market share which Holdens retained until after 1900. The running of the French mills was entrusted for many years to Holden's nephews. They continued to be entirely successful and between 1864 and 1877, for example, their combined average annual trading profit totalled £130,000. The Reims factory ceased operation in 1914 and Croix in 1938.

Square Motion comb (courtesy of Dr J Iredale).

After the closure of the St Denis mill, Holden in 1860 returned to Yorkshire where he established a works in Bradford. This quickly led to the creation in 1864 of a purpose-built mill of considerable size, Alston Works, which was able to process in excess of five million kilogrammes of combed wool per annum. (These premises are still used for wool scouring, but the Holden company disappeared, in 1964, as a result of a take-over by Woolcombers Ltd). Both in Bradford and France Holden largely followed the practice of commission combing (generally more common in the UK than in France), using the Square Motion Comb. The invention of this comb, like most other wool-combing machines, is uncertain. It was claimed to be the best machine for fine wools. The comb was, however, only used in the factories owned by Holden or by his family connections, the Illingworths. Of the important nineteenth century wool combs the Square Motion Comb is now the only one which has been entirely abandoned by the modern industry.

The re-orientation of interests to Bradford which took place in the first few years of the 1860s coincided with a double marriage in which Angus Holden was united with Margaret Illingworth and Angus's sister, Mary married Margaret Illingworth's brother, Henry. This was not the end of the linking of the two families, for six years later the eldest of the Illingworth 'children', Alfred, married the youngest of Isaac Holden's daughters, Margaret.

During the early years of the 1860s Isaac Holden also moved his residence from the mill house at St Denis to Oakworth House near to Keighley, which he had had re-built; the original previously belonged to the family of his second wife, Sarah née Sugden (ca 1804-90).

The pressures of the massive reorganisation and refurbishing of the Holden Mills which had taken place in the early 1860s took their toll on Isaac Holden's health and his doctors insisted on an entire change of occupation. As a Liberal of long-standing he was approached to adopt a parliamentary career and, in July 1865, he was elected MP for Knaresborough. In November 1868 he resigned the seat in favour of his son-in-law, Alfred Illingworth. Then he unsuccessfully contested the Eastern Division of the West Riding (1868), the Northern Division (1872 by-election), the Eastern Division (1874). In 1882 he won the Northern Division seat in a by-election caused by Lord Frederick Cavendish's assassination. In 1885 he was elected for Keighley and in 1892 his seat was not contested by the Conservatives 'out of consideration and respect for Isaac Holden not his political beliefs' {*The Herald* 10 June 1892}; he retired from parliament in 1895. He was created a baronet in 1893.

Holden's very considerable success as an entrepreneur at a relatively late stage in life could be attributed to his long association with the textile industry and the resultant thorough understanding of the associated technology; to his despatch by Lister to France at an opportune time; to the choice of capable subordinates; a useful second marriage; and finally to that degree of luck which is necessary for any business.

Holden's investments were both varied and global. Little financial detail appears to remain, but in 1874 his total assets were in excess of half a million pounds. On his death his personal estate was £317,635. Holden supported the idea of death duties but is reputed to have distributed £2 million to members of his family before his death.

As a philanthropist, Isaac Holden particularly supported those organisations with which he had connections in his earlier years. The Wesleyan Methodist Church, of which a large number of his relatives and friends were members, was a frequent recipient of considerable financial assistance. Encouragement of technical education spread from the Mechanics Institute movement, of which as a young man he had experience both as a student and a teacher, to the provision of Technical Colleges. His support extended to the Continent and in Reims a library still bears his name.

An indication of his influence in business is the description of Isaac Holden as one of the five men who dominated the West Riding wool textile industry in the nineteenth century. He led an active life almost up to the end, dying suddenly in his ninety-first year on 13 August 1897.

JOHN A IREDALE *and* J MALCOLM TRICKETT

Writings:

British Patent:

1847 (11,896).

Sources:

Unpublished

Bradford University, Holden papers.

Leeds University, Holden papers.

Information from Jordan Goodman and Katriona Honeyman.

Jack Reynolds, 'Great Men Connected with the Bradford Textile Industry', paper to Textile Institute, Yorkshire Section, 25 Mar 1975.

Elizabeth Jennings, 'Sir Isaac Holden (1807-97): The First Comber in Europe' (Bradford PhD, 1982).

J Malcolm Trickett, 'A Technological Appraisal of the Isaac Holden Papers' (Bradford MSc, 1977).

Published

James Burnley, *The History of Wool and Wool Combing* (Sampson Low & Co, 1889).

DNB.

HOLLAND, William Henry

1st Lord Rotherham

(1849-1927)

Textile manufacturer

William Henry Holland was born in Manchester on 15 December 1849, the younger of the two sons of William Holland, a warehouseman's son, and Ellen, daughter of Samuel Robinson, a coachman. William Holland (1823-92) had achieved affluence and social recognition through his own endeavours initially as a mill manager then as proprietor of his own cotton spinning mills — from 1854 at Salford and from 1868 in new and larger premises at Miles Platting in Manchester. Besides achieving success as a businessman he became a JP, a prominent Wesleyan lay supporter, Overseer of the Poor for Salford and a Lancashire County Councillor. His second son, William H Holland was educated at Manchester Grammar School and Bramham College, Tadcaster. At the age of eighteen he entered his father's business and in 1872, with his elder brother Samuel, was admitted as a partner into the family firm which then became William Holland & Sons.

The new partners participated in the repeated expansion of the business and although the principal activity was the spinning of Egyptian and Sea Island cotton William was responsible in 1877 for introducing the spinning of 'French Cashmere Yarn' and in 1878 a mill for worsted spinning was erected. The Hollands were strict disciplinarians but reputedly displayed a fairness which brought them an apparent immunity from labour troubles. By the 1890s the firm, employing some 1,000 hands, was one of the largest in Manchester; 170,000 spindles in their Victoria mills were devoted to cotton and 24,000 in the Albert mills to worsted. The growth of the Hollands' firm was matched elsewhere in the trade and brought over-production and cut-throat competition. In 1898 the family's cotton mills were amongst the first to be merged into the Fine Cotton Spinners' & Doublers' Association Ltd (FCSDA), subsequently the country's largest manufacturing company. Although the elder Holland brother, Samuel, was to be nominally responsible for the management of the Holland firm within the new Association, William's links with the family concern were broken. Instead he took a wider part within the FCSDA, from 1898 as vice-chairman and as chairman from 1908 until 1917.

Holland, because of his family firm's size, would undoubtedly have played an influential role in the decision to establish the FCSDA; as a director from 1897 to 1910 of Williams Deacon & Manchester & Salford Bank Ltd, one of the FCSDA's bankers, he may also have played a part in the financial structuring of the new firm. For eighteen years he was a regular participant at general board meetings and more importantly at the weekly meetings of the seven-man executive board which effectively guided and managed the Association. Like Sir William Houldsworth (qv), the first chairman, he was the effective link between the general and executive boards and kept an eye on the policies pursued by A H Dixon (qv), the managing director and company's lynchpin. Holland made a particular contribution to the firm as its European representative, for example when the purchase of French and German firms was being considered. In the board room he was generally a firm supporter of expansion, and conciliation with labour, and he was a strong advocate of the British Cotton Growing Association. His succession to Houldsworth as chairman of the Fine Spinners ensured that this large firm continued to have one of Manchester's principal commercial statesmen at its head. His contacts with Government were a considerable advantage to the firm during the First World War.

Outside the FCSDA Holland sustained a wide range of commercial and political interests. As a director of the Manchester Chamber of Commerce from 1886 he forged working relationships with leaders of Manchester's business community. His work on its various sub-committees — Tariffs, Education, Limited Liability and particularly the Bombay and Lancashire Cotton Spinning inquiry (1888) — provided him with a valuable apprenticeship in the cut and thrust of committee work which bore fruit in a later parliamentary career; he also took an active part in the formation of the Conciliation Board for dealing with trade disputes. The Chamber brought other opportunities; in 1881 and 1891 Holland was selected to give expert evidence in London before the committees considering the French treaty negotiations, whilst in 1898 he was appointed a member of Sir Henry Fowler's Indian Currency Committee. On this committee he stoutly defended the monetary status quo, rejecting the bimetallist nostrums, one of whose prime advocates was, ironically, Sir William Houldsworth, chairman of Fine Spinners. He also served as a commissioner at the Brussels, Paris and Milan exhibitions. The esteem of his peers was reflected in his election as president of the Manchester Chamber of Commerce, 1896-98, as member of the Machinery Users' Association, 1908-10, the Association of Chambers of Commerce, 1904-7 — an important link between Government and the business community — the Institute of Directors and as first president of the Textile Institute, 1910-12.

Commercial recognition went hand-in-glove with a moderately successful parliamentary career. Although he first developed an interest in politics during the 1874 general election it was only in the 1880s that his active work began. He established himself in local government and served as an alderman of the City of Manchester (1889-99). In 1885 he was made president of the East Manchester Liberal Association and subsequently became president of the Manchester Reform Club (1895) and a member of the executive of the National Liberal Federation. He was selected for the Salford North constituency in 1888 and was elected in 1892. He rapidly emerged as an active member specialising in industrial and commercial questions but he was defeated by six votes in the 1895 general election, suffering for his support of Home Rule and Indian Cotton duties. His strong Manchester connections and commercial expertise kept him before the public eye and in 1899 he was returned to Westminster, this time as a member for the Rotherham division of Yorkshire. He continued as a forceful advocate of Lancashire's Liberal interests, particularly of free trade — the *Manchester Guardian* later reported that 'he did much towards the winning of the Liberal triumph of 1906 in the industrial North'. He also used his status to advance particular interests — machine rating, limited partnership reform, and the Channel Tunnel Bill of 1907. Though an articulate and pointed speaker and serving, sometimes as chairman, on a number of committees he failed to achieve government office and remained a respected back-bencher. In February 1910 he took the Chiltern Hundreds making his safe Rotherham seat available for J A Pease, then Chancellor of the Duchy of Lancaster. Six months later, perhaps as a political reward, he was raised to the peerage; though less active he was still to use his parliamentary status in furtherance of commercial interests.

Elevation to the Lords coincided with an expansion of Holland's business interests. In 1910 he became a director of the Royal Exchange Assurance Co Ltd; in 1911 a director of the London, City & Midland Bank Ltd; and in 1912, of the Yorkshire Penny Bank Ltd. Holland was now intent on diversification beyond cotton and finance. In 1913 he became a director of the Eagle Oil Transport Co Ltd, a charter-ship company for the shipping of Mexican oil whose chairman was Lord Cowdray (qv). By the time of the First World War he was engaged in riskier ventures; he became interested in an electric light company in Africa, oilfields in Russia, a colliery in Wales and land in Canada. He also participated in loss-making stock exchange dealings and, what was to be his undoing, speculative ventures in Manchuria and with Japanese bonds. These latter, combined with losses caused by the war, forced him to turn to moneylenders who, in July 1917, seeking satisfaction, applied for a receiving order against him. In anticipation of being gazetted he had earlier resigned his board appointments, including that to which he had given most — his chairmanship of the FCSDA. His assets, at first count

£6,105, were totally inadequate to meet liabilities initially assessed at £332,516 but later ranked at about £125,000. Aided by a donation of £8,500 from the Association (who also took a half share in Holland's Albert Mill), arranged by his successor as chairman, A H Dixon, he was able to raise sufficient to satisfy in part his creditors and so obtain release from bankruptcy with a composition of 6s in the pound. A discharged bankrupt, Holland's career was in ruins.

Building upon his own earnings as a partner in the family firm, sharing in his father's £211,000 will, and receiving £160,000 in cash and shares as his share of the sale of William Holland & Sons to the FCSDA, Holland might have died a rich man if he had stayed in cotton and banking. From 1898 to 1917 his income was £20,000 to £25,000 a year of which £4,000 was in directors' fees. But his financial adventures brought oblivion. Holland attributed his downfall to the large sum of money he received from the sale of the family firm to Fine Spinners in 1898. He once remarked 'I was surrounded by honest and honourable men all my life in the North and when I came to London I was too trustful' {*Times* 28 Dec 1927}.

Drawing on the prosperous start provided by his father and on his own abilities, Holland had scaled the heights of business, commercial and political achievement. He had not been ungenerous with his time or wealth and had contributed to Mancunian and Indian charities. Public recognition was showered upon him: he was JP for Manchester and Cheshire; a Freeman of the Borough of Rotherham; Officer of the Order of Leopold, Belgium; knighted in 1902, created baronet in 1907 and made First Lord Rotherham of Broughton in 1910. Holland was received into the Roman Catholic Church in 1924 (following his wife who joined in 1905). Though he somehow received sufficient income to keep up his family home at Lothersdale, Rottingdean, Sussex, on his death on 26 December 1927 Holland left a mere £25 gross. His wife Mary, the eldest daughter of James Lund of Malsis Hall near Bradford, whom he married in 1874, died in 1931 leaving £2,031 gross. They had three children and their only son, a Harrow- and Oxford-educated soldier, succeeded to the title and became an inspector in the Ministry of Pensions. Since he was childless, the peerage became extinct on his death in 1950.

J J MASON

Writings:

Salford Reporter 25 June 1892, 6, 13 July 1895.

PP, Report of the Commercial Intelligence Committee of the Board of Trade (1898) C 8962.

PP, Report of the Committee Appointed to Inquire into the Indian Currency (1899) C 9421, C 9087.

presidential addresses *Reports of Annual Meetings* of the Association of British Chambers of Commerce, 1904-7.

Times 19 Jan 1905, 6 Dec 1907, 6 Feb 1909.

The Cotton Industry and the Fiscal Question. Speeches by Sir W H Holland and Mr William Tattersall (Free Trade Union, 1909).

presidential addresses *Journal of the Textile Institute* 1910.

Sources:

Unpublished

British Library, Herbert Gladstone papers BL Add MS 46061 and Campbell-Bannerman papers BL Add MS 41240 and 41242.

Courtaulds, Northern Spinning Division, Fine Cotton Spinners' & Doublers Ltd, General Board Minutes, 1898-1918; Executive Board Minutes, 1898-1910 and Annual Reports.

PrC of William Holland.

Information from Dr A C Howe.

Published

Peter F Clarke, *Lancashire and the New Liberalism* (Cambridge: Cambridge University Press, 1971).

Complete Peerage 13.

The Fine Cotton Spinners' & Doublers' Association Ltd, *The Fine Cotton Spinners' and Doublers' Asociation* (Manchester: pp, 1909).

J R Hay, 'Employers and Social Policy' *Social History* 4 (1977).

E Helm, *Chapters in the History of the Manchester Chamber of Commerce* (Manchester, 1898).

Henry W Macrosty, *The Trust Movement in British Industry: A Study of Business Organisation* (Longmans Green & Co, 1907).

Manchester Chamber of Commerce, *Bombay and Lancashire Cotton Spinning Inquiry* (1888).

Manchester Guardian 14 Nov 1892, 28 Dec 1927.

W T Pike and W B Tracy, *Manchester and Salford at the close of the 19th Century: Contemporary Biographies* (Brighton 1899).

Spy 12 July 1895.

T Swindells, *Manchester Streets and Manchester Men* 5th ser (Manchester, 1908).

Times 31 Oct, 7 Nov 1917, 30 Jan, 27 Feb, 6 Mar 1918, 28 Feb, 4 Apr 1919, 28 Dec 1927, 11 Sept 1928, 15 Aug 1931.

WWMP.

WWW.

HOLLINS, Denis Machell

(1880-1952)

Textile machinery manufacturer

Denis Machell Hollins was born at Mansfield Woodhouse, near Mansfield, Nottinghamshire on 20 August 1880, the fourth of the five children of Henry Ernest Hollins (qv) and Mary Anne née Gibson. His paternal family had been closely involved with the pioneering of the mechanised cotton-spinning industry (spanning four generations and in association with the Oldknows) and his father, a dominant entrepreneurial figure in the Mansfield-based firm of William Hollins & Co, had been instrumental in the development of the famous 'Viyella' brand of fabric. His maternal antecedents, on the other hand, were prosperous landowners and bankers of the Lune Valley — a family which could proudly trace their ancestry back to the early fifteenth century. This mixed background of 'trade' and landed gentry ensured an affluent early upbringing: before proceeding to Haileybury College in 1891, Denis would spend part of the year in the imposing house lying close by the large mill at Pleasley Vale, and the remainder — the grouse-shooting and fishing seasons — on the extensive family estate at Barbon in Westmorland.

Immediately after completing his public school education, young Hollins joined his father's firm at their weaving sheds in Glasgow, recently acquired, in 1899, with the firm of Alexander McNab & Co. It was there that Hollins became acquainted with the automatic loom, since the company were amongst the first British concerns to import the new Northrop innovation, developed between 1889 and 1894, from the Draper Corporation of Hopedale, Massachusetts, USA. An immediate and enduring fascination with the technical properties of this revolutionary machine, and the realisation that his elder brother, Arthur, was being groomed for the William Hollins 'succession', prompted Denis Hollins to join the newly-founded firm of British Northrop Ltd. He was probably invited to do so by a family friend and business associate of his father, Henry P Greg (qv), a director, and later chairman, of Ashton Bros & Co of Hyde, who, along with William Livesey of Henry Livesey & Co, the Blackburn loom-making enterprise, and Edward Tootal Broadhurst (qv), had been chiefly responsible for the establishment of Northrops in the UK in June 1902.

Hollins's career with Northrops probably began in the early part of 1903. Later that year William Livesey, who had been appointed first managing director, died and Hollins succeeded him. He remained managing director for the next fifty years, and was also chairman from 1945 until his death. He was undoubtedly the key managerial figure behind the growth of the firm from its humble origins as a tiny sub-assembly shop in Harewood Street, Blackburn, to one of the largest manufacturers of automatic looms in the world producing 10,000 looms per annum in 1952.

This growth was neither steady nor continuous. Before the Second World War the major market was overseas (especially Europe), with only about a quarter of total sales destined for Lancashire itself. Ironically enough Blackburn, one of the world's great weaving centres, bought hardly any Northrop looms. Whatever may have been the reasons for this failure to invest in new technology, a subject which still excites considerable controversy, the small Northrops' sales staff (numbering no more than 15 in the 1930s, excluding overseas agency men not directly employed by the firm) found it extremely difficult to make any real headway. The enormous American market was closed by the terms of the original agreement between Northrops and Drapers. The company grew by fits and starts, and in this period never made more than a small trading profit: before 1938, the year when Northrops went public, dividends never exceeded 7.5 per cent.

During the war the works were made over entirely to the manufacture of armaments, but afterwards a period of really rapid expansion began. The Government urged the firm (at first by persuasion, later by threatening to open a rival factory in Scotland) to put down plant at a rate considerably in excess of Hollins's intentions, but did not provide any additional finance. This rapid increase in productive capacity led to the kind of trading success which Hollins had worked towards for so long, but it was comparatively short-lived: within a decade of his death Northrops began to decline, and by the late 1960s had shrunk to a small workshop, housed in the original premises of 1905-7 and employing barely a tenth of its peak work force.

In each of these three phases of British Northrops' commercial life — the jerky growth between 1907 and 1939, the intensive enlargement of the late 1940s and early 1950s, and the subsequent contraction — Denis Hollins played an important role. His managerial style was frankly dictatorial, and in the words of one of his fellow directors: 'he was a man who had always had a complete say in the details of the production and management ... he did not easily delegate responsibility ... and the rest of the Board would get nowhere with the shareholders ... without full support from Mr Hollins' (PRO, BT 64/3015 SUPP 14/388, notes of a discussion with J Hunter, 21 Sept 1949). Somewhat surprisingly for a man of his family background, Hollins was single-minded in his devotion to his work, largely shunning social intercourse and showing little outward interest in either the great issues of the day (in marked contrast to his father, a prominent Liberal), or the more parochial civic concerns of Blackburn (despite Northrops being the town's largest employer, he was an almost anonymous member of the local Chamber of Commerce).

This obsessive attitude inspired great respect and loyalty amongst his workforce and, in turn, his classic paternalism (which, unusually, did not run to hostility to trade-unionism) led to the building-up of a relatively generous welfare scheme. He took a real interest in the well-being of the employees, prided himself on knowing something about their personal lives and proved to be a generous benefactor to the men whenever they suffered unexpected hardship and distress. He began an in-house journal, the *Northrop News*, in the 1920s in order to encourage close contact between staff.

However, his social reticence (in part caused by poor eyesight) meant that he did little personally to publicise the virtues of the new loom, and this is rather curious in view of the great pre-war need to get the product recognised both at home and abroad. Hollins himself appears to have been much more enthusiastic about purchasing, especially machine-tools, and the organisation of production than he was about sales. Three further character traits had a real impact upon Northrops' fortunes. Firstly, he was never convinced about the need to invest in R&D and he was wary of the Shirley Institute, the cotton industry's research institute; this is particularly ironic in view of his perpetual frustration with Lancashire's unwillingness to adopt the automatic loom. Hollins begrudged the expenditure of even very nominal sums on future projects (much to the chagrin of the Draper Corporation, which retained an important interest as shareholder). Although the Evershed Report of 1947 stated unequivocally that the late 1940s models were technically as good as any being produced throughout the world, this short-sighted policy cost the company dear in the long run because continental competitors (especially the Swiss and Belgians) were busy developing a completely new generation of shuttle-less weaving devices. Secondly, Hollins was quintessentially a 'cotton man' and was quite unable to foresee the true significance of artificial fibres: he even fought a long rear-guard action against the development of a loom specifically geared for rayon production, for which Courtaulds were pleading. Finally, in the last few years of his life, he was undecided about the future leadership of the company: in the end he created a dual structure that pleased no one. A nephew, I F E Hollins, and the long-serving sales director, H de G Gaudin, were made joint managing directors: this undoubtedly provoked many managerial problems foreseen by Drapers. This fault, that of many absolute rulers, clearly proved detrimental to the firm. Nevertheless, damaging though they were, the effects of these prejudices and shortcomings were far from being irreversible, and must be set against Hollins's basic achievement — the patient nurturing and then the careful fostering to full maturity of a problematic enterprise.

At the comparatively late age of forty-eight, in 1928, Denis Hollins married Mrs Lucy Jamieson née Stowell. After a protracted, if not completely debilitating, illness, he developed cancer of the liver in the spring of 1952 and died on 23 October 1952 in his Blackburn home, leaving his widow and two step-children. His estate was proved at £99,155 gross.

COLIN SIMMONS

Writings:

'The Automatic Loom' *Journal of the British Association of Managers of Textile Works* 8 (1916-18).

'To my Fellow Workers' (British Northrop Ltd, 1918).

'The Economic Unit in Textile Factories' *Journal of the British Association of Managers of Textile Works* 11 (1920-21).

'Fellow Workers' (British Northrop Ltd, 27 Aug 1945).

Sources:

Unpublished

British Northrop Ltd, *Contract: Adopting Agreement between the Northrop Loom Co and the British Northrop Loom Co Ltd* 5 Sept 1902.

PRO, BT 96/142, Post-War Reconstruction: Textile Machinery Files, Jan 1943-Apr 1944; BT 64/207, minutes of meetings of Machinery and Plant Sub-Committee of the Cotton Industry Working Party, Nov 1945; BT 64/2708, Report of the Machinery and Plant Sub-Committee of the Cotton Industry Working Party, Jan 1946; BT 64/3015 SUPP 14/388, Ministry of Supply Committee on Industrial Productivity, Mar 1947-Jan 1948.

Wm Hollins & Co Ltd, Pleasley, Derbyshire, archives, especially Directors Minute Book, 11 May 1897-4 Dec 1903.

BCe.

MCe.

PrC.

Private papers of H de G Gaudin, relating to British Northrop.

Interviews and correspondence with J N B Cardwell (sales manager, British Northrop), H de Gaudin (formerly joint managing director, British Northrop), J Gibson (nephew and former director, British Northrop), Miss A Hawkins (formerly industrial nurse, British Northrop), Mrs A M Hollins (widow of nephew), F E Hollins (formerly joint managing director, British Northrop), Miss N Jamieson (step-daughter), Mrs M King (niece), T Yates (formerly sales representative, Henry Livesey & Co).

William Lazonick, 'Industrial Organisation and Technological Change: The Decline of the British Cotton Industry', Harvard Institute of Economic Research, Discussion Paper 794, Oct 1980.

William Mass, 'The Adoption of the Automatic Loom 1890-1920' Paper for the Twenty-first Annual Cliometric Conference, USA, April 1980.

Published

James B Aitken, *Automatic Weaving* (Manchester: Columbine Press, 1964).

Derek H Aldcroft, 'The Entrepreneur and the British Economy, 1870-1914' *Economic History Review* 2nd ser 17 (1964).

Amalgamated Weavers' Association, *Northrop Weaving, Replies to Questions* (1911).

Blackburn Times 26 July 1902, 5 Oct 1928, 19, 26 Aug, 2 Sept 1933, 21 Aug 1950, 1 Aug, 31 Oct 1952.

British Northrop Ltd, *Automatic Weaving: The Northrop System* (Blackburn: British Northrop Ltd, 1942).

—, *Information for the Press* (1959).

Burke's Landed Gentry.

William H Chase, *Five Generations of Loom Builders: A History of Draper Corporation* (Hopedale, Massachusetts: Draper Corporation, 1950).

HOLLINS Denis Machell

Cotton Industry Working Party Report (HMSO, 1946).

Daily Mail 15 May 1930.

Douglas A Farnie, 'The Textile Industry: Woven Fabrics' in Singer *History of Technology* 5.

Irwin Feller, 'The Draper Loom in New England Textiles, 1894-1914: A Study of Diffusion of an Innovation' *Journal of Economic History* 26 (1966).

Alan Fowler, 'Trade Unions and Technical Change: The Automatic Loom Strike 1908' *North West Labour History Bulletin* 6 (1979-80).

Marvin Frankel, 'Obsolescence and Technical Change in a Maturing Economy' *American Economic Review* 56 (1966).

Hugh de G Gaudin, 'A Reply to the Evershed Report' *Textile Mercury and Argus* 12 Dec 1947.

—, 'British Northrop: Reply to R Rothwell' *Journal of the Textile Institute* Jan 1976.

Robert Gibson, *Cotton Textile Wages in the US and Great Britain* (New York: King's Crown Press, 1948).

Lancashire Cotton Corporation Ltd, 'Official Report Concerning a Test of Automatic Looms, etc, made in 1931' *Journal of the Textile Institute* 33 (1932).

Manchester Guardian 25 Oct 1952.

Northern Daily Telegraph 24 Oct 1952.

Stanley Pigott, *Hollins: A Study of Industry* (Nottingham: William Hollins & Co, 1949).

Report of a Committee of Investigation, Cotton Textile Machinery Industry vol 2 *Weaving Machinery* (chairman Sir F R Evershed) (Ministry of Supply, 1947).

Roy Rothwell, 'British Northrop: A Case Study of Decline and Renaissance' *Journal of the Textile Institute* Nov 1975.

Lars G Sandberg, *Lancashire in Decline: A Study in Entrepreneurship, Technology and International Trade* (Columbus, Ohio: Ohio State University, 1974).

Stock Exchange Official Year-Book 1937-60 passim.

Frederick A Wells, *Hollins and Viyella: A Study in Business History* (Newton Abbot: David & Charles, 1968).

William F Whittaker, 'The Northrop Loom' *Journal of the Manchester School of Technology Textile Society* 1 (1908-9).

HOLLINS, Sir Frank

(1843-1924)

Cotton manufacturer

Frank Hollins was born in Stockport on 16 April 1843, the fourth son of Edward Hollins (1805-86), a cotton manufacturer, and his wife Margaret Harding formerly Woody. A sleeping partner in Wm Hollins & Co of Pleasley Vale, Edward Hollins had been active in Manchester textiles since 1832, and had later joined his brother-in-law Henry Marsland (MP for Stockport, 1835-47; d 1864) in setting up the Park Mills in Stockport, where Frank was born. Edward Hollins migrated about 1847 to Preston, where he took over the Sovereign Mills, and soon gained a reputation for the weaving of the finest calicoes, earning a gold medal at the Paris Exhibition of 1855. It was this firm which Frank, although originally destined for university and the professions, joined at the age of nineteen, after an education at Bridgnorth Grammar School and Rossall.

But the family firm at this point was experiencing a caesura in its fortunes. Edward Hollins publicised his chagrin at failing to win a gold medal at the International Exhibition of 1862 and having perhaps suffered as a result of the cotton famine, he was in 1866 obliged to come to an arrangement with his creditors. Yet he remained in business and it was with his father as salesman, traveller and partner that Frank Hollins entered the cotton trade.

Hollins soon built up a wide trade connection, facilitated by his geniality of manner but backed up by the still reputedly high quality of Hollinses' cloth. On the retirement of his father ca 1871 he was left in partnership with an elder brother, Edward, and George Galloway of Preston (d 1912). Frank now became the mainspring of the firm, and in the 1870s was responsible for a radical departure from the commercial norm when he initiated the practice of direct trading with retailers. After some doubts, this proved a resounding success. Nevertheless, Hollins emerged as the head of the firm only after a bitter management tussle (resolved ultimately at the Nottinghamshire Assizes in 1879), as a result of which Edward was forced out, allegedly for incompetence. In the meanwhile two other brothers joined the Nottingham firm of Wm Hollins & Co, as did a fourth brother later.

Having consolidated his control of Hollins Bros, Hollins embarked on the greatest gamble of his career when in 1885 in a reverse takeover, he amalgamated his relatively small firm (ca 650 looms, 350 operatives) with its Preston neighbour, the ailing giant Horrockses, Miller & Co, a firm which twenty years earlier under Edward Hermon (qv) had led the industry. This was a vital lifeline for Horrockses: as Sidney Hermon urged, 'the old traditions of the concern must be put on one side. It would be suicidal for us to let ... this amalgamation fall through' {Lancashire RO, Horrockses Business Records, S A Hermon to F Styles, 12 Apr 1885}.

Equally emphatically, Hermon wrote to his brother Samuel, 'Whatever you do do not let these negotiations fall thro — you have no idea the weak state we are in in Preston and how we are eaten up with high-salaried nonentities' {ibid, S A Hermon to Samuel Hermon 12 Apr 1885}. Some feared that Horrockses would prove a deadweight, dragging the smaller firm down with it. However, Hollins, a man of great confidence, ambition and ideas, as well as an adept commercial diplomat, ably supported by his partners, George and W W Galloway (1854-1936), pulled the two dissimilar firms into an effective whole. Hollins Bros was able to offer modern weaving machinery (Horrockses were 'out and out behind the times' {ibid}), technical expertise and entrepreneurial vigour; Horrockses possessed reputation, an established market position at home and abroad, and a large capital base. Horrockses' assets were threatened by managerial incompetence but the new company, with a joint capital of £750,000, provided the opportunity to marry size with talent. Hollins, as managing director and leading spirit of the new firm, pressed home this advantage. Hollins's system of direct trading was now successfully applied to the vaster custom of Horrockses, a major innovation in a trade dominated by the 'home trade' warehouse. This rupture of established practices created some discomfort, especially in London. There was also an assimilation of discounts on home and foreign trade in order to provide an incentive to shipping. The shipping business itself was transferred from London to Manchester, both to cut costs, and, more importantly, to take it out of the hands of the reputedly incompetent and lazy London office. Along with managerial and technological changes at Preston, the new firm had thus taken decisive steps to counter the depression from which the textile industry was beginning to suffer.

The second stage in Hollins's ambitious merger policy was not long delayed, for by January 1887 negotiations were under way for an amalgamation with the Bolton firm of Crewdson, Cross & Co. Crewdsons itself had resulted from the amalgamation in 1864 of the Bolton firm J Cross & Co, with the Manchester firm of Crewdson & Worthington. Its head, J K Cross (1832-87), MP for Bolton, 1874-85, Under-Secretary of State for India, 1883-85, was only nominally involved in the firm, but his partners A Crewdson and his brother Edward Cross (1834-90) welcomed the merger, 'alive to the many advantages which might be derived from the removal of competition and of the joint-working of the two firms' {ibid, E Cross to Hollins, 9 Jan 1887}. The merger was to some extent defensive on both sides. W B Secretan of Horrockses believed that, on existing sales figures 'we shall ... be laughing Crewdson Cross & Co's competition and amalgamation to scorn perhaps after all,' and that given two more years' profits of £30,000 'we could readily convert into a *public* limited ... we could then leave Crewdsons to flounder' {ibid, Secretan to Hollins, 20, 19 Jan 1887}. Nevertheless the merger offered solid advantages, given fears which even Secretan shared as to whether there existed enough retail business for both concerns. Hollins saw in it the opportunity to improve prices, while achieving economies of production and distribution. Crewdsons were one of the best-known firms in the white calico trade, with a reputation for high quality and an extensive world trade. Although their spinning mill (42,700 spindles) was outdated, their weaving shed at Farnworth (built 1877) was colossal, with 2,000 looms, said to be without a peer in Lancashire. In May 1887, therefore, Horrockses, Crewdson & Co Ltd, was formed with 200,000 spindles, 6,600 looms, and about 6,000 operatives, with gross assets valued at £912,950. The firm under Hollins's control had thus grown to eight times its original size in only three years.

Although chairman only from 1891, Hollins's leadership of this 'proto-corporation' was ensured by his own drive, together with the support of vigorous lieutenants who were able to offset the overstaffing which initially resulted from the mergers. Machinery was modernised and production rationalised: thus the older part of Crewdsons was closed down, while low-quality work was centred at Bolton, fine quality at Preston. As a result, not only did profitability increase, but the new firm was able, between 1887 and 1914, to regain the leadership of the cotton trade lost to Rylands in the 1870s. Economies of scale were effected and amalgamation with Crewdsons represented a major extension of home and foreign trade. The efficient distribution network which resulted was subsequently used to market 'Viyella', pioneered by Frank Hollins's brother Henry (qv) at Pleasley in the early 1890s. New factories were built in 1895 (the Centenary Mill) and 1913, while in 1900 another long-standing rival of Horrockses, the Preston firm of Swainson & Birley, was taken over. The range of Horrockses' products was also extended, including for example, the introduction of hemmed, ready-to-use sheets, catering for the 'modern woman ... not much given to needlework' {*Illustrated London News* July 1909, XIV}. By 1913, the firm employed ca 6,500 workers, 7,500 looms and 300,000 spindles (94,000 of them ring spindles). Capital had grown correspondingly, with gross assets in 1911 totalling £1.62 million.

During the First World War, Horrockses' prosperity was maintained, boosted in part by war demand, and by 1919 capital assets were valued, internally, at £3 million, having almost doubled since 1911. However, in the post-war boom, the market value of Horrockses was estimated at £4.5 million and it was, presumably, the highly attractive, if highly inflated, offer of £5.25 million from the company promoter S B Joel (1865-1931) which encouraged Hollins and a majority of shareholders to sell out to the Amalgamated Cotton Mills Trust in 1919. The participation of Hollins in this most astonishing of post-war take-overs is itself curious, but perhaps, his earlier instinct for amalgamations had been revived. Now aged seventy-seven, he remained a director of the Amalgamated Cotton Mills Trust and chairman of Horrockses, although effective control passed to the new managing-director N Seddon-Brown (1880-1971).

Before his energies had been engrossed by Horrockses, Hollins had been an early supporter of the Manchester Ship Canal; when it was eventually constructed Horrockses became one of the first to use it. Later, Hollins played an important role in the reconstruction of the Calico Printers' Association, where his knowledge both of manufacturing and of amalgamations provided valuable advice for this difficult company. He sat on the shareholders' committee of 1902 and was to remain a director until 1912. Hollins was also for many years a director of the Manchester & County Bank, although he failed to achieve the most prized of outside directorships, that of the London & North Western Railway. The British Cotton Growing Association found in Hollins an early and enthusiastic supporter, and his firm became heavy institutional subscribers, as indeed did his workforce, inspired by his advocacy. Horrockses were also the largest shareholders in the British Northrop Loom Co Ltd of 1902, run by D M Hollins (qv), a nephew; Sir Frank was for a time a director of Northrop.

Even so, outside Horrockses, Hollins's major contribution to the cotton industry probably lay in the sphere of industrial relations. In the mid-nineteenth century Preston had been at the centre of bitter industrial strife, which the Hollins firm had not escaped. Sir Frank's conciliatory disposition, gentlemanliness and courtesy, however, not only developed amicable relations with his own workforce but helped to underpin industrial peace in North Lancashire, where between 1894 and 1917 he was chairman of the Master Spinners' Association. Always willing to negotiate with trade union officials, he worked patiently for compromise and arbitration, providing a moderating influence most successfully in the Preston district but also within the broader Cotton Spinners' and Manufacturers' Association, and its political wing, the Cotton Employers' Parliamentary Association. The illuminated address with which he was presented in December 1923 by the Preston cotton unions thus signified not the token esteem of a deferential workforce but the genuine respect of organised labour.

An Anglican in religion, politically Hollins was a convinced Liberal, and unswerving free trader. His father had been an Anti-Corn Law Leaguer in the 1840s; and in 1883 Frank emerged as a bitter critic of another monopoly, the Liverpool toll bar; in 1904 he was a member of the Free Trade League, and as late as the election of 1923 he was equally ready to oppose Protection. He acted as president of the Preston and Blackpool District Liberal Association and was active in its reconstruction preceding a rare Liberal victory in the election of 1906. Suitably, the Liberal Government awarded him a baronetcy in 1907. (He was also one of Asquith's potential peers, to be created, if necessary, for the passing of the Parliament Bill in 1911.) As Preston's leading businessman, he became the first chairman of the Chamber of Commerce in 1917 until his death. He acted as JP for county and borough, welcoming working men, including his own, as colleagues; he was also a governor of Rossall. A keen sportsman (W G Grace was a friend), he was chairman of both Preston North End Football Club, and the Lancashire County Cricket Club (1919-20). At his country home in Bridgnorth he was well known as a supporter of local charities.

Hollins had married in 1875 Dora Emily Susan Cox, OBE, daughter of Caleb Cox, a Wimbledon Collector of Customs and Excise. Of their four sons, two were to become directors of Horrockses and the Amalgamated Cotton Mills Trust and one a clergyman; three were to be Oxbridge blues, and two Lancashire cricketers. At his death on 27 January 1924 Hollins's estate of £325,824 gross, even though depleted by the transfer of shares to his sons, compared favourably with the value of his partnership share in Hollins in 1884, £28,383, and was handsome indeed by the standard of his father's meagre £50 (net) in 1886.

A C HOWE

Writings:

The Liverpool Toll Bar (reprinted from *Manchester City News* 1883).

Sources:

Unpublished

Bodleian Library, Oxford, Bryce papers.

Lancashire RO, Preston, Horrockses Business Records (DDHs).

Manchester Central Library, Calico Printers' Association, secretary's correspondence, 1902-12.

North Lancashire Cotton Spinners' Association, minutes, 1894-1920; Textile Employers' Association records.

PRO BT6/153, BT31/14866/24541.

Tootal Group PLC, Manchester, Calico Printers' Association, minutes, 1902-12.

In private possession: Hollins family papers and miscellanea, Cross family papers, and miscellanea.

PrC; Will.

Published

Bolton Weekly Journal 7 May 1887.

Bridgnorth Journal 2 Feb 1924.

Sir Charles Brown, *Origin and Progress of Horrockses, Crewdson & Co* (Preston: Preston Guardian, 1925).

Concerning Cotton: A Brief Account of the Aims and Achievements of the Amalgamated Cotton Mills Trust Ltd (Wilson, 1921).

The Cotton Factory Times 16 Feb 1923.

The Draper's Record 15 Sept 1888.

History, Origin and Development of the Firm of Horrockses, Crewdson & Co Ltd 1791-1912 (np: Horrockses, 1913).

Illustrated London News 10 July 1909.

Stanhope Joel, *Ace of Diamonds: The Story of Solomon Barnato Joel* (Frederick Muller, 1958).

Lancashire Daily Post 28 Jan 1924.

London Gazette 11 Dec 1866, 19 July 1867, 10 Oct 1871, 14 Nov 1873.

Manchester Guardian 30 Aug 1862, 28 Jan 1924.

Gale Pedrick, *The Story of Horrockses* (Preston: Horrockses, 1950).

Stanley Pigott, *Hollins: A Study of Industry 1784-1949* (Nottingham: Hollins, 1949).

Preston Guardian 2 Feb 1924.

Preston Herald 2 Feb 1924.

Textile Mercury 2 Feb 1924.

Textile Recorder 15 Feb 1924.

Times 15 Aug 1862, 30 Apr, 3 May 1887.

Times Textile Number 27 June 1912.

WWW.

HOLLINS, Henry Ernest

(1842-1920)

Cotton and garment manufacturer

Henry Ernest Hollins was born in Stockport, Cheshire, on 17 April 1842, the third child (of twelve) of Edward Hollins and Margaret Harding formerly Woody. Although retaining a financial interest (in the form of a 'sleeping' partnership) in the family textile firm of Wm Hollins & Co of Pleasley Vale, Mansfield, his father had set up as a cotton manufacturer in his own right, first in Stockport (Park Mills, a spinning enterprise) in the 1830s, and subsequently in Preston (Sovereign Mills, a weaving concern). Hollins's mother came from a medical family from the Tamworth area. There is only scanty and somewhat conflicting information about Henry's childhood, education and early manhood. The weight of the evidence suggests a comfortable upbringing, some private tuition, and a brief grammar school education at Rossall. Between leaving school and his twenty-third birthday it is likely that he helped his father in some junior capacity, as did one of his younger brothers, Frank (qv).

In 1865 Hollins joined his uncle William Hollins at the Pleasley works in order to learn the business of hosiery yarn spinning. Within five years of his appointment he succeeded W B Paget (whose family, together with the Hollinses and the Oldknows, had been at the core of the firm since the late eighteenth century), as second assistant manager to the mills at nearby Radford and Lenton, whilst his elder brother Richard, and younger brother Claude, helped to run Pleasley. William's own two sons were also inducted into the firm, but of these five aspirants to the succession it was Henry who undoubtedly stood out, and when the principal began to withdraw from active management in the early 1870s on account of ill-health, Henry — rather than his cousins or Richard — was singled out as heir-designate to the head of the executive. In 1873 he was made a partner and from that point emerged as the dominant entrepreneurial figure. He was the first managing director of the new private limited company

Staff photograph of Hollins, Henry Ernest Hollins, chairman and managing director, seated centre (taken from F A Wells Hollins and Viyella. A Study in Business History Newton Abbot: David & Charles, 1968).

formed in 1882, an office he held until 1916, and in 1908 he became the first chairman when the company went public (William had died in 1890), only resigning from this post in the last few months of his life.

In the years that 'H E H' (as he was usually known) controlled the reins of the firm, Wm Hollins & Co was transformed. From a relatively modest and essentially locally-orientated business supplying yarn to the Nottingham hosiery trade, it became a substantial multi-process, multi-product and multi-million pound vertically-integrated organisation with world-wide market outlets and a famous trade-mark, 'Viyella', harnessed to an equally well-known advertising slogan, 'Day and Night Wear'. The responsibility and credit for effecting a change of this magnitude and scope goes far beyond that of a single individual, however talented, forceful and enterprising, but there can be little doubt that Hollins played a decisive, if not a crucial, entrepreneurial role. His contribution did not lie in the area of invention or any special command over the technical conditions of supply (indeed there are doubts about his engineering competence), nor did it involve any unusual degree of financial wizardry; rather, it was Hollins's qualities as an innovator and a co-ordinator of the factors of production that were outstanding. He possessed the ability to foresee new demand opportunities that were opening up as a result of a rising standard of living and alterations in taste, and he had the courage to pioneer new methods and products. He had considerable organisational skills, and unlike his son, Richard Arthur, who succeeded him at the end of the First World War, Hollins had the gift of working harmoniously with his colleagues and workforce. Richard's resignation in the mid-1920s severed the Hollins family's connection with the company.

During the first half of Henry Hollins's regime the firm made steady — but hardly spectacular — strides forward. Output in the traditional lines of cotton and some woollen yarn for hosiery, knitting and sewing expanded. Two smallish enterprises, the Via Gellia Mills (whence the name 'Viyella' was derived, although, paradoxically, none was ever made there) which were near Cromford, and the Cockcroft Mills at Huddersfield were bought out to eliminate their increasingly intense competition, and capacity at Pleasley was gradually enlarged. The private limited company was reorganised in 1890, with a paid-up capital of £330,000 (about £100,000 more than in 1883). The breakthrough occurred with the development of a radically new product, Viyella, in the early 1890s. The vagaries of fashion had begun to render cotton-based hosiery somewhat unpopular, at least amongst the upper echelons of the market, and from as early as the 1870s, Hollins sought to confront this trend by increasing output of worsted yarns. The disadvantage of this strategy as far as the mass-market was concerned was the relatively high cost of the merino raw material, and he therefore went a step further by requesting his more technically competent spinning staff to experiment with a cotton and wool mix. There were formidable technical obstacles in the way of producing a suitably fine yarn with two quite different natural fibres. After almost three years of painstaking labour, with Hollins himself overseeing the project and offering encouragement, a Mr Hardwick and two brothers named Sissons arrived at the solution: this centred upon marrying specially selected breeds of wool and cotton into a compatible twist, and determining a highly specific combination of proportions between the two (which remained a closely guarded secret until very recently) yielding the distinctive soft, yet hard-wearing, yarn. The decision to commence full-scale production was taken in November 1893. Not all the members of the board were as enthusiastic about Viyella's prospects as Hollins, and at first many of the firm's traditional hosiery customers proved to be highly sceptical. It was only through the good offices of Frank Hollins (now the chairman of Horrockses, Crewdson & Co) who instructed his travellers and representatives to 'push' the yarn, that Viyella became known within the trade.

This early market apathy was broken down in two ways. First, Hollins began to think of extending the range of goods by a process of vertical integration — a virtually unprecedented strategy in the highly differentiated world of textile production and distribution. To this end he established close contact with two well-known Glasgow weaving enterprises, Renison McNab & Co and John McMath & Co, with the view to deploying their expertise in cloth-making to produce Viyella. During the 1890s their weaving shed personnel (especially in the former company) succeeded in turning out a satisfactory woven fabric and at the end of the decade both were formally taken over by Wm Hollins: they were run as the 'Glasgow Cloth Department' and the most modern looms (including Northrop automatics) were installed. In addition to producing ever-increasing quantities of Viyella yarn and cloth, which shortly after 1900 became the largest single item in the turnover, Hollins decided to make ready-made garments. To this end the mills at Huddersfield and Radford were enlarged, modernised and completely refitted, and a chief designer was introduced to head a small specialist team. By the outbreak of war in 1914 over £100,000 worth of male and female attire was being sold a year.

The second aspect of Hollins's marketing offensive was his novel approach to selling. He realised that an entirely fresh policy was needed to market the Viyella range. The relatively expensive raw materials required meant that the unit price charged could never be 'cheap'; he therefore consciously fostered an image of high quality, and long life. After completely reorganising the small and somewhat staid sales department in the 1890s, Hollins opened up large warehousing and office premises both at home (London and Manchester) and in the chief overseas markets (the USA, Canada and Australia). He then embarked upon a major advertising campaign, regularly taking full- and half-pages in the national press, especially the *Daily Mail*. By the end of the war expenditure on advertising amounted to well over £20,000 a year. A noteworthy characteristic of these campaigns was the emphasis given to brand names, first Viyella, and then a number of offshoots such as the 'Clydella' (aimed at the 'utility' end of the market and devised partly out of necessity during the war when the supply of wool was scarce) and 'Zephyr' ranges. These steps paved the way for Hollins's radical break with existing distribution practices. Following the example of Horrockses he dispensed with wholesaling, directly negotiating selling contracts with individual retail shops and stores. The Viyella agency soon conferred a much sought-after status upon even the humblest of outlets and there was fierce competition for the possession of a locally 'exclusive' agreement. In turn, Hollins was anxious to protect shop proprietors handling Viyella from 'unfair competition' which, pirating problems aside, really meant price-cutting by the larger High Street establishments. From as early as 1896 Hollins insisted upon a clause in all new agreements which fixed a 'minimum retail price' on both cloth and garments — one of the first instances of what became known as Resale Price Maintenance. As a result of these efforts the annual value of sales rose from just under £250,000 in the early 1880s to over £5 million in the year of Hollins's death.

Like most of his immediate family, Hollins was a committed Liberal, Free Trader, and Unitarian (although towards the end of his life he attended the Pleasley Parish Church). His interest in politics, however, was always secondary to his business life and although he was a steadfast and concerned member of the local Liberal party, serving as chairman and president, and representing the Mansfield Woodhouse ward on the County Council for a number of years, he never became a prominent public figure in the mould of his uncle. His one outstanding contribution to the civic community was his work on behalf of the Mansfield and District Hospital, serving as chairman of the board of management for twenty-nine years, and championing the cause of expansion and improvement. Paternal benevolence was also at the heart of Hollins's attitude towards labour: he donated a considerable amount of time and effort to extend the various welfare schemes that William had inaugurated: the mutual aid society; the two small village communities which had grown up around Pleasley and Radford (cottages for the foremen at peppercorn rents, a farm, and a co-operative store); the 'Penny Bank'; trips to the sea-side; and a profit-sharing scheme begun in October 1917 which started off in a small way although Hollins placed great faith in its future potential. In keeping with this general philosophy, Hollins saw little point in trade unionism and frowned upon it in his own business.

Hollins married twice: firstly, in 1875, to Mary Anne Gibson, with whom he had five children; and five years after she died in 1903, to May Gaythorne Wilson; there were no children of the second marriage. Mary

Anne, whom Hollins met on a walking holiday in Switzerland (walking, a passion for natural history and the new sport of cycling, formed his main recreations), brought him a large country house and estate in Westmorland. Her diaries reveal him as immensely hard-working, an indefatigable traveller in pursuit of business, and a somewhat remote father. Hollins died on 15 March 1920, leaving an estate proved at £198,999.

COLIN SIMMONS *and* HELEN CLAY

Sources:

Unpublished

Wm Hollins & Co Ltd, Somercotes and Pleasley Vale, Nottinghamshire, archives: company papers 1860-1920, including directors' minutes, accounts, memoranda, articles of association (1890 and 1908) and wage books.

MSS Diaries of Mary Anne Hollins, 1871-1902, in possession of Mrs Alison Hollins.

PrC.

Interviews and correspondence with Joseph Gibson (grandson); Mrs Alison M Hollins (widow of Ian F E Hollins); H E Hollins (grandson); Kate Hollins (daughter of the late Ian F E Hollins); R J D Hollins (grandson); H A Peck (former personnel officer, Wm Hollins & Co).

Published

The Drapery Times 21 Nov 1908.

Mansfield Advertiser 19 Mar 1920.

Mansfield Chronicle 18 Mar 1920.

Mansfield Reporter 19 Mar 1920.

Nottingham Daily Guardian 17 Mar 1920.

Nottingham Evening News 16 Mar 1920.

Stanley Pigot, *Hollins: A Study of Industry* (Pleasley: W Hollins & Co, 1949).

F Arthur Wells, *Hollins of Viyella* (Newton Abbot: David and Charles, 1968)

W F M Weston-Webb, *The Autobiography of a British Yarn Merchant* (Cayne Press, 1929).

HOLLOWAY, Thomas

(1800-1883)

Patent medicine manufacturer

Thomas Holloway was born at Plymouth Dock (later Devonport) on 22 September 1800, the son of Thomas Holloway, a retired militia warrant officer who turned to baking in Plymouth and later became landlord of the *Turks Head* in Penzance. He was educated at Camborne and Penzance until 1816. That year his father died and Holloway gained his first commercial experience when, with his mother and a brother, he took over a grocery and bakery shop in the Penzance marketplace. Still unmarried and seeking greater fortune, he left Cornwall in 1828 and moved from one job to another in London for eight years, during which time he suffered a bankruptcy. In 1840 he married Jane Driver (1817-1875), the daughter of John Driver, a shipwright. His wife was to become an influential aid in his business and philanthropic affairs. They remained childless.

A turning point in his career occurred in 1837 while he was a merchant and foreign commercial agent at 13 Broad Street Buildings. A client, Felix Albinolo, a vendor of leeches (for therapeutic purposes) and of a medicinal ointment, asked for aid in marketing his medicine in Britain. Holloway introduced him to the authorities at St Thomas's Hospital and obtained for him testimonials of the ointment's use and efficacy, a common and necessary practice for patent medicine marketing at the time. The episode showed Holloway just how potentially profitable patent medicines could be. He quickly produced a competing product of similar composition, and announced 'Holloway's Family Ointment' for sale in 1837. It too was vouched for by 'medical experts' but attracted a vehement response from Albinolo in a published accusation of theft and fraud. The Italian disappeared before pursuing any action. Holloway soon began producing pills, and in 1839 the entry 'Thomas Holloway Patent Medicine Warehouse, 244 Strand' appeared in the *London Directory*.

Holloway's entry into the patent medicine field was well timed, because it was a period of increasing interest in self-medication, using preparations less harsh than those prescribed by physicians, but still available in shops. By exploiting an advertising style already widespread among patent medicine makers, and by employing a network of foreign agents, Holloway was able to expand his efforts to colonial and native overseas markets. He spent all he could on advertisements and to gain a wider market he is said to have visited the docks daily to offer samples to the captains of vessels and passengers sailing to all parts of the world. This was not very successful until he increased his investment in printed advertisements which rose from £5,000 in 1842 to £10,000 in 1845, £20,000 in 1851 and £50,000 in 1883. This increased expenditure, along with his strategy for international marketing, was boosted by a policy of using foreign language package labels and directions in Chinese, Turkish, Armenian, Arabic, most of the dialects of India, among other languages. Advertisements were also placed by agents in newspapers in all parts of the world.

In the midst of the spectacular growth of his firm, fuelled by a steadfast determination to make money, Holloway was inhibited by a number of problems. In 1850 he felt compelled to obtain an injunction against his brother, Henry, who had begun selling 'Holloway's pills and ointment' at a nearby address, 210 Strand, and in 1860 he tried unsuccessfully to introduce his products into France through an agent, Dr Sillen, but the collapse of this venture brought further litigation. His premises at 244 Strand were demolished in 1867 to make way for new law courts, whereupon he moved to 533 (later numbered 78) Oxford Street. His accounting methods were relatively simple and in his business transactions he relied on business with ready money, perhaps as a result of his earlier experience with bankruptcy. This extended to the practice of paying his employees daily, which he did throughout his career. He is said to have employed nearly 100 people after his move to Oxford Street, almost doubling the size of the Strand works. For a while he continued to live on the premises and work very long hours alongside his wife at the warehouse. This pattern of life ended in the late 1860s when he built a lavish country house at Tittenhurst, Sunninghill, Berkshire and began to concentrate more on investing an increasingly large proportion of what may have been as much as £50,000 a year in profits from the patent medicine business alone. Around that time he also started a successful but short-lived bank, which reportedly earned almost £100,000 in profits a year during the late 1870s.

His mastery of what was already a well-established genre of advertising among patent medicine sellers was always the keystone of his success. He adroitly played upon the fears, hopes, vanity, and sense of social place of the middle and working class by conveying the message that users of Holloway's pills were enlightened people. His advertisements emphasised the imperial and international character of his clientele and the mysterious origins of his uniquely efficacious concoctions. One advertisement combined the images of Britannia, Queen Victoria, a sailor and a guardsman, surrounded by a Red Indian, a Zulu, a turbaned Oriental, and veiled Moslem ladies along with traditionally-dressed Chinese women. Although his business was larger than other British patent medicine manufacturers at the time, his practices were similar, relying as they did on simple compounding procedures.

Holloway spent most of his career concentrating on business and experienced an awakened sense of social responsibility only in later life. His first effort at philanthropy led to the refusal of his benefaction by his home town, so modelling himself after the American, George Peabody and soliciting advice widely, he accepted Lord Shaftsbury's suggestion that he build a sanatorium for the mentally afflicted among the lower middle class. When his wife died in 1875 he dedicated to her the result of his £350,000 donation, the Holloway Sanatorium at Virginia Water. The next year he began to work on his college for the education of women at Mount Lee, Egham Hill, Surrey. Unconventional in that it demanded no religious commitment by its staff or students and required no set preparatory education, the college reflected his belief in a special providence rather than organised religion, and rather romantic notions of self-improvement. He had only vague, though grandiose, ideas of how the college was to differ from the two Cambridge women's colleges and from institutions limited to training teachers. By the time Royal Holloway College was opened by Queen Victoria in 1886, three years after his death, some £800,000 of his money had gone into it, including a rather large investment in Victorian pictures.

Holloway died on 26 December 1883 leaving an estate proved at £596,335 gross, and his business quickly declined, but did not disappear until much later. Even after the distribution of over £1 million, his will provided more than £550,000, plus 'considerable freehold property' to his wife's sister, Mary Ann Driver, and her relatives. In 1887 this will was unsuccessfully contested by his sister, Mrs Caroline Young. He attracted rather little attention during his life, was non-political and seemed to want no title.

JONATHAN M LIEBENAU

Sources:

Unpublished

MCe.

Published

Annual Register 1883.

DNB.

Illustrated London News 5 Jan 1884, 20 June 1885, 3, 10 July 1886.

Medical Circular 1853.

David E Owen, *English Philanthropy 1660-1960* (Cambridge, Massachusetts: Harvard University Press, 1964).

Pall Mall Gazette 28, 29 Dec 1883, 16, 19, 25 Jan 1884.

William D Rubinstein, *Men of Property* (New Brunswick, New Jersey: Rutgers University Press, 1981).

Saturday Review 1 Oct 1887.

Times 28 Dec 1883, 1, 3, 5 Jan 1884, 28 May 1887.

Alfred Holt (taken from F E Hyde, Blue Funnel *Liverpool, Liverpool University Press, 1956).*

HOLT, Alfred

(1829-1911)

Shipowner

Alfred Holt was born in Rake Lane, Liverpool, on 13 June 1829, the son of George Holt, a merchant, and his wife Emma Durning, daughter of a wealthy Liverpool merchant. Alfred's father had come to Liverpool in 1807, from a textile background in Rochdale (his father being a small dyer); apprenticed to the rising cotton broker, Samuel Hope, George Holt became his partner within five years. His marriage in 1820 brought him into the important group of Unitarian business families in the town. George left the Hope partnership in 1823 and continued in cotton broking, helped to found the Bank of Liverpool and the Liverpool & London Assurance Co and built on his own account the first Liverpool office building, India Buildings. Like his sons after him he made major contributions to Liverpool's municipal government and educational charities.

Alfred Holt, the third son, early showed an interest in machines and after education at a private Unitarian school he was apprenticed as an engineer to the Liverpool & Manchester Railway, where he was put in charge of several important projects. At the end of his apprenticeship he was temporarily unable to find engineering work and spent some time in the shipping offices of Lamport & Holt, for whom he did work on new steamships. In 1852 he set up as a consulting engineer in India Buildings and soon picked up marine engineering work. In 1853 he began to act for and collaborate with Thomas Ainsworth of Cleator, for whom he became agent as well as engineer. Ainsworth and George Holt invested in a ship, the *Cleator*, designed by Alfred, which made good profits in the Crimean War and then in a second vessel which Alfred and his brother Philip (still with Lamport & Holt) put into the West India trade. Eventually they had five vessels in this trade but were pressured into selling out to a large rival in 1864.

They therefore looked to a trade which was undeveloped by steamers, and chose that to China. Alfred Holt put a new vertical compound tandem engine of his design in the *Cleator*; this engine, which used the then-remarkable boiler pressure of 60 lbs psi, was highly economical both of fuel and space and was put into an iron-hulled screw-driven steamer. Three new steamers, *Agamemnon*, *Ajax* and *Achilles*, were laid down by the brothers with tandem compound engines, 70 lbs pressure, 945 indicated hp and 2,280 gross tons. *Agamemnon* sailed for China in April 1865 under Isaac Middleton, a master long connected with Holts. She was able to reach Mauritius in thirty-seven days without refuelling; soon a Holt ship was to reach China and return as far as Singapore on her Liverpool bunkering. The Holt family held 51 per cent of the shares of these vessels and the others were held by a close circle of mainly

The First Agamemnon (taken from F E Hyde, Blue Funnel *Liverpool, Liverpool University Press, 1956).*

Nonconformist friends. Naturally there were teething troubles, and the odd 'immensely disgusting accident' which upset Alfred as an engineering perfectionist, but soon the brothers could claim that the 'mechanical part of the problem' was solved, 'the commercial one remains' — that of exploiting the complex and difficult China trade. Briefly, the major influence was the wise appointment of agents. John Swire (qv), of Butterfield & Swire, acted as Shanghai agent from 1867; tirelessly energetic, analytically penetrating, cuttingly candid, a radical thinker, he counterbalanced Philip Holt's tough orthodoxy. Holt assisted him in developing the China Navigation Co, an important feeder to the main line, and they joined him later in the Taikoo Sugar Co and investment in the Taikoo Shipyards. The Singapore agency was as splendidly served by Walter and George Mansfield and run from 1873 by their partner Theodore Bogaardt, who played an important part in building up feeder line services to many parts of Indonesia and to Bangkok.

The opening of the Suez Canal was influential in bringing other lines, Glens, Shires, and Castles, into the trade which had hitherto been highly profitable to Holts, while existing mail lines, P&O and Messageries Maritimes, expanded their operations. Larger and faster ships competed with the Holt vessels which Alfred and Philip continued on the slower but economical earlier pattern, built however to strict specification ('Holt's Class'). Competition became desperate, and Swire eventually overcame the free-trade liberal ethic of the Holts and the line entered the China Outward and Homeward Conference in 1879 under Swire's chairmanship. Instinctively, however, Holts were against it, and they occasionally broke ranks in the early days, eventually causing Swire's resignation as chairman. The Conference advantages were affected by the creation of the independent China Shippers' Mutual Navigation Co in 1882, which built triple-expansion and steel vessels, and was at times outside the Conference. In Alfred Holt's last two decades, however, he became again willing to countenance notable innovation. From 1891 new, faster ships were ordered of larger size to allow for the newer, heavier cargoes and the decline of the China tea trade; new, younger managers came in to strengthen the administration; and the direct trade with the Dutch colonies was secured by the formation of the Nederlandsche Stoomvart Maatschappij Oceaan (NSMO) under Dutch registration, while the local feeder services developed by Bogaardt became the East India Ocean Steamship Co. Chinese crews were increasingly used. A vigorous building policy between 1894 and 1902 added 22 steamers, all triple expansion and some over 7,000 tons, the China Mutual Co was bought out, an important Australian trade was begun, useful working arrangements entered into with the Koninklijke Paketvaart Maatschappij (KPM), and the EIOS Co sold to North German Lloyd while retaining most of its advantages. Trans-Pacific trade including Japan, the USA and Canada developed, particularly after the purchase of China Mutual. As Alfred Holt's chairmanship ended in 1904 after nearly forty years, new vessels of advanced design were being put into service (with H B Wortley as naval architect) having holds with reduced pillar obstruction, new types of derricks to increase cargo handling by the ships, and innovative stern frames and propellor shafts.

Alfred Holt's career was somewhat paradoxical. His intensely innovative early period was followed by a period of conservatism, only to be succeeded by a period when progress was again encouraged in younger managers at India Buildings. He supported the development of the Suez Canal when it was scorned by many British engineers and shipowners. He opposed the Manchester Ship Canal on the ground that it would not need to be built if the Mersey Docks & Harbour Board and the railways would act more liberally, and tried to counter it with his Lancashire Plateway scheme; when the Manchester Ship Canal was built he used it frequently. He laid down new ships most usually in slack times with a large advantage in capital costs. At first Holt opposed Merchant Shipping Acts because he did not believe that forcing good shipbuilding by law was the best way, but he himself always built to standards well beyond any regulations, and all his cargo vessels were built to passenger-carrying standards. He disliked the casual labour system on the Mersey docks, and his nephew and successor, Lawrence Holt, was a principal actor in the reforms instituted in 1911-12.

Alfred Holt retired in 1904 from the management of what had, after initial resistance on his part, become a limited liability company in 1902 with a nominal capital of £425,337, though in 1903-4 the capital employed was £1.8 million.

Alfred Holt, married firstly, Catherine Long, daughter of John Long, in 1865 and secondly, Frances Long, daughter of Henry Long, in 1871; he had three sons and a daughter. He died in 1911 leaving £155,566 gross. Philip Holt married Hannah Booth (sister of Alfred Booth) in 1856; they did not have any children and Philip died in 1914, leaving £235,852 gross.

J R HARRIS

Writings:

Cromwell's Burial Place (Liverpool: pp, 1899).

(ed) *Merseyside* (British Association, 1923).

Sources:

Unpublished

MCe.

PrC.

Published

Francis E Hyde and John R Harris, *Blue Funnel, A History of Alfred Holt and Company of Liverpool from 1865 to 1914* (Liverpool: Liverpool University Press, 1956).

Francis E Hyde, *The Senior, John Samuel Swire 1925-98* (Liverpool: Liverpool University Press, 1967).

WWW.

HOOLEY, Ernest Terah

(1859-1947)

Company promoter

Ernest Terah Hooley was born at Sneinton, Nottinghamshire, on 5 February 1859, the son of Terah Hooley, a lacemaker, and his wife Elizabeth née Peach. He is said to have gone to school at Draycott in Derbyshire, and then worked for his father who had established a factory in Long Eaton sometime before 1870. By 1880, Ernest became his father's partner and took control of the firm's Nottingham office.

Hooley's early years were exemplary. After marrying in 1881, he lived quietly with his wife, Annie Maria née Winlaw, the daughter of a baker, and their increasing family at Park Street, Long Eaton. A life-long teetotaller and non-smoker, Hooley was deacon and organist at Station Street Baptist Church and on the local Board of Guardians. He applied himself so well to his father's business (though rumour says that he also inherited £35,000 from his mother) that by 1888 he was able to buy Risley

Hall for £5,000. His father thought the purchase a gross extravagance and predicted bankruptcy, but Hooley's first venture into landed property was significant. Neither Irishman nor Jew, as later gossip insinuated, Hooley came of a line of farmers who had been in the area since 1780, and he had a dream of farming, but on a grand scale. There was not enough money in lace-making to make this possible, and so in 1889 he left the family partnership and set up as a stockbroker in Nottingham.

Hooley's property deals at this time were many but unremarkable, except perhaps the acquisition for £25,000 of the Amner estate near Sandringham, a strategic move for Hooley, who became on familiar terms with the Prince of Wales. The increasing scale of manufacturing and the emergence of new industries offered widening opportunities for stockbrokers in the 1890s. Hooley and his partner Martin Rucker, a cycle enthusiast and business man, bought up small cycle firms and refloated them as public companies, selling the shares at a substantial profit. Foremost among these deals was the purchase early in 1895 of the Humber Cycle Co of Beeston, Wolverhampton and Coventry, from which they made £25,000.

Hooley grasped the principle that it was perfectly legal to buy up a firm with money one had not got, so long as one could sell it at a higher price before the initial payment had to be completed. But to do this the company promoter had to inspire confidence in the public. Hooley had £100,000, but he must seem to have far more; for this purpose he moved to London in April 1896, taking a floor at the Midland Grand Hotel, St Pancras. He had probably already begun negotiating for the purchase of the Dunlop Tyre Co, for two years earlier Rucker had missed the chance of buying the patent through lack of confidence, and Hooley knew that the tyre would transform cycling — would make him 'the man who put the world on wheels' {Hooley (1925) 71}. Now with Rucker he bought the company for £3 million, refloating it with a capital of £5 million, and the name of an earl, allegedly bought for £25,000, on the prospectus. The deal caught the public imagination, applications for stock totalled £9 million and Hooley's career in big business was launched.

From then on he had only to be connected with an enterprise for the public to compete for shares. His name worked like magic, but the only magic about Hooley was his personal charm. The rest was careful calculation and quick thinking. Knowing the veneration in which the aristocracy was held, he was careful to have at least one titled name on each of his directorates: the 'guinea pig', who got lunch and travelling expenses and a guinea for each board meeting he attended. Hooley gave generously to charity and to party funds. He plunged further into landed property by purchasing the Papworth Hall estate for £70,000, and entertained there lavishly, with fabulous quantities of wine and cigars, although he himself did not drink or smoke. He threw himself into the district's local life, becoming High Sheriff of Cambridgeshire. At the Midland Grand Hotel he gave audience to financiers, inventors and any interested party, acting with great speed when he was convinced of the value (and validity) of a patent or project, so that a company was usually launched within a week. It was said that prospective clients would pay up to £500 to those near him for an audience with the great man. By 1896 he was a millionaire.

Of the companies Hooley promoted over these years, several were in the cycle industry, either the manufacture of cycles (notably Raleigh, Singer and Swift) or of components (the Cycle Manufacturers' Tube Co and Pedersen's Cycle Frames). But other companies included Bovril and Schweppes, and by 1898 he had diversified into armaments (the Lee Metford Small Arms & Ammunitions Co and the United Ordnance & Engineering Co). He realised early the importance of foreign subsidiaries, launching Humber & Co (Russia) and (Portugal) in 1895 and the Dunlop Pneumatic Tyre Co (France) in 1896, while the Bovril Co, 1897, was British, foreign and colonial. Possibly his second most sensational deal, however, was in property: the purchase of the Trafford Park estate in 1896, which he claims in *Confessions* to have heard of through a delivery error and to have bought under an assumed name, to be cut up and sold at a profit of £740,000. 'I always did these deals in the same way. The deposit was paid over to the vendor or his agent, and I then had three months to cut up the estate and make my profit' {*ibid*, 271}.

In his day, many companies failed through under-subscription; Hooley's promotions were usually over-subscribed. However, once floated, they were saddled with a high debt burden because of the inordinate sums owing to Hooley and the vendors. Many felt he watered the stock of the companies he promoted to such an extent that they survived despite his intervention, as the burden of interest and dividends on the excessive capital made it less easy to plough back funds for future expansion. Nevertheless some of the companies he floated, notably Bovril, Humber and Schweppes, did survive and went on to prosper.

Hooley's bankruptcy in 1898 shook the world of finance. According to him, it all hinged on a cheque for £70 and a blackmailer, and he filed his petition out of pique, scarcely realising the consequences, but the investment boom was over and he was living on a knife edge. He had a certain flair for finance, but he had no training in accountancy, and, belonging to no professional body, he lacked the protection which membership could give. His highly-placed friends deserted him, which is not surprising: what was surprising was the number of small investors who rallied to his aid.

Hooley was permitted to trade after his bankruptcy, on the understanding that he furnished his trustee with a statement of profit and loss, to enable him to pay off some of his creditors. He freely admitted that he never kept any proper books, and could not have done so without embarassing some of those to whom he made payments. With his private property so disposed that it could not be touched, he lived in as much style as before and earned the name of the 'magnificent Bankrupt'. He held on to Papworth Hall until 1909, and on to Risley to the end of his life. Unfortunately he continued speculating, and his Siberian Goldfields project in 1904 led to an unsuccessful charge of fraud. A shady property deal in 1911 led to his second bankruptcy and twelve months' imprisonment for fraud; his promotion of Jubilee Mills in the cotton boom of 1919 brought about his third, in 1921, and a sentence of three years. His final bankruptcy came in 1939, when his original debts were still undischarged.

Hooley's handling of his estates was as vigorous and expansive as his promotion of companies. He was no farmer, but on the principle that if investment could help industry it could help farming, he poured it into wagonloads of fertiliser for his impoverished fields and unprecedented increases in wages for his labourers; over the latter it took all his charm and hospitality to mollify the local farmers. On the Papworth estate he was held in high esteem, and left a reputation for kindness and charity which, together with the 'new model cottages' he built, has survived to the present day (1982).

He ended his life poor, dependent on his seven children, but respected in the town of Long Eaton and taking part in its public life. He died on 11 February 1947. There is no trace of any estate in the probate records.

KENNETH *and* MARGARET RICHARDSON

Writings:

The Hooley Book (John Dicks, 1904).

Hooley's Confessions (Simpkin, Marshall, Hamilton, Kent & Co Ltd, 1925).

Sources:

Unpublished

Derbyshire CRO, Matlock, Hooley case papers.

BCe.

MCe.

James B Jeffreys, 'Trends in Business Organisation in Great Britain since 1856, with Special Reference to the Financial Structure of Companies, the Mechanism of Investment, and the Relations between the Shareholder and the Company' (London PhD, 1938).

Published:

Ernest Gaskell, *Derbyshire Leaders: Social and Political* (pp, 1907).

A E Harrison, 'Joint Stock Flotation in the Cycle, Motor Vehicle and Related Industries, 1882-1914' *Business History* 23 (July 1981).

Long Eaton Advertiser & South Derbyshire Chronicle 15 Feb 1947.

Hubert A Meredith, *The Drama of Money Making* (Sampson Low & Co Ltd, 1931).

Henry Osborne O'Hagan, *Leaves from My Life* (2 vols, John Lane, 1929).

Rowland Parker, *On the Road* (Cambridge: Pendragon Press, 1977).

Times 13 Feb 1947.

Weston F M Weston Webb, *The Autobiography of a British Yarn Merchant* (Richards & Toulmin, 1929).

Sir Frederic Hooper (courtesy of Cadbury Schweppes).

HOOPER, Sir Frederic Collins

(1892-1963)

Professional manager and soft drinks manufacturer

Frederic Collins Hooper was born at Bruton, Somerset, on 19 July 1892, the only son of Frederic Stephen Hooper, a wine and spirit merchant, and his wife Annie née Collins. He attended Sexey's School, Bruton and then University College, London, where he did not distinguish himself and graduated in botany with a wartime degree in 1916. On the outbreak of war he was commissioned into the Dorset Regiment and served on the western front, becoming in 1918 Camp Commandant and ADC to General Sir Reginald Pinney, commander of the 33rd Division.

After the First World War Hooper spent two years in Athens with the Ionian Bank. Then in 1922 he was brought to Lewis's, the Liverpool department store, by Frederick James Marquis, later Lord Woolton (qv). Marquis had been recruited by Rex Cohen, son of the firm's late-nineteenth-century owner, Louis Samuel Cohen (1847-1922), in order to brace management and restructure the firm in readiness for expansion. Hooper was one of several new senior managers who participated in the inter-war development of the store which had branches in Manchester and Birmingham. By 1928 he was general manager of the Bon Marché, Liverpool, a fashion store in the Lewis's group, and in 1934 was made a director of Lewis's Investment Trust, the holding company of Lewis's Ltd. Though he could be very bad-tempered and could become very emotional Hooper related successfully to his staff. With other managers he supported Marquis (who had been warden of Liverpool University Settlement and was familiar with the social problems of his employees), when Marquis replaced the company's arbitrary and paternalistic controls 'by the organised relations more appropriate to the social framework of an increasingly democratic society' {Briggs (1956) 164}. Before Hooper arrived, a new wage structure and salary scale had been adopted in 1920 and a Welfare Department set up the next year. These were elaborated with medical facilities, a pension scheme (1928), provision of sports clubs and social activities.

When economic conditions improved somewhat in the mid-1930s, Lewis's directors, intent upon bettering working conditions and finding no minimum standards in the distributive trades, negotiated with the Shop Assistants' Union (the Government declining to provide a Trade Board) and produced a Shop Assistants' Charter in February 1937. This laid down wage rates, hours of work, a two week annual holiday with pay and arrangements for medical treatment; it also recognised in each store a staff council which, with a new joint consultative council of management and staff, relayed staff opinions and ideas to management. Although these innovations had earlier appeared in manufacturing firms, like those of George Cadbury or Joseph Rowntree (qqv), 'it is difficult to comprehend what a revolution all these changes represented in the traditional relations between employer and employed in retail distribution.' {*ibid*, 166} For Hooper they provided an integral component of his management philosophy, what he later called 'the climate of work' {Hooper (1948) 61}.

During the inter-war period Lewis's expanded fast, opening branches in Glasgow (by taking over John Anderson's drapery store in 1929), Leeds (1933), Hanley (1935-36) and Leicester (1936). Net assets rose from £2,231,885 to £5,123,145 and pre-tax profits from £396,732 to £740,006 between 1925 and 1939. By 1939 the firm employed 12,000 people. In 1940 Hooper became joint managing director of Lewis's Ltd but after two years, and now aged fifty, he sought a political career.

At the invitation of Sir Kingsley Wood, Chancellor of the Exchequer, he set up the Political Research Centre, forerunner of the Conservative Central Office, with the task of shaping Conservative policies in a post-war world. The death of Wood in 1943 and the dissolution of the PRC in 1944 took Hooper on a futile quest for adoption by a Conservative constituency association.

In the 1940s he did some broadcasting on the 'Brains Trust' and other programmes. Then in 1945-46, as director of business training at the Ministry of Labour, he organised the resettlement of ex-servicemen. This done, he formed a business consultancy firm. One of its first clients was Schweppes, the mineral water company which in May 1948 invited Hooper to investigate and advise on the selection and training of personnel. That report, Hooper's record with Lewis's and his reputation as a management expert — enhanced in 1948 with the publication of his wide-ranging *Management Survey* — persuaded the Schweppes directors to invite him onto their board as joint managing director. Hooper accepted on condition that a modest salary be supplemented by a percentage of the company's annual profits. In November 1948 James W Joyce, the managing director, resigned leaving Hooper in sole managerial control. Fifteen years later, on the eve of his own impending retirement, Hooper was reputed to be earning in excess of £100,000 a year from his commission on annual profits. This remarkable success started from the perplexities of the post-war situation.

During the Second World War, in order to economise on power, transport and factory space, the Minister of Food, Lord Woolton, ordered the concentration and rationalisation of the soft drinks industry. Between 1943 and 1948 it was run by the Soft Drinks Industry (War Time) Association which was chaired by J W Joyce of Schweppes, the industry's biggest single manufacturer. Products were standardised under a common label and profits were pooled and distributed to each member firm according to average profits for the three years 1938-40. Schweppes was therefore striving to rebuild itself and its market share when Hooper arrived. Under Joyce manufacturing equipment had been ordered and installed and Hooper found production arrangements efficient. His considerable talents were applied in particular to the company's organisation, selling arrangements and industrial relations. In these three areas he applied his ideas and energies with characteristic vigour.

He commenced by destroying the cumbersome centralised control of the firm which had existed for generations. The head office was reorganised on a functional basis, with four main departments: production, sales, accountancy and personnel. 'The Production and Sales Controllers were appointed as staff officers to myself as Managing Director. But the operation of the business as a whole was to depend on the executive Branch Managers, who were responsible directly to me for production and sales. The Head Office controllers, as senior staff officers, were to have no control over the branches except through the Managing Director' {Hooper (1952) 3}. Branch managers were now rewarded with commissions on sales and, in addition, statistical controls were vastly simplified.

On the selling side Hooper inherited 'a constant merchandising policy. This policy was to turn out a mineral water of the very highest quality which had never been allowed to diminish whatever the economic conditions' {ibid, 2}, except for the adoption of the standard formula during the war years. For generations 'the company had been the manufacturers of a drink for gentlemen, run by gentlemen' {*ibid*}. Hooper decided that in future he would tap mass markets whilst maintaining the old standards of quality and appointed L M Alexander, a chartered accountant then jointly in charge of production, as his sales manager. The sales force was motivated by raising salaries and introducing a commission system related to turnover. Within two years, instead of the projected three, sales caught up with the 80 per cent budgeted increase in production capacity projected in 1948.

To boost sales Hooper also pursued new advertising devices. Garlands, who had the Schweppes account when Hooper arrived, in 1946 created the 'Schweppervescence' slogans with their 'amusing literary approach' {Simmons (1983) 135}. Hooper paid £150 for rights to the word when he moved the Schweppes contract to Bloxhams, an advertising agency set up by Clifford Bloxham whom he had known while at Lewis's. Hooper, though suspicious of some market research techniques, took a close personal interest in advertising. During a snooker game at the Savile Club between himself and Stephen Potter, the humorist and inventor of Oneupmanship, Gamesmanship and Lifemanship, the imaginary county of Schweppshire was born. The map of Schweppshire was unveiled in spring 1951 and 'for fourteen years Potter annually produced six fresh insights into this idiosyncratic county, much assisted by an artist, usually George Him' {*ibid*, 138}.

In the area of industrial relations Hooper strongly believed in devolving 'all sorts of functions of a human and personal order. Of these discipline, the power of the sack, and therefore individual security are among the most important' {Hooper (1948) 86}. At Schweppes, following his experience at Lewis's, he set up a system of joint consultation between workers and management at both branch and company levels. He introduced his scheme with a disarming frankness: at the first company joint council he presented a simplified balance sheet for the year and invited discussion about the distribution of profits between workers and shareholders, adding that the directors, who would make the final decision on distribution, had not yet seen the accounts. This dramatic demonstration of confidence won over the employee representatives.

Similarly Hooper re-applied the industrial relations approach he had helped to forge at Lewis's: he replaced the existing paternalistic arrangements for sickness benefits, bonuses and promotions with

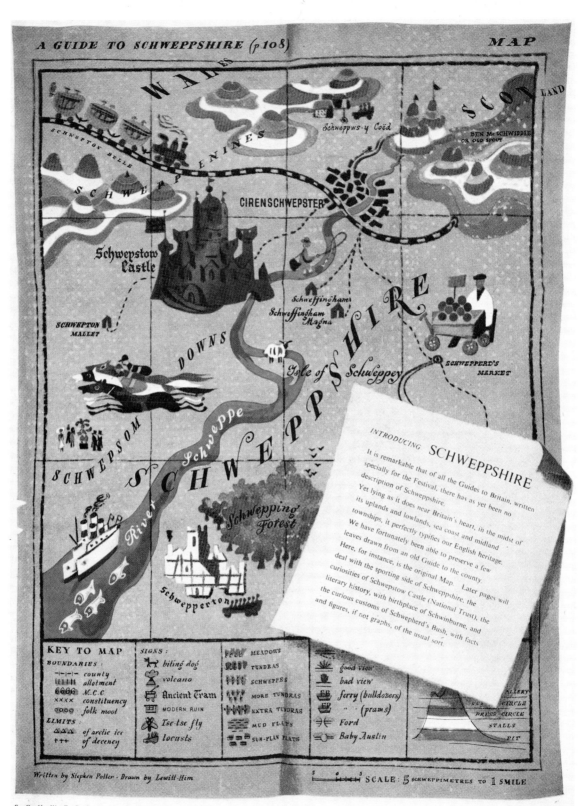

Map of Schweppshire (courtesy of Cadbury Schweppes).

regularised schemes to which employees had entitlement by right, rather than at the behest of managers or directors. He succeeded triumphantly by collaborating with Arthur Deakin, head of the Transport and General Workers Union. Company and union officials adopted a Code of Employment which was signed in May 1950. Sickness payments were related to an employee's length of service by means of a 'Health Bank' scheme, started in February 1950. Pension rights under the old insurance scheme of 1932 were improved for every employee under a new scheme introduced in September 1950. And all employees had access to a management training scheme which progressed from part-time study to learning-by-doing in junior management positions — in its first two years 22 people went through the course with 13 reaching junior management positions, including a stoker, two van drivers and an electrician. Hooper was also extremely concerned about security of employment for his workers. The principle of 'reasonable security' {Hooper (1952) 7} was tested in 1956 when a very wet summer hit sales drastically. Despite this no-one was laid off.

Within four years Hooper's policies produced dramatic results. Trading profits rose from £293,003 in 1948 to £619,816 in 1951 and labour turnover fell from 200 per cent to 20 per cent. With the company reinvigorated, Hooper embarked upon a policy of expansion and diversification. In 1948 Schweppes was the only UK soft drinks manufacturer with an international foothold, with branches in Australia (established 1877), and subsidiary companies in Belgium (1923), South Africa (1925) and France (1928). Hooper expanded Schweppes' national and international market share by granting franchise bottling appointments to carefully selected reputable firms, commencing with Messrs Simonds-Farsons-Cisk Ltd for the island of Malta (by the 1970s over half Schweppes' mineral waters were sold this way).

The American situation was rather different. The lifting of sugar rationing, the last of Britain's wartime controls in the soft drinks industry, early in 1953, opened the way for the giant American beverage companies — Canada Dry, 7-Up, Coca Cola, Pepsi-Cola — to invade the British soft drinks market. Therefore in 1952 Hooper pre-empted the new competition by negotiating two marketing agreements with the Pepsi-Cola Co which became operative in May 1953. One bolstered Schweppes' UK position; the other took the firm into the North American market. Under the English agreement (still in force in 1983) Schweppes bottled and sold Pepsi-Cola in England, Scotland and Wales. Under the American agreement (terminated in 1957, in order to give Schweppes access to other North American bottlers) Pepsi-Cola bottled and sold Schweppes' products in the USA and Canada. Schweppes (USA) was formed as a wholly-owned subsidiary of Schweppes (Overseas) Ltd to operate the agreement. Hooper appointed Commander Edward Whitehead to take charge of the American company. With his distinctive red naval beard Whitehead effectively projected an image of English quality and for twenty years figured in Schweppes' American advertisements. By 1955 it was estimated that 70 million drinks in the USA were annually mixed with Schweppes Tonic.

As sales expanded at home Hooper ensured that production kept pace by investing heavily in new equipment and plant. While he was managing director six major new factories were commissioned — at Aintree, Fareham, Birmingham, Bristol and Gateshead and, most technically advanced of all, at Sidcup in Kent (opened in 1961). The factories at Hendon and Leeds were extended and, following the Pepsi-Cola agreement, the Park Bottling Co (a Schweppes' subsidiary) took over the Pepsi factory at Park Royal, London.

Hooper simultaneously in the 1950s developed Schweppes' product range, partly by developing new soft drinks, partly by moving into the food industry by means of takeovers. New products included comminuted citrus drinks (produced in 1953, following J Lyons & Co's franchised manufacture) and Bitter Lemon (1957) which was a rapid and lasting success. Aquisitions at first comprised smaller firms in the soft drinks industry: the firm which owned rights to Apollinaris Spring Water, in 1955; Jewsbury & Brown Ltd of Manchester, in 1955; and L Rose & Co Ltd, the famous lime juice manufacturers, which cost £1.8 million through an exchange of shares, in 1957. Hooper failed to secure the 'Corona' manufacturers, Thomas & Evans Ltd founded by William Evans (qv), in 1958, but bought R Fry & Co Ltd of Portslade, Sussex in 1961, gaining its subsidiary Ingram & Royle Ltd. He took his first steps towards diversification in 1959, buying Chivers & Sons Ltd of Histon, Cambridge, built up by John Chivers (qv); Wm P Hartley Ltd of London and Aintree, founded by William Pickles Hartley (qv), both manufacturers of jams, marmalades, canned fruits and vegetables; and Moorhouse & Sons Ltd, specialising in jams, lemon cheese and mincemeat, and costing together £5 million. Hooper formed a management company, Connaught Food Products Ltd, to reorganise and consolidate these food acquisitions but this formidable task, coupled with low profit margins of food products, brought some losses until 1964.

The result of all this activity was continued growth, with group net profits before taxation moving from £779,000 in 1952 to over £3 million in 1958 and, with a small setback in 1961, up to £4,446,000 in 1963 when Sir Frederic (he was knighted in 1956 and made a baronet in 1962) died in office. Abroad Schweppes had made remarkable progress, selling 15.5 million units (a dozen bottles normally) of mineral water in 1956 and more than four times that amount in 1963. Yet Hooper left some major tasks unfinished. The food companies had yet to be absorbed into the group and Sir Frederic's decentralisation policies, as the group had grown (in 1963 it had 22 subsidiaries), had significantly diminished the strategic role of the main board.

Outside Schweppes, Sir Frederic Hooper had numerous involvements. Besides speaking and writing about management, he sat on a number of government bodies including the Committee of Enquiry into the Organisation of the RAF, 1954; the Committee on Servicing Aspects of the RAF, 1955 (deputy chairman); the Committee on Employment of National Servicemen in the UK, 1956; and the Advisory Board to the Regular Forces Resettlement Service at the Ministry of Labour and National Service, 1957-60 (chairman). He was advisor on recruiting to the Ministry of Defence, 1960-63. In addition he was a governor of the Ashridge Trust, 1958-63; chairman of the Royal Academy of Dancing; and chairman of the finance committee of the Royal College of Nursing. Besides his knighthood (for services to government departments) (1956) and baronetcy

(1962) his honours included the fellowship of his old college, University College, London (1957).

Though he worked hard, Hooper refused to allow business to monopolise his life. In 1949 he declared 'Mine is a thoroughly enjoyable week in which business occupies an average of some eight well-packed hours a day Monday to Friday, but most of my evenings are strictly my own, and Saturday and Sunday find me as far away from business as a garden and congenial company can take me' {*Leader Magazine* 30 July 1949}. A tall stocky man, Hooper was nimble on the dance floor and tennis court. He collected modern pictures and loved the ballet and his 20 acres of cherry orchard at Tenterden, Kent. Among his strong dislikes were 'tax fiddlers, pop singers, ostentation, and the fizzy drinks upon which the prosperity of his firm depended' {*DNB*}.

Hooper married twice: first in 1918 to Eglantine Irene, daughter of Thomas Augustine Bland of Yelverton, Devon. They had a son, Anthony Robin Maurice (b 1918) who succeeded to the title, and a daughter. After his first marriage was dissolved in 1945 he married Prudence Avery, daughter of Basil Elliott Wenham of Barnt Green, Worcestershire. They had a daughter.

Sir Frederic Hooper planned to retire in 1962 but stayed longer to cover the induction of his successor Harold (later Viscount) Watkinson. Sir Frederic died overnight on 4 October 1963, following the Schweppes' half yearly management conference. He left £109,387 gross.

DAVID J JEREMY

Writings:

Management in the Public Services: A Portrait of the Public Administrator (Institute of Public Administration, 1948).

Management Survey: The Significance of Management in the Modern Community (Pitman, 1948).

Nationalised Audit Service (BIM Conference series II, 1949).

LCC Committee of Inquiry on Sadlers' Wells. Report of the Independent Committee of Inquiry Set Up to Advise the London County Council (London County Council, 1959).

Sources:

Unpublished

BCe.

PrC.

Information from University College, London, Registry, Professor Z A Silberston, Douglas A Simmons.

Frederick Collins Hooper, 'The Development and Organisation of Schweppes Ltd' (Edwards Seminar paper 120, 28 Oct 1952).

Viscount (Harold) Watkinson, 'Schweppes Ltd — in Retrospect and Prospect' (ibid, 377, 6 Dec 1966).

Published

Asa Briggs, *Friends of the People. The Centenary History of Lewis's* (B T Batsford Ltd, 1956).

DNB.

Leader Magazine 30 July 1949.

Lewis's. A Cavalcade, 1856-1937 (pp, the firm, 1937).

Douglas A Simmons, *Schweppes. The First 200 Years* (Springwood Books, 1983).

WWW.

HOPKINSON, John

(1849-1898)

Electrical engineer

John Hopkinson was born in Manchester on 27 July 1849, the eldest son of John Hopkinson, a millwright, a partner in the substantial firm of Wren & Bennett. The family were Congregationalists, and their religion played an important part in their lives. The father was resourceful and enterprising in business, a Liberal in politics, interested in the conditions of workpeople and more generally in civic affairs. He became an alderman in 1872 and was elected Mayor of the City of Manchester in 1882.

Hopkinson was educated initially at a private school in Cheshire, the headmaster of which, Charles Willimore, was an educationalist of unusual insight and ability. When, in 1864, Willimore was appointed to Queenswood School, a boarding school in Hampshire, young Hopkinson went with him. Here the boy's ability for mathematics first showed itself. As the eldest son, John was destined for the family business. Traditionally, the craft of the millwright required some five years of apprenticeship starting at the age of fourteen, but a new pattern of engineering education at university had been evolving for some years. Hopkinson went to Owens College, Manchester, which at that time prepared students for the examinations of the University of London. There he came under the influence of the mathematicians Sandeman and Barker, both Cambridge senior wranglers. Barker suggested that he might go to Cambridge to read for the mathematical tripos, and in 1867 he took first place in the competition for a mathematics scholarship to Trinity College. In 1868 he passed the BSc examinations of the University of London, and won a Whitworth Exhibition. The year before the tripos, he sat the examinations, at that time wholly written and without thesis, for the degree of DSc in the University of London. In June 1871 Hopkinson's name appeared in the tripos lists as senior wrangler. Shortly afterwards he took first place in the Smith's prize. He was elected to a fellowship at Trinity but held it for only a short period, as he maintained his intention to make his career in engineering.

Returning to Manchester, Hopkinson began to acquire responsible practical experience in his father's works. Within a few months, however, his father was approached by James Chance (qv), head of the Birmingham firm of optical glass manufacturers, with the suggestion that John should take up the appointment of engineer and manager of their lighthouse department. This post he held for five years, dealing competently and effectively not only with the technical problems of optical system design but with matters of management, finance and labour relations.

By the time Hopkinson joined Chance Bros the electric arc was being used as a high intensity illuminant for lighthouses. He thus became involved in the provision of electrical equipment. It was during his service with Chance that Hopkinson made a very simple but quite important invention, that of group flashing lights. This was achieved by rearranging the angular distribution of the rotating lens panels to form groups. By this means, two, three, or four flashes at short intervals could be obtained, separated by longer intervals of darkness. Electrical generators for lighthouses prompted Hopkinson to make careful investigations of the behaviour of the machines, using alternating current and direct current, which were then available. He devised a graphical method of representing performance, which became known as 'characteristic curves' and he developed the theoretical explanation of the phenomenon of the stable parallel running of alternators. Hopkinson's mathematical ability was devoted always to practical ends. During his service with Chance he carried on at home experiments upon the residual electric charge of the Leyden Jar. Based upon these, he evolved a simple theory of dielectric behaviour which provided a theoretical description of the phenomenon of dielectric absorption.

Hopkinson left Chance Bros in 1877, and set up in practice as a consulting engineer in London. In 1878 he was elected FRS. It was just at that time that Edison and Swan (qv) successfully 'divided the electric light', by producing the vacuum incandescent lamp. Their success stimulated the promotion of many schemes for public electricity supply, and the rapid development of electric generators. Hopkinson served as a consultant to many of the major electricity supply developments, including that for his native city of Manchester. With his brother Edward, also an electrical engineer and a Cambridge graduate, he co-operated in two pioneer developments of electric traction, the Bessbrook & Newry Tramway in Ireland and the City & South London Railway, the first underground electric railway in the world. The major part of Hopkinson's income was, however, derived not from consulting work, but from his service as an expert witness in patent litigation, an activity for which he showed an astonishing aptitude.

HOPKINSON John

Early in 1882, the recently-formed English Edison Co appointed Hopkinson one of their consulting engineers. From this resulted two of his most notable contributions. The first was a technical one, the re-design of the Edison dynamo, in which connection Hopkinson devised the important concept of the magnetic circuit. The second was a commercial one, the principle of the Two Part Tariff for electricity supply. Hopkinson also made two inventions, both very simple in principle, which had wide commercial application: the three-wire system of electricity supply and the series-parallel connection of electric traction motors.

Throughout his life, Hopkinson carried on experimental scientific research along with his engineering work, and he published in all some 60 papers. His work on the dynamo prompted him to make valuable fundamental investigations on the magnetic properties of iron. Keenly interested in education and with a firm belief in the value of examinations, Hopkinson encouraged the development of the engineering school in Cambridge and during the last five years of his life he was professor of electrical engineering in King's College, London.

In 1873 Hopkinson married Evelyn, daughter of Gustave Oldenbourg, a merchant; she was a friend of his sister Ellen. They had several children. His life ended in one of the most tragic of Alpine accidents, when, together with his son Jack and his daughters Alice and Lena, he was killed in a fall on the Petite Dent de Veisivi near Arolla on 27 August 1898. He left an estate proved at £74,672 gross.

Shortly before his death, Hopkinson had promised Alfred Ewing, professor of engineering in Cambridge, to open a subscription list for a proposed extension to the engineering laboratories. His widow gave immediately £5,000 as a memorial.

JAMES GREIG

Writings:

Many scientific and technical papers collected in:

Original Papers on Dynamo Machinery and Allied Subjects (Whittaker & Co, 1893).

(Bertram Hopkinson, ed) *Original Papers by the Late J Hopkinson, with a Memoir* (2 vols, Cambridge: Cambridge University Press, 1901).

Sources:

Unpublished

MCe.

PrC.

Published

DNB.

James Greig, *John Hopkinson, 1849-1898* (reprinted from *Engineering* 1950).

—, *John Hopkinson, Electrical Engineer* (HMSO, 1970).

Mary Hopkinson, *Memories of John Hopkinson* (Manchester: pp, 1902).

Proceedings of the Institution of Civil Engineers 135 (1898).

WWW.

HORLICK, Sir James

(1844-1921)

Food and drink manufacturer

James Horlick was born at Ruardean, Gloucestershire on 30 April 1844, the third son of James Horlick (d 1875), a saddler, and Priscilla née Griffiths. James and his brothers gained their first experience of business by helping in the small family saddlery firm, before going to boarding school at Andover in Hampshire. In 1862 James went to London to work for a Mr Keene, homeopathic chemist of Bond Street, and qualified as a pharmacist in 1869, the year his younger brother William emigrated to the USA. Following his marriage in 1873 to Margaret Adelaide (d 1925), eldest daughter of William Burford of Leicester, a builder, James and his new wife joined his brother in Chicago.

While there James Horlick intended to manufacture powdered baby food, drawing upon the extensive knowledge of the chemical properties of malt he had gained while working for the Mellin Co, who made a dried infant food from malt and bran. Failing to obtain a partner for this venture, he persuaded William to join him in the partnership of J & W Horlick, established late in 1873. A year later a US patent in their joint names was granted for their 'New Food for Infants, Dyspeptics and Invalids'. This food was made by soaking wheat flour and malted barley in water, extracting the water and finally pulverising the residue of solid matter. James concentrated his energies upon marketing the product by canvassing doctors and pharmacists, while William, who had mastered accounting as book-keeper and company secretary to the Racine Stone & Gravel Co in Wisconsin, took responsibility for production and financial matters.

The new food proved highly popular and in 1876 the brothers built a factory at Racine for its manufacture in larger quantities. James developed an efficient sales network across the USA and Canada and began to export to England, so that by 1882 the factory had to be extended to keep pace with demand. At this point William proposed expanding their business by selling 'malted milk', a beverage composed of an extract of malted barley and wheat mixed with milk, and then packaged in a powdered form. Although several physicians were enthusiastic about a drink for infants and invalids which was more digestible than ordinary cows' milk, James was pessimistic about its sales potential and William had to patent it himself in 1883. James quickly changed his opinion in view of the strikingly favourable response to the new product, and then contributed half of the costs of launching it. 'Malted milk' accelerated the growth of the firm, and in 1885 the Horlicks Food Co was incorporated in Wisconsin with James as president and William as secretary.

James returned to live in England in 1890, opening a London office of the company and promoting its products on the Continent and throughout much of the British Empire. His growing interest in country pursuits was exemplified by his acquisition of a large estate at Cowley, near Gloucester, in 1898. He eventually persuaded his reluctant brother to invest in building a British factory by agreeing to share equally any profits it should make but bearing sole responsibility for meeting any losses it might incur. In 1906 James began building a factory at Slough. The new undertaking prospered, with Horlicks Malted Milk being supplied as rations to Polar explorers such as Amundsen and Byrd, and being used extensively by the army during the First World War.

Horlick's business success was complemented by growing social recognition. He was appointed a JP in 1900, served as High Sheriff for Gloucestershire in 1902 and was made DL for that county in the same year. He was created a baronet in June 1914. Horlick was a keen patron of rural associations like the Gloucestershire Root, Fruit and Grain Society, served as president of the Gloucestershire Agricultural Society and exhibited Shorthorn cattle and Oxford Down sheep bred at Cowley and his Sussex estate, but his principal recreation was shooting. Politically a Conservative, he was an ardent supporter of Tariff Reform and was a member of the Carlton and Constitutional Clubs. Horlick had three sons: Ernest Burford Horlick (1880-1934), who succeeded to his title and his share of the business; James Nockells Horlick (1886-1972), who was later Unionist MP for Gloucester, 1923-29, and became the fourth baronet; and Major Gerald Nolekin Horlick (1888-1918), who died on active service. A devout Anglican, James Horlick commemorated his dead son by restoring the organ of Gloucester Cathderal in 1920. His last years were clouded by ill-health and he died in his London home on 7 May 1921, leaving an estate proved at £450,481 gross.

CHRISTOPHER MURPHY

Sources:

Unpublished

MCe.

PrC.

P Campbell, 'A Brief History of Horlicks' (typescript, 1969).

Published

DAB.

E Gaskell, 'James Horlick Esq., DL, JP', in *Gloucestershire Leaders, Social and Political* (Queenhithe Printing & Publishing Co, nd).

'James Horlick, JP, DL' *Men of the Day No 1162*, supplement to *Vanity Fair* (nd).

Times 22 June, 26 Oct 1914, 3 Dec 1915, 16 Feb, 1 Dec 1916, 12 July 1918, 16 Nov 1920, 10 May 1921, 25 Nov 1925.

Who Was Who in America 1, 1897-1942 (Chicago: A N Marquis, 1943).

WWW.

HORNBY, Frank

(1863-1936)

Toy manufacturer

Frank Hornby, taken from Meccano Magazine *XXI no 11, November 1936 (courtesy of Merseyside County Museums and John Mills Photography Ltd).*

Frank Hornby was born in Liverpool on 15 May 1863, the son of John Hornby, a provision merchant, and his wife Martha née Thomlinson. Leaving school at sixteen, he worked for seven years as a clerk in his father's firm before obtaining employment with D H Elliott, an importer of American meat and livestock, for whom he eventually became managing clerk.

Hornby was raised as a Methodist and became prominent in the Band of Hope temperance society in his local church. He met his wife-to-be, Clara, the daughter of William Godefrey, a customs officer, while both were members of the choir of the Liverpool Philharmonic Society. They married in 1887 and had two sons, Roland and Douglas, and a daughter, Patricia Elliott, who died at the age of fourteen.

As a youth Hornby became keenly interested in engineering, reading a great many books and manuals on the subject during his leisure time. Inspired above all by Samuel Smiles's *Self-Help*, he practised his hobby in a small work-room in his parents' home and became a skilled amateur engineer.

Hornby also built various toys for his children, most of which, he noticed, were quickly discarded. By about 1900, after much experimentation, he had developed the idea of producing re-constructable mechanical toy kits consisting of thin metal strips perforated at half-inch

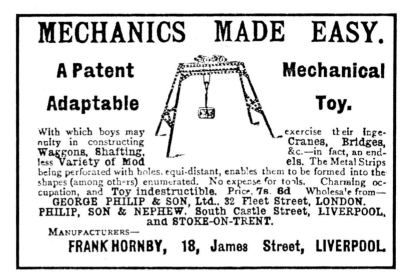

Early Mechanics Made Easy *trade card, c 1903, taken from* Meccano Magazine *XVIII no 2, February 1933 (courtesy of Merseyside County Museums).*

intervals, together with connecting rods, cog-wheels, brackets, and nuts and bolts.

At first, Hornby was unable to obtain support for his idea from manufacturers, who were unimpressed by his lack of capital and the crude nature of his home-made kits. However, with the help of a letter of recommendation from Professor Hele-Shaw, professor of engineering at Liverpool University, he eventually gained the necessary financial backing, notably from his employer, D H Elliott.

Having obtained the first British patent for his invention in January 1901, Hornby set up a spare-time business in partnership with D H Elliott in a small rented room at 17 James Street in the centre of Liverpool. In this room Hornby and one female assistant boxed sets made up of parts produced by various manufacturers. For several years Hornby wrote all of the construction manuals himself. The first kits were marketed under the title 'Mechanics Made Easy', later shortened to 'Meccano', a trade name officially registered in 1907. In 1908 the rapidly-expanding business was incorporated as Meccano Ltd, with an initial share capital of £5,000. At this time Elliott withdrew from the enterprise and Hornby assumed full control.

In order to promote the standardisation of his product, Hornby decided to set himself up as its sole manufacturer in a former motor car factory at 274 West Derby Road, Tuebrook, Liverpool. Later, in 1910, he bought five acres of land in the Old Swan district of Liverpool, and built, to his own specifications, the Binns Road factory, which opened in 1911. It remained the head office of Meccano until its closure in 1979. The major expansion of business which followed the move to Binns Road continued up to and throughout most of the First World War. Under Hornby's shrewd guidance the remarkable success of Meccano in Britain was quickly duplicated abroad, with associated companies being established in the fiercely competitive markets of Germany and the USA by 1914. Despite repeated legal wrangles over patents, particularly in the USA,

THE
HAPPIEST
BOYS IN THE WORLD

Meccano advertisement 1929, taken from Meccano Magazine *XIV no II (courtesy of Merseyside County Museums).*

Meccano soon outstripped all competitors to become widely acknowledged as 'The World's Most Famous Toy'.

A major innovation was the publication in September 1916 of the first edition of the *Meccano Magazine*. Deriving from a single sheet newsletter written by Hornby himself in order to advise users of Meccano, the magazine, with its emphasis on engineering and informative articles of general interest, soon gained a very wide readership. Hornby remained editor until 1924, by which time approximately 100,000 copies were being sold worldwide every month. It was largely due to the success of the magazine that Hornby later founded the 'Meccano Guild' (1919) and the 'Hornby Railway Company' (1928), both of which became extremely popular co-ordinating organisations for enthusiasts.

Hornby responded to the precarious economic conditions of the post-war era by diversifying the company's product range. In 1920 he took advantage of the prevailing weakness of the German toy industry to enter the clockwork train business. Five years later he introduced Hornby electric trains and accessories, featuring the famous 'o' gauge. Sales of Hornby trains, especially in Britain, almost immediately rivalled and surpassed those of Meccano. Among other products introduced during this period were constructional motor car and aeroplane outfits and chemical and electrical kits. The introduction in 1934 of the 'Dinky Toys' series of model figures and vehicles, introduced as 'Modelled Miniatures' for use with the Hornby railway system, placed the seal on the creative output of the company.

It is a measure of the success of Meccano Ltd in the UK alone during the lifetime of Frank Hornby that its initial share capital of £5,000 in 1908 was increased to £100,000 in 1921 and £300,000 in 1932. In 1910-11 the business made a net profit in Britain of £3,094, rising to a pre-war peak in 1913-14 of £54,034. Its net profit was £43,897 in 1925-26 and £40,109 in 1935-36.

Gentle in private, inspiring respect and affection among his employees, Hornby also possessed the vision and tenacity to convert what was virtually a one-man enterprise into an internationally successful concern within very few years. The invention of Meccano was of inestimable value to children around the world, providing them with endless enjoyment and practical education in basic mechanics. Meccano, however, was the product of a practical mind rather than a truly inventive genius. Hornby achieved most as a salesman and manufacturer. His boyish enthusiasm for his inventions and belief in the quality and value of his products were the main foundations of his business success. Although of strictly limited business experience at first, he learned from each new venture and eventually became an extremely accomplished businessman.

Hornby was not much involved in public life, until between 1931 and 1935 he served as Conservative MP for the Everton division of Liverpool, where he had spent part of his early life. He was also a member of the Rotary Club of Liverpool. Frank Hornby died in Liverpool on 21 September 1936. His will was proved at £231,536 gross.

ALAN J SCARTH

Writings:

'The Life Story of Meccano' *Meccano Magazine* XVII, no 1 (Jan 1932) to XVIII, no 2 (Feb 1933) (12 articles in all; not in XVII, no 9).

Sources:

Unpublished

Merseyside County Archives, Liverpool, Meccano archives (D/ME), Articles of Association of Meccano Ltd 1908; Meccano Ltd Annual Balance Sheets, 1910-11, 1913-14, 1925-26, 1935-36; 'Bill of Complaint: Meccano Ltd v John Wannamaker, New York. In District Court of the United States, for Southern District of New York (9 July 1918)'.

BCe.

MCe.

PrC.

Published

Maurice P Gould, *Frank Hornby: The Boy Who Made $1,000,000 with a Toy* (New York: Meccano Company Inc, 1915).

'Histories of Liverpool Companies: No 17, Meccano Ltd' *Illustrated Liverpool News* Dec 1963.

B Ikin, 'Happiness Unlimited' *Liverpool '68* no 15 (City of Liverpool Public Relations Office, 1968).

Liverpool Echo 21 Sept 1936.

'Meccano Ltd' in Edwin Thompson (ed), *Excursions and Visits to Works. British Association for the Advancement of Science, Liverpool 1923* (Liverpool, 1923).

Meccano Magazine XXI, no 11 (Nov 1936).

Gustav Reder, *Clockwork, Steam and Electric: A History of Model Railways* (Allan, 1972).

Times 22 Sept 1936.

WWMP.

WWW.

HORNE, Robert Stevenson

Viscount Horne of Slamannan

(1871-1940)

Railway and industrial company chairman

Robert Stevenson Horne was born at the mining village of Slamannan, Stirlingshire on 28 February 1871. He was the youngest son of Rev Robert Stevenson Horne, minister of the parish of Slamannan, and his wife Mary, the daughter of Thomas Lochhead of Toward, Argyllshire.

The family had sufficient means (the father left £740 on his death in 1887) to send Horne to George Watson's College, Edinburgh, and then to the University of Glasgow. There he distinguished himself by achieving a first class degree in mental philosophy (1893) and by becoming president

HORNE Robert Stevenson

Sir Robert Horne (taken from E J Cocks and B Walters A History of the Zinc Smelting Industry in Britain *George G Harrap & Co Ltd, 1968).*

of the University Conservative Club (1891) and of the Students' Representative Council a year later. After a brief academic career he decided to study the law and was admitted as a member of the Faculty of Advocates in 1896. His connection with Glasgow assisted the early success of his practice, especially in commercial and shipping cases. In 1910, aged thirty-nine, he took silk and came to occupy a position among the leading half-dozen members of the Scottish Bar. But according to Harold Macmillan, a close political friend, fellow director of the Great Western Railway in the 1930s and on whose small executive committee of the Industrial Reorganisation League (1934) Horne sat, he was not a dedicated lawyer: the law was 'rather a means of livelihood and advancement than delight' {*DNB*}. He continued to cultivate his political interests and contacts, trying in vain in 1910 to enter parliament as a Unionist for Stirlingshire.

It was the First World War that eventually gave Horne the opportunity to enter a wider field. After a minor appointment as secretary to the agricultural section of the National Service Department, Horne became involved in railway organisation at the front with the rank of lieutenant-colonel under Eric Geddes (qv), the director-general of railways in France. In 1917 he was promoted to the post of assistant inspector-general of transportation and later in that year, at the suggestion of Geddes (now at the Admiralty) he became the director of the department of materials and priority at the Admiralty. Then, in 1918, still at the Admiralty, he directed the department of labour and held the position of Third Civil Lord. He was created KBE in 1918 (and CBE in 1920).

In December 1918, he was returned to parliament as the Unionist member for the Hillhead division of Glasgow and, unusually, achieved cabinet rank immediately as Minister of Labour. He owed this to the high opinion of his ability formed by Lloyd George during the conflict. In that flush of post-war idealism that characterised the early months of the new Government, Horne opened the National Industrial Conference (27 February 1919) which promised, but hardly realised, better relations between workers, employers and the state. In fact Horne devoted much of his time to the immediate problems of industrial unrest, from which experiences he became increasingly afraid of the prospect of 'direct action' by the workers. His major legislative contribution was the Unemployment Insurance Act (1920) which, with its actuarial optimism conceived in boom conditions, brought the number of insured persons to nearly 12 million out of an economically active population of approximately 19 million. In 1920 he was moved to the presidency of the Board of Trade, where he decided to give effect to the Government's pledges towards new or fragile industries, the bill for which (the Safeguarding of Industries Bill) was successfully introduced by his successor, Stanley Baldwin. In a cabinet reshuffle of March 1921, Horne succeeded Austen Chamberlain as Chancellor of the Exchequer, where he was rigidly orthodox and according to Sir Frederick Leith-Ross 'really out of his depth ... and what is more, tended to show it' {Leith-Ross (1968) 81}.

On the dissolution of the Coalition Government in October 1922, Horne's friendship with Lloyd George and disgust with the back-bench Unionist revolt, which ended the Liberal Unionist coalition, prevented him from accepting office in the new Conservative administration of

Bonar Law. Although Baldwin, who apparently despised Horne, offered him the Ministry of Labour in November 1924, he refused it and soon after resigned his seat on the board of Baldwins Ltd. While he never held office after 1922, he retained his seat in the Commons until 1937, when he was raised to the peerage as Viscount Horne of Slamannan. Moreover, he was active within the upper reaches of the party, especially on matters such as Empire free trade and protection, the financial crisis of 1931 and rearmament (he was one of the malcontents concerned about the nation's defences in the late 1930s).

It was after leaving the Exchequer at the age of fifty-one, that Horne was absorbed into the business élite as a director of a number of major companies. With his political connections, legal training and wartime administrative experience he was a valuable asset to the companies he served. He was always on the board of at least ten companies and at his death in 1940 of 15: National Smelting Co Ltd, chairman, 1923-40; Burma Corporation Ltd, chairman, 1926-40; Zinc Corporation Ltd, chairman, 1926-40; Imperial Smelting Corporation Ltd, chairman, 1929-40; New Broken Hill Consolidated Ltd, chairman, 1937-40; Union Corporation Ltd (Mining); Great Western Railway Co, chairman, 1934-40; Peninsular & Oriental Steam Navigation Co; British India Steam Navigation Co Ltd; Suez Canal Co; Lloyds Bank Ltd; Bay Hall Trust Ltd, chairman, 1937-40; Commercial Union Assurance Co Ltd; Samuel Hodge & Son Ltd (construction); and Grease Proof Paper Mills (wholly owned by Wiggins Teape (1919) Ltd). Of these, he attached the most importance to the National Smelting Co and its off-shoots, and the Great Western Railway.

The urgent need for zinc for war purposes led to the formation in 1917 of the National Smelting Co, a private company but supported in various ways by the Government. However, in the post-war flurry of jettisoning government-sponsored wartime projects, only Lloyds Bank, which had lent heavily to Richard Tilden Smith (qv) who possessed a controlling interest in the firm, was afraid that the Avonmouth project for a major smelting complex, as yet (1923) unfinished, would be worthless. Horne was drawn into the efforts to save the enterprise and to reconstruct it as a public company through his association with Lloyds, of which he was a director. He acted as a mediator between the bank and the Government to produce an arrangement that freed the firm of its financial obligations to the Government, and facilitated its survival during a period of very difficult trading conditions. Moreover the arrangement appealed to Horne's deeply-felt 'imperial sentiment' for, apart from Lloyds, the British Metal Corporation, and Tilden Smith's interests, the Zinc Corporation and other Australian concentrates suppliers were represented on the board, which he chaired from 1923. The importance of the Australian connection was reflected also in his chairmanship later of the Zinc Corporation and Broken Hill Consolidated, and in the strong support that Australian non-ferrous mining companies gave to the Imperial Smelting Corporation. In 1929 the board of National Smelting found it necessary to form another company, Imperial Smelting, to take over National Smelting as a prelude to expansion. Horne became its chairman. Imperial Smelting had an authorised capital of £7 million (just under £4.5 million raised initially), an assured supply of raw materials after the Government's wartime contract with Australian interests expired in 1930, and sales from its valuable portfolio of investments, especially in the Burma Corporation. It grew and diversified and, having survived the collapse of prices between 1929 and 1932, emerged with international interests and markets as the sole producer of zinc in Britain.

Horne joined the board of the Great Western Railway in 1923 and was unanimously elected chairman in 1934, with a fee of £6,000 a year, in succession to Viscount Victor Spencer Churchill. While the GWR ranked third in size of the four systems created under the Railways Act of 1921, it was in 1934 an immense and complex concern, with a paid-up capital in excess of £149 million, a net revenue of £5.5 million and a workforce of around 96,000. However, in common with the other mainline railways at this time, it laboured financially during Horne's chairmanship: net revenue fell far short of standard revenue (£8.5 million) set in 1928; the return on capital expenditure varied between 2.5 per cent (1938) and 3.5 per cent (1937); and the dividend on ordinary stock fell below 3 per cent for the first time. The decline of the staple industries of South Wales, the growth of competition from road transport and the cyclical hesitations of the economy generally, imposed external constraints on the company's prosperity and raised important questions about its social responsibilities and public policy. For example, faced with a dismal return on the company's extensive docks in South Wales, where receipts were insufficient even to cover working expenses, Horne carefully examined the legal and political costs involved and decided to recommend the closure of Penarth Dock from 6 July 1936. 'South Wales' he said 'could not expect to succeed by bleeding the Great Western Company' {Channon (1981) 215}. Horne was also energetic, using his political and business connections in the moves made by the railways to persuade the Government, industrialists and the public, that the industry was severely handicapped by the burden of obsolete restrictions and obligations, when confronted with road competitors who were virtually free from such hindrances. Following the Railways' 'square deal' campaign, in 1939 the Minister of Transport agreed that there was a prima facie case for some relaxation in the railways' terms of reference but the Second World War forestalled any action.

A logical thinker, as would be expected of a man who had been a university lecturer in philosophy and practised at the Bar, Horne had a 'supreme conventional competence' that was applied to whatever task he tackled during the varied phases of his life {DNB}. 'Bertie' was a much-favoured after-dinner speaker who, with his debonair appearance and sociability, was adept at telling amusing, sometimes dirty, stories, an ability that some admired while others, like Stanley Baldwin who once called Horne 'that rare thing — a Scots cad', plainly did not {Middlemas and Barnes (1969) 282}.

Viscount Horne died on 3 September 1940 at Farnham, Surrey, after an appendix operation. A memorial service was held at Westminster Abbey a week later. As he was unmarried, the peerage became extinct. In addition to drawing fees from the many companies he served, he had an income from a wide portfolio of investments in which, as might be expected, the Empire was heavily represented. He left an estate valued at £64,923 gross.

GEOFFREY CHANNON

Sources:

Unpublished

House of Lords RO, London, Bonar Law Papers; Lloyd George papers.

PRO, Great Western Railway, reports and accounts, minutes, memoranda and letters.

Scottish RO, General Register House, Edinburgh, Elibank papers.

Communications from G E Flack, assistant to the managing director, RTZ Chemicals Ltd, Avonmouth, Bristol.

Published

Theodore C Barker and Christopher Savage, *An Economic History of Transport in Britain* (3rd ed, Hutchinson, 1974).

Geoffrey Blainey (ed), *If I Remember Rightly: W S Robinson's Memoirs* (Melbourne: Cheshire, 1967).

Geoffrey Channon, 'The Great Western Railway Under the British Railways Act of 1921' *Business History Review* 55 (1981).

P K Cline, 'Eric Geddes and the "Experiment" with Businessmen in Government, 1915-22' in K D Brown (ed), *Essays in Anti-Labour History* (Macmillan, 1974).

Edward J Cocks and Bernhardt Walters, *A History of the Zinc Smelting Industry in Britain* (Harrap, 1968).

DD 1918-40.

DNB.

Ian M Drummond, *Imperial Economic Policy 1917-1939* (Allen & Unwin, 1974).

Financial News 4 Sept 1940.

Financial Times 13 Jan 1941.

Bentley B Gilbert, *British Social Policy 1914-39* (Batsford, 1970).

Sir Frederick Leith-Ross, *Money Talks: Fifty Years of International Finance* (Hutchinson, 1968).

Rodney Lowe, 'The Erosion of State Intervention in Britain, 1917-24' *Economic History Review* 2nd ser, 31 (1978).

Harold Macmillan, *Winds of Change 1914-1939* (Macmillan, 1966).

J M McEwen, 'The Coupon Election of 1918: The Unionist Members of Parliament' *Journal of Modern History* 34 (1962).

Robert Keith Middlemas and John Barnes, *Baldwin: A Biography* (Weidenfeld & Nicolson, 1969).

Modern Transport 6 Sept 1940.

Oswald S Nock, *History of the Great Western Railway. Vol 2, 1923-48* (Shepperton, Surrey: Ian Allan, 1971).

Railway Gazette 6 Sept 1940.

Christopher J Schmitz, *World Non-ferrous Metal Production and Prices 1700-1976* (Cass, 1979).

Stock Exchange Year-Book 1918-33.

Stock Exchange Official Year-Book 1934-40.

Times 4, 11, 12 Sept 1940, 13 Jan 1941.

WWMP.

WWW.

HOULDER, Edwin Savory

(1828-1901)

Shipowner

Edwin Savory Houlder, the youngest of seven children, was born on 19 December 1828. His father, William, deserted the family home in Sussex soon afterwards, leaving Edwin's upbringing to his mother. To what extent this inauspicious start influenced his early career is not known, but Edwin enthusiastically entered business in 1844 when he joined Ionides, Sgouta & Co, who rewarded his ability and enterprise in 1849 when they provided finance and accommodation in London for his own shipbroking business. Edwin later brought his brothers Alfred (in 1856) and Augustus (in 1867) into the partnership, as Houlder Brothers & Co.

Houlders diversified business along familiar lines from shipbroking to insurance and, in time, shipping and forwarding, with some success as merchants on their own account. Attention focused on Australia where emigration and an expanding outward trade promised well. Houlders chartered tonnage and by 1861 had extensive shipowning interests, advertising a regular packet service to Australia with clippers bought cheaply from the United States. By the end of the century Houlders became firmly established in the Australian meat trade with London, after first developing return cargoes in guano, phosphate and copra from the Pacific, and had developed regular links with India and South Africa, loading coal and cement and shipping supplies for the British Government during the Boer War.

These routes alone did not satisfy the rapid commercial expansion which Houlder sought. In 1881, he visited Argentina to stake a claim in the expanding meat business and from the 1890s, with the trade assured and refrigeration techniques improved, Houlders launched a modern fleet of steamships, enabling them to become firmly entrenched under long-run contracts with the meat packers. In Britain, too, the firm extended their representation — at Manchester, where they loaded for Australia via the Ship Canal, and at Newport, where Houlders inaugurated coal shipments to Buenos Aires.

Such developments demanded adjustments to Houlder Brothers' organisation. The original partnership had ended when Alfred died in Hawaii in 1876, and Augustus in 1884. But Edwin continued as senior partner with Ebenezer Cayford, his nephew who had long worked in the house, and his son Frank. Houlders formed separate companies averaging some £40,000 in £100 shares for each ship, all managed by the firm. Then in 1898 Houlder Brothers & Co Ltd assumed the partnerships' management responsibilities, the partners selling their interests and becoming directors in the new concern which raised £20,000 equity and £145,000 in preference and debenture stock. In 1899, the 10 single ship companies (totalling some 23,000 tons) merged into Houlder Line Ltd, managed by the parent company, with capital of £500,000 to buy out existing shareholders and finance expansion.

Edwin Houlder represents a type of successful shipowner building up a business from modest means, well-known in nineteenth-century Liverpool but less characteristic, perhaps, of London. While it is difficult to distinguish the man from his company, his influence from that of his partners, he appears to have been a shrewd, hard-working, thrusting man, quick to exploit a diversified range of commercial opportunities and flexibly prepared to switch to more promising activities. In some respects Houlder's management might be considered conservative. The firm long preferred to charter, rather than own, tonnage, which reduced risks and capital requirements. It did not pioneer the adoption of steamships or technological change, but instead clung to clippers well into the 1880s, letting others make the expensive experiments. Nor did the firm enthusiastically embrace modern company formation until the very end of the century. Nonetheless, such caution should not be confused with entrepreneurial failure.

Houlder was twice married, to a Miss Booth by whom he had two children and, after her death, to Mary Elizabeth Amos, by whom he had five more children. He lived at Sutton in Surrey, first at 'Fernwood' and then at 'The Grange', the suffix of the name of most of Houlder's later steamers. Towards the end of his life he moved to Ingress Abbey, Greenhithe, sold on his death but later purchased by the Thames Nautical Training College (HMS *Worcester*) with which he had been closely associated. He died on 29 July 1901, after suffering a heart attack while defending company policy at a shareholders' meeting. In addition to his English property, Houlder owned land in Argentina and left an estate in England of £128,382 gross.

ROBERT GREENHILL

Sources:

Unpublished

C Reg: Houlder Brothers (55,805).

HOULDER Edwin Savory

PrC.

Published

Fairplay 16 Mar 1899, 19 July 1900, 1 Aug 1901.

South American Journal 17 June 1899, 27 July 1900.

Edward F Stevens, *One Hundred Years of Houlders* (pp, 1951).

Times 30 July 1901.

HOULDSWORTH, Sir Hubert Stanley

(1889-1956)

Chairman of the nationalised coal industry

Hubert Stanley Houldsworth was born at Heckmondwike, Yorkshire on 20 April 1889, the son of Albert Houldsworth, a manufacturing chemist, and his wife Susannah née Buckley. After the death of his father seven years later, Houldsworth was supported by his mother, who worked as a rug-binder in a factory at Heckmondwike. His family had neither private means nor connections. He won a scholarship to Heckmondwike Grammar School and then Leeds University where Houldsworth took a BSc in physics, with first class honours in 1911. The following year he obtained an MSc and after a few years as a science master in Castleford Secondary School, returned to Leeds University where he joined the staff in 1916 and obtained a DSc in 1925.

Academic science was not wholly to his taste, however. As a boy he had wanted to become a lawyer and while still at Leeds read for the Bar. He was called to the Bar at Lincoln's Inn, taking silk in 1937, becoming a bencher in 1943 and, finally, Recorder of Doncaster, 1946-48. At an early stage he specialised in the legal problems of the coal industry, and eventually became 'one of the two or three leading authorities on mining law' {*Times* 2 Feb 1956}. His connection with the coal industry began in 1936 when he was appointed independent chairman of the District Co-ordinating Committee of the Midland (Amalgamated) District (Coal Mines) Scheme of 1930, a post he held until 1942. These district schemes, established under the Coal Mines Act, 1930, had the dual — and partly conflicting — tasks of allocating quota production limits to collieries (to control coal over-supply) and to encourage company amalgamations (to promote efficiency). Now only one step removed from immediate management, Houldsworth increased his involvement at the outbreak of the Second World War. In 1939 he became Joint Coal Supplies Officer for the Midland area and, from 1941, added the duties of Fuel and Power Controller for the North East region. All of these appointments terminated in 1942 when he became Regional Controller (for South and West Yorkshire) of the Ministry of Fuel and Power. In 1944 he rose within the Ministry to become Controller-General, thus taking a major role in the direction of coal supply and consumption during the last two years of the war. He was awarded a knighthood in 1945.

Upon the enactment of the Coal Industry Nationalisation Act 1946, Houldsworth became chairman of the NCB's East Midlands Division. Whether or not this had actually been his ambition, he had progressed steadily from the legal fringe of the coal industry to control directly its most successful operating division, and it is thought that his five years in this capacity were among the happiest of his working life. Not that chairmanship of a well-favoured group of collieries caused any relaxation on his part; on the contrary, Houldsworth pushed the development of his mines so that they exceeded all others in productivity and profitability.

East Midlands was already dramatically more successful than any other division, producing in 1947 19 per cent of British coal from 10 per cent of Britain's collieries. Manpower productivity was 50 per cent above the British average and more than 20 per cent above the next best operating division. Tonnage lost due to labour disputes was less than a tenth of the national percentage. All of these parameters were maintained or enhanced during Houldsworth's regime. Up to 1951, when Houldsworth left the Division, the East Midlands had shown a growth in tonnage of 24 per cent (against a British average of 14 per cent), a 54 per cent growth in revenue (British average 44 per cent) and a 39 per cent growth in production per colliery (British average 24 per cent).

In 1951 the service contracts of the 1946 appointees to the national board expired and, either from this cause or due to earlier resignations, the composition of the National Coal Board changed almost entirely in this year. Only two new men were appointed from the Divisions, and one was Houldsworth, who became chairman of the NCB.

As chairman he attempted to put into effect the lessons he had learned in the East Midlands. Essentially these were the benefits of good geological conditions (about which he could, of course, do nothing), and of good labour relations. The latter dominated his remaining years, as he attempted to bring national standards up to those he had enjoyed in the East Midlands.

Here he underestimated substantially the obstacles in the way of success. The NCB at this time was still trying to put in order its own organisation, which after five years was still only partly workable. The days of 'coal at any price' had gone and the first threats to coal's market dominance were apparent, with detrimental changes on the railways, in the gas industry, in exports and in alternative domestic fuels. Controlling and directing an organisation the size of the NCB required, above all, a supremely able administrator. Houldsworth was not that; indeed it is doubtful that he ever understood the importance of administration. The virtue which served him so well in the East Midlands — a love of people —

proved his Achilles' heel as NCB chairman. In pursuit of better communications and labour relations, he relied too much on personal intervention which took up a great deal of his time, but did not achieve his objective, and this was a source of disappointment to him. The report, published in February 1955, of the independent advisory committee on the National Coal Board, chaired by Alexander Fleck (qv), criticised the policy of relative autonomy for the Divisions which Houldsworth had favoured, and recommended firmer direction by the national board. This criticism was another blow to him.

He had nevertheless achieved something. During his time as chairman, the last arrears of maintenance due to wartime postponement were dealt with, and the first real developments for a modern industry were initiated. By 1955, little of the effects of the latter were noticeable, for production had fallen slightly, and profitability was down by 60 per cent compared to 1951. But he had made it plain to the NCB, then and for the future, that unless there was accord between the pitman and every level of management, real progress would be impossible.

A lifelong Liberal, Houldsworth unsuccessfully contested Pudsey and Otley in the 1929 general election. He was deputy chairman of the West Riding Quarter Sessions, and became pro-chancellor of Leeds University in 1949. He was given a baronetcy in the New Year Honours of 1956 only a few weeks before his death.

Houldsworth married in 1919 Hilda Frances, daughter of Joseph Clegg of Cleckheaton, Yorkshire; they had one son. Sir Hubert Houldsworth died six months before he planned to retire, following a heart attack; he left an estate proved at £18,208.

C G DOWN

Writings:

Speech at Opening of NCB Summer School at Oxford, Monday 27 August 1951 (National Coal Board, 1951).

Statement ... at a Luncheon to Industrial and Labour Correspondents and the Editors of the Coal Trade and Technical Press, Tuesday 2 January 1952 (National Coal Board, 1952).

(and others) *Efficiency in the Nationalised Industries* (Allen & Unwin, 1952).

Speech to NUM Annual Conference, Hastings, 8 July 1953 (National Coal Board, 1953).

The Pits of Britain (Manchester: Manchester Statistical Society, 1953).

Speech to NUM Annual Conference, Blackpool, 7 July 1954 (National Coal Board, 1954).

Opening Address at NCB Summer School, Oxford 1954 (National Coal Board, 1954).

Britain's Coal Industry (National Coal Board, 1954).

The Future of British Coal (National Coal Board, 1954).

Power for Prosperity (National Coal Board, 1955).

Speech to NUM Conference 1955 (National Coal Board, 1955).

He also contributed papers to the *Transactions of the Ceramic Society* and to the *Journal of the Society of Glass Technology.*

Sources:

Unpublished

PrC.

Published

Burke's Peerage and Baronetage.

Coal Feb, Aug 1951, Mar 1956.

Colliery Guardian 9 Feb 1956.

DNB.

Hugh A Clegg and Theodore E Chester, *The Future of Nationalisation* (Oxford: Basil Blackwell, 1953).

Times 2 Feb 1956.

WWW.

Sir William Houldsworth (taken from E Gaskell Lancashire Leaders Social and Political *The Queenhithe Printing and Publishing Co Ltd).*

HOULDSWORTH, Sir William Henry

(1834-1917)

Cotton and iron manufacturer

William Henry Houldsworth was born in Manchester on 24 August 1834, the fourth son of Henry Houldsworth, at that time manager of his uncle Thomas's extensive fine-spinning mills at Newton Street, Manchester. After attending Mr Jackson's school at Broughton, Manchester, where in the 1840s he presented 'a very attractive example of a school companion' {Hayes (1905) 70}, Houldsworth completed his education at St Andrew's University under the Professor of Logic, William Spalding, a Shakespearean scholar of some distinction. Partnership followed in Thomas Houldsworth & Co, of which his father was now head, having inherited this firm (founded in 1796) together with extensive interests in iron works and land at Coltness, Lanarkshire, on the death of Thomas Houldsworth in 1852. At the Newton Street works, William displayed some adeptness in the mechanical improvements which his father had keenly pursued, particularly in combing machines. However, Henry soon retired from active management, leaving William as the leading partner in the firm at a relatively young age, although with experienced and able lieutenants in Joseph Higginson, the works manager and Charles Ling, William's 'commercial godfather'.

Houldsworth himself seems to have contributed much of the energy and vision with which the firm was, in 1865, relocated from central Manchester to the outlying area of Reddish, near Stockport. Although the Manchester works was retained (as was a country mill at Rocester, Staffordshire until about 1875), Reddish, besides offering the advantages of cheap land, good communications, and, possibly, cheaper labour, provided above all an opportunity to modernise plant and working habits. The mill, a model of architecture and arrangement, was equipped with fully-modernised machinery, with self-acting mules finally replacing the hand mules which had long survived in fine spinning. In 1870 a second mill was built by the same partners, but organised, fashionably, as the Reddish Spinning Co Ltd, with a capital of £50,000 (later £75,000). In all, by the 1880s, these mills employed about 1,000 operatives, and their prosperity put Houldsworths back in the forefront of the fine-spinning sector. In 1892 Thomas Houldsworth & Co was incorporated in limited liability form, with fixed assets valued at £206,618 (excluding the Newton Street works). The mills employed a total of 296,000 spindles in the 1890s giving Houldsworth control of probably the largest number of fine-spinning spindles in the trade; certainly when the two companies became part of the Fine Cotton Spinners' & Doublers' Association in 1898, they were, at £546,896, the most highly-valued of the founding firms.

However, an integral part of Houldsworth's vision in removing to rural Reddish was the creation of a factory community. Strongly aware of his responsibility as an employer, he sought to provide for the working-man the best conditions he could; in return for such 'sacrifice' of immediate profits, he looked for adaptability of the workers in respect of machinery, hours, and if necessary, wages, in order to maintain the firm's competitive position. In the light of these ideas, Houldsworth devoted considerable resources to providing workmen's houses and a school, together with a recreation ground, while engaging Alfred Waterhouse (qv), the leading Manchester architect of the day, to construct a working-man's club, parsonage and, in 1883, the church of St Elisabeth's, a rare example of Waterhouse's quality as an ecclesiastical architect. In this 'Philanthropic Venture' Houldsworth met some disappointment: the community was for many years bitterly divided, with one mill a union one, the other not, and the latter working longer hours than the former. Nor did the working-men support Houldsworth's institutions with the degree of commitment he looked for. Nevertheless he persevered, with annual addresses and treats for the workers (for example, picnics at his Cheshire home, Norbury Booth Hall). By 1887 the community was reported to be reunited, and good feeling restored. It was, therefore, a qualified success, deserving to rank alongside better-known examples of later nineteenth-century factory communities such as Saltaire or Port Sunlight.

The development of Thomas Houldsworth & Co under William's personal supervision established his reputation as a sound man of

The Reddish Mills, Stockport, T Houldsworth & Co Ltd (courtesy of Dr A C Howe).

business, with an interest in his workers' welfare. The firm's growth and its large dimensions provided 'the best proofs that experience and knowledge of affairs have been liberally expended upon it' {*Momus* 25 Mar 1880}, while, 'knowing more of ledgers and profit-sheets than of Huxley or Carlyle' {*The Free Lance* 19 Oct 1877}, Houldsworth was well-placed to enter Manchester politics, and was soon marked out as their 'coming man'. Although many of his views were acceptable to, and it was claimed, indistinguishable from, those of the Liberals, it was as a Conservative that Houldsworth was defeated as candidate for Manchester in 1880. But Manchester Conservatism at this period had begun to see the rapprochement between the industrialists and the working-class which was essential to its success. Houldsworth, well-known for his attention to the condition of the working-class, set out vigorously to cement this alliance, underpinning it by organisational changes, and extending its appeal by drawing national politicians, such as Lord Randolph Churchill, to Manchester as speakers and, potentially, candidates. As president of the Manchester Conservative Association, he shaped its brand of Tory democracy, and was duly elected to succeed Hugh Birley in the Manchester by-election of 1883. In 1885 he won the newly-created seat of North-West Manchester, which he was to retain until 1906. Bolstered by plural votes and reneging Liberals, this seat was a secure bastion of business Conservatism rather than of Tory democracy, a theme to be toned down after 1884. In that year Houldsworth played an important part as a leader of provincial Conservatism in the National Union and its struggles, although now as an opponent of Lord Randolph Churchill. He was to remain, for the most part, a loyal supporter of Salisbury and

Balfour. His important contribution to the Tory revival in Lancashire was recognised by Salisbury with a baronetcy in the Jubilee Honours of 1887.

As an MP, Houldsworth's interests were commercial and social. After initial doubts, he became an important backer of the Manchester Ship Canal in its many legislative demands. Working closely with the Manchester Chamber of Commerce (of which he was a director for many years), Houldsworth promoted and supported many bills in its interest — for example, those for the amendment of the Limited Liability Acts, and the Rating of Machinery. (He was also president of the Machinery Users' Association, 1889-1904.) A strong advocate of the Union, and the Empire, he supported intervention abroad in favour of British trade and sternly resisted Indian import duties as an infringement of the free trade principles essential to the interests of Lancashire. He became the acknowledged leader of the 'commercial party' in the House of Commons, chairing several Select Committees, and if, as was occasionally mooted, a Department of Commerce had been created, he was thought likely to have been its head. Houldsworth, however, was not without his usefulness to labour. In advance of local opinion, he supported the reduction of factory hours, the extension of the age of half-timers, and the tightening-up of employers' liability; in 1890 he served as a British plenipotentiary at the Berlin Labour Conference. His attitudes were nevertheless broadly orthodox within the framework of political economy, and as a member of the informal Parliamentary Social Reform Committee of the 1880s, he saw more good in temperance and emigration than in 'collectivist' social policies. Significantly, although a persistent free trader in the 1880s and 1890s, in 1903 Houldsworth supported Tariff Reform, a decision which precipitated his retirement from active politics, although he contributed evidence to the Tariff Commission's Textile Inquiry in 1904 and lent his name to the Cotton Tariff Reform Association in 1910.

It was, however, the promotion of currency reform which most distinguished Houldsworth's political career. As a member of the Royal Commission on the Depression of Trade and Industry in 1886, he became convinced that the depression since 1873 was real rather than mythical, although unsure of its causes or remedies. This uncertainty was removed by his membership of the subsequent Royal Commission on Gold and Silver (1888) which convinced him that the cause of depression lay in falling prices, the solution in international bimetallism.

The merits of the bimetallist case were, of course, widely challenged, although they had much in common with the Currency School which had dominated monetary policy in the 1840s. Nevertheless, the bimetallists had strong and too often neglected appeal in Lancashire and Houldsworth entered the currency lists with verve and gusto, a dogmatic crusader for economic truth. In 1888 he emerged as a leading light of, and subscriber to, the Bimetallic League, chairman of its parliamentary committee, an active and voluble propagandist in the country at large, frequently addressing meetings, canvassing politicians, corresponding with academic economists, writing extensively in the Press and publishing numerous pamphlets. At the peak of the movement, he seconded Samuel Smith's bi-metallist resolution in the crucial debate of May 1890. In 1892 he was appointed by Goschen as one of the British delegates to the Brussels International Monetary Conference, a meeting long-sought by the

Bimetallic League. The accession of the Liberal Government in July 1892, however, stacked the cards further against any bi-metallist success at the conference, for Houldsworth was swamped in a delegation of ultra-orthodox monometallists led by Bertram Currie, while Harcourt, the new Chancellor of the Exchequer, was markedly unsympathetic. To Harcourt's annoyance, Houldsworth did manage to secure agreement to reconvene the conference in May 1893 but this was the extent of the bi-metallists' success; even this meeting failed to take place, given American indifference.

In 1893, Houldsworth's attention was turned to the closing of the Indian mints to silver — in effect, the imposition of a gold exchange standard on India. The reimposition of Indian import duties on Lancashire cotton goods in 1894 added fuel to the controversy as Houldsworth linked the duties with the fiscal needs of an Indian Government facing interest payments in appreciated gold. He urged international conferences, committees of monetary experts, the re-opening of the Indian mints, but to no avail. After 1896 monetary questions narrowed into those of Indian currency rather than international bimetallism. Houldsworth, whose knowledge of India was not great (it was not an important market for fine spinners), relegated his interest in bimetallism to an academic one, becoming, with the assistance of L L Price, the Oxford economist, expert on index numbers.

Indeed, in the late 1890s Sir William's efforts to restore prosperity in British industry through the global nostrum of bimetallism gave way to his leadership of initiatives for the internal reconstruction of particular industries. This was a necessary corollary to the bimetallists' failure, if the effects of falling prices were to be countered, but paradoxically, the long-awaited upturn in prices after 1896 provided an additional stimulus.

In 1897 Houldsworth gave his support to the projected amalgamation of fine-cotton spinning firms in an effort to resolve the problem of undercutting, by removing internal competition. No nostalgic cotton king, he eschewed individualistic rivalry in favour of mutual working and co-operation, in order to raise standards of production while lowering costs and restoring profitability. Amalgamation, he believed, could lead to the efficiency of production which abroad was encouraged by tariff-defended home markets. In May 1898 he therefore became chairman of the Fine Cotton Spinners' and Doublers' Association Ltd, in which Thomas Houldsworth & Co and the Reddish Spinning Co together represented about 13 per cent of the purchase price of the 31 firms in the combination. The energy and ideas behind the Fine Spinners came from A H Dixon (qv) and Scott Lings, both proteges of Houldsworth, but his role as chairman until 1908 (vice-chairman, 1908-10) was not merely decorative. He encouraged the emergence of the executive board rather than the directors as the power-house of the firm, and placed full trust in its members, on whom the success of the firm largely depended. Nevertheless, Houldsworth kept a close eye on executive policy, making available his ripe experience and knowledge of trade, and providing an ideal link as elder statesman between the relatively youthful executive and the board. Executive policy was largely the work of Dixon, but on particular issues Houldsworth exerted crucial influence: for example, it was on his insistence that the Fine Spinners joined the Bolton Master Cotton

Spinners' Association rather than the Manchester Cotton Employers' Association of Charles Macara (qv), as Dixon preferred. Houldsworth's connection with the Coltness Iron Co was also of value in providing expertise and capital for the Fine Spinners when they came to develop their own colliery, at Bradford, Manchester. Ironically, however, the policy of rationalisation pursued by the Fine Spinners led, in 1899, to the closure of Houldsworth's Newton Street mill. Ill-health forced Houldsworth to end his regular attendance at the board in 1907, but by the time he formally retired in 1908, the Fine Spinners had emerged as the largest manufacturing company in Great Britain, employing over 30,000 workers, with net assets of £8.63 million, and with average dividends since 1899 of 8.67 per cent, including record pre-war profits in 1908. It had thus been one of the most successful of the experiments in industrial organisation which marked turn-of-the-century entrepreneurship.

Concurrently, Houldsworth was actively involved in the reconstruction of the Coltness Iron Co. Founded in 1836 by his grand-uncle, this firm had become, under the control of Sir William's brother, Thomas, the second largest Scottish iron company, with a nominal capital of £360,000 in 1872. Sir William was sporadically active in its affairs, a partner in the 1870s, and a director, 1881-83. In the 1890s he pressed, from outside the board, for a revaluation of the firm's capital, and greater concentration on coalmining as the market for iron fell. After rejoining the board in 1897, Sir William became chairman in 1902 until his death. Under his lead the company was reorganised in 1899 with a nominal capital of £800,000 (raised to £1 million in 1900): at this point it comprised nine blast furnaces, 20 coal mines, important interests in Spain through the Alquife Mine & Railways Co (of which Houldsworth was also chairman), in Cumberland through the Millom & Ashom Haematite Iron Co, and from 1902 in the Warwickshire coalfield, through the Warwickshire Coal Co Ltd (chairman, 1902-17). The prosperity of the Coltness branch of the family's interests owed much to Sir William's ideas, and the leadership which he retained 'by reason of this steadiness of aim, reliability of judgement and determination of purpose' {Carvel (1948) 98}. As at Reddish, Houldsworth was noted for his keen interest in the welfare of the firm's employees.

As a businessman, therefore, Houldsworth played a unique and crucial role in both the Scottish iron and coal, and the Lancashire cotton industries. These, however, were by no means the sum of his interests. Between 1895 and 1905, he was a director of the London & North Western Railway, a position esteemed by many of his business peers above a seat in the House of Commons. He served on the boards of the National Bank of Scotland, 1911-17, and of the Manchester Ship Canal, 1885-87. He was also a leading subscriber to, and vice-president of, the British Cotton Growing Association from 1905. In this diversity of interests, Houldsworth was essentially building on his inheritance from his father (whose estate at his death in 1868 was valued at £388,000, comprising cotton, coal, iron, railway and banking assets), yet his success was informed by his own entrepreneurial flair, breadth of vision, boundless energy and application.

Moreover, Houldsworth's ambitions extended beyond business and politics. His experiment in community-building at Reddish in the 1860s was but one sign of his philanthropy, which appeared above all in his support for temperance and the Church of England. As an MP, like his predecessor Hugh Birley, Houldsworth was prominent among the small band of temperance advocates in the Conservative party, and was president in the 1890s of the National Conservative Temperance Union. As a leading parliamentary spokesman for the Church of England Temperance Society, Houldsworth persistently urged its policy of Sunday closing, equitable compensation for the loss of licences, and more representative licensing authorities. Temperance legislation he believed to be in accordance with 'the wishes of the great majority of the working-classes' {*PD*, HC, 2 Apr 1884, col 1417} and he welcomed piecemeal legislation towards this end in preference to waiting for 'heroic measures' {*ibid*, 7 Apr 1902, col 1215}. He served on the Peel Commission into the Liquor Licensing Laws (1896-99), signing its Minority Report. While backing Conservative licensing legislation in 1904, he found it unsatisfactory. Increasingly, he believed that the 'guerrilla war' between 'a Trade, which exists for the purpose of business and profit' and 'a Licensing System which seeks to restrict that business and profit to arbitrary dimensions' was irresolvable {Houldsworth (1901-2) 51}. He therefore became an advocate of public house trust companies, which would eliminate private profit from the drink trade and establish popular control of licensed houses. He chaired the Manchester, Salford and District Public House Trust Co, 1905-13.

Houldsworth was a distinguished Manchester Churchman, espousing a liberal-minded, moderate High Churchmanship. Sunday, he proclaimed, was not to be a day of gloom and deprivation, but one of religious and social enjoyment. He supported the Sunday opening of libraries and museums as fully compatible with the true Christian Sabbath. A firm supporter of church extension, he believed that beauty could play its part in recapturing the working masses for the Church. At Reddish his church, while not quite escaping Romanesque gloom, was enlivened by Gregorian chants, and rich stained glass made by F J Shields, who had also adorned Houldsworth's private chapel at Coodham. Manchester Cathedral, where he was churchwarden, 1866-69, benefited from Houldsworth's generosity, particularly in the gift of the organ in 1872, but so too did many churches, as far afield as Bristol. His religious exuberance might be ascribed to recent conversion from the Nonconformity of his fathers, but his religious antecedents are by no means clear: his grand-uncle was a cheerful, horse-racing Anglican, his father supposedly a stern Presbyterian, yet William was undoubtedly baptised in the Church of England (at St Thomas's, Ardwick).

Houldsworth contributed to many aspects of Manchester life. He was, for example, a conspicuous supporter of Owen's College (through its extension fund and as a life-governor under the Act of 1862), and of its transformation by charter into the University of Manchester, becoming a member of its first Court and receiving an honorary LLD. A supporter of many working men's social clubs, he also held office in numerous institutions, among them the YMCA, the Diocesan Board of Education, the Gentlemen's Concert Hall and Manchester Grammar School and the Manchester Statistical Society. In 1905 his abundant local services were recognised in the Freedom of the City of Manchester. He also served the county of Lancashire as a JP (as for Cheshire) and councillor (for Heaton Norris), acting as vice-chairman of the council, 1892-1906.

After 1906 Houldsworth, for the most part, retired to Scotland, where his 600-acre Coodham estate, purchased in the 1870s as a summer residence, became his home. He took a keen interest in agricultural improvement, enjoying good relations with his tenants. Here too he was a generous patron of local institutions, as well as JP and DL for Ayrshire. He pursued his favourite recreations of golf, shooting, and fishing, and remained an enthusiastic organ-player.

Houldsworth had married in Scotland in 1862, Elisabeth, daughter of Walter Crum, FRS, the eminent calico-printer of Thornliebank, Renfrewshire. Their eldest son, Henry, was at one time nominally connected with the family firm and Manchester politics (being Conservative candidate for Prestwich in 1900), but Scottish acres and Highland regiments held a greater attraction for him, as they did for the Houldsworth's second surviving son, William. For such ambitions, Sir William had provided a sufficient fortune, which, although depleted by philanthropy in his prime and war taxation in his dotage, remained a healthy £467,489 at his death, on 18 April 1917.

A C HOWE

Writings:

Evidence in *Minutes of Evidence Given By Proponents and Opponents of the Manchester Ship Canal Bill* (6 vols, pp by Waterlow & Sons, 1883-85).

Mr W H Houldsworth MP on the Contagious Diseases (Animals) Bill (Manchester, 1884).

PD, 3rd ser, 284-356 (1884-91), 4th ser 1-140 (1892-1904).

'The Conditions of Industrial Prosperity' in *Industrial Remuneration Conference, Report of Proceedings and Papers* (Cassell & Co, 1885).

'Sunday Observance: Closing Public Houses on Sunday' *Church Congress, Manchester, Report* (Manchester, 1888).

'On Colonisation' *Transactions of the Manchester Statistical Society* 1888-89.

Bimetallism and the Depression in Trade (Preston, 1889).

Bimetallism: An Address to the Members of the Carlton Club, Manchester (Manchester: Bimetallic League, 1889).

The Future of the Cotton Trade: An Address (np, 1889).

Address in *Proceedings of the Bimetallic Conference, December 1888* (Manchester, 1889).

Address in *The Bimetallic Question; Deputation to the Prime Minister and Chancellor of the Exchequer, 30 May 1889* (Manchester: Bimetallic League, 1889).

PP, RC Liquor Licensing Laws, Reservations by Sir William H Houldsworth (1889) C 9379.

PP, HC 1892 (237) XVIII, Watermen's and Lightermen's Compensation Bill and Barge Owners' Liability Bill.

Address in *Bimetallic Question; Deputation to the Marquis of Salisbury et al 11 May 1892* (Effingham, Wilson, 1892).

Address in *Discussion on International Bimetallism at the Manchester Chamber of Commerce, 1892* (Manchester, 1892).

Contribution to *Conférence Monétaire Internationale, 1892: Procès-Verbaux* (Bruxelles, 1892).

Address to *Bimetallic League: Report of the Proceedings at the Annual Meeting, Manchester, 27 January 1893* (1893).

'On Bimetallism: A Reply' *New Review* 8 (1893).

Comments on the Debate and Division on Monetary Reform in the House of Commons, 28 Feb 1893 (E Wilson, 1893).

On the Present Depression in the Iron Trade as Affected by Currency Questions (Vacher & Sons, 1893).

'Closing of the Indian Mints' *National Review* 21 (1893).

The Currency Question and its Relation to Trade: An Address (Effingham, Wilson & Co, 1894).

The Fall in Prices of Commodities, with Special Reference to Trade Depression and Bimetallism (E Wilson & Co, 1894).

The Church of England Temperance Society Bill: Compensation or Equitable Consideration (Church of England Temperance Society, 1894).

Address in *Bimetallism as Affecting the Cotton Industry: Deputation from the Bimetallic League to the Federation of Master Cotton Spinners, 26 October 1894* (Manchester, 1894).

The Bimetallist 1895-1898, passim.

'The Currency Question for Laymen. II. Trade and Industry' *National Review* 25 (1895).

PP, HC 1896 (233) VIII, SC Belfast Corporation and Londonderry Improvement Bills.

'Index Numbers and the Course of Prices as Indicated by Them during the Last Fifty Years' *Transactions of the Manchester Statistical Society* 1896-97.

'Bimetallism' *ibid* 1897-98.

'Public-House Licences' *ibid* 1901-02.

The Tariff Commission Reports vol 2 *The Textile Trades* Pt I. *The Cotton Industry* (P & S King & Son, 1905).

Sources:

Unpublished

BL, Balfour papers, Add MSS 49791, 49850-52.

BLPES, Tariff Commission papers, TC3 1/159.

Bodleian Library, Oxford, Sir William Harcourt papers.

Churchill College, Cambridge, Lord Randolph Churchill papers.

Courtaulds, Manchester, Northern Spinning Division, Fine Cotton Spinners' & Doublers' Ltd, board minutes, 1898-1910.

Guildhall Library, London, Antony Gibbs papers.

HOULDSWORTH Sir William Henry

Hatfield House, Hatfield, Hertfordshire, Third Marquess of Salisbury papers.

PRO: BT 31/1558/5045 Reddish Spinning Co Ltd; BT 31/5371/36890 T Houldsworth & Co Ltd.

Reddish Records, The History of the Church and Parish of St Elisabeth, Reddish Green (MS Notes in possession of the Rector).

PrC.

P A Hayes, 'The Houldsworth Cotton Mill and its Community, 1866-1976' (typescript in Stockport Public Library, 1976).

Information from Sir Reginald Houldsworth (great-grandson).

Published

The Bimetallist 1895-1900.

John L Carvel, *The Coltness Iron Co* (Edinburgh: pp, 1948).

Church of England Temperance Society Annual Reports 1887-1906.

Church of England Temperance Society, *Our Legislative Policy, 1862-1908* (1908).

Peter Clarke, *Lancashire and the New Liberalism* (Cambridge: Cambridge University Press, 1971).

Cotton Factory Times 20 Apr 1917.

DNB.

The Fine Cotton Spinners' and Doublers' Association Ltd (Manchester, 1909).

Free Lance 19 Oct 1877.

Ernest Gaskell, *Lancashire Leaders: Social and Political* (Queenhithe Printing & Publishing Ltd, 1908).

Louis M Hayes, *Reminiscences of Manchester* (Manchester: Sherratt & Hughes, 1905).

The Jubilee Distaff, 1898-1948 (Manchester: pp, 1948).

Kilmarnock Herald 20 Apr 1917.

Kilmarnock Standard 21 Apr 1917.

William H Macleod and Sir Henry H Houldsworth, Bt, *The Beginnings of the Houldsworths of Coltness* (Glasgow: Jackson, Son & Co, 1937).

Manchester City News 21 Apr 1917.

Manchester Evening News 18 Apr 1917.

Manchester Faces and Places 10 Oct 1889.

Manchester Guardian 19 Apr 1917.

Manchester Weekly Times 21 Apr 1917.

John D Marshall (ed), *The History of Lancashire County Council, 1889-1974* (Martin Robertson, 1977).

Momus 25 Mar, 25 July 1878.

W T Pike and W B Tracy, *Lancashire at the Opening of the Twentieth Century: Contemporary Biographies* (Brighton: W T Pike & Co, 1903).

Samuel Smith, *My Life Work* (Hodder & Stoughton, 1902).

Stockport Advertiser 1 July, 11 Nov 1887, 20 Apr 1917.

Textile Recorder 15 May 1917.

Times 19 Apr 1917.

Transactions of the Lancashire and Cheshire Antiquarian Society 25 (1917).

Philip J Waller, *Democracy and Sectarianism: A Political and Social History of Liverpool 1868-1939* (Liverpool: Liverpool University Press, 1981).

WWMP.

WWW.

HOUSTON, Sir Robert Paterson

(1853-1926)

Shipowner

Robert Paterson Houston was born in Bootle, Liverpool, on 31 May 1853, the only son of Robert Houston of Renfrewshire. Educated at Liverpool College and privately, Houston seemed destined for the Church, but instead followed his father into marine engineering. After a four-year apprenticeship in the engineering and shipbuilding trades, at the remarkably early age of twenty-one he was appointed superintendent engineer of one of Liverpool's smaller transatlantic companies, the National Line. But, as Houston himself admitted, his ambition was to be a successful shipowner and, after part-owning the *Athlete* (356 tons) in 1877, he loaded his first vessel from Liverpool in 1881. From this modest start there quickly developed a successful business, managed by R P Houston & Co. The timing, if accidental, was decisive. Houston was one of many shipowners who widely adopted iron, and later steel, screw-driven steamships powered by fuel-saving engines without incurring the development costs of these innovations. This was also the decade when British trampship owners, prepared to go anywhere for cargoes, exploited the commercial opportunities of expanding international trade. At first, his small fleet loaded for the Far East, brought construction materials to the Panama Canal and handled freight contracts for West Africa. As well as these favourable economic factors, Houston's own qualities, energy, enterprise and attention to detail, added to his success. Unlike many firms, his gave a complete service from supply and transport, to providing ancillary services for a c i f price.

In addition to progress in the construction of ocean-going steamships, improved refrigeration techniques (developed by Alfred Haslam (qv)) had reached a point where it was becoming feasible to transport frozen meat from the southern hemisphere to the markets in Western Europe. Houston's early interest in South American cargoes soon developed into a regular fortnightly service between the River Plate and Liverpool, which loaded machinery and equipment for railroad construction outwards and shipped the products of Argentina's pastoral industry homewards. In 1884, after visiting Buenos Aires, Houston contracted with Argentina's pioneering meat packer, Sansinena, for regular shipments in four specially constructed steamers, at the same time inaugurating the livestock trade from the Plate. Once established, Houston's vigorous and energetic style of competition in the cargo trades, still more his entry into passenger business, raised protests from the regular Conference Lines — the cartel of established shipowners on that route — with whom he fought a prolonged rate war. His approach to the Argentine Government in 1887 for a subsidised weekly line aroused further opposition. In 1889 he opened a link between New York and the Plate.

More controversy marked Houston's subsequent entry into the South African trades when the Boer War provided the opportunity to run government transports for troops, horses and supplies. Houston also loaded vessels from New York and Buenos Aires to Cape Town but faced accusations inside and outside parliament of profiteering and ignoring load limits. Then, anticipating a boom in South Africa with the declaration of peace, Houston embarked upon a bitter eighteen-month conflict with the Conference lines in which all his fighting qualities were displayed, despatching the aptly-named *Hostilius* from Middlesbrough as his opening shot. As well as taking on the Conference at several points and threatening to enter the passenger trade, Houston also resorted to the courts, where he used the experienced and enterprising solicitor George Hankey and the legal skills of F E Smith, later Lord Birkenhead. Houston emerged in triumph in 1904 to be admitted to the South African Conference, withdrawing his lawsuits and cancelling plans for competing services. Far from bringing South African merchants the permanent benefit of cheaper transport, freight rates rose once again and, as officials noted, far from aiding British trade, his sailings from New York encouraged American competition. Houston ended his River Plate link with South Africa in 1906, starting instead a service to German South West Africa, which ran until 1912.

Houston's basic business shrewdness and engineering background were never more in evidence than in building his fleet. Like all firms, Houstons chartered when necessary but, unlike many small shipowners, he preferred new ships to cheaper, second-hand steamers — although the needs of his South African adventure did force him to buy old tonnage. His eye for a bargain meant that he engaged no regular builders but shopped around the yards of the UK to obtain basic 13 or 14 knot freighters. Additionally, at Cape Town, Houston operated small cargo carriers, feeders to the main line steamers, which loaded at restricted berths in South Africa's congested ports. Until his last new tonnage was ordered before 1914, Houston's policy was to reinvest profits in modernising his fleet while selling his older vessels. His steamers, each named after a classical deity starting with H, were well-manned, Houston taking pride in his all-British crews, who were paid union wages, and his accident record was exemplary. By 1914 his fleet comprised some 20 steamers (80,000 tons), the oldest built in 1898, operating mainly cargo services from New York and the UK to the River Plate and South Africa.

The financial management of Houston's business followed a more predictable pattern. At first R P Houston & Co, a partnership which included Alfred Collard (from 1893) and later E Farrar, managed single-ship companies but in 1898 the firm floated the British & South American Steam Navigation Co to take over the steamers and finance new construction. The firm marked time immediately before the First World War. During the war, like those of all British owners, Houston's ships were requisitioned for transport work and the frozen meat trade, and seven (some 28,000 tons) were lost to enemy action. In 1918, with his ageing and depleted fleet worn out by war work, and facing spiralling replacement costs, Houston preferred to sell up for a reputed £2 million to the Clan Line run by Cayzer Irving & Co, ironically one of his arch rivals in the South African rate war. Cayzer Irving subsequently sold the River Plate interests in 1926 to Kaye & Sons of London and later joined Union-Castle to form the British & Commonwealth Line.

Houston was also abrasive in his public career. Entering parliament in 1892, he represented West Toxteth, his seat for thirty-two years until ill-health forced his retirement, and despite his undoubted local popularity — he liked to portray himself as labour's friend, with a reputation for helping dockers — his extreme views and plain speaking scarcely endeared him to fellow Conservatives. His brand of working-class Toryism, his fierce Protestant loyalties, his sectarian approach to Liverpool's religious issues and his bitterness towards political opponents lowered the tone of public life. An enfant terrible in the House of Commons, he spoke for shipping and for commercial and Imperial interests, and in the First World War was a persistent critic of muddled wartime bureaucracy which interfered with the shipowner's freedom. He also represented the Liverpool Shipowners Association upon the Mersey Docks Board.

Created a baronet in the 1922 New Year's Honours List, Houston's later years were equally controversial. For many years a confirmed bachelor, he married Lady Fanny Lucy Byron, widow of the Ninth Lord Byron, in December 1924. He spent his last days in Jersey (notwithstanding his several addresses in London and Liverpool), where he died after a period of ill-health on 14 April 1926, leaving no heir. The gross probate value of his estate in England was £6.843 million. Houston remained as contentious in death as in life, his will becoming subject to litigation as the Inland Revenue sought to extract death duties, while one of the chief beneficiaries, his close friend Lord Birkenhead, was omitted at the last moment owing, it is said, to an injudicious remark to Lady Houston. Four-fifths of his estate was bequeathed to her.

Not among the country's largest shipowners, Houston still remains a complex, colourful, even eccentric figure, who enjoyed an influence out of proportion to the size of his business. Dubbed the 'Robber Baron' by Dewar, the whisky magnate, Houston's critics unflatteringly represented him as the arch-exponent of free-wheeling capitalism, tough, bull-headed and determined, part of the labour mythology. Feared rather than liked, his remorseless methods, questionable ethics and litigious dealings with government departments and conference officials gained him few friends. Yet his undoubted business success against far more powerful commercial rivals, his reputation for decisive action and an enviable record as an enlightened shipowner running well-managed steamers also won him a grudging respect. He had a real pride in Liverpool, enjoyed twisting the tails of London's shipowners and officials, and was capable of personal kindness and loyalty.

ROBERT GREENHILL

Writings:

Many speeches in the House of Commons: eg *PD* 4th ser 153, cols 1141-4 (13 Mar 1906); 185, cols 635-8 (3 Mar 1908).

Sources:

Unpublished

PRO: Ministry of Transport papers, MT9 (1903-7).

C Reg: Houston Line Ltd (261,826).

PrC.

Published

Lord Birkenhead, *FE: The Life of F E Smith; First Earl of Birkenhead by His Son* (Eyre & Spottiswoode, 1959).

F C Bowen, 'Seventy Years of Houstons' *Nautical Magazine* 163 (Mar 1950).

James Wentworth Day, *Lady Houston DBE: the Woman Who Won the War* (Allan Wingate, 1958).

DNB.

Fairplay 23 Sept 1887, 22 Apr 1926.

Percy Harley, *My Life in Shipping, 1881-1938: An Impression of Some of the Matters and Men I Have Met in It* (pp,1939).

Liverpool Post and Mercury 2 Jan 1922.

J McRoberts, 'The Houston Story' *Sea Breezes* 44 (Mar-May 1970).

PD, 4th ser 79, cols 360-1 (19 Feb 1900), cols 1267-68 (27 Feb 1900).

Porcupine 6 June 1896, 18 Sept 1899, 24 Apr 1909, 30 Jan 1915.

PP, RC Shipping Rings (1909) Cd 4685.

Stanley Salvidge, *Salvidge of Liverpool: Behind the Political Scene, 1890-1928* (Hodder & Stoughton, 1934).

V E Solomon, *The South African Shipping Question 1886-1914* (Cape Town, 1982).

South American Journal 17 Sept 1887, 26 Mar 1898, 11 Feb 1899.

Times 15 Apr 1926.

Philip J Waller, *Democracy and Sectarianism: A Political and Social History of Liverpool, 1868-1938* (Liverpool: Liverpool University Press, 1981).

WWMP.

WWW.

HOWARD, James

(1821-1889)

Agricultural machinery manufacturer

James Howard (courtesy of the Institute of Agricultural History, Reading).

James Howard was born at Bedford in 1821, the eldest son of John Howard, the proprietor of a modest agricultural implement firm in High Street, Bedford, founded in 1813. James was educated at Bedford public school and then joined his father in business around 1837. The firm opened new premises at this time, which enabled an expansion into plough production, a particular interest of James. In 1839, James was given overall charge of production, leaving his father to concentrate on commercial matters. Two pioneering types of iron plough, introduced in 1839 and 1841, laid the foundation for Howards' rapid expansion during the 1840s. By 1850 John Howard & Son had become one of the three leading UK plough producers, alongside Ransomes & May at Ipswich and Richard Hornsby & Son at Grantham. In the same year, John Howard retired from the partnership to be replaced by James's younger brother, Frederick. The new concern was known as James & Frederick Howard, with James as the senior partner responsible for production and overall policy, and Frederick handling the bulk of the commercial work.

During 1850-89, James Howard successfully maintained the firm's new-found prominence as plough makers, supplying designs adapted to both home and export market conditions. Annual plough sales were already averaging 6,000 in 1860, with both partners travelling widely to promote business. By the 1870s Howards had an extensive export trade in Russia and Eastern Europe (helped by the absence of tariff barriers that restricted sales in Western Europe and North America) as well as with the colonial market in India, Australia and South Africa. Howard tried to extend the firm's range of products into corn-harvesting machinery, but the competition from other UK producers, such as Samuelsons and Hornsbys, as well as North American manufacturers, proved to be too strong. Howard also became interested in steam cultivation in the 1850s and the firm produced steam cultivating machinery throughout the remainder of the nineteenth century, notable for both its technical diversity and its commercial failure. It was one thing for Fowlers, the leading UK steam plough makers, to manufacture such equipment as part of a range of sophisticated steam engineering products. It was quite another thing for a conventional plough maker to move into the production of steam ploughing machinery.

Howard was interested in both the production and application of agricultural implements. In 1862 he purchased the Clapham Park Estate of over 1,000 acres where, in addition to breeding livestock, he set up a large trial ground for the scientific application of agricultural technology, and in particular steam ploughing. Howard's other public contributions to agriculture included the establishment of the Farmers' Alliance in 1879, while he was at various times a president of the Agricultural Engineers Association, a council member of the Royal Agricultural Society of England, a president of the London Farmers Club and a director of the Agricultural Hall Ltd. The 16-acre site occupied by Howards' Britannia Works, built during 1856-59, dominated Bedford and made the firm into the leading employer in the town. Howard accordingly held various local offices, including the mayoralty, 1863-64. In addition Howard was an ardent advocate of patent law reform, doubtless influenced by some acrimonious litigation with Fowlers in the early 1860s, as well as chairman of the Bedford & Northampton Railway.

Howard published various works on farm management and tenant farming, an interest also evident when, as Liberal MP for Bedford, 1868-74, he introduced a bill on tenant-landlord reform. He represented South Northamptonshire, 1880-85, and spoke frequently on agricultural topics in the House.

The few descriptions of Howard's character reveal a technically inventive mind, a fair degree of business acumen and a well-developed social conscience, though tempered by a streak of stubbornness.

In 1846 Howard married Mahala Wendon Thompson of Brooke House, Great Bentley, Essex, the daughter of Peter Thompson, a merchant; they had two sons and three daughters. When he died on 25 January 1889, leaving an estate of £82,703 gross, Howards were still as firmly committed to plough production as they were in the 1840s and second only to Ransomes of Ipswich among UK plough makers.

D C PHILLIPS

Writings:

A Trip to America: Two Lectures (Bedford, 1867).

Continental Farming and Peasantry (1870).

A Paper on Impediments to the Development of British Husbandry (Bedford, 1873).

Our Meat Supply (1876).

The Railway Commissioners and the Companies (1878).

The Tenant Farmer: Land Laws and Land Lords (1879).

Practical Politics (1881).

The English Land Question: Past and Present (Birmingham, 1881).

Local Rates as They Affect the Farmer (1882).

The Farmer and the Tory Party (Birmingham, 1883).

Gold and Silver Supply: Or the Influence of Currency upon the Price of Farm Produce (Bedford, 1887).

The Science of Trade: Free Trade or Fair Trade? (Luton, 1887).

Sources:

Unpublished

MCe.

PrC.

Published

'The Britannia Ironworks, Bedford' *The Engineer* 30 (1870).

The Engineer 67 (1889).

The Implement and Machinery Review 14 (1888-1889).

'Men of Mark. Mr James Howard, MP' *ibid* 8 (1882-1883).

WWMP.

HOWLEY, Richard Joseph

(1871-1955)

Road transport company executive

Richard Joseph Howley was born in 1871 at Rich Hill, County Limerick, Ireland, the son of Lieutenant Colonel John Howley, DL. He was educated at Oscott College, the Jesuit establishment outside Birmingham, and at Dublin University, and trained as a civil engineer, concentrating on dock and railway construction.

In August 1899 Howley joined British Electric Traction, the company with which he was to remain throughout a long and distinguished career. As assistant permanent way engineer he was associated with the tramway side of the business rather than with electricity generation; in January 1901 he became assistant construction engineer, and subsequently served as permanent way engineer with several subsidiary companies. He did not remain a specialist manager for long, however, being appointed joint manager (with C H Dade) in 1912, a position which he held until 1919. He served on the Tramways Committee of the Board of Trade, and from 1917 to 1919 was a member of the Railways Priority Committee, for which service he received the CBE. In 1919 he was a founder member of the Institute of Transport.

In 1923 Howley joined the BET board, with responsibility for organisation, and in 1929 he took over from Emile Garcke (qv) as head of the executive, becoming deputy chairman in 1930. In 1942 he succeeded J S Austen as chairman, and the duties of head of the executive were taken over by J Spencer Wills (qv). After handing the chairmanship to H C Drayton (qv) in 1946, Howley remained an active member of the board until retiring in 1953.

Richard Howley was a quiet man, who never married, and whose contribution to the development of the bus industry could easily be underrated. He was not unsociable, as is shown by his place as vice-captain of the BET cricket eleven in 1901. Fulford speaks of his early influence on the company, and comments on his singleness of purpose. C F Hayward, who was editor of *Motor Transport*, referred to a 'rare occasion' when he found Howley 'annoyed', the subject being a letter of Sir J Frederick Heaton's (qv) to the *Times*, which he described as 'rot' {*Modern Transport* 11 July 1955}. The Minutes of Evidence of the Royal Commission on Transport of 1929-1931 reveal a depth of understanding of the bus industry that has rarely been equalled, and it was as much Howley's evidence as anything that decided the Commission (and hence the Government) to make bus licensing the responsibility of regional Traffic Commissioners rather than give powers to any class of local authority. At the same time, his evidence was clearly designed to favour the larger firms, causing Major H E Crawfurd (a member of the Commission) to accuse him of 'going dangerously near telling us a monopoly is less efficient than those with whom you are competing' {*Minutes of Evidence RC on Transport*, II 391}. The point was not pressed by the chairman of the Commission.

When BET was still largely a tramway group, Howley was an early supporter of the motor bus, along with Sidney Garcke (qv). He was chairman of the Birmingham & Midland Motor Omnibus Co Ltd, the largest of the BET subsidiaries, during a period when it was judged inappropriate to appoint a general manager over its two warring chief officers — O C Power as traffic manager and L G Wyndham Shire as chief engineer. (Contrary to every textbook rule, they each reported directly to the chairman, and the business flourished.) His professional activities were recognised by the award of the Institute of Transport's Road Transport (Passenger) Medal.

Howley died on 2 April 1955, leaving £230,710 gross, having left his mark both upon British Electric Traction and upon the statutory control of the bus industry to the present day.

JOHN HIBBS

Writings:

Minutes of Evidence Taken Before the Royal Commission on Transport (3 vols, HMSO, 1929-30) 2.

Sources:

Unpublished

PrC.

Published

Roger Fulford, *Five Decades of BET* (pp, 1946).

—, *The Sixth Decade* (pp, 1956).

Modern Transport 11 July 1955.

WWW.

HOZIER, Sir Henry Montague

(1838-1907)

Secretary of Lloyd's

Sir Herbert Hozier (courtesy of Mr T Atkins).

Henry Montague Hozier was born in Lanarkshire on 20 March 1838, the third son of a Scottish landowner and barrister, James C Hozier (1791-1878), and Catherine Margaret (d 1870), second daughter of Sir William Fielden, First Baronet of Feniscowles Hall, near Blackburn, Lancashire. His eldest brother William Wallace Hozier (1825-1906), a Lanarkshire magnate, who was created Lord Newlands in 1898, left £1,504,279 gross in 1906. Henry attended Rugby School in 1851, and later the Edinburgh Academy and Royal Military Academy at Woolwich. His education was punctuated by frequent Continental tours. He joined the Royal Artillery in 1856, saw service in China, passed first into and out of the Staff College and transferred to the Life Guards in 1863. He participated in the Schleswig-Holstein War of 1864; acted as war correspondent for the *Times* in the Austro-Prussian War of 1866; assisted Lord Napier of Magdala in the Abyssinian War, one of the most shocking and discreditable colonial campaigns of the nineteenth century; became Controller at Aldershot in

1870; was attached to the German army in the Franco-Prussian War of 1870-71, receiving the Iron Cross from the Kaiser; and returned to the War Office in 1874. Hozier's extensive military experiences were later documented in his numerous writings on campaigns and army tactics.

Hozier was appointed secretary by the Committee of the Corporation of Lloyd's on 13 March 1874 (after the post had been advertised in the London press). He started work on 1 April and a week later presented his suggestions for a thorough reorganisation of Lloyd's management, a swift adumbration of the efficiency with which he was to run the Corporation's affairs for the next thirty-two years. A born autocrat who demanded instant obedience, Hozier proved to be a gifted and energetic administrator. However, he was a good judge of men and, despite his high-handed attitude towards the Committee, he commanded its confidence for most of his career at Lloyd's. In 1882 the Committee thanked him for his extraordinary services and asked him to accept a gift of 500 guineas as a mark of their appreciation, raising his salary from £1,000 (at which he was appointed) to £2,000.

One of Hozier's major innovations at Lloyd's was the system of paying cargo claims at foreign ports, which he organised in 1886. It removed the necessity of transacting all the paperwork in London and greatly expanded Lloyd's business. He also improved the provision and dissemination of shipping intelligence which may not have benefited the underwriters directly but certainly established Lloyd's as the centre of the world's shipping news. By the end of the century he had established a chain of some 40 coastal signal stations in the UK and 118 in the colonies and in foreign countries, all either controlled or allied to Lloyd's. From its inception Hozier took an immediate and intense interest in Marconi's wireless telegraphy system obtaining an operating licence from the Government for Lloyd's signal stations. The revocation of this licence in 1906, following a dispute with the Marconi Co, was a bitter disappointment to him at the end of a highly successful career. Hozier's feelings can be gauged by his reaction to the criticisms of Sydney Buxton, the Postmaster General in the Liberal Government in 1906, who withdrew Lloyd's wireless licence: he challenged Buxton to a duel.

Hozier's career was not above criticism. He concentrated his power and influence by performing many of the duties of the Lloyd's chairman (usually a figurehead who rarely attended the Royal Exchange) and by carefully filtering information submitted to the Council, Lloyd's ruling body. He spent extravagantly: over forty-five years his signal station projects cost the Corporation £140,000, of which £25,500 went on his own overseas travelling expenses. In 1902 Sidney Boulton was elected to the Committee and soon challenged Hozier's policies, the accuracy of his figures and the value of his telegraph stations. Nevertheless even his bitterest critics admitted that Hozier, by his skills as an organiser and a diplomat, by his claim-settling service and by his signal stations, had greatly strengthened Lloyd's marine insurance facilities, made its shipping intelligence services unrivalled and confirmed its prestige with Government and shipowners alike. When the revocation of Lloyd's wireless license prompted Hozier's resignation in 1906 Lloyd's made him an honorary member, a rare distinction.

Hozier was unsuccessful Liberal parliamentary candidate for Woolwich in 1885, but after the Irish Home Rule debate, he became honorary secretary for the Liberal Unionist party. He was deeply involved in freemasonry, being Senior Grand Deacon of England, member of the Grand Lodge of Scotland, past master of the Ubique Lodge, a founder of the Lutine Lodge at Lloyd's, and a member of the Westminster and Keystone and Household Brigade Lodges. His nephew the Second Lord Newlands (1851-1929) was grand master mason of Scotland in 1899-1903. Hozier's recreations were yachting, shooting and hunting and he was a member of several clubs, including the Turf, Junior United Service, City, Beefsteak, New (Edinburgh), Western (Glasgow), and several yachting organisations. He was knighted in 1903.

He was married twice, both marriages ending in divorce, and Hozier never mentioned his wife or children in reference books. His second wife, whom he married in 1878, was Lady Henrietta Blanche Ogilvy (1852-1924), first daughter of Earl Airlie. They had one son, who committed suicide, and two daughters, one of whom, Clementine, later married Winston Churchill. Hozier was estranged from his wife for many years and she died abroad in straitened circumstances.

Even after his retirement Hozier continued travelling abroad on Lloyd's behalf. He visited Panama, despite the fact that the climate was unwholesome for a man of his age, and died there from pyaemia fever on 28 February 1907.

T ATKINS

Writings:

Organisation, Composition, and Strength of the Army of Great Britain (War Office, 1863).

Equipment of Cavalry (War Office, 1865).

Equipment of Commissariat Staff Corps (War Office, 1865).

Equipment of Military Train (War Office, 1865).

Der Feldzug in Böhmen and Mähren (Berlin, 1866).

The Seven Weeks' War (2 vols, 1867).

The British Expedition to Abyssinia (1869).

(with Trevenen J Holland) *Record of the Expedition to Abyssinia* (2 vols, 1870).

(ed) *The Franco-Prussian War; Its Causes, Incidents, Consequences* (2 vols, 1870-72).

(with Col Von Wright and translator) *The Campaign of 1866 in Germany* (War Office, 1872).

The Invasions of England (2 vols, 1876).

The Russo-Turkish War (2 vols, 1877-79).

Hints to Captains of the Mercantile Marine (Lloyd's, 1885).

(with E Puttock) *Lloyd's General Report* (Lloyd's, 1885).

Turenne (Chapman & Hall, 1885).

The Channel Tunnel (C F Roworth, 1888).

Hozier's Duplex Code for Reporting Movements of Vessels (Lloyd's, 1900).

The King's Weigh House Lectures to Business Men (Lloyd's, 1901).

Sources:

Published

David E W Gibb, *Lloyd's of London* (Macmillan, 1957).

Mary Soames, *Clementine Churchill* (Cassell, 1979).

Times 2 Mar 1907.

Windsor Magazine Oct 1895.

Charles Wright and C Ernest Fayle, *A History of Lloyd's* (Macmillan, 1928).

WWW.

HUGHES, John William

(1843-1917)

Shipowner

John William Hughes was born in Liverpool on 13 April 1843, the son of Thomas Hughes, a Welshman and a contractor of some repute who constructed stations for the Chester to Holyhead Railway. The eldest of a family of two sons and one daughter, he was comparatively young when his father died. Hughes was educated at the well-known school run by Rev John Brunner, the Swiss-born father of Sir John Brunner (qv), the chemical magnate. He later spent a period at the Pension Marais, a school at Le Havre, France, where he learned to speak French fluently, a skill which proved a considerable asset in his business career.

In about 1860 he was apprenticed to the shipping firm of T & J Harrison, which managed a number of sailing ships and steamships, at that time principally engaged in the wine and brandy trade with the Charente area of France, and which was to become the Charente Steamship Co in 1871. He became the firm's bookkeeper and from 1866 began to accumulate shares in the company's ships. The firm's partners, the brothers Thomas and James Harrison (qqv), allowed him and his younger brother, Thomas, also in the firm, to purchase shares on generous deferred terms. Clearly the Harrison brothers discovered his talents early and thought of him as a potential future partner.

When the Charente Steam Ship Co became a limited liability concern, managed by the private company, T & J Harrison, in 1884, both J W Hughes and his brother were subscribers. He was the moving force behind the Harrison firm's advancement to a position of international prestige and influence.

Hughes's great strength, frequently noted by his contemporaries, was his accounting ability. He was able to work out with great precision the investment potential of the firm's capital, much of which was invested in its ships. In 1914 the fleet consisted of 57 ships, reckoned to be worth some £3 million, largely carrying its own risk, the 'insurance account' being used as a reserve fund. He led his firm 'to seek out and exploit new trades in those parts of the world where, given a strong and well-organised commercial system, potentially large returns could be expected from expanding economies' {Hyde (1967) 44}.

The entry of Thomas and James Harrison into the Gulf of Mexico cotton trade, the Indian and Ceylon, the Brazilian and Caribbean trades, has been mentioned in the biography of the brothers (qqv). In 1902 they entered the South Africa trade and in 1910 the East Africa trade with a view to capturing the import trade in Empire-grown cotton. That same year they commenced a service to the North Pacific ports of North America, via the Straits of Magellan, and, in due course, via the Panama Canal.

J W Hughes had been fully behind the firm's participation in the conference system, believing it to be the logical answer to unfair discrimination, rate wars and sharp practices. He became its leading champion when attacks on it came to a head in the appointment of a Royal Commission on Shipping Rings (1909). Harrisons belonged to seven conferences. In evidence given before the Royal Commission, Hughes argued that while stability of rates and services was maintained, healthful competition was still possible and the best service still won; that the system enabled efficiently-organised bodies of merchants to get the best terms from the most efficient shipping companies and that far from being a tool for the abuse of united strength on the shipowners' part, they were flexible associations which could be used to discipline their own members and alter freight rates to suit changed trading conditions. He defended the much criticised 'deferred rebate', which conference lines granted to loyal shippers and argued powerfully that no monopoly was established.

Hughes vastly improved his firm's bookkeeping, making it a model of its kind and a cardinal element of the firm's eminence in the shipping world, enabling it to maintain a policy of steady growth in fleet size, by two new ships a year in the 1890s and by three new ships a year in 1900-10. Ships were built as needed, not when costs were low. The vessels incorporated the latest improvements in design and equipment. In 1893 Harrisons had introduced a new type of ship of 7,000 tons gross, costing £70,000 and producing a net annual income of £7,000 with a life of twenty years. The capital was expected to be recovered over thirteen years. By 1899 they employed three classes of ships, ranging from those of 10,000 tons deadweight for the Calcutta and New Orleans routes, to those of 5,000 tons, employed on routes where a shallow draught was needed. There was a good deal of flexibility in deployment. Harrisons considered it worthwhile to pay 10 per cent more for their ships from 1908 onwards, to secure the most modern improvements in their vessels.

Harrisons purchased a number of whole fleets, for example, in 1889 that of the Star Line from Rathbone Bros & Co paying £135,000 for both ships and goodwill, and in 1911 that of Rennies of London, who managed a direct line to South Africa, consisting of seven ships. One of J W Hughes's last transactions was the purchase of the Rankin, Gilmour fleet of 12 ships in 1917, at an average price of £160,000 per vessel. Even so the Harrison fleet only amounted to 39 vessels in 1918, owing to war losses. Hughes was clearly determined to keep up the strength of the firm's fleet, despite the extraordinary set-backs of the First World War and also proved his confidence in the financial soundness of the firm he had built up. He was looking for even further progress after the war, whose end he did not live to see. He died in office, never contemplating retirement.

Hughes took a leading part in associations bearing on the shipping industry. He was elected a member of the Mersey Docks & Harbour Board, serving on all principal committees and on a number of very important special committees. He was chairman of the Works Committee for twenty-one years, from 1896, and for a long period was deputy chairman of the Board. In this capacity he master-minded the modernisation of the South Docks, the Pier Head development which gave Liverpool its distinctive waterfront, and the new docks at the North End, of which the Gladstone system was the culmination. In 1905 he was nominated to a seat on the board of the Suez Canal Co, where his vast experience was deeply appreciated, as was his fluent French. He became president of the Liverpool Steam Ship Owners Association in 1887, president of the Liverpool Shipbrokers' Benevolent Society in 1900, as well as a founder trustee, president of the American Chamber of Commerce in Liverpool, and a member of the Liverpool Underwriters' Association. He was also a director and vice-chairman of the Liverpool Grain Storage and Transit Co and of the Pacific Steam Navigation Co.

In civic affairs he served as a member of the committee of the Royal Infirmary, of the Board of Management of the Merchant's Guild, vice-president of the Liverpool Workshops and Home Teaching Society for the Outdoor Blind, vice-president of the Liverpool Clerks' Association, chairman of the Liverpool Geographical Society and a member of the Committee of the Royal Liverpool Seaman's Orphan Institution.

Hughes was a generous donor to many schemes of social value, often anonymously. In conjunction with his partners he contributed to the £40,000 endowment of the Harrison-Hughes Engineering Laboratories, specially equipped for the study of the internal combustion engine. He gave lavishly to the Anglican Cathedral scheme and many other church and educational causes. Through his beneficence, the Bluecoat School was moved from its original eighteenth century buildings in the centre of the city of Liverpool to the outstanding elegant and modern building in the semi-rural suburb of Wavertree.

A man of strong convictions, which he expressed brusquely, he nonetheless had a reputation for integrity, modesty and geniality. Unlike many of the shipowners, he was remembered also for his cordial relations with the Dock Labourers' Union. He was a Liberal Unionist, a member of the Reform Club, and a loyal Anglican.

Hughes married in 1872 Elizabeth Watson, the niece of John Waite, a partner in a well-known merchant house; she was ten years his junior. Their married life seems to have been a very happy one. He died on 20 November 1917. He was survived by his wife, three sons, of whom one, T Harrison Hughes, reached an equally distinguished position in the shipping world, and two daughters. The gross value of his estate was £542,733.

J GORDON READ

Writings:

PP, RC on Shipping Rings (1909) Cd 4685.

Sources:

Unpublished

T & J Harrison, Mersey Chambers, Covent Garden, Liverpool, records.

Merseyside County Archives, Liverpool, Liverpool Steam Ship Owners' Association, records. Mersey Docks & Harbour Co, Liverpool records.

PrC.

Published

Fairplay 29 Nov 1917.

Francis E Hyde, *Shipping Enterprise and Management, 1830-1939. Harrisons of Liverpool* (Liverpool: Liverpool University Press, 1967).

—, *Liverpool and the Mersey* (Newton Abbot: David & Charles, 1971).

Journal of Commerce 22, 23 Nov 1917.

Liverpool Courier 22, 26 Nov 1917.

Liverpool Daily Post 22, 23 Nov 1917.

Shipping World 28 Nov 1917.

Syren and Shipping 28 Nov 1917.

HULTON, Sir Edward

(1869-1925)

Newspaper and periodicals proprietor

Edward Hulton was born in Hulme, Lancashire, on 3 March 1869, the second son of Edward Hulton, a bill-setter on the *Manchester Guardian*, and Mary née Mosley, a woman of severe and puritanical convictions. In 1871 Edward Hulton Sr went into the newspaper publishing business in partnership with a stockbroker called E O Bleakley. Originally in 1871 their daily *Sporting Chronicle* was a one-page issue printed on a handpress. It flourished, and was joined by a weekly, the *Athletic News*, in 1875. In 1885 Hulton launched a Sunday newspaper, the *Sunday Chronicle*, and about this time he took his son Edward away from St Bede's Roman Catholic College, Manchester, where he was educated, and set him to learn the business. He was a stern disciplinarian at his office, although on the whole a more relaxed and kindly character than his formidable wife.

The boy gained experience of all aspects of the newspaper trade, and by the mid-1890s was taking a large part in running the business. His father was devoted to him, and increasingly admired both his business acumen and smart manner. In 1897 Edward Jr was largely responsible for founding a new halfpenny evening paper, the *Manchester Evening Chronicle*, which eventually secured the largest evening circulation in the country. Its success encouraged Hulton to found a daily morning paper, the *Daily Dispatch*, in 1900. One journalist who worked for the *Evening Chronicle* at this time recalled that Teddy Hulton 'excelled in marvellous silk ties and waistcoats cut very low'. He took many of his ideas from Alfred Harmsworth (qv), 'adapting them to local needs', and cultivated Northcliffe's habit of unexpectedly appearing in departments to check that everything was at concert pitch.

> With many contradictory elements in his personality, naïveté and shrewdness, impulse and caution, crowding in and disputing with one another, the younger Hulton constituted a rare find for the connoisseur of character. Except when annoyed he had, like his father, a pleasant, soft voice and an inviting, bland manner. But attempt to presume on that superficial gentleness and off blew your head! He was particularly down on people who came to him with schemes for which they made out all sorts of specious claims. He would listen until they had finished, his patience unruffled, his demeanour apparently friendly; induce them once more to repeat their confident assertion that success was a certainty; then, if it was a particularly bad case of bluffing, would turn on his smooth-tongued visitors with the withering taunt, 'You *must* think I'm a damned fool'. {Falk (1951) 21-23}

By the time Edward Sr died in 1904, leaving £557,000, the Hultons were by far the biggest newspaper proprietors outside London. Two of Hulton's sisters, Aggie and Theresa, thinking his intemperate life would make him unfit to match this success, withdrew their money from the business after their father's death; two others, Maggie and Mary, supported him.

In 1909, Hulton followed the example of the *Daily Graphic* and the Harmsworths' *Daily Mirror* by founding a daily illustrated paper, the *Daily Sketch*. Like all of Hulton's papers until then, this was founded in Manchester, but it soon became clear that most photographs of interest to the *Sketch* were to be taken in or near London. In addition, the *Daily Mirror* 'gradually but most effectively began to invade the Midlands and the North; straight into the hitherto unchallenged Hulton territory ... Mr Hulton did not like the intrusion in his field, so he came to London with the *Daily Sketch*, a tabloid rival of the *Mirror*' {Blumenfeld (1933) 146}. About this time, Hulton himself moved south, perhaps under pressure from his common-law wife. He was however a proud Mancunian and Lancastrian who was notably reluctant to take London journalists at their own high self-evaluation.

In 1915 he extended his London newspaper interests by buying from Davison Dalziel and Alexander Henderson (qqv) the *Evening Standard and St James's Gazette* (reputedly for £50,000). In 1915 Hulton determined to start a Sunday companion to his *Daily Sketch*, and hearing of this, Harold Harmsworth (qv), in a pre-emptive strike, rushed out the *Sunday Pictorial* a week or so before Hulton's *Sunday Herald* (later called the *Sunday Graphic*) was due to be launched. Hulton was very bitter at this, and accused Harmsworth of exploiting confidential information obtained through trade associations to whom the Hulton group had applied for use of wartime publishing facilities. His son recalls him at this time as 'tormented ... by the Victorian, Puritan urge to get up early and work hard, and always be doing something "useful". He was a conscientious worker to an almost pathetic degree, being ... too suspicious to delegate' {Hulton (1952) 133}.

> His goal was not money. It was efficiency ... His face spoke of a completely indomitable will, of honesty of purpose, but also of a certain amount of sadism ... He had somewhat high cheekbones, and there were two cruel-looking lines right down his face, which looked extraordinarily like Red Indian war-paint. The prominent, rather handsome, hooked nose, though its fleshiness was perhaps a little sensual-looking, also testified to a quite unusual strength of will. The mouth was rather small and precise ... often kept firmly shut with an almost incredible firmness. It was a somewhat ugly but handsome face, almost terrible-looking, yet attractive to women {*ibid*, 134}.

Ill-health, which had dogged Hulton for twenty years, finally prompted him to sell all his publications in 1923. By then E Hulton & Co Ltd, a private company, owned eight newspapers and a number of periodicals. The average circulation in the first six months of 1923 of his morning papers was 1,267,343, of the evening papers 868,639, and of the Sunday and weekly publications 4,518,349. Average profits before tax for the previous five and a half years were £377,702, despite a loss in 1920 of £216,433; profits for 1922, which included fifteen months of the profits of Empire News Ltd (Hulton had bought a Manchester paper called the *Umpire*, changing its name to *Empire News*) were £818,438. After negotiating for some time with W E Berry (qv) and coming very near to concluding a deal with him, Hulton sold his papers to Lord Beaverbrook (qv) for £6 million. Beaverbrook offered only about £100,000 more than the Berrys had done, but paid cash. Half of the proceeds went to Hulton's sisters Maggie and Mary, who kept their money in the business after their father's death. Beaverbrook then resold the Hulton group to Rothermere for the same price, keeping a 51 per cent stake in the *Evening Standard* as commission.

Hulton's interest in newspapers was entirely commercial: in the age of Northcliffe, Rothermere and Beaverbrook he seldom used his papers to publicise his own personal opinions, or to win political influence. When he did intervene on editorial policy, as over his papers' attitude to the Montagu-Chelmsford proposals for Indian constitutional reform, it was not from personal conviction, but under pressure from Lloyd George Coalition Government supporters, from whom he was probably then seeking an hereditary honour. His own political convictions were those of a moderate Conservative. His papers were popular and unpretentious, providing simple news stories rather than party politics, with particular emphasis on sporting news, and puzzles, competitions and serial stories.

His main interests outside his business were horseracing and greyhound coursing. He registered his racing colours in 1906, under the name of H Lytham (using this assumed name so his mother would not hear of it), and invested considerable sums in building up a fine racing stable, which met with some success, although the only classic race his stable won was The Oaks in 1924, which went to his filly, *Straitlace.* He was also an enthusiastic collector of Chinese porcelain, and built up a major collection of eighteenth century English mezzotints. Eighteenth century history was of particular interest to him, and he had a large library. He was captain of the Golf Club at Lytham St Anne's in Lancashire, and a director of several race-courses. Although he never hunted, he enjoyed riding himself as well as shooting and fishing.

According to one Fleet Street editor, 'Money-making was a Hulton attribute, but he was also to be credited with the production of some good newspapers' {Blumenfeld (1933) 146}. The biographer of Edgar Wallace, whom Hulton appointed in 1913 as editor of two of his periodicals, *Ideas* and the *Story Journal*, calls the proprietor 'an unpredictable man' and disagreeable employer.

> Uncouth, dour, brutal and suspicious, he was a curious person to find running publications ostensibly devoted to popular lightheartedness ... One of the trials to which the staff ... had to submit was the formal reading aloud to Hulton of the weekly joke page; at the climax of each witticism he would fire the reader a hostile stare and observe crushingly 'I see nothing funny in *that*.' He was violent in his criticisms, and undoubtedly enjoyed making his employees writhe ... brutal criticism and contempt ... were Hulton's favourite weapons {Lane (1964) 197}.

Hulton's years of serious ill-health may have contributed to his egregious temper. Towards the end of his life he was met at Ascot by a former employee who congratulated him on his improved appearance. 'You are wrong', replied Hulton, 'I am dying and I am the most miserable man on earth' {Falk (1951) 23}.

His private life was mercurial. He married first, the daughter of Mr Turnbull, a Manchester solicitor, but separated from her, and went to live with Millicent Warris, alias Lindon or Warris-Lindon. They had a son,

Edward (b 1906), and a daughter Betty (1910-1932) who were reared as Roman Catholics. Hulton's first marriage seems to have been dissolved in 1915, for in June of that year, after an approach by Hulton (whom he had never before met), Northcliffe instructed his editors not to allude in any way to the forthcoming divorce (which is not even listed in the *Times*). Hulton subsequently married Millicent Warris, whose antecedents and age are mysterious (when she died at Taormina in 1940 as Baroness Sklenar von Schaniel, she was erroneously said to be aged only fifty). A former actress, she was socially ambitious, revelled in Mayfair life and disliked her husband's Lancashire roots: she organised the Great Victory Ball at the Albert Hall in 1918, appearing at midnight in a classical chariot, garbed as Peace, releasing doves from her bosom.

Lloyd George recommended Hulton for a barony in 1918, but the latter 'preferred a Baronetcy in the hope that his son would be made the legitimate heir to the lesser honour' {HLRO, Lloyd George papers F4/6/14}. Hulton accepted his baronetcy in 1919 on the understanding that it would carry a special remainder enabling his son to inherit, although born out of wedlock; but Lloyd George then receded from this agreement (obtained through Beaverbrook), and as Hulton vainly wrangled for three years, the patent of the baronetcy was not issued until 1921.

Hulton died at his house at Leatherhead on 23 May 1925, leaving £2,195,125. His son became a magazine publisher of *Hulton's Weekly* and *Picture Post*, and was knighted in 1957.

CHRISTINE SHAW *and* R P T DAVENPORT-HINES

Sources:

Unpublished

HLRO, papers of Lord Beaverbrook, C/180 and Lloyd George, F4/6/14.

PrC.

Published

Ralph D Blumenfeld, *The Press in My Time* (Rich & Cowan, 1933).

DNB.

Thomas E N Driberg (Lord Bradwell), *Swaff, the Life and Times of Hannen Swaffer* (MacDonald, 1974).

Lord Camrose, *British Newspapers and Their Controllers* (Cassell, 1947).

Bernard Falk, *Bouquets for Fleet Street* (Hutchinson, 1951).

Sir Edward G W Hulton, *When I Was a Child* (Cresset Press, 1952).

Margaret Lane (Countess of Huntingdon), *Edgar Wallace* (Hamish Hamilton, 1964).

H Simonis, *Street of Ink* (Cassell, 1917).

Kurt von Stutterheim, *The Press in England* (Allen & Unwin, 1934).

Times 25 May 1925.

WWW.

Sir Nutcombe Hume (courtesy of Standard Telephones and Cables PLC).

HUME, Sir Hubert Nutcombe

(1893-1967)

Financier and merchant banker

Hubert Nutcombe Hume was born in Southgate, North London, on 4 September 1893, the elder son of Frederick Nutcombe Hume, then medical Superintendent of the Northern Fever Hospital, and Catherine Mary née Walton. He was sent to Westminster School, and went on to Sandhurst through the generosity of relatives who paid his way after his father's death. Lack of funds prevented him from pursuing an army career, and in 1912 he went to Canada to seek his fortune. In the two years he was there he worked his way across the country in a variety of jobs, including those of schoolteacher, cook, motor mechanic and land surveyor. He returned to England at the outbreak of war in 1914 and served with distinction as an officer in the Hampshire regiment. He was wounded in action in 1916, and was subsequently mentioned in despatches and awarded the MC.

Soon after the Armistice, Hume left the army and after a difficult period during the 1921 slump, joined the new issue business of George Clare & Co. By temperament he was independent, and valued the challenge of doing business on his own. The swashbuckling environment of the post-war City offered salutary lessons and during the next few years Hume gained valuable experience in gauging the market and the relative strengths of the businesses he encountered. His chance came in 1925, when, together with Sir Arthur Marshall, Liberal MP for Huddersfield, and Sir Arthur Wheeler (qv), the well-known and powerful outside broker, (to whom Hume had been introduced by Harry Clifford-Turner (qv), George Clare's legal advisor), he formed the Charterhouse Investment Trust.

The Trust, which had an issued capital of 300,000 £1 ordinary shares, was set up to handle new issues, and was one of many such companies established at about the same time. Hume was managing director, but Sir Arthur Marshall succeeded Wheeler as chairman in 1928 after the conduct of Wheeler's brokerage business began to give his two colleagues cause for concern. In 1931, the Macmillan Report called attention to the need for the institutional provision of finance to small- and medium-sized private companies. Hume, with his now considerable experience of the needs of such companies, formed the Charterhouse Industrial Development Co to meet those needs in 1934, at a time when finance for development on a long-term basis was virtually unobtainable. He was thus the first to take direct action to fill what came to be known as 'the Macmillan Gap', more than a decade ahead of the government-sponsored Industrial & Commercial Finance Corporation, set up for the same purpose after the Second World War.

During the war, Hume took up the post of Director of Finance

(Commercial) at the Ministry of Supply at the personal request of Patrick (later Sir) Ashley Cooper, the Ministry's Director General of Finance. He returned to Charterhouse in 1945 and became chairman a year later on the retirement of Sir Arthur Marshall. Charterhouse continued to expand under Hume's leadership, purchasing the merchant bank and accepting house S Japhet & Co in 1954, establishing subsidiaries in Canada and Australia, and, after a major reorganisation, assuming the title of the Charterhouse Group in 1959. Hume remained chairman until his retirement in 1964, and president until his death.

Hume combined his active role in the management of Charterhouse with a number of notable outside appointments. During 1948-53 he was a director of the Colonial Development Corporation (now the Commonwealth Development Corporation) and was deputy chairman, 1953-1959 and chairman, 1959-60. He served as chairman of the National Film Finance Corporation, 1956-64. He was also a Council member of the Confederation of British Industry, having previously been a vice-president of the Federation of British Industries. For many years he was a governor of the English-Speaking Union, and a British correspondent of the National Industrial Conference Board of America. He also gave much time and support to the Salvation Army, heading its advisory board. In addition he held appointments on the boards of a number of companies, including Associated British Maltsters, Metropolitan Estate and Property Corporation, Associated Book Publishers and Slough Estates.

During his long career, Hume was responsible not only for nurturing many companies that showed potential, but many men as well. His enthusiasm was infectious and over the years he became a respected as well as a rumbustious city figure. Hume was awarded the CBE in 1946 and the KBE in 1956. He married firstly Vera Lilian née Hope and secondly, in 1927, Jessie Annie (d 1975), a divorcée and daughter of the late Donald Campbell. Sir Nutcombe Hume died on 22 December 1967 leaving £38,504 gross.

LAURIE DENNETT

Sources:

Unpublished

The Charterhouse Group, London, papers including the minute books of the Charterhouse Investment Trust and the Charterhouse Industrial Development Co.

BCe.

MCe.

PrC.

'The Finance of Industrial Development in Current Conditions' (Edwards Seminar paper 51, 22 Feb 1949).

'Preparation and Handling of New Issues of Capital' (*ibid* 239, 24 Feb 1959).

HUME Sir Hubert Nutcombe

Nutcombe Hume,

—

Published

Laurie Dennett, *The Charterhouse Group 1925-1979. A History* (Gentry Books, 1979).

John Kinross, *Fifty Years in the City: Financing Small Business* (John Murray, 1982).

WWW.

HUNSDON, 1st Lord Hunsdon
see **GIBBS, Herbert Cokayne**

Sir Ellis Hunter from a portrait by A W Davidson Houston for the British Iron & Steel Federation (courtesy of the British Steel Corporation).

HUNTER, Sir Ellis

(1892-1961)

Steel company chairman

Ellis Hunter was born at Great Ayton, Yorkshire, on 18 February 1892, the younger son of William Hunter, headmaster of the village school, and his wife Alice née Davison. His paternal grandfather was a farmer on Teesside at Newport (which the new town of Middlesbrough was building). To his father Hunter certainly owed something of the powers of intense concentration and meticulous accuracy that permeated all his thought and activities. He had a countryman's reserve of manner which he never lost and a realism about human nature, but he always retained, throughout the political and economic trials he was to endure, a countryman's deep fund of idealism.

He was educated at Middlesbrough High School. From there he went to a local firm of accountants, with whom he qualified in 1914. In the First World War he was a temporary civil servant in the Ministry of Munitions, where (he later said) he had an opportunity of 'seeing the muddle made by the government of the whole business of factory extensions for wartime production' {Wilson (1962) 11}. In the post-war slump he was back in the North East again, as a local partner from 1922 with the accountants W B Peat & Co. His competence became locally famous. In 1928 he became a general partner in the newly-formed partnership of Peat, Marwick, Mitchell & Co.

It was at this point that new horizons opened, for amongst the ailing clients of his new partnership were Dorman, Long & Co. Under the dynamic, but not always well-advised, leadership of Arthur Dorman (qv), this large steel-making firm had become an empire in the North-Eastern world of iron and steel, absorbing the pioneers of Cleveland steel making, Bolckow Vaughan, Bell Bros, kings of the iron industry, Samuelsons, and a number of structural iron and bridge builders. A vast and diversified empire, but one that faced a world of domestic and foreign rivalry for shrinking markets, guided — but guided uncertainly — by an almost geriatric management. Dormans, in short, were in sore straits in a depressed economy. In 1935 it was Ellis Hunter's unenviable task to become secretary of the Dorman Long Debenture Holders' Association, that is, the watchdog for those who had lent capital to Dormans. Within three years they had come to regard him as indispensable. In 1938 he became deputy chairman of Dorman, Long & Co. Soon afterwards, he became managing director, a position he retained until the year of his death; from 1948 he was also chairman.

On taking charge of Dorman, Long his actions were swift, immediate and effective. By the time war broke out in 1939 Hunter was boss of one of the largest coal, iron and steel concerns in Britain. It produced every kind of semi-finished and finished steel, including rails and structural steel. As head of Dorman, Long, Hunter was ineluctably drawn into the national counsels of the whole iron and steel industry. By 1945, when the vice-president of the Iron and Steel Federation died suddenly, he found himself presiding not only over the future technical structure of the British iron and steel industry, but also over the blistering political debate about its control and ownership.

In June 1945 the new Labour Government addressed itself more peremptorily to the Iron and Steel Federation which represented the entire industry. Its tone was chilly. Hunter knew as well as the Government that state planning, controls and regulations were as much a part of the national life of the day as queues and rationing. Accordingly, Hunter and the Federation lost no time in setting up a steering committee, whose duty was to prepare a seven-year plan for the renovation and expansion of the national steel industry. A stickler for punctuality himself, Hunter applied the same principles to others: six months to the day he personally presented his report to the Minister. It covered the activities and future of 300 companies, large and small, engaged in every form of iron and steel manufacture. They employed more than 300,000 workers. Their products were valued at about £500 million, vital to the engineering, construction, motor car, shipbuilding, railway, coal mining and scores of other industries: in short the life blood of the nation's economy.

Over the next three years vital differences of opinion, not least within the Labour Government itself, were to emerge. The ministers all shared a jaundiced view of the industry as it stood, but little else. Faute de mieux, nationalisation won. The chief of the Iron & Steel Corporation of Great Britain was to be Stephen Hardie, whose knowledge of the industries concerned was minimal and who held his meetings down to 1951 mainly at the Dorchester Hotel.

Meanwhile Hunter, as president of the BISF, and Sir Andrew Duncan (qv), the independent and indomitable chairman of its executive committee, representing 'the public interest', attempted to observe the rules of the game with constitutional rigour. Duncan died in March 1952. But meanwhile the Attlee Government, exhausted and distracted, had also passed away. Churchill, back at No 10, received Hunter at his room in the House. Tradition has it that the interview ran thus:

> PM: I hear that you still want us to denationalise steel.
> Hunter: Yes, Sir.
> PM: Very well, we will. {*ibid* 33}

The Bill that followed incorporated, as no other document ever did, Hunter's basic ideas of a privately-*owned* industry combined with public and parliamentary supervision by a strengthened Iron and Steel Board. Gone were Lowthian Bell's (qv) dreams of a laissez-faire, free trade economy of iron and steel. But gone too were his predecessor's, Arthur Dorman's (qv), dreams of a simple protectionist economy of iron and steel. His work done, Hunter stepped down in 1953 from his long occupancy of the presidency of the BISF. His ideas

> marked a change of outlook in an industry essentially individualistic in its approach ... and established for the first time a truly corporate view, an acceptance of public accountability and a disposition, reluctant at first, to submit individual company policies to the test of natural need. In achieving this change Ellis Hunter's appreciation of the probable trend of public opinion and national requirements was a significant factor. {*Times* 22 Sept 1961}

At the root of his ideas was his collaboration with Sir Andrew Duncan, wartime Minister of Supply, a formidable administrator, negotiator and business diplomatist. Duncan and Hunter shared a view of the British steel industry that was essentially new: neither laissez-faire in the British tradition nor state-organised in the German tradition. It took institutional shape from 1932 onwards under the Import Duties Act, which enabled the Advisory Committee for the industry to recommend a special tariff and negotiate with the European Steel Cartel for a limitation of their imports into Britain and a fair share of world markets for British iron and steel producers. A forceful sentence from Hunter's report of 1944 to the Minister of Supply, might be taken as their joint text for steel policy: 'The industry, while depending on certain actions of the community, accepts the right of the community to make sure that any facilities granted are used in the public interest'. {Wilson (1962) 18} It was a phrase he often repeated.

Hunter had begun life as an accountant, orderly and meticulous. His training was the basis of the strictly analytical methods which he deployed to such effect in his management of Dorman, Long. But they never restricted the play of his imagination. A few years before his death he gave up membership of his original profession to show (as he said) that he 'had made steel his life' {*ibid*, 47}. The claim was not excessive. After his unplanned excursions into public affairs, he returned to the firm he had put on its feet two decades earlier, to reorganise and develop a vast complex of giant new coke ovens, blast furnaces, rail and beam mills at Lackenby, Redcar and Cleveland. A South African subsidiary, new structural steel and bridge building organisation, new managerial training schemes, plans for promotion to high office on merit: all these and many other plans occupied his later years. They proved that his long and testing period of service in London on behalf of the whole steel industry never weakened his interest or faith in his own firm in Middlesbrough. Economical, even ascetic himself, his policy of modest dividends provoked criticism but it made possible his company's £100 million development programme after 1945. One of his first acts on becoming managing director of Dorman, Long was to abolish their London headquarters. To him it seemed lavish and dispensable. Middlesbrough was the proper centre for Dorman, Long. His own office in London was, and remained to the end, a modest, almost dingy room.

Hunter never pretended to be a technologist or a salesman, though he knew more of both than he would admit. He disliked the jargon and vulgarity of the (temporarily) affluent commercial society. He distrusted politicians who gambled with fortunes that were not theirs to gamble with. To the British Millers' Association in 1958 he gave a striking address which combined formal courtesies to trade associations in general with some sharply-edged reminders that such institutions were justified only if they developed the confidence of their consumers and showed a proper regard for the public interest. (Hunter had not forgotten that the president of the Association was Archibald Forbes, former chairman of the Iron and Steel Board.)

Hunter was, at first acquaintance, shy, almost dour, but beneath this facade he remained a man with a quiet sense of humour. At heart he was a countryman who grew roses, and loved the hills and moors of his childhood. Tall and spare, he looked more like a country solicitor or doctor than an entrepreneur — perhaps most like a public servant. And that, perhaps, was how he regarded himself.

Ellis Hunter married Winifred Grace, daughter of John Steed, a commercial traveller, in 1918; they had two daughters. He was knighted in 1948, and received the GBE in 1961. He died at his country home in Yorkshire on 21 September 1961, leaving an estate proved at £106,884 gross.

CHARLES WILSON

Sources:

Unpublished

Messrs Dorman, Long, papers.

BCe.

MCe.

PrC.

Published

Duncan L Burn, *The Structure of British Industry: A Symposium* (Cambridge: Cambridge University Press, 1958).

James C Carr and Walter Taplin, *A History of the British Steel Industry* (Oxford: Basil Blackwell, 1962).

Sir Norman Chester, *The Nationalisation of British Industry 1945-1951* (HMSO, 1975).

Hugh Dalton, *High Tide and After: Memoirs, 1945-1960* (Frederick Muller, 1962).

Manchester Guardian 17 May 1960.

Observer 4 Feb 1951.

Times 22 Sept 1961.

Edward Francis Williams, *A Prime Minister Remembers: The War and Post-War Memoirs of the Rt Hon Earl Attlee* (Heinemann, 1961).

Charles Wilson, *A Man and his Times: A Memoir of Sir Ellis Hunter* (Newman Neame, 1962).

HUNTER, Sir Ernest John

(1912-1983)

Shipbuilder

Sir John Hunter (courtesy of Mr J F Clarke).

Ernest John Hunter was born at Newcastle upon Tyne on 3 November 1912, the second son of George Ernest Hunter (1875-1954) and Elsie née Edwards (1881-1957), and grandson of Sir George Hunter (qv). His father, an engineer, became a director of Swan, Hunter & Wigham Richardson Ltd in 1903 and worked for the company all his life.

The young Hunter was educated at Oundle School and then became an apprentice in the shipyard (1930-31), with take-home pay of 7s 4d. This followed a tradition of many North-East Coast employers for their sons. He studied for a year at St John's College, Cambridge, and then moved to Durham University, where he graduated in 1935 with a BSc. For the next two years Hunter worked as a draughtsman earning £2 a week, enhancing his knowledge of shipbuilding, and then in 1937 went as assistant manager to Barclay Curle, the Scottish subsidiary of Swan, Hunters, for a salary of £5 a week.

Throughout the Second World War and for many years afterwards the Tyneside drydocks of Swan, Hunter were John Hunter's main responsibility, firstly as assistant manager and from 1943 as general manager. He very successfully managed the heavy and complex ship repair demands of wartime. He was appointed a director of the company in 1945. In 1948 the departments under his control repaired in dock 321 ships exceeding 2.2 million tons in all and a further million tons of shipping afloat. These were enjoyable years for John Hunter and his departmental profits increased vastly. His experience was enlarged by a visit to the USA in 1949. In the 1950s a new dry dock, at 715 feet long, the largest possible size given the constraints of the site, was planned and constructed under his direction.

In 1956 Hunter was elected president of the Shipbuilding Employers' Federation, facing serious industrial troubles in his year of office. Labour relations have never been easy in shipbuilding, and John Hunter over many years attempted to improve working agreements so as to minimise industrial stoppages in a situation later complicated by various company mergers. In 1971 it was said 'very real progress' had been made 'in standardising conditions of service and ending demarcation squabbles' {*Newcastle Journal* 27 Aug 1971}, three years after the 'Workers' Charter' agreed in 1968.

Following the death of J W Elliott (1887-1957), Hunter was elected chairman of Swan, Hunter in May 1957; at that time the company's profit (before taxation) exceeded £3 million. In the following months Hunter's responsibilities were extended to the chairmanship of the brassfounders, M W Swinburne & Sons and the Hopemount Shipping Co, as well as board membership of Wallsend Slipway & Engineering Co, Barclay Curle and the Glasgow Iron & Steel Co.

Hunter's policy for investment had resulted in an expenditure of £13 million by 1960, when he stated that 'we are employing all the latest techniques' {*Shipbuilding & Shipping Record* 1960, 477}. Shipbuilding was moving into difficult times: British output for 1962-64 was less than 68 per cent of 1956-58. To help to meet these difficulties, Hunter advanced the policy of combining the separate engine works and shipyards. Following the Geddes Inquiry into shipbuilding of 1965-66 the company acquired by merger the capital of Smiths Docks Co, which had shipyards on the Tyne and the Tees. This was followed by the inclusion in the Swan Hunter group of the Tyneside shipyards of Readheads, Clelands and Hawthorn-Leslie and the Teesside yard of Furness, bringing approximately 40 per cent of British shipbuilding under a single management control.

An important step in diversification was the acquisition of the Newcastle civil engineering company of Brims, who had played a major part in the post-war reconstruction of North-East shipyards. During the 1960s there were substantial overseas developments in ship repairing: through Swan Hunter International as the managing agency, the Malta Drydocks were converted for merchant shipping work, followed by

Sembawang Shipyard, formerly the British Naval Dockyard and the Keppel Drydock at Singapore. Ship repairing facilities were operated in South Africa jointly with Dorman, Long; there were also ship repairing works in Trinidad.

Hunter led the team charged with the formidable task of bringing together the different accounting systems and practices of the newly-acquired companies. The workforce in 1968 was 20,500, with approximately another 10,000 in overseas establishments and the Group turnover exceeded £62 million. The issued capital was £11,501,000, of which in 1968 Hunter himself held a modest 11,102 shares, although he increased his holding threefold by the end of 1974. When many shipyards were failing the Group held a steady trading position, even increasing their workforce despite massive losses in 1969 and 1970. During the years of turmoil and extensive negotiations with the Government, Sir John Hunter (he was knighted in 1964) was ably assisted by his vice-chairman and joint managing director Thomas McIver; policies as ambitious as a joint venture in shipbuilding in South Korea and the take-over of the Belfast Harland & Woolf shipyard were explored. Hunter's salary as chairman and joint managing director was £40,000 in 1971; in 1973 he gave up his post as joint managing director and his salary as chairman became £20,000.

The threat of nationalisation did not deter investment. Hunter devoted considerable efforts to securing the best compensation for his shareholders, and indeed argued that the Swan, Hunter grouping could claim much success as a shipbuilding and ship repairing company. He was chairman of a group with 14 wholly-owned subsidiaries and a further nine associated companies. Following nationalisation, Sir John resigned as head of the company in 1979 after forty-eight years service.

He also held directorships of Newcastle & Gateshead Water Co, the Newcastle upon Tyne Electricity Supply Co Ltd, Common Brothers Ltd and the Midland Bank. Always active in employers' organisations, Hunter held the chairmanships of the Tyne Shipbuilders' Association, 1956-57, the North East Coast Ship-repairers' Association, 1957-58, the Dry Dock Owners' and Repairers' Central Council, 1961-62 and the Shipbuilders' and Repairers' Association from 1968. During Hunter's term of office, 1962-64, as chairman of the British Employers' Confederation talks began with the Federation of British Industry which led to the formation of the Confederation of British Industry in 1965. He was appointed to the National Economic Development Council on its formation in 1962, and served for three years on the British Railways Board.

The well-being of the young and the training of craftsmen were always of special interest to John Hunter. In the late 1950s his company employed 800-900 apprentices and in 1961 a school was established for pre-apprenticeship training. In 1964 Hunter became the first chairman of the Central Training Council.

Technical issues, too, were always of interest to Hunter. He was an active member of the North East Coast Institution of Engineers and Shipbuilders, served for many years on its council and was president, 1958-60. Besides a knighthood, he was awarded the CBE in 1960. In 1968 he received an honorary DSc from the University of Newcastle upon Tyne, and became DL of Northumberland. Four years later he was made a

Freeman of the Borough of Wallsend and in 1977, in recognition of his services, he was awarded a fellowship of the Sunderland Polytechnic. He was a JP, and a Liveryman of the Company of Shipwrights.

In 1937 Hunter married Joanne Winifrid, daughter of Cornelius Garbutt Wilkinson, a shipbroker; they had one son. After a divorce, in 1949 he married Sybil Malfroy, the divorced wife of Camille Enright Malfroy, and daughter of a London stockbroker, Charles William Gordon; there were one son and a step-daughter of the second marriage. Sir John Hunter died on 19 December 1983.

J F CLARKE

Writings:

'Shipgrafting — Certain Wartime Repairs' *Transactions of the North-East Coast Institution of Engineers and Shipbuilders* 64 (1948-49).

'Presidential Address' *ibid* 75 (1959-60).

Sources:

Unpublished

Newcastle upon Tyne City Library, Swan Hunter Group newspaper clippings, 6 vols.

Swan Hunter Annual Reports 1945-78.

Tyne & Wear Archives, North-East Coast Ship Repairers' Association; Swan-Hunter Archives; Tyne Shipbuilders' Association.

BCe.

MCe.

Information from the subject.

Published

Brian W Hogwood, *Government and Shipbuilding — The Politics of Industrial Change* (Farnborough: Saxon House, 1979).

Newcastle Journal 27 Aug 1971.

Shipbuilding and Shipping Record 1945-79.

Times 21 Dec 1983.

WW 1982.

HUNTER, Sir George Burton

(1845-1937)

Shipbuilder

Sir George B Hunter (courtesy of Mr J F Clarke).

George Burton Hunter was born at Sunderland on 19 December 1845, the third son of Thomas Hunter (1805-1887) and Elizabeth, the eldest daughter of master mariner William Rowntree of Sunderland. Thomas Hunter was first apprenticed as a potter, but failing to find work in this trade, he mastered the skills of the shipwright and went to sea. After acquiring the small sum of capital needed to build wooden ships, he constructed, and then traded in, a small vessel. By 1853 Thomas Hunter was the owner of a barque of 454 tons and in it he took his eight-year-old son George round the world, no doubt trading on the way.

The young George had little formal schooling and did not learn to read until he was ten. He left school at thirteen to serve two years as apprentice to Thomas Meek, the River Commissioners' engineer, and 'In his leisure moments he diligently perused "Cassel's Popular Educator"'{Rutherford (1934) 31}. His life's work began when he was apprenticed to the famous W Pile, Hay & Co, who were about to start building iron ships. The young man displayed such talents that at the age of twenty he was given charge of the drawing office and outside work. During the following four years more than 40 ships in iron and 'composite' were launched from the shipyard. George then secured valuable experience by working in the distinguished Scottish Govan shipyard of Robert Napier as assistant to William Pearce.

In 1871 Hunter returned to Wearside as manager of Pile's yard, but only two years later the business collapsed on the death of William Pile. Hunter then became junior partner to S P Austin, who had built his first wooden ship in 1831. The new firm of Austin & Hunter built and repaired iron ships. Output in the first year was a mere two vessels of 2,300 tons but reached 5,225 tons in 1878. At the end of the following year Hunter ended the partnership. The tragic death of C S Swan, who was managing a shipyard at Wallsend which was jointly owned by Charles Mitchell (1820-1895), Charles Swan and his brother, Henry Frederick, offered Hunter a fresh opportunity. A new partnership was formed with Swan's widow under the title C S Swan & Hunter.

About 700 men and boys worked on the seven-acre site of the Wallsend shipyard. Six cargo ships of 8,532 tons were built in the first year under Hunter. Output reached 20,000 tons in the boom of 1883 and ten years later, when more than 2,000 were employed, the output of 31,088 tons was the largest on the River Tyne. Extra land had been acquired and the site expanded to 23 acres. While on the Wear, Hunter played a major part in advancing the general use of water ballast by the cellular construction used on the SS *Fenton* in 1876; at his new yard he led the way on the Tyne in using mild steel for ship construction and in adopting triple expansion engines. Over the years 1880-88 profits averaged £7,301. In 1889 the yard built the first of many oil tankers and in the following year their first refrigerator ship. In 1895 a major innovation was introduced into Hunter's yard which was not followed for many years by others: two berths were enclosed with a glass roof of steel girders, which also supported overhead travelling cranes.

A private limited company was formed in September 1895 with Hunter as chairman; he was now able to share the burdens of management with well-chosen, able colleagues. Two years later the premises of the shipbuilders Schlesinger, Davis & Co were taken over and on these there began the building of the first of many notable self-docking floating graving docks. Hunter organised in 1903 the formation of Swan, Hunter & Wigham Richardson Ltd, and this new company acquired a controlling interest in Wallsend Slipway & Engineering Co; to this combination was added the Tyne Pontoons & Dry Dock Co Ltd. The new company had a registered capital of £1.5 million (£700,000 in 5 per cent cumulative preference shares); the initial issue was just over £994,000. In 1913 the capital was increased to £2 million. The launching of the *Mauretania* in 1906 highlighted Hunter's great ability in winning this order for the Tyne, and in successfully organising the design and production of 'one of the two largest, swiftest mail steamships afloat' {*Shipbuilder* (1906) 61}. The company's scope was extended before the First World War by the acquisition of a shipyard on the Wear, and in 1912 of the Clyde shipbuilders and engineers Barclay, Curle & Co Ltd, which was founded in 1818.

The scale of the new enterprise of which Hunter was chairman is indicated by a workforce of about 6,000 in 1906 and an output of ships of 126,921 tons, together with engines totalling 141,640 hp; net profit for the year was £114,807. Despite the depression in shipbuilding over the next four years profits averaged more than £364,000 and during the remainder of Hunter's chairmanship from 1911 to 1928 an average annual profit of £294,389 was made.

In the boom following the First World War, Hunter led the company in securing control of the Glasgow Iron & Steel Co Ltd, in order to guarantee steel supplies, and of the North British Diesel Engine Works, which opened opportunities for the new type of marine engine. There were associated companies in New York, Londonderry, Swansea and Dartmouth as well as on the Clyde, Wear and Tyne in the 1920s; and prior to the Depression about 10,000 were employed. In those years, with almost no profits to be made in new ships 'the favourable results' were due 'to the conservative policy ... as regards investment and the careful management of assets' {Swan Hunter Annual Report 1924}. Hunter resigned as chairman of the board in 1928, but 'remained active in his interests to the last' {*Newcastle Journal* 22 Jan 1937}.

Hunter's capacity for work was almost legendary, leading to suggestions that he grew a beard to save the time spent in shaving; he himself described his recreation as 'change of employment' {*WWW*}. He was a lifelong abstainer from alcoholic drink and a national vice-president of the Society of Non-Smokers; these were not just passing interests but matters of continuous concern to him, and he supported a petition to parliament for prohibition. He was an ardent advocate of spelling reform. Widely

View of part of the Swan Hunter shipyard, Wallsend on Tyne (courtesy of Mr J F Clarke).

recognised as a controversialist, he was a forceful speaker and frequent writer to newspapers in defence of his views. Normally a free trader, the Depression led him to conclude that 'arguments for safeguarding and protecting our industries and our workers in the present world conditions' are 'overwhelming' {Rutherford (1934) 130}.

High wages were regarded by Hunter as a major part of Britain's industrial difficulties, and he had little sympathy with trade union restrictions, but he did maintain good relations with many trade union leaders. Indeed his only attempt to be elected to parliament was as a joint Liberal candidate with the general secretary of the Shipwrights' Union, Alex Wilkie, at Sunderland in 1900. He was very concerned with his local community and lived in Weston Villa, Wallsend for ten years before moving to the more fashionable Jesmond. A keen Rotarian, he was president of the Wallsend Club. He served on the Local Board of Health, later the Wallsend Urban District Council, and was the second mayor, 1902-3, when the district became a borough. He donated park land to the local authority, as well as supporting local hospitals and the erection of St Luke's Church. From childhood he was a devoted Anglican, and in later years supported the Evangelical movement.

Soon after his arrival in Wallsend, Hunter became very actively involved in efforts to improve the opportunities for the young men of the district. He was assisted by technical staff who were educational enthusiasts in classes held at the Wallsend Café. This building, opened in 1883, provided refreshments, rooms for meetings and a lecture hall, in addition to a large open space for Boy Scout meetings and other activities. The company also had a very active sports programme. Hunter played an important part in the development of Armstrong College, and was awarded an honorary DSc in 1906 for his services by the University of Durham.

George Hunter was a founder member of the North East Coast Institution of Engineers and Shipbuilders and served on its council for many years. He was elected to the council of the Institution of Naval

Architects in 1900, and was also a member of the Institution of Civil Engineers. He was never over-keen to write technical papers, but contributed usefully to the work of all these institutions and served on Lloyd's Technical Sub-committee. In recognition of his services during the First World War, Hunter was created KBE in 1918.

In 1873 Hunter married Ann (1845-1927), daughter of Charles Hudson of Whitby and niece of the 'railway king' George Hudson. There were two sons and three daughters of the marriage. Sir George Burton Hunter died on 21 January 1937, leaving an estate proved at £152,363 gross.

J F CLARKE

Writings:

'Large Cargo Steamers' *Institution of Naval Architects* 41 (1899).

(with E W De Rusett), 'Sixty Years of Merchant Shipbuilding on the North East Coast' in *Transactions of the North East Coast Institution of Engineers and Shipbuilders* 24 (1908-9).

National Prosperity in 1914 and after the War (Greenock: 'Telegraph' Printing Works, 1917).

(with E T Good) *Trade Unions and Trade Unionism* (Hutchinson, 1926).

Wages and Purchasing Power (Newcastle upon Tyne: Easey & Best, 1931).

Sources:

Unpublished

Tyne & Wear Archives Department, Tyne Shipbuilders Association archives, Swan Hunter archives.

BCe.

PrC.

Published

DNB.

David Dougan, *The History of North East Shipbuilding* (Allen & Unwin, 1968).

Engineering 1907, 1937.

Engineer 1937.

An Historical Retrospect of Swan Hunter (Swan Hunter, 1932).

Institution of Naval Architects 79 (1937).

Mid-Tyne Link 1-2 (1904-6).

Newcastle Journal 22 Jan 1937.

William Richardson, *History of the Parish of Wallsend* (Newcastle upon Tyne: Northumberland Press, 1923).

Wilfred Rutherford, *The Man Who Built the 'Mauretania' ... the Life Story of Sir George B Hunter* (Hillside Press, 1934).

Shipbuilder 1906-37.

Swan Hunter & Wigham Richardson Ltd, Engineers and Shipbuilders (Swan Hunter, 1929).

Swan Hunter & Wigham Richardson Ltd, *Launching Ways* (Wallsend-on-Tyne: pp, 1953).

WWW.

HUNTING, Sir Percy Llewellyn

(1885-1973)

Shipping and aviation companies' chairman

Percy Llewellyn Hunting was born at Deep Dene House, Newcastle upon Tyne on 6 March 1885, the elder son of Charles Samuel Hunting (1853-1921), a Tyneside shipowner, and Agnes Mona née Arthur. Educated at Loretto (where he became head boy), Percy was sent to Paris in 1903 to become fluent in French. He was then apprenticed at North Eastern Marine Engineering Co Ltd at Wallsend, and studied marine engineering part-time at Armstrong College, Newcastle. In 1906 he joined the family shipowning group, Hunting & Son. This had been founded in 1874 by Percy's grandfather, Charles Hunting (1823-99), chiefly to provide a career for his son, Charles Samuel. The partnership began with two sailing ships, the *Sylvia* and the *Genii*, but by 1899 there were 13 ships in the fleet, all of them steamers. The first of many oil-tankers, the *Duffield*, had been purchased in 1893 and was being run by a newly-established subsidiary, the Northern Petroleum Tank Steamship Co, run in conjunction with James Duffield of Workington. In the years before 1914, however, the firm was no longer growing. In 1912 Percy and his younger brother, Gerald Lindsay (1891-1966), were sent on a visit to America, where they travelled to Mexico and into Canada, investigating the possibilities for overseas investment, especially in oil. Although nothing came of this venture, it was a foretaste of what was to come.

As a member of the TA Percy was mobilised in 1914 in the 4th Northumberland Fusiliers, but after two years, during which he was not posted abroad, he volunteered for the RFC, and after training as a wireless officer was posted to Mesopotamia.

At the end of the war only two ships of the Hunting fleet remained. After their father's death in 1921, Percy and Lindsay began to rebuild the fleet, chiefly with oil tankers, and by 1939 it comprised more than 100,000 tons. In 1925 they purchased the London shipbroking firm, E A Gibson & Co, with which Hunting had been associated for a long time, and thus began the diversification away from simple shipowning and from Tyneside. In 1926 the partnership, of which Percy had been head since 1921, was turned into a private limited company and he became chairman, a post he was to retain until his retirement in 1961. Badly hit by the depression and with all the Group's ships laid up in 1932, Hunting decided to leave Tyneside for London. He became a name at Lloyd's, but this was not to be a long-standing interest, and as the economy revived he began to look for new areas into which to develop. In particular he looked to oil and aircraft as important industrial sectors of the future. Huntings made several attempts during the 1930s to become involved in oil production, taking a share in the British Oil Development Co, of which Percy was a director, and having some success through the purchase in 1937 of the Brazos Young Oil Co of Texas. They also purchased a retail company, the City Petroleum Co of Preston, with filling stations in Lancashire and Yorkshire.

The move to London had clearly widened Percy Hunting's commercial horizons, and in 1938 Huntings made its first step into the rival field of aviation, when it took a minority interest (a majority was obtained in 1939) in Rollasons, a small aircraft servicing company at Croydon, then London's airport. War led to expansion of its interests, especially the manufacture of aircraft parts under licence. In 1941 total control of the company was obtained and its name changed to Field Air Services (one of the Hunting Group's shipping companies had earlier taken the name Field, which was the suffix of all its vessels). Airframe components for several military aircraft, including Lancasters and Wellingtons, were manufactured at Croydon and newly-established factories elsewhere, and to cope with demand the North East Aircraft Co was set up in disused slate sheds near Llanberis, North Wales. Percy was much involved with the latter development, which at its peak about 1943 employed 3,000 workers, and also with the many official visitors to the North Wales plant. These visits encouraged him to establish a company which purchased three local hotels for accommodation of visitors.

At the end of the war the North Wales operation closed, but Fields continued to expand in aircraft servicing and the Hunting Group had already laid plans for diversification. In 1944 Percival Aircraft of Luton was purchased from Lord Londonderry, opening the way for aircraft manufacture proper. Under the name of Hunting Aircraft it was to obtain an enviable reputation for the design and manufacture of trainer and communications aircraft. Among the trainers were the Prentice, Provost (1950) and its development the Jet Provost (still (1983) in use with the RAF), the world's first ab initio jet trainer. These were purchased by many air forces overseas, as were the Prince and Pembroke survey and communications aircraft. In 1960 the company was merged with British Aircraft Corporation, which was to produce the successful civilian BAC One-Eleven, on which Hunting had done the initial design work as the H107.

A second diversification began in 1945 with the setting up of an airline, Hunting Air Travel, which was to make the first post-war independent commercial flight in the UK. The company had difficulty in obtaining routes, but had some success in developing flights to Africa, and in 1954 it joined with Clan Line to provide stronger financial backing in forming Hunting-Clan Air Holdings, the first independent airline to fly Viscounts. The company was frequently in difficulty with UK aviation authorities and was eventually amalgamated in British United Airways. Allied to the development of African routes, Field Air Services developed an African subsidiary, together with another in Canada.

A third diversification commenced in 1938 when Huntings purchased a minority share in the Aircraft Operating Co, which controlled Aerofilms. In 1942 Huntings took complete control of this aerial survey and mapping company, which was initially government-controlled for war purposes. At the end of the war, as Hunting Aerosurveys, it began to develop a complete range of survey services, such as geophysics, forestry and soil surveys, which came to be used throughout the world, and which was particularly renowned for its surveys in Antarctica. Subsidiaries and joint companies with local interests were set up in Africa, Canada and New Zealand.

Apart from his involvement with group companies, Percy Hunting was also a director of Dixon & Corbitt & R S Newall & Co Ltd, rope manufacturers of Tyneside, until the firm was sold to British Ropes, and of Berry Wiggins & Co Ltd and the London Steamship Owners Mutual Insurance Association Ltd. He was much involved with the British Chamber of Shipping and was chairman of its Oil Tanker Committee, 1935-40. A fellow of the Institute of Chartered Secretaries, he was also a member of the Institute of Petroleum Technology, the Royal Aeronautical Society, the Photogrammetric Society of Great Britain and of the Society of Naval Architects and Marine Engineers (of the USA).

On 3 February 1910 he married Dorothy Edith, daughter of Daniel Birkett, headmaster of Sevenoaks School. They lived at the Glebe House, Edmondbyers, Northumberland, near to Slaley Hall which had been built by his father. Shortly after his move to London he purchased Old Whyly, East Hoathly, Sussex, where he took a great interest in village life. In 1946 he took over the local building firm, Alfred Trill & Sons Ltd, to save it from closure, and developed it to become a significant housebuilder in the area.

Hunting and his wife had two sons, of whom the elder, Charles Patrick Maule, took over the chairmanship of the Hunting Group in 1962. Their second son was killed in action in 1941. Hunting's first wife died on 1 January 1958 and on 1 October 1960 he married her sister, Evelyn Birkett. In the latter year he received a knighthood. He listed his recreations as arboriculture and travel, and the two were combined at Old Whyly, where he planted many trees gathered from the various countries he visited around the world on Group business. He was a member of the Travellers' and RAF Clubs. He died at Old Whyly on 2 January 1973 and left an estate valued at £468,032 gross.

D J ROWE

Writings:

The Group and I. An Account of the Hunting Group with Which Is Interwoven My Own Life and Thoughts (The Hunting Group of Companies, 1968).

Sources:

Unpublished

BCe.

MCe.

PrC.

Published

Hunting Fleet Magazine 80, *Centenary Review* (1974).

The Hunting Fleet of Ships Past and Present (2nd ed, Newcastle: Hunting & Son Ltd, 1961).

Times 3 Jan 1973.

WWW.

HURCOMB, Cyril William
Lord Hurcomb of Campden Hill

(1883-1975)

Nationalised transport industry chairman

Cyril William Hurcomb was born in Oxford on 18 February 1883, the son of William Hurcomb, a bookseller, and Sarah Ann née Castle. He was educated at Oxford Grammar School and St John's College, Oxford. Hurcomb entered the Surveyors' Department of the Post Office in 1905. A series of promotions and transfers soon led him to the post of Private Secretary to the Postmaster General, serving a succession of Postmasters General between 1911 and 1915.

His long association with transport began when he went to the newly-formed Ministry of Shipping in 1915. He was an able addition to a brilliant team which included John Anderson (later Lord Waverley) and Arthur Salter (later Lord Salter). He worked first as Deputy Director of

Commercial Services under Sir Percy Bates of the Cunard Line, who became one of his closest friends, and then succeeded him as Director of Commercial Services with responsibility for planning the civil import programme for Britain. He was awarded a CBE in 1918.

After the war he moved to the newly-formed Ministry of Transport. As Director of Finance and later, in 1927, as Permanent Secretary, he was renowned for his great energy and determination, despite the strain of working in a department under constant threat of abolition with a very rapid turnover in Ministers. During his service at the Ministry he received a CB in 1922 and a KBE in 1929.

In 1937 he moved to the Electricity Commission, initially as a Commissioner. Later that same year he was appointed chairman, in a difficult period of discussions about reorganisation which, however, came to nothing. He was given a KCB in 1938.

At the outbreak of war in 1939, a new Ministry of Shipping was set up to control the operation of shipping, and Hurcomb was appointed its Director-General. He immediately set about planning for the expected shipping shortage and took steps to enable the Ministry to gain control of all British ships and to charter all the foreign vessels possible. The Ministries of Food and Supply and the Board of Trade drew up plans of imports required, and the Ministry of Shipping arranged the shipping programmes. Hurcomb felt that shipping had to be controlled by an independent department, and resolutely rebuffed repeated attempts to interfere with his control of the merchant fleet. Without his foresight and driving energy, Britain's supplies of food and materials might have been jeopardised. When in 1941 Churchill amalgamated the old Ministry of Transport with the Ministry of Shipping to form the Ministry of War Transport under Lord Leathers, Hurcomb was appointed Director-General of the new Ministry. Here, though with wider responsibilities, he was still concerned with the maintenance of supplies from overseas. The Labour Government which came to power in July 1945 was committed in sweeping, though vague, terms to the nationalisation of all public transport. Hurcomb formed an excellent relationship with the Labour Minister of Transport, Alfred Barnes, and effectively supervised the drafting of the Transport Act, 1947. This implemented the Government's election pledge by creating a vast public corporation, the British Transport Commission, charged with the duty of providing an efficient, adequate, economical and properly integrated system of public inland transport and port facilities within Great Britain for passengers and goods. Once the Act had become law, Barnes invited Hurcomb, although already of retiring age, to become chairman of the new undertaking. Hurcomb was also offered the deputy chairmanship of the new British Electricity Authority. He recorded in some 'Autobiographical Notes' later that he had 'felt bound to leave myself in the Government's hand', and Barnes's offer met with Cabinet approval. Hurcomb later wrote 'I felt equal to the strain and my wife's death in the preceding February made an absorbing job more attractive' {Autobiographical notes}.

Leading the British Transport Commission in the directions laid down by the Act was both an exacting and a frustrating task. Hurcomb's long experience and formidable reputation within the Civil Service were of only limited value to him in directing the whole of this very diversified group of businesses. The railways, above all, now managed by a Railway Executive nominally responsible to the Commission, showed a very independent attitude. The nationalisation of road goods transport proceeded apace, but the approach to 'integration' was pitifully slow and little had been achieved before the change of Government in October 1951. He was awarded the GCB in 1946, and elevated to the peerage in 1950.

The new Conservative administration soon outlined the radical changes it had in mind, including the de-nationalisation of road haulage, insisted upon by Churchill. Hurcomb's initial term of office expired in 1952, but he agreed to continue for one more year until the provisions of the Transport Act, 1953, which drastically changed the constitution and objectives of the Commission, took effect. Hurcomb was by then over seventy, and he retired with some relief. The financial performance of the Commission had not been a source of much comfort to him. A loss of £39.5 million for the period 1948-50 was only partially offset by profits of £12.3 million in the period 1951-53.

His life-long interest in fishing was given free rein after his retirement, as were his other passions, bird watching and the conservation of nature. Whilst chairman of the BTC he took on the chairmanship of the Committee of Bird Sanctuaries in the Royal Parks and the presidency of the Society for the Promotion of Nature Reserves, and in 1954 he accepted appointment as vice-president of the International Union for the Conservation of Nature and Resources. He was president of the Royal Society for the Protection of Birds, president of the Field Studies Council, founder-president of the Council of Nature, and chairman of the Nature Conservancy from 1961 to 1962.

Hurcomb's character was a complex one. In the Civil Service he inspired more admiration than affection, though those who worked directly under him as Private Secretaries or Personal Assistants had a great regard for him. He was often impatient and direct in personal contacts, yet cautious and ultra-diplomatic on paper. He had a remarkable memory for detail, and a masterly command of official English, improving any draft submitted to him with rapid pencil emendations. He was shy, and for a long time disliked making public appearances; yet towards the end of his active life he seemed to relish the publicity arranged for him by the BTC's chief public relations and publicity officers. He had no illusions about politicians though he handled them skilfully, and he often appeared to find it difficult to trust fully even those who served him loyally. Austere and economical in his own tastes, he seemed to have a sneaking admiration for some business tycoons whose way of life was very different from his own. In every way he was a man of contradictions.

Hurcomb married Dorothy (d 1947), daughter of an Oxford accountant, Alfred Brooke in 1911. They had two daughters. Hurcomb died on 7 August 1975, aged ninety-two, leaving an estate proved at £45,521 gross.

KERRY HAMILTON *and* MICHAEL BONAVIA

Sources:

Unpublished

British Railways Board, Porchester Road, London, British Transport Commission Minutes 1948-53. British Transport Commission *Reports and Accounts* 1948-53; Railway Executive Minutes 1948-53.

BCe.

MCe.

PrC.

Autobiographical notes of Lord Hurcomb in private possession.

Published

Philip S Bagwell, *The Transport Revolution from 1770* (Batsford, 1974).

Michael R Bonavia, *The Organisation of British Railways* (Shepperton: Allan, 1971).

Leslie Hannah, *Electricity before Nationalisation* (Macmillans, 1979).

Times 8 Aug 1975.

WWW.

HYDE, Sir Robert Robertson

(1878-1967)

Promoter of industrial welfare

Sir Robert Hyde (taken from Sir Robert Hyde, Industry was my Parish*).*

Robert Robertson Hyde was born at Clapham, London, on 7 September 1878, the second of the five children of Robert Mettam Hyde, a civil engineer, and Marjory née Robertson, who were both Scots. Financial difficulties soon caused the family to take a small house in Forest Gate, in East London, and there the father died, when Robert was aged nine, leaving the family in poverty. Robert attended the local elementary school, but when the family's fortunes improved he was sent to various private schools. At fourteen he began work in the first of a number of 'dead-end' clerical jobs, studying part-time, and then full-time at King's College, London, for ordination in the Church of England.

His work for boys' welfare, with which his name became synonymous in later years, began in earnest in 1903 when he was sent to St Saviour's Church, Hoxton. In Hoxton, he became acquainted with some of the poorest members of the community, working in 'sweated industries' such as boxmaking, clothing, and shirtmaking. When Seebohm Rowntree (qv) invited him in 1916 to join the Welfare Department at the Ministry of Munitions, Hyde accepted, with his views on what needed to be done already formed.

His task, as he saw it, was to prevent the degeneration of young persons, to increase efficiency, to improve industrial relations and to create a tradition of welfare supervision. His methods were those of persuasion: he showed industrialists what could be done (that is, what was already being done by enlightened employers), and appealed to their humanity and their common sense to improve conditions in their own factories. Hyde's methods of working did not appeal to the civil servants in the Ministry, and he left early in 1918. By May 1919, he had established the independent Industrial Welfare Society, through which he exerted an influence on the attitudes of British industrialists towards the men and boys in their employ for the next thirty years.

The Society aimed to become a vehicle for disseminating and improving good practice in the management of men. For example, member organisations were persuaded to provide accounts of their welfare schemes, apprenticeship arrangements, joint consultation committees, pension schemes, and so on, for loan to others. Conferences were arranged for special interest groups — welfare officers and the directors who employed them, editors of house magazines, canteen managers, doctors engaged in industrial medicine. A magazine and confidential monthly bulletin kept members informed, especially on points of industrial law. The Society published brochures providing guidance on, for example, pension schemes, works committees, and savings funds, at a time when such guidance was not generally available.

Opposition to welfare, and to the men and women who promoted it, was strong amongst unions and many employers during Hyde's early years as director of the Industrial Welfare Society. It was seen as divisive by the unions, and as gross interference by the employers. Hyde's success lay in his first-hand knowledge of welfare programmes in companies with good industrial relations; in effective campaigning techniques (he aimed at winning over the boardroom, without whose support he felt no welfare scheme would succeed); and in the support of Prince Albert, Duke of York. In 1950 Hyde retired from the directorship of the Industrial Welfare Society, whose council gave him the title of founder.

Together with the Duke of York, Hyde organised the Duke of York's camps, summer camps where boys from industry and from public schools met together. The last of these camps was held at Balmoral in 1939, after the Duke had succeeded to the throne as George VI. George V in 1932 made Hyde a member of the Royal Victorian Order for his services to the Duke. In 1949 George VI gave his friend Hyde a KBE; Hyde's acceptance of the honour led to his being forced by the Archbishop of Canterbury to relinquish holy orders, a cause of great sorrow to him.

In 1918 he married Eileen Parker, daughter of Dr George Parker of Cuckfield. They had two children — a son Ian, killed in action in 1943, and a daughter, Jean. Robert Hyde died on 31 August 1967, leaving an estate proved at £32,503.

SHIRLEY KEEBLE

Writings:

'The Boy: East End and West End' *Ways and Means* 5 Apr 1919.

'Boys' Welfare Work' *ibid* 28 June 1919.

The Boy in Industry and Leisure (Social Service Library, 1921).

The Camp Book (Ernest Benn, 1930).

Industrial Welfare (Loughborough: Association of Technical Institutions, 1936).

Medical Services in Industry in Great Britain (1945).

Industry Was My Parish (The Industrial Society, 1968).

Sources:

Unpublished

BCe.

PrC.

Edward F L Brech, 'Robert R Hyde: Founder and Director of the Industrial Welfare Society, 1918-1950' (np, nd, copy held by *DBB*).

Published

DNB.

Helen Jones, 'Employers' Welfare Schemes and Industrial Relations in Inter-war Britain' *Business History* 25 (1983).

Times 1 Sept 1967.

WWW.

HYNDLEY, 1st Viscount Hyndley
see HINDLEY, John Scott

I

ILIFFE, Edward Mauger

1st Lord Iliffe of Yattendon

(1877-1960)

Newspaper and periodicals proprietor

Edward Mauger Iliffe was born at Coventry on 17 May 1877, the younger son of the three children of William Isaac Iliffe, a printer, and his wife Annette, daughter of James Coker of Guernsey. William Iliffe, anticipating the development of the infant cycling and motor car industries, founded a number of trade journals for these industries, such as *Cycling* (launched in 1891) and *Autocar* (1895), and in 1891 founded the *Midland Daily Telegraph* (later known as the *Coventry Evening Telegraph*). It is not recorded where Edward was educated. Later in life he often said he learned his alphabet from a printer's typebook, and he showed an active interest in printing and publishing from an early age. Edward Iliffe joined his father's firm at the age of seventeen, and was trained in all aspects of it. He and his brother, William Coker Iliffe (1874-1942), took part in running the business. Among the journalists recruited for the flourishing trade journals was the young Alfred Harmsworth (qv), who worked for Iliffe & Sons in 1885-87. William Iliffe refused to back Harmsworth's scheme for a magazine, *Answers to Correspondents*, although he did allow him credit to have the first issues printed on Iliffe presses. By the outbreak of the First World War, the Iliffes had one of the largest periodical publishing concerns in the country, as well as their Coventry newspaper interests.

In 1915 Edward Iliffe was appointed Deputy Controller of the machine tool department of the Ministry of Munitions, and became Controller in 1917. He was given a CBE for his services in 1918, and knighted in 1922.

William Iliffe died in 1917, and Edward and William Coker inherited the business. They worked happily together, though Edward was clearly the driving force. They moved the headquarters of the periodical company, Iliffe & Sons Ltd (which had been incorporated in 1898), to London. According to Bernard Falk, after a while they decided to separate to forestall difficulties amongst the next generation; they valued the business

Lord Iliffe (on the right) at a meeting of the Governors of the Shakespeare Memorial Theatre, Stratford with Sir Fordham Flower (courtesy of Coventry Evening Telegraph*).*

at £500,000, and it was arranged that whoever remained in charge should pay the other his half in a debenture for £250,000. Coker preferred that Edward should remain the active proprietor, but before anything was settled, they were approached by Sir William Berry (qv), who offered £1 million and they accepted his offer. The *Coventry Evening Telegraph* and its associated weekly, the *Coventry Standard*, were not included in the deal, and remained in the possession of the family. Berry asked Iliffe to continue to look after the periodicals for at least a year, and was very reluctant to let him go at the end of that period. As an inducement to him to stay, Iliffe was allowed to acquire a share in the Berrys' other interests. This subsequently became an equal share with the two brothers in all their future ventures. (This account of the beginning of the association with the Berrys differs substantially from that given in the history of the *Sunday Times*, which is erroneous: unfortunately, the entry on the Berry brothers in this *Dictionary* follows that account).

In October 1923 the Associated Iliffe Press Ltd, a private company, was registered to acquire the business of Iliffe & Sons Ltd, which had a share capital of £600,000. Associated Iliffe Press had an issued ordinary capital of £100,000 and 500,000 $7\frac{1}{2}$ per cent £1 cumulative preference shares, as well as £500,000 $6\frac{1}{2}$ per cent debentures. Iliffes had a wholly-owned subsidiary, the Cornwall Press, with printing works in Stamford Street in South East London which printed their own and other journals. Kelly's

Directories Ltd, which had been acquired by Sir William Berry and his brother Gomer in 1921, acquired for £979,000 all the preference and 75,000 of the ordinary shares of the Associated Iliffe Press Ltd. Sir Edward Iliffe was chairman of the Associated Iliffe Press, and his brother also joined the board. Sir Edward became a director of Allied Newspapers when the Berrys formed it in 1924 to take over the former newspaper interests of Sir Edward Hulton (qv), which they had just acquired from Lord Rothermere (qv), and the *Sunday Times*, which they had owned since 1915. He also became a director of the periodical company, the Amalgamated Press, acquired from Rothermere in 1926, and became a partner with the Berrys in the *Daily Telegraph*, when they bought that in 1927. In 1930 he joined the board of Kelly's Directories Ltd, which then owned all the shares of Associated Iliffe Press.

Iliffe and the Berrys seems to have worked together very amicably; there were no indications of any major disagreements over policy, or clashes of personality throughout the years of their association. After the acquisition of the *Daily Telegraph*, the three partners had offices on the same floor in the new Daily Telegraph building, and lunched or dined together on most days. Iliffe's expertise in provincial newspaper publishing and trade periodicals must have been of great help in the expansion of the provincial interests of Allied Newspapers Ltd. However, Iliffe, like Gomer Berry, was to some extent under the shadow of William Berry, Lord Camrose, though so close was the harmony in which they worked that it is impossible to assign clear divisions of responsibility and function to the partners.

In January 1937 the Berry brothers (now Lords Camrose and Kemsley) and Iliffe (who had been given a barony in 1933) decided to separate their interests, which together comprised the largest publishing concern in the country. Iliffe took Kelly's Directories Ltd, with its subsidiary, the Associated Iliffe Press. He became chairman of Kelly's Directories (with Kemsley as vice-chairman). In 1939, however, Iliffe announced his 'retirement from active business' {*Birmingham Mail* 26 July 1960}. He had already resigned from the board of Kelly's Directories at the end of 1938 — and he sold back Kelly's to Camrose and Kemsley, with his other remaining interests in the Berry companies.

During the Second World War, Iliffe became chairman of the Duke of Gloucester's Red Cross and St John's Appeal Fund, and travelled the country widely, raising money. Over £50 million was raised during his chairmanship, to June 1945, and the final total was £57 million, a fact of which he was justly proud. In 1946 he was given the GBE for his services.

Iliffe had always retained very close links with Coventry and the Midlands, and despite his supposed retirement from active business and commitments to the Red Cross Appeal Fund, in 1943 he bought a group of Birmingham papers from the executors of Sir Charles Hyde for £2.25 million. Iliffe considered this a low price; it had been calculated on the basis of profits, and these had been depressed during the later years of Hyde's ownership, partly because he had refused to increase the price of his papers from 1d to 1½d, as many of his rivals did (including the *Coventry Evening Telegraph* from 1942 to 1945). Hyde, who died in 1942, had instructed his executors to sell only to buyers with local interests and unconnected with any of the larger newspaper concerns. The Birmingham

'Kellys' from W. H. Beable, The Romance of Great Businesses *(Heath Cranton, 1926).*

Post & Mail Ltd was incorporated in 1944, with Iliffe as chairman, and his son, Edward Langton Iliffe, as director.

By 1948, at the time of the Royal Commission on the Press (to which Iliffe gave evidence), the Yattendon Investment Trust Ltd, Iliffe's family investment company, owned Coventry Newspapers Ltd, a private company which owned the *Coventry Evening Telegraph* and controlled Coventry Standard Newspapers Ltd, a private company which owned two weekly newspapers; it also owned the *Cambridge Evening News*. The Yattendon Investment Trust also controlled the Birmingham Post & Mail Ltd, holding all of the 750,000 £1 ordinary shares of the £1.75 million issued capital. As well as the morning *Birmingham Post* and the evening *Birmingham Mail*, this public company owned the *Birmingham Weekly Post*, and controlled J & W Griffin Ltd, a small private company which owned the *Walsall Observer*. The *Birmingham Post*, which had been losing money under Hyde, was restored to profitability by Iliffe. By 1948, its circulation had been increased by one-third, while the *Birmingham Mail* had increased its circulation by a half, to over 300,000; it had the third largest circulation in the provinces. The *Coventry Evening Telegraph*, the only evening paper in the city, had a circulation of about 85,000. By the early 1950s, Iliffe's elder son, Edward Langton, was taking much of the responsibility for the running of these papers; he was vice-chairman of the Birmingham papers. Lord Iliffe retired from the chairmanship of the Birmingham Post & Mail Ltd in 1957, becoming president of the company. He maintained his close personal interest in the *Coventry Evening Telegraph*.

Iliffe was one of the least flamboyant of the press barons. Atypical in his concentration on trade journals and the provincial press (only through his association with the Berrys did he have any part in the national press), he never regarded his papers as a vehicle for his own views. This is not to say he did not have firm opinions, and his papers did reflect his own Conservative politics. He sat as MP for the Tamworth division of Warwickshire from 1923 to 1929, when he resigned to provide a safe seat for his friend Sir Arthur Steel-Maitland. His barony in 1933 was given for 'public and political services' {*Coventry Evening Telegraph* 26 July 1960}.

Nevertheless, he believed strongly that a provincial paper, if it was to serve its community properly — and not leave the field open for rivals — must reflect all points of view. Proper service to the local community was, to Iliffe, an important feature of the provincial press and one intimately bound up with its success. Small advertisements, for example, he saw as a valuable service to readers, as well as one of the foundations of his papers' profitability. He criticised those critics of the press who seemed to him to imply that all that was needed to establish a paper was money. 'Money does not really matter as much as is generally supposed. It is ability to run a paper, to know what the public wants, enterprise, energy and all that kind of thing.' {*PP* (1947-48) Cmd 7473, 9} After his acquisition of the Birmingham papers, he said

> I never looked upon the acquisition of these great Midland newspapers as merely a financial transaction. It was for that reason I declined to go in as a partner with anyone else. I had offers. If I had done so, I should, of necessity, for the sake of my partners, have had to keep an eye constantly on profits. I think, however, those who run newspapers have a greater responsibility to the community than that. I realise my own responsibilities have increased, but the possibiliities of service have increased, too.
> {*Birmingham Mail* 26 July 1960}

Iliffe retained strong links with Coventry throughout his life. He was interested in the preservation of its ancient guilds, such as the Drapers and Cappers, and at one time was president of the Coventry Chamber of Commerce. In the late 1930s he gave his former home, Allesley Hall, and 52 acres of grounds to the city (he had moved to Yattendon in Berkshire, an estate he bought in 1926), and his other gifts to Coventry included a £50,000 donation to the rebuilding of the cathedral after the Second World War. He was a JP for Warwickshire and vice-president of Warwickshire County Cricket Club.

His business interests outside publishing included membership of Lloyd's. He was chairman of the Guildhall Insurance Co, a director of London Assurance and chairman of the House Property & Investment Co Ltd. Active for many years in the Association of British Chambers of Commerce, he served as chairman of the finance and taxation committee and, in 1932, as president. He served as Master of several City livery companies, including the Stationers and Newspaper Makers (1937) and he was president of the Periodical Proprietors' Association in 1935-38. He was an Officer of the Légion d'Honneur and a Knight of the Order of St John.

A kindly, courteous man, with a good sense of humour, he seems to have earned the genuine respect and affection of those who worked for him, although

> As a young man, his brilliance and keenness of mind made him formidable. He was impatient of stupidity, and could never tolerate attempts to justify what was not justifiable. But he never blamed anyone for being wrong, provided there had been a properly thought-out attempt to be right. And when he delegated a job, he left it to those responsible to bring the job to completion. {*Coventry Evening Telegraph* 26 July 1960}

In his youth, Iliffe was an active sportsman, playing tennis for Warwickshire. He was a member of the All-England Tennis Club, president of the International Lawn Tennis Club of Great Britain and a member of the Royal Yacht Squadron. He was an enthusiastic pioneer motorist, and he was a life member of the Royal Automobile Club and a founder member of the Midland Automobile Club. His greatest cultural interest was the Shakespeare Memorial Theatre at Stratford on Avon; he was an active president of the board of governors of the theatre from 1933 to 1958.

Iliffe married in 1902 Charlotte, daughter of Henry Gilding, of Liverpool. They had two sons, Edward Langton, who succeeded his father, and Richard (d 1959), and a daughter. Lord Iliffe died on 25 July 1960 at the Middlesex Hospital, after he had fallen and injured his head on board a ship returning from the USA. He left an estate proved at £510,368 gross.

CHRISTINE SHAW

Writings:

PD, HC, 5th ser 178-228.

PD, HL, 5th ser 88-139.

PP, RC on the Press (1947-48) Cmd 7473.

Sources:

Unpublished

C Reg: Kelly-Iliffe Ltd (52,790).

PrC.

Published

Birmingham Mail 26 July 1960.

Birmingham Post 26 July 1960.

Burke's Peerage and Baronetage.

Viscount Camrose, *British Newspapers and Their Controllers* (Cassell, 1947).

Coventry Evening Telegraph 26 July 1960.

DNB.

Bernard Falk, *Bouquets for Fleet Street: Memories and Musings Over Fifty Years* (Hutchinson & Co, 1951).

Harold Hobson, Philip Knightley and Leonard Russell, *The Pearl of Days: An Intimate Memoir of the Sunday Times 1822-1972* (Hamish Hamilton, 1972).

PP, RC on the Press (1948-49) Cmd 7700.

Stock Exchange Official Intelligence 1924, 1931.

Stock Exchange Official Year-Book 1937, 1939.

Stock Exchange Year-Book 1924, 1925, 1927.

Times 26 July 1960.

Times *Prospectuses* 65 (1923), 98 (1939-46).

WWMP.

WWW.

ILLINGWORTH, Alfred

(1827-1907)

Worsted spinner

Alfred Illingworth was born in Kent Street, Bradford, Yorkshire, on 25 September 1827, the elder son of Daniel Illingworth (1792-1854) and his wife Elizabeth, daughter of Michael Hill of Bradford. Alfred's grandfather, Phineas Illingworth, had been employed by James Buckley, the first man to try (unsuccessfully) to start a steam-powered factory in Bradford and followed him to Todmorden. Miles Illingworth (Phineas's eldest son) returned to Bradford after a short time and in 1820 was joined by Daniel who helped set up a new textile business. A new partner, William Murgatroyd, brought a good deal of fresh capital into the business in 1827 and the firm expanded into new premises in Union Street. Murgatroyd retired in 1834 and Miles took over complete control, Daniel being employed as the firm's chief cashier and bookkeeper. In 1837 Daniel started his own business at the Providence Mill in the Goit off Thornton Road.

Alfred and his brother Henry (b 6 November 1829), with whom Alfred worked closely in later life, went to a private academy in Little Horton, run by Joseph Hinchcliffe, a Moravian, a man of very considerable intellectual distinction and public spirit. A number of Bradford's earliest industrial entrepreneurs including Henry Ripley, the dyer, and Charles Stead, later one of the principal directors of the great Salt enterprise, started their education here. The school aimed to meet the needs of boys from the growing number of middle class dissenting families who would not or could not use the Bradford Grammar School. Its curriculum included both modern and commercial subjects in addition to the traditional 'grammar school' syllabuses. Soon after 1839 the two boys went to the newly-opened Huddersfield College, a public institution under a committee of trustees, intended for Nonconformists in the West Riding of Yorkshire who had not succumbed to the lures of the 'traditional' public schools and whose sons needed education for a business career. The classics were taught but the prospectus emphasised that particular attention would be paid to modern languages, writing, commercial arithmetic and bookkeeping. Both Alfred and Henry appear to have distinguished themselves from time to time in the school examinations.

Alfred left school in 1843 when he was sixteen and entered his father's business immediately. Henry joined them two years later. We have no details of the firm's operations nor any information about the boys' industrial training. Presumably they worked through the various departments under the guidance of a senior overlooker. It was a successful business exploiting in the boom years of the Bradford economy (1848-74) the special advantages which the development of machine wool-combing gave the large specialist firms. Wool-combing remained substantially a domestic industry until the 1850s. The first effective advances in mechanisation came in 1843 and during the next twenty years the trade was gradually transformed into a mechanised, factory-based process. Machine combs were expensive and for a number of years in the 1850s excessively so. Samuel Cunliffe Lister (qv), one of the inventors of an efficient machine comb, held all the patents for several years, restricted production and charged a monopoly price. But machine combing cheapened production costs enormously. Many firms were therefore happy to leave the operation of combing and the production of the 'tops' required for spinning in the hands of the specialists. It was also easier for many of them, particularly the medium-size and smaller firms, to leave the production of yarns with the specialists; most of them needed to use a variety of different qualities and types and did not want to deal with the difficulties and expenses this involved. As the most important pioneer in the use and development of machine combing, the Bradford trade always had a considerable business in semi-manufactured products and this increased to enormous size as the international markets expanded after about 1840.

By the mid-1860s, Lister's patent rights were exhausted and a new range of cheaper combs became available. About this time the Illingworth brothers decided to expand their business premises and built a new and modern factory a little further up the Thornton Road. After their father's death in 1854, the two brothers took over as joint partners, continuing to use the name Daniel Illingworth & Sons. The factory, Whetley Mills, was opened in 1865. It was one of the largest in Bradford, employing in 1873 946 'mill-hands' and operatives — 296 of them were half-timers under twelve years of age, and altogether over 600 of them were under eighteen. Alfred Illingworth had charge of the woolbuying and marketing. Henry took over the internal management of the firm. The firm remained a private company until it became part of the new Illingworth, Morris amalgamation in 1922. It became one of the largest of the specialist combing and spinning firms in the town of Bradford, which during Illingworth's lifetime became the capital of the international worsted textile industry.

By the time the Whetley Mills were opened, the Illingworths formed part of a powerful alliance of great importance in the political and social life of Liberal Bradford. Alfred and Henry Illingworth married respectively Margaret (in 1866) and Mary Holden (in 1860), two of the daughters of Isaac Holden (qv), and Angus Holden (the girls' brother) married Margaret Illingworth, the oldest sister of the Illingworths (in 1866). Holden's new mill in Bradford stood about a mile away from the Whetley Mill. The three brothers-in-law lived within walking distance of each other all their lives and within walking distance of their works: Alfred at Daisy Bank in Allerton, Henry at Lady Royd next door and Angus at Woodlands in Manningham. Thus the Illingworths retained their close connection with Bradford. They were one of the few very successful entrepreneurial families of the nineteenth century who did not put a great deal of distance between their homes and the sources of their wealth. Alfred, however, had a country house at Stanbury near Haworth where he is said to have entertained his friends at weekends, lavishly, and where he indulged in what appears to have been his only recreations — a little gentlemanly shooting and billiards. The strength of the alliance was shown several years later. In 1885, three of its members were MPs. Alfred sat for Bradford West where the family factories and homes were and where most of their employees lived; Angus Holden sat for Bradford East and Isaac Holden for Keighley. Angus also represented West Ward and later East Ward on the town council and was mayor of the borough from 1878 to 1881 and again in 1886-87.

It was as a politician rather than as a businessman that Alfred Illingworth was to make his mark on local and national events. By the time he was thirty-eight, he was one of the two or three most important local members of the Liberal-Radical interest and between 1885 and 1895 was its undisputed leader — the most powerful politician in Bradford. He sat as MP for Knaresborough between 1868 and 1874 and for Bradford from 1880 to 1895. During these years his business activities were much reduced, the firm being managed by his brother, Henry, until he died in 1895 and it was then taken over by Alfred's sons and nephews.

Illingworth's politics were the natural extension of his social and business experience and illustrate the philosophy and the methods by which a Liberal Nonconformist millowner exercised authority within the community. Brought up in the Baptist faith, he had vivid memories of his father's part in the Church Rates controversies of the 1830s and 1840s.

Though never in adult life a full member of any religious community, he was a militant radical in the politics of religion, placing the disestablishment of the Anglican Church in a position of first importance. At the national level he was one of the most active members of the Liberation Society, national treasurer for a number of years and a close friend and colleague of Edward Miall, secretary to the Society and editor of the *Nonconformist*. Relying on the support of the powerful Nonconformist communities in Bradford he brought the religious issue to the centre of Bradford politics between 1867 and 1874. In these years his influence lay behind the election of Miall as one of the MPs for Bradford. He was also the most powerful voice in the opposition to the other Bradford MP, W E Forster, and the Education Act of 1870 of which Forster was the progenitor.

In political economy he was a pure Manchester school Liberal. For him the concept of free trade was a moral as much as an economic issue. Individualism, the freedom of every man to determine his own way, was a passionately held and often bitterly argued principle; government intervention in all and any of the affairs of men was to be kept to a minimum and taxation was to be as low as possible. He was a man of peace, a long time member of the Peace Society and a determined opponent of the many warlike undertakings pursued by the British Government from the Crimea to South Africa and the borders of India. Unmerited privilege was anathema, and landlordism a simple denial of justice. He remained until his death committed to the urgent need of freedom for Ireland.

Illingworth's career illustrates very precisely the dilemma that Radical middle class employers faced in dealing with the problems of the working classes. He was one of the leading exponents in Bradford of the necessity of an alliance between middle class Radicals and the workers. He threw himself into the struggle for reform of the franchise — the secret ballot and the working class vote. His early enthusiasms for manhood suffrage had diminished during the Chartist troubles, and he settled like many others for the cautious gradualism of household suffrage and a registered lodger suffrage. He expected leadership to flow from middle class to working class, from employer to employee, from those who had shown their worth to those who (in the middle class language of the day) still needed the moral, social, and intellectual improvement which education and effective leadership could provide. He took the lead in Bradford in institutionalising the political activities of the new voters created by the Reform agitation of the 1860s. In 1860 he helped to organise the Bradford Working Men's Reform Committee, designed to appeal to 'the most intelligent and judicious ... men of integrity and character ...' (in practice the better paid). {*Bradford Review* 28 July 1868} In 1868, his was the most important influence in the creation of the Bradford Liberal Association which brought into a single body all the Liberal and Radical associations in the town. In it, effective power lay with an executive of 24 men of whom four were working men. For years in Bradford it was a fertile source of what was known there as 'Illingworthism'.

His attitude towards labour as such was also revealing. He believed that the arrangements made between employer and employee were matters for individuals and that individual contracts should be made with the least possible interference from the state or from trade unions. Attempts to limit hours of work by law or to get equalisation of wages in firms and industries through the trade unions were an invasion of the employers' rights and a challenge to the dignity of working men. In addition to their 'friendly society' role he thought trade unions might have useful functions in helping to organise the labour market and in educating their members in the principles of the market economy. He accepted the right of trade unions to a legal existence, but voted in the House of Commons with those who wanted severe restrictions on their powers.

As the century drew to a close, however, Illingworth's type of Liberalism came under serious challenge. A new radicalism demanded a degree of social generosity in dealing with the problems of working class life. Illingworth remained a Manchester Liberal opposed to any sort of intervention in the market; he either rejected outright or blew cold on all proposals for social reform. He was found rejecting proposals for the eight-hour day, defending female labour and the half-time system as the only means by which working class people could improve their living standards, and avoiding discussion about old age pensions by denying that any sensible scheme had yet appeared.

He did nothing to help the campaign for direct working class representation in town council and in parliament. He had supported the candidature of James Hardaker, a stone-mason put up by the Trades Council in the election of 1874, but his intention had really been to keep such indications of working class independence under control. A more widely diffused threat appeared in the 1890s — the local Labour Electoral Association which wanted to see more workingmen standing as Liberal nominees. Although it guaranteed its loyalty to the Liberal party, it got scant encouragement. Illingworth, however, reserved his fiercest hostility for an entirely new body, the Independent Labour Party just emerging between 1891 and 1893. Both its appearance and its ultimate success in Bradford owed a great deal to the intransigence of Illingworth and his friends.

His dissatisfaction with the way Liberal policy was developing hardened between 1892 and 1895 and he retired from the House of Commons. For several years he continued his battle against the Labour party but, disgusted with the 'New Radical' attitude to Labour, withdrew from politics totally in 1900. He came back again between 1903 and 1906. He tried unsuccessfully to impede the Balfour Education Act (1902) which, he thought, strengthened the position of the Anglican Church in education. He tried once again to rally the opposition to the new party, for F W Jowett, Bradford's leading Socialist, had been nominated as parliamentary candidate in what had really been for years the Illingworth 'pocket' constituency — Bradford West. Jowett was elected and became Bradford's first Labour MP.

After 1900, and his first retirement from Liberal affairs in Bradford, Illingworth had lived quietly. He travelled abroad a little and spent a good deal of time at his country house at Stanbury. In 1902 he was made a freeman of the City of Bradford. He died on 2 January 1907 in his

ILLINGWORTH Alfred

eightieth year, leaving personal assets of £172,470 gross. He was survived by his wife (d 1919) and his six sons. Two of them, Hampden Holden Illingworth and Eustace Holden Illingworth entered the family firm, Daniel Illingworth & Sons, along with two cousins, Henry's sons; Alfred Holden Illingworth became a partner in the firm of Fraser & Co, of Liverpool, Bradford and Buenos Aires; Francis Holden Illingworth became a solicitor; Norman Holden Illingworth entered the medical profession; Dudley Holden Illingworth became a partner in the firm of Cole, Marchant & Morley Ltd, engineers.

As a businessman Illingworth enjoyed the success which a capable man, joint inheritor of a well-established firm, was likely to earn in the boom conditions of the Victorian economy. A parliamentary colleague recalled him as

> A man too seldom humorous, and perhaps too often passionate and bitter; one interested in few things but profoundly interested in these; with few emotions but strong ones, proud and reserved; overscornful if anything but immediately combative once challenged by any sort of antagonist {*Yorkshire Daily Observer* 2 Jan 1907}.

As important as the claim for personal freedom was, his bitter antagonism against almost any intervention in industrial affairs, left him open to the challenge that his views in the final analysis were dictated by his circumstances. He sat in the House of Commons primarily as the representative of Bradford's business interest and simply wanted to retain as much as he could of the once absolute authority of the millowner and manufacturer. There is no doubt that the expression of his views strengthened in incalculable ways the appeal of the new Labour Party in Bradford.

JACK REYNOLDS

Writings:

Fifty Years of Politics: Mr Alfred Illingworth's Retrospect (Bradford: Bradford Printing Co, 1905).

Sources:

Unpublished

MCe.

PrC.

Brian S Diggle, 'Illingworthism, Alfred Illingworth and Independent Labour Politics' (Huddersfield Polytechnic MA, 1984).

Published

William Cudworth, *Manningham, Heaton and Allerton (Townships of Bradford) Treated Historically and Topographically* (Bradford: pp, 1896).

Eustace H Illingworth (ed), *The Holden-Illingworth Letters* (Bradford: Lund, Humphreys, 1927).

Keith Laybourn and Jack Reynolds, *Liberalism and the Rise of Labour 1890-1918* (Croom Helm, 1984).

Jack Reynolds, *The Great Paternalist, Titus Salt and the Growth of Nineteenth Century Bradford* (Temple Smith, 1983).

Eric M Sigsworth, *Black Dyke Mills, a History* (Liverpool: Liverpool University Press, 1958).

David G Wright and James A Jowitt, *Victorian Bradford, Essays in Honour of Jack Reynolds* (Bradford: City of Bradford Metropolitan Council, 1981).

WWMP.

WWW.

INGLIS, Sir James Charles

(1851-1911)

Civil engineer and railway executive

James Charles Inglis was born in Aberdeen on 9 September 1851, the only son among the three children born to James Inglis and his wife Jane née Smith. His father, brought up in Mosstodloch near Fochabers in Morayshire, settled in Aberdeen in 1836. He became the proprietor of two baker's shops and leader in the local trade association, the Bakers' Corporation; he was also a leading member of the Free Church.

James Charles Inglis attended Aberdeen Grammar School and then Aberdeen University, 1867-70, where he studied natural science and mathematics, taking prizes in both. He did not complete the degree, having decided after working in the shop of a village millwright during the vacations that he wished to train as an engineer. After two years in the workshops of Messrs Norman, Copeland & Co, millwrights of Glasgow, he became a pupil (1871-74) of James Abernethy of London, a sometime president of the Institution of Civil Engineers, and soon became engaged in docks and harbour construction, notably at Newport, South Wales (the Alexandra Docks).

This professional training gave Inglis a lot of career mobility, in particular it enabled him to move from fee paying assignments to salaried positions and back again. Thus in 1875 he took the position of salaried assistant to the chief engineer of the South Devon Railway, which within a

423

year was for practical purposes absorbed by the Great Western Railway. Under Peter Margary he was engaged in the construction of Plymouth station, the Harbour Railway at Plymouth and the widening of the Newton Abbot-Torquay line. In 1877 he became the resident engineer at the company's docks at Millbay, Plymouth. Between 1878 and 1892 he returned to private practice, mainly accepting commissions in the South West of England. However, he retained his association with the GWR and supervised the building of the Princetown (1881-83) and Bodmin (1887) branches.

In June 1892, at the age of forty-one, he rejoined the GWR as a salaried employee, remaining with the company until his death in 1911. He was appointed as the assistant engineer to Louis Trench during the final stage of the conversion of the company's broad gauge track to narrow (standard) gauge in the four remaining counties of the South West. Trench, who was the only outsider ever to be appointed to such a senior position in the engineering department, was overbearing towards his divisional officers. After a disagreement with the board over his managerial style, Trench resigned and returned to the London & North Western Railway. Inglis replaced him in October 1892 at a salary of £1,200 a year. Over the following decade, as the company's engineer, he was responsible for a considerable annual budget. This fluctuated between £1.2 million and £2.6 million and always exceeded £2 million between 1898 and 1903, as the investment decisions made on the basis of transient high profits and low interest rates in the late 1890s were realised. The emphasis was upon the replacement of timber viaducts in Cornwall and 'cut-offs' to reduce the length of mainline journeys so as to improve the company's competitive edge. Altogether 230 additional route miles were built, making a total network of 2,695 route miles which the engineering department maintained in 1903.

In June of that year Inglis became the company's general manager, succeeding Sir Joseph Wilkinson (qv) who had died in office. Tradition was thus maintained by the decision to appoint an insider. In other respects, however, his appointment was exceptional. He was the first general manager in the company's history to have attended university and the only one to have an engineering background. In this second respect the GWR followed the recent precedent of the Lancashire & Yorkshire Railway and heralded a slight departure from the common practice whereby the majority of general managers in Britain had a background in traffic or administrative departments. Also unusually, Inglis combined the office of general manager, for which he was paid £3,000 a year, with that of the company's consulting engineer, for which he received £500 and then (1904) £1,000 a year. He therefore preserved his status as a professional engineer while fulfilling the responsibilities of the chief executive of the third largest railway company (judged by traffic receipts) in the country.

Inglis assumed office at a time when there was a good deal of public and company discussion about railway management, in particular its efficiency and the related issues of its recruitment and training. In common with British railways generally, the preceding few years had seen a rise in the GWR's operating ratio (the contemporary yardstick for efficiency) from around 55 per cent to 62 per cent and a decline in the ratio of net receipts to capital expended. Inglis continued and developed the forward policies of his predecessor with regard to staff training, the promotion of express and long distance trains, improved advertising and the introduction of road and rail motor services; he was also an advocate of pooling agreements to moderate inter-company competition. Further 'cut-off' lines were built and Inglis, in his engineering capacity, designed a major harbour development, at Fishguard, and established a connecting service of high-speed turbine steamers with Rosslare in Ireland. Between 1903 and 1911 total operating receipts rose by 21.2 per cent; the operating ratio was stabilised and the ratio of net receipts to capital expended showed, in the final two years of Inglis's life, a modest improvement.

Inglis was not satisfied. He believed that the company's efficiency and financial results were being damaged by the intransigent attitude of the heads of department to his plans for improved interdepartmental co-ordination and accountability through the general manager. As the company's engineer he had been aware of the damage inflicted on the permanent way by the heavier, faster trains that were being assembled by the superintendent of the line; yet neither the general manager nor the board seemed easily able to handle the problem. As general manager it appears that he had difficulty in containing the expenditure plans of the brilliant locomotive engineer, G J Churchward, and was unaware of the excessive provision for locomotive depreciation that the chief accountant was ascribing as a liability in the general balance sheet, which therefore gave an exaggerated picture of the growth of expenditure. The root of the trouble was the direct access that departmental heads had to the board or its subcommittees, disregarding therefore the general manager and his small office (42 staff in 1911). Inglis tried to bring the company into line with the practice of the other leading railways but failed: his organisation chart showing the general manager as the focus of executive decision-making, while approved by the board in 1910, lacked practical substance. The stress that such internal conflicts imposed on Inglis probably contributed to his death a year later at the age of sixty.

Inglis was the second general manager of the GWR to receive a knighthood (1910), an honour that, by the early twentieth century but not before, was more often than not awarded to the chief executive of a leading railway. In his case the honour was in part recognition of the service he gave as a member of several public bodies, including the following: the Royal Commission on Canals and Inland Navigation (1905-9); the Engineering Standards Committee (1905), when he represented the Institution of Civil Engineers; a government mission that went to Malaya to advise on the purchase of Tanjong Docks as a naval base; and the Board of Trade Railway Conference which considered working agreements, pools and other combinations between railways. His profession also honoured him for, having served on the council since 1897, he achieved the rare distinction of being elected to the presidency of the Institution of Civil Engineers in two successive years, 1908 and 1909.

Sir James, a bachelor, died on 19 December 1911 at Rottingdean, Sussex. His personal estate was valued at £124,554 gross, including £18,732 in the Canadian Pacific Railway and £12,437 in the Powell Duffryn Steam Coal Co Ltd. He left £5,000 towards the cost of a new building for the

Institution (then being built in Great George Street, Westminster), a last gesture that signified his lifetime commitment to a strong, centralised professional body for civil engineers which he hoped, as a Liberal Unionist, would promote their interests throughout the British Empire.

GEOFFREY CHANNON

Writings:

'The Design of Permanent Way and Locomotives for High Speeds' *Engineering* 75 (1906).

Presidential Address *Proceedings of the Institution of Civil Engineers* 175 (1908), 176 (1909).

PP, RC Canals and Waterways, 1905–9, Fourth and Final Report (1910) C 4979.

Various contributions to the *Great Western Railway Magazine*.

Sources:

Unpublished

PRO, Kew, Great Western Railway Co reports and accounts, minutes and memoranda, in particular: Analysis of the accounts 1882-1912, RAIL 266/14; Reports on broad gauge conversion 1872-92, RAIL 254/49; general manager's fortnightly reports to the board from 1903, RAIL 250/429, etc; reorganisation of the engineering department 1904, RAIL 267/259; report on motor car services 1904, RAIL 267/258.

PrC.

Communication with the Rector of Aberdeen Grammar School, Robert D Gill.

Published

Engineer 112 (22 Dec 1912).

Engineering 92 (22 Dec 1912).

T R Gourvish, 'A British Business Elite: The Chief Executive Managers of the Railway Industry, 1850-1922' *Business History Review* 47 (1973).

Great Western Railway Magazine 23 (1911), 24 (1912).

E T MacDermot, *History of the Great Western Railway* (rev edn by C R Clinker, 2 vols, Ian Allan, 1964).

John Marshall, *Biographical Dictionary of Railway Engineers* (Newton Abbot: David & Charles, 1978).

Felix J C Pole, *Felix J C Pole: His Book* (Reading, 1954, privately circulated; Bracknell: Town & Country Press, 1968).

Harold Pollins, *Britain's Railways: An Industrial History* (Newton Abbot: David & Charles, 1971).

PP, Report of Board of Trade Railway Conference (1909) Cd 4677.

Proceedings of the Institution of Civil Engineers 187 (1911-12).

Railway Yearbook 1904.

Jack Simmons, *The Railway in England and Wales 1830-1914* (Leicester: Leicester University Press, 1978).

WWW.

INMAN, William

(1825-1881)

Shipowner in transatlantic emigrant and passenger trades

William Inman was born in Leicester on 6 April 1825, the fourth son of Charles Inman and Jane née Clay. His father came of a Lancashire family and had been in cotton and American business at Liverpool before moving to Leicester in 1818 to join the firm of Pickford & Co, the well-known carriers. He managed their Midlands business until 1838, when he left the firm and returned to Liverpool. William was educated at Leicester Grammar School, Liverpool Collegiate Institute, and Liverpool Royal Institution. He was then apprenticed as a clerk to Messrs Cairns & Co, provision merchants, moving on later to Cater & Co, and finally to Richardson Brothers & Co. The brothers were Irish Quakers engaged in the linen and provision trades. From 1846, William Inman managed the Richardson sailing packets which traded between Liverpool and Philadelphia. He gained an intimate knowledge of the transatlantic emigrant trade, and in January 1849 he became a partner in the firm.

In 1850 Inman followed with interest the voyages of the *City of Glasgow*, an iron screw steamship recently built at Glasgow by Tod & McGregor. The vessel was only the third iron screw steamer to cross the Atlantic, and she made good passages between Glasgow and New York. Inman persuaded his partners to buy the *City of Glasgow* from her builders, who had been running the vessel on their own account. Thus began a long association between Inman and Tod & McGregor. The *City of Glasgow* became the first vessel of the newly-formed Liverpool & Philadelphia Steam Ship Co. On 11 December 1850, she sailed from Liverpool carrying 400 emigrants, and took twenty-two days to reach Philadelphia owing to rough weather. For the first time emigrants had been taken across the Atlantic by steamship. The vessel's homeward passage was only thirteen days sixteen hours, just one day and sixteen

Inman Line's berth, Pier 45, New Harbour, from the Inman Line Guide, 1878.

hours longer than a contemporary passage by a Cunard paddle steamer on the appreciably shorter homeward run from Boston.

Until Inman took this bold initiative and introduced steamships into the emigrant trade, there were two very different ways of carrying passengers across the Atlantic. The richer passengers went in the wooden paddle steamers of the British Cunard and the American Collins lines, firms subsidised by mail contracts from their respective Governments. The emigrants made the voyage in wooden sailing ships, often enduring long passages and appalling conditions. It was believed that steamships were so costly to run on the North Atlantic route that only government subsidies in the form of mail contracts could make such shipping lines profitable. Inman believed that he could run a profitable transatlantic steamship line without government support by using the latest marine technology — the

INMAN LINE

(ESTABLISHED 1850).

ROYAL MAIL STEAMERS.

LIVERPOOL to NEW YORK, Tuesdays and Thursdays,
NEW YORK to LIVERPOOL, Thursdays and Saturdays,

Calling at QUEENSTOWN each way.

	Tons		Tons
CITY OF BERLIN	5491	CITY OF NEW YORK	3500
CITY OF RICHMOND	4607	CITY OF PARIS	3081
CITY OF CHESTER	4566	CITY OF BROOKLYN	2911
CITY OF MONTREAL	4490	CITY OF LIMERICK	2536
CITY OF BRUSSELS	3775	CITY OF ANTWERP	2391

The first Transatlantic Line to adopt Lieut. MAURY'S LANE ROUTES, taking the Southerly course between the months of January and August.

These Steamers are built especially to meet the requirements of the Admiralty, and are fitted with watertight compartments.

They are among the strongest, largest, and fastest on the Atlantic, reducing the passage to a minimum, giving thereby especial comfort to passengers.

The saloons are large, luxuriously furnished, especially well lighted and ventilated, and take up the whole width of the ship amidships.

The principal staterooms are amidships, forward of the engines, where least noise and motion is felt; and all the cabins are particularly light and airy, and replete with every comfort, having all latest improvements, double berths, electric bells, &c.

The cuisine has always been a specialité of this line.

Ladies' cabins and bathrooms, Gentlemen's smoking and bathrooms, Barbers' shops, pianos, libraries, &c., provided.

Experienced Surgeons and Stewardesses carried.

SALOON PASSAGE—FIFTEEN, EIGHTEEN, and TWENTY-ONE Guineas, according to accommodation. Return Tickets at Reduced Rates.

THROUGH BOOKING.

Passengers booked to all parts of the UNITED STATES and CANADA, as also to SAN FRANCISCO, CALIFORNIA, AUSTRAILA, NEW ZEALAND, INDIA, CHINA and JAPAN, by Union Pacific Railway and Pacific Mail Steamers at lowest through rates.

Inman Line advertisement, from the Inman Line Guide, 1878.

iron-hulled screw-driven steamship — to lower costs and by ensuring a large and constant flow of passengers to bring in revenue. Inman found his market among the slightly better-off emigrants who were ready to pay a little extra in return for a faster passage and better conditions than could be provided by the sailing packets.

Profit was Inman's goal, but he was also concerned to improve conditions for the emigrants. In the early days of his line, he and his wife made a transatlantic crossing in steerage to see how the lot of the emigrant passenger could be improved. One of the main improvements was simply the faster passage. The sailing packets took around thirty-five days, Inman vessels fourteen or fifteen. They were still not as fast as Cunard or Collins ships, but the new passage times were a great improvement. A faster crossing was welcome, but Inman still charged eight guineas for a steerage passage from Liverpool to Philadelphia, nearly twice the cost of passage in a sailing ship. He therefore had to provide further benefits for the emigrant, such as better accommodation, regular food, hot water, and, most important of all, the assurance of good health on voyage, for Inman refused to allow sick emigrants aboard his vessels and so avoided the epidemics which had often ravaged the sailing packets. The Inman vessels always carried a number of wealthier cabin passengers, and over the years increasing efforts were made to cater for that market, but the emigrant trade remained the backbone of the business. By the time of Inman's death in 1881, his line had carried more than one million emigrants from the British Isles to America.

Inman's gamble was rapidly successful. In 1851 he acquired a second iron screw steamship and placed orders for several others with Tod & McGregor. Then, in 1854, Inman suffered two blows. First the *City of Glasgow* disappeared at sea with nearly 500 passengers and crew, the worst marine disaster involving a steamship up to that time, and then the latest addition to his fleet was wrecked off Newfoundland on her maiden voyage, but without loss of life. Inman's fleet was thus reduced once again to a single vessel, and although two others were under construction at Glasgow, the future of the line seemed to be in doubt. Inman was rescued by the outbreak of the Crimean War which offered lucrative employment for his ships as transports on charter to the Government. The one obstacle was that Inman's partners, the Richardson brothers, were Quakers and opposed the use of their vessels for warlike purposes. Inman was thus forced to buy them out. Because he disliked the terms offered by the British Government, Inman hired his sole existing ship to the French Government in 1854, and she was followed by the two Glasgow vessels when they were completed in 1855. Inman also bought a fourth steamer which was already under contract as a transport to the British Government.

Inman did not resume his transatlantic service until his four ships ended their transport duties in 1856, and after some initial difficulties his ships began to achieve good earnings. By this time it was clear that New York was the chief port by which emigrants entered America, so in 1857 Inman switched most of his sailings there and changed the name of his firm to the Liverpool, New York & Philadelphia Steam Ship Co. Soon after this change, there arose what seemed to be a great opportunity for Inman. In 1858, the Collins line went out of business and Inman took over its sailing days from New York and also agreed to carry United States mails for ocean postage only. Inman offered to carry British mails on the same terms, but the British Government refused to break Cunard's monopoly. Then Inman learned, to his fury, that a new transatlantic steamship line, the Galway Line, was to be established, and that it would have a

City of Berlin *passenger steamer,*
from the Inman Line Guide 1878.

government mail contract and be able to poach his emigrant trade by
taking emigrants direct from Ireland to America with no necessity for
them to go to Liverpool. As a reaction to this threat, Inman's ships began
to make regular calls at Irish ports on their transatlantic voyages, and
Inman himself demanded that the Galway Line should lose its privileges.
He pointed out that in 1858 his fleet of iron screw steamers, totalling
11,000 tons and built at a cost of £300,000, had carried more passengers to
and from America than any other transatlantic steamship line. Partly as a
result of Inman's pressure, the Galway Line lost its mail contract in 1861,
and when there was talk of reviving it in 1863, Inman renewed his attacks,
pointing out that his line was far more important than the Galway
company. In 1862 Inman ships had carried 29,000 people across the
Atlantic, about a third of all passengers conveyed by steamships, and
Inman believed that if anybody should have a mail contract it should be
he.

Neither the Galway Line nor Inman received a mail contract, but this
scarcely mattered to the latter. Inman's business prospered during the
American Civil War, and in 1865 Inman could look back on a considerable
achievement. In the nine years since his ships had returned to the North
Atlantic after the Crimean War, sailings had increased from one a
fortnight to two a week, and the fleet had grown from four ships to 13. At
the end of the American Civil War transatlantic emigration boomed, but
this brought increased competition as more shipping companies entered
the lucrative North Atlantic passenger trade. At the end of 1867, Inman
won his first British mail contract, to Halifax, Nova Scotia, and then one
to the United States in 1868. Although Inman had sought British
transatlantic mail contracts at various times after 1858, he had always
boasted that his line had prospered without government subsidies. Also,
by the late 1860s, British Governments had made mail contracts less
attractive in financial terms. Why then was Inman so keen to obtain mail
contracts at this time?

No doubt it was partly the pressure of increased competition on the
North Atlantic routes which made Inman glad of any financial support he
could obtain. Also, a mail contract would help Inman to escape the
Passenger Acts. These acts laid down that all vessels carrying emigrants

were to be closely inspected before they left British ports, and Inman hated them because they slowed down his vessels. Royal Mail ships were usually exempt from such inspections so that the mails would not be delayed. Equally importantly, Inman told the 1869 parliamentary committee on mail contracts that one of the chief reasons he wanted such contracts, so often lavished on Cunard, was to set the seal on his company's achievement.

The year 1870 probably marked the zenith of the Inman Line. Inman had a fleet of 18 ships, totalling nearly 40,000 tons; he had British and American mail contracts; and he dominated the North Atlantic passenger trade. In that year his ships, in 68 voyages, landed 3,635 cabin passengers and 40,465 steerage passengers at New York. Inman's total of 44,100 passengers carried exceeded that of any other transatlantic steamship line to date.

The North Atlantic passenger trade continued to boom in the early 1870s, and competition became even more intense, especially after the appearance of the White Star Line in 1871. Inman, along with the other established transatlantic lines, began to lay down new vessels to match the White Star ships, but in 1873 boom gave way to slump. By 1875, Inman was cutting back his sailings, but even without this, the cost of building four large ships between 1872 and 1875, as well as rebuilding older vessels, put a considerable strain on the company's finances. Each of the four new vessels cost over £100,000, and the last one, the 5,500 ton *City of Berlin* of 1875, cost nearly £200,000, and was the largest merchant ship afloat in the world when built, the *Great Eastern* having been laid up. Because of these financial burdens and the continuing depression, the old firm was wound up in 1875, and a company, the Inman Steam Ship Co Ltd, was set up in its place, partly in the hope of attracting new capital.

The transatlantic passenger trade remained depressed, and despite a deal with White Star about sailings in 1876, the Inman Line was not in a good state by 1879. The firm had some 12 ships, with work for only seven. Five were sold. Since only four of the remainder were less than ten years old, new investment in at least one new vessel was necessary. This was the 8,500 ton *City of Rome* which was launched in 1881 shortly before Inman's death. He was fortunate not to see her go into service as she proved to be a commercial failure and was returned to her builders. After Inman's death, the company got into increasing financial difficulties. New vessels were needed to match those built by rival firms, but the necessary capital could not be obtained. In 1886, the Inman Line was taken over by American interests, and in 1893 the remaining ships were put under the American flag.

Whatever its official title, the firm run by William Inman was known to the public as the Inman Line from a very early period in its history. However, Inman was never rich enough to have complete control of his company. In 1867, the Liverpool, New York & Philadelphia Steam Ship Co had some 15 proprietors, and although William Inman had the largest individual share, the Inman family share was smaller than that of the Birley family. Three members of the Birley family were proprietors, giving their occupations as owners of flax and cotton mills in Lancashire. Then came the Inman family group, comprising William Inman, his brother Charles, a Liverpool banker, and another brother, Thomas, a

Liverpool doctor. The third largest group of proprietors was the three members of the Lepper family of Belfast, who owned flax mills. Among the other proprietors were Tod & McGregor, the Glasgow shipbuilders, a Durham coalowner related to William Inman's wife, a Belfast banker, a London gentleman, and a number of Lancashire gentlemen. The proprietors generally enjoyed good dividends, for the company paid an annual average of £67,000 over the fifteen years 1860-74. The best year was 1862 with a dividend of £179,000, and there was a loss in only one year, a serious debit of £97,000 in 1874. This latter blow was one of the reasons the old firm was liquidated in 1875 and replaced by a public company, Inman Steam Ship Co Ltd. Most of the shares in the new company were held by the old proprietors, with the Birleys still having a bigger holding than the Inmans, but some new investors were brought in to provide more capital.

William Inman was one of the founding members of the Liverpool Steamship Owners Association in 1858, and was its chairman in 1862 and 1868-69. He was also a member of the Mersey Docks & Harbour Board and sat on the local marine board. Inman was a member of the first Liverpool School Board, a JP in Cheshire, and a captain in the Cheshire Rifle Volunteers. He took a hand in Tory politics, but was never an MP. Inman was an Anglican by religion and built churches at the villages of Upton and Moreton in Cheshire and a mission hall for seamen in Liverpool.

William Inman married Anne Brewis Stobart, daughter of William Stobart of Picktree, County Durham, on 20 December 1849; they had nine sons and three daughters. Once he was successful, Inman moved out of Liverpool and lived at Upton in Cheshire. He also had a house called the Abbey at Windermere, with a number of steam launches on the lake. William Inman died at Upton Manor on 3 July 1881, leaving a personal estate worth £121,359 gross (resworn at £20,252 gross in 1883, according to an annotation on PrC).

ALAN G JAMIESON

Writings:

PP, HC 1860 (530) XIII, SC on Merchant Shipping.

PP, HC 1868-69 (106) VI, SC on Mail Contracts.

The Loss of the 'City of Boston'. Inman v Jenkins. An Action for Libel Trial at Liverpool Assizes (Liverpool: Lee & Nightingale, 1870).

PP, HC 1874 (227) X, SC on Merchant Ships (Measurement of Tonnage) Bill.

Sources:

Unpublished

Liverpool RO, papers of Inman Steam Ship Co Ltd (387 INM).

PrC.

Published

Noel R P Bonsor, *North Atlantic Seaway* (Prescot: T Stephenson & Sons, 1955).

DNB.

The Inman Steamship Company Limited Official Guide (Thomson Bros, 1878).

Clement W Jones, *Pioneer Shipowners* (2 vols, Liverpool: Birchall & Sons, 1935, 1938) I.

William S Lindsay, *History of Merchant Shipping and Ancient Commerce* (4 vols, Sampson Low, 1874-76) 4.

PP, HC 1859 (230) (Sess I) XVII, Postal Communication with North America.

PP, HC 1863 (68) XXX, Correspondence on the Subject of the Restoration of the Galway Subsidy.

PP, 1867-68 (42) XLI, Papers Relating to North American Mail Contracts.

David B Tyler, *Steam Conquers the Atlantic* (New York: D Appleton-Century Co, 1939).

INSTONE, Sir Samuel

(1878-1937)

Coal, shipping and airline entrepreneur

Samuel Instone was born at Gravesend, Kent, on 16 August 1878, eldest of the three sons of Adolphe Instone. He attended a school at Tunbridge Wells and another at Boulogne-sur-Mer. He left there to enter the family shipping business and soon became an expert on trade between Great Britain and the Continent. Sometime before the First World War he set up S Instone & Co Ltd, at Cardiff (which went public in December 1921 with a capital of £500,000, £300,000 issued) to provide coal shipping services on the Antwerp-London and Antwerp-Cardiff routes. Quick to seize chances of cutting expenses, before the war he bought the Bow Creek site of the London Iron Works and established the Instone Wharf there with direct connections to what would become the London & North Eastern Railway, so avoiding the time-consuming passage of goods through the busy East End and the City of London. In his business activities Instone worked closely with his brothers, Theodore and Alfred.

After the First World War, he was most anxious to speed up the movement of bills of lading so that his ships were not kept in demurrage while the paperwork was being processed, and for this reason he started

Vickers Vulcan City of Antwerp *1922 (courtesy of Professor Robin Higham).*

the Instone Air Line (registered as a company on 21 December 1921) on 13 October 1919. At first it carried only documentation, but later passengers were taken from London to Paris and shortly thereafter the services expanded to include also Brussels, the Riviera, Cologne, with plans for Prague, Baghdad and India. By prudent management, including the sponsorship for the DH-34 single-engined passenger aeroplane, the Instone Air Line managed to survive with subsidies totalling £119,234. In the year 1922-23 the Instone Air Line had passenger revenues of £21,683 and a government subsidy of £38,789. Run like the shipping company, it made money by developing freight and other sidelines. The Instone Air Line was closed down as a result of the Hambling Report of 1923 which recommended that Britain create 'a chosen instrument' (named Imperial Airways after being formed) which would compete with foreign subsidised airlines. Instone had owned or still had on charge 20 aircraft in March 1924 when it was absorbed into Imperial Airways, in which Instones had a £46,000 share, partly in stock. Sir Samuel Instone (he was knighted in 1921) joined the IA board and remained an active member until his death — the dominant force on the board was Sir Eric Geddes (qv).

In the meantime, Instone's shipping interests led him into the coal trade, coal being one of his principal cargoes. He bought into the Askern Coal & Iron Co Ltd of Yorkshire, and the Bedwas Navigation Colliery Co (1921) Ltd of South Wales, becoming chairman of each. Facing a depression in coal prices in the 1920s, along with geological difficulties, the Bedwas collieries ran into a financial crisis which took Instone into the limelight of a series of industrial relations conflicts. The company borrowed £300,000 from the parent company, S Instone & Co, and £1 million from Barclays Bank which in 1928 appointed an adviser to the management. In an effort to reduce labour costs, price lists (piece rates for miners) were cut and work was contracted out. A strike followed in 1933 when over a thousand men turned out, leaving 60 at work. With unemployment high, the company had no difficulty in recruiting miners from other localities and formally recognised the less militant South Wales Miners' Industrial Union, the alternative to the South Wales Miners' Federation. The strike soon broke and men went back to reduced wages. Over the next three years the labour situation festered, fed by a torrent of propaganda from all sides and including a pamphlet, reprinted in the regional newspaper in 1936, by Sir Samuel Instone. Instone vehemently resisted appeals to recognise the South Wales Miners' Federation, the majority but more militant union in the industry, despite pressure from the Government's Mines Department. His obstinacy was rooted in a refusal to concede control of the colliery's working conditions, won since 1933; 'profit was', he openly admitted, 'the principle' {Francis and Smith (1980) 331}. The Bedwas Company's reported debt burden of £1 million and depletion of the Miners' Federation strike fund forced a compromise in 1936 when 'the Federation ... accepted the management's rule in the pit (with some safeguards) in return for the vital recognition of the SWMF' {*ibid*, 338-39}.

As a coal proprietor Sir Samuel Instone combated falling coal prices not only by reducing his labour costs but by a vigorous pursuit of technical innovation. In 1928 he formed British Benzol & Coal Distillation Ltd with an authorised and issued capital of £250,000. He brought Sir Arthur Duckham (qv) onto the founding board and the £290,000 contract for building the plant (35 ovens and associated retorts for producing coal by-products, particularly coke, gas, tar, benzol) went to the Woodall Duckham Co. Unfortunately the venture was ill-timed, though excusably so: the depression after 1929 weakened or removed many of the main customers for coke, in the iron and steel industry. A variety of cost-cutting exercises enabled the company to survive the worst years of the 1930s but in the process Instone fell out with Duckham over the causes of technical difficulties, with Instone blaming defects in the cleaning plant and Duckham coal quality. The controversy lasted throughout the decade, long after Duckham's early death, but the sales agents, the most independent witnesses, felt that Instone expected too much from his coal.

Beyond his company interests, but not unrelated to them, Instone was long concerned about the congestion of London's streets and proposed a system of waterbuses on the Thames to relieve traffic. In private life he was much attached to his brothers. A similar closeness characterised his very happy family life. He married in 1910 Alice Maud, daughter of Edward Liebman; they had five daughters, with whom Samuel spent musical evenings. He also enjoyed bridge and sailing.

Instone was known for his generosity, humour, approachability and inquisitive mind, always searching for industrial improvements. He loved all things mechanical, habitually examining them and making models of them.

Sir Samuel Instone died suddenly as a result of surgery on 9 November 1937 and was buried in the Jewish Cemetery, Beaconsfield Road, Willesden, North London. He left £1,034 gross.

ROBIN HIGHAM

Writings:

'The Bedwas Colliery: The Truth' *Western Mail* 22 Aug 1936.

Sources:

Published

Hywel Francis and David Smith, *The Fed: A History of the South Wales Miners in the Twentieth Century* (Lawrence & Wishart, 1980).

Robin Higham, *Britain's Imperial Air Routes, 1918-1939* (G T Foulis, 1960).

Graeme M Holmes, *Fifty Years of British Benzol: A History of British Benzol and Coal Distillation Ltd* (Cardiff: pp, the company, 1979).

Alfred Instone, *The Early Birds* (Cardiff: Western Mail & Echo Ltd, 1938).

David Smith, 'The Struggle against Company Unionism in the South Wales Coalfield, 1926-1939' *Welsh History Review* 6 (1972-73).

Times 10, 11, 12 Nov 1937.

WWW.

IRVIN, Richard

(1853-1920)

Trawler owner and fish salesman

Richard Irvin was born at North Shields on 23 February 1853, the eldest son of John Irvin, a shipwright, and his wife Sarah née Drummond. Richard's formal education was short as he started work in the family marine store business while a boy. At the age of eighteen he bought a second-hand sailing trawler and established himself as a fish salesman at North Shields, auctioning the catches of other boats as well as those of his own. Eventually he became one of several fish salesmen who revolutionised the sale of fish on Tyneside.

In 1877 Irvin converted a paddle tug into a trawler and became one of the first to change successfully from sail to steam. During the next ten years he built up a fleet of steam trawlers which fished as far north as Aberdeen.

The difference between Irvin and many of the other early owners was that he sought to organise the activities of his fleet. To this end he established an Aberdeen office in 1887. His decision to set up in Aberdeen was not due to chance; it was then the northernmost first-class railhead in Britain. It was also the city nearest to the northernmost fishing grounds of the North Sea. In practice this meant that his trawlers working from

IRVIN Richard

Richard Irvin auctioning fish (courtesy of Richard Irvin & Sons Ltd).

Aberdeen could land their catches fully two days earlier than trawlers from Hull or Grimsby.

Irvin's other striking characteristic was his willingness to innovate. By the early 1890s he was operating a new fleet of purpose-built 'sidewinder' trawlers. These used the new otter trawl, instead of the cumbersome beam trawl used by the old paddle trawlers, and were equipped with steam winches for hauling the net.

The successful manager of his own fleet, and drawing on his own experience in the family chandlery business, Irvin was soon selling management services to other owners. In 1905, for example, the Aberdeen office was acting as agent for a number of them. At the same time the North Shields and Aberdeen offices were supplying the industry with nets, sails, ropes and other gear.

Yet it took more than luck and an eye for the main chance to create a modern trawling fleet with bases at Aberdeen, North Shields, Scarborough and Milford Haven from a small beginning. By all accounts Irvin was a man of exceptional energy and 'the ardent Presbyterian', as he was known in old age, had a single-minded devotion to hard work and thrift. He was a regular attender at the Howard Street Chapel, North Shields, where he later became an elder.

He married Ann Driver, daughter of John Driver, a farmer, in 1873; they had five sons and four daughters. Four sons worked in their father's office and were encouraged to buy and run their own trawlers. (Another son, David, unlike the rest of the family, made a career in the Indian Army.) This, plus a number of judicious takeovers, accounts for the rapid expansion of the family fleet. By 1904 Richard Irvin & Sons had 60 trawlers under their management or ownership. By 1907 the fleet had grown to 80 vessels worth an estimated £275,000 — making Irvins one of the largest firms in the industry at that time. As their fleet expanded so did the family's interests in subsidiary industries. Richard Irvin was one of the driving forces behind the development of North Shields. He was a major shareholder in the ice factory, local canning factory, offal works and ship repair yard.

In 1905 the family began a new venture when one of Irvin's sons, George, left North Shields, with five of the family's trawlers, bound for Cape Town. Four years later Irvins, in partnership with C O Johnson, of Cape Town, set up the Irvin & Johnson Ltd Southern Whaling & Sealing Co of North Shields, with an authorised capital of £100,000. This company exploited Johnson's whaling and sealing expertise on a grander scale by moving operations from the South African coast to Antarctica. At the same time it seemed to be a profitable way to employ Irvin's surplus capital. They made an immense investment in a new whaling fleet and in equipping a land station on South Georgia. Unfortunately the company's first four seasons were not a success. Indeed, Southern Whaling was one of Irvin's least successful ventures, for it was to prove to be profitable only in the artificial conditions of the First World War and its aftermath.

In 1907 Richard Irvin & Sons was formed into a limited liability company with a capital of £200,000 of which £127,261 were issued. This amalgamated the fishing interests of the Irvin family and their associates. Local boards were established at Aberdeen, North Shields, Fraserburgh, Peterhead and Great Yarmouth. In consequence of this reorganisation John Irvin became joint managing director along with his father; later he pioneered the firm's investment in the Scottish herring fleet.

By 1912 the Irvins had 140 fishing vessels under their management, ranking them among the largest firms in the fisheries industry. As with others of his class, commercial success brought Richard Irvin municipal power and responsibility. A stalwart Liberal, Irvin was elected to Tynemouth borough council in 1890 and was mayor in 1897 and 1898. He served on a number of local authorities such as the Tyne Improvement Commission and the Tyne Salmon Conservancy — and took his duties seriously. In addition he was an active patron of local charities too numerous to mention.

During the First World War the capture and internment by the Germans of his eldest son John Irvin forced Richard, in spite of failing health, to assume full responsibility for the company's affairs. The loss of his son Thomas, who was killed in action, affected him deeply and, in 1919, he became seriously ill. He never regained his strength and, despite major surgery, Richard Irvin died in the Jubilee Infirmary, Tynemouth, on January 1920 leaving £270,000 gross.

After their father's death the three surviving Irvin brothers reorganised the company. The most important consequence of this was the sale of Southern Whaling to Lever Bros for £360,000. At the same time, some smaller parts of the company were sold off and the two divisions of the company were expanded to three: Scotland, England, and South Africa. These increasingly tended to function as separate concerns.

GEORGE MUIRHEAD

Sources:

Unpublished

BCe.

MCe.

PrC.

Published

Fishing Port of North Shields (North Shields, 1911).

Illustrated Guide to the Borough of Tynemouth (Tynemouth, 1899).

Gordon Jackson, *The British Whaling Trade* (A & C Black, 1978).

Alec Meek, *With a Deep Sea Trawler to the Grounds off Fair Isle* (Newcastle: Northumberland Sea Fisheries Committee Reports, 1898).

Newcastle Daily Journal 19 Dec 1920.

Newcastle Evening Chronicle 18 Jan 1971.

Newcastle Evening News 16 Mar 1956.

W T Pike (ed), *Contemporary Biographies* (Brighton: W T Pike, 1905).

PP, RC Sea Fisheries (1883) 3596-1.

PP, SC Sea Fisheries Bill (1904) Cd 356.

Paul Thompson et al, *Living the Fishing* (Routledge & Kegan Paul, 1983).

Sir Henry Irving (courtesy of the National Portrait Gallery).

IRVING, Sir Henry

(1838-1905)

Actor-manager

John Henry Brodribb (who adopted the name Henry Irving when he went on the stage) was born at Keinton Mandeville in Somerset on 6 February 1838, the son of Samuel Brodribb, a travelling salesman for a large country store and his wife Mary née Behenna, the daughter of an improvident farmer from Cornwall. Samuel Brodribb was an amiable, but rather ineffectual man; his strong-willed wife, who combined vivacity and enthusiasm with devout Methodism, exerted much more influence on their son. The store where Samuel Brodribb worked closed in 1842, and he and his wife went to live in Bristol, sending Henry to live with his mother's sister Sarah, who was married to Isaac Penberthy, a 'captain' of four mines near St Ives; there Henry attended a dame school. When Isaac Penberthy died in 1848, Henry returned to his parents, who were now living in London. His father's sources of income are obscure at this period, though he earned enough to send Henry to a good school, the City Commercial School, where the fees were a modest £6 a year. Henry disliked lessons, except for elocution (he had a stammer, which he worked hard to eradicate). He was already showing a love of recitation and drama that his mother could not approve.

At the age of twelve, Henry was sent as a junior clerk to a firm of lawyers, Paterson & Longman, in Cheapside, and then moved to Thacker, Spinke & Co, East India merchants of Newgate Street. While working as a clerk he stinted on food to buy books, attend lessons at the City Elocution Class and go to the theatre. In 1856 his uncle, Thomas Brodribb, gave him £100 (the proceeds of a paid-up insurance policy) which he used to buy theatrical props and costumes and to launch himself as an actor. He found an engagement at the Royal Lyceum Theatre in Sunderland where he was to be paid no wages until he proved himself useful. His mother was horrified at his decision and never forgave him, believing his soul was damned.

Henry Irving (as John Henry Brodribb was known henceforth) worked as an actor in the provinces for several years, 'a tall, thin, interesting, gentle young man' {Hollingshead (1895) I, 204}, learning his trade as a 'walking gentleman' and 'general utility' actor and graduating to juvenile lead. By the 1860s, he was earning £3 a week but was paid only when he was working; his total earnings for 1865 were £75. Having played some 630 parts in twelve years, and beginning to acquire a reputation as an actor in melodrama and tragedy, in April 1871 he signed a contract with Hezekiah Bateman, a theatrical manager, for three years, to act at the Lyceum Theatre in London (whose lease Bateman had just taken) or any other theatre in the United Kingdom. He was to be paid £15 a week for the first year, £17 a week for the second, and £19 for the third. The Lyceum

Theatre, which had been the ruin of several previous lessees, had a reputation for bad luck. Bateman, too, began his tenure in September with a couple of failures. Irving saved the situation by suggesting a production of the melodrama *The Bells*. 'Mathias', his leading role in this play, was to become one of his most famous roles. *The Bells* was a great success with critics and audience. Irving's growing reputation filled the theatre; his *Hamlet*, produced in 1874, ran for two hundred nights, an unprecedented length of run for Shakespeare. Col Bateman died after the party celebrating the hundredth night of this production, but his widow kept the lease and Irving continued with the company. By 1878, Irving felt he could no longer act with the Batemans' daughter, Isabel, as his leading lady and Mrs Bateman generously proposed that he should take on the remaining three years of the lease.

Engaging Ellen Terry as his leading lady and a Dublin civil servant, Bram Stoker, as his business manager, Irving spent nearly £4,000 on renovations to the theatre and a further £4,000 on production costs and rehearsals; he had an overdraft of £12,000 by the opening night of his first production as an actor-manager, which was *Hamlet*.

Irving was now free to realise fully his own conceptions of stage production. His meticulous attention to details of costume, scenery, music and stage properties and lavish expenditure to achieve his aesthetic purposes, were the hallmarks of his productions. Some critics accused him of paying too much attention to the trappings, rather than letting the play speak for itself, but Irving was unrepentant: nothing but the best he could afford and achieve would match his high conception of the dignity of the drama. But 'He considered that the first duty of an actor manager was to make his theatre pay and thereby to win liberty of action to pursue whatever policy he chose' {Irving (1951) 359}, and used popular melodrama (which he unquestionably enjoyed producing and acting) to help with the costs of his productions of Shakespeare, which were not always successful.

Irving treated his company well, insisting on discipline on stage, but seeing to their comfort off stage. He set up a provident and benevolent fund for them and acted as a trustee. (With Squire Bancroft (qv) and H I Toole he set up the Actors' Benevolent Fund in 1882, presiding over it until his death and ensuring its success. He was also president of the Actors' Association, founded in 1891, which he guided and held together.) He paid himself a salary of £70 a week, and Ellen Terry £200 a week. The first season brought receipts of £39,881 against expenditure of £32,869, and his debts were further reduced by a legacy of £5,000 from an admirer that he received at the time, the only financial help in his career. The second and third seasons each produced a profit of about £10,000. In 1881, Irving was offered the freehold of the theatre for £100,000 but he refused it, arranging instead a long lease at £4,500 a year. In 1882, at a cost of £12,000, he altered the Lyceum so that more spectators could be admitted, thus increasing the maximum receipts from £228 a night to £420.

In 1881 Irving made the first of a series of highly successful provincial tours on which he took the full Lyceum productions, bringing the standards of London theatre to the provinces and pioneering the full-scale railway tour (taking scenery as well as casts). His first tour of North America was made in 1883; there too he and his company enjoyed considerable success. The profits from these tours became ever more necessary, as the costs of running the Lyceum steadily mounted. Not only were his productions becoming, if anything, even more lavish, and even more expensive, but there were a steadily increasing number of people who had been found little jobs about the theatre by the ever-charitable Irving. He was aware of the mounting costs, and tried to suggest economies, but was unwilling to sacrifice standards in any aspect of his productions. By 1892, when he put on *Henry VIII*, theatrically a great success, but with production costs of nearly £12,000, the average weekly running costs of the theatre were £1,800. That season showed a loss of £4,000. Eventually the Lyceum Co was employing 600 people including 60 gasmen, 60 carpenters and 40 property men.

Too much of the responsibility for the success of the company, financially and theatrically, rested on Irving's shoulders. He had worked hard all his life, and the strain on his health was beginning to tell. His performance of *Richard III* in 1896 was a triumph, but after the first performance he severely damaged his knee and his recovery was set back by his general physical exhaustion. The season showed a loss of £10,000, which was nearly recovered by the profits of that year's provincial tour. Disaster struck in 1898, when 260 pieces of scenery, the setting for 44 plays, were destroyed by fire. They had been insured for £10,000 but Irving, in his attempt to economise, had reduced the insurance to £6,000. In fact, these productions had cost over £30,000 and would cost much more to replace. Irving had been relying on these old productions as a provision for his old age, when he would no longer have the energy to mount new productions each season, and he could revive old successes at comparatively little expense. Irving took this severe blow philosophically, his only comment was that 'he thought the fire might have been caused by a spark of the moral indignation of those playgoers who insisted that to produce plays without scenery was the highest development of the simple life' {Irving (1951) 619}.

Another blow followed. A few weeks into the provincial tour of 1898 Irving fell ill with pneumonia and pleurisy: his company continued the tour without him, but without Irving, the profits were only £500.

While his spirits were still low and he was physically weak, he was approached by an old friend Joseph Comyns Carr, who had formed a syndicate which proposed forming a company to relieve Irving of all financial responsibility in return for his services and the transfer of his interests in the Lyceum. The Lyceum Theatre Co would take over the remaining eight years of the lease, Irving was to give at least 100 performances a year at the Lyceum, bearing 60 per cent of the cost of new productions, paying all stage expenses and half the cost of the advertising. He was to play on tour in the UK or the USA at least four months a year; 25 per cent of the profits of these tours would go to the company. Irving was to receive £26,000 cash and £12,000 in shares. Bram Stoker, his business manager, was dismayed at these terms when he heard of them, but he was unable to do more than persuade Irving to ask for the payment of his £70 a week salary, as before. Stoker was still more dismayed when the company not only issued £100,000 preference and £70,000 ordinary share capital, but £120,000 mortgage debentures to the freeholders of the theatre, thus grossly over-capitalising the company. The inequity of the contract between Irving and the company soon become apparent. Staging a new production, *Robespierre*, his share of the expenses were over £1,000 a week, but his share of the gross takings, although these were higher than for several previous seasons, often fell below that. By the end of the season he had made a loss of about £4,000 (less the salary Stoker had insisted upon for him) while the company made a handsome profit. Tours in the USA and the provinces were more rewarding for Irving — his share of the profits for the 1899 US tour was £24,000. Between 1879 and 1898 the Lyceum company made profits of £66,516 in the USA and £73,166 in London against losses of £35,156 in London. However, on his return to England from his seventh US tour in 1902 (on which he made a profit of about £12,000) he found that the London County Council was insisting on alterations at the Lyceum for it to conform to new standards for fire safety. The over-capitalised company, whose shares were now worthless, could not find the £20,000 needed for these alterations and was forced to close the theatre at the end of Irving's season and call in the Receiver, though Irving was not bankrupt, as was commonly thought.

Irving was hurt and angry at the failure; he tried to raise capital to help the theatre but failed. The Lyceum became a music hall. Against all advice, he staked over £12,000 on an ambitious production, an adaptation of Dante's *Divine Comedy*. So expensive was this to mount and run, it would have made a loss even if it had been a success — which it was not, either in the UK or the USA. Irving planned an extended farewell tour of the provinces and North America, but fell ill again on the initial provincial tour and had to disband his company, making a loss of £2,000. After some successful engagements in London, he embarked on another provincial tour, but collapsed and died at Bradford on 13 October 1905.

As an actor, Irving was a controversial figure. To some, he was the greatest actor of his day with a rivetting and magnetic personality on stage. Others thought of him as an actor 'whose physical disabilities for his calling were not only marked but in the opinion of many, absolutely insuperable. It was often said of him that he could neither walk nor talk' {*Morning Post* 14 Oct 1905}. His 'mannerisms, his peculiar pronunciation, his halting gait, the intonations of his never-very-powerful or melodious voice, the often excessive slowness that grew upon him with the years, were welcome to some as the result and expression of his personality; others they inspired with a feeling that might be described as a desire to laugh if they dared' {*Times* 14 Oct 1905}. His success as a manager was more generally acknowledged. Although there were criticisms that he staged very few new plays, and that he had perhaps encouraged others towards 'the abuse of decoration' {*Morning Post* 16 Oct 1905}, yet it was widely accepted that 'he succeeded in recalling to the theatre the intelligent public, in making play-going fashionable among all classes, and in accustoming the thousands of new and old playgoers, whom he attracted, to look to the theatre for more than empty amusement' {*Times* 14 Oct 1905}. He had, it was said, done for tragedy what Squire Bancroft and his wife had done for comedy.

But his greatest achievement, it was felt, and one which not even his severest critics disputed, was, by the standards he set and by his success, to raise the status of the theatre as an art and of acting as a profession. He gathered round him superb supporting players who deferred, on stage and off, to his unquestioned authority as leader of his profession. Gladstone came so frequently backstage at the Lyceum that a special chair was set aside for him in the wings. Irving's company was summoned to Windsor more than once to give special performances for Queen Victoria and the Prince of Wales was a great admirer and friend. His knighthood, the first ever given to an actor, was granted to him in 1895 in personal recognition by Victoria of his services to art; it was seen as a token of recognition to his profession, as well as to him as an individual. His honorary degrees, from Trinity College, Dublin, in 1892 and from Cambridge in 1898, were similarly the first given to an actor.

The theatre was Irving's life. The little time he spent away from it was passed in the company of a few close friends; only his manservant was admitted to his home. He married in 1869 Florence O'Callaghan, the daughter of the Surgeon General who was serving in India. Her family had been opposed to the match, but Florence had determined she would have him for her husband. It was very soon apparent that she had a harsh temper and a bitter tongue; she disliked his theatrical friends and, worst of all, derided his acting. They separated within months of the birth of their first son, Henry; an attempted reconciliation did not succeed, and they had parted for good before the birth of their second son, Laurence, in 1871. Both sons became actors themselves, though their father had hoped for other careers for them. Irving wanted to marry Ellen Terry, his leading lady, but she knew the scandal and trouble his divorce would cause, and in any case felt they would probably not be happy together. He had several friendships with older women, but they were replacing the loss of his intimacy with his mother, and not his wife. Irving was essentially a lonely, reticent and secretive man, though his warmth and charm gave some the illusion they knew him well.

He died virtually penniless. Most of his estate of £20,527 gross was the result of the sale of his pictures, books and memorabilia, which fetched a total of £18,853.

CHRISTINE SHAW

Writings:

The Stage. Address Delivered … at the Perry Barr Institute (1878).

English Actors. Their Characteristics and Their Methods (Oxford: Clarendon Press, 1886).

PP, HC 1892 (240) XVIII, SC on Theatres and Places of Entertainment.

The Drama. Addresses (W Heinemann, 1893).

Sources:

Unpublished

BL, 'Death of Henry Irving' (a collection of newspaper cuttings).

Information from Dr Michael Sanderson.

Published

Academy 21 Oct 1905.

Squire and Marie Bancroft, *The Bancrofts: Recollections of Sixty Years* (John Murray, 1909).

Daily Chronicle 24 Oct 1905.

Daily Telegraph 14 Oct 1905.

DNB.

Percy Fitzgerald, *Henry Irving: A Record of Twenty Years at the Lyceum* (Chapman & Hall, 1893).

John Hollingshead, *My Lifetime* (2 vols, Sampson Low, Marston & Co, 1895).

Laurence Irving, *Henry Irving: The Actor and His World* (Faber & Faber, 1951).

Morning Post 14 Oct, 5 Dec 1905.

Walter Herries Pollock, *Impressions of Henry Irving Gathered in Public and Private During a Friendship of Many Years* (Longmans, Green & Co, 1908).

Times 14 Oct, 20 Dec 1905.

Truth 26 Oct 1905.

WWW.

ISAACS, Godfrey Charles

(1866-1925)

Developer of wireless telegraphy

Godfrey Isaacs (from H Montgomery Hyde's Lord Reading *Heinemann, 1967).*

Godfrey Charles Isaacs was born in 1866, the fourth son, and seventh of nine children, of Joseph Michael Isaacs (1832-1908) of Norwood and Sarah (1835-1922), daughter of Daniel Davis. His father was a fruit merchant and shipbroker who left £7,600 while his uncle Sir Henry Aaron Isaacs (1830-1909) was Lord Mayor of London, 1889-90 and left £6,411. Godfrey was educated at Hanover and Brussels universities, travelling extensively in Europe on his father's business before starting on his own in the 1890s. He then joined various private syndicates of a speculative character.

He was director of a Transvaal prospecting company, but resigned after finding a discrepancy between the prospectus and the engineer's report on their properties. He was interested with the Randlord Sir Lionel Phillips in a Welsh granite quarry, and backed the Hibernian Development Co which tried unsuccessfully to mine zinc and copper in Tipperary. He helped to finance a social gossip newspaper, the *Sovereign*, and in 1900 started *British Mining*. His other interests included Welsh gold-mining: he invested up to £4,000 in the St Davids Gold & Copper Mines Co and the St Davids Mining Development Co. He also put £1,750 into Gwyn Mines, and was active in the Mining Machinery Improvement Co and the Veel Mining Co. Altogether companies with which he was connected recovered Welsh gold worth £213,312 and after 3.5 per cent royalty to the Crown, and £101,182 in wages and working expenses, dividends of 80 per cent were paid.

He was a shareholder in the Transit Syndicate of Davison Dalziel (qv) which introduced motor taxicabs to London. He was a director of the City and Suburban Motor Cab Co from its formation in 1905, and of its successor after 1907, the United Motor Cab Co, in which he invested £250. In 1908 he invested £200 in the Provincial Motor Cab Co and joined the board, but resigned in 1911 over a policy disagreement. He also became a London director of the Australian Motor Cab Co in 1909.

In that year Isaacs was introduced to Guglielmo Marconi, the inventor of wireless telegraphy, managing director of the Marconi Wireless Telegraph Co. The latter had little aptitude for the commercial side of business, his interest being in scientific development, and the company paid no dividends in 1897-1910. Although he had made startling demonstrations of his system by land and sea, he had failed to secure government contracts to erect stations, while the implications of his invention were imperfectly understood. Marconi was impressed by Isaacs's hustling salesmanship and invited him to run the company's business affairs. In January 1910 Isaacs became joint managing director with Marconi, and after familiarising himself with operations, became sole managing director in August 1910.

Marconis applied to the Colonial Office in March 1910 for twenty-year licenses to operate a network of 18 wireless stations in Asia, Africa, Australia and the West Indies linking the British Empire. No answer was received until November, when Isaacs was told that the matter would be considered at the Imperial Conference of June 1911. This reply dissatisfied Isaacs, who knew that his German rivals Telefunken were seeking to erect a world-wide range of stations: at that period it was impossible to build stations within several hundred miles proximity without constant interference and he was anxious lest Telefunken forestall him. He maintained his pressure, and in May 1911 the Cables (Landing Rights) Select Committee recommended that six stations, using the Marconi system, should be established under government ownership. The Imperial Conference endorsed this proposal, and negotiations directed by the Postmaster General, Herbert Samuel, led to the signature in March 1912 of a preliminary agreement between the Post Office and Marconis. Stations costing £60,000 each were to be built in England, Egypt, East Africa, South Africa and Singapore, with Marconi receiving 10 per cent royalty for twenty-eight years on the gross takings of each station. Meanwhile Marconi shares rose from £2 8s 9d in August 1911 to £3 6s 3d in December; in March they were £6 15s 0d and next month they peaked at £9.

The preliminary agreement was soon strongly attacked from two quarters. In political circles it was traduced as unbusinesslike, with the suggestion that Isaacs had procured unduly favourable terms in a Jewish conspiracy between himself, his elder brother Rufus (then Attorney General with a seat in the Cabinet) and Herbert Samuel. In the City the rise in Marconi shares led to stories that the market was rigged and that Government ministers had speculated in Marconi shares using privileged information. One rumour suggested that Rufus Isaacs had made £160,000 and Samuel £250,000.

This outcry led to the appointment in October 1912 of a Parliamentary Select Committee of investigation under Sir Albert Spicer (qv). Shortly afterwards Isaacs stated that in view of the delay this entailed, with the cost of keeping engineers idle and escalating material costs, he regarded the agreement of March as terminated. During the next months it transpired that Rufus Isaacs had dealt in shares of Marconi's American subsidiary, and had sold 1,000 of them to both Lloyd George, the Chancellor of the Exchequer, and the Master of Elibank, the former Liberal Chief Whip then working in the oil business for Weetman Pearson (qv). The Select Committee's report split on party lines, but only the most pertinacious Liberal apologists could pretend that Rufus Isaacs and Lloyd George had shown judgement, discretion or candour in their handling of the scandal.

A new Marconi contract with the Post Office ratified by parliament in August 1913 was cancelled by the Government in December 1914 because of the war. The company had then already partly completed three stations, had spent £140,000 of its money and had declined other contracts in order to press on with the work. They therefore sued for breach of contract, but the lawsuit lasted until 1919, when £600,000 compensation was paid.

Isaacs nevertheless won other orders for the company. The value of contracts in hand rose from £250,000 in July 1911 to £1 million in 1912; by June 1913 the company had 1,600 telegraph stations on board merchant ships, had supplied 163 military field-stations and up to 300 land-stations. In June 1913 the company employed 3,000, including 200 skilled engineers.

Isaacs began a vigorous commercial war with German Telefunken. In 1912, after the Australian and New Zealand Governments had contracted with a Telefunken subsidiary to erect a chain of coastal wireless stations, he sued the German company and the Australian Government for infringing patents, and forced a new arrangement in which the work was executed by a company controlled by Marconi with minority German participation. An agreement between Telefunken and Marconi in 1912 provided for an exchange of patents, but an element of 'vindictive animosity' {Baker (1970) 135} remained in Isaacs's attitude to the Germans. For this reason he supported the attempts of Dudley Docker (qv) to obtain consular reforms and to reorganise British exporters on a corporatist basis. Isaacs was a founding member of the Executive Council of the Federation of British Industries in 1916, and was one of the seven members of the first Organising Committee appointed on 12 September. He was an original member of the Consular and Overseas Trade Committee (November 1916); in September 1917 he and Sir Vincent

Caillard (qv) were delegated to see the Prime Minister to urge the denunciation of existing commercial treaties; and in 1918-19 he sat on the FBI's Terms of Peace Committee considering the industrial provisions of the peace treaty. These activities reflected his pre-occupation with Anglo-German trade rivalry, but he was also a signatory of the FBI report on labour policy (November 1917) whose enlightened and imaginative recommendations enraged Sir Allan Smith (qv) of the Engineering Employers Federation. Isaacs was always progressive in such matters: the Marconi company introduced a retiring age and contributory pensions fund as early as 1913.

Isaacs was very litigious, which initially was a strength to Marconi. From the outset in 1910 he determined to enforce and preserve the company's patent rights. In 1911 he won judgement against the British Radio Telegraph & Telephone Co for infringements, and in 1912 he obtained verdicts against the Clyde Steamship Co and the United Wireless Co (subsequently bought by the American Marconi interests). Also in 1912 he forced Siemens to acknowledge the validity of Marconi patents and there was bitter litigation over the patent of Lee de Forest's triode. This tendency became a liability after the Marconi scandal, when his naturally aggressive personality seems to have been touched by paranoia. In 1913 he successfully prosecuted for criminal libel the anti-semitic journalist Cecil Chesterton who had displayed newspaper placards proclaiming 'Godfrey Isaacs' Ghastly Record'. In 1914 he was defendant in a complex and costly suit brought by two malicious busybodies connected with the Conservative Central Office, Oliver Locker-Lampson and Peter Wright, each of whom had bought one share in the Marconi Co. Later in 1914 Isaacs won a case for breach of contract brought by Samuel Seger because the judge ruled that Seger had blackmailed Isaacs into making the contract; but in 1916 Isaacs lost Hamilton's case of wrongful dismissal. Then in 1916 a commission agent, Thomas Jackson, was gaoled for blackmail after trying to force Isaacs to buy 35,000 shares in the *Financial News* to stop adverse comment on Marconis. He next sued for libel Sir Charles Hobhouse, who had denied Isaacs's allegation that when Postmaster General he had tried to get Telefunken to compete with Marconi in Britain. The judge commented that either Hobhouse or Isaacs 'is committing blackest perjury' {*Times* 20 July 1918}, and the jury found against Isaacs, who thereupon offered to resign from Marconi. Finally there was Marconis' action for breach of contract against the Government which lasted from 1915 to 1919.

This desperately unfortunate publicity reacted on the company. Their offer in 1919 to supply a wireless system connecting all parts of the British Empire was rejected in 1920, when the Post Office was asked to create a scheme to prevent a private monopoly. A series of government schemes were discussed and abandoned in 1921-24 without consulting Isaacs or Marconi. Other Dominion Governments were less dilatory, or less prejudiced against Isaacs. A big contract was signed with South Africa in 1924, and in 1923 an equally valuable concession was secured in Australia. Then in 1924 Guglielmo Marconi revolutionised telegraphy by developing a much cheaper system of shortwave directional transmission and reception, and a contract was signed for an Imperial network that was completed by 1927.

At the same time Isaacs secured other foreign business. His Peking agent, E F Birchal, a 'damned scallywag' who 'couldn't go straight if he tried' {NSWL, G E Morrison diary, 24 Dec 1912, 27 May 1915} negotiated in 1914 a £2 million contract to erect eight stations in China which 'would have gone through if it had not been for the [British] Legation's personal opposition to Birchal' {ibid, 13 May 1918}. Telefunken instead secured the contract which was cancelled after the outbreak of European war. Marconis' later negotiations were hurt by the brutal tactlessness of the British Minister in Peking, but a new contract was signed in 1918 to erect Marconi stations across China. A loan of £600,000 was issued in London by Birch Crisp (qv) for the Chinese to pay for this work; it was known as the Marconi Loan, although the company was not legally responsible for it, and when the Chinese predictably defaulted, Marconis' reputation was further injured.

The siting of the League of Nations Assembly at Geneva led Isaacs to open a station there in 1920; subsequently Marconis supplied another station at Berne and the wireless equipment for Geneva aerodrome. They also obtained in 1921 a contract of twenty-one years' duration to run the entire postal, wireless and telegraph service in Peru. Under the direction of Sir William Slingo a Peruvian postal and telegraphic deficit of £70,000 in 1920 was turned into a surplus for 1925-26 of £396,975. Total revenue earned by the Peruvian services (1921-26) was £2,391,186. In 1928 Marconis sought a similar contract with Portugal, where they had previously secured a concession to build and operate for forty years five stations throughout the Portuguese Empire. With effect from 1926 Marconis also won a contract of twenty-five years' duration to operate Bolivia's posts and telegraph.

There was long-standing tension in the company between its engineers and head-office administrators. Guglielmo Marconi was passionately and exclusively loyal to the engineering caste, and his technical assistants were antagonistic to the formal controls and administrative duties which were essential in a multinational business. This was not the only trouble. Isaacs had a gambler's instinct and a grandiose imagination which enmeshed Marconis in some bizarre investments. Over £3 million was transferred from reserves in 1923-24 to write down the book value of assets, and yet by late 1924 the company was still interested in 56 other companies, of which twelve were unconnected with the wireless business. Thus, as part of the wartime anti-German movement to organise the British Trade Corporation of Lord Faringdon (qv) and George Manzi-Fé's British-Italian Banking Corporation, Isaacs launched the British-Hungarian Bank (or Angol-Magyar Bank Részvénytársaság). He was probably drawn to Hungary by its goldmines suggesting his earlier Welsh successes. After discussions in 1919 with Faringdon, Marconi in 1920 bought 42.5 per cent of the Hungarian Trading Bank at Budapest, which was renamed the British-Hungarian Bank with Isaacs as co-president. Later in 1920 Isaacs and Angol-Magyar jointly established the British-Danubian Trading Co. These ventures were unsuccessful, and in 1927 Marconis wrote off £225,000 invested in the British-Hungarian and the Compass Allgemeine Guarantee banks. Other interests of Isaacs were the Carreg-y-Llam slate quarries, a tin-making company called Gauntlets and a company for making artificial coal, Hamonite.

Isaacs's influence was evident, for example, in Marconis' failure to win

Baltic orders. Their agent there, Leon Aisenstein, appeared 'to lack business experience' and held a 'perfunctory interest' in wireless schemes, preferring to prospect 'for the formation of a National Export Company to undertake general commercial business in the Baltic ... in which ... the Marconi company would be interested' {PRO FO 371/6738, despatch 102 of Sir Ernest Wilton, Riga, 12 Dec 1921}. Aisenstein was further handicapped by anti-semitism in Latvia and Estonia and by his employment of Mme Reiss, 'a Jewess of Russian origin ... known ... as a Bolshevik agent and as an intermediary of the Germans', who leaked Marconis' plans to Telefunken and Siemens {PRO FO 371/6738, Wilton to Sir Hubert Montgomery, 22 Nov 1921}. Isaacs sent an unsuccessful sales mission to Russia in 1924 under a former signals officer, Major General Sir Graham Bowman-Manifold.

Under Isaacs's 'reckless mismanagement' of Marconi, 'substantial profits were reported, inordinately large fees paid to certain directors, and shareholders lulled into a false sense of security by receiving appreciable dividends ... [when] the company was in fact suffering heavy losses by unwise investments ... and by foolish speculation in foreign currencies' {*Times* 16 Mar 1927}. He was responsible for losing some £6 million, and in November 1924 left the Marconi board.

A team of accountants was put in to save the group. After they reported in 1927 a further £2,766,168 was written down: £1,059,262 on advances to associate companies, £772,623 on shares in associate companies, £373,856 on obsolete equipment, £275,690 on depreciated foreign currencies and £237,955 on claims arising from an Argentine lawsuit. Isaacs's successor at Marconi, Frederick Kellaway, was a former Liberal Postmaster General selected because, despite peremptory and autocratic manners, he was more acceptable than Isaacs in official circles.

Isaacs became a director in 1920 of the Aircraft Disposal Co formed by F Handley Page (qv) to dispose of the Ministry of Munitions' surplus aircraft, with Lt Col John Barrett-Lennard (1863-1935) as managing director. Of the machines initially supplied, 113 were broken or otherwise unsaleable, and after threats of legal action a new and more lucrative contract with the Ministry was obtained in 1922. Aircraft Disposal Co was a major supplier of second-hand aeroplanes and parts to minor powers in the 1920s. Isaacs was also appointed a director of the British Broadcasting Corporation in 1923.

In February 1913 Isaacs was invited to stand as Liberal parliamentary candidate for mid-Essex, where Marconi had a factory, but he withdrew in December 1913. His eldest brother Henry (1858-1950) was prospective Liberal candidate for the Isle of Thanet until 1914, and having succeeded to the family fruit business, sat on the government committee on orange imports in 1916.

Having suffered much anti-semitism in 1912-13, Isaacs entered the Roman Catholic Church. He died after a brief illness, hastened by overwork, on 17 April 1925 at his house at Virginia Water. He was survived by his widow, Leah, and two sons, Marcel Godfrey and Dennys Godfrey; he left £195,490 gross.

R P T DAVENPORT-HINES

ISAACS Godfrey Charles

Writings:

letter on telegraph delays and Calais railway accident *Times* 27 Jan 1914.

letter on Berlin wireless telegraph service *ibid* 12 Sept 1914.

letter on telegraph transmission delays *ibid* 27 Feb 1915.

letter on defective cables *ibid* 26 Feb 1919.

letter on wireless telegraphy at sea *ibid* 30 July 1919.

letter on government failure to grant licences for Marconi stations *ibid* 5 Feb 1923.

Sources:

Unpublished

New South Wales State Library, Sydney, papers of George Ernest Morrison.

PRO, Foreign Office papers; Ministry of Munitions papers (especially Mun 4/6020, 6178 and 6217).

University of Warwick, Modern Records Centre, papers of Federation of British Industries.

West Sussex CRO, Chichester, papers of Leo Maxse.

PrC.

Published

W J Baker, *A History of the Marconi Company* (Methuen, 1970).

Charles Bright, 'Inter Imperial Telegraphy' *Quarterly Review* 220 (1914).

Burke's Peerage and Baronetage.

Richard Davenport-Hines, 'Vickers' Balkan Conscience: Aspects of Anglo-Romanian Armaments 1918-39' *Business History* 25 (1983).

—, *Dudley Docker* (Cambridge: Cambridge University Press, 1984).

Lady Donaldson of Kingsbridge, *The Marconi Scandal* (Hart-Davis, 1962).

Murray Goot, 'Sir Ernest Fisk' *Australian Dictionary of Biography* 8 (Melbourne: Melbourne University Press, 1981).

Journal of Royal Society of Arts 70 (1922).

'The Marconi Affair' *Quarterly Review* 219 (1913).

National Review 60-61 (1912-13).

Marquis of Reading, *Rufus Isaacs, First Marquis of Reading* (2 vols, Hutchinson, 1942).

Alice Teichova and Philip L Cottrell (eds), *International Business and Central Europe 1918-1939* (Leicester: Leicester University Press, 1983).

WWW.

ISHERWOOD, Sir Joseph William

(1870-1937)

Naval architect

Joseph William Isherwood was born in Hartlepool on 23 June 1870, the son of John Isherwood and Mary Ellen née Dobinson. His parents kept a grocer's and beer retailer's business. He was educated at Luggs School, and at the age of fifteen was apprenticed as a ships' draughtsman to the local shipbuilders, Edward, Withy & Co Ltd. At the end of his apprenticeship he continued to work for the firm until 1896 when he became a ship surveyor in Lloyd's Register of Shipping at Hartlepool. His work earned him transfer to London where he worked under the chief ship surveyor at Lloyd's and it was his experience in classifying vessels and examining the results of shipping accidents that led to his first major contribution to naval architecture. He became convinced that the traditional method of transverse construction of cargo vessels (with plates attached to pairs of ribs placed at regular intervals along the keel) was unsatisfactory. In 1906 he patented what was to become known as the 'Isherwood system' throughout the shipbuilding world. Although not the first attempt at a longitudinal system of construction (where the lateral frames were replaced by longitudinal girders) it was certainly the first successful system. It was rapidly adopted on a large scale, especially for oil tankers which had previously been prone to breaking their backs under the old system of construction. Isherwood returned to the North East to put his theories into practice and the first-fruit was, appropriately enough, an oil tanker, the *Paul Paix*, built in 1908 by R Craggs & Sons Ltd of Middlesbrough, of which firm Isherwood became a director, having resigned from Lloyd's Register in 1907. As well as offering an increase in ship safety, the longitudinal system offered a reduction in building costs and an increase in cargo space as compared with the transverse system.

After a brief spell with Craggs, Isherwood set up his own firm of naval architects, J W Isherwood & Co Ltd with offices in Leadenhall Street and Lloyds Avenue in London and subsequently in New York. During the First World War he worked for the Government on ship design and for his services was created baronet in 1921. After the war he made further major contributions to ship design, including the 'Isherwood bracketless system' (1925), especially for oil tankers, which overcame the problems which had occurred with bracket connections to the bulkhead, and the 'Isherwood locked steel interchangeable hatchway covers' (1931). Finally, in 1933 he made another outstanding contribution with the 'Arcform' vessel, as a result of his experiments on hull shape in the tank of the National Physical Laboratory at Teddington. It had previously been held that beam should be narrow in relation to length (with length exceeding beam by at least seven times). Isherwood reduced this ratio to almost six to one and cut away the wedge of the hull to produce an arc. The result was an increase in speed of vessel and a reduction of fuel costs. Isherwood backed his theory by having a number of vessels produced to the new design for his own account, including the first, the *Arcwear*, built by Short Bros Ltd of Sunderland in 1934.

Isherwood's working life was entirely concerned with the problems of ship design. He was a liveryman and member of the Court of Assistants of the Worshipful Company of Shipwrights, and associate member of Lloyd's Register of Shipping and member of its technical committee, and member of the Institution of Naval Architects, the North East Coast Institution of Engineers and Shipbuilders, the Cleveland Institution of Engineers and the American Society of Naval Architects and Marine Engineers. By the time of his death around 2,500 vessels of more than 20 million deadweight tons had been constructed on the 'Isherwood system'.

Isherwood married in 1892 Annie Mary, daughter of Matthew Robson of Fleetham, and they had one son and one daughter. He listed his recreations as riding and motoring and was a member of the RAC, the Cleveland in Middlesbrough and the Whitehall in New York. He lived at 'Raggleswood', Chislehurst and died at his London home, in Grosvenor House, Park Lane, on 24 October 1937. He left an estate valued at £176,639 gross.

D J ROWE

Writings:

'A New System of Ship Construction' *Transactions of the Institution of Naval Architects* 50 (1908).

The Isherwood System of Ship Construction (1917).

Register of Vessels Built on the Isherwood System (Liverpool: C Birchall, 1919).

'The Isherwood "Bracketless System" for Oil-Carrying Ships' *Shipbuilder* 33 (1926).

(with W Isherwood) 'Merchant Shipbuilding: The Bracketless System' *ibid*.

'Do the Rules of Classification Societies Tend to Improve Shipbuilding and Engineering in this Country?' *Transactions of the North East Coast Institution of Engineers and Shipbuilders* 45 (1928-29).

'The Arcform Ship: Trials and First Voyage Performances' *ibid* 50 (1933-34).

Sources:

Unpublished

PrC.

Published

DNB.

Shipbuilder 44 (1937).

Transactions of the North East Coast Institution of Engineers and Shipbuilders 54 (1937-38).

WWW.

T H Ismay (courtesy of Merseyside County Council).

ISMAY, Thomas Henry

(1837-1899)

Shipowner

Thomas Henry Ismay was born at Maryport, Cumberland, on 7 January 1837, the eldest son of Joseph Ismay and his wife Margaret née Sealby. Seagoing enterprise was already in the family. Ismay's great-grandfather, Joseph Middleton, owned one of the earliest shipbuilding yards in Maryport; his grandfather, Henry, was a sea-captain and had married Charlotte, a daughter of Joseph Middleton; his own father was a foreman shipwright in Middleton's yard, then a timber merchant and shipbuilder on his own account and Maryport's first shipbroker, dealing with the Liverpool firm of Imrie, Tomlinson, to which Ismay was soon to be apprenticed. Joseph Ismay had done well for himself and clearly expected his son to do even better.

After local elementary schooling, Thomas was sent in 1849 to Croft House School, Brampton, near Carlisle, an extremely advanced school for its time, with a considerable emphasis on science. Although Ismay's father died when he had only been at the school a year, he was able to continue there until he was sixteen, and did well. He took special lessons in navigation, spending nearly all his spare time building model ships (also picking up the habit of chewing tobacco). In 1853 he was apprenticed, through the introduction of his uncle, Isaac Middleton, to the Liverpool shipbrokers, Imrie, Tomlinson & Co. William Imrie, Jr, son of the partner, who was the same age as Ismay, was also serving his apprenticeship then. The two became life-long friends.

By the time Ismay had served his term, he had gained a reputation with the Liverpool merchant community for efficiency in business. In 1856 he sailed to Chile for a Maryport firm as supercargo. His diaries reveal great powers of observation, a zest for living and a love of adventure. He spent a whole year away.

By 1857 he was already part-owner of two ships. That year he opened a partnership in shipbroking with a retired sea-captain also originating from Maryport, Philip Nelson. The articles could not be formally signed until 7

January 1858 when Ismay attained his majority. Nelson was old and cautious, whereas his junior partner was both very young and very progressive. So the arrangement was ended in April 1862 and Nelson retired. Not, however, before Ismay had persuaded his partner to commission the building of an iron brigantine.

Ismay now moved into an office in 10 Water Street, under the style of T H Ismay & Co. This was to be the head office of his firm until 1898, by which time his name was well-known throughout the maritime world.

The commissioning of his first iron ship coincided with Ismay's marriage to Margaret Bruce, daughter of Luke Bruce, master mariner and shipowner, on 7 April 1859 at St Bride's Church, Percy Street. The marriage was a very happy one, producing nine children; the oldest son, Joseph Bruce (b 1862), succeeded his father as chairman of the White Star Line and later survived the *Titanic* disaster. In 1865 the Ismays moved into Beech Lawn House, Waterloo, which still stands. This commanded a fine view over the Mersey. Here he built hothouses and laid out a romantic sunken garden known as the Grotto.

Meanwhile Ismay's business, running cargo ships mainly to Central and South America, was forging ahead. In 1864 Ismay broke into the steam ship trade by becoming a director of the National Steam Navigation Co, originally founded to carry cargo and steerage passengers to the Southern States. The ships were transferred to the New York route after the Civil War. By 1866 Ismay was the owner of 12 vessels. In 1867 he performed a master stroke. For £1,000 he bought the flag and goodwill of the bankrupt White Star Line of sailing clippers to Australia. He then put his own iron ships in the Australian and New Zealand trade.

Among the directors of the National Line was one George Hamilton Fletcher, who owned a fleet of sailing vessels trading with India. It seems clear that both he and Ismay were hoping for an opportunity to enter the North Atlantic passenger trade, despite the fact that at least five major British firms were already firmly established in it.

The opportunity came in 1869, when Ismay was invited to a dinner party at the home of Gustavus C Schwabe, a Liverpool merchant and financier whose nephew Gustav Wolff (qv) had recently entered into a partnership with Edward Harland (qv), in a shipbuilding business in Belfast. Schwabe had a big stake in the Bibby Line and had been impressed by the design of the iron ships which Harland & Wolff had built for their Mediterranean trade. He wanted to put more capital into shipping, and his suggestion was that if Ismay would agree to form a transatlantic shipping line he would back it providing all ships were ordered from Harland & Wolff. G H Fletcher was in charge of negotiations. Six vessels were ordered. On 6 September 1869 the Oceanic Steam Navigation Co Ltd was registered with a capital of £400,000, in £1,000 shares. The first 100 shares were taken up by Ismay and Fletcher, 50 each; Schwabe took 12, as did several other wealthier merchants. William Imrie, Sr meanwhile, had died and his son, Ismay's one-time fellow apprentice, came into the partnership and from 1870 the shipping line was managed by Ismay, Imrie & Co, Imrie being in charge of the sailing fleet, Ismay of the steamer fleet.

On the 27 August 1870 the first ship was launched, the *Oceanic*. Revolutionary in design, it instantly outclassed vessels of other shipping lines. The ships were designed more like a yacht than the traditional liner. The ratio of length to beam was 10:1, in contrast to the normal ratio of the time, 8:1. Such proportions had been pioneered by the Liverpool-built blockade runners in the American Civil War, such as the *Banshee*, which was probably the first steel ship to cross the Atlantic. Also, in the *Oceanic* iron railings replaced the traditional high bulwarks, enabling the sea to flow freely off the deck. All the state rooms and first class accommodation were placed amidships, farthest from engine noise and motion in the after part, which had been the traditional place for passenger accommodation. The state rooms were now much more spacious, better lit and ventilated. Comfort and safety for the passengers, rather than speed, was the objective of the line. Captains were given firm instructions in this respect. The convenience of all passengers, including steerage, was equally the management's concern, to the extent that in 1872 an agent travelled steerage incognito to report on conditions. Improvements were accordingly made in the vessels of lines controlled by Ismay; for example White Star ships were the first to provide bedding and eating utensils and proper family accommodation for the third class. Although White Star stressed safety and comfort rather than speed, *Adriatic* made a record westbound Atlantic passage in May 1872. From then on White Star held its own with all other transatlantic lines, even Cunard.

In April 1873 Ismay suffered a blow when the *Atlantic* was wrecked near Halifax, Nova Scotia, with the loss of over 500 lives. He and his partner, G H Fletcher, left no stone unturned to vindicate the company. It says much for the soundness of the management that nonetheless the line still prospered. Some of the loss was offset by selling two steamships used in the South American trade.

The firm increased its capital to £750,000 in December 1875, so as to add two more ships, *Germanic* and *Britannic*, both launched in 1874. *Germanic* was not broken up till 1950, a tribute to its good workmanship. No more capital was put into the company during Ismay's lifetime. Not until 1902 did the firm publish its accounts. But Ismay kept a careful account of the earnings of his rivals, the Cunard and Inman lines. Never did the company pay an annual dividend of less than 7 per cent during Ismay's lifetime, whatever the vicissitudes of the shipping industry.

Ismay's keen opportunism was seen in 1874, when, faced with spare tonnage, he took advantage of the founding of a new company by the American George Bradbury, a former president of the Pacific Mail Steamship Co, which had fallen out with the railroad companies of the USA. Bradbury was now backed by the railroads in the formation of a new company, the Occidental & Oriental Steamship Co, which was to provide a service across the Pacific from the Far East, linked with American railways. Spare White Star ships were chartered to this company and the Ismays themselves went to Hong Kong via the Suez Canal in 1875, on their own pioneer vessel *Oceanic I* in its new role.

The firm had a unique relationship with Harland & Wolff. All its ships were built by them on a 'cost plus profit' basis. They were built to the highest standards, Ismay and Sir Edward Harland working closely together on details. So close was their mutual relationship and confidence that no contract was ever signed. The closeness between builder and owner facilitated Ismay's pursuit of innovations. Some, such as the

Ismay Presentation Plate (courtesy of Merseyside County Council).

lighting of *Celtic* by gas and fitting an adjustable propellor to *Britannic* were unsuccessful, but showed a very progressive attitude.

When faced by excess shipping tonnage and something of a slump in the mid-1880s, Ismay pursued sensible reciprocal arrangements to reduce wasteful competition. The attempts of his rivals, Cunard, to bring about an amalgamation, however, he politely but persistently rebuffed, since the two firms' policies and standards were at variance on a number of key issues.

Ismay wished to replace his older vessels on the Atlantic run. In 1878 he had responded to the apprehension of danger from the Russian Fleet by putting his ships at the Admiralty's disposal. Now, ten years later, he proposed that he should build merchant vessels under Admiralty supervision, subsidised by the Government, so made that they could be quickly converted into armed merchant cruisers in an emergency. The Government accepted these proposals. Ismay and Harland & Wolff reacted promptly and provided two magnificient vessels, *Teutonic* and *Majestic*, each of 10,000 tons, capable of 30 knots. These were modern-looking vessels, relying wholly on their twin-screw engines, carrying no sail whatever. The Prince of Wales visited *Teutonic* while in the Harland & Wolff Yard at Belfast in 1889. The conversion of the vessel into an armed merchant cruiser was carried out in the Mersey in twenty-four hours. She made a lasting impression at the Naval Review at Spithead, not least on the German Emperor.

In 1891 Bruce and James Ismay (who had been apprenticed in the firm) became partners with their father in the firm. At the end of the year Ismay resigned 'from the firm' but remained chairman. He was able thus to devote more time to wider and more public interests, although he steadfastly refused to stand for parliament.

In 1893 he visited the United States, to see the Chicago Exposition. He also had an interview with the President at the White House. In 1897, the Queen's Diamond Jubilee Year, Ismay was offered a baronetcy. Though strongly urged to accept it, he finally declined, though deeply appreciative of the proffered honour. At the Naval Review that year he and Bruce took a trip on Charles Parsons's (qv) revolutionary turbine vessel, *Turbinia*. Both were impressed, but did not think the extra speed warranted the expense. Meanwhile the grand luxury liner, *Oceanic II*, was about to be built at Belfast. Norman Shaw, the eminent architect had been called in to design the firm's palatial offices (still standing in 1984) near the Liverpool waterfront, opened on the first day of 1899. He was now consulted on the décor of the new liner, giving it a truly grand touch, probably making it the world's most luxurious vessel, as well as the largest, to date.

Ismay left a firm not only prominent in the transatlantic passenger trade, at least the equal of, and in some ways excelling Cunard, but also leading in the transport of refrigerated meat from New Zealand, through the Occidental & Oriental Steamship Co, and of cattle and cargo across the Atlantic. In August 1899 the *Medic* had begun the White Star Service to Australia. Many of the ships could be adapted from cargo to passenger usage. By 1899 his fleet's total tonnage was 163,291 tons, composed of 21 large steamers and two tenders.

Ismay's other commercial interests were directorships of the London & North Western Railway Co and of the Royal Insurance Co and the Sea Insurance Co. He was active in professional circles, as chairman of the Liverpool and London Steamship Protection Association and of the Audit Commissioners of the Mersey Docks & Harbour Board. As a leading user of the port, he proposed many bold ideas, such as a scheme to make Liverpool a free port, believing it would add immensely both to its trade and its general prosperity and that the Dock Board's system of raising loans upon bonds should be replaced by the conversion of most of the debt into stock. He also pressed hard for the establishment of Riverside Railway Station on the Quayside for the convenience of sea travellers. He served on many government advisory bodies. In 1884, he was a member of Lord Ravensworth's Admiralty Committee to inquire into the contract system as compared with the dockyard system of building and repairing the ships of the Royal Navy. He sat on the Royal Commission on the administration of the Army and Navy, in 1888; as chairman, on the Board of Trade Life Saving Appliances Committee, under the Merchant Shipping Acts in 1889; he served on the Admiralty Committee on the Naval Reserves in 1891; and in the same year was appointed to the Royal Commission on Labour. In 1895 he served on the Board of Trade

Committee on Side Lights. Just before his death, he was nominated by the Prince of Wales, as president, to serve on the Royal British Commission for the Paris Exhibition in 1900. His ability as a chairman to produce a balanced and unanimous report was outstanding. He declined the chairmanship of the London & North Western Railway Co, offered to him in 1891.

He was a member of the *Indefatigable* Training Ship committee and for over twenty-five years its chairman and treasurer. This institution trained orphans of sailors and other healthy destitute boys for merchant navy service, giving training in seamanship as part of a normal school curriculum. He was also a director of the British Workman Public House Co, founded to provide non-alcoholic refreshments for dock workers and seamen in 1875.

Ismay's fundamental probity and basically kind nature seem never to have been disputed. He was a man of action rather than words. Hence his refusal of political involvement, although he held Liberal Unionist sympathies and was a member of the Reform Club. He was, however, a magistrate for both Lancashire and Cheshire and was High Sheriff of Cheshire in 1892. His modesty ensured that much philanthropic activity was unseen. He consistently remembered his birthplace, Maryport, and Bootle Hospital, in his giving.

Although not naturally an ostentatious man, his position in the business world led him to build a mansion at Dawpool in Cheshire, overlooking the Dee. He originally bought the estate in 1877, for use mainly as a holiday home. In 1884 the Ismays marked their silver wedding by moving into a magnificent new mansion there which Norman Shaw had designed for them in Elizabethan style, costing £53,000. It was, however, over-ornate and oppressive, and lacking in modern comforts such as central heating and bathrooms, with the result that none of the family wished to live there after Mrs Ismay's death. In 1926 it was demolished. It was adorned with a notable collection of pictures and trophies of the Ismays' travels.

In a sense this mansion was typical of the man, reflecting his sternness and aloofness. Bruce Ismay's widow recalls the restraint of the Ismay household, particularly as it affected the young ladies of the family, who were not even allowed access to newspapers! Meals were conducted in silence, unless 'Papa' opened the conversation. Prayers, compulsory for the whole household, were conducted by Ismay himself at 7.30 am, promptly, necessitating a 6.30 am rise in freezing bedrooms. At 8.00 am, Ismay walked to Thurstaston station from his home, as part of his constitutional regime. If he saw a fallen leaf in the drive he placed a stone on it. If, on his return, it was still there, he would soundly reprimand his ten-man corps of gardeners!

A devout Anglican, he attended church every Sunday and in his private diary regularly recorded his thanks to God for his prosperity (in 1888 for example, he wrote 'May God's blessing rest on the work of the year, and grant that I may be useful to others not for my own glory, but in acknowledgement of God's great goodness to me' {Oldham (1961) 102}). His life was governed by a compassionate sense of duty. On his retirement, for instance, he took 200 deaf and dumb children for a cruise on the *Teutonic*. When he accepted the presidency of Bootle Hospital at about the same time, he gave £1,000 to start an endowment fund. To give them work he transported some of Liverpool's unemployed workmen to Dawpool to weed the heather. Frequently he helped young men needing a start in life, businessmen on the verge of bankruptcy, and any cases of obvious need who came to him. He was noted for magnanimity towards business rivals, not least because he believed it was better to sustain a weak competitor than let a stronger one in!

Ismay had only just returned from the launching of his new vessel, *Oceanic II*, in 1899 when symptoms of a fatal combination of weaknesses were observed. Although he recovered sufficiently to go to Belfast to receive the freedom of the city in July, his health continued to deteriorate. A series of heart attacks and an abscess on the liver (the latter necessitating two operations) together brought about his death on 23 November 1899, at the age of sixty-two.

Ismay's estate was valued at £1,297,882 gross. He left legacies to his firm's staff and to his domestic staff. A large number of charitable bequests were also made, including a special prize fund for those boys of the *Indefatigable* training ship selected 'by the general body of boys on the ship as being those whose character and conduct they consider most worthy of esteem, admiration and imitation'. {*Daily Post* 12 Mar 1900}

J GORDON READ

Writings:

PP, Board of Trade Life Saving Appliances Committee, under the Merchant Shipping Act (1889) C5762 (chairman).

PP, RC Administration of the Army and Navy (1890) C5979.

PP, RC Labour (1892) C6708.

PP, Board of Trade Committee on Side Lights (1895) C7908.

Sources:

Unpublished

Merseyside County Archives, Liverpool: Philip Nelson, letter book 1856-64 (D/N); G H Fletcher, diaries, notes and extracts, compiled by S A Hamilton-Fletcher, 1865-79 (DX/174); T S *Indefatigable* Reports, 1865-81 (D/B, Box 115 N); Presentation Volume accompanying Ismay's silver-gift presentation service, 1885; White Star Line, miscellaneous legal records, ca 1890-99 (D/B, Box 174 et seq); Mersey Docks and Harbour Board, archives, 1858-99; *S S Teutonic* (Photo Album), 1897 *National Maritime Museum*; T H Ismay, diaries 1856; Margaret Ismay, diaries 1881-99.

Published

Roy Anderson, *White Star* (Prescot: Stephenson & Sons, 1964).

Noel R P Bonsor, *North Atlantic Seaway* (Prescot: T Stephenson & Sons, 1955).

DNB.

Fortunes Made in Business. Life Struggles of Successful People (Sampson, Low & Co, 1901).

Clement Jones, *Pioneering Shipowners* (Liverpool: C Birchall & Sons Ltd, 1935).

Journal of Commerce 24 Nov 1899.

Liverpool Courier 24 Nov 1899.

Liverpool Mercury 24 Nov 1899.

Liverpool Post 24 Nov 1899, 12 Mar 1900.

Manchester Guardian 24 Nov 1899.

Wilton J Oldham, *The Ismay Line* (Liverpool and London: C Birchall & Sons Ltd, 1961).

Shipping Telegraph 24 Nov, 1 Dec 1899.

Shipping World 29 Nov 1899.

Syren and Shipping 29 Nov 1899.

J

JACKSON, Sir John

(1851-1919)

Engineering contractor

John Jackson was born in York on 4 February 1851, the son of Edward Jackson, a goldsmith, and his wife Elizabeth née Ruddock. After education at Holgate Seminary, York (for seven years), he studied engineering, surveying and levelling and political economy at Edinburgh University, for two sessions, 1869-71. Afterwards he had three years' engineering training in workshops at Newcastle upon Tyne, presumably including the workshops of Sir W G Armstrong (qv). He finished his engineering training with his brother.

When only twenty-five years old, Jackson set up on his own in Newcastle upon Tyne in the risky market of the Victorian engineering contractor. To succeed in this business it needed 'great skill in estimating cost, aided to some extent by good fortune and by ... ability to make a good bargain' {*PP*, Cd 8518 (1917) 7}. By dint of his theoretical and practical background, his sharp mind, forceful personality and great energy, Jackson possessed many of the basic prerequisites for succeeding as a contractor. However, it is not clear how he secured his first and vital contract, crucial because it established his 'reputation for smartness and thoroughness' {*Western Morning News* 16 Dec 1919}. The contract, for the completion of the Stobcross Docks, Glasgow, was finished in three years — six months ahead of time and despite a problem with quicksand. In rapid succession there followed dock contracts at Middlesbrough, Hartlepool and North Sunderland, to meet the needs of the expanding North East's iron, steel and coal industries. In 1881 Jackson was one of the five contractors invited to offer tenders for the foundations of the first Forth Bridge, a contract he did not secure. He did however lay the foundations of Tower Bridge, London (built 1886-94) and afterwards completed the last eight miles of the Manchester Ship Canal (opened by Queen Victoria on 21 May 1894). For finishing his section of the Canal in two-thirds of the estimated time Jackson was knighted in 1895.

Dockwork became Sir John's speciality. For the War Office he extended seawards the fort at the end of the Admiralty Pier at Dover and also built the Prince of Wales Pier for the Dover Harbour Board, though his great rival, Weetman Pearson (qv), was the main contractor at Dover when it was extended in 1897-1909 to accommodate the growing shipping services with the Continent. In addition Jackson constructed docks and basins at Swansea, at Methil and at Burntisland, both in Fife, and the deep water lock at Barry, South Wales, which was still one of the largest of its kind in the 1920s. Sir John Jackson's major work in England, however, was the Naval Dockyard Extension at Keyham, Plymouth.

Ordered by the Admiralty because of the rapidly growing size of capital ships, the Keyham Extension (comprising a tidal basin, a deep-water entrance lock, three graving docks and a 35-acre closed basin) covered 120 acres and more than doubled the size of the Devonport Dockyard. It took eleven years to complete, being opened in February 1907, and cost £4.5 million. To remove the 10 million tons of spoil and to construct the basin walls, some of which went down 120 feet in order to rest on rock, 150 engines and boilers and 25 locomotives were employed. At its height, 3,700 workmen worked on the scheme, toiling day and night, with the aid of electric arc lights. Jackson put up 200 houses for some of his men (many other houses being built by private builders) and also supplied a mission hall and chaplain. When a shortage of granite workmen jeopardised the supply of Cornish granite, Jackson imported a third of his needs from Norway. And, further indication of his resourcefulness in cutting costs and meeting completion dates, he set up on site a 'complete mechanical engineering factory, not only for their repairs, but for the manufacture of cranes and other plant, which proved a great advantage to the firm during the very busy and expensive times of 1898, 1899 and 1900' {*Western Daily Mercury* (Supplement) 21 Feb 1907}. When the Extension was finished, Devonport Dockyard could at any one time have two Dreadnoughts under construction, four more and five cruisers in drydock and 'within its closed basins could be comfortably berthed the entire Channel fleet' while the rest of the British Navy could be moored on the Hamoaze waterway 'with perfect convenience and security' {*ibid*}.

Britain's imperial commitments took Jackson's firm into other naval dock work: for the Admiralty, the harbour at Simonstown in the Cape Colony, a contract worth £2 million completed in 1911; for the Straits Settlements Government, Singapore Harbour works, worth £2 million; and for the Dominion Government of Canada, a breakwater at Victoria, British Columbia.

Foreign powers also called upon Sir John Jackson. He advised the Austro-Hungarian Government on the extension of arsenal works at Pola and docks at Trieste. For the Spanish Government he built a drydock and deepened the harbour at Ferrol. In Chile he won the £3 million contract to build a railway from Arica on the coast to La Paz the capital of Bolivia, a distance of 300 miles but reaching an altitude of 14,500 feet in crossing the Andes. French engineers consulted him about the practicability of a bridge from Dover to Calais and American engineers about a Nicaraguan canal. At the outbreak of war in 1914 Jackson's firm had made surveys and proposals to the Russian Government for a second Trans-Siberian Railway estimated to cost over £20 million. Another major overseas contract halted by the First World War was for a series of irrigation schemes, involving dams across the Euphrates, aimed at cultivating 3.5 million acres for the Turkish Government.

By the late 1890s Sir John Jackson's firm was one of the largest engineering contractors in the country, rivalling the businesses of Sir John Aird (qv) and Weetman Pearson among others. In 1898 Jackson (now an associate member of the Institution of Civil Engineers) converted his firm into a limited liability company, Sir John Jackson Ltd, with a capital of £1 million. He and his family held 90 per cent of the shares, the rest being 'presented' to leading members of the firm's staff {*Western Morning News* 16 Dec 1919}. In 1907 the firm was working on a series of contracts, including the Devonport Dockyard extensions and the Simonstown Naval harbour, together valued at between £8 and £10 million sterling. On these large contracts Sir John reckoned his firm would receive a minimum commission of 10 per cent, and in the cases of the Ferrol Harbour and the Mesopotamian irrigation scheme his firm's commission was well over 10 per cent — which British authorities regarded as 'improvident' contracts on the part of the foreign powers {*PP* Cd 8518 (1917) 7}. As governing director of his firm Sir John's salary was £6,000 per annum by 1916-17, at which point a wartime scandal struck the firm and its founder.

The scandal had its origins in a letter Sir John wrote to Lord Kitchener on 7 August 1914, offering 'to place at Lord Kitchener's disposal any engineering assistance which he or the Company's staff at their head office were able to give' {*ibid*, 3}. Kitchener accepted the offer and Sir John's firm built three army camps and a permanent depot, at Grantham, Rainham and Ormskirk, for over 18,000 men and 5,000 horses and costing £429,139; later they put up the enormous Salisbury Plain and Wylye Valley hut camps and Brockenhurst Hospital, together costing £3,299,648. When Jackson insisted on being paid a commission of 5 per cent (half his peace-time commission rate) for the Wiltshire camps the War

Office objected and the dispute went before the parliamentary Public Accounts Committee. Taking advice from an ad hoc committee of the Institution of Civil Engineers, the Public Accounts Committee concluded in August 1916 that Sir John's insistence on a 5 per cent commission was extortionate. When the Public Accounts Committee's evidence was published and Sir John was identified under the newspaper headline 'A War Contractor's Claim. £170,000 Commission on Camp Work. Evidence before the Committee' {*Times* 11 Oct 1916}, he had little option but to respond: by implication, his patriotism and integrity, the reputation of his firm and his fitness for public office (he was then MP for Devonport) were all called into question. On 10 October 1916, he wrote to the Financial Secretary to the War Office demanding a judicial inquiry, independent of parliament, so that he could answer the charges. Asquith decided that it should take the form of a Royal Commission. Appointed on 18 November 1916, the Commission comprised Sir Arthur M Channel (formerly a High Court judge), Sir Frank Crisp (a distinguished company solicitor) and Sir Alexander R Stenning (a past president of the Surveyors' Institution), all septuagenarians. They sat in public and reported on 30 March 1917. Sir John was exonerated, but not entirely. A patriotic motivation behind his original offer to Kitchener was vindicated and he was not found to have inflated the wage rates or materials' prices as some suggested. Further, the War Office was criticised for not postponing the settlement of terms. However, Sir John's insistence on 4 or 5 per cent commission (he came down to 4 per cent in negotiations in autumn 1916) was regarded as inconsistent with his first offer and the level of that commission was described as 'greatly excessive':

> His career as a successful contractor making large profits in work requiring large capital and with risks which fortunately seem never in his case to have led to disaster, seems to have given him an altogether inflated idea of the market value of the services of his firm when rendered under different circumstances which involved no risk whatever, and the providing of no capital {*PP* Cd 8518 (1917) 9}.

A year later Sir John retired from parliament, besmirched if not broken.

Sir John Jackson began to move towards political involvement while living in Devonport and working on the Keyham project. He accepted the invitation to join the Royal Commission appointed in 1903 to investigate the military preparations for the war with the Boers in South Africa. In its Report he revealed his belief in strong government, arguing that an extra £10 million ought to have been at the disposal of the War Office, subject only to cabinet approval, on the eve of the Boer War. A Unionist, he unsuccessfully contested one of Devonport's two parliamentary seats in 1904 and 1906 (in 1904 he clumsily offered to give the local hospital £1,000 if it could be proved that he was a supporter of Joseph Chamberlain (qv)). Eventually he was elected for Devonport in 1910. Before retiring in 1918, his contributions to Commons proceedings amounted to only a dozen questions. Nearly all related to naval and dockyard matters and some, like his questions about contracts for dry docks and floating docks in 1910, might have concealed a commercial interest. After 1913 Sir John asked no more Commons questions, though his hostility to the Liberals' progressive direct taxation was reported in the *Times* in 1914. His election agent later recalled, 'Sir John was a man of deeds rather than of words, and the dreary drip of declamation in the House of Commons bored him beyond words'. {*Western Morning News* 16 Dec 1919}

Besides his knighthood, Sir John Jackson received various other public accolades. A JP for Devon, he was made CVO in 1911 when the Duke of Connaught opened the Simonstown naval harbour. Sir John was elected FRS of Edinburgh in 1894. He received an honorary LLD from Edinburgh University in 1903 (and four years later he provided £4,000 to set up Professor P G Tait's Memorial Fund, in memory of his old university teacher and to advance 'physical research'). In recognition of his firm's engineering work, Sir John held the Grand Cross of Naval Merit of Spain and the Chilean Order of Merit, First Class.

From his school days Jackson evidently enjoyed most water sports. A strong swimmer, while at Newcastle he was a founder member of the Volunteer Life Brigade, formed to assist the coastguard. Fond of small boat sailing, he often raced on Plymouth Sound during the Keyham project. He belonged to the Royal Yacht Squadron, Cowes, and the Royal Western Yacht Club and, for some time, was commodore of the Royal South-Western Yacht Club, Plymouth. 'After he reached his sixtieth year Sir John often sculled on the Thames, and did a steady pull of 12 to 15 miles without feeling the exertion' {*ibid* 16 Dec 1919}. Constantly an active man, he always drove his own motor car.

At the outset of his career, in 1876 he married Ellen Julia of Clapham Road, South Lambeth, Surrey, younger daughter of the late George Myers. They had five daughters, four of whom married naval or army officers. 'Lady Jackson was an indefatigible social worker during the whole time her husband associated with Devonport. For 17 years she carried on a Girls Club at St Aubyn Street, and only relinquished it in June 1917, when she handed over the premises to the YWCA who have since conducted it as a Patriotic Club, with Lady Jackson as president.' {*ibid*} Until 1914 Sir John lived at Pounds on the outskirts of Devonport; after its lease expired he and his wife moved to Henley Park, Oxfordshire, though kept a residence in Devonport and another in Belgrave Square, London.

Sir John Jackson died of 'heart failure' {*ibid*} on 14 December 1919. He was buried at Norwood Cemetery, a memorial service being held at St Peter's, Eaton Square. He left £520,474 gross.

DAVID J JEREMY

Writings:

'Notes by Commissioners: Note by Sir John Jackson' *PP*, RC War in South Africa, 1903 (1904) Cd 1789.

'On Practical Engineering' *Times* 19 Dec 1908.

'Comment on the Future of British Industry' *ibid* 19 June 1914.

Sources:

Unpublished

BCe.

MCe.

PrC.

Information from Edinburgh University Library and West Devon Area Central Library.

Published

Edinburgh University Calendar 1908-9.

Robert K Middlemas, *The Master Builders: Thomas Brassey; Sir John Aird; Lord Cowdray; Sir John Norton-Griffiths* (Hutchinson, 1963).

National Review 43 (July 1904).

PD, 5th ser 16, cols 21-22 (4 Apr 1910), 766 (7 Apr 1910), 1560 (14 Apr 1910), 2073-74 (20 Apr 1910); 35, cols 1050 (13 Mar 1912), 1407 (14 Mar 1912), 1535 (18 Mar 1912); 36, col 1050 (2 Apr 1912); 38, col 38 (6 May 1912); 43, cols 1235-36 (6 Nov 1912); 46, cols 1651 (13 Jan 1913), 2091 (15 Jan 1913); 56, cols 2490-91 (13 Aug 1913); 85, col 2477 (22 Aug 1916); 86, col 387 (17 Oct 1916).

PP, RC War in South Africa, 1903 (1904) Cd 1789, 1790, 1791.

PP, 1916 (115) III Reports from the Committee of Public Accounts.

PP, RC Sir John Jackson Ltd (1917) Cd 8518.

Proceedings of the Royal Society of Edinburgh 40 (1919-20).

Times 19 June 1914, 11, 16 Oct, 16 Nov 1916, 16 Dec 1919.

Western Daily Mercury 21, 22 Feb 1907.

Western Morning News 21, 22, 23 Feb 1907, 16 Dec 1919.

Edward Leader Williams, 'The Manchester Ship Canal' *Minutes of Proceedings of the Institution of Civil Engineers* 131 (1898).

WWMP.

WWW.

William Lawies Jackson, Lord Allerton (courtesy of Leeds Central Library).

JACKSON, William Lawies

1st Lord Allerton of Chapel Allerton

(1840-1917)

Tanner, currier and leather merchant

William Lawies Jackson was born at Otley, near Leeds, on 16 February 1840, the eldest son of William Jackson 'a tanner' {MCe} (1815-58). He was educated at a private school in Adel and the Moravian School in Fulneck. In the late 1840s his father moved to Leeds which was becoming the country's second largest leather centre, and set up in business as a tanner and leather merchant. At his death in 1858, the firm produced 20,000 hides a year. During the next twenty years, his son, a first-rate administrator and an inventor, took advantage of a buoyant market to build up 'the largest tanneries in England' {*Industries of Yorkshire* 121}; they eventually covered an area of nine acres, employed 200 workmen, produced 300,000 hides a year, and integrated tanning with currying. Jackson's meteoric success not only made him the leader of the Leeds leather industry; it also provided him with the means for a career in politics.

In 1869 Jackson was elected to the Leeds Town Council and for the next eleven years represented the Headingley Ward. Although a Conservative in a Liberal-dominated Council, he was made chairman of the Finance Committee and framed the financial reforms of the 1877 Local Improvement Act. Under his chairmanship the profits of remunerative municipal undertakings were passed on to consumers through lower prices instead of being channelled into consolidated revenue. In 1876, he became leader of the Leeds Conservative party and stood, unsuccessfully, for parliament. Four years later he was elected to Westminster and, after the Redistribution of Seats Act of 1885, represented North Leeds until 1902.

Highly esteemed for his public service in Leeds and for his stand on national issues, Jackson soon came to the fore in the Conservative party. In the early 1880s he promoted higher education by serving on the council of the newly-founded Yorkshire College, defended the role of the Church in elementary schooling, supported Imperialism, preferred free trade and became master of a masonic lodge. Described by Arthur Balfour as 'that rara avis, a successful manufacturer who is fit for something besides manufacturing' {Egremont (1980) 101}, Jackson was appointed by Randolph Churchill as Financial Secretary to the Treasury (1885-91) and in the last nine months of Salisbury's second Government (1891-92) he reached the peak of his political career as Chief Secretary of Ireland. In 1890, Jackson was made a Privy Councillor and in the following year was elected an FRS. In 1893, he was installed as the Provincial Grand Master of the West Riding Masonic Order and two years later became the first Conservative to be nominated mayor of Leeds.

In his subsequent parliamentary career Jackson served on numerous Select Committees and chaired a Royal Commission. With the exception of the Jameson raid inquiry of 1896-97, these investigations were mainly concerned with financial and commercial issues: financial relationships with India, Indian railways, war office contracts, bankruptcy law and coal supplies. His business interests now included directorships of the East Lincolnshire Railway, the Forth Bridge Railway and the Eastern Telegraph Co, and he was a trustee of the Submarine Cables Trust. As chairman of the Great Northern Railway after 1895 he introduced capital works programmes to modernise the company, and when he concluded a Working Agreement twelve years later with its competitor, the Great Central Railway, he was nominated to chair the joint-committee to manage the two companies, a proposal extinguished by parliament. However, his fortunes as a tanner waned with the decline of the Leeds leather trade and made him a protectionist. At the end of the nineteenth century this industry was no longer the model of modernity that it had been in the 1860s. Its competitive strength had been sapped by inadequate investment and out-dated marketing strategies. As Jackson's sons did not enter the business a manager was brought in from outside, and in May 1912 the firm was closed following Jackson's retirement.

Although he purchased Park Hill Estate near Doncaster, Jackson continued to live at Allerton Hall in Leeds and participated in public life. He was created a baron in 1902. Two years later he was awarded an honorary DL from the new University of Leeds and acted as its Treasurer from 1912 to 1917. In 1908 the Freedom of the City of Leeds was conferred upon him. A devout churchman, he became chairman of Bishop Boyd Carpenter's Commission and served on the Board of Management of the Leeds Church Extension Society.

Jackson married in 1860 Grace Tempest (1841-1901), the only daughter of George Tempest, a butcher of Otley. They had two sons and five daughters. The elder son succeeded to the title: his brother, educated at Harrow and Trinity, played cricket for county and country, and followed a military career.

Lord Allerton died on 4 April 1917, leaving £91,014 gross.

W G RIMMER

Sources:

Unpublished

Leeds City Library, Newspaper Cuttings, Leeds People 2.

MCe.

Published

Max Egremont, *A Life of Arthur James Balfour* (Collins, 1980).

R F Foster, *Lord Randolph Churchill — A Political Life* (Oxford: Clarendon Press, 1981).

Derek Fraser (ed), *A History of Modern Leeds* (Manchester: Manchester University Press, 1980).

Ernest P Hennock, *Fit and Proper Persons* (Edward Arnold, 1973).

Industries of Yorkshire I (Historical Publishing Co, 1888).

Leeds Mercury 5 Apr 1917.

W G Rimmer, 'Leeds Leather Industry in the Nineteenth Century' *Publications of the Thoresby Society, Miscellany* 13.

Times 27 Sept 1881, 5 Apr 1917.

John Wrottesley, *The Great Northern Railway* (3 vols, Newton Abbott: David & Charles, 1979–81).

WWMP.

WWW.

Yorkshire Daily Observer 5 Apr 1917.

Yorkshire Evening Post 4, 7 Apr 1917.

Yorkshire Post 27 Oct 1910, 5 Apr, 5, 14 May 1917.

Lord Jackson (courtesy of Lady Jackson).

JACKSON, Willis

Lord Jackson of Burnley

(1904-1970)

Electrical engineer and research director

Willis Jackson was born in Burnley, Lancashire, on 29 October 1904, the only son of Herbert Jackson, a parks superintendent, and Annie née Hiley. He was educated at Burnley Grammar School and Manchester University where he obtained the degrees of BSc (1925) and MSc (1926) in electrical engineering.

Jackson taught at Bradford Technical College until 1929 when he began a long association with the Metropolitan-Vickers Electrical Co by joining its College Apprentice Scheme at its Trafford Park Works. Metropolitan-Vickers was deeply committed to the establishment of new products, maintaining a large research section. From its outset the company had been concerned with the education of its employees and developed several apprenticeship schemes (from craft to graduate levels) which relied on close collaboration with local educational institutions. Having completed his apprenticeship and spent a brief period teaching at Manchester

TELEGRAMS: METROVICK, MANCHESTER.

FORM 1703 B

TELEPHONE: TRAFFORD PARK 2431 (20 LINES)

METROPOLITAN-VICKERS ELECTRICAL CO., LIMITED

SUBSIDIARY OF
ASSOCIATED ELECTRICAL INDUSTRIES LIMITED

Trafford Park
Manchester. 17

REGISTERED OFFICE:
NUMBER ONE, KINGSWAY,
LONDON, W.C.2.

DIRECTORS:
SIR FELIX J. C. POLE
W. C. LUSK, (U.S.A.)
G. E. BAILEY
K. BAUMANN, (SWISS ORIGIN)
A. J. BOYD
A. P. M. FLEMING
J. S. PECK, (U.S.A.)
H. C. PIERSON
C. S. RICHARDS
A. S. RINDER
H. N. SPORBORG, (U.S.A.)
P. S. TURNER
CAPTAIN H. VIVIAN.

Letterhead of Metropolitan-Vickers (courtesy of Lady Jackson).

College of Technology, Jackson undertook research at Oxford University, for which he was awarded a D Phil in 1936.

Jackson then returned to Metropolitan-Vickers as a research engineer. However, through his association with Arthur Fleming (qv), the company's director of research and education, Jackson rapidly developed an interest in the provision of technical specialists for industry; this interest being conditioned by the experience of Metropolitan-Vickers in developing the partnership between industry and educational institutions.

Jackson remained at Metropolitan-Vickers until 1938, leaving to become Professor of Electrotechnics at Manchester University. He stayed there throughout the war and further increased his involvement with the organisation of scientific manpower through his work with the Hankey Radio Bursary Scheme and the Institution of Electrical Engineers. In 1946 he became Professor of Electrical Engineering at Imperial College, London. He made a major impact on the organisation and research of his department, but spent less time on his own research, concentrating more on the policy issues which were shaping the post-war expansion of higher education.

In 1953 Jackson was made an FRS. In that year also he left Imperial College and returned to Metropolitan-Vickers to become director of research and education, Fleming having retired in 1951. The 1950s were a period of expansion for Associated Electrical Industries (of which Metropolitan-Vickers was a part) but there were also pressures to reorganise Metropolitan-Vickers' research section — a problem with which Jackson had to contend. At the same time he was able to supervise a growth in the company's educational programme with important new developments occurring at the undergraduate and graduate levels.

However, Jackson planned only a relatively limited return to Metropolitan-Vickers for his life was not wholly absorbed by the company. His public life, concerned with science and engineering educational policy, and centred largely on London, took more of his time as he served on a great many government, professional, academic and industrial committees. While Jackson advocated the expansion of these forms of education he always maintained that it should be geared to the needs of the economy. Thus he was not only concerned with the production of graduate or professional engineers but also with technicians and craftsmen. Moreover, for the higher levels of education he continually stated the need for qualitative changes which would enable the universities and colleges to produce more useful employees for industry. According to Jackson, this required the development of new courses which gave different mixes of scientific/engineering theory and practice, but which would all be based on the collaborative effort of industry and education. In this way Jackson sought wider support for the practices which had been institutionalised at Metropolitan Vickers and a few other manufacturing companies.

In the early 1960s changes were occurring in Associated Electrical Industries which prompted Jackson to return to his previous post at Imperial College where he remained from 1961 until his death. In 1967 he became Pro-Rector of the College and was made a life peer.

At Imperial College Jackson became even more a leading figure in the national science advisory apparatus, and continued to advocate educational change which sought to combine the demands of industry with the needs of science. But perhaps his most important contributions revolved around his chairmanship of the Committee for Manpower Resources for Science and Technology. This Committee was an important part of the 1964 Labour Government's attempt to provide a framework for the modernisation of British industry. The Committee, with strong representation from science-related industries, reflected Labour's promise to supervise a technological revolution in Britain.

Under Jackson's control this Committee had two main aims: to bring about changes in the use and training of scientific manpower, and to develop methods of manpower planning. These objectives were not always seen as compatible, but the Committee was responsible for an integrated series of reports on aspects of technical manpower. While these reports attracted much attention, the assumptions and institutional connections which had underpinned the Committee were being eroded. Thus, in 1968, when Jackson, suffering from deteriorating health, announced his retirement, the Committee was quietly dissolved. Nevertheless, if much of the Committee's and Jackson's more general propositions about science education and manpower and industrial growth no longer attracted high-level government support, their sentiments continued to be reflected in subsequent attempts made to link higher education and industrial employment.

Lord Jackson died on 17 February 1970, leaving £30,339 gross. He was survived by his wife Mary Elizabeth, the daughter of Robert Oliphant Boswall DSc, whom he had married in 1938; they had two daughters.

RICHARD BREWER

Writings:

'Dielectric Loss in Single Layer Coils at Radio Frequencies' *Explaining Wireless* 5 (1928).

'High Frequency Resistance Measurement by the Use of a Variable Mutual Inductance' *Journal of the Institution of Electrical Engineers* 68 (1930).

'The Analysis of Air Condenser Loss Resistance' *Proceedings of the Institute of Radio Engineers* 22 (1934).

'Conductivity-Temperance Studies on Paraffin Waxes' *Transactions of the Faraday Society* 31 (1935).

(with A P M Fleming), 'The Training of University Graduates for the Engineering Industry' *Engineering* 22 Oct 1937.

'Post-Advanced Education' *ibid* 22 Sept 1939.

'Field Strengths' *Journal of the Institution of Electrical Engineers* 88 Part I (1941).

'The University Education and Industrial Training of Engineers, with Particular Reference to Telecommunications' *ibid* 90 part 3 (1943).

High Frequency Transmission Lines (Methuen, 1945).

'Recent Developments in Dielectric Materials' *Journal of the Institution of Electrical Engineers* 94 part 3 (1947).

(ed of series), *Monographs on the Physics and Chemistry of Materials* (Oxford: Clarendon Press, 1948-).

Advanced Courses in Electrical Engineering (Association of Technical Insitutions, 1950).

(ed), *Symposium on Information Theory; Report of Proceedings* (Ministry of Supply, 1950).

(ed), *Communication Theory* (Butterworths, 1953).

(ed), *The Insulation of Electrical Equipment* (Chapman & Hall, 1954).

'The Changing Pattern of Part-Time and Full-Time Courses in the Technical Colleges' *Report of the Technical Colleges and Industry Conference* (Federation of British Industries, 1954).

'The Education and Training of Russian Technologists' *Journal of the Institution of Electrical Engineers* 2 (1956).

Report of the Second National Conference between Industry and Technical Colleges (Federation of British Industries, 1957).

'The Partnership between Industry and Education. Presidential Address to the Education Section of the British Association' *Advancement of Science* 15 (1958).

'The Making of Professional Engineers' *Proceedings of the Institution of Electrical Engineers* 107 B (1960).

'Some Human Aspects of Engineering Progress. 1961 Viscount Nuffield Paper Delivered to the Institution of Production Engineers' *Production Engineer* 40 (1961).

'The Partnership between Science and Electrical Engineering. Inaugural Lecture as Professor of Electrical Engineering', in *Inaugural Lectures 1960-61 and 1961-62* (Imperial College of Science and Technology, 1962).

Scientific, Technological and Technical Manpower, Tenth Fawkey Foundation Lecture (Southampton: University of Southampton, 1963).

'Commonwealth Education Conference, Ottawa' *Technical Education and Industrial Training* 6 (1964).

JACKSON Willis

'Reflections on the Robbins Report' *British Association for Commercial and Industrial Education Journal* 18 (1964).

'Manpower Resources for Science and Technology' *Science Journal* Nov 1966.

'Science Technology and Society. Presidential Address to British Association' *Advancement of Science* 24 (1967).

The Problems of Engineering and Scientific Manpower and their Implications for National Policy. Fourteenth Graham Clark Lecture (Council of Engineering Institutions, 1968).

'Manpower For Engineering and Technology. First Annual Willis Jackson Lecture' *British Association for Commercial and Industrial Education Journal* 23 (1969).

This bibliography is by no means a complete record of Jackson's many scientific and educational publications, and it omits his speeches in the House of Lords, newspaper articles and the reports of the Committees on which he served. More complete records of Jackson's writings are given in the two biographies cited below.

Sources:

Unpublished

Imperial College, London, papers.

Papers held by Lady Jackson, Oxford.

BCe.

MCe.

PrC.

R I Brewer, 'The Life and Work of Lord Jackson of Burnley: An Investigation of Science and Engineering Education Policy Formation' (Manchester MSc, 1979).

Published

G K Gabor and M Brown, 'Willis Jackson' *Biographical Memoirs of Fellows of the Royal Society* 17 (1971).

WWW.

Lord Jacques (courtesy of Lord Jacques).

JACQUES, John Henry

Lord Jacques of Portsea Island

(1905-)

Co-operative society manager and administrator

John Henry Jacques was born at Ashington, Northumberland, on 11 January 1905, the eldest son of the six children of miner Thomas Dobson Jacques and his wife Annie née Bircham. He had an early connection with the Co-operative Movement through attending junior classes at the local society. He left school at the age of thirteen and worked in a local coalmine. After two years as a miner, he joined the Ashington Co-operative Society as a grocery apprentice. Here he extended his earlier education by participating in classes which were held for employees. While taking required correspondence courses and participating in Co-operative summer schools, John Jacques came under the influence of R J Wilson (author of the standard text on general management in Co-operative societies, and later MP for Jarrow) and W R Rae (chairman of the Education Executive of the Co-operative Union). As a result of Rae's persuasion, John Jacques, at the age of nineteen, went to the Co-operative College as a full-time student.

On completion of one year's study, Jacques joined the Moorsley Co-operative Society, first as secretary and later as managing secretary. He held the post until 1929 when he returned to the Co-operative College as a tutor. He remained in teaching for the next thirteen years, and at the same time completed a BA (Com) degree at the University of Manchester (Victoria University) by means of evening classes, and was responsible for the production of three important texts on co-operative accounting procedures. Such were his interests in the practicalities of retailing, however, that in 1942 he left the academic world for the post of accountant at the Plymouth Co-operative Society. Three years later, he moved into general management when he joined the Portsea Island Society as secretary. Soon after, the unexpected departure of the chief executive officer opened the door to his leadership of the Society.

With the Portsea Society, which covered the Portsmouth area, John Jacques made his reputation in retailing. Despite the difficulties of immediate post-war trading (still dictated by wartime controls) the Society's performance was an unqualified success in the five years after 1945. Membership increased from 62,217 to 80,459, and annual turnover was more than doubled from £2.3 million to £4.7 million in a conurbation whose population rose from 180,000 to 240,000 over the same period. Moreover, this dynamic performance was maintained throughout the next fifteen years despite the fierce competition from multiple retailers which threatened to erode the competitive position of the Co-op as a whole.

The rapid progress of Portsea Island under the direction of John Jacques

Lord Jacques opening 1st self service shop in Great Britain (courtesy of Portsea Island Co-operative Society).

owed much to his capacity for confident, incisive examination of retailing problems and his determination to ensure that action followed analysis. His observation, for example, that following the adoption of a shorter working week and a relatively high minimum wage, high labour costs threatened the efficiency of Co-operative service, led him to adopt after 1947 self-service operation, following the false start of Jack Cohen (qv) of Tesco. Innovation and modernisation were facilitated by the necessity and opportunities of reconstruction following wartime air raids which severely damaged one-third of Co-operative properties in Portsmouth. In March 1954, Jacques revealed that during the period 1947-53 Portsea's grocery trade had increased by 141 per cent, an achievement he attributed largely to the establishment of self-service units.

The Portsea Society also highlighted the need of the Co-operative movement to cater more rigorously for the broadening demands of its

PORTSEA ISLAND MUTUAL CO-OPERATIVE SOCIETY LIMITED

THESE
PREMISES WERE
CONVERTED
IN MARCH 1948
TO BECOME THE
FIRST
SELF SERVICE SHOP
IN
GREAT BRITAIN

Plaque to commemorate the opening of the first self service store in Great Britain (courtesy of Portsea Island Co-operative Society).

clientele. While many societies cautiously concentrated their activities in the traditional area of food retailing, Jacques promoted the expansion of the service enterprises of the Society. Success was particularly marked in the field of hairdressing where, by 1960, Portsea was responsible for almost 12 per cent of Co-op hairdressing turnover.

This adventurous approach to business displayed by John Jacques was successfully complemented by his prudent day-to-day management of affairs. Close supervision of selling space, standardised stacking, reluctance to over-capitalise and monthly analysis of accounting figures established a firm financial base for the Society (his accounting procedures, in particular, became widely utilised within the Co-operative Movement).

He also confronted a perennial problem of Co-operative organisations, the role of the democratically elected board of directors. A common accusation was that boards were encroaching on the day-to-day management of societies by attempting, in committee and sub-committee meetings, to share the function of detailed management with their full-time officials. Such interference was seen as tantamount to reducing the Co-op's ability to compete with private opposition free from such constraints. The Portsea Island Society solved this difficulty by initiating a small board system (nine members) with directors responsible for long-term policy making and with no sub-committees. This newly-defined role for the board was supported by the Co-operative Independent Commission Report which affirmed that the proper role of elected officers was not to interfere in management but to concentrate on 'deciding and sanctioning major policy' {*Co-operative Independent Commission Report* (1958) 56}.

When John Jacques retired from the Portsea Island Society in 1965 he left arguably the most successful Co-operative operation in Britain. Membership stood at 193,771, direct sales at £20 million, net surplus at £1.8 million and the Society continued to pay a dividend of 1s 8d, a figure much above the contemporary Co-operative average. Such was the strength of the Portsea dividend policy that Jacques, in his presidential address to the Co-operative Congress at Scarborough in 1961, commented that

> Dividend is the Movement's greatest attraction and subject to satisfactory service and reasonable prices a Society's efficiency in the public mind is measured by the rate of dividend it pays {*Report of the Annual Co-operative Congress* (1961) 236}.

Unfortunately, for many societies the paying of a reasonable dividend on purchases was becoming an impossibility. The steady erosion of retail price maintenance meant that any retailer prepared to cut margins could sell below the recommended price and the multiples were increasingly willing to do this. In addition, the dividend appeared less pertinent to the needs of modern consumers who often demonstrated a preference for lower prices at the time of purchase rather than a payment delayed until the end of the accounting period.

Despite the problems associated with dividend the success of Portsea Island Society confirmed the ability of Co-operative societies to withstand even the strongest competition. It also confirmed the strength of its chief executive's far-sighted approach to trading. His talent for problem solving, though, was not limited to retail activities, since he exhibited similar astuteness in examining the Movement's wholesale operations. His minority report, with E Turner, on the Co-operative Wholesale Society in December 1953, achieved little at the time but it did contain the seeds of future changes. The view, for example, that the CWS should reorganise to act as a buying agency rather than as a warehousing wholesaler was, in 1965, supported by the influential Joint Reorganisation Committee, of which John Jacques was himself a member. Moreover, the minority report suggestion, that the banking activities of the Movement should be contained within a separate bank, foreshadowed the creation, in 1971, of the Co-op Bank Ltd, which in 1975 became the first new member of the London Clearing House for thirty-nine years.

On his retirement from the Portsea Island Society, John Jacques concentrated his attentions on a new role as chairman of the Co-operative Union Ltd, a post to which he was elected in 1964. His time at the Union, the main administrative body of the Co-operative Movement was, perhaps, characterised by greater caution and less innovation than he displayed at the retail level. This attitude appears to derive from a concern for maintaining a relatively low level of society subscriptions to the Union, no doubt prompted by the financial difficulties faced by many societies, and some uncertainty about the future role of the Union. Nevertheless, he continued to serve the Union with typical dedication until 1970. During his term of office the first Regional Plan for the amalgamation of societies was adopted.

Retirement from active service in the Movement did not, however, signal the end of his career. In 1968 he had been made a life peer by Harold Wilson, an honour which marked the beginning of his political career. As a Lord in Waiting (Government Whip) 1974-77 and again in 1979 he was Labour Party Spokesman on, and was particularly concerned with, Treasury and economic affairs. Between 1971 and 1975 he was president of the Retail Trades Education Council, and throughout the period he continued to serve as a Portsmouth JP. More recently he has been an active campaigner against Sunday trading on social grounds, although it is an indication of his willingness to accept compromise that he has lent his support to the policy of opening until 1.00 pm.

Lord Jacques, now a Deputy Speaker, continues to attend the House of Lords as often as is possible, travelling regularly from his home in Portsmouth where he lives with his wife Constance née White, daughter of Harry White, a warehouseman, whom he married in 1929, and his daughter Ann who is a teacher. He also has two sons, Philip, an aeronautical researcher in San Francisco, and Paul, a doctor in the East Midlands.

STEPHEN LAWRENCE

Writings:

Co-operative Bookkeeping — Elementary (Manchester: Co-operative Union, 1940).

Co-operative Bookkeeping — Intermediate (Manchester: Co-operative Union, 1941).

Co-operative Bookkeeping — Advanced (Manchester: Co-operative Union, 1942).

Presidential Address in the *Report of the Annual Co-operative Congress* (Manchester, 1961).

Co-operative Democracy (Manchester: Co-operative Union, 1966).

Management Accounting for Retail Co-operative Societies (Manchester: Co-operative Union, 1966).

(ed), *Manual on Co-operative Management* (Manchester: Co-operative Union, 1969).

Sources:

Unpublished

Reports of the Annual Co-operative Conferences.

BCe.

MCe.

Information from Lord Jacques and Dr R C Marshall, former principal of the Co-operative College and long-time acquaintance of John Jacques.

Published

Co-operative Independent Commission Report (Manchester: Co-operative Union, 1958).

Co-operative News.

Co-operative Statistics.

Christina Fulop, *Competition for Consumers* (André Deutsch, 1964).

P Greer, *Co-operatives. The British Achievement* (New York: Harper, 1955).

Sir William Richardson, *The CWS in War and Peace 1938-1976* (Manchester: Co-operative Wholesale Society, 1977).

WW 1982.

JENKINS, William

(1825-1895)

Iron and steel company manager

William Jenkins was born at Dowlais on 23 February 1825, the second of the two sons and the six children of Thomas Jenkins, schoolmaster of the John Guest School at Dowlais in South Wales, and his wife Jane née Thomas. Before the age of ten he was educated at the school run by Taliesin Williams, the son of the celebrated poet and antiquarian Iola Morganwg, and there he became a close and lasting friend of W T Lewis (qv). He continued his education on a part-time basis, under the general direction of his father, a noted Welsh literary scholar, after entering employment with the Dowlais Iron Co in 1835.

Jenkins's business training was of a purely practical nature. From starting as office boy and messenger he worked his way, in various capacities, through all the administrative and commercial departments of the massive Dowlais coal, iron and steel complex. By 1852, at the age of just twenty-seven years, he had completed his managerial training and was pressing the directors for more pay and responsibility. Following the death of Sir John Guest in that year he was placed in charge of all Dowlais commercial operations. Under the managerial leadership of George Thomas Clark (qv), Jenkins, together with the famous engineer William Menelaus (qv), helped to guide Dowlais into new fields of production. Notably the production of iron rails was progressively run down following the inauguration of steel rail manufacture in 1858.

William Jenkins (courtesy of Dr Charles Harvey).

As an influential member of the Dowlais management team Jenkins soon acquired a national standing in the iron and steel trades. He was especially noted for his sensitivity to changing conditions in the market for iron and steel and his success in profiting from them. Widespread recognition of his ability to identify and clinch favourable deals predictably brought offers of employment from other large iron and steel concerns, but for a long time Jenkins resisted all such offers. He and his wife Rosina, the daughter of mining engineer George Kirkhouse, whom he had married in 1851, were strongly attached to Wales and the Dowlais community. They were active workers of the local episcopalian Church of Wales at the village of Pant and sought to contribute to the well-being of the local community.

A strong desire to advance his career and family fortunes eventually brought Jenkins to leave South Wales. In 1869 he was appointed general manager of the Consett Iron Co at a salary of £1,500 per annum. Under the managing director, David Dale (qv), the company had been formed five years before Jenkins's arrival in County Durham to take over the Consett iron works and coal mines which since 1840 had been operated without financial success by various concerns. When Jenkins took charge of the enterprise it was in the middle of a minor crisis. The previous general manager had been dismissed for alleged inefficiency. Much of the plant was in a state of disrepair, the blast furnaces urgently needed reconstruction and profits were well below the level projected when the company was formed in 1864. Under the management of Jenkins and Dale, however, Consett established itself during the next twenty-five years as one of the largest and most profitable coal, iron and steel enterprises in Britain. The programme of expansion which began with the reconstruction and enlargement of the blast furnaces continued with the acquisition by Dale of iron ore mines in northern Spain (in partnership with Dowlais, Krupp of Essen and local Spanish interests) and additional coal mining rights, the erection of new plant to manufacture steel ingots and plates and the construction of a new angle mill. The result was a doubling of coal and pig iron capacity between 1870 and 1894 and the creation of a very large new business in steel manufactures. In the same period the company's annual net profit, expressed as a percentage of total capital employed, averaged 20.5 per cent, compared with a figure of 10.4 per cent for the years between 1864 and 1869.

Scholars who have attempted to explain the financial success of Consett have attached importance to the managerial skills of William Jenkins. He was an enthusiastic and inspiring worker who exercised a tight control over all aspects of the business whilst taking a particular interest in sales, purchasing, labour and business strategy. His letters and costing books reveal a manager fully committed to a constant search for cost reductions and marginal revenue gains. This search involved the close scrutiny of the comparative cost and price data which came to form the basis for decision-making at Consett. He involved senior managers in all departments in the quest to maintain the financial health of the business, encouraging technical staff in particular to keep themselves fully informed of new developments in their fields through active membership of professional associations. Yet the relentless manner in which Jenkins communicated the need for financial vigilance did not sour relations between the general manager and his staff. He was seen by the management team as firm but fair in his judgements and was liked for his kindness, consideration and tact in personal dealings. A strong sense of loyalty was built up at Consett with the result that many managers spent the greater part of their careers with the company.

The same positive sense of association with the business also extended to the workforce as a whole. In spite of the speed with which Jenkins enforced reductions in wages whenever iron and steel prices began to fall, relations between management and labour were never particularly strained and strikes occurred rarely. Bad feeling towards the company was restricted by the fact that Jenkins was equally ready to grant pay increases whenever wage levels began to rise in other iron and steel districts. Moreover, other aspects of the firm's labour and welfare policies convinced the majority of workers that periodic wage reductions and lay-offs were the result of commercial necessity rather than managerial malevolence. (It should also be said that the reputation of Jenkins's superior, David Dale, as an industrial conciliator spread far beyond the North East.) During Jenkins's time as general manager the firm paternalistically extended its commitment to improving the quality of working class life. Thousands of company houses were built at Consett and surrounding villages together with schools, reading rooms, hospitals and churches. Roads and pavements were made up and a park laid out. Various clubs and societies were encouraged, adult education classes organised and relief for the poor provided in times of depression. With Dale, William Jenkins was the moving spirit behind many of these schemes for social improvement and care.

Jenkins served as a member of the Benfieldside and Leadgate Local Board and was for many years chairman of the Consett School Board. After 1888, when the Durham County Council was formed, he was elected member for Consett and became an alderman in 1890. In the wider political sphere he campaigned for the Liberals, conscientiously giving support to the local MP in constituency affairs. The energy and sincere concern which Jenkins displayed in public affairs won him the respect of the community at large. In 1890 he completed twenty-one years' service with the firm, and the people of Consett and surrounding villages, as a mark of their esteem, presented Jenkins with a life-sized portrait and an album of photographs of the Consett works and district. He retired as general manager of the Consett Iron Co in 1894 to become a director of the firm. He died on 14 May 1895, just a few days after the death of his wife. The bodies of the couple were taken by train for burial in the churchyard at Pant near Dowlais. They were survived by three daughters and one son. Six other Jenkins children had died at early ages. William Jenkins left an estate valued at £92,522 gross.

CHARLES E HARVEY

Writings:

Description of the Consett Iron Works (Newcastle upon Tyne: Mawson & Co, 1893).

Sources:

Unpublished

British Steel Corporation, Middlesbrough, Northern Regional Records Centre, Consett Iron Co papers.

Glamorgan CRO, Cardiff, Dowlais Iron Co letter books.

MCe.

Notes on 'William Jenkins of Dowlais and Consett' prepared for the author by D J Lewis of Cardiff.

A S Wilson, 'The Consett Iron Company Limited: A Case Study in Victorian Business History' (Durham MPhil, 1973).

Published

Consett Iron Co, *Leaves from the Consett Letter Books 1887-1893* (Consett: pp, 1962).

Consett Lions Club, *The Consett Story* (Consett: pp, 1963).

R M Hornsby, *History of the Consett Iron Company* (Consett: pp, 1958).

Peter L Payne, *Colvilles and the Scottish Steel Industry* (Oxford: Clarendon Press, 1979).

Newcastle Daily Chronicle 13 July 1891, 15 May 1895.

Newcastle upon Tyne Weekly Chronicle 19 Sept 1877.

Northern Echo 17, 19 July 1872.

'Presentation to Alderman William Jenkins' *Consett Guardian* 31 Oct 1890.

H W Richardson and J M Bass, 'The Profitability of Consett Iron Company before 1914' *Business History* 7 (1965).

JENKINSON, Sir Mark Webster

(1880-1935)

Accountant and industrialist

Mark Webster Jenkinson was born at 263 Pearl Street, Ecclesall Bierlow, Yorkshire, on 31 July 1880, one of the seven sons of Mark Jenkinson (1856-1942), a Sheffield accountant (who left £7,198), and his wife Hannah Elizabeth née Mansell. In later life he obscured the date of his birth,

Sir Mark Webster Jenkinson
(courtesy of Vickers Ltd.)

which was usually given as 1878. He was educated at Wesley College, Sheffield, and privately. In 1901 he was first prizeman in the Finals of the Institute of Chartered Accountants (of which he became a fellow in 1908). As a young man he practised accountancy in Sheffield, and published a series of popular guides, beginning with *Bookkeeping for Retail Grocers* (1905). He edited the *Accountants' Journal* for a period, and also contributed to the *Accountant*. He became well-known as a lecturer to student societies, taking a keen interest in matters affecting accountancy students. It was largely due to him that the Institute of Chartered Accountants established a fund to help students returning from war service after 1918.

After the outbreak of war, Webster Jenkinson's Sheffield background was utilised in dealing with armament contracts, and in September 1915 he joined the Ministry of Munitions, where he remained until March 1920. Appalled by the wasted expenditure which the Ministry was incurring, he served successively as Director of Factory Accounting, and as Controller of the Department of Factory Audits and Costs. He later boasted that he cut the cost of one of the first contracts submitted to him by £1 million. As one example of the waste which Jenkinson's persistent and exact mind had to extirpate, he found that hitherto, both in peace and war, the audit of Woolwich Arsenal had never counted the cash, which fluctuated between £70,000 and £250,000.

With the cessation of hostilities, Webster Jenkinson became Chief Liquidator of Contracts at the Ministry of Munitions. The magnitude of the transactions which he directed during 1919-20 was unprecedented in British history. One of the members of the Ministry's Advisory Council on Liquidations was Dudley Docker (qv), and when in 1921 Docker formed a private investment bank, the Electric & Railway Finance Corporation (Elrafin), Jenkinson was recruited as its secretary. Docker's talent in picking younger men, and promoting them to high responsibilities, was well-known, and Webster Jenkinson fully justified the confidence of his mentor. Elrafin was not only involved with British railways and electro-technology, but also with Docker's internationally ramified interests in such Belgian investment trusts as Sofina. The electrical supply interests of Lord Cowdray (qv) were represented on Elrafin's board by his brother Sir Edward Pearson, and after the latter's death, by Sir Clarendon Hyde.

In April 1920 Docker had resigned as director of Vickers after criticising its improvident financial policy, but he maintained sizeable interests in the company, retaining great influence through his nominees on the board. In the winter of 1921-22, when Vickers's position had further deteriorated, Docker contrived for Webster Jenkinson to report to the Vickers board on the company's position. Vickers had expanded very rapidly in 1918-19, adding electro-technology, rolling-stock, optical instruments and general engineering to its steelworks and shipyards. Jenkinson's conclusion that 'trusts can only be successful if confined ... to one type of production or its subsidiaries' {Scott (1962) 157} was based on an accurate analysis of Vickers's problems; but the values of the companies which Vickers had acquired during the boom of 1919 had already so depreciated, that Vickers were unable or reluctant to sell many of their new subsidiaries. Vickers paid only 5 per cent dividends in 1921 and 1922, thereafter passing their

HM Repair Ship Resource, fitted with Parsons Geared Turbines and Yarrow Boilers built by Vickers-Armstrong (from Brassey's Naval and Shipping Annual *1929).*

dividend until 1927. They were declining into bankruptcy, and in June 1925, under conditions of high secrecy, appointed an advisory committee on reconstruction, comprising Sir William Plender (qv) the accountant, Dudley Docker and Docker's confrère, Reginald McKenna (qv), chairman of the Midland Bank. This trio did not make detailed examinations, but relied instead on Jenkinson's scrutiny and calculations. The report was in every sense Jenkinson's work, and following the principles of his advice of 1922, recommended that the group's assets be written down by £12,442,366. The issued share capital was reduced from £12,315,483 to £4,105,161; fixed assets were written down by £4,254,994; and the book value of subsidiaries by £5,488,316. This bold and acute document was published in December 1925. It earned Jenkinson a knighthood in 1926 and a reputation as 'one of the ablest financiers in the country' {*Financial Times* 5 Nov 1935}.

He resigned as secretary of Elrafin to join Vickers's board. During 1926 he implemented his own recommendations that the bulk of the subsidiaries be sold, and that Vickers revert from being a vertical combine of various supplementary, allied industries into a more compact group manufacturing steel and ships. Both the Vickers board and management were restructured, and instead of the inexact delineations of responsibility which had prevailed before, Jenkinson designed a new structure. The

Vickers board, with overall control, was sub-divided into three management boards, with executive responsibility (armaments and shipbuilding; finance management; and industrial management, the latter with further sub-divisions). He long argued that the evolution of business organisation necessitated the divorce of control and management, and that rationalised companies should have two boards of directors, 'control' chiefly comprising outsiders, and 'executive' comprising the operating managers of the different divisions.

Webster Jenkinson was a zealot about the purity and accuracy of accounts, urging that every public company should be obliged to employ an official to explain its accounts intelligibly to shareholders. He faulted Vickers's existing audit and accounts procedures as antiquated, unreliable, and unable to give a clear record of all transactions. He re-designed these procedures, establishing full and accurate flows of internal information. In the autumn of 1927, after a discreet power struggle, Jenkinson became finance comptroller of Vickers, attaining unrestricted scope to implement his principles of scientific management. He introduced formal procedures and systematic planning: his ascendancy terminated the ramshackle and intuitive leadership of the Vickers old guard, which had been successful before 1914, but had proved unequal to post-war complexities. His attitude to his colleagues was implicit in his view that public companies should be forbidden to have more than one-third of their directors aged above sixty. As he warned, 'So long as boards of directors are constituted without regard to the qualifications of those selected, so long as shareholders prefer a man "with a name" to a man "with a future" — so long will other nations continue to beat us' { *Times* 1 March 1932}.

Webster Jenkinson had served in 1923-24 on the departmental committee to reform Army accountancy systems, chaired by General Sir Herbert Lawrence (qv), who was chairman of Vickers in 1926-37. Between them, Jenkinson and Lawrence dominated Vickers's strategy in the decade after 1925, although Docker remained influential until the spring of 1928. Vickers's acquisition in 1927 of the armaments and shipbuilding capacity of Armstrong, Whitworth was marginal to the main plan of Jenkinson and Lawrence, although it enabled Jenkinson to develop his idea of executive and control boards. Vickers became a holding company, whilst the newly-formed Vickers-Armstrongs company operated executive functions in the various shipyards, steelworks and engineering factories. Ruthless in his negotiations with Armstrongs during 1926-27, Jenkinson would not have minded their collapse. He agreed with Lawrence that Vickers should not pay cash for Armstrongs, as Vickers's laboriously reconstructed cash position was a main element of their new-found strength. Jenkinson and Lawrence attached far greater strategic importance to their deal with W L Hichens (qv) of Cammell Laird, implemented with effect from 1 January 1929, whereby the two groups' rolling-stock interests were merged in the Metropolitan-Cammell Co and their steelworks united in the English Steel Corporation (ESC). Although ESC was unlucky in starting operations on the eve of the Depression, and suffered from the backwardness of much of its plant, unlike most steel-makers, it carried no debenture charges. Its strong cash position made it the only steel company to pay preference shareholders in 1931.

Vickers's co-operation with Cammell Laird was one of the most vaunted

RMS Orford, *built by Messrs Vickers-Armstrong, at the naval construction works, Barrow-in-Furness, for the Orient Line (from* Brassey's Naval and Shipping Annual *1929).*

examples of industrial rationalisation in the period, and Webster Jenkinson was strongly identified with its development. When, by 1926, it had become clear that Britain's return to the gold standard was not the panacea for industrial recovery that had been promised, 'rationalisation' became the new shibboleth among politicians, industrialists, financiers and Whitehall officials. Jenkinson was foremost in urging the rationalisation movement: so much so that, in 1931, when he was a member of Lord May's (qv) committee on the national economy, one Treasury official complained that he had 'an amalgamation complex' {PRO Cab 21/384, Sir Percival Waterfield to Sir Maurice Hankey, 3 July 1931}.

Jenkinson was critical of British financial institutions' facilities for furthering rationalisation. His evidence, in 1930, to Lord Macmillan's Committee on Finance and Industry was based on the difficulties which Vickers had experienced since 1918. He recommended the formation of a financial trust with its capital invested in gilt-edged securities, which would provide capital for industry and actively involve financiers in industrial management. He also propounded a Contracts Guarantee Scheme to enable British manufacturers to take contracts on deferred terms from Central and Eastern Europe. Finally Jenkinson advocated the institution of Industrial Banks to assist the rationalisation of different industrial sectors, speaking in terms which resembled the ambit of the Bankers Industrial Development Co of C Bruce Gardner (qv). More generally, he deprecated the loose co-ordination between the City and most of industry.

Jenkinson was intimately involved in Vickers's foreign armaments contracts. These were usually with minor powers, to whom the financial facilities of the package (involving payment by instalments over a term of several years) were at least as important as the technical performance of the weaponry offered. British armourers were at a disadvantage to their Continental competitors as armaments were excluded by the Trade Facilities Act of 1921 from receiving Export Credit Guarantees from the

Launch of the Captain O'Brien, *first post-war submarine for the Chilean Navy (from Brassey's* Naval and Shipping Annual *1929).*

Government. Very fine calculations were involved: in 1932 Jenkinson was obliged to visit Ankara to settle questions about deferred payments by Turkey for anti-aircraft equipment.

He was an early proponent of the future of civil aviation, and although he shared partial responsibility for the formation and expansion of Vickers Aviation in 1928, he was unable to prevent the long-standing friction between Vickers Aviation and Vickers-Armstrongs. Apart from his directorship of Vickers, Vickers-Armstrongs and ESC, he was on the board of several of their subsidiaries, including Broadway Finance & Investment, Whitehead Torpedoes, and the optical instrument makers, Cooke, Troughton & Simms. He was also a director of several foreign concerns in which Vickers were interested, such as the Spanish arsenal La Placencia, and the Cie Européenne de Participations Industrielles, a holding company to which Vickers's Yugoslav and Romanian interests were transferred. CEPI, at its inception in 1934, was the third financial company ever registered in Monaco, the others being the Prince's private trust, and a holding company for the Credit Anstalt Bank. He also acted as deputy-chairman of Car & General Insurance, and of Motor Union Insurance.

His expertise was sought outside the Vickers group. He was active in trying to strengthen the colliery and metallurgy interests of the Earl of Dudley (qv), and was vice-chairman of the latter's Baggeridge Colliery and his Round Oak Works. When Birmingham Small Arms sustained a loss of £797,928 in 1932, they sought the advice of Dudley Docker, who in turn arranged for Jenkinson to report on the structure of BSA. His recommendations that BSA's capital be written down, and their subsidiaries amalgamated, were neglected amidst the board-room rows of 1932-34.

He sat on several government committees, including those on Night Baking and on the Cost of Housing. The Lawrence Committee on Army Administration and the May Committee on Economy have already been mentioned. The latter's report, published on 31 July 1931, was called by Keynes 'the most foolish document I have ever had the misfortune to read' {Harrod (1951) 438}. It certainly exaggerated the difficulties facing the national economy; its recommendation that unemployment relief be cut by 20 per cent, to save £96 million, was widely resented. The role of the May Committee in the collapse of the Labour Government, and the formation of a National Government later in 1931, is well-known.

In character Jenkinson remained a compulsively industrious Sheffield accountant, and self-confessed devotee of the Victorian spirit, Victorian living and genuine Victorian cooking. Some of his more cosmopolitan Vickers co-directors thought him unpolished. This was ungrateful, for his contribution to the organisation was immense, and he almost literally gave his life for the company. After many warnings that he was over-working, he developed heart disease in the summer of 1935, and died on 4 November 1935, at his house, Woodside, Smallfield, Surrey. He was apparently unmarried. For many years he was the companion of Mrs Nina Stokes, and indeed, his affection for Sir Basil Zaharoff flowered after the latter had shown gallantry to Mrs Stokes during a visit to Paris. She and one of Jenkinson's brothers (a Sheffield accountant) were joint executors of his will executed in 1924, and under its terms, she inherited most of his estate, worth £10,918 in 1935.

R P T DAVENPORT-HINES

Writings:

Bookkeeping for Retail Grocers and Other Tradesmen (Gee, 1905).

The Elements of Bookkeeping (Arnold, 1906).

Cost Accounts for Small Manufacturers (Gee, 1907).

Bookkeeping and Accounting (Arnold, 1910).

The Promotion and Accounts of a Private Limited Company (Gee, 1911; 3rd edition, 1931).

The Promotion and Accounts of a Public Limited Company (Gee, 1912).

Some Notes on Bankruptcy (Gee, 1915).

Costing at National Factories: A Lecture Delivered at the London School of Economics 9 October 1918 (Gee, 1918).

JENKINSON Sir Mark Webster

The Workers' Interest in Costing (Gee, 1919).

The Value of a Balance Sheet (Gee, 1928; 2nd edition 1929).

Some Aspects of Rationalisation (Gee, 1929).

Some Dangers of Rationalisation (Gee, 1929).

PP, Committee on Finance and Industry, chaired by Lord Macmillan, 1929-31 (1931) Cmd 3897.

Sources:

Unpublished

House of Lords RO, papers of Sir Patrick Hannon.

PRO, papers of Ministry of Munitions (Mun 4/6375, minutes of Jenkinson's evidence, 20 January 1919, to 5th meeting of the sub-committee on Costs of Departmental Committee of Enquiry into the Royal Ordnance Factories, Woolwich, chaired by Rt Hon Thomas McKinnon Wood MP); papers of Cabinet Office; Board of Trade (BT 56/2, Jenkinson memorandum on Steel Industry, July 1929).

Vickers House, Millbank, microfilm collection and J D Scott's research notes.

BCe.

PrC; Will.

Richard Davenport-Hines, 'The British Armaments Industry during Disarmament 1918-1936' (Cambridge, PhD 1979).

Published

Richard Davenport-Hines, 'Vickers' Balkan Conscience' *Business History* 25 (1983).

—, *Dudley Docker* (Cambridge: Cambridge University Press, 1984).

Economist 12 Dec 1925 (for text of Report of Advisory Committee on Vickers).

Financial Times 5 Nov 1935.

Sir H Roy F Harrod, *The Life of John Maynard Keynes* (Macmillan, 1951).

Robert H Parker, *British Accountants: A Biographical Sourcebook* (New York: Arno Press, 1980).

Richard S Sayers, *The Bank of England 1890-1944* (3 vols: Cambridge University Press, 1977).

John D Scott, *Vickers, a History* (Weidenfeld & Nicolson, 1962).

Times 1 Mar 1932, 5 Nov 1935.

Vickers News 1925-35.

WWW.

Sir Harry Jephcott (courtesy of Glaxo).

JEPHCOTT, Sir Harry

(1891-1978)

Pharmaceutical manufacturer

Harry Jephcott was born at Tardebigge, Redditch, Worcestershire, on 15 January 1891, third and youngest son of John Josiah Jephcott (1853-1929), of Redditch, a train driver and former miner, and his wife Helen (1849-1930), daughter of Charles Matthews, of Coundon, Warwickshire. He was educated at King Edward Grammar School, Camp Hill, Birmingham, and with the financial help of his eldest brother Charles (1879-1961) trained as a pharmacist. He was apprenticed in 1907 to the pharmacist J Thornton at Redditch, and afterwards worked for a pharmacy called Hunt's at Winchester. In 1911 he came third in the Pharmaceutical Society's John Bell scholarship examination, and as only two scholarships were offered, he instead joined the Customs and Excise Department of the Civil Service in 1912. He specialised there in the analysis of tobacco, and in 1914, after qualifying as a chemist and druggist, was seconded to the Department of the Government Chemist. Having previously studied at West Ham Technical College, in 1915 he gained a BSc degree with first class honours in chemistry at the University of London. He gained the diploma of pharmaceutical chemist in 1916, was awarded the Pharmaceutical Society's silver medal in 1917, and became an associate of the Royal Institute of Chemistry in 1916, being elected to fellowship in 1920. He took his MSc degree in 1918, submitting a thesis on tobacco.

In April 1919 Jephcott left the civil service for private industry. The Anglo-New Zealand mercantile and trading firm of Joseph Nathan had, since 1908, been marketing dried milk for infants and invalids under the trade name of Glaxo. The quality of the milk supplied from New Zealand for marketing in Britain fluctuated considerably, and Jephcott was recruited by Alec Nathan (1872-1954) to monitor the quality and set standards. His first laboratory was a tiny room in a warehouse off Harrow Road in West London, and he was regarded by other members of the Nathan family as 'Alec's bloody folly' {Jephcott (1969) 91}. Nevertheless, he soon gained the confidence of the London partners, and in 1920-21 was sent by them to New Zealand and Australia to review the productive methods and standardise the quality of their milk supplies. The success of this mission established his standing with the Nathan family. Product quality was his first concern with Glaxo dried milk in 1919, and quality of products and people remained paramount considerations throughout his life.

Glaxo milk powder suffered a serious contraction of demand in 1922, but in the next year Jephcott laid the basis for the revival after 1926 of the fortunes of the Glaxo department of the Nathan firm. He persuaded the Nathans to send him, as Glaxo's chemist, to the International Dairy Congress held in Washington, DC, in 1923. While in the USA, Jephcott seized the chance to visit Professor Elmer V McCollum and Dr Theodore Zucker to discuss their recent work on 'accessory food factors'. At a time when no vitamin had been isolated, and nothing was known of their chemical nature, Jephcott, on Glaxo's behalf, had conducted a series of experiments to test the antiscorbutic value of dried milk — a question which was often raised with the company by pediatricians and anxious mothers. McCollum demonstrated to Jephcott his recent discovery that there were two vitamins, A and D, while Zucker had devised a process to extract Vitamin D from fish-liver oil. Jephcott immediately realised that Glaxo powder fortified with anti-rachitic Vitamin D would have an almost immeasurable advantage over its competitors, and at his instigation, the Nathan company secured a licence under Zucker's process. Thus, within five years of joining the business, he laid the foundation for its development as a pharmaceuticals manufacturer. In 1928 Dr Harry Steenbock of Wisconsin University patented his process for irradiating foods containing ergosterol to raise their Vitamin D content, and after refinements, Steenbock's process superseded Zucker's, with Nathans obtaining the first British licence. This development ultimately led to the production of Vitamin D as a pure substance (calciferol) in 1931.

In 1924 the Nathans' Glaxo department began production of Ostelin, the company's first pharmaceutical product, and the first vitamin-concentrate to be made on a commercial scale in Britain. Jephcott's visits to the USA led him to realise that his work as a commercial chemist would be inseparable from the intricacies of international patent law, and in his spare time he read for the Bar. He was called to the Middle Temple in 1925, but never practised law. His contribution to the Nathans' profits was recognised by his appointment as general manager of the Glaxo department in 1925, and by his election as a director of the parent company, Joseph Nathan & Co, in 1929. He became managing director of their new subsidiary, Glaxo Laboratories Ltd (GL) in 1935, succeeding Alec Nathan as managing director of the parent company in 1939.

After Ostelin, GL began marketing other vitamin products, such as Adexolin (Vitamins A and D), Berin (B$_1$), Celin (C), Viteolin (E) and Kapilon (K). They began manufacturing purified anti-anaemic liver extracts in 1936, by which date Jephcott was transforming GL into a pharmaceutical company.

The Second World War gave further impetus to GL's growth and to Jephcott's career. Jephcott was Adviser on Manufactured Foods to the Ministry of Food in 1941-43 and chairman of the Therapeutic Research Corporation during 1943. He visited the USA on behalf of the Ministry of Supply in 1944 to report on penicillin production, and was sent as advisor to the Indian Government on milk powder production in 1945.

Jephcott had been quick to realise in the 1930s the fantastic developments that were occurring in chemo-therapeutic substances. He had the vision to foresee the large and exciting business opportunities that awaited as fine chemicals replaced galenicals. This conviction had been evident in his strategy for GL during the 1930s; around 1938 he had contemplated resigning to become a New Zealand fruit farmer when he was particularly discouraged at Glaxo's continuing commitment to unexciting and only moderately profitable food subsidiaries such as Trengrouse & Nathan Ltd. However, by 1943 he persuaded his colleagues

Bombay factory extension, 3 August 1938 (courtesy of Glaxo).

that their organisation of fine chemical production should be developed and given priority. This was his reason for resigning in that year from the Ministry of Food. In 1944 he seized the opportunity to propel this strategy forward by securing for GL the leading position in Britain's adoption of American deep fermentation techniques for the production of penicillin in Britain. As a chemist he well understood the magnitude of the problem of determining the structure and synthesis of penicillin. Jephcott led GL to construct a purpose-built antibiotics factory at Barnard Castle, County Durham (1944), and another at Ulverston in Lancashire (1946); he also visited the USA in 1945 to negotiate licensing agreements with Merck and Squibb which enabled GL to use deep culture techniques for the production of penicillin. He never lost sight of the chemical, scientific and technological fundamentals of his business. Within days of succeeding Alec Nathan as chairman of Glaxo Laboratories in October 1945, he left on another tour of the USA, New Zealand, Australia and India. GL achieved a major research success in 1948 when a team under Dr E Lester Smith isolated vitamin B_{12} (the anti-pernicious anaemia factor) in the liver. This vitamin was so potent that its dosage was measured in micrograms: its injectable solution was marketed as Cytamen.

In 1947 Jephcott arranged that Glaxo Laboratories should go public and divest itself of the many non-pharmaceutical interests of its parent, Joseph Nathan & Co. Simultaneously he began establishing or extending local production in several overseas markets previously served wholly or largely from Britain. The overseas marketing of Glaxo products during Jephcott's chairmanship was concentrated in Commonwealth countries, (especially Australia, India, Pakistan and South Africa), together with Italy and South America, but some crucial foreign markets such as Japan and the USA were scarcely broached. Although there were then excellent commercial reasons for this (including American cross-licensing agreements and British Treasury restrictions on overseas investment), it set limits on GL's growth capacity which Jephcott's successors later had to surmount. The company co-operated with the Medical Research Council in work on cortisone production, and in 1950 introduced the first commercial cortisone produced in Britain. In the same year GL started developing a commercial synthesis of cortisone made entirely from materials available within the British Commonwealth's sterling area. Their discovery that waste-juice from sisal was a copious source of hecogenin led to GL's development of a cortisone synthesis and to a successful series of Glaxo corticosteroids, such as Cortelan, EF-Cortelan, Delta-Costalan and Delta-EF-Cortelan. This break-through conversion by GL was one of the most complex series of chemical processes ever brought to production scale.

Jephcott had numerous interests outside Glaxo. GL had been a major customer for many years of Metal Box, and Jephcott, who became a friend of its redoubtable chairman Sir Robert Barlow (qv), was a director of Metal Box in 1950-64. The Ministry of Housing and Local Government appointed Jephcott in 1953 as chairman of a committee on synthetic detergents, which reported in 1955. He was a member of the Government's Advisory Council on Scientific Policy in 1953-56, and after retiring from executive office as GL's managing director in 1956, chaired the Council for Scientific and Industrial Research (CSIR) in 1956-61. But as non-executive chairman of GL after 1956, Jephcott nevertheless remained an important and often decisive figure in the counsels of the group, and continued to travel widely in its overseas operations even after becoming life president. For some time Jephcott had felt concerned that the influence of the foreign-owned pharmaceutical companies was becoming excessive, and that this was due in part to the number and smallness of many British companies. In July 1957 he discussed his feelings with certain directors of Allen & Hanburys and there was mutual agreement that a merger between Glaxo Laboratories and Allen & Hanburys might be to the advantage of both and would strengthen the British-owned sector of the industry. Discussions proceeded and in April 1958 Glaxo acquired a controlling interest in Allen & Hanburys. Other companies acquired in this period were Dextran, manufacturers of Intradex blood plasma, and Murphy, makers of horticultural insecticides and pesticides, in 1952 and 1955 respectively, and later Evans Medical, Edinburgh Pharmaceutical Industries, Farleys and British Drug Houses.

Jephcott was knighted in 1946 on the Ministry of Food's recommendation and created a baronet in 1962 after retiring as chairman of CSIR. He held many other professional offices and honours. He was chairman (1947-52) and president (1952-55) of the Association of British Chemical Manufacturers. In 1948, when the Pharmaceutical Society completed the transfer of its School of Pharmacy to London University, he was elected chairman of the School's Council, which position he retained until 1969. He was president of the Royal Institute of Chemistry in 1953-55, and held honorary fellowships of the Royal College of General Practitioners (1960), the Royal Society of Medicine (1961), and the School of Pharmacy, London University (1966). He received an honorary DSc from Birmingham University in 1956, was made Freeman of Port Fairy in Victoria in 1964, was admitted to the court of patrons of the Royal College

Glaxo medical list September 1945 (courtesy of Glaxo).

of Surgeons in 1965, and was awarded the Pharmaceutical Society's charter gold medal in 1970.

Jephcott was governor of North London Collegiate School from 1957 and of the London School of Economics in 1952-68, where respectively his wife and elder son were educated. He endowed several charitable trusts, including the annual Jephcott lecture at the Royal Society of Medicine in 1958 and a post-doctoral fellowship at the School of Pharmacy in 1971. The most important of his benefactions was perhaps the Triangle Trust, which was first formed in the 1930s by Jephcott and two Glaxo co-directors, Colonel E A Rose and Archie Sandercock. The original objectives of the Trust might have prejudiced its eligibility for charitable status and in 1949 Jephcott revived the Trust as sole settlor, to assist needy employees or former employees of the British pharmaceutical industry, or their dependants. He lived from 1928 at the same house at Pinner in Middlesex, but also owned a house and farms at East Portlemouth in south Devon. He gave and endowed 35 acres of the coastline there to the National Trust in 1966.

'He was a formidable person, most business-like in negotiation, mindful yet confident of the technical problems to be solved and entirely a realist in the use and need of capital resources and human skills', so Sir Frank Hartley wrote, adding that Jephcott was an exceptional

example of hard work, devotion to duty, economical use of time and energy, fearless approach to challenge, compassion to his fellow men and generosity to those suffering from adversity ... he never ceased to amaze me by his fantastic intuitive sense of what was possible in our industry ... He could divine the right course to take and rationalise his decision afterwards. He understood how to use wisely the expertise of others and never ceased to emphasise the possibilities of application of science. He could recognise and encourage capacity in applied chemistry and therein lay much of his success as an industrialist {*Pharmaceutical Journal* 3 June 1978}.

A forthright man, he was of imposing appearance (almost six-and-a-half feet tall), but always kind-hearted and considerate. He brought zest and enthusiasm to everything he did, and found his own rewards in doing a job well. A shrewd judge of character, he had an exceptional capacity for inspiring colleagues or subordinates with dedication, enthusiasm and personal devotion. Although a perfectionist, he was never cantankerous or unreasonably demanding. He was an indefatigible overseas traveller, and an inveterate walker, who took an evening 'constitutional' of at least five miles whenever possible, sometimes to the physical distress of those who were expected to accompany him when he was visiting Glaxo establishments overseas.

As a young man he was an ardent photographer, developing, printing and enlarging all his own negatives, and in the mid-1930s he usually took a rather bulky 16mm movie camera on overseas business trips. With the post-war growth of colour photography he reverted to still cameras and left the processing to Kodak. He maintained an interest in carpentry and cabinet-making until the Second World War, and in the spring of 1939 personally built a reinforced concrete air-raid shelter in his garden. Jephcott was a lifelong gardener, particularly interested in cultivating apples, pears and gladioli, and in constructional activities such as erecting greenhouses and laying paths. With the aid of a fellow Glaxo director, Colonel Rose, Jephcott built his own radio receiver around 1927, and would not countenance television until colour became available in 1968. On a visit to Chicago in 1936, he bought a Hammond electronic organ which was the first to be imported to southern England. It appealed both to his scientific mind and to a musical taste nurtured in youth upon the Three Choirs Festival, the great oratorios and Midlands church music. Although he was never an accomplished organist, he bought a series of these electronic instruments, and made generous contributions through his charitable trusts to rebuilding church and cathedral organs in New Zealand and England.

Jephcott married in April 1919, at Hampstead, Doris (born 1893), daughter of Henry Gregory, builder, of Swiss Cottage, London. She had been the first woman to win the Pharmaceutical Society's Fairchild scholarship in 1915, gaining the pharmaceutical chemist's diploma in 1917, in which year she also won the Pharmaceutical Society's bronze medal. They had two sons. Sir Harry Jephcott died on 29 May 1978 leaving £2,011,589 gross.

R P T DAVENPORT-HINES

Writings:

(with Alfred L Bacharach) 'The Anti-Scorbutic Value of Dried Milk' *Biochemical Journal* 15 (1921), reprinted as *La Valeur Antiscorbutique du Lait Sec* (Brussels: Cl Denis, 1924).

'Estimation of Fat, Lactose and Moisture in Dried Milks' *The Analyst* 48 (1923).

(with R F Hunwicke and Norman Ratcliffe) 'The Attainment of Bacterial Purity in the Manufacture of Dried Milk' *Proceedings of World Dairy Congress* 2 (1923).

(with N Ratcliffe) 'Fat in Commercial Casein' *Proceedings of World Dairy Congress* 2 (1923).

(with R F Hunwicke) 'The Destruction of Bacteria in the Roller Process of Milk Drying' *Journal of Dairy Science* 8 (1925).

(with A L Bacharach) 'L'Effet de la Dessication sur les Vitamines du Lait' *Le Lait* 6 (1926).

(with A L Bacharach) 'A Rapid and Reliable Test for Vitamin D' *Biochemical Journal* 20 (1926).

(with A L Bacharach) 'The Quantitative Estimation of Vitamin D' *ibid* 22 (1928).

(with A L Bacharach) 'Vitamin D and Fecal Reaction' *Journal of Biological Chemistry* 82 (1929).

letter on penicillin supplies to Poland *Times* 15 Jan 1946.

(part author) *Report on the Chemical Industry* (Association of British Chemical Manufacturers, 1949).

'The Glaxo Research Organisation', chapter nine in Sir John D Cockcroft (ed), *The Organisation of Research Establishments* (Cambridge: Cambridge University Press, 1966).

The First Fifty Years: An Account of the Early Life of Joseph Edward Nathan and the First Fifty Years of His Merchandise Business that Eventually Became the Glaxo Group (Ipswich: Glaxo, 1969).

Sources:

Unpublished

London School of Economics, Business History Unit (temporary deposit), papers of Glaxo and Sir Harry Jephcott including Edwards Seminar papers.

Information from Doris, Lady Jephcott; Sir Anthony Jephcott; Dr Louis Bieder; Mrs Gillian Lewis; Sir John Hanbury; Roy Stagg.

Published

Burke's Peerage and Baronetage.

Pharmaceutical Journal 3 June 1978.

David Wilson, *Penicillin in Perspective* (Faber, 1976).

WWW.

JOBLING-PURSER, Ernest Joseph

(1875-1959)

Glass manufacturer

Ernest Joseph Jobling-Purser was born in Ireland in 1875. His family's connections with North-East England led to his apprenticeship with the Tyneside engineering firm, C A Parsons Ltd. He pursued a career in electrical engineering, first with Parsons and later with Ferranti, until 1917, when at the age of forty-two he joined his uncle, James A Jobling, as the managing director of the Sunderland glass firm, Greener & Co.

James A Jobling had taken over Greeners (a small glass firm manufacturing pressed glass table ware) in 1915 as a bad debt. Although the firm had enjoyed some prosperity during the twenty years following its foundation in 1869, by 1915 it was suffering from the competition of cheap foreign glass and the inadequacies of its own outdated equipment. Jobling-Purser succeeded in reversing the firm's decline largely through securing, in 1922, the exclusive British manufacturing rights to the new heat-resistant boro-silicate glass developed in America by Corning Glass Co. Jobling-Purser's foresight in recognising the potential of boro-silicate glass is underlined by the lack of enthusiasm showed by other British glass firms; Cornings had previously tried to interest other British firms in the new glass but without success.

The production of boro-silicate glass at Sunderland rapidly expanded. By the 1930s the firm's ranges of domestic and industrial glass ware included oven-door panels, laboratory and scientific equipment, insulators, globes and chimneys, traffic signal lenses, car headlight glasses, and — most importantly — 'Pyrex' oven and table ware. Ordinary pressed glass continued to be produced and the firm had some success with its range of 'Weardale' table ware. The glass firm became James A Jobling &

JAMES A. JOBLING & COMPANY LIMITED

Wear Glass Works, Sunderland

England

Telephone: 57251   Telex: 53146   Telegrams: Greener, Telex

Pyrex trademark of James A Jobling & Co Ltd (courtesy of Miss C Ross).

Co Ltd in 1925 on its amalgamation with Jobling's other business interests in Newcastle: the Tyne Mineral Works, the Tyne Oil & Grease Works and the Basic Slag Grinding Mills at Benwell. In 1928 Jobling-Purser was made the governing director and he continued to play an active part in the firm, taking out a number of patents during the 1930s.

In 1949 he retired to his native Ireland. He died at his home, Rathmines Castle in Dublin, on 23 November 1959, leaving £3,541 gross.

CATHERINE ROSS

Writings:

British Patents:

1933 (401,710)
1937-38 (442,882)
1938-39 (482,266)
1949-50 (626,000)

Sources:

Published

Glass Technology Feb 1960.

Sunderland Echo 24 Nov 1959.

Sunderland as an Industrial and Residential Centre (Sunderland Corporation, 1927).

Sunderland Official Industrial Handbook (Sunderland Corporation, 1937).

JOHNSON, Claude Goodman

(1864-1926)

Automobile and aircraft engine manufacturer

Claude Goodman Johnson was born at Datchet, Buckinghamshire, on 24 October 1864, the sixth child of William Goodman Johnson, a glover, and his wife Sophia Fanny née Adams. His father was regarded as an unsuccessful man who spent most of his life as an official in the Science

JOHNSON Claude Goodman

Claude Goodman Johnson (courtesy of Rolls-Royce Ltd).

Museum, Kensington, where he worked for thirty years. But he passed on to his son most of his Victorian virtues, a remarkable energy, a love of good music, especially Bach, and a relentless determination to succeed. Between September 1878 and April 1882 Claude Johnson attended St Paul's School where he became a foundation scholar and specialised in drawing. On leaving school he attended the Royal College of Art for a short period, but decided quickly that his abilities were outmatched by his tastes and turned to administration.

Most great men will admit to an important element of luck in their lives, though the word is one which is ill-defined. Johnson was presumably introduced by his father to Sir Francis Philip Cunliffe-Owen (1828-94), the director of the Museum and a great organiser of exhibitions. He gave Johnson his first job, to organise a Fisheries Exhibition in 1883. This was followed by Health, Inventions and the Colonial and Indian Exhibitions, in rapid succession. The Prince of Wales had been persuaded to set up what later became known as the Imperial Institute and Johnson was made the Chief Clerk of the new venture, which very nearly failed despite the Prince's patronage. The background and experience of this work was clearly invaluable, for the range of his contacts and experience was much broader than that offered by most conventional careers open to a young man of his age.

Johnson's first contact with the chrysalis world of the automobile started when he arranged the first national car exhibition, entitled, with typical Victorian self-confidence, the International Exhibition of Motors and their Appliances. This brought him into contact with F R Simms (qv), the founder of the Automobile Club, who invited Johnson to become its first secretary, at a salary of £5 a week plus a bonus of 10s for every new member. This, too, very nearly failed, but the challenge gave Johnson the opportunity to develop his remarkable flair for publicity. He organised and ran exhibitions, trials and other automobile clubs at a time when the motor car was not only a rich man's toy but regarded as a dangerous innovation which, in Britain, was preceded by the legendary red flag. He became, simultaneously, the first secretary of the Aero Club, founded by a group of balloonists, and should probably be remembered as much for the fact that, in a letter to the committee of the Automobile Club, he proposed and set out what would today be recognised as the first clear design for a motorway — a road specially built for motor vehicles which avoided cities, had width, good surface, bridged minor roads, would carry 'fruit to London', would be paid for partly by tolls and partly by 'government subsidy', and would allow 'unlimited speed'. Here were the strong indications of that most fundamental quality of all great entrepreneurs — vision.

Having increased the membership of the Automobile Club from 163 to 2,000, Johnson was tempted into his second move, a stage nearer the exotic world of the automobile. In June 1903 Paris Singer launched his 'City and Suburban Electric Car Project' and persuaded Johnson to join him. Within a few months Johnson moved again, into partnership with the Honourable C S Rolls (qv), whom he had met frequently on Automobile Club occasions. Rolls had the British agencies for Panhard and Levassor and Minerva cars and was one of the best known motorists of the Edwardian era. Within months Rolls's search for an equivalent British

The Silver Ghost (courtesy of Rolls-Royce Ltd).

vehicle brought him into contact with F H Royce (qv) and his unique 10 hp 'Royce', which he had built to improve the engineering quality of a French Decauville. Rolls and Royce had both refused to travel to meet each other, but in May 1904 a meeting was finally arranged between the twenty-seven-year old scion of the Llangattock family and the forty-one-year old crane engineer who had turned his hand from electric motors and cranes to the motor car. On his return Rolls went straight to Johnson's flat and announced that he had 'found the greatest engineer in the world'. Even he, in his enthusiasm, probably had little idea how accurate his forecast was to prove, but when Rolls acquired the exclusive agency for the 'Royce', Johnson's publicity talents were offered a wide scope. Trials, shows, press-runs, TT races followed hot on the heels of one another as the Royce demonstrated its almost unique reliability and performance. His enthusiasm was harnessed to persuade Lord Llangattock (Rolls's father) to put up the capital and in 1905 a customer, A H Briggs, proposed a merger of the Rolls and Royce interests. C S Rolls & Co of London and Royce Ltd of Manchester merged in March 1906, with a capital of £60,000. Johnson became managing director (at £750 per annum and 4 per cent of the surplus profits) and Royce's partner A E Claremont, chairman. From this time Claude Johnson proved to be the real architect of Rolls-Royce's development and success.

Rolls-Royce might easily have foundered on a policy mistake which was to plague so many other British car manufacturers before the First World War — multiplicity of types and models. Royce, in rapid succession, built 10, 20 and 30 hp engines and chassis, in four, six and V-8 cylinder configurations. The 30 hp was a great success but Johnson sensed, accurately, that there was a market niche which Rolls-Royce was well qualified to fill by past reputation and future promise — the 'best car in the world'. He persuaded Royce to design and produce the now legendary 'Silver Ghost' 40/50 hp, a vehicle far in advance of most of its rivals, and decided to standardise its production. To achieve this objective, Rolls-Royce had to go public and raise new capital. Rolls Royce Ltd was floated in December 1906 with an authorised capital of £200,000, £100,000 initially issued, but the minimum subscription of £50,000 was under-subscribed by £9,000. The outcome hung in the balance until a woollen manufacturer and banker, Arthur Harry Briggs, came up with a personal loan of £10,000 and joined the board.

This gave Johnson the resources and opportunity he was seeking. At this stage of his life he had become well known as an organiser, rally driver and author, having published, with Lord Montague of Beaulieu, one of the first road guide books ever published in Britain, entitled *Roads Made Easy*. He developed, in the first 'Silver Ghost' 40/50 hp, a car of the highest quality and performance and exploited it to the full. He had become very friendly with Alfred Harmsworth (qv), proprietor of the *Daily Mail* and the two men frequently discussed the car, the industry and publicity. Harmsworth described himself as 'one of the Rolls-Royce salesmen' and owned several cars. He volunteered a good deal of frank advice and never withheld constructive criticism of Rolls-Royce policy or products. Johnson must certainly have benefited from this, for he forged ahead rapidly with such innovations as a school for chauffeurs and paintings of the car commissioned from top artists of the day. One of these, the *Spirit of Ecstasy* by Eric Sykes, ultimately formed the basis of the famous 'Silver Lady' mascot which appeared as an optional extra on the radiators of Rolls-Royce cars after 1911.

The optimism of the era and the success of the product led to the building of a new factory on a site outside Derby. This was opened in July 1908 and was designed essentially for the production of the Silver Ghost chassis. The marque and the name flourished together and shortly afterwards an attempt (the first of many) was made to take over the company. Johnson organised a skilful rearguard action and survived intact. Within two years, however, he had to endure two massive setbacks. Rolls was killed in a flying accident in 1910 and shortly afterwards it became clear that Royce's health would not survive the strain of a continued close association with both the design and the production work at Derby. Johnson acted at once with his characteristic imagination and drive. He had a small house at Le Canadel in the South of France and persuaded Royce to move down there with a small design team. Johnson built him his own villa in the grounds and eventually this became the design office of the company and was used continually as such until Royce died in 1933.

The First World War broke upon a firm whose board and managing director were evidently not expecting the extraordinary impact which this appalling event had on the life, industry and social structure of Britain. Johnson adapted somewhat slowly at first but eventually turned disaster into opportunity and employed the Derby factory on armoured cars, shells and aero-engines. By the end of 1918 the company had become the world's largest manufacturer of aero-engines and the horizons of its management had extended far beyond the limited activities of 1913. Johnson himself played a vital part in the organisation of the Rolls-Royce war effort, both in Britain and the USA, where the production of Rolls-Royce 'Eagle' aero-engine parts had been organised on a large scale. The company had developed broad and complex relations with all the service and supply departments of Government and Johnson was recognised as one of the foremost men in the new and important aero-engine industry. He was offered a knighthood but declined the honour, suggesting that this should go to Royce instead.

Johnson presided with a sure and firm judgement over the complexities of the transition to peace and the recovery of the market which the company regarded as its own. He was by no means immune to the immediate post-war gloom and pessimism, but nevertheless decided that the 40/50 production line should resume.

The Rolls-Royce board had to consider many other problems in 1919. Johnson's experience of the United States during the war had convinced him that this was an immense market for the luxury car and he was certain that he could build the 40/50 hp chassis out there. A new company, R R Inc was formed which acquired a factory in Springfield, Massachusetts, where several hundred Ghosts and Phantom I's were eventually to be manufactured. But the business plan was not successful and despite herculean efforts the company did not succeed and was eventually put into liquidation shortly before the depression. This was Johnson's biggest commercial failure, but he did not live to know that the American company had failed. Rolls-Royce continued to thrive in England, despite the burden imposed by the ailing performance of the American subsidiary. The first non-stop flight across the Atlantic by Alcock and Brown had been powered by Rolls-Royce engines and Royce was beginning to turn his mind to the design of the great V-12 engine that was eventually to power the Schneider Trophy world-speed record breakers and, ultimately, the Hurricane and Spitfire. Between 1907 and 1920 the net worth of the firm rose from £109,502 to £1,220,266 and net profits from £5,390 to £202,835. Turnover by 1920 stood at £3,409,695 and by 1926 £5,676,121.

Johnson did not conform in any way to the modern stereotype of the industrial 'tycoon'. He was a sensitive man who had a passion for music, especially that of Bach and Debussy, discovered and promoted the young French organist, Marcel Dupre, relished the company of artists such as Ambrose McEvoy (whose portrait of him hangs in the Conduit Street showroom of Rolls Royce Motors), entertained lavishly and generously in his home, Villa Vita, on the Kent coast, which he loved so much, and booked large blocks of seats in the Grand Theatre in Derby for Rolls-Royce employees. He was not a man who lived for his work, but one whose work served his purpose and vision. He enjoyed life and shared that enjoyment with others, whether in the South of France, the Hotel Meurice in Paris, or on his two large motor-boats.

His merit and contribution were certainly recognised by his

contemporaries. In a letter to Max Aitken (qv) Lord Northcliffe described the Rolls-Royce business as 'a delicate orchid which owes its success entirely to Johnson' {Oldham (1967) 96}. Years later Royce, in a letter thanking him for the statue which Johnson had had erected in the Arboretum at Derby, expressed the same sentiments in the phrase 'the pros and cons of the small pieces of metal could not have come to much without your great guiding genius' {*ibid,* 155}. That from a man who was himself undoubtedly an engineer of immense talent, if not genius, was an obviously sincere tribute.

Johnson married twice. On the first occasion in 1891, he eloped with Fanny May, daughter of James Stuart Morrison, an army surgeon; they had eight children, including twins. Only one child, a daughter, Elizabeth, survived this marriage, which was not a happy one. The tragedy of losing seven children left its mark. Little is known about the first Mrs Johnson, but the second marriage was, by all accounts, a very happy one. By his second wife Johnson had a daughter, known as 'Tink'. There were no surviving sons of either marriage.

Claude Johnson died at his flat in London from an attack of pneumonia on 11 April 1926, leaving £43,647 gross.

IAN LLOYD

Writings:

(with Lord Montagu of Beaulieu) *Roads Made Easy by Picture and Pen* (*Car Illustrated,* 1907).

(ed) *The Works of Ambrose McEvoy from 1900 to May 1919* (2 vols, Chiswick Press, 1919).

The Early History of Motoring (E J Burrow, 1927).

Sources:

Unpublished

BCe.

MCe.

PrC.

Published

Robert B Gardiner (ed), *Admission Registers of St Paul's School, 1876-1905* (George Bell & Sons, 1906).

Ian Lloyd, *Rolls Royce: The Growth of a Firm* (Macmillan, 1978).

—, *Rolls Royce: The Years of Endeavour* (Macmillan, 1978).

—, *Rolls Royce: The Merlin at War* (Macmillan, 1978).

Wilton Oldham, *The Hyphen in Rolls-Royce* (G T Foulis, 1967).

Stock Exchange Official Intelligence 1907.

WWW.

Ernest Johnson (courtesy of Dr S M Gaskell).

JOHNSON, Sir Ernest James

(1881-1962)

Pottery and sanitary ware manufacturer

Ernest James Johnson was born at Gnosall, Staffordshire, on 15 February 1881, the third son of Robert Lewis Johnson, who then described himself as a 'Farmer' {BCe}, and his wife Sarah née Stubbs. Robert was one of the founders of H & R Johnson Ltd, tile manufacturers of Tunstall, but in 1887 he joined Johnson Brothers, a firm of earthenware manufacturers formed in Hanley four years earlier. In 1888 Robert Johnson went to the USA, taking his family with him, in order to manage the firm's American business. He achieved such success that he returned to the Potteries in 1890 in order to advise on production matters and the enlargement of the business.

Ernest Johnson was then educated at Newcastle-under-Lyme High School and Rugby School, where his attainments were pre-eminently sporting. Afterwards he briefly studied law in Manchester, but in the autumn of 1899 he joined the firm of Johnson Brothers. He became a director ten years later; succeeding as managing director after the First World War, he remained at the head of the firm until 1959. For over fifty years, therefore, he was responsible for the development and direction of the firm.

In this he was very much in the tradition of the Potteries where manufacture depended on the enterprise of family business, reflecting the limited demands on both capital and technical expertise in this labour-intensive industry. In the early twentieth century the basic unit of organisation was the medium-sized pottery employing between 300 and 1,000 persons. Johnson Brothers comprised five such units in Hanley and Tunstall (Trent Sanitary Pottery, Alexandra Pottery, Imperial Pottery, Hanley Pottery and Charles Street Pottery). This organisation remained intact and independent until the 1960s. It specialised in earthenware, along with sanitary ware, and by the time of his death Ernest Johnson had established the firm as the largest British earthenware manufacturers, employing nearly 3,000 people and with net assets of over £2.5 million.

In part this reflected the changing balance of the pottery industry over the course of this century, with domestic ware counting by 1963 for 47 per cent of the industry measured by output and 61 per cent measured by employment. It was, however, an achievement aided significantly, in two respects, by Johnson. In the first place, he appreciated the need to respond to changing artistic appeal and changing market requirements. By the 1920s demand was strongest for a popular-priced range of dinner and tea wares suitable for the needs of a world mass market. This was a quite different problem from the hand-decorated wares made for the upper end of the market. The new ware had to be easy to stock, to cater for the average taste while retaining distinctiveness and to have a certain permanency in terms of fashion. Ernest Johnson decided that the right answer to this complex problem was a single coloured body without decoration except that of moulded forms. Wedgwood had manufactured this in the eighteenth century on a handicraft basis. With the aid of tunnel firing and control of glazes Johnson in 1928 introduced the mass-produced 'Dawn' series which was such a success that, by the outbreak of the Second World War, there were over 120 different shapes in three colour series, securing Johnson Brothers a place in world markets. This international dimension was Ernest Johnson's other major contribution to the development of the firm. Johnson Brothers had long established overseas outlets, as evidenced by Robert Johnson's work in America, and in the late nineteenth and early twentieth centuries much of the advertising and publicity for both earthenware and sanitary ware products was geared to colonial markets. Ernest Johnson built on this basis and in the inter-war years he was in advance of competition in consolidating the share of the firm's European market, particularly in Germany; after 1945 he encouraged the development of subsidiaries in Canada, Australia and South America. Design and production were geared to markets which responded readily to the traditional products for which Johnsons had become well-known.

Ernest Johnson was largely responsible for this achievement and for the establishment of a firm reputation for supplying good quality wares at a reasonable price. His perception of marketing and design factors meant that the company was well placed to face the changing technological and organisational structure in the pottery industry of the post-war era.

Sensitive to the needs of the pottery industry as a whole and to the need for combined strength, he served as president of the British Pottery Manufacturers Federation (founded in 1919) from 1934 to 1946, during which period the Federation became accepted as speaking with authority for the industry as a whole and began to make an effective contribution to concerted sales promotion. This position amongst his professional colleagues was reflected more generally in the close-knit society of the Potteries. He joined the North Staffordshire Royal Infirmary Committee in 1923 and was president from 1927 to 1931 and again from 1945 to 1948. He was president of the Leek & Moorlands Building Society from 1938 onwards; he was appointed a JP for the county in 1929 and was a member of the Willingden Mission to South America in 1940. He played cricket in North Staffordshire for nearly thirty-one years and held office as president of the North Staffordshire District League for many years. He was president of the Stone Conservative and Unionist Association from 1933 to

1953 and president of the North Staffordshire Political Union from 1936 to 1952. His public and professional services were recognised with the award of a knighthood in 1937.

By his wife Anna Shepard (elder daughter of Alfred Boote of East Orange, New Jersey, USA), whom he married in New Jersey in 1906, he had three sons and one daughter.

Sir Ernest Johnson died at Stone, his home for most of his life, on 21 December 1962, leaving £86,029 gross.

S MARTIN GASKELL

Sources:

Unpublished

BCe.

PrC.

Published

Ceramics Sept 1968.

Philip W Gay and R L Smith, *The British Pottery Industry* (Butterworths, 1974).

Geoffrey A Gedden, *Illustrated Guide to Mason's Patent Ironstone China* (Barrie & Jenkins, 1971).

Johnson Bros (Hanley) Ltd, *Foreign Gross Price List* (Burslem: Warwick Savage, 1923).

—, *Catalogue of Lavatories* (Hanley: Johnson Bros, ca 1900).

Donald J Machin and R Leslie Smith, *The Changing Structure of the British Pottery Industry 1935-1968* (Newcastle-under-Lyme: University of Keele, 1969).

Pottery and Glass Apr 1950, Feb 1951.

Tableware International Sept 1976.

Times 22 Dec 1962.

Times Weekly Review 15 May 1958.

VCH Staffordshire 2.

WWW.

JOHNSON, Henry

(1866-1938)

Textile manufacturer

Henry (generally known as Harry) Johnson was born in Macclesfield on 20 March 1866, the son of William Jackson, a small silk throwster, and his wife Elizabeth née Martin. Both his parents and his grandparents worked in the local silk industry. After leaving school at the age of twelve he had various jobs including working at his father's mill. In 1895 he joined Samuel Courtauld & Co in Essex, first as assistant and then, in the following year, as manager of their silk throwing mill at Braintree. His work there earned the approbation of the new power in the company, H G Tetley (qv), who in 1904 secured for Courtauld & Co the patent rights to the viscose process of making rayon. A new factory was set up at Coventry and in 1907 Johnson took over as manager from the failing original appointee to that post. He proved to be highly successful, and in 1914 was put on the board of the newly-formed Courtaulds Ltd. When Tetley became chairman in 1917 Johnson was made a managing director and remained the dominant voice in the control of the company's rayon yarn spinning mills until his death in 1938.

At the pioneer rayon plant in Coventry Johnson's role as manager was crucial to the success of the company's new venture. A blunt and outspoken character and an admirer of Tetley, he imparted vigour and a sense of purpose at a time when the enterprise was trembling on the brink of failure. He contrived both to drive and to lead; he expected hard work and long hours from others and did the same himself; he enforced strict discipline, got to know everybody by name and distributed cash bonuses to those who earned his approval. There was a good deal of rough and ready justice. His methods were essentially those of the old-type mill boss; he had little time for the rights of the workers and still less for unions; he was ignorant of science and believed that chemists should be 'kept in their place'; as he alienated some, so at the same time he created for himself a faithful band of followers. Crude though they were, these methods proved effective, for in the first five years after he took over there was not only a great increase in output but also improvements in yarn quality, in productivity, and in organisation.

As a director after 1914 he became the undisputed boss of the company's yarn mills in the Midlands and North-West, operating from a power base in Coventry and ruling over a world remote and different from that of the London head office. His knowledge and experience and 'man-on-the-spot' methods were very real assets which were put to good use in the early 1920s when he effected substantial improvements in performance and organisation at the yarn mills of Courtaulds' US subsidiary, American Viscose Corporation. By the 1930s, however, his limitations became evident: resistance to innovation, contempt for theory and research, and, to give a specific example, a tenacious belief that costs were not the concern of the plant managers. His hostility towards labour organisations, which ran in complete contrast to the views of his own chairman, Samuel Courtauld (qv), was an element in bringing about bad labour relations in the yarn mills. Amongst those who had been put into positions of power in local management and under-management were a number of representatives of the type of hard-driving, bullying foremen that he favoured. Such minions were often his personal cronies; accusations of corruption and favouritism were rife. It was left to younger directors, including his son, Henry L Johnson, who had been put on Courtaulds' board in 1933, to try to clear up the mess. But the legacy remained for some years after Harry Johnson's death. New directors who came to the company at the end of the Second World War commented upon the poor calibre of local management in the yarn mills, the hostility towards the London office, and the implacable resistance to any changes which threatened those who were the beneficiaries of Johnson's system of patronage. Thus did a man who had been effective and successful by methods which sufficed in one phase of a firm's growth cause harm by perpetuating them in changed circumstances.

Harry Johnson died on 11 June 1938. His will was proved at £558,889 gross.

D C COLEMAN

Sources:

Unpublished

BCe.

PrC.

Published

Donald C Coleman, *Courtaulds. An Economic and Social History* (3 vols, Oxford: Clarendon Press, 1969–80) 2.

JOHNSTON, George Lawson

1st Lord Luke of Pavenham

(1873-1943)

Food manufacturer

George Lawson Johnston was born at 2 Blacket Place, Edinburgh, on 9 September 1873, the second son of John Lawson Johnston (qv) and his wife Elizabeth née Lawson. His parents moved to Canada and he was educated privately there; on their return to England he attended Dulwich College for one year and when aged sixteen went to Blair Lodge, Scotland, a highly respected public school. He was strongly influenced by his father's strict teetotalism and Presbyterianism, although he moved to the Church of England, and throughout his life remained a devout Christian. His training was entirely 'on the job': he first helped in Bovril Ltd when only fifteen, initially as a private secretary to his father and then for six months or so, between schools, in charge of the French business based in Paris. On leaving full-time education he went into Bovril Ltd, learning all aspects of the business and travelling extensively to the main sources of raw materials in South America.

By 1896, when Bovril was bought and relaunched by E T Hooley (qv), Johnston had become a director of the company and his father's right hand man, concentrating on the financial and raw material side of the business and travelling regularly to the Argentine. On his father's death in 1900 he became vice-chairman of the company and was the driving force, as the chairmen like the Earls of Arran and Erroll were essentially figureheads. In 1916 he became chairman of the company and in 1932 joint managing director; he retained both positions until his death in 1943.

He addressed himself to three major problems facing Bovril in this period: the legacy of over-capitalisation created by Hooley's intervention; the need to ensure raw materials' supplies by integrating backwards into extract manufacture and cattle raising; and the need to diversify from essentially a one-product company.

Hooley's re-launch of Bovril in 1896 had capitalised it at £2.5 million. Because of its capital structure the company had to find £102,500 per annum to service the fixed interest capital; to pay a dividend to the deferred shareholders, who had been promised a return of about 10 per cent, would have meant a further charge on profits of £75,000. In fact in the early years they received no such return, having to make do with 2 or 3 per cent; nevertheless the directors needed to find nearly £130,000 from profits each year simply to service their capital. Since Hooley had stripped all cash reserves from the company before refloating it, to find working capital to continue business and expand the firm's activities taxed Johnston's financial ingenuity. Initially the company existed on an unsecured loan of £150,000 from Johnston's father; on the latter's death the trustees required security and so Johnston launched a new company, Estates Control Ltd, with Bovril holding all the ordinary shares, and the preference shares were taken up partly by the trustees of John Lawson Johnston's estate and partly by the public. The funds so raised were used mainly to buy raw materials.

In order to diversify backwards into the source of raw materials Johnston set up separate subsidiaries of Bovril — first, Argentine Estates Ltd, in 1908 and then Bovril Australian Estates Ltd in 1909 — to buy land, breed and raise cattle, and establish local factories for initial processing, namely slaughtering, rendering down and concentrating of beef extract and other raw materials. Bovril Ltd held controlling interests in these subsidiaries and raised capital by issuing some shares to the public.

He bought vast estates in Argentina for Bovril to breed and fatten cattle; by 1943 these exceeded 1.5 million acres; he acquired a factory at Santa Elena which was improved and updated, for example, providing an adequate electricity supply and adding freezing facilities; he initiated a programme to improve the quality of the beef by introducing prize bulls and champions from Buenos Aires shows and the UK; he actively encouraged the improvement of local transport facilities, the company owning a number of cattle boats, capable of carrying several hundred head apiece, which plied up and down the river Parana. He visited the Argentine every other year, touring the company's estancias and inspecting the Santa Elena factory. Bovril owned 10,000 square miles of territory at Victoria River Downs in Australia to breed and fatten cattle but it was never as successful or profitable as the Argentinian operation, because rainfall was inadequate and the distance to a factory too great, given the lack of transportation, necessitating cattle drives of up to a thousand miles.

Once the immediate problems of finance and raw materials had been solved, he set about diversifying the company's product base. This had begun in 1899 when 'Virol' was introduced as a malt tonic food; in the early years of the twentieth century 'Stelna' corned beef was introduced to the market, a by-product of meat extract manufacture; then, and later as Bovril Corned Beef, it sold more extensively in the USA than the UK. The shift came in the 1920s when Bovril bought into the 'Marmite' company which made a yeast extract with vegetable flavouring meant to appeal to a vegetarian segment of the market, and the 'Ambrosia' company which manufactured a range of milk-based baby foods; in 1936 it launched 'Ambrosia Creamed Rice' which enjoyed remarkable success after the Second World War.

Under Johnston's firm hand Bovril grew and prospered. Sales records were continually being broken and net profits grew from £125,000 in 1899 to nearly £400,000 per annum in the late 1920s; he built up a reserve fund of over £1 million by 1940 having started with £30,000 in 1899. The profits were generated overwhelmingly by Bovril itself, but by the 1920s the subsidiary companies were contributing £60,000-70,000 a year. This steady growth allowed him to increase the dividend paid on the deferred shares to 8 per cent or more after 1920, so increasing stock market confidence in the company that he was able to raise fresh capital via new issues of all three classes of shares in the 1920s and by medium term loans (Eight-Year Notes). In 1934, after paying off both the debentures and

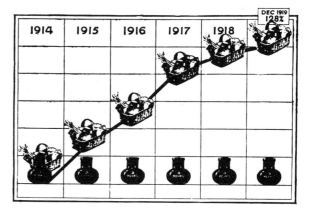

The RISE in The Price of FOOD

| 1914 | 1915 | 1916 | 1917 | 1918 | DEC 1919 128% |

No Rise in the Price of BOVRIL

WHILE practically all the things you put in your shopping basket have doubled in cost, Bovril remains the same price as in July, 1914, and it is not only the same price; *it is the same quality.* Bovril Ltd. have succeeded in their determination not to increase prices, a smaller profit per bottle on increased sales and skill in keeping down the cost of production have enabled them to achieve what probably has not been achieved in the case of any other popular food—namely, the maintenance of pre-War price and quality.

Yet people would have paid almost any price for Bovril. There were times when it could have been sold for a sovereign a bottle. But the policy of Bovril Ltd. was *not* to take advantage of the people's necessity, but to *help* in that necessity, and to consider it as a National Trust. That is why the price of Bovril is the same as in July, 1914.

That is why
Bovril did not PROFITEER

The Body-building Power of Bovril has been proved by independent scientific investigation to be from 10 to 20 times the amount taken.

Advertisement for Bovril 1919-20, at a time when there was much public indignation at wartime profiteering (courtesy of Bovril Limited).

Eight-Year Notes, he introduced pre-preference shares carrying two votes apiece, mostly taken up by the Lawson Johnston family in an effort to increase their control over the company as their shareholding amounted to only about 10 per cent of issued capital.

Johnston undoubtedly left Bovril in a much stronger position than he found it despite some export problems in the 1930s. He was very much the decision-maker in the firm and was certainly no mere figurehead. As well as taking control of the financial and raw material side, he insisted on

From a concert party programme August 1936 (courtesy of Bovril Limited).

vetting personally all of Bovril's many advertising campaigns, and no batch of Bovril might be bottled until he had tasted it and given approval. Early in the Second World War, anticipating shortages through lack of shipping, he laid in sufficient quantities of raw materials, at advantageous prices, to ensure Bovril production through the whole of the conflict.

He held many directorships outside the Bovril group. He was a director of the *Daily Express* from 1900 to 1917 by virtue of being the largest single shareholder, especially after Arthur Pearson's (qv) withdrawal in 1908; Luke sold his interest to Max Aitken (qv), later Lord Beaverbrook, in

November 1916. He held directorships in Sir Isaac Pitman & Sons Ltd, which was owned by a son-in-law, and Lloyds Bank, 1933-43; he was director from 1914 and deputy chairman from 1920 of Ashanti Goldfields Corporation, in which he was a large shareholder. He was a director also of the Australian Mercantile, Land & Finance Co Ltd and the Forestal Land, Timber & Railways Co. He was also chairman of the British National Committee of the International Chambers of Commerce and in that capacity attended a number of the general congresses.

Johnston was never an active politician but in his early life, like his father, was an ardent Liberal. He worked readily with the Government in the First World War, serving in the department of the Surveyor General of Supply at the War Office, as a member of the Leather Control Board, and as chairman of several committees in the Raw Materials Department of the War Office. In recognition of these services he received the KBE in 1920. During the 1920s with the split of the Liberal Party, Luke switched allegiance to the Conservative Party, helping to found the Conservative Central Office Research Unit.

Johnston was a great benefactor of hospital charities, serving in honorary roles on many hospital committees, introducing novel ways of raising funds, one in particular being a competition to judge the most popular of many famous Bovril posters, and reorganising hospital flag days. He served on the committee of King Edward's Hospital Fund for London from 1901, as one of the honorary secretaries from 1929; he was honorary treasurer of the Royal Northern Hospital, 1909-23. In 1922 he was chairman of the combined appeal which raised over £480,000 for London's voluntary hospitals, and in 1936 was chairman of the committee which reduced London's 77 hospital flag days to two while ensuring the income increased. He became honorary secretary of the Thankoffering Fund for the recovery from illness of King George V and for this he was elevated to the peerage as the First Lord Luke of Pavenham in 1929. The title was chosen partly from the parish church close to which he worked (St Luke's, Old Street) and partly because St Luke was the patron saint of physicians, and hence hospitals. In the House of Lords he moved amendments to the Traffic Acts of 1929 and 1933, to make it possible for hospitals to obtain payment from insurance companies for treating road accident victims. In 1935 he introduced the Voluntary Hospitals (Paying Patients) Bill and successfully re-introduced it in 1936 when it was enacted.

Luke was chairman of the Ministry of Health's Second Advisory Committee on Nutrition from 1935. This was the first British attempt to consider a national food policy. It produced a first report in 1937, but its work had no immediate effect, for although it instigated long term investigations into diet, income levels, and the incidence of disease, by means of family budgets, dietary surveys, medical examinations, and a revision of the cost of living index, work ceased on the outbreak of war in 1939, although the committee did not officially lapse until 1941. Luke was also chairman of the Ministry of Information's Advisory Committee on the Appointment of Advertising Agents from February 1941 until his death, chairing 24 meetings in less than two years.

A devout and active Christian, he was on the committee of the Religious Tract Society for more than twenty years, and after the Society joined with the Christian Literature Society in 1935 to become the United Society for Christian Literature he continued to serve, latterly as president. He took a keen interest in the *Boy's Own Paper* and *Girl's Own Paper* which were owned by the Society, and was instrumental in establishing in 1941 a separate company, Lutterworth Periodicals, to publish them; he was chairman of its board until his death. In the 1920s he endowed a philanthropic trust, the income from which was to be devoted to Christian charities, and bequeathed a substantial additional sum to this fund, which became known as the Luke Trust.

Luke was a governor of the Polytechnic, Regent Street, from 1915 until his death, and served in many public roles in Bedfordshire, his adopted county, where he was a JP, High Sheriff in 1924, and from 1936 Lord Lieutenant.

In 1902 he married the Honourable Edith Laura St John, fifth daughter of the Sixteenth Lord St John of Bletsoe. They had four daughters and two sons, Ian St John and Hugh de Beauchamp, both of whom entered Bovril Ltd, the former as chairman from his father's death in 1943 to 1970, the latter on the board, 1946-72, and briefly as chairman in 1971, before the company was involved in a takeover.

Lord Luke died on 23 February 1943 in London, leaving an estate of £411,606 gross.

JOHN ARMSTRONG

Writings:

Report of the Post Office Advisory Council on the Postal Cheque System (HMSO, 1928).

Sources:

Unpublished

Guildhall Library, Stock Exchange reports: Commercial Section; MS 14164/1-7, Ashanti Goldfields Corporation.

PRO, MH 56/49, 79/343, 79/345; INF 1/341.

C Reg: Bovril (50,220); London Express Newspapers (141, 748).

BCe.

Conversations with Hon Hugh de B Lawson Johnston, 29 Mar, 28 Apr, and 7 July 1983 and with Rt Hon Lord Luke, 26 July 1983.

George Lawson Johnston, 'John Lawson Johnston 1873-1896' (typescript, nd).

—, 'The Development and Organisation of Bovril Ltd' (Edwards Seminar Paper 339, 1 Dec 1964).

Published

Boy's Own Paper Apr 1943.

Viscount Camrose, *British Newspapers and Their Controllers* (Cassell, 1948).

JOHNSTON George Lawson

DNB.

Dulwich College Register 3223 (1887).

Evening Standard 23 Feb 1943.

Gordon Hewitt, *Let the People Read* (Lutterworth Press, 1949).

Polytechnic Magazine Mar 1943.

The Polytechnic Prospectuses.

Alan J P Taylor, *Beaverbrook* (Hamish Hamilton, 1972).

Times 22, 24 Feb, 1 July 1943.

E S Turner, *Boys Will Be Boys* (Michael Joseph, 1948).

JOHNSTON, John Lawson

(1839-1900)

Food manufacturer

John Lawson Johnston (courtesy of Bovril Limited).

John Lawson Johnston was born in Roslin, Midlothian, Scotland, on 28 September 1839, the eldest son of William and Jane Johnston. William (1813-57) was employed in the nearby gunpowder works until he was injured in an explosion; he later worked as a cobbler. Lawson Johnston was educated in Edinburgh with a view to entering the medical profession following in the footsteps of his maternal grandfather, Dr J O McWilliam, who went out as senior surgeon on an expedition to the Niger in 1841. He was apprenticed to, and virtually adopted by, an uncle who owned a butcher's shop in Cannongate, Edinburgh. Here he received his early business training and developed an interest in dietetics and food chemistry which led to contact and friendship with Lyon Playfair, then the Professor of Chemistry at Edinburgh University.

In 1874 he won a contract from the French Government to stock the French forts with a three-year supply of food, comprising one million one-kilo cans of beef, against future emergencies, the Government believing that the lack of such supplies had hastened their defeat in the Franco-Prussian War. To execute this commission he went to Canada, selling the butcher's shop in Edinburgh he had inherited from his uncle. While in Canada, he sent the first consignment of frozen poultry and meat from Canada to Liverpool and helped to pioneer the tomato canning industry in Canada. At the same time he invented 'Johnston's Fluid Beef', a blended meat extract which was first commercially produced in 1874 at

Sherbrooke, Quebec. Initially the product was sold mainly as a beverage, diluted with hot water, for Lawson Johnston was an ardent teetotaller throughout his life and saw this as an alternative to alcoholic drinks. By 1880 the product had become so popular, helped in part by the Scott Act of 1878 which increased the demand for temperance beverages, that he moved to a larger factory in Montreal. He already had a selling agency over the border in the USA run by William A Shoemaker. An early marketing technique was to offer free tastings at the ice carnivals organised in Montreal during the winter. After a fire destroyed Lawson Johnston's Montreal factory in 1884, he sold his business in Canada to William Clark and returned to England.

By 1886 Lawson Johnston had established a factory at 10 Trinity Square, London, to sell 'Johnston's Fluid Beef (brand Bovril)'. Bovril was a development of Johnston's Fluid Beef, being thicker and more concentrated than the Canadian product. Johnston's marketing techniques included free tastings at the Colonial and Continental Exhibition at South Kensington that year. At the 1887 exhibition Lawson Johnston built a facsimile of the Montreal Ice Palace in frosted glass to promote the product; sales were so impressive that Spiers & Pond, the restaurant owners, hoteliers and caterers, who had the overall catering franchise for the exhibition, undertook to sell cups of hot Bovril in their outlets, including their railway refreshment rooms. This success was repeated at the 1888 American Exhibition at Earls Court. Bovril's sales and profits rose steadily: by 1888 sales exceeded £60,000 and profits £16,500, a very attractive return on sales.

In March 1889 Bovril became a limited liability company with a nominal capital of £150,000 and a paid up capital of £100,000, soon increased to £120,000 by a further call on shares. Lawson Johnston received £50,000 in shares and £25,000 in cash for the business. The issue was heavily over-subscribed. Andrew Walker, a friend from Edinburgh days, who had made about £20,000 in cotton and then 'retired' in Manchester, came onto the board as managing director, buying several thousand shares. Larger premises were acquired in Farringdon Street.

From its inception Bovril was heavily advertised in a variety of newspapers, journals and posters. Much of the early success of Bovril was a result of striking advertising including famous name testimonials and offers of rewards if a claim could be disproved. An essential part in this success was played by S H Benson (qv), who worked as factory manager of Bovril's Bath Street premises in London, after being invalided out of the Royal Navy. In 1893 Benson set up his own 'advertisers agency' in Fleet Street, with Bovril as his first client. The rapid growth of Bovril owed much to his energy and creative brilliance. Profits rose above £20,000 in 1894 to nearly £90,000 in 1896. Dividends varied between 7.5 per cent in 1892 and 20 per cent in 1895. The capital was increased in early 1896 to £400,000 by a scrip issue of three new shares for every one fully paid, to reflect the real value of the assets. In 1896 Bovril was sold to the notorious company promotor, E T Hooley (qv) who bought the company for £2 million or £5 6s 8d per £1 share. Frank Harris, who acted as Hooley's negotiator with Lawson Johnston, claims in his memoirs that Lawson Johnston would have been willing to accept a price of £1.3 million, but that he, Harris, was outbid by another of Hooley's agents, W D Ross of

The first known Bovril display advertisement, Ladies Pictorial *1889 (courtesy of Bovril Limited).*

the *Black and White* periodical. Despite this, Harris claims to have convinced Hooley's financial backers of the value of Bovril, and to have written the prospectus. It is an indication of Hooley's methods that Harris informed the financiers that Bovril was making annual profits of nearly £150,000 when in fact for 1896 it made less than £100,000. Harris received his fee partly in deferred shares of the company. Hooley relaunched Bovril with a total capitalisation of £2.5 million made up of £500,000 4.5 per cent debenture stock, £500,000 5.5 per cent preference shares, £750,000 7 per cent ordinary shares and £750,000 deferred shares.

After the capital reconstruction Lawson Johnston remained the single largest shareholder, the vice-chairman and very much the directing and controlling influence, since the shareholding was widely dispersed with only a couple of dozen shareholders owning more than one thousand shares. Before Hooley became interested in Bovril, Lawson Johnston recruited as chairman Lyon Playfair (then Lord Playfair and previously associate of Liebig in his pioneering work on the chemistry of food). Another director was Dr Robert Farquharson, a medical man and MP interested in dietetics and health. Obviously such names subtly advanced Bovril's image as medically and dietetically sound. After Hooley joined the board, ornamental aristocratic directors followed, such as Viscount Duncannon.

New, purpose-built premises were opened in 1897 in Old Street, with a capacity three times that of the Farringdon Street factory and profits soared in that year to over £160,000. For the rest of the century the directors of Bovril, usually through Lawson Johnston, continued to report vast increases in sales per annum, for example 30 per cent between 1895 and 1896, 50 per cent between 1896 and 1897 and 122 per cent between 1899 and 1900. This growth resulted from large-scale national advertising; the re-purchase of the goodwill to manufacture Bovril in Canada (sold by Lawson Johnston in 1884 when he quit the Dominion); the extension of the company's activities into complementary areas such as army rations and hospital food; a significant export drive; and the removal of competing firms either by buying them out (for example Vimbos Ltd) or by using legal action to prevent them imitating Bovril's product (for example Bouillion Fleet Ltd). Bovril continued to use eminent dieticians as advisors, such as Professor Sir Edward Frankland who became the company's consulting chemist in 1897. Likewise every opportunity was seized to advertise Bovril products. For example, great play was made of Bovril's value to the troops in the Boer War when whole page advertisements were taken in the *Daily Mail*, testimonials from Baden-Powell and Rudyard Kipling were publicised, and the Bovril War Cables Scheme introduced. In 1899 Bovril branched out into another health food, Virol, a malt tonic. Initially it was produced and sold by Bovril, but as demand rose a separate company was established in the early 1900s.

Throughout these years and until his death in 1900 Lawson Johnston remained the moving force in Bovril. After 1898, with Lyon Playfair's ill-health and death, Johnston became chairman in name as well as in fact. One of his strengths was the ability to delegate. Much of Bovril's success came from the able men Lawson Johnston picked to run aspects of the business such as Benson in advertising; Walker the managing director, in charge of day-to-day administration and bookkeeping; his eldest son, William, who was a competent chemist and took charge of the laboratories; and his second son, George (qv), who was a brilliant financier. Lawson Johnston himself was a compulsive, creative chemist whose breakthrough with Bovril was to combine the nutritive value of beef with the stimulant beef tea by including beef powder, peptones and albumenoids. He was also a persuasive and inventive salesman, but tended to be less interested in the financial and administrative aspects of the business.

Although never an MP, Lawson Johnston was an ardent Liberal and was invited to stand for election on more than one occasion, but declined for health reasons. He was awarded the Royal Humane Society's gold medal for saving life from drowning on three occasions and during the Boer War was instrumental in establishing the War Employment Bureau which found work for the wives and dependants of reservists called to the colours. He acted as chairman of the Bureau and provided the bulk of its costs from his own pocket, Benson (the advertising agent) and Gibson (one of the secretaries at Bovril) acting as joint honorary secretaries. Lawson Johnston also served on the boards of Gordon Hotels Ltd and Apollinaris & Johannis Ltd, the mineral water manufacturer. He was a committed Presbyterian throughout his life, in youth attending Brighton Street Evangelical Union Church, Roslin, Edinburgh, and in the 1880s and 1890s Upper Norwood Presbyterian Church.

Lawson Johnston married Elizabeth Lawson in 1871. She was the daughter of the baker, confectioner and biscuit manufacturer George Lawson, of Newington, Edinburgh. They had thirteen children including seven sons, two of whom joined Bovril; one, George Lawson Johnston became Bovril chairman in 1916.

John Lawson Johnston died on his yacht *White Ladye* in Cannes Harbour on 24 November 1900, at the age of sixty-one. The probate valuation of his estate was £850,000 gross, though his real worth was much greater, some of his capital having been invested in Argentina and other large sums being given to his children in his lifetime.

JOHN ARMSTRONG

Sources:

Unpublished

Guildhall Library, ST 405-7, loans and company prospectuses.

C Reg: Bovril Ltd (50,220).

Interviews with the Hon Hugh de B Lawson Johnston, 3, 29 Mar and 28 Apr 1983.

George Lawson Johnston, 'John Lawson Johnston 1873-1896' (np, nd).

Published

Daily Express 7 Dec 1900.

John Dicks, *The Hooley Book: The Amazing Financier His Career and His Crowd* (John Dicks, 1904).

Economist 21 Nov 1896.

Grocery Feb 1900.

Peter Hadley, *The History of Bovril Advertising* (Bovril Ltd, 1972).

Frank Harris, *My Life and Loves* (W H Allen, 1964).

Ernest T Hooley, *Hooley's Confessions* (Simpkin, Marshall & Co, 1925).

Illustrated Mail 1 Dec 1900.

Midlothian Journal 4 Jan 1901.

Newcastle Journal 27 Nov 1900.

Norwood Review 8 Dec 1900.

Saturday Review 23 May, 17 Oct, 21 Nov 1896.

The War Story of Bovril (Bovril, 1946).

Times 5 Mar 1889, 7 May, 21, 29 July, 24 Oct, 15 Dec 1896, 6 Jan, 20 Feb 1897, 5 Feb 1898, 4 Feb, 11 Aug, 17 Oct 1899, 10 Feb, 26 Nov 1900.

WWW.

James Joicey (courtesy of Lord Joicey).

JOICEY, James

1st Lord Joicey of Chester Le Street, County Durham

(1846-1936)

Coal mine owner

James Joicey was born at Tanfield in County Durham on 4 April 1846, the younger son of George Joicey, an engineer, and his wife Dorothy, daughter of Jacob Gowland of Wrekenton, near Gateshead. His father was head and co-founder of the Newcastle engineering firm of J & G Joicey, and his uncle, James Joicey, was the founder of the private coal firm of Joicey & Co to which James, the nephew, was eventually to succeed as head.

James was educated at Gainford School near Darlington, and in order to gain business experience was found a position as a clerk in offices at the quayside in Newcastle with a wage of 40s a week. He entered the family business at the age of seventeen in 1863 and became a partner four years later. At the death of his uncle John Joicey in 1881 he gained control of the family firm. This consisted of collieries in County Durham with a total output in 1872 of 1.25 million tons, making it roughly fourth in the hierarchy of Durham coal producers.

Joicey's business career lay in the consolidation and extension of this empire. The firm of James Joicey & Co adopted limited liability in 1886, though it remained a private enterprise with most of the shares held by family members. Between 1886 and 1911 the firm had a nominal capital of £500,000 of which £430,000 was paid up. James Joicey's most important achievement came in 1896 when he formed a new company to purchase the Lambton collieries from the Earl of Durham. These had a combined output of 2.25 million tons. The purchase price was low, reflecting the current depression, though the transaction was completed prior to a boom which greatly enhanced the value of the collieries. In 1913 Lambton

Collieries Ltd had a paid-up capital of £900,000 and a nominal capital of £1.2 million. Joicey acquired the Hetton collieries (purchased in 1911) and Silksworth collieries (purchased from the Marquess of Londonderry in 1920) both in County Durham. In the inter-war period he was probably the only man in Europe to command an annual output of coal in excess of six million tons. In 1924 James Joicey & Co was sold to Lambton Collieries Ltd and the firm's name was changed to Lambton, Hetton & Joicey Collieries Ltd.

Joicey became a millionaire. At his death his personal holdings in coal companies comprised shares to the value of £200,000 each in James Joicey & Co and in Lambton Collieries Ltd (both being heavily undersubscribed). He was also a shareholder in the East-Midlands Shirebrook Colliery Co in which he owned shares to the value of £270,000 in 1898 and £120,000 in 1913. As a leading North-East businessman he became a director or partner in many enterprises including the North Eastern Railway Co; George Angus & Co Ltd; the Montevidean & Brazilian Telegraph Co Ltd; and the Dunrobin Shipping Co Ltd. In addition he was president of the Mining Association of Great Britain and the proprietor of three North-Eastern newspapers, the *Newcastle Daily Leader*, the *Evening Leader* and the *Northern Weekly*. An acquaintance recalled 'In business he was shrewd, sagacious and far sighted. He was of a handsome presence, an engaging personality, and had an optimistic outlook on life'. {*DNB*}

Joicey also enjoyed an active political career, becoming a JP for Northumberland, Durham, Montgomeryshire and Newcastle upon Tyne, DL for County Durham, and in 1885 Liberal MP for Chester-le-Street. In politics he was originally an 'advanced Liberal' and Home Ruler. He was created a baronet in 1893 and retired from the Commons on being created Baron Joicey in 1906. (He also received an honorary DCL from Durham University.) During later life his politics underwent a marked move to the right. He opposed the enfranchisement of women, joined the Conservative Party in 1931, and expressed public support for Mussolini and the politics of dictatorship.

Joicey married twice, firstly in 1879 to Elizabeth Amy, daughter of Joseph Robinson, JP, a shipowner of North Shields, and secondly in 1884 (following his first wife's death in 1881) to Margaret Smyles Drever, only surviving daughter of Colonel Thomas Drever of the Bengal Army, a deceased army surgeon. He had two sons by his first wife, and by his second a further two sons and one daughter. These last three children all predeceased their father; his successor to the title of Baron Joicey was James Arthur (1880-1940), the elder son of his first marriage. Joicey's recreations were listed as hunting, shooting, cycling, golf and tennis. He lived at Longhirst Hall near Morpeth in Northumberland, but in 1907 purchased Ford Castle near Berwick-on-Tweed, becoming a wealthy landowner in his own right. He also possessed homes in Cadogan Square, London and Gregynog in Montgomeryshire.

He died at Ford Castle on 21 November 1936 aged ninety, leaving an estate of £1,519,717 gross.

A A HALL

Sources:

Unpublished

Newcastle Upon Tyne City Library, local newspaper cuttings vol 70; R W Martin (comp), 'Northern Worthies' Vol II (1932).

PRO, BT 31/36829/48510.

MCe.

E I Waitt, 'John Morley, Joseph Cowen and Robert Spence Watson. Liberal Divisions in Newcastle Politics, 1873-1895' (Manchester PhD, 1972).

Published

Burke's Peerage 1980.

DNB.

J Jamieson, *Northumberland at the Opening of the Twentieth Century* (Brighton, 1905).

Newcastle Weekly Chronicle 28 Nov 1936, 30 Jan 1957.

WWMP.

WWW.

J H Jolly (courtesy of Guest, Keen & Nettlefolds).

JOLLY, James Hornby

(1887-1972)

Industrialist

James Hornby Jolly was born at Preston, Lancashire, on 26 February 1887, the son of William Jolly, a 'book-keeper' {BCe} and later coal agent in Preston, and his wife Ellen Jane née Hornby. James was educated at Baines's Grammar School, Poulton Le Fylde. Serving his articles with the Blackpool practice, Bowman & Grimshaw, Jolly qualified as a chartered accountant in 1909. Possibly because of his father's connections, he then moved to Cardiff, the principal port in Wales for the export of coal, where he was employed as a clerk in the accountancy firm of W B Peat & Co, at 3 Dock Chambers, Bute Street, working there for two years.

In 1911 he was instructed to compile a report on the Blaenavon Co, a steelworks with colliery interests, and having recommended managerial changes asked Peats whether he could leave to carry them into effect. He remained at Blaenavon until 1918 when Jolly became Guest Keen & Nettlefolds (GKN) secretary. Edward Steer (1851-1927), who lived nearby in Monmouthshire, then a director (and who was later to serve as the company's chairman, 1920-27), knew that their current secretary H Probyn suffered from poor health and suggested that Jolly should join GKN's head office in Smethwick as his replacement. As a professional accountant Jolly was surprised by the company's antiquated methods of keeping financial records, insisting as a result that he be made chief accountant as well as secretary. He proceeded to appoint a small number of qualified assistants so that they could reorganise GKN's accounts. His success in this field, in part, explained his promotion, at the age of forty-three to the main board in October 1930 and then his rise to managing director in August 1934. In this post he was responsible for handling the sale of GKN's coal holdings (which formed a major part of Welsh Associated Collieries) to Powell Duffryn in 1935. Jolly subsequently became one of GKN's deputy chairmen in April 1943 and its chairman in October 1947, until July 1953 when he retired from the chair, to be followed by Sir Kenneth Peacock (qv). Long experience on the board was valued, however, and Jolly continued to serve as a director until 1957. In addition, he was chairman of the several companies formed to run the Dowlais-Cardiff steelworks at East Moors between 1946 and 1957.

Unusual for the time, Jolly represented the advancement of chartered accountancy into the highest ranks of management, a career particularly remarkable in that it occurred in an industry characteristically headed during the inter-war years by wealthy families. His rise to power in the 1930s owed much to the vacuum created by the unexpected death of Henry Seymour Berry, Lord Buckland (qv) in 1928. When GKN amalgamated with John Lysaght in 1920, Berry, who had been the latter's chairman, eventually took control of the merged company. The Keen, Nettlefold, Guest and Lysaght families, though often represented on the various boards and administrative committees, no longer ran the business and Jolly — following in the footsteps of Sir Samuel R Beale (1881-1964), chairman 1935-47 — assumed command after a considerable period of service on the main board. A professional manager with a special interest in steel, Jolly summarised his business philosophy succinctly: if you expand, expand into something which links up with the main business. This policy was manifested in the acquisition of Brymbo steelworks in 1948 (its special steels being needed by GKN's forgings companies) and Somerset Wire Co in 1950, which consumed the coil produced at the Castle Rod Mill in Cardiff. Similarly, as managing director from 1934, he had supported the extensive modernisation of East Moors in 1934-36, which was achieved by merger with Baldwins. Jolly became a director of the new company (Guest Keen Baldwins Iron & Steel Co) on its formation in 1930, and succeeded Sir Charles Wright (qv) as its chairman in 1946. After denationalisation in 1954 the name was altered to Guest Keen Iron & Steel Co, Jolly resuming his post as chairman until retirement in 1957.

As an accountant Jolly failed to implement any form of consolidated accounts until compelled to do so by the 1948 Companies Act. Other more enlightened groups had perceived the value of devising accounts which fully documented the holding-subsidiary company relationship. Given the size and diversity of the GKN group during the 1930s, some consolidation

An aerial view of the Dowlais-Cardiff Steelworks, East Moors in July 1949 when it belonged to Guest Keen Baldwins Iron & Steel Co, of which J H Jolly was chairman. Roath Dock is visible in the distance where shipments of iron ore were unloaded (courtesy of Aero Films).

would have been necessary to obtain a precise and detailed understanding of its overall financial performance. It remained, in common with much of British business, a highly devolved organisation throughout which subsidiaries retained a high degree of autonomy, preparing their own financial statements for individual analysis at the centre, each being judged on its own merits. Jolly was not opposed to the principle of consolidation but gave it a low priority, preferring to improve GKN's management and reporting policies by recruiting a number of qualified accountants during the late 1930s to work at head office and in the major manufacturing units.

A cautious, conservative chairman, Jolly did not make any strategic changes of direction. His contribution was to hold the group on a steady

JOLLY James Hornby

course during a period of growth, so that pre-tax profits rose from £1.96 million in 1947 to £7.67 million in 1953 on a turnover of £84.69 million. Whilst this approach reflected his personality, it may also have resulted from a pre-occupation with nationalisation. Pledged to take steel into public ownership, the Labour Government had much of GKN's plant in its sights. To minimise potential losses, in 1948 Jolly formed two holding companies — GKN (Midlands), which embraced the screw works at Smethwick and bolt works at Darlaston, and GKN (South Wales), which took over the re-rolling mills and wire and nail works at Cardiff — in an attempt to divorce threatened subsidiaries from steel-making operations. Although Brymbo, East Moors and Normanby Park (Lysaghts' former steelworks at Scunthorpe) together with GKN (South Wales) were nationalised in February 1951, a change of Government meant that GKN was able to re-purchase them all from the Iron & Steel Holding & Realisation Agency by 1955 and the practical impact of this short period of public ownership was limited.

J H Jolly also served in 1947-67 as a director of the Midland Bank — GKN's principal bankers with whom there had existed strong links from the days when Arthur Keen (qv) had been chairman of them both.

In 1912 Jolly, then a Wesleyan Methodist, married Elizabeth née Parkinson, the daughter of a corn merchant; they had one son, who became a flying officer and was killed in 1944 (his death prompting Jolly's interest in psychic research) and a daughter. J H Jolly's brother, Thomas Jolly, entered GKN in the early 1920s direct from school and, having spent time in America and worked at Port Talbot steelworks, rejoined the company in 1942 when he became general manager of East Moors steelworks, later rising to become its joint managing director; another brother, W A Jolly, served as managing director of another GKN subsidiary, W A Bonnell (1924) Ltd, the London timber importers, from April 1938 to March 1958.

An austere man of few words, J H Jolly's taciturn nature concealed a decisive mind and a determination to solve problems. His hobby, fell walking, was reflected in the name of his home 'Langdale,' Barnt Green, near Birmingham. James Hornby Jolly died on 25 July 1972, aged eighty-five, leaving £63,492. The exceptionally short obituary in the *Times* failed to do justice to a long and successful career as an industrialist.

EDGAR JONES

Sources:

Unpublished

BCe.

Information from GKN departments.

Published

Guest Keen Baldwins Iron & Steel Co Ltd (1937).

Times 29 July 1972.

WWW.

Sir Alfred Lewis Jones (from E Gaskell, Lancashire Leaders The Queenhithe Printing & Publishing Co Ltd, 1914).

JONES, Sir Alfred Lewis

(1845-1909)

Shipowner

Alfred Lewis Jones was born in Carmarthen, South Wales, on 24 February 1845, one of the nine children (most of whom died young) of Daniel Jones, a currier or leather worker, reputedly once the owner of a local newspaper, *The Welshman,* and his wife Mary née Williams, eldest daughter of Rev Henry Williams, Rector of Llanedi, South Wales. While his parents were not particularly affluent they were well respected in the district and although Daniel suffered from intermittent ill-health, which later reduced his earning power, it is unlikely that Alfred ever experienced serious hardship.

When Alfred was three years of age his family moved to Liverpool and here he spent the rest of his life. He received a sound education at local schools where he displayed a great aptitude for mathematics. His family's financial circumstances compelled him to leave school at the age of fourteen when he obtained a position as a cabin boy with the African Steam Ship Co. He made only one voyage to West Africa, for on his return he was recommended to the company's Liverpool agents who gave him a job as a junior clerk.

The office of William & Hamilton Laird (later known as Messrs Fletcher & Parr) was a small one but the staff contained several individuals who were destined to make important contributions to the economic development of British West Africa. These included Alexander Elder who acted as superintendent engineer, John Dempster who was then the chief clerk and John Holt, at that time an apprentice but destined to establish a major firm of West African merchants.

Alfred Jones remained with the Liverpool agents of the African Steam Ship Co until 1877, gradually increasing his status and earning power. The following year, at the age of thirty-three, he established his own firm of Alfred L Jones & Co and this proved to be highly successful in the fields of shipping and insurance broking. His company also chartered a number of small sailing vessels to carry cargoes to and from West Africa and in 1879 it hired a steamer for the same purpose. This had immediate repercussions with his former colleagues, Elder and Dempster, who by then were managing agents of the British & African Steam Navigation Co which was also serving the ports of West Africa. The result was an offer of a junior partnership and within five years Jones had manipulated events to such good effect that he had become the senior partner and both Elder and Dempster had been encouraged to leave the firm that they had created.

Having achieved control Jones faced two main problems. These were the maintenance of friendly relations with the African Steam Ship Co and the British & African Steam Navigation Co, together with the elimination of lines or individual ships that attempted to enter the trade. Separately

Statue to commemorate Sir Alfred Jones on Liverpool's pierhead (courtesy of Dr P N Davies).

these were substantial difficulties but fortunately for Jones they tended to cancel one another out. Thus by keeping on the closest terms the two British lines were able to put up a solid barrier against any outside threat and Jones made it clear to them not only how much could be gained by co-operation but also how rivalry could only ensure disaster.

The success of Jones's policies in this respect then enabled him to enhance Elder Dempster's position in the trade. By 1890 Elder Dempster were managing agents of both British shipping firms so he was able to begin the process of integrating the two fleets and extracting the maximum economies of scale from joint operations. He gradually eliminated all other competition on the British-West African route and made an agreement with the Woermann Line of Hamburg whereby the Continental-West Africa trade was shared. This latter understanding was formalised by the setting up of the West African Lines shipping conference in 1895.

After this date Alfred Jones was in a position to control effectively the external communications of British West Africa and he used this authority to expand and diversify his interests in many ways. For example Jones acquired the surf and boating companies in West Africa, he instituted many branch line services, he provided tugs, lighters and river craft: all to supplement and support his external communication system. His other subsidiary companies provided hotels, workshops, cold-storage and victualling facilities and, in time, he created a complete network of integrated concerns that helped to channel the produce of West Africa to his mainline ships. Jones also established the Bank of British West Africa to help ease financial transactions; he assisted in the establishment of the cotton growing industry by initially providing free transport in his ships (and in 1902 founded and became first president of the British Cotton Growing Association); he invested in the exploration for mineral wealth and he purchased two collieries in South Wales to provide fuel for his growing fleets and coaling stations.

The need to provide bunkering facilities for his ships at the Canary Islands (halfway to West Africa) encouraged a further aspect of Jones's enterprise. Seeking to fill any unoccupied space on vessels that called for fuel in Grand Canary or Tenerife, Jones pioneered the export of bananas to the UK. This expertise later led in 1900 to an invitation from Joseph Chamberlain (qv), then Colonial Secretary, to assist in conjunction with the firm of Edward Fyffe (qv), the development of the banana industry in the West Indies. This subsequently grew into a very large, distinctive business and Jones's interests were then hived off and he became the largest shareholder in the new firm of Elders & Fyffes Ltd. A special fleet of vessels was developed for this trade and was operated by two new companies, Elders & Fyffes (Shipping) Ltd and the West India Direct Mail Service Co Ltd. Jones also operated his ships on a number of routes which were not concerned either with West Africa or the West Indies, the most important of these being the trades from the UK to the Gulf and to Canada, and that between South Africa and Canada.

The result of all these activities was that Jones enjoyed great, but not absolute, power. He could not afford to upset the West African merchants in case they combined against him and in spite of his duopoly with the Woermann Line he could not fix rates at too high a level in case he encouraged an interloper to enter the trade. The need to keep the tacit approval of the British and colonial Governments meant that he had to act in what appeared to be a reasonable manner at all times and this implied, in turn, that he had to make sure that he did not alienate public opinion.

The most direct and obvious consequence of Jones's success in regulating the West African shipping trade was the growth in the size of the fleets which he controlled. Thus when he became senior partner of Elder Dempster in 1884 the combined fleets owned by the African Steam Ship Co and the British & African Steam Navigation Co amounted to 35 ships totalling 53,310 gross tons. By 1909, just before his death, the vessels under the control of his companies comprised 101 ships totalling 301,361 gross tons.

Jones's success in promoting Elder Dempster's interests led almost inevitably to an enhancement of his own personal situation and ultimately to a KCMG in 1901. He invested heavily in the African Steam Ship Co and at the time of his death on 13 December 1909, he owned 75 per cent of its issued capital. He also possessed a controlling interest in the British & African Steam Navigation Co after it was reorganised in 1900. These and his other assets were assessed at a gross valuation of £583,500 when his estate was settled in 1910 but this figure almost certainly under-valued his shipping interests, for when they were sold to a consortium consisting of Sir Owen Philipps (later Lord Kylsant) and Lord Pirrie (qqv), no allowance was made for goodwill.

Alfred Lewis Jones never married (he always claimed he was too busy) but he did make considerable provision in his will for his sister, Mrs Mary Isobel Pinnock (and her family), who had acted as his housekeeper for many years. Most of his estate, however, was left to charities which were mainly concerned with West Africa, the sea or Liverpool. During his lifetime, Jones helped to establish the Liverpool School of Tropical Medicine in 1899 (in recognition of which he was elected an honorary fellow of Jesus College, Oxford) and also funded its Alfred Jones chair in tropical medicine. This school, together with the 'Alfred Jones Memorial Hospital' also benefited from his will. He is buried at Anfield Cemetery and is commemorated by a large statue on Liverpool's Pier Head.

P N DAVIES

Writings:

'The West Indies' *The Empire and the Century* (New York, 1905).

'Our Greatest Industry, The World's Cotton Supply' *Daily Mail* 24 May 1909.

Sources:

Unpublished

Jones's grand-niece, Mrs Florence Norah Mocatta, currently holds his few remaining papers and artifacts.

Published

Peter N Davies, *The Trade Makers. Elder Dempster in West Africa 1852-1972* (Allen & Unwin, 1973).

— (ed), *Trading in West Africa, 1840-1920* (Croom Helm, 1976).

—, 'The Impact of the Expatriate Shipping Lines on the Economic Development of British West Africa' *Business History* 19 (1977).

—, 'Group Enterprise: Strengths and Hazards' in Sheila Marriner (ed), *Business and Businessmen* (Liverpool: Liverpool University Press, 1978).

—, *Sir Alfred Jones: Shipping Entrepreneur Par Excellence* (Europa, 1978).

DNB.

A H Milne, *Sir Alfred Lewis Jones, KCMG* (Liverpool: Henry Young & Sons, 1914).

WWW.

Sir Henry Jones (courtesy of Mr G Battison).

JONES, Sir Henry Frank Harding

(1906-)

Gas company engineer and director

Henry Frank Harding Jones was born at Paddington, London, on 13 July 1906, the first and only son, in a family of four children, of Frank Harding Jones (1873-1954), a civil engineer {BCe} of Housham Tye, Harlow, Essex, and his wife Gertrude Octavia née Kimber. For three generations the family had been engineers in the gas industry. Henry's great grandfather Robert Jones (1812-95) came from an established Chester family, was the manager of the Chester gas undertaking before moving to Wolverhampton and was also consultant to several other gas companies. In 1850 he moved to London where he became engineer to the Commercial Gas Co. Robert's son, Henry Edward Jones (1843-1925), served an apprenticeship at the GWR Works at Swindon and then joined his father in the Commercial Gas Co, later becoming engineer of the Wandsworth & District Gas Co. He established a firm of consulting gas and civil engineers, H E Jones & Son, which acted as consultant to the European Gas Co and to many British and some other overseas gas companies; in 1917 he became president of the Institution of Civil Engineers. Henry's son, Frank Harding Jones, born in 1873, was articled, after leaving Rugby School, to the eminent engineer Sir J Wolfe Barry (qv) and worked on the

Tower Bridge in London and the Subway (underground railway) in Glasgow. As a qualified civil engineer he then joined the family firm, H E Jones & Son. The firm flourished and Frank Jones became a director of a number of gas companies including in 1912 the large South Metropolitan Gas Co (which had developed under the chairmanship of Sir George Livesey (qv)), of which he became president (chairman) in 1937.

Henry was educated at Harrow and Pembroke College, Cambridge, where in 1927 he obtained a first class degree in the mechanical sciences tripos. After graduating he was articled to the distinguished consulting engineer George (later Sir George) Evetts, who had come to provide much of the driving force for H E Jones & Son with Frank Jones, the other partner, only occasionally acting as a consultant. As George Evetts's junior assistant in what was a very small firm, Henry Jones worked on several overseas projects. Among them was a large Belgian gas and coke works which suffered a foundation failure while under construction which George Evetts was called in to deal with, thereby gaining an important new client. In 1929 he won an Institution of Civil Engineers' Miller prize for a student paper entitled 'Long-Distance Gas Transmission'.

The other strong influence in Henry's early career was his father, who impressed upon him the importance of the balance sheet and of effective marketing. Good engineering was basic but commercial success resulted from proper financial control and Henry learned the importance of cost control in gas management.

Much of his earlier work involved the design and construction of gasworks plant, but he also undertook work on both parliamentary and rating and valuation matters, including methods of charging for gas in gas tariffs. More significantly, he participated in the integration of gas companies into more economic units. For several years after 1927 Frank Jones was still using the firm's office if, as occasionally happened, he accepted consulting work, and Henry Jones would then work for him as well as for George Evetts. But eventually Frank Jones gave up all consulting work and Henry Jones was appointed to a number of directorships of gas companies where his father was chairman, and also to other companies with which his father had no connection, notably the British Gas Light Co and the United Kingdom Gas Corporation Ltd, a holding company established to obtain control of gas companies by agreed purchases of all their shares. In the early days of the company he advised negotiators on the takeover value of some of the companies acquired, but as the number of companies owned grew Col W M Carr OBE, TD, well-known as manager of the Stretford gas undertaking and as a consulting engineer, was appointed managing director. Under his leadership the corporation expanded rapidly with groups in Yorkshire, Lancashire, Bedfordshire and South Wales. The British Gas Light Co was an old-established gas company supplying gas in Hull and Norwich under statutory powers, but also owning by share purchase many gas companies in East Anglia and a few elsewhere.

By the mid-1930s Henry Jones was no longer an employee of George Evetts, but kept in close touch with him, on one occasion in 1937 making a report for him on a new process for making oil and other products from coal, operating at Nuremberg.

In 1939 Henry Jones, who had been in the Regular Army Reserve of

Officers since his Cambridge days, was called up. He went to France and Belgium as a lieutenant in the Essex Regiment and was evacuated from Dunkirk. For two years he was Brigade transport officer and later staff captain of the 25th Infantry Brigade and then in 1942 went to India to become a major on the staff of 14th Indian Division. He served in India and Burma for the remainder of the war, being demobilised in 1945 with the rank of brigadier and the military MBE (awarded in 1943).

By 1948 Henry Jones was deputy chairman of the Wandsworth & District and Watford & St Albans Gas Cos, and a director of many others. In 1946 he had become a member of the Institution of Gas Engineers (president in 1956-57) and in 1948, after the necessary examination and professional interview, the Institution of Civil Engineers. He joined the Institution of Chemical Engineers in 1955.

Henry Jones's experience of linking gas undertakings and of imposing sound managerial and financial controls over large groups made him an eligible candidate for appointment in the new nationalised structure imposed on the gas industry by the Labour Government in May 1949. He became the first chairman of the newly-formed East Midlands Gas Board, having been appointed a member of the Gas Council, the industry's central authority (which had ultimate responsibility for the economic performance of the industry), in the previous November.

The task of unifying the 100 gas undertakings which passed from the ownership of gas companies and local authorities to become part of the East Midlands Gas Board on vesting day, was not easy, but from the outset Henry Jones gave priority to the feelings of the individuals concerned. 'Every man and woman should be treated as a human being and not as a cog in a machine' he told officials of gas undertakings in the East Midlands on 25 February 1949, and this was repeated later that year to the first Area Conference of the East Midlands Gas Board at Skegness, a meeting of officials struggling to adjust to the new circumstances. It was sincerely meant because Henry Jones has a strong sense of the rights of others and a gift for extracting loyalty. To some degree this conflicted with his natural reserve which has on occasion been misinterpreted as remoteness. Apart from a keen intelligence and a natural authority, perhaps his most outstanding characteristic is a transparent honesty; it was one of the qualities which enabled him to achieve sweeping changes during this and later stages in his career, carrying with him his employees' trust.

In 1952 the success which had attended his efforts in the East Midlands Gas Board resulted in his appointment as deputy chairman of the Gas Council; in 1960 he became chairman.

It was a critical period for the gas industry which had for some years been struggling to remain viable in the face of a feedstock which had risen steadily in price. The National Coal Board, believing the gas industry to be a captive customer, was in process of raising the price of high-quality coking-coals to a level which threatened to put gas out of business. Competition from electricity (which could fire its boilers with relatively cheap coal) and from oil was intensifying. Carbonisation demanded the maintenance of a market for the gas industry's chief subsidiary product, coke, and revenue from this source was, to say the least, unreliable. Moreover, dependence on coal as a feedstock necessitated the employment of a large labour force and the operation of complex purification processes. Since gas manufacture was still largely conducted in relatively small undertakings, possessed of an image which was no more attractive to the prospective employee than it was to the public at large, prospects for the future appeared bleak.

In the circumstances it is remarkable that the gas industry survived as it did during the late 1940s and early 1950s; one reason was undoubtedly a very energetic selling policy in the domestic market and the creation of a generous back-up technical service in industrial markets where gas was under even greater pressure from electricity and propane.

Without the vision and determination of a small number of men (amongst whom were certainly Henry Jones and his predecessor Colonel Sir Harold Smith) it is doubtful if the industry could have achieved anything more than a gradually slowing momentum and an eclipse over perhaps twenty years. It was that small band of pioneers which harnessed the research machinery which had been set up in 1939 under the title of the Gas Research Board, and in due course enabled the Gas Council to take over all its assets and personnel. Research stations were set up to conduct investigations into various aspects of the industry's operation.

Clearly, if the gas industry were to survive it had to break away from its dependence on coal, and although research continued to be conducted into more sophisticated coal plants which gasified the feedstock without leaving a residue of coke and tar, it was to the chemical industry that the Gas Council turned for its salvation. The availability of large quantities of light petroleum distillate led to the development of a catalytic rich gas process and the gas recycle hydrogenator process. This produced a cheaper therm and made possible not only the preservation of threatened gas markets but the establishment of an important new one — domestic gas central heating.

Henry Jones's chairmanship was well timed to permit these developments to be advanced with all possible speed and during the 1960s a considerable number of oil gasification plants were built. As an engineer he was well able to recognise the need for the industry to pursue this path and to match its growing sophistication in gas manufacture with a parallel upgrading of marketing techniques.

Whether or not the gas industry would have continued to prosper into the 1970s and beyond as an oil-based industry we shall never know because gas manufacture was overtaken by events. Again it was the farsightedness of Henry Jones which put muscle behind the first experiments in bringing seaborne liquid methane to this country. The first shipments (from Louisiana) arrived in 1959 and by 1963 two specially-built tankers were making regular deliveries of natural gas from the Sahara to Canvey Island. In January 1966 the Gas Council announced the establishment of three new departments, including one for Production and Supplies of which Denis E Rooke (now Sir Denis) was the first Director — and was appointed a full-time member of the Gas Council in August 1966.

Thus the new gas industry was born, but its potential could not have been fully realised without the national transmission system which was another of the major achievements of Henry Jones's chairmanship. In an unprecedented burst of engineering activity this system grew from 74,000 miles at nationalisation to 127,000 by 1973. Turnover also soared, from

£233.5 million in 1950-51 to £401.9 million in 1960-61 and then to £787 million in 1971-72.

For the first seven years of his chairmanship his deputy was W K (later Sir Kenneth) Hutchison with whom he forged a particularly constructive partnership. Sir Kenneth was the elder of the two and on his retirement the deputy chairmanship passed to A F (later Sir Arthur) Hetherington (qv), with whom Henry Jones worked towards the creation of the British Gas Corporation. In 1967 Sir Henry Jones (he was knighted in 1963) took the advice of McKinsey & Co, the management consultants, who recommended changes in the structure of the Gas Council, essentially strengthening the industry's management structure. The members of the 12 Area Gas Boards, set up in 1949, were directly appointed by the Minister and the Boards reported annually and directly to him. The Area Board chairmen formed the Gas Council (together with the Council chairman and vice-chairman). With the expansion of the industry in the 1960s a more centralised structure became necessary, with much more power vested in a new central authority (the British Gas Corporation, created in 1973). While the Minister continued to appoint members of the central authority, the 12 Area Boards were replaced by regional managers chosen by the central authority. Sir Henry paid special attention to the industry's recruitment of top and middle managers, keeping files on promising individuals both within and outside the gas industry. Over a period this led to an atmosphere in which talent was allowed to flower and to a significant improvement in the quality of middle management. Consequently the gas industry gained an envied reputation for management progression. By 1972, when Sir Henry retired, the gas industry had undergone a complete technological and organisational revolution. It was larger, much more efficient and was well launched on its ten-year programme of conversion from manufactured gas to town gas. After he retired Sir Henry joined the boards of the Benzene Marketing Co and Benzole Producers Ltd, serving as chairman of both during 1972-77. He was an active representative of the Gas Industry on the World Energy Conference, being chairman of the British National Committee from 1968 to 1971 and a vice-chairman of the International Executive Council from 1970 to 1973. While popular as a speaker and author of papers to a wide variety of engineering and scientific bodies, his prime interest was the Institution of Gas Engineers: he became its president in 1957, delivered one of the Centenary Addresses in 1963, received its Birmingham medal in 1964 and became one of its honorary fellows in 1970.

Sir Henry Jones was made KBE in 1965 and GBE in 1972. In 1972-73 he was Master of the Clothworkers Company, of which he became a liveryman in 1928. He is a fellow of the Institution of Gas Engineers, the Institution of Civil Engineers, the Institution of Chemical Engineers, the Fellowship of Engineering and the Royal Society of Arts. He was awarded honorary doctorates by the universities of Leeds (LLD, 1967), Leicester (DSc, 1970) and Salford (DSc, 1971). He served as a member of the Royal Commission on Standards of Conduct in Public Life, 1974-76, and was chairman of the Economic Development Committee for the Chemical Industry.

Currently Sir Henry Jones lives quietly at his Buckinghamshire home, but he continues to attend occasional gas industry functions and maintains his interest in energy matters on a global scale, like his involvement with Energy International NV (of which he was for a number of years a member of the Advisory Committee and to which he had presented several papers over a decade).

He married in 1934 Elizabeth née Langton, the daughter of Spencer James Langton; they have three sons, Richard Harding (b 1936), John Harding (b 1938) and Antony Harding (b 1946), and one daughter, Priscilla Mary McDougall (b 1940).

GEOFFREY BATTISON

Writings:

Presidential address to Institution of Gas Engineers *Transactions of the Institution of Gas Engineers* 106 (1956-57).

'Fuel and Power — the Mainsprings of Industry' *The British Foundryman* July 1962.

'Good Engineering (a Centenary Address)' *Journal of the Institution of Gas Engineers* 3 (1963).

'The Future of Fuel' *Powell Duffryn Review* Aug 1963.

'The Future of the Gas Industry' *Transactions of the Institution of Engineers and Shipbuilders in Scotland* 10 Dec 1963.

'The Gas Industry — Today and Tomorrow' *Journal of the Royal Society of Arts* Apr 1964.

'Re-organisation of the Water Supply Industry' *Transactions of the British Waterworks Association* June 1972.

'Gas for Industry' European Industrial Research Management Association (European Research Management Association, 13-14 Mar 1974).

Sources:

Unpublished

BCe.

MCe.

Information from Sir Henry Jones.

Published

Sir Norman Chester, *The Nationalisation of British Industry, 1945-51* (HMSO, 1975).

PP, White Paper on Fuel Policy (1967) Cmd 3438.

Trevor I Williams, *A History of the British Gas Industry* (Oxford University Press, 1981).

WW 1982.

JONES, Theodore Brooke

(1827-1920)

Accountant

Theodore Brooke Jones was born on 3 September 1827, probably in London, the son of Orlando Jones, public accountant and patent starch manufacturer in the City of London, and his wife Anne Elizabeth née Lamphier. Jones was the grandson of Edward Thomas Jones (1767-1833), author of *Jones's English System of Bookkeeping* (Bristol, 1796) and proprietor of Waunfawr Colliery, Risca, from 1796 to 1811, who founded an accounting practice in London in 1821.

Following his father's death in 1843, he trained as a public accountant with his uncle, Theodore Jones, later becoming his partner. In 1860 he married Euphemia Turnbull of Glasgow, daughter of Thomas Turnbull, bleacher. They had nine children, including Theodore Shaw Jones, who later assumed responsibility for the London office, and Cecil Lamphier Jones, who was the last member of the family to practice accountancy.

Although London-based, the practice had an unusually strong industrial bias, with clients as far away as Glasgow, Manchester and South Wales. Jones was a close friend of William Foster (qv), the worsted manufacturer. Towards the end of the 1860s, Jones began to restructure the firm by creating a network of local partnerships such as one finds in twentieth century accountancy, although he did not follow the modern practice of using the same name for all offices. In 1867 Arthur James Hill joined the London office. A circular to clients observed that this would enable the firm to undertake 'the management and improvement of estates and the negotiation of sales by private contract' {Brotherton Library, circular of Sept 1867}, activities which were soon banned by professional rules of conduct. By 1870 offices had been opened at Leeds (Theodore B Jones & Co) and Manchester (Jones, Crewdson & Co), to be followed later by a Belfast office. Reportedly Jones also had offices in America and Russia but there is no hard evidence of this.

New articles of partnership were drawn up for the London partners in 1873. Theodore was released from full-time work and would retire in 1877. His nephew Theodore Brooke Jones now moved to Harrogate and lived there for the rest of his life. In 1879 Theodore Jones (now of unsound mind due to old age) commenced a Chancery suit in which it was alleged that his former partners had failed to account for some sums due to him, both from the firm itself and in respect of profits on E T Jones's copyright works.

A second major dispute occurred ten years later when Arthur Hill left the partnership, taking with him W E Vellacott (who joined the firm in 1882) and founding Hill, Vellacott & Co. The reasons are not known, but may be connected with Jones's authoritarian attitude and changing personal interests. The incident certainly seems to mark a turning point in the fortunes of the family practice, for although Jones continued to

JONES'S

ENGLISH SYSTEMS

OF

BOOK-KEEPING,

BY

SINGLE AND DOUBLE ENTRY,

IN TWO PARTS,

BY THE LATE

EDWARD THOMAS JONES.

SIXTEENTH EDITION.

WITH NUMEROUS ILLUSTRATIONS AND EXPLANATIONS,

BY

THEODORE JONES.

LONDON:
PUBLISHED BY THEODORE JONES AND CO.
GENERAL ACCOUNTANTS, 1, FINSBURY CIRCUS, E.C.;
AND BY SIMPKIN, MARSHALL AND CO.,
STATIONERS'-HALL-COURT.

[*Entered at Stationers' Hall.*]

Title page of E B Jones's English
System of Book-keeping *with
illustrations and explanations by T
B Jones (courtesy of the Institute of
Chartered Accountants).*

dominate the firm until his death, he delegated the day-to-day running of
the London office to his son, Theodore Shaw, and showed little interest in
expanding the practice.

It is clear that Jones's creative urge had now found other outlets.
Although he joined both the Institute of Accountants and its successor, the
Institute of Chartered Accountants in England and Wales, he did not take
any notable part in the affairs of either body. Instead, he opened a
Plymouth Brethren Mission Room in Harrogate and turned his mind to a
multitude of practical problems as well. Between 1879 and 1911, he
obtained provisional patents for a series of inventions, ranging from

bookkeeping and music holders to communication platforms for railway carriages, sewage treatment and invalid chairs.

Although not an original accounting thinker, he continued to develop his grandfather's ideas, mainly by publishing account books for special purposes. An undated price list issued by Theodore B Jones & Co, Chartered Accountants, Standard Buildings, Leeds, details the following publications:

> *Jones's Improved Sales and Bought Ledger Balance Books*
> *Jones's Weekly Balance Ledger for Retail Houses*
> *Jones's Every Man his Own Landlord*
> *Jones's Tables and Rules for Building Societies* and
> *Jones's Commercial Account Books*

His influence on textile accounting is apparent from G P Norton's *Textile Manufacturer's Bookkeeping* (1889), which is strongly Jonesian in places. Jones's accounting methods were introduced into Australia by one of his clerks, John Scouller, author of *Practical Bookkeeping* (1880).

Theodore Brooke Jones died on 21 October 1920, having divested himself of his property earlier in life.

JOHN R ETOR

Writings:

Rules of the London and Provincial Permanent Building Society (1864).

Jedermann Hauseigenthümer (Nach TJ) Das bewährteste System Englischer Baugenossenschaften ... bearbeitet ... mit einer Einleitung von L Sonnemann. Herausgegeben von Dr F A Lange (Duisburg, 1865).

Jones's Table, and Tables for Calculating Interest at All Rates Per Cent (1872).

Jones's Lunar Monthly Tables for the Use of Building Societies (1877).

Sources:

Unpublished

Brotherton Library, University of Leeds, papers of John Foster & Son, correspondence between William Foster and Theodore Brooke Jones.

PRO, Statements of Claim and Defence in *Theodore Jones v Theodore Brooke Jones* (1879) and *Theodore Jones v Theodore Brooke Jones and Arthur James Hill* (1879).

Family papers, genealogies and reminiscences in the possession of Rev T Garnett Jones (son of Cecil Lamphier Jones).

Published

L Goldberg, 'The Search for Scouller: An Interim Report' *Accounting and Business Research* Summer 1977.

Sir Walter Benton-Jones (courtesy of Sir Simon Benton-Jones).

JONES, Sir Walter Benton

(1880-1967)

Steel manufacturer

Walter Benton Jones was born at Cannock, Staffordshire, on 26 September 1880, the son of Frederick John Jones (1854-1936), the chief executive of the Rother Vale Collieries and his wife Annie Elizabeth née Benton. Frederick later became chairman of the Mining Association and in 1919 received a baronetcy for his services to coal industry labour relations during the First World War. Walter spent most of his childhood in Treeton, Yorkshire, near a colliery and mining village, much under the influence of his father, who soon became a widower. He went to Repton, then Trinity College, Cambridge, where he read history, and travelled briefly abroad before joining Rother Vale Collieries in 1902. There he underwent a long tutelage in general management under his father, becoming secretary of the company in 1906, a director in 1909 and managing director in 1915. This formation in the coal industry encouraged a sense of financial realism and a keen eye for operating efficiency which were to persist. The proximities to the men in the pits, in both his childhood and his early career, were unusual for someone of his social class. According to some who knew Benton Jones well, they helped to form his social consciousness, an important influence in later years.

After Rother Vale Collieries became part of the new United Steel Cos in 1918, the two Joneses made substantial contributions to the latter's early development, Sir Frederick as vice-chairman and chairman of the finance committee, Walter Benton Jones as executive director in charge of colliery operations. During Albert Peech's troubled chairmanship of United Steel in 1920-27, Walter became increasingly involved in strategic policy discussions. Already, he showed signs of a determination to reform, but also to preserve largely intact, the sprawling new combine, in some ways an industrial equivalent of the Habsburg empire. Although still somewhat overshadowed by his father, he contributed much analytical ability and commonsense, helping to counterweigh an impulsive chairman and the marked centrifugal tendencies within what was then a highly confused organisation. These were anxious years for United Steel, loaded as it was with heavy indebtedness, bold expansions which had turned sour in the depression and a long tail of commercially declining operations, its leadership dogged rather than inspired.

In late 1927 Maxmilian Mannaberg, a strong internal critic of Peech on the board, engineered a palace coup in the midst of a severe financial crisis for the firm. As a result, Walter Benton Jones became chairman and a managing director was appointed, Robert Hilton (qv). There followed a creative period of dual leadership by Benton Jones and Hilton until 1939.

Never an outstanding entrepreneur, Benton Jones nonetheless emerged as an assiduous chairman in terms of both policy thinking and the human aspects of organisation. He played a leading role in financial policy, particularly in a critical reconstruction in the early 1930s and in capital raising, and he continued to be directly in charge of colliery operations. However, it was primarily the more forceful Hilton who directed the classic turn-round in United Steel's fortunes between 1928 and 1932 by means of rationalisation, centralisation, infusions of new management, and productivity schemes. The relationship between the two men was sometimes uneasy. To a considerable extent, though, they complemented each other, with Benton Jones as the more reflective and conciliatory figure while Hilton spearheaded the astringent tasks of getting on top of the organisation and keeping tight control. Moreover, despite some obvious temperamental differences, on most areas of policy they agreed.

The Benton Jones-Hilton regime had four main characteristics. First, a strong emphasis on productive and organisational efficiency, continuing well beyond the 1928-32 turn-round, increasingly made the company an exemplar in productivity promotion, planning, budgeting and control systems, and management training and development. Second, there was much caution on, and little propensity for, strategic expansion. Through the 1930s United Steel expanded no more than broadly in line with the industry's general recovery, despite showing much technical progressiveness. In its competitive strategy with regard to mergers, inter-firm diplomacy and key product developments the firm was frequently outmanoeuvred, particularly in the important 'Midland Corridor' and notably by Stewarts & Lloyds. Both Benton Jones and Hilton had decided limitations on these fronts. Third, the firm genuinely pioneered, relative to the industry, in its social policies. Benton Jones painstakingly cultivated shop-floor goodwill, supported the introduction of works councils, advocated worker pensions (introduced in 1936) and threw his weight behind the maintenance of economically marginal activities, notably in West Cumberland. Attitudes of social obligation played an important role in these policies, particularly the last. A fourth important feature was the firm's vigorous support for the idea of a strong central organisation and industry-wide co-operation in iron and steel throughout the national reorganisation efforts of 1932-35. Although United Steel became restive over certain aspects of the new British Iron and Steel Federation regime under Sir Andrew Duncan (qv) after 1935, its mainly 'co-operative' stance towards industrial and public policies throughout the 1930s, in contradistinction to other firms' 'passivity' or 'separatism' {Boswell (1983) ch 9} owed much to Benton Jones's preferences for stability and for a collective rather than individualistic ethos.

In 1939 Hilton relinquished the managing directorship, a change facilitated by his appointment as president of the BISF but also partly engineered by Benton Jones and by some restive younger dynastic elements in the firm. While still continuing as chairman, Benton Jones then took on the managing directorship in 1941 and a joint managing directorship in 1945. During this peak period of his power until about 1947, he concentrated on four principal tasks: the organisation of war production; the formulation of plans for post-war reconstruction; a process of internal decentralisation (now desirable, it seemed, but also easier because of the previous centralising phase under Hilton); and the preparation of a new generation of leadership from among the original family elements. In 1947 he handed over the managing directorship to Gerald Steel, son of Harry Steel, the man who had spearheaded the formation of United Steel in 1916-18. Although Benton Jones's indulgence towards dynastic influences was sometimes misplaced, in this case his choice appeared to be sound. Gerald Steel emerged as a very capable chief executive so the previous approximation to a dual monarchy was restored.

Benton Jones continued inordinately long as chairman, not retiring until 1962: he even outlasted Gerald Steel, who died prematurely in 1957. On his retirement he became president of United Steel. During this long period his capacities showed signs of weakening. Apart from symbolising continuity, his main contributions lay in counselling caution over expansion, where his influence was now often conservative (although Steel also strongly adhered to an efficiency-promoting rather than expansionary emphasis). But significantly, too, he still actively represented United Steel's public service orientation and its role as a socially-conscious employer. Benton Jones's overlong retention of the chairmanship had elements of pathos. It largely reflected decades of absorbed dedication to the firm and his twenty-nine years of solitude as a widower so that psychologically he found it hard to contemplate anything else. After Gerald Steel's death in 1957, his continuance also reflected a dutiful desire to play in the latter's still partly-unprepared successor, A J Peech.

Benton Jones performed well the monarchical aspects of chairmanship. A slight, dapper, bow-tied figure, he exuded much dignity, dedication and high-minded purpose. Despite streaks of imaginative impulsiveness in the realm of ideas, Benton Jones was essentially cautious as a businessman. This reflected his long formation in the coal industry, the scars left by the depression years, and both temperamental and ideological preferences for order and moderation as opposed to aggressive cut-and-thrust. His long, painstaking memoranda reveal persistent pursuits of tidiness, good organisation, improved housekeeping. Yet he could also sometimes exhibit an excessive zeal for facts and figures, a rambling verbosity particularly in the later years, and minor extravagances, for example over head office amenities and guest houses. Benton Jones never played an outstanding role in the national leadership of the industry even though United Steel was highly participative in its counsels and even though his own style and concepts contributed to its political evolution during the 1930s. He was dedicated to pacification as well as efficiency; sometimes laborious and slow in decision-making; a quiet provincial industrialist who was suspicious of nouveau riche acquisitiveness and of the City; a devotee of the ideas of wealth-as-stewardship and industrial co-operation. A high-minded upbringing, Anglican religious convictions and probably too, the early links with mining communities were influential in encouraging a humanitarian social idealism. For example, working conditions should show 'higher standards ... than have ever been reached in any works of our kind'; health provisions should be well in advance of the law; the workplace should be 'a community' and a source of 'happiness'; 'people were more important than things' {Benton Jones (1941)}. At the same time managerial objectives should include 'social responsibility' overall and 'maximum employment' particularly in dependent communities {Andrews and Brunner (1952) 274}.

Benton Jones made a substantial contribution to co-operative marketing schemes in the Midland coal industry in the late 1920s and early 1930s. In his later years he was an assiduous non-executive director of the Westminster Bank, and also devoted much time to church affairs and to the Trevelyan Scholarships, which helped students from state schools to pursue imaginative courses of study at Oxford and Cambridge.

Benton Jones married in 1907 Lily, daughter of James Dixon Fawcett of Sheffield. Devoted to his wife and to their somewhat reclusive domesticity, he never fully recovered from her death in 1938 after a long disabling illness. They had two daughters and a son, Peter Benton Jones. The latter became a director, a member of the top management and operating head of the United Steel's ore mining and chemicals-from-coal interests, although he never emerged as a powerful force.

Sir Walter Benton Jones died on 5 December 1967, leaving £36,631 gross.

JONATHAN S BOSWELL

Writings:

Three Elementary Things. Talks Addressed to Officers of the United Steel Companies Ltd (pp, 1941 and T Nelson & Sons, 1942).

'The History and Organisation of the United Steel Companies Ltd' in Ronald S Edwards and Harry Townsend (eds), *Business Growth* (Macmillan, 1966).

Sources:

Unpublished

Bank of England, Securities Management Trust and Bankers' Industrial Development Corporation papers.

British Steel Corporation Midland Regional Records Centre, Irthlingborough, Northamptonshire, National Federation of Iron and Steel Manufacturers' and British Iron and Steel Federation records.

British Steel Corporation North East Regional Records Centre, Middlesbrough, Cleveland, United Steel Cos' records particularly Directors' Minutes, Annual General Meetings, Central and Finance Committee Minutes, Sir Frederick Jones's Correspondence, Chairman's Investigations, Robert Hilton's copy letter books, and special files on, for example 1927-28 reorganisation, iron ore resources, amalgamations, and financial and organisational matters in the 1930s.

PRO, BT/56/14, 21, 37; BT/55/38; Import Duties Advisory Committee papers BT/10.

PrC.

Interviews mainly in 1981, with ex-officials of United Steel: P Beynon, H P Forder, D Ward Jones, T S Kilpatrick, R M Peddie, A J Peech, R Scholey, J Y Lancaster, also with Sir M Finniston, S Gray, Mrs R Kydd (née Benton Jones).

Written information from T S Kilpatrick, R M Peddie, E T Sara.

Philip W S Andrews and E Brunner, interview notes 1950 for their *Capital Development in Steel* (by courtesy of the late Professor E Brunner).

Steven Tolliday, 'Industry, Finance and the State: An Analysis of the British Steel Industry in the Inter-War Years' (Cambridge PhD, 1979).

Published

Philip W S Andrews and Elizabeth Brunner, *Capital Development in Steel: A Study of the United Steel Companies Limited* (Oxford: Basil Blackwell, 1952).

Jonathan S Boswell, 'Hope, Inefficiency or Public Duty? The United Steel Companies and West Cumberland, 1918-39' *Business History* 22 (1980).

—, *Business Policies in the Making, Three Steel Companies Compared* (George Allen & Unwin, 1983).

Duncan L Burn, *The Economic History of Steelmaking 1867-1939* (Cambridge: Cambridge University Press, 1940).

—, *The Steel Industry 1939-59* (Cambridge, Cambridge University Press, 1961).

James C Carr and Walter Taplin, *A History of the British Steel Industry* (Oxford: Basil Blackwell, 1962).

John Jewkes and W A Winterbottom, *An Industrial Survey of Cumberland and Furness* (Manchester: Manchester University Press, 1933).

Bernard S Keeling and Anthony E Wright, *The Development of the Modern British Steel Industry* (Longmans, 1964).

Maurice W Kirby, *The British Coalmining Industry 1870-1946* (Macmillan, 1977).

J Y Lancaster and D R Wattleworth, *The Iron and Steel Industry of West Cumberland, an Historical Survey* (Workington: British Steel Corporation, 1977).

R M Peddie, *The United Steel Companies* (Sheffield, 1967).

John E Vaizey, *The History of British Steel* (Weidenfeld & Nicolson, 1974).

WWW.

JOSEPH, Sir Maxwell

(1910-1982)

Hotel, brewing and entertainments company chairman

Max Joseph (in later years he adopted the name of Maxwell) was born in Whitechapel, London, on 31 May 1910, the son of Jack Joseph, a journeyman ladies tailor and his wife Sarah née Orler. As a boy Maxwell failed the entrance examination to the Regent Street Polytechnic and, despite private tutoring, showed no grasp of any subject until his father,

JOSEPH Sir Maxwell

Sir Maxwell Joseph (courtesy of Grand Metropolitan plc).

'in sheer desperation' {Erdman (1982) 128} sent him to Pitman's Business School. There he did very well in examinations in shorthand, typing and bookkeeping. His first job was with Ernest Owers, estate agents in West Hampstead, at 30s a week. No commission was paid to the staff for selling houses but a small commission was paid for every 'For Sale' or 'Sold By' board which was put up. According to Erdman, Joseph concentrated on putting up boards, with or without the permission of the owners of the property concerned. Next, he worked for Ernest Durbridge in Thayer Street, Manchester Square and later for Dudley Samuel & Harrison, estate agents with a determinedly commercial attitude to their business. At one time or another their employees included a number of future entrepreneurs, including Edward Erdman and Harry Hyams. Joseph did not work for them long, however, because Dudley Samuel expected quick results which Joseph failed to provide. In 1928, at the age of nineteen, with money lent by his father (£100 according to one account, £500 according to another), he set up his own estate agency, Connaught Hooper in Bayswater, and a small private property company. He seems to have financed his property dealings by borrowing; by 1939 he owed William Deacons Bank £40,000. The bank did not press for reduction of this debt until after the war; Joseph was always grateful to it for this forbearance, and remained closely associated with it for the rest of his career.

Failing in his application for a commission in the RAF, Joseph spent the war as a lance-corporal in the Royal Engineers. In later years he relished the reference given to him by the army on his demobilisation in 1946, 'This man might be able to assume some responsibility in civilian life' {*ibid*, 129}.

After the war, he resumed property dealing and began from about 1948 to concentrate on buying small hotels in Kensington, such as the Milestone, and in the West End, like the Mandeville in Wigmore Street. His acquisition of the Mount Royal Hotel, Marble Arch (later renamed the Grand Metropolitan) for £1 million in 1957 later appeared to him to be the turning point of his career.

Joseph was also dealing in rented property at this time. In 1958 he bought a block of 1,200 flats, Dolphin Square, 'believed to be the largest block of flats in Europe' {Times *Prospectuses* (1959) 107}, built by R R Costain (qv). Following on the restoration of an effective market in residential property by the lifting of rent controls, this was the largest deal in such property in London for some years. Joseph paid £2.5 million for Dolphin Square. In 1959 he exchanged the whole of the issued share capital of 2,000 £1 shares of Dolphin Square Ltd for 3.5 million 5s shares in Lintang Investments Ltd (out of a total of 6.3 million issued 5s shares); Lintang also took over a debt of £100,000 owed to Joseph by Dolphin Square Ltd. Later that year Joseph and other major shareholders sold their controlling interest in Lintang to H Jaspar & Co, which was acting on behalf of one Friederich Grunwald. However, Grunwald did not actually have sufficient resources to pay for these shares and some complicated financial transactions took place with Joseph lending £1.5 million against collateral of 3.3 million shares in Lintang and 500,000 shares in Reliable Properties. Grunwald also borrowed £3.5 million from the State Building Society, not all of which could later be accounted for. The transaction became one of the largest post-war financial scandals and resulted in the

544

Sir Maxwell Joseph's favourite hotel, the Carlton, at Cannes (courtesy of Grand Metropolitan plc).

prosecution and conviction of Grunwald for fraud and some changes in company law. Joseph himself was recognised to be innocent of any malpractice, and had only failed to ensure that Grunwald did in fact have enough cash to pay all the shareholders of Lintang. He had lent Grunwald the £1.5 million because he was anxious the deal should be concluded to the satisfaction of all Lintang shareholders. In 1964 he devised a scheme to try to clear up the remaining problems, making an offer through a specially created company, Baker Street Realisations, to shareholders of the various companies caught up in the deal, who were not themselves concerned in the transactions. Joseph himself stood to lose about £500,000 by this scheme. Dolphin Square was sold by Lintang to Westminster City Council for £4.5 million in 1963.

In the 1960s Joseph was still primarily a London hotelier. By 1960 Grand Hotels (Mayfair) Ltd (which he and some associates had taken over in 1957), with an issued capital of £511,833 and group assets of £835,846, owned 11 medium-priced hotels and two restaurants in London: several of the hotels were recent acquisitions, and Joseph was known to be looking for more. (The Mount Royal Hotel was owned by a separate private company, Mount Royal Ltd, with an issued capital of £300,000.) The tourist industry in Britain, especially to London, was flourishing and he was confident that reduced air fares would increase the number of visitors still further. His confidence was justified: the total spent by foreign visitors to Britain rose by 80 per cent from 1958 to 1963. Increasing business travel and entertaining and conferences also promoted growth in the hotel industry. In 1962 Joseph brought Mount Royal Ltd and Grand Hotels (Mayfair) Ltd, into one group, Grand Metropolitan Hotels Ltd. By 1965 Grand Metropolitan Hotels claimed to be the largest hotel group in the world by profits (pre-tax profits for the year to September 1964 had been £1.6 million); Trust Houses, under the chairmanship of Geoffrey Crowther (qv), was probably the largest by number of rooms. The growth of Grand Metropolitan was attributed to the initiative of its management. In the years after the war, 'while the rest of the industry carried on much as it always had, Mr Maxwell Joseph and Mr Fred Kobler [joint managing director with Joseph of Grand Metropolitan] evolved a new conception of hotel management. They have aimed for the upper-middle class hotel price bracket. The technique has been to collect a handful of well-located hotels in London's West End. This permitted bulk buying of nearly all foodstuffs. The group pioneered the idea of a permanent sales organisation for both tourists and industrial business. And it has shown no hesitation in turning space over to other uses (such as shops or offices) where it is unsuitable for hotel use' {*Economist* 20 Mar 1965}.

The conscious effort to organise the selling of hotel rooms centrally (rather than leave it to the managers of individual hotels to fill their rooms) was an important factor in the continued prosperity of Grand Metropolitan Hotels. Its objective was to find new ways of marketing hotel rooms to avoid the seasonal fluctuations that left many rooms empty for part of the year. In the mid-1960s the group began the promotion of 'mini-holidays' (usually weekends) which were priced to cover only the hotel's marginal costs, and were so successful, despite the initial opposition of travel agents, that sometimes Grand Metropolitan had to place customers in the hotels of their rivals, because their own were completely full. By 1974 over 140,000 customers annually were taking mini-holidays with Grand Metropolitan, and although by that time there were about 35 competitive schemes, the company reckoned to have 70 per cent of this market. Efforts were thus being made to think up new ways of keeping hotels full all year round, like meetings for crossword enthusiasts or choral competitions.

Until the mid-1960s, Joseph had shown little interest in developing the catering side of his hotel business. However, in 1966 he declared that he was not in fact uninterested in catering and demonstrated this by the acquisition, by an exchange of shares in Grand Metropolitan, of Levy & Franks. Best known for its chain of Chef & Brewer pubs in London, Levy & Franks were also involved in wholesaling and warehousing of drink, for which Grand Metropolitan hotels provided a ready market.

This beginning of diversification of interests may have been prompted also by Joseph's increasing misgivings about the prospects for the British tourist and hotel industry. He complained that the Government was failing to recognise the importance of the hotel industry as an earner of foreign exchange, and was penalising it by excluding it from incentives offered to other industries, such as investment allowances. He was particularly critical of Selective Employment Tax, which, he argued, by forcing hotels to raise their prices could have a disastrous effect on

Interior of the Palm Beach Club, London (courtesy of Grand Metropolitan and London Clubs Limited).

tourism. In 1966 he announced the cancellation of projects totalling £3.5 million. He began to extend Grand Metropolitan's interests abroad; his acquisitions included three of the best hotels in Paris in 1967 which, with the two hotels the group already owned there, made the largest hotel group in France (most hotels in France being owned individually). In 1969 Joseph also bought the Royal Manhattan Hotel in New York, partly because he believed that giving Grand Metropolitan a physical presence in the USA would help the sales of rooms in its European hotels to American tourists.

Aided by the devaluation of the pound in 1967, the British tourist industry had not suffered as badly from the unhelpful attitude of the Government as Joseph had feared. Indeed, there was a distinct boom in tourism in the late 1960s, from which Grand Metropolitan benefited, with other hotel companies. Joseph once again planned extensions to its British hotel interests, aiming to increase Grand Metropolitan's 7,000 beds in London to 12,000 (the Group had a further 3,000 beds outside London). A major part of these plans was a project to build a giant hotel with several thousand rooms, combined with an air terminal for TWA, in West London, which mercifully was dropped. The flourishing tourist industry (over 5 million tourists came to Britain in 1969, making it the most popular tourist destination in the world), encouraged others to plan and build new hotels too, and Joseph became worried that they would spoil the market. In 1970 he warned that 'gross overcharging' by some of London's newer hotel groups would harm the image of Britain's hotel industry: 'many new hotels are now being planned by property developers and inexperienced operators, some with little or no financial backing. These hotels can only operate profitably by gross overcharging during the present boom conditions which the industry is now experiencing in London' {*Times* 12 Feb 1970}.

The diversification of Grand Metropolitan which had begun with the acquisition of Levy & Franks, continued in earnest in 1969, with the takeover of Express Dairies for £32 million. Rather than arguing any advantage of supply to his hotels, Joseph gave as his reason for the takeover, that he thought the milk industry had been slow in exploiting the basic milk run business. The following year saw the acquisition for £15 million of the Berni Inns, with 130 steak-houses and 15 hotels, and of the Mecca group of betting-shops, dance halls, and bingo houses for £33 million. Next, Joseph made a bid for the Cunard shipping line in 1971, but soon dropped that bid to go after the brewery Truman Hanbury Buxton. A difficult and rather ill-natured takeover battle followed, as a rival brewery, Watney Manns, put in a counter-bid. Joseph found Trumans an attractive proposition because its 1,200 public houses were concentrated in and around London (the company had just pulled out of the North of England, closing its loss-making brewery in Buxton, exchanging its public houses in the North for a number of Courage houses in London, and re-building its major brewery in the East End of London). Truman's products could be sold through Grand Metropolitan's hotels and catering outlets at a significant saving. In late August 1971, Watneys conceded defeat. Joseph's 'success marked the first large scale incursion of an outside group of interests' {*ibid* 24 Sept 1982} into the conservative brewery business, still dominated by a few inter-related families.

The take-over of Trumans significantly strengthened Grand Metropolitan's assets and expanded its share capital to over £80 million, allowing Joseph to pursue still bigger acquisitions. Even before the Trumans deal was completed it had been suggested that Watneys might be his next target and this proved to the case. Watneys itself had been interested in Trumans because of the new brewery Trumans was building. Watneys was planning to close four of its eight breweries, and to modernise its production, but needed additional capacity, such as that new brewery could provide, to help while the reorganisation took place. When he bid for Trumans, Joseph said he did not want a brewery with interests spread over a wide geographical area; on bidding for Watneys, just six months afterwards, he was seeking to acquire a company with eight breweries spread from Edinburgh to Trowbridge, over 7,000 licensed premises in the UK and over 3,000 in Belgium. This takeover bid was the second biggest ever in the UK, and attracted some unfavourable comment. It was said Joseph could do little to improve Watneys' performance, that the size of the bid might damage the interests of Grand Metropolitan's shareholders, and there were some unpleasant 'beerage' murmurings in some sections of the City; Joseph's bid, the *Economist* austerely commented, 'does not deserve to succeed' {*Economist* 20 May 1972}. The success of his bid of about £435 million roughly doubled the size of the group.

The warnings of the pundits proved to have some degree of justification. Borrowing had provided much of the funds for this rapid expansion, and high capital investment was needed to continue the essential reorganisation of the brewery groups and to keep Grand Metropolitan's hotels competitive. Joseph had never been afraid of expanding his business on borrowed capital, but as he later said 'what we could not possibly have foreseen was the high interest rates which we had to pay after the takeover' {*Sunday Times* 25 Aug 1981}. By 1975, Grand Metropolitan had a debt of over £500 million, and the interest charges of £54.3 million were greater than the pre-tax profits of £41.96 million. Joseph's policy of using available cash to acquire appreciating assets was one whose appeal to shareholders could only be long-term, but short-term considerations had a stronger effect on the market. During 1972 Joseph himself bought nearly 900,000 shares in Grand Metropolitan 'because I thought the price was too low' {*Times* 22 Feb 1973}. In February 1973, he held nearly 8.1 million shares, with a market value of about £13-15 million. A year later, he held 10.25 million, 4.25 per cent of the company's equity, but with the share price then standing at about 72p, worth only £7.5 million.

Despite the difficulties, Joseph still sought to expand Grand Metropolitan's operations, but by arranging to provide management for hotels, on a profit-sharing basis, with property developers. By 1975 the group had 13 hotels in continental Europe and 55 in Britain. Joseph was still not entirely optimistic about the prospect for the hotel industry in Britain. With domestic commercial traffic, the backbone of much provincial hotel trade, declining, and an increasingly competitive international market for tourism, the hotel industry, he warned, could not afford to let standards slip. However 'inflation, restricted profits and high interest and enormous general rate increases in seasonal and country areas, mean that many hotels are faced with the alternative of either properly maintaining their hotels or making a reasonable return on capital. This is a shocking state of affairs and must result in a decline in standards in future years.' {*Times* 14 July 1977}

Joseph's gloom at this time might have been increased by the demands of the income tax authorities on his personal income. In May 1977, he was obliged to sell 400,000 Grand Metropolitan shares to meet tax bills (he had apparently already dispensed of some, as he was said to hold about 7.25 million after the sale, as against the 10.25 million he held in 1974). While he declared he was not selling any more in any circumstances, a few months later he sold 1 million shares. He then sold the Gainsborough portrait of Sir Benjamin Truman, the founder of Trumans' brewery, which had hung in Trumans' boardroom. Joseph had bought the portrait when, after a review of unproductive assets, the board had decided to sell it; he had left it hanging, on loan, in the boardroom, and was said to be reluctant to sell it 'because he would not have bought it if he had not wished to preserve it where it was' {*ibid* 21 Oct 1977}.

By 1980, however, Grand Metropolitan's position had improved, and Joseph was able once again to pursue his liking for takeovers (or his 'merger mania' as some of his critics described it {*ibid* 24 Sept 1982}). In that year Grand Metropolitan took over the Liggett Group Inc, of the

USA, a tobacco and drinks company which had diversified into pet foods and sports goods. Liggetts opposed the bid, even having recourse to the courts, but Joseph succeeded, paying £210 million cash. The prime motive for the acquisition of Liggetts was their liquor interests, as Grand Metropolitan wanted a direct interest in the US liquor business to protect the distribution of their J & B Rare Scotch Whisky, the biggest-selling Scotch whisky in the US market. Soon after the conclusion of the bid, Joseph began bidding for Coral Leisure, the gambling (betting, bingo and casino) and holiday group. Grand Metropolitan already ran four London casinos, as well as managing those on board Cunard's passenger liners. Had the Coral bid succeeded, the company would have had eight of the 21 casinos licensed in London. However, the proposed takeover was referred to the Monopolies Commission, and the bid lapsed.

As one of the largest companies in Britain (the 12th biggest by turnover) any attempt to expand substantially by merger in the UK could run into a similar obstacle as the Coral bid. Furthermore, Joseph again foresaw more difficult times ahead for the UK hotel industry, with cheap flights encouraging travellers to go further afield for their holidays and a stronger pound discouraging foreign visitors to Britain. As major airlines, several of which had set up hotel chains, were troubled by rising oil prices, and forced by increased competition for declining traffic to cut their fares, Joseph realised that one or other of these hotel chains might be coming up for sale. In July Grand Metropolitan 'expressed interest' {*Sunday Times* 23 Aug 1981} in Pan Am's Intercontinental group of 83 hotels in 46 countries (six of the hotels were directly managed; the rest operated under leases or long-term management contracts). Pan Am was not particularly anxious to sell, but in the throes of a financial crisis, they came under pressure from their financial backers to reduce their growing debt. Grand Metropolitan's offer of £270 million was accepted. Together, Grand Metropolitan and ICH Ltd had 43,000 rooms, making them the ninth largest hotel group in the world. The acquisition of Intercontinental Hotels was financed by borrowing; even before the deal, Grand Metropolitan's debt had stood at £600 million; now, it had risen to £900 million. The shareholders, particularly the institutional shareholders who held about 60 per cent of the company's equity, were not entirely happy with this. However Grand Metropolitan's past record and continuing profitability (pre-tax profits for 1981 were £74.8 million on a turnover of £1,827 million) encouraged them not to sell, and the share price did not suffer, as it had done during the period of high borrowing in the 1970s. A rights issue of about £125 million, to help cut Grand Metropolitan's overdraft, was well received in the City.

One reason for the City's confidence in the future of the company was that Joseph had already taken steps to ensure a smooth succession after his retirement. He did not suffer from the common failure of successful but ageing entrepreneurs, of not knowing when to go. Announcing in 1980 that he was likely to retire in five years' time, Joseph had named Stanley Grinstead, who had been joint managing director of Grand Metropolitan for sixteen years, as his probable successor and in March 1980 Grinstead became deputy chairman and group managing director. Grinstead's colleague as managing director had been Ernest Sharp, who now resigned without acrimony. One director of Grand Metropolitan, Peter Hughes, who had come onto the board after the takeover of Trumans, of which he had been a director, once said that 'when you've got an entrepreneur like MJ, what you really need is a lot of bureaucrats' {*Times* 5 Jan 1973}. However, Joseph took pride in the quality of management of Grand Metropolitan, to which he attributed much of the success of the company and looked at the managers of companies he proposed to take over as carefully as he looked at their assets and balance sheets. For all his business drive and the aggression displayed in his policy of expansion, Joseph believed in, and practised, delegation; he claimed (with some exaggeration) to work only four hours a day, four days a week. Yet until his resignation as chairman of Grand Metropolitan in July 1982 (he remained a director) 'he had retained a firm control of the group's strategic decisions, through his chairmanship and through directorships within the group, even when the running began to be made by younger colleagues at the centre' {*ibid*, 24 Sept 1982}.

Although Joseph was not fully persuaded of the virtues of formal management education, he used graduates of hotel schools to staff the important centralised booking operations of Grand Metropolitan. At head office 'A consciously muscular air of get-up-and-go and being generally untrammelled pervades the atmosphere' {*ibid*, 16 Sept 1974}. Joseph's chosen successor, Stanley Grinstead, was described as 'very tough, very bright, a number cruncher ... if you like' {*ibid*, 26 May 1982}. By contrast, Joseph himself was a shy, reticent, reserved man, urbane, never raising his voice in the office. One manager that did not fit into the group was Eric Morley, who had done much to build up the Mecca entertainments group, was chairman of Mecca from 1969 and joined the board of Grand Metropolitan after the 1970 takeover. A flamboyant man, he was the creator and organiser of the Miss World contests, but his somewhat brash style brought him into conflict with Joseph, and in 1978 he left Grand Metropolitan and Mecca, with £200,000 compensation.

Grand Metropolitan was undoubtedly Joseph's main, but not his only business interest. He was also involved with a number of property and finance companies. One such was Giltspur Investments. In 1965, through a subsidiary of Giltspur, the Montrose Trust, he acquired a controlling interest in Home & Continental Investment Trust, which in turn controlled two merchant banking companies, Robert Fraser & Partners and Robert Fraser & Partners (Finance). In 1966 he became chairman of these banks and of Home & Continental Investments. In that year he also became joint chairman of Lombard Banking, in which he had acquired a substantial interest, and in 1969, became chairman of Union Property Holdings, which owned inter alia the Classic Cinema chain. Union Property Holdings was taken over in 1970 by the property company, British Land, of which Joseph became deputy chairman. The takeover gave Joseph a 4.5 per cent holding in British Land, though he disposed of some of these shares, retaining shares worth over £1 million. He resigned as deputy chairman of British Land, saying he wished to concentrate on Grand Metropolitan and his two other major interests, Giltspur Investments and Robert Fraser.

Some of the smaller companies in which Joseph was interested also owned hotels. In 1968 he bought shares, said to be worth about £250,000, in Mount Charlotte Investments, a hotel and restaurant group, but left the board and sold his shares (worth about £300,000) in 1974 to reduce his non-executive commitments. In 1971, he bought 20 per cent of the equity of Norfolk Capital Hotels for about £1.4 million from British Land. Under Joseph this group began to expand. Its biggest single takeover was made in 1973, when Associated Hotels and Kensington Palace Hotels were acquired for £6.5 million. The company was then reorganised, becoming an investment holding company. On the whole, Joseph only went onto the boards of companies in which he had a personal shareholding. In 1966 he was invited to join the board of Cunard, which wanted his advice on the development of their passenger liners. He resigned after the board had accepted a takeover bid from Trafalgar House Investments which he thought inadequate and later told Nigel Broackes, the chairman of Trafalgar House, that he would never again join the board of a public company, unless he was chairman. He never became part of the City establishment, and indeed sharply criticised what he described as the City's 'own kind of establishment, clannish and snobbish' {*ibid*, 24 Sept 1982}. Exclusiveness was one aspect of the British way of life he would often criticise in private; another was inefficiency.

Outside his business, one of his chief relaxations was stamp collecting; his collection of Cape of Good Hope triangular stamps was famous and won a gold medal at the International Stamp Exhibition in Washington in 1966. The collection fetched over £1 million when it was sold at Sothebys after his death. He also liked to gamble, sometimes heavily. While he did not participate in public charitable work, he 'gave generously, but quietly and privately, to charities and good causes' {*ibid*}. He was knighted in the New Year's Honours List of 1981.

Joseph married in 1932 Sybil Nedas, daughter of Harold Samuel, a clothier. They were separated in 1953, and divorced in 1981, when he married Eileen Olive, a divorcée, daughter of Arthur Scott Warrell, a clerical officer. Sir Maxwell Joseph died on 22 September 1982 and left an estate of £17,313,831 gross, the bulk of which was left to his second wife.

CHRISTINE SHAW

Sources:

Unpublished

BCe.

MCe.

PrC.

Information from Grand Metropolitan plc.

Published

Nigel Broackes, *A Growing Concern: An Autobiography* (Weidenfeld & Nicolson, 1979).

Economist 22 Nov 1958, 3, 10 Oct 1959, 12 Mar, 9 Apr, 4 June, 30 July 1960, 15 Apr, 2 Dec 1961, 26 Jan 1963, 29 Aug 1964, 20 Mar 1965, 23 July 1966, 22 Apr 1967, 31 Aug 1968, 11 Jan, 8 Mar, 26 July, 23, 30 Aug 1969, 21 Feb, 7 Mar 1970, 16

Jan, 3, 17, 24 July, 28 Aug 1971, 18 Mar, 20 May, 24 June, 8 July 1972, 19, 26 Apr, 10, 17 May, 6 Sept 1980, 29 Aug 1981, 22, 29 May, 17 July, 4 Dec 1982.

Edward L Erdman, *People and Property* (B T Batsford Ltd, 1982).

Stock Exchange Official Year-Book 1957-82.

Sunday Times 23 Aug 1981.

Times 24 Mar 1962, 4 Jan, 14 May, 4, 5 June, 28 Aug, 18 Sept 1964, 30 Jan, 30 Dec 1965, 1, 10, 11 Mar, 5, 30 May, 26 Aug, 23 Nov 1966, 4 May, 27 June, 15 Aug 1967, 9, 10 Aug, 15 Oct 1968, 4, 16 Apr, 18 Aug 1969, 12 Feb, 29 May, 31 July 1970, 7 June, 2, 23 Aug, 2 Oct, 26 Nov 1971, 13 Mar, 8 July 1972, 5 Jan, 22 Feb, 10 Apr, 30 May 1973, 19 Feb, 4 May, 16 Sept 1974, 20 Sept 1975, 24 Jan, 24 Mar 1976, 2 Feb, 13 May, 14 July, 10 Sept, 11, 24 Oct 1977, 22 Sept, 9, 10 Oct 1978, 15 Feb, 15 Mar, 15 Apr 1980, 26 May, 22 July, 24, 25 Sept, 27 Nov 1982.

Times *Prospectuses* 120 (1957), 124 (1959), 131 (1962).

JOWITT, John

(1811-1888)

Wool stapler

John Jowitt was born at Kendal, Westmorland on 15 September 1811, the eldest child of Robert and Rachel Jowitt of Carlton House, Leeds. His father, a cloth manufacturer and wool stapler, was the son of an earlier John Jowitt and prominent member of the Society of Friends. His mother was the daughter of Thomas and Cicely Crewdson of Kendal, who were also Quakers. John was educated at Mr Mercer's day school in East Parade, Leeds and then, in 1823, was sent to Josiah Forster's school at Tottenham, London, a Friends' School.

In 1826 John Jowitt joined the family business in Leeds. The firm was founded at Churwell near Leeds in 1776, although the family had for long been engaged in the wool textile trade. He soon gained a reputation as an astute businessman. As the firm's records show he very assiduously monitored the state of his industry and developed a reputation for his speed and accuracy with figures. Within a few years he entered into partnership with his father and was described by his son as having provided new life to a somewhat somnolent business. Under his leadership the firm expanded in the home wool trade and was at the forefront of the provision of wool supplies to Europe from New Zealand, Australia and South Africa. Branches of the firm were opened in the latter two countries.

In 1837 John Jowitt decided to leave the Society of Friends and to become a Congregationalist at the Leeds Salem Chapel, a chapel which produced four Liberal MPs. For the rest of his life he was heavily involved in religious, social and educational activity in Leeds. He became a deacon at East Parade Church and superintendent of the Sunday Schools. He helped found the Leeds Town Mission in 1837, acting as its secretary for over forty-three years, and then as its president. He also worked for the Bible Society, the Religious Tract Society, helped establish Ilkley Hospital, and was a founder committee member of Cookridge Convalescent Hospital and the Reformatory at Adel. In 1870 he joined the first Leeds School Board, becoming vice-chairman and then chairman.

Although John Jowitt's personal interests were mainly in religious and philanthropic work, he also undertook some voluntary commercial and political activity. He was an early member of the Leeds Chamber of Commerce and its vice-president for many years. For a short period he was a member of Leeds City Council. In politics he was an inactive Liberal. He became a West Riding JP in 1870.

In May 1836 John Jowitt married Deborah Benson, the eldest daughter of Robert and Dorothy Benson of Parkside, Kendal, another Quaker family. They had eleven children, five of whom died soon after birth. John Jowitt's first and only surviving son, Robert Benson Jowitt, born on 24 May 1839, became a partner in the business by 1874, allowing his father, whose health was failing, to retire gradually. John Jowitt died on 30 December 1888 leaving £111,735 gross. Robert Benson Jowitt was joined in the business by his sons F McCullock Jowitt, Edward Maurice Jowitt and Robert Jowitt who moved the business from Leeds to Bradford in 1911. In 1919 the private partnership ceased and a private limited company was formed, with F Mc C Jowitt as the first chairman. The firm still survives in 1982 and rightly claims to be one of the oldest in the wool trade.

D T JENKINS

Sources:

Unpublished

Brotherton Library, University of Leeds, business records of Robert Jowitt & Sons Ltd.

Published

A Barnard, 'Wool Buying in the Nineteenth Century: A Case History' *Yorkshire Bulletin of Economic and Social Research* 8 (1956).

R B Jowitt, *Reminiscences of John Jowitt by his Children* (Gloucester: pp, John Bellows, 1889).

W R Millmore, 'Traders in Wool for nearly Two Centuries' *Wool Record* 79 (1951).

R J Morris, 'The Middle Class and the Property Cycle during the Industrial Revolution' in T C Strout (ed), *The Search For Wealth and Stability* (Macmillan, 1979).

'150 Years in the Wool Trade: Unique Record of a Bradford Firm' *The Wool Record and Textile World* 30 (23 Sept 1926).

Edward T Judge (courtesy of E T Judge).

JUDGE, Edward Thomas

(1908-)

Steel industry manager

Edward Thomas Judge was born at Leicester on 20 November 1908, the only son of Thomas Oliver Judge, a master jeweller, and his wife Florence née Gravestock. He was educated at Worcester Royal Grammar School and St John's College, Cambridge, where he graduated in mechanical sciences.

In 1930, at a time when Dorman Long & Co of Middlesbrough was undergoing extensive reorganisation, Ted Judge joined the company as a member of a newly-formed technical group to advise on improving the efficiency of existing iron and steel works and applying new technical developments. By 1937 he was chief technical engineer in charge of the Central Engineering Department and that year started a 'day release' scheme for selected apprentices to attend the Constantine Technical College. He was appointed a special director in 1944, chief engineer in 1946, and a director of Dorman Long & Co Ltd in 1947.

During the period 1945-58 Ted Judge was responsible for carrying through far-sighted proposals he had put forward for transferring Dorman Long's iron and steel operations from the congested 'iron masters district' of Middlesbrough to spacious adjacent sites alongside deep water near the mouth of the Tees at Redcar, where long-term major iron and steel plant developments could be ideally accommodated. New coke ovens and blast furnaces and rolling mills at Cleveland Works and a new steelworks at Lackenby were brought into production by 1953. Dorman Long's Universal Beam Mill, the first to be erected in Britain, was commissioned at Lackenby in 1958. Major plant investment continued until nationalisation, finance being secured through normal private enterprise channels with the support of the Finance Corporation for Industry, of which Ted Judge in due course became a board member.

In 1959 he was appointed assistant managing director, Dorman Long (Steel) Ltd, moving up to become joint managing director in 1960. In 1961 he became chairman and general managing director of the parent company, Dorman Long & Co Ltd. He was also a director of the South African subsidiary, Dorman Long Vanderbijl SA, 1959-79. During these years his knowledge of the steel industry and technical ability made him a valued member of the executive committee of the British Iron and Steel Federation. He was the Minister of Transport's Representative on the Tees Conservancy Commission, 1951-66, a part-time member of the North Eastern Electricity Board, 1952-62, and a governor of the Constantine College of Technology, Middlesbrough. His technical achievements and services to the industry were recognised in 1967 when he was awarded the Bessemer gold medal of the Iron and Steel Institute (of which he was a vice-president).

Rolling a large beam in the Universal beam and heavy section mill, Lackenby (courtesy of E T Judge).

During his presidency of the BISF in the years 1965, 1966 and 1967 he sought a solution to the problem of the ownership and organisation of the steel industry which would be acceptable to all political parties, as an alternative to nationalisation. In his presidential speech in March 1966 he announced the setting up of a Development Co-ordinating Committee under the independent chairmanship of Sir Henry Benson (qv) to examine technical requirements up to 1975, and to consider the organisational changes that would be required. At this time, although the Labour Government had the clear intention of nationalising steel, implementation was delayed by lack of an overall majority on this issue. When the general election of April 1966 ensured that the industry would be nationalised the work of the Benson Committee (of which Ted Judge was himself a member) was curtailed and only the technical survey ever emerged. Just prior to nationalisation Ted Judge negotiated the merger of Dorman Long with two other steel companies, South Durham and Stewarts & Lloyds, as British Steel & Tube Ltd, but this move proved too late to have any effect on the Government's intentions.

Before nationalisation of the steel industry (which took 14 major steel firms into public ownership) in June 1967, Ted Judge had been succeeded as president of the BISF by A J Peech, but he was asked to continue to lead for the Federation in discussions with the Government on nationalisation and associated matters.

The identity of the first chairman of the British Steel Corporation was a particularly well-kept secret and prior to the announcement of the appointment of Lord Melchett (qv) there was speculation in the Press that Ted Judge, amongst others, might be in the running. In the event, Judge did not accept any appointment. In 1968 he became deputy chairman, and in 1969 chairman, of two leading heavy electrical engineering companies on Tyneside, A Reyrolle and C A Parsons. As chairman and chief executive of these two companies in 1969-74, he was responsible for their merger, together with Bruce Peebles, into Reyrolle Parsons. He also established close ties with Clarke Chapman and thus prepared the way for the formation of Northern Engineering Industries Ltd in 1977. He was president of British Electrical Allied Manufacturers Association Ltd in 1970-71.

Judge married Alice Gertrude, daughter of Edmund Matthews, in 1934; they have two sons. Ted Judge is currently (1984) a director of ETJ Consultancy Services, Zenith Electric Co Ltd, Weldall Engineering Ltd and the Cleveland Scientific Institution. Through ETJ Consultancy Services, Ted Judge was retained by companies for advice on technical and organisational matters and in particular as a non-executive director he supported the growth at home and overseas of both Pilkington Bros and BPB Industries during the period 1967-1979.

M M ARMSTRONG

Sources:

Unpublished

BCe.

MCe.

Information from Mr Ted Judge.

Published

David W Heal, *The Steel Industry in Post War Britain* (Newton Abbot: David & Charles, 1974).

Journal of the Iron and Steel Institute 205 (Jan-June 1967).

Bernard S Keeling and Anthony E G Wright, *The Development of the Modern British Steel Industry* (Longmans, 1964).

Keith Ovenden, *The Politics of Steel* (Macmillan, 1978).

John E Vaizey, *The History of British Steel* (Weidenfeld & Nicolson, 1974).

WW 1982.

K

KAPP, Gisbert

(1852-1922)

Consulting electrical engineer

Gisbert Kapp ca 1920 (courtesy of Professor D G Tucker).

Gisbert Kapp (no evidence has been found that he had the middle names of John Edward, despite numerous attributions of these names after his death) was born at Mauer near Vienna on 2 September 1852; his father was a senior civil servant and his mother a professional singer who later attained international repute. He was educated at schools in Vienna and Prague and gained an engineering diploma at the Federal Polytechnic in Zurich in 1871. He acquired varied experience as a mechanical engineer for the next ten years and travelled widely. He took up electrical engineering in 1881 and achieved outstanding success in this field, being president of the Institution of Electrical Engineers, 1909-10.

In 1881 electrical power engineering was in its infancy; ideas of public supply from central generating stations were just beginning to emerge, and electrical generators were still being designed on an empirical basis. R E B Crompton (qv) had set up his important electrical manufacturing firm at Chelmsford and in 1882 appointed Kapp as manager. Kapp immediately began to apply quantitative design processes to all aspects of electricity supply systems and Crompton's business flourished. However, Kapp left Crompton in 1884 to set up as a consulting electrical engineer and retained his practice for the rest of his career. He supervised the electrical department of W H Allen & Co during 1884-1890, undertaking the design of dynamos himself; one of his design notebooks — that for 1885 — survives. He did much other consulting work, including acting as the head of the dynamo department of Johnson & Phillips, and was also London editor of the technical weekly *Industries* from 1886 to 1889. It was during this period, in 1886, that his most notable and influential technical paper was published: this set out his concept of the magnetic circuit (a concept developed independently at the same time by John Hopkinson (qv)), which put dynamo design on a thoroughly sound theoretical basis for the first time.

In the 1890s Kapp undertook much major design work, including a very large electrical lighting system at Arundel Castle and the whole of the new

Gisbert and Teresa 'Treasy' Kapp and their two sons, 1894 (courtesy of Professor D G Tucker).

electricity supply system of the Bristol Corporation (opened in 1893). Towards the end of the decade he was consultant to the Brush organisation.

From 1894 to 1905 Kapp was based in Germany as general secretary of the Verband Deutscher Elektrotechniker (VDE) and editor of its journal *Elektrotechnische Zeitschrift*. In this capacity he was very influential; for example, it was through his agency that the Emperor's scientific adviser, Privy Counsellor Slaby, was introduced to Marconi's work on radio in 1897. While in Germany he was also involved in teaching at the Technische Hochschule at Charlottenburg in Berlin.

In 1905 Kapp was appointed professor of electrical engineering at the University of Birmingham, retiring in 1919. At this stage he was something of an elder statesman, and got drawn into business and trading politics. Nevertheless, throughout his career he maintained a lively interest in research and new design techniques, and his flow of original publications was almost continuous.

An alternator designed by Gisbert Kapp, giving an output of 60 kw. From The Electrician *23, (1889).*

A small dynamo designed by Gisbert Kapp, giving an output of 9.6 kw, from The Electrician *18, (1887).*

Kapp's contribution to business and industry was mainly as an engineer. He made a contribution to both the manufacturing and the electrical supply sides. He was in continuous contact with the industry and his advice was much sought after. He helped to establish sound design principles for electrical machinery, and in this respect can be regarded as a pioneer. He was a modest entrepreneur, however, and probably did not make much of a fortune.

Gisbert Kapp became a naturalised British citizen on 5 December 1881. In 1884 he married Teresa Mary née Krall aged twenty and of English birth. They had two sons, one of whom became a professor of electrical engineering. Their marriage endured but was none too happy. Kapp died on 10 August 1922, leaving an estate valued at £11,210 gross.

D GORDON TUCKER

Writings:

A fairly complete list is found in D Gordon Tucker, *Gisbert Kapp* (Birmingham: University of Birmingham, 1973). The most important are:

Transformers for Single and Multiphase Currents. A Treatise on Their Theory, Construction and Use. Translated From the German by the Author (Specialists Library, 1885).

'Modern Continuous-current Dynamo-electric Machines and their Engines' *Proceedings of the Institution of Civil Engineers* 83 (1886).

Electric Transmission of Energy, and Its Transformation, Subdivision and Division (Whittaker & Co, 1886).

Dynamos, Alternators and Transformers (1893).

(with W W Beaumont) *Practical Electrical Engineering* (1894).

Electricity (Home University Library, 1911).

The Principles of Electrical Engineering and Their Application (Edward Arnold, 1916).

'The Improvement of Power Factor' *Journal of the Institution of Electrical Engineers* 61 (1923).

Sources:

Unpublished

Institution of Electrical Engineers London archives, National Archives for Electrical Science and Technology 11 and 42.

University of Birmingham archives.

PrC.

Information from Dr James Brittain, Behrend papers, Clemson University, USA.

Published

C Brooks, *The History of Johnson and Phillips* (Johnson & Phillips, 1950).

Engineering 18 Aug 1922.

D G Tucker, 'The Beginnings of Electrical Supply at Bristol: 1889-1902' *Journal of the Bristol Industrial Archaeology Society* 5 (1972).

KEARLEY, Hudson Ewbanke

1st Viscount Devonport

(1856-1934)

Retailer and first chairman of the Port of London Authority

Hudson Ewbanke Kearley was born at Uxbridge, Middlesex, on 1 September 1856, the youngest son of George Ewbanke Kearley, then a 'plumber' {MCe}, later a builder and contractor, and his wife Mary Ann

KEARLEY Hudson Ewbanke

Hudson Ewbanke Kearley (courtesy of the National Portrait Gallery).

Hudson, the widow of Josiah John Barrow. He left the Surrey County School at Cranleigh aged fifteen and, after failing the Civil Service examination, was found an unpaid post with a London coffee merchant. From there he moved to Tetley & Sons Ltd, tea merchants, as a counting clerk and by the age of twenty had been promoted to company salesman.

In this post he embarked on a profitable sideline, buying in bulk from Tetley's and selling to numerous shopkeepers too small to place direct orders. This led in 1876 to the establishment of his own firm, although soon afterwards, he went into partnership with Heseltine, an acquaintance from Tetley's, who provided an initial capital of £500. They were subsequently joined by G A Tonge, also of Tetley's. Heseltine retired from the firm in 1887; Tonge remained a director until his death in 1927.

From this small operation the enterprise grew rapidly and within two years sufficient capital was available to finance the opening of a shop in Brentford. With a secure base Kearley could take advantage of the flood of cheap imported foodstuffs and expand both the range of produce sold and the number of retail outlets. By 1880 he had opened ten shops under the name of International Tea Company's Stores and was one of the leading exponents of multiple retailing in the grocery trade. His shops were unique in selling a large range of provisions cheaply; most of the other multiples with national coverage were specialists distributing a limited range of products in bulk. Accordingly the wholesale side of his business had to adapt rapidly to meet this multifarious demand. The policy of direct distribution was followed where possible, large scale purchases from importers and producers being supplemented by manufacturing and processing within the enterprise.

Throughout the 1880s the firm catered increasingly for the national market: in 1885 it had 100 branches, adding a further 100 by 1890. Lipton Ltd and the Home & Colonial Tea Co Ltd, the other leading multiple grocers, did not pass the 100 branch mark until after this latter date. In 1888, with prosperity assured, he married Selina, daughter of Edward Chester, a carpenter of Blisworth, Northamptonshire. The couple had two sons and one daughter. Thereafter he travelled extensively abroad, often with his wife, to establish new business connections. In 1895 the company went public with a nominal capital of £900,000 to finance future expansion, a flotation which was apparently assisted by the company promoter, Osborne O'Hagan (qv).

Kearley was a pioneer at the heart of the retailing revolution. With the altered conditions of supply and demand, new methods of food distribution were needed. Kearley was one of the first to take advantage of these conditions by establishing multiple grocery stores, catering for the mass market. He explored the possibilities of vertical integration, moving forwards, from his wholesale base, into retailing and backwards into production and processing, exhibiting a readiness to take risks, and a determination to bring his innovations to fruition.

Like many successful businessmen of his time he turned to politics. At first a Conservative, in 1890 he became a Liberal, attracted by Gladstone's Home Rule for Ireland policy, and was elected Liberal member for Devonport at the age of thirty-six, representing it between 1892 and 1910 when he retired from the Commons. He soon became known for his persistent attacks on the administration of the Royal Patriotic Fund, a relief fund, supervised by a Royal Commission, to provide for the widows and orphans of soldiers and seamen. Kearley bitterly opposed the parsimonious actions of the Commissioners and was a member of a Select Committee of Inquiry in 1895 on this subject. He had partial success, a new Patriotic Fund Corporation being appointed in 1904, of which he was a member, but many of the old attitudes remained. Reflecting his constituency interests, he chaired the Departmental Committee on the Supply and Training of Boy Seamen for the Mercantile Marine in 1906-7. In 1905 he was appointed Parliamentary Secretary to the Board of Trade and in this capacity supervised the purchase of London's docks in 1909. He subsequently renounced his political ambitions to become first chairman of the Port of London Authority. Made a baronet in 1908 and sworn to the Privy Council in 1909, he was raised to the peerage as Baron Devonport in 1910. Hilaire Belloc in an unpublished poem mischievously marked the event:

> He might have had, we understand, the title of Lord Sugarsand;
> Or then again he might have been Lord Underweight of Margarine;
> But being of the nobler sort he took the name of Devonport. {text provided by Professor Jack Simmons}

He maintained personal control over the Port until March 1925 and important reconstruction and development were carried out under his forceful guidance. In this capacity he was involved in some particularly acrimonious labour disputes, notably the 1911 dock strike, when he maintained a dogged anti-union stance throughout.

His work at the Port was interrupted in December 1916, when he was summoned by Lloyd George to take charge at the newly-constituted Ministry of Food Control. He was neither popular nor effective in this role, although he did lay the groundwork of a national rationing system before resigning through ill-health in May 1917, an action which might soon have been forced upon him. In the same year he was elevated to a viscountcy. During the war he was also chairman of the Royal Commission on Sugar Supplies, 1916-17.

On retiring from the Port of London Authority he returned to business affairs. By 1920 the International Tea Co had over 400 stores. However, in 1927 G A Tonge, who had taken charge of the daily running of the company after Kearley moved into politics, died. Devonport decided to dispose of his own interests and in December of that year sold his shares for £4 million to Major Cooper, who afterwards acquired the Tonge interest.

Viscount Devonport was now free to devote time to gardening at his home in Wittington, Marlow, as well as hunting and shooting in Scotland and Wales. He died on 5 September 1934 on his estate of Kinloch, Perthshire, and was buried in Hambledon Cemetery, near Marlow. He left £1,897,818 gross.

JULIE G STARK

Writings:

PP, 1895 (347) XII and 1896 (368) XIII, SC on the Royal Patriotic Fund.

PP, Departmental Committee on the Supply and Training of Boy Seamen for the Mercantile Marine, 1906-7 (1907) Cd 3722-3723 (chairman).

The Travelled Road. Some Memories of a Busy Life (Rochester: for private circulation, 1935).

Sources:

Unpublished

BCe.

MCe.

PrC.

Published

Robert D Brown, *The Port of London* (Lavenham: Terence Dalton, 1978).

DNB.

James B Jeffreys, *Retail Trading in Britain, 1850-1950* (Cambridge: Cambridge University Press, 1954).

Peter Mathias, *Retailing Revolution: A History of Multiple Retailing in the Food Trades Based upon the Allied Suppliers Group of Companies* (Longmans, 1967).

Henry Osborne O'Hagan, *Leaves from My Life* (2 vols, John Lane, 1929).

Times 6 Sept 1934.

WWMP.

WWW.

KEARTON, Christopher Frank

Lord Kearton of Whitchurch, Buckinghamshire

(1911-)

Industrialist

Christopher Frank Kearton was born at Tunstall, Stoke-on-Trent, on 17 February 1911, son of Christopher John Kearton, a 'bricklayer (journeyman)' {BCe}, and his wife Lilian née Hancock. From Hanley

High School he went to St John's College, Oxford, where he graduated with first class honours in natural science. In 1933 he joined ICI and went to that company's Billingham division. As an up-and-coming young chemical engineer, he was seconded to the Atomic Energy Project and worked, both in the UK and in the USA, on the problems associated with the construction of gaseous diffusion plants. He was awarded the OBE in 1945 in recognition of this work. He returned to ICI but in 1946, at the instigation of A H Wilson, he went to head the chemical engineering research deparment of Courtaulds Ltd, to the board of which company Wilson had recently been appointed as director in charge of research and development. Kearton remained at Courtaulds for almost thirty years, being appointed director in 1952, a managing director in 1957, a deputy chairman in 1961, and chairman from 1964 to 1975.

In the twenty-three years that he spent on the board, Courtaulds' net assets rose from just over £90 million to nearly £760 million and its profits from around £10 million to £120 million. A very substantial part of that formidable expansion came from 1957 onwards and was largely a product of Kearton's leadership. The expansion had four main components though its progress was not as premeditated or logically thought out as it may seem in retrospect. The four components were: the absorption of the other British rayon companies and the extension of Courtaulds' own productive capacity to include other fibres; the creation of a vertically integrated fibres-to-textiles group, mainly achieved by acquiring spinning, knitting, weaving, dyeing, as well as wholesaling and retailing capacity; diversification into areas chemically related to man-made fibre production, namely, paint, plastics and packaging; and a programme of investment in modernisation. Much of the finance and administration of this expansion was the responsibility of A W Knight (qv) but the driving force came from Kearton. He brought to the company qualities of vigour, determination and aggressiveness which its chairman from 1946 to 1962, J C Hanbury-Williams (qv), was wholly incapable of stimulating, as well as a wide intellectual grasp of relevant concepts, a quickness both in assimilating masses of detail and in integrative thought. Expansion was accompanied by a reorganisation of the managerial structure and the creation of a series of divisions and 'profit centres'. That this reorganisation did not bring as thoroughgoing a delegation of authority as it might have, was substantially due to Kearton's own highly individual and personal way of exercising power.

He first came to the attention of a wider public by his role as one of a group of younger directors who led Courtaulds's successful defence against the takeover bid launched by ICI in 1961-62. But he had already captured some public imagination by having played an active part from 1958 onwards in fostering Courtaulds's exports of complete man-made fibre plants to the USSR and other Eastern bloc countries, an activity which culminated in the sale of an acrylic fibre plant to China in 1965. His knighthood in 1966 was indeed awarded for services to export. From 1966 to 1968 he was chairman of the Industrial Reorganisation Corporation, created by the Labour Government of the day, and in 1970 was made a life peer.

By this time he had become one of Britain's best-known businessmen; and he was certainly not averse to publicity. Within Courtaulds his path to the chairmanship and his period of rule from 1964 to 1975 left a number of battered egos, not to speak of retirements and resignations amongst which was that of Wilson himself, chairman-designate at the time of the ICI bid. Not all of Kearton's investments proved, in retrospect, to have been wise; some were scrapped by his immediate successor; and since 1979, under the impact of general economic depression particularly severe in textiles, some part of the vertical fibres-to-textiles structure has been dismantled. A fluent talker, a volatile personality who could swing rapidly from charm to abuse and back again, Kearton made enemies as well as gained admirers. Nevertheless, it was his very real achievement to have transformed and revitalised a firm much in need of a boost to its morale and a thorough shake-up in its procedures. The year of his departure saw the highest profit in the firm's history.

He left to become, in 1976, chairman and chief executive of the British National Oil Corporation. Oil presented him with some very different problems. Instead of radically changing an existing entity he had to create a new one and, moreover, to do so in the face of the opposition of the oil companies. BNOC was the brain-child of the Labour Government. Although many of its opponents recognised that some form of nationally-controlled organisation to exploit North Sea oil was desirable, and although BNOC represented to them something preferable to the feared outright nationalisation, it remained true that the appointment necessarily had political overtones and that the appointee needed to be tough and resourceful. Kearton was seen as just the man for such a job. In practice neither his personality nor his tactics endeared him to the oil industry. But, as in Courtaulds, his achievement was very real, for by the time he left in 1979 he had successfully built up an efficient organisation and secured the co-operation, albeit reluctant, of the oil industry.

As a man who has left his mark both on the scientific side of business (he was elected FRS in 1961) and on its structure and profitability, it was inevitable that his services should be in demand on many governmental and professional bodies. Although sundry efforts to attract him back full-time to work on atomic energy proved fruitless, he served as a part-time member of the UK Atomic Energy Authority, 1955-81; of the Central Electricity Generating Board, 1974-80; the Electricity Supply Research Council, 1954-77 and of the National Economic Development Council, 1965-71. Other such bodies on which he served have included the Special Advisory Group on the British Transport Commission in 1960. Acknowledgement of his achievements has come from numerous professional and academic bodies: St John's College, Oxford, made him an honorary fellow in 1965; and he received honorary degrees from the Universities of Aston, Bath, Heriot-Watt, Keele, Leeds, Oxford, Reading, Strathclyde and Ulster. Since 1980 he has been Chancellor of the University of Bath.

In 1936, he married Agnes Kathleen Brander, daughter of Samuel Brander a schoolmaster, and has four children (two sons and two daughters).

D C COLEMAN

Sources:

Unpublished

BCe.

MCe.

Published

Donald C Coleman, *Courtaulds. An Economic and Social History* (3 vols, Oxford: Clarendon Press, 1969 and 1980) 3.

Margaret Gowing, *Independence and Deterrence. Britain and Atomic Energy 1945-52* (2 vols, Macmillan, 1974).

Douglas Hague and Geoffrey Wilkinson, *The IRC. An Experiment in Industrial Intervention* (Allen & Unwin, 1983).

KEAY, Sir John

(1894-1964)

China clay industrialist

John Keay was born at Stoke-on-Trent, on 31 March 1894, the son of John Keay, a railway locomotive fireman, and his wife Alice Seling née Allman. On leaving school, he was articled to a local firm of accountants, Bourner Bullock & Co in Hanley, and part of his duties included visits to St Austell in order to carry out the audit of William Varcoe, the china-clay merchants. He was immediately attracted to Cornwall and the Cornish and made a private vow to live and work there at the first opportunity. During the First World War he served with the Civil Service Rifles, and on demobilisation returned to the Potteries to complete his articles and to qualify as an accountant. He was placed third in the final examination of the Institute of Chartered Accountants of England and Wales in February 1921, a considerable distinction in view of the number of candidates. He had already announced his intention of leaving the Potteries and setting up in practice on his own in St Austell but in order to retain his services, Bourner Bullock opened a branch office in St Austell and Keay became its resident manager and partner. His work there for a number of clay producers and merchants gave him an invaluable insight into the problems of what was then, in the 1920s, a very fragmented and far from prosperous industry.

The largest company within the industry was English China Clays, which had been incorporated on 9 April 1919 by the amalgamation of three of the largest producing companies, Martin Bros, the West of England & Great Beam Clay Co, and the North Cornwall Clay Co. ECC continued to absorb other companies during the 1920s including, in 1929, Varcoes. In that year John Keay joined the ECC board as secretary. There were those who were surprised by his decision to abandon a prosperous and secure career and to commit himself to an industry which appeared to have such poor prospects that he was able to buy the ECC shares he was required to have as a director for only 7s 10½d each.

Keay became assistant managing director in 1931. By then the china-clay industry was doing worse than ever and the need for further rationalisation had become obvious. In 1932 ECC merged with its two principal competitors, Lovering China Clays and H D Pochin & Co. It then became, as from 12 October 1932, a holding company, its assets being transferred to a new trading company, English Clays Lovering Pochin & Co.

The survival of the ECLP business between then and the end of the Second World War and its remarkable growth during the late 1940s and the 1950s was largely due to Keay's energy and foresight. During the war years, a detailed scheme was worked out for the complete reorganisation and modernisation of the company. This, the 'Post-War Development Plan', recognised that china-clay production was a backward and in many ways primitive industry and called for the establishment of mass-production techniques in place of the existing small-scale methods. These changes were initiated by John Keay, who became chairman of English China Clays in 1947 and chairman of ECLP in 1953 (as well as managing director of that company). Between 1947 and 1963 (when he retired) the authorised capital of ECC was increased from £2 million (£1,895,661 issued) to £12 million (£10,549,716 issued). For his achievements in laying the foundations of an efficient, modern industry, John Keay was knighted in 1950.

John Keay had a workshop at his home in St Austell where he enjoyed carrying out experiments in clay processing. His true bent may well have been towards engineering and science, rather than accounting, but his rare combination of financial expertise and strong technical interests made him an exceptionally suitable person to guide the fortunes of ECC and ECLP. By the time he retired, ECLP was practically synonymous with the industry.

Keay's deserved reputation for prudence and unshakeable honesty stood the company in good stead, especially during the slump years of the 1920s and 1930s when the temptation to make money at any cost was very great, and in the period of enormous demand for china clay after the Second World War. He believed firmly in his own company and showed this in a very personal way. He bought ECC shares steadily over the years and never sold them, being convinced that the Group was certain to prosper. He had a sound instinct for growth. The late 1950s were a period of immense progress for ECC and its associated companies, both on the china clay side and in those other activities — building, civil engineering, transport and quarrying — which had begun merely as fringe enterprises, but soon became large and thriving businesses in their own right.

He retired from his executive positions in ECLP in 1960 and in 1963 from the chairmanship of all Group companies. In acknowledgement of his services over a period of thirty-five years, he was then elected president.

Throughout his years in Cornwall, John Keay took a keen interest in social and community activities, especially those in which ECC and its employees were directly involved. He was justifiably proud of the fact that, by the time he retired, ECC had become the largest single employer in Cornwall and even more proud of the company's excellent labour relations and welfare arrangements. He listed two recreations in his *Who's Who* entry: golf and beekeeping. Keay married Agnes, daughter of Charles Arthur Cooper, a carriage builder, in 1917; they had one son and two daughters. Sir John Keay died on 20 August 1964, leaving £107,478 gross.

KENNETH HUDSON

Sources:

Unpublished

BCe.

MCe.

PrC.

Published

English China Clays Review Autumn 1963, Autumn 1964.

Kenneth Hudson, *The History of English China Clays* (Newton Abbot: David & Charles, 1968).

Institute of Chartered Accountants of England and Wales, *List of Members*.

Rex Winsburg, 'English China's Inexhaustible Clays' *Management Today* May 1967.

WWW.

Arthur Keen (courtesy of Guest Keen & Nettlefolds).

KEEN, Arthur

(1835-1915)

Nut, bolt and steel manufacturer

Arthur Keen was born in Cheshire, on 23 January 1835, the son of Thomas Keen, a yeoman farmer and innkeeper, who died in November 1867 leaving £450.

After a comparatively brief education, he joined the LNWR at Crewe. Hard work and determination led to Keen's appointment as the railway company's goods agent at Smethwick. Possibly in 1856 Keen formed a partnership with Francis Watkins, an American who had come to Britain in that year to sell a patent nut-making machine but being unable to find a purchaser decided to set up as manufacturer. The introductions had been effected by Thomas Astbury, a wealthy iron-founder, whose daughter, Hannah, Keen married at Smethwick Chapel (Church of England) on 2 September 1858. Watkins & Keen took offices at Victoria Works, Rolfe Street, neighbours to Thomas Astbury & Sons and within two years were employing 500 workers. In 1858, however, the latter occupied part of the London Works, Smethwick, formerly the premises of Fox, Henderson & Co, manufacturers of the pre-fabricated iron components for the Crystal Palace. It seems that Watkins & Keen followed them there around 1860, and then, in 1866, moved into that part of the works formerly used by Astburys.

In April 1864 Watkins & Keen was floated as a limited liability company with a capital of £200,000. The conversion was arranged by David Chadwick (qv), a Lancashire accountant, who specialised in company promotions, this being his first outside the Manchester-Sheffield region. In January 1865 Keen, who was soon able to purchase his partner's share of the business, arranged a merger with Weston & Grice, owners of the Stour Valley Works, West Bromwich (a bolt works with its own rolling mills for railway fasteners, fish bolts, fang bolts, and spikes) and the Cwmbran Iron Works, near Newport. The firm had been founded in 1853 by Joseph (later Sir Joseph) Dodge Weston (1822-1895) and James Grice (d 1889) who had bought the rod rolling mills from Messrs Gregory & Pearson. Joseph Weston became the chairman and Arthur Keen the managing director of the new business, registered as the Patent Nut & Bolt Co and capitalised at £400,000. This too was arranged by Chadwick and by May 1865 66.9 per cent of the shareholding came from the West Midlands, the North West (with 22.5 per cent) providing the second-largest input of funds. The amalgamation of these three units secured a measure of vertical integration and was based on certain common products. For Cwmbran (which in 1871 comprised 20 puddling furnaces, 10 balling furnaces and 2 blast furnaces employing 800 men) manufactured bolts, nuts and railway fasteners, whilst its foundry produced cast-iron pot sleepers for colonial railways, rail chairs, fish plates and sole plates. Blast furnaces were fed by coke made from coal mined in the company's two collieries, Cwmbran and Viaduct.

The success of the Patent Nut & Bolt Co's operations in their London Works, Smethwick, was attributed to 'the division of labour' {*The Engineer* Sept 1865} and the application of self-acting machines, which were 'principally attended by boys and girls as but slight manual exertion is required. A number of skilled machinists are, however, employed to look after the tools' {*ibid*}. Both this plant and the Stour Valley Works each employed around 1,000 workers.

When Sir Joseph Weston (then a civic leader and industrialist in Bristol and MP for Bristol East) died in 1895, Keen succeeded him as chairman of the Patent Nut & Bolt Co. The business performed sufficiently well by 1899 for him to open negotiations with Ivor Guest, Viscount Wimborne (1835-1914) to take over the Dowlais Iron Co, which had recently built an integrated steelworks at East Moors, Cardiff. The Guest family who had wholly owned the business for most of the nineteenth century and entrusted its control latterly to G T Clark (qv) wished to spread their financial responsibilities. By using the accumulated funds of the Patent Nut & Bolt Co, Keen could acquire the Dowlais and Cardiff works and so gain a major productive capacity for pig iron and steel, together with a substantial holding in coal (both for coking and domestic sales) and an interest in the Orconera Iron Ore Co, Bilbao, Spain, which guaranteed supplies of hematite. The purchase price of the Guest properties was fixed at £1,530,000 and that for the Patent Nut & Bolt Co (whose capital was still only £400,000, the firm having pursued a conservative financial policy of ploughing back profits) at £1 million. The merger, concluded in 1900, produced Guest, Keen & Co with an issued share capital of £2.53 million, only £380,000 in preference shares and debentures being sold to the public, the balance going to Lord Wimborne, his family and the Patent Nut & Bolt shareholders. Arthur Keen, the chairman, appointed three joint managing directors including his two sons, Arthur Thomas Keen (1861-1918) and Francis Watkins Keen (1863/64-1933), together with E P Martin (1844-1910), general manager of Dowlais since 1882. The rationale for the merger had been, as Keen declared to the shareholders, 'to give the company a position of complete independence and to enable it to hold its own in competition with the whole world' {Macrosty (1907) 38}. Having pursued a policy of retaining undisclosed profits for extensions or acquisitions, Keen had now obtained a secure hold over his raw material needs and henceforth would be able to sell or stockpile iron and steel to compensate for market fluctuations.

Arthur Keen then turned his attention to his close neighbours in Smethwick, Nettlefolds Ltd, developed by Joseph Chamberlain (qv), whose screw works occupied a site on the opposite side of Heath and Cranford Streets. He led Nettlefolds to believe that the London Works was about to enter the woodscrew market (and went so far as to purchase a small number of screw-making machines from America, which he repeatedly ferried into his plant). By this deception he was able to persuade them to join his group in 1902 to form Guest, Keen & Nettlefolds. Keen declared that the removal of competition was the principal motive for the merger, arguing that 'Messrs Nettlefolds were not only screwmakers but manufacturers of goods so similar to their own in many cases that the line of demarcation between the two was so obscure that it could hardly be explained. In addition to that they were steelmakers on no small scale, and, in many instances, produced the same classes of steel which Guest, Keen & Co manufactured, and they had been regularly selling in competition with one another' {*ibid* 38-39}. This was scarcely true. Nettlefolds were primarily woodscrew manufacturers, made few nuts and bolts, and had only limited steel-making plant (acid Bessemer converters at their Castle Works, Rogerstone), whilst Guest, Keen & Co had hardly ventured beyond the market for rails, nuts, bolts and railway fasteners — Cwmbran's output of woodscrews being very limited. With the acquisition in the same year of Crawshay Brothers, Cyfarthfa, Ltd (a rival steelworks in Merthyr Tydfil), GKN's issued capital rose to £4,535,000. Keen's offices at London Works became the headquarters for the new group, a reflection of his determination to be master of the whole organisation. The success of these mergers may, in part, be measured by the group's profits which averaged £419,224 over the five years from 1901, the variation between the highest and lowest figures being a mere £43,000. In 1915, the year of Keen's death, the consistency of these earnings was revealed by a reported profit of £384,400.

To protect himself against the rising tide of competition from overseas, Keen had travelled to America in 1900 in an abortive attempt to conclude a merger with the United States Steel Corporation. It was possibly the collapse of this scheme which turned his attention to Nettlefolds. With their purchase, however, his desire to expand was not satisfied and in 1905 a proposal was made to merge with the Ebbw Vale Steel, Iron & Coal Co but without effect. Throughout 1914-15 he held discussions with Dudley Docker (qv) of the Metropolitan Carriage Co to bring about an amalgamation that would have dominated the Midlands' industry. Yet Keen's death in 1915 and the nervousness of his son, who inherited the negotiations, together with the disruption caused by the First World War, aborted any possible union.

In April 1880, as a leading industrialist, Keen became a director of the Birmingham & Midland Bank and offered continuous support for its expansionist policy. In 1891 to signify the removal of the head office to London the name was changed to the London & Midland Bank and, to strengthen its operations there in 1898 it merged with the City Bank to form the London, City & Midland Bank. In September 1898 Keen was elected chairman, a post he retained until 1908. Although something of a figurehead for the chief general manager Sir Edward Holden (qv), Keen, as a leading businessman closely associated with the Midlands, provided the bank with a sound manufacturing image. He authorised and assisted the takeovers initiated by Holden, including those of the Sheffield Union Bank and the Yorkshire Banking Co, both in 1901.

Arthur Keen also held a number of directorships in industrial concerns, including the chairmanship of Muntz's Metal Co, manufacturers of alloy tubes, bolts, nuts and casings, situated in Smethwick, and of the New Cransley Iron & Steel Co, while he also sat on the boards of the Loddington Ironstone Co and of Bolckow, Vaughan & Co.

He was for twenty-five years a member of the Local Board of Health for Smethwick, for fifteen years serving as its chairman. During this period a number of public buildings were erected, municipal gas supplies provided, Victoria Park acquired and baths and free libraries built in a district dominated by manufacturing and populated by workers living in densely-planned terraced houses. Nevertheless, Keen's benefactions were not confined to Smethwick as he was chairman of the canvassing committee of Birmingham University and was instrumental in securing an endowment fund (to which he subscribed £1,000) and later became a life governor. In 1869, when it was proposed to hold a Working Men's International Exhibition, Keen seconded the motion and then joined the committee formed to promote the enterprise. He was a JP for Staffordshire and for a period regularly sat on the bench at the police courts held at Handsworth and Smethwick.

In politics Keen voted for the Liberal Unionists and was a strong supporter of tariff reform, advocated by Joseph Chamberlain. Before the redistribution of seats, he was treasurer of the Liberal Association for the East Staffordshire Division and in 1886 helped to form the Handsworth Liberal Unionist Association and became its vice-president. In 1904 Keen was appointed a member of the Tariff Commission's iron and steel committee serving until 1911, though pressure of work seems to have reduced his effective contribution. Although several opportunities presented themselves for a parliamentary career, business commitments remained paramount for Keen, yet he did take an interest in labour questions and was for many years a member of the Midland Iron and Steel Wages Board.

He became a member of the Iron and Steel Institute in 1885, joining the council in 1891 and four years later was elected as a vice-president, a post he retained until his death. Similarly, Keen joined the Institution of Mechanical Engineers in 1869, serving on the council from 1891 to 1897 when he was elected as a vice-president, an appointment he resigned in 1911.

A self-made man of great determination and energy, he was both the creator of Guest, Keen & Nettlefolds and one of its outstanding chairmen. Neither an innovative engineer nor an expert on the manufacture of steel, Keen was in essence a tough businessman with a passion for growth whether internally generated or by acquisition. He possessed a shrewd eye for take-overs and through his network of contacts in industry, finance and the various professional bodies Keen was able to build a mighty empire from modest beginnings. A failing, common to many powerful leaders and exacerbated by his death during office, was to leave GKN without a suitable successor. Arthur T Keen, who followed him, found the pressures intolerable and Francis W Keen refused the post, the vacuum being filled by Edward Ponsonby, the Earl of Bessborough (1851-1920), who remained something of a figurehead chairman.

By Hannah Astbury (d 1904) Arthur Keen had ten children, four sons and five daughters surviving him. Of these, Arthur and Francis both became directors of GKN; the former, who had been called to the Bar, practising for a short time before entering the Patent Nut & Bolt Co, succeeded him as chairman in 1915, but died unexpectedly three years later. Francis Keen, who had been articled as a mechanical engineer and draughtsman to the Patent Nut & Bolt Co in 1883, managed the Stour Valley Works and remained on the main board of GKN until his death in 1933, having been appointed as joint deputy chairman and managing director in 1918. A third son, Harry A Keen, also entered the business but lived in London. Arthur Keen died on 8 February 1915 aged eighty, leaving £1 million gross.

EDGAR JONES

Sources:

Unpublished

BLPES, Tariff Commission Collection, TC6 1/19, A Keen's correspondence, 1903-14.

Midland Bank Archives, Edward Holden's Diaries and Board Minutes.

PRO, BT 31/958/1311 c.

Scottish RO, Edinburgh, Steel-Maitland papers, GD 193/165/544.

MCe.

PrC.

Information from various GKN departments, including annual reports and balance sheets, 1901-15.

Published

James C Carr and Walter Taplin, *History of the British Steel Industry* (Oxford: Basil Blackwell, 1962).

Philip L Cottrell, *Industrial Finance 1830-1914* (Methuen, 1980).

Richard P T Davenport-Hines, *Dudley Docker* (Cambridge: Cambridge University Press, 1984).

The Engineer 15 Sept 1865 ('The Works of the Patent Nut & Bolt Co Ltd'), 21 Apr 1933 (obituary, F W Keen).

Edwin Green, *The Making of a Modern Banking Group, A History of the Midland Bank Since 1900* (St George's Press for Midland Bank Ltd, 1979).

Samuel Griffiths, *Griffiths' Guide to the Iron Trade of Great Britain* (1873).

Guest, Keen & Nettlefolds, an Outline History of this Group of Companies (Birmingham, ca 1925).

The Ironmonger Apr 1864, Jan, May 1865, Dec 1868.

Journal of the Iron and Steel Institute Part I (1915).

Henry W Macrosty, *The Trust Movement in British Industry, a Study of Business Organisation* (Longmans Green & Co, 1907).

Proceedings of the Institution of Mechanical Engineers 88 (1915).

Earl B Thomas, 'Guest, Keen & Nettlefolds Group of Companies' *Steel Review* 17 (Jan 1960).

WWW.

Sir Ambrose Keevil (courtesy of Mr A Clement A Keevil).

KEEVIL, Sir Ambrose

(1893-1973)

Food retailer and wholesaler

Ambrose Keevil was born at New Malden, Surrey, on 13 November 1893, the twelfth child of Clement Keevil, a descendant of a long line of dissenting (Particular Baptist) Wiltshire yeoman farmers, and Emma née Long. Ambrose's father appears to have been the dominant influence in his early life, instilling in his son a love of farming and horse-breeding, planning his education at University College School and later in Paris, and organising his entry into the family business when he was about eighteen. Launched by Clement in 1872 and trading under the style of Keevil & Weston, the firm sold English poultry, game, eggs and pigs in Smithfield, London. The newcomer was made an office boy at a salary of £1 a week, but soon began dabbling in buying and selling foreign exchange for the firm and in New Zealand and Australian meat buying. His inexperience and over-confidence in the latter led to a loss of £2,000, inviting his father's sardonic comment that it was about the cost of a Cambridge or Oxford education and had probably taught him more!

The First World War and service with the Royal Munster Fusiliers interrupted Ambrose Keevil's business career. He was demobilised in 1921, having been awarded the MC in 1917 (Bar 1918) and MBE in 1918, and immediately re-joined the family firm. Now Keevil & Keevil, the business was increasingly under the able management of his older brother C Percy Keevil, since his father had virtually retired to devote himself to breeding stud shire horses. Together the two brothers began to build a wholesale provision concern which was to establish Keevils as one of the foremost poultry importers in the country. Ambrose concentrated on the Continental poultry trade and until the Second World War headed an informal organisation of traders to set maximum buying prices. Clement died in 1925 and his two sons took the opportunity to form a limited company. Within four years profits had doubled and they continued to rise even during the difficult years of the Depression, reaching a peak in 1932. Ambrose attributed the success to Percy's contacts with other major distributors such as Fitch & Son and to a wise policy of non-speculation in an era when the poultry business was very uncertain. By 1936, though, the business had lost its attraction for them: Percy wished to take up farming and Ambrose was offered the chance to become an MP. But their plan to sell the firm had to be shelved due to the war.

At this time Ambrose was increasingly active in the national affairs of the food industry. He was president of the Metropolitan Market Clerks Benevolent Institution, 1934-36; chairman of the London Provision Exchange, 1938-39; Master of the Worshipful Company of Poulters, 1938-39 (he was to serve again in 1958-59); chairman of the Co-ordinating Committee of Produce and Provision Exchanges of the UK, 1938-41; chairman of the London Area Committee, Ministry of Food, 1941-42; and chairman of the Co-ordinating Committee of London, Southern, Eastern and South Eastern Areas, Ministry of Food, 1941-42. The main function of the last-named was to ensure continuity of supplies in the event of the wartime destruction of the warehouses and buildings of the wholesale provisions and grocery trade. By his own admission, however, Ambrose lacked the temperament to make a good civil servant and he was happy to join the army again in 1942 as a commander of the Home Guard Sector of the London District. A CBE followed in 1944.

As the war and wartime controls dragged on, the profits of Keevils suffered, and the idea of selling the business was again considered. As Ambrose Keevil's son Clement had been demobilised and indicated a willingness to join the company, Ambrose and Percy decided to continue the business but to seek to merge with a public company. Fitch & Son, a secondary wholesaling organisation established in Bishopsgate, London in 1784, became interested through a director Hervy S Rowlandson and in 1946 a majority of shares in Keevils passed to Fitch. The arrangement satisfied both parties: under Fitch and Rowlandson, Keevils's profits swiftly began to improve and soon reached £100,000. Ambrose not only purchased Fitch's shares at a low price but was also asked onto the Fitch board to direct their provision companies.

Fitch was now poised to begin a dramatic climb which would take it from a small family provisions firm to one of the principal companies in the food trade involved in retailing, baking and timber. A post-war reorganisation of Fitch allowed it to take full advantage of the general growth of the food industry. Profits for the year ending March 1947 were £218,000, rising to £294,000 in 1948 and £424,000 in 1949, compared to only £7,500 in 1939. By 1957-58 Fitch's profits reached £629,000, with a turnover of about £14 million, and net assets of over £3 million.

The expansion was partly a reflection of Ambrose Keevil's plan, which he had formulated as early as 1936, for a widely-based company embracing importing, wholesaling, manufacturing and retail divisions. H S Rowlandson had supported the idea and it was adopted as part of Fitch's policy. In 1955 Ambrose thought that the time had come for the board to develop its policy of expansion in greater detail. Accordingly, he drew up a memorandum which was presented to the board on 15 June 1955 and approved in principle. Meanwhile, Ambrose's eye had settled on Lovell & Christmas Ltd, another large, widely-spread wholesaling firm located in the Smithfield area. It had been built up by the dynamic Victorian entrepreneur John Carey Lovell who, taking advantage of growing markets and advances in packaging and food preservation, had opened up a massive international business, firstly with France, and later with New Zealand, the Argentine, Denmark and Canada. By the 1950s, however, Lovell & Christmas lacked working capital, for it had over-extended and carried heavy stocks. In 1957-58 profits were only £325,000, from a turnover of about £49 million, with net assets of over £3 million. A merger between the two — forming Fitch Lovell Ltd — was therefore agreed in August 1958, bringing into existence the type of wholesaling organisation Ambrose had envisaged. Sir Graham Rowlandson, formerly chairman of Fitch & Son, became chairman of the merged companies with Rolande Wall and K O G Huntley nominated by Lovell & Christmas and Ambrose Keevil, R E Blanning, N F Lambourne and Clement Keevil by Fitch as the first directors. Later in 1958, after a reorganisation, Ambrose took charge of the general provisions firms, which comprised the following: Fitch & Son with its attendant small companies; Keevils and the market firms; Bywaters; the meat retailers Layton & Burkett and Hale & Partners; and the grocery retailers Robsons of Bournemouth and Impey & Dyke. Fitch Lovell's authorised capital was raised to £3 million by 1959 when profits exceeded £1 million for the first time. At this point Rowlandson resigned and Ambrose was invited to take the chair.

Under Ambrose Keevil's chairmanship Fitch Lovell's momentum of growth, after an initial period of consolidation, continued. In 1960 an important step forward was taken in the retail meat division when Fitch Lovell acquired 100 meat and 30 provision shops of R Gunner Ltd. Greens, the stores group, joined which marked Fitch Lovell's expansion into supermarkets (a policy that was to culminate in the founding of Key Markets); large-scale poultry production was initiated by the takeover of W D Evans Golden Produce and the Golden Produce distributors, Henry Gillham; the sausage and pie manufacturing business was greatly strengthened by the purchase of the Dorset firm Millers; and fancy cheese and delicatessen lines were started through Auguste Noël. The chairman found himself increasingly involved in administrative matters and the constant round of business lunches prevented him from making the personal visits to the company's numerous subsidiaries which he considered so essential. To deal with the increasing complexity special committees, sophisticated budgetary controls, and group boards of directors were instituted.

After a hectic period in office and approaching his seventieth birthday, Ambrose Keevil resigned on 24 May 1963, handing over to his loyal vice-chairman, Sir Rolande Wall, and accepting the post of company president until 1969. Reflecting upon his chairmanship in his published company history of Fitch Lovell, Keevil remarked that his main fault was that he was a 'lone wolf'. 'Also I possibly came to high office too late in life' {Keevil (1972) 131}. In his opinion the test of a chairman's work is the company's results in the first six years after his retirement. In 1963 net profits before tax surpassed £2 million for the first time and by 1969 the profits of Fitch Lovell (which included over 50 subsidiary firms) were nearly £3.5 million.

Ambrose Keevil was appointed Chevalier of the Ordre de Mérite Agricole in 1939, and a Chevalier of the Légion d'Honneur in 1956. Knighted in 1952, he was made a KBE in 1962. He was a member of several Conservative associations and in 1953-61 served as vice-chairman of the Conservative Central Board of Finance. He also took an active interest in the affairs of his village of Upper Warlingham, Surrey; he was appointed DL of Surrey in 1944 and High Sheriff in 1956-57. A dog lover (he was a Kennel Club championship judge and once had a kennel of 80 Dalmatians), he also belonged to various horse and rifle societies.

He married in 1918 Dorothy Pearsall, daughter of Arthur Andrews JP, of Ryde, Isle of Wight. They had one daughter and one son, Clement, who joined the board of Fitch Lovell in 1958.

Sir Ambrose Keevil died on 9 February 1973 leaving £500,805 gross.

GEOFFREY TWEEDALE

Writings:

The Story of Fitch Lovell 1784-1970 (Phillimore, 1972).

Sources:

Unpublished

BCe.

MCe.

PrC.

Private information from Mr A Clement A Keevil.

Published

Times 10 Feb 1973.

WWW.

KEMNAL, Sir James

(1864-1927)

Heavy engineering equipment manufacturer

Sir James Kemnal (courtesy of Babcock International plc).

James Hermann Rosenthal (as James Kemnal was known before he changed his name in 1915) was born in London on 16 August 1864, the son of David Ferdinand Rosenthal, a naturalised British subject, and a glass and china dealer, and his wife Elizabeth née Marshall, of Scottish descent. He received his early education in London and later studied at Cologne University, before serving an apprenticeship at the works of the Belgian State Railways. On completing his training he joined the engineering staff of the Anderston Foundry Co Ltd, Glasgow.

At about this time, in 1881, Babcock & Wilcox of New York established a branch office in Britain under Charles A Knight. In about 1883 Rosenthal joined the British office as draughtsman. The American partnership had been formed in 1867 when George H Babcock and Stephen Wilcox set out to pioneer the production of water-tube boilers: the devices raised steam without the necessity of heating a large quantity of water as in the older shell-type boiler. Glasgow was initially selected as the organisation's European headquarters and the first boiler was manufactured at Glasgow

Model of a Babcock WIF boiler of around 1900 (courtesy of Babcock International plc).

at the plant of the Singer Sewing Machine Co. In 1884 offices were established in London, Manchester and Sydney, and shortly afterwards others were opened in Paris, Brussels and Berlin. By 1890 the European side of the business had grown to such an extent that the New York company had outrun its available capital. Consequently, in June 1891, a completely independent British firm, Babcock & Wilcox Ltd, was formed with purchase-money of £190,000 to acquire from the American business the patents, goodwill, and rights to manufacture throughout the world outside the USA and Cuba. During the 1880s Rosenthal had supervised the London office where he was described by George H Babcock, on his visit to Europe in 1888, as 'a good engineer, an excellent salesman and very reliable in all points' {Babcock & Wilcox archives, Presidential Report, 19 Sept 1888}. When the new company was formed in 1891 Rosenthal became the London managing director alongside Knight, who was the general managing director.

The business was well placed to take advantage of several important economic and engineering developments. The use of electricity, then in its infancy, was growing rapidly, so increasing the demand for larger and more efficient boiler plant. The introduction of the steam turbine in 1884 not only resulted in a rapid expansion of electricity, particularly in the field of power as against lighting, but also ensured the water-tube boiler's adoption for marine purposes because of its savings in weight and space. Since the steam turbine demanded higher pressures, cast iron boiler parts were replaced with steel headers, drums and tubes: using Scottish steel Babcock & Wilcox's works at Renfrew, established in 1895 with less than 100 men, led the way in this development.

Increasingly under Rosenthal's direction the company expanded rapidly, especially into the European market. In 1898 branch companies were opened in France (La Société Française des Constructions Babcock &

Wilcox at La Courneuve, near Paris); and in Germany (Deutsche Babcock & Wilcox Dampfkesselwerke AG at Oberhausen in the Rhineland). Prior to the First World War other works were established in Poland, Italy, and Japan. Knight made way for his more pushful colleague in 1898, though he was to remain a board member until his death in 1928, and in 1900 the company was re-registered with an authorised and issued capital of £630,000 with Rosenthal as sole managing director, a position he was to hold until 1927. Henceforth, Rosenthal was the directing force behind the firm's affairs. Recalled a colleague:

> [He was] head and shoulders above us all in drive and ability ... His power of application was immense, he could deal personally with his correspondence in German and French, and his English letters were so concise and perfectly phrased that there was never any difficulty in understanding the exact meaning of whatever he wished to convey ... yet he was a hard taskmaster. He kept a strong hold on the affairs of the Company as well as on the personnel; he never spared himself and made equally heavy demands on others. Only the highest service was good enough for him.
> {Metcalf (1943) 37}

Such was his hold on the company that other board members, notably Sir John Dewrance (qv), complained that the managing director was too secretive. The company's high profitability, however, may explain why Kemnal was given such a free hand. Babcock & Wilcox, noted one observer, has 'enjoyed an exceptional state of prosperity throughout its career' {Statist 2 May 1914}. Between 1898 and 1914 dividends never fell below 14 per cent, while only on six occasions was the rate below about 20 per cent (a bonus issue of 1 for 2 in 1905 and 1 for 1 in 1912 must also be taken into account).

As the firm expanded in the 1920s Kemnal's responsibilities grew to include, besides the overseas subsidiaries and the Renfrew works, a tube works at Dumbarton, and the boiler works of Edwin Danks & Co, Oldbury, and Clayton & Shuttleworth Boiler Works, Lincoln. By his death capital had increased to £4.6 million and Babcock & Wilcox had over 10,000 employees world-wide.

Kemnal also found time to serve on the boards of Power Securities Corporation, Balfour, Beatty & Co Ltd, and the Power & Traction Co (Poland) Ltd. He was also the chairman of Worthington-Simpson Ltd of London and Newark, and was president of the British and Latin-American Chamber of Commerce. Though in his early days he was said to have had the typical working engineer's contempt for the professional man, he became increasingly involved with technical societies, becoming a member of the Institution of Mechanical Engineers, the Institution of Electrical Engineers, the Institution of Marine Engineers, and a fellow of the Royal Society of Edinburgh. In the 1920s he contributed numerous papers on steam generating practice and became one of the earliest advocates of higher working pressures.

James Kemnal was knighted in 1920. He was a liveryman of the Worshipful Company of Shipwrights, a freeman of the City of London, a JP for Glasgow, and had he lived, an LLD would have been bestowed upon him by Glasgow University.

Kemnal's first marriage in 1889, was to Amelia, daughter of Richard

Marshall, a manufacturer: they were later divorced. In 1905 he married Linda Larita, daughter of August de Leuse, Nyallo, Victoria, formerly of Nice: they had one son.

Sir James Kemnal was taken ill at his home, Kemnal Manor, Chislehurst, in 1926 and died on 8 February 1927 at Sandbanks, near Poole, Dorset, leaving £452,726 gross.

GEOFFREY TWEEDALE

Writings:

'Advantages of the Use of the Water-Tube Boiler in Merchant Ships' *Transactions of the North-East Coast Institution of Engineers and Shipbuilders* 37 (1920-21).

'A Review of the Introduction of the Babcock & Wilcox Boiler for Electricity Supply' *Journal of the Institution of Electrical Engineers* 60 (1922).

'Water-Tube Boiler and Crane Construction' *Proceedings of the Institution of Mechanical Engineers* 1923.

'Present Tendencies of Steam Generation' *Transactions of the Institute of Marine Engineers* 36 (1924-25).

'Steam Generation' *Transactions of the First World Power Conference* (1925) 2.

'The Development of Increased Efficiency in Steam Application for Marine Purposes' *Transactions of the Institution of Engineers and Shipbuilders in Scotland* 69 (1925-26).

Sources:

Unpublished

Babcock & Wilcox International PLC, London archives, information and typescripts supplied by R W M Clouston.

BCe.

MCe.

PrC.

Sir Kenneth Hague, 'The Development and Organisation of Babcock & Wilcox Ltd' (Edwards Seminar Paper 230, 18 Nov 1958).

Published

Engineer 143 (11 Feb 1927).

Journal of the Institution of Electrical Engineers 65 (1927).

Henry E Metcalf, *On Britain's Business* (Rich & Cowan, 1943).

Statist 57 (1906), 80 (1914).

WWW.

KENNING, Sir George

(1880-1956)

Car distributor

George Kenning was born at Clay Cross, Derbyshire, on 21 May 1880, the second son of the eight children of Francis Kenning, a dealer in china and earthenware, and his wife Ann née Whitworth. His father came from Blyth but the family moved to Clay Cross where the developing coal and iron mines offered employment. Francis Kenning worked in the local colliery but following an accident in the pit in 1878 he had set up as an oil and hardware merchant.

George Kenning left school at the age of eleven to help his father selling paraffin, pots, matches and soap, in local markets and from door-to-door with a horse and dray, the firm trading as F Kenning & Sons. Paraffin was drawn direct from railcars into horsedrawn tankers. The firm were distributors in central Derbyshire on behalf of various companies such as the Anglo-Caucasian Oil Co (from 1903), Consolidated Petroleum Co and British Petroleum (a subsidiary of the Deutsche Bank and other Continental groups, formed in 1906).

Francis Kenning died in 1905 and following the death of his elder brother two years later, George Kenning, now twenty-four years old, assumed control of the business, assisted by his younger brother Herbert. The business prospered, but it still remained essentially local although its scope widened. He hired bicycles to the oil companies for their travellers and horses to draw the tank wagons. Sales followed, first bicycles, then petrol and eventually motor vehicles. His imagination had been fired by the prize of a motor car offered by a soap company to the person sending in the largest number of soap wrappers. As his firm was already distributing this brand, he persuaded his dealers and customers to let him have the wrappers and so he won his first motor car.

George Kenning secured his first motor agency as a distributor for BSA Royal Enfield motor cycles in 1910. The Ford agency followed in 1916 and thereafter in quick succession, and by 1922, he held agencies for Morris, Austin, Karrier, Guy, Laurin & Clement Concessionaires and the first agency granted by the Dennis brothers (qv) who made trucks. In the 1920s F Kenning & Sons was the only company to hold both Austin and Morris distributorships.

George Kenning first met William Morris (qv) in 1919; 'although at that time he had neither the cash to pay for them nor Morris the resources to produce them' {*Methodist Recorder* 16 Feb 1956}, he asked for and secured the sole agency for Morris cars in Derbyshire. Not long afterwards he negotiated the sale of the first fleet of Morris cars (140 Bull-nosed Morris Oxfords) to Shell. Morris required some convincing before he released the major part of his production to a single customer who, in his turn, was wary of whether Morris could undertake an order of that magnitude. The

Illustration from an old catalogue by courtesy of Kennings (Harrogate) Ltd.

"When the nobleman's choice was the drag or park coach."

In the spacious days of elegance the gentry took
pride in owning vehicles of ornate design and superior
finish—craft productions, each lovingly cared for
by paid retainers.
To-day, mass-produced complicated vehicles
throng the roads. Gone is the old hand craftsman
and the loyal retainer, and in their place has
developed the modern garage that supplies the wide
needs of the modern road user.
The Kenning Motor Group gives a complete motoring
service with over 100 depots throughout the country
and still retains pride of craftsmanship and
personal service as in those leisurely days of yesteryear.

Over 100 depots in 28 counties represent
the nation-wide contribution to the maintenance of road transport by the Kenning
Motor Group—identified by the Kenning
Shield, a guarantee of an efficient service.

Kenning
THE
MOTOR GROUP

Est. 1878

Regd. Office: Gladstone Buildings, Clay Cross, Derbyshire.

WELL OVER 100 DEPOTS IN 28 COUNTIES

Advertisement for Kenning Motor Group (from Who's Who in the Motor Industry*).*

business relationship between Kenning and Morris later developed into a firm personal friendship.

Clearly by then the motor business had become the dominant side of the family firm, although the hardware business remained and still remains (1984) in Clay Cross. George Kenning grasped the economic advantages of supplying as comprehensive a range of services as possible to motor vehicle owners as well as marketing the vehicles themselves. He sold petrol, set up companies for handling bodywork and hire purchase, and also sold various accessories, becoming one of the first agents in the country for Lucas (qv). The development of the tyre business was greatly assisted when he obtained the first concessionaireship for the Tyresole system of remoulding in 1936. Tyres grew as a specialised business from then on. He took on the concessionaireship for the Fisk tyre from UniRoyal in 1955.

Kenning had many other interests in various companies and founded the Midlands Counties Motor Finance Co, a public company in the field of motor car hire-purchase which was later acquired by Bowmaker. He was also a director of Adamant Engineering Co Ltd, Pirelli Ltd, Stevensons (Dyers) Ltd and other companies.

Kennings Ltd was registered as a private company in 1930 with a capital of £100,000. When conversion to a public company was made in 1939 the authorised capital was increased to £500,000. At this date the company had four subsidiaries and five associated companies and claimed to be the largest organisation in the provinces for the distribution of motor cars and commercial vehicles. It had depots at Burton on Trent, Chelmsford, Clay Cross, Derby, Doncaster, Ilkeston, Leigh-on-Sea, London (Edgware Road), Manchester, Matlock, Sheffield, and Walsall.

> All depots have recently been re-equipped with the most modern service plant, including specialised equipment for the rapid and economical repair of cars and commercial vehicles. Constant liaison with the Service Departments of the manufacturers is maintained by the Directorate, so that expert advice and methods of repair are immediately available to the public. This side of the business continues to develop rapidly. At the Sheffield and London depots two of the latest type of continuous-process car valeting equipments have been installed. These cleaning plants are unique and enable a car owner to have his vehicle washed, greased, vacuum-cleaned and polished in eight minutes. The London installation has a capacity of 500 cars per day and is claimed to be the best equipped car valeting station in the world. {C Reg: Prospectus 23 Jan 1939}

In the 1939 prospectus it was also reported that since its formation in 1878 the company had never sustained a trading loss. Profits between 1934 and 1938 averaged £48,861 per annum and the dividends declared had climbed from 6 per cent in 1935 to 40 per cent in 1937, falling back to 15 per cent in 1938. That year total assets were £385,000.

During and immediately after the Second World War the company expanded greatly and by 1956, when George Kenning died, it covered 18 counties including most of the North Midlands, East Anglia and Essex, employing well over 2,000 people and with an annual turnover of over £20 million (and a pre-tax profit of £489,000 in 1955). Its authorised capital was then £1.25 million. In the 1930s the company operated a contributory life assurance and pension scheme for the whole of the staff and holidays with pay were granted.

George Kenning's private interests included aviation (he entered a plane in the King's Cup Air Race in the 1930s and by the 1950s went on business trips in his own aircraft piloted by one of his sons) and football (he was vice-chairman of Chesterfield Football Club). He was on the board of management of Chesterfield Royal Hospital until it was incorporated into the National Health Service. He was also a notable benefactor in a wide range of large charitable causes and Lord Nuffield said of him 'He has done so much more than people may know' {*Sheffield Telegraph* 7 Feb 1956}.

He was JP and chairman of the Alfreton Bench, and over a period of nearly thirty years was member and chairman of the Clay Cross UDC and member and alderman of Derbyshire County Council. A prominent Liberal between the wars, he became president of the Hallamshire National Liberal and Conservative Association though he declined invitations to stand for parliament. He was knighted in 1943 for public and political work in Derbyshire.

Kenning was also deeply concerned with the Methodist Church in which he was a 'pillar of support' {*Derbyshire Times* 10 Feb 1956} at Clay

Cross and gave time and money to the YMCA. A freemason, he belonged to the Hardwick Lodge; he was also a president of the Chesterfield Rotary Club. From the perspective of a Methodist Church leader, Dr W E Sangster remembered him 'as unlike the popular idea of a self-made man as anyone could be. He was gentle and unassertive, humble and astonishingly kind, ready to defer to the judgement of others and at ease in all strata of life' {*Times* 16 Feb 1956}.

In 1911 George Kenning married Catherine Bogle Buchanan, formerly an assistant mistress at Clay Cross Higher Grade School and daughter of a family from near Londonderry; she supported her husband both in business activities and in public life and was herself a county councillor. They had four sons, three of whom survived their father: Frank, George and David (1920-1982). In the 1930s George Kenning lived at Kenwood Bank, Sheffield; by 1939 he had moved to Eastwood Grange, Ashover, Derbyshire (which he sold at a nominal figure for use as a conference centre by the British National Temperance League, of which he was vice-chairman); in 1947 he moved to Stumperlowe Hall, Sheffield. Here Sir George Kenning died on 6 February 1956, leaving an estate proved at £333,478 gross.

DAVID KENNING *and* FRANCIS GOODALL

Sources:

Unpublished

C Reg: Kenning Motor Group (249,065).

BCe.

PrC.

Published

Derbyshire Times 10 Feb 1956.

Economist 4 Feb 1939, 5 Jan 1952, 2 Jan 1954.

Methodist Recorder 16 Feb 1956.

Sheffield Telegraph 7 Feb 1956.

Times 16 Feb 1956.

WWW.

KENRICK, William Edmund

(1908-1981).

Hardware manufacturer

William Edmund Kenrick was born at Edgbaston, Birmingham, on 21 September 1908, the second child and eldest son of Wilfrid Byng Kenrick and his wife Norah née Beale. His father was chairman of the family cast iron hollow-ware business of Archibald Kenrick & Sons Ltd which had been founded in West Bromwich in 1791. William was educated at Rugby and Balliol College, Oxford, where he read classical Greats.

Entering the business in 1930, he was first attached to the newly-opened cost department and subsequently placed in charge of the sales department. He described this period as one in which he was allowed to write letters (all of which went in those days from the private office) but with no authority to do anything in particular. Throughout this time he got to know the customers and the market and formed the view that the firm's sales policy, aimed at cutting out the wholesaler but not following up the implications by providing the right goods and service, was utterly wrong.

Alongside William's business life went an involvement in public life which he ascribed to a Unitarian tradition going back two hundred years. In 1941 he became a Commissioner of Taxes. Given the condition of the business, due in part perhaps to excessive diversion of effort towards external activities, he thought that public service must initially be in fields related to the business. In 1944 he began his association as a Guardian of the Standard Wrought Plate, with the Birmingham Assay Office, and was chairman of the Guardians Committee, 1975-79. Faced with the virtual collapse of the family business after the war ended in 1945, following unfortunate plans to modernise the bath foundry, John Donkin, an engineer, was appointed to take charge of production, sharing with William the title of joint general manager. Subsequently, William became sole managing director of the business which by this time was in hardware, no hollow-ware being produced.

Kenricks itself, however, was drifting towards bankruptcy. William was so determined, nevertheless, to continue that he had decided that had the bank 'finally decided to shut us up I would buy from the liquidator one or two die-casting machines and try to get Donkin with me to set up a small business' {Personal communication to author}. In the event, he pushed for the closure of the foundry, further development of the die-casting process, and the introduction of modern management methods. In the 1950s William Kenrick took the major step of introducing manufacture of the Shepherd furniture castor, a labour-saving device for the housewife. This retrieved the firm's fortunes: of total sales, which rose from £250,000 in 1950 to £1.25 million in 1965, Shepherd castors accounted for a proportion which rose to 71 per cent; gross profits in 1965 were 9 per cent on sales. Paradoxically, it was a step which in the longer term might have left it over-dependent on a single product. William Kenrick was aware of this, certainly by the latter period of his chairmanship of the company (1963-78), though it was his eldest son Martin, his successor as chairman, who presided over subsequent diversification into the leisure industry, computers and a process of making cheap dies for prototypes.

In the 1950s William Kenrick emerged as a leading figure in the trade, becoming president of the National Institute of Hardware, 1950-53 and of the National Hardware Alliance in 1957. His involvements therefore progressed through trade associations, trade education, the local Chamber of Commerce and then non-trade bodies like the Birmingham Polytechnic. From the first two steps, therefore, William moved towards the vice-presidency of the Birmingham Chamber of Industry and Commerce and then became president in 1962. Under his presidency there occurred the initial discussions with the City Council which foreshadowed establishment of the National Exhibition Centre at Bickenhill. Under his guidance the Chamber also sent its first trade mission to Japan. During 1966-78 he was vice-president of the Association of British Chambers of Commerce and evinced a strong interest in the implications of the EEC.

William Kenrick's interest in education led to his role as a governor of the College of Art and Design from 1962 to 1970 (during which he became chairman of the governors), and hence in forming the Polytechnic in Birmingham of which he was a governor, 1970-79 (chairman, 1971-78): he was also a life governor of Birmingham University and a member of Convocation of Aston University. He was made an honorary LLD of Birmingham University in 1972 and was elected a fellow of the Royal Society of Arts in 1973. Until 1972 he was a member of the West Midlands Advisory Committee for Aviation.

He retired from the firm in 1978 after a career in which it can be said that every organisation of which he became head appeared to be at a point of change. It became his task to effect and guide that change. He was a Midlands industrialist in a firm which in certain respects is pure Black Country: yet he himself was in other ways strikingly different in his Rugby and Balliol background. His interest lay to a dominating extent in his own firm but he influenced the hardware trade more widely, largely through his sedulous pursuit of the Kenrick tradition of encouraging and participating in trade associations.

His personal interests included his membership from 1933 of the British Trust for Ornithology; he was probably considered a founder member. After his retirement he became involved with the Black Country Museum at Dudley and in particular with the cataloguing of their historical pieces.

He married in 1939, Elizabeth, daughter of Lieutenant Colonel Francis Loveday, and they had three sons (one deceased) and a daughter (deceased). William Kenrick died in a road accident on 20 June 1981. He left £101,929 gross.

A L MINKES

KENRICK William Edmund

Sources:

Unpublished

BCe.

MCe.

PrC.

Conversations and correspondence with W E Kenrick and M J Kenrick.

Published

Birmingham Post Year Book.

Roy A Church, *Kenricks in Hardware: A Family Business, 1791-1966* (Newton Abbot: David & Charles, 1969).

Times 9 July 1981.

WW 1981.

KEYNES, John Maynard

Lord Keynes of Tilton

(1883-1946)

Economist and City chairman

John Maynard Keynes (courtesy of the National Portrait Gallery).

John Maynard Keynes was born in Cambridge on 5 June 1883, the elder son of John Neville Keynes, the Cambridge philosopher, economist and university administrator, and his wife Florence Ada, daughter of Rev John Brown, a Congregational minister. Educated at Eton and King's College, Cambridge, where he was twelfth wrangler in the mathematics tripos of 1905, he spent two years in the India Office before returning to Cambridge to lecture in economics. He became a fellow of King's College in 1909 and maintained that connection until his death. Both World Wars found him in the Treasury, largely concerned with Britain's overseas financial relations. In recognition of these services he was raised to the peerage in 1942.

Apart from a brief involvement in the rationalising of the Lancashire cotton industry during 1926-27, Keynes's main business connections were with the world of finance. This financial career began in earnest in 1919, after he had resigned from the Treasury in protest over the Peace Treaty with Germany. At a personal level, this career took his own net assets from just over £7,000 at the end of 1918 to £411,238 at the end of 1945, excluding his collections of pictures and books. At the public level, it saw him as a bursar of King's College (1919-46), and, through Geoffrey Marks (qv), a director of the National Mutual Life Assurance Society (1919-38, chairman 1921-38), the Provincial Insurance Co (1923-46), the Independent Investment Co (1924-46) and two small investment companies, the AD Investment Trust (1921-27) and the PR Finance Co (1923-35, chairman 1932-35). In all of these firms, he was in the beginning closely associated with Oswald Toynbee Falk, a part-time Treasury colleague of 1917-19, but the two men parted ways in the course of the 1929 slump, though both remained on the National Mutual board until Keynes's resignation in 1938.

In all his financial connections, Keynes was noted for his advocacy of an aggressive investment policy. In the 1920s, he — and Falk — believed that such a policy entailed taking advantage of changes in the relative prices of long- and short-term fixed interest securities and equities over the course of the credit cycle. Such a strategy proved to be only partly successful: indeed it meant that he and Falk lost control of the Independent, whilst Falk's AD Investment Trust, with which Keynes ceased his connection in 1928, failed and Keynes's PR Finance Co, which he took over from Falk in 1932, almost failed before Keynes nursed it back to health and wound it up in 1935. After 1930, Keynes changed the emphasis of his preferred strategy towards a greater concentration on the long-term performance of a limited portfolio of shares of established companies which he believed to be undervalued by the market. With the shift in emphasis, he was more successful.

In the life insurance world, and later in the City generally, Keynes's speeches as chairman to the National Mutual's annual meeting became important events. His emphasis on an active investment policy with a substantial concentration on commercial and industrial equities was new to the world of insurance, as it was to Oxbridge colleges. So too was his emphasis on investment results, less conservative valuations of life assurance liabilities and more frequent bonus declarations. Despite the setbacks of 1929-32, these changes in emphasis were on the whole successful for the National Mutual which over the years of Keynes's chairmanship normally stood at the top of the industry's league tables of returns to policy holders. At the National Mutual under Geoffrey Marks there was also a less successful raft of new policies to attract policy-holders from specific segments of the market, such as house purchasers, and new pension and profit-sharing arrangements for employees. The Provincial and King's College also prospered. An active investment policy along either of Keynes's lines required a larger degree of day-to-day discretion than normal and, especially in the inter-war period, strong nerves. Where he had the most discretion, at King's, Keynes was at his most successful as an investor. When he did not get the necessary discretion and investment policy led to seemingly endless argument, he tended to withdraw from the company concerned. This was one of his reasons for leaving the National Mutual in 1938, although it also appears that he was less happy with the management after Geoffrey Marks's retirement and was glad to use his recent heart attack as an excuse for reducing his commitments. Similar reasons led to his assuming control of the PR Finance Co in 1932. Despite such difficulties, the general consensus amongst contemporaries was that Keynes was 'fun' to invest with — and in the long run successful.

As well as his financial activities, Keynes did a modicum of consulting. His first (again with Falk) was for Sir Ernest Debenham between 1920 and 1924. In the 1930s he maintained long-standing connections with W S Robinson in Australia and Case, Pommeroy & Co of New York, but he also for a time provided regular memoranda for Philips of Eindhoven and the Scottish Investment Trust Co. His fees varied. With Case, Pommeroy & Co he seems to have provided his views in exchange for the firm's own information on American conditions, while for Debenham his fee ran to £500 per annum and for Phillips averaged £12.50 per memorandum, which he was free to (and did) use elsewhere. For an individual consultation or memorandum he normally received £50-£75. However, he was much more inclined to consult for Governments for nothing than to advise businessmen for a fee, which is not surprising given his professional interest as an economist.

In 1925 Keynes married Lydia Lopokova, a ballerina who had made her reputation with Diaghilev. There were no children. Lord Keynes died on 21 April 1946 at Tilton, his country home near Firle, Sussex, leaving £484,864 gross.

D E MOGGRIDGE

Writings:

In his lifetime Keynes produced ten books and several hundred articles. All of his published writings, his evidence and contributions to nine Royal Commissions and official committees, plus much unpublished material appears in Elizabeth Johnson and Donald Moggridge, *The Collected Writings of John Maynard Keynes* (30 vols, Macmillan, 1971-). The material on Keynes's financial activities appears in vol 12.

Sources:

Unpublished

BCe.

MCe.

PrC.

Published

DNB.

Roy F Harrod, *The Life of John Maynard Keynes* (Macmillan, 1951).

Elizabeth Johnson and Donald Moggridge (eds), *The Collected Writings of John Maynard Keynes* (30 vols, Macmillan, 1971-) 12.

Eric Street and R Glenn, *The History of the National Mutual Life Assurance Society, 1830-1980* (National Mutual Life Assurance Society, 1980).

WWW.

Sir Hew Kilner (courtesy of Vickers Ltd).

KILNER, Sir Hew Ross

(1892-1953)

Aircraft manufacturer

Hew Ross Kilner was born in Marylebone, London, on 9 September 1892, the son of Charles Harold Kilner, lieutenant (later Colonel) in the Royal Horse Artillery, and his wife Helen née MacGregor. He was educated at Cheltenham College, 1906-10, and at the Royal Military Academy, Woolwich. Following in his father's footsteps, he was gazetted in the Royal Artillery in 1911. During the First World War he served as a gunner for a short time in Hong Kong and then for the rest of the war on the Western Front in France and Belgium, winning the MC and rising in rank to acting major by the age of twenty-four.

After the war he continued his career as a regular soldier and, from 1919 to 1923, was an instructor in anti-aircraft gunnery with the Army of Occupation in Germany. In 1923 he moved to the War Office in London where he held an appointment as staff captain until 1927. In 1927-30, he passed with distinction the advanced course at the Military College of Science, then at Woolwich.

Kilner must have been disappointed with his prospects in the Army because in July 1930 he resigned his major's commission. By then, however, he must have become known in the armaments industry as an up-and-coming young officer likely to go far and it was, no doubt, because of this that he received an invitation from Sir Nigel Birch (qv), also an ex-gunner who was on the Vickers board, to join the company as an armament and ballistics specialist. In his new job, Kilner continued his particular association with anti-aircraft artillery and he must have quickly made a good impression because the following year, when the Vickers Southern Works at Crayford were reorganised, he was appointed manager and later general manager, an appointment he held with success throughout the 1930s.

In 1936, Kilner was given a seat on the board of Vickers-Armstrongs Ltd, the Vickers subsidiary concerned with armaments, general engineering and shipbuilding, which controlled the Crayford Works. In

1938, Vickers-Armstrongs also took control of the company's aviation interests consisting of Vickers (Aviation) Ltd at Weybridge and the Supermarine Aviation Works (Vickers) Ltd at Southampton. Soon after the take-over and following the resignation of the former chairman and managing director, Sir Robert McLean (qv), the new chairman Commander Sir Charles Craven appointed Alexander Dunbar to be general manager at Weybridge. Dunbar, previously accountant at head office, did not stay long at Weybridge, and was succeeded there by Kilner in 1940.

Kilner was much more of a technical man than he was usually given credit for (he was never, for example, granted corporate membership of the Royal Aeronautical Society) but he had had no previous experience of aircraft, other than a flight in an early military Farman in 1912, when he was appointed early in the war to the highly responsible job of running Vickers's aviation activities. This appointment shows in what high regard he must have been held by the Vickers board, and particularly by Craven, on the evidence of his performance at Crayford. It probably also reflected Craven's view that aviation is just another branch of engineering requiring no special management expertise.

Despite his lack of aviation experience, Kilner's technical military background and his experience of production problems at Crayford stood him in good stead, as did his flair for picking able assistants who found him to be lively, cheerful and imaginative, as well as a kindly and considerate leader who inspired loyalty and, by example, could get people to work very hard. When changes in senior management were required, these were achieved quickly and smoothly. Throughout the war years, Kilner skilfully guided the course of the great Vickers aviation organisation. Production of a total of 11,500 Wellingtons and 20,000 Spitfires is some measure of the achievement under his direction.

The leading position Kilner quickly assumed in the aircraft industry is demonstrated by his election in 1943 as president of the Society of British Aircraft Constructors — he had been a member of the SBAC Management Committee since 1941 and continued to be a member until 1952. In 1944 he was promoted to managing director of the Aircraft Division of Vickers-Armstrongs, being given a seat on the Vickers main board the following year. This appointment was overdue; under the part-time chairman, Sir Archibald Jamieson, who was a financier not an industrialist, Kilner had already been the most influential figure responsible for Vickers's aviation interests for the previous five years. When Sir Robert Micklem, head of the Vickers shipbuilding and engineering activities, was appointed chairman of Vickers-Armstrongs in August 1946, Kilner was made deputy chairman in charge of all aviation activities as well as chairman of the Vickers subsidiary Cooke, Troughton & Simms Ltd, the optical instrument manufacturers. He was knighted the following year.

The return of peace reduced the scale of operations but, under Kilner's shrewd guidance, Vickers quickly rationalised and redirected its aviation activities in a period of rapid technological change. A most successful series of transport aircraft for civil and military use was developed, culminating in the famous Viscount, the world's first turboprop airliner, which first entered service with British European Airways in March 1953. Less satisfactory was the lack of opportunity to apply the results of prolonged research into variable geometry and major difficulties with the new Swift jet fighter programme at Supermarine.

Kilner's health began to fail in 1952 and he had finally to retire on 30 June 1953. During the last months of Kilner's illness, Major General Charles Dunphie deputised for him. Dunphie was later to become chairman of Vickers-Armstrong and later still of the Vickers main board. The day-to-day running of the aircraft business was in the hands of George Edwards (qv), who was appointed general manager and chief engineer in February 1953 and managing director in September. Building on foundations laid by Kilner, Edwards was to lead the company and its successor, British Aircraft Corporation, to further successes and disappointments during the following twenty-two years.

Kilner in 1919 married Elizabeth, daughter of John Harmstone Coulson; they had one daughter. Sir Hew Kilner died on 2 August 1953 at the age of sixty.

PETER W BROOKS

Sources:

Unpublished

BCe.

Discussions at Weybridge with contemporaries.

Correspondence with Sir George Edwards, 16 Dec 1980, 13 Jan 1981.

Published

Aeroplane 10 July, 7, 21 Aug 1953.

Flight 7 Aug 1953.

John D Scott, *Vickers. A History* (Weidenfeld & Nicolson, 1962).

Times 4, 12 Aug 1953.

WWW.

KIMBER, Cecil

(1888-1945)

Motor car manufacturer

Cecil Kimber was born at West Dulwich, Surrey, on 12 April 1888, the son of Henry Francis Kimber, a partner in the family firm of Kimber Brothers of Manchester who made printing ink, and his wife Frances (Fanny) Newhouse née Matthewman, a talented watercolourist who had trained at the Slade School. Educated at Stockport Grammar School, Kimber left to join the family business, selling printing ink and earning £1 a week. A bad motor cycle accident left him permanently lame (and prevented active war service) but he used his £700 compensation to replace his motorbike with a Singer 10 car, refusing to put the rest into the family business. The episode estranged him from his father and Cecil Kimber entered the engineering industry.

During the First World War he worked as a design engineer on airships for Sheffield-Simplex and as buyer for A C Cars at Thames Ditton. At his first marriage in 1915 he described himself as 'Departmental Manager, Motor Works' {MCe}. In 1918 Kimber joined the staff of E G Wrigley, Birmingham, the car component suppliers. He became sales manager of Morris Garages, Oxford, in 1921 and in the next year, following the suicide of their general manager, E Armstead, Kimber succeeded to this post. For some years he had been interested in car design and he now began to design bodies which could be fitted to standard Morris chassis. In 1924 he began to order modified chassis and the famous octagonal MG (Morris Garages) symbol appeared in advertising. Kimber's creative initiatives triggered a conflict of loyalties, which surfaced with the racing successes of the early 1930s and led eventually to Kimber's premature retirement from the Nuffield MG Group. The evolution of the MG car as a separate concept took place throughout the second half of the 1920s: in 1925 Carbodies of Coventry built the first distinctive MG sports car body on a modified Morris chassis. Production took place at the Longwall Garage in Oxford until a new factory was built in Cowley in 1927. The success of the MG Midget, introduced in 1928, meant that MG production was moved to Abingdon in September 1929 (remaining here until closed in 1980), and in 1930 the MG Car Co was registered with Kimber as managing director and Sir William Morris (qv) as governing director.

There followed several years in which MG obtained favourable publicity from record-breaking and racing successes. In February 1931 Captain George Eyston reached 103 mph in an experimental MG and the company then produced 14 C-type 'Montlhéry' Midgets for the Brooklands 24-hour race that year. Competitive successes and record-breaking had obvious advantages in projecting the public image of the marque, but there were two major attendant disadvantages, the obvious one of cost, and the less obvious but very real problem created by success itself, the need to keep production models up to the expectations raised by the special record-breaking and racing models. The J2 introduced at the 1932 Show found the right formula, but sales fell in the first half of the 1930s in part due to the economic depression: from 2,400 in 1932 to 1,250 in 1935 (but recovered to 2,850 in 1937, the best year of the decade). Greater use of Nuffield resources was imposed: in the autumn of 1933 Morris Bodies replaced Carbodies as suppliers of MG coachwork and the order to use as many Nuffield components as possible followed the company's enforced withdrawal from racing in 1935. Kimber, however, continued to design MG bodies, such as that of the 2-litre which made its debut in October 1935, and record-breaking attempts continued, for example, with the Railton-bodied MG Midget in 1938.

After 1936, preparation for war increasingly occupied the motor industry and in September 1939 MG car production ceased for the conversion of the works to a war footing, although Kimber found it necessary to seek contracts himself, including one to manufacture the front part of the Albemarle bomber. The appointment of Miles Thomas (qv) as Nuffield vice-chairman in 1941 led to an increased insistence on the centralisation of war production within the Nuffield Group and Kimber left MG. He went first to Charlesworth Bodies, which he reorganised, then to Specialloid Piston Rings as works director.

His first wife Evelyn Irene Phyllis née Hunt (daughter of Charles William Hunt, an engineer of Withington near Manchester), whom he had married in 1915 and who had been closely involved in the early days of MG, had died in 1938 after a long illness which led to their separation. There were two daughters of this first marriage. Kimber married his second wife, Muriel Lillian Dewar 'Gillie', a widow and daughter of Frank Reeves Greenwood, a musician, in 1938. Cecil Kimber was killed in a railway accident whilst travelling on Specialloid business on 4 February 1945. He left £20,382 gross. In his daughter's words, he was 'an adventurous idealist, brilliant as designer, innovator, works organiser and as a manager of men, a father-figure to the MG concern'.

RICHARD STOREY

Sources:

Unpublished

BCe.

MCe.

PrC.

Information from Mrs Jean Cook, daughter of Cecil Kimber.

Published

F W McComb, *MG* (Osprey, 1978).

G Robson, *Motoring in the 30s* (Cambridge: Patrick Stephens, 1979).

T Willard et al, 'The MG Story' *Birmingham Post and Mail* July 1980.

KINDERSLEY, Robert Molesworth

1st Lord Kindersley of West Hoathly

(1871-1954)

Merchant banker

Robert Molesworth Kindersley was born at Wanstead, Essex, on 20 November 1871 {BCe}, the second son of Edward Nassau Molesworth Kindersley, then described as a 'manufacturing chemist' {*ibid*}, of the 19th Regiment of Foot, and Ada Good, daughter of John Murray, a London solicitor. His education at Repton ended when his father could no longer afford it, and at fifteen he started work at Millwall Dock Co, transferring to the Thames Ironworks (the last constructor of large warships on the Thames) where he was assistant secretary and private secretary to the chairman, Arnold Frank Hills (1857-1927). From there he migrated to the City, becoming a member of the Stock Exchange in 1901. The next year he became a partner in the stockbroking firm of David A Bevan & Co, where he remained until he joined Lazard Brothers in 1906 as a partner. When Lazards became a limited company in 1919, Kindersley became chairman.

By then, Kindersley was a substantial City figure. He was a director of the Bank of England (1914-46) and governor of the Hudson's Bay Co (1916-25). In 1916 he became involved in attempts to mobilise small savings as chairman of the War Savings Committee and presided over its successor, the National Savings Committee, between 1920 and 1946. In the 1920s he was active in international financial affairs as a member of the Bankers' Committee on German Finance (1922) and senior British representative on the Dawes Committee on Reparations (1924). However, he also retained domestic connections as chairman (1921-25) of the advisory committee set up under the Trade Facilities Act.

In the 1930s his outside activities declined somewhat, although he was an active chairman of the foreign exchange committee set up by the Bank of England to help manage sterling on a day-to-day basis from the late stages of the 1931 financial crisis onwards. During that crisis, he was 'unusually active' {Sayers (1976) 388} not only because he was involved in negotiating the £25 million credit from the Bank of France in the early stages, but also because Lazards itself was in dire straits. The firm's problems had their origin in a loss of £6 million in the Brussels office, but to avoid its closing its doors completely on 20 July the Bank of England had to come to its aid with a loan of £3.5 million. Further assistance from the Bank followed in 1932. A condition for the 1931 assistance was that Lazards close its overseas offices, although links with the Paris firm of the same name continued. These difficulties abroad, plus the cessation of British overseas lending after 1929, meant that the firm moved much more extensively into the finance of British industry.

In all his activities Kindersley used his immense capacity for work, attention to detail and powerful personality and unfailing courtesy to good effect. As the *Times* put it, 'Here, at a glance, was a man with whom it would be safe to go tiger hunting and whom it would probably be unprofitable to oppose' {*Times* 21 July 1954}. Yet with this presence and capacity went a strong streak of creative thought and imagination. It is thus no accident that this same figure is well-known to students of economic history for a series of 11 articles in the *Economic Journal* between 1929 and 1939 on British overseas investments (forerunners of official statistics on the subject) or, less well-known, that one of his phrases, 'the rules of the game" casually dropped before the Macmillan Committee on Finance and Industry on 6 February 1931 (Question 1595), has passed into the language of international economists, who often attribute it to Keynes. His work for the National Savings Movement, which saw the country save £9,000 million during the Second World War, was recognised by a barony in 1941 (he was appointed KBE in 1917 and GBE in 1920). In 1928-29 he was High Sheriff of Sussex.

In 1896 Kindersley married Gladys Margaret, daughter of Major General James Prinsep Pattle Beadle RE. There were four sons and two daughters of the marriage. His eldest son was killed in action in 1917, but his second son survived to succeed him as chairman of Lazards and as a director of the Bank of England. Never retiring from Lazards, he died at East Grinstead, Sussex on 20 July 1954, leaving £388,885 gross.

D E MOGGRIDGE

Writings:

'A New Study of British Foreign Investments' *Economic Journal* 39 (Mar 1929).

'British Foreign [Overseas] Investments in 1928 ... 1938' *ibid* 40-49 (June 1930-Dec 1939) annual reviews.

PP, Committee on Finance and Industry 1929-31 (1931) Cmd 3897.

Sources:

Unpublished

BCe.

MCe.

PrC.

Information from Dr John Orbell.

Published

DNB.

Richard S Sayers, *The Bank of England 1891-1944* (3 vols, Cambridge: Cambridge University Press, 1976).

Times 21 July 1954.

WWW.

James Kitson, Lord Airedale (courtesy of Leeds Central Library).

KITSON, James

1st Lord Airedale of Gledhow

(1835-1911)

Ironmaster and locomotive manufacturer

James Kitson was born in Leeds, on 22 September 1835, the second son of James Kitson (1807-85) and his wife Ann, daughter of John Newton of Leeds. His father served an apprenticeship in a dye works, attended the Leeds Mechanics Insititute and pioneered locomotive manufacturing at the Airedale Foundry in Hunslet in partnership with David Laird, a farmer with capital, and Charles Todd, a former apprentice of Matthew Murray. A second partnership in 1842 with Thompson and Hewitson which lasted for sixteen years laid the foundations of the family's fortune. With prosperity, Kitson became a Unitarian and a Liberal, and served on Leeds Town Council from 1854 to 1868. At his death in 1885 he left a personal estate declared at £100.

James Kitson Jr was educated at Wakefield Proprietary School and University College, London, where he studied principally chemistry and natural sciences between March 1852 and 1854. With his elder brother, Frederick William Kitson, he managed Monkbridge Iron Works which his father had acquired in 1854 to obtain a supply of 'best Yorkshire' iron. In 1858 Monkbridge was amalgamated with the Airedale Foundry and the family controlled the enterprise, notwithstanding the formation of a limited liability company in 1886 with a capital of £250,000 (but not marketing its shares until 1911), until the appointment of a receiver in 1934. After 1862 James Kitson became the effective head of the firm, assisted by his younger brother Hawthorn Kitson (1843-99), his son E C Kitson, and a nephew, F J Kitson.

With six other manufacturers, Hunslet became Britain's second largest locomotive producer in the nineteenth century. Almost 6,000 engines were built at the Airedale Foundry for 48 railway companies at home and 80 companies in 28 countries abroad. Although the firm concentrated on locomotives, some diversification took place through the manufacture of stationary engines for agricultural machinery and steam engines for tramways. At Monkbridge, steel was produced from the 1880s on a small scale by the Siemens-Martin open-hearth process, and after 1900 the foundry was equipped with electrical motors. In 1912 the company employed 2,000 workmen.

James Kitson attained prominence in business circles as the town's largest steam engine manufacturer. He became president of the Leeds Chamber of Commerce (1880-81), president of the Iron and Steel Institute (1889-91), and recipient of its Bessemer medal (1903); a member of the council of the Institution of Civil Engineers (1899-1901); and president of the Iron Trade Association. He was also chairman of the Yorkshire

Engine shop in the Airedale foundry (courtesy of Leeds Central Library).

Banking Co, the London & Northern Steamship Co, and the Baku Russian Petroleum Co and a director of both the London City & Midland Bank and the North Eastern Railway Co.

For fourteen years Kitson was a Sunday School teacher and superintendent at Mill Hill Unitarian Chapel, and later became chairman of the Chapel's trustees. In public life, he followed in his father's footsteps although he never sat on Leeds Town Council before he became mayor in 1896-97. He participated in a model dwelling scheme for workmen, was a governor of the Leeds Infirmary, supported the Yorkshire College from its inception, served in the Leeds Volunteer Rifle Corps, founded the Hunslet Mechanics Institute, and acted as secretary of the Yorkshire Union of Mechanics Institutes. In 1870 he gained public recognition for the part he played as secretary of the Leeds branch of the National Education League in the debate on the Education Act. An orthodox Liberal on national issues, Kitson's main political contribution was in party organisation. As president of the Leeds Liberal Association in 1880 he played a major role in W E Gladstone's election campaign in Leeds, and from 1883 to 1890 was president of the National Liberal Federation. Converted to Home Rule by Gladstone, Kitson, who was knighted in 1886, ensured that the Leeds Liberal party remained loyal after the split on Home Rule, and he accepted the Newcastle programme 'practically in its entirety' {Hargrove (1911) 15}.

Casting a cylinder at the Airedale works (courtesy of Leeds Central Library).

From 1890 to 1907, Sir James Kitson represented the Colne Valley in parliament. As Liberal party support was eroded by its opponents, he became downcast, criticising the Socialists for attempting 'to make themselves a separate class with distinct interests' {*ibid*, 7}. In industrial relations he opposed shorter hours and advocated higher wages, and he supported the introduction of old age pensions, becoming president of the National Old Age Pensions League in 1894.

Many honours were bestowed on the 'foremost Liberal patrician' {Fraser (1980) 327} of Leeds towards the end of his career: an honorary DSc was conferred by the University of Leeds in 1904; he became an honorary colonel in the West Yorkshire Regiment, 1905; he was made a Privy Councillor and received the Freedom of the City of Leeds, 1906; and he was created Lord Airedale of Gledhow in 1907.

In 1860 Kitson married Emily Christiana Cliff, daughter of Joseph Cliff, a fire brick manufacturer of Wortley; she died in 1873; they had three sons and two daughters. He married in 1881 Mary Laura Smith, daughter of Edward Fisher Smith of the Priory, Dudley, by whom he had a son and a daughter. Lord Airedale died on 16 March 1911 leaving £1,130,907 gross.

W G RIMMER

Writings:

'A Horizontal Compound Lever Testing Machine of 15,000 powers, with Further Recording Lever of 150,000 Powers' *Journal of the Iron and Steel Institute* 1888.

'Address at Paris' *ibid* 1889.

Address to Iron and Steel Institute *ibid* 1889.

'Address as president at New York meeting of the Iron and Steel Institute' *ibid* 1890.

'Address at Pittsburgh' *ibid* 1890.

'Iron and Steel Industries of America' *Contemporary Review* 59 (1891).

Preface to the *Iron and Steel Institute in America in 1890. Special Volume of 'Proceedings'* (E & F N Spon, 1892).

An Address Given to the Students at a Prizegiving at the City of Birmingham Municipal Technical School 31 Oct 1902.

Sources:

Unpublished

University College London, Registry, Registers of Students.

MCe.

PrC.

Published

Edwin K Clark, *Kitsons of Leeds 1837-1937* (Locomotive Publishing Co, 1938).

Complete Peerage.

DNB.

Charlotte J Erickson, *British Industrialists: Steel and Hosiery 1850-1950* (Cambridge: Cambridge University Press, 1959).

Fortunes Made in Business (3 vols, Sampson, Low & Co, 1884) 3.

Derek Fraser (ed), *A History of Modern Leeds* (Manchester: Manchester University Press, 1980).

C Hargrove, *In Memory of James Kitson, First Baron Airedale of Gledhow* (Leeds: J Whitehead & Sons, 1911).

Ernest P Hennock, *Fit and Proper Persons* (Edward Arnold, 1973).

Leeds Mercury 17 Mar 1911.

R J Morris, 'The Rise of James Kitson: Trades Union and Mechanics Institution, Leeds, 1826-1851' *Publications of the Thoresby Society* 53 (1973).

H Spender, 'A Great Captain of Industry: Kitson of Leeds' *Pall Mall Magazine* 40 (1907).

Times 17, 23, 29 Mar 1911.

WWMP.

WWW.

Yorkshire Observer 17 Mar 1911.

Yorkshire Post 10 Nov, 8 Dec 1896.

A D Klaber (courtesy of Roneo Alcatel Ltd).

KLABER, Augustus David

(1861-1915)

Office machinery manufacturer

Augustus David Klaber was born in 1861. His parents had emigrated from Prague, then the capital of Bohemia. No details are known of his early life until his employment in his early twenties as a stationer's assistant by Partridge & Cooper of Chancery Lane. There he met David Gestetner (qv), seven years his senior and a stationery assistant for another firm in the same area. Gestetner had already patented the cyclostyle — a wheel pen for stencil perforation that was to revolutionise office duplicating — and was about to begin its manufacture. Klaber left for New York in 1882 to open a small business in office supplies and when he returned briefly to England in 1884 Gestetner recruited him as his sole agent to market the cyclostyle in the USA, where Gestetner had patented the wheel pen in 1882.

The market in office machinery was a highly competitive one and numerous inventors became involved with duplicating devices. In America Klaber kept a close eye on the latest developments, often providing Gestetner with ideas for his own patents. Klaber himself, perhaps in return for such favours, was allowed by his partner to take out an American patent in 1886 for a flat-bed duplicating apparatus based on Gestetner's own design in London. Other Klaber patents soon followed both in the USA and Britain and indicated his emergence as an inventor in his own right.

In 1888 Gestetner patented an improved pen, the Neo-Cyclostyle, which could be used at a normal writing angle. At Klaber's request the product was marketed in the USA as the Neostyle, a name which Klaber himself appropriated in 1893 when he opened a New York company to sell stationery and other products as well as those from Gestetner. As Klaber's independence grew the business relationship deteriorated and Gestetner began to rely on others to market his products.

At about this time the need for more rapid methods of copying led to the invention of rotary duplicators which held the stencil on a revolving drum. The most sophisticated version was patented by Harry W Lowe of Omaha in 1897. Within two years Klaber had acquired exclusive rights and began manufacturing and selling the duplicators, called Rotary Neostyles, in America.

In 1900, however, Klaber returned to London, having in the previous year sent ahead his two American associates, Augustus S Newmark, his future son-in-law, and S King, to run a newly-founded firm in rented premises off St Martin's Lane. The business had been registered in 1900 as the Neostyle Manufacturing Co with a nominal capital of £10,000 and had adopted amongst its trademarks the word 'Roneo'. The beginnings were modest: parts had to be shipped in from New York for assembly, King soon left, and apart from Newmark the staff consisted of one salesman and an office boy. Nevertheless, the machines, especially the rotary duplicator, sold well and a promising demand appeared from government departments. When Klaber returned to London he offered the chairmanship to William T Smedley, the chairman of Bio-Trust Ltd, an accountant, and a man with useful City contacts. Smedley, who was to remain in the chair until 1933, put up half the capital for the venture, which was under Klaber's management. Edmund T Williams, chairman of the Gramophone Co Ltd, makers of His Master's Voice players and records, also became a director, as did Newmark. Within a year staff and workforce had grown to 30 people and Klaber, sensing a growing demand, despite shortages of capital opened agencies in Birmingham, Liverpool, Dublin, Paris, and Cape Town, and established two Roneo companies in Australia. In London larger premises were acquired in Great Eastern Street.

In 1903 the use of the Roneo trademark was ensured when Gestetner successfully contested Klaber's right to use the word Neostyle. (Klaber's tit-for-tat was to have the name Cyclostyle removed from Gestetner's pen, on the basis that the law did not allow a descriptive word to be used as a trademark.) In 1904 the Roneo mark was stamped on a best-seller — the D10, which automated many of the features of Lowe's original duplicator. It became the basis of the firm's reputation and was proudly displayed at the new Roneo offices and showroom on Holborn Viaduct. Even more successful was Klaber's automatic 'dry' Roneo Copier marketed in 1906. Based on the traditional letter copying book process, the Copier launched the firm on a period of spectacular world-wide expansion. Within a year an American organisation was set up in New York under Klaber's son, Emile, and a factory was opened near Syracuse, New York. Other agencies followed in Canada, most of the leading European cities, and Russia, India, and Japan. A Roneo journal likened all these overseas branches and agencies to 'a nest of hungry sparrows all clamouring for food' {Dorlay (1978) 18}, and the company's productive capacity was quickly outstripped. In 1907, therefore, manufacturing activity was transferred to Romford, Essex, using the old factory of the Ormond Cycle Co, part of the financial empire of E T Hooley (qv). To raise money the company went public in 1908 as Roneo Ltd with a capital of £175,000 in £1 shares, one-third of which were taken as part payment by the vendors of the Neostyle Manufacturing Co, the remaining two-thirds being offered to

KLABER Augustus David

The Roneo Sales Organisation in Japan in 1907 (courtesy of Roneo Alcatel Ltd).

the public. The prospectus showed that annual sales had increased from £14,000 in 1900 to about £105,000 in 1907.

Another round of expansion followed. In 1909 the highly popular Roneotype machine was introduced: marketed until 1950 it fulfilled the need for multiple copies set in facsimile typewriter characters. Pencil sharpeners and dictating machines were other new lines. Moreover, in 1911 the company acquired a 45 per cent share in the Art Metal Construction Co Ltd, which gave it a major interest in the revolutionary introduction of steel office furniture. Once again capital grew short and in 1909 £50,000 was raised by the issue of 6 per cent debentures. Two years later the call was for £100,000 in 6 per cent cumulative preference shares of which half was to redeem the debentures and the remainder to be added to the working capital. A substantial interest (33 per cent) in Deutsche Roneo was also sold to local interests for cash and a percentage on local sales. The measures were only temporarily successful and in 1913 it was necessary to pass the dividend on the ordinary shares. But Klaber did not live to deal with these problems — they were left as a legacy to his elderly chairman and weak management, who postponed resolution of them until the Midland Bank placed its own director, Arthur Chamberlain, in control in the 1930s.

Klaber married in 1882 in Paris, where his bride's parents lived: they had two sons, Emile, who became a managing director of Roneo, and Emil Hertz (later Edward Henry Kinnard), and two daughters.

Klaber died suddenly after an operation on 29 June 1915, leaving £84,592 gross.

GEOFFREY TWEEDALE

Sources:

Unpublished
PrC.

Published
John S Dorlay, *The Roneo Story* (Roneo Vickers, 1978).
W B Proudfoot, *The Origin of Stencil Duplicating* (Hutchinson, 1972).
Times *Prospectuses* 36 (1908).

Alexander Drake Kleinwort (courtesy of Kleinwort Benson Ltd).

KLEINWORT, Sir Alexander Drake

(1858-1935)

Merchant banker

Alexander Drake Kleinwort was born in Camberwell, London, on 17 October 1858. He was the second son and fourth child of Alexander F H Kleinwort, a merchant banker, who came originally from Hamburg, and who established his own firm in London in 1855. His mother Sophie Charlotte née Greverus was the daughter of an Antwerp merchant who settled in London during the 1820s.

Kleinwort was educated at home until the age of twelve, when he was sent abroad to improve his knowledge of foreign languages. He went first to the Real Gymnasium in Karlsruhe, where he became fluent in German, and then to the Institut Supérieur de Commerce in Antwerp, where he studied French and commercial subjects as a basis for a career in the family firm.

He entered the family bank, then styled Kleinwort, Cohen & Co, in 1877, at the age of nineteen. After three years learning the London end of the bank's business, Kleinwort went on an extensive world tour to meet the bank's correspondents and to build up contacts for the future. He returned to London and to his father's firm in 1883. He became a partner in the bank at the beginning of 1884, joining his father and elder brother Herman in the partnership which was restyled Kleinwort, Sons & Co.

When their father died in 1886 (leaving a personal estate of £701,334), the two brothers took over the direction of the bank. Herman, being the elder, became senior partner, although Alexander was always more active in the bank's affairs. Herman retired from active participation in the bank's management in 1914 because of ill-health. Alexander Kleinwort continued to direct the firm's policy until his death and was also closely involved in the day-to-day running of the firm. He knew many of the bank's customers and their businesses personally and had a detailed knowledge of the important features of their accounts.

Kleinwort, Sons & Co were primarily an acceptance house during the nineteenth century. Under Kleinwort's guidance the business grew in size and the scope of the firm's activities was widened to include other types of financial work. He encouraged new links with American companies, both for the provision of commercial credits and for foreign exchange business. These new links enabled Kleinworts to develop new business placing American share issues in the London market, as well as to expand their established activities.

After the First World War Kleinwort led the firm in a reappraisal of the type of work they undertook, to deal with the changed economic circumstances they faced in the post-war world. As a result of this the firm began to extend its non-acceptance business. Bullion trading, stock exchange arbitrage and foreign exchange work were all built up during the 1920s.

Kleinwort had few business interests outside his firm. He argued that such involvements would leave less time for his own business and might affect his view of the credit-worthiness of potential customers. Nevertheless he became a director of the North British & Mercantile Insurance Co Ltd in 1884 and chairman of the company in 1928. He was also a director of the Railway Passenger Assurance Co and of the Ocean Marine Insurance Co Ltd, becoming chairman of both in 1928. In addition, Kleinwort was an underwriting member of Lloyds, elected in 1886.

Kleinwort made many donations to a range of charities, particularly to hospitals. He was a supporter of the Liberal party and was created a baronet in 1909. He died on 8 June 1935, being survived by his wife Etiennette née Girard, daughter of Etienne Girard, a merchant, whom he married in 1889, and by five children. Two of his sons, Ernest (qv) and Cyril, were partners in the bank and continued the firm after his death. Kleinwort left an estate valued at £616,328 gross.

STEFANIE DIAPER

Sources:

Unpublished

Kleinwort, Benson Ltd, London, papers.

BCe.

MCe.

PrC.

Published

Burke's Peerage and Baronetage.

WWW.

Ernest Kleinwort (courtesy of Kleinwort Benson Ltd).

KLEINWORT, Ernest Greverus

(1901-1977)

Merchant banker

Ernest Greverus Kleinwort was born at his parents' home in Cuckfield, Sussex, on 13 September 1901. He was the sixth of seven children of Sir Alexander Kleinwort (qv), a London merchant banker, and his wife Etiennette née Girard. He was educated at home with his brothers, and then in 1920 went up to Jesus College, Cambridge, where he read French, German and economics and gained a first class degree. After university he went to work in his father's merchant bank, Kleinwort, Sons & Co, and together with his younger brother Cyril, became a partner in the firm in January 1927, at the age of twenty-five. Kleinwort was actively involved in the management of the business after this until the 1960s, apart from wartime service in the RAFVR from 1942 to 1945.

Kleinwort entered the management of his family firm during a difficult period for the merchant banks. The prosperity of the early 1920s was beginning to fade and the disruption of the world trading system, which the Wall Street Crash and the German banking crisis of 1931 caused, seriously affected the business of the merchant banks. Kleinwort built up a large acceptance business with German companies during the 1920s, and in 1931 approaching half of the firm's acceptances were on German account. Because of this heavy involvement in Germany, Kleinwort, Sons & Co was one of the merchant banks hardest hit by the 1931 default. Kleinwort played a leading part in steering his firm through the crisis, and he was also involved in the discussions among the merchant bankers to consider the German Standstill agreement in 1931 and its subsequent renewal during the 1930s. He was also involved in the negotiations which took place during this period to reschedule the commercial debts of Austria, Romania, Hungary and Czechoslovakia.

After his father's death in 1935, the work of running the firm fell more and more upon Kleinwort and his brother, since one of their remaining partners had already retired from day-to-day duties, and the other was considering retiring. The merchant banks as a whole found business much harder to come by in the 1930s than they had done in the 1920s, and Kleinworts' experience mirrored this general trend. Their acceptance business halved between 1929 and 1933, to approximately £8 million, and continued at this lower level until the outbreak of war, which reduced the acceptance business available to the merchant banks to almost nothing as trade was taken under government control.

When the war ended Kleinwort and his partners made several trips abroad to re-establish contact with old clients and to try to rebuild their acceptance business. Progress was slow as the merchant banks had to operate within the prevailing world trade situation and the Exchange Control Regulations, and it was not until 1951 that Kleinwort and his colleagues managed to do as much acceptance business as they had done before the war. New tax laws, which made it difficult for partnerships to build up reserves, and a desire for increased security, persuaded Kleinwort and his brother to convert their firm into a private limited company in 1948. Although the two brothers worked very closely together in managing their business, Ernest Kleinwort, as the senior of the two, became acting chairman of the new company.

Kleinwort, Sons & Co specialised in acceptances, but after the war Kleinwort and his brother decided to diversify their interests, and to move into the growing field of corporate finance work. This was a difficult area to enter because clients tended to remain loyal to their traditional advisers. By the end of the 1950s Kleinwort and his fellow directors were considering the possibility of a merger with a firm already established in the field, as a way of both building up their corporate finance interests and also increasing their capital base. Kleinwort took a leading part in the discussions with the investment bankers, Robert Benson, Lonsdale Ltd, which led up to the merger of the two companies in 1961. He became chairman of both the new bank, Kleinwort, Benson Ltd, and the new holding company, Kleinwort, Benson, Lonsdale Ltd, which were formed as a result of the merger. He retired as chairman of the bank in 1966, at the age of sixty-five, but continued as the chairman of the holding company until 1968.

Kleinwort was a keen gardener, and was also very interested in wildlife and conservation. He became trustee of the British National Appeal of the World Wildlife Fund in 1962, and served on the International Board of Trustees of the Fund, 1967-76. He was a member of the Council of the Wildfowl Trust, 1967-77, and became vice-president in 1970. In 1974 he was made a Commander of the Netherlands Order of the Golden Ark for his work for conservation. He gave money to several hospitals and charities and to the Cheshire Homes, and made possible the building of a home for retired district nurses, which was named after his wife.

He was survived by his wife Joan Nightingale née Crossley, daughter of Arthur W Crossley, a doctor of science, whom he married in 1932, and by a son and daughter. When he died on 7 November 1977, he left an estate valued at £730,666 gross.

STEFANIE DIAPER

Sources:

Unpublished

Kleinwort, Benson Ltd, London, papers.

BCe.

MCe.

Prc.

Published

WWW.

KNIGHT, Alfred Edward
========================

(1898-1974)

Pianoforte manufacturer

Alfred Edward Knight was born in Camberwell, South London on 26 December 1898, the son of Alfred Edward Knight and his wife Florence Jane née Liversage. He was educated at West Square Central Boys' School, Southwark. Piano-making was a family tradition (his great-great-grandfather had worked in the Broadwood factory in Westminster). Young Alfred earned 'very good' grades in practical handicraft in wood and metal, and while a schoolboy was allowed to spend his evenings helping in the Hicks piano factory in the New Kent Road. On leaving school at fourteen he entered an apprenticeship with Hicks.

In 1919, out of his indentures, he joined the distinguished workshop of Squire & Longson in Medlar Street, Camberwell. That firm, run at this time by C E 'Clarrie' Lyons and his brother-in-law H V 'Bert' Shepperd, were making fine pianos under their own 'Cremona' brand name, but were also making 'Welmar' pianos for the British agents of Blüthner, and

Alfred Knight testing one of his upright pianos (courtesy of Mr David Wainwright).

'own name' pianos for music retailers throughout the country. The piano trade doubled the value of its exports between 1921 and 1924 (in the latter year 6,542 pianos were exported, worth £315,000). However, the British manufacturers were coming under challenge from other countries and from other sources of entertainment, notably radio, the electric gramophone, and the cheap motor car.

A fire destroyed the Squire & Longson factory in 1929. It was rebuilt, but two years later, at the height of the depression, Alfred Knight found a factory at Carysfort Road, Stoke Newington, and began business as Booker & Knight. In 1935 he bought out his partner and became sole proprietor of the Knight Piano Co. Soon he was exporting all over the world, and by the beginning of the Second World War was manufacturing 1,000 instruments a year.

'Alfie' Knight was a bustling, cheerful Londoner with a brisk line in chat, a consummate salesman as well as a fine craftsman. He was gregarious and loved meeting people. He enjoyed travelling the world, making business contacts and building up licensing arrangements in North America, South Africa and Australia, which stood him in good stead as tariff barriers were raised against British products. He relished being made a knight of the Honourable Order of Kentucky Colonels and was proud of being a freeman of the City of Santiago and an honorary citizen. Unusually among piano manufacturers he played the instrument well, having studied music with Tracy Robson at Steinways, and played with bands and in a cabaret.

He believed firmly that children should be taught to read music as readily as words, and undertook many lecture tours of schools.

> 'Music is something you can do and appreciate for the whole of a lifetime,' he said. 'When parents give their children a musical education they are giving them the greatest gift possible. The playing of a musical instrument and appreciation of music is about the only thing left that can be done from nine to ninety'. {Personal interviews}

For his services to music and musical education (he was president of the Association of Blind Piano Tuners) he was awarded the OBE in the New Year Honours, 1966.

In 1955 he took his company from Central London to a new factory of 50,000 square feet in Loughton, Essex. He was one of the first manufacturers to recognise that plastics could be more effective than wood in piano actions, particularly in conditions of high temperature and humidity. He conducted a personal research programme and found that nylon impregnated with glass fibre and graphite served best. Soon afterwards the Knight Piano Co took a major American award for piano manufacture, and the combined plastic-and-wood action was produced by British Piano Actions, in Llanelli, South Wales. Alfred Knight took the lead in the fortunes of British Piano Actions, of which he was a director. In 1958, recognising that the Americans were attempting to achieve a monopoly in the manufacture of piano actions worldwide, he enlisted support from companies in Australia, Canada, America and South Africa to keep the South Wales factory in being. Although the company went into receivership in the recession of 1983, the piano action was still highly regarded.

The upright pianos manufactured by Alfred Knight were acknowledged throughout the trade to be of skilful design and high quality, perhaps the best manufactured in Britain since the Second World War. Many people regretted that he never attempted to manufacture a grand, to challenge the dominance of imported pianos on the concert platform.

Alfred Knight married Florence Jenny Slodden, daughter of Alfred George Slodden, a machinist, in 1923; they had two daughters. He died on 3 September 1974, inventive to the last: in his final months he was working on the production of a fibre bush to replace wood as the housing for the tuning pin. This proved highly successful and has been adopted by many piano manufacturers. He left an estate valued at £35,612 gross.

His daughter Sylvia (who succeeded her father as chairman of Alfred Knight Ltd) married John York (also a director of the company). Their daughter Gillian worked for the company until her marriage, and their son Michael took charge of the technical side of the business and became general manager of the firm.

DAVID H E WAINWRIGHT

KNIGHT Alfred Edward

Sources:

Unpublished

BCe.

MCe.

PrC.

Personal interviews with Alfred Knight.

Information from Mrs Sylvia York.

Published

David Wainwright, *The Piano Makers* (Hutchinson, 1975).

KNIGHT, Sir Arthur William

(1917-)

Synthetic textiles company chairman

Sir Arthur Knight (courtesy of Sir Arthur Knight).

Arthur William Knight was born in London on 29 March 1917, son of Arthur Frederick Knight, a steel hardener in Enfield Royal Ordnance Factory (and later a railway porter), and Emily née Scott. He received his schooling at Tottenham County School. On leaving, at the age of sixteen and equipped with a certificate of matriculation, he went to work as a clerk for the grocery business of J Sainsbury & Co at Blackfriars. Whilst so doing he attended the London School of Economics as an evening student and in 1938 graduated B Comm with first class honours. He was awarded a Leverhulme Research Studentship by LSE and spent a year in the Department of Business Administration. In 1939 he took a job as junior economist in the London offices of Courtaulds Ltd, at that time the world's largest rayon producers. The onset of the Second World War soon found him in the army, in which he served from 1940 to 1946, finishing in the Finance Division of the Control Commission for Austria with the rank of lieutenant-colonel. Returning to Courtaulds he went into the company's overseas investment department. He successfully scaled the rungs of the managerial hierarchy to become senior executive in that department and, in 1958, to be elected to the main board of directors. Although continuing to have some concern with the firm's North American interests he soon became involved with C F Kearton (qv), then recently made a managing director, in diversification schemes which the latter was launching. Knight's evident abilities in financial matters made him the obvious candidate for the new post of finance director, to which he was appointed in 1961 only a few months before ICI made a take-over bid for Courtaulds in December of that year.

In the ensuing battle Knight played a prominent part, along with Kearton and others of the younger directors, in defeating the ICI onslaught. From this engagement he emerged in a strong position on a reconstructed board. That position was strengthened by his contribution to the negotiations which resulted in 1964 in Courtaulds and ICI disengaging from their reciprocal financial interests. Kearton succeeded to the chairmanship of the company in the same year; Knight's voice remained very influential on the board. When Kearton's reign came to an end in 1975 Arthur Knight became chairman of Courtaulds, by this time a very large multinational company with much vertical integration in its man-made fibre and textile activities as well as substantial interests in paint and plastics. He had been knighted shortly before his appointment as chairman, in which capacity he remained for four years, retiring at the age of sixty-two in 1979.

As a businessman his concern was largely with finance and organisation. Some lucid, percipient and shrewd reports on the functioning of overseas subsidiaries, made before he became a director, marked his path to the main board. Once there, his was the expertise which transformed the financial structure of the firm as it expanded and diversified largely by taking over other companies. In the seventeen years between his appointment to the board and his assumption of the chairmanship, Courtaulds's net assets multiplied (in monetary terms) over four-fold, its sales more than ten-fold, its profits over eight-fold, its workforce in the UK alone more than doubled. The driving power had been provided by Kearton; Knight advised, negotiated, forecasted, and steered the financial procedures by which this expansion was achieved. His was also the necessary voice of caution which from time to time prevented headlong rushes into potentially disastrous investments. With a personality totally different from that of Kearton, Knight was also the resilient buffer which absorbed the periodic onslaughts so often the concomitant of aggressive entrepreneurship. Their co-operation provided a classic example of a type of partnership by no means uncommon in business; and the significance of those who play the less public role is too often underestimated.

He took over the chairmanship just as the economic recession began to bite. Profits were the highest ever achieved in the year of Kearton's retirement; in the first year of Knight's rule they fell by 60 per cent. He initiated a new concern for good relations with customers and encouraged a participative management style. Under the pressure of adverse economic winds, he intensified the drive for increased productivity to which his predecessor had given momentum and rapidly scrapped some of the latter's more expensive ventures. During his brief reign as chairman, the UK workforce was cut by 14 per cent but sales increased and profits, though not reaching the 1975 peak, recovered substantially. As chairman his willingness to take tough decisions and his ability to consult his colleagues and communicate his views earned the admiration of many and

Sir Arthur Knight presenting prizes to French knitwear designers at the 'Salon du Maille' in Paris 1979 (courtesy of Sir Arthur Knight).

dispelled the reputation of being remote which he acquired in some quarters.

On his retirement he confined his business activities — apart from a temporary one-year spell as chairman of the National Enterprise Board in 1979-80 — to continuing work within the CBI and to a non-executive directorship of Dunlop. He continued to play an active part, as he had earlier, on various bodies concerned with management education and public affairs. The Manchester Business School, the Royal Institute of International Affairs, the Court of Governors of the London School of Economics, the National Institute for Economic and Social Research were amongst the many such bodies on which, at one time or another from 1964 onwards, he served in various ways. He also sat on some official committees of enquiry, notably in 1968-70 on the Roskill Committee on the siting of a third London airport and the Cairncross (Channel Tunnel) Committee in 1974-75. Since retirement he has been particularly active in helping to initiate the Business History Unit at LSE and in running there a series of seminars on problems of business management and administration. It was wholly in character that he should have been one of the very few leaders of British business ever to publish a serious analysis of one of the most important aspects of modern business enterprise. His *Private Enterprise and Public Intervention: The Courtauld Experience* was published in a series sponsored by the London Business School whilst he was deputy chairman of the company.

Sir Arthur Knight married first, in 1945, Beatrice Joan Osborne née Oppenheim. They had one son and three daughters. After his first wife's death in 1968, he married in 1972 Sheila Whiteman.

D C COLEMAN

Writings:

Private Enterprise and Public Intervention: The Courtauld Experience (Allen & Unwin, 1974).

'UK Industry in the Eighties' (1980 IFS Lecture) *Fiscal Studies* vol 2, No 1 (Mar 1981).

'Industrial Policy' in Frances Cairncross (ed), *Changing Perceptions of Economic Policy* (Methuen, 1982).

'Wilson Revisited: Industrialists and Financiers' *Policy Studies Institute*, Discussion Paper No 5, 1982.

'Ideas and Action: How to Improve Industrial Performance?' The Fairbairn Lecture, Jan 1983 *Policy Studies* 3 (1983).

Sources:

Unpublished

BCe.

Published

Donald C Coleman, *Courtaulds. An Economic and Social History* (3 vols, Oxford: Clarendon Press, 1969-80) 3.

WW 1982.

E B Knobel (courtesy of Mr R J Hercock).

KNOBEL, Edward Ball

(1841-1930)

Analytical chemist and photographic materials manufacturer

Edward Ball Knobel was born in Marylebone, London, on 21 October 1841, the son of William Edward Knobel, a solicitor at Lincoln's Inn Fields, and his wife Emily née Roberts. The father and grandfather of his mother were Clerks of the Pells in succession to Addington and Barré. Edward was educated at La Chapelle and Stockwell Grammar School. On leaving school he studied law for two years and then in 1861 entered the School of Mines in Jermyn Street to study geology. Passing his examinations after two years, he was advised by Professor A W Hoffman to apply for a vacancy for an analytical chemist with Bass & Co, the brewers at Burton-on-Trent. He stayed with them thirteen years and rose to become manager and head brewer. He transferred in 1875 to Courtaulds, under Samuel Courtauld III (qv), at Bocking in Essex as manager and chief dye chemist, where he remained until he moved to Ilford in 1893 to become a director and scientific expert in Alfred Harman's (qv) photographic materials manufacturing firm, at a salary equivalent to £1,200 per annum under a profit sharing scheme. For five years he was the only scientist employed by the firm.

During his first years, besides his work as director and analytical chemist, he was involved with improvements to printing-out and bromide papers and isochromatic plates and the use of formaldehyde as a hardening agent for gelatin. Five new brands of plates were introduced and backed plates were made available. He also interested himself in the economics of production. In 1894, when Harman retired, Knobel was made managing director. A new production unit was completed in 1895, with new plate and paper coating machines and automatic plate cutting machines. At the same time a steam engine and dynamo were installed and for the first time the factory was lit by electricity. Knobel in 1898 engaged three more chemists who formed the nucleus of a research department, which is essential for a photographic manufacturer. During these years the firm prospered. In 1897 the profit was 50 per cent higher than in 1892 and a dividend of 27.5 per cent was paid.

Harman sold the business in 1898 to the Britannia Works Co Ltd (renamed Ilford Ltd in 1900) for £380,000. He retained £120,000 shares in the new company, receiving cash for the balance of the price. The other £260,000 shares making up the authorised capital were offered to the public at par in May 1898. Knobel retained his position of managing director in the new company.

By 1900, the factory was no longer surrounded by green fields and in order to escape the atmospheric pollution a new factory was opened at Brentwood in 1904. Meanwhile, a method had been found of cleaning the air at Ilford before it entered the factory so the old factory was retained.

When George Eastman of Kodak suggested the amalgamation of the two companies, Knobel and Harman supported the proposal, but were overruled by the shareholders. Eager to seize market opportunities, the Ilford directors decided to form a subsidiary company in Japan. Knobel left for Japan in 1906 to investigate the possibilities. Unable to raise enough capital or to conclude satisfactory agreements with any Japanese company he returned home after two months. The failure of his Japanese mission led to disagreement with the board and he was dismissed in 1907, aged sixty-six.

In addition to his busy life in commerce, Knobel was also a gifted amateur astronomer and published measurements on the brightness of stars and the separation of double stars. In 1879 he published a translation of a Persian manuscript of Ulugh Beg's star catalogue which inspired him to collate Greek, Latin and Arabian manuscripts on Ptolemy's 'Algamest', which was published in 1915. He followed this with the translation of another thirty Persian manuscripts which was published in 1917. As early as 1873 he was elected a fellow of the Astronomical Society and served on its committee from 1876 to 1922. In 1910 he was invited to become president of the British Astronomical Society.

He was also an excellent violinist and performed at many public concerts.

He married Margaret (d 1922), daughter of Henry Whitehead, a solicitor, in 1869. Edward Knobel died on 25 July 1930, leaving £9,279 gross.

R J HERCOCK

Writings:

On a Catalogue of Stars in the Calendarium of Mohammad al Achsasi al Monakket (Spottiswoode & Co, 1895).

(with C H F Peters) *Ptolemy's Catalogue of Stars, a Revision of the Almagest* (Washington DC: Carnegie Institution of Washington, 1915).

Ulugh Beg's Catalogue of Stars (Washington DC: Carnegie Institution of Washington, 1917).

Sources:

Unpublished

BCe.

MCe.

PrC.

Published

R J Hercock and G A Jones, *Silver by the Ton, the History of Ilford Limited, 1879-1979* (McGraw-Hill Book Co (UK) Ltd, 1979).

WWW.

2nd Viscount Knollys (courtesy of Vickers Ltd).

KNOLLYS, Edward George William Tyrwhitt

2nd Viscount Knollys of Caversham

(1895-1966)

Airline executive

Edward George William Tyrwhitt Knollys was born in St James's Palace, London, on 16 January 1895, the elder son of Francis Knollys, Private Secretary to the Prince of Wales (later King Edward VII), and then to King George V, 1870-1913, and his wife the Honourable Ardyn Mary Tyrwhitt, elder daughter of Sir Henry Thomas Tyrwhitt, Bt, and Baroness Berners. His father was created Viscount Knollys of Caversham in 1911. As a boy Knollys was page of honour to Edward VII and to his godfather, George V. He was educated at Harrow and New College, Oxford.

This unusual background for a businessman was followed by military service in the First World War, during which he served with distinction in the 16th London Regiment (TA) and in the Royal Flying Corps (flying as an observer), being awarded an MBE and a DFC.

After demobilisation from the RAF in 1919, Knollys joined a leading firm of chartered accountants, Deloitte, Plender, Griffiths & Co and then worked for some years for Barclays Bank, being appointed local director in Cape Town of Barclays Bank (Dominion, Colonial & Overseas) in 1929. He succeeded his father as Viscount Knollys in 1924 and returned to England in 1932 to become a director of the Employers' Liability Assurance Corporation, of which he became managing director the following year at the early age of thirty-eight. He was to maintain a close association with this company for the rest of his life.

Not long before the outbreak of the Second World War, Knollys became Civil Defence Deputy Commissioner for the South-East Region and he continued to hold this post for the first two years of the war during a period when England was being subjected to heavy air raids.

As Governor and Commander-in-Chief of Bermuda, 1941-43 (the first civilian to hold this post), he improved Anglo-American relations following the destroyers-for-bases deal, by exploiting his experience in dealing with Americans which he had acquired in the 1930s during frequent visits to the USA in connection with the Employers' large insurance interests there.

His success in Bermuda led to his appointment in 1943 to the newly-open post of full-time chairman of the state-owned British Overseas Airways Corporation. BOAC had been formed in 1940 from a amalgamation of the two principal British private airlines and, under war conditions, had made little progress towards becoming a viable commercial organisation. Under Viscount Knollys's leadership, and in a new atmosphere, the management was re-organised under Brigadier General A C Critchley (qv) as Director General and plans laid for post-war development. After the war, a start was made on these before Knollys's four-year appointment ended in 1947 and he resumed his private business career as managing director of the Employers' and director of Barclays Bank. It was said that Knollys's resignation from BOAC was because of the appointment of a Select Committee to enquire into the administration of civil aviation. He considered this and criticism in the House of Commons of BOAC's heavy losses to be a reflection on his chairmanship.

In 1951-52 during the Korean War, when sudden re-armament created major shortages, Knollys was loaned to the Government as Minister at the British Embassy in Washington responsible for raw materials and as UK representative at the International Materials Conference.

On his return home he joined the Vickers board. In 1954 he retired as managing director of the Employers' Liability Assurance Corporation, being promoted to chairman. The following year he became deputy chairman of Vickers and in 1956 succeeded Sir Ronald (later Lord) Weeks (qv) as chairman.

His selection for this appointment, which he filled with some success despite his lack of previous industrial experience, for six difficult years, was no doubt based on his strong, if somewhat aloof, personality and on his extensive background and contacts in commerce, banking and administration. These had, after all, been gained in a thirty-seven year career of quite unusual versatility, in both private and public sectors, during which he had shown an immense capacity for hard work, and an outstanding intelligence.

As chairman of Vickers, Viscount Knollys ('Edgey' to his friends) demonstrated considerable skill at policy-making, negotiation and judgement of men. This was done with an unsentimental charm, invariable courtesy at first meeting and omniscient air of amiable authority which came naturally to him. He operated as a chairman should but was never so far removed from what was going on to be caught by surprise when, as inevitably happens from time to time, something goes wrong.

He drove his people hard but no harder than he drove himself, while he had a remarkable capacity for dealing in a day with a range of matters well beyond the powers of most people. He believed nevertheless that affairs should be conducted with elegance and style. Although this led sometimes to criticism for extravagance — notably, for example, in transferring the company's headquarters from the dingy old-fashioned offices in Broadway to the new Millbank Tower — this was in fact appropriate to the traditions and long-established status of Vickers.

During his time with the company, he created central planning and research departments and organised a series of senior management conferences which, although also criticised for their cost and expenditure of management time, helped the board in formulating effective new policies. Important advances were also made in arrangements for staff training and career development.

The whole of Knollys's time as Vickers chairman was under a Conservative Government. This removed all nationalisation worries but, on balance, Vickers's performance deteriorated during his regime and the company was moving into a difficult period as it ended. Successful years under the previous chairman, Sir Ronald Weeks, had culminated in exceptionally good results in 1955. Things started going less well soon after Knollys took over: several new ventures were unsuccessful although shipbuilding did well and a move into office equipment was rewarding. Government pressure for the reorganisation and consolidation of the aerospace industry, faced as it was by greatly increased needs for capital in modern technological development, led to major changes at Vickers.

Aircraft and guided weapons represented one of the four major areas of Vickers activity and it was under Knollys that, in 1960, the aerospace subsidiary was hived-off under the leadership of Sir George Edwards (qv) to form, in amalgamation with the aircraft and guided weapons activities in Bristol, English Electric and Hunting, the new British Aircraft Corporation in which Vickers had a 40 per cent holding. BAC was to become one of the two principal elements of the nationalised British Aerospace seventeen years later. But the 1960s, during and following Knollys's chairmanship, were a difficult period for BAC. The Vanguard and VC 10 airliners did not sell in sufficient numbers for commercial success, while cancellation of the TSR2 bomber in 1965 was a heavy blow.

After retirement from the Vickers chairmanship in 1962, Knollys continued as a Vickers director until 1965. Meanwhile, he was chairman of the Vickers subsidiary English Steel Corporation, 1959-65, and, in 1960, became chairman of Northern & Employers after merger of the Employers' with the Northern Assurance Co. He was also chairman of Merchants' Marine Insurance.

Between the wars, his numerous charitable interests included: honorary treasurership of the Radium Institute and of Mount Vernon Hospital and, from 1953, chairmanship of the RAF Benevolent Fund. He was also a member of the finance committee of the British Empire Cancer Campaign, of the management committee of the Harefield and Northwood Group Hospitals and of the council of the King Edward VII Sanatorium at Midhurst.

His later honours included KCMG (1941) and GCMG (1952). Viscount Knollys died on 3 December 1966 at the age of seventy-one after nine months of illness. He was survived by his wife, Margaret Mary Josephine, daughter of Sir Stuart Coats, Bt, whom he married in 1928, and by a son, David Francis, who succeeded to the title. He left £62,572 gross.

PETER W BROOKS

Sources:

Unpublished

BCe.

PrC.

Correspondence with Sir George Edwards 16 Dec 1980, 13 Jan 1981.

Published

Burke's Peerage and Baronetage 1980.

Harold Evans, *Vickers: Against the Odds, 1956-77* (Hodder & Stoughton, 1978).

Flight 8 Dec 1966.

John D Scott, *Vickers — a History* (Weidenfeld & Nicolson, 1962).
Times 5 Dec 1966.
WWW.

KNOTT, Sir James

(1855-1934)

Shipowner

James Knott was born in the small village of Preston on north Tyneside on 31 January 1855. He was the eldest of the two sons of Matthew Knott, a customs searcher, and his wife Margaret née Dobson. The family moved to Willington Quay, Newcastle, in his early youth, where his father bought a small public house. Thus the young James grew up with ships on his doorstep, and soon became fascinated by the adventure and romance of the sea.

He was educated at the Scotch School in North Shields and at the age of thirteen took a job in a small shipbroker's office on Newcastle Quayside. Just six years later he started out on his own account as a shipbroker. He became convinced however, that the advantages of shipowning far outweighed the advantages of shipbroking, and in 1878 he purchased 16 of the 64 shares of the collier brig *Pearl*, with some money borrowed from a friend. His share cost him £185, and was enough to make him managing owner. That year too he married Margaret Annie, daughter of Rev Thomas Garbutt.

The returns of the *Pearl* were good, and in the following year he purchased shares in six more brigs. The collier brigs usually ran down the coast with coal returning to the Tyne in ballast, or with whatever cargo was available. Knott made large profits out of the brigs, and at one point had over 20 under his control, but by 1887 the last had been sold off. He had fully utilised his knowledge of shipbroking and the coal trade, so as to get the best from the last years of sail, before he devoted himself to the age of steam and a fleet of worldwide ocean-going steamers.

Knott's first steamship was the *Saxon Prince*, delivered by Swan Hunter in 1881; from this ship right up to the present day, Prince liners have always carried the fleur-de-lis emblem and the *Prince* nomenclature. During the next two years, the North East yards turned out a further eight steamships for Knott. These vessels were first engaged in tramping. In

1883 Knott went against the generally depressed state of the shipping industry and formed the Prince Steam Shipping Co. By 1886 he owned 17 steamships. As the fleet continued to expand and regular routes were established, Knott formed the Prince Steam Shipping Insurance Association in 1887; the company was formed with a view to cheapening the insurance of the growing number of vessels, which he either owned as managing director of PSSC, or as major shareholder of the 64-share ownership vessels.

In 1895 the Prince Line (1895) Ltd was set up to administer all the vessels that were owned under the 64-share arrangement. It was not until 1898 that the three firms were amalgamated under the banner of Prince Line Ltd. The nominal capital of the company was increased to £1 million, and it is from this organisation that the future Prince Line took shape.

During these early years particularly Knott's entrepreneurial abilities flowered. In seventeen years he had managed to build a steamship fleet of 35 vessels, incorporated into a large, growing and financially healthy company. His success seems to come down to the knack of predicting market movements so that he could be just one jump ahead.

Through these years Knott gained entrance to several trades. In 1886, two years after the world's first purpose-built ocean-going tanker was launched, Knott introduced his first tanker *Russian Prince*. He found the tanker trade extremely profitable, and it was not until 1918 that Princes' tanker interests were sold off. He also made large profits from the North Atlantic trade, carrying Italian emigrants to New York, Boston and Philadelphia, until the Italian Government restricted the franchise to Italian companies in 1907.

Knott gained entry to the Spanish Main services (Europe to the West Indies, Gulf ports and Mexico) with considerable difficulty, and it was under hard conditions that these routes were maintained for about twelve years. Competition in the trade was well established, and the ports were ill-equipped. Knott was forced to institute cut throat price policies, and never really secured a profitable position before the services were abandoned in 1910.

He had far more consistent good fortune in the River Plate run between North and South America. As usual his policies were aggressive; in the early days of trying to grasp a place, he would carry coffee from Santos to New York at 5 cents a bag, about the cost of loading the cargo alone. Knott also profited from the Mediterranean services, one of the Prince Line's oldest interests, and the only service still operating today.

In 1902 Knott set up lines from North America to South Africa, India and the Far East. In 1914 those were extended to the successful development of a round-the-world service.

The start of the First World War saw Prince Line at the height of its development as a maritime power; Knott owned some 45 vessels, and was well established on four routes. The war was to wreak havoc upon the company ashore and afloat. Knott was finding the business more and more of a personal strain, especially with the absence of his three sons, serving abroad. Although his eldest son Thomas Garbutt was something of a reprobate, the younger sons were actively involved in the running of the company. His favourite son, James Leadbitter Knott, was deputy managing director, and had been largely responsible for the development of the company's American business. All three sons went abroad in the war, and it was, apparently, the tragic deaths of Henry Basil and James Leadbitter within a year of each other that prompted his decision to sell Prince Line to Furness Withy in August 1916.

Knott's interests ranged far beyond shipping. He was also a large general merchant and colliery owner. He was called to the Bar at Gray's Inn in 1889. A Unionist, he unsuccessfully contested the Tyneside division of Northumberland in 1906 and was elected MP for Sunderland in 1910, holding the seat until he retired in December that year. His philanthropic work in the North East was considerable. He built a church in Newcastle; supported the rights of the local fishermen; built blocks of flats and Servicemen's homes; and set up a trust fund that still operates from Jersey today, to the benefit of the North East. His policy of building vessels in Tyneside and Wearside yards along with jobs in his fleet, provided considerable employment for the North East.

Knott's baronetcy was announced in 1917, by which time he had moved with his wife to Samarès Manor, Jersey. Lady Knott died aboard their yacht in Cannes in 1929; but only three years later Knott married his second wife who was only twenty-five. Sir James Knott died on 8 June 1934.

JERRY HARRIS

Sources:

Unpublished

A J Henderson, 'Feathers on the Funnel' (1957).

Prince Line Centenary History 1983.

Prince Line papers, local North East archives.

BCe.

Published

A J Henderson, *Progress of the Prince Line* (1949).

WWMP.

WWW.

KORDA, Sir Alexander

(1893-1956)

Film maker

Alexander Korda was born at Túrkeve, a small market town in Hungary, on 16 September 1893, as Sándor Kellner, the eldest child of Henrik Kellner, a soldier and a retired sergeant of the Hussars who became an estate manager of the Salgo family's estate outside Túrkeve, and his wife Ernestine. His father died penniless in 1906 leaving Alexander to support a mother and two younger brothers, Zoltán and Vincent. In 1908 while a part-time student at a commercial school in Budapest, Alexander was given a temporary job with the *Független Magyarország* ('Independent Hungary') a prestigious liberal daily. Because he was still a student he wrote under the pseudonym 'Sursum Corda' ('Lift up your Hearts'). A year later he had substituted the Kellner 'K' for the Latin 'C' and appeared in print for the first time as 'Korda Sándor' — Alexander Korda. It was while a student in Budapest — he was educated at the Reformist College and the Royal University — that he developed his passion for the cinema and by 1912 he was co-editor with Lajos Biró (Hungarian dramatist and novelist) of Hungary's first film journal, the weekly *Pesti Mozi* ('Budapest Cinema'). Two years later, in 1914, he directed his first film *A Becsapott Úisagiró* ('The Duped Journalist'). By 1917 Korda owned in partnership his own studios and production company, Corvin, and had produced and directed over 20 feature films. However, as a result of the political upheavals in the wake of the First World War, he left Hungary with his wife, the film star, Maria née Farkas (whom he married in 1919), and for the next ten years they travelled extensively, making films in Vienna, Berlin, Hollywood, and Paris.

In 1920 while in Vienna he formed a small production company, Corda Film Consortium, partly to exploit his wife's growing reputation in Europe, partly to finance his work from her earnings. However, he quickly exhausted his sources of finance in Vienna and so in January 1923 he moved with his wife to Berlin. Virtually penniless during this period, Korda went through an extravagant ritual in order to attract financial backers: he would take the largest and most expensive suites, order the best wardrobe for himself and his wife, and he would dine out every night at the most expensive restaurants. None of this was paid for but it gave the impression of wealth and confidence and generally succeeded in attracting the finance necessary to produce a number of relatively successful small budget pictures. In 1926 Korda accompanied his wife to Hollywood where she had been signed under contract to First National. His first stay in Hollywood was brief and generally unhappy. Having produced and directed his own films for twelve years he found it difficult to work in the rigid American studio system, dominated by the major Hollywood moguls. His only memorable product of these years was *The Private Life of Helen of Troy* (1927), a historical romance that did, however, set a pattern for many of his later films.

After a brief interlude in Paris in 1930, he completed the film *Marius* (1931) in record time for Paramount, and then proceeded to shoot it over again with a German cast as *Zum goldenen Anker* — effectively presenting the American parent company with two films for the price of one. As a result he was offered the job of running Paramount's ailing British studios. Thus at the age of thirty-eight he settled in England. Within a year of his arrival he had set up his own production company, London Film Productions, demonstrating once again his ability to attract financial supporters in a foreign country. London Film Productions was formed in 1932 with the assistance of several British financiers, including Leopold Sutro, a city banker, whose son John became one of the company's directors. Korda therefore had little difficulty in assembling a distinguished board of directors who opened the way to even more lucrative financial sources.

As founder and head of London Film Productions, he infused new life into an ailing British film industry with much-needed creative and business energy. As a producer, he employed nepotism sensibly, making full use of the considerable talents of his brothers Zoltán and Vincent. The quality and good taste that were the hallmarks of his products resulted in a series of opulent productions which revealed Korda's gift for gauging public tastes. The first, *The Private Life of Henry VIII* (1933), was in many ways an epochal film and its success decisively established Korda as a force to be reckoned with. It was completed in five weeks for a mere £60,000, was premiered in New York and earned back more than half its production cost in a week. It eventually grossed $2.5 million, won Charles Laughton a best actor Oscar (the first awarded to a British actor in a British film), re-established the vogue for historical films in Britain, won Korda his place on the United Artists board and provided a direct stimulus to film production in Britain. Rarely has a single film been so influential. Other lavish productions followed, including *The Scarlet Pimpernel* (1934), *Sanders of the River* (1935), *Rembrandt* (1936), and *Things to Come* (1936).

The initial success of London Film Productions earned Korda a partnership in United Artists which guaranteed London Films a distribution vehicle in America and made it the first British motion picture company to have a reliable major American outlet. British financiers were so impressed with his Continental panache that even the traditionally cautious Prudential Assurance Co agreed to finance London Films, thus enabling Korda to build Denham Studios, which opened in 1936 and rivalled Hollywood in its grandiose facilities.

Alexander Korda brought two major innovations to British film-making, both of which had been widely applied in Hollywood. The first was a basic method of accounting which had hitherto been ignored in Britain. Unfinished films, literary properties that would never be made into films, even completed films that were too bad to be released, all were used as a means of improving London Films' balance sheet by simply listing them as 'assets'. He even bought up foreign films which were then deposited in Denham's vaults never to be distributed but which were registered as recurring assets enabling London Film Productions to obtain further capital. Secondly, Korda decided to buy the screen rights to almost every literary property that came on the market, though seldom with the intention of making a movie. He reasoned that in the long term these properties (and they included works by Wells, Shaw, and Maugham) would be a major source of profit for him. Not only did the purchase of these screen rights give Korda clear title but in addition they could be carried as assets — provided nothing was ever done with them (for example he paid £10,000 for the screen rights to Winston Churchill's *The Life of Marlborough*, which he had no plans to make into a film!). Twenty years later City investors and the British Government were still trying to puzzle out exactly what his assets were, complaining that the more money he lost, the more he seemed able to borrow. As his nephew and family biographer explained, 'He had contrived to make an asset of his extravagance' {Korda (1980) 105}.

Korda's boost to British film production was spectacular, and his reputation was never higher, but by 1938 he had over-extended himself and his financial backers. The Denham Studios venture was too ambitious and he had expanded London Films beyond the resources of even his main backer, the Prudential, which had advanced £2 million and were financing a payroll of £20,000 a week. They now acted swiftly and Denham was removed from Korda's control. He then spent the first part of the Second World War in Hollywood finishing *The Thief of Bagdad* (1940) and making *Lady Hamilton* and *Lydia* (both in 1941), the latter starring his second wife Merle Oberon (Merle O'Brien Thompson whom he married in 1939). In 1942 he returned to England and received the first knighthood given to a film-maker, as much for his war services as for his contribution to the British cinema. It has subsequently been revealed that MI6 had discreetly used London Films over a long period as a commercial cover for their foreign activities. Indeed, Sir Claude Dansey, deputy director of the service, was even given a seat on the board.

In 1944 Korda disposed of his holdings in United Artists for nearly £1 million and bought back for a ridiculously low price his films from the Prudential. At the same time he refloated London Films, initially in partnership with MGM and then as an independent company. For once he was financing himself. He began by purchasing Shepperton Studios and in order to ensure distribution for his films he bought a controlling interest in British Lion, and again set about assembling a distinguished team of independent film-makers: among them Carol Reed, David Lean and Michael Powell. Although *An Ideal Husband* (1947) was the last film directed by Alexander Korda, he was responsible for producing some of the most notable productions of the post-war years including *The Third Man* (1949), *Hobson's Choice* (1954) and *Richard III* (1956). However, he must also be held partly responsible for losing almost £3 million lent by the Government to British Lion in 1948 when they were attempting to expand the domestic film industry. By 1951 the Government was faced with the prospect of either making good British Lion's losses or allowing the country's largest distribution company to go under. The loan was extended but Korda was persuaded to give up control and to confine himself to London Films.

The problems of British Lion were not altogether of Korda's making, but he was personally attacked for his extravagance in the Commons during the debate on the Cinematograph Bill. Perhaps if he had not provided such a ready-made flamboyant scapegoat in an age of austerity the Government might have accepted British Lion's losses more easily. However, by 1954 the company was sliding inevitably into bankruptcy with the result that most of the original £3 million loan was now irrecoverable. The loan was called in and a receiver appointed. Korda resigned and is reputed to have lost £500,000. He bravely announced that he would continue to produce films through his own company, London Films, but died suddenly on 23 January 1956. His will was proved at £385,684. After numerous bitter legal battles the bulk of his estate went to his third wife, Alexandra Irene Boycun (whom he married in 1953 after his second marriage was dissolved) and his son from his first marriage, Peter.

Alexander Korda was frequently blamed for the flamboyance of his business methods and he was undoubtedly a manipulator of money. London Films, for example, was very much a one-man operation, and after his death in 1956, the company ceased production. The name London Films was revived in 1961 for a company distributing Korda's films.

DAVID WELCH

Writings:

(with others) *The Private Life of Henry VIII* (Methuen, 1934).

(with others) *Alexander Korda's The Thief of Bagdad. Authorised Edition Adopted from A Korda's Technicolor Production* (Akron, NY: Saalfield Publicity Co, 1949).

Sources:

Unpublished

PrC.

Information from Jeffrey Richards.

Published

DNB.

Michael Korda, *Charmed Lives: A Family Romance* (Allen Lane, 1980).

Karol Kulik, *Alexander Korda: The Man Who Could Work Miracles* (W H Allen, 1975).

Paul Tabori, *Alexander Korda* (Oldbourne, 1959).

Nigel West, *MI6: British Secret Service Intelligence Operations 1909-45* (Weidenfeld & Nicolson, 1983).

WWW.

Victor Kullberg (courtesy of Mr A C Davies).

KULLBERG, Victor

(1824-1890)

Chronometer manufacturer

Victor Kullberg was born in 1824 in Visby, on the island of Gotland, Sweden. At the age of sixteen he was apprenticed to a leading Swedish watch and chronometer manufacturer. In 1843 he moved to Copenhagen to work for the celebrated Danish chronometer maker, Louis Urban Jürgensen. After visiting the Great Exhibition in 1851 he stayed on in London, and gained employment as an outworker, making chronometer escapements for leading English makers. In 1856 he established his own firm in Islington (eventually located, after some moves, at 105 Liverpool Road), where he made stem-wind watches and chronometers of the highest quality. From 1860 onwards his firm and that of Thomas Mercer (qv) produced the bulk of British chronometers. These were sold either directly to customers or to other 'makers' or finishers in the trade who engraved their own names and numbers on what was a basic Kullberg or Mercer instrument. Kullberg's personal and business reputation was based upon consistent successes in open competition at international industrial exhibitions, and at annual trials of chronometers held for the Admiralty at Greenwich Observatory. He became a leading supplier and repairer of chronometers to the British and other European navies, and he supplied a world-wide network of retailers and customers in major port cities. In an industry in which methods of production were still pre-industrial, involving extensive sub-division of labour and an elaborate putting-out system, Kullberg's annual output exceeded 200 instruments only in peak years of demand: between 1868 and 1918 output averaged ca 150 per annum. Because of the extraordinary durability of their instruments much of the firm's business was repair work: between 1890 and 1920 the manufacturing and repair workshop handled business worth annually about £4,000.

Kullberg's reputation as a master instrument maker rested upon his skills as a maker of escapements, springs, and balances, and the fine-tuning of these in the final assembly of the instrument. He invented an auxiliary balance, and published related technical articles in the *Horological Journal*, the organ of the British Horological Institute of whose council he was a member for thirty years. Although he took first place at Clockmakers' Company trials in 1881, and was consequently made a member, and although he was universally acknowledged as Britain's pre-eminent chronometer manufacturer, he did not become a freeman of the Company, because of his foreign birth. Kullberg died of pleurisy on 7 July 1890 leaving £13,555, and is buried at Highgate Cemetery.

He never married, but had two illegitimate sons, one in Sweden and the other in England. The sons and Kullberg's nephew Peter John Wennerstrom inherited his property. The latter bought the interests of the sons, and with his own son successfully carried on the business until the industry collapsed after the First World War. The firm then rapidly declined, making few new instruments in the 1920s and 1930s, and handling a decreasing volume of repairs until its demise in 1943.

ALUN C DAVIES

Writings:

'On the Causes of Acceleration in New Chronometers' *Horological Journal* 1 (1859).

'Keyless Split Seconds Watch' *ibid* 13 (1871).

'On the Polishing of Pinions' *ibid* 15 (1873).

Translation of Urban Jürgensen, 'On the Isochronism of the Vibrations of the Balance and the Cylindrical Spring' *ibid* 19 (1877).

'Fusee Keyless Work' *ibid* 26 (1883).

'Centrifugal Force and Isochronism' *ibid* 30 (1887).

Sources:

Unpublished

Kullberg's business archives are deposited in the Guildhall Library, London. Principally they comprise his manufacturing books (1868-1943), ledgers (1857-92), outletter books (1871-1927) and other miscellaneous records.

Published

Paul Chamberlain, *It's About Time* (New York: R R Smith, 1941, repr Holland Press, 1964).

Alun C Davies, 'The Life and Death of a Scientific Instrument: The Marine Chronometer, 1770-1920' *Annals of Science* 35 (1978).

—, 'The Rise and Decline of Chronometer Manufacturing' *Antiquarian Horology* 12 (1980).

KYNOCH, George

(1834-1891)

Ammunition manufacturer

George Kynoch was born at Peterhead, Aberdeenshire in 1834, the youngest son of John Kynoch, a journeyman tailor, and his wife Margaret née Ballantine of Edinburgh. He attended the local National School and on leaving went to work in a Glasgow insurance office. From there he moved to Worcester where he obtained a post as bank clerk. Shortly afterwards he moved to Birmingham and a new post as ledger clerk in a bank. He is said to have rapidly come to the conclusion that he was unsuited to a lifetime in banking and, in his early twenties, entered the employment of Pursall & Phillips, percussion cap makers of Whittall Street in the heart of Birmingham's gun quarter. Late in 1859 the factory was totally destroyed in an explosion which killed 19 of its 70 employees, including a number of children. The business moved to other premises in the town but the censure of both the coroner and the press led to pressure to move away from the densely populated area, which was considered unsuitable for 'places where gunpowder or detonating substances were used' {*The Owl* 25 June 1886}.

In September 1861 Pursall sought a licence to erect a powder magazine and percussion cap factory at Witton. Pursall was informed that before a licence could be granted he would have to notify the local residents of his intentions by fixing notices on to church doors. No objections were recorded and the licence was granted. Pursall leased a four-acre plot at a rental of £32 per annum and the factory, which at first consisted of no more than two wooden sheds, commenced production in 1862. Kynoch was made manager and within a year was recognised as proprietor. Possibly he was assisted financially by his future father-in-law, Samuel Birley, a jeweller, whose daughter, Helen, Kynoch married in 1863. The factory staff consisted of one man and 12 girls.

Kynoch entered the ammunition trade at a period when arms technology was changing rapidly. There was a reasonably assured demand for the percussion cap both at home and abroad in 1862 since the British Government still insisted that it was unsafe to incorporate the cap with the cartridge. The muzzle-loading Enfield rifle developed to government specifications required a new type of cartridge and by the end of 1863 Enfield paper cartridges were being made at Witton. In 1864 the War Office decided to convert the Enfield into a breech loader but no existing cartridge was found to be satisfactory and it was admitted that what was needed was 'a strong, fast, tight cartridge containing its own means of ignition' {*ibid*}. The Boxer cartridge consisting of thin coils of brass held together with paper with a brass cap chamber proved to be the answer.

The design of ammunition with its inherent safety problems both in manufacture and use, could be a source of considerable tension between the War Office, the contractor and the customer, whether a foreign Government or a private agent. When, in 1869, the War Office selected the Martini-Henry as its standard service rifle, the coiled cartridge was modified in a manner considered by Kynoch and others to be potentially dangerous. Private firms and foreign Governments on the other hand were being supplied with solid brass drawn cases. It was not until twelve years later during the campaign in the Sudan that the War Offce accepted the solid drawn case. However this held more gunpowder than the coiled case. Such an increase in charge was not permitted but all attempts to reduce the capacity failed. George Kynoch solved the problem by inserting a continuous paper lining in the cartridge which not only reduced the powder capacity but, by preventing the powder from being in contact with the walls of the case, prevented its deterioration. Kynoch recommended the standardisation of sporting gun cartridge sizes but opposition from the gun trade prevented any formal attempts until the end of the century.

Within five years of its establishment Kynoch's works consisted of several distinct ranges of single storey workshops housing different departments, each of which was headed by a foreman or forewoman. A form of internal contract by which the foreman employed his or her own labour operated at Witton. In 1872 the post of head of the percussion cap department was given to a forewoman aged twenty-two. Mrs McNab became a legend at Witton. In the 1860s an order for 5 million caps was regarded as large but by the late 1870s Mrs McNab could take a contract for 150 million and her peak contract was for 449 million. Mrs McNab had a reputation for workshop safety and in thirty years there were no serious accidents. Cartridge loading, which was largely done by children, had a poorer safety record and in 1870 an explosion injured 28 people, of whom eight died. Kynoch, sensitive to public opinion, responded to critical comments in the press by announcing that cartridge loading had been suspended until a safer method of performing the task had been found. He went on to describe an experiment which had indicated such a method and concluded by inviting the press to witness the procedure. His invitation was not accepted.

By the early 1880s, George Kynoch owned the second largest ammunition factory in Britain. The valuation of the business in land, buildings, machinery and stock was over £100,000. There were depots or agencies in London, Liverpool, Glasgow and 30 cities around the world. The capacity of the Witton factory was claimed to be 400,000 cartridges a day and approximately 800 people were employed there. Kynoch was, moreover, proprietor of a brass rolling mill, a patent lamp business and a print works and was shortly to buy a gun factory.

By this period George Kynoch had amassed a personal fortune of between £60,000 and £80,000 and he was living in a large mansion, Hamstead Hall, Handsworth, Staffordshire, set in a wooded 300-acre park. He was 'flamboyant, energetic, likeable and randy' {Reader (1970) I, 145}. He had political ambitions and was nominated Unionist candidate for Aston in 1886. Kynoch claimed, 'although I am strongly conservative in my political ideas, I am not a party man' {*The Owl* 25 June 1886}. A contemporary political satirist observed that 'to intense political zeal Mr Kynoch adds an element of personal popularity, especially amongst the section of the community interested in athletic sports' {*ibid*} — he had become president of Aston Villa Football Club. An opponent describing himself as a 'conservative clergyman' was less generous: 'Apart from its numerous grammatical errors, his harangue of last evening displayed evidence of a coarseness and vulgarity such as one would hardly expect from the maudlin lips of the lowest pothouse politician' {*Under Five Flags* 27}. Kynoch held the Aston seat from July 1886 until his death.

Kynoch's business began to suffer, as interest in politics, public service and society began to demand more time and money. Kynoch took steps to convert his business into a private limited company, a move he accomplished in 1884. Kynoch acted as managing director at £500 per annum plus 10 per cent of the profits. The board, under the chairmanship of Viscount Bury, consisted of six members who rarely visited the works. A bank overdraft was negotiated, new stores and mechanics shops were erected and the company tendered for and obtained a government contract for the supply of 10 million loaded rifle cartridges, 1 million shells and half a million uncapped cases. However, quality control was poor and tests at the Royal Arsenal failed to confirm the results obtained at Witton. By 1886 contracts had dropped sharply and the marginal trading profit had become a loss which by 1888 had quadrupled.

Kynoch could not accept the divorce of ownership from control. A heavy investment programme continued whilst the board blamed poor results on a recession in the cartridge trade. Co-operation between Kynoch and the board was almost non-existent; moreover Kynoch, by retaining other business interests closely connected with and dependent upon Witton, was in a dubious ethical position. He had retained ownership of metal rolling mills supplying Witton as well as agencies in South Africa handling Witton products. An independent view of the situation was sought and in 1887 the board recorded that the constant supervision required at Witton was incompatible with the duties which devolved upon an MP.

Early in 1888 the shareholders formed a Committee of Investigation which soon identified the lack of co-operation between Kynoch and the board as the source of the problem. Proposals recommending the appointment of three local directors with more frequent board meetings in Birmingham were accepted and by the end of the year Arthur Chamberlain (qv), J P Lacy and S Leitner became board members. The three newly-elected Birmingham directors took the unprecedented step of presenting the board with a formidable list of the company's shortcomings, most of which were directly or indirectly attributable to Kynoch. Kynoch was asked to resign and did so within a fortnight on health grounds. Shortly afterwards he left for South Africa, neglecting to apply for the Chiltern Hundreds, thereby leaving his constituents in a predicament over parliamentary representation. He owed the company over £14,000 which was only settled by an order of the Queen's Bench enabling the company to sell sufficient of Kynoch's shares to offset the debt. George Kynoch was by this time a sick man. He died in comparative poverty in Johannesburg on 28 February 1891.

JENNIFER TANN

Sources:

Published

Birmingham Post 31 May 1962.

The Owl 25 June 1886.

William J Reader, *Imperial Chemical Industries. A History* (2 vols, Oxford University Press, 1970–75) 1.

Under Five Flags: The Story of Kynoch Works, Witton, Birmingham 1862-1962 (Birmingham: Kynoch Press, 1962).

WWMP.

L

Sir James Laing (courtesy of Mr Joe F Clarke).

LAING, Sir James

(1823-1901)

Shipbuilder

James Laing was born in the house built at the end of his father's shipyard at Deptford, Sunderland, on 11 January 1823. The Laings were farmers in Fife but in the 1790s James's father, Philip (1770-1854), after training for some time as a doctor went to work with his brother John in his South Shields shipyard. The Laings traded in timber and were shipowners as well as builders. James was the only son of Philip Laing's second wife, Anne (1785-1852), the daughter of John Jobling and the widow of a Durham solicitor. After some schooling he served a normal shipyard apprenticeship.

At the age of twenty in 1843 James was put in charge of the yard. The Deptford shipyard already had a good reputation and the first vessel launched under him was the *Agincourt* for Duncan Dunbar. During the next ten years one or more ships were supplied annually to this shipping line. He displayed technical initiative in the diagonal strengthening of wooden ships with metal strips (and later persevered with the introduction of gas furnaces for heating ships' plates). Laing was deeply impressed by the iron-built *Great Britain* during a visit to Liverpool and he took the lead in building iron ships on the River Wear. In 1853 he launched his first iron vessel, six years before anyone else on the Wear. However, Laing continued to build in wood as well as iron and it was not until 1866 that his last wood ship, the *Parramatta* (1,521 tons) was launched. Joseph Conrad's *Torrens*, launched in 1875, was but one of the many splendid composite clipper ships built at Laings' yard.

Laings was one of the largest shipyards on the Wear and built more than 2,000 tons in 1851. Soon after this Laing played a leading role in dealing with a major strike by the independent-minded shipwrights in 1853 and he became chairman of the employers' association which was then formed. A short-lived but successful conciliation board was established and the wage rates and conditions it agreed endured for many years. Thirty years later in 1883 Laing played a major role in the very successful Wear Conciliation Board, whose activities were not matched in any other shipbuilding port.

A patrician figure in appearance, James Laing was not particularly sympathetic to trade unions but worked satisfactorily with the local leadership of the workers. His general concern for his work-force was expressed in the 1880s by the inclusion of a large dining room and a commodious gymnasium, for the youths he employed, in the new building extensions. These new facilities augmented the long-established 'British Workman': a self-supporting ($\frac{1}{2}$d a week subscription) club which provided a library, meeting rooms and non-alcoholic drinks.

Output doubled during the 1850s and in January 1863 the *Sunderland Herald* wrote of Mr Laing's 'enterprise and farseeing sagacity' marking 'him out as the pioneer of the new trade' of iron shipbuilding {*Sunderland Herald* 9 Jan 1863}. The output of the Deptford shipyard exceeded 7,600 tons in 1864 and averaged 15,000 tons in the early 1870s. By then there were only 15 shipbuilders compared with the 70 builders when Laing took charge of his yard; he had survived and expanded while many others failed.

By the early 1880s Laing operated two shipyards totalling about 30 acres, and about 23,000 tons were launched in both 1882 and 1883. Only two Wear shipyards launched a greater tonnage and they both suffered more severely in the ensuing slump. Already 300 ships had been built under Laing's direction, including the largest passenger vessel built on the North East coast up to that date, the 4,670 ton *Mexican*. However, more typical output was of high-quality cargo vessels with passenger accommodation. The two graving docks, a long-established tradition with the Laings, provided regular income from repair work, which in one year amounted to 60,000 tons. The company also developed, under the guidance of one of Laing's sons, an extensive and highly efficient brass and copper works. This works employed about 300, supplying not only the Laings' yards with propellors and other requirements but also other yards and the Navy with similar equipment.

Laing was elected to the River Wear Commissioners in 1859 to represent the shipowners and he served as chairman of the Commission, 1868-1900. As president of the Chamber of Shipping of the United Kingdom he 'championed the cause of the shipowners against the Suez Canal board' {*Engineering* 20 Dec 1901}. Laing was the first chairman of Sunderland's Hendon Docks and the Roker Pier was described as 'a lasting tribute to the zeal displayed by Sir James in the interests of the Port' {*Newcastle Daily Chronicle* 16 Dec 1901}. In the early years of the Sunderland Chamber of Commerce Laing played an important part and served as the second president of the Chamber.

During the 1890s the Laings built many oil-carrying ships, including in 1898 the *Tuscarora*, with a capacity of 2 million gallons. At the turn of the century in a shipyard with its own central electric power house their output exceeded 40,000 tons, equal to 15 per cent of the total output on the River Wear. The enterprise became a limited liability company in 1898. During his sixty years in the shipbuilding industry, while it passed through the phases of construction in wood, iron and steel, and from using almost exclusively hand tools to electrically-driven machinery, it may fairly be stated that no one else equalled his contribution to shipbuilding on the Wear. However, Laing did fail in his final years to create a management team that could carry his great business forward. Within eight years of his death the company went into liquidation, though it was then reconstructed by James Marr (qv).

Laing held many directorships, including those of the Suez Canal Co, the North Eastern Railway and such local companies as the Sunderland Gas Co and the Sunderland & South Shields Water Co. James and his children held shares in many shipping companies, such as the Dale Line, the Columbia Steam Navigation Co and the Neptune Steam Navigation Co.

A Unionist in politics, Laing unsuccessfully fought the North Durham parliamentary seat in 1880. He was a JP in both Durham and Northumberland and served as High Sheriff of Durham as well as being a DL of the county. He was knighted in 1897. Laing was a governor of the local infirmary and orphanage and generally supported medical charities. In religion he was a staunch member of the Church of England.

Unlike most local shipbuilders he was never a member of the North-East Coast Institution of Engineers and Shipbuilders, although two of his sons, James Jr and Hugh, were active members. He was first elected to the council of the Institution of Naval Architects in 1885 and re-elected six years later. He served on the Bulkhead committee and contributed to discussions on this subject. He also served as vice-president of Lloyds Load Line committee.

James Laing married twice, firstly in 1847 to Mary (1816-50), fourth daughter of Henry Tanner; they had two children, Phillip (1849-1907) who was concerned with managing some of the family's shipping interests, and Mary born in 1848. Secondly in 1855 he married Therese, eighth daughter of Thomas Peacock; they had five sons and eight daughters. James Jr (1862-95) was given a shipyard training like his father but Hugh (1871-1930), after education at Wellington College and Cambridge, later became manager of the shipyard, retaining the position for twenty-nine years.

Sir James Laing died on 15 December 1901, leaving an estate valued at £129,558 gross.

J F CLARKE

LAING Sir James

Writings:

PP, RC on Labour (1893-94) C 6894-VII.

Sources:

Unpublished

Sunderland Public Library, Corder MSS.

Tyne and Wear Archives, Sunderland Chamber of Commerce Minute Book, 1879-1898; Wear Commissioners papers; Wear Shipbuilders Association papers.

J F Clarke, 'Labour Relations in Engineering and Shipbuilding on the North East Coast c1850-1900' (Newcastle upon Tyne MA, 1967).

Published

J F Clarke, 'Shipbuilding on the River Wear 1780-1870' in R W Sturgess (ed), *The Great Age of Industry in the North East* (Durham: Durham Local History Society, 1981).

Concerning Ships (Sunderland, 1933).

Engineer Dec 1901.

Engineering 20 Dec 1901.

Amy C Flagg, *Notes on the History of Shipbuilding in South Shields* (South Shields: South Tyneside Borough Council, 1979).

Newcastle Daily Chronicle 16 Dec 1901.

David Pollock, *Modern Shipbuilding and the Men Engaged in It* (Spon, 1884).

J W Smith and T S Holden, *Where Ships Are Born* (Sunderland:Thomas Reid & Co, 1953).

Sunderland Echo.

Sunderland Herald 9 Jan 1863.

Transactions of the Institution of Naval Architects 29 (1921), 33 (1925), 44 (1936).

Turnbull's Shipping Register passim.

WWW.

Sir John Laing (courtesy of John Laing & Son plc).

LAING, Sir John William

(1879-1978)

Builder and civil engineering contractor

John William Laing was born in Carlisle on 24 September 1879, the third but only surviving son of the seven children of John Laing (1842-1924) who headed a small, third-generation firm of builders originating with migrant Scottish stonemasons. His mother, Sarah née Wood, a strong-willed woman, came from a Cumbrian farming family. The Laings, like the family of Jonathan Dodgson Carr (qv), strongly supported the Brethren Assembly in Carlisle and John William Laing early in life decided to become a Christian in a tradition emphasising personal piety and evangelism. After education at Sedbergh School and Carlisle Grammar School, Laing entered the family firm at the age of fifteen and served a three years' apprenticeship as bricklayer-mason.

In 1908 he took over the firm's management and in 1910 became sole proprietor. Early on he perceived the importance of accurate costing for tender and of control of performance during construction. He appointed a tendering manager, William Sirey (also a member of the Carlisle Brethren), in 1903 and he himself, by work-study methods, mastered control of labour costing on his building sites. During the boom construction decade, 1900-9, Laing took on two sizeable civil engineering projects, the Uldale reservoir and the Barrow outfall sewers. In the former he worked with a navvy gang of 200 men, which widened his sympathies for the construction labourer. The Barrow project involved him in unforeseen and costly natural hazards and led to litigation with the Barrow corporation. Although Laing won the action, it occasioned a spiritual crisis in which he vowed to make God 'as seen in Jesus Christ ... the centre of my life' and 'to live my life in a less ruthless manner' {Coad (1979) 51-52}. He drafted and followed a financial programme by which he saved half his income and, on a graduated system, gave away an eighth to a third, living on £150 to £500 a year.

His encounters with civil engineering proved valuable after 1914 when he secured wartime contracts from the War Department (prefabricated timber army huts), Ministry of Munitions (part of Gretna Green town and munitions factory complex), Control Board (state-managed inns) and Air Ministry (Crail aerodrome, Fife). These wartime demands partly explained his firm's growth from around 50 employees in the early 1890s to 4,000 in 1917, with turnover rising from £11,000 in 1912 to £500,000 in 1920.

In the face of pent-up housing demand and government building subsidies, Laing organised for expansion. In 1920 he converted his business into a private company, John Laing & Son Ltd (authorised capital, £60,000), selling his assets to the new company for just over £5,000 in cash and £41,209 in £1 ordinary shares. Business expanded in the North of England and North Wales but wider prospects lay in the South: by 1931, 40 per cent of UK building employment was located in Greater London and the South East. To reach the fastest growing house-building market, Laing opened an office in London in 1921 and then in 1926 moved his company's headquarters with many of its staff of nearly 30 from Carlisle (where a branch office remained) to Mill Hill, North West London. Two years later he formed a second company, Laing's Properties Ltd, to acquire and manage houses, flats, shops and factories which it owned or leased.

Laing tried to overcome the post-war shortage of skilled labour by building in situ concrete cavity walls with an unskilled method of handling shuttering, which he patented as Easiform in 1924. With this and, much more as the labour supply situation eased, with brick, the firm built housing estates in South Wales and the West of England, and in the 1930s, in London's spreading suburbs. Laing's houses, designed in a traditional style by professional architects, met specifications of a high standard. His estates were carefully planned, with trees preserved and shrubs lining road verges. Each estate was served by a parade of shops, the freeholds to which remained with his property company. Laing deliberately sought quality as well as efficiency in his speculative building and to counter shoddy work he supported the formation of the National House Builders' Registration Council, formed in 1937, which registered builders and guaranteed their houses. To extend his market he and other prominent builders promoted the builders' pool system, an arrangement with the building societies led by Harold Bellman (qv) which reduced the cash deposits required for house mortgages. The consequent growth of John Laing's firm, especially in the 1930s, is apparent in turnover figures: the post-war peak of £500,000 was again exceeded in 1924 and then grew to £1.1 million in 1930, £2 million in 1936 and £3 million in 1938. Net profits rose from £10,000 in 1920 to £156,000 in 1938.

Laing exercised a benevolent paternalism over his workers. Apart from his numerous individual acts of charity, he introduced a scheme for worker shares, in July 1922. Of the 48,652 ordinary shares issued, 8,451 went to 11 of his employees comprising managers, agents, surveyors, clerks and cashiers. Laing himself assigned the shares in numbers and to employees of his own choice, but always to men ranking as gangers or foremen and above. Often the shares were purchased in instalments through the company secretary and not infrequently Laing gave employee shareholders shares as part of his distribution of profits. Shares had to be sold back to the firm when the employee left.

The failure of an attempt to regionalise the company's organisation in the early 1920s confirmed Laing's faith in a centralised firm structure over which he preserved strict personal control. He supplemented a hand-picked office staff with a handful of trusted and experienced building managers who travelled out from London to the major sites. Since John Laing rarely needed more than four or five hours sleep a night, his subordinates were hard-pressed to keep up with his extensive probings and checks, recorded in a series of black notebooks, on labour costs and site progress. But the firm's work certainly never occupied all his waking hours. At the age of forty-seven, having reached a reasonably secure position, he decided to spend half his time in the firm and half on

*Interior view of Coventry Cathedral
(courtesy of John Laing & Son plc).*

Christian activities. He organised an assembly for the Christian Brethren
in Mill Hill, for which he built Woodcroft Hall at Burnt Oak, and devoted
a great deal of effort and money to youth movements such as the
Crusaders' Union (whose camps he regularly officered), the Covenanters
and Inter-Varsity Fellowship, besides financing numerous Brethren halls
and chapels.

The Second World War brought massive expansion and the firm
engaged in a wide variety of construction: 54 airfields, the underground
headquarters of RAF Bomber Command, munitions factories and sections
of the D-Day Mulberry harbour. Wartime conditions also intensified site
level controls. Head of one of the largest firms in the building industry
and a leader among building employers, John Laing served as consultant
to wartime Governments. He sat on the Committee of Wartime Building
(March 1940) and on the Central Committee of Works and Building where
the Minister of Works, Lord Portal (qv), heavily relied on him and
Godfrey Mitchell (qv) of Wimpey for professional advice.

Confronted with a chronic housing shortage after 1945, Laing launched
his company into Easiform construction again, supporting it with a
thorough R & D programme. Utilising concrete technology, Laings
built 10,000 Easiform houses between 1945 and 1949. During the
reconstruction years Laing sat on the Cost of Housebuilding Committee
(which reported under J G Girdwood in 1948) and suggested a yardstick

Berkeley Nuclear Power Station (courtesy of John Laing & Son plc).

house in order to facilitate standardisation in costing and the assessment of innovations.

The rapid growth of his firm in the war and post-war years posed problems for John Laing. It became clear that he could no longer exert centralised control if the firm were to expand. Despite his characteristic reluctance to delegate, in the late 1940s he slowly transferred the firm's management to his sons, William Kirby (b 1916) and John Maurice (b 1918) and allowed them to share in entrepreneurial decisions. By 1950 the first experiment in a regional organisational structure commenced at Bristol. It led to financial and managerial decentralisation, implemented by Ernest C Uren, an accountant responsible for the firm's financial functions. Further expansion required increasing the firm's capital resources and to do this the business was converted in 1952 into a public company with an authorised capital of £1.3 million of which nearly £927,000 was issued. The public company, John Laing & Sons (Holdings) Ltd, took over John Laing & Sons Ltd, its subsidiaries, and Laing's Properties Ltd, with a combined net asset value of £4,412,555. The prospectus advertising the intended flotation showed the group's profits for 1951 before tax to be £1,258,741 (on a turnover, calculated by Roy Coad, of £17 million) of which a high proportion were ploughed back, in line with John Laing's long-practised refusal to distribute high dividends (indeed in the period 1941-51, after taxation, some 35 per cent of the profits were retained in the business and only 5 per cent distributed to shareholders). The Laing family and their charitable trusts held sufficient ordinary shares in the public company to maintain control of the firm; John Laing became chairman (at a salary of £5,000 per annum) and his sons, joint managing directors. Employee shareholders held 23 per cent of the ordinary shares.

Besides housing, the firm now engaged in more complex civil engineering works, like Windscale nuclear plant and Fawley oil refinery, Prestwick and Glasgow airports. Laing commenced his firm's overseas expansion in 1947 when he opened a South African branch. Shortly before John Laing retired from the chairmanship of the holding company in 1957, the firm won contracts for the rebuilding of Coventry Cathedral (all the profits on which the firm returned to the Cathedral) and the building of Berkeley nuclear power station. The year after he retired the firm won the contract for the first 50-mile section of the M1 motorway, a new activity in which it became a national leader and which derived from its wartime airfield construction experience. By 1953-54 his firm was, with Wimpey, the largest in the British building industry with net assets of £6.6 million, though its consolidated profits before tax in 1954, at £1,238,447, were half those of Wimpey (a profit level which hardly changed relatively or absolutely before Laing retired); turnover in 1954 was £19.3 million. That year Laings employed 15,000 men. For his services to the industry, John Laing was appointed CBE in 1951 and knighted in 1959.

John Laing married Beatrice Harland (1885-1972), daughter of William Harland (chartered accountant and member of the Stockton-on-Tees Brethren asssembly), in 1910. Their two sons attained distinction in the business world, Kirby becoming president of the Institution of Civil Engineers and Maurice a director of the Bank of England and of Rolls Royce, both being knighted in the 1960s.

To the end of his life Laing, supported by his wife, remained a generous benefactor of evangelical Christian enterprise. In 1922 he gave nearly 40 per cent of his personal ordinary shares in the company to a Brethren charitable holding foundation, the Steward's Company Ltd. This applied its income to missionary, evangelistic and poor relief work. Besides the Brethren, a wide range of Christian interdenominational organisations benefited from Laing's support: among them, those mentioned earlier; the London Bible College, which he and Philip Henman (qv) heavily funded and helped to set up; the British and Foreign Bible Society; the Missionary Aviation Fellowship; Fact and Faith Films; and the Billy Graham crusades.

Politically Laing was a Conservative, and a visit to Russia in 1935 strengthened his fears of Communism, but faith not politics dominated his outlook. On principle he always opposed speculative profits, on shares or land. Once, in the mid-1930s, he even made a public statement in favour of the gradual state ownership of land, a solution he rejected after the war.

Paternalistic and dominating, Laing gained a reputation for straightness in his personal and business dealings. Pursuit of efficiency and quality and close personal control marked his business style. So did frugality, evidenced in his policy of extensively ploughing back profits, and his preference for the works canteen or sandwiches instead of an expensive restaurant. In some ways he was socially narrow: he once sacked a man for going to a pub at lunchtime. A strong-willed optimist, he worked immensely hard, long enjoyed physical fitness and held a simple, bold

Christian faith until his death at the age of ninety-nine on 11 January 1978. He left an estate valued at £74,592 gross.

DAVID J JEREMY

Writings:

House Building, 1934-6 (1934). This has been listed in Jackson (below) but has not been located.

Modern Methods of House Construction, paper read to the General Meeting of the Chartered Surveyors' Institution, 3 Dec 1945.

'A Bible Message' repr in Godfrey Harrison, *Life and Belief in the Experience of John W Laing CBE* (Hodder & Stoughton, 1954).

British Patent:

1924 (250,993)

Sources:

Unpublished

Laing Archives, Mill Hill, London, research notes compiled by Roy Coad.

C Reg: John Laing & Son Ltd (172,161); Laing's Properties Ltd (235,250); John Laing & Son (Holdings) Ltd (511430).

BCe.

MCe.

PrC.

Interviews with Roy Coad, K G Jerrard, John J G Michie, E J Miles, E C Uren (all in spring, 1980).

John Maurice Laing, 'The Construction Industry: Its Prospects, Problems and the Need for Change' (Edwards Seminar Paper 342, 19 Jan 1965).

John William Laing, 'The Economics and Organisation of Building and Civil Engineering Contracting' (ibid 160, 7 Dec 1954).

Published

Marian Bowley, *The British Building Industry: Four Studies in Response and Resistance to Change* (Cambridge: Cambridge University Press, 1966).

H F R Catherwood, 'Development and Organisation of Richard Costain Ltd' in Ronald S Edwards and Harry Townsend (eds), *Business Growth* (Macmillan, 1966).

Roy Coad, *Laing. The Biography of Sir John W Laing, CBE (1879-1978)* (Hodder & Stoughton, 1979).

Godfrey Harrison, *Life and Belief in the Experience of John W Laing, CBE* (Hodder & Stoughton, 1954).

Wallace Haughan, 'Death of Sir John Laing' *Team Spirit* Jan 1978.

Alan A Jackson, *Semi-Detached London. Suburban Development, Life and Transport, 1900-39* (George Allen & Unwin, 1973).

National Institute of Economic and Social Research, *A Classified List of Large Companies Engaged in British Industry* (NIESR, 1955).

Harry W Richardson and Derek H Aldcroft, *Building in the British Economy Between the Wars* (George Allen & Unwin, 1968).

Serving a Nation at War, 1939-45: A Review of the Building and Civil Engineering Work of John Laing & Sons Ltd. London and Carlisle (John Laing & Sons Ltd, August 1946).

Stock Exchange Official Year-Book 1953.

Teamwork. The Story of John Laing & Sons Ltd (John Laing & Sons Ltd, July 1950).

Times 12 Jan, 3 Apr 1978.

Times *Prospectuses* III (1951).

WWW.

LANCASTER, Arthur Henry

(1841-1928)

Lead manufacturer

Arthur Henry Lancaster was born on 13 January 1841, the third son of William James Lancaster of Stamford Hill. He was intended to become an architect and enter the office of Gilbert Scott (qv) but, probably because his elder brothers took little interest in it, he was taken into the family firm, Locke, Lancaster & Co, lead manufacturers. With works at Limehouse and Bridge Road, Millwall, this was among the largest London blue lead manufacturers, smelting lead ores and desilverising and refining mainly imported pig lead and producing lead sheet and pipe. After his father's death in 1866 he took on considerable responsibility and was managing partner from 1883 on the death of his uncle, Samuel Lancaster. In this period A H Lancaster expanded the firm and introduced up-to-date technology, including the first mechanically-charged lead blast furnace in the UK, using the 'bell and cone' principle borrowed from the iron industry.

In 1894 he amalgamated his firm with another London company, W W & R Johnson & Sons Ltd, which was chiefly involved in the complementary manufacture of lead chemicals. The amalgamation and formation of a large limited company was a response to growing competition in the lead industry and Lancaster threw his efforts behind schemes of amalgamation and cartelisation in the trade. In 1897, together with the Tyneside firm of Cooksons (led by Norman Cookson (qv)), he attempted to buy out and close a rival manufacturer, Locke, Blackett & Co Ltd. His firm and several others amalgamated in 1924 as Associated Lead Manufacturers Ltd.

In 1872 Lancaster married his cousin Martha Anne, daughter of Captain James Rigby Lancaster; they had two daughters, Eveline and Elsie. After living in Kensington and at 'Honeylands', Waltham Abbey, he purchased in 1895 the estate of Sendholme, Send in Surrey. He became the benefactor of the village, building and endowing the Village Institute and Hall, becoming churchwarden, holder of the advowson, and making many charitable donations in the area. He was also responsible for donations to many charities, including the Missions to Seamen in 1924. Arthur Lancaster died at Sendholme on 11 February 1928, leaving a gross estate of £527,731.

D J ROWE

Sources:

Unpublished

MCe.

Published

E C Fâche (comp), *Lancaster & Locke. A Pedigree* (pp, 1934?).

D J Rowe, *Lead Manufacturing in Britain. A History* (Croom Helm, 1983).

Sir Allen Lane (courtesy of Penguin Books Ltd).

LANE, Sir Allen

(1902-1970)

Publisher

Allen Williams (he changed his name by deed-poll to Lane in 1919) was born in Bristol on 21 September 1902, the eldest son of Samuel Allen Williams, a municipal architect, and Camilla née Lane. He was educated at Bristol Grammar School. At the age of sixteen Allen was taken into the firm of a distant cousin, John Lane (known to him always as Uncle John). John Lane was the founder and proprietor of the distinguished and, in its earlier days, pioneering house of John Lane: The Bodley Head, publishers of *The Yellow Book*, of Oscar Wilde, Francis Thompson, Alice Meynell, Anatole France and of many another leading author of the fin de siècle and Edwardian periods. John Lane, a childless man, hoped for an heir to the notable but crumbling empire he had created. Allen's alacrity as an apprentice-publisher offered to Uncle John the chance to make substantial his dreams and, at the same time, to satisfy his strong sense of family. When not only Allen but also his parents and all their family took to themselves Uncle John's surname, Allen's status as heir-apparent was made certain. He went to live at the Lanes' house in Lancaster Gate Terrace. There, not altogether to his liking, he was regularly present at the John Lanes' salon-evenings.

At the Bodley Head he worked in the warehouse, made deliveries, and then became the firm's London traveller. In 1924 Allen was promoted to the board of the Bodley Head.

Though John Lane had himself started work as a railway-clerk he had acquired with determination the gloss of aristocracy and it was under his scrupulous tutelage that Allen shed all traces of his plebeian origins and took on that social sophistication which was a notable part of his persona. As publisher, too, John Lane was an excellent tutor but when he died, early in 1925, Allen's grief was short-lived. He admired John Lane for his past achievements, and he remained throughout his life grateful to his memory for early indoctrination in the trade, but already he was unsympathetic to Lane's archaic methods and impatient with his dedication to a tradition which, in Allen's opinion, could no longer hold the Bodley Head in the advance-guard of publishing, or even keep it solvent.

Allen was soon in conflict with his seniors and with other directors, his contemporaries, who had been brought in largely because it was hoped that their wealth would underpin the firm's shaky finances. When Annie Lane died in 1926 she left most of her Bodley Head shares to Allen. His position was now unassailable and, at the age of twenty-four, he became managing director of the Bodley Head.

In terms of prestige it was a rich inheritance; in terms of immediate reward anything but munificent; and as prelude to a successful career scarcely promising. Allen brought in soon as directors his younger brothers, Richard (a shrewd manipulator of their limited funds) and John (like Allen an energetic and bold salesman). The three of them, generally against opposition from the rest of the board, worked hard to recover the former glories, and the former prosperity, of the firm. At the same time they set up in Talbot Square, London, a bachelors' residence which, if in a manner far from the staid elegance of Uncle John's Lancaster Gate Terrace, nevertheless perpetuated the salon-tradition. Here, at a series of hilarious parties, there came together many of the convivial in the new generation of writers, publishers, painters and artists.

Impatient with the timidity of their colleagues the Lanes decided to establish a private kingdom within the Bodley Head empire. Their first venture in this kind, a collection of cartoons by the American Peter Arno, could not be regarded as sensational even by those on the board who had some reason to doubt Allen's business acumen. Even so the board insisted that, though the Lanes could use the Bodley Head imprint and services, all losses must be born by the brothers. Allen countered by demanding all profits, and the profits were large. For its fears about the second venture, the publication for the first time in Britain of James Joyce's *Ulysses*, the opposition had some justice. Though this miraculous work had been acclaimed by critics from the day Harriet Weaver first published a few chapters in serial form in Paris, it had been suppressed, burnt and successfully prosecuted all over the world and Joyce had earned from it not one penny in royalties. The Bodley Head directors demanded a further surety; £20,000 against potential legal costs. The Lanes somehow found that money but still the board dragged its feet. When finally *Ulysses* was published, in October 1936, the Lanes had gone from the Bodley Head, set on their seminal adventure, the launching of Penguin Books.

There was in truth nothing original in the notion of producing books at a price which made them accessible to a vast readership. The experiment had been attempted many times and in many places during a century and a half, but no earlier pioneer had been so determined, so persistent or so original in his methods as was Allen Lane. Perhaps, too, none had been situated in a market so certainly prepared for this wondrous novelty as was Allen in a Britain made hungry for good books of all kinds in inexpensive form by an explosion of adult education.

Allen saw his chance and seized it, but against the opposition of most publishers (who forecast and prayed for his damnation), most booksellers (who foresaw no profit to themselves in the meagre returns on books sold at sixpence, if sold at all, and which otherwise wasted space on their shelves), and even authors (none other than George Orwell pronounced Penguins anathema, and the end of literature).

Somehow Allen scraped together a list of ten titles for reprinting as the first Penguins, still under the Bodley Head imprint. It was planned to print only 20,000 copies of each title; the break-even point for each title was estimated at 17,000-18,000 copies. He and his brothers stumped the country with a dummy copy of Eric Linklater's *Poet's Pub* (Penguin No 3). Advance orders from conventional booksellers were disappointing and it was not until Allen decided to go outside the customary market for books, to Woolworths, that the project was made viable. Woolworths ordered 63,000 copies, so that this order alone brought the first batch of Penguins within reach of breaking-even.

First Penguin Book to be published on 30 July 1935 (courtesy of Penguin Books Ltd).

On the August Bank Holiday of 1935, the first ten Penguins, headed by André Maurois' *Ariel*, appeared in the shops and immediately the response of the public confounded the gloomy (or hopeful) prognostications of the book-trade.

Penguin (the origin of the name is obscure and disputed but undoubtedly the choice had something to do with Allen's perennial wish to give his books 'dignified impertinence') became almost immediately too much for the Bodley Head to handle. For a while the relationship was ambiguous. Allen was still Bodley Head's managing director but he also took an office in Great Portland Street and storage space in the crypt of a nearby disused church. On New Year's Day 1936 the uneasy marriage was dissolved. With a capital of £100 (the product of an insurance claim for a burglary at Talbot Square) and with £5,000 borrowed from a brave and far-sighted manager of Martin's Bank, the firm of Penguin Books Ltd was established. Allen resigned from the Bodley Head, just before it went into liquidation.

From the outset Allen insisted on quality, not merely in editorial selection but also in the appearance of his books, and it was this insistence which granted to him, for the first time in the history of publishing, the advantage of selling 'by the mark'. The simple cover-design and the jolly colophon made a Penguin immediately identifiable and, immediately, the public came to recognise that, whether its author was famous or unknown, whether the subject-matter was popular or abstruse, anything that came from Penguin was worth sixpence, and probably much more.

Yet, though the history and success of Penguin must be measured from 1935, the most significant innovation came two years later, with the publication as a Penguin of a new edition of the *Intelligent Woman's Guide* by Bernard Shaw, an author who, rare among his fellows, had from the first recognised the seismic significance of Lane's infant venture. The possibilities inherent in commissioning new works for first-time publication by Penguin aroused Lane to establish a new series, Pelicans, composed of original and authoritative works on a multiplicity of subjects by scholars, some already famous, others whose fame would be founded, for the most part, on their inclusion in the Pelican list. From Pelicans there stemmed over the years a number of other notable series; among them Specials, Penguin Classics, The Buildings of Britain, and there followed also the handsome King Penguins, Penguin Pocket Scores, and, in a different kind but almost inevitably, books for children, Puffins and Puffin Picture Books. Throughout Lane's life, and still to an extent today, Penguin's emphasis on originals distinguished it from other paperback houses.

Just before the Second World War Lane set up a headquarters for his rapidly growing organisation some 15 miles west of the centre of London, at Harmondsworth. The new buildings were hardly occupied before they had to be evacuated to make room for a war-time operation.

The war years made phenomenal a success that was already considerable. Paper-rationing was calculated on pre-war production, and as Lane had published more titles than any other publisher and in much longer runs, and the authorities were conscious of the value of his books as morale-boosters, he never suffered as did others from shortage of paper. Even more significant to his immediate prosperity and to the long-term and especial affection in which the public held Penguins, hundreds of thousands of men and women, civilians at home and in the Services at home and abroad, deprived of most other forms of entertainment, took to reading and notably to the reading of Penguins. His books were portable, amenable to parcelling, and their variety and cheerful appearance gave to them a notable quality that helped to lighten the gloom and horror of war.

Lane himself worked tirelessly. Several of his small staff joined the Services, among them both his brothers (John was killed). Lane founded the Forces Book Club and a similar operation for the Canadians. He travelled widely. Like many another book-publisher before him, he moved into periodical-publishing, and particularly with *Penguin New Writing* (edited by John Lehmann), made of it, for the moment at least, a mainspring of literary influence.

Already before the war Lane had been accused of Left-Wing sympathies, and the Penguin Special list above all had served to support this notion. But it is likely that he and his senior editors were old-fashioned radicals and that he was less concerned with any political dogma than with the conviction that the reading public was intelligent and ready to accept any form of enlightenment, however unpopular or unconventional so long as it was presented with clarity and, if possible, with elegance. Nevertheless, Clement Attlee commented that his road to Downing Street was paved with Penguins, Pelicans and Penguin Specials.

The decade that followed the war was Penguin's golden era. As yet Lane had few imitators, and hence little competition. In Britain his only effective rival was Pan Books, and Pan piped an editorial tune so utterly dissimilar that the two could live happily in the same market. In the United States in 1937 Robert de Graff had emulated Lane with his Pocket Books and, during the war, he had been followed by several other imitators, three of them fugitives from Penguin. Yet there was, even in America, still room for Penguin Books Inc (set up as Allen Lane Inc in 1949) and all over the English-reading world (as occasionally in areas using other languages) Lane set up his outposts — in Australia where Penguin Books Proprietary Ltd was established in 1946 with lasting success. Subsidiaries in Canada and South Africa were less successful, and had both ceased trading by the end of 1958.

Lane's bold editorial policies in this period were epitomised in 1949 by the publication of the first Penguin Million: ten volumes of Shaw, each in editions of 100,000 copies, published in one day, Shaw's ninetieth birthday. This was followed by several other Millions. One, the D H Lawrence Million published in 1960, brought down upon Lane a prosecution for publishing an obscene book. The *Lady Chatterley* case served to enshrine his reputation, and to sell several millions of a title for which he had ordered a run of only 150,000. Even an antagonistic judge could not but recognise the integrity and distinguished reputation of Penguin: Lane was excused the humiliation of sitting in the dock. And thousands who had never before heard of either Lawrence or Lane followed the case as if it were the Cup Final, and then bought the book.

Between 1951 and 1960, annual sales increased from 9.8 million books to over 17 million, from £592,000 to £1,588,000. While sales had risen steadily, profits had been less secure. Despite increased retail prices, profits before tax had fluctuated, reaching their lowest point in 1951 (£19,471), and their highest in 1957 (£135,372), apart from the record £288,096 of 1960, for which *Lady Chatterley's Lover* could take much of the credit. It was only about 1960 that Lane came to appreciate the potential financial success of his firm. He began to consider turning Penguin into a public company. First, however, in March 1961 the authorised share capital of the private company was increased from £262,500 to £500,000, and Lane's brother Dick sold his 43,750 £1 ordinary shares to Allen for £220,000. The following month, Penguin became a public company, and 690,000 4s ordinary shares were offered to the public at 12s each, with a further 60,000 shares reserved for the 270 employees. Lane himself held 1,275,000 4s ordinary shares (a further 475,000 were held by trustees for his daughters), and he had a contract to serve the new company as chairman and managing director for seven years. His control of Penguin had hardly diminished.

By this time, however, Lane himself was tiring. The business was now too complex to be directed, as virtually it had been previously, by one man. Lane was prepared to delegate but only to a degree. Whenever, by his own decision, one collaborator threatened to become too powerful he somehow rid himself of the potential rival to his hegemony. The situation was further confused by Lane's reluctance to establish a succession to his throne. In June 1941 he married Lettice, the daughter of Sir Charles Orr, a distinguished Colonial official, and they had three daughters. But Lane could not accept a girl as heir-apparent, or for that matter anyone else. Many times he brought in a Prince of Wales, often chosen after consulting astrologers and graphologists. None lasted more than a few months.

Penguin was also faced by heightened competition. The paperback revolution which he had begun now threatened his downfall as dozens of hardback publishers, reluctant to see all the fat from their efforts going into Lane's store, set up their own paperback lists. Lane attempted to stem the tide against him by making deals with hardback publishers for the first choice of reprints from their lists. To a considerable extent, his Penguins had already replaced text-books in schools and colleges. Now he founded a Penguin educational list.

In the 1960s schisms within the firm further unsettled the Lane empire. The most sensational was a dispute about cover-designs. Lane had always held to the doctrine that clean design was no less integral to Penguin philosophy than sound editorial selection, and indeed his contribution to public awareness of design in all kinds was no less important than his gift to general literacy. Now, or so argued his adjutants, in order to meet the competition Penguins must follow the example of those same competitors and appear, as Lane put it, 'decorated with bosoms and bottoms'. For the first time in Penguin history, Allen Lane: King Penguin was defeated by his courtiers.

His health was failing but not yet his energy. In an act that was not uncharacteristically sentimental (for he was, despite his ruthlessness, much given to sentimental gestures) he founded a hardback firm, called with nostalgic echoes Allen Lane: The Penguin Press, and with its offices in the building where he had begun his career with John Lane: The Bodley Head. At last (though the final act was not sealed until his death) he conceded virtual control of Penguin to S Pearson & Co (who already owned the publishing house of Longman, with which he had an alliance). Just before his death in 1970, S Pearson & Co bought Penguin for £15 million.

Lane was knighted in 1952 and in 1969 he was made a Companion of Honour. He died on 7 July 1970, leaving an estate proved at £1,216,474 gross.

Ebullient, devious, ruthless, and yet at times unbelievably benevolent, Lane in his life-time made a lunatic-seeming venture into a national and international institution. Against competition from new and pervasive forms of communication he made the book, for the first time in its history, one of the mass-media. He pioneered a world-wide revolution that made literacy and book ownership accessible to millions. More than any other individual, he changed the face of formal and informal education. He was the authentic original book-publisher of his generation, and of this century. He was perhaps the most-respected, the most-imitated, the most-hated and, perversely, the most-loved publisher, of our century.

J E MORPURGO

Sources:

Unpublished

BCe.

MCe.

PrC.

Published

DNB.

J E Morpurgo, *Paperbacks Across Frontiers* (Bowater, 1962).

—, *Allen Lane: King Penguin* (Hutchinson, 1979).

Penguins Progress (Harmondsworth: Penguin, 1960).

C H Rolf, *The Trial of Lady Chatterley* (Penguin, 1960).

Edmond Segrave, *Ten Years of Penguins* (Harmondsworth: Penguin, 1945).

Times 8 July 1970.

Times *Prospectuses* 128 (1961).

William E Williams, *The Penguin Story 1945-56* (Harmondsworth: Penguin, 1956).

—, *Allen Lane: A Memoir* (Bodley Head, 1973).

WWW.

LANE, Frederick

(1851-1926)

Shipbroker and oilman

It is not known exactly when and where Frederick (usually known as Fred) Lane was born and nothing is known of his family or of his education. His early career was in a London shipbroker's business. In the early 1880s Lane and a colleague went into business on their own, establishing the firm of Messrs Lane & MacAndrew. The firm specialised in shipping kerosene oil. In 1884 Lane chartered a tanker to bring a cargo of Russian oil to London — the first delivery to Britain by bulk tanker. He became closely associated with the French Rothschilds, who had recently acquired large oilfields in Russia and formed an oil company, the Société Commerciale de Naphte Caspienne et de la Mer Noire, known as BNITO (from its Russian initials), and he was soon playing the leading role in BNITO's export strategy.

Perhaps the essence of Lane's success lay in his astute perception of business opportunities, combined with his ability to act as an intermediary between various interests. Lane was widely regarded as completely honest and fair, and this reputation helped him over the two decades after 1885 to arrange a series of increasingly important business transactions which made a fundamental impact on the European oil industry. In 1890 he approached Marcus Samuel (qv), a London Jewish merchant who had participated in a syndicate with Wallace Bros and Jardine Matheson which had marketed BNITO case oil in the Far East, with the radical proposal to market Russian oil in bulk in tankers instead of in cases. This method would make the oil sufficiently cheap to break the monopoly of Standard Oil of the United States. After investigating the matter, Samuel was persuaded, and in 1891 Lane arranged a supply contract between the French Rothschilds and Samuel. A large trade was soon established, and on this basis the Shell Transport & Trading Co was founded in 1897. Lane was one of the original directors.

Lane's involvement in the petroleum industry deepened after 1897. He had organised two oil distribution companies, the Kerosene Co and the Tank Storage & Carriage Co, for the French Rothschilds in Britain in the late 1880s, and he carried this work further in 1897 with the formation of the Anglo-Caucasian Petroleum Co. An important new development came in the summer of 1901, when Lane met Henri Deterding, the dynamic manager of the Royal Dutch Petroleum Co. They were deeply impressed with each other: Deterding later described Lane as the cleverest man he had ever met. In 1902 Lane brought together the Royal Dutch, Shell Transport and the Rothschilds into a marketing alliance in the East, an arrangement formalised by the setting-up of the Asiatic Petroleum Co in London in 1903. Lane was appointed the English representative of the Rothschilds on the board of the Asiatic. He had already resigned from the board of Shell Transport at the end of 1902, having lost patience with its managerial amateurism. From 1903 Lane was closely allied with Deterding, though he remained friends with Samuel.

In the next few years Lane's influence was at its height. His role as BNITO's agent for the British Empire, as well as his close relations with Deterding, gave him a unique position in the European oil industry. In 1906 he pulled off his two greatest coups. On the Continent, he united the Rothschild, Nobel and Deutsche Bank oil interests in a giant marketing cartel, the European Petroleum Union (EPU). Lane became a director of the British Petroleum Co, the United Kingdom marketing company founded by the EPU. However, it was Lane's key role in the merger negotiations between Shell Transport and Royal Dutch in 1906 which was to prove of the greatest significance for the British oil industry. By the end of the year it was agreed that the two companies would be united, with the Dutch having a 60 per cent interest and Deterding in complete control. Deterding subsequently remarked about the merger that 'he could not have done it without Lane' {Jones (1981) 30}.

After 1906, Lane became a director of Asiatic and Shell companies operating in several countries. He was involved in forming companies for the exploitation of oil in, among other places, Trinidad and Russia. Lane facilitated the Shell Group's entry into the lubricating oil trade of Western Europe by arranging the Group's purchase of the Schibaieff Petroleum Co. He was one of the three original directors of the 'sGravenhage Association, a syndicate formed in 1912 including the Shell Group and the French Rothschilds, with the aim of buying oil lands in Illinois and Oklahoma. He facilitated Shell's purchase of the Rothschilds' Russian interests in 1912, and he played a role in the negotiations aimed at winning an oil concession in Mesopotamia. He became a director of the Turkish Petroleum Co when it was formed in 1912. Meanwhile, the firm of Lane & MacAndrew continued to expand. In 1912 the firm chartered 80 per cent of the total tank steamer tonnage chartered throughout the world.

After 1906 Lane also began to interest himself in the development of the diesel engine. The pioneering work done in Germany on the internal combustion engine attracted relatively little interest in Britain. British shipbuilders in particular were wedded to the steam engine, and left the adaptation of the diesel engine to marine propulsion to others. Lane was appalled by this parochialism. He watched the development of the diesel engine on the Continent at first hand, and determined as a hobby, as he told a Royal Commission in 1912, to push the oil engine in Britain. In Russia he had been impressed by the use of diesel-engined oil tankers on the Caspian and Volga Seas. In 1909 he persuaded the Shell Group to order a small ocean-going tanker with diesel engines, which was built in Holland (subsequent orders were placed at British shipyards). Lane wrote to trade journals advocating the new type of engine, and in 1913 he promoted the formation of a diesel-making firm, the North British Diesel Engine Co, with a capital of £1 million and a factory on the Clyde. He used his Continental contacts to purchase the British rights to Krupps' diesel engines, and before the war the factory began the manufacture of two stroke-cycle diesel engines.

After 1914 Lane began to take a less active role in the oil industry. However, he advised the Admiralty on the running of their tanker fleet during the First World War, and he continued to function as the French Rothschilds' special oil representative. In this capacity he participated in the liquidation of the old Asiatic Petroleum Co in 1919, when Deterding bought out the Rothschilds' interests in the company. Lane retired from active business about the middle of 1921, and went to live in Norfolk, where he became involved in charitable work. He died on 24 September 1926 at the age of seventy-five, leaving two sons and a daughter. He left an estate valued at £571,510 gross.

Lane exercised an enormous influence on the development of the British and European oil industries before 1914. Brilliant, imaginative, phenomenally hard-working, an entrepreneurial risk-taker par excellence, Lane was described many years after his death by another oilman, Calouste Gulbenkian, as the father of the British oil industry, yet he always remained, said Gulbenkian, a modest man who never coveted honours or any fame.

GEOFFREY JONES

Writings:

letter to *Petroleum World* Sept 1912.

Sources:

Unpublished

Archives Nationales, Paris, Rothschild Archives.

PRO, ADM 116 120, 819, evidence of Frederick Lane to RC on Fuel and Power 1912-13.

Shell Group Archives, London and the Hague.

DCe.

PrC.

Published

Sir Henri Deterding, *An International Oilman* (Ivor Nicholson & Watson, 1934).

Frederik C Gerretson, *History of the Royal Dutch* (4 vols, Leiden: E J Brill, 1953-57).

Robert Henriques, *Marcus Samuel, First Viscount Bearsted and Founder of the 'Shell' Transport and Trading Company 1853-1927* (Rockliff, 1960).

Geoffrey Jones, 'The Oil Fuel Market in Britain 1900-1914: A Lost Cause Revisited' *Business History* 20 (1978).

—, *The State and the Emergence of the British Oil Industry* (Macmillan, 1981).

Oil and Petroleum Manual 1910-26.

Petroleum Times 9 Oct 1926.

LASCELLES, William Henry

(1832-1885)

Builder and pioneer of prefabricated concrete construction

W H Lascelles, photograph by Lombardi & Co (courtesy of Miss Helen Brooks).

William Henry Lascelles was born in Exeter in 1832, the second of four children of Henry Lascelles and his wife Sarah née Hutchings. The Lascelles were a well-known Exeter family; a direct ancestor was Master of the Worshipful Company of Weavers, Fullers and Shearmen of Exeter in 1792. Henry served his apprenticeship as a fuller, receiving his indentures in 1828, but the serge trade was waning and in 1845 his son, William Henry, was apprenticed by the Company under 'Crispin's Charity' to John James White, a local joiner.

In 1852, now a journeyman carpenter, Lascelles left Exeter for London and joined Cubitt & Co in Gray's Inn Lane as a builder's clerk, soon rising to foreman. After two years he moved to Newman & Mann of 12 Peter's Hill, EC (builders) and in 1856 he joined the well-established firm of Charles William Waterlow, high-class joiners and horticultural builders, 121 Bunhill Row, Finsbury. He must have felt this to be a secure position for at St Sidwell's Church, Exeter, on 7 June 1856, he married Mary Hill Pollard, a dressmaker, daughter of a local innkeeper.

In December 1859 the senior partner of Waterlows retired and the firm was sold up. Lascelles, with Alexander Clerihew, a foreman, continued the business under the name of Clerihew & Lascelles, Finsbury Steam Joinery Works, but early in 1861 Clerihew died and Lascelles found himself, at twenty-nine, the sole owner of the firm.

During the next ten years he concentrated first on efficiency in his workshops, his ingenuity enabling him to adapt many of his woodworking machines to produce finer, more intricate and meticulous work. Industrious, inventive and a shrewd business man, Lascelles expanded the firm (reputedly the oldest piece-work house in the trade), increased his work-force, changed the name to W H Lascelles and then established himself as a builder.

In 1870 he registered his first patent, 'an improved construction of Office Table' where articles stored within the frame could be brought to hand without disturbing the writer. In 1872 he erected a new office building with showrooms at Bunhill Row, much publicised for the incorporation of a fully glazed vinery which covered the entire roof area; anticipating his second patent in 1874 for 'constructing steamed curvilinear wooden framings for the roofs of horticultural structures'. A prototype conservatory was erected for a Croydon nurseryman.

During 1872 the family moved to 'Middleheath', Sydenham Road, Croydon, an old house with a long garden and much undeveloped land in the vicinity. A keen horticulturist himself, he erected curved-wood lean-to temperate and tropical plant houses round three sides of his garden. Although he never exhibited professionally his plant houses were much visited and well known in horticultural circles.

By 1873, and now a builder of repute, Lascelles had become one of the most favoured contractors of the foremost domestic architect of the day, Richard Norman Shaw, for whom he built 'Hopedene' at Holmbury St Mary, Surrey (1873-75) and many London houses including Lowther Lodge (1873-75), now the Royal Geographical Society, and Shaw's own house in Ellerdale Road, Hampstead (1875-76).

Whilst building for the rich, Lascelles became acutely aware of the need for cheaper and faster building methods to provide housing for the working classes. He had long had an interest in concrete and in 1875 he devised and patented an entirely new method of house construction using pre-cast concrete slabs screwed to a timber framework. The slabs, 3 feet by 2 feet by 1.25 inches, composed of crushed coke and Portland cement and faced with a fine concrete, stained red, were cast in wood moulds, the face fashioned to simulate hung tiles. Screwed at the corners to a timber frame with uprights 3 feet apart, this cladding formed both outer and inner walls, while plain surfaced slabs, laid on a network of wood beams, served as ground floor ceiling and bedroom floor combined.

Lascelles invited Shaw to make sketches for the module and proceeded to build experimental cottages near his home in Croydon after overcoming early disapproval by the local Board of Health.

In 1877 his last patent, also using red concrete, concerned bricks, blocks and tiles, ornamented or plain, cast in moulds and thus eliminating the distortion caused by firing.

28 sketches, signed R Norman Shaw RA, were published by W H Lascelles on 1 May 1878, the opening day of the Paris International Exhibition. Two hundred tons of exhibits, including concrete slabs and bricks, were transported to Paris. Two of the Shaw/Lascelles concrete slab houses were erected and the 'Jury House', with a 'Queen Anne' facade, also by Shaw, was built by Lascelles using plain and ornamental red concrete bricks. Among Lascelles's many exhibits were furniture designed by Shaw and a spectacular dome-shaped conservatory, using his patent curvilinear steamed-wood framing. Both Shaw and Lascelles were awarded the Cross of the Légion d'Honneur for their contributions to the Exhibition.

Lascelles was invited several times to the Royal Institute of British Architects to describe (with examples) his slab construction and his works were visited twice (1877 and 1881) by members of the Architectural Association. He exhibited at the Sanitary Congress at Croydon in 1879 and at the Building Trades Exhibition in 1881, 1882, and 1883.

He continued to build in Croydon, now pairs of houses 'of a better sort', with cavity walls (slabs on both sides of the timbers) and containing the firm's excellent joinery, the last pair as exhibition show houses (1882).

His health was now declining and in a 'farewell' letter to the *Builder* in 1882 he announced his partial retirement. Summing up his experience over thirty-seven years in the industry he wrote that he agreed with trade unions, believed in compromise, had never had a strike, and considered that 'no body of men ever worked harder or did a fairer day's work than the British workman at the present time' {*Builder* 21 Oct 1882}. In spite of his failing health he gave evidence to the Royal Commission on Working Class Housing in 1884.

Lascelles's eldest daughter, Mary, died in 1875 (aged fifteen), and the death of his only son, William in 1883 (aged twenty-six) affected him deeply. He died at home on 25 October 1885 at the early age of fifty-three. He was buried at Croydon Cemetery. His wife and two daughters, Minnie and Amy, survived him. He left an estate valued at £17,776 gross.

HELEN BROOKS

Writings:

letter on foreign joiners' work in England *Builder* 4 Dec 1869.

'Wooden Curvilinear Conservatories' *Garden* 7 Nov 1874.

comments on Alexander Payne, 'Concrete as a Building Material' *Transactions of the Royal Institute of British Architects* 26 (1876).

letter on glass roofs for London *Builder* 16 Dec 1876.

letter on scarcity of cottages in Ipswich *ibid* 30 Dec 1876.

Sketches for Cottages and Other Buildings Designed to Be Constructed in the Patent Cement Slab System of W H Lascelles from Sketches and Notes by R Norman Shaw RA (W H Lascelles, 121 Bunhill Row EC, 1 May 1878).

comments on Arthur Cates, 'Concrete and Fire Resisting Construction' *Transactions of the Royal Institute of British Architects* 28 (1878).

letter on fireproof floors *Builder* 3 Nov 1879.

letter on waterproof roofs *ibid* 22 Nov 1879.

letter on weatherproof walls *ibid* 8 Dec 1879.

letter on the treatment of concrete *ibid* 8 Apr 1882.

letters about house building *ibid* 20, 27 May 1882.

letter about peach growing *ibid* 1 July 1882.

letter about employers and employed *ibid* 21 Oct 1882.

PP, RC on the Housing of the Working Classes (1884-85) C4402.

British Patents:

1870 (3,276)
1874 (2,324)
1875 (2,151)
1877 (1,535)

Sources:

Published

Builder 31 Oct 1885.

Building News 30 Oct 1885.

'Concrete Houses' Croydon Local Board of Health Report *Croydon Chronicle* 14 Aug, 11 Sept 1875.

LASCELLES William Henry

'Concrete Slab Cottages' *Builder* 14 Aug 1875.

Beatrix E Cresswell, *History of the Weavers, Fullers and Shearmen of Exeter* (Exeter: William Pollard & Co, 1930).

Croydon Advertiser 31 Oct 1885.

Croydon Chronicle 31 Oct 1885.

Everyday Uses of Portland Cement (The Associated Portland Cement Manufacturers (1900) Ltd, 2nd ed, 1912).

'The Finsbury Steam Joinery Works' *Building News* 23 Mar 1877, *Builder* 24 Mar 1877.

Garden 31 Oct 1885.

Gardener's Chronicle 31 Oct 1885.

'Housetop Conservatories' *Building News* 20 Feb 1874.

Journal of Horticulture and Cottage Gardener 5 Nov 1885.

'Jury House. Paris Exhibition' *Building News* 14 June 1878.

Samuel Knight, 'The Influence of Business Requirements on Street Architecture' *Transactions of the Royal Institute of British Architects* 27 (1876).

'Livre d'or W H Lascelles' *Paris Exhibition of 1878 Illustrated Weekly Review. English Edition* 12 (7 Feb 1879).

'Mr Lascelles' Housetop Garden' *The Garden* 31 Jan 1874.

'Mr Lascelles's Specialities in Concrete Building and Decoration' *Builder* 21 May 1881.

'Mr Ley's Nursery, Croydon' *The Garden* 17 Oct 1874.

A E J Morris, *Precast Concrete in Architecture. W H Lascelles and 'Improvements in the Construction of Buildings' 1875* (Godwin, 1978).

'Ninety-year-old Precast System' 1882. Croydon Houses in Patent Slab Construction *Concrete* 6 No 4 (Apr 1972).

Andrew Saint, *Richard Norman Shaw* (Yale University Press, 1976).

George A Sala, *Paris Herself Again 1878-79* (2 vols, Remington & Co, 1880) 2.

'Sanitary Congress, Croydon' *Croydon Advertiser* 1 Nov 1879.

'Two Old Bridges and Three Ancient Houses' *Concrete* 7 No 4 (Apr 1973).

'A Visit to Mr Lascelles' Works' *Building News* 20 May 1881.

Edward Bryan Latham (courtesy of Mr E Michael Latham).

LATHAM, Edward Bryan

(1895-1980)

Timber merchant

Edward Bryan Latham was born in Walthamstow, on 7 May 1895, the eldest son of Edward Locks Latham (1865-1951), timber merchant, and Emily née Chappell, the daughter of a London tailor. The family consisted of two daughters and three sons, Bryan (as Edward Bryan was known), Russell and Douglas.

Lathams had grown in the two homes of the English timber trade, London and Liverpool. The first James Latham established himself as a dealer in exotic hardwoods in Liverpool in 1757. His son Henry moved to London at the end of the eighteenth century, shortly before the opening of the West India Docks, and by mid-century the firm was firmly established in the timber trading business in Shoreditch, East London. The large Latham families ensured that there was no shortage of recruits for what has always been a quintessentially family concern. Bryan Latham's father joined the firm in 1881 and was occupied with his father in handling the growing hardwood business and in supervising the various sawmills and wharves. The firm adopted limited liability in 1900, with the title James Latham Ltd.

Bryan was educated at Felsted School, Essex, and though he showed some desire to continue his studies, his father brought him into the business in 1912. A year later he was joined by his brother, Russell. At the outbreak of the First World War, Bryan fought in France, won the MM, and was then commissioned in the Tower Hamlets Rifles. Bryan and Russell, both demobilised in 1919, promptly rejoined the firm, and were appointed directors in 1921, under the chairmanship of their father.

Thereafter the company entered upon a decade of profitable business. An interest was acquired in a number of logging concessions in Nigeria, and later these areas were consolidated into a subsidiary, the Nigerian Hardwood Co Ltd. The Nigerian connection ensured that the firm was in the forefront of one of the most important timber developments after the war, the introduction of decorative timbers from colonial forests. In the inter-war period the company also established itself in the wholesale plywood trade by developing a new site at Mount Pleasant Hill on the River Lea. Lathams had a considerable interest in the veneer trade, supplying not only veneers but also veneered panels, and shortly before the Second World War it bought the veneer business of Richard Graefe Ltd at High Wycombe, a major centre of the furniture-making industry.

The outbreak of war in 1939 seriously depleted the five-man Latham board. After mobilisation Bryan and his father remained to run affairs, while Russell left to work at the Timber Control, which was responsible for the direction of the industry in wartime. It was a period of great activity. Lathams, now firmly situated in Mount Pleasant Hill, Clapton,

Aerial view of James Latham Ltd, Mount Pleasant Hill, Clapton, London ca 1960 showing the company's timber yards and warehouses on the River Lea (courtesy of James Latham Ltd).

after the closing of the Shoreditch premises, were heavily involved in the manufacture of aircraft plywood: with government encouragement a factory for its manufacture was set up at the Mahtal Works, High Wycombe. In 1942 the firm acquired the old-established home-grown timber business of Rowland Bros of Bletchley.

After the war Lathams, with the return of the board members, was reconstituted and reorganised to cope with the upsurge in demand for hardwoods, following the lifting of government restrictions. In 1947 Bryan toured the USA and Canada to reopen the channels of trade which the company had enjoyed with its North American suppliers. After his father's death in 1951, Bryan Latham was made chairman of both James Latham Ltd and the Nigerian Hardwood Co Ltd, with Russell as deputy chairman of the former and Douglas as deputy chairman of the latter. James F Latham also played a considerable part in the activities of the board.

The final years of Bryan Latham's chairmanship were a period of both consolidation and expansion of James Latham Ltd and its subsidiaries.

Notable features included the mechanisation of the Leeside, Middlesex, and Mahtal Wharves; the maintenance of the firm's output from Nigeria, despite political changes; and the introduction of bonus incentive schemes to increase productivity. Upon Bryan's retirement from the business in March 1971, Douglas Latham took over until 1973, when Michael Latham, Bryan's eldest son who had joined the firm in 1948, succeeded.

Bryan Latham was closely involved with the national organisation of the industry. Following in his father's footsteps, he held successively the offices of chairman of the London Sawmill Association, 1940-42; chairman of the National Sawmilling Association, 1942-43; chairman of the then Timber Development Association, 1943-45, later being elected a vice-president and, in 1973, president of its successor the Timber Research and Development Association; vice-president of the Timber Trade Federation of the United Kingdom, 1943-45, then its president, 1945-47. In 1944 he was elected to the Council of the Commonwealth Forestry Association of which he later became chairman, and in 1948 joined the Council of the Timber Trades Benevolent Society, subsequently being elected president. Interested in developing the scientific side of timber production he became founder-chairman of the Institute of Wood Science in 1956-58, and a member of the Furniture and Timber Training Board, 1965-71. He was appointed a Forestry Commissioner in 1957, serving until 1963. He was made a CBE in 1964.

He maintained a life-long interest in education, and regretted that in his younger days he had been unable to attend university. After his retirement he graduated BA (Hons) in history and social studies from the Open University in 1974. He was a contributor to various forestry and wood journals, such as the *Timber Trades Journal*. He found time to write two books on the development of the industry in which his family had played so prominent a role, and also a history of the Timber Trade Federation. His interest in collecting Victorian Staffordshire portrait figures led him to write a short study of the subject.

In 1927 he married Anne Arnot Duncan, the daughter of an Edinburgh auctioneer. They had two sons, Michael and Christopher, the former the present chairman of the company. Bryan Edward Latham died in Plymouth on 7 February 1980, leaving £199,449 gross.

GEOFFREY TWEEDALE

Writings:

Victorian Staffordshire Portrait Figures for the Small Collector (Alec Tiranti, 1953).

Timber, Its Development and Distribution. An Historical Survey (George G Harrap, 1957).

Wood from Forest to Man (George G Harrap, 1964).

History of the Timber Trade Federation of the United Kingdom. The First Seventy Years (Ernest Benn Ltd, 1965).

Sources:

Unpublished

Private information from Michael Latham.

Published

John L Oliver, *The Development and Structure of the Furniture Industry* (Oxford: Pergamon Press, 1966).

Times 12, 28 Feb, 21 Mar 1980.

WWW.

LATHAM, Sir Thomas Paul

(1855-1931)

Silk and rayon manufacturer

Thomas Paul Latham was born at Chorlton, Lancashire, on 19 June 1855, the son of Samuel Latham of Manchester and his wife Ann née Barlow. After education at Manchester Commercial School and Manchester Grammar School, he went to work in textiles and became in time a salesman and agent for various firms including the big Yorkshire firm of Lister & Co and the Essex-based silk business, Samuel Courtauld & Co. In 1893 the directors of the latter firm, recently converted into a private limited liability company, were actively seeking new managerial talent to revive what had become a rather moribund family business. They engaged H G Tetley (qv), then head of the silk manufacturing department at Lister's Manningham Mills. He in turn brought in Latham, who in January 1894 was appointed sales manager of S Courtauld & Co at a salary of £1,250 per annum plus an annual commission of 0.75 per cent on all business in excess of that of 1893. In 1895 Tetley became a director of the company; in 1898 so did Latham. For a quarter of a century after their appointments these two men totally dominated the Courtauld business.

During the first decade of his work at S Courtauld & Co Latham was mainly concerned with trying to improve the company's flagging sales of silk mourning crape (the staple and very profitable output of the firm until the market for it collapsed in the early 1890s) and to push its new lines of coloured silks, chiffons, crêpe de chine, and the like. He had some limited success with the former, especially in promoting exports to continental Europe, particularly France, and the USA; and considerable success with the latter, the value of the sales of coloured fabrics rising from approximately £10,000 to £250,000 over the period 1894-1904, with the bulk of them going to the home market. Despite these advances the company's general profitability remained much lower than it had been in the 1870s and 1880s, though it was financially sound. In search of a new source of profit Tetley persuaded his fellow directors to buy the patent rights for the viscose process of making rayon — 'artificial silk' as it was then called. After a successful flotation of the business as a public company, this was done in 1904. In this venture Latham supported Tetley against the views of a minority of their older colleagues and the two of them became the managing directors of the new company. By 1911 the main technical and organisational problems at the new factory in Coventry had been overcome, much of the credit being due to the manager there, Harry Johnson (qv), and Latham was increasingly shifting his attention to marketing the new rayon yarn.

Between 1906 and 1912 the value of the company's yarn sales rose from approximately £7,500 to £686,000. In the process Latham's commission rose from a mere £1,319 in 1906 to no less than £43,966 in 1912. Although Courtauld & Co had a UK monopoly of the viscose process, these sales were achieved in competition not only with natural fibres but with the two main existing types of rayon yarns produced, mainly in France and Germany, by the nitrocellulose and cuprammonium processes. Viscose yarn soon proved to be better suited for weaving than its rivals, which were much used for braids and trimmings. The network of agents already marketing the company's textiles helped in yarn sales; in addition, new agents were appointed specially to market yarn in the textile towns of the Midlands and North and, in 1908, in the USA. Latham attended to all these commercial matters: it was he who appointed agents, arranged terms of sales, advised on the creditworthiness of jobbers and dealers, and considered the appropriate levels of prices. As viscose yarn proved its weaving superiority over its rivals Latham made sure that full advantage was taken of this sellers' market, pursuing discriminatory pricing techniques and getting, in effect, monopoly prices whenever possible. It was Latham, too, who made representations to the Government over tariffs, and, most important, worked with Tetley to get inside the US tariff and to bring about the purchase in 1909 of the US viscose patent rights in order to start manufacturing in America. With the successful launch of the American subsidiary, Latham pursued similar lines of commercial policy there. An international consortium of rayon producers had by this time come into being and Courtauld & Co were members of it, but they could afford to be fairly indifferent to their competitors. Latham's approach is clearly evident in a letter which he wrote to the American agent in 1911:

> ... as the position is one of great strength, the consortium production for a considerable period forward being very largely sold, we have decided against import of viscose yarn at less than Coventry rates ...
>
> We shall be glad of a report ... as to the possibility of advancing Coventry rates by say 3d per lb without too serious disturbance ... {Coleman (1969) II, 115}.

On the reorganisation of the company into Courtaulds Ltd in 1913, Tetley and Latham between them held 18.5 per cent of the £2 million equity of the new company. They remained as managing directors, with Latham increasingly taking major decisions on financial and organisational as well as commercial matters. When Tetley became chairman in 1917, Latham appropriately became deputy chairman, and when Tetley died in 1921 the chairmanship was offered to Latham. He declined it, however, and relinquished the deputy chairmanship but remained on the board for another decade. Henceforth he attended meetings, with some decline in frequency, was consulted and advised especially on overseas matters, but took little or no active part in the running of the business.

Latham's partnership with Tetley provides a classic example of the successful co-operation of opposites. The noisy, vigorous, bullying, innovative Tetley was matched by a quiet, tactful, reserved and efficient Latham. The latter showed no particular mark of originality; he followed generally middle-of-the-road courses; his actions were shrewd but cautious. Without Tetley, Latham would probably have been very competent and effective but little more; on the other hand he may well have prevented Tetley from blundering into disaster. In the business Latham was reputed to have combined meanness with a certain charm of manner which undoubtedly had value in negotiations. On more than one occasion he calmed down those ruffled by Tetley and was expert in deploying soothing phrases in courteous letters. His business life brought him wealth and he used it to buy social status for his family, to whom he was said to be generous. While Tetley remained little loved and little known outside business, the more personally agreeable Latham acquired a baronetcy in 1919, nominally for public and local services particularly in the Ministry of Pensions, though there is nothing to suggest that his role therein was of any particular consequence.

In 1888 Latham married Florence Clara Walley, daughter of William Henry Walley, a solicitor, of Manchester. They had one son and two daughters. Sir Thomas Latham died on 26 October 1931, leaving £778,504 gross. The baronetcy passed to his son Herbert Paul.

D C COLEMAN

Sources:

Unpublished

BCe.

MCe.

PrC.

Published

Donald C Coleman, *Courtaulds. An Economic and Social History* (3 vols, Oxford: Clarendon Press, 1969-80).

Debrett.

Times 27 Oct 1931.

WWW.

LAVERTON, Abraham

(1819-1886)

Woollen manufacturer

Abraham Laverton was born at Trowbridge, Wiltshire, in 1819, the third son of a master weaver whose forebears, some of them in the cloth trade, came from Shepton Mallet in Somerset. One of his first cousins was Sir Isaac Pitman (qv), the inventor of phonography and the founder of an important printing and publishing firm in Bath, while one of his brothers founded a leading furniture-making concern in Bristol.

Laverton first worked in Edgells' Trowbridge cloth factory where he was a clerk. In 1838 he moved to Frome to work for the much larger clothmaking firm of Sheppards, which soon promoted him to the responsible post of manager of their kerseymere department.

Abraham Laverton's move to Westbury, the scene of his work as an independent manufacturer, came in 1849, in which year he bought the fine late Georgian Angel Mill, first used for finishing cloth but later employed as a flour mill. Laverton used it again for the making of woollen cloth, and in 1856 he bought the older Bitham Mill, not far away in the same town, using both buildings for the making of high-quality cloth; for a few years Laverton also operated a third cloth mill, also near Westbury.

What distinguished Laverton's operation as a cloth manufacturer was his insistence on high-quality production; this won his firm high awards in the London Exhibition of 1862 and at Paris in 1867. He had also exhibited in the Great Exhibition of 1851, laying emphasis on his determination to improve and invent. He was one of the founders of the trade in 'broad fancy coatings' which soon became a prominent feature in the output of the woollen industry. Unlike some contemporary makers of West of England cloth he was always ready both to install up-to-date machinery and to extend his buildings in his two mills at Westbury, when this became necessary.

Abraham Laverton's great wealth cannot, however, be explained solely by his activity in the cloth trade. At Westbury his interests were by no means confined to his cloth mills. He was a shareholder in, and a director of, the Westbury Gas Works and of the important Iron Works which in his time flourished at Westbury thanks to the presence of ironstone deposits less than two miles away. He was the proprietor of a brick, tile and pottery works at Westbury and he was a substantial shareholder in the Great Western Railway which served Westbury, Frome and Trowbridge. His local interests also extended to agriculture and he owned a large farm at Sutton Veny near Warminster.

Laverton's interests, financial and otherwise, in railways formed a large part of his business activity, bringing him into contact, as a co-director and also as a parliamentary colleague, with one of the most ambitious and dynamic of Victorian businessmen. One of Laverton's obituary notices made the point that he engaged in speculation in the money market and especially in railway shares. A railway in which he had a large holding, with £66,000 of its ordinary stock in 1874, was the Manchester, Sheffield & Lincolnshire (later extended to London and renamed the Great Central) whose chairman, Sir Edward Watkin (qv), has been described as the last of the 'railway kings'. The dividend record of the MS&LR was always poor, and Laverton's interest in it could never have added much to his income. But from 1874 until his death Laverton was one of this railway's directors, this being the period when the MS&LR made important additions to the docks at Grimsby, and when it was largely responsible for the development of neighbouring Cleethorpes as a seaside resort. The 1880s also included the first scheme for the MS&LR's London extension and for its link, via the Metropolitan Railway of which Watkin was chairman and in which Laverton had shares, to the South Eastern Railway (another concern of which Watkin was chairman) and hence via Watkin's favoured project of the Channel Tunnel, to the French railways and so to Paris.

Laverton also entered public life, starting as a member of the Wiltshire bench, qualifying as a magistrate in 1859 and being commissioned as a JP in 1864. It is clear, from various papers and letters, that some of Laverton's fellow magistrates drawn from the long-established gentry, looked upon this self-made man as something of an upstart. In 1868 Laverton contested the Westbury, or West Wiltshire, constituency as a Liberal and although his Conservative opponent was unseated, on petition he won the seat in a second election held the next year. But in 1874 Laverton won the Westbury seat and for six years sat in parliament as a Liberal MP and a strong supporter of Gladstone. His political work was reinforced by various benevolent activities in Westbury. In 1872-73, soon after some employees of another cloth firm had been discharged for voting for Laverton, he built the enclosure of model cottages, known as Prospect Buildings and designed by W J Stent of Warminster, to provide homes for workers who could live there for low rents and without fear of eviction. In 1873 he paid for the building, again to Stent's designs, of the Laverton Institute which could house various social facilities and was seen, by his opponents, as a vote-catching gesture. Just before his death he opened the Westbury Infant School built at his expense. He also arranged for some extra dwellings near Prospect Buildings to be set aside as almshouses for retired clothworkers.

Laverton's charitable donations disregarded religious differences. He regularly supported hospitals and the Müller Orphan Homes in Bristol, and he left money to a variety of causes. He himself was a member of the Church of England, served as a churchwarden of Westbury church and, along with his sister Charlotte, gave a pulpit and windows to that same church.

On the loss of his parliamentary seat in 1880 Abraham Laverton retired from public life, left Westbury and moved a few miles away, to the mock-mediaeval 'castle' at Farleigh Hungerford. He lived there as a country gentleman until his death on 31 October 1886. He had never married and left £47,417 gross; his nephew William Henry Laverton, who for a time carried on the Westbury business, was his residuary legatee. The Wiltshire papers printed long obituaries. One of them, a Liberal organ, described Laverton as a thorough businessman and expected that his name would take high place among those of our merchant princes.

BRYAN LITTLE

Sources:

Unpublished

Wiltshire CRO, Laverton papers.

PrC.

Information from Mrs Sylvia Laverton.

Bryan Little, 'Sarum Fine Woollens' (Lavertons of Westbury and Tucker's of Frome) (typescript, 1954).

Published

Alfred Baker, *The Life of Sir Isaac Pitman* (centenary ed, 1913).

George Dow, *Great Central (1864-1899)* (3 vols, Locomotive Publishing Co, 1959-65) 2.

Julia de L Mann, *The Cloth Industry in the West of England from 1640 to 1880* (Oxford: Clarendon Press, 1971).

Trowbridge Chronicle 6 Nov 1886.

Wiltshire Times 6 Nov 1886.

WWMP.

LAWRENCE, Sir Herbert Alexander

(1861-1943)

Banker and industrialist

Herbert Alexander Lawrence was born at Southgate, Middlesex, on 8 August 1861, the fourth son of Sir John Lawrence, GCB, GCSI, PC (1811-1879) and his wife Harriette Katherine (1820-1917), daughter of Rev Richard Hamilton of Donegal. His father was Viceroy of India, 1864-68, was created Baron Lawrence of the Punjab in 1869 and left under

667

Sir Herbert Lawrence (courtesy of Vickers Ltd).

£140,000. Lawrence was educated in the headmaster's house at Harrow in 1875-79, and went to the Royal Military Academy at Sandhurst before being gazetted as a lieutenant in the 17th Lancers in 1882. He was posted to India where he remained until 1891. As a subaltern he devoted himself to steeplechasing, polo, racquets and cricket, but acted as an adjutant in 1890-94 and was promoted to captain in 1892. In the same year he married Isabel Mary (1862-1941), eldest surviving daughter of Charles Henry Mills, First Lord Hillingdon, head of the banking firm of Glyn Mills Currie. He had two sons, who were both killed in the First World War, and a daughter.

Lawrence, who was nicknamed 'Lorenzo' by fellow officers, passed with distinction from the Staff College at Camberley in 1896 and joined the German section of the War Office's Intelligence Branch. He was promoted Deputy Assistant Adjutant General in 1898, and on the outbreak of the Boer War in 1899 was sent to South Africa as senior intelligence officer with the cavalry. He served there until 1902, ending as a brevet lieutenant-colonel commanding the 16th Lancers, but he resigned from the Army in 1903 and went to work in the City of London. His brother Charles Napier Lawrence (1855-1927), who was created Lord Lawrence of Kingsgate in 1923, was a member of Price & Pierce, City merchants in Clements Lane, a director of several investment companies, and chairman of the North British & Mercantile Insurance Co (chartered 1809), the London & North Western Railway in 1921-23 and of the London, Midland & Scottish Railway in 1923-24.

Initially Herbert Lawrence collected South African mining directorships, and by 1906 he was on the London committee of such companies as Bantjes Consolidated Mines and Vogelstruis Consolidated Deep (both developing goldmines discovered by the prospector Jan Gerritze Bantjes, 1843-1914), Bibiani Goldfields, the Main Reef group of mining companies (absorbed by the Consolidated Main Reef Mines & Estates Co in 1909), the Marievale Nigel Gold Mines & Estates Co, Witwatersrand Deep and others. In 1907 Lawrence became a partner in Glyn Mills Currie following the collapse in health of his brother-in-law, Lord Hillingdon. He had previously, in 1906, joined the London committee of the Imperial Ottoman Bank, on which Hillingdon also sat; this bank had been established in 1863 under firman from the Turkish Government, and on the outbreak of war in 1914 was placed under British governmental supervision. Lawrence succeeded Hillingdon around 1908 on the London committee of the Anglo-Austrian Bank (established in Vienna, 1863), but resigned on the outbreak of war in 1914. He was a director of the Midland Railway from 1912.

Lawrence received a command in Egypt after the outbreak of war in 1914, and was posted in 1915 to the Dardanelles where he showed conspicuous coolness and ability. He was in command at the Battle of Romani (1916) whereby the British won control of the Sinai desert, and in 1917 was put in charge of the intelligence branch at GHQ in France. Early in 1918 he was made chief of general staff to Haig's army in France, 'the greatest Army ever deployed by the British Empire in one theatre of war' {*Times* 27 Jan 1943}, and won wide renown for his calm judgement and administrative capacity. His success was despite the initial hostility of Lloyd George: 'PM much dismayed by Lawrence ... whose obvious

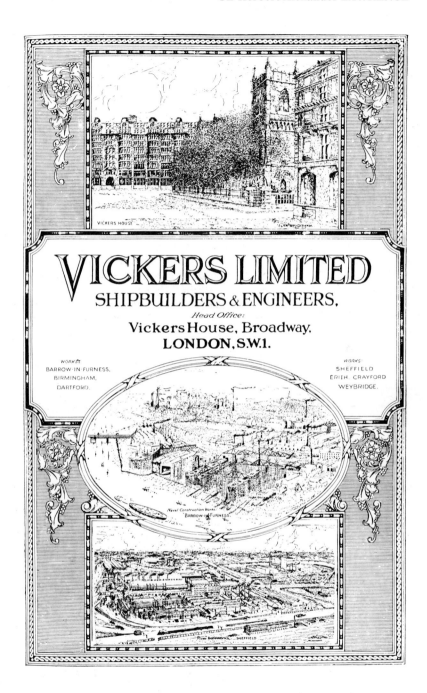

Advertisement for Vickers Ltd (from Brassey's Naval Annual 1923).

intellectual inferiority struck him at once', it was reported in January 1918 {Amery (1980) 202}. Although there was a longstanding mutual antipathy between Lawrence and Haig, they worked efficiently together. Lawrence was promoted to major general in 1915, lieutenant general in 1918 and general in 1919. He was appointed CB in 1916, KCB in 1917 and GCB in

1926. He received the Légion d'Honneur from France and the Serbian Order of Karageorge in 1916, the French and Belgian Croix de Guerre (1918), the American Distinguished Service Order (1918), the Grand Cross Crown of Romania (1918), the Grand Cross of St Benedict of Aviz (1918), the Grand Cordon Crown of Belgium (1919) and the Japanese Order of the Rising Sun (1921).

He returned to the City in 1919 to become managing partner of Glyn Mills. During the war the partnership had been continued, somewhat insipidly, by Lord Wolverton, Algernon Mills (1856-1922), Laurence Currie and the sickly Maurice Glyn (1872-1920). Lawrence directed the bank with appreciably more enterprise and energy. It had a longstanding connection with the Army, and in 1923 merged with Holt's Bank, headed by Sir Vesey Holt (1854-1923). From Holts GMC acquired a valuable connection as army agents, as well as a lucrative West End branch to complement Glyns' traditional City base. Following this amalgamation the bank was briefly known as Glyn, Mills, Currie & Holt, becoming the largest remaining private bank.

The death of the Earl of Jersey in 1923, obliged his executors to meet death duties by offering for sale Child's Bank, in which he was senior partner and which had been founded by one of his ancestors in 1673. Negotiations with Lloyds Bank were almost complete when Montagu Norman (qv), Governor of the Bank of England, who was a friend and confidant of Lawrence, intervened to declare that he would not countenance the deal. Instead, in 1924, GMCH absorbed Child's Bank, henceforth it was known as Glyn Mills. Their first branch outside London was opened at Carfax, in Oxford, in 1932, while the Lombard Street head office was re-built in 1933.

In much of this expansion Lawrence was aided by his protégé, Colonel Sir Arthur Maxwell (1875-1935), who became general manager and managing partner of the bank. In 1939 control of Glyn Mills was sold to the Royal Bank of Scotland because many of its partners were young men: it was felt that if some of them were killed in the war that was then imminent, the payment of death duties on their family holdings would create formidable difficulties. Lawrence remained chairman and managing partner of Glyn Mills until his death over three years later.

Glyn Mills had long been bankers to the armaments company of Vickers, and in 1921 Lawrence joined their board at a critical moment during their cash crisis. In 1926, following the financial and organisational reconstruction of Vickers instituted by Dudley Docker and Reginald McKenna (qqv), Lawrence became chairman. In 1927 he obtained the replacement of Sir Vincent Caillard as finance director by Sir M Webster Jenkinson (qqv), and together they completely overhauled the group.

It was the policy of Lawrence and Jenkinson to put Vickers in a strong cash position by disposing of their many unprofitable and unmanageably diversified subsidiaries acquired during the boom of 1919-20, and by rationalising all their productive facilities. Several of the smaller works were shut or sold in 1926-29, and the group's electrical subsidiary, Metropolitan-Vickers, was sold for £1,299,905 in 1928. Somewhat against Lawrence's financial instincts, the armaments and shipbuilding business of Armstrong Whitworth, rendered insolvent by the mismanagement of Sir Glynn West (qv), was absorbed in 1927, and a new company Vickers-

Orient Liner Orontes, *built by Vickers-Armstrongs Ltd, Barrow-in-Furness (from Brassey's* Naval and Shipping Annual *1930).*

Armstrongs was formed, with Vickers henceforth acting as a holding company. Lawrence insisted throughout negotiations for Vickers that 'Our cash position is one most important element of our strength' and he 'always disliked having to give Armstrongs cash' {Vickers microfilm R323, Lawrence to Jenkinson, 11 Sept 1927}. He yielded on national grounds to the proposed merger, but only after he and the Bank of England had arranged for Sun Insurance to issue a policy of five years' duration at a premium of £400 per annum, whereby if the profits of the new Vickers-Armstrongs fell beneath £900,000 in any one year, Sun would contribute a sum that would bring them up to that figure, subject to a maximum contribution of £200,000. It typified Lawrence's ruthless thoroughness in negotiations that Vickers held out for this guarantee: Sun duly paid £200,000 a year in 1928-32. Lawrence attached more importance to rationalising Vickers' rolling-stock factories and steelworks than to the Armstrongs deal. Negotiations were entered with Lionel Hichens (qv) of Cammell Laird which led to the unification of their rolling-stock facilities and the formation of the consolidated English Steel Corporation with effect from January 1929. Though the performance of these reconstructed companies was marred by the onset of world economic depression, it was an undoubted source of strength that Vickers-Armstrongs (unlike its competitors in steel) carried no debenture charges whatsoever.

Although armaments accounted for as little, on average in 1930-34, as 46 per cent of Vickers' turnover, the company remained 'the only organisation of its kind in the British Empire'. As Lawrence wrote: 'Practically every requisite of the three fighting services is manufactured by Vickers, and large research and experimental establishments are maintained' {PRO Supp 3/43, PSO 358, Lawrence to Sir Maurice Hankey, Secretary of Committee of Imperial Defence, 7 Oct 1932}. Its manufacturing reserve fell into desuetude during the disarmament era of 1918-35, and consequently its work in rearmament after 1936 was all the harder. He often criticised the Government's inconsistent treatment of the company:

> The British Government often asks Vickers 'What can you produce, and in what time in the event of war?' The answer to this question must be a constantly diminishing quantity unless a steady flow of work can be maintained in the factories. Large technical staffs must be kept in idleness, and the upkeep of empty, or practically empty, factories is heavy. Orders which Vickers have passed owing to restrictions have undoubtedly been placed abroad, and Britain is poorer in consequence, her national defence has suffered, and her ability to secure commercial and armament trade abroad weakened. Foreign firms have no fine feelings when in search of armament orders {ibid}.

As chairman of Vickers, Lawrence was personally attacked in the 1930s by radical pacifists such as Fenner Brockway, Philip Noel-Baker and Dorothy Woodman. In 1936 he gave detailed evidence to the Royal Commission on the Private Manufacture of and Trade in Arms. He did not fit into the 'merchants of death' demonology: 'No-one could be in his presence for five minutes without realising he was an honourable, straightforward man whose word could be relied upon absolutely', Sir Edward Peacock (qv) of the Bank of England recalled in 1958, 'he was a man of good ability, but no genius ... very likeable, although rather formidable and aloof in appearance' {Vickers file 63}. On his retirement from Vickers in 1937, he received a personal letter of thanks from Duff Cooper, then Secretary for War.

Apart from becoming a director of Vickers in 1921, he also joined in that year the head board of Dalgety & Co, a finance house of Australian origins whose funds were then chiefly used in making advances on land, livestock and wool. He joined the London board of the Liverpool, London & Globe Insurance Co in 1921, but had resigned by 1923 when he became a director of Sun Insurance and of Sun Life.

In 1922 he became chairman of the re-constituted Anglo-Austrian Bank, whose business in Czechoslovakia was transferred to the new Anglo-Czechoslovakian Bank. This move was 'accounted for by the British government's attempts from 1916 to foster overseas banking in Europe on a German model, together with the Bank of England's desire to liquidate its £1,665,000 claim on the bank ... coupled with Montagu Norman's particular European plans' {Cottrell (1983) 330}. There were various local and managerial obstacles to prosperity. In 1926 Anglo-Austrian absorbed the British Trade Corporation (BTC) of Lord Faringdon (qv), and was reconstructed as the Anglo-International Bank, of which Lawrence was first chairman. The Austrian assets of Anglo-Austrian were sold to the Rothschilds' Credit-Anstalt in July 1926, while the Italian assets were transferred to George Manzi-Fé's Banca Italo-Britannica. Anglo-International, however, retained its interests in the Croatian Discount

Bank and the Anglo-Czechoslovak Bank until the latter was absorbed by the Prague Credit Bank in 1930. The subsequent collapses of Banco Italo-Britannica in 1929 and Credit-Anstalt in 1931 indicate the precarious nature of Anglo-Austrian's business. BTC's other main interests were in Turkey and the Balkans, where Lawrence had cognate financial concerns. He was a director of the Bank of Roumania Ltd, which had been registered in 1903 to take over a company which had been working a banking concession granted by the Roumanian Government in 1866. Lawrence remained a London director of the Imperial Ottoman Bank, succeeding Lord Goschen as its chairman when the Turks extended the firman for ten years until 1935 (when its name was changed to the Ottoman Bank). The latter also owned the Agricultural Bank of Cyprus Ltd.

Lawrence's military and business colleague Guy Dawnay (qv) wrote that he

> had in a very exceptional degree a mind capable of ... strip[ping] any subject of non-essentials and irrelevancies ... With this was combined a notable lucidity of expression, leaving no loophole for doubt or indecision. He had ... forcefulness and determination, even ... a measure of ruthlessness ... his courage was as unflinching as his line of action, once determined, was unswerving. Underlying all was a great kindliness based on a very human understanding. Small follies stirred his dry humour; real foolishness his — silent — contempt; but anything really unworthy evoked his grim and icy disgust. He was singularly devoid of ... self-seeking {*Times* 27 Jan 1943}.

Lawrence's name was mooted for appointment as Viceroy of India in 1920, as Chief of Imperial General Staff in 1922 and as Field Marshal in 1932-36. He was made honorary colonel of the Manchester Regiment in 1925, trustee of the War Graves Endowment Fund from 1926, and of the Bulgarian Refugee Loan from 1926. He became treasurer of the Douglas Haig Memorial Homes in 1928, and through Montagu Norman's influence was appointed in 1930 to the Advisory Council of the Bankers Industrial Development Corporation run by Charles Bruce Gardner (qv). He chaired a War Office committee on reforming the Army accountancy system in 1924-25, and sat on the Royal Commission on the Coal Industry during 1925. With this expertise he gave valued advice to Stanley Baldwin, the Prime Minister, and Sir Arthur Steel-Maitland, the Minister of Labour, during the prolonged coal strike of 1926. A governor of Wellington College from 1921, he received honorary degrees of LLD from St Andrews University in 1922 and of DCL from Oxford in 1929.

Lawrence died on 17 January 1943 at Woodcock, Hertfordshire, leaving £107,207 gross.

R P T DAVENPORT-HINES

Writings:

Chapter in Charles S Goldman, *With General French and the Cavalry in South Africa* (Macmillan, 1902).

PP, RC on the Private Manufacture of and Trading in Arms (1936) Cmd 5292.

LAWRENCE Sir Herbert Alexander

Sources:

Unpublished

Cambridge University Library, papers of Earl Baldwin of Bewdley.

House of Lords RO, papers of Viscount Davidson, letter of Sir John Davidson, Lord Trenchard and Sir Noel Birch to Davidson, 19 May 1936.

Imperial War Museum, papers of Guy Dawnay (eg 69/21/5).

National Library of Scotland, Edinburgh, military papers of Sir Herbert Lawrence.

PRO, papers of Ministry of Supply, Treasury and War Office.

Vickers House, Millbank, London, Vickers microfilm.

Richard P T Davenport-Hines, 'The British Armaments Industry during Disarmament 1918-36' (Cambridge PhD, 1979).

Published

Leo C M S Amery, *Diaries 1896-1929* (Hutchinson, 1980).

Burke's Peerage and Baronetage.

Philip Clarke, *The First House in the City* (pp, Child's Bank, 1973).

Philip Cottrell, 'Aspects of Western Equity in the Banking Systems of East Central Europe' in Alice Teichova and P L Cottrell (eds), *International Business and Central Europe 1918-1939* (Leicester: Leicester University Press, 1983).

Richard P T Davenport-Hines, *Dudley Docker* (Cambridge: Cambridge University Press, 1984).

DNB.

Sir Roger T B Fulford, *The History of Glyns* (Macmillan, 1953).

John D Scott, *Vickers* (Weidenfeld & Nicolson, 1962).

WWW.

LAWRENCE, Sir Joseph

(1848-1919)

Industrialist

Joseph Lawrence was born on Zante, the southernmost of the Ionian Islands, on 23 September 1848. His father, Philip Lawrence, was connected with the commercial and military life of the small British

Sir Joseph Lawrence (courtesy of the Linotype Machinery Co).

community therre. Raised in Manchester, Joseph Lawrence left school in 1861, although later in the 1860s he took an evening course in political economy at Owens College, Manchester.

In 1861 Lawrence joined the secretary's department of the Manchester, Sheffield & Lincolnshire Railway Co. Seventeen years later, with the full support of his employers (who had a financial interest in his new firm), Lawrence became secretary of the Hull Dock Co. Situated 20 miles from the mouth of the Humber, Hull was entirely dependent on two monopolies — the North Eastern Railway and the Hull Dock Co — to maintain its position as the third largest port in Britain. Lawrence arrived in Hull when the last of the several local attempts to break these monopolies was gaining momentum. Within a year he had left his new job to work for several dissident directors of the Hull Dock Co as secretary of what became the Hull, Barnsley & West Riding Junction Railway & Dock Co. Largely due to Lawrence's indefatigable labours, the shares of the new company were oversubscribed nearly two-and-a-half times. Yet, within three months of this considerable triumph and as a result of a dispute over the inadequacy of his salary of £500, Lawrence had resigned and gone to Southern Africa.

After spending less than a year in Cape Town, where he had a stormy tenure as sub-manager of the Colonial Railways, Lawrence returned to England. In September 1882 he was appointed manager of the provisional committee for the proposed Manchester Ship Canal. He wrote and spoke incessantly in an endeavour to create and sustain a widespread and favourable local climate of opinion for this long-cherished Mancunian scheme of ending the city's dependence on Liverpool as its port. In London he masterminded the lobbying of MPs in August 1885 during the three lengthy attempts necessary to gain parliamentary approval for the proposal. Again, however, at the very moment of his apparent triumph, Lawrence resigned, embittered at the refusal of Daniel Adamson (qv), chairman of the provisional committee, to accord him the public recognition he sought for bringing the scheme so successfully to fruition.

Realising the potential of linotype, the greatest advance in printing since Gutenberg's invention of the mould and the matrix, was Joseph Lawrence's most significant contribution to the commercial life of Britain. After spending two years in America Lawrence returned to London in 1887 where he began publishing two railway trade journals. The expense of this endeavour, however, readily led him to investigate the potential of Ottmar Mergenthaler's revolutionary typesetting invention, the linotype machine, which had first been used by the *New York Tribune* in 1886. Lawrence became the moving force behind a syndicate led by his friend from Ship Canal days, Jacob Bright MP, to purchase the linotype patents from their American owners. Capital of £1 million was sought in London to cover the £820,000 spent in acquiring the patents for the British Empire; the resultant share issue in July 1889 was a complete failure. Ultimately the members of the original syndicate had to take up £800,000 worth of shares themselves.

Joseph Lawrence was a director of the Linotype Co from its inception and soon became deputy chairman. In 1896 he was made chairman and managing director at a salary of £2,000; this was increased to £3,500 in 1898 and £5,000 in 1901. As the largest shareholder in the company, he

benefited handsomely from its rapid growth; net profits increased from
£2,118 in 1892 to £273,996 in 1899. Financial success in this decade was
not, however, effortlessly achieved. Most customers were, initially, highly
sceptical of claims advanced for linotype. To them it was simply another
in a long line of inventions which had promised, unsuccessfully in each
case thus far, to revolutionise typesetting in the newspaper and magazine
industry. Customer scepticism was reinforced by the natural hostility of
many workers in the printing trade. Any machine which could do the
work of three to six men, which could be leased for £100 a year or bought
for £350 and which could pay for itself in eighteen months raised serious
questions for hand compositors. Lawrence's firm was caught in a dilemma
of its own making. Anxious to obtain the goodwill of the unions in order to
increase sales without fear of industrial strife, the company was equally
concerned to see as low a piece rate as possible for compositors in order to
make linotype more attractive to potential customers. As early as 1900 it
was clear that Lawrence had presided over a technological revolution in
the printing of British newspapers and magazines. Indicative of the
success of Lawrence's company was the opening in 1899 of a new factory
employing up to 2,300 at Broadheath, Altrincham. The Broadheath plant
(still (1983) largely intact) was regarded as a model for the times; 170
cottages (yielding a 5 per cent return) were also built for employees on this
40-acre industrial estate.

Success led Lawrence in new directions. He became a country squire,
was elected to the Surrey County Council and was a minor patron of the
arts. He was a founding director of British Westinghouse, a subsidiary of
the American electrical manufacturers who established a factory in
Manchester. A personal friendship with Thomas Edison led Lawrence to
organise a company to purchase Edison's patents for the recovery of low
grade ores for iron and steel production; he was deputy chairman (1902-6)
and subsequently chairman (1906-9) of the Dunderland Iron Ore Co.
However, the Edison process, untested on a mass production basis, proved
when tried in Norway to be a disastrously inefficient and extremely
expensive way to extract ore, at the very moment when world prices of ore
were steadily falling. Angry shareholders finally forced two independent
examinations of Dunderland's activities. As a result the company was
placed in receivership in 1909 and Lawrence was forced to resign both as
chairman and director.

The year 1909 also saw a change in the fortunes of the Linotype Co after
a decade of distressing results. Increased competition, particularly from
the United States and Germany, the need to service an ever-increasing
burden of debt, combined with a persistent decline in the growth of the
printing industry, dramatically reversed the success of Linotype's first
decade. Net profits fell from £273,966 in 1899 to £31,295 in 1909. In 1908,
determined to end calamitous competition in the industry, the
Mergenthaler Linotype Co of America bought its German rival and
purchased 95 per cent of the shares of Linotype & Machinery (formed in
1903 by the merger between Linotype Co Ltd and Machinery Trust Ltd).
Lawrence remained chairman of Linotype & Machinery and also became
chairman of International Linotype Ltd, the holding company established
to control the new multinational.

Lawrence was also active politically. Narrowly defeated in his first attempt to gain a seat for the Conservatives at Cardiff in 1900, he was returned at a by-election in Monmouth Boroughs in 1901. Although he spent £25,000 on his election campaigns, Lawrence was not a House of Commons man except for rare but penetrating interventions on patent matters. He did not contest the 1906 election, although he remained politically active. Early in 1906, acting as a stalking horse for Joseph Chamberlain (qv), Lawrence was largely responsible in the City of London Conservative Association for forcing one MP to give up his seat to make way for Arthur Balfour, the defeated party leader, and driving the other, Sir Edward Clarke, a Unionist Free Trader, from his seat. Lawrence was a key member of the Tariff Reform League almost from its inception; he campaigned for the cause at every opportunity and was particularly active in the 1910 elections and several by-elections. As honorary treasurer of the National Union of Conservative and Unionist Associations for many years, a founding member of the Federation of British Industries, Lawrence was also a prominent figure in the right wing anti-Labour business group, the British Commonwealth Union. Elected Sheriff of the City of London in 1900, he was knighted in 1902 and rewarded for his years of political service with a baronetcy in 1918.

A lapsed Catholic, Lawrence married Margaret Alice Jackson of Southport in 1873; their only child, a daughter, was born in 1877.

Sir Joseph Lawrence died on 24 October 1919, leaving an estate proved at £26,600 gross.

J O STUBBS

Writings:

Cape of Good Hope, Votes and Proceedings of Parliament (1882), Appendix III: Reports of Select Committees, SC on Railway Management.

(under the pseudonym 'Cottonopolis') *The Manchester Ship Canal. Why It Is Wanted! and Why It Will Pay! With Observations in Reply to Recent Objections, and Including Appendix to the Bridgewater Navigation Company* (Manchester, 1882).

(under the pseudonym 'A Supporter of the Canal') *The Manchester Ship Canal: A Reply to Mr A Provand's Adverse Criticism* (Manchester, 1883).

(under the pseudonym 'By a Shareholder') *The Linotype Composing Machine: A Retrospect and a Prospect: Being an Enquiry into the Economic Possibilities of this Great Invention; with some Data as to the Probability of Dividends on the Share Capital of the Linotype Company, Limited* (1889).

Some Figures and Facts on the Depreciation in the Value of Securities and Investment of British Capital Abroad in Recent Years, with Other Economic Data (King, Sell & Olding, 1907).

The New Patents Act. Its Genesis (King, Sell & Co, 1908).

The New Patents Act. Its Origin and Its Authors (King, Sell & Olding, 1908).

LAWRENCE Sir Joseph

Sources:

Unpublished

Birmingham University Library, Joseph Chamberlain MSS, JC 18/15/1-83, JC 18/19/1-60, JC 19/7/1-87, JC 20/4, JC 21/2.

British Museum, A J Balfour MSS, Add MSS 49,758, 49,764, 49,791, 49,858; Cecil of Chelwood MSS, Add MSS 51,158.

House of Lords RO, Andrew Bonar Law MSS, 18/2/23, 18/4/78, 26/3/3, 27/1/8, 64/G/8, 83/5/15, 83/6/6, 84/3/8, 84/7/57.

Lancashire RO, Manchester Ship Canal, correspondence and papers, 1882-87, DDX/101, papers, plans, pamphlets, 1881-1925, DDBe.

Joseph Lawrence MSS (in private possession).

Linotype & Machinery Ltd, Altrincham, Cheshire, minute books of the Linotype Ltd and Linotype & Machinery Ltd.

Manchester Central Library, and Cheetham's Library, Manchester, Manchester Ship Canal, miscellaneous materials.

PRO, Hull, Barnsley and West Riding Railway & Canal Co Ltd, RAIL 312/2-3, 7, 57; Manchester, Sheffield & Lincolnshire Railway Co Ltd, Minutes and Reports (Shareholders and Directors) MSL 1; Staff Records MSL 15.

PrC.

John O Stubbs, 'Sir Joseph Lawrence, 1848-1919' (typescript, 1975).

Published

Bernard W E Alford, 'Business Enterprise and the Growth of the Commercial Letterpress Printing Industry, 1850-1914' *Business History* 7 (1965).

Keith J Allison (ed), *A History of the County of York, East Riding* vol 1 *The City of Kingston Upon Hull* (Oxford University Press for the Institute of Historical Research, 1969).

Neal Blewett, *The Peers, the Parties and the People: The General Elections of 1910* (Macmillan, 1972).

John Child, *Industrial Relations in the British Printing Industry* (Allen & Unwin, 1967).

Frank E Cornwall, 'Early Pioneers — Joseph Lawrence' in William B Tracy (ed), *Port of Manchester: A Sketch of the History and Development of the Manchester Ship Canal, and Formation and Growth of the Cotton Association* (Manchester: Hind, Hoyle & Co, 1901).

James L Garvin and Julian Amery, *The Life of Joseph Chamberlain* (6 vols, Macmillan, 1932, 1969) 5 and 6.

Kenneth Hoole, *The Hull and Barnsley Railway* (Newton Abbot: David & Charles, 1972).

Ellic Howe, *Newspaper Printing in the Nineteenth Century* (pp, 1943).

— (ed), *The London Compositor: Documents Relating to the Wages, Working Conditions and Customs of the London Printing Trade 1785-1900* (Oxford University Press, 1947).

Sir Bosdin T Leech, *History of the Manchester Ship Canal* (2 vols, Manchester: Sherratt & Hughes, 1907).

Kenneth O Morgan, *Wales in British Politics, 1868-1922* (Cardiff: University of Wales Press, 1970).

Albert E Musson, *The Typographical Association: Origins and History up to 1949* (Oxford University Press, 1954).

Richard A Rempel, *Unionists Divided: Arthur Balfour, Joseph Chamberlain and the Unionist Free Traders* (Newton Abbott: David & Charles, 1972).

John Southward, *Type Composing Machines of the Past, Present and Future: Paper Read Before the Balloon Society of Great Britain, 3 October 1890* (Truslove & Shirley, 1890).

Souvenir Inauguration of the Linotype Works, Broadheath, 14 July 1899.

Stock Exchange Year-Book passim.

Alan Sykes, *Tariff Reform in British Politics 1903-1913* (Oxford: Clarendon Press, 1979).

Transcript of Proceedings of a Commemorative Luncheon at the Connaught Rooms, London, 17 October 1918 in Honour of Sir Joseph Lawrence's Seventieth Birthday (London, 1918).

John A Turner, 'The British Commonwealth Union and the General Election of 1918' *English Historical Review* 93 (July 1978).

WWMP.

WWW.

LAWSON, Edward Levy

1st Lord Burnham of Hall Barn

(1833-1916)

Newspaper proprietor

Sir Edward Lawson (from Lord Burnham, Peterborough Court. The Story of the Daily Telegraph *Cassell & Co 1955).*

Edward Levy (he adopted the additional surname Lawson in later life) was born in London on 28 December 1833, the eldest of the eight children of Joseph Moses Levy (1811-88), a printer and his wife Esther, daughter of Godfrey Cohen of London. Edward Levy was educated at University College and then worked as a drama critic on the *Sunday Times* which his father owned at that time.

In July 1855 Joseph Levy became the printer to the *Daily Telegraph and Courier*, whose first issue came out on 29 June of that year. The proprietor of the paper was one Colonel A B Sleigh, who founded it in order to pursue through its columns a private feud with the Duke of Cambridge. Sleigh, whose own modest financial resources were rapidly becoming exhausted by the expenses of launching a newspaper, pledged his shares in it to Levy as collateral. Within weeks of Levy's becoming printer, he had taken over the newspaper. He raised £4,000 capital, largely from family resources; half came from his brother Lionel, Joseph Levy himself contributed one-quarter, Edward Levy one-eighth, and the remainder came from George Moss, who seems to have been machine manager at the printing works.

The *Daily Telegraph and Courier* (the *Courier* was dropped from the title after about eighteen months) had been issued at 2d, when most newspapers cost 5d. Undeterred by the tiny circulation and the exiguous advertising revenue, Joseph Levy reduced the cover price to 1d. Thus, the *Daily Telegraph* became the first penny newspaper in the country (although it would not have been possible for any newspaper to appear at 1d before June 1855, when the stamp tax on newspapers was repealed). The public's response was immediate, for within a week of the price reduction, the *Daily Telegraph* claimed the largest circulation of any London morning newspaper, except the *Times*, then in its heyday. In January 1856 the *Telegraph* claimed a circulation of 26,000 copies.

The Levys aimed to produce an entertaining newspaper, but a well-written one, and recruited writers (many of them not professional journalists) of some literary ability. One of their best-known contributors, the ebullient journalist, George Augustus Sala, later recalled, 'The idea of the proprietors was that it should be not only a thoroughly comprehensive newspaper, but also a miscellany of humorous and descriptive social essays' {Sala (1895) I, 393}. By 1860, when the repeal of the duties on paper (Joseph Levy had led a deputation to Downing Street appealing for their abolition) cut the costs of the *Telegraph* by £12,000 a year, it was firmly established as a leading London daily. The offices and production were moved that year to larger premises at 135 Fleet Street, with buildings behind which covered the old Peterborough Court, from which the offices took their name.

Joseph Levy had clear ideas about what sort of newspaper he wanted, but he was perhaps more concerned with advertising and production than with the editorial side. He invented the device of the 'box number' and he particularly liked to see what he called a 'black newspaper', that is, one with plenty of remunerative small advertisements. He left much of the editorial responsibility to his son, Edward, after he had ensured that Edward had gained experience in every department of the paper. Soon Edward combined many of the functions of editor and general manager. His staff recognised his outstanding ability as a newspaper man and did not see his direction as interference. His competitors criticised the 'vulgarity' of his approach to the production of a daily newspaper — his search for human interest in stories, his inclusion of copious reports of divorce cases, and of crime and sport. 'Politics', he once said, 'are fearfully dull and it is not good forcing them when there is a superabundance of social matter immediately calling for attention' {Koss (1981) 157}. He regularly warned his staff against 'the unforgiveable sin of lack of variety in the paper' {Falk (1951) 201}. He shared his father's horror of a dull paper, and would say to his staff that while it was easy enough to produce

IMPERIUM ET LIBERTAS.

Sir Edward Lawson in the editorial chair (from Lord Burnham, Peterborough Court. The Story of the Daily Telegraph *Cassell & Co, 1955).*

a good paper when exciting news was plentiful, the test came when such news was lacking. He urged them to have a reserve of interesting articles on hand, and thus began the 'silly season' topic. One favoured method was to encourage a correspondence on topics such as 'Do We Believe?' or 'Is Marriage a Failure?' He also helped make news by sponsoring expeditions, including that of the archaeologist George Smith to Assyria and, jointly with the *New York Herald*, Henry Stanley's expedition seeking the sources of the Congo river.

By present-day standards, the paper in layout and tone was staid and unappealing, and even at the time the verbose and florid style of its staff writers gave rise to the expression 'Telegraphese'. However, in its time it was lively and interesting, and brought into being a new and much-wider public for daily newspapers. In 1870, circulation reached 196,855 and in 1877, 242,215. In that year new buildings were erected, to house machinery which, it was announced, was 'capable of printing 168,000 copies per hour, every copy being Bound, Cut and Folded, so that henceforth there will appear advertisements and News Always Together' {Burnham (1955) 90}. In the 1880s, the *Telegraph* printed every day the statement: 'Largest circulation in the world. The sale of the *Daily Telegraph* amounts to an average which, if tested, will show an excess of half-a-million copies weekly over any other morning paper'. No figures were produced to support this claim, but it was not challenged until the rise of Alfred Harmsworth's (qv) *Daily Mail*. According to office records, the *Daily Telegraph* touched 300,000 in 1888.

The capital of the *Telegraph* was held by many members of the Levy Lawson family, who were principally interested in their dividends. After the death of Joseph Levy and his brother Lionel Lawson, their shares were divided among numerous relatives. Edward Lawson held the largest single share, but still less than half. For many years, whatever the actual profits had been (and the *Daily Telegraph*, even in its troubled years after Edward Lawson died and before Harry Lawson sold it to the Berry brothers (qv), never made a loss), a fixed dividend of £124,000 was paid. No adequate provisions were made for renewal of plant and development; the old steam-driven rotary presses remained in use until after the First World War. Edward Lawson himself was no business man, and took no pains to conceal the fact. When 'the cashier ... brought him a balance sheet he would say "Take the damned thing away, my boy, I don't understand anything about it". He was gratified and often surprised at their financial success, but ... he did [not do] anything constructive to achieve it, except to make every effort to produce a good and readable newspaper. Only an obstinate popularity carried the paper through the haphazard methods of management'. {Burnham (1955) 171-2}

Politically, Edward Levy (who took the name Lawson in 1875 by Royal Licence 'in respect of a deed of gift from his uncle Lionel, who had also added Lawson to his surname' {*ibid* 2}) was a supporter of William Gladstone for many years. To the *Daily Telegraph*, Gladstone was 'The People's William', and to Gladstone, Lawson was, at one time, 'the only man who knew how to support a Minister in the London press' {Koss (1981) 293}. But when Gladstone made that remark, in 1886, the days of full support for Gladstone from the *Daily Telegraph* were long since over. Gladstone's withdrawal from the Liberal leadership in 1875, his Olympian inaccessibility, and his opposition to the Turks after the massacres of Bulgarian Christians, brought Lawson to support Disraeli (who used to mock his paper as the 'Delirium Tremens'). Lawson was castigated by the Liberals, particularly by Labouchere, who vilified him in the magazine *Truth* as an apostate from his religious as well as his political faith. (Lawson had become a Christian on his marriage in 1862 to Harriette (d 1897), only daughter of an actor-manager, Benjamin Webster.) Lawson sued Labouchere for libel, but lost his case. He relieved his feelings in 1879 in a bout of fisticuffs with Labouchere on the steps of the Beefsteak Club, which brought them both (temporary) expulsion from the club. Henceforth, the *Telegraph* was 'to all intents and purposes' Conservative {*ibid* 203}, though Lawson denied this, and preferred to describe it as 'Imperial'. The loss of the *Telegraph* was a severe blow to the Liberals, for 'The giant of Fleet Street, it addressed the multitudes beyond the perimeters of Clubland' {*ibid*}, and it had been the only major London daily to support them. Lawson was a familiar figure in the lobby of the House of Commons and shared with John Thadeus Delane of the *Times* the rare privilege of standing at the bar of the House of Lords with MPs.

Edward Lawson came to be considered as one of the best newspapermen of his day. Northcliffe would often say, as he passed the *Daily Telegraph* building, 'Sitting in a room upstairs is an elderly gentleman who can teach us all our business' and would also describe him as 'the greatest journalist of us all' {Falk (1951) 199}. Lord Camrose considered that 'there can be no doubt that Edward Lawson was the originator of morning journalism as we know it today' {Camrose (1947) 28}. In 1913, on his eightieth birthday, Northcliffe presented him with a congratulatory address signed by hundreds of journalists, describing him as 'Father of the Press and doyen of his profession' {*ibid*}. He was president of the Royal Institute of Journalists, 1892-93 and of the Empire Press Union from 1909 to his death.

In later years, however, Lawson (who was given a baronetcy in 1892) withdrew to an increasing extent from the direction of the paper. He spent much time entertaining, with charm and generosity, at his country home, Hall Barn in Buckinghamshire. When Alfred Harmsworth launched the *Daily Mail*, which rapidly became the largest circulation daily newspaper, Lawson did not rise to the challenge by undertaking any major reforms of his paper, which was becoming a little set in its ways. When Harmsworth brought out a Sunday edition of the *Mail* in 1899, Lawson did respond with a *Sunday Telegraph*, but public pressure from Sabbatarians forced them both to withdraw after a few weeks. But at the *Daily Telegraph*, the old staff continued in the old way.

Lawson's son, Harry, took an increasing share of responsibility for the direction of the paper, and in 1903, when Lawson was created a baron, taking the title Lord Burnham of Hall Barn, he handed over active control to Harry completely. However, Harry's principal interest was really his political career in which he was encouraged by his mother, who saw in him a future Prime Minister, and did not want him to spend his career in newspapers. Harry Lawson sat as Liberal MP for St Pancras, 1885-92, for East Gloucestershire, 1893-95 and the Mile End division of Tower Hamlets, 1905-6 and 1910 until 1916, when he succeeded his father as Lord Burnham. His political contacts provided valuable information and insights, but he took his politics seriously and this was reflected in a duller newspaper.

Like his father, Harry Lawson was loyal to old staff. John Le Sage, who started as personal assistant to Edward Levy in 1863, ended his career as editor of the paper, staying in that post, adamantly refusing to use the telephone, and issuing instructions to reporters in longhand, until 1923, when he was eighty-six years old. Although the paper continued to attract classified advertising, it lost much display advertising and its circulation steadily fell; by 1927 circulation had dropped below 100,000. In 1927 the *Daily Telegraph* was sold to the Berry brothers, whose new measures, men — and machinery — soon revived it.

Edward Lawson was a convivial soul and though many politicians, it has been said, 'despised Lawson yet grovelled to him' {Koss (1981) 254}, he had a wide circle of friends, ranging from Lord Rowton, Disraeli's secretary for many years, to Sir Henry Irving (qv), one of a number of friends from the theatre (he was a trustee of the Garrick Club). He was a member of the circle of Edward, Prince of Wales, who visited him at Hall Barn every year from 1892 until his death. The King gave Burnham a

KCVO in 1904. Burnham owned about 4,000 acres of land and enjoyed country pursuits, particularly riding, shooting and golf. He served as High Sheriff for Buckinghamshire in 1886, was a DL and JP for Buckinghamshire and an alderman of Buckinghamshire County Council. For all his political interests, he never spoke in the House of Lords.

Lord Burnham died in London on 9 January 1916 leaving £267,871 gross. He was survived by his sons Harry, who succeeded to the title, and William, who became the Third Lord Burnham, and his daughter, Edith.

CHRISTINE SHAW

Sources:

Unpublished

PrC.

Published

Burke's Peerage and Baronetage.

Lord Burnham, *Peterborough Court: The Story of the Daily Telegraph* (Cassell & Co, 1955).

Lord Camrose, *British Newspapers and Their Controllers* (Cassell & Co, 1947).

William L Courtney, *The Passing Hour* (Hutchinson & Co, 1925).

DNB.

Bernard Falk, *Bouquets of Fleet Street: Memories and Musings over Fifty Years* (Hutchinson & Co, 1951).

Stephen Koss, *The Rise and Fall of the Political Press in Britain. Volume 1: The Nineteenth Century* (Hamish Hamilton, 1981).

Alan J Lee, *The Origins of the Popular Press 1855-1914* (Croom Helm, 1976).

George Augustus Sala, *Life and Adventures* (2 vols, Cassell & Co, 1895).

WWMP.

WWW.

LAWSON, Henry John

(1852-1925)

Bicycle manufacturer and company promoter

Henry John Lawson was born on 23 February 1852 in the City of London, the son of Thomas Lawson, a brass turner, and his wife Ann Lucy née Kent.

Early in life Lawson appears to have acquired direct experience in the cycle trade in Brighton and in 1876 he patented a low bicycle, preceded in 1873/74 by his safety bicycle which Caunter describes as the 'first authentic design of safety bicycle employing chain-drive to the rear wheel which was actually made' {Caunter (1955) 34}. The 1876 Likeman & Lawson bicycle had a large rear wheel, powered by pedals and levers; a few were made by Haynes & Jeffries of Coventry. Lawson's third design, the Bicyclette, was patented in 1879; this still echoed the Ordinary, having a front wheel of much greater diameter than the rear, but the smaller size of the machine, improved distribution of the rider's weight, and chain-drive entitled Lawson to a place amongst the several pioneers of the safety bicycle. He was by now manager of the Tangent & Coventry Tricycle Co, but does not appear to have made any immediate decision to manufacture his new design. It was not until 1884 that he approached BSA, who made two prototypes for him, but declined to manufacture his design. In the same year he took out a patent, 13,078 (of 1884), for a ladies' safety bicycle. In 1885 the direct fore-runner of the modern safety bicycle appeared, designed, not by Lawson, but by John Kemp Starley (qv), and Lawson turned to cycle company finance, transforming the Haynes & Jeffries business into the Rudge Cycle Co in 1887, in collaboration with the Coventry solicitor, George Woodcock (d 1891).

It is, however in conjunction with Ernest Terah Hooley (qv) that Lawson reached the peak of his activity as company promoter, following the Humber & Pneumatic Tyre Co schemes with one which was intended 'to create a motor car industry in the country and to control it himself' {Richardson (1977) 17}. The envisaged, although not the actual, scope of his concerns is indicated by the titles: in 1895 the British Motor Syndicate Ltd (subsequently the British Motor Co Ltd, then the British Motor Traction Co Ltd) and in the following year the Great Horseless Carriage Co Ltd (subsequently the Motor Manufacturing Co Ltd). The British Motor Syndicate had an original capital of £150,000 (which Lawson unsuccessfully tried to refloat for £1 million after the repeal of the Red Flag Act, raising road vehicle speed to 14 mph, in November 1896). It acquired the Daimler patents from the Daimler Motor Syndicate of F R Simms (qv) in 1895 and sold them to the Daimler Motor Co in the following year. The Daimler concern (reformed in 1904) was the only enduring result of Lawson's motor industry projects.

The Daimler rights were the most important, but by no means the only ones acquired by Lawson. Those of the American, E J Pennington (1858-1911), were amongst the least valuable. Pennington, who has been characterised as 'a glib promoter with some mechanical talent' {Rae (1965) 12}, organised with Lawson the Anglo-American Rapid Vehicle Co in the USA in 1899. After the collapse of this scheme to merge British and American companies Pennington faded from the automobile scene.

The end of Lawson's attempt to control the development of the UK motor industry through patents came with Mr Justice Farwell's decision in the High Court in July 1901, dismissing an action by the British Motor Traction Co Ltd for alleged infringement of Maybach's carburettor patent (16,072 of 1893). Farwell found that both Edward Butler and George Wilkinson had anticipated the method patented by Maybach. Within two years, in February 1903, a receiver was appointed to the British Motor Traction Co.

In the following year Lawson was indicted with Hooley for conspiring to defraud Alfred John Paine, a speculator, and shareholders and creditors of the Electric Tramways Construction & Maintenance Co Ltd. Lawson was charged with making false statements to induce persons to buy shares or lend money. Hooley's defence by Rufus Isaacs was to depict Paine as a businessman and gambler, who might presumably have been expected to understand the risks he was taking. Hooley was acquitted but Lawson, who conducted his own case, was sentenced to one year's hard labour.

Despite his successes in attracting the titled to add lustre to the prospectuses of the companies he promoted, by the time Lawson sought to manipulate the nascent UK motor industry, the press was loud in proclaiming its doubts and dislike of his methods. He was also mistrusted by his colleagues in the motor world. The Motor Car Club which he had founded towards the end of 1895 was a thinly-disguised commercial operation and F R Simms and others found it desirable to create an independent body, the Automobile Club of Great Britain & Ireland (later the RAC), in July 1897.

After the Electric Tramway case, Lawson seems to have faded from the changing motor world — he was after all by then in his fifties. In August 1921 the *Autocar* carried letters from him, commenting on the early years of the industry, but it is significant that an article in the *Motor* shortly after his death, whilst charitably commenting that his chief fault was that 'his optimism was twenty-five years before the times' should also epitomise him as 'poor' Harry J Lawson. Lawson, who was married (his son Thomas E Lawson is named on DCe), died at Harrow, Middlesex, on 12 July 1925. He left £99 gross.

RICHARD STOREY

Writings:

letters to *Autocar* 20, 27 Aug 1921.

Sources:

Unpublished

BCe.

DCe.

PrC.

Published

C F Caunter, *The History and Development of Cycles as Illustrated by the Collection of Cycles in the Science Museum* Part I (HMSO, 1955).

A E Harrison, 'Joint-stock Company Flotation in the Cycle, Motor Vehicle and Related Industries 1882-1914' *Business History* 23 (1981).

St John C Nixon, 'H J Lawson, the Would-be Dictator of the British Motor Industry' *Veteran and Vintage Magazine* Jan 1957.

R D F Paul, 'Selling Cars in the '90s' *Motor* 29 Jan 1929.

John B Rae, *The American Automobile. A Brief History* (University of Chicago Press, 1965).

Gerald Rufus Isaacs, Marquess of Reading, *Rufus Isaacs, First Marquess of Reading by his Son* (2 vols, Hutchinson, 1942).

Kenneth Richardson, *The British Motor Industry 1896-1939* (Macmillan, 1977).

A Ritchie, *King of the Road* (Wildwood House, 1975).

Times 30 July 1901.

Geoffrey Williamson, *Wheels Within Wheels* (Bles, 1966).

LAYBORN, Thomas Alec Edwin

(1898-)

Assurance company executive

Thomas Alec Edwin Layborn was born at Chiswick on 30 November 1898, the son of William Edwin Layborn, a wine merchant who retired early, and his wife Mary Ellen née Stevens, who came of Essex farming stock. He was educated at Latymer Upper School, which he left in 1914 on the death of his father. He worked briefly for the Car & General Insurance Co Ltd before being appointed in 1915 to the Liverpool & London & Globe Insurance Co Ltd as a junior clerk. At the age of seventeen, he

LAYBORN Thomas Alec Edwin

T A E Layborn (courtesy of Professor Hugh Cockerell).

volunteered for the Artists' Rifles. He was later commissioned in the Royal Flying Corps and the Royal Air Force.

On demobilisation Layborn rejoined the Liverpool & London & Globe but after a few months obtained a position as a junior inspector with the Legal & General Assurance Society Ltd, an eighty-three-year-old company which was planning to expand and was taking powers to transact fire and accident insurance as well as life business. He served successively as a general inspector of agents in the East End, as chief fire and accident inspector at the City office, as City accident manager (1925) and as the Society's first West End manager (1926). While in the latter capacity he was sent in 1931 to South Africa to negotiate (successfully) a pension scheme for the Victoria Falls Power Co. In 1933 he was appointed group manager to control and expand group life and pensions business, of which the society was seeking to make a speciality, and in 1937 he became agency manager, one of the most senior positions in the society's hierarchy.

When Layborn joined the Legal & General, the society had only about 40 employees at its head office in Fleet Street. In the space of twenty-six years it was to become one of the most important life insurers with branches all over the country. Its rapid rise was in no small measure due to Layborn's success in selling, and in organising the sale of group life and pensions business. The task was facilitated by the purchase in 1933 of the UK pensions business of the Metropolitan Life Insurance Co of New York, which was the leader in the field but decided to withdraw from the UK in order to concentrate its attention on the US. Layborn's method was to appoint salesmen as resident inspectors with the promise that if the business they obtained was sufficient, they would soon be given a sub-branch to manage and ultimately a full branch. He took a personal hand in selling many large pension schemes, for example to the Austin Motor Co Ltd and the flour milling industry. By 1938 the Legal & General provided cover in group life and pensions schemes for 190,000 workers. Its leadership in this field is shown by the growth in its life fund from £25 million in 1933 to £41 million in 1938, although the number of policies issued to individuals did not rise. This increase in the fund exceeded that achieved by the leading company (the Prudential) in its ordinary life fund. From 1933 to 1945 the Legal & General's fund increased nearly threefold, and the growth was to continue. Concentration on group life and pensions schemes was the secret of success. By 1978 the aggregate premium income of insurance companies from group business exceeded for the first time that on ordinary life assurances issued to individuals. Group schemes then had a membership approaching 10 million. Layborn's marketing skills coupled with the actuarial abilities of Harold Ernest Raynes laid the foundation for the continued ascendancy of the Legal & General in this growth area.

He combined capacity for hard work with a gift for inspiring confidence in all he met. Thus his connection with Austins led to his becoming a director of the British Motor Corporation. His special knowledge of the pension field led to his appointment to the Mitchison Committee which was charged to report on the state of the Ministry of Pensions in view of the extra work imposed on it by the outbreak of the Second World War. In 1947 he was appointed to the Industrial Injuries Advisory Council on which he served for many years, and in 1960 he became a member of the committee set up by the Minister of Agriculture to consider and advise on the problem of fowl pest. His various activities received official recognition, a CBE in the 1944 Birthday Honours.

The combination of business and public duties during the Second World War, which involved very long hours of work, led to a state of severe physical and mental exhaustion which resulted in his retirement from the Legal & General in 1945. A few months of enforced rest gave him renewed energy and he set up in 1946 as an insurance consultant in life and pensions business in the name of Layborn & Son Ltd. (In 1920 he had married Helen Field, a teacher, daughter of John Field, a paymaster; they had a son and a daughter but the son died in 1948.) When Layborn started this business there were few such intermediaries. His success was such that in 1953 his business was acquired for a substantial sum by C T Bowring & Co (Insurance) Ltd and he became deputy chairman of the renamed C T Bowring & Layborn Ltd for whom he has continued to work until well over the age of eighty, still (1984) coming regularly to his office at 9.00 am.

In 1961 Layborn was appointed president of the Insurance Institute of London, the first insurance broker to hold that office since the Institute's foundation in 1907. He was the first president of the Corporation of Insurance Brokers' Society of Pension Consultants on its formation in 1958.

Starting without capital, connections or academic qualifications, he rose by virtue of the chance he found to exercise his personal gift of inspiring confidence in a rapidly-growing field of endeavour — the pensions industry.

HUGH COCKERELL

Writings:

'Practical Problems in Group Life and Pension Business' *Journal of the Chartered Insurance Institute* 39 (1936).

'New Thoughts on Pension and Group Schemes' *ibid* 50 (1953).

'Presidential address' *Journal of the Insurance Institute of London* 50 (1962).

Sources:

Unpublished

BCe.

MCe.

Interview with T A E Layborn 16 July 1980 and letters of 27 June, 17 July 1980.

Published

'President for 1961-62 — T A E Layborn, CBE, FCIB' *Journal of the Insurance Institute of London* 50 (1962).

Sunday Telegraph 30 June 1963.

H G Lazell, from a portrait by Dorothy Wilding (courtesy of Mr Paul Lazell).

LAZELL, Henry George Leslie

(1903-1982)

Pharmaceutical entrepreneur

Henry George Leslie (known as Leslie) Lazell was born in London on 23 May 1903, the elder son of Henry William Lazell, a wine merchant's manager, and his wife Ada Louise née King. At birth he was registered by mistake as a girl, but he never troubled to have this absurd error corrected. A year later his father, who had moved with the family to a post in Bombay, died, soon after the birth of another son. Mother and boys returned to London, where they lived frugally but contentedly with her parents who kept a railwaymen's lodging house in Camden Town; the mother later remarried and had two more sons. Leslie attended an LCC elementary school there, and at the age of thirteen-and-a-half left to become an office boy in the Inland Revenue at Somerset House.

In 1918 he failed the examination for a permanent civil service post: 'the greatest bit of luck that could possibly have befallen me', he afterwards admitted {Lazell (1975) 3}. That failure not only set his life in the direction of business but also gave him a resolve to succeed — a resolve put to the test during the next twelve years of unremitting application by day and in the evenings. He took a job in a bookmakers and was subsequently a ledger-keeper with Allen & Hanbury Ltd, pursuing his professional studies at night-school. After qualifying in bookkeeping, he passed the examinations of the Association of Certified and Corporate Accountants and the Chartered Institute of Secretaries; he later became a fellow of both these bodies.

Increasingly dissatisfied with what he regarded as the backward-looking management of Allen & Hanbury, in 1930 he accepted an offer from (Sir) Alexander Maclean, founder of the toothpaste and stomach powder firm, to become its accountant; then only twenty-seven years old, he passed himself off as thirty. There he introduced a sorely-needed budgeting system, and in 1936 was made a director. As the company's representative on various trade associations, he got to know the chairmen of the British subsidiaries of international companies and grasped the vulnerability of British firms to American competition and the consequent need to develop research facilities so as to counter this threat.

During 1938 Macleans Ltd was bought by Beechams Pills Ltd, the chairman of which was the financier Philip Hill (qv). Lazell greatly admired Hill for his integrity and courage. Hill in turn appreciated the same qualities in this diligent and independently-minded young man. In 1940 he appointed Lazell to the Beecham board and made him managing director of Macleans.

For Lazell the years of the Second World War gave him a crash course in management, when he learnt that the inevitable improvisation measures could be successfully carried out only within the framework of a clear business strategy. Backed by his chemist colleague Walter McGeorge, in 1943 he gained Philip Hill's ready consent to the establishment of a company research organisation, and in 1945 Beecham Research Laboratories Ltd was set up. At first this concentrated on research for consumer products, but Lazell's ultimate goal was the discovery of some really important drug that would be in great public demand, and as a result of some work the company undertook for the forces during the war, he fixed on penicillin. Brockham Park, near Dorking, was opened in 1947 as the company's research laboratory, and was for a number of years under Lazell's direct managerial control. The laboratory's expenses were met entirely from the earnings of Lucozade, a glucose drink manufactured by a firm which he had persuaded Beecham to acquire, and which then contributed one-third of Beecham's profits.

For the Beecham group, the period from Philip Hill's death in 1944 to 1951 was an unhappy one. The new chairman, Sir Stanley Holmes (later Lord Dovercourt), was very busy as a politician and practising accountant, and executive responsibilities were at various times divided between the managing director and three assistant managing directors. The group comprised no less than 105 companies, only partly co-ordinated; hence there was little overall corporate strategy, and an atmosphere of intrigue overhung the group. Moreover, the introduction of the National Health Service in 1948 seemed to herald the demise of the old proprietary medicine trade in Britain. At first the group diversified in the wrong direction, into wholesale groceries, which yielded only narrow margins and in which the group lacked the necessary expertise; many of the low-earning acquisitions later had to be sold off.

The main shareholders were then Philip Hill Investment Trust Ltd and the Eagle Star Insurance Co Ltd, and in 1949 Kenneth (later Lord) Keith joined the Beecham board to represent these institutions' interests. Although in reasonable shape, Beecham did not enjoy a particularly high standing in the City of London. To provide the strong top direction that was clearly needed, Keith in 1951 induced Lazell to become group managing director.

Now that he had a free hand in the Beecham group, Lazell's object was to turn the company into an international science-based and marketing-orientated firm: something that was all too rare in British industry of the early 1950s, when the country's products tended to be technologically backward and its companies lacked marketing consciousness. Most fundamentally, he was able to promote a massive research effort, in which — despite all his other duties — he took much personal interest and which he kept supplied with the necessary funds.

Perhaps uniquely among British companies in those days, Beecham made use of eminent scientists as outside consultants, notably Sir Charles Dodds (1899-1973), Sir Ernest Chain (1906-79) and Sir Ian Heilbron (1886-1959). Commercial development of penicillin had taken place mainly in the United States, and in 1955 Beecham reached the decision to investigate the possibility of producing new and improved penicillins by chemical means. It received technical help first of all from Chain's own research institute in Rome and later from the American pharmaceutical company Bristol-Myers Co. After the Beecham group scientists had succeeded in isolating the basic core of penicillin, in 1959 it launched its first semisynthetic penicillin Broxil, and also concluded an important licensing agreement with Bristol-Myers. Other pharmaceuticals — notably Penbritin in 1961 — followed during the next decade. Some years passed before the expenditure on developing these products was recouped, but these discoveries gave Beecham an important position in the world antibiotic market.

To turn Beecham into an international company, the overriding need was to break into the market of the United States, one which required considerable financial and management resources. Lazell had regularly to cross the Atlantic to help achieve that breakthrough. In the 1950s two products above all were successful there: Brylcreem, and Maclean's tooth paste. Brylcreem took six years before it became profitable there; Macleans took three years, gaining 8 per cent of the US toothpaste market. In other products there were costly reverses. By the mid-1960s Lazell was planning a campaign to market pharmaceuticals on a large scale in America. In 1968-69 the Western Hemisphere (including Australia and New Zealand) accounted for almost a quarter of the group's sales and nearly a third of its profits.

The group's exertions in the United States were necessarily at the expense of efforts in the European market, which had to be held back until the mid-1960s. Thereafter Europe — with the development of the EEC — became its main growth area. In 1968-69 Europe contributed 14 per cent of sales and over 20 per cent of profits; equivalent figures in 1983-84 were 26 per cent of both sales and profits.

As to marketing generally, Lazell had been interested in sales techniques ever since his early days at Macleans. However, it was his hard-won experience in the American market, aided by some very able managers, that helped the Beecham group to become one of the earliest British companies making use of the new medium of television.

In 1958 Lazell became group chairman. He later claimed that the beginning of 1962 was a watershed in the group's affairs when the 'tide of success, previously running strongly along the advertised proprietary products channel, altered course and thereafter ran with increasing strength along the pharmaceutical channel'. {Lazell (1975) 151} While proprietary products continued to account for the greater proportion of sales, pharmaceuticals were from then on to be the big profit-earners.

On the organisation side, his great achievement was to assemble the large number of disparate companies into a coherent group. In 1962 he reshaped it into the three divisions of food and drink, toiletries, and pharmaceuticals. By 1968, when he retired at the age of sixty-five, group turnover (for 1968-69) was £133.9 million and profits £25.2 million, a ratio of 18.8 per cent; turnover in 1951-52 had been £25.4 million and profits £2.6 million, a ratio of 10 per cent. He was appointed president of the Beecham group, and remained as chairman of the US Beecham Inc until 1972.

Leslie Lazell belonged to the last generation in British history of men who could rise, without even full-time secondary education, to the highest ranks of domestic and international business. In some ways, therefore, he was a throw-back to the self-educated and idiosyncratic nineteenth-century entrepreneur. He staunchly supported the competitive system, and was a founding subscriber to the Institute of Economic Affairs. At the same time, he expected the highest ethical standards in business and refused to claim more for his own products than he felt they genuinely deserved; he played an influential role in the setting up of codes of conduct for advertising in Britain.

His analytical mind allowed him to secure a layman's grasp of such matters as pharmaceutical research and sophisticated product marketing. This mental receptiveness and voracious reading — especially of autobiographies — in his limited spare time engendered in him an eclectic view of life, one which turned him away from the British establishment: it was no coincidence that he received no recognition from the state or from a university. His time as an office boy in Somerset House and wartime wranglings with the bureaucracy gave him a lifelong distaste for the civil service mentality. Outspoken to a fault, he was prepared to be tough and decisive within the group, particularly when inefficient management had to be changed. He believed in singlemindedly building on a company's strengths and cutting out its weakest parts.

A slightly-built man of medium height, his energy and enthusiasm marked him out in any company, and he was able to do as much as he did because of the support of a happy family life. His outside activities were carefully chosen and actively pursued. From 1966 to 1968 he was a non-executive director of ICI, where he was a persistent critic of what he saw as that company's bureaucratic and top-heavy structure. He was chairman of the board of governors of Ashridge Management College and a council member of the Institute of Directors, and the appeal president of the British Heart Foundation. After his retirement he spent much of his time in Bermuda, enjoying his favourite pastime of sailing. As a young man he had been an enthusiastic cricketer, playing for a local team in Ealing.

Leslie Lazell died in London on 17 November 1982: fifty-four years to the day after he had married Doris Beatrice Try, by whom he had one son.

T A B CORLEY

Writings:

'The Years with Beechams' *Management Today* Nov 1968.

From Pills to Pencillin: The Beecham Story (Heinemann, 1975).

Sources:

Unpublished

Beecham Group, PLC, Annual Reports 1944/45 onwards, tribute (1983) by chairman, Sir Graham Wilkins.

BCe.

MCe.

DCe.

Information from Margaret Ackrill, Ronald Halstead, Lord Keith, Paul Lazell and Sir Graham Wilkins.

H G Leslie Lazell, 'Development and Organisation of the Beecham Group Ltd' (Edwards Seminar paper 252, 23 Feb 1960).

Published

Sir Ernest Chain, 'Thirty Years of Penicillin Therapy' *Proceedings of the Royal Society of London. Biological Sciences* 179 (1971).

Chemist and Druggist 218 (27 Nov 1982).

Times 19 Nov 1982.

Sir Graham Wilkins, obituary of H G L Lazell *Pharmaceutical Journal* 11 Dec 1982.

Walter Leaf (from The Institute of Bankers 1897–1929 *Blades, East & Blades, 1929).*

LEAF, Walter

(1852-1927)

Clearing banker

Walter Leaf was born at Norwood, South London, on 26 November 1852, the eldest son of Charles John Leaf, merchant, and his wife Isabella Ellen, daughter of John Tyas of the *Times*. Charles Leaf was a partner in Leaf & Co, wholesale and export merchants and warehousemen. Established in 1790, Leaf & Co was then probably the largest house in London dealing in silks, ribbons and velvet. Walter Leaf's education was characteristic of the social rise of the large London merchants in the mid-nineteenth century: Harrow, followed by Trinity College, Cambridge, where Walter Leaf distinguished himself in classics, being awarded a scholarship in 1871 and, after graduating in 1874, a fellowship in 1875; he was to remain a distinguished classical scholar for the rest of his life.

Despite his love of classics and an intended career at the Bar, Walter Leaf entered the soft goods trade in 1874, a year which saw the death of both his grandfather and uncle, thus leaving his father, also in worsening health, as sole partner. Consequently, Walter was asked to join the family firm. After apprenticeship as a junior partner, he became a full partner three years later in 1877, at the age of twenty-five. Walter Leaf started with the firm at a difficult period. His father was not just the only surviving partner, but also the executor for his own father and brother and thus the trustee of the whole family fortune. The business was burdened with heavy commitments to legatees of the deceased partners. Walter Leaf was then of the opinion that his father should have converted the firm into a limited company, but could not persuade him to take this step until 1888.

The difficulties of the business during the late 1870s and 1880s, with its very low rate of profit, would ultimately lead in 1893 to an amalgamation with a rival house, Pawsons & Co, under the name of Pawsons & Leaf Ltd. Walter Leaf decided to retire from active management of the new firm, only retaining a seat on the board.

It was as a partner of Leaf & Co that Walter Leaf was in 1891 elected to the board of the London & Westminster Bank, an appointment which surprised and gratified him. The London & Westminster Bank was then the third largest bank in the country, measured by its deposits, and certainly was the most prestigious, apart from the Bank of England. Its board was mainly composed of the most distinguished merchants and merchant bankers in the country, very often partners in firms represented on the Court of the Bank of England and in the other major London joint-stock banks. As Leaf stressed in his autobiography, his years spent as a partner in a commercial firm gave him a wealth of experience which provided him with a good basis in his new career. A merchant on the board of a joint-stock bank was no mere figurehead, particularly in the case of banks such as the London & Westminster Bank and the London & County Bank, which were extremely conservative and whose boards held daily meetings, closely controlling the activities of their managers. Moreover, without being technicians in banking operations, merchants knew the quality of the bills and their experience as well as their City connections were a very useful asset to their banks. Herein lies the true ambiguity of the profession of banker in English banking: bank directors were weighty City men, with seats also on the boards of insurance companies and probably investment trusts, but whose main concerns were with their private business, who collectively supervised the working of their bank.

Walter Leaf's appointment to the London & Westminster Bank in 1891 coincided with the acceleration of the amalgamation movement. The provincial newcomers, Lloyds, and the Midland (under Edward Holden (qv)), invaded the City and were becoming threatening; as a result of their vast and ambitious amalgamation policy, by the beginning of this century they surpassed in size the London & County Bank and the London & Westminster Bank. Another danger came from the 'Quaker connection', and the foundation of the modern Barclays Bank in 1896. This increased competition led to the amalgamation of the London & County Bank and the London & Westminster Bank. Leaf was in the chair at the extraordinary general meeting of the London & Westminster Bank and stated very clearly that both banks regarded size as an important element in bringing new openings for a bank's activity, and that prestige was a most valuable asset. The new bank would now need a permanent chairman and vice-chairman. Leaf, who had devoted more and more of his time to banking since his retirement from his commercial firm, was elected vice-chairman, the chairman being the Second Viscount Goschen, son of the statesman. The amalgamation between the London & County Bank and the London & Westminster Bank was the first between two banks of truly prime importance. The more common practice had been for large joint-stock banks to absorb a smaller joint-stock or private bank. The new bank regained its position amongst the largest in the country, with deposits amounting to £70,198,000 and total assets of £83,795,000.

With the First World War, Leaf was quickly obliged to assume the chairman's functions, Lord Goschen being called to other duties. His career, if not as a banker, but as the real head of a large bank, had now started. However, he was officially elected chairman of the bank only in 1917, a position he retained until his death in 1927. Leaf's name is linked with the definite shape that the Westminster Bank acquired as one of the 'Big Five' after the war. In 1917, the London County & Westminster Bank acquired the Ulster Bank (which continued to operate under its own name) by an exchange of shares, and more important, early in 1918, it amalgamated with Parr's Bank, then the sixth largest bank in the country; changing the bank's name to London County Westminster & Parr's Bank Ltd. In 1923 the name was shortened to Westminster Bank Ltd. Similar steps were simultaneously undertaken by the four other major joint-stock banks.

As head of one of the 'Big Five' Leaf was involved in the economic problems of the post-war period, the peace conference, and the problem of reparations. Apparently, he fulfilled his functions very satisfactorily, without, however, exerting any more influence than that of other chairmen of large banks, or making any particular theoretical contribution. On political economy, his views were representative of the banking sector. He remained a free trader all his life. In 1925 he favoured an early return to gold and was not particularly worried about its effects on industry; and when in 1924, with the first Labour Government, the question of nationalising the banks arose, he was not surprisingly a firm opponent. His *Banking* published in 1926 in the Home University Library series is an excellent little handbook but its innovations are concerned only with practical aspects of the post-war period. In fact Leaf's literary contributions are more important, particularly his translation of Homer's *Iliad*. Leaf belonged to that category of English bankers whose semi-amateur status allowed them freedom to attend to other interests. Sir John Lubbock, later Lord Avebury (qv), is probably the most famous example. However, a generation younger with more professional commitments, Leaf, besides being a Homerist, was widely knowledgeable, particularly in languages, psychology, mathematics and astronomy.

Leaf also played a prominent role in the associations connected with his profession. As a merchant, he was a founder of the London Chamber of Commerce in 1882, becoming deputy chairman in 1885-86 and chairman in 1887. After the war he was associated with the International Chamber of Commerce from its inception, being one of the British delegates, as president of the Institute of Bankers, to its initial meeting in Paris in 1920. He was elected a vice-president in 1923, and president in 1925. It was as chairman of the Westminster Bank that, in 1919, he was elected president of the Institute of Bankers for two years. Similarly, he came to preside over other banking associations: the Committee of London Clearing Banks, of which he was deputy chairman in 1917 and chairman in 1918, and the Central Association of Bankers when it merged with the Country Bankers Association to form the British Bankers Association. His various interests also brought him honorary posts in several other institutions, including the presidency of the Classical Association in 1921 and appointments as a governor of Harrow School and Marlborough College. Politically, Walter Leaf was in harmony with the general banking community: Liberal, then Liberal Unionist after 1886. He seems to have considered standing for Parliament, but served only at the local level, being member of the London County Council for East Marylebone, 1901-4.

Walter Leaf belongs to that small group of men who have moulded the English banking system into its present form. While becoming professional bankers, that is devoting most of their time to a large joint-stock bank and not to a private firm, these men retained an amateur, gentlemanly style characteristic of the English upper class.

Leaf married in 1894 Charlotte Mary, daughter of the author John Addington Symonds; they had a son and a daughter. Walter Leaf died on 8 March 1927 leaving £125,740 gross.

YOUSSEF CASSIS

Writings:

Walter Leaf wrote little on banking but a great deal on classical subjects; in the latter field only his most important studies are listed here.

(ed) *Iliad* (with English Notes and Introduction) (2 vols, Macmillan, 1886-1888).

Troy, a Study in Homeric Geography (Macmillan, 1912).

Homer and History (Macmillan, 1915).

(ed) *Strabo on the Road* (With Translations and Commentary) (Cambridge: Cambridge University Press, 1923).

Banking (Williams & Norgate, 1926, 4th edition 1943).

'Some Chapters of Autobiography With a Memoir' in Charlotte Leaf (ed), *Walter Leaf* (below).

Sources:

Unpublished

BCe.

MCe.

PrC.

Speeches as chairman of the London County & Westminster Bank, the London County Westminster & Parr's Bank and the Westminster Bank, 1915-1927.

Walter Leaf, Inaugural Addresses to the Institute of Bankers London, 1919 and 1920.

Published

Bankers' Magazine 1927.

DNB.

Edwin Green, *Debtors to Their Profession. A History of the Institute of Bankers 1879-1979* (Methuen, 1979).

Theodore E Gregory, *The Westminster Bank through a Century* (2 vols, Oxford University Press, 1936).

Charlotte Leaf (ed), *Walter Leaf* (John Murray, 1932).

Donald E Moggridge, *British Monetary Policy 1924-1931* (Cambridge: Cambridge University Press, 1972).

WWW.

James Leathart (courtesy of Dr G Leathart).

LEATHART, James

(1820-1895)

Lead manufacturer

James Leathart was born at Alston, Cumberland, on 25 November 1820, the son of John Leathart, a mining engineer and lead miner, and his wife Margaret née Setree. James was educated at Alston Grammar School until the age of fourteen and soon afterwards he was sent to Newcastle where he started work as a clerk for Locke, Blackett & Co. This firm of lead manufacturers had been set up in the 1790s by a London lead merchant and Christopher Blackett, agent for the Blackett/Beaumont lead mines in the northern Pennines. Although the business was owned by partners descended from the founders, they took no active part in the business, which was controlled by managers. It was, in the 1830s, a medium-sized firm with a broad range of lead products, refining pig lead to obtain silver and manufacturing red and white lead for use as pigments, lead sheet and pipe and also producing lead shot by dropping it into a deep shaft in place of the normal use of a shot tower.

James's hours of work at the firm were long, but, encouraged by his father, he began to read widely in scientific subjects, especially chemistry and metallurgy, in order to obtain a better understanding of lead manufacturing. In his early twenties his efforts began to be rewarded as he was given increasing management responsibilty and in 1846 he was made responsible for the erection and subsequent running of a works which the firm had decided to establish at St Anthony's on the Tyne for the smelting and refining of imported Spanish ores. By contemporary standards this was a large lead works with almost 100 employees in the early 1850s and 150 by the end of the decade.

Leathart's successful establishment of the new works gained him a partnership in the firm by 1851 when he was joint managing partner with a salary of £250 per annum; this was raised to £450 per annum in 1857 when he became sole managing partner of the firm, which then had a total capital of £80,000. Leathart's share of the partnership was one-eighth, although he had actually paid up only a little over £4,000 and was to be allowed to finance the remainder out of his share in future profits. At partnership renewals in 1864 and 1874 Leathart injected new capital, again financed from his share in future profits, in order to raise his share to one-quarter and then one-third of the firm, whose total capital was by 1874 £130,000; by that time his salary was £600 per annum.

Leathart was entirely responsible for the expansion of the firm, which included the purchase of the Wallsend Lead Smelting Works in 1874. By this time, Locke, Blackett & Co, with three works, was probably the largest lead manufacturing firm on Tyneside, which was the dominant centre of the industry. In addition the firm was in the van of technical progress, being the first Tyneside business to adopt the Parkes process for desilverising pig lead and adopting exclusive Tyneside licences to work several newly-patented lead manufacturing processes. In the late 1870s and early 1880s however, the firm got into financial difficulties as a result of overcapacity and having to write off losses from the failure of some of its new processes. The works were sold to a public limited liability company in 1891, the old partners receiving only £29,000 for their assets. Leathart became managing director of the new company, in which he owned 10 per cent of the ordinary share capital. Reorganisation did little for the firm, profits being less than £6,000 per annum in the early 1890s, despite sales of 6,000 tons of lead chemicals, 8,000 tons of metal products and half a million ounces of silver annually.

Leathart had few interests apart from his work, although he was a director of the Tyne Steam Shipping Co, and of William Cleland & Co, a JP for Gateshead and secretary of Newcastle Art School. He was an active Anglican, and was churchwarden of St Helen's Church, Low Fell, Gateshead for some years. He was a Liberal, though he took no active role in local or national politics. His major interest was his collection of contemporary paintings, chiefly of pre-Raphaelites, which was described by *The Athenaeum* in 1873 as the most important private collection of modern paintings in the neighbourhood of Newcastle. It included a portrait of Leathart by Ford Madox Brown and of Mrs Leathart by D G Rossetti. In June 1858 Leathart had married Maria, eldest daughter of Thomas Hedley (qv), the Tyneside soap manufacturer. They had fourteen children who spent much of their childhood in a playhouse at the end of their father's garden, built so that he could have undisturbed contemplation of his collection of pictures and china.

James Leathart died on 9 August 1895, leaving an estate valued at £14,924 gross.

D J ROWE

Sources:

Unpublished

Tyne and Wear RO, records of Locke, Blackett & Co.

MCe.

Family papers in private hands.

Published

Newcastle Daily Chronicle 12 Aug 1895.

Oils, Colours and Drysalteries 15 May 1895.

Paintings and Drawings from the Leathart Collection 7 October-18 November 1968 (Newcastle upon Tyne: Laing Art Gallery Catalogue, 1968).

Penny Magazine supplement 13 (Aug 1844).

D J Rowe, *Lead Manufacturing in Britain. A History* (Croom Helm, 1983).

W White, *Northumberland and the Border* (Chapman & Hall, 1859).

LEBUS, Harris

(1852-1907)

Furniture manufacturer

Harris Lebus was born in Sculcoates, Hull, on 21 May 1852, the eldest son of Lewis {BCe} or Louis Lebus and his wife Eleanor née Fletcher. His father had moved from Breslau to Hull in 1840 and set up in business as a furniture-maker on his own account. The family, which eventually comprised five sons and three daughters, moved to Whitechapel in London in 1857 where they established a furniture-making business and then in 1862 to Willclose Lane in London, taking over larger premises.

Harris Lebus joined his father in 1868 as a cabinetmaker but left him in 1873 after a quarrel and worked for a year with the antiques dealer D L Isaacs. Afterwards he returned to the family business which now employed 30 craftsmen. In 1879, on the death of his father, he took sole charge of the business, producing furniture for the domestic market. His brother Solomon (Sol) joined him in 1881 as joint owner of the firm, the other brothers and sisters choosing to emigrate to California. The growth of the company from this point was rapid. In 1885 larger premises at Tabernacle Street, Finsbury, were acquired and when they were burnt down in 1894 as a result of a fire next door, they were rebuilt to provide 121,000 square feet of manufacturing space. By the late 1890s there were some 1,000 craftsmen employed, controlled by 45 staff, making it the largest furniture manufacturer in the country. Turnover had risen from £34,000 per annum in 1887 to £223,000 in 1898. So great was this expansion that in 1900 the Ferry Lane site in Tottenham was acquired which eventually covered 51 acres and was, for over fifty years, the largest furniture manufacturing plant in the world. By 1907 this site was fully operational and employed over 3,000 on the manufacture of domestic furniture. There was always a close link with Maples stores and the sales analysis of 1910 shows these percentages on sales of £380,000: Maples 11.8 per cent, London 21.3 per cent, country areas 41 per cent, overseas 25.9 per cent.

Harris married Sarah Mayers, daughter of Andrew Mayers, a cigar maker, in 1878; they had at least two children.

Harris Lebus died on 21 September 1907, leaving £510,436 gross.

HEW REID

Sources:

Unpublished

Family records.

BCe.

MCe.

PrC.

Information from Anthony Lebus.

LEBUS, Sir Hermann Andrew

(1884-1957)

Furniture manufacturer

Hermann Andrew Lebus was born in Whitechapel, London, on 1 June 1884, the second son of Harris Lebus (qv) and his wife Sarah née Mayers. He was educated at the City of London School and privately. After his father died in 1907, Hermann and his elder brother, Louis (1883-1963) succeeded their father in the family business, being joined by their cousins Louis Solomon and Robert, sons of Solomon Lebus, Harris's brother.

The company dominated the domestic furniture market throughout the first half of the century, though growth in size was not on its nineteenth century scale; nevertheless the output of the factory rose until 1939 when the turnover was close to £2 million. In normal times the main business of the firm was the manufacture of household furniture of good quality which, as a result of scientific mass and flow production techniques, was sold at prices suitable to the medium and low income groups.

Wartime production of furniture was negligible and the factory was turned over to aircraft production and Lebus were the major producers of the Albermarle, Hotspur Glider, Horsa Glider, and the Mosquito. The other major area of wartime production was landing craft of all sizes and descriptions. The firm's net profits (but pre-income tax) moved from £280,411 in 1937 to £159,874 in 1939 and peaked during the war at £494,241 in 1942; by 1946 they were back above £350,000.

In 1947 the firm became a public company, Harris Lebus Ltd, with an authorised capital of £4 million, of which £2 million was issued in ordinary stock and £1 million in cumulative preference stock. Its fixed assets were £1.5 million and net assets £3 million; net profits (pre-income tax) were £428,983. Hermann became chairman and managing director and the other members of the family on the board were L S Lebus, Bob Lebus and the sons of Louis H Lebus, Anthony and Oliver Lebus.

In the post-war period the company's productivity continued to grow though the labour force remained around the 3,000 mark and in 1960 turnover was £11,600,000 with a profit of £646,000.

Lebus's influence extended beyond the family concern. He was chairman of the Furniture Industry Postwar Reconstruction Committee; a member of the Board of Trade Utility Furniture Advisory Committee, 1942-49; and served on the Furniture Development Council, 1949-57. He was a liveryman of the Worshipful Company of Coopers since 1910. A JP, he was made a CBE in 1920, and was knighted in 1946.

He married in 1912 Ethel, daughter of Charles Hart of Chicago; they had two sons and a daughter.

Sir Hermann Lebus died on 15 December 1957, leaving £165,325 gross.

HEW REID

Sources:

Unpublished

Family records.

BCe.

PrC.

Information from Anthony Lebus.

Published

Times 17 Dec 1957.

Times *Prospectuses* 101 (1947).

WWW.

Henry Lee (courtesy of Manchester Central Library).

Sir Joseph C Lee (courtesy of Manchester Central Library).

LEE, Henry   *and*   LEE, Sir Joseph Cocksey

(1817-1904)   (1832-1894)

Cotton manufacturers

Lee Lee, a muslin manufacturer of Chorley, Lancashire, suffered badly in the depression of 1826, yet continued to combine cotton manufacturing with farming until, at his death in 1837, he left a modest fortune of £300, together with outstanding business debts. Despite such inauspicious origins, within the next century three of his grandsons had headed major textile companies in Lancashire, the Calico Printers' Association (L B Lee (qv)), the Fine Cotton Spinners' & Doublers' Association (H W Lee) and Tootal Broadhurst Lee Co Ltd (Harold Lee, 1852-1936). Among Lee Lee's numerous immediate progeny, the most outstanding were Henry, his second son, born 29 November 1817 and Joseph Cocksey, his ninth and youngest son, born 18 January 1832. In harness with Henry Tootal Broadhurst (1822-96), they were responsible for the emergence of Tootal Broadhurst Lee & Co Ltd (hereafter Tootals) as one of the great late-nineteenth century textile firms of Lancashire; in turn, they founded a remarkable business dynasty.

Henry Lee, during the period of his father's prosperity, spent his ninth year at the school of the Congregational minister Rev J T Price, but returned home in 1826. Thereafter he helped in his father's business, while benefiting from the deep influence, particularly in his religious life, of his mother Anne, daughter of Joseph Cocksey, 'gentleman', of Bolton. Later he served an apprenticeship with John Goodair, cotton manufacturer of Preston, but formerly a warehouseman at Chorley, where, like Lee Lee, he attended the Congregational Chapel in Hollinshead Street. About 1835 Henry Lee entered the warehouse of Robert Gardner, who, having also been a muslin manufacturer in Chorley in the 1820s, had become by the 1830s one of Manchester's leading cotton entrepreneurs, partner in the spinning of fine cotton with Thomas Bazley (at Manchester and Bolton) and in the manufacture and shipping of white cotton goods with William Atkinson. It was the latter branch which Lee entered, and with which he remained when ca 1842 Gardner was succeeded in the partnership by the silk manufacturer Edward Tootal. Atkinson, Tootal & Co was to provide the crucial opening for Lee's talents. Besides the Manchester warehouse, the firm operated in the 1840s and 1850s as cotton and muslin manufacturers at Preston (in close association with Gardners) and as muslin manufacturers at Bolton. Lee, as purchaser of cloth and as salesman, was rigorous in his insistence on high-quality workmanship, a policy to become distinctive of Tootals in later years. The retirement of William Atkinson in 1848, and the diversion of Edward Tootal's energies to railways paved the way for Lee to emerge as the leading partner by 1855, together with Tootal's nephew, Henry Tootal Broadhurst, in the firm which thus became styled Tootal Broadhurst &

Lee. In 1859 the partnership was enlarged with the entry of Robert Scott, cashier, and Joseph C Lee, Henry's brother, who benefiting from his brother's success, had joined the firm at sixteen, after an education at Manchester Grammar School, and had since travelled extensively on the firm's behalf.

The main basis for the rise to prominence of Tootals was their success in the manufacture by powerloom of fine and fancy fabrics, hitherto the preserve of hand-labour. This transition from hand to power was largely accomplished through the erection of the firm's Sunnyside Mills at Rumworth, Bolton, between 1862 and 1865. In supervising the establishment of these mills, Henry Lee found full scope for his resourcefulness and ingenuity as a manufacturer. A quarter of a century later his achievement evoked the eulogies of contemporaries. The Sunnyside Mills were thus, 'in every respect model mills, and the most perfectly organised concern we have ever seen. For rapid, efficient and economical production, under complete and easy control, they stand supreme' {British Trade Journal 1 June 1887}. The first mill had concentrated on weaving, with its number of looms rising from 960 in 1865 to 2,529 by 1881. In 1870, a spinning-mill was erected, which by the 1880s contained 60,000 spindles and spun about 2 million lb of raw cotton per annum. In 1880 the old Bee Hive Mill had been purchased and equipped with 16,364 ring-spindles. Net capital employed rose rapidly from the initial £7,000 to £209,701 in 1884, while gross assets rose from £8,901 to £341,125. Profitability was sufficient not only to pay for investment and renewals but to add over £200,000 to the resources of the Manchester 'parent company' over these years. Losses were recorded only once between 1862 and 1885, while net profits averaged £17,380 per annum. This level of profitability attests to Henry Lee's success as an entrepreneur, a success which must, in part, be ascribed to his personal qualities.

Lee was thus widely praised for the foresight and vigour with which he set up Sunnyside during the Cotton Famine, while the mills themselves revealed much organisational skill. They were remarkable for their order, cleanliness and systematic working, with great economy in the use of materials and machinery. Lee's fertile mechanical brain contributed a whole series of improvements to powerlooms for fancy fabrics between 1869 and 1886, while self-acting mules, American ring spindles, and electric stop motions kept the spinning side at the forefront of technological innovation. The need to keep ahead of competitors was constantly urged by Henry Lee. By the 1880s the Bolton works also had its own foundry, machine shops, and a fully up-to-date bleaching-house. The yarn produced, ranging in fineness from 40 to 60 hanks per lb, was destined for export, doubling, and sewing thread as well as for the firm's weaving side, which produced a wide variety of fabrics from plain shirtings to fancy dress goods, noted for excellence of quality. Productivity was bolstered not only by technological change but by Lee's 'enlightened' approach to labour. Imbued with a keen sense of business as a God-given vocation, he devoted much attention to the moral, spiritual and material welfare of the workforce. In addition to providing some workmen's cottages, the Sunnyside Institute provided adult and child education, while dining-rooms and baths were available. Lee was also a generous benefactor of local churches and chapels. He earned the workers' fulsome praise for 'that constant presence and vigilance of a master which ensures order, regularity and harmony among the men', and for his 'anxiety for our moral well-being and advancement' {Illuminated Address, Sept 1867}. Such 'benevolence' was rewarded by a workforce noted for its stability and loyalty. Labour relations were generally good; for, although the 1887 list of prices led to a strike, disputes were normally settled by 'friendly conference'. The 'spirit of good fellowship' at which Lee aimed was bolstered by his introduction of Saturday half-time in advance of legislation and by his assuring constancy of employment. No theory of industrial management nor any 'labour strategy' lay behind Lee's entrepreneurship — merely the dictates of a well-developed Nonconformist conscience, which urged that 'one of the major obligations of wealth is to devote it to the service of God, by using it in the service of Man' {Illuminated Address, 15 May 1886}.

With Sunnyside Mills as the main centre of manufacturing success and profitability, Tootals built up a series of interlocking mills. The Preston works, having been moved from Kay St to Bamber Bridge in 1869, were abandoned by 1877 but in 1865 and 1872 land had been purchased at Newton Heath, Manchester, and this became the site of the 900-loom Ten Acres Mill, devoted to the manufacture of the finest quality cotton and mixed fabrics. In 1881, the Black Lane Mills at Radcliffe were purchased and re-equipped with modern machinery, embracing 55,000 spindles and 470 looms. In 1884, the range of Tootals' products was extended by an ultimately ill-fated venture into the manufacture of sewing thread, a 'boom' industry in the 1870s and 1880s in home and foreign markets. Largely under J C Lee's auspices (but in association with Wm Waller & Co), the Lee Spinning Co was established at Dan Lane, Atherton. It was equipped with the most up-to-date machinery, with 45,000 doubling spindles in a mill which was 'everything that is best' {*British Trade Journal* 1 June 1887} in arrangement. Here the Lees aimed to produce high quality sewing-cotton from yarn spun at Black Lane and Rumworth. Finally, at the Cornbrook Works, Manchester, the Lee Spinning Co's thread was spooled, but this factory also employed a large number of girls hemming handerkerchiefs, 'with sewing-machines of special invention', and 'apparent prosperity and cheerfulness' {*British Trade Journal* (1887) 431}. By 1887 these diverse manufacturing operations employed in all ca 5,000 operatives, 172,000 spindles and 3,500 looms. Tootals were thus the third largest of the great combined firms of Lancashire, after Rylands and Horrockses; however, there may have been some truth in their claim that, in the extent and variety of their products, they stood 'at the head of the trade' {PRO FO 27/2531}.

The finishing of the firm's goods was undertaken partly at Sunnyside but calico-printing was carried out by the Rossendale Printing Co at Loveclough, Rawtenstall, which was owned by J C Lee, Henry's brother. A small-scale firm employing only 164 workers in 1840, this printworks had been modernised and enlarged by J C Lee in the 1870s. It remained under his sole proprietorship, not that of the Tootal partnership. J C Lee was thus to play some role in schemes for price-fixing among calico printers in the early 1890s. On his death in 1894, the firm passed to his eldest son, L B Lee. In 1899, it became the fifth-largest of the Lancashire calico-printing firms joining the Calico Printers' Association, with a gross valuation of £351,520.

Tootals' warehouse and offices in Mosley Street, Manchester, co-ordinated its dispersed manufacturing and finishing operations with those of the merchanting side. For Tootals, unlike most manufacturing firms, continued to market extensively (in the years 1888-91, merchanting contributed ca 50 per cent of total profits), and unlike, for example, Rylands, looked more to exports than to the home trade. Offices and warehouses were also established at Bradford, Belfast and Paris, while a series of agencies directed the firm's goods world-wide, although more particularly to the sophisticated markets of Europe and the United States, the latter an outlet which Henry Lee had assiduously cultivated. Tootals were, therefore, almost uniquely strong in their degree of vertical integration at the upper end of the market, a reflection, in turn, of their 'personnel' with 'an all-round power possessed by very few houses' {*British Trade Journal* 1 July 1887}. Within this team, productive efficiency was largely the forte of Henry and his sons who were to follow him in the Bolton Mills' management, while Joseph, particularly by the 1880s, provided the commercial genius responsible for the quality of products, their penetration of overseas markets, and the administrative skills necessary to organise an increasingly complex empire.

Tootal's market reputation was built up largely on its fancy dress goods, in which quality, design, taste and skill were all-important. Here J C Lee's fertility of mind lay behind the vast array of different fabrics and designs which the firm produced; Joseph held diversity to be the key to saleability in increasingly overstocked markets. Tootals' merchanting was thus crucial as it ensured a close link between the market and manufacturer which other firms lacked. Lee's personal interest in design was considerable; he owned a large collection of decorative textiles and himself contributed many designs. He, and the firm, also became important patrons of the movement for improved technical and artistic education, which revived in Manchester in the 1870s. He thus became president of the Manchester School of Art, chairman of the Whitworth Institute and vice-president of the Manchester Technical School. Such institutions, he believed, were essential to improving the quality of labour, itself vital to British competitiveness. On the same grounds, those of discouraging skill, Lee disapproved of trade unions, while seeing guilds as a defence of craftsmen, as well as an expression of the joint interests of masters and men. Lee also sought to improve public taste, leading in the 1880s a movement for popularising calico prints for ladies' wear. It was thus a stimulus both to the improvement of labour and taste, as well as a celebration of the achievements of industry, that he acted as chairman of the Executive Committee of the Manchester Royal Jubilee Exhibition of 1887. This was, in many ways, Lee's most ostensible and outstanding contribution to the civic life of Manchester. His interest in the application of art to industry also led to his participation in the Antwerp and Paris Exhibitions of 1885 and 1889 respectively.

Joseph C Lee also contributed to the success of the firm, and to national commercial policy through the vast fund of commercial knowledge of which he became the repository. His expertise in the field of tariffs was invaluable to the firm in a period of tightening trade barriers, when the difference between success and failure was the ability, as he noted, 'to work between the lines of the tariff' {PRO, FO 27/2583 Bateman to Dilke, 4 Jan 1882}. Painstaking in these detailed questions, he guided Tootals' goods behind the tariff walls of Europe and America, although not able to prevent a considerable drop in volume to the latter. Lee's unrivalled knowledge of cotton manufacturing and trade led to his becoming ex-officio tariff consultant to the Board of Trade and the Foreign Office. In 1881-82 he played a leading role in the largely abortive negotiations for the renewal of the Anglo-French Treaty of 1860, although Manchester was not displeased with the most-favoured nation clause which resulted. His services were rewarded with a knighthood from Gladstone in 1882. In 1883-84, Lee was closely involved in commercial negotiations with Turkey. As a result, he became a strong advocate of a permanent committee of experts to advise Government on trade and treaty questions, preferring such a committee to a politically-volatile Minister of Commerce. It was, therefore, with some satisfaction that he served on the Trade and Treaties Committee of the Board of Trade, 1890-92, although Rosebery declined his proposal, through the Manchester Chamber of Commerce, to make this body permanent. Lee's concern in these years with tariffs was part of his general belief that improved efficiency in the distribution of British goods was a more secure way to prosperity than the nostrums of fair traders and currency reformers.

Less orthodoxly, Lee, in his evidence before the Royal Commission on the Depression in Trade and Industry, 1886, upheld the value of chartered companies as a means to bolster British trade. Significantly, both he and Henry Lee had taken a leading part in the affairs of the North-West African Co, promoted in 1879 by Donald MacKenzie to extend commerce and Christianity in the area around Cape Juby, a disputed territory south of Morocco. The aspiration was that typical of the Victorian imperialist: to open up the supposed wealth of Central Africa and the Niger region, while simultaneously exposing the native population to the benefits of European civilisation. The brothers Lee put up most of the capital for the company, with Henry becoming its chairman. Henry, from 1880 MP for Southampton, and Joseph, as confidant of the Foreign Office, were well placed to put pressure on Government to grant the company a royal charter. They were not slow to urge the dangers of foreign intervention to the detriment of British trade in Africa, the philanthropic opportunity to abolish the slave trade locally, and the general commercial importance of the area; Joseph indeed was to raise the spectre of Bismarck, 'rambling about the world picking up odd lots of property' {Parsons (1958) 144}. Yet the Government remained unpersuaded, while the commercial results were disheartening. Ultimately, therefore, the company were bought out by the Sultan of Morocco, at a price estimated to have reached ca £100,000 by the time of final withdrawal in 1895. However, by this date, the company had become a source of considerable financial embarrassment to the brothers, who, as a result of its activities, were heavily indebted to the Tootal company. The episode was clearly a failure, the result of some idealism but much misplaced commercial and political risk-taking. Incidentally, it seems that, largely as a by-product of their interest in the North-West African Co, the Lee brothers became influential patrons of the Manchester Geographical Society. Founded in 1884, Henry later became its president and Joseph the not entirely disinterested contributor of a paper, in 1886, on the 'North-West Coast of Africa'.

Even without the complications brought by the North-West African Co, Tootals had, by the mid-1880s, become an organisation of some complexity with thirteen partners responding to its varied interests and managerial needs. The addition as partners of the younger Broadhursts and Lees and the growth in family members financially interested in the firm, combined with the impossibility of endlessly sub-dividing partnerships and profits, produced growing pressure, as in so many firms, to convert from partnership to limited liability. Sir Joseph Lee, therefore, despite his declared aversion to this form of company, emerged in January 1888 as chairman of Tootal Broadhurst Lee Co Ltd. Shareholdings (£250,000 preference, £302,260 ordinary) remained confined to the partnership families, although debentures (£300,000) gave access to the wider capital market. The company, with a nominal capital of £1.1 million and gross assets valued at £1 million (at this point the Lee Spinning Co was fully integrated with its parent), was thus roughly comparable in size to the recently-amalgamated Horrockses, Crewdson & Co Ltd, although its assets were only a quarter of the value of those of Rylands.

The successful launching of Tootals as a limited company owed much to Sir Joseph's administrative skills and financial acumen, although he was by this time turning his energies towards the Manchester Ship Canal. Henry provided an experienced deputy, while day-to-day management increasingly devolved on able lieutenants, notably Harold, son of Henry Lee, and Edward Tootal Broadhurst (qv). Nevertheless, under the seven-year rule of Sir Joseph, the firm's fortunes were meagre. Capital assets grew only slowly, to £1.2 million in 1894, while profitability was poor, averaging only £19,517 per annum in fluctuating trading conditions. This was insufficient to pay share dividend regularly, save out of future anticipated profits, a dangerous policy when they subsequently failed to materialise. Moreover, the company, although not paying for goodwill on formation, took over heavy book debts which were to prove fictitious assets. At the same time, the Lee brothers and Robert Scott were heavily indebted to the company on account of the North-West African Co. Promises to pay outstanding debts (£59,578 in 1888, £62,553 in 1891) were not met, and, as a result, the board was riven between the interests of the two companies, and, in turn, the two families of Lee and Broadhurst. This conflict remained for a number of years with directors' debts the subject of much astringent criticism by the auditors. Henry Lee seems to have been the worst culprit in this respect, and even after the scheduling of repayments in 1895, his debts were still the subject of concern in 1900. The problems of the firm in these early years were compounded by its sewing-cotton venture, once a bright prospect for future profits, but increasingly in an overstocked field a source of losses. Progress was hampered by the unreliable quality of cotton, yet determined efforts to improve this, to cut prices, and to advertise, all failed to create a market, while the firm declined to join price-fixing combinations.

In other respects, sounder foundations for future growth were laid. The firm's dispersed production sites were consolidated, with the sale of the Cornbrook works in 1891, while machinery was fully modernised, with a sizeable depreciation fund in reserve. Marketing was aggressive, with a 'continental policy' of numerous agencies, commercial investigations in South America, Australasia and India, and an office opened in New York in order to develop direct trading with retailers in an effort to stem falling American sales. Interestingly, this was pursued against Sir Joseph's advice, but combined with his strategy of selling fewer but better goods, it enabled Tootals to retain their hold on the American market.

Sir Joseph's leadership in these years was more and more undermined by ill-health and he ceased to attend the board regularly after June 1891. On his death in 1894, Harold Lee succeeded to the chair, while his father, Henry, remained active on the board and its Mills Management Committee until 1901. These years continued to be lean ones of transition. Sewing-cotton was finally abandoned in 1897, after the formation of the all-but impregnable Coats combine in 1896. Patents were accordingly exchanged for shares in Coats' rival, the English Sewing Cotton Co Ltd, and the Atherton works sold to the Fine Spinners & Doublers in 1898. In 1902 the Bradford warehouse was also closed. However, trade debts were gradually written off and partners' debts repaid, even if dividends were, for the most part, foregone. As a result, the company was successfully 'turned round', with record profits in 1900 and 1903. This was some solace for Henry Lee whose death in 1904 ended sixty-nine years' 'magnificent services' in 'a connection almost unique in the history of any commercial undertaking' {Manchester CL, TBL board minutes, 3 Jan 1905}. The connection was perhaps overlong. But, if to some extent the financial stability of Tootals had been jeopardised by the Lees' African gamble, the company's strengths were also of their making. Sir Joseph's 'exercise of energy and capacity' {ibid, 8 Jan 1895} had indeed raised the firm to a high commercial position on the basis of the essential manufacturing expertise provided by his elder brother. Tootals as a result had unique strengths as a large, vertically-integrated firm, specialising in better-quality goods in which British exports could expect to remain competitive. The company was thus well-placed not only to withstand the entrepreneurial travails of the 1890s but also to enter the twentieth century with a capacity to survive and adapt which most old 'family' firms and many new 'combines' lacked.

The business leadership of the Lees was not confined to textiles. Henry was for many years a director of the Manchester & Salford Bank, and Joseph of the Lancashire & Yorkshire Bank. Although only a minor shareholder, Henry was also a director of Bolckow, Vaughan & Co Ltd, Britain's largest iron and steel manufacturer, and its chairman between 1898 and 1900, testimony to the respect his business qualities commanded very late in life. This role was far from nominal but it did not devour energy as did the all-consuming Manchester Ship Canal of which Sir Joseph was director and deputy-chairman, 1885-1894.

The canal project, launched in 1882, had suffered from persistent doubts as to its engineering feasibility and its commercial viability, from the opposition of powerful vested interests, from legislative difficulties, and, not least, from inability to raise enough capital. Sir Joseph, a firm believer in the Canal on commercial grounds, joined its board at a time when it sought a much-needed boost in public esteem through the addition of prominent Manchester men. The Canal company lacked not only confidence but also funds. In 1885-86, therefore, Lee assisted in negotiations with Rothschilds in order to hold off financial collapse. Yet his efforts foundered on what he saw as the 'cheeseparing' policy of the board, and its chairman, Daniel Adamson (qv). Lee then became a vigorous supporter of the idea of a Consultative Committee to review the whole Canal scheme in the autumn of 1886. The report of this committee paved the way both for the reconstitution of the board and for new capital raising operations. The somewhat visionary Adamson resisted both, placing his faith in the existing board and working-class sources of funds. More realistically, Lee preferred a new board, with aristocratic leadership and plutocratic finance. He was therefore instrumental in the deposition of Adamson in February 1887 and the election of Lord Egerton of Tatton to the chair. Lee, as deputy chairman, now successfully undertook the raising of the necessary capital, partly through the capitalists of Lancashire and the North but additionally through the City of London, for, after delicate negotiations, Rothschilds and Barings agreed to raise £4 million. Lee's financial acumen and diplomatic skills were, therefore, crucial in the floating of the Canal company. Moreover, he played a critical role in re-negotiating the engineering contracts and, as head of the executive, in supervising the short-term financing of the works once begun. He also helped publicise the cause through the Manchester Jubilee Exhibition, and the Fourth International Inland Navigation Conference at Manchester in 1890. The complexities of the Canal's affairs continued to demand his constant vigilance. Engineering delays, the over-running of financial estimates and the voracious capital needs of the Canal threatened by 1891 to exhaust the patience and the confidence of the private capital market but Lee successfully negotiated recourse to the City of Manchester for capital support. 'Anxiety and overwork' {Leech (1907) II, 123} fatally undermined Lee's health, so that even before the opening of the Canal in January 1894 he had ceased to play an active role on the board. Yet if Adamson's ideas and enthusiasm had launched the Canal, Lee's 'financial genius' {*ibid*, 237} had ensured its cutting and completion.

Sir Joseph retired in the spring of 1894 to the valetudinarian air of St Leonard's-on-Sea, a self-confessed, 'broken-vessel'. He died there on 19 December 1894, after a life dominated by the demands of business, which left little time or inclination for political or philanthropic activities. He had been a director of the Manchester Chamber of Commerce, 1890-94, and JP for Cheshire, Derbyshire and Lancashire. Recreation featured little save for travel, itself often dictated by the imperatives of health or commerce, although Lee was once a president of the Altrincham Dramatic Society. As his political allegiance had bent in 1886 towards Liberal Unionism (he presided briefly over the Manchester Liberal Unionist Association), so too he turned towards the Established Church, despite having married in 1861 Henrietta, the daughter of Rev James Hill, president in 1860 of the Congregational Conference. Among their seven children, the eldest, Lennox Bertram, succeeded to the Rossendale Printworks and became for decades the chairman of the Calico Printers' Association, while Noel was a director of Tootals. Sir Joseph's personal fortune was a sizeable but not spectacular £206,600.

Sir Joseph, in entrepreneurial style and public image, provided a neat foil for his elder brother. Both displayed the energy, foresight, and shrewdness essential to success. Sir Joseph exuded the polished qualities of the business statesman, full of tact, charm and urbanity, Henry epitomised the earlier generation of rugged, Nonconformist entrepreneurs, a model of industry, method, and conscience. While Joseph accepted a knighthood and strayed dangerously towards the Salisburian Establishment, Henry remained resolute in his native Congregationalism and Gladstonian Liberalism. A precocious petitioner against the Test and Corporation Acts in 1829, he became in the 1840s a deacon of Richmond Chapel, Salford, following a secession from the Chapel Street Chapel, under the leadership of the Anti-Corn Law Leaguer, Rev J W Massie. Richmond Chapel's fortunes rose with those of Lee, and he was instrumental in setting up, as an offshoot, the Broughton Park Chapel, a rich Nonconformist Gothic cathedral. Lee's Congregational loyalties were deeply-rooted. The Established Church, he believed, violated conscience and hindered the extension of Christ's Kingdom on earth. Like his Congregational business peers such as John Rylands and Samuel Morley (qqv), it was in the Bible that he found the only source of real experience, and the spreading of its precepts, through Congregationalism, would, he believed, promote both the temporal and the spiritual welfare of mankind. Impelled by these beliefs, he was an active supporter of the British and Foreign Bible Society, 'the most valuable in England' {speech, *Salford City Reporter* 23 Apr 1904}; for many years an active Sunday School teacher, especially among adult working men ('working-women' he found 'the weak point in all their Christian organisations'); a keen promoter of chapel extension in Lancashire, and of the Lancashire Independent College, for the supply of ministers. Lee was also an important lay influence within the Congregational Union, particularly in its attempts to centralise its finances so that rich localities might support poor in an effort to maintain the quality of the ministry and its geographical coverage. A forceful advocate of business methods in Church administration, he thus became treasurer of the Church Aid Society in 1878. Lee also contributed to the vitality of his denomination through numerous journeys abroad on which he subsidised leading ministers as his companions. With Rev R W Dale he toured Egypt and the Holy Land in 1873, and the United States in 1877. In 1888, with Dr Hannay, secretary of the Union, he visited Australasia. Finally, as a leading Free Churchman, Lee had been a founder member and leading subscriber to the Liberation Society.

Lee's political career, in which the cause of religious freedom was further promoted, began with his election in 1865 and 1866 to Salford town council. He was, however, defeated on contesting the Salford parliamentary seat in 1874, making little headway against the Tory-Anglican, W T Charley, 'the darling of the unwashed' {Joyce (1980) 288}. Forced to look further afield, he declined to contest Northampton with Bradlaugh, but headed the poll at Southampton in 1880. Here he espoused vigorously the Liberal principles of peace, retrenchment and reform. In the House of Commons, he proved a reliable Gladstonian, speaking infrequently but lending his support to the causes of religious and commercial freedom. But disadvantaged by redistribution in 1884 and failing to canvass in person, Lee was defeated in 1885. In 1886 he challenged, unsuccessfully, William Houldsworth (qv) for the newly-created North-West Manchester seat but thereafter relinquished his political ambitions.

Yet he remained active in other spheres. A director of the Manchester

Chamber of Commerce from 1878 until his death, he was its president between 1889 and 1891, elected as a stalwart free trader and reliable gold-standard man in the face of a growing minority in the Chamber sympathetic to fair trade and bimetallism. On other issues, Lee was more open-minded: he favoured a Board of Conciliation for labour disputes (this was set up in 1891 but was rarely used), promoted an important scheme for the encouragement of commercial education and inaugurated the Chamber's publication, the *Monthly Record*. The Chamber was also now organised into sections, with their own committees, a change which increased its flexibility and efficiency.

Among his other public and philanthropic activities, Lee served as JP for Lancashire and Salford, and as deputy-chairman of the Governors of Manchester Grammar School. Education was probably his foremost secular interest, seen, above all, in the Sunnyside Institute, but also in his presiding over the Bolton branch of the National Education League, and serving on the Bolton School Board, 1870-73, after he had been converted from voluntarism by his first-hand experience of the American common school system. But if Lee accepted the role of the state in education, his philanthropy was directed by an essentially individualistic ethic. Lauding the virtues of temperance and thrift (he was closely associated with the Manchester and Salford Penny Bank), Lee aimed to heighten men's sense of their own responsibility, while providing the means, and encouragement, for them to realise their own material, moral and spiritual destinies. The ethic was the one by which Lee had raised himself in discouraging circumstances, but which even he found exacting later in life. Indeed, at the beginning of the twentieth century, it was a social creed heard uneasily by progressive intellectuals, even if it still dominated the thinking, and, sometimes, the practice of grey-haired Nonconformist businessmen.

Henry Lee died on 2 December 1904 after a career which had striven, not without success, to reconcile 'the man of business' with the 'man of God'. His religious idealism had been reinforced by marriage in 1846 to Ann, daughter of John Dracup, wholesale draper and deacon of Richmond Chapel. Among their eight children, besides Harold, the eldest and chairman of Tootals (1894-1907), the second son, Arthur, tiring of plain-weaving at Sunnyside, found aesthetic vent for his entrepreneurial talent in establishing A H Lee & Co Ltd, furnishing fabric manufacturers of Birkenhead, while Lennox, the third son, became a director of Tootals. Both Arthur and a sister, Helen, married into the Armitage family, consolidating one of the most successful and distinguished of Lancashire's Nonconformist cousinhoods. At his death, Lee left only a small fortune, £60,970, depleted perhaps by unwise investments but, as he noted in his will, he had 'given very largely during my lifetime according to my means to philanthropic and religious institutions' {Will}.

A C HOWE

Writings:

Henry Lee, Preface to Rev C Chapman, 'The Act of Uniformity and its Immediate Effects' in *Chester Bi-Centenary Papers* 1862.

PD 3rd ser, 257-284 (1881-84).

'The Church Aid and Home Missionary Society' and 'Speech' in *Jubilee of the Congregational Union, Manchester, 1881* (1882).

'Inaugural Address' *Journal of the Manchester Geographical Society* 1886.

'Introductory Article' *Monthly Record* (Manchester Chamber of Commerce) 1890.

Joseph Lee, 'The North-West Coast of Africa' *Journal of the Manchester Geographical Society* 2 (1886).

PP, RC Depression of Trade and Industry (1886) C 4797.

Sources:

Unpublished

Bolton Public Library, Tootal Broadhurst & Lee, Sunnyside Mill business records.

Greater Manchester RO, Manchester Ship Canal Co, board minutes, 1885-1895; Executive Committee, 1887-89.

House of Lords RO, minutes of evidence, Manchester Ship Canal Bills, 1884, 1887, 1891.

Manchester Central Library, (microfilm) registers, Hollinshead Chapel, Chorley; Inland Navigation Conference, 1890; Sir J Lee's autograph book; Manchester Chamber of Commerce, Proceedings, 1885-94; Jubilee Exhibition Manchester, minutes, Executive Committee, 1886-88; Tootal Broadhurst Lee Co Ltd board minutes, 1888-1905.

PRO, BT 31/30986/17653 British Alizarine, 1882-88; FO 27, 78, Commercial Negotiations, 1881-84.

Tootal Group PLC, Manchester, illuminated addresses, 1867, 1886, 1897, 1917.

MCe.

PrC; Will.

Published

Altrincham Divisional Advertiser 21 Dec 1894.

Altrincham Guardian 22 Dec 1894.

Herbert H Bassett (ed), *Men of Note in Finance and Commerce A Biographical Business Directory 1900-1.* (1901).

Clyde Binfield, *So Down to Prayers* (Dent, 1977).

Bolton Journal & Guardian 22 May 1886, 30 Dec 1904.

Sir Alfred W W Dale, *The Life of R W Dale of Birmingham* (Hodder & Stoughton, 1898).

'The Editor's Travels' *The Congregationalist* 1874-76.

The Examiner 5 Jan 1905.

A Few Aspects of the Tootal Organisation (Manchester: pp, 1939).

Roger Fulford, *Glyn's, 1753-1953* (Macmillan, 1953).

Patrick Joyce, *Work, Society and Politics: The Culture of the Factory in Later Victorian England* (Harvester, 1980).

LEE Henry and LEE Sir Joseph Cocksey

'Lee Spinning Company' *British Trade Journal* 1 June 1887.

Sir Bosdin Leech, *History of the Manchester Ship Canal from its Inception to its Completion, with Personal Reminiscences* (2 vols, Manchester: Sherratt & Hughes, 1907).

Manchester Chamber of Commerce *Monthly Record* 1890-1905.

Manchester Chronicle 19 Dec 1894.

Manchester Faces and Places (8 vols, Manchester, 1890-97) 5.

Manchester Guardian 19 Dec 1894, 28 Dec 1904.

'Mr Henry Lee, MP' *The Biograph and Review* 3 (1880).

'Mr Henry Lee, MP' *The Congregationalist* 1880.

Benjamin Nightingale, *Lancashire Nonconformity* (6 vols, Manchester: J Heywood, 1890-93).

—, *The Story of the Lancashire Congregational Union, 1806-1906* (Manchester: J Heywood, 1906).

Frederick V Parsons, 'The North-West African Company and the British Government, 1875-95' *Historical Journal* I (1958).

Alfred Temple Patterson, *A History of Southampton, 1700-1914* (Southampton: Southampton University Press, 1975).

Samuel Pearson, *Henry Lee, 1817-1904: Address and Sermon* (Manchester: Palmer, Howe & Co, 1905).

Albert Peel, *These Hundred Years: A History of the Congregational Union of England and Wales, 1831-1931* (1931).

PP, Trade and Treaties Committee, 1st and 3rd Reports (1890-91) C 6286, C6349.

Arthur Redford, *Manchester Merchants and Foreign Trade* (2 vols, Manchester: Manchester University Press, 1956) 2.

Richmond Congregational Church, Bazaar Handbook (Manchester, 1911).

Salford City Reporter 31 Dec 1904.

Albert D Shaw, *Extracts from a Special Report on the Cotton Goods Trade of Lancashire* (Manchester: A Ireland & Co, 1883).

A Short History of Tootal Broadhurst Lee Company Limited (Manchester: pp, nd).

'Sir Joseph Lee', *Manchester City News* 13 Jan 1917.

Herbert S Skeats and C S Miall, *History of the Free Churches of England, 1688-1891* (Alexander & Shepheard, 1894).

Joseph Thompson, *Lancashire Independent College, 1843-93* (Manchester: J E Cornish, 1893).

'Tootal Broadhurst Lee & Co' *British Trade Journal* 1 July 1887.

William B Tracy, *Manchester and Salford at the Close of the 19th Century: Contemporary Biographies* (Brighton: W T Pike & Co, 1899).

WWMP.

LEE, Lennox Bertram

(1864-1949)

Calico printer

Lennox B Lee (taken from 50 Years of Calico Printing. A Jubilee History of the CPA *Manchester: Calico Printers' Association Ltd, 1949).*

Lennox Bertram Lee was born at Broughton, Salford, on 18 August 1864, the son of Sir Joseph Lee (qv) and his wife Henrietta née Hill. He was educated at Thorpe Mandeville and Eton before serving for two years with the Sherwood Foresters (1883-85). After 1885 he travelled widely, particularly in North-West Africa, a region of great financial and commercial importance to his family. In 1889, Lee returned to his father's calico-printing firm, the Rossendale Printing Co, one of the best of contemporary printworks; here he acquired the training which by 1899 had given him the reputation of one of the first-class 'practical men' in the trade. This decade also provided Lee with a clear demonstration of the difficulties faced by the calico-printers — those of undercutting in a highly competitive industry, of relations with the merchants (80 per cent of printing was done on commission) and of profitability in a trade which required heavy capital outlay yet faced uncertain prices in fluctuating, and in the long term declining, markets. The remainder of Lee's business career was largely devoted to the solution of these problems.

The Rossendale Printing Co had taken part in various schemes of co-operation and price regulation in the 1890s, and it was therefore natural that Lee, having inherited the firm on his father's death in 1894, should in 1899 take it into the Calico Printers' Association (CPA). This amalgamation of 46 printing firms and 13 merchanting firms sought to restore profitability to the printing trade by reducing competition and costs through greater centralisation and concentration of production. Lee rapidly became the leading member of the executive of the CPA (1899-1902; chairman of the executive, 1902-4; and director with special executive functions, 1904-8), and provided one factor of continuity amidst the ever-shifting personnel of the CPA in its early years (the years 1899-1908 saw the resignation of three chairmen). The formation of the CPA provided an opportunity to solve the underlying problems of the industry since it embraced 85 per cent of capacity. The wasting of this opportunity may not, however, be attributed to Lee, for the problems the CPA faced were enormous: the firms it comprised varied widely in size, efficiency and in the marketability of their goods. More importantly, the structure of the CPA made for immobility. A top-heavy directorate of 84 members, representing the vendors and still in charge of individual works, stood over the executive which was attempting to impose some form of central control without suppressing the individuality of the firms. Yet it was the executive which took the blame for poor results while lacking the power to impose its policies. This conflict Lee identified as crucial to the future of the CPA. At his instigation, a shareholders' committee of reconstruction was formed in 1902, leading to the reduction of the board to six members, and the simultaneous strengthening of the executive's powers. Lee's managerial policies henceforward centred on the problems of overproduction, excessive costs and competition between firms within the CPA. Capacity was substantially reduced (23 works, with 258 printing machines, that is, 31 per cent of the capacity taken over by the CPA in 1899, and valued at £763,000, had been closed by 1905); overlapping agreements, both 'offensive' and 'defensive' were negotiated with the Bleachers' and Bradford Dyers' Associations, while a research department was set up in 1905 as a result of William Mather's (qv) recommendation in 1902. The years 1903-7 witnessed a marked improvement with the average gross trading profits rising by 75 per cent, compared with 1900-2, the result of managerial success and better trading conditions.

The retirement of R P Hewit in 1908 opened the chairmanship to Lee, the Association's ablest director as well as its largest shareholder. Lee, however, had no intention of abandoning his managerial role: under his chairmanship the board now exerted much closer control over the executive, composed of relatively junior men, who became the instruments to carry out policies forged by Lee and the directors. (No managing director of the CPA was to be appointed until 1949.) Lee's major concern was how to improve the trading position of the CPA, whose share of exports had fallen to 40 per cent. Under the new management scheme of 1909, and the market scheme of 1913, markets, not works, became the basis of the CPA's organisation. Attempts were also made to introduce more direct trading. This was in an effort to resolve a dilemma which the CPA persistently faced, and even by 1947 had not resolved, whether it was to be a vertical organisation, with its own manufacturing (in 1899 the Association had included 6,656 looms and 277,264 spindles which accounted for only a small proportion of yardage printed), printing and selling, or whether it was to work essentially on commission for the Manchester merchants. Movement in the former direction normally resulted in the loss of outside business, while movement in the latter exposed the Association to price-cutting and over-specialisation. The Association's percentage of real productive capacity was nearer to 50 per cent than its nominal 85 per cent so that it remained exposed to under-cutting by external competitors and to under-pricing by merchant houses. Central control of selling within the CPA also met internal resistance by threatening the important link between merchant, salesman and printer. Nevertheless, up to 1914 the CPA continued to improve in efficiency and to maintain profitability, a prosperity complemented by the opening of its new offices in St James Building in 1912, then the largest steel-framed building in Britain.

The First World War brought peculiar problems for the calico-printing industry, given its dependence on imported, notably German, dyes. The government-sponsored solution, the formation of the British Dyestuffs Corporation, was, however, not one which found favour in Lee's eyes. Such a corporation, he believed, could neither adequately nor efficiently supply industrial needs; Swiss manufacturers should therefore be encouraged rather than English ones whom Lee believed to be motivated by the prospect of large, immediate profits not the 'future general needs of the industry and welfare of the country' {CPA correspondence, Lee to Sir William Plender, 13 Oct 1914}. Moreover, rather than set up a new

Roller printing machine (taken from 50 Years of Calico Printing. A Jubilee History of the CPA *Manchester: Calico Printers' Association Ltd, 1949).*

Feeding the colour boxes (taken from 50 Years of Calico Printing. A Jubilee History of the CPA *Manchester: Calico Printers' Association Ltd, 1949).*

company, he preferred to see Government co-operating with the colour-users (such as the CPA and BDA) to organise the existing 'mass of producing power' {ibid}. Lee's attitude to the 'Dyes Question' continued to be informed not only by the interests of the CPA but by his distrust of bureaucratic interference in industry, and his preference for management by 'businessmen in whom we could have confidence and who are accustomed to deal with large interests and controlling a large staff' {Manchester CL, CPA correspondence, Lee to P Ashley, Board of Trade, 18 Nov 1914}. When British Dyes Ltd was set up in 1915, the CPA subscribed only against Lee's advice, and for the rest of the war he remained a reluctant participant in the various government licensing schemes. In a succession of abandoned schemes, 1915-18, Lee saw only the ignorance of the 'official mind' {ibid, Lee, 'A Review of the Colour Position' 18 Jan 1916}. After the war he became an insistent advocate of a return to normalcy and to 'free trade' in dyestuffs, heading in 1922 efforts to secure the repeal of the 1920 Dyestuffs Act, and participating in moves to revive trade links with I G Farben.

War and its aftermath also resulted in other changes in CPA policy. Somewhat suspiciously Lee was prepared, after several meetings with Addison at the Ministry of Reconstruction, to support a 'Whitley Council' for the finishing trades. An employee benefit fund was also set up, a gesture to improve labour relations, although it remained on an ad hominem rather than a systematic basis. Trading schemes were also more fully undertaken. Wartime had also seen the formation, mooted since 1912, of the Federation of Calico-Printers, a trade association which attempted to regulate prices, in which the CPA was naturally a dominant voice. To some extent, however, Lee preferred the Association to rely upon its own power rather than to depend on price-support arrangements whose effect was normally only temporary.

The CPA badly needed a new business strategy. After the war, the CPA had not only to counter competition at home, but growing international competition in overseas markets, a threat perceived before 1914, although the speed with which the CPA's markets and those of British textiles generally fell away, was unforeseen. Exports of printed goods were, for example, to fall from the pre-war peak (1911) of 1,242 million linear yards to 683 million in 1919, to 322 million in 1931; the ten year average, 1911-20 was 944 million yards, that for 1921-30, 618 million yards. The CPA's peak value of exports was attained in 1920 and their peak dividend (12.5 per cent) paid in 1922-23. (Dividends, 1908-29, averaged 5.65 per cent.) Lee himself was quick to recognise the long-term problems facing the CPA in these years, and five major elements provided a recipe for survival. Firstly, the market selling scheme of 1913 was partially abandoned, while an aggressive marketing and advertising campaign was undertaken at home and abroad. Secondly, unprofitable works were disposed of, including the French Malaunay works in 1924, in an effort to reduce capacity in line with trading results; at the same time, however, the policy of concentrating production meant that some obsolete works were rebuilt to provide the most modern and economical means of production: for example, in the late 1920s, the Strines works was rebuilt while the Scottish works of the CPA were being closed. Thirdly, in a policy which Lee particularly favoured, the CPA turned its attention to the possibility of building works abroad, near their markets. In 1917 Lee had received reports on the possibility of a printworks in the Far East to overcome Japanese competition, and in 1924 a site was purchased in China although its development was slow, the board lacking Lee's enthusiasm for the project and his keen perception of business trends. Fourthly, research, slowed down by war, was revived, largely dealing with the development of printed rayons as a regular product. Finally, a concerted effort was made to reduce further the costs of production. Here, Lee, whilst critical of high wages, reserved his maximum fire for government policy, inveighing against rising taxation and 'reckless and wasteful civil expenditure' {*Times* 19 Sept 1924}. With an invective inherited from the heyday of laissez-faire, he urged the 'abandonment of professed social reform' and a return to self-respect, individual responsibility, private enterprise and free trade, 'the system which in the past brought us world-wide trade and great prosperity' {*Times* 17 Sept 1925}. Taxation, he urged, deprived industry of the capital necessary for investment, a plausible argument perhaps, but not one which applied in the CPA's case, as its resources were mounting, and in 1923 its investments in outside securities totalled more than £2.5 million, betokening a desire for financial security over and above risking capital.

Until 1928, these policies, backed up by minimum prices through the Federation of Calico Printers, were, by and large, successful but only as a holding operation, enabling the Association to retain its market share and maintain dividends. To some extent, the CPA had come to rest on minimum price agreements rather than its inherent strength. By the late 1920s, it attracted criticism for its failure of imagination, its rigid

Finishing room (taken from 50 Years of Calico Printing.
A Jubilee History of the CPA *Manchester: Calico Printers'
Association Ltd, 1949).*

*One of the largest printing machine rooms in the world (taken
from* 50 Years of Calico Printing. A Jubilee History of the CPA
Manchester: Calico Printers' Association Ltd, 1949).

organisation and inability to make headway against its competitors at
home: medium-sized firms such as Mitchells & Barlow could outsell it
abroad in some markets, while firms such as Turnbull & Stockdale held
their own at home. However, the steep fall in overseas markets after 1929
and the disappearance of profits necessitated a thorough re-fit of the CPA
if it were to chart the dangerous waters ahead. That it achieved this
relatively successfully was in part due to Lee's vision.

The CPA's response to depression and its ability to recover hinged on
three policies. Firstly, the continuance of the post-war strategy; secondly,
the adoption of large-scale rationalisation in the industry as a whole, with
government support; thirdly, the fulfilment of the policy of overseas
expansion. In line with the first, the concentration of production in the
most efficient units was continued, with the result that the CPA had only
11 printworks in operation in 1935. Merchanting at home was
reinvigorated with the launching of 'Cepea' silk fabrics and a clearer
demarcation between the 'merchanting' and 'commission' groups with the
company. A greater degree of vertical integration and increased
production of the better class of textile goods remained important
objectives. Lee himself was closely associated with moves to broaden the
fashionability of the CPA's cloth, for example, through the Dress
Advisory Council. At the same time, closed works agreements with the
Bleachers' and Bradford Dyers' Associations were strengthened by an
overlapping agreement with the former in 1931.

Yet the need for a longer-term solution to the problems of the calico-
printing sector, and of the cotton industry as a whole, became insistent in
Lee's mind, sharpened perhaps by his membership of the Macmillan
Committee on Finance and Industry, 1929-31, and by the economic
collapse of 1929-32, which ended, among other things, the Federation of
Calico Printers' price-agreement. In 1929, in their evidence before the
Civil Research Inquiry on the Cotton Trade, the CPA had argued that the

merchanting system largely explained falling sales and high costs, since the merchant houses insisted on constant novelty in design and production, and on maximum returns, while minimising the cost-cutting possibilities of mass production. The CPA advocated 'some form of partnership between the Producers and the Merchant' {Manchester CL, evidence of the CPA before the Cotton Enquiry Sub-Committee of Civil Research, Oct 1929} to reduce competition and costs by making possible more standardised production. Lack of capital and expertise deterred the CPA itself from the risk involved in more extensive merchanting, but in an effort to strengthen the producers, in 1930, Lee had been one of the prime movers of an attempt to create in a new combine a complete monopoly of calico-printing, with a capital of £16 million. This idea failed to command widespread support. In 1931-32, financial crisis meant that marking-time and survival were the only objects in view, but in 1933 Lee in two far-sighted articles in the *Manchester Guardian* advocated a full-scale rationalisation of the cotton trade. He urged co-operation by all sections of employers (merchants, manufacturers, finishers) and the trade unions on the domestic front, to be followed by international agreements in order to balance production and world demand. Cartels he defended as preferable to tariffs, largely because the former were run by businessmen, the latter by Government. But while fearful of meddlesome Governments with respect to tariffs, Lee now became an advocate of 'right-minded' government support, that is, legislation which put into effect collective self-regulation by businessmen. In practical terms, rationalisation would mean more large vertical combinations linking merchants and producers, together with redundancy schemes for excess capacity. Lee's vision was perhaps too radical, and certainly outran the perspectives of the trade and the Government of the day. Nevertheless, the FCP, with much work done by Forrest Hewit of the CPA, consistently urged legislation for the print trade, seeking reorganisation tied to a quota scheme, on the lines of the Spindles Act of 1936. These proposals were eventually rejected, a disappointment to Lee, and although he emerged as a champion of the general Cotton Enabling Act belatedly passed in 1939, this lacked the 'pool and quota' scheme which the CPA and FCP had sought.

The limited success of this 'rationalisation' campaign made more urgent the CPA's policy of overseas expansion, which, faute de mieux, now became their major strategy to counter-attack in overseas markets. The Shanghai printworks had operated since 1928, and a manufacturing side was added in 1935. Lee himself visited these works (valued at £820,000) in 1938, and was able to report that they were now in the forefront of standard work in China, although their future would depend on British foreign policy, whose 'outstanding feature ... in the Far East was to temporise' {ibid, L B Lee, Report on China Visit, Mar 1938}. The China works was followed by joint-venture schemes in Egypt in 1934 and India in 1936, and the policy was furthered during the Second World War with works in Java, Australia and South Africa. Ironically, therefore, it was the Second World War which saw the culmination of a policy Lee had pushed in the First. The intention behind this policy had been to recapture trade lost permanently or to take advantage of foreign Governments' determination to erect national industries. Its pursuit represented an important reorientation of the CPA away from Lancashire but this was a

*Head Office, St James's Building,
Oxford Street, Manchester (taken
from 50 Years of Calico Printing.
A Jubilee History of the CPA
Manchester: Calico Printers'
Association Ltd, 1949).*

change essential to long-term survival, and perhaps Lee's major contribution to the firm, although its implementation 'on the ground' owed much to C R Hargreaves, later managing director (1949-57).

During the Second World War, Lee was no longer the linchpin of policy-making but he remained a dominant presence in the board room, and albeit reluctantly, he now accepted the direction coming from a younger management team in his son, R M Lee, C R Hargreaves and N G McCulloch. A thorough review of the structure of the CPA also led to important organisational changes, with the directors relieved of much routine work in order to concentrate on the policy-making which was now increasingly slipping into their hands. A renewed effort was also made to extend the Association's vertical structure, selling more of its own manufactures. Wartime was also to see a major contribution to the medium-term fortunes of the CPA, in the culmination of its research policy with the discovery of terylene by J R Whinfield and J T Dickson at its Broad Oak laboratory in 1941. Ironically, the Association lacked the capital to exploit this discovery which it was left to ICI to develop under licence. Nevertheless, the royalties of terylene were to provide an important revenue cushion for the CPA in the post-war period.

If Lee's involvement in day-to-day administration was diminishing in these years, his views on industrial questions were still highly respected. Two themes dominated his wartime reflections as distilled to the CPA's annual general meetings, the impact of wartime controls and the possibility of post-war recovery. Lee firmly believed in the capacity of British textiles to regain world markets after war, but linked this capacity to the absence of governmental controls. Prosperity would depend on leadership in design and taste, on efficiency encouraged by reorganisation on scientific lines with full liberty to exploit all cost-reducing methods, and maximum co-operation with trade unions and between sectors of the trade. The success of government-led export drives, he believed, could only be transient 'for they are built on the power of an overriding control which is anathema to Lancashire's tradition and initiative' {*Manchester Guardian* 26 Sept 1940}. Lee's case was clear and incisive but restated traditional recipes from which in the 1930s he had sought to break free; it was the creed of an octogenarian, elegiacally recalling past success but convincing neither within the CPA board room nor the wider business world.

Lee in the 1940s, essentially autocratic, somewhat irascible, and always aloof, was increasingly distanced from his colleagues; the separation was to come when having secured the familial succession with the pre-election of his second son, R M Lee (his elder son having died in the First World War), to the chair in January 1947, Lee resigned in June of that year. R M Lee (1902-72) was to remain chairman until 1964, an unusual display of hereditary talent within the modern corporate economy. His father continued briefly as a director, with responsibility for the CPA overseas companies (for which he was preparing a holding company scheme), the Estates Department, and Staff Pension Fund, and finally, at his own suggestion, he was preparing a Jubilee History of the Association. However, Lee was divided from many of his colleagues on CPA participation in the FCP redundancy schemes and retired in September

1947. Even so, he visited South Africa on the Association's behalf in 1948, and lived to see the Jubilee of the Association in December 1949.

By 1949, the CPA was undoubtedly very different from the Association Lee had helped create in 1899. It had fallen far short of its initial aims; the 'power of the merchants' had never been satisfactorily tamed, and if redundancy in the industry had been reduced, it was in a manner more drastic and dramatic than ever envisaged. In 1946 the Association employed a mere 6,000 workers, rather than the 12,000 of 1930 and the 20,500 of 1903. In 1907, it had been the fifth largest of all industrial companies, with a capital valuation of £8.2 million; by 1919, it had shrunk to twenty-fourth but with assets, in 1918, of £13.13 million. Thereafter, the relative decline had been rapid; in 1949, it was valued at £17.8 million. Lee, however, had the satisfaction of seeing the company restored to profitability: ordinary dividend payments suspended since 1929, were resumed in 1947. The companies' overseas ventures, with the results of efficiency and rationalisation at home, and the boom of terylene royalties were to ensure the survival and renewed profitability of the CPA. That it survived as long and as well as it did was, in no small measure, due to Lee's protective custody of the sickly infant he had nurtured since 1899. Yet against this, his custodianship had been overlong. His thirty-nine years in the chair had led to the loss of talented ambitious men (for example J S Addison to Courtaulds, J G Nicholson to ICI), a haemorrhage of ability unstaunched from outside, given Lee's insistence on the 'right man' and internal recruitment. Lee's authority had therefore never been challenged from below, with a board of mostly 'second eleven' directors.

Lee held various directorships outside the CPA but most were closely related to its interests. For example, he was, until its purchase by ICI in 1931, a director, and for many years chairman of British Alizarine Co Ltd which his father had helped found for the supply of synthetic colours to the textile industry, and in which Lee and the CPA held large stakes. He was also a director of the British Trade Corporation, 1916-26, set up in order to boost British exports after the war. Otherwise, Lee's directorships were all direct offshoots of the CPA, for example, St James Buildings Co and International Textile Printers Association. Exceptionally, Lee was briefly a director of the Manchester Chamber of Commerce before 1914 and was between 1921 and 1945 a director of the Manchester Royal Exchange, on whose building, erected in 1924, his name remains inscribed.

Manchester public life held little attraction for Lee, but he participated in industrial politics at the highest level. An early supporter of the Federation of British Industry, he succeeded Sir Herbert Dixon (qv) as president of its Manchester branch in 1922. Throughout the 1920s, he was active on the FBI's most important committees. His knowledge of its workings, and 'his great experience and wide vision' as chairman of the CPA {Modern Records Centre, FBI Records, R T Nugent to Viscount Ebbisham, 8 Feb 1928} recommended him as its president in 1929, the only Lancashire textile industrialist to achieve this position. His presidency coincided with three major issues in the FBI's inter-war history — the Mond-Turner talks, the Macmillan Committee on Finance and Industry, and the discussion of fiscal policy preceding the return to protection. On none was he a formative influence. He led the FBI in joint talks with the TUC and National Confederation of Employers' Organisations in April-December 1929, indecisive as these were, without attempting to develop policies beyond a mere distillation of unenlightened employers' attitudes. As president of the FBI, Lee also sat on the Macmillan Committee, although he contributed almost nothing to its deliberations. He was, however, disappointed by the evidence initially put forward by the FBI ('It seems to be rather parochial. The Federation claims to represent industry ... yet is unwilling to give a lead or information to a committee that requires its expert assistance' {ibid, EI/1/7 Lee to Walker, 11 Mar 1930}) and encouraged it to expand its frame of reference, particularly on the issue of distribution. Lee stressed this issue in his Addendum to the Committee's Report, in which he also urged close co-operation with trade unions in the reorganisation of industry. Lee's ideas on fiscal policy, for he remained a stalwart free trader, increasingly separated him from the protectionist sentiment swelling in the ranks of the FBI. The end of his presidency was thus to see the re-opening of this issue and a rapid swing towards tariffs, a remedy Lee wholly discountenanced. For, by embracing protection, the FBI had turned away from the large-scale co-operation in, and rationalisation of, industry, which Lee had continually urged as a substitute for 'the devastating individualism which cannot bring itself to sink its suspicions or its jealousies and work with others towards a common end' {*Manchester Guardian* 10 Apr 1930}. He resigned as president of the Manchester FBI in 1931, and it was only with difficulty that the CPA itself was persuaded to remain within that organisation.

Lee's career as an industrial leader was combined with the life of a country gentleman in Herefordshire. After his marriage in 1892 to Edith McLellan of Glasgow, by whom he had two sons and a daughter, Lee lived for a while in Cheshire before acquiring in about 1900 the estate and manor of How Caple Court, to which he endeavoured to retreat weekly from Wednesday night until Sunday evening. He acted as JP for the county (from 1905) and was its High Sheriff in 1915. He was active as a farmer (at one time known as a breeder of Welsh pigs), and in 1927, a vice-president of the Woolhope Naturalists' Field Club. Completing the family's transition from Independency to Anglicanism, Lee was an enthusiast for beauty in ecclesiastical architecture, patron of How Caple and Sollers Hope churches, a noted benefactor of Hereford Cathedral, and for many years, treasurer of the Cathedral's 'Friends'. Such pursuits, some might aver, distracted Lee from single-minded devotion to industrial responsibilities and were hence symptomatic of British industrial decline; a more generous judgement would suggest that Lee had successfully fused the elements of North and South, calico-printing and Eton, industry and landownership. His reward was meagre financially; at his death on 14 December 1949 Lee left £282,556 gross, scarcely more than his father fifty years before.

A C HOWE

Writings:

letter to the *Times* 17 Sept 1925.

'World Trade' *Lloyds List and Shipping Gazette* 31 Dec 1929.

PP, Report of Committee on Finance and Industry (1931) Cd 3897, Addendum IV.

'Reorganising Industry. 1. The Cotton Trade' *Manchester Guardian* 10 Mar 1933.

'Reorganising Industry. 2. The Cartel' *Manchester Guardian* 11 Mar 1933.

Sources:

Unpublished

Manchester Central Library, CPA Secretariat Records (Secretary's correspondence 1901-49, press cuttings 1929-49, miscellaneous items); CPA Board Minutes, 1899-1949.

University of Warwick, Modern Records Centre, FBI Records, especially 1929-31.

BCe.

PrC.

Published

British Industries 1929-31.

[A Clegg] 'An Old Calico Printer', *Some Thoughts on the Calico Printers' Association* (Manchester: George Falkner & Sons, 1929).

P Lesley Cook, *Effects of Mergers: Six Studies* (George Allen & Unwin, 1958).

Fifty Years of Calico Printing (Manchester: CPA, 1949).

Hereford Citizen 16 Dec 1949.

Hereford Times 17 Dec 1949.

Herefordshire Portraits (Hereford: Jakeman & Carver, 1908).

Elizabeth Johnson and Donald E Moggridge (eds), *The Collected Writings of John Maynard Keynes* vol 20 (Cambridge: Cambridge University Press, 1981).

Henry W Macrosty, *The Trust Movement in British Industry* (Longmans & Co, 1907).

Manchester Evening News 15 Dec 1949.

Manchester Guardian 16 Dec 1949.

Monopolies Commission Report on the Process of Calico Printing (HMSO, 1954).

William J Reader, *Imperial Chemical Industries: A History* (2 vols, Oxford University Press, 1970-75).

Ross Gazette 22 Dec 1949.

Textile Mercury 2 Mar 1929.

Times 19 Sept 1924, 16 Dec 1949.

Geoffrey Turnbull, *A History of the Calico Printing Industry of Great Britain* (Altrincham: J Sherratt & Son, 1951).

WWW.

LEES, Sir William Clare

(1874-1951)

Chairman of textile finishing conglomerate

William Clare Lees was born in Ashton-under-Lyne on 9 December 1874, the son of William Lees (1840-1916) and his wife Emma, daughter of Dr William Clare. He was educated at Cambridge and on graduation joined in business with his father, who was a director of the Buckton Vale Printworks. This plant was part of the cotton empire of John H Gartside & Co, a firm engaged both in manufacturing and finishing cotton. At the time of Clare Lees's introduction to the business world Gartside was among those actively involved in setting up the Calico Printing Association and Clare Lees's involvement in these activities earned him the description of one of 'John Henry Gartside's young men'. At the age of twenty-six he became one of the 82 original directors of the Association but he left in 1901 to become manager of the River Etherow Bleaching Co. In 1906 this company was purchased by the Bleachers' Association for £475,000 and Clare Lees became a director.

The Bleachers' Association had been formed in 1900 to acquire the business of 53 firms engaged in the bleaching trade. Although the Association did not suffer from the top-heavy organisational structure which bedevilled the early years of the CPA it was not without its initial teething problems. A number of firms had entered the Association with inefficient plant and equipment, a poor profits record and inefficient management. An expensive programme of restructuring was embarked upon, which by the outbreak of the First World War had brought important results. Apart from a weak year in 1909, profits improved from 1907, peaking in 1913 when the Association paid an ordinary dividend of 6 per cent. Between 1907 and 1914 reserves more than doubled to just over £1 million. Clare Lees gained considerable administrative and organisational experience in the restructuring programme in a company which at the time of his appointment was Britain's ninth largest by capital.

During the First World War Clare Lees did not see active service but he did gain further administrative experience which was considerably to broaden his career in the post-war years. In 1917 he was appointed deputy chief executive officer of the War Department (Cotton Textiles Section), a post he held until 1919. In that year he participated in the World Cotton Conference at New Orleans and four years later was appointed commercial adviser to the British delegation to the International Conference on Customs Formalities at the League of Nations. His public role as an international representative for the cotton trade was further extended in 1929 when he went to South America as a member of the British Economic Mission. These international duties were matched by active participation in domestic public activity. Between 1922 and 1924 he was president of the Manchester Chamber of Commerce and his long and close association with the Chamber was in later life to lead to his appointment as an emeritus director. In 1925 he became president of the Manchester Statistical Society and between 1924 and 1927 was a member of the Board of Trade Advisory Council. The public appointment which impinged more directly on his rising business role with the Bleachers' Association (he had become a managing director in 1925) was his membership of the Balfour Committee, 1924-29. This Committee of Inquiry was established to investigate the conditions and prospects of British industry and commerce, with special reference to the export trade.

Unfortunately for Clare Lees, evidence presented before the Committee proved to be the source of some embarrassment. Representatives of the spinning, weaving and merchandising sections of the cotton trade objected strongly to what they claimed to be the monopolistic pricing policy of the finishing trades, which led to excess profits and restricted the consumption of British cotton goods. This attack necessarily implied criticism of the Bleachers' Association, given its quasi-monopolistic position in bleaching. It was further pointed out that the Bleachers' Association had recorded a higher annual rate of profit in the post-war years (8.3 per cent from 1920-21 to 1926-27) than in the immediate pre-war period (6.4 per cent from 1910-11 to 1913-14). Yet the higher post-war profit record had been achieved on a smaller volume of trade; between 1912 and 1924 the fall in cotton piece goods bleached, but not dyed or printed, was 26.9 per cent. A Bleachers' representative defended the company's policy by arguing that the high costs of the reconstruction programme in the pre-war years had depressed profits during those years and it was consequently unfair to compare them with post-war results. The long term result of the programme was a more efficient company, which allowed stability of prices, improved customer services and the ability to absorb the rise in costs associated with the war without unduly raising prices. Clare Lees found himself in rather a delicate position; on the one hand an impartial member of a public committee, on the other the director of a company strongly criticised in the course of the committee's inquiries.

The outcome of the inquiry was a lame and tentative set of conclusions relating to the finishing trade. The only recommendation made was that the question of the alleged monopolistic pricing policies of the finishing section should be explored and settled by the parties concerned acting in concert.

That Clare Lees supported such a recommendation may be deduced from the fact that Bleachers were stung into more positive action and in January 1928 announced certain reductions in bleaching charges on types and widths of cloth (made from medium and coarse counts) which had suffered most heavily from foreign competition. In the short-term this did not harm Bleachers' performance. Indeed trading profits improved in the late 1920s and a dividend of 10 per cent was paid to ordinary shareholders in 1927-28 and 1928-29. Net profits collapsed, however, in 1930-31, falling from £466,391 in the previous year to only £4,576 and the dividend was passed. Although the profit position recovered in the early 1930s, throughout the decade trading profits remained well below the 1929 level. Taking 1929 trading profits as 100, they averaged only 37 per annum, 1930-38. The underlying problem was the falling volume of bleached goods, in particular the intense competition the Association met in its traditional foreign markets. In a survey of their principal foreign markets Bleachers found that during 1929-33 these markets had reduced their imports of bleached cotton piece goods by 30 per cent, yet more than doubled their imports from Japan. In face of this intense competition Bleachers adopted a three-pronged strategy: a rationalisation programme involving the closing-down of unprofitable plant and the concentration of production in the more efficient works; a research and development drive which looked to new processes especially in the field of artificial fibres; and a stabilisation policy in relation to their major foreign markets, especially the vital Indian market. It was with the third strategy that Clare Lees was most closely associated. In 1933 he went to India as the head of a British trade mission and came back with the Clare Lees-Mody Pact, his major contribution to the fortunes of the Bleachers' Association. Apart from Japanese competition Bleachers faced a further threat in their Indian market, the growing imposition of tariffs against British cotton piece goods as the Indian authorities strove to protect their domestic cotton industry and to establish fiscal autonomy. In 1931 the Indian Finance Act raised duties substantially and British cotton goods paid 20 per cent, raised in September 1931 to 25 per cent. Against the background of growing Japanese competition Clare Lees negotiated with Bombay mill owners, seeking, among other objectives, a preferential tariff. The outcome was the Clare Lees-Mody Pact signed on 28 October 1933. The Bombay mill owners accepted the principle of preference as fair and desirable and in accordance with the Pact the Indian Government introduced new cotton duties in 1934. These continued the British preferential rate of 25 per cent and the foreign rate of 50 per cent for two years, after which time the rates might be adjusted. The Pact incorporating the principle of Imperial Preference in cottons was more favourable to Lancashire producers than the Indian Tariff Board Report of 1932-33 which had recommended higher protective tariffs and no Imperial Preference. Commenting on the Clare Lees initiative, Walter Runciman, the President of the Board of Trade, observed: 'The work of the delegation ... has gone some way in justifying the government in their belief that the best approach to the problem of international industrial cooperation is the method of discussion between industrialists' {Drummond (1971) 134}.

In broad terms the result of the Clare Lees mission was to enhance the degree of mutual understanding between Lancashire and Bombay. On his return to Britain, the Joint Committee of Cotton Trade Organisations, in conjunction with the Indian section of the Manchester Chamber of Commerce, set up a special Indian Trade Relations Committee to represent all the producing as well as merchandising interests. Clare Lees was appointed the first chairman of this committee and was a strong advocate of the need for Lancashire producers to purchase a larger volume of Indian cotton. In more direct economic terms the Pact went some considerable way in stemming the flood of Japanese exports into the Indian market, although British cottons still faced substantially higher duties at the Indian frontier than they had in 1929.

The significance of the agreement for the Bleachers' Association was highlighted by the chairman, Sir Alan Sykes (qv), when he informed shareholders in 1935 that nearly 75 per cent of the exports of bleached goods went to Empire markets, and of that quantity 90 per cent was affected by quotas operating in Britain's favour by the limitations of imports of foreign cloth. During 1934-35 the exports of bleached goods to colonial markets where quotas were in operation nearly doubled and by 1936 exports were almost three times their 1934 level. However, while Clare Lees's diplomacy had stabilised the Association's position, particularly in the vital Indian market, outside the Empire the full weight of Japanese competition was felt. Bleachers' position in non-colonial markets deteriorated sharply and there was no overall increase in its volume of trade. Indeed the chairman in his 1939 report, announcing improved profit margins, explained the rise not in terms of an increase in trade volume but as a direct consequence of the rationalisation programme which had significantly cut operating costs. The success of the rationalisation strategy was related to the organisational abilities of the top management team, particularly the managing directors. Clare Lees's diplomatic initiative must therefore be read in the light of the internal policy of the Association, which throughout the 1930s sought to adjust capacity to the falling volume of sales and it was in his role as chairman of the managing directors that he made a more direct contribution to the long-run survival of the Association.

In 1933 Clare Lees was appointed chairman of the managing directors, who met weekly to discuss a variety of issues ranging from the mundane (bathers trespassing on company property) to key areas of policy. The rationalisation scheme was a priority and Clare Lees was actively involved in the 1930s in visiting various plants, making recommendations on closure and supervising the transfer of work from one branch to another. Between 1934 and 1938 nine branches were closed and their work transferred to other plants. While this policy was crucial in placing Bleachers on a more secure footing Clare Lees's role was not confined to retrenchment. In 1935 he met with executives of the Calico Printers' Association and the Bradford Dyers to discuss the proposed establishment of plants in three Indian centres, Bhoped, Sind and Madras. Clare Lees favoured starting all three but after lengthy discussions it was decided to proceed with two works in Bhoped and Sind. A holding company, Overseas Industries, was established by the three Associations. This also invested in Egypt, committing Bleachers to a capital sum of £50,000.

By the late 1930s and early 1940s Bleachers were sufficiently confident to embark on a programme of diversification and acquisition. Clare Lees strongly pushed this policy and used his position on the Association's finance committee (to which he was invited as chairman of the managing directors) to seek authorisation of capital funding. The main area of diversification was in laundry and dry cleaning services. The Association had already acquired some small laundries at the end the 1930s and as the Second World War came to an end were ready to launch a more ambitious programme. In January 1945 Clare Lees gained approval for a long-run expansion policy entailing the purchase of eight to ten laundries. The first stage of the expansion involved the purchase of two or three laundries at an estimated cost of £50,000 and by the late 1940s the programme was firmly established. In 1949, for example, a large laundry and dry cleaning company was acquired for £72,500. Sir William was also involved in a number of other company acquisitions. In 1945 he was instrumental in Bleachers' purchase of the North British Chemical Co for £30,000 and led the negotiations with Robinsons of Chesterfield (the leading firm in surgical and medical cotton) which in 1949 committed the two concerns to a capital investment of £149,250 in a plant to be jointly managed.

In 1946 Clare Lees was appointed deputy chairman and was closely involved in the finance committee's discussions of the capital reconstruction of the Association. In 1947 a capitalisation scheme was introduced which reduced authorised capital by nearly £2 million, reflecting the rationalisation of the Association's bleaching plant. In the late 1940s the Association's profit position showed steady improvement and in its jubilee year in 1950 it paid a 5 per cent dividend to its ordinary shareholders plus a special jubilee bonus of 2.5 per cent and a sum of £25,000 for the payment of a bonus to its employees.

It was in the jubilee year that Clare Lees attained, after forty-four years' service, the chairmanship of Bleachers. In his jubilee speech he argued that heavy taxation was undermining the efficiency and progress of all manufacturing industry and he was particularly scathing about profit tax. This tax he saw as effectively distributing away from industry its working capital and the funds required to maintain fixed capital. The result was a standard of living in excess of what was justified by the volume of national production. From his appointment as chairman of the managing directors in 1933 to his death in office in 1951 Bleachers' trading profits had more than doubled from £535,851 to £1,244,211, but on a fixed asset base, which as a result of the policy of plant rationalisation had shrunk from £7,976,970 (1933) to £5,709,294 (1951).

Clare Lees also served as a director of a number of other companies, particularly in Manchester. He was a director of the Manchester Ship Canal Co and of Lloyd's Packing Warehouses Ltd, a deputy chairman of Martin's Bank Ltd and chairman of the Manchester district board of Martin's Bank and of the Manchester board of the Phoenix Assurance Co. He served as a vice-president of the Court of Arbitration of the International Chamber of Commerce and of the FBI, was president of the Association of British Chambers of Commerce in 1931-32, and of the Textile Institute in 1933. In 1939 he was a member of Lord Weir's Conference on War Damage to Property.

Clare was a man of deep religious feeling in common with his brother, who became Archbishop of Melbourne, and his brother-in-law, the Bishop of Bristol. He took a great interest in the welfare of Hollingworth St Mary's Church and served actively on the board of management of the YMCA in Manchester. Politically he was a lifelong supporter of the Conservative party. A member of the Mottram and District Agriculture Society, he was fond of fishing and shooting. He took an interest in art and was considered to be something of an expert on ceramics and antiques. In 1922 he joined the Court of the University of Manchester, became a member of its council seven years later and for the last ten years of his life was the honorary treasurer of the University. Lees was knighted in 1924 and received a baronetcy in 1937.

He married Kathleen, daughter of John Nickson, a merchant of Liverpool, in 1901; they had a son and a daughter. Sir William Clare Lees died on 26 May 1951, leaving £129,822 gross.

ROGER LLOYD-JONES

Writings:

Presidential Addresses to the Manchester Chamber of Commerce 5 Feb 1923 and 11 Feb 1924. Trade with South America 4 Nov 1929.

Some Economic Developments During the Past Hundred Years and Their Reactions Upon the Cotton Trade (Manchester, 1934) (Reprinted from the *Transactions of the Manchester Statistical Society).*

Sources:

Unpublished

Manchester Central Library, Box 290 (dyeing, bleaching and finishing); Clare Lees microfiches; Manchester Chamber of Commerce, minutes.

Quarry Bank Mill Museum, Styal, Cheshire, Bleachers Association, minute books of managing directors and finance committee.

BCe.

MCe.

Published

Committee on Industry and Trade: Part III *Survey of Textile Industries* (HMSO, 1928).

P Lesley Cook (ed), *Effects of Mergers: Six Studies* (George Allen & Unwin, 1958).

Ian M Drummond, *British Economic Policy and the Empire 1919-1939* (George Allen & Unwin, 1971).

Henry W Macrosty, *The Trust Movement in British Industry* (Longmans & Co, 1907).

Manchester Guardian commercial 14 Feb 1924.

Arthur Redford and Brian W Clapp, *Manchester Merchants and Foreign Trade* (Manchester: Manchester University Press, 1956).

WWW.

LEESE, Sir William Hargreaves

(1868-1937)

City solicitor and solicitor to the Bank of England

William Hargreaves Leese was born in Guildford, Surrey, on 24 August 1868. He was the grandson of one of Lancashire's 'Cotton Kings' and the eldest son of Sir Joseph Leese (1845-1914), Recorder of Manchester, 1893-1914 and MP for Accrington, 1892-1910, and his wife Mary Constance née Hargreaves of Surrey. William Leese was educated at Winchester and Trinity Hall, Cambridge, where he took his degree in 1890. Following his father's wishes, rather than his own inclination for a military career, Leese was called to the Bar of the Inner Temple in 1893. In that year he married Violet Mary, daughter of Albert G Sandeman, whose family wine firm was well known in the City and who was also a director of the Bank of England from 1866 until 1918, taking the Governor's chair, 1895-97.

Leese's early career at the Bar prospered; he acted as junior counsel to Sir Charles Matthews on behalf of the Bank of England in a number of forgery cases. In 1906, however, Leese accepted an invitation to leave the Bar and join Freshfields, solicitors to the Bank of England. At that time the senior partner of a family firm of nearly a century's standing, Dr Edwin Freshfield (qv), was seventy-four and neither of his junior partners, his son and his nephew, showed a sufficient dedication to the practice.

From the time he joined the firm, Leese worked on the affairs of the Bank of England and in 1916 Sir William (he succeeded to his father's baronetcy in 1914) was appointed joint solicitor to the Bank with Dr Edwin Freshfield and his son Edwin Hanson Freshfield. After the death of Dr Freshfield in 1918 and the early retirement of his son in 1921, Sir William became senior partner. He set about reorganising the firm and brought in new partners, some from other firms. For the first time, able assistant solicitors working for the firm were offered the partnerships which previously they had had to leave Freshfields to find.

From 1914 onwards, Leese bore the main burden of the Bank of England's legal work. In the 1920s and 1930s this responsibility was particularly heavy as the Bank, under Montagu Norman (qv), was led into activities and initiatives unparalleled in its history. Through the Bank's involvement with international financial reconstruction, Leese acted for the trustees of the Dawes and Young loans designed to solve the problem of German reparations; subsequently he was concerned with the flotation of the various international loans made under the auspices of the League of Nations and intended to promote financial stability in Central Europe.

At home, the Bank of England's participation in the reconstruction of the cotton, engineering and steel industries — 'one of the oddest episodes in its history' — led to the formation of a private subsidiary company, Securities Management Trust and, in conjunction with other banks, the

Bankers' Industrial Development Corporation, both of which were advised by Freshfields.

As the first non-family partner admitted for forty years he had brought Freshfields through a difficult period when the family line was failing and 'had established for himself a leading position among the solicitors in the City' {*Times* 22 Jan 1937}. His strength lay in his interest 'in finding a commonsense solution to a problem' rather than in 'complex legal technicalities' {*ibid*}. Leese's distinction in his profession was reflected in his membership of the Council of the Law Society and its major committees. However he also served the community in a wider sphere. Remarkably for a leading City solicitor, for many years he gave free advice at Cambridge House in the East End and he took a keen interest in the Boy Scout movement. He sought relaxation in cricket, acting, golf, horse-racing and fishing.

Sir William died suddenly on 17 January 1937 while on holiday at Sidmouth, leaving £53,951. He was survived by his wife (d 1947), a daughter and three sons. He was succeeded in the baronetcy by his eldest son who, accomplishing his father's own early ambitions, was the distinguished soldier, Lieutenant-General Sir Oliver Leese.

JUDY SLINN

Writings:

Port of London Act 1908 ... together with ... a Summary of the Principal Acts Affecting the Chief Dock Companies ... (Effingham Wilson, 1910).

Sources:

Published

Judy Slinn, *A History of Freshfields* (pp, for Freshfields, 1984).

Times 22 Jan 1937.

WWW.

William H Legge, Lord Dartmouth (from Representative British Freemasons *Dod's Peerage, 1915).*

LEGGE, William Heneage

6th Earl of Dartmouth

(1851-1936)

Coalowner

William Heneage Legge was born at Mayfair, London, on 6 May 1851, eldest son of William Walter Legge, Fifth Earl of Dartmouth, by Lady Augusta Finch, eldest daughter of Fifth Earl of Aylesford, and granddaughter of Second Earl of Warwick. Styled Viscount Lewisham from his father's succession to the peerage in 1853 until the latter's death in 1891, Legge was educated at Eton in 1865-69 and matriculated at Christ Church, Oxford, in 1869.

As a youth Lewisham was a great traveller and shortly after obtaining his majority went on a world tour; while in the Holy Land in 1878 he was recalled to England to fight a by-election; thereafter he was Conservative MP for West Kent (Sevenoaks) in 1878-85, and after the constituency was divided, sat as Conservative MP for Lewisham (where his family owned valuable property) from 1885 until his succession to the peerage in 1891. The Kentish influence was strong in Conservative party organisation; the Marquess of Abergavenny (living near Tunbridge Wells), Disraeli's principal party manager, and Sir William Hart Dyke, Disraeli's Chief Whip and Patronage Secretary, led 'the Kent gang' {Chilston (1961) 4} which dominated the principal staff appointments of the party. Lewisham, as a junior member of the gang, served as a Conservative Whip in the House of Commons until June 1885. He was then sworn of the Privy Council and became an agricultural spokesman while serving as Vice Chamberlain of the Royal Household which office he held (with an interval in 1886) until November 1891. As such he was an obscure member of Lord Salisbury's first and second administrations.

The Sixth Earl typified the passive coal and urban property proprietor of the late nineteenth-early twentieth century. His grandfather had participated directly in the development of the South Staffordshire field. Yet even he had leased the working of the minerals to professional coal masters, and the Fifth and Sixth Earls relied on their agents as influential intermediaries in negotiations with the Sandwell Park Colliery Co, which exploited deep seams on the family's estate on the edge of West Bromwich from the 1870s. By the following decade coalmines accounted for 56 per cent of the estate revenues compared to 14 per cent in the 1850s. The Fifth Earl had also leased land for urban development in order to relieve his mortgage burden, incurred after the family bought a more rural family seat, Patshull Hall, in 1848. As royalty owner the Sixth Earl — following the example his father had set in the 1870s — cooperated with the coal firm in overcoming difficulties involved in sinking a new pit at the turn of the century. Nevertheless, while remaining influential, the economic role of the son, like the father, was more permissive than entrepreneurial. In 1891 the Sixth Earl inherited estates which, excluding his London properties, covered 19,578 acres and which in 1883 had yielded £58,657. These included 8,024 acres around Huddersfield in the West Riding of Yorkshire, 7,316 acres in Staffordshire, 391 in Kent (worth £10,470 a year in 1883 and much more later) and 42 in Middlesex (worth £3,350 in 1883). The Fifth Earl left £119,811 but the Sixth Earl, unlike many other landowners, was not obliged by Edwardian taxation to sell any of his property, including Sandwell Park, one of the three largest collieries in South Staffordshire, employing 250 men underground.

Although Dartmouth's position was encumbered in 1891 by lingering debt and the burden of supporting relatives this was steadily redressed as the value of his properties in Lewisham and St Pancras, and of his Black Country coalmines, rose in the 1890s.

Until the mid-1890s Dartmouth was a director of Exchange & Hop Warehouses Ltd, registered in 1881 to acquire the Hop Exchange in Southwark. Other directors included Aretas Akers-Douglas MP (Viscount Chilston), a Kentish friend of Dartmouth who had been a colleague in the Whips office and in Abergavenny's gang.

Although active for many years in the House of Lords, Dartmouth focussed his interests on county affairs, primarily in the West Midlands. A useful but not brilliant cricketer, he was president (later trustee) of the Middlesex County Cricket Club in 1893, and president of Staffordshire County Cricket Club for over forty years. He served as Lord Lieutenant of Staffordshire in succession to his father from 1891 until 1927 and as an alderman of the county council. He was also president of the county agricultural society and chairman of the County Territorial Association 1908-22. Active in Midlands Conservative politics, he was president of the Wednesbury Conservative Association until succeeded by Dudley Docker (qv). He was also prominent in West Bromwich politics and charities. Dartmouth was Provincial Grand Master of the Freemasons of Staffordshire from 1893. He was a magistrate in Staffordshire and Shropshire, a Freeman of the Skinners' Company and president of the William Salt Archaeological Society of Stafford. He was honorary colonel in 1891-1908 of the first volunteer battalion of the South Staffordshire Regiment (Volunteer Decoration, 1904), and of the fifth territorial divisional train of the Royal Army Service Corps in 1908-28 (his successor being Herbert Austin (qv)).

> Lord Dartmouth belonged to a type which unfortunately is fast passing away ... which gave sturdy qualities and enrichment to our country life. He was content to live on his property at Patshull, and was exact in fulfilling, modestly and efficiently, the duties and responsibilities of his position as a territorial nobleman. With a strong sense of duty he combined sound judgment and a capacity that might well have qualified him for higher office than it was his fortune — or perhaps his ambition — to hold ... his genial, humorous disposition made him welcome all through his career. {*Times* 12 Mar 1936}

He was created KCB (civil) in 1917 and GCVO in 1928.

Dartmouth married in 1879, at Holkham, Norfolk, Lady Mary Coke (1849-1929), fourth daughter of the Second Earl of Leicester, and granddaughter of Samuel Whitbread the brewer. They had three sons (of whom the second was killed in action in 1915) and two daughters. Dartmouth died at his seat, Patshull, near Wolverhampton, on 11 March 1936, leaving unsettled estate worth £123,221 gross.

R P T DAVENPORT-HINES

Writings:

letter on attitude of Church Association to general election *Times* 5 Feb 1906.

letter on House of Lords *ibid* 2 May 1907.

letter on Agricultural Holdings Act *ibid* 28 Dec 1907.

letters on Territorial Army and artillery *ibid* 21 Mar, 8 May, 20 Aug 1908, 17 Dec 1910.

letter on Stratford-on-Avon by-election *ibid* 20 Apr 1909.

letter on Lloyd George budget *ibid* 9 Oct 1909.

letter on Unionist policy to Parliament Bill *ibid* 31 July 1911.

letter on appointing magistrates *ibid* 25 Dec 1911.

letter on Welsh Church disestablishment *ibid* 23 May 1912.

letter on Irish home rule *ibid* 5 Oct 1912.

letter on modern dancing *ibid* 23 May 1913.

Sources:

Unpublished

PrC.

Information from Dr R Trainor.

Published

John Barnes and David Nicholson (eds), *The Leo Amery Diaries 1896-1929* (Hutchinson, 1980).

Viscount Chilston, *Chief Whip* (Routledge & Kegan Paul, 1961).

Complete Peerage.

Richard Davenport-Hines, *Dudley Docker* (Cambridge: Cambridge University Press, 1984).

Old Public School Boys' Who's Who: Eton (St James's Press, 1933).

R W Sturgess, 'Landowners, Mining and Urban Development in Nineteenth Century Staffordshire' in J T Ward and Richard G Wilson (eds), *Land and Industry* (Newton Abbot: David & Charles, 1971).

Times 12 Mar 1936.

Richard Trainor, 'Peers on an Industrial Frontier: The Earls of Dartmouth and of Dudley in the Black Country ca 1810-1914', in David Cannadine (ed), *Patricians,*

Power and Politics in Nineteenth Century Towns (Leicester: Leicester University Press, 1982).

VCH Staffordshire 2.

WWMP.

WWW.

LESLIE, Andrew

(1818-1894)

Shipbuilder

Andrew Leslie (courtesy of Swan Hunter Shipbuilders Ltd).

Andrew Leslie was born at Garth, Dunrossness, Shetland Islands, on 1 September 1818, the youngest child and only son of Andrew Leslie and Christina née Allison. His father was a crofter who, after being displaced from his land, worked as a cartman and occasionally on coastal ships out of Aberdeen, where the family moved when Andrew was still an infant. In 1829, the family moved back to the Shetlands after the death of the father, but two years later Andrew was back in Aberdeen, where he served an apprenticeship as a boilermaker.

As a craftsman Andrew Leslie impressed his employers, John Vernon & Co, so that they promoted him to foreman; at this time he studied in the evenings, learning engineering drawing from Charles Mitchell (1820-95), who was also to establish an iron shipyard on Tyneside. Early in the 1840s, Leslie established his own business in Aberdeen as a boilermaker, later adding the description 'general blacksmith'. In 1853 he moved to Tyneside, with £198, seeking a site for an iron shipyard. He chose a piece of land east of Hebburn Quay, largely open country with a large ballast hill nearby. There followed a brief partnership with J H Coutts, another Scot who began on the Tyne in 1840, but Leslie soon became sole owner of the shipyard he had constructed.

Leslie recruited the bulk of his skilled craftsmen and foremen from Scotland and many of these stayed at the Hebburn shipyard for the whole of their working lives. Soon he was employing about 200 workers. He was one of the pioneers of iron shipbuilding on the North East Coast and his ability to impress potential customers was such that his first order was for the 1,000 ton *Clarendon*, in which the principal shareholder was W S Lindsay, MP for Tynemouth. However, for the first nine years annual

LESLIE Andrew

Calais-Douvres—twin hulled cross channel steamer (courtesy of Mr Joe F Clarke).

output averaged about 2,000 tons and during this time Leslie speculatively built some ships without orders, hoping to sell them on completion; when this failed he would trade with these ships until a buyer was found. At this time he lived in a house adjacent to his shipyard, with his foremen in houses nearby. Little detail is known of his various commercial investments but in the early 1860s he had financial problems, which caused him to seek a new partner who would bring fresh funds into the business. Leslie valued his business at £90,000 in the negotiations with Thomas Coote, who was making the investment for his son Arthur (1841-1906). The young Coote, who served his apprenticeship at the famous Dunbarton shipyard of Denny & Co, became Leslie's partner in 1863 and later married the adopted daughter of the Leslies, who were childless.

Over the period 1863-75 new tonnage launched averaged more than 10,000 tons a year; turnover was about £200,000 a year at the outset of this period and in the best year probably reached £400,000. Andrew Leslie was an excellent salesman and established early connections with Russia. Of his first 20 ships, 12 were for Russian owners and in Britain he found his main customers in Liverpool. From 1861 it was rare for a year to pass without the Hebburn shipyard supplying Holts' shipping line with at least one vessel and in many years Holts' orders accounted for more than 40 per cent of the yard's output. One of the Holts' ships, the *Smyrna*, was the first on the Tyne to be fitted with twin compound engines.

Leslie's final ten years, 1876-1885, saw the yard's output average almost 16,000 tons and peak in 1881 at 23,500 tons. In the depression of the mid-1880s, while shipbuilding output nationally fell below 40 per cent, at Hebburn output never fell below 50 per cent and in 1885 exceeded 66 per cent of the peak year. Three ships were built in excess of 3,000 tons: the *Vega* in 1879 and the *Capella* and *Red Sea* in 1882; in all 260 ships were built before Leslie retired in 1885. At the end of 1883 there was an abortive attempt to form a limited liability company with the engine builders North Eastern Marine and others, but Leslie played no part when the Hebburn shipyard became part of R & W Hawthorn, Leslie & Co Ltd in 1886 under Benjamin Browne (qv). The valuation of the Hebburn enterprise in July 1885 was £275,800 (including housing at £38,640), which is a measure of Leslie's success as a businessman. In his best years he probably employed many more than the 2,000 men whose annual wage bill in 1885 totalled £130,000.

Labour relations were not always happy for Andrew Leslie. He had little patience with trade unions, as he made clear in written evidence to the Royal Commission on Trade Unions (1867-69) and would resort to the courts to discipline workers. In 1872 he personally intervened to resolve a strike by the young rivet heaters and joined the short-lived Tyneside Shipbuilders Conciliation Board (1875-76) but was one of the first employers to withdraw. The strength of the Boilermakers Society was such that they could not be ignored by any iron shipbuilder and so they gained a grudging recognition by this proud, independent-minded Scot. Many of his men clearly held him in high regard and they contributed to his lifesize portrait at his retirement; this loyalty was reflected by his first draughtsman, John Skinner (1836-1920), who designed ships at Hebburn for thirty years before he established his own shipyard in 1884 and also by the many foremen who remained despite undoubted job opportunities in the expanding iron shipbuilding industry.

Leslie played a major part in developing the town of Hebburn and its social life. He built 400 houses for his workers and these were a steady source of income (certainly £2,000-£3,000 a year) apart from helping to attract and retain workers. Leslie chaired the first meeting of the Hebburn Co-operative Society in 1866 and gave a room in shipyard property to provide the first classroom. Later he contributed to the cost of constructing a school and a workmen's Institute. The gas produced at the shipyard was supplied to both the Co-operative Society and the local Presbyterian Church at very favourable rates. A life-long Presbyterian, Leslie, through a gift of £9,000, was responsible for the building of St Andrew's Church, a very short distance from the shipyard gates.

From 1859 Leslie lived at Wallsend, in a house which gave him a clear view of his shipyard across the Tyne. He was the most active member of the Wallsend community and promoted the establishment of a local board of health on which he later served. He was vice-chairman of the first Wallsend School Board and he served for thirteen years as a River Tyne Commissioner. A Unionist in politics, he was a JP for both Northumberland and Durham.

There were few members from the North East in the Institution of Mechanical Engineers when Leslie joined in 1858. His patent (no 2,842) of the following year was later incorporated into the *Great Britain*. Only in 1882 did Leslie join the Institution of Naval Architects but was elected to their Council almost immediately.

Leslie's wife Margaret Jordan was the daughter of a Leith merchant. Andrew Leslie died on 27 January 1894 and left £161,275 gross.

J F CLARKE

Writings:

PP, RC on Trade Unions (1867-69) 4123-I.

British Patent:

1859 (2,812)

Sources:

Unpublished

Tyne and Wear Archives, records of Hawthorn-Leslie.

Papers collected by John Gascoigne of Hebburn.

Joseph F Clarke, 'Labour Relations in Engineering and Shipbuilding on the North-East Coast c 1850-1906' (Newcastle uponTyne MA, 1967).

Published

Joseph F Clarke, *Power on Land and Sea ... a History of Hawthorn-Leslie* (pp, the company, 1977).

Francis E Hyde and John R Harris, *Blue Funnel: A History of Alfred Holt and Company of Liverpool from 1865 to 1914* (Liverpool: Liverpool University Press, 1956).

Newcastle Daily Chronicle 29 Jan 1894.

Proceedings of the Institution of Mechanical Engineers 1894.

W Richardson, *History of the Parish of Wallsend* (Wallsend, 1923).

South Shields Daily Gazette 29 Jan 1894.

LETTS, Charles John

(1839-1912)

Diary publisher

Charles John Letts was born near London Bridge, South East London, on 30 July 1839, the son of Thomas Letts (1804-1873), a stationer, and his wife Harriet née Cory. His grandfather John Letts (1772-1851) was a stationer and printer in the Royal Exchange, London, who in 1812, identifying a need among City merchants, produced his *Letts Diary or Bills Due Book and Almanack*, generally regarded as the world's first commercial diary. Under John and Thomas Letts the business grew, selling maps and pocket books as well as diaries.

Like his older brother Thomas Alton Letts, who later emigrated to New York, Charles entered the family business, but he became dissatisfied with the way it was run, especially after the retirement of his father in the 1870s. Evidently, he resented the influence of directors from outside the

The first product Charles Letts & Co produced in 1883, an Old Almanack, entry for January (courtesy of Charles Letts & Co Ltd).

family. This process of disenchantment culminated in 1881 when he left Letts Son & Co Ltd and set up in business on his own account.

The founding of Charles Letts & Co was a bold enterprise by a father of four children with only £500 capital to his name (he was able to borrow a further £700 from a close relative). His credit, however, was good with his banker and suppliers. The new company, located in the Royal Exchange, with a warehouse off Farringdon Street, had small beginnings. Charles Letts's eldest son Harry later recalled: 'My father's staff in those early days, so far as I can remember, consisted of himself, a traveller, an order clerk, and one apprentice, plus a warehouseman' {Beable (1926) II, 216}.

The misgivings felt by Charles Letts about the old family firm were soon vindicated. Minus the Letts family, Letts Son & Co Ltd was wound up in 1885, although the right to publish Letts Diaries was bought by Cassells. Charles was therefore careful to promote himself in an early catalogue of his products as 'the only Letts now in the Diary Trade — and for many years Editor of the Original Series'.

Charles Letts's Diaries.

These Diaries are compiled by Mr. Charles Letts—the only Letts now in the Diary Trade—and for many years Editor of the Original Series. They are admitted to be the cheapest in the world, *contain several novel improvements, are got up in the most modern style—the Paper, Blotting, Printing and Binding being all above the average—and are in use in most Government, Railway and Insurance Offices.*

Best Cloth-Bound Diaries.

Extra Thick Paper, very strongly Bound, with Monthly Cash Summary and Ribbon Register.

21 VARIETIES

OF BEST

CLOTH-BOUND
DIARIES.

FOUR SIZES.

Folio	-	8¼-in. × 13¼-in.
Quarto	-	8¼-in. × 10⅝-in.
Imperial 8vo.	-	7¼-in. × 11-in.
Large 8vo.	-	5⅝-in. × 8¼-in.

No.		s.	d.
151.	Imperial Octavo 1-day Diary, cloth lettered, with monthly summary	7	0
161.	Folio 1-day Diary, stout paper, with monthly summary, cloth lettered	9	0
161B.	The same Diary, interleaved blotting paper ..	12	0
162.	Folio 2-day Diary, stout paper, with monthly summary, cloth lettered	5	0
162B.	The same Diary, interleaved blotting	6	6
163.	Folio 3-day Diary, stout paper, with monthly summary, cloth lettered	3	6
163B	The same Diary, interleaved blotting	4	6
163C.	Folio 3-day Diary, Dr. and Cr. in the opening, cloth lettered	5	6
171.	Quarto 1 day Diary, with monthly cash summary, cloth lettered	8	0
172.	Quarto 2-day Diary, with monthly cash summary, cloth lettered	5	0
172B.	The same Diary, interleaved blotting	6	0
173.	Quarto 3-day Diary, stout paper, with monthly summary, cloth lettered	3	0
173B.	The same Diary, interleaved blotting	4	0
173C.	Quarto 3-day Diary, Dr. and Cr. in the opening, cloth lettered	5	0
181.	Octavo 1-day Diary, stout paper, with monthly summary, cloth lettered	4	6
181B.	The same Diary, interleaved blotting paper ..	5	0
182.	Octavo 2-day Diary, stout paper, with monthly summary, cloth lettered	3	6
182B.	The same Diary, interleaved blotting paper ..	4	0
183.	Octavo 3-day Diary, stout paper, with monthly summary, cloth lettered	2	6
183B.	The same Diary, interleaved blotting	3	6
183C.	Octavo 3-day Diary, Dr. and Cr. in the opening, cloth lettered	4	0

25

Catalogue of diaries 1887 (courtesy of Charles Letts & Co Ltd).

The rise of the new firm was not quite as rapid as the decline of the old. At the end of the first year's trading Charles Letts showed a loss of £355, and not until the late 1880s did he record a profit. His was by no means a one-product firm: initially he sold more papers, pens and inks than diaries, although the range of diaries grew to the three-figure mark. The enterprise of Charles Letts showed in the development of the specialist diary and record books, some early favourites being his *Ideal Medical Visiting List, Pew Rent Register* and *Wine Bin Book*.

By the time Charles Letts retired from active business in 1909 sales of his diaries were close to three quarters of a million. The new family firm, which passed to his sons, was set on a course of steady growth.

Charles Letts was married three times: firstly in 1866 to Sarah (1840-1876), the daughter of Thomas Ashworth, a flannel manufacturer. They had four children, Henry Vaughan (1868-1952), Norman Ashworth, Charles Hubert and Daisy. After his first wife's death in 1876 he married in 1878 Eliza, 'Lizzie', daughter of James Petrie, a machinist. After his second wife's death he married Helena, daughter of John Tidy, in 1901.

Charles John Letts died on 11 June 1912, leaving £21,315 gross.

ANTHONY A LETTS

Writings:

This is a list of the subject's compilations (all published by his firm), nearly all annuals.

An Olde Almanack in Forme of a Book of Reference ... Newlye Sette Forthe by Charles Letts (1883).

Some Notes on Celebrated Diarists and Their Diaries (Letts & Co, 1888).

Charles Letts's Cyclists' Diary and Note Book for 1891 (1890) for 1892 (1891).

Charles Letts's Ideal Medical Diary and Daily Visiting List.

Charles Letts's Improved Office Diary and Note Book for 1891 etc (1890 etc).

Charles Letts's Improved Scribbling Diary and Note Book for 1892 etc (1891 etc).

Charles Letts's Indispensable Universal Postal Calculator (1890).

Charles Letts's Ladies' Year Book and Housekeepers' Diary for 1892 etc (1891).

Charles Letts's Stationers' Diary and Trade Book of Reference.

Sources:

Unpublished

Charles Letts & Co Ltd, London, archives.

BCe.

MCe.

Published

William H Beable, *Romance of Great Businesses* (2 vols, Heath Cranton Ltd, 1926) 2.

LETTS, Sir William Malesbury

(1873-1957)

Motor vehicle distributor

William Malesbury Letts was born at Brackley, Northamptonshire, on 26 February 1873, son of William Edward Letts, a coachman and domestic servant, and his wife Sarah née Ward. Letts began his working life in the motor trade and industry as a young man. In 1898 he visited the United States, working there for a few years and becoming familiar with American business practice and acquiring in particular a knowledge of the Locomobile steam car. He returned to the UK with the agency for the Locomobile Co until 1903, selling 400 of its steam runabouts in 1900-1. Soon after in 1903, he joined Charles Jarrott, the well-known racing driver, to found the distributorship Charles Jarrott & Letts Ltd and on Jarrott's retirement, in 1909, he assumed full control of the business. The firm sold Oldsmobile and De Dietrich cars, Jarrott being particularly associated with the latter marque as a racing driver. It also undertook marketing of the Crossley car, which the stationary engine manufacturers, Crossley Bros Ltd of Manchester, founded by Francis Crossley (qv), introduced in 1904.

In 1910 Letts joined Sir Kenneth Crossley in Crossley Motors Ltd, Manchester, taking control of manufacturing as managing director. He remained a director of the company until his death. Jarrott & Letts was bought up by Crossley as their distributor. In 1912 Crossley Motors developed their first commercial vehicle, which proved to be highly successful as an RFC tender, based on the 25/30 hp car. Only 58 had been delivered by the outbreak of the First World War, but production was 3,000 a year during the war, vehicles being supplied through Jarrott & Letts, at which point any last minute adjustments were made.

During the First World War Letts set up for the Government the No 3 National Aircraft Factory at Heaton Chapel, near Stockport. He received the CBE in 1918 and was knighted in 1922.

Letts's involvement in motoring organisations began in the early days of the industry. He was, together with Jarrott, an original subscribing member of the Society of Motor Manufacturers & Traders convened by F R Simms (qv) in 1902. He was first chairman of its agents' section, 1907-10, served on various committees over a long period and was president 1925-26. He was one of the founders of the Motor Trade Association, and the firm of Jarrott & Letts was closely involved in the establishment of the Automobile Association (originally the Motorists Mutual Association) in 1905, assisting with staff and offices in its early days, although Letts did not become a member of its committee. He remained a director of Crossleys until his death but otherwise played a less prominent role in business after the 1920s. Letts married Edith Annie Pearson. He died on 25 February 1957, leaving £230,190 gross.

RICHARD STOREY

Sources:

Unpublished

BCe.

PrC.

Published

Hugh Barty-King, *The AA. A History of the First 75 Years of the Automobile Association* (Basingstoke: The AA, 1980).

G N Georgano (ed), *Complete Encyclopaedia of Motorcars* (2nd ed, Ebury Press, 1973).

— (ed), *Complete Encyclopaedia of Commercial Vehicles* (Iola: Krause Publications, 1979).

Charles Jarrott, *Ten Years of Motors and Motor Racing* (Grant Richards, 1912).

D Scott-Moncrieff, *Veteran and Edwardian Motor Cars* (Batsford, 1963).

Charles Smith, 'I Worked at Jarrott & Letts' *Motor Sport* 59 no 2 (Feb 1983).

Times 27 Feb 1957.

WWW.

LEVER, William Hesketh

1st Viscount Leverhulme of the Western Isles

(1851-1925)

Soap and food manufacturer

William Hesketh Lever was born in Wood Street, Bolton, Lancashire, on 19 September 1851, the elder son of James Lever, a retail grocer of Bolton who moved up to wholesaling in 1864, and his wife Eliza, daughter of William Hesketh, a cotton mill manager of Manchester. He went to a

William Lever, Lord Leverhulme (from W H Lever, 2nd Viscount Leverhulme Viscount Leverhulme *George Allen & Unwin, 1927).*

church school (the Church Institute, Bolton) because his father admired the headmaster, but the Levers were Congregationalists. All his life he believed in self-help and Free Trade, and his hero in politics was Gladstone. There could be no more representative member of the trading middle class which created so much of the wealth and set so much of the tone of Victorian England. All the roots of Lever's being sprang from it and all its precepts and ideals were his.

Lever might have become a doctor — his mother wished him to — but instead, after a conventional school career for a boy of his time and social class, he went at sixteen into the family business. His father took him into partnership at the age of twenty-one, with the very high income of £800 a year, and he married at twenty-three, laying the first foundations of his art collection soon after.

Until he was about thirty-five he was in business as a wholesale grocer, increasingly independent, it appears, of his father, and expanding the business, its geographical extent, its range of products, and its sources of supply, as he saw fit. He took a keen interest in his customers' customers, the working-class housewives of Lancashire, observed their habits and mentality, and was aware that their standard of living was rising. He observed also, at a distance, the methods of American business men dealing with consumers whose standard of living was rising. He noticed that they sold their products under brand names supported by heavy advertising and sales promotion schemes, and he studied their techniques very closely. By trade Lever was a grocer, and by profession a marketing man.

He applied his marketing skill, from the 1880s onward, not to the varied stock-in-trade of a wholesale grocer, but to Sunlight Soap, which he soon began to manufacture for himself because no soap-maker would manufacture it satisfactorily for him. He withdrew some money from the grocery business, and with that and loans from the family got together about £27,000 for the establishment of his new enterprise. In 1885 the new firm purchased the soap works of Winser & Co in Warrington. He did not invent Sunlight soap, for he had no technical knowledge. He did recognise its outstanding quality: that it saved work for the housewife. He gave the soap its brand name and he put it in a package which protected it, guaranteed it, and gave it individuality. He advertised and promoted his product by all the means in his power, creating a demand which no retailer dared ignore. His competitors deeply resented his methods, and copied them.

The demand for Sunlight Soap grew rapidly and manufacturing was begun in January 1889 at a new centre on the Mersey, near Bebington, Cheshire, named Port Sunlight. In 1890 Lever Bros was made a limited company, and in 1894 this company went public with a capital of £1.5 million, divided equally into preference and ordinary shares. The first issue of the preference capital was heavily over-subscribed, whilst Lever himself gradually acquired nearly all the ordinary shares. Amalgamation with other soap-making firms soon followed, beginning with the acquisition of Benjamin Brooke & Co in 1899, and Lever attained the leading position in the soap industry. An attempt, in 1906, to build a combine of soap firms was defeated by Lord Northcliffe (qv), fearful of losing advertising revenue for his newspapers, but Lever launched a series

Aeroplane view of Port Sunlight (from W H Lever, 2nd Viscount Leverhulme Viscount Leverhulme *George Allen & Unwin, 1927).*

of libel actions which gained him £141,000 in damages, at that time a record sum.

By 1906 Lever was at his zenith. He had transformed the nature of with factories already in half-a-dozen countries and many more to come. He had repeatedly been a parliamentary candidate, and in 1906 won a seat, as a Liberal, in the Wirral, but he only held it until 1909 — he scarcely had the temperament of a democratic politician. He owned an estate at Thornton Hough, where he largely rebuilt the house and village, opening out an ambitious road system which, when the local authority would not take it over, he closed again. He was an enthusiastic builder and alterer of houses, and his collecting enthusiasm provided him with furniture, paintings and ceramics. 'Short and thickset in stature', says Sir Angus Watson (qv), a contemporary, 'with a sturdy body set on short legs and a massive head covered with thick, upstanding hair, he radiated force and energy' {Watson (1937) 140-41}.

Lever's 'force and energy', from the 1880s until his death in 1925, went principally into the development of Lever Bros Ltd (James Darcy Lever, completely overshadowed by William, became an invalid and died in 1910) from a small soap firm in Lancashire to the controlling company in a world-wide business of remarkable diversity. In expanding his activities Lever showed on the one hand the optimism, self-confidence, imagination and will-power without which no entrepreneur is likely to succeed, and on the other an almost paranoid fear of being held to ransom by monopolist suppliers of raw materials.

Insofar as there were unifying principles underlying the growth of Lever Bros, apart from the personality of the founder, they were, first, reliance on oils and fats as raw materials and second, the supply of household necessities and minor luxuries of sound quality and moderate price, to the great advantage of the mass of consumers. These principles led not only to the making of a wide range of soaps and washing products generally but also, very early on, to oil-milling and the manufacture of animal feedingstuffs, and in 1914 to the manufacture, with indifferent success, of margarine. It led Lever also to seek control of his own supplies of oilseeds, and here both his positive and his negative motivation — his constant search for new activities, on the one hand, and his fear of monopolists, on the other — joined forces with spectacular results. From 1902 onward Levers became plantation owners in the Solomon Islands and from 1911, on a much larger scale, in the Belgian Congo. In Nigeria, in 1910, Lever took the first step towards building up what became the largest group of merchant businesses in West Africa, and in 1916 he went into shipping, with six ships, to protect Lever Brothers' interests on the route between Liverpool and the West African coast.

Lever Brothers' success made Lever very rich. His personal assets were valued at £1.5 million in 1897: in 1912 at almost £3 million, and he had income to match. Yet he denied that he worked at business only for the sake of money. 'I am not a lover of money as money', he once told a journalist, 'and never have been. I work at business because business is life. It enables me to do things' {Wilson (1954) I, 187}.

This might be mere pious platitudinising, but examination of some of the 'things' suggests that it is not. He meant what he said, and his motives were more complex than simply the maximisation of profit.

Looked at from this point of view, three projects stand out, from the early, middle and late phases of Lever's career. The first is the creation of the village of Port Sunlight, alongside his soap factory, between 1888 and 1914. The second is the establishment of palm oil estates, rather like black Port Sunlights, in the Belgian Congo from 1911 onward. The third is the attempt to rehabilitate the economy of the Western Isles — the Outer Hebrides — where in 1917 Lever bought an estate to provide him with occupation in his retirement. They all demonstrate Lever's lifelong passion for planning, for building, and for regulating people's lives for their own good as he saw it.

In Port Sunlight he was very consciously the paternalist employer, the benevolent despot acting in a manner highly unfashionable in our day, widely admired in his own. He once explained that the village was a form of prosperity sharing. 'If I were to follow the usual mode of profit sharing', he said, 'I would send my workmen and work girls to the cash office at the end of the year and say ... "You are going to receive £8 each; you have earned this money: it belongs to you. Take it and make whatever use you like of your money." Instead of that I told them: "£8 is ... soon spent, and it will not do you much good if you send it down your throats in the form of bottles of whisky, bags of sweets, or fat geese for Christmas. On the other hand, if you leave this money with me, I shall use it to

Lever Brothers' first factory at Warrington, 1886 (from W H Lever, 2nd Viscount Leverhulme Viscount Leverhulme *George Allen & Unwin, 1927).*

provide for you everything which makes life pleasant — viz nice houses, comfortable homes, and healthy recreation. Besides, I am disposed to allow profit sharing in no other than that form" {*ibid*, I, 146}.

There are indications that as Port Sunlight came to maturity Lever's early enthusiasm for it may to some extent have been replaced by his new-found fascination with the Congo, where much the same motives came into play but the horizons were wider. He felt himself a pioneer. 'We have got hold of somethng we can employ all our talents and energy upon for the next quarter century', he wrote in 1913, 'and still find plenty to do' {*ibid*, I, 176}. He visited the Congo twice in great state, once in 1912-13 at the age of sixty-one and again in 1924-25 when he was seventy-three. Both visits were probably foolhardy. His wife, who went with him the first time, died soon afterwards and he died soon after his second visit. The juxtaposition may be coincidental, but it looks sinister.

Lever's activities in the Hebrides had originally nothing to do with Lever Bros. He had conceived a romantic affection for the islands when he and his wife, as a young couple, visited them on holiday, and when first Lewis, in 1917, and then North and South Harris, in 1919, came on the market, he bought them, intending to reconstruct the islands' distressed economy by putting capital — his own capital — into the development of fishing. This was purely his private hobby, but in pursuing it he launched MacFisheries and acquired a group of food companies, including T Wall & Sons, makers of sausages, pies, and ice cream, to complement the fishmongering business. Local opposition to his plans, limited but tiresome, caused him to withdraw from the Western Isles in 1922. Having no further use for the MacFisheries group, and being in need of the capital invested in it, he sold it to Lever Bros. When Levers merged with the

Margarine Union in 1929 to form Unilever, MacFisheries came with them as part of the package. Unilever thus found itself with a substantial stake in the food industries as a result of the failure of William Lever's plans to find himself occupation in retirement: one of the more surprising results of the impact of a strong personality on big business.

Neither the building of Port Sunlight, the establishment of the Congo plantations, nor the Hebridean venture was an orthodox commercial proposition launched mainly with an eye to profit. The Congo came nearest to being one, but if Lever had simply been concerned to secure his supplies of palm oil he could have found easier and quicker ways of doing it than opening up plantations in virgin forest which could not be expected to yield a worthwhile return for a quarter of a century. The Congo enterprise, as from time to time he came close to admitting, was an expression of his innate romanticism. All these projects were of immense importance to him, for each provided an outlet, alongside the outlets provided by his normal business activities, for the immensely varied creative force of his many-sided character.

Lever's tragedy was that he could not be obliged to retire. He remained in power too long and towards the end of his life his judgement, distorted by megalomania, led him into serious errors. The worst was his rash decision, at the beginning of 1920, to commit Levers to buying control, for over £8 million, of the Niger Co, Lever Bros' greatest rivals in West Africa. He could not have chosen a worse moment. The decision nearly ruined his life's achievement, clouding his last years with black anxiety which even his resilience and will-power could not entirely control. His business was rescued by Francis D'Arcy Cooper (qv), who from 1921 onward exercised discreet control over the running of Lever Bros and after Lever's death became its chairman. Nevertheless, by 1924 the capital of Lever Bros amounted to nearly £57 million and it was the largest industrial undertaking of its kind in the world.

Lever married in 1874 Elizabeth Ellen, daughter of Crompton Hulme, a linen draper in Bolton. Only one of their children grew up: William Hulme Lever (1888-1949).

Lever was created a baronet in 1911 and in 1917 was raised to the peerage as Baron Leverhulme. In 1922 he became a viscount and added to his title 'of the Western Isles'. Viscount Leverhulme died at his house in Hampstead on 7 May 1925, leaving £1,625,409 gross.

W J READER

Writings:

Following the Flag. Jottings of a Jaunt Round the World (Simpkin & Marshall, 1893).

An Address to ... the Port Sunlight Men's Meeting (Port Sunlight: Lever Bros, 1903).

The Buildings Erected at Port Sunlight and Thornton Hough (Thornton Hough, 1905).

Land for Houses (Port Sunlight, 1905).

(ed) *Port Sunlight* (Square Peals, 1909).

Co-partnership. An Address ... to the Members of the Agricultural and Horticultural Association ... 13 June, 1912 (Port Sunlight: Lever Bros, 1912).

Co-partnership and Efficiency. An Address ... Delivered ... in the Mason College of Birmingham University (Port Sunlight: Lever Bros, 1912).

Art and Beauty in the City. Three Addresses (Port Sunlight: Lever Bros, 1915).

Day by Day — That's All. Each Other's Burdens and Fast Asleep: Three Addresses (Port Sunlight: Lever Bros, 1916).

Girls and Boys; Harmonising Capital and Labour: and Industrial Administration: Three Addresses (Port Sunlight: Lever Bros, 1916).

Output and Intake: Three Addresses (Port Sunlight: Lever Bros, 1917).

Standardising Welfare (Port Sunlight: Lever Bros, 1917).

(Stanley Unwin ed) *The Six Hour Day and other Industrial Questions* (George Allen & Unwin, 1918).

Tools to the Men Who Can Use Them: An Address at Hudddersfield (Port Sunlight: Lever Bros, 1918).

Higher Wages and Shorter Hours (1919).

Reconstruction after War (Port Sunlight: Lever Bros, 1919).

'Prevention of Strikes' in *Labour and Capital after the War* (1919).

Capital and Capitalism (Port Sunlight: Lever Bros, 1920).

The Six Hour Shift and Industrial Efficiency (New York: H Holt & Co, 1920).

Co-partnership. Laying the Three Ghosts, Unemployment, Sickness, Death (Port Sunlight: Lever Bros, 1922).

Sources:

Unpublished

BCe

MCe.

PrC.

Published

William Henry Beable, *Romance of Great Businesses* (2 vols, Heath Cranton, 1926) I.

DNB.

W P Jolly, *Lord Leverhulme. A Biography* (Constable, 1976).

Andrew Knox, *Coming Clean* (Heinemann, 1976).

William Hulme Lever (2nd Viscount Leverhulme), *Viscount Leverhulme* (George Allen & Unwin, 1927).

Sir Angus Watson, *My Life: An Autobiography* (I Nicholson & Watson, 1937).

Harley Williams, *Men of Stress* (Cape, 1950).

Charles Wilson, *The History of Unilever* (2 vols, Cassell, 1954) I.

WWMP.

WWW.

LEVINSTEIN, Ivan

(1845-1916)

Chemical manufacturer

Ivan Levinstein was born at Berlin-Charlottenburg, Germany, in 1845. Nothing is known of his background and early life, except that he went to school and to university, where he read chemistry, in Berlin. He left Berlin in 1864 without completing his studies, and came to England where he established aniline dye works at Blackley in Manchester.

For many years the business made aniline colours, and though small was quite successful. In 1882 or 1883 Levinstein introduced a red azo-dye, 'Blackley Red', which the German company BASF claimed to be identical with their patented dye. BASF sued Levinstein, and after losing in the Appeal Court took the case to the House of Lords, where it won (1884-87). The case attracted much attention and turned Levinstein into a patent law reformer.

It also led him to associate with two other German dye-makers, Friedrich Bayer & Co and Agfa of Berlin, to enlarge his enterprise and increase the range of azo-colours. The business was sold in 1890 to a newly-incorporated company, Levinstein & Co Ltd, with a nominal capital of £150,000. Levinstein, Bayer and Agfa each held one-third of the shares. A new factory was built at Crumpsall in north Manchester. However, Levinstein quarrelled with his German partners, and when the agreement came up for renewal in 1895, and a new company, Levinstein Ltd, was formed they put up very little of the capital and by 1897 had completely withdrawn. Levinstein once more had problems raising capital, the preparation of dyes did not pay and the loss of exports of dyestuffs intermediates to Germany was a serious blow; only the outbreak of the First World War saved the business.

By then Ivan Levinstein had handed over direction of the company to his second son, Herbert, to devote himself to his other interests. These included at one time an ammonia-soda and salt works, Murgatroyd & Co, at Middlewich in Cheshire, which was sold to Brunner, Mond & Co in 1895. Brunner, Mond offered Levinstein a directorship, but an agreement between Brunner, Mond and the Salt Union forbidding Brunners to appoint a director concerned with the salt trade meant the offer had to be withdrawn. In 1908, together with Arthur Chamberlain (qv), Levinstein founded the Ammonia Soda Co at Plumley, Cheshire, which was sold to Brunner, Mond after his death.

Levinstein's public activities attracted wide attention. He saw himself as the champion of chemical manufacturers against the unfair trade practices of foreigners (especially Germans). As he enjoyed controversy, was not discountenanced by defeat and was a skilful litigant, he had a measure of success. The solution to the industry's problems, for which he campaigned tirelessly for more than twenty years, was to strengthen its bargaining position vis-à-vis overseas enterprises. This was to be achieved first by co-operation, next by better research and application, thirdly by a thorough reform of the patent law (in particular by the compulsory working of foreign patents in the UK) and, in the 1900s, by the introduction of a tariff. He aired these opinions in *The Chemical Review* which he founded and edited, and when that finished, in the *Journal of the Society of Chemical Industry*.

In his position as vice-president and later president of the Society (1897-1900, 1901-6), he lobbied vigorously on behalf of the chemical industry and influenced the drafting of the Patent Law Amendment Act (1902) and the Patent Act of 1907. He supported Chamberlain's Tariff Commission from 1903 onwards and was a vice-president of the Tariff Reform League. Levinstein also took a keen interest in the development of Manchester University and for many years was a governor of the Manchester College of Technology (now UMIST). Apart from an honorary MSc from the University, he received no public distinction. Nothing is known of his private life. He died on 15 March 1916 and was survived by three sons and left an estate of £113,884 gross.

L F HABER

Writings:

Levinstein contributed frequently to the *Journal of the Society of Chemical Industry* which also reprinted his presidential addresses. See in particular 17 (1898) and 19-22 (1900-03).

(ed) *The Chemical Review* Oct 1871-Apr 1891.

Sources:

Published

Guardian 16 Mar 1916.

Lutz F Haber, *The Chemical Industry 1900-30. International Growth and Technological Change* (Oxford: Clarendon Press, 1971).

Journal of the Society of Chemical Industry 35 (Apr 1916).

William J Reader, *Imperial Chemical Industries. A History* (2 vols, Oxford University Press, 1970-75).

David Lewis (from Asa Briggs, Friends of the People *BT Batsford Ltd, 1956).*

LEWIS, David

(1823-1885)

Retailer

David Lewis was born in London in 1823, the son of Wolfe Levy, a small Jewish merchant. He arrived in Liverpool, a growing city, at the age of sixteen and served his apprenticeship with a lively firm of tailors and outfitters in Lord Street, Benjamin Hyam & Co, which was already operating a branch system in several cities. It followed explicitly two rules which Lewis himself was to adopt when he set up his own business. 'All goods are marked in figures at the lowest selling price from which no abatement can be made' was the first. 'Any garment bought and taken away, if not satisfactory, will be exchanged, if not worn or injured' was the second. These were two of the rules which were to transform retailing in more than one country in the nineteenth century: they were followed, for example, by the pioneer Aristide Boucicaut, who set up his first small Bon Marché store in Paris in 1852, in the same decade as Lewis.

Within eighteen months of joining Hyams, Lewis was promoted to be its Liverpool manager, and within three years he was supervising existing Hyams branches and opening new ones.

At the age of thirty-three, in 1856, he commenced as a small shopkeeper on his own account, in Ranelagh Street, Liverpool. He dealt at first, like Hyams, only in men's and youth's clothing, most of it manufactured in his own workshop — knickerbockers were his speciality — and it was not until 1864 that he began to sell women's clothes also. By then, however, he had moved (in 1859) to new and more imposing premises in Bold Street and had become as well-known locally for his advertising as for his clothes. His women's coats and bonnets were advertised as 'the finest make of London and Paris fashions'.

In 1856 Lewis married Bertha Cohen, the daughter of a rabbi, but they had no children, and it was for this reason that he eventually invited his nephew Louis Samuel Cohen (1847-1922), who had been born in Australia, to join him in what he thought of as a family business. The shop premises were gradually extended in a series of often difficult property deals, and new merchandising departments were added until Ranelagh Street had been transformed into a department store. It was one of the first of its kind. By the 1870s Lewis's were manufacturing not only clothes but shoes and were selling toiletry, patent medicines, stationery and tobacco. In 1880 tea was lavishly added to the list, in 1882 the 'Penny Readings' of miscellaneous literature, and in 1884 watches.

As the development of his department store proceeded — according to no prefabricated plan — Lewis turned increasingly for his products to a number of manufacturers from whom he bought direct in large quantities at low prices, cutting out middlemen. He made the most of his advertising, of his own low retail prices, his small profit margins, his ready

Advertisement for Boys School Wear, 1880 (from Asa Briggs, Friends of the People BT Batsford Ltd, 1956).

money principle, and his rapid turnover, and, like Boucicaut, organised spectacular sales. He was a remarkable combination of organiser and showman, and his last exploit in this second capacity, the envy of P T Barnum, was to acquire the famous steamship, the *Great Eastern*, just before his death.

By then he had extended his business inside and outside Liverpool as well as the departmental range at Ranelagh Street. Family influences shaped his first move. His wife's sister Thérèse was married to a doctor in Paris, and it was through this connection that Lewis learned of Boucicaut and the new Bon Marché which was opened in 1869. In 1867, he himself acquired what he called a Bon Marché store in a 'superior area' in Bold Street, Liverpool, where, as in Paris, all kinds of goods, with a stress on nouveautés, were on display. It successfully tempted visitors into becoming customers: its clock tower became a Liverpool landmark. Yet its management was deliberately kept separate from Lewis's Ranelagh Street store and a cluster of other stores which Lewis acquired in other provincial cities, and it was there rather than in the Bon Marché that he made his own somewhat distinctive contribution to retailing, appealing to all kinds of customer in democratic language, priding himself that his business was 'essentially with the masses' and that Lewis's were 'the Friends of the People'.

Lewis's 'provincial empire' had its first outpost in Manchester. In the same year, 1877, as he leased the Bon Marché premises, he acquired an attractive site in Market Street, Manchester, and three years later opened a brand new store there. Very soon, it was claimed in characteristic advertisments, more than 100,000 people a week would be shopping there. With six merchandising departments, it would serve, it was also claimed, as a substantial acquisition for the city. Competitors did not see it in this way. Local shopkeeper rivalries led Lewis to be prosecuted, like William Whiteley (qv), for blocking the thoroughfare, and when he was found guilty and merely bound over, this only added to free publicity. He was spending 10 per cent of his gross sales on advertising at this time. Not all merchandising ventures succeeded, however. An attempt to sell coal, which Lewis claimed would last longer than coal sold by any other merchant, failed in 1884. Nor did a Food Department, introduced a year later, last for very long.

A new store opened in Waingate, Sheffield in 1884 was not a success either — it was to close in 1886 — but trumpets were sounded in 1885, when a further department store — and this time a highly successful one — was opened in Birmingham in Corporation Street, two years after Lewis had acquired a site in this important new thoroughfare, the pride of Joseph Chamberlain (qv). Much was made in this case of the fact that the new store was American in concept and style, one of the first instances when American rather French influence on British retailing was deliberately stressed. Lewis died only a few weeks after it opened, and it was left to Louis Cohen, a more cautious man, to consolidate its success.

Lewis himself was the archetypal great retailer of his time, ploughing back his profits into the business, justifying his belief that sales bred sales. He was devoted to charity, however, and set up a David Lewis Trust, the capital of which was wholly invested in the business: it was to provide Frederick Marquis, First Lord Woolton (qv), with his own introduction to the Lewis concern twenty-three years after Lewis's death, when he became warden of the David Lewis Men's Clubs and the University Settlement. At his death on 4 December 1885 David Lewis left £125,081 gross.

ASA BRIGGS

Sources:

Unpublished

PrC.

Published

Asa Briggs, *Friends of the People: The Centenary History of Lewis's* (BT Batsford Ltd, 1956).

LEWIS, Sir Edward Roberts

(1900-1980)

Manufacturer of records and electronics equipment

Edward Roberts Lewis was born at Derby on 19 April 1900, the only son of Sir Alfred Edward Lewis (1868-1940), of Fir Royd, Ilkley and Coneybury, Lower Kingswood, and his wife May, daughter of William Roberts, of Chapel Allerton, near Leeds. Sir Alfred Lewis was a Birmingham banker who was sometime general manager of the National Provincial Bank, and whose other directorships included the Bank of British West Africa and the Yorkshire Penny Bank. Edward Lewis was educated at Rugby in 1914-18 and matriculated in 1919 at Trinity College, Cambridge, but did not take a degree.

He went to work as a stockbroker in 1923, was admitted to the London Stock Exchange in 1925, and formed his own firm, E R Lewis & Co. His stockbroking career was, however, subject to an unusual diversion as a result of his firm participating in the public share issues made by the Decca Record Co in 1928-29. Until 1928 the Decca business had been a family firm, Barnett Samuel & Sons Ltd. Established in 1832 as steel pen and watch makers they had later included musical boxes in their range, and were subsequently one of Britain's leading musical instrument wholesalers. In the early Edwardian period the Samuel firm acquired English agencies for the Edison phonograph, the Italian Fonotipia classical gramophone records and for Carl Lindstroem AG of Berlin, who pioneered cylinder dictating machines and double-sided discs. Barnett Samuel began producing their own records under the Jumbo label, and sold Dulcephone cabinet gramophones. In 1914 they patented the first portable gramophone, using the name 'Decca' which had been carefully chosen as pronounceable in all languages and recognisable even by illiterates.

Before 1914 the total turnover of the business had been £60,000; by 1928 it was £419,000. This sevenfold growth was largely accounted for by the sales of Decca portable gramophones, home and export sales of which in the year to March 1928 were worth respectively £190,000 and £166,000. Nearly 22 per cent of the total number of gramophones exported from Britain in 1927 were made by Decca, who also had a small research laboratory. The Samuel cousins, however, wished for different reasons to retire from their business, which in 1928 they sold to the British Equity Investment Co preparatory to a stock exchange flotation. In September 1928 Lewis was the broker when 370,000 ordinary shares worth £185,000 were issued to the public.

At an early stage Lewis was struck by the peculiarity that Decca sold large quantities of gramophones but only a negligible number of gramophone records. When the new company encountered difficulties in 1929, Lewis urged that they buy a record company; when Decca's new board demurred from further expenditure, Lewis himself raised the money to buy the ailing Duophone Record Co to secure a sales organisation for Decca.

Lewis joined the Decca board, but the records diversification was inauspiciously timed, as there was an international collapse of demand in the records business during the Depression. Within a short time Lewis ousted Decca's existing chairman, and against all advice, cut prices and started an aggressive marketing campaign with the slogan 'Leading Artists — Lower Prices'.

Apart from its perilous finances Lewis recognised that Decca was handicapped by its inability to reach the crucial American recording repertoire on which Decca's rival, EMI (headed by Alfred Corning Clark (qv)), had a stranglehold through licensing deals. To surmount this problem, Lewis arranged in 1932 for Decca to buy the moribund US record company, Brunswick, whose official Jack Kapp had the crooner Bing Crosby under personal contract. When, in 1933, Lewis tried the Brunswick purchase with a new Decca share issue worth £123,000, only £23,000 was subscribed by the public, and the Lewis family took up the rest. This increased his personal power over the Decca company.

In 1934 Lewis formed the American Decca Co with Jack Kapp as president and Crosby as its leading star. Once again he cut record prices to stimulate sales, and by the end of the decade, Decca was the leading American popular music record company. Nevertheless, in Britain the finances of the group remained precarious for some years. Brunswick's chief engineer, Henry Schwarz, developed a process for directing ships and aircraft by radio, as a result of which Decca expanded into the radar business during the Second World War. The famous Decca Navigator was used in the Normandy landings of 1944, and after 1945 the group's research and development of navigational equipment led to profitable contracts from the Ministry of Defence.

Lewis was a quintessential financier who fervently believed in competition and the profit motive. His informal memoir of Decca is entitled 'No CIC', an allusion to his conviction that Decca would probably not have survived the 1930s if the Capital Issue Committee controls over prospectuses for share issues worth above £10,000 had been introduced before 1946. Although Lewis ran Decca from 1933, he did not become chairman until 1957, and never drew salary or expenses. Nevertheless, with friends and family he commanded the group's voting shares and as late as November 1979 major non-family shareholders like the Kuwait Investment Office (with 9.9 per cent) and Prudential Corp (with 7.4 per cent) were effectively powerless. This mattered increasingly, for although Lewis was a shrewd judge of the record business, his touch was less successful after 1963. He took all major decisions himself, and worked a good deal on personal instinct: personal relations mattered to him, and one contemporary who felt affection for Lewis recalled, 'he would do business with you if he liked you, but not otherwise' {Oral, John H Davenport}.

Until then American popular musicians had made the running, and by careful sorting of new singles and small independent recording companies, Decca's London American label scored an outstanding success in American rock'n'roll and often bested EMI. But Decca, who turned down a contract with the Beatles, were less adept at handling the British pop boom. Although they did sign up the Rolling Stones, senior management were too conservative and elderly to keep up with trends. Lewis rewarded old employees who had shown loyalty in the troubled 1930s: one favoured old hand was Hugh Mendl, cousin of Sir Edward Manville (qv) and son of Lewis's nominee chairman of Decca, Sir Sigismund Mendl. Another such colleague was Decca's commercial director, William Townsley, who often boasted that he had been sacked by Lewis in the early 1950s, but never left. Youth was essential in the record business, but by March 1979 Decca's youngest director was born in 1927, and the average age of its directors was sixty-nine. Decca's market share declined sharply by the 1970s, and failed to attract new musical talent.

At one stage Lewis was pressured into appointing an outsider, Ken East, as managing director to the record division developing long-term strategy; but he was unable to trust East, or to delegate power to him, and the arrangement proved unworkable. Decca were reduced to back catalogue sales and a few random hits. Its share of the British album record market dropped from 18.5 per cent in 1968 to 6 per cent in 1978; the singles' market share declined from 8 per cent to 1.1 per cent in the same decade. Correspondingly the sales force and distribution system to retailers fell into desuetude.

Lewis had had the vision to recognise the post-war growth potential for Decca in marine navigational systems, airborne radar and the hugely successful marine radar, and for years the profits of Decca's Navigator and Electronics/weapons divisions helped to carry the group. But even these divisions faltered after 1977, when Decca's pre-tax profits peaked at £16 million. The company entered a dizzy and almost frightening decline. A net profit of £4.1 million in the year to March 1978 was transformed in the following twelve months into a net loss of £5.3 million. Decca's debt/equity ratio at 31 March 1979 was 71.5 per cent. While both executives and institutional shareholders pleaded for either a massive internal reorganisation, or a sale of the company, Lewis seemed to remain unmoved.

Having received several previous overtures, late in 1979 Lewis agreed to sell Decca's record interests to the German-Dutch combine, Poly-Gram, for a sliding price of between £5.5 and £15.5 million (dependent on subsequent sales) and the military electronics and communications divisions to Racal for £65 million in shares. Within a few days of this deal being settled, Lewis was dead. General Electric, under Arnold Weinstock, subsequently tried to outbid Racal, who eventually secured the relevant part of Decca's business for over £100 million. To some this price seemed excessive for a company with net assets of only about £60 million and current borrowings of £66 million.

Lewis had brought considerable nerve and ingenuity to saving Decca in the 1930s, and his long post-war success should not be obscured by the final catastrophe. Lewis's last year at Decca, in 1979, had all the elements of personal tragedy: as one of his staff recalled,

> In January, Sir Edward would drive in early in the morning, park the car and walk quickly across the car-park to the Albert Embankment offices. By spring the car was being parked closer to the side entrance. Then a chauffeur drove the car in, then came the walking frame and in the last few months Sir Edward had to be lifted into his chair {Hardy (1980) 14}.

LEWIS Sir Edward Roberts

Lewis was a benefactor of Middlesex Hospital and Rugby School. Knighted in 1961, he received the Albert gold medal of the Royal Society of Arts for his contribution to the development of electronics.

He married first in 1923, May Margaret (1900-68), daughter of Rev George Dickson Futton of Dunbar; they had two sons (of whom the elder, John, was drowned at Rugby in 1943). His surviving son Richard remains (1984) a partner in his father's stockbroking firm. Lewis remarried in 1973 to Jeanie Smith, daughter of Thomas Henry Smith, a farmer. Sir Edward Lewis died on 29 January 1980, leaving £1,104,730 gross.

JENNY DAVENPORT

Sources:

Unpublished

MCe.

PrC.

Edgar Samuel, 'The History of Barnett Samuel 1832-1928' (unpublished ms).

Information from John H Davenport.

Published

Economist passim.

Arthur C Fox-Davies, *Armorial Families* (2 vols, Hurst & Blackett, 1930).

Phil Hardy, 'It's All Over Now' *Time Out* 22-28 Feb 1980.

Times *Prospectuses* 76 (1928).

Times 30 Jan 1980.

WWW.

LEWIS, Frederick William

1st Lord Essendon

(1870-1944)

North-East industrialist and shipowner

Frederick William Lewis was born at West Hartlepool on 25 May 1870, the only child of Edmund Lewis of West Hartlepool and Elizabeth, daughter of John Dent of Weardale. His father was employed as a cashier at a local ironworks, but later in life held a 'confidential position' with the steel, shipbuilding, engineering, and shipping magnate, Christopher Furness (qv). Furness promised Edmund Lewis when he was seriously ill in 1882 that he would give Frederick a start in life. Consequently, young Lewis joined C Furness & Co as an office boy the following year.

In 1890, Furness opened an office in London and placed Lewis in charge. Nine years later Lewis was elected to a seat on the board of Furness, Withy & Co Ltd, as Furness's was styled after its amalgamation with Edward Withy & Co in 1891. During the course of his career, Lewis remained at the London office and under his management the turnover of that branch became the largest in the firm by 1902. In addition to being a very successful manager, he was an able negotiator, conducting the bargaining for some of the principal acquisitions made by Furness, Withy before the outbreak of the First World War.

Following the death of Stephen Wilson Furness, a nephew of Furness who succeeded him as chairman, Lewis became deputy chairman in 1914 under Marmaduke, the Second Lord Furness (qv), who was thirteen years his junior. During the war, Lewis was a member of the Ships Licensing Committee (1915-17), eventually becoming its chairman. In 1916, he joined the Shipping Control Committee under Lord Curzon and also served in the Ministry of Shipping until after the conclusion of hostilities. For his service to the nation Lewis was created a baronet in 1918.

With his full-time duties at the Ministry concluded in 1919, Lewis resumed work at Furness, Withy. Upon his return to the company, Lewis discovered that Viscount Furness (as Marmaduke Furness became in 1918) had pursued policies of which he did not approve and it soon became apparent that the two men had very different visions of the future development of the group. Consequently, Lewis arranged to have the subsidiaries of Furness, Withy purchase the interest of the Furness family. Viscount Furness, who accepted the securities held in numerous coal, engineering, steel and shipbuilding companies as part payment, went on to pursue his interest in the industrial sector, while Lewis succeeded him as chairman of Furness, Withy which retained all of the shipping interests of the group.

During this second phase of his career, Lewis presided over the development of Furness, Withy's West Indian trades and the acquisition

Frederick Lewis, Lord Essendon aboard the SS Asturias *(Royal Mail Lines) with the Master, Captain Arthur Cocks, in 1938 (courtesy of Major Andrew Napier).*

of the Cairn Line in 1928. Following the breakup of Lord Kylsant's (qv) Royal Mail Group in 1929, Furness, Withy acquired Shaw, Savill & Albion, the Royal Mail Steam Packet Co and the Pacific Steam Navigation Co from the stricken group, but failed in its efforts to purchase the White Star Line which Cunard took over. By 1930, Lewis was also a director of 31 companies including Sun Life, Sun Insurance and Barclay's Bank.

Perhaps Lewis's most remarkable business skill was in negotiation. His early letters reveal a shrewd mind with a keen ability to find the weaknesses in the position of his opponents. Lewis was highly imaginative in seeking out new areas for business development and possessed formidable analytical powers in assessing their potential. He was a competent organiser and pursued a consultative rather than dictatorial approach to decision-making.

During the inter-war period, Lewis continued his public service, being a member of the advisory council to the Board of Trade, 1921-23, chairman of the Departmental Committee on Co-operative Coal Selling in 1926, a member of the Channel Tunnel Committee, 1929-30, a member of the Obsolete Tonnage Committee, 1930-31 and chairman of the Development (Public) Utility Advisory Committee, 1930-32. Lewis was also elected president of the Chamber of Shipping in 1922-23 and served as JP and High Sheriff of Hertfordshire in 1926-27. In recognition of his services Lewis was elevated to the peerage as Lord Essendon in 1932. He was also a Commander of the Légion d'Honneur and was awarded the orders of the Crown of Italy and the Crown of Belgium and the Grand Cross Crown of Roumania.

He married Daisy Ellen, daughter of Captain Robert Henry Harrison of West Hartlepool, in 1896 and had one daughter, Frieda, and one son, Brian Edmund. Lewis died on 24 June 1944, having served Furness, Withy for sixty-one years.

GORDON BOYCE

Sources:

Unpublished

British Maritime Trust Co Ltd, London, records.

Furness, Withy & Co Ltd, London, records.

National Maritime Museum, Greenwich, Furness, Withy & Co Ltd records.

Published

Burke's Peerage and Baronetage.

Arthur J Henderson, *Under the Furness Flag* (Liverpool: C Birchall & Son, 1951).

WWW.

John Lewis, taken in 1910 (courtesy of John Lewis Partnership).

LEWIS, John

(1836-1928)

Department store founder and proprietor

John Lewis was born in Shepton Mallet, Somerset, on 24 February 1836, the fifth child and first son of John Lewis, 'a cabinet maker' {MCe}, and his wife Elizabeth Speed. He was orphaned at seven, and was brought up locally with his five sisters by an unmarried aunt, Ann Speed. After attending the local grammar school Lewis was apprenticed at fourteen to Tasker, a draper in Wells. Four years later he moved on to Nicholls, another drapers in Bridgwater; and after a brief stay in Liverpool, he moved to London in 1856 to work for Peter Robinson of Oxford Circus as a salesman, and later buyer for silks and woollen dress materials.

In 1864 he set up on his own as a draper and haberdasher in a single little leasehold shop at 132 (later 286) Oxford Street, on the north side just west of Holles Street. Weekly takings were at first only around £100, and the life was 'so hard and dreary' that Lewis later told his son that 'he doubted if he could bring himself to go through it again' {Lewis (1948) 14}. But the situation was a good one and John Lewis's simple but unexceptional trading policy — honesty, and a wide assortment of merchandise, clearly priced and giving good value to the customer — proved attractive and profitable there.

He concentrated on offering a wide choice of colours and qualities in silks, woollen and cotton fabrics, together with sewing threads and ribbons, laces and other trimmings. He diversified later from dress fabrics by the yard ('dress piece goods') into women's and children's ready-made clothing and accessories such as hats, gloves and shoes; and from furnishing fabrics into household supplies including carpets, furniture, china, glass and ironmongery. He did not sell food; and he did not advertise. His sales reached £25,000 in 1869-70 and about £70,000 ten years later. From 1875 he gradually leased more houses on Holles Street and Oxford Street until in 1895 he was able to rebuild. The new shop had retail showrooms on the first and second floors as well as the ground floor, with lifts, space for wholesale trading (never fully used) on the third floor and a customers' restaurant as well as dining-rooms for the staff of some 150. About 100 girls were housed in a hostel in Weymouth Street nearby.

John Lewis exploited his own skill with long hours of personal work over many years. He took no one into partnership until his two sons were of age, and never incorporated his business into a limited company. His only attempt at expansion outside Oxford Street was the acquisition of Peter Jones Ltd, Chelsea, the control of which he had bought in 1906 when he had walked from his store to Sloane Square with £20,000 in banknotes in his pocket. When the need to invest spare capital became pressing, John Lewis would watch the property advertisements in the newspapers, cut out and file anything that interested him, and later put in a bid, often without having seen his purchase. By the end of his life he had made over a hundred shop and property investments, all bought without any clearly defined policy. Always an outspoken and colourful character, John Lewis engaged in a running battle with his landlords (the Portland Estate, owned by Lord Howard de Walden) and in a wider public campaign to redress what he considered was the great imbalance in market power between landlord and tenant and the injustice of many leasehold covenants; he spent some weeks in Brixton Prison in 1903 for contempt of court.

By his own terms John Lewis's life was a great success. By 1924 sales had reached £921,000. He lived in a large house on the edge of Hampstead Heath, drove a pair of horses, and later a Rolls Royce. On the other hand his conservative business style became increasingly inappropriate for twentieth century conditions and he appears as less than dynamic in comparison with other contemporaries such as William Whiteley (qv), Frederick Gorringe, and Owen Owen. His son, John Spedan Lewis (qv), who was eventually to inherit the store, though he paid tribute to his father's success in building the business up, provided a withering portrait of his parsimonious father and his unimaginative methods in his account of the John Lewis Partnership.

> Altogether it was glaringly obvious ... that, however great had been at some time past the general efficiency of the business — and in earlier years it must have been very great indeed — my father had [by the 1900s] got himself into the position of being the captain of a big ship much under-engined and with those engines much under-fuelled. As a whole his staff were not nearly good enough and they had no sufficient motive to do their best. My father was more or less conscious that great parts of the floor-space were idle or nearly so and, so far as he was conscious of it, of course the thought vexed and worried him. But that consciousness was almost unbelievably small. As was shown by his amazement, when he read in

An impression of the first small drapery shop opened in Oxford Street by John Lewis in 1864 (courtesy of the John Lewis Partnership).

Peter Jones establishment, after first rebuilding ca 1899 (courtesy of the John Lewis Partnership).

newspapers the fortunes that had been made in some other careers like his own, he was extremely out of touch with what was happening outside his own business {*ibid*, 5}.

Tactless and high-handed attitudes towards his staff, which provoked a strike in 1920, persistent mismanagement of Peter Jones, which resulted in losses during the years 1906-14, and the refusal to relinquish personal control almost until his death, which effectively prevented for fifteen years the infusion of fresh ideas from his son, John Spedan, were the other features of the founder's rule.

John Lewis served on St Marylebone Vestry (later Borough Council), 1888-1919; and was elected Liberal representative for the West Marylebone division of London County Council in 1901 and 1904.

He married in 1884, Eliza Baker, daughter of a 'yeoman' {MCe}, a schoolmistress from a drapery family in the West Country who was one of the first students at Girton College, Cambridge, and eighteen years his junior. They had two sons, John Spedan and Oswald, both of whom went into the family business. John Lewis died on 19 September 1928, leaving £84,661 gross.

GEOFFREY TWEEDALE

Sources:

Unpublished

MCe.

PrC.

Published

John Spedan Lewis, *Partnership for All* (Kerr-Cros Publishing Co, 1948). Reissued with an additional appendix, 1952.

LEWIS, John Spedan

(1885-1963)

Department store owner and founder

John Spedan Lewis was born in Marylebone, London, on 22 September 1885, the elder son of John Lewis (qv), the founder and proprietor of the

John Spedan Lewis (courtesy of John Lewis Partnership).

John Lewis department store in Oxford Street, London, and his wife Eliza née Baker. By his own admission his upbringing was narrow: he was a day boy in a preparatory school and at Westminster (Queen's scholar), his father seldom entertained, and he and his brother, Oswald (1887-1966), rarely stayed away from home except at the house of their aunt at Weston-super-Mare. Nevertheless, he appears to have soon developed a strong social conscience and his education was far wider than that of his father, who had been apprenticed at the age of fourteen.

John Spedan joined his father's Oxford Street business when he was nineteen, in preference to going up to Oxford University. On their twenty-first birthdays he and Oswald were each given £50,000 capital (a quarter of the capital of the business) and a partnership carrying one-quarter of the profits after 5 per cent had been paid on the capital. His entry into the business, however, brought disillusionment. 'At home [his father was] regarded ... as a superman, virtually infallible in matters of business', so it came as a shock to his son to find that 'his business was in fact no more than a second-rate success achieved in a first-rate opportunity' {Lewis (1948) 3}. On examining the store's accounts he found that his father, he and his brother were drawing £10,000 a year in interest from the business — as much as the total outlay for the whole staff. Though his father had an ample fortune and customers were well served, all of the profits were generated on the ground floor and part of the first floor; other departments were trading at a loss, and the whole of the third floor was simply used for storage. Management was ruthlessly close-fisted: wages were low, employment decisions arbitrary, there were no pensions, and catering and housekeeping for staff who lived in were inefficient and inadequate. Recalled Spedan Lewis:

> The more I considered all this, the more utterly unreasonable did it seem to me. There on the one side was my father and on the other side his staff — my father with over a hundred separate pieces of property that he never saw and that were nothing but a bother to him, and with an income so far larger than the cost of his very comfortable way of living that the surplus was constantly obliging him to make more and more of those investments: the staff with an employment that was extremely insecure and that gave them a living so meagre that they were very far less happy than they perfectly well could have been, a happiness that would have increased very greatly both the soundness of the business and the real happiness of my father's own life. {*ibid*, 18}

As an emotional response to these inequalities and his father's repressive attitudes, Spedan began to devise the idea of business Partnership. The plan, which owed nothing to Owenite precursors or co-operative theorists, crystallised when he was recovering from a serious riding accident in a nursing home soon after his twenty-fifth birthday, when it occurred to him that shares (or stock) could be distributed to the workers instead of cash. Simple in conception, however, it was some time before the idea could be put into effect. His riding accident left one lung permanently damaged and he also had to work against the implacable opposition of his father. Horrified at any suggestion that might reduce his hard-won fortune (he had earlier reacted very strongly to his son's frivolous idea of going to the opera once a week), his father poured scorn upon the Partnership idea by

Peter Jones, Sloane Square (courtesy of the John Lewis Partnership).

asking: 'Who do you suppose would bear the carking cares of business for such a miserable remuneration as this would mean?' {*ibid*, 20}.

Spedan Lewis's chance came in 1914 when his father handed over to him the chairmanship of Peter Jones. He was to be given a free hand providing he did not go to Sloane Square before 5.0 pm — a condition that made the work extremely physically taxing and effectively destroyed his leisure time. Nevertheless, the fortunes of Peter Jones, which had suffered under his father's antiquated business methods, were reversed and a 12 per cent growth in sales was recorded after the first six months. Spedan was able to introduce the Partnership idea by means of the committees between the rank and file and principal management, which he had tentatively tried out the year before at John Lewis. But his father, alarmed at these experiments and contemptuous of his son's abilities to regenerate a failing business, demanded the return of the controlling interest. His son refused. When his father warned that if he did not comply his partnership at Oxford Street would be ended, Spedan replied that he would accept in exchange for it the remainder of his father's interest in Peter Jones. For Spedan it was a calculated risk: an exchange of a quarter-partnership in one of the soundest businesses in England against the prospect of being his father's sole heir for a controlling interest in what was, at that time, a rather run-down drapery trading establishment. Against the advice of his mother, the opposition of the auditors, and the Midland Bank which declined to take the Peter Jones account, he pressed on. Working at home as much as possible to foster devolution, Spedan improved wages, catering and hostelling arrangements, and increased the efficiency of the store by separating the management of sales and buying. By 1919 the annual turnover of Peter Jones had increased five-fold to £500,000. In five years the turnover of the best year of Peter Jones himself (half as large again as the level at which the elder Lewis had passed control to his son) had been more than doubled and a yearly loss of about £8,000 had been converted to a profit of £20,000.

Slowly the Partnership ideal took shape. On 16 March 1918 the first issue of *The Gazette* appeared, which incorporated the revolutionary publication of detailed weekly statements on sales and profits. In 1919 came the first meeting of an elected council, which was later to become the central council, and the first meeting of the committee for claims. In 1920 profit-sharing was implemented after Spedan won over the shareholders to an alteration in the articles of association. He held £35,000 of debentures and almost all of the £60,000 (nominal) of the ordinary shares, but few of the £60,000 (nominal) of preference shares belonged to him and their cumulative dividend of 5.5 per cent was far in arrears. It was proposed that the arrears should be forgone in consideration of a permanent increase of 2 per cent in the rate of the preference dividend and of a reduction of the rights of the ordinary shares so that the profit would go to the employees. At this point, his father, impressed by his activities at Peter Jones, invited his son to rejoin the partnership at Oxford Street, on condition he kept Peter Jones a separate affair. Until his father's death in 1928, however, Spedan felt it would be unwise to issue Partnership benefit in the form of a security that could be sold on the Stock Exchange, so bringing the experiment to his father's notice. Consequently, share promises were issued instead of actual shares or stock. These were redeemed in 1929 by an issue of shares saleable on the Stock Exchange: by then their total nominal value was £76,632.

On his father's death he became sole owner of a business worth over a million pounds, having by that time also acquired his brother's interest. One of his first decisions was to expand the business by taking over T J

Harries & Co Ltd, with its extra space and desirable Oxford Street frontage. To raise fresh capital the store went public in September 1928, forming John Lewis & Co Ltd; it raised over £1.5 million. Shortly afterwards the John Lewis Partnership Ltd was formed with a capital of £312,000. Spedan then instituted a first trust settlement, which amounted to selling the right to the income from the whole of his property in Peter Jones and John Lewis to all who worked there, and all who were to work there in the future, in the John Lewis Partnership Ltd. He did this by making what was in effect an interest-free loan to the Partnership of more than £1 million which was to be paid back to him over thirty years. The effect of this was to give the Partners some of the benefits they would have had if he had been able to start the system a generation earlier. In addition both he and his wife renounced their directors' fees and other remunerations. He later calculated that had he and Mrs Lewis sold out and invested in sound securities their fortune would have produced an income of over £40,000 a year besides the freedom from the anxieties of running a large business. But the Partnership was not quite complete: Spedan retained a controlling interest which allowed him to bring the experiment to an end should it be a failure. In 1935 the business was again expanded by the acquisition of buildings owned by D H Evans Oxford Street on the west side of his father's original store. A new policy of branch trading was introduced which added Jessop & Son in Nottingham, Lance & Lance in Weston-super-Mare (later sold), Tyrrell & Green in Southampton, Selfridge Provincial Stores, and Knight & Lee in Southsea to the business. These stores became of vital importance when the Oxford Street premises were bombed during the Second World War. Devolution and decentralisation were continued, a pension fund and sports clubs were set up, and the chairman experimented with the Partnership's own adult education college. By 1950, with the signing of the second trust settlement, Spedan was ready to complete his design (though he publicly stated that he regarded the results of his 'experiment' as inconclusive, since he felt that the dynamic potentialities of his system had not yet been released). He renounced his right to bring the experiment to an end, and the equity interest in the business was vested in a trust company of five directors, three of whom were elected by the central council. Thereafter the Partnership belonged in essence and in fact to all who worked in it; and its principles and the rights of Partners were set out in the articles of the constitution.

The chairman retired, as he promised, on his seventieth birthday. He regretted the decision to retire — and said so — and later unsuccessfully attempted to regain a part in the control of the Partnership. The central council gave a dinner in his honour and representatives from all the branches were among the 2,460 Partners who attended his farewell meeting at the Central Hall, Westminster. O B Miller, whom he had appointed as his successor, presented him with £10,000 to mark his retirement, a sum with which he established the John Spedan Lewis Trust for the Advancement of the Natural Sciences — a reflection of his passionate enthusiasm for ecology. He was fond of music, was president of the Classical Association in 1957, and was an ardent supporter of the Glyndebourne Opera, the continuance of which he secured in 1949 by guaranteeing losses of up to £12,500. He had few interests apart from

The present John Lewis department store in Oxford Street, London. It replaced the original department store destroyed by a fire bomb in the London blitz but was not completed until 1964 (courtesy of the John Lewis Partnership).

these, having declined a number of invitations in his early twenties to stand for parliament. The Partnership was a full-time occupation: spare moments were spent in writing for *The Gazette* and in reviewing the achievements and feasibility of the Partnership in more substantial works such as *Partnership for All.*

In 1962, the year before he died, profits distributed to Partners or applied for their benefit amounted to £1.5 million; since the formation of the Partnership in 1929 they totalled £11 million. By 1962 the total Partnership numbered 16,000 and the capital had risen to £30 million. In 1962-63 the turnover of the John Lewis Partnership, which by then included John Lewis & Co, Suburban & Provincial Stores Ltd, John Lewis Properties Ltd, and Bainbridge & Co Ltd (acquired in 1953), exceeded £50 million.

John Spedan Lewis in 1922 married Sarah Beatrice Mary Hunter (1890-1953), daughter of an architect and one of his numerous women graduate recruits, who had joined the Partnership from Somerville College, Oxford, because of a sympathy with its aims. She was at various times editor of *The Gazette*, goodwill director, head of the department of staff advice (later the Partners' Counsellorship), chairman of the committee for administration and chairman of the education committee. She became the Partnership's first deputy chairman and it was expected that she would succeed her husband. They had three children. The eldest, to his parents' great distress, died of meningitis at the age of eight. The two others, Elizabeth Marion ('Jill') and Edward Grosvenor, were both to work in the Partnership for a time; Jill was general editor of *The Gazette* and Edward became a barrister.

John Spedan Lewis died on 21 February 1963 at The Burrow, Longstock Park, Stockbridge, Hampshire, leaving £127,557 gross.

GEOFFREY TWEEDALE

Writings:

Partnership for All (Kerr-Cros Publishing Co, 1948). Reissued with an additional appendix, 1952.

Fairer Shares (Staples Press, 1954).

Inflation's Cause and Cure (Museum Press, 1958).

Sources:

Unpublished

BCe.

MCe.

PrC.

John Spedan Lewis, 'The Development and Organisation of the John Lewis Partnership' (Edwards Seminar paper 140, 20 Oct 1953).

O B Miller, 'The John Lewis Partnership — Ten Years On' (Edwards Seminar paper 329, 25 Feb 1964).

Published

DNB.

Allan Flanders, Ruth Pomeranz and Joan Woodward, *Experiments in Industrial Democracy. A Study of the John Lewis Partnership* (Faber & Faber, 1968).

The Gazette of the John Lewis Partnership 2 Mar 1963.

Times 23, 25 Feb 1963.

WWW.

Sir William Thomas Lewis (courtesy of Mr T O Lewis).

LEWIS, William Thomas

1st Lord Merthyr of Senghenydd

(1837-1914)

Coal owner

William Thomas Lewis was born at Merthyr Tydfil on 5 August 1837, the second son of Thomas William Lewis, engineer at Anthony Hill's Plymouth ironworks at Merthyr, and his wife Mary Anne, daughter of Watkin John. The family had already been connected for several generations, as contractors, agents and engineers, with the iron industry of South Wales.

After a brief formal education until he was thirteen, William Lewis became articled to his father as an engineer. This training led to his appointment in 1855, at the age of eighteen, as assistant to W S Clark, the chief engineer to the Welsh estates of Lord Bute. On the death of Clark in 1864 he became (at £1,000 a year, plus a residence at The Mardy, Aberdare) the chief mining engineer for the Bute estates. In 1880 he assumed complete control of all the Bute Welsh estates.

William Lewis became a dominant figure in the expanding industrial and commercial life of South Wales, particularly during the last quarter of the nineteenth century. He was seven times chairman of the powerful South Wales Coalowners' Association (1879-84 and 1887), and was for eighteen years (1880-98) chairman of the Joint Sliding Scale Committee which regulated wage changes in the industry. He was also elected president of the Mining Association of Great Britain (1880) and of the Iron and Steel Institute (in 1908, when he turned it down as he was 'too busy', and in 1910), and of the Institute of Mining Engineers. He was also chosen, implicitly as the representative of the employers of South Wales, to serve on a number of Royal Commissions: those on Accidents in Mines (1879-81); Action of Coal Dust in Mines (1891-94); Mining Royalties (1890-91); Labour (1891-94); Coal Supplies (1901-5); Trades Disputes (1903-6); and Shipping Combination (1906-7). He was additionally involved, usually to represent the Bute interest, in a large number of select committee hearings on Welsh railway and dock bills.

The sources of Lewis's pre-eminence were basically three-fold: his own industrial interests; his position as controller of Bute's Welsh estates from the 1880s; and the force of his character and temperament. His direct industrial interest started in his early thirties when, probably in 1868, he became the part-owner (with John James and William Williams) of the small Coedcae house-coal colliery in the Lower Rhondda valley. By 1873, when the Monmouthshire and South Wales Collieries' Association was formed, the output of Coedcae had just reached 100,000 tons, less than 1 per cent of the total output of the members of the Association. Lewis persistently expanded his activities as a coal owner: he sank the Lewis Merthyr colliery in the 1870s and bought Hafod colliery in 1881. Both of these were in the Rhondda and, with Coedcae, were amalgamated in 1881 to form the Lewis Merthyr Navigation Colliery Co Ltd, which in 1900 became Lewis Merthyr Consolidated Collieries. At that time, his company contributed about 850,000 tons from four collieries to the total Association output of 30 million tons. Besides the Rhondda valley, the firm also extended into the Ogmore valley (Rhondda Main colliery) and the Aber valley (Universal colliery at Senghenydd, where in October 1913 427 men were killed in South Wales's worst mining disaster). In 1913 the Lewis Merthyr company owned seven collieries and employed 7,000 men out of the coalfield total of 233,000. At each period there were many coalowners controlling substantially larger outputs.

Lewis was also involved in other industrial ventures. In 1873 he was active in the Forest Iron & Steel Co at Pontypridd, but this concern was tiny compared to such giants as Dowlais and Ebbw Vale. He also, almost unavoidably, acquired a number of directorships but in most of these — as in the case of the International Steam Coal Co from 1902 onwards, or the South Wales Electric Power Co in 1900 — both his financial commitment and managerial participation were small. Lewis's general prominence in industrial South Wales was largely due to the importance of the Bute connection, and Lewis's own energies and character. The Bute interest was central to the industrial and commercial development of South-East Wales. A great deal of the coal was extracted from under Bute lands; some of the iron-works (in particular, Dowlais) were built on Bute land; the main town of Cardiff grew rapidly on Bute property; the docks at Cardiff had been, in a unique enterprise, built and owned solely by the Second Marquess of Bute; and the family was, to varying degrees, involved with several of the railways of the region. Consequently, any major servant of the Bute estate necessarily occupied a strategic position in the region. During Lewis's career, however, this influence was greatly intensified, because the estate officials were given a very high degree of executive authority. The Second Marquess of Bute had played an extremely active part in running the estate, but the Third Marquess who had succeeded when he was less than a year old, in 1848, even after his long minority, preferred to leave the conduct of the estate to others. Lewis's career thus coincided with a period when the power and wealth that went with the vast Bute property were largely wielded by the officials of the estate; and from 1880 onwards he was — and this, too, was an innovation in the management of the estate — placed in overall control of all its aspects (mineral development, agricultural land, urban properties, docks and railways).

The mineral and urban estates were already widely developed and much of the development of mineral leases had long been Lewis's responsibility. The income from each continued to expand. Most of the mineral land was already leased but rising output automatically brought higher royalty incomes. Nonetheless, Lewis was in the 1880s actively engaged with Professor Galloway in proving the steam coals at workable depths on the Bute estate at Llanbradach in the Rhymney valley. The urban rentals increased because of new building and also because high standards of layout required by the estate commanded high ground rents.

The docks, however, earned a low direct rate of return on the capital employed. Despite this, Lewis was, somewhat reluctantly, compelled to expand the Bute dock facilities substantially by building the Roath Dock (opened 1887) and the huge Alexandra dock (opened 1907). These additional undertakings had to be made to meet the growing competition (especially with the opening of the Barry Dock & Railway in 1889), to assure that Cardiff continued to attract a growing trade. To some degree, Cardiff docks had a captive trade. The requirement to ship at the Bute docks had long been a standard clause in Bute mineral leases, and the Rhymney Railway (essentially a Bute undertaking on the construction of which Lewis had worked during his early years in the Bute service) ensured a flow of Monmouthshire coal to Cardiff rather than Newport. The competition of other ports, however, kept down the rates which Cardiff could charge and made a high volume of traffic economically essential. Lewis attempted to meet the problem of a low return in several ways. First, he initiated or welcomed several attempts to sell the docks (to the Taff Vale Railway, to Cardiff Corporation and to a Harbour Trust). All failed, perhaps because he pressed for too hard a bargain. Secondly, he reduced the extent of direct Bute involvement by, in 1886, incorporating the Bute Dock Co to take over the hitherto privately-held undertaking. Thirdly, he attempted to diversify the trade, to reduce the dependence on coal and iron. He was particularly active in this respect and achieved some success, especially in encouraging imports of grain and meat. He failed, however, in attempts to make Cardiff into a shipbuilding port (it did a great deal of ship-repairing) and into a centre for ocean passenger traffic.

The two main streams of his activity — as controller of the Bute estates and as the moving force in the Coalowners' Association — were brought together in his handling of industrial relations. Respectful, and sometimes fearful, contemporary comment accorded him great credit as an industrial peace-maker and conciliator. It is difficult to sustain such a view. Certainly by the turn of the century conciliation in labour affairs required a greater flexibility of attitudes than he possessed. He was unbending in his opposition to 'outsiders' coming between masters and their men and passionately believed in 'free' labour. Such views, whatever their intrinsic merits, barred him from any conciliation which required some acceptance of the growing trend towards trade unionism; whilst his frequent high-handedness was incompatible with conciliation through tactful diplomacy. In the Cardiff dock strike of 1891, for example, when six coal tippers refused to load the *Glen Gelder* because its master would not engage any members of the seamen's union, Lewis asserted, reasonably, that the affairs of the seamen's union were none of his concern, but then promptly threw the full weight of the Bute Dock Co behind the Shipowners' Federation. He took out summonses against the tippers who had struck, and quickly and easily used 'free' labour to replace the other dockworkers as they came out piecemeal. He refused to negotiate with union leaders, saying that the men had left their employment voluntarily and been replaced. The strike, which had already collapsed, was called off and, with the dockers neutralised, the seamen also capitulated to the shipowners.

Lewis always claimed that he did not care whether his men were union members or not — in this dispute he said that former workmen if they applied for any vacant jobs would not be asked whether they were, or had been, union members — but that he could only meet and talk with workers in his own employment and not with union officials. The men saw this as merely a way to render any union ineffective. His unbending attitude also tended to antagonise the public but Lewis seemed oblivious of this; it is doubtful if by the 1890s such lofty indifference to public attitudes was wholly wise.

The 1898 coal strike demonstrated much more sharply Lewis's strengths and weaknesses in industrial relations. In one sense the conflict was a remarkable success for his principles and leadership: in a rising market the miners were totally defeated and the owners gained some cost-reducing concessions. In particular, the men were forced to give up their cherished holiday on the first Monday on each month ('Mabon's Day'). Yet from almost every other perspective, Lewis was the loser. For nearly a quarter of a century the Welsh miners had been little organised — there were numerous autonomous valley unions, mostly weak, loosely connected and with only tenuous contacts with their English counterparts — but within months of the abject defeat of 1898, the South Wales Miners' Federation was launched and affiliated to the Miners' Federation of Great Britain. These moves were made under the same moderate leaders who had so long resisted them. Lewis's best allies in his principled resistance to stronger unionism had long been the existing miners' leaders, and his best instrument the sliding scale which tied wages to prices. His intransigence sacrificed both. The 1898 scale had been forced down the miners' throats and they would not accept another. The settlement had humiliated the leaders, and thus they made no attempt to defend a settlement 'not based on justice and good will' {*South Wales Daily News* 3 Sept 1898}. Within a year, in June 1899, Lewis resigned as chairman of the Joint Sliding Scale Committee. He relinquished (or was driven from) his controlling position in the Coalowners' Association because most of its members were, despite the victory, dissatisfied at Lewis's conduct of the dispute. They disliked his penchant for legalism, his dictatorial attitude to workmen, his abrupt refusal to allow any questioning of his actions, and his insensitivity to public opinion. He had repeatedly challenged the authority of the men's leaders, refusing to discuss matters until they could wrest from the miners' delegates conference full plenary powers to settle on any terms they wished, and had refused to consider any attempts at outside concilation, whether offered privately by Lord Dunraven or by the Board of Trade under the new Conciliation Act of 1896. Even the *Western Mail*, the coalowners' paper, was dismayed at his abrupt dismissal of Sir Edward Fry, the government conciliator; indeed he simply ignored a universally hostile press.

Lewis had a long-standing feud with D A Thomas (qv), whose scheme for controlling the output of Welsh coal was effectively obstructed by Lewis, and whose refusal to act with the Coalowners' Association in the 1898 strike was bitterly resented by Lewis. When, in 1899, the Association accepted Thomas's application for membership, Lewis was so incensed that he resigned from that body for a time.

Lewis was not, either as an engineer or businessman, a significant innovator, although he was in 1887 part-inventor of the Lewis-Hunter crane for coal-loading which he then introduced to Cardiff docks, and the introduction of the sliding scale system of wage regulation into South Wales was claimed for him. But essentially his frame of mind — orderly, clear and powerful — lacked the imagination of an innovator. He was a man of undoubted stature but with an impervious, haughty and autocratic approach: even an admirer described his manner as 'terrifying'.

In 1880 Lewis stood unsuccessfully for Merthyr as an Independent Conservative. He opposed local option on licensing laws (Welsh Sunday closing) and the workmen's compensation bill, advocating instead voluntary Permanent Accident Funds (he played a prominent part in the founding of the South Wales Miners Provident Fund in 1881). He was active in establishing hospitals at Merthyr and Porth, and aided many other charitable institutions. In these and other respects he was warmly sympathetic to the workmen — but on his own terms. He was a member of the Aberdare Board of Health, the Merthyr Board of Guardians and the Glamorgan County Council.

He was knighted in 1885, granted a baronetcy in 1896, and a barony in 1911, when he took the title Lord Merthyr. He was given a KCVO in 1907 and a GCVO in 1911. A JP for Glamorgan, Monmouthshire, Pembrokeshire and Breconshire, he was given the freedom of the city of Cardiff in 1905, and was the first freeman of the borough of Merthyr in 1908.

In 1864 Lewis married Anne, daughter of William Rees, a colliery owner of Lletyshenkin, Aberdare, and thus became directly linked with a family which had a special place in the coal industry of the region, since Anne's grandparents were Robert Thomas of Waun Wyllt and Lucy Thomas who, as his widow, was known as 'the mother of the Welsh steam-coal trade' because she was reputed to have initiated the sale of steam-coal from Cardiff to London. William and Anne Lewis had two sons and six daughters. Lord Merthyr died on 27 August 1914, leaving £615,522 gross.

L J WILLIAMS

Sources:

Unpublished

MCe.

PrC.

Published

Burke's Peerage and Baronetage.

John Davies, *Cardiff and the Marquesses of Bute* (Cardiff: Verry, 1981).

DNB.

D M Richards, *Some Episodes in the Career of Sir William T Lewis* (Merthyr Tydfil, 1908).

Shipping World July 1907.

South Wales Coal Annual 1905.

South Wales Daily News 3 Sept 1898 and passim.

Times 28 Aug 1914.

Western Mail passim.

L J Williams, 'The New Unionism in South Wales, 1889-92' *Welsh History Review* I (1963).

—, 'The Strike of 1898' *Morgannwg* 9 (1965).

WWW.

*Sir Arthur Lasenby Liberty
(courtesy of Liberty and the Victoria
Museum).*

LIBERTY, Sir Arthur Lasenby

(1843-1917)

Department store founder

Arthur Lasenby Liberty was born in Chesham, Buckinghamshire, on 13 August 1843, the eldest of eight children of Arthur Liberty, who owned a drapery shop in Chesham High Street, and his wife Rebecca née Lasenby, a farmer's daughter. When he was eight years old the family moved to Nottingham where an uncle had a lace warehouse, and where Arthur Liberty became a lace manufacturer.

His career began inauspiciously when at sixteen he was apprenticed to an old-fashioned draper in Baker Street, London. To Arthur Liberty, whose extra-curricular interests when a boarder at Nottingham University School had been in the theatre and scene painting, this was less an opening to a career than a slamming of the door. After two years he obtained a less uncongenial position at Farmer & Rogers' Great Shawl & Cloak Emporium in Regent Street, a prestigious establishment where he handled beautiful shawls from India and China. It was the year of the International Exhibition of 1862, at which the arts and crafts of Japan were for the first time shown to the Western world; when the exhibition closed, Farmer & Rogers bought up most of the Japanese section to form the nucleus of an oriental warehouse next door to their main shop. Liberty was one of the two young men chosen to staff it, and two years later was appointed manager. He served the pre-Raphaelite painters who came seeking soft, pale, oriental silks to drape on their models; he absorbed their tastes, their philosophy of 'art for art's sake', and declared that if only he could have a shop of his own, he would change the whole look of fashion in dress and interior decoration.

After twelve years, during which Liberty made the oriental warehouse the most profitable side of Farmer & Rogers' business, he asked to be taken into partnership. When this was refused, his fiancée, Emma Louise

PROTECTIVE MIMICRY.

ABDUL THE CHAMELEON (on *Young Turkey Carpet*). "I THOUGHT I COULD MANAGE SOMEHOW TO TAKE THE COLOUR OF MY SURROUNDINGS, BUT I'M NOT AT ALL SURE THAT THESE LIBERTY DESIGNS WON'T BE TOO MUCH FOR ME."

Punch cartoon for 28 April 1909 (courtesy of Liberty and the Victoria Museum).

Blackmore, persuaded her father, who owned a tailoring business in Brook Street, to lend Liberty £1,500 and back a bill for £1,000 from Henry Hill, a tailor of Bond Street. This enabled him to take a lease, in 1875, of half a shop at 118A Regent Street. Within eighteen months he repaid the loans and also acquired the second half of the shop. His oriental silks had become an influential element in the Aesthetic Movement; and when F C Burnand's comedy *The Colonel* and Gilbert and Sullivan's *Patience* were produced, both satirising the aesthetes, Liberty silks were used for the costumes. At D'Oyly Carte's newly-built Savoy Theatre, Liberty decorated a reception room for the Prince of Wales; and this led to similar work at Covent Garden, the Haymarket Theatre, Drury Lane and the Lyceum. When *The Mikado* was in preparation, Liberty sent envoys to Japan to select exactly the right fabrics for costumes and stage sets. Soon he was increasing his stocks by importing oriental silks in the raw state to be dyed in England and then hand-printed with reproductions of old Indian prints at Littler's block-printing works on the River Wandle at Merton in Surrey. Liberty bought these print works from Littler in 1904.

By 1883 the shop had become too congested for the variety of merchandise handled, and another property was taken further south in Regent Street for carpets and furnishings. The basement housed an Eastern Bazaar and Curio Department for oriental antiques; an Arab Tearoom with a ladies' cloakroom was a much appreciated innovation. A furnishing and decorating studio was inaugurated, and Liberty furniture and interior woodwork (panelling, doors, staircases, etc) were made in a nearby cabinet factory. Contracts were executed in private mansions and official buildings, while work of a more temporary nature was done for charity bazaars, balls, and exhibitions. In 1884 a costume department was opened under the direction of the architect and theatrical designer E W Godwin, who was an expert on historic costume. He believed modern dress should be designed upon the same principles as classic Greek costume; and it was intended to 'initiate a renaissance that would challenge the heretofore all-powerful and autocratic fiat of Paris' {*Liberty Lamp* Oct 1931}. In 1889 the challenge was flung down in Paris itself, a Maison Liberty being opened in the Avenue de l'Opéra, with couture salons and workrooms for aesthetic gowns and children's artistic dresses à la Kate Greenaway, as well as a boutique selling Liberty silks by the metre, cushions, bedcovers, men's ties and dressing-gowns. Marcel Proust bought ties chez Liberty, and a duvet which proved to be bad for his asthma.

Liberty's achievement was not simply that of outstanding business success from humble beginnings; more importantly, he was the first retailer to instigate and influence changes of fashion in dress and interior decoration. Involved in the Aesthetic Movement of the 1870s and 1880s, he was a friend of the pre-Raphaelite painters and later a patron of leading designers in Art Nouveau silver, pewter, furniture and fabrics. His shop brought all that was avant garde to the attention of ordinary customers as well as to the cognoscenti of art movements. More effectively than his contemporary, William Morris (qv), he showed that the aesthetically acceptable could be made commercially viable.

In 1894 the firm became a public company, with an authorised capital of £200,000 in shares of £10 which were all taken up at a premium of 10s per share. There were only two directors besides the founder, neither from outside, and all the shares were held by members of the Liberty and Blackmore families. Arthur Liberty was now a member of the Royal Society of Arts and received silver medals for papers on 'The Industrial Arts and Manufactures of Japan' (1890) and 'English Furniture' (1900). He was a member of the Royal Institute and of the Organising Council of the Japan Society; a fellow of the Asiatic Society, the Royal Historical Society, the Royal Statistical Society, the Zoological Society; council member of the London Chamber of Commerce, director of the British Produce Supply Association, master of the Glass Sellers' Company, president of the English Monumental Inscription Society, and freeman of the City of London. He moved from Cornwall Terrace, Regent's Park, to The Lee Manor near Chesham, travelling to London by train every day. His holidays were spent abroad seeking unusual merchandise and he planned many connoisseur exhibitions at the shop: of, for example, antique embroideries, historic lace, ancient prayer rugs from Eastern palaces. He was influential in a revival of the British silk industry, holding an

East India House, Regent Street, late 1890s (courtesy of Liberty and the Victoria Museum).

exhibition by Spitalfields weavers, instituting an improved school of design, and helping to form the Silk Association of Great Britain, of which he was vice-president.

By the turn of the century, Liberty's contract department was involved with furnishing and decorating commissions all over Europe, in the Far East, and in South Africa. In the doomed summer of 1914, one of the Liberty team was learning Russian preparatory to supervising a contract for the Czar Nicholas at St Petersburg; and a contract was actually in progress for the Archduke Franz Ferdinand of Austria when he was assassinated.

Arthur Liberty was knighted in 1913 for his services to the applied and decorative arts of the country. By this time he was giving more of his attention to his role as country squire. He then owned over 3,000 acres with many farms, cottages, and other properties. He gave The Lee village, near Chesham, a green, financed extensions to the church, planted avenues of trees. He had been High Sheriff of Buckinghamshire, and was a JP, DL and county councillor. Having no children, he made his nephew Captain Ivor Stewart his heir, requesting him to take the name of Stewart-Liberty. Sir Arthur Liberty died on 11 May 1917, leaving £343,505 gross. After Sir Arthur's death Lady Liberty's nephew Harold Blackmore became chairman of Liberty & Co, until 1950, when Ivor Stewart-Liberty succeeded upon Blackmore's retirement.

ALISON ADBURGHAM

LIBERTY Sir Arthur Lasenby

Writings:

De Libertat: A Historical and Genealogical Review, Comprising an Account of the Submission of the City of Marseilles, in 1596, to the Authority of Henry of Navarre: and the Lineage of the Family De Libertat, from the XIVth to the XVIIIth century. Compiled from Historical Manuscripts (T Pettit & Co, 1888).

'The Industrial Arts and Manufactures of Japan' *Journal of the Royal Society of Arts* 38 (1890).

'English Furniture' *ibid* 48 (1900).

Springtime in the Basque Mountains ... with Illustrations by Emma Louise Liberty and Others (Grant Richards, 1901).

'Pewter and the Revival of Its Use' *Journal of the Royal Society of Arts* 52 (1904).

Inaugural address of His Oddship, Brother Arthur Lasenby Liberty, craftsman, delivered 24 Oct 1905.

(ed) *Japan. A Pictorial Record by Mrs Lasenby Liberty* (Adam & Charles Black, 1910).

A Day in Tangier ... Pictured by John Hassall. Photographs by Lady Liberty and Others (Adam & Charles Black, 1913).

The Treasure Hunt: The Conspirators in Constantinople (Liberty & Co, 1915).

Sources:

Unpublished

Westminster Library, Buckingham Palace Road, London, Liberty & Co archives.

BCe.

PrC.

Published

Alison Adburgham, *Liberty's. A Biography of a Shop* (George Allen & Unwin, 1975).

DNB.

The Liberty Lamp staff magazine, Feb 1925-Jan 1932.

WWW.

LIDBURY, Sir Charles

(1880-1978)

Clearing banker

Charles Lidbury was born in Middlewich, Cheshire, on 30 June 1880, son of Frank Albert Lidbury, a school teacher, and his wife Emily née Harding, also a school teacher. He left school at the age of thirteen and joined the branch of Parr's Banking Co at Winsford, Cheshire. While his brother won a scholarship to Owens College, Manchester (later Manchester University) and went on to become a world authority on phosphorus, Charles improved himself by night-school studies for banking and educational qualifications and by working formidably hard during the day: as he later said 'I am a bank clerk and a damn good one too!' {*National Westminster Magazine* Oct 1978}. Remarkable powers of concentration constituted one of his characteristics: later he could 'remove himself at a moment's notice from a discussion and apply himself to the writing of a paper oblivious of the continuing contention around him' {*ibid*}.

After a series of minor promotions he was appointed in 1908 to investigate the affairs of the Whitehaven Joint Stock Banking Co prior to its absorption by Parr's Bank that year. Six years later he was made joint manager of the Iron Gate, Derby, branch of Parr's Bank. In 1919 he was promoted to Inspector of Foreign Branches, of which there were then ten; four years later he was made Superintendent of Foreign Branches.

Lidbury became a joint general manager of the Westminster Bank in 1927, and between 1930 and 1947 was chief general manager. The Westminster Bank was one of the 'Big Five' London clearing banks. In 1918 the London County & Westminster Bank had amalgamated with Parr's Bank to form a 700-branch bank with wide representation throughout England. After 1919 there was a series of mergers with smaller banks, such as the Nottingham & Nottinghamshire Bank and Beckett's Bank of Leeds and the East Riding, which added to the regional representation of the group (which adopted the name of the Westminster Bank in 1923). Lidbury presided over the consolidated banks, and he also encouraged the further extension of the branch network. By 1939 the Westminster Bank, which ranked fourth among the 'Big Five' London clearing banks in terms of deposits, had 1,000 branches throughout England, though two of its constituents, Parr's and London & County, retained their individuality at their head offices in the City.

Lidbury was closely involved with the foreign activities of the Westminster Bank. In 1913 the Bank had established a subsidiary, the London County & Westminster Bank (Paris) Ltd with an office in Paris. This bank opened further branches in Bordeaux in 1917 and Lyons and Marseilles in 1918. In 1912 the parent bank also opened branches in Madrid and Barcelona, and in the following year branches opened in Antwerp and Brussels. In 1919 Lidbury conducted an inspection of the

Paris branch. He revealed a potentially dangerous situation, caused by the Bank's too rapid expansion into an unfamiliar banking market. His report in effect halted the Bank's programme of continental expansion and led to his appointment as the first Superintendent of Foreign Branches. He held the position of general manager of the Westminster Foreign Bank Ltd from 1928 to 1947. His general policy was one of extreme caution, and he exercised tight centralised control over the continental branches. Lidbury's policies meant that the Westminster Bank's growth on the Continent was stunted, but this probably saved his bank from the bad debts and difficulties experienced in the inter-war years by several of the other English clearing banks with continental branches.

He was well aware that the business and reputation of the Westminster Bank were much involved with personal and professional accounts, and though he did not neglect industrial accounts, he was least interested in industrial clients. Nevertheless he was drawn into the Bankers' Industrial Development Corporation which, under government supervision and the encouragement of the Bank of England, gave loans to ailing British export industries in the 1930s, so that they could rationalise and restructure themselves. But his dealings with industry inclined him to the belief that market forces rather than government intervention or even persuasion should determine banking policy.

Lidbury's banking principles can be characterised as conservative and reflecting the cartelised and uncompetitive nature of banking in this period. He was an opponent of innovation in the financial sector. Lidbury, for example, attempted to block the formation of the Industrial and Commercial Finance Corporation (ICFC), established after the Second World War on the Bank of England's initiative with the job of filling the 'Macmillan gap' by providing funds for small and medium-sized businesses. During the late 1940s Lidbury unsuccessfully attempted to limit the activities of ICFC.

In spite of limited venturesomeness Lidbury's quick mind, ready grasp of alternatives, and his forceful personality won him the esteem, if not always the affection, of his colleagues. To work directly for him was an education in itself. To win his approval, as three future chief general managers did, was to be marked for rapid promotion. Lidbury had very firm views about the separation of the roles of directors and managers of the bank: he was very much in control not only of day-to-day management, but also of investment policy and in particular the purchase of gilts. He was made a director of the Westminster Bank in 1936, while still chief general manager, and held that directorship for twenty-six years. He was undoubtedly, during his days as chief general manager, the most powerful man in the Westminster Bank. Yet while he did not encourage 'interference' by the board, he liked some of its members, and to a degree admired their life-style and emulated it.

Lidbury was an able and formidable man, and was widely respected in the English banking world. During the Second World War he was president of the Institute of Bankers, and he was also chairman of the Chief Executives' Committee of the Clearing Banks. In these roles he made an appearance before the Cohen Committee which considered company law amendment during 1943-44. On the destruction of his home in 1941 Lidbury took up residence in the basement of the Westminster

Bank's headquarters, in Lothbury in the City, and he remained there until the war ended, on hand to inspect immediately any London branch damaged by enemy action, prodding rubble with his walking stick to find anything worth salvaging. For his services to finance he was knighted in 1941. After he retired in 1947 he retained his seat on the Westminster board until 1962.

He enjoyed chess, backgammon and golf, loved the theatre, and revelled in the countryside after retiring to Melbury Abbas, Dorset. For many years he was honorary treasurer of the British Empire Cancer Campaign.

He married in 1909, Mary, daughter of George Moreton of Kinderton Hall, Middlewich. They had two daughters who cared for their father after their mother died in 1939.

Sir Charles Lidbury died on 25 July 1978 aged ninety-eight, leaving £246,522 gross.

GEOFFREY JONES *and* MARGARET ACKRILL

Writings:

PP, Evidence to the Company Law Amendment Committee, 1944 (1945) Cmd 6659.

Sources:

Unpublished

BCe.

MCe.

Published

Theodore E Gregory, *The Westminster Bank through a Century* (2 vols, Oxford University Press, 1936) 2.

Geoffrey Jones, 'Lombard Street on the Riviera: The British Clearing Banks and Europe 1900-1960' *Business History* 24 (1982).

John Kinross, *Fifty Years in the City: Financing Small Business* (John Murray, 1982).

National Westminster Magazine Oct 1978.

Richard Reed, *National Westminster Bank: A Short History* (privately published, 1983).

Times 27 July 1978.

Antony W Tuke and R J H Gillman, *Barclays Bank Limited, 1926-1969* (Barclays Bank, 1972).

WWW.

William Lidderdale (courtesy of Dr Sheila Marriner).

LIDDERDALE, William

(1832-1902)

Central banker and merchant

William Lidderdale was born in St Petersburg on 16 July 1832. The Lidderdale family has been traced back to the sixteenth century in the Scottish Lowlands. They included several successful merchants operating in Britain, North America and the East and West Indies as well as members of the legal and medical professions. William's father John, a merchant, was the seventh of nine children of William Lidderdale (1730-1819) of Castle Dykes, Kirkcudbrightshire, and Elizabeth (1745-1823). It is not known when John went to St Petersburg but he was certainly there in 1828. On 26 December 1829 he married Ann (1806-1844), daughter of a St Petersburg merchant, William Morgan (ca 1774-1810) and Mary Ann (ca 1778-1808). John and Ann had five sons, William being their second.

William grew up in the British commercial community in St Petersburg. John Lidderdale is said to have been a prosperous merchant but there is no record in the minute books of the Russia Company of his becoming a freeman. In 1837 John lost most of his money in a Scottish bank failure.

The three eldest boys were sent to England to be educated at the Academy, Hamilton Square, Birkenhead, watched over by Aunt Morgan and E N Heath, a Russia trader. A letter from John Lidderdale to the headmaster early in 1844 shows that William was already a good German scholar. John asked that the boys should be taught modern languages and other subjects necessary for 'a mercantile life' because unless they showed exceptional talents in other directions they were destined for mercantile careers.

When the Lidderdale boys were in their teens disaster struck the family. Their mother Ann died in 1844. Their father, so short of money that he was living in two rooms in St Petersburg, died months later on 4 January 1845. William inherited very little money: in April 1845 one of John's executors anticipated that the estate might only realise about 8,000 roubles. Friends, however, helped the boys; further, their uncle, Halliday Lidderdale, died in February 1845, and left them £250 each. Their guardians, Loder, Gwyther and Heath, were all Russia traders. The boys spent school holidays with their uncle James Lidderdale of Lochbank, Castle Douglas. He probably influenced their upbringing and careers. A solicitor and successful businessman who gained the agency for the Bank of Scotland in Castle Douglas, he was described as firm, decisive, austere but kindly, methodical and prudent.

William finished his formal education when fifteen but later learnt some Italian; in the 1860s he studied economics when in New York. Meanwhile in 1847 he had entered one of his guardians' firms, Heath & Co, a

Liverpool merchant house trading to Russia. Nothing is known of his next few years except that he eventually became cashier to Rathbone Bros & Co, a long-established Liverpool merchant house with extensive trading, shipping and financial business. From 1857 to 1863 he worked in their New York agency at a salary of £900 per annum and in 1864 he became a partner, establishing and becoming responsible for Rathbones' London house, which was particularly concerned with finance and with the tea trade. In 1870, at the age of thirty-eight, with extensive mercantile and financial experience, he became a director of the Bank of England. He became Deputy Governor in 1887, and from 1889 to 1892 he was Governor.

Much attention has been paid to William Lidderdale's involvement in the so-called Baring Crisis of 1890 and to a lesser extent to his other measures to strengthen the Bank's control over the monetary system, but his three years as Governor should be seen as the natural culmination of a lifetime's experience. His whole life seemed to have been a training for the problems he then tackled. When young he must have been impressed by the disastrous effects of bank failure when his father lost all his money. Throughout his career within Rathbones he learned to gear business operations closely to business fluctuations. Partners' letters related both specific and general decisions to trading conditions after the last crisis or to that next expected. For example, on 17 October 1873 Lidderdale wrote in a routine business letter to a partner that the British banking and monetary systems were complicated and interdependent: 'the system of taking enormous sums on deposit at call or short notice on which interest has to be paid and which there is almost a necessity to employ if serious losses are to be avoided is one which carries risk in its face ... and throws on the Bank of England the onus of providing a reserve adequate to the needs of its competitors as well as its regular customers' {University of Liverpool Library, Rathbone Papers XIV-1-24, William Lidderdale to Henry Cair, 17 Oct 1873}. He also pointed out that the Bank's own reserves were always particularly low in October and raising Bank Rate would not remedy the fall though it might hasten recovery. On 20 October 1873 he clearly recognised the ineffectiveness of Bank Rate: 'The Poverty which causes 7 per cent to be the official rate is limited to the Bank of England and the British Government' {ibid, 20 Oct 1873} — the money market generally was not affected.

Such comments appear frequently in his letters and in those of his partners. It is hardly surprising that when he became Governor he sought to remedy what he regarded as weaknesses in the financial system. On 15 October 1889 he wrote to one of his partners that on the one hand there were already 'most of the elements of a crisis, with the additional danger that our collective liabilities are enormously increased with a small increase in the central cash reserve of the country' compared with twenty years earlier. On the other hand it had become easier to attract gold, and also financiers had 'learnt to work together for their own safety' {ibid IX-8-12, William Lidderdale to William Rathbone, 15 Oct 1889}.

Clearly therefore he wanted to strengthen the system, and persuaded public and semi-public authorities to deposit surplus reserves in the Bank to give it greater control over credit. Bill brokers were readmitted to regular borrowing and rediscount facilities for the first time since 1858 and he sought closer co-operation from the commercial banks and the

Treasury. He tried thereby to make Bank Rate more effective and to gain greater control over foreign exchanges and gold movements.

When therefore Baring Bros realised early in November 1890 that by over-issuing South American loans, and by undertaking too much acceptance business, they could not meet immediate liabilities, it was to the Governor of the Bank that they turned. The Bank itself could not rescue them but if Barings' difficulties had become public a disastrous crisis would have ensued. William Lidderdale asked the Chancellor of the Exchequer, Goschen, to underwrite Barings' debts: Goschen refused but told the Governor to 'prevent such a disaster' himself {Papers in the possession of J D L Lidderdale, Edward Lidderdale to Mary Martha Lidderdale, 6 Apr 1911}. William Lidderdale instituted an investigation into Barings' position by B W Currie and Benjamin Buck Greene and was convinced that when their assets were ultimately realised they would be sufficient to cover their liabilities. A guarantee fund was therefore organised, whereby the Bank of England was covered against losses in liquidating Barings' liabilities to the tune of over £17 million by guarantees given by commercial and merchant banks. Furthermore, Lidderdale arranged for the import, partly by purchase partly by loan, of £4.5 million of gold from Russia and France to strengthen the Bank's reserves. By the time Barings' difficulties were made public the crisis was over.

There has been some controversy about the relative contributions of those involved, especially about those of Currie and Lidderdale in the organisation of the guarantee fund. Lidderdale left no account of the events but he did write about them to his eldest son Edward, who used his father's letter to write to his mother on 6 April 1911 after reading a review of a book of Lord Goschen's life. Edward Lidderdale asserts quite categorically that 'the Guarantee fund was his own idea. It is nonsense that he should share credit with ... Lord Rothschild and Mr Currie'. {ibid} Rothschild's brother helped to obtain gold from France and Currie's main contribution was going through Barings' accounts with Greene. Certainly it does seem that Lidderdale was deeply involved at every stage though naturally other people gave help and support.

At the time he was widely praised and heaped with honours. Having refused a baronetcy because he did not believe in hereditary honours or primogeniture, he accepted a Privy Councillorship in the Queen's Birthday Honours List on 30 May 1891 and was also given the freedom of the City of London. He was asked to serve as Governor for three years instead of the normal two, partly to ensure continuity in negotiations with the Treasury about charges for government business.

His five years as Deputy Governor and Governor marked the zenith of his business career, but he set aside his personal business affairs, and his personal finances suffered severely. Rathbone Bros & Co made heavy losses throughout the 1890s; when their London house closed in 1897, Lidderdale ceased to be their partner. He seems to have lost all his capital; for income he relied on three directorships in American railway companies and on his wife's income, derived partly from property settled on her in 1897.

In 1868 he had married Mary Martha, elder daughter of a Russia merchant, Wadsworth Dawson Busk and Elizabeth née Thielcke. Mary

Martha had been born in St Petersburg in 1843, probably just before William left to come to school in England; she died in 1924. Their marriage was exceptionally happy: they lived first in Cambridge Square, London, then from ca 1894 at 42 Lancaster Gate and eventually at 55 Montagu Square where William died on 26 June 1902. There were four sons (all educated at Winchester) and three daughters. None of the sons entered the Bank of England but a nephew, William Kennedy Lidderdale, served the Bank for some years.

One of his sons describes his father as having grey eyes, darkish hair and a fresh complexion. Though serious by nature he was fond of humorous quotations from such sources as *The Pickwick Papers* and Mark Twain. He devoted much time to reading leading newspapers, but also enjoyed Scott, Burns, Thackeray and Dickens. He was keen on music (particularly Russian and Scottish music and Mendelssohn), played the piano, visited the opera and the theatre and subscribed to the Saturday 'Pops' at St James's Hall. His favourite pastime was shooting in Scotland. In 1887-88 he took Yaldham Manor, Kemsing, near Sevenoaks to be near to London. In 1892 he went to America and on a European tour. His club was the Windham, St James's Square.

William Lidderdale died on 26 June 1902, leaving £9,338 gross.

SHEILA MARRINER

Sources:

Unpublished

The Bank of England Archives does not apparently have any biographical material relating to William Lidderdale.

Guildhall Library, London, Diocese of London, Foreign Registers; Register of the Chapel of the British Factory at St Petersburg, MS 11,194/1. As the Russians still used the Julian calendar, dates given in the register have been revised to allow for the twelve-day discrepancy between the Julian and Gregorian calendars at this time.

Liverpool University Library, Rathbone Papers.

Family papers in the possession of J D L Lidderdale (who is compiling a history of the family), including the written reminiscences of William Lidderdale's son Alan W Lidderdale.

PrC.

R H Lidderdale, 'An Account of the Lowland Scots Family of Lidderdale'.

Interviews with J D L Lidderdale (cousin) and Sir David Lidderdale (grandson).

Published

Sir John Clapham, *The Bank of England, a History* (2 vols, Cambridge: Cambridge University Press, 1944) 2.

DNB.

Hon Arthur D Elliott, *The Life of George Joachim Goschen, First Viscount Goschen 1831-1907* (2 vols, Longmans, Green & Co, 1911).

Roger Fulford, *Glyn's 1753-1953* (Macmillan & Co Ltd, 1953).

Sheila Marriner, *Rathbones of Liverpool 1845-73* (Liverpool: Liverpool University Press, 1961).

E Victor Morgan, *The Theory and Practice of Central Banking 1797-1913* (Frank Cass & Co Ltd, 1965).

Leslie S Pressnell, 'Gold Reserves, Banking Reserves and the Baring Crisis of 1890' in C R Whittlesey and J S G Wilson (eds), *Essays in Money and Banking* (Oxford: Clarendon Press, 1968).

Richard S Sayers, *The Bank of England 1891-1944* (3 vols, Cambridge: Cambridge University Press, 1976).

WWW.

*David A E Lindsay ca 1910
(courtesy of Mr Donald Anderson).*

LINDSAY, David Alexander Edward

27th Earl of Crawford and Balcarres

(1871-1940)

Coalmine proprietor

David Alexander Edward Lindsay was born at Dunecht, Aberdeenshire, on 10 October 1871, the eldest son of the Twenty-sixth Earl of Crawford and his wife Emily Florence, daughter of Colonel the Hon Edward Bootle-Wilbraham. Dunecht was at that time one of the family's Scottish seats. Both his father and his grandfather had been chairman of the Wigan Coal & Iron Co, which the family had controlled almost since 1870, five years after its formation.

David went to Eton and Magdalen College, Oxford, where he read history. When he succeeded his father as chairman of the Wigan Coal & Iron Co Ltd, on the Twenty-sixth Earl's death in 1913, the company was working 23 collieries in the neighbourhood of Wigan, as well as Clock Face Colliery at St Helens and Manton Colliery in Nottinghamshire. The output of the Wigan pits alone, which employed 10,000 men, amounted to 2.5 million tons per annum; at that time famous Wigan seams such as the Cannel and the Arley were still being worked. There were saleyards and agencies in 14 towns covering every part of Britain and Ireland.

The company's iron and steel works at Kirkless, near Wigan, comprised four batteries of patent coke ovens and 10 blast furnaces for the production of pig iron. The steel works produced 1,300 tons of steel a week in five basic open-hearth furnaces, the rolling mills making every variety of

Kirkless Iron & Steelworks, Wigan Coal & Iron Co Ltd, Wigan ca 1900 (courtesy of Mr Donald Anderson).

section. Steel forgings and castings were also produced. In connection with the ironworks, a concrete flag and tarmacadam works made use of the blast furnace slag. The company also produced 6 million pressed bricks annually, including blue engineering bricks and firebricks.

The archives show that the Earl took a great personal interest in this vast concern and his advice was constantly sought by senior officials of the firm. It was during his chairmanship that the important Parsonage Colliery at Leigh, Lancashire, was sunk. At 1,008 yards, it was the deepest pit in Britain at the time it was completed (1920) and during the 1930s coal was being extracted at a depth of 1,500 yards; these were said to be the deepest coal workings in the world.

When the Coal Mines Act of 1930 encouraged amalgamations of the colliery firms, Lord Crawford, unlike most other coalowners, concurred and amalgamated the Wigan Coal & Iron Co, Pearson & Knowles Coal & Iron Co, Rylands Bros, Whitecross Co and Wigan Junction Colliery Co to form the Wigan Coal Corporation and the Lancashire Steel Corporation. He was actively engaged as chairman of the Wigan Coal Corporation, which employed over 11,000 men at its 12 collieries, until his death. He was also a director of the Lancashire Steel Corporation which owned very large works at Irlam and Warrington.

Unionist MP for the Chorley Division of Lancashire as Lord Balcarres from 1895 until his succession to the title in 1913, he held appointments as

LINDSAY David Alexander Edward

Former Manchester Collieries, Astley Green (courtesy of Mr Donald Anderson).

Junior Lord of the Treasury, 1903–5, President of the Board of Agriculture and Fisheries, 1916, Lord Privy Seal, 1916–19, Chancellor of the Duchy of Lancaster, 1919–21, First Commissioner of Works, 1921–22, and Minister of Transport and member of the Cabinet, 1922.

During the early part of the First World War Lindsay served as a private in the RAMC, until summoned home from France to become President of the Board of Agriculture and Fisheries, then President of the Mining Association of Great Britain and head of the Government Wheat

Parsonage Colliery, Leigh, Manchester (former Wigan Coal & Iron Boys) (courtesy of Mr Donald Anderson).

Production department. In 1925 he was chairman of the Broadcasting Committee whose recommendations led to the setting-up of the BBC.

His interest in the preservation of the arts was reflected in the multitude of public appointments he held and committees and societies of which he was an active and inspiring leader. He was a trustee of the National Portrait Gallery and of the British Museum, a member of the Council of the British School at Rome, and chairman of the Royal Fine Arts Commission and of the National Arts Collection Fund. He was secretary of the Society for the Protection of Ancient Buildings for twenty-three years, and president of the Ancient Monuments Society from 1924 until his death. He was president of the Society for the Preservation of Rural England from its foundation in 1926, and was from 1924 to 1929 president of the Society of Antiquaries. A member of the Council of the National Trust, of the Commission on Historical Monuments and of the Royal

LINDSAY David Alexander Edward

Commission on Historical Manuscripts, he had the rare distinction of being an honorary fellow of the Royal Institution of British Architects. He was elected FRS in 1924 and held honorary degrees from the universities of St Andrews (1911), Manchester (1923), Cambridge (1924), Edinburgh (1926) and Liverpool (1928). He was elected an honorary fellow of Magdalen College, Oxford in 1923 and chancellor of Manchester University from that year. He was KT.

In 1900 he married Constance Lilian, daughter of Sir Henry Carstairs Pelly; they had two sons and five daughters. The Twenty Seventh Earl of Crawford died on 8 March 1940, leaving £514,799, of which £125,734 was in settled land. The funeral service was held at Wigan Parish Church, where his coal mining ancestors had been buried for centuries, although he was interred at Balcarres, Fife.

D ANDERSON

Writings:

PP, RC on Wheat Supplies, First and Second Reports (1921) Cmd 1544, (1924–25) Cmd 2462 (chairman).

PP, Committee on Broadcasting (1926) Cmd 2599 (chairman).

Centenary address *Transactions of the Manchester Statistical Society* 1933–34.

He also published extensively on the history of art.

Sources:

Unpublished

BCe.

MCe.

Published

Burke's Peerage and Baronetage.

Colliery Year Book & Coal Trades Directory 1923–30.

DNB.

Transactions of the Lancashire and Cheshire Antiquarian Society 54 (1939).

WWMP.

WWW.

LING, Reuben Herbert

(1864-1939)

Paper company manager

Reuben Herbert Ling was born in Greenwich, London, on 9 September 1864, the son of Reuben Ling, a music seller, who later worked for Longmans, Green & Co in the publishing department, and his wife Anna née Ford. Nothing is known of his schooling, but he probably received at least a sound elementary education, for by the age of fifteen he was considering taking orders — indeed he had declared his intention of rising to be Archbishop of Canterbury. Instead, his father took him to see Frank Pratt Barlow, a partner in John Dickinson & Co, a firm linked to Longmans by long-standing business and family connections. Pratt Barlow offered him a clerkship in John Dickinson's London office at the Old Bailey. Here Ling stayed from 1879 to 1890, in the sales department.

The late 1880s were a difficult time for Dickinsons, and for the paper trade generally. Only stationery manufacture yielded any profits for the firm at this period. It was therefore a mark of considerable confidence in him that in April 1890, at the age of twenty-six, Ling was appointed manager of their major stationery factory, Apsley Mills in Hertfordshire. Nearly 700 people were employed at Apsley, over half of the total Dickinson workforce of 1,200. In 1894, the supervision of two other mills, Home Park and Nash, were added to his charge.

Ling amply justified the confidence shown in him. At a time when profits were low, and capital difficult to raise (in November 1892 the auditors reported the financial position of the company was very serious, although not fatal), Ling persuaded the board to sanction improvements and extensions to Apsley, and steadily increased production and sales there. One of his first acts as manager was to obtain the board's permission to advertise the products of the firm — the first time this had been done. In January 1904 the London Stationery Department, moved from the Old Bailey offices to Upper Thames Street, was put under Ling's management; the Paddington Wharf was added eighteen months later. By this time Dickinsons were employing over 3,000 people and sales had increased to £1.1 million (from £260,000 in 1886-87). 1,500 were employed at Apsley alone, and Apsley continued to receive the largest share of the firm's capital investment. By 1914 2,500 were employed there. The war put an end to this progress, because part, and then all, of the mills at Apsley were commandeered by the Government.

1918 was an important year for Dickinsons and for Ling. In October 1918, Dickinsons took over one of their most powerful stationery rivals, Millington & Sons (the makers of 'Basildon Bond' and the only manufacturers in England of 'window' envelopes). Louis Evans, the last 'family' chairman of the company, retired, but not before Ling was appointed managing director in January 1918. Evans had championed

Ling's schemes and proposals against the cautious conservatism of most of his colleagues on the board for many years. He was succeeded as chairman by A H Godfrey, who had come from Millingtons and still largely concerned himself with running that business. Ling was therefore the virtual head of Dickinsons, a position formally recognised by his appointment as chairman on Godfrey's death in November 1924 (he retained the post of managing director).

Ling, largely self-educated, vigorous, plain-speaking and ambitious, had made enemies within the firm (Evans may have had to fight to secure his appointment to the board). However, he was as ambitious for the company as for himself, and if he often clashed with those close to him in the hierarchy, he had the ability to win the loyalty and obedience of those below him.

Ling thought of the problems of manufacturing in terms of sales promotion and the management of labour, and not in terms of technology and technique as his predecessors had done. In the difficult commercial conditions of the 1920s his qualities were needed badly. He instituted an economy campaign and revised the costing system to help the company through the post-war trade recession. When better trading times came, he continued the policy of building and modernising the mills he had consistently urged before the war. Little attempt was made to integrate Millingtons into the Dickinson organisation, but the popularity of 'Basildon Bond' was stimulated by an advertising campaign. A new overseas trading policy was developed to surmount the difficulties of competition between exports from Dickinson's factories in England, and those in India, South Africa and Australia.

Labour relations were the most pressing post-war problem of all. When the National Union of Printing and Paper Workers first tried to organise Dickinsons' workers, Ling had been set against recognising the union, but he had changed his mind when he sensed the support for it in the mills. In 1919 he ordered the managers of the mills to encourage their workers to join. Hours and rates of pay were negotiated with the union, but Ling also continued Dickinsons' tradition of making their own arrangements for employees' welfare. A scheme was started to allow employees to buy shares in the company, and a pension fund set up. The closing of the mills in the General Strike of 1926 brought to fruition a scheme Ling had been contemplating, for a company union to replace the NUPPW, one which would embody his vision of Dickinsons as 'a united family ... governed by a Stewardship that secures for all the just reward of their labour'. {Evans (1955) 200} It flourished; through its institution Ling made perhaps his most enduring contribution to the smooth running of the company for many years to come.

In May 1927 Ling's health broke down; he was unable to attend board meetings much of the time before his resignation in December 1929.

Ling seems to have had few interests outside his business life, and no charitable or public work is recorded. He married Catherine Oliver, daughter of Joseph Whittal, a secretary, in 1890; they had two daughters. He died on 15 May 1939, leaving £124,116 gross.

CHRISTINE SHAW

Sources:

Unpublished

John Dickinson & Co, archives.

BCe.

MCe.

PrC.

Published

Harold Cox and J E Chandler, *The House of Longman. With a Record of Their Bicentenary Celebrations 1724-1924* (Longmans, Green & Co, 1925).

Joan Evans, *The Endless Web: John Dickinson & Co Ltd 1804-1954* (Jonathan Cape, 1955).

LIPMAN, Michael Isaac

(1902-1978)

Industrialist

Isaac (he later took the forename of Michael) Lipman was born on 26 September 1902 in Leeds, son of Hyman Lipman, a master tailor, and Rachel née Rajinski, Russian immigrants who had come to Britain in 1892 and set up an independent tailoring business. They had changed their name from Lipnik to Lipman soon after their arrival in Britain. He was their fifth born (after four daughters). His intelligent and precocious mind flowered in the atheistic and anarcho-socialist atmosphere of the family household. Lipman was educated at elementary schools and socialist Sunday schools in Leeds, and, during the First World War, at the Leeds Central High School (from which he was briefly expelled in 1916 for distributing anti-war propaganda). After a year with engineering companies, and another year training in the workshops of Bradford Technical College, he read engineering at the University of Leeds.

Finding it difficult to get a job in 1924, he set up his own electrical retailing and contracting business with a partner, to whom he sold his share of the business in 1928 for £800. He then moved to London to marry a Mrs King, whom he had met when she was assistant to the head of the Biology Department at Leeds. Lipman became a sales engineer representing the German electrical giant AEG. In 1930 he joined a rapidly growing radio firm, Ekco of Southend founded by E K Cole (qv), then, after a brief period with the Zenith Co (a US radio manufacturer established in Britain in 1932), he returned to Ekco to develop their car radio range and a Belgian factory. During the war, he established an Ekco factory producing radar and other RAF equipment at Malmesbury, and was awarded the MBE in 1944. Although he might have been expected to head Ekco after the war, his political views and personal abrasiveness appear to have militated against this, and he left the company in 1946.

Lipman had retained the socialist views of his childhood, despite a successful career in business, but he denied being a Communist Party member, of which his rivals in business sometimes accused him. He was, however, an active left-wing socialist, despising traditional labour leaders, believing passionately in public ownership and planning, and promoting socialist education by chairing the local Left Book Club in Southend in the 1930s and, late in life, founding the Lipman Trust with an initial donation of £50,000. His socialism did not blind him to the short-sightedness of the unions as well as employers, or to the problems of Communist states. It was compatible with membership at various times of groups like the New Britain Movement and the Fabian Society, and bore the heavy imprint of ideas of social engineering and 'technocracy' which were prominent among radically-minded engineers in the 1930s. His impatience with financiers and competition, and preference for technical matters and planning, became all the more uncomfortably evident when in 1946 he took a City job which separated him from technical production matters and made him deeply unhappy.

His socialism and engineering training did, however, determine the direction of the Wogau Group, which he and a partner then started up. Initially exporting textile machinery to Yugoslavia, they broadened the business into selling chipboard machinery to other Eastern European countries. By the 1960s, the Wogau group, now half-owned by the merchant bank Guinness Mahon (to whom the partners had turned for working capital), was also exporting machinery to the USSR. Following a personal disagreement with his former partner, who left, Lipman became managing director of the Wogau Group. Not always easy to get on with, he was nevertheless recognised as one of the most skilled negotiators in the highly-specialised business of selling all kinds of machinery to Communist buyers.

He retired early, becoming for a time an active farmer in Kent, where he died on 10 November 1978. He left £121,831 gross.

LESLIE HANNAH

Writings:

Memoirs of a Socialist Business Man (Lipman Trust, 1980).

Sources:

Unpublished

PrC.

Published

Mass Observation, *War Factory* (Gollancz, 1943).

Sir Thomas Lipton (courtesy of Argyll Stores Ltd).

LIPTON, Sir Thomas Johnstone

(1850-1931)

Grocer

Thomas Johnstone Lipton was born in Crown Street, Glasgow, on 10 May 1850, the only surviving son of Thomas Lipton, a Protestant labourer who had migrated from Clones, County Monaghan, in Ireland, because of the potato famine, with his wife Frances, daughter of Frank Johnstone of Kilrid, Clones. In Glasgow his father successively worked in a warehouse and a cotton mill before setting up a small grocer's shop in which Thomas began to work at the age of nine.

After several jobs outside the family shop, he booked his passage to New York in 1865 at the age of fourteen. In the following four years Lipton's energies were taxed by working in the South for tobacco and rice producers, though he was employed by a large New York grocery store when, in 1869, he decided to return to Scotland. He had gained experience of keeping accounts and learned something of American go-ahead methods when he returned to Glasgow with $500 saved from his endeavours.

The legend of Thomas Lipton's ostentatious drive down Crown Street in a cab laden with a rocking chair and a barrel of flour gave some indication of what was to follow. Despite the apprehensions of his parents, Lipton opened his own shop in Stobcross Street in 1871 on his twenty-first birthday. He followed his father by beginning as a provision merchant selling 'Irish produce', chiefly ham, butter, and eggs. The success of this venture led to a second shop in 1874 in the High Street, and by 1878 he had four shops all known as 'Irish markets' in Glasgow. The next step was to move to other Scottish towns, beginning with Dundee in 1878 and Paisley in 1879. A relentless expansion into England followed during the 1880s: first in Leeds (1881), then the other provincial centres, and Lipton's first

London shop in 1888. The speed of Lipton's expansion amazed the retail trade; six branches in London alone were opened in 1889 and within ten years he had 72 shops in the capital. He had a total of over 100 branch shops in Britain by 1891, rising to 242 in 1898 (though Lipton claimed to own more than 400 shops across the world at that time).

The growth of this immense retail organisation was dependent upon the creation of a London headquarters (to which Lipton moved in 1891) and by large-scale backward integration, notably in meat and tea. Until 1889, Lipton's success was due to the Irish and, later, American provisions trade, for grocers and provision merchants still handled separate goods. The ham and butter windows of Lipton's shops still reflected the basis of his success but he was among the leaders in breaking down this retailing specialisation. In 1889, Lipton began to move into the grocery trade by selling tea and soon became known in the South principally for this item. During the 1890s, sugar, jam, cakes, biscuits, confectionery, and coffee became new lines in Lipton's shops and with this diversification the modern food-retailing shop began to emerge. Such developments depended upon the growth of the network of Lipton's shops and they in turn relied upon Lipton's delight in outrageous and innovative marketing techniques: cartoons and comic pictures, street processions of pigs, monster cheeses and elephants, the use of trick mirrors, imitation £1 notes, and leaflets scattered from balloons all aroused intense excitement among the public and created a mythology of Lipton's activities that found further expression in newspaper articles and on the music-hall stage. Although this was free publicity, Lipton's advertising outlays reached £40,000 a year by the 1890s and over £50,000 per annum before war broke out in 1914.

Thomas Lipton's financial success over the first quarter century of his business matched the rate of expansion of his trading activities. Starting from his £100 capital in 1871, the firm's turnover had passed £200,000 per annum at the beginning of the 1880s and was well in excess of £1 million before the decade ended. During the years 1890-96, profits averaged nearly £94,000 and from May 1897 onwards there was much speculation that Lipton intended to make a public offer of the company on the Stock Exchange. The flotation in March 1898 was based on 242 shops, a number of factories and warehouses plus a contract trade to institutions and the armed forces, and a large number of agencies at home and in as many as 38 countries abroad. It valued the company at £2.5 million in one million £1 5 per cent cumulative preference shares, one million £1 ordinary shares (to be placed at a 5s premium), and £500,000 of 4 per cent debenture stock (redeemable from 1920). Lipton retained one-third of each category of shares and further allocations to his managers, employees and friends meant that almost one-half of the issue was kept back from the general public. There followed 'the Lipton scramble' as over £40 million was subscribed by the public for the remaining shares. As chairman of Thomas J Lipton Ltd for the next ten years, Lipton received £5,000 per annum and one-quarter of any profits over and above the dividend when this reached 12 per cent (up to a maximum of £5,000). He retained complete ownership and control of his activities in North America (which included two meat packing factories in Chicago) and part of his tea enterprise in Ceylon.

As his fiftieth birthday approached, Lipton for the first time allowed interests outside the firm to divert him. He was still a bachelor and essentially alone since his mother's death in 1889. It was his gifts to charity in the 1890s, notably his 'anonymous' donation to the Princess of Wales's Jubilee Appeal in 1897 and his support for the Alexandra Trust for feeding London's poor that brought him a knighthood in 1898, but it was his new status as a millionaire (he had received £1.63 million in cash from the flotation) which enabled him to develop the interest in yacht-racing which remained with him until the end of his life. His first challenge for the America's Cup in 1899, with his yacht *Shamrock I,* brought him enormous publicity on both sides of the Atlantic. By the turn of the century he was a public figure in London society, having been created Lord Lieutenant of the City of London in 1897, and being a close friend of the Prince of Wales who as King Edward VII installed him as KCVO in 1901 and baronet in 1902.

Sir Thomas Lipton remained chairman of Liptons until September 1927 when the successful takeover bid by Van den Berghs forced him into retirement at the age of seventy-seven. Between the public flotation in 1898 and 1927, Liptons never repeated the dynamic growth of the 1870s and 1880s. Profits remained around £200,000 per annum until 1914, with dividends tending to slip from 11 per cent to 6 per cent. When the First World War came, no dividends were paid for two years, from 1914 to 1916. There seems little doubt that the company was over-capitalised in its original incorporation and that further capital issues in 1909, 1919, and 1921 increased the problems of paying dividends for a firm which lacked adequate cash reserves. Lipton retained his policy of centralised control over the company after incorporation but he was less successful in marketing new lines in his shops. Sales of wines and spirits, begun in 1898, failed to meet expectations and were barely covering costs in 1914; Lipton's beef extract products failed to divert customers' preference for Bovril; schemes to import Siberian pork and vegetable oil (in the form of copra) were failures; and some of Lipton's manufacturing operations proved to be more costly than buying in from outside suppliers. Finally, in the 'canteen scandal' trial at the Old Bailey in 1914, the firm received much adverse publicity though its loss of War Office contracts was only temporary.

After the shock of the early war years, Liptons found new prosperity which concealed the inherent difficulties that burdened the firm. Sir Thomas Lipton had failed to solve two problems of management: he had not been able to create a decentralised system to which he was prepared to delegate authority nor, in his later years, had he been able to choose the kind of management staff needed to run the firm. With age he became obstinate and grew increasingly to distrust his staff. Dividends of 12.5 per cent were paid on ordinary shares until 1923 and turnover reached £11 million. The number of shops rose from 500 in 1919 to over 600 by the mid-1920s. However, Lipton's new plans for expanding manufacturing, particularly of breaking into the margarine market, and for the development of a teashop chain were overtaken by the economic adversities of the inter-war years. With losses in overseas business and increased capital burdens, dividends could not be sustained from 1924 onwards. When, in 1926, it appeared that the preference dividend could not be met, Lipton's effective control of the company passed to Sir John

Ferguson of Lloyds Bank as vice-chairman. In 1927 Van den Berghs obtained control of Lipton Ltd by paying Sir Thomas £600,000 for his shares which amounted to roughly one-quarter of the issued capital. Lipton became the life president and chairman of the reconstructed company but the dominant influence was that of Meadow Dairies run by George Beale (qv).

Lipton turned to the scene of his greatest popularity, issuing further challenges for the America's Cup with *Shamrock IV* in 1920 and *Shamrock V* in 1930. His attempts to win the cup in 1899 and, subsequently, in 1901 and 1903, had endeared him to the American public and in 1930 they presented him with a gold cup in recognition of his sportsmanship. Lipton's election to the Royal Yacht Squadron in 1931 was the ultimate accolade and during that summer the success of *Shamrock V*, now under the White Ensign, in British waters was a final triumph. Full of plans for *Shamrock VI* and a new challenge in 1932, Sir Thomas caught a chill at the end of September and died on 2 October 1931 at the age of eighty-one years. He had never married and had no living relative. Osidge, his house near Southgate, Middlesex, was left for a nurses' home and his estate of £600,105 gross was bequeathed to the City of Glasgow for the poor and sick. His trophies and collections of photographs and press-cuttings are held in that city.

DEREK ODDY

Writings:

The Terrible Truth about Serbia ... with Serbia's Fight for Freedom by "Shamrock" (British Red Cross Society, 1915).

(with William Blackwood) *Leaves from the Lipton Logs* (Hutchinson & Co, 1931).

Sources:

Unpublished

PrC.

Published

DNB.

Peter Mathias, *Retailing Revolution. A History of Multiple Retailing in the Food Trade Based upon the Allied Suppliers Group of Companies* (Longman, 1967).

Alec Waugh, *The Lipton Story* (Cassell, 1951).

WWW.

Sir Percy Lister (courtesy of Mr James Lister).

LISTER, Sir Charles Percy

(1897-1983)

Diesel engine manufacturer

Charles Percy (known as Percy) Lister was born at Dursley, Gloucestershire on 14 July 1897, the third son of Charles Lister (1871-1965) and his wife Laura Emeline née Browning. He was educated at Mill Hill School and Sandhurst and in 1919 entered the family firm of R A Lister & Co Ltd of Dursley in Gloucestershire after service in the First World War with the 18th Queen Mary's Own Royal Hussars.

The firm was started in 1867 by Robert Ashton Lister (1845-1929), himself the son of the owner of a medium-sized engineering firm manufacturing woollen machinery in Dursley, but estranged from his father. Ashton Lister's firm started by selling and servicing agricultural machinery, moving into manufacturing later. It remained a small-scale agricultural engineering concern until in 1889 it began to sell, and then make, cream separators. It expanded rapidly and in the 1900s, with Ashton's sons Charles and Austin (1873-1934) now actively associated in the management, added generating sets, sheep shearing sets and stationary petrol engines to the product range. By the 1920s Listers employed over 1,000 men at Dursley. Exports, mainly to the Dominions, the Continent, and the Argentine, took some 50 per cent of output, a reflection of Ashton's active salesmanship. He is said to have introduced the cream separator to railless Western Canada using a three-horse buggy, and he and his sons made frequent overseas visits, arranging agencies and in some countries starting subsidiary sales companies.

Charles Lister's sons Percy, George (b 1893), Robert (b 1894), Frank (b 1898) and Cecil (b 1905) entered the firm from 1917 onwards. In 1925 Percy became managing director, ousting his father Charles from that position. This episode may have been connected with management problems in the early 1920s when heavy losses were incurred. Austin Lister was chairman from Ashton's death until 1934, when Percy became chairman as well as managing director. In the late 1920s the firm developed a range of small stationary diesels with the help of H Ricardo, a leading consulting engineer. The firm's growth from then on was rapid. It was based on diesels, which gradually became central to the firm's activities, although the older product ranges remained and others were added. In 1930 Listers made an agreement with Ruston & Hornsby Ltd, the agricultural machinery manufacturers, whereby the two firms agreed to rationalise their combined range of engine production; Percy Lister joined the board of Rustons as a result of the agreement. It was terminated in 1935. Air-cooled diesels, of which the firm were innovators and were and are (1984) market leaders in Britain, first appeared in 1954. Hawker Siddeley took over the company in 1965 and two years later Percy Lister retired.

Percy Lister was a dynamic leader of the firm. He was primarily a salesman, making long and frequent trips abroad, and developing in the inter-war period important sales outlets in, inter alia, the USA and Mexico. After the war he started manufacturing subsidiaries or associates in Australia, Colombia, and Mexico. He constantly stressed expansion of the product range, adding large diesels and a range of harvesting machinery in 1936 by a takeover of Blackstones of Stamford, and new types of farm machinery after the war. At times his ideas went further than his brothers wished, and if this happened, he deferred to them. His brothers were all directors, and each had significant managerial responsibilities. Although the family's control was close, they are remembered for recognising talent and delegating where appropriate.

Ashton Lister was an orthodox paternalist in relations with the workforce. Percy Lister was more innovative. Listers introduced a week's paid holiday in 1926; other inter-war developments included medical and dental care. Most notable was the 'Joint Board', set up in 1926 and consisting of company directors and elected employees. In spite of its name this did not consider significant policy matters, but concerned itself with subjects such as waste of materials. It resembled the Works Councils proposed in the Whitley Report but rarely set up. His relatively advanced ideas on employer-employee relations notwithstanding, Percy Lister did not have strong views either for or against trades unions.

In quantitative terms the firm's growth was rapid. It became a private limited company in 1893. In 1922 the capital was £200,000. In 1932 the firm went public, originally with an issued capital of £600,000, which was increased over the years. The brothers retained shareholdings, but did not have a controlling interest. The number of employees rose from about 1,500 in 1930 to about 7,000, world-wide, in 1965; profits from about £80,000 per annum pre-tax in the early 1930s to over £1.5 million by 1964; and production of diesel engines to over 50,000 per annum in the mid-1960s, at which time 70 per cent of total turnover was exported. The final takeover consideration was £19 million.

The firm's success, both under Percy and earlier, was based on the attention paid to sales and to the service network, although this was backed up by an adequate level of investment in production facilities. The overseas subsidiaries formed one part of the sales effort; from 1924 overseas agents were linked by a journal; and home and overseas agents were regularly invited to Dursley. Existing products were developed for diverse uses: thus marine diesels were produced from the early 1930s. The firm were rarely innovators in design. They developed their own new engine ranges from the 1930s but most of their new products originated outside the firm.

Percy Lister had a number of outside interests. During 1940-45 he was chairman of the United Kingdom Commercial Corporation, an organisation concerned with purchasing raw materials and promoting British exports, travelling 300,000 miles in this role. He was knighted in 1947 for his wartime services.

Lister was a member of the Capital Issues Committee, 1946-47, of the Dollar Exports Council, 1949-64, and the Iron and Steel Board, 1953-58. He was a director of Armstrong, Whitworth and Broom & Wade, and latterly of Hawker Siddeley. He was also active in the Institute of Directors.

In social and religious outlook the Lister family exhibited contrast and continuity. Ashton was an active Congregationalist and keen Liberal. Percy was Church of England and a Conservative. The family exhibited continuity in their attention to local affairs. Ashton Lister lived some 200 yards from the works; all his grandsons lived locally. Ashton was for many years a county councillor, and was knighted in 1911 for his services to the locality. Percy gave strong support to the Slimbridge Wildfowl Trust and Gloucester County Cricket Club, although his chief recreation in earlier life had been hunting. On a personal level, his most remembered characteristics were his energy and his wit.

Percy Lister married in 1933 Peggy Broom, the daughter of Harry Broom of Broom & Wade, air compressor manufacturers. There was one son of the marriage. They divorced and in 1953 he married a widow, Mrs Geraldine Hilda Florence Bigger. Sir Percy Lister died in Cheltenham on 7 March 1983.

CHARLES MORE

Sources:

Unpublished

BCe.

MCe.

R A Lister & Co Ltd, Annual Reports 1933-64; Report on R A Lister & Co Ltd by Binder Hamlyn & Co, 1930.

Interviews with James Lister and staff of R A Lister & Co Ltd.

Published

David E Evans, *Listers, the First Hundred Years* (Gloucester: Alan Sutton, 1979).

Industrial Welfare Dec 1929.

Lister Standard 4 No 4 (Dec 1927), 6 No 4 (Dec 1929), Centenary Issue 1967.

Times 7 Dec 1929, 2 Apr 1965, 12 Mar 1983.

WW 1982.

Samuel Cunliffe Lister (courtesy of Dr J Iredale).

LISTER, Samuel Cunliffe

1st Lord Masham of Swinton

(1815-1906)

Textile and textile machinery manufacturer

Samuel Cunliffe Lister was born at Calverly Hall near Bradford on 1 January 1815, the fourth son of Ellis Cunliffe Lister, a manufacturer of Manningham Hall, Bradford, and the second of his three wives, May née Kay. Originally intended for the church, after education at a private school at Balham Hill, Clapham Common, Samuel chose instead to gain experience with Sands, Turner & Co, merchants of Liverpool, whence he visited America on several occasions. In 1836, he entered partnership with his brother John as a wool spinner in a worsted mill built for them by their father. Because of the death of Ellis Cunliffe, John retired from the partnership after two years to run the family estate.

Samuel took other partners (such as J Ambler and later J Warburton) and became interested in the potential profits of wool combing by machine; he purchased certain patent rights from George Edmund Donisthorpe and together they produced a workable machine. These machines were then sold at considerable profit. Other patents followed. In 1847 Lister was joined by Isaac Holden (qv), who was also interested in the development of machine combing. Partnership followed and together they set up three wool-combing factories in France, Lister remaining in England.

In this period Lister was involved with the development of at least three wool-combing machines, each with several variations. His strategies included the purchasing of other combing patents and employing other inventors in his own workshops. He also continued his commercial activities and in 1855 had an interest in three factories in France, all wool-combing, five factories in Yorkshire and one in Germany; these textile undertakings involved a total of six partners. Lister derived considerable income from certain of his factories and from the sale of his combing machines, but he was always short of capital to finance his development and commercial activities, and in 1857 his Halifax factory failed. One consequence of this was his being called by the Bank of England to explain his financial position.

In 1858 his partnership with Holden ended, as did his major involvement in wool combing; Lister sold his share to Holden for £74,000. At about this time, Lister became interested in exploiting the processing of silk waste and in association with another of his partners succeeded in developing new forms of dressing (or combing) the material. As with the wool combs, a large amount of money, approximately £250,000, was spent in development costs but eventually this resulted in very considerable profits. Between 1864 and 1874, the silk business made sufficient money to

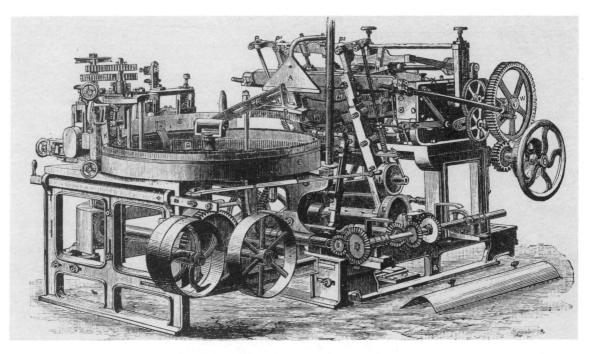

Lister comb (courtesy of Dr J Iredale).

rebuild and equip the (present) Manningham Mills, the previous building having burnt down in 1871.

Lister's next area of interest was with an improved loom to weave plush. Again in association with its inventor, success was achieved, and as a result Manningham Mills was working at a profit of £200,000 a year in the early 1880s.

Because of his many and varied patents (over 150 were taken out in his name), Lister was embroiled in numerous legal disputes. One of his earliest was with Heilman, a Frenchman and also an inventor of a wool comb. The suit concerned the use of a nip mechanism which Lister had also used in one of his combs; Lister lost. He then bought Heilman's patent for wool combing in England, but ignored a clause not to sell it on the Continent. A further legal battle took place and Lister settled out of court. Lister experienced considerable difficulties in his relationships with most of his partners and managers. To his death he was disputing Holden's claims regarding the invention of the Square Motion Comb.

In 1889, Lister turned Manningham Mills into a public company, although retaining a large number of shares. This coincided with the McKinley tariff which made severe restrictions on exports to America and reduced annual profits by 75 per cent to £50,000. The reduction in profits was followed by a reduction in wages and a strike lasting twenty-one weeks. In 1893 there were severe labour troubles at a coalmine, Ackton colliery at Featherstone, Yorkshire, which he had purchased some years before; there were riots, during which the colliery buildings were destroyed and troops fired on the rioters, killing some. However, under Lister's proprietorship the output of the colliery increased twelve-fold.

Lister sold the Manningham estate to the city of Bradford in 1870 for the nominal sum of £40,000, for it to be made into a park, now known as Lister Park. In 1883 he bought the Swinton estate (north of Ripon) for £400,000, and four years later he purchased the adjoining Jervaulx estate for £310,000.

A JP for the North and West Ridings and a DL, Lister was appointed High Sheriff of Yorkshire in 1887. In the same year he was offered a baronetcy, which he declined. From about 1874, Lister was active in politics, describing himself first as a Conservative-Liberal, later as a Liberal-Conservative. He stood for parliament in 1874 and 1885, but was unsuccessful on both occasions. He was granted a barony in 1881, taking the title Masham of Swinton. He was given an honorary LLD by Leeds University, and in 1886 was awarded the Albert medal of the Society of Arts.

Lister married in 1854 Anne (d 1875), daughter of John Dearden of Hollins Hall, Halifax; they had two sons and five daughters. His main recreations were sport, particularly shooting and coursing, and collecting pictures: among the artists represented in his collection were Reynolds, Romney and Gainsborough. Lord Masham died on 2 February 1906, aged ninety-one, leaving a gross personal estate of £633,637.

JOHN A IREDALE *and* J MALCOLM TRICKETT

Writings:

Free Trade and Reciprocity: A Series of Letters (Bradford, 1879).

Lord Masham's Inventions (Lund, Humphries & Co Ltd, 1903).

Sources:

Published

Burke's Peerage and Baronetage.

DNB.

WWW.

Henry Littleton ca 1885 (courtesy of Novello & Co Ltd).

LITTLETON, Henry

(1823-1888)

Music publisher

Henry Littleton was born in the parish of St Margaret's, Westminster, on 7 January 1823, the eldest and only surviving son of James Littleton, a saw maker, and his wife Elizabeth née Whildon. Descended from an old Cornish family, his grandfather William came to London in the last quarter of the eighteenth century. Henry joined the firm of London music publishers, Novello (Vincent and J Alfred, father and son), in 1841 as a collector, that is, a pick-up and delivery man.

Exactly when Littleton became Alfred Novello's primary assistant is not known. He had been brought 'in house' as a shopman by 1844. Novello had no children of his own, and his consideration for Littleton was marked out very early by a special regard. Certainly by 1856, when Novello retired to Italy, Littleton was effective head of the firm. On 1 November 1861 the two men made a partnership agreement enabling Littleton to purchase the firm for £50,000 over a period of ten years. In the event he paid off the debt in just five years, becoming sole proprietor of the firm in 1866. At the time of his takeover, publishing and printing were carried on, respectively, in 69 Dean Street and Dean's Yard, 21 Dean Street. A second publishing house in the City was located at 35 Poultry.

In the early summer of 1867 Littleton purchased J J Ewer & Co, music publishers in Regent Street, for £15,000. The firm was styled Novello Ewer & Co. This judicious move brought Novello copyrights on several of Mendelssohn's finest works, including the oratorio *Elijah* and his violin concerto. The firm had acquired and profited by the copyright of Mendelssohn's *St Paul* oratorio in 1837, and in 1867 there would have been no doubt about the wisdom of acquiring works by this popular composer. Copyrights for various books of his *Songs Without Words* were bought by Ewer for 15 guineas and 25 guineas in 1841. In 1869, Littleton paid £200 for the eighth book in this collection.

The awkward task of trying to run the business from three locations (Dean Street, Poultry and now Regent Street) led Littleton to announce a consolidation. The City office was retained but the rest of the publishing concern was moved in December 1869 to 1 Berners Street. Printing had a short stint there as well, but was soon returned to the old Dean Street premises.

In another enterprising move that same year he decided to offer a wholesale 50 per cent reduction in the prices of Novello's popular *Octavo Choruses*. These comprised 318 part-songs (vocal scores with keyboard accompaniment), a small but significant segment of the catalogue. The reduced prices ranged from 1d to 4½d, most being offered at 1d or 1½d. Good music at a cheap price: this was the legacy inherited by Henry Littleton. Alfred Novello had identified a vast provincial market for sacred

The music room, Westwood House ca 1885 (courtesy of Novello & Co Ltd).

choral music and campaigned around the country to supply Novello editions to the growing number of enthusiasts for amateur choral singing. His 'grass roots' approach brought the firm an affectionate place in the hearts of English people countrywide. Littleton retained the popular markets of his predecessor, but chose also to bring his firm into the realm of 'high culture' by concentrating heavily on the international market. Gounod (in 1871), Verdi (in 1875), Dvorak (1884), Liszt (1886) and others were shrewdly invited to England by the firm to conduct their music, usually in exchange for British, if not exclusive, copyright on the works performed. Littleton himself was abroad in Europe at least three times, seeking and finalising contract agreements with composers, and recruiting apprentices for the firm. In the music market the Novello firm appears to have been the major beneficiary of changing tastes and patterns of arts consumption in Victorian England.

In an ambitious experiment begun in 1867, Littleton and his talented musical adviser, Joseph Barnby, combined musical and entrepreneurial efforts by organising several concert series in London, Barnby conducting his own choir. An association of the firm with subscription concerts at the Royal Albert Hall began in 1872. Daily concerts given in Passion Week and short seasons of oratorio concerts were among several schemes offered there between 1872 and 1875. Six or seven price categories, most under £1, were offered, and a cheap 1s admission was available. Concert management may have proved more ambitious than profitable. It was tried again in the 1880s, after which it was dropped for good.

Two premises were leased at 111 and 113 Southwark Street in 1877 to accommodate a new side of the business — bookbinding. Now, except for the actual production of paper, the firm was vertically integrated, undertaking to publish, print, bind, advertise and sell its printed music, books on music and periodical magazines. A so-called general printing branch which took in outside jobs, unrelated to music, and an extensive music lending library (acquired in 1867 with the purchase of Ewer) were further related businesses of the firm.

Henry Littleton retired on 31 December 1886. The firm then occupied eight premises in and about London (1 Berners Street, 80 and 81 Queen Street, 69 and 70 Dean Street, and 111, 113 and 115 Southwark Street) at an annual rent of £1,776 1s. Outside London there was a branch in New York City which had been set up in 1852 by Alfred Novello. This office was run intermittently by the firm, or managed by an outside agency. Littleton transferred the business to his two sons, Alfred Henry (1845-1914) and Augustus James (1854-1942), and his two sons-in-law, Henry William Brooke and George T S Gill. The purpose of the move to a joint partnership from Littleton's point of view was motivated by two concerns: he wanted to guarantee the 'line of succession' for his descendants in the firm, and he wanted to guarantee financial security for himself and his wife. He succeeded in both. He had an annuity payable until his death, by the firm, of £7,500. If he pre-deceased his wife, she was to receive £3,000 a year in her lifetime. Littleton was not trained in music, but he knew the value of good advisers and he chose them well. He was also lucky in his offspring. Alfred worked closely with his father preparing for the general management of the firm. Henry's second son and his two sons-in-law capably looked after much of the bookbinding and printing.

Quantitative measures of the firm's growth under Henry Littleton are limited. Very few business records, and no account books survive. When the firm was incorporated in 1898, the joint partnership was valued at £272,250. The firm's share capital of £270,000 has remained unchanged to the present day (1984). Two complete catalogues of music published by the firm in 1858 and 1893 show a great leap ahead in both number and variety of works offered. *The Musical Times*, the chief organ of communication in the music world in England, was owned and published by Novello and boasted a circulation of 14,000 in December 1870 — a readership that included amateurs, professionals and the trade, countrywide. Advertising increased steadily along with the size and scope of the journal. The firm's staff must have increased significantly under Henry for in 1898 the entire staff of 270 was kept on after incorporation.

Novello thoroughly absorbed Henry Littleton. Its success was his success — the means by which he was able to break out of the world of shopmen and sawmakers. He bought Westwood House, in Sydenham, in 1874, and lived there after it had been extensively renovated, in comfortable magnificence until he died. He acquired works of art and literature including the famous Roubiliac statue of Handel (now at the Victoria and Albert Museum). He retained a 'crusty' exterior, but learned to move in the cultured and socially aristocratic circles associated with the firm in its connection with the fine arts.

Henry Littleton married Sarah Eliza, daughter of William Law, an attorney's clerk, in 1844. They had four children, the two sons, and two daughters, Elizabeth Ann and Amy Eliza. Littleton died on 11 May 1888, leaving a personal estate of £8,650 and four properties: the freehold mansion, Westwood House in Sydenham, Lewisham; 'a piece of land ... forming part of the demesne of Westwood House' {Novello & Co, Deed of Assignment, 1889}; Dunedin House, also in Lewisham; and 7 Victoria Mansions, in Hove, Sussex.

CAROLE TAYLOR

Sources:

Unpublished

Leeds University, Novello Cowden Clarke Collection, J Alfred Novello/Henry Littleton Agreement, 1866.

Novello & Co Ltd, Borough Green, private library files (uncatalogued).

Westminster Abbey Muniment Room, St Margaret's, Westminster, Register of Baptisms, 1822-1824.

MCe.

PrC.

Information from Michael Hurd 16, 23 Nov 1983.

Published

Joseph Bennett, *A Short History of Cheap Music as Exemplified in the Records of Novello, Ewer & Co* (Novello, 1887).

'Henry Littleton' *Musical Times* 29 (June 1888).

'Henry Littleton' *ibid* 64 (Jan 1923).

Michael Hurd, *Vincent Novello — and Company* (Granada Publishing Ltd, 1981).

'Liszt in London, 1886' *Musical Times* 27 (May 1886).

Sir George Livesey (from The Gas World *vol 49 July-December 1908).*

LIVESEY, Sir George Thomas

(1834-1908)

Gas company manager

George Thomas Livesey was born in Islington, North London, on 8 April 1834 the eldest of the three children of Thomas Livesey (1806-1871) and his wife Ellen née Hewes. At that time Thomas Livesey was a clerk with the Gas Light & Coke Co (of which his uncle became deputy governor) at Shoreditch, but moved south of the Thames in 1839 to join the South Metropolitan Gas Co as company secretary, becoming secretary and general manager from 1842 until his death in 1871.

George Livesey was brought up in and around the gas works and recalled swimming in the canal used by the coal barges. He started work with the South Metropolitan Gas Co at the age of fourteen in 1848; he was appointed assistant manager in 1857, engineer in 1862 and on his father's death was appointed engineer and company secretary. Although he had no formal engineering or chemical training, he was 'an exceptionally able engineer' {Everard (1949) 254}, patenting a number of improvements, including the Livesey washer for gas purification, his most important technical innovation (patented 1867) and he became the foremost gasholder constructor of his time.

However, his main contribution to the industry was to exploit to the full the commercial possibilities of the existing technology. As demand for the South Metropolitan's gas rose in the second half of the nineteenth century, with the growth of London and the adoption of gas lighting, he was closely involved in the complete reconstruction of the Old Kent Road gasworks and the major expansion of the company's manufacturing capacity. Assisted by his younger brother Frank (d 1899), who succeeded him as engineer when George joined the board of directors in 1882, he was responsible for the purchase of a large site on the Greenwich marshes and the construction of the East Greenwich works which opened in 1887. The gasholder at East Greenwich, which George Livesey himself designed, was large enough to accommodate the Albert Hall.

The first stages of this massive engineering programme were completed in the lifetime of his father, Thomas, who, however, always acknowledged George's leading role. Thomas, it was said, left a reconstructed works, a 10 per cent dividend which had been maintained for over ten years, a low price (3s 2d per 1,000 cubic feet), loyal staff and the best managed gas works in the Metropolis. In view of later labour problems, it is noteworthy that a workmen's contributory sick benefit fund (with 40 per cent of the contributions from the employer) was established in 1842, a superannuation fund in 1885 and a week's holiday with pay in 1860.

Government regulation of the industry came first with the Gasworks Clauses Act of 1847 which restricted dividends to a maximum of 10 per cent per annum in line with railway and water undertakings and, although procedures were established for reduction of prices where excess profits were being made, this proved inadequate and ineffective. Individual companies generally enjoyed monopoly powers unless their territory was shared. George Livesey recalled one dramatic case in the Walworth Road, South London, where four companies were competing in 1853; each had a main on both sides of the road and the customers were constantly switching between gas suppliers which caused general inconvenience and loss to the companies concerned. In that year informal agreement was reached by the South London companies for each to have its own exclusive district of supply. Four years later similar informal agreements were reached north of the Thames and in 1860 these were formalised by act of parliament. This act also set a maximum price for gas, but took no account of changes which would arise from savings or economies of manufacture, or through amalgamations. In consequence, customers were aggrieved at gas prices, but without remedy. In his presidential address to the Institution of Gas Engineers in 1874, George Livesey advocated adoption of a direct link between the price of gas to customers and the allowable level of dividend and within two years his company had been authorised by parliament to adopt this scheme and almost all gas company acts of parliament thereafter included a similar provision. For every penny reduction in the price of gas below a standard price, the dividend could be increased by $\frac{1}{4}$ per cent; if the price charged exceeded the standard price the dividend had to be reduced correspondingly. In 1867 and for the next decade, the company's price was lower than that of any other metropolitan company. This was significant for the future of the South Metropolitan Co as its neighbour north of the Thames, the Gas Light & Coke Co, had embarked upon an expansionist policy to take over all the London companies. Seven companies were swallowed up between 1870 and 1876, in which year the Gas Light & Coke Co approached Livesey and the other two South London companies, the Phoenix and the Surrey Consumers'. Livesey pointed out that the basis of the offer, that his customers should pay Gas Light prices (then 3s 2d per 1,000 cubic feet compared with South Metropolitan's 2s 10d) and that his shareholders should receive a flat 10 per cent, was an unacceptable proposition. By the time a further approach was made a couple of years later, Livesey had himself made arrangements to take over the Phoenix and the Surrey Consumers', establishing an organisational pattern for gas supply in London and also a rivalry which survived beyond nationalisation in 1949. The price differential between north and south of the river remained a bone of contention for customers and a cause of animosity between the two companies. Matters were not helped when, in 1886, George Livesey offered to take over the Gas Light Co; his offer was declined. In 1898 the Gas Light was charging 3s per 1,000 cubic feet and the South Metropolitan 2s 3d. At a government committee of enquiry that year Livesey appeared as the principal technical witness on behalf of the customers; he made a vitriolic attack on the Gas Light's over-capitalisation, inadequate engineering skill and incompetent buying of coal, and much of what he said was true. The change in the Gas Light's fortunes thereafter was in no small measure due to David Milne-Watson (qv).

An attempt was made to unionise gas stokers in 1872 and there were widespread strikes, but the South Metropolitan was the only company unaffected as regular Sunday working was stopped in that year and a weekly 1s 6d good time money bonus was given. The union was crushed when the Gas Light Co brought conspiracy charges against the leaders. In March 1889 Will Thorne set up the Gas Workers' Union whose main objectives were to establish an eight-hour day for stokers instead of the twelve-hour day then being worked. The eight-hour day was agreed in July by Livesey who also reluctantly agreed to double-time for Sunday working but, as he pointed out, no regular Sunday day shift had been worked by his company since 1872, although it was commonplace elsewhere in London. On the issue of a closed shop for stokers, raised in September 1889, Livesey was not prepared to agree. In view of general unrest in gas works throughout London Livesey prepared contingency plans to recruit additional workers but at the same time proposed (30 October) to the board

> Could not the Company instead of fighting the men use their money and efforts in making them their friends? Let the money that would be spent in a strike form the beginning of a fund for the men's benefit to be increased in future by giving them a share in the profits of the company in addition to their wages. In short I would apply the sliding scale to them so that they as well as the public and the shareholders should have a share in the benefits resulting in the reduction of the price of gas {evidence of George Livesey to the RC Labour (1893) C 6894}.

This was adopted by the board and put to representatives of the men who at first showed little enthusiasm. However, when the stokers in the union turned the scheme down, other men decided they had nothing to lose and several hundred applied to join the scheme. The board then agreed that it would enter into individual agreements with its staff offering a guarantee of employment for twelve months, no reduction in pay and 1 per cent bonus for every 1d reduction in gas price below 2s 8d. Three stokers applied to join the scheme and the union demanded that they should be dismissed and the scheme withdrawn. Livesey refused and strike notice was given in December 1889. The two-month strike was bitterly contested. New men were taken on to man the retorts but had to lodge within the gas works to avoid violence outside, and up to 3,000 police were required to maintain public order. Following a threat by the union secretary to dispense with notice in any future strike, contrary to the law, Livesey incorporated a condition in his scheme to exclude trade unionists from participation.

Livesey and his co-partnership scheme have been held up as a dramatic example of paternalism by the employer. Livesey himself was a devout Anglican (and Sunday School superintendent for ten years); and he saw co-partnership creating a new relationship between worker and employer. He quoted Mazzini with approval on many occasions. 'The ultimate position of the labourer which was orginally slavery, then serfdom, next the wage earner must ultimately be that of partner' {*Co-partnership Journal* 1 (1904) 3}; 'Co-partnership is Christianity in Business' {*ibid*, 5 (1908) 3}. In his last few years he used the co-partnership scheme as a platform to commend to his staff the virtues of temperance (he was himself a lifelong abstainer), to warn of the evils of gambling and money lending and to commend the virtues of house ownership. He was closely associated with

The funeral procession of Sir George Livesey (from The Gas World *vol 49 July–December 1908).*

the Metrogas Building Society (founded 1886 and still operating in 1984) and some of the co-partnership bonus left invested in the company at 4 per cent interest (when debenture holders received 3.5 per cent) was channelled into home loans. In 1905 in declaring a 9.75 per cent bonus on salaries and wages for co-partners he said the bonus of over £42,000 'would buy 140 houses at £300 apiece' {*ibid*, 2 (1905) 137}. That year the debenture holders received £55,452 and the ordinary shareholders £343,750. From 1896 the co-partners elected three worker directors to the board. At the end of 1907, £347,727 in stock and deposits was held by the company on behalf of 5,003 co-partners.

Livesey enthusiastically promoted his co-partnership ideals and read a number of papers to the Insitition of Gas Engineers on the subject. At the time of his death about 40 companies in the gas industry representing about half the total capital employed had adopted co-partnership schemes. It is a tribute to Livesey's personal standing in the gas industry that his scheme, which never found great favour elsewhere, was a major factor in the good labour relations experienced in the industry for half a century.

Despite his advocacy of co-partnership, Livesey was first and foremost a practical gas engineer and manager with a world-wide reputation. He was always willing to advise and help gas engineers elsewhere in the country and overseas. Where appropriate and economic, he favoured the use of machinery — but only introduced stoking machinery, which had been available for about twenty years, following the 1889 strike, to redress the increased labour costs of the eight-hour day and to enable the company 'to recover its rightful control' {Livesey (1908)}.

He was appointed chairman of the South Metropolitan Gas Co in 1885. Between 1871 and his death in 1908 the company's price of gas was reduced from 3s 2d to 2s 3d per 1,000 cubic feet. The capital employed increased from £250,000 to £7 million (1908) and gas sales rose from 350 million cubic feet (1862) to 12,520 million cubic feet (1908). Its workforce rose from under 500 to around 6,000 in 1908, making the South Metropolitan Gas Co second in output only to the Gas Light & Coke Co.

As well as his membership of the Institution of Gas Engineers (whose highest award, the Birmingham medal, he received in 1882) he was also a member of the Insititutions of Mechanical and Civil Engineers. He was a member of the Royal Commission on Labour 1891-94 (to which he also gave evidence on the 1889-90 gas strike) and other committees. He was a generous benefactor to religious and philanthropic movements. He erected at his own expense, the Livesey Library, the first public library in Camberwell (since 1974, the Livesey Museum). He gave the testimonial collection made for him following the strike, for the purchase of a public recreation ground at Telegraph Hill, Hatcham. He was a keen cyclist, walker and early motorist. He was knighted in 1902.

He married in 1859 Harriet (b 1836) daughter of George and Harriet Howard; there were no children and she died in 1909. Sir George Livesey died on 4 October 1908, leaving £161,326 gross.

FRANCIS GOODALL

Writings:

Livesey contributed many technical papers and papers on co-partnership, in particular to the Institution of Gas Engineers.

(with Frank Livesey) 'The New Works of the South Metropolitan Gas Company at East Greenwich' *Journal of Gas Lighting* 1886.

PP, RC Labour 1892–94 (1893) C 6894.

'Paper on the Profit-Sharing Scheme of the South Metropolitan Gas Co' Co-Partnership Conference of the Labour Association, 14 Oct 1899 (McCorquodale & Co, 1899).

Co-Partnership — Paper Read before the Institution of Gas Engineers June 16 1908 (King Sell & Olding, 1908).

LIVESEY Sir George Thomas

Sources:

Unpublished

London Borough of Southwark, Local Studies Library, Livesey collection.

PrC.

Published

Walter T K Braunholtz, *The Institution of Gas Engineers. The First Hundred Years 1863-1963* (Institution of Gas Engineers, 1963).

Dean Chandler and A Douglas Lacey, *The Rise of the Gas Industry in Britain* (British Gas Council, 1949).

Philip Chantler, *The British Gas Industry* (Manchester: Manchester University Press, 1938).

Roy A Church, 'Profit Sharing and Labour Relations in England in the Nineteenth Century' *International Review of Social History* 16 (1971).

DLB sv William James Thorne.

DNB.

Stirling Everard, *The History of the Gas Light & Coke Company 1812-1949* (Benn, 1949).

Gas World 49 (July-Dec 1908).

Walter T Layton, *The Early Years of the South Metropolitan Gas Company 1853-1871* (Spottiswoode Ballantyne & Co Ltd, 1920).

Robert B Perks, 'Real Profit Sharing: William Thomson & Sons of Huddersfield 1886-1925' *Business History* 24 (1982).

South Metropolitan Gas Company, *A Century of Gas in South London* (pp, 1924).

—, *Co-Partnership Journal* 1-6 (1904-).

Statist 5 Sept 1908.

Transactions of the Institution of Gas Engineers 1908.

Trevor I Williams, *A History of the British Gas Industry* (Oxford University Press, 1981).

James Livesey (courtesy of Mr David Wainwright).

LIVESEY, James

(1833-1925)

Consulting civil engineer

James Livesey was born at Preston, Lancashire in 1833, the youngest of three sons of Joseph Livesey (1794–1884) a cheesefactor, and his wife Jane née Williams. His father became a leading temperance reformer in the 1830s and between 1844 and 1859 was the proprietor of the *Preston Guardian* newspaper. James early showed an aptitude for engineering and mechanical drawing, and after education at a Mr Isherwood's day school in Preston he was apprenticed at the age of fourteen to Isaac Dodds and worked on the construction of the Caledonian Railway. As a boy in lodgings in Glasgow, James Livesey made his first invention. He bought an alarm clock incorporating a weight attached to a chain, which as it dropped struck a wax match against emery paper; this lit the lamp, and also began to heat a tin of coffee lodged above it. After two years he entered the Bolton works of Musgrave & Co, engineers specialising in land engines, mill machinery and bridge buildings.

At the request of his father and brothers he devised a machine to cut out the laborious business of folding newspapers. Immediately successful, it was first introduced in the print room of the *Preston Guardian*; a second model was built for the *Manchester Guardian*, and a third for the stand of the *Illustrated London News* at the Great Exhibition of 1851 (where the young Livesey presented a folded newspaper to Queen Victoria). W H Smith thereafter ordered eight machines, and Livesey contracted with Ainscow & Tomlinsons to make them in Preston. Orders came from all over the country, and while still an apprentice, Livesey was financially independent at eighteen.

In search of further experience he spent two years (1853-54) in the great locomotive works of Beyer, Peacock & Co of Manchester. During this period, with some friends, he installed compound engines and a tubular boiler in a small steam yacht, and almost lost his life when, on a trip to the Isle of Man, fire nearly engulfed the ship.

Through an associate in the construction of the Caledonian Railway he was invited in 1857 to manage the locomotive department of the Isabel Segunda Railway from Santander to Alar del Rey in Spain. During the ceremonial opening run, with Livesey at the engine controls, a bank of earth gave way and the engine rolled down the slope. Livesey survived, though with his clothes and flesh burnt by the firebox coals; two young British engineers who had been standing beside him were killed. Shortly afterwards he returned to England to marry, but soon returned to Spain with his young bride. Their son was born in Santander on 30 May 1860, and christened on board the liner *Himalaya* in Santander Harbour: George Hudson, the 'railway king', stood godfather.

Livesey returned to England in 1862, determined to manufacture his newspaper folding machine on his own account, and become an engineering agent. He set up in business at 29 Corporation Street, Manchester. His first agency was for the Imperial Tube Works of Birmingham, whose Manchester business he substantially increased. He became friendly with the family of W Owen of Rotherham, whose business was manufacturing railway wheels and axles; the Owen family suggested that he should take up their agency in London, and Owen agreed to underwrite him. This change of direction took Livesey into the new world of iron and steel, and the technological innovations that were affecting railways.

He began to do considerable business with the railway contractors Brassey, Ogilvie & Evans. Livesey designed a cast iron sleeper and had models made by the Muirs' Anderston Foundry in Glasgow. Ogilvie arranged for one hundred yards of these sleepers to be laid by the Great Eastern Railway. They proved a great success. Soon afterwards Livesey was invited to advise the Buenos Aires Great Southern Railway, which at that time had 70 miles of track but was shortly to have 3,000. Livesey became chief engineer to that railway.

Almost simultaneously he had met Andrew Carnegie, who was planning to manufacture steel rails in his Pittsburgh steelworks. When in London, Carnegie frequently discussed the problems with Livesey, who records that 'one day we were standing on St James's railway station platform soon after the opening of the District Railway. I called his attention to the rails and told him they were a new kind of rail with the top of the rail as hard as if made of steel' {Livesey (nd)}. As a result of these discussions Livesey was invited to tour the new railways of the United States and Canada, with letters of introduction from Carnegie and from (Sir) Sandford Fleming, with whom he had earlier worked as an engineer on the construction of Canadian railways.

As a consequence of this experience, Livesey (who had London offices at 9 Victoria Chambers, Westminster, and subsequently at 28 Victoria Street) became designer and engineer to railways in Argentina, Brazil, Chile and Peru, including the Transandine Railway. Many of these enterprises were backed financially from London by Sir Alexander Henderson (qv). Livesey designed the Bessemer Steel Works of the Freedom Iron & Steel Co, Pennsylvania; two large timber saw mills at Corunna and Bilbao, Spain; and improvements in railway construction such as the switch-lock for facing points.

While in South America he also designed and constructed an innovative grain elevator at Caracarana on the River Plate in the Argentine. This was designed to store some 2,000 tons of grain, which had to be constantly moved so as not to heat and deteriorate. Livesey designed a honeycomb of hexagonal iron bins 40 feet deep and 10 feet in diameter. The grain could be drawn from each of these bins on to wide travelling bands, and thus conveyed by buckets to any other part of the building. Finding that no engineer could advise him on the necessary thickness of the iron on the bin sides Livesey experimented with sacks, and discovered that so little lateral movement occurred that the bins could be made of thin sheet iron. This was done, and the grain elevator proved a commercial success.

His inventiveness spanned many fields. In London in 1875 he was disturbed by inexplicable sickness suffered by his family in their Kensington house. He attributed this to the drains, and redesigned the drainage and sanitation system. This cured the problem, and he wrote an account of his ideas in the journal *Engineering*, which had an influence on the general design of domestic sanitation in Britain.

James Livesey's son Fernando Harry Whitehead (afterwards Sir Harry Livesey (1860-1932)) acted as assistant to his father in the construction of the Buenos Aires Great Southern Railway, the Central Uruguay Railway, the Buenos Aires and Rosario Railway and their extensions, the Uniao Mineira Railway of Brazil, the Taltal Railway of Chile, La Guaira and Caracas Railway, Venezuela Central Railway, Lombardy Roads Tramways, the Macuto Railway of Venezuela, Entre Rios Railways, and the Puerto Cabello Railways of Venezuela.

Harry Livesey joined in partnership with his father in 1885 when the firm became James Livesey & Son. In 1891 they took into partnership Brodie (afterwards Sir Brodie) Henderson (1869-1936), youngest brother of Livesey's financial backer Alexander Henderson, and the company became Livesey, Son & Henderson with offices first at Broad Street Avenue, and from 1902 at 14 South Place, London EC2.

James Livesey was elected an associate of the Institution of Civil Engineers in 1867, and became a full member in 1878. He was also a member of the Iron and Steel Institute. He retired from full participation at the age of sixty in 1893 (when the firm became Livesey & Henderson), occupying his time at his estate at Rotherfield, Sussex, and his villas at Beaulieu, France, and in Norway, though remaining active and inventive until his death at Whitehall Court more than thirty years later, on 3 February 1925. His estate was proved at £304,308 gross.

Sir Harry Livesey was as inventive as his father, and took out several engineering patents in the years up to 1914 when he was senior partner. In 1911 he commissioned a steam yacht of 1,023 tons from John Brown & Co on Clydebank: up to the First World War he cruised in the Mediterranean on the *Jeanette* from October to March. During the war the yacht was employed by the Admiralty to detect submarines. In 1917, at the request of Sir Eric Geddes (qv), Sir Harry became Director of Contracts at the Admiralty. After the war he resumed his cruises, sailing occasionally to South America. He died on board the yacht in Monte Carlo harbour on 21 June 1932, leaving £212,340 gross. He was unmarried.

His partner Brodie Haldane Henderson travelled widely in South America and East and South Africa on engineering work. In 1914 he was commissioned into the Royal Engineers and became Deputy Director-General of Transportation in France. He retired from the Army as a brigadier-general, was mentioned four times in despatches and awarded a number of decorations. He was president of the Institution of Civil Engineers in 1928-29. He was a governor of the Imperial College of Science and Technology, a member of the Delegation of the City and Guilds College, and Honorary Consulting Engineer to the Imperial War Graves Commission. He died on 28 September 1936. Two of his sons, Neil Brodie Henderson (1904-83) and Andrew Brodie Henderson (b 1913) became partners in Livesey & Henderson, as did his nephew the Honorable Philip Henderson (1881-1939), fourth of six sons of the First Lord Faringdon.

DAVID H E WAINWRIGHT

Sources:

Unpublished

PrC.

J Livesey, 'From Youth to Old Age' (MS nd) in the possession of the author.

Published

DNB sv Joseph Livesey.

Minutes of Proceedings of the Institution of Civil Engineers 50 (1869-70), 67 (1881–82).

WWW.

LLEWELLYN, Sir David Richard

(1879-1940)

Coalmine owner

David Llewellyn (courtesy of Sir Harry Llewellyn).

David Richard Llewellyn was born at Aberdare on 9 March 1879, the eldest of five sons of Alderman Rees Llewellyn (1851-1919) of Bwllfa House, Aberdare, and his wife Elizabeth née Llewellyn. Rees Llewellyn spent a long period in the coal industry, being articled in 1868 as a surveyor at Hirwaun, becoming manager of the Bwllfa Colliery, Cwmdare, in 1872 and later joining with Edward Arnott and others to form the Bwllfa & Merthyr Dare Steam Collieries (1891) Ltd. When he retired from the position of general manager of the Bwllfa & Merthyr Dare Collieries in November 1918, one of his sons, William Morgan Llewellyn, succeeded him as general manager.

After education at Aberdare Higher Grade School and at Llandovery College, David Llewellyn began his career in the coal industry as a mining surveyor like his father, being articled to R Vaughan Price at the Main Collieries near Neath. On completing his articles, he studied at the mining department at University College, Cardiff, qualifying as a mining engineer in 1903. Subsequently he went to America to study mechanical mining and could have stayed there either as a mining engineer or in another post which was offered to him of chief engineer for the state of British Columbia. However, his prospective wife refused to leave Britain. On his return to Wales in 1905, he married Magdalene, the younger daughter of Rev H Harries of the Libanus Baptist Church, Treherbert. In the same year he acquired and developed the Windber Colliery in which he used electrically-driven coal cutters, reputed to be the first imported into South Wales from the USA where Llewellyn had seen them working. Windber was a small drift mine composed of three very thin seams, the largest of which was only two feet six inches thick. By 1913 annual output had increased to rather over 60,000 tons.

With the outbreak of the First World War Llewellyn joined the army where his expertise made him an obvious recruit for the Royal Engineers. When he was about to move to France he was prevented from serving by the authorities: because of the difficulties being experienced with the output and supply of coal in Britain, they considered him more valuable in Wales. In 1916 he became chairman of the Gwaun-cae-Gurwen Co, an appointment which marked a turning-point in his career since it brought him into contact with Henry Seymour Berry (qv) when Berry opened negotiations to acquire Gwaun-cae-Gurwen on behalf of the 'Cambrian Combine'. Between 1916 and 1922 Llewellyn's rise to prominence as a coalowner was rapid, so much so that *Who's Who in Wales* (1921) stated that 'he owns or controls one-seventh of the South Wales coalfield'. His importance in the coal industry, particularly in the mining of anthracite, the promotion of coal sales and his connection with Berry and the Cambrian Combine, was recognised by the conferment of a baronetcy in 1922.

In 1916 H S Berry was clearly interested in the potential of the anthracite coalfield, an optimism which Llewellyn shared. When making the chairman's speech at the annual meeting of Gwaun-cae-Gurwen in December 1918, Llewellyn said that the company was one of the very few anthracite companies which had been able to keep going on a profitable basis throughout the war. He thought that now that world markets were reopened there were good prospects for the coal trade and especially for anthracite, since South Wales was practically the only anthracite coalfield in Europe. In the event, the 'Cambrian Combine' link with anthracite remained limited to Gwaun-cae-Gurwen and Llewellyn expanded his own interests independently in the anthracite coalfield in the 1920s. In October 1921 he repeated his optimism about anthracite, saying that a strong demand for anthracite was coming to stay and that huge resources in the Vales of Neath had hardly been tapped on an extensive scale. His main anthracite interest was in the Vale of Neath Colliery Co together with the Rock, Penhydd and Aberpergwm collieries. Following a marked trend in the 1920s towards combination in the anthracite coalfield, his own anthracite interests and the Gwaun-cae-Gurwen Co (then in the ownership of Guest Keen & Nettlefolds) were sold in 1928 to the Amalgamated Anthracite Colliery Co under the chairmanship of Sir Alfred Mond, Lord Melchett (qv) with Sir David Llewellyn joining the board of Amalgamated Anthracite as deputy chairman. In that capacity he became the effective head of the mining section of AAC and among the changes brought about under his aegis were the pooling of wagons, the creation of a centralised stores agency and the adoption of a uniform system of accountancy.

His prominence in the promotion of coal sales began in October 1918, when together with H H Merrett he acquired a block of offices in Mountstuart Square, Cardiff Docks. A coal marketing organisation, Llewellyn, Merrett & Price Ltd, was formed in January 1919 and it was to have a relatively successful existence as a sales agency, reaching a peak during the 1920s in handling between 12 and 13 million tons per annum. In 1926 it merged with L Guéret Ltd (founded by Louis Guéret (qv)). The managing director of the new firm, Guéret, Llewellyn & Merrett, was Herbert Henry Merrett (1886-1959) who was Sir David Llewellyn's main marketing adviser throughout his career. The coal sales agency was to handle sales for most of the collieries controlled by Llewellyn and Merrett, which already in 1919 included Bwllfa & Merthyr Dare, Cwmaman Coal Co, Graigola Merthyr Co and Ynisarwed Colliery Co. Llewellyn's later colliery interests included the formation of D R Llewellyn & Son and chairmanship of the Graigola Merthyr Co and of North's Navigation Collieries (1889) Ltd.

Llewellyn's connection with H S Berry and the 'Cambrian Combine' began in 1916. The most important episode in that connection for Llewellyn's subsequent career was the acquisition of John Lysaght Ltd in 1919 and the subsequent sale of Lysaght to Guest Keen & Nettlefolds in 1920. As a result, Llewellyn not only became deputy chairman of John Lysaght but also, in his new position on the board of GKN, had the virtual direction of all the collieries now owned by GKN, including such important firms as D Davis & Sons Ltd, Consolidated Cambrian Ltd and Meiros Collieries. He became chairman of GKN's colliery committee. He remained a director of GKN until his death and eventually became chairman of John Lysaght for a brief period in 1940, although GKN virtually divested themselves of colliery interests during the 1930s. The first stage of reorganisation began in 1930 when GKN, D R Llewellyn & Sons and Guéret, Llewellyn & Merrett Ltd joined in the formation of Welsh Associated Collieries Ltd with Sir David Llewellyn becoming chairman. Five years later in 1935 there followed the fusion of Welsh Associated Collieries Ltd with Powell Duffryn Steam Coal Co Ltd under the title of Powell Duffryn Associated Collieries Ltd, with Sir David Llewellyn becoming vice-chairman of the overall body under the chairmanship of Edmund L Hann (1881-1968), who also joined the board of GKN.

Although Llewellyn was an important coalowner, his activities in the politics of the mining industry were not usually designed to cultivate publicity. On balance, he comes over as one of the more enlightened coalowners, a view subject to challenge because of the highly controversial nature of the industry's management. Critics might point to his statement in March 1921 when he put forward the owners' viewpoint in saying that absolute decontrol would make it possible for the owners to manage their pits economically as they used to do before the war: 'once we get wages reduced we shall be better able to compete for foreign or Continental markets' {Kirby (1977) 63-64}. Equally, in the meetings of the Monmouthshire & South Wales Coalowners' Association he was a strong supporter of the approach of Evan Williams (qv) towards the problems confronting coalowners, in the years 1925-26, and in December 1926 Evan Williams paid him a tribute for 'help of a most important character' {National Library of Wales, Monmouthshire and South Wales Coalminers' Association minutes, Dec 1926}. Llewellyn was resolute in 1925-26 that coalowners should stand firm for an eight-hour day, even if he admitted that it should not be made a strike issue. He was, in fact, a long-serving member of the regional Coalowners' Association, serving continuously either on the Cardiff District or latterly on the Swansea District of the Joint Conciliation Board until 1935. From 1929 to 1936 he was one of the South Wales representatives on the executive council of the Mining Association of Great Britain.

Nevertheless, his most active period in the regional Coalowners' Association lay in the years 1925 to 1930 and he served as chairman in 1929-30. There is evidence from that period that he was one of the more moderate coalowners and his support for Evan Williams was probably to avoid the impression of divisions existing on the coalowners' side. In fact, he disagreed on more than one occasion in the regional Coalowners' Association with those like Sir Samuel Instone (qv), whom he considered to take an unrealistic hard-line attitude. The diaries of Thomas Jones provide an unsolicited tribute that compared with 'the Powell Duffryn Co which had been screwing the men down mercilessly for a long time [there] was very much better feeling in the pits of Sir David Llewellyn and his brother William who moved among their workmen and knew them personally' {Middlemas (1969) II, 14}. Equally, the diaries give evidence that he was willing in August 1926 to meet miners' representatives alone with Lord Wimborne, until Evan Williams raised objections. In September 1926, 'D R' agreed with Churchill that it would not be possible for the owners to refuse to negotiate nationally with the miners and he met with Churchill also in September when Churchill's attitude was much more flexible than actions early in the previous May, during the General Strike, would indicate. Another important incident was in November 1926 when he interceded on behalf of Arthur Jenkins (father of the Rt Hon Roy Jenkins) who had been given a sentence of nine months which 'D R' considered 'most harsh ... Arthur Jenkins is quite a moderate and sensible leader ... a man of strong character and fair minded' {*ibid*, 95}. The diaries show also an attitude of resignation or fatalism towards the problems of the industry: 'D R L thinks the suspicion and hatred are such that permanent good relations with the men are impossible. He rather counts on a very prosperous spell during which a lot of money can be made, then a moderate spell, then bad times. He regards this as an inevitable sequence in the coal trade' {*ibid*, 89}. His son Harry claims that a significant indication of his good attitude towards his employees lay in the experience of the Windber colliery where in twenty-eight years under 'D R''s ownership there was no time lost in industrial disputes' {Llewellyn (1980) 33}.

Apart from his activities as a coalowner he followed his father for a time in interesting himself in the local government of Aberdare, where he was a member of the Aberdare District Council, becoming chairman in 1920. His politics were Liberal. In 1922 he donated £30,000 to University College, Cardiff, became the College treasurer, and then the president in 1924. In July 1929 he was made an honorary Doctor of Laws in the University of Wales.

In personality he was warm-hearted and affectionate, if sometimes inclined to be impulsive and impatient. Besides shooting, horses were his one great leisure interest, a passion which he inherited from his father. Like their father, both he and his brother, W M Llewellyn, were at times master of the Bwllfa Hunt. Sir David was himself a racehorse owner but was inclined to bet rather heavily and impulsively on his own horses, a fact not always appreciated by his second son Henry Morton (Harry), who rode *Ego* in the Grand National to finish second in 1936 and fourth in 1937. Among Sir David's four sons the eldest son and heir Rhys Llewellyn became managing director of the Graigola Merthyr Co and succeeded to the baronetcy in 1940 but it was Harry who achieved national distinction as a gold medallist for equestrian events in the 1952 Olympic games at Helsinki. Harry, knighted in 1977 for services to Wales, succeeded to the baronetcy in 1978 on his brother's death.

Sir David R Llewellyn died on 15 December 1940, leaving £714,131 gross. He was survived by his widow Magdalene, four sons and four daughters.

GRAEME HOLMES

Sources:

Unpublished

National Library of Wales, Monmouthshire and South Wales Coalminers' Association manuscripts: Minute Books MG17-MG21; Press Cuttings Files CB13 et seq.

BCe.

MCe.

PrC.

Interviews with Sir Harry Llewellyn.

Published

James C Carr and Walter Taplin, *History of the British Steel Industry* (Oxford: Basil Blackwell, 1962).

Colliery Guardian 20 Dec 1940.

Charlotte Erickson, *British Industrialists: Steel and Hosiery: 1850-1950* (Cambridge: Cambridge University Press, 1959).

A E C Hare, *The Anthracite Coal Trade of the Swansea District* (Swansea: University College, 1940).

Harry Llewellyn, *Passports to Life* (Hutchinson, 1980).

Michael W Kirby, *The British Coalmining Industry: 1870-1946* (Macmillan, 1977).

Keith Middlemas (ed), *Thomas Jones: Whitehall Diary* (3 vols, Oxford University Press, 1969) 2.

Times 16 Dec 1940.

Western Mail 16 Dec 1940.

Who's Who in Wales (1st ed 1921, 3rd ed 1937).

David J Williams, *Capitalist Combination in the Coal Industry* (Labour Publishing Co, 1924).

WWW.

LLOYD, Edward

(1815-1890)

Newspaper proprietor and paper manufacturer

Edward Lloyd was born at Thornton Heath, Surrey, on 16 February 1815. His father had come there from Wales hoping to seek his fortune but he died when Edward was still a child and Edward was brought up by his mother in London.

After an elementary education he started work in a solicitor's office and also studied shorthand at the London Mechanics' Institute. When still a boy he opened a shop where he sold cheap literature and in 1833 he compiled and printed *Lloyd's Stenography*. Before he was twenty Lloyd moved to Shoreditch and subsequently published penny numbers of popular stories or 'imitations', including plagiarisms of Dickens' works, aimed at the urban working classes.

His business grew and he moved to Salisbury Square off Fleet Street. Here he made various attempts to circumvent the tax on newspapers imposed by the Stamp Act, which he disliked as a Radical and a champion of popular education and, no doubt, as a publisher. One important attempt at avoidance was his publication in 1842 of *Lloyd's Penny Illustrated Newspaper* but his contention that this paper did not contain news was not accepted by the Stamp Office and he had to continue it as a stamped paper without illustrations. It became *Lloyd's Weekly London Newspaper* or *Lloyd's News*; priced at $2\frac{1}{4}$d (later 3d) it was the first of the cheap weeklies. In April 1852 Douglas Jerrold became editor and in 1853 the circulation averaged about 90,000. The readers, a large proportion of whom were female, belonged especially to the expanding lower middle class but there was also a considerable working class readership. The price was reduced to a penny in 1861 and the paper forged ahead to develop the largest circulation of any paper in the country. On 16 February 1896 *Lloyd's News* reached the circulation figure of a million, the first paper to do so.

In 1876 Lloyd bought the *Daily Chronicle* for £30,000 and after spending over £150,000 succeeded in transforming it from a suburban paper into a London daily.

It was characteristic of Lloyd's pioneering attitude that when in 1856 he introduced Hoe's American printing presses he was among the first in England to do so. With similar enterprise he began to manufacture newsprint and in 1861 he set up a mill with two machines at Bow. Later, after he had taken over the *Daily Chronicle*, he moved to Sittingbourne in Kent where he laid out a mill with two machines to which he soon added a 125 inch machine, the biggest erected up to this date. Sittingbourne not only produced newsprint for Lloyd's two newspapers and for export but also a large range of other paper for a general wholesale stationery business. Lloyd experimented with several fibres, but particularly with esparto grass for which he acquired property and rights to collect in Algeria and southern Spain.

Edward Lloyd's career foreshadowed that of Northcliffe (qv). In his publications he anticipated, over a generation earlier, what the Harmsworths were to do on a larger scale. Like Lloyd, also, but again later, the Harmsworths turned to manufacturing their own paper.

Before his death in 1890 Lloyd was in process of forming Edward Lloyd Ltd as a private company and the matter was completed by his executors. He sold to the new company his businesses and assets as newspaper proprietor, paper manufacturer and stationer and in return the company agreed to allot at his direction £250,000 in ordinary shares — the original share capital of the new company — and £260,000 in mortgages and debentures. Lloyd, who married twice and had nineteen children, left the direction of his large business to four of his sons making Frank (qv), the eldest by his second marriage (to Maria née Martins), chairman and managing director. Edward Lloyd died on 8 April 1890, leaving a personal estate sworn at £563,022.

RACHEL LAWRENCE

Writings:

Lloyd's Stenography (1833).

Lloyd's Reciter (1846-47).

Lloyd's Song Book (1846-47).

Sources:

Unpublished

Bowater Paper Corporation, archives.

Notes from Major D P J Lloyd (great-grandson).

Virginia S Berridge, 'Popular Journalism and Working Class Attitudes, 1854-1886: A Study of Reynold's Newspaper, Lloyd's Weekly Newspaper and The Weekly Times' (London PhD, 1976).

Published

British & Colonial Printer & Stationer 11 July 1889.

Thomas Catling, *My Life's Pilgrimage* (John Murray, 1911).

Daily Chronicle 9 Apr 1890, 6 May 1911.

DNB.

East Kent Gazette 18 Nov 1922.

'The Father of the Cheap Press. The Interesting Story of Mr Edward Lloyd' *Fortunes Made in Business: Life Struggles of Successful People* (Harmsworth Bros, 1901-2).

Paul Hoggart, 'The Pirates of Charles Dickens' *Times* 28 Mar 1981.

Illustrated London News 19 Apr 1890.

Lloyd's Weekly News Souvenir Copy 6 June 1909.

Thomas P O'Connor, 'The Lloyds' *Sunday Times* 29 May 1927.

Paper-Maker & British Paper Trade Journal Nov 1902.

Paper Trade Review 31 Jan 1890.

William J Reader, *Bowater: A History* (Cambridge: Cambridge University Press, 1981).

Sell's *Dictionary of the World Press* 1891.

Times 9 Apr 1890.

LLOYD, Frank

(1854-1927)

Newspaper proprietor and paper manufacturer

Frank Lloyd (courtesy of Bowater plc).

Frank Lloyd was born at Acton Vale, London, on 18 September 1854, the son of Edward Lloyd (qv), newspaper proprietor and newsprint and paper manufacturer, and his wife Maria née Martins. He was educated at the Wick School, Brighton, and at Guignes in France. Edward Lloyd had four sons in his business and before his death in 1890 he chose Frank, the eldest son by his second marriage, to succeed him by becoming chairman and managing director of Edward Lloyd Ltd. Frank had gone straight into paper-making after leaving school, first at his father's mill at Bow and then at his mill at Sittingbourne in Kent where he became manager. He had his father's keen business sense, enthusiasm for new technology and mastery of figures but in character he was very different. 'Hardness ... was the impression you got of the father, gentleness and sweetness of the son' {*Sunday Times* 29 May 1927}.

Under Frank the two Lloyd newspapers, *Lloyd's News* and the *Daily Chronicle*, continued to flourish and *Lloyd's News* reached the circulation figure of a million in 1896, being the first English newspaper to do so. Frank gathered a team of good journalists for the *Daily Chronicle* and developed the literary and artistic side of the paper. In 1904 the price was reduced from one penny to a halfpenny and Robert Donald became editor. Lloyd stipulated a broad Liberal policy, and although the paper was entirely independent of party control it was an advocate of the Liberal programme. At the same time Frank Lloyd was extending the Sittingbourne paper mills and before the end of 1902 he was manufacturing woodpulp — now essential raw material — at two mills in Norway.

Death deprived Frank Lloyd of the services of two of his brothers and in 1911 he formed a separate company, United Newspapers, for the newspaper side of the business. Robert Donald, who by now was editing both papers, was made managing director and given very full control. In the same year Edward Lloyd Ltd, now concerned only with paper manufacture and wholesale stationery, went public. The company, with net assets at this date of about £1.5 million, continued expansion at Sittingbourne and Frank Lloyd now started building a dock and wharves at Ridham on the Swale.

In 1915 Donald and Frank Lloyd made an abortive attempt to launch a new evening paper, but the *Echo and London Evening Chronicle* lasted only six weeks and Lloyd was said to have lost between £60,000 and £100,000. After the First World War he decided to concentrate his energies on paper manufacture. He sold United Newspapers for £1.6 million to a Liberal syndicate headed by Sir Henry Dalziel and in 1923 he embarked on a new mill at Kemsley near Sittingbourne. By his death in 1927, Kemsley had been equipped with two new wide machines and a third was being installed. A new power house was in course of construction and Lloyd had also installed an experimental groundwood mill, the first in this country. These developments were mainly financed from internal resources. By the end of 1927 production of newsprint at Sittingbourne and Kemsley was in excess of 4,000 tons a week and Lloyds were the largest manufacturers of newsprint in the country.

Frank Lloyd was a Liberal and a free-trader. He was also a paternalist of the Victorian school. He provided Sittingbourne with a sports ground and a clubhouse with cinema and library and at Kemsley he was building a model village for a population of 3,500. He was a generous benefactor to local institutions.

Lloyd married Helen Julia Mills, daughter of Robert Mills 'gentleman' {MCe} in 1881, and they had one daughter. When he died, on 20 May 1927, the company's ordinary shares were sold to the Berry brothers (qv) for £3.2 million. The Berrys kept the company on the course of expansion which Frank Lloyd had set and when Bowaters acquired Edward Lloyd Ltd in 1936 they took over a business both larger and more diverse than their own. Frank Lloyd left unsettled property valued at £679,923, with bequests to charities of over £48,000.

RACHEL LAWRENCE

Sources:

Unpublished

Bowater Paper Corporation, archives, including Reports and Accounts and Minutes of Edward Lloyd Ltd.

BCe.

MCe.

PrC.

Notes from Major D P J Lloyd.

Virginia S Berridge, 'Popular Journalism and Working Class Attitudes, 1854-1886: A Study of Reynold's Newspaper, Lloyd's Weekly Newspaper and the Weekly Times' (London PhD, 1976).

Published

Thomas Catling, *My Life's Pilgrimage* (John Murray, 1911).

Daily Chronicle 6 May 1911, 21, 25 May 1927.

East Kent Gazette 29 Mar 1919, 18 Nov 1922, 25, 28 May 1927.

Lloyd's Weekly News Souvenir Copy 6 June 1909.

Thomas P O'Connor, 'The Lloyds' *Sunday Times* 29 May 1927.

Paper-Maker & British Paper Trade Journal Nov 1902, 1 Jan 1919.

Paper Trade Review 31 Jan 1890.

William J Reader, *Bowater: A History* (Cambridge: Cambridge University Press, 1981).

H A Taylor, *Robert Donald* (Stanley Paul, 1934).

Times 18 Aug 1927.

LLOYD, Howard

(1837-1920)

Clearing banker

Howard Lloyd was born at Poole, Dorset, on 16 August 1837, the fifth son of Isaac Lloyd, a branch manager with the Wilts & Dorset Bank, and his wife Mary née Rigg. From his grandfather, the Birmingham banker Samuel Lloyd (1768-1849), the private banking business had devolved upon Howard Lloyd's cousins, Sampson Samuel Lloyd and George Braithwaite Lloyd. The fact that Howard Lloyd became the chief executive officer of a bank which bore his surname should not disguise the

Howard Lloyd (courtesy of Lloyds Bank plc).

fact that he was from a cadet branch of the family and his entry into the bank was on the same formal, negotiated and probationary basis as that of any other junior clerk of the period.

After education at private schools, Lloyd worked in London in underwriting and marine insurance. After a year in his brother's business, Lloyd & Lloyd, tube manufacturers near Birmingham (forerunners of Stewarts & Lloyds), he then joined the private bank of Lloyds & Co, as, in his own words, 'a sort of Secretary or assistant to the partners' {Lloyds Bank, Lloyd, 'Notes and Reminiscences', 1}. In the bank's eyes he was a confidential clerk on six and, later, twelve months' trial. This lowly start, involving practical experience in all the clerical roles of banking, was responsible for the knowledge of bookkeeping and concern for the welfare of personnel which were the hallmarks of his later managerial career. He became joint manager and secretary in 1865 and general manager in 1871 of the newly-formed Lloyds Banking Co Ltd, the joint-stock reconstitution of the private bank. He held the post of general manager until 1902 when he retired and was elected a director.

Of languid appearance, the result of poor childhood health, Lloyd nevertheless had a commanding presence and displayed the strength of character and depth of moral conviction associated with a Quaker upbringing. His own religious leanings, however, were more towards the Church of England, for whom he helped found a college at Five Ways (Edgbaston), as well as new churches.

Lloyd made a memorable contribution to banking history in the form of unpublished 'Notes and Reminiscences ... Indited at Various Times, and ... Transcribed August 1917'. At once business-like and anecdotal, the 'Notes' provide an insight into Lloyd's character while recording the bank's growth, explaining why the private bank became a joint-stock company and taking occasion to comment on events of wider banking significance, such as the Overend, Gurney failure (1866) and the Baring crisis (1890).

Lloyd emerges from this history, and from the many volumes of his business correspondence, as a tireless administrative banker, often combining the roles of inspector, controller of advances, and head of personnel with that of general manager, whilst accepting that J Spencer Phillips, chairman from 1898, had some executive responsibility. It would appear that Lloyd scrutinised the books of amalgamating banks and found new positions when advisable for certain of their management, while Phillips negotiated merger terms on the basis of Lloyd's assessments. A further key role, from 1884, was his supervision and co-ordination of the bank's two centres of business, in Birmingham and London. Another conclusion from the 'Notes' is that Lloyd played little part in seeking out new business among Midlands industrialists. He saw growth in terms of amalgamations and the result was a sense of detachment from the markets which they introduced. For example, he liked Rugby, as 'a small, pleasant, clean country town' before it 'extended and degenerated into a large manufacturing centre' {*ibid* 25}, although this industrial development brought in substantial new business, following the take-over of Butlin's Bank in 1868. He speculated about why Coventry became the centre of the cycle and motor trade, rather than Wolverhampton or Birmingham, with what he called their equal facilities, energy and capital; but he did not quantify the increase in business brought about by the purchase of a Coventry bank.

The administrative complexity of managing 267 branches did not rob Lloyd of his interest in staff and he was reputedly responsible for accepting all recruits, whether to the board or to the branches. He adopted a basis of mutual confidence with clerks; 'never exacting any undertaking of secrecy, he shook hands and said 'I trust you'' {Lloyd's Bank, Rev Sylvanus Fox Lloyd, 'Reminiscences'}. His last letter to head office in 1920 expressed his delight in the new Widows and Orphans Fund.

A recurrent theme in the 'Notes' is the benefit to be acquired from good premises. Lloyd was often dismayed at 'mean' and 'absurdly sited' buildings acquired by amalgamation and he is reported to have toured with Joseph Chamberlain (qv) in a hackney cab, securing corner sites.

Lloyd married in 1867 Mariabella Howard, daughter of John Eliot Howard, FRS, of Tottenham. They had eight children between 1868 and 1881. In 1902 Lloyd retired to Grafton Manor, Bromsgrove, taken on lease. Although an active member of the Lloyds board until 1917, he devoted himself increasingly to local life, becoming a JP for Worcestershire and living in rural tranquillity. Howard Lloyd died on 17 September 1920, leaving £54,987 gross. His wife died five months later and both were buried at Stoke Prior, near Bromsgrove.

JOHN BOOKER

Sources:

Unpublished

Lloyds Bank PLC, archives, including Howard Lloyd's unpublished 'Notes and Reminiscences ... Indited at Various Times ... Transcribed August 1917'; Walter Barrow, 'Reminiscences', 1953; Rev Sylvanus Fox Lloyd, 'Reminiscences of My Childhood at Cannon Hill House Between 1885 and 1900'.

BCe.

PrC.

Published

Dark Horse (Lloyds Bank Staff Magazine) Oct 1920.

Richard S Sayers, *Lloyds Bank in the History of English Banking* (Oxford: Clarendon Press, 1957).

Times 20, 23 Sept 1920.

WWW.

LOCKWOOD, Sir Joseph Flawith

(1904-)

Industrialist

Joseph Flawith Lockwood was born at Southwell, Nottinghamshire, on 14 November 1904, the son of Joseph Agnew Lockwood, a miller who had married his employer's daughter Mabel née Caudwell. His mother's family had been millers for five generations. On a visit to Manchester to consult with Henry Simon (qv) on the question of building a mill at Newark-on-Trent, his father developed appendicitis and died at the age of twenty-seven. Joseph was then six and his mother was left with four sons to bring up. Joseph won a scholarship to preparatory school at Lincoln and from there went to Newark Grammar School. On leaving school he went into his grandfather's mill but his uncle had two sons destined to become millers, so at the age of nineteen in 1924 Joseph went to Santiago, Chile, to manage a flour mill.

He returned to England in 1928 and joined Henry Simon Ltd. He was sent almost immediately to Brussels, and became technical manager of établissements in Henry Simon Ltd in Brussels and Paris, from 1928 to 1933. During the next five years he became a director of the company's subsidiary in Buenos Aires, chairman of the Australian branch and finally, chairman and managing director of the British-based Henry Simon Ltd. It was during this period that Lockwood visited Minneapolis at the invitation of the millers. He remarked that the flour mills he saw were out-dated compared with the best European ones and Henry Simon Ltd was engaged to modernise a number of American and Canadian mills as a result.

Using his wealth of technical experience Lockwood wrote a standard text on provender milling, published in 1939; and another on flour milling, published after the war. During the Second World War he organised the protection of vulnerable factories, warehouses, docks and other installations in the North West Civil Defence region against fire bombs, and towards the end of the war soon after the Normandy landing and after the end of hostilities for a further year was heavily involved with the working party which planned essential food supplies for the liberated peoples of Europe. One of his plans was to make mobile flour mills in England for use in Europe where the milling capacity of the liberated countries was unknown. As a civilian officer with SHAEF he supervised the rehabilitation of devastated flour mills and the handling and transport of wheat in Western Europe.

Lockwood was appointed a director of the National Research Development Corporation in 1951, remaining a director until 1967. It was whilst on that body that merchant banker Sir Edward de Stein approached him with the invitation to become chairman of EMI, the gramophone company built up in a large part by Alfred Corning Clark (qv). Lockwood

Sir Joseph Lockwood standing next to the original Barraud painting which became the HMV trademark (courtesy of Sir Joseph Lockwood).

accepted in 1954, taking responsibility for a company reputed to be losing half a million pounds a year.

EMI had a fine reputation in the field of classical music recordings. It was, moreover, an innovative firm, having been in the forefront of the development of television and, towards the end of Sir Joseph's term as chairman, it developed the scanner. But the company was not sufficiently profit-conscious. Eventually, the firm headed by Jules Thorn (qv), was licensed to make HMV television sets and Lockwood, recognising that pop music was a growth area, expanded in that direction. When the opportunity arose, he bought Capitol Records, then a small company which after a period of rapid growth became for a few years the largest music company in America. The Beatles recorded for EMI; Frank Sinatra and Dean Martin for Capitol, and the value of both EMI and Capitol shares rose rapidly.

Joseph Lockwood was asked, whilst chairman of EMI, for his views on leadership; he listed eight necessary qualities: the ability to understand human beings came first, followed by common sense, interest in the job and the desire to succeed. Judgement was deemed important as were good health, intelligence and drive. He added that it was difficult to rank the qualities 'but I think that intelligence, though essential, comes quite a long way down in the list' {Rupert (1967) 6}.

Lockwood was a member of the Engineering Advisory Council of the Board of Trade, in 1959; of the Export Council for Europe, 1961-63; and of the Export Credits Guarantee Advisory Council in 1963-67. He was a member of the Industrial Reorganisation Corporation, 1966-71 and chairman, 1969-71. For public services he was knighted in 1960.

Sir Joseph's directorships included Smiths Industries, 1959-79; British Domestic Appliances, 1966-71 (serving as chairman, 1966-70); Beechams, 1966-75; and Hawker Siddeley, 1963-77. He has been a member of the board of Laird, from 1970 to present (1983) and although he retired from the chairmanship of EMI on his seventieth birthday in 1974, he remained a member of the board.

Sir Joseph has made important contributions in the field of the arts, particularly theatre and ballet, as well as to racing and cancer research. He was chairman of the governors of the Royal Ballet School from 1960 to 1977 and has been chairman of the Royal Ballet since 1971. He is also vice-president of the Central School of Speech and Drama of which he was chairman from 1965 to 1968. Sir Joseph was a member of the Arts Council from 1967 to 1970 and has been a member of the South Bank Theatre board, which was responsible for building the National Theatre, since 1968, being appointed chairman in 1977. He was chairman of the Young Vic Theatre Company in 1974-75, during the period of its separation from the National Theatre and its establishment as a separate body, and he remains a director of the Young Vic. In 1977 he was asked by the Royal Opera House Covent Garden to help with their ambitious building programme. He was treasurer of the British Empire Cancer Campaign from 1962 to 1967 and has been a director of several racecourse management companies. Sir Joseph was a member of the Council of the Imperial Society of Knights Bachelor.

JENNIFER TANN

Writings:

Provender Milling — the Manufacture of Feeding Stuffs for Livestock (Liverpool: The Northern Publishing Co Ltd, 1939).

Flour Milling (Liverpool: The Northern Publishing Co Ltd, 1945).

The Tradition of Scholarship; an Inaugural Address Delivered at University College, London 24 May 1946.

Sources:

Unpublished

Interview with Sir Joseph Lockwood 7 Apr 1983.

Published

EMI Biography — Sir Joseph Lockwood (1978).

Anthony E Rupert, *Leaders on Leadership* (Pretoria, 1967).

WW 1982.

LOCOCK, Sir Guy Harold

(1883-1958)

Director of the Federation of British Industries

Sir Guy Locock (courtesy of CBI).

Guy Harold Locock was born at Croydon, Surrey, on 10 July 1883, second son of Herbert Locock (1837-1910), of Frensham Grove, Surrey, and only child of his second marriage to Adelaide (1849-1929), daughter of James Fraser, and widow of Captain Hugh Allen Mackey (d 1877), of the Royal Artillery. His half-brother Hugh J A Mackey (1876-1927) became a brigadier general in the Royal Artillery. His grandfather Sir Charles Locock (1799-1875) was created a baronet in 1857 for his services as physician accoucheur to Queen Victoria, while his father was a colonel in the Royal Engineers who served as Deputy Inspector General of Fortification at Headquarters, 1887-96, and left £57,412 in 1910.

Locock was educated at Wellington (1897-99), and after passing a competitive examination, was appointed a clerk in the Foreign Office in April 1906. (His uncle Sidney Locock had been Envoy and Minister Resident in Serbia during 1881-85.) He worked in the Consular Department, made a tour of inspection of consular posts in the USA in 1912, and was then Secretary General to the International Conference on Safety of Life at Sea held in London in 1913. He was private secretary to three successive Parliamentary Under-Secretaries for Foreign Affairs, Rt Hon Francis Dyke Acland (1913-15), Hon Neil Primrose (1915), and Lord Robert Cecil (1915-17). In the latter years he was much concerned in the blockading of Germany. On the formation of the new Department of Overseas Trade, he was appointed private secretary to its zealous first chief, Sir Arthur Steel-Maitland, in October 1917, and became acting head of the Foreign Section of that department in January 1918. The DOT had been formed to lead and co-ordinate post-war British export policy, and was intended particularly as a weapon in the Anglo-German trade war. However, the Government was faint-hearted in its backing of the DOT, which was housed in small and unsuitable offices in Leadenhall Street, and suffered gross understaffing. Control of the DOT was divided between the Board of Trade and Foreign Office, who proved to be jealous and antagonistic towards the young department. Intolerable working conditions and departmental politicking broke the health of Steel-Maitland and his chief assistants, William Clark and F G A Butler. Locock was 'the first to lead the revolt from the DOT' {Scottish RO, Steel-Maitland papers 193/115/11, Butler to Steel-Maitland 16 Aug 1919}, resigning from the civil service a week after the Armistice in November 1918 to become Assistant Director of the Federation of British Industries, responsible for overseas policy.

The FBI had been founded in 1916, under Roland Nugent (qv) as Director, with the organisation and prosecution of a British 'selling campaign' as one of its chief aims {PRO, BT 55/10, FBI evidence to Balfour of Burleigh committee on post-war trade policy, 16 Feb 1917}. From the outset it worked intimately with the DOT, and took a keen part in consular and diplomatic reform; but above all the FBI sought to disseminate information on foreign markets and opportunities among manufacturers, to introduce them to overseas customers, to compile an export register service for member firms, and to improve the financial facilities for exporters. In the latter context, Locock had many dealings with the British Trade Corporation of Lord Faringdon (qv), and served as a director of its associated Levant Co (1919-26) and Trade Indemnity Co (1919-58), the latter of which provided credit insurance for exporters. Locock was also involved in 1920-21 with Sir James Kemnal (qv) in attempts to form a British-Chinese Trade Corporation under FBI aegis. On all matters within his remit, he showed tact and tenacity, and was friendly and unruffled in his dealings, however frustrating they proved.

The range of Locock's work as FBI's Overseas Director was wide. He was concerned in publishing their Anglo-South American handbook, their journal *British Industries*, and other propaganda and advertising activities. German reparations, and Russian debts and refugees were areas of high policy which he touched, and for example in 1932 he held discussions with Sergei Bessonov, newly-appointed Soviet deputy trade representative in London. But he was also concerned in remedying international postal delays and obstructions to Rhine navigation; in attempts to negotiate commercial treaties with countries as diverse as Spain (1921) and El Salvador (1927); in the administration of the Chinese Boxer Indemnity (1924-32); and in reducing discriminatory tariffs. During the course of ten years he complained to the Foreign Office about matters as diverse as Romania's prohibition of silk imports (1921), French duties on potable spirits and cotton yarn (1921), Belgian tariffs on motor-vehicles and wallpaper (1921-22), regulations on disinfecting straw used in packing merchandise for the USA (1923), Austrian duties on leather (1924), Spanish tariffs on balata belting, Portuguese duties on hats, Polish tariff classification of canned kippered herrings, Italian export duty on crude tartar, Yugoslavia's duty on cotton bandages (all in 1925), Hungary's duty on hacksaw blades (1926) and Dominica's duty on soya bean oil (1928).

A Greek delegation of businessmen visited London at the FBI's invitation in September 1918, and was followed by a Brazilian delegation in 1919, American hoteliers (1926), the King of Afghanistan's entourage (1928), and many others. Locock handled these missions, and was also responsible for the Federation's overseas commercial and intelligence work. Colonel Thoroton was appointed as the FBI's trade commissioner at Madrid in January 1919, and shortly afterwards Colonel Edmund Kennard was sent on a long tour to report on business prospects in the Balkans. Other FBI representatives were appointed during 1919 for the east coast of South America, the East Indies, and Scandinavia (Montagu Villiers, former Commercial Attaché in Madrid), while confidential correspondents were appointed for China and Japan (respectively C A Middleton-Smith, Professor of Engineering at Hong Kong University, and S H Somerton, editor of *Eastern Commerce*). Thereafter Locock steadily expanded the FBI's overseas intelligence function, despite severe financial stringency from 1920 onwards.

As early as 1917 the FBI had established reciprocal facilities with organisations like the National Union of Manufacturers (USA), the Swedish Industries Association and the New Zealand Association of Manufacturers and Traders, and Locock continually developed the Federation's relations with its overseas counterparts. Among other foreign tours, he visited the USA with the FBI president F V Willey (qv) in 1925, Germany (1926), Poland (1927) and Manchuria (1934). He maintained intimate relations with his former colleagues at the Foreign Office, and indeed in 1926 was permitted to wear diplomatic uniform. He was British delegate to the diplomatic conference at Paris on limiting international exhibitions of 1928, represented the International Chamber of Commerce at the League of Nations' Statistical Conference, was alternate industrial adviser to the World Economic Conference during 1933 and attended the Anglo-German Industrial Conference at Düsseldorf in March 1939 upon which Neville Chamberlain placed some hopes.

In April 1932 Locock succeeded Nugent as Director of the FBI, remaining in that post until December 1945. The main concerns confronting the Federation in those years were the economic depression and its aftermath, the rearmament crisis of 1936-39, and the world war. Much responsibility at the FBI for the first category lay with its economic adviser, Roy Glenday, but its calculatedly uncontroversial stance in economic policy undoubtedly reduced its influence. It was unable to exercise leadership in the rationalisation movement associated with men like Sir M W Jenkinson (qv), because FBI membership included many of the ineffective and marginal producers which rationalisation would eliminate; as representative of Britain's existing industrial structure, the Federation was necessarily cautious about rationalisation and defended the status quo. It was prominent in rearmament after 1935, and held a primary role as an intermediary between Government and industry under the vast wartime system of central State control over industrial production. After his retirement Locock was made vice-president of the FBI and listed as an Adviser.

Locock was appointed in 1931 as a member of the committee on the British Industries Fair chaired by Sir Gilbert Garnsey (qv), in 1932 to the British Committee on Empire Trade, to the Civil Aviation Committee in 1934 and to the Census of Production Committee in 1935. He became British representative on the Council of the International Chamber of Commerce around 1938, and was deeply involved in wartime munitions administration. He was a member of the Anglo-French Industrial Council from February 1940, Board of Trade representative on the London and South East Area Munitions Board, and went with Sir Alexander Roger (qv) on the Ministry of Supply mission to India of 1940-41, serving as a delegate at the Eastern Group conference at New Delhi. In 1941 he was nominated FBI representative on the Central Joint Advisory Committee to the War Cabinet's Production Executive, and in the following year he became a member of the National Production Advisory Council and of the government committee on Regional Boards. He served with C B Gardner (qv) on the Reconstruction Joint Advisory Council, and was a member of the committee on the admission of women into the Foreign Service (1945) and of the Civil Service Commission Selection Board during 1945-49. He was an organiser of the British Exhibition at Copenhagen in 1948. He was a director (sometime vice-chairman) of Doulton & Co until 1956.

Locock was created CMG in 1918 and knighted in 1942; he was also a Commander of the Greek Order of the Redeemer (1920) and of the Danish Order of Dannebrog (1935), and received a Swedish decoration in 1925. He married in 1906, at St Mary Abbots, Kensington, Esther Mary Eleanor (d 1955), only child of William James Reade (1856-1942) of Kensington and Folkestone. They had a son, who died in 1945 of illness contracted while serving with the Royal Engineers in Burma, and a daughter. Sir Guy Locock died on 25 August 1958 at Queens Gate, Kensington, leaving £11,738.

R P T DAVENPORT-HINES

Writings:

letter on *Popolo Romano*'s criticism of British business methods *Times* 10 Oct 1921.

(with Colonel the Hon F Vernon Willey) *Report on Visit to the United States of America* (Federation of British Industries, 1925).

article on Federation of British Industries *Times* 1 Nov 1932.

letter on public works contracts *ibid* 13 Jan 1933.

letter on Levant Fair *ibid* 22 Mar 1934.

letter on television *ibid* 28 Apr 1939.

letter on exports *ibid* 21 Sept 1939.

letter on Munich agreement *ibid* 27 Oct 1939.

letter on the *Marseillaise ibid* 11 Mar 1940.

tribute to Dudley Docker *ibid* 11 July 1944.

letter on FBI report on industrial organisation *ibid* 28 Oct 1944.

Sources:

Unpublished

British Library, papers of Viscount Cecil of Chelwood.

House of Lords RO, Hannon papers 12/6, Locock report dated 5 Feb 1919 of political visit to Paris.

PRO, Foreign Office papers.

Scottish RO, Edinburgh, papers of Sir Arthur Steel-Maitland.

University of Warwick, Modern Records Centre, papers of Federation of British Industries.

Published

Burke's Peerage and Baronetage 1949.

Sir William Clark, 'Government and the Promotion of Trade' *Journal of Public Administration* 1 (1923).

R P T Davenport-Hines, *Dudley Docker* (Cambridge: Cambridge University Press, 1984).

FBI Review Sept 1958.

Sir Robert H Bruce Lockhart, *Your England* (Putnam, 1955).

Percy F Martin, 'British Consuls and British Trade' *Financial Review of Reviews* 23 (Dec 1918).

Robert Keith Middlemas, *Politics in Industrial Society* (Deutsch, 1979).

Simon Newman, *March 1939: The British Guarantee to Poland* (Oxford University Press, 1976).

G Springer, 'To Organise Foreign Trade' *Ways and Means* 17 May 1919.

Sir Charles B L Tennyson, *Stars and Markets* (Chatto & Windus, 1957).

WWW.

LONGLEY, Sir Norman

(1900-)

Builder

Norman Longley was born at Crawley, West Sussex, on 14 October 1900, the eldest son of Charles Longley (1862-1931) by his second wife Anna Gibson née Marchant, the daughter of a prosperous Eastbourne farmer. Charles Longley had worked in the family building firm of James Longley & Sons since leaving school and was concerned with its first major contracts: the new Christ's Hospital at Horsham, 1897-1901 and the King Edward VII Sanatorium at Midhurst, 1903-6.

LONGLEY Sir Norman

Sir Norman Longley (courtesy of Sir Norman Longley).

Norman went to school at Clifton and after a false start training as an electrical engineer, joined the firm in 1923 at the age of twenty-two. The business, which had been at a virtual standstill during the First World War, was readjusting to peace-time conditions when it was nearly ruined in 1924 by a devastating fire that destroyed most of its premises, including the important joinery works. Norman Longley and his brother Basil (1904-79) soon found themselves the leaders of the private limited company, of which Norman was made one of the three directors with his father and uncle George Longley, when it was set up in November of that year. The company bought the assets of the partnership, which were valued at approximately £20,000. More responsibility devolved on Norman after his father became an invalid in 1925 and his uncle George died in 1926. On the death of his father in 1931, Norman became chairman of the company, serving until 1970. He was also joint managing director, with his brother Basil, until 1967. The output of the company, valued at around £500,000 in 1930, was worth £10 million in 1970.

The firm revived in the 1930s, partly due to the ploughing-back of profits and partly because, under Norman's guidance, Longleys concentrated on good-quality work for established architects and revived their pre-war speciality of church building and other work demanding a high standard of craftsmanship. In 1935 Norman and Basil appointed Eric White, a qualified architect with a special knowledge of ecclesiastical work, to their staff. In collaboration with White they encouraged the development of carpentry skills in the re-built joinery works at Crawley. Contracts, such as that for All Saints' Church, Hockerill, in 1936, and St Dunstan's home for the blind, Rottingdean, 1937-39, showed the firm to be equally at home in traditional and innovative practice.

During the Second World War Longleys undertook building work throughout the South and West of England: factory, camp and aerodrome construction from 1939 onwards, coastal defences after the fall of France, and further aerodrome work resulting from the entry into the war of the United States and after 1942, pontoons for Bailey bridges. The firm had already experimented with Air Ministry contracts in 1938, offering low tenders to gain experience. Many building sites were subject to enemy air attacks. Norman Longley's gift for leadership and his commanding figure made him a natural focus for a community, which extended beyond his business to include his family (enlarged by evacuees), the local forces of the Special Constabulary, and the civilian and military population of Crawley. Fascinated by the prospects for a fairer society in the post-war world, he believed strongly in worker participation in industry. He established a works council for the firm in 1943, a sports and social club in 1948, and experimented with profit-sharing.

From 1948 to 1958 Longleys played a major part in constructing the public, educational and industrial buildings of the Crawley New Town and in 1953 began its long involvement in construction and civil engineering work at Gatwick international airport. In the same period and into the 1960s it built large shopping stores in Plymouth, Southsea, Bristol, Bromley, Hastings, Gloucester and Guildford. Work on schools (Eton and Tonbridge) and universities (the new campuses of Sussex, Surrey and the microbiology building and department of engineering at Oxford) was also begun under Norman Longley's direction. With the

St Dunstan's convalescent and holiday home for blind ex-servicemen, under construction by James Longley & Co on the South Downs near Rottingdean ca 1938 (courtesy of Sir Norman Longley).

assistance of White, he encouraged the joinery works to undertake fine wood carving for such tasks as the restoration of the choir stalls of Henry VII's Chapel, the organ casings (1952-55) and the feretory above Edward the Confessor's tomb (1958-60) in Westminster Abbey. In 1948 the firm's joinery works were converted from steam to electric power and in 1957-61 the company headquarters at Crawley were modernised and largely rebuilt including a new mill extension.

Norman Longley communicated his enthusiasm for his firm's achievements in the editorials and other items he wrote for the *News Sheet*, a lively house journal he had initiated in the war years. In the January 1959 issue he listed the company's aims and objectives, in which goodwill, fair dealing, team-work, efficiency, quality, craftsmanship and prudence were stressed. By prudence he meant the 'build[ing] up of reserves wherever possible, so that in difficult trading periods there is a fund of strength to ensure continuity' {Smith (1983) 64}. However, the use of the word itself is significant and shows how his pre-war experience affected his thinking at this time.

The post-war successes of his firm gave Norman Longley the opportunity to play a part in the affairs of the industry as a whole. He had originally been shy of public speaking but he soon developed a laconic and humorous style, and his words carried weight because of the experience upon which they were based. He was president of the National Federation of Building Trades Employers, 1949-50, and of the International Federation of Building and Public Works Contractors, 1955-57. In the latter office he secured the adoption of an international form of contract for tenders for civil engineering works, which was accepted by the World

Bank. He was treasurer of the National Federation, 1954-60, chairman of the Federated Employers Press, 1956-65, trustee of the National Federation Pensions Fund, 1954-76, and a member of the Joint Contracts Tribunal, 1954-64. His work for technical education, both in his own firm and in Sussex, made him a natural choice for the chairmanship of the Construction Industry Training Board, which he held from 1964 to 1970. He was a member of the Wilson Committee on Noise, 1961-64, of the Building Regulations Advisory Committee, 1963-65, and of the Industrial Disputes Tribunal Employers' Panel, 1960-70. Recognition for his achievements came with a CBE (1954), a knighthood (1966), an honorary doctorate from Heriot-Watt University (1968), the Insignia award in technology from the City and Guilds of London Institute (1969), and honorary fellowship of the Institute of Builders (1975).

Norman Longley was elected to Crawley Parish Council in 1928; to the Horsham Rural District Council in 1933 (serving as chairman of the Housing Committee, 1946-48 and being much involved in war damage repair assessment); and to the West Sussex County Council, from 1945 to 1961, when he steadfastly refused to accept a party label. Keenly interested in education, he sat on the County Education Committee, 1945-60, and was deputy chairman of Crawley College of Further Education. He was a county alderman of West Sussex, 1957-61, and has been a DL of West Sussex since 1975.

He continues (1984) the work for Crawley Parish Church and the diocese of Chichester he began in 1931. With the assistance of his wife, Dorothy Lilian née Baker, whom he married in 1925, he takes a special interest in the welfare of the aged. Gardening has been a life-long pursuit: he has been a fellow of the Royal Horticultural Society since 1945 and of the Royal Society of Arts since 1959.

When his sons, Peter (b 1927) and Michael (b 1929), together with Basil's son Oliver (b 1933) took over the direction of the firm in the 1970s, more adventurous, albeit riskier, policies tended to be adopted. By 1983 Longleys had become the tenth largest private construction firm in the United Kingdom with an annual turnover valued at £40 million.

D G C ALLAN

Writings:

Editorials and other contributions to *Longley's News Sheet* (later *Longley Times*) published biannually, 1943- .

A Record of Longley's Activities 1939-45 (Crawley: the firm, 1945).

A Year as President of the National Federation of Building Trades Employers (Crawley: the firm, 1950).

(with Michael Longley) *The Development of the Joinery Works of James Longley & Co Ltd, Crawley* (Crawley: the firm, 1984).

Sources:

Unpublished

Information from Sir Norman Longley.

Published

Charles Longley, *Recollections* (Brighton: pp, 1923).

James Longley & Co Ltd, *A Royal Occasion* (Crawley: the firm, 1958).

—, *Longleys of Crawley* (Crawley: the firm, 1963).

Rhonda Smith, *Longleys of Crawley: A Pictorial History* (Crawley: the firm, 1983).

Bertram Newton, *The First Ten Years of the Construction Industry Training Board 1966-76* (Construction Industry Training Board, 1976).

WW 1982.

LONGMAN, Charles James

(1852-1934)

Publisher

Charles Longman (courtesy of Philip Wallis).

Charles James Longman was born in Paddington, London, on 14 April 1852, the second son of William Longman and his wife Emma Pratt née Barlow. Charles was a member of the fifth generation of Longmans, a bookselling and publishing family business which was established at the Sign of the Ship and Black Swan in Paternoster Row in the City of London by Thomas Longman in 1724. His father was the publisher of Macaulay's *History of England* and Roget's *Thesaurus*, among other landmarks in publishing history. Charles went to a preparatory school at Winchester, from where he remembered being taken by his father to visit John Keble when William went to verify some facts in the great Charles Kingsley-Newman controversy before the publication of Newman's *Apologia*. This early introduction to editorial care in the relationship between author and publisher must have impressed the young boy. His education was continued at Harrow and University College, Oxford, where he read theology and law (BA, 1874) and gained a blue for association football in two successive years, 1872-73. Longman joined the family business in 1874 and became a partner three years later on the death of his father.

LONGMAN Charles James

The book trade during a large part of the nineteenth century still followed the pattern of earlier times when heads of family businesses were fiercely independent in their methods, having little regard for the general health of the trade and of bookselling in particular. The gradual separation of publishing from selling to the public, accelerated by the growth of readership, created new problems. In response to these Charles Longman, with Frederick Macmillan (qv) and John Murray, in the 1890s pioneered the famous Net Book Agreement (signed in 1901) which required stock-holding booksellers to sell at the net price recommended by the publisher; educational books were excluded from the agreement. Longman was elected as the first president of the Publishers Association in 1896, holding office for two years, and served a second term in 1902-4.

In spite of these wider activities Longman still found time to edit *Longman's Magazine* for more than twenty years. It succeeded in bringing both regular and casual contributors to the publisher's list, including such famous names as Andrew Lang, Rider Haggard, Stanley Weyman and R L Stevenson. In the 1870s and 1880s Longman formed a close personal friendship and publishing connection with Andrew Lang and Rider Haggard which lasted for forty or more years until their deaths.

Longman was quick to appreciate that the 1870 Education Act would lead to a growing demand for school books at primary and secondary levels, and eventually for universities. In 1884 he appointed J W Allen, who came from the Liverpool School Board with teaching experience, to take charge of that side of the business, as head of the newly-formed Education Department. Allen quickly got to work with a series of readers, geographies and histories. Many of these were still selling forty years later. His own *Junior School Arithmetic* sold over 2 million copies. But Allen's greatest contribution was to pioneer the expansion of Longman's educational publishing overseas in India and South Africa. This growth of business made it essential to open branches in Bombay (1895), Calcutta (1906) and Madras (ca 1918). Shortly before Allen retired in 1933 he opened up new territory in West Africa. There is no doubt that foundations were laid by him on which the future prosperity of the firm was to depend to an ever-increasing extent.

Meanwhile Charles Longman, aided by his cousin Thomas Norton Longman, fostered the growth of publications in many other fields: general literature, history (including the works of G M Trevelyan who followed the Macaulay family tradition), philosophy, science and religion. In 1890 the renowned house of Rivington was purchased which added a fine list in theology and classical education.

By the end of the First World War Charles Longman was sixty-six and had done his best work; his cousin had retired but members of the sixth generation of the family were beginning to play their part. To meet the needs of the post-war era Longman took steps to strengthen the financial stability of the company. Kenneth Potter joined the staff in 1921 after training in accountancy. Potter had been educated at Winchester and after distinguished service in the First World War went up to New College, Oxford. In 1926 the old family partnership became a private limited company, Longmans, Green & Co Ltd, and Potter was appointed a director. Through his family, who prospered in the shipping business, he was able to provide much-needed finance but more than that, he brought a first-class financial mind which was used to its fullest extent during the Depression of the 1930s, and even more positively after the Second World War when reconstruction and expansion were the order of the day. There are few data of firm size until the firm went public. Between 1906 and 1914 turnover fluctuated between £150,000 and £175,000. By 1947 the reputation of the firm was sufficiently strong for it to be converted into a public company, when the issued share capital was increased from £177,902 to £273,480. Potter was president of the Publishers Association in 1959-61 and chairman of the National Book League for a number of years.

Another step taken by Charles Longman and his fellow directors was to find a successor to J W Allen in educational publishing. C S S Higham came to the firm in 1926, a history scholar of Trinity College, Cambridge, and a lecturer at Manchester University. Higham, then aged thirty-six, discovered that the home market was rapidly contracting in the early 1930s and launched new initiatives for fresh overseas expansion. For thirty years he travelled throughout the world on long and exhausting journeys in pursuit of new markets in the developing world, where there was a growing demand for educational books both in English and in the local vernacular. Higham, incidentally, inspired G M Trevelyan to write his famous *English Social History*.

Mention has been made of these three non-Longman directors (Allen, Potter, Higham) to illustrate Charles Longman's foresight in appointing men who would carry forward and enrich the tradition of two centuries of publishing in a new and rapidly changing world. Longman himself retired at the end of 1928. Until his death six years later he compiled a comprehensive bibliographical history of his firm (1724-1800). This entailed years of research at the British Museum and elsewhere, aided by his own private collection of Longman books published during that period, a remarkable achievement for an old man of over eighty.

In 1880 Longman married Harriet Ann Evans, the daughter of Sir John Evans (qv). They had two sons and a daughter. Named after the great Whig statesman Charles James Fox, and coming from a family with strong Whig views, Longman maintained the radical tradition. Yet in his private life he was extremely conservative; he spurned electric light in his London home at Norfolk Square, Paddington, and was never known to use the telephone in his office. There is no doubt that he was a formidable character, not suffering fools gladly, but once his confidence was gained great kindness and understanding were shown. Many young men who survived his strict training rose to positions of responsibility in the firm.

Charles Longman died on 17 April 1934 at his country house, Upp Hall, Braughing in Hertfordshire, at the age of eighty-two, leaving £61,624 gross. His elder son, William Longman, succeeded him as chairman of the company.

PHILIP WALLIS

Writings:

Longmans Magazine Nov 1882-Oct 1905.

(with Col H Walrond) *Archery* (Longmans Green & Co, 1894).

(ed) *The Days of My Life, an Autobiography by Sir H Rider Haggard* (Longmans Green & Co, 1926).

A Letter of Dr Johnson and Some Eighteenth Century Imprints of the House of Longman (pp, 1928).

The House of Longman, 1724-1800. A Bibliographical History with a List of Signs Used by Booksellers of that Period (ed) John E Chandler (Longmans Green & Co, 1936).

Sources:

Unpublished

Reading University Library, Longman archives.

BCe.

MCe.

PrC.

Published

Cyprian Blagden, 'Longman's Magazine' *A Review of English Literature* 4 (1963).

Harold Cox and John E Chandler, *The House of Longman with a Record of Their Bicentenary Celebrations, 1724-1924* (pp, 1955).

Times *Prospectuses* 101 (1947).

Philip Wallis, *At the Sign of the Ship, Notes on the House of Longman, 1724-1974* (pp, 1974).

WWW.

LONGRIDGE, Robert Bewick

(1821-1914)

Promoter of engineering insurance

Robert Bewick Longridge was born in Bedlington, Northumberland, on 2 January 1821, the fourth of eight children of Michael Longridge (1784-1858). Michael, who inherited control of the Bedlington Ironworks from his uncle Thomas Longridge in about 1810, entered partnership with George and Robert Stephenson in 1823 and shared in the management of their locomotive-building concern, Robert Stephenson & Co.

Robert Longridge was indentured as an apprentice at the Bedlington Ironworks in January 1835. After the statutory seven years he studied at Edinburgh University, although his grandson reported that 'he told me that he attended fencing lessons more often than lectures' {Edwards (1978) 13}. He subsequently toured Europe, but returned in the mid-1840s to become manager of the Bedlington Ironworks Locomotive Department, which had been established in about 1837. The Locomotive Department was not competitive and in 1854, the year after Michael Longridge's retirement, the Ironworks was wound up.

The collapse of the Bedlington partnership and the death of his wife in the same year — leaving three infant sons — forced Robert Longridge to search for a more secure, salaried appointment. In March 1855 he applied for the post of chief inspector of the 'Association for the Prevention of Steam Boiler Explosions and for Effecting Economy in the Raising and Use of Steam'. This association, subsequently renamed the Manchester Steam Users' Association, had been established at Manchester earlier in the same year, in response to mounting public anxiety over the casualties and damage caused by high-pressure boiler explosions. The Association's main objective was the systematic inspection of boilers and the setting up of an advisory service for members. The prime mover in the Association was William Fairbairn, the Manchester engineer, and its supporters included the cotton spinner Henry Houldsworth (qv) and Joseph Whitworth (qv) the engineer.

Longridge was selected from amongst 80 applicants for the post: possibly Fairbairn and his colleagues were influenced by his working knowledge of boiler construction and his father's links with the Stephensons. His salary was £500, and his main duties were the inspection of steam boilers owned by the 500 members of the new Association. One of the founder members, Thomas Forsyth, general manager of Sharp Stewart & Co's locomotive works, soon convinced Longridge that the principle of inspection should be linked to the insurance of boilers. Longridge, despite support from Fairbairn and Whitworth, failed to persuade the Association to introduce an insurance scheme. However, when Forsyth was killed in an explosion at the Atlas Works in July 1858, the proposal for boiler insurance was taken up by Benjamin Fothergill, a former partner in Sharp Stewart. Fothergill approached Longridge, encouraged him to resign from the Association, and promised him the managership of a new company dealing solely with boiler insurance. The new company, the Steam Boiler Assurance Co, was formed in January 1859. Fothergill was elected chairman and Longridge was appointed chief inspector and general manager at a salary of £800. The new company was quickly successful, and by 1864 it was insuring 9,000 boilers in comparison with the 1,415 boilers under inspection by the Association. The total had risen to 22,000 by 1871, despite competition from the National Boiler Insurance Co, established in Manchester in 1864. Even the Association had become a competitor for boiler insurance. When the Association offered a 'guarantee' to its members in 1865, Longridge's original argument that insurance would not encourage carelessness amongst boiler owners was vindicated.

Before the formation of the Steam Boiler Assurance Co, fire insurance offices had usually refused to pay claims arising from boiler explosions.

LONGRIDGE Robert Bewick

Longridge's first priority was therefore the settlement of a workable structure of rates and premiums for boilers. Yet by the 1870s he felt that boiler insurance was too narrowly based. In 1873 he urged that company (which had been renamed the Boiler Insurance & Steam Power Co in 1865) to underwrite engine and machinery risks as well as boilers. Engine insurance was introduced as an experiment in 1875, but two years later, as the result of a heavy claim, it emerged that the company's articles of association did not allow for this type of business. Longridge recommended that the company should be reconstructed with wider powers. When the directors prevaricated, he lost patience and resigned in March 1878. The company appointed Longridge's son, Robert Charles (1849-1936), who had been recruited in 1872, to take his place as chief engineer and manager.

As in 1858-59, Longridge was more concerned with the development and refinement of insurance cover than with loyalty to a particular company. This characteristic, relatively rare in the higher echelons of nineteenth century insurance offices, reflected the restlessness and independence of his engineering background rather than the increasingly bureaucratic style of the insurance industry. He now established an entirely new company as the vehicle for his plans for insuring engines and machinery. The new company, the Engineer & Boiler Insurance Co, began business in November 1878 close to the Boiler Insurance Co's office in King Street, Manchester. Longridge became chairman and managing director at a salary of £500 and a commission of 5 per cent of annual profits, and he appointed his nephew Michael (1847-1928) chief engineer. Robert Charles Longridge joined the new company in the following year; the Boiler Insurance Co had dismissed him when his father had refused to agree not to underwrite boiler risks.

Competition between the old and new companies was extremely acrimonious. Although it was not until the end of 1882 that the new company moved into profit, Longridge had a strong following amongst the engineers and manufacturers of Manchester. The original capital of £10,000 and the new company's first customers were drawn from the contacts which Longridge had built up at the old Association and at the Boiler Insurance Co. As before, customers were given an inspection service as well as insurance for their boilers and engines. Initially profits were relatively low, reaching only £25,000 by 1887 and £42,000 in 1897. In 1898, however, the scope for business was greatly enlarged when Longridge initiated the insurance of electrical plant. The Factory and Workshops Act of 1901, which made the inspection of boilers and machinery compulsory, was a further stimulus, and profits rose to £80,000 in 1907 and £142,000 ten years later.

Longridge retired from the chairmanship of the company in March 1913. His son Robert Charles, who had taken over as managing director in 1900, succeeded him as chairman; in 1936 R C Longridge's son Harry Morgan Longridge (1880-1967) became the third generation of the family to serve as chairman.

Longridge created and developed the concept of engineering insurance, combining his practical engineering experience with the zeal for safety which he had inherited from Fairbairn and Forsyth. Although this class of business remained a relatively small part of the insurance market, his achievements as a company promoter were considerable. The old Steam Boiler Assurance Co, renamed Vulcan Boiler & General Insurance in 1896, continues as part of the National Vulcan Engineering Group, a subsidiary of Sun Alliance Group. The Engine & Boiler Insurance Co, renamed British Engine Boiler & Electrical Insurance Co in 1904, is a subsidiary of Royal Insurance.

Robert Bewick Longridge died at home at Over Tabley, Knutsford, on 31 July 1914 and was buried at Bedlington, Northumberland. He left an estate valued at £90,435 gross.

EDWIN GREEN

Sources:

Unpublished

British Engine Insurance Ltd, Longridge House, Manchester, minutes and reports of British Engine, from 1878, and Manchester Steam Users' Association, 1854-1927.

PrC.

Published

William H Chaloner, *Vulcan: The History of One Hundred Years of Engineering and Insurance, 1859-1959* (Manchester, 1959).

Hugh A L Cockerell and Edwin Green, *The British Insurance Business 1547-1970. An Introduction and Guide to Historical Records in the United Kingdom* (Heinemann Educational, 1976).

W A Dinsdale, *History of Accident Insurance in Great Britain* (Stone & Cox, 1954).

N Edwards, *One Hundred Years of British Engine* (pp, 1978).

W Fairbairn, *The Life of Sir William Fairbairn, Bart* ed W Pole (Longmans, 1877, repr 1970).

Robert C Longridge, *Reminiscences* (pp, 1932).

Cornelius Walford, *Insurance Cyclopaedia* (6 vols, C & E Layton, 1871-80).

LORD, Cyril

(1911-1984)

Textile and carpet manufacturer

Cyril Lord was born in the Droylsden district of Manchester on 12 July 1911, the son of Richard Lund Lord, a Co-operative Society stores clerk (and later retail manager) and his wife Kate née Hackney.

After attending the Central School, Manchester, Lord's first job, obtained by his father, was as a clerk with the CWS Bank. It was hoped he would make his career in the bank, but after two weeks, and with a decisiveness which was to become a familiar trait in his later business career, Lord left what he evidently decided was boring work, moving into the textile industry as an apprentice with Ashworth Hadwen, a local spinning and weaving firm.

It was in his late teens that Lord laid the basis for his subsequent ascendancy in the industry: a mastery of textile production technology, gained at night classes in the Manchester College of Technology, which he attended in the evenings after a full day's work at the mill.

In 1935 at the age of twenty-four Lord joined the London laboratories of a firm of wholesalers and converters, Scott & Son. In 1939 he started his own converting firm, Hodkin & Lord, which he sold a year later, joining the state Cotton Board as an adviser with the job of helping to match greatly reduced supplies of yarn to very strong demand, under the wartime utility scheme.

During the same year he was sent to Northern Ireland to help the weaving industry with the technical problems involved in switching from flax as a raw material to cotton, and it was during this period that he formed his link with his long-time business associate William McMillan, a Belfast solicitor.

In June 1945, with the help of a £20,000 bank loan, Lord started another textile merchant firm, Cyril Lord Ltd, in Belfast, with William McMillan. From 1949 he began to acquire established textile businesses. By 1952 he owned six mills in Lancashire, spinning and weaving cotton and rayon and other synthetic fibres, employing 2,200 with sales of £7.5 million, and was engaged in a vigorous programme of expansion and acquisition. Technical work carried out by Lord in these years brought an honorary LLD from Florida Southern College in the USA. Cyril Lord Ltd was converted into a public company in 1954, when £1 million 6.5 per cent redeemable cumulative preference shares were offered to the public; all the £1 million ordinary shares were held by Lord and McMillan. The issue of shares was made to repay the bank loans incurred in purchasing Lily Mills Ltd in 1951 (for about £1.2 million) and the Soudan Mill Company (Holdings) Ltd, in 1953, for about £900,000. The profits of Lord's company (and its subsidiaries), which then employed 2,900 workers, had risen from £15,443 in 1946 to £566,174 in 1952.

With the immediate post-war boom beginning to fade by the early 1950s, and with new suppliers entering the market, Lord began to involve himself, as the decade proceeded, in the textile industry's political issues and in particular in industry lobbying against imports. The main threat at this stage was posed by Japan, which had become a major exporter of cloth to British Empire markets such as India. Demands for protection were backed by Lord with a series of letters from his Harley Street offices in London to newspapers, and by other more unconventional measures. In 1952 he organised a mass rally at the Manchester Free Trade Hall as part of a personal campaign entitled 'Save Lancashire through the Empire'. In a publicity gimmick for which he was to attract some notoriety, Lord disguised himself as a journalist in order to be able to heckle the trade minister, Toby Low, at a meeting. On another occasion MPs were presented with a long-playing record of Lancashire workers demanding import controls. The campaign, in which other textile figures were also prominent, led ultimately to the Cotton Industry Act of 1959 which set out a framework for the rationalisation of the sector.

Sensing, however, that the UK textile industry would have to learn to live with imports and strong competition in its traditional markets (a judgement that has proved sound), Lord also launched himself with characteristic vigour into another field. Cyril Lord Carpets Ltd was formed in 1955, employing 200 people to experiment in making tufted carpets from the new man-made fibres then coming on the market. Others had gone into the much more economical tufting method of making carpets ahead of Lord but with his technical expertise he played a major role in overcoming the problems to create a mass market product. Possibly sooner than anyone else, Lord saw that the tufted carpet, which could be produced much more quickly with far fewer operatives than the conventional woven carpet, would make it possible for ordinary families to enjoy the luxury of fitted carpets throughout their homes.

With his strong Northern Ireland connections (he still had his home in the province) Lord took his plans to the Ulster Government, which at the time was engaged in a vigorous campaign to attract new industry to cater for a rising population and to counter the decline in older sectors. A generous twenty-one year £2.8 million loan from the Northern Ireland authorities provided Lord with most of the capital he needed to set up a new plant at Donaghadee, and the final seal of approval was an official opening in 1957 by the then Prime Minister of Ulster, Lord Brookeborough.

Already a comfortably wealthy man, Lord added greatly to his fortune as a result of the boom in tufted carpet sales from the late 1950s onwards, and always a showman at heart, his riches brought him into contact with a wider social milieu which he clearly enjoyed. In Northern Ireland he bought a castle which he converted into a hotel. He indulged his passion for tennis and yachting, acquired a racehorse and speedboat, which he used to cross the Irish Sea on occasion, and ran a Bentley car. He also gave fabulous parties at his Northern Ireland home to which he brought over his new friends from the world of showbusiness, among them Jack Hawkins, Dickie Henderson, Joan Turner and Gracie Fields. As if to emphasise the appeal which the showbusiness world had for him, Lord, a bald and plump five feet three inches, appeared in a Batman film as the Karpet King of Europe, the Holy Matman.

LORD Cyril

While the Carpets Group (which since 1961 had become a subsidiary of Cyril Lord Ltd) prospered, the other activities of the company were in decline. The main merchant converting business was discontinued in 1957, and textile wholesaling and retailing, reduced since 1959, ceased altogether by 1964. Weaving had been discontinued in Lancashire by the end of 1962, and from that year spinning was concentrated in five mills in Lancashire. Some weaving was still carried on in Northern Ireland, at a factory in Rathgael acquired in 1962. Despite the 'very patchy record of the company' {*Economist* 27 Mar 1965}, there was a big response to an offer to the public to subscribe to shares in the company and the price rose to put a valuation of £4 million on the group (at one point the shares and debentures had a market value of about £8 million). Profits in 1966 were £769,000 with the company at the time claiming some 10 per cent of the carpet market. Public confidence in Lord's prospects appeared well justified, but less than two years later the company had crashed with liabilities of more than £5 million.

With the benefit of hindsight commentators have not found it hard to offer explanations for the company's failure. Even before the collapse, two of Lord's ideas had failed, having major flaws in their planning, for which Lord's own impetuous nature and over-confidence must take much of the blame. With prospects for making cotton textiles in the UK poor, Lord organised a deal with the South African authorities in 1962 for manufacturing facilities to be set up in a Bantu area. Demand for the factory's output was overestimated, in 1965 production was switched from poplins to coarser cotton cloths, and Lord lost interest in the project.

Lord had also embarked on another new project, Cyrilawn artificial turf, but its spectacular launch preceded by some distance the solution of many technical, marketing and other problems surrounding the product, one of them being chemical instability in the dye which changed it from green to blue. Other ill-fated attempts at diversification, where Lord's enthusiasm overcame his judgement and swept aside the doubts of advisers, were an artificial astrakhan he wanted to make after a visit to Russia and a move into the already over-crowded vinyl flooring market.

The collapse came in 1968 following the devaluation of the pound, under the Labour Government of Harold Wilson, which was accompanied by austerity measures to restrict consumer demand. The Cyril Lord Group's vulnerability to a downturn in demand was increased by a move made earlier by the group into carpet retailing. Through a subsidiary, Cyril Lord Carpets Sales Ltd, sales were made directly to the public, largely in response to expensive, large-scale advertising campaigns in the national and local press. By 1965, the company had about 6,000 part-time agents, 200 full-time representatives and 46 retail shops throughout the UK; about 60 per cent of the Carpets Group sales were handled by the shops and full-time representatives. This retail network was an ideal channel for moving the product from the factory to the home in buoyant times but became a liability in times of difficulty. Like others before him, Lord was exposed to the hazards of trying to be both a manufacturer and a retailer and of understanding both businesses.

The first open recognition of the problems confronting the company came in September 1967, when Lord and McMillan cut their salaries by half, and waived their dividends; the showrooms were put up for sale.

Lord himself retired from direct control of the business because of ill-health, handing over the chairmanship to McMillan several months before the final collapse of the company in November 1968. He moved to the West Indies, where he lived quietly. In 1974 he unsuccessfully sued the *Sunday Telegraph* for libel in an article of 17 November 1968, dealing with his sale of shares in the company prior to its collapse.

Lord married three times; firstly, in 1936, to Bessie Greenwood, a newsagent's daughter; there were two sons and two daughters of this marriage, which ended in divorce in 1959. In 1960, he married Shirley Hussey, a journalist twenty-two years his junior. Following the dissolution of his second marriage Lord married in 1974 Aileen, widow of Val Parnell (qv). Cyril Lord died on 29 May 1984 at his home in Barbados.

RHYS DAVID

Writings:

letters in *Financial Times* 19 Aug 1954, 25 Aug 1955, 1, 25 Apr, 13 May 1958.

letter on protectionism for home cotton industry *Economist* 6 Nov 1965.

Sources:

Published

Daily Telegraph 13, 14, 15, 19 Nov 1974.

Economist 27 Mar 1965, 16 July 1966, 9 Sept 1967.

Financial Times 19 Nov 1974.

Stock Exchange Official Year-Book 1955, 1967, 1968.

Sunday Telegraph 17 Nov 1968.

Sunday Times 4, 11 May 1969.

Times 19 Nov 1974, 4 June 1984.

Times *Prospectuses* 114 (1954), 136 (1965).

WW 1982.

LORD, Leonard Percy

Lord Lambury of Northfield

(1896-1967)

Motor vehicle manufacturer

Leonard Percy Lord was born in Coventry, Warwickshire, on 15 November 1896, the son of William Lord, a baths superintendent {BCe} (1867-1911) and his wife Emma, daughter of George Swain of Coventry. He attended Bablake School in Coventry, leaving at the age of fifteen. His early career followed a pattern familiar in an area of specialised machine-building and metal-working. He joined Courtaulds in 1912 as an apprentice engineer. During the evening after his work at Courtaulds he gave courses at technical college to earn extra money for his widowed mother.

In 1922 Lord joined the Hotchkiss armaments company as an engineering draughtsman. When William Morris (qv) bought the Hotchkiss factory and converted it to Morris Engines Ltd, Lord stayed on. He became part of a team of production engineers under F W Woollard, one of the major innovators in production layout and Taylorism in Britain in the 1920s. It was here that Lord was introduced to a range of new ideas on rationalised production and specialised machine-tooling.

Woollard made Lord machine tool engineer responsible for buying machinery for the new Morris Engines plant. When tools could not be bought Lord arranged their design, undertaking some of the work promptly and inventively. When Woollard's automatic transfer machinery proved too unreliable because of failures in electrical components and hydraulic equipment, Lord recommended a new machine-tool layout using individual tools rather than a continuous track, but achieving high savings in time and materials nonetheless. In 1927 he moved to Morris's new acquisition, the Wolseley Co, as a full production engineer. He was partly responsible for Wolseley's rapid recovery in the late 1920s, distinguishing himself in the eyes of Morris by designing a successful side-valve engine for the Morris Minor.

In the early 1930s the Morris companies experienced a short-term crisis caused largely by a failure of product policy with ageing and inappropriate models, and also by the increasingly incoherent nature of the business organisation. Morris decided that Lord should be invited to the central works at Cowley to reorganise production as he had at Wolseley. In 1933 Lord became managing director, replacing E H Blake and Woollard. He promised Morris that he would expand sales to peak levels and re-establish the lead Morris had enjoyed in the popular car market for most of the 1920s. He restructured the companies that Morris had acquired along more rational lines, introduced modern line-assembly methods in a major investment programme carried out in 1934, and rationalised the system of selling and distribution. He also had considerable say on product selection, abandoning the unsuccessful and experimental lines of the Depression period. Morris production was concentrated on a new series of popular cars, such as the Morris 8 and Morris 10 which recaptured the market lead Morris wanted. But in 1936, at the end of an acrimonious relationship with the ageing Morris, who was reluctant to forego control over his business, Lord resigned. The final decision was taken partly because Lord was dissatisfied with the amount of money he was being paid and his lack of a financial stake in the companies he was running, partly because of Morris's high-handed attitude to the Air Ministry in the rearmament 'shadow-factory' scheme set up under Lord Austin (qv).

For a year Lord withdrew from the industry, travelling abroad extensively and then in January 1937 taking up an appointment to run the Special Areas Trust Fund set up by Morris, now Lord Nuffield, to cope with the effects of unemployment in the most depressed regions. He travelled extensively in the United States to study new production methods. In 1938 he was approached by the Austin company, which was suffering from the effects of Lord's rationalisation of Cowley, with a view to joining its board of directors. Lord accepted enthusiastically. His brief was the same as it had been under Nuffield: to reorganise and revitalise an ailing, arthritic industrial organisation. Lord preferred the Austin group to Morris Motors because of its engineering bias; Morris had placed much more emphasis on buying-in components and on selling. Lord embarked at once on a rationalisation drive at the Longbridge works, which was interrupted by the outbreak of war in 1939.

During the war Lord was co-opted by Lord Beaverbrook (qv) as Government Controller of Boulton & Paul Aircraft Ltd, and was also in charge of aero-engine and airframe production at Austin's converted factories. In 1941 he became joint managing director of Austin and in 1945 managing director and chairman. After the war the rationalisation of Austin continued, with large modernisation investment and the introduction of car models with increased standardisation and American styling. He campaigned vigorously after 1945 against the Labour Government's industrial controls, demanding 'freedom of competition ... and freedom to make as many motor cars as we can' {Motor Trader Apr 1950}. During the 1940s Austin's market position was further eroded by the General Motors and Ford subsidiaries in Britain. Austin's net assets increased from £3.5 million in 1938 to £11.25 million in 1950, while output increased from 89,745 vehicles in 1937 to 157,628 in 1950. In 1948 he undertook the first tentative efforts to arrange technical collaboration with the Morris company, despite Nuffield's hostility. In 1949 the limited agreement that had been secured was terminated, due to a great extent to Morris's reluctance to pool technical experience when they were in a stronger market position than Austin. But by 1950 the market share of Austin and Morris together had fallen to 40 per cent from over 50 per cent in the mid-1930s. Encouraged to persevere by Nuffield's personal secretary, Lord re-established contact and in December 1951 reached agreement for a merger between the two companies to form the British Motor Corporation.

Lord claimed that BMC was created to boost car exports, increase standardisation, and achieve significant economies of scale. While it certainly achieved the latter, both in home and foreign markets the group continued to see its market share slowly eroded. The merger was in fact largely defensive, designed to protect both companies from American and British competition. In the first four years of BMC Lord spent £25 million on expansion and modernisation, while he oversaw the introduction of a range of advanced car models, including the 'Mini' in 1959, which temporarily restored BMC's market prospects in the early 1960s. Over this period Lord revolutionised productive performance. In 1939 a workforce of 19,000 at Austin produced 1,700 cars a week. In 1960 23,000 workers each week produced 6,750 cars. During his period as head of BMC the firm's performance was very uneven. Net profits in 1952-53 were £3.8 million, in 1962-63 £9.4 million, but they were higher in the mid- and late-1950s than in the early 1960s. Output figures, however, showed a steady increase, from 278,840 vehicles in 1952-53 to 748,470 in 1962-63. Market share remained approximately the same over the whole period, 38 per cent in 1954, 39 per cent in 1964. Net assets for Morris and Austin in 1951 were £29.7 million; BMC assets in 1956 were valued at £62.6 million and by 1963 stood at £107 million. Lord became chairman and managing director of BMC on Nuffield's retirement in 1952. In 1961 he surrendered the chairmanship to George Harriman (qv), remaining president and consultant for the company until 1966.

Lord lived for a long time in the shadow of Nuffield and Austin. His own meteoric rise in the motor industry was due not to making millions quickly, nor to designing a remarkable car, but to his perception that the long-term competitiveness of motor firms depended on production innovation and organisational skills. These factors had to be blended with an appropriate selection procedure for new models and sound finances, but neither of these on their own guaranteed economic survival. During most of his years in business Lord relentlessly rationalised production processes, the supply of materials and components, and corporate administration. His priority was not the financial success of the enterprises he worked for, but extracting the maximum from the material and labour resources available to him.

Lord also changed the managerial style of the businesses which he reformed, moving away from the autocratic style of Nuffield towards a more rational and co-operative system of supervision. He was more of a chief-of-staff than a general, willing to delegate responsibility where he had no expertise himself. Yet in some respects he was a difficult man to get on with. He was very ambitious, a ruthless pursuer of efficiency and production goals, a strong opponent of organised labour and left-wing politics. His brusqueness and directness were qualities that won respect rather than affection. He was determined from the start of his career to rise to the top. 'If the door isn't open', he was reported as saying, 'then you kick it open' {Turner (1963) 183}. He became a leading industrialist not just because of his skills as a production engineer, which were easy to exploit in a relatively conservative engineering environment, but because of his forceful personality and general managerial skills: his willingness to get others to do what he was not technically skilled enough to do himself. The major drawback to his emphasis on production was that car design remained more cautious than it might have been, and that sales, particularly abroad, and after-sales service received less attention than they deserved. These were both problems that BMC inherited from the period of Lord's stewardship.

Lord single-mindedly pursued his career in business. He was not a 'political' industrialist like Nuffield, though he was involved in charitable projects. In 1949 he set up the Junior Car Factory in South Wales to provide work for ex-miners suffering from pneumoconiosis. He was made a KBE in 1954, the same year in which he was elected president of the Institution of Production Engineers. He was a life governor of the University of Birmingham. Lord was created Baron Lambury of Northfield in 1962, and remained closely involved in the affairs of BMC up to his death. He was a successful spare-time farmer in his later years. His chief diversion was oil-painting. In every other respect Woollard considered him to be 'the ideal executive' {*Motor* July 1955} entirely committed to the business in hand, his ambitions confined to the market performance and productivity of the businesses for which he worked.

Lord married in 1921 Ethel Lily, daughter of George Horton of Coventry, who was in the motor trade. They had three daughters. Lord Lambury died on 13 September 1967.

RICHARD OVERY

Sources:

Unpublished

BCe.

MCe.

Published

Philip W S Andrews and Elizabeth Brunner, *The Life of Lord Nuffield* (Oxford: Basil Blackwell, 1955).

Roy A Church, *Herbert Austin* (Europa, 1979).

Robert Jackson, *The Nuffield Story* (Frederick Miller, 1964).

Motor Trader Apr 1950.

William Miles Thomas, *Out on a Wing* (Michael Joseph, 1964).

Times 14 Sept 1967.

Graham Turner, *The Car Makers* (Eyre & Spottiswoode, 1963).

Frank W Woollard, 'Sir Leonard Lord KBE' *Motor* 86 (July 1955).

WWW.

Noble Lowndes (courtesy of Noble Lowndes & Partners Ltd).

LOWNDES, Noble Frank

(1896-1972)

Insurance broker and employee benefit consultant

Noble Frank Lowndes was born in Gisborne, New Zealand, on 28 August 1896 and was the eldest of six brothers. His father, Frank Forbes Lowndes, after inheriting a small coastal shipping line, had set up a cartage and transport firm based on the wool trade from the outback; his mother, Laura Louisa Lowndes, had emigrated from England with her parents at an early age. So that Noble could contribute as early as possible to the administrative side of his father's business, his education was restricted to attendance at the local primary school. After working in Gisborne for some years, he went to a large export firm in Auckland to gain greater business experience.

Always an enthusiast for the military life, Noble volunteered for the army at the outbreak of the First World War, when he was seventeen-and-a-half years old. He was despatched to German Samoa, where he has been credited with being the first to raise the Union Jack. After six months in action he was invalided home with tropical fever, but was later a member of the ANZAC force sent to England. It was on this visit that Noble contracted his great love of English culture and the English countryside. Wounded in action on the Western Front, he was recuperating when the Armistice was signed.

Noble returned to New Zealand with plans to expand his father's transport business. He was thwarted, however, by the latter's determination to market his patented 'Lowndes safety keel rail'. This involved a commercially disastrous trip to England in an effort to promote the invention — particularly with a view to persuading the Government to make it a compulsory shipping safety feature. The ultimate result, combined with the effects of post-war depression, was the dissipation of the Lowndes family capital. The transport business went bankrupt and Noble was left without employment.

Forced to find his own vocation, Noble became an industrial assurance salesman in Auckland. It was here that he first demonstrated the outstanding natural selling ability upon which he was to base his own ventures. Having been made head of the firm's pension unit (ca 1924-25), Noble attempted to develop more progressive insurance contracts. He succeeded, for example, in selling a combined pension, life assurance, sickness and accident scheme to a Gisborne newspaper, but his company refused to underwrite it. Frustrated at what he regarded as inexcusable inertia, he resigned and joined the New Zealand branch of an Australian insurance company, Mutual Life & Citizens (MLC), where he was mainly involved in life assurance. His success there resulted in his becoming the first member of the Million Dollar Round Table of the National Association of Life Underwriters (USA) from the southern hemisphere.

Lowndes was made manager of the new London branch of the MLC in 1932, but soon felt that his plans for expansion and development in the field of underwriting were not properly appreciated. He set up his own brokerage firm in Gracechurch Street, London, EC3, in 1934 (which became Noble Lowndes & Partners), initially specialising in 'Estate Duty Conservation Policies' and financial services for individuals. The first pension scheme broked by Noble was set up in April 1936 and was based on individual endowment assurance contracts underwritten by the Australian Mutual Provident Society. About this time, he was joined by two former colleagues, Alec Simpson and Colin Stewart, and his brother Colin. This constituted the team which was to build the foundations of the firm. In 1938 the business was moved to 38 Lowndes Street. This was more than mere coincidence, since one of Noble's ancestors (William Lowndes) had been Chancellor of the Exchequer during the reign of Queen Anne, and it was after him that Lowndes Street and Lowndes Square were named. In this sense, the New Zealander was returning to his roots in his mother country.

Noble contributed a great deal to the pensions scene in Britain. He was particularly enthusiastic about non-contributory endowment assurance schemes, in contrast to the typical contributory group life and pension scheme of the 1930s — an American import. Under a non-contributory scheme, Lowndes argued, the whole of the premium paid by the employer could be offset against Income Tax, Profits Tax and the Excess Profits Levy, thus allowing a scheme to be set up at virtually no cost. Under a contributory scheme, and in contrast, the employee could only enjoy a limited degree of tax relief on his contributions. Lowndes was also responsible for the drawing-up of a revolutionary 'Master Policy' for the Odhams Press Ltd Pension Scheme (effective from October 1941), which covered endowment assurance and life assurance, and gave guaranteed surrender and paid-up policy values. Under this policy, the Life Office (in this case, Eagle Star) granted automatic life cover on normal terms without medical examination or evidence of health ('free cover'). The combination of these provisions marked the birth of a new, much more comprehensive endowment assurance scheme. Other innovations included Noble's persuasion of certain insurance companies to grant full war-risk cover on all schemes arranged by his business, through a process of reassurance involving Eagle Star, Legal & General and the Guardian.

After the war, Lowndes set up a corporate trusteeship company, Lowndes Associated Pensions Ltd, which formed the basis of the 'LAP Superannuation Scheme' (a central Master Pension Scheme with LAP acting as trustees). The first clients were Kosmos Photographics Ltd and the Industrial Management Research Association (1946). The innovation was an evident success: in 1959 alone, for example, corporate trusteeship facilities were adopted in respect of 451 schemes. Perhaps Noble's most famous invention, however, was the notorious 'Top Hat Scheme' (1946). Designed for directors and senior executives, the employee's potential salary was reduced and the difference was paid by the employer in the form of a premium to a Life Office under an endowment assurance contract. The object was to avoid a situation in which the employee paid income tax and surtax at the high rate on the upper part of his income and then used the small remaining net amount to purchase a pension. Under

Advertisement for Noble Lowndes which appeared in the Anglo-American *October 1962.*

the Top Hat Scheme, the full gross amount of the premium went towards provision for the employee at no extra cost to the employer. The Scheme was interpreted as a primary method to retain top management personnel and often involved substantial sums. The 1947 Finance Act first gave official statutory approval to the endowment assurance scheme, but limited the amount that could be taken in the form of a tax-free capital sum to one-quarter of all the member's benefits at retirement. Despite this, the post-war period saw a remarkable growth in the number of endowment schemes and other pension plans broked by Lowndes. By 1957 total new sums annually assured under schemes devised and administered by the Noble Lowndes Pension Service were exceeding £60 million. The cumulative total at the end of 1959 was £350 million. By then (according to a survey quoted in the *Times* on 13 January 1960) one in four major British companies had a pension scheme devised and administered by Noble Lowndes — the largest firm of pension consultants in the world at that time.

Obviously, such success was based on co-operation with the insurance companies, but Noble's relationship with them was ambivalent. On one hand, he had a special affiliation with the so-called 'Panel Offices' to deal with such things as free cover — and obviously brought a lot of underwriting business to the Life Offices (many of his senior employees were attracted to his business from the insurance companies). On the other, he often resented the latter's behaviour in the pensions market. Symptomatic of this suspicion was the formation of Noble Lowndes Annuities, which was specifically designed to prevent joint action by the insurance companies to push up immediate annuity rates. (Under endowment assurance contracts, the underwriting insurance company guaranteed immediate annuity rates on the maturing of the policy — 'minimum pension option' — but pension scheme trustees could buy pensions elsewhere.) In 1954, as a prominent member of the Chartered Insurance Brokers Society of Pension Consultants, Noble took particular exception to the Life Offices Commission Agreement. Under this, the commission payable to brokers on endowment assurance schemes (which had been far in excess of that on comparable deferred annuity schemes) was reduced by about a half. The agreement did not discriminate between 'ordinary' brokers and those like Lowndes which offered more extensive services including the formulation of special schemes and general administrative assistance.

By the mid-1950s, Noble Lowndes' reputation was such that it was the only firm of pension consultants to give both written and oral evidence to the Millard Tucker (No 2) Committee on the Taxation Treatment of Provisions for Retirement. Noble played a prominent part in encouraging pension schemes to contract-out of the Boyd-Carpenter graduated state pension scheme inaugurated by the National Insurance Act of 1959 and brought into operation in 1961 (and, partly as a result, new pension business rose to £125 million in 1960).

Noble Lowndes & Partners became a limited company in 1949 (prominent members of the board included Lord Beveridge). Noble Lowndes did not become chairman (the first chairman of the company was Alec Simpson), and from this point appears to have been a 'back-seat driver'. He was particularly active in assessing suitable areas for international expansion. Overseas development began in 1947 when the Irish Pensions Trust Ltd was set up in Dublin. By 1956, Noble Lowndes had established subsidiary companies in Australia, New Zealand and South Africa (subsequently spreading to other parts of Africa) as well as a network of branches throughout the United Kingdom. The 1960s saw expansion into France, Germany, the Far East and eventually the United States (with the first office in New York). Noble Lowndes also took a prominent part in the company's relations with the Government and the Life Offices. The base of the business was extended to include privately administered funds (as opposed to merely insured ones) and personal financial services were offered to directors and senior executives who had largely been introduced to Noble Lowndes through their pension schemes. In 1960 the company set up its own life office (the life fund exceeding £40 million by 1969), and a formal 'Personal Consultant Service' appeared in 1969.

Noble Lowndes himself retired at the age of seventy in August 1966 and the company was shortly after (January 1969) taken over by the merchant bankers, Hill Samuel. At this time the chairman of the Noble Lowndes organisation was another of Noble's brothers, Roy — the three between them held about one-fifth the company's shares. According to the *Times*, Roy claimed that the union with Hill Samuel would mean 'a rounded organisation able to offer a complete insurance service' {*Times* 22 Jan 1969}. The business was bought for £14 million — premium income handled by the brokerage side had exceeded £50 million in 1968. Noble's obituary in the *Times* stated that he had been 'intensely proud of British traditions' and saw himself as 'the wild colonial boy' who had come back to the mother country to make good {*Times* 10 May 1972}. This aggressive sales technique was encapsulated in his motto: 'No one ever buys life insurance; it is sold'. Although he was to be most famous for his promotion of schemes for senior staff, Noble did have a paternal concern for less exalted employees. He believed, for example, that their pensions should be considered as deferred wages, and hence that they should not be expected to contribute towards them. Within his own organisation, staff circulars addressed employees as 'Dear Friends'. They were also given shares in the company.

Despite his aggressiveness in the business world, Noble enjoyed relatively sedate pastimes — gardening and bridge were particular favourites. He was married twice, firstly about 1928, to Maisie Hennessy, from Gisborne, and after this marriage had ended in divorce, secondly to Jane Hose; this second marriage produced a son, Charles, and a daughter, Sarah. Noble Lowndes died in Jersey in the Channel Islands, on 9 May 1972.

HUGH WOOLHOUSE

Sources:

Unpublished

Life Offices Association, London, archives.

Interviews with Michael Pilch of Noble Lowndes and Colin R Lowndes.

Noble Lowndes brochure 'Noble Lowndes — The Top Name in Employee Benefits'.

'The Story of Noble Lowndes' — a History of Noble Lowndes & Partners up to 1959' (typescript, nd, Noble Lowndes).

Published

Financial Times 28 Oct 1961.

Times 13 Jan, 24 Feb 1960, 15 Jan, 22 Jan 1969, 10 May 1972.

LOWOOD, John Grayson

(1835-1902)

Refractory materials manufacturer

John Grayson Lowood (from Men of the Period *Biographical Publishing Co, 1896).*

John Grayson Lowood was born in the house of his uncle, John Grayson of Spink Hill near Deepcar, a refractory-stone and colliery owner, in 1835. Curiously the identity of his parents is unrecorded. John Lowood had a sound education and became a clerk in the employ of the Sheffield & Rotherham Bank, until his uncle retired from his small business in 1868 and asked his nephew to take it over.

The immense increase in steel production and hence in the market for refractory materials for furnace linings from the mid-nineteenth century, together with the continuing development of the local ironfounding industries, led to the development in the Sheffield area of an important and largely new industry, that of furnace brick-making.

The old works were at some distance from main-line railway transport and indeed from the local turnpike road, but in 1873 the genesis of a new works at Deepcar, located close to both supplies of ganister, fireclay and coal and to the railway and turnpike, were under construction on an ample site leased from Lord Wharncliffe.

Lowood's uncle had produced firestone, an obviously non-mouldable material, but Lowood himself produced, indeed inaugurated, a much wider range of purpose-orientated and moulded products, more suited to the customers' changing needs. In 1899 it was reported that,

> The principal producers of fire resistants are Messrs J Grayson Lowood & Co Ltd. Their business was established over thirty years ago for the manufacture of various materials required in the construction of Siemens Crucible and Siemens-Martin Open hearth melting furnaces, Blast furnaces, Bessemer converters, Heating furnaces, Puddling, Balling and Mill furnaces, Gas, Chemical and Glass works, Copper refinery and Copper smelting furnaces, Coke ovens etc, etc. To this firm belongs the proud distinction of having brought the production of this invaluable material to the highest state of perfection, and of having adapted it to uses unthought of even a few years ago {*Sheffield and Neighbourhood* (1899) 238}.

Lowood's success was so great in the new location that it was possible to write in about 1900 that

> From every point of view the business of Messrs J Grayson Lowood & Co Ltd, is one of the most important industrial undertakings in Sheffield, and affords a splendid field for the energy and enterprise of Mr Lowood, in whose hands the administration of the concern is marked by such vigour and capacity ... [and] the era of development which he inaugurated has been chiefly characterised by the substitution of ganister and silica for the firestone of former times, and an entirely new complexion has thus been given to the industry, while the greatly increased usefulness of its products has enormously expanded the scope of its operations. {*Men of the Period* (1896) 89}

Lowood's first lease at Deepcar was signed in May 1873, being taken from Lord Wharncliffe and relating to both the works site and what was to become known as Lowood's Wharncliffe Colliery; the first 'castings' or mineral surveys of coal got were made in July 1874, just over an acre of coal having been mined and a mineral rent of £150 an acre being paid. The mine proved quite safe, and there was only one fatal accident during the years 1868-88. About 1873 the main drift of the Deepcar ganister mine was driven by Lowood, and a lease of May 1876 provided that he should spend at least £650 in building houses or retail shops at Deepcar. In July 1876 Lowood leased a stone quarry from Wharncliffe at Deepcar, at a minimum rent of £50 a year.

By the early 1880s the Lowood concern at Deepcar was growing, and in 1881 a new lease was negotiated for a forty-year period to allow for considerable capital expenditure and return upon it, and with 'enlarged powers', the production being planned to rise from the then capacity of 40,000 ganister bricks to 120,000 a week. In January 1882 Lowood had a scheme in mind, which was apparently implemented later that year, for erecting six of the new continuous kilns, invented by James Dunnachie, with Wilson gas producers to provide them with heat. These kilns were usually in banks of ten (two rows of five), with chambers ranging in state of preparedness from empty-and-ready-for-filling to being emptied of the finished bricks. At that time the ganister bricks were used in Siemens and Bessemer furnaces; puddled iron and mill furnaces; in copper smelting; in glass works and in coke ovens.

Lord Wharncliffe was asked in the 1880s to provide a further advance of £1,000 towards the new works, and ultimately £3,000 (in addition to the earlier £3,000) was provided, again through Lord Wharncliffe, from the British Linen Bank at Dundee.

The Deepcar works were now the largest in the district, the basic raw materials coming from Lowood's own (leased) mines. Beaumont's Colliery in Wharncliffe Wood near Oughtibridge was also transferred to Lowood (from March 1883), and pot clay mine workings — the clay used for steelworkers' pots — are first mentioned in 1886. In July 1889 a major fire occurred at the works and new capital was required for their reconstruction. Lowood was usually chronically short of working capital, and as early as 1886 he had written to his landlord's agent that he 'must either go forward and keep pace with the requirements of his customers or his trade would necessarily decrease, other manufacturers being ready to step in with a supply' {City of Wakefield MD Libraries, John Goodchild

Loan, MSS, J G Lowood MSS}. Wharncliffe was, of course, now intimately concerned in the fate of the works, because of his loans and the substantial rents which he was drawing from the properties leased by Lowood: meetings and negotiations went ahead during 1890 and it was ultimately agreed to 'go public', to enable the necessary working capital for extensions, repairs and reserves to be available. The public company (J Grayson Lowood & Co Ltd) was registered in 1890. A new lease, covering a roughly rectangular area some three-and-a-half by one-and-a-half miles, was envisaged under the new arrangements, and the works were valued at £18,072. The draft prospectus described the advantages of the business: the railway communications; increasing trade and great demand for the firm's specialities; and the successful exhibits and favourable notice of the manufacturing press (Lowood's firm obtained prize medals for its products at internal trade exhibitions between 1885 and 1897); and the overseas markets for refractory materials (which by 1919 included India, China, Japan, Egypt, Italy, Spain, France, Belgium, Russia, Sweden and Canada).

The new company was successfully floated in July 1890, Lord Wharncliffe (who had become an Earl in 1876) offering a subscription of between £10,000 and £15,000 on behalf of himself and his friends. By 1899 the firm was manufacturing ganister or silica bricks; Bessemer tuyères, stoppers, nozzles; steel moulders' composition; ground ganister; and glazed and buff bricks for architectural, ornamental and sanitary purposes.

One of Lord Wharncliffe's relatives had written in March 1898 that 'Lowood & Co fail to get all the orders they might get for want of effective canvassing' {ibid}, but the influential directorship (including Lowood, Wharncliffe and successive members of the coal-owning Roberts family of Sheffield) ensured that the business went ahead. By 1899 the works at Deepcar and the offices and works in central Sheffield, at Attercliffe Road, had been supplemented by works at Middlesbrough. The coal and clay workings at Deepcar were becoming very extensive, and in 1899 the underground ganister workings alone had reached at least one-and-a-half miles from the works and the adit entrance, and in 1900 a new ganister seam was planned at Oughtibridge. The numbers of employees in the mines fluctuated, largely in relation to output and (consequently) to dividends. In 1901 the Wharncliffe ganister mine had 189 employees producing coal, fireclay and ganister, in 1903 the same mine employed 170.

John Grayson Lowood involved himself in a number of civic and social interests. He was a member of the Stocksbridge Local Board, established in 1872, and for some time was its chairman. He was elected to Sheffield Corporation in 1893 after an unsuccessful attempt two years earlier, serving as a member of the Highways and the Watch Committees until defeated in 1896. He was also a fellow of the Imperial Institute, a member of the Sheffield Club and of the Conservative and Constitutional Association of Sheffield, and a trustee of the Upper Chapel (Unitarian) in Sheffield, to which last office he was appointed in January 1891. He was, in addition, recorded as being a 'generous and unostentatious' {Sheffield Daily Independent 2 Aug 1902} supporter of local charities and institutions. In a professional capacity he was a member of the the Iron and Steel Institute, and an associate member of the Institution of Mechanical Engineers.

Lowood retired both from his positions as chairman and managing director of the company and from his home in Glossop Road in Sheffield to live at Swinton Hall, beyond Rotherham, in about 1900. He was twice married, having four daughters and one son; the son was only eight at the time of his father's death. John Lowood died on 1 August 1902, after a very short illness, surrounded by the collections of objets d'art and pictures — the latter of 'exceptional merit' {*Sheffield Daily Telegraph* 2 Aug 1902} — which he had formed. He left an estate of £141,156 gross.

JOHN GOODCHILD

Sources:

Unpublished

City of Wakefield Library, MD Libraries Headquarters, John Goodchild Loan MSS, index cards and notes.

PrC.

Published

'J G Lowood, The Ganister King' in *Old West Riding* 2 (1982).

Men of the Period (Biographical Publishing Co, 1896).

Sheffield and Neighbourhood (Sheffield: Pawson & Brailsford, 1899).

Sheffield Daily Independent 2 Aug 1902.

Sheffield Daily Telegraph 2 Aug 1902.

LOYD, Samuel Jones

Lord Overstone of Overstone and Fotheringhay

(1796-1883)

Banker

Samuel Jones Loyd was bred to banking, being born at Lothbury in the heart of the City of London on 25 September 1796. His father, Lewis Loyd, had trained originally as a Welsh Unitarian preacher and teacher but in 1792 had entered the small Manchester banking firm of John Jones & Co. The following year he married Sarah Jones, daughter of the bank's founder, and then proceeded to transform the fortunes of this bank. A small office had already been established in London, in order to facilitate the Manchester bank's business there, and it was this branch that Lewis Loyd developed to make Jones, Loyd & Co into one of the most successful private banking firms in the country. By the end of the Napoleonic wars, Jones, Loyd & Co had become established as an important and wealthy private bank in London, actively engaged in taking up government loans and providing trade credit, while Lewis Loyd himself had made a fortune through dealing in government stock.

Samuel Jones Loyd was educated at Eton and Trinity College, Cambridge. Although he was made a partner in the bank in 1816, at the age of twenty, he initially took no active part in the business, even after his formal education was complete. In 1819 he became MP for Hythe, a seat he held until 1826; and in 1821 he undertook the 'Grand Tour' of the Continent, visiting France, Italy and Switzerland. It was at the end of that year, when his uncle William Jones, the senior partner in the bank, died, that Samuel Jones Loyd found himself drawn into the bank's affairs at the age of twenty-five. He was the only heir to the banking business conducted by his father and maternal uncles and thus the only one of his generation available to carry on the bank.

The bank that Samuel Jones Loyd joined was a well-established one, operating in both Manchester and London. In Manchester it conducted a general banking business, accepting deposits and providing credit, particularly to the large trading community. It was of major importance within Manchester, as Loyd himself recognised: ' ... I could at any time convulse Manchester by gross mismanagement of my banking business' {O'Brien (1971) Overstone to C Wood, 4 June 1847}. However, increasingly this branch of the bank's business was left to Lewis Loyd's brother, Edward Loyd, to manage, with Samuel Loyd and his father only exercising minimal intervention from London. Eventually, in 1848, the Manchester and London businesses were formally split, with Samuel Loyd retaining no financial interest in the Manchester bank. It was the London branch of the bank that absorbed his attention, as it had that of his father. This bank not only conducted a deposit and lending business, including the provision of credit for those engaged in foreign trade, but also undertook a number of specific functions, reflecting its position as a trusted and safe London bank. Jones, Loyd & Co were the London agents for a number of other country banks, apart from their own Manchester branch. As such they were always ready to supply these country banks, or their customers, with credit or employ remuneratively any funds entrusted with them. This involved the bank extensively and actively in the London money market, where it subscribed to government issues and undertook discount operations.

In the management of this London bank, Samuel Loyd took an increasing share of responsibility, though his father did not retire until 1844 and remained active until 1846, while other partners were progressively introduced, including Samuel's first cousin, Lewis Loyd. The permanent staff, his father, and later the other partners, undertook most of the day-to-day running of the bank, allowing Samuel Loyd to

enjoy frequent and prolonged absences from the bank. His control was in
the field of the general policy of the bank rather than in its everyday
business. Always conscious of the risks involved in banking, even though
he did not have to cope with the problems of note issue and the sudden
threat of redemption, he followed a very conservative policy. A large
margin was maintained between assets and liabilities, further enhanced by
his own and his father's great wealth, as the partners in a private bank
were without limitation of liability. In addition, the bank always sought to
minimise risks by being cautious about the nature and duration of loans. It
was this policy of caution that Samuel Loyd stamped upon Jones, Loyd &
Co.

As a result, he ensured that the bank, under his influence, never
experienced a year of loss, as it had in the past, and that the fluctuations
between good and bad years were minimised. During the 1820s the profits
produced by Jones, Loyd & Co in individual years ranged from as low as
£9,693 to as high as £212,038. In contrast, in the 1840s the range was from
a low of £48,747 to a high of £106,511. However, the cost of this change to
a more conservative policy was that the profits produced in each decade
stagnated. As a result of this stable performance, Jones, Loyd & Co came
to be regarded as one of the safest banks in the country and attracted
rather than lost funds during a crisis, as depositors were confident that
their money would be safe there.

On the other hand, during Loyd's career the nature of banking was
changing as new opportunities became available and old ones disappeared.
The Government, for example, became much less important as a borrower
and alternative uses for funds had to be sought. At the same time the
absorption of individual country banks by joint-stock banks, with their
own London offices and extensive branch networks, removed the need for
London agents. Jones, Loyd & Co could have joined this trend, but
Samuel Loyd opposed the principle of joint-stock banking, as he felt that it
removed the personal control and responsibility which he considered
essential in banking. Similarly, he opposed limited liability, as it removed
a restraint which encouraged caution. Alternatively, Jones, Loyd & Co
could have developed as an exclusive private bank, catering for the
interests of the very wealthy, or become a merchant bank, actively
involved in the finance of trade and industry. However, neither Samuel
Loyd nor those who followed him adopted any of these plans and,
eventually, both the Manchester and London banks were absorbed by
joint-stock banking enterprises when the partners wished to retire. In 1863
the Manchester branch was acquired by the Manchester & Liverpool
District Bank for £437,500 and in 1864 the London branch was taken over
by London & Westminster Bank, for £187,500.

Samuel Loyd ensured the survival and prosperity of Jones, Loyd & Co
during his years of control but, unlike his father, he did not set it upon a
new course which would ensure its continued growth and independence.
As a friend and fellow London banker, W G Prescott (of Prescott,
Dinsdale & Co) noted in 1863,

> He was perhaps of too cautious a character to have created the business, but
> his judgement in managing the banks which were established by uncles and
> his father was unrivalled. He used the large deposits at his disposal with
> great skill and while he kept free from hazardous transactions he did not

shrink from large bold operations when they could be undertaken with a due respect to safety {O'Brien (1971) 1,024}.

No-one doubted Loyd's intellectual capabilities, his knowledge of banking, and his thorough familiarity with financial and economic affairs. However, his wider knowledge and perspective made him all too aware of risks, and so unwilling to experiment in new fields, as his father had done, while he refused to recognise what was happening within banking. This left the initiative to others, so that the bank he controlled was gradually eclipsed and left behind a business which was increasingly being dominated by large national concerns.

Throughout his life Samuel Loyd's real interest was clearly outside banking, in the wider field of economic and financial affairs. He was involved in numerous government commissions into such topics as banking reform, decimalisation, and the plight of the handloom weavers, and was closely connected with the Great Exhibition of 1851, and the development of the National Gallery and of London University. He was also president of the Statistical Society, 1851-53. Apart from these posts, his influence was much more general and persuasive. Particularly during the 1840s and 1850s he was regularly consulted by Prime Ministers, Chancellors of the Exchequer, and writers on economic affairs concerning economic policy and his advice had considerable weight, helping to influence the decisions of Governments and the ideas of his contemporaries.

Samuel Loyd was always much more interested in the theoretical implications of money and credit than the day-to-day operations of a bank or the practical considerations of banking policy in a competitive business world. As a result, the bank which he controlled slowly lost its position as one of the leading concerns in the country, being overtaken by others run by men who knew less about banking but more about how to create, manage and expand a business. His real success lay on the wider stage, in his contribution to government policy making and the intellectual debate. Only a third of his life was actually spent in business, and much of that with great reluctance, only out of respect for his father. When Loyd was created Baron Overstone of Overstone and of Fotheringhay in March 1850, he ceased to have any further direct involvement in the family bank or any other business. He invested most of his wealth in his extensive landed estates, which fell in value with the onset of the agricultural depression of the 1870s.

Loyd married in 1829 Harriet (d 1864), daughter of Ichabod Wright of Mapperley Hall, Nottingham, a banker. He died in London on 17 November 1883, aged eighty-seven, leaving securities valued at £2,118,084 and land worth £3,114,262. This was inherited by his only surviving child, Harriet Sarah (b 1833), who had already received a substantial portion of his wealth when she was married in 1858 to Robert James Lindsay, who changed his surname to Loyd-Lindsay. She became, eventually, Lady Wantage when her husband was created Baron Wantage in 1885. They had no children and the direct line ended in 1920 with her death.

RANALD C MICHIE

LOYD Samuel Jones

Writings:

Reflections Suggested by a Perusal of Mr J Horsley Palmer's Pamphlet on the Causes and Consequences of the Pressure on the Money Market (P Richardson, 1837).

Further Reflections on the State of the Currency and the Action of the Bank of England (P Richardson, 1837).

Remarks on the Management of the Circulation, and on the Condition and Conduct of the Bank of England and the Country Issuers (1840).

Thoughts on the Separation of the Departments of the Bank of England (1844).

PP, HC 1857-58 (381) V, Operation of the Bank Acts.

(ed John R McCulloch) *Tracts and Other Publications on Metallic and Paper Currency* (1858).

A number of other publications, mainly speeches, letters and tracts, are listed in the BL and NU catalogues. The definitive edition of Loyd's correspondence is:

Denis P O'Brien (ed), *The Correspondence of Lord Overstone* (3 vols, Cambridge: Cambridge University Press, 1971).

Sources:

Unpublished

An index to unpublished material is to be found in P Kelly, *The Overstone Papers: A Handlist* (University of London Library, 1972).

Published

DNB.

P H Emden, *Money Powers of Europe in the Nineteenth and Twentieth Centuries* (Sampson & Law, 1937).

Theodore E Gregory, *The Westminster Bank through a Century* (2 vols Oxford University Press, 1936).

L H Grindon, *Manchester Banks and Bankers* (Manchester, 1877).

P Martin, *Stories of Banks and Bankers* (Cambridge, 1865).

Ranald C Michie, 'Income, Expenditure and Investment of a Victorian Millionaire: Lord Overstone, 1823-1883' *Bulletin of the Institute of Historical Research* (forthcoming).

Lady Wantage, *Lord Wantage: A Memoir* (Smith, Elder & Co, 1907).

John Lubbock (courtesy of Lord Avebury and Bromley Borough Council).

LUBBOCK, John

1st Lord Avebury of Avebury, Wiltshire

(1834-1913)

Banker

John Lubbock was born in Eaton Place, London, on 30 April 1834, the son of John William Lubbock, later the Third Baronet, of Lammas, Norfolk, and his wife Harriet, daughter of Lieutenant Colonel George Hotham. His father, who was senior partner in the banking business of Lubbock, Foster & Co, was a mathematician and astronomer as well as a banker: his 'Theory of Probabilities' and his pioneering work on the tides earned him a considerable scientific reputation. He was a fellow, and for some years the treasurer, of the Royal Society.

His son was to prove more distinguished than the father, both as a banker and a scientist. He left Eton when he was fourteen and joined his father in the bank. Sir John's two partners were gravely ill, and in fact soon died, so the boy's help — he was immediately made a partner — was welcome, while his father in any case regarded with disfavour Eton's exclusively classical curriculum that excluded science, mathematics and living languages. At first the boy 'found the City very lonely. No doubt, however, beginning so early gave me a sort of instinct for business' {Hutchinson (1914) I, 23}.

He learned quickly. In his early twenties he suggested, and was entrusted with, setting up a country cheque clearing, for the benefit of banks outside London who were so far denied the use of the London Bankers' Clearing House. At twenty-nine he was appointed honorary secretary to the London Bankers' Committee (which was later to be known as the Committee of London Clearing Bankers), an office which he retained for twenty-four years. His suggestion, made at the age of thirty-three, that the Clearing House returns should be published weekly was adopted without opposition.

In 1870 Lubbock was elected Liberal MP for Maidstone. He took a number of statutes of banking significance through parliament: the Falsification of Accounts Act, 1874, the Companies Colonial Registers Act, 1883, the Companies Acts Amendment Act, 1880, the Limited Partnership Act, 1906, and two longer surviving Acts: the Bills of Exchange Act, 1882 and the Bankers Books of Evidence Act, 1879. 'All sorts of small and in many cases vexatious pieces of parliamentary and other business for the proper conduct of which bankers were concerned were managed by Lubbock', acting together with the representatives of banking interests in the Commons {*Times* 29 May 1913}.

In 1882 Lubbock gave up daily attendance at the bank, but this in no way meant retirement from the City. In 1879 when the Institute of Bankers was founded he was the founders' obvious choice as first president; from 1874 he was prominent in the counsels of the Council of Foreign Bondholders, and became chairman in 1890, its president in 1900. From 1897 he was chairman of the Central Association of Bankers, and from 1898 chairman of the Committee of London Clearing Bankers, retaining both offices until his death. In the last years of his life he was concerned with the developing trustee business of banks: in 1911 he introduced a Trustee (Corporate Bodies) Bill, which passed the Lords but fell in the Commons.

In parliament, first in the Commons and from 1900 in the Lords, he was also active in social reform. His best known parliamentary achievement was his Bank Holidays Act of 1871, the real purpose of which was not widely recognised by fellow members: Lubbock said 'If we had called our Bill the General Holidays Bill or the National Holiday Bill I doubt not it would have been opposed' {Hutchinson (1914) II, 66}. The public at large were in no doubt as to its effects; for many years the first Monday in August was known as 'St Lubbock's Day'. No such easy passage was given Lubbock's efforts to ease the life of shop workers. A Bill of 1872 was effectively blocked and its substance had to await his piecemeal Acts of 1880, 1900, 1904 and 1908.

Lubbock was responsible for many other enactments, some of them useful formal legislation — the College of Surgeons Act, for example — some of them on matters of personal concern — the Wild Birds Protection Act, 1880, the Open Spaces Act, 1890, and perhaps particularly the Ancient Monuments Acts of 1882 and 1901: the Avebury of his title reflected his association with the area which he had personally saved from speculative building.

Despite his active parliamentary career, his principal interest outside banking was scientific enquiry and experiment. As a boy his scientific bent had been encouraged by Charles Darwin, who was a near neighbour of the family in Kent. He was twenty-one when he found the first fossil musk-ox recorded in Britain and concluded that the river gravel containing it was laid down in a glacial period. He was elected an FRS at the age of twenty-four, and when *The Origin of Species* was published in 1860, Lubbock and T H Huxley were Darwin's principal supporters in the controversy that followed. Darwin was later to say that he valued the opinions of Huxley and Lubbock above 'that of any other man in England' {*ibid*, I, 49}.

Lubbock's studies were wide ranging. He was the first man to recognise the effect of the relationship between insects and flowers on their evolution, to use a maze as a technique for studying the learning ability of animals, to discover that ants follow a path dependent on the angle at which light is shining on them, and to distinguish between Palaeolithic and Neolithic cultures (it was he who so named them).

He was a prolific writer, producing some 30 books and innumerable lectures and papers. His first publication, *Prehistoric Times*, appeared in 1865, when he was thirty-one. His writings covered all his interests: anthropology, geology, zoology, entomology and botany, politics, education and, of course, banking.

His books were popular: his concern was always to spread his own enjoyment of knowledge amongst the growing number of readers produced by wider schooling. In the area of popular education his *Pleasures of Life* (1887-89) and *Beauties of Nature* (1892) were best sellers for many years and were widely translated; and his *Hundred Best Books*, listed first in a Working Men's College lecture in 1885, eventually became a popular guide for two decades of self-education. The list set a higher standard than we should expect today, including Marcus Aurelius, Epictetus, Spinoza and Confucius.

Lubbock remained a personal friend of Gladstone after he had parted political company with him over Home Rule. But he was not party-politically minded. He never sought political office, devoting his remarkable energy in parliament to his private member legislation (it may be questioned whether any other private member has ever achieved as much as he did), and outside parliament to his multifarious interests and the innumerable associations that sought his services. He was president of the Proportional Representation Society, in the cause of which he campaigned and wrote. From 1872 to 1880 he was vice-chancellor of London University, and in 1860 became MP for the University. Among very much else he was first president of the Anthropological Institute, vice-president of the Royal Society, first president of the International Institute of Sociology, president of the International Library Association and president of the British Association in its jubilee year. He was president of the London Chamber of Commerce, 1888-93, and a member of the London County Council, 1889-92, its vice-chairman, 1889-90, chairman, 1890-92 and alderman, 1892-98.

Lubbock found time for relaxation as well; he played cricket and golf, and was fond of whist. Contemporary record shows that his concern for social reform was based on an exceptionally kindly nature: affection combined with admiration for a man of extraordinary ability who sought no personal aggrandisement. On his death, the *Bankers' Magazine* said 'he had come to be regarded almost in the light of the father of banking in the City, and we would fancy that there would be few of the most prominent bankers of the present day who would not have been prepared at all times to yield precedence to the late Lord Avebury' {*Bankers Magazine* 1913}.

Lubbock married in 1856 Ellen, daughter of Rev Peter Hordern of Chorlton-cum-Hardy in Lancashire; they had three sons and three daughters. After his first wife's death in 1879, he married in 1884, Alice, daughter of Lieutenant General Augustus Pitt-Rivers, the archaeologist; they had three sons and two daughters. Lord Avebury died of heart failure, following influenza, on 28 May 1913, at his house on the Kent coast, Kingsgate Castle (his family home was High Elms, Downe, in Kent). His estate was proved at £315,137.

P EYNON SMART

Writings:

This list excludes his natural history and political works and his numerous prefaces and introductions to other authors' works.

PD, 3rd ser 199-4th ser; *PD*, HL 5th ser 1-13.

On the Bank Act of 1844 (1873).

LUBBOCK John

Fifty Years of Science (Macmillan & Co, 1882).

Representation (Swan Sonnenschein & Co, 1885).

The Pleasures of Life (2 vols, Macmillan & Co, 1887-89).

Sir J Lubbock's Hundred Books (C Routledge & Sons, 1891).

The Use of Life (Macmillan & Co, 1894).

'The History of Money' in *The King's Weigh House Lectures to Business Men* (Macmillan & Co, 1901).

A Short History of Coins and Currency (John Murray, 1902).

Free Trade and British Commerce (Cobden Club, 1902).

Essays and Addresses, 1900-3 (Macmillan & Co, 1903).

Municipal Trading (Industrial Reform League, 1903).

Happiness and Thrift: An Address to the Members of the Booksellers' Provident Institution (Macmillan & Co, 1905).

On Municipal and National Trading (Macmillan & Co, 1906).

'The Case for Free Trade' *Financial Review of Reviews* Apr 1908.

Peace and Happiness (Macmillan & Co, 1909).

Sources:

Unpublished

MCe.

PrC.

Published

Bankers' Magazine 96 (1913).

DNB.

The Hon Mrs Adrian Grant Duff (ed), *The Life-Work of Lord Avebury* (Watts & Co, 1924).

Horace G Hutchinson, *Life of Sir John Lubbock, Lord Avebury* (2 vols, Macmillan & Co, 1914).

Proceedings of the Royal Society 87 B (1913-14).

Times 29 May 1913.

WWMP.

WWW.

LUCAS, Joseph

(1834-1902)

Lamp manufacturer

Joseph Lucas (courtesy of Lucas Industries plc).

Joseph Lucas was born in Birmingham on 12 April 1834. His father described himself as a brazier of plated wares, and Joseph followed the same trade initially, becoming in due course an electro-plater journeyman.

A craftsman by heredity, Joseph Lucas also had a strong streak of independence and enterprise. In 1860 he set up in business on his own account, buying and selling — and later manufacturing — various items of household hollow-ware, as well as selling paraffin (which had just been introduced) from door-to-door in the neighbouring streets. In 1869 his name appeared for the first time in *White's Birmingham Directory* as a lamp and oil dealer.

It was as a manufacturer of lamps that Joseph Lucas established himself in the early 1870s, producing a wide range of oil and candle lamps and lanterns. The most important was the 'Tom Bowling' ship lamp, a name Joseph also used for the small two-storey workshop in Little King Street into which he moved in 1875.

By the mid-1870s a vast new market for lamps was provided by the rapidly increasing popularity of the bicycle. Joseph eagerly seized this opportunity, producing his first bicycle lamp, 'The King of the Road', for the penny-farthing in 1875.

In 1872 Lucas was joined by Harry, his seventeen-year-old eldest son, who was to prove an invaluable assistant. When Harry had completed ten years of training Joseph decided to take him into formal partnership, changing the trade name of the business from Joseph Lucas to Joseph Lucas & Son. During the next fifteen years father and son took the maximum advantage of the bicycle boom, ploughing back their profits into the business and expanding their catalogue of Lucas bicycle lamps and accessories. More production space was needed as sales rose from £47,000 in 1894 to over £125,000 in 1897; the annual profit averaged £23,000 in these three years. The payroll had risen to nearly 700 with more hands being taken on during the season. New factory premises were developed on the site around Great King Street which is still (1984) the central headquarters of the modern Lucas group.

To pay for all this construction work and new plant Joseph Lucas & Son was converted into a public company in 1897. The new company, Joseph Lucas Ltd was incorporated with a capital of £225,000. The two partners were paid £170,000 for their business in cash and shares and remained in charge as chairman and joint managing director.

Joseph Lucas died on 27 December 1902, aged sixty-eight, after catching typhoid fever when the ship in which he and his wife were cruising in the Mediterranean called at Naples. He was survived by his third wife, Mary Anne (née Owen), whom he had married the year before, and six children

The original Lucas 'Tom Bowling' lamp (courtesy of Lucas Industries plc).

by his first wife, Emily (née Stevens), who died in 1885. He left an estate valued at £92,163 gross.

HAROLD NOCKOLDS

Writings:

A Fireside Chat on the Commercial Side of Life (pp by Mary Anne Lucas, 1906).

Sources:

Unpublished

Lucas Industries Ltd, archives.

PrC.

Published

Harold Nockolds, *Lucas — The First 100 Years* (2 vols, Newton Abbot: David & Charles, 1976-78).

Sir Edwin Lutyens (courtesy of the National Portrait Gallery).

LUTYENS, Sir Edwin Landseer

(1869-1944)

Architect

Edwin Landseer Lutyens was born at Kensington, London, on 29 March 1869 and was named after his godfather Sir Edwin Landseer, the painter. He was the tenth of the thirteen children of Charles Henry Augustus Lutyens (1829-1915), a painter of horses and hunting scenes, and his wife Mary Teresa née Gallwey (1833-1904), sister of Thomas (later Sir Thomas) Gallwey, who became Governor of Bermuda. A victim of rheumatic fever, Edwin did not join his brothers at public school and university and he was educated by a governess. Home life in Surrey allowed him to develop a passionate interest in domestic buildings, crafts, and materials, and by the age of fifteen it was assumed that he would become an architect. He enrolled at the Kensington School of Art (now the Royal College of Art) in 1895 but gave up the course a year later to become apprenticed to Ernest George & Peto, a successful architectural practice. In 1889, on the strength of a commission to build a house for Arthur Chapman at Crooksbury, near Farnham, he set up his own practice at 6 Gray's Inn Square.

Edwin Lutyens's early reputation and first contacts with clients relied heavily upon his family's Surrey neighbours. He had been introduced to Chapman by the Webbs of Milford, near Godalming, and the Chapmans in turn introduced him to Gertrude Jekyll (1843-1932), the garden designer. Miss Jekyll commissioned him to build a cottage and house at Munstead Wood, near Godalming, and in subsequent years Lutyens and Gertrude Jekyll collaborated in a series of over 50 major garden designs. Miss Jekyll's patronage also brought Lutyens into a circle of important clients, notably the Jekyll and Horner families and Princess Louise. The most influential of his new contacts was Edward Hudson, proprietor of *Country Life* magazine which he founded in 1897. In addition to commissioning Lutyens for Deanery Gardens, Sonning, Berkshire (1899), Lindisfarne Castle (1903), and the Country Life Building in Tavistock Street, London (1904), from 1900 Hudson also gave Lutyens generous coverage in his new magazine and in a companion series of books. *Country Life*, tailored specifically for wealthy property-owners, was the ideal market-place for Lutyens's style of country houses. Some of his most distinctive work was carried out for Hudson's friends and readers. These commissions included Marsh Court, Hampshire (1901) for the stockbroker Herbert Johnson, and Dormy House, Walton on the Hill, Surrey (1906), for George Riddell (qv), chairman of *News of the World*.

Whereas before 1900 Lutyens had won commissions from a relatively small circle of friends and neighbours, after 1900 the *Country Life* connection was essential to maintain a steady flow of commission income. In 1897 he had married Lady Emily Lytton, daughter of the First Earl of Lytton (1831-91), a former Viceroy of India. Before consenting to the marriage, the Lytton family insisted that he insured his life for £10,000 and that he should maintain a net annual income of at least £1,000. These were heavy demands, which Lutyens himself reckoned would require contracts worth at least £29,000 each year. Large outgoings for their home at 29 Bloomsbury Square and for their family of five children — one son and four daughters (born between 1898 and 1908) — rapidly increased his burden. In response, Lutyens took on over 120 new commissions in the first ten years of his marriage, and his net income increased to nearly £2,900 by 1904. His original staff of one assistant increased to eight when the office was moved to Bloomsbury Square in 1898. The appointment of A J Thomas as office manager in 1902 simplified the administration of the practice.

By 1909, when his practice was twenty years old, Lutyens was recognisably 'the leading architect of country houses on the ample scale' {Richardson (1973) 6}. Some of his competitors attributed his success to his wife's connections, but with very few exceptions his clients were introduced through the Jekyll circle or through the *Country Life* following. His clients were predominantly from the worlds of finance, industry and the arts rather than from the aristocracy. They included, for example, the bankers Henry Farrer (The Salutation, Sandwich, Kent, 1911) and Lord Revelstoke (qv) (Lambay Castle, Dublin, 1905-12), the tobacco magnate W G Player (qv) (Ednaston Manor, Derbyshire, 1912-13) and Julius Drewe (qv), founder of Home & Colonial Stores (Castle Drogo, Devon, 1910-30). Even private clients in politics and Government such as Alfred Lyttelton, Lord Haldane and Reginald McKenna (qv) were linked with the Jekyll and Horner families rather than with the Lyttons.

Successful as Lutyens had been in attracting commissions for country houses, the tax and death duty provisions in Lloyd George's 1909 Budget brought an end to the age of large and plentiful private contracts. Lutyens now found himself 'frequenting the market-place more than had been his wont, convincing committees, dealing with politicians and administrators' {Hussey (1950) 186}. He was nervous about his prospects in these new conditions, especially after his failure in the London County Council's prestigious competition for the County Hall in 1908: 'I imagined all sorts and kinds of horrible ignorant and unsympathetic men, though they very seldom are' {Lutyens (1980) 84}. These fears were misplaced. From about 1910, when the practice was moved next door to Hudson's house in Queen Anne's Gate, the major part of Lutyens's income came from public or commercial projects.

One of Edwin Lutyens drawings, from the RIBA drawings collection.

The centrepiece of these projects was his work on New Delhi. Reginald Blomfield, then president of the Royal Institute of British Architects, recommended him to the Indian Government shortly after King George V had announced the creation of the new capital in 1911. With Herbert Baker, Lutyens was one of the two principal architects for the scheme and his responsibilities included the Viceroy's House and its Mogul Garden and the government records office. The project was politically, financially and artistically controversial, most obviously in Lutyens's case in his long and bitter feud with Baker over the siting of the approach to the Viceroy's House. Yet the scale and duration of the project transformed Lutyens's practice. Before his appointment in 1912 his office expenses were apparently only half those of Baker. After his appointment, it was necessary to establish a separate office to handle the Delhi work. In addition to expenses, Lutyens and Baker both received advisers' fees of £1,000 each year until the scheme was completed in 1931, but Lutyens's net total income for architects' fees for Delhi was only £5,000 between 1912 and 1929. For the first fifteen years of the project both he and Baker were working at a loss. The New Delhi project was not the only factor in the expansion of the practice. His work on Hampstead Garden Suburb (1908-20) and New Delhi made him a first choice for public commissions during and after the First World War. With Blomfield and Baker, he was appointed a Principal Architect to the Imperial War Graves Commission in 1918. He was directly or indirectly responsible for 126 war cemeteries, including the Memorial to the Missing of the Somme at Thiepval (1927-32). At Lloyd George's invitation he also designed the Cenotaph, Whitehall, in 1919, an achievement which 'suddenly made him into the most famous architect in the British Empire' {Amery and Richardson (1981) 149}.

In the 1920s the Delhi and War Graves projects continued to provide the practice with an enormous volume of work at very low margins of return. Lutyens's financial position was also jeopardised by a number of time-consuming commissions for which he received little or no payment. The Doll's House for Queen Mary, which earned thousands of pounds for charity at the British Empire Exhibition in 1924, was intended as a gift, while all his work for Lady Sackville was an expensive loss. This generosity was combined with an extremely vulnerable tax position, eventually forcing him to pay £10,000 in back taxes in 1930. Savings which he had built up before the war were barely maintained and throughout the 1920s he suffered 'aching anxiety' from the twin threats of tax claims and a large bank overdraft. He was not helped by his refusal to employ an accountant either in his practice or in his increasingly complex family finances.

These anxieties increased when the New Delhi project came to an end in 1931 and the Depression effectively stopped the thin trickle of country house commissions. The Delhi office was closed and the practice moved to a single office at 5 Eaton Square. His position was only relieved by a series of commercial building projects, particularly Britannic House (1920-24) for the Anglo-Persian Oil Co and four buildings, including the head office at Poultry, for the Midland Bank, where Reginald McKenna was then chairman. After 1929, however, the practice was dominated by work on the proposed Metropolitan Cathedral of Liverpool, for which he was appointed architect in 1929. The crypt was completed in 1941, but by 1953 the original estimates of £3 million had increased to £27 million and the project was abandoned. His other later projects included the Page Street housing scheme, Westminster (1929-30), Reuter's building in Fleet Street (1935), the Bressey-Lutyens Highway Development Report (1935-39), the post-war London reconstruction scheme (1942-43), and schemes for a National Theatre on the South Bank.

Edwin Lutyens saw himself as an architect, craftsman and designer rather than as a businessman, and he would have denied that he was a business leader. His career was shadowed by financial uncertainties and misjudgements, and many of his large projects were bedevilled by errors in the building estimates. Nevertheless he was unrivalled in his success in attracting work, first as a country house designer, later as the architect of major public and commercial buildings. Of the total of over 750 works which he carried out (including memorials, cemeteries and unexecuted designs), a very high proportion were cases where Lutyens was commissioned as a matter of prestige. His leadership of the architectural profession was not in doubt, especially after the First World War.

Knighted in 1918 and created KCIE in 1930, he became a Royal Academician in 1920 and president of the Academy in 1938. When he was awarded the Order of Merit in 1942, he was the first architect ever to join the Order.

Lutyens was still at work on the Liverpool Cathedral scheme when he died of lung cancer on 1 January 1944. After a long period of financial strain, his savings had dwindled to £18,000. The estate was eventually valued at £42,271 gross. His office, which had been moved to his house at 13 Mansfield Street in 1939, was taken over by the architectural practice of his son Robert, with whom Lutyens had collaborated since the departure of his assistant A J Thomas in 1935.

EDWIN GREEN

Writings:

Ministry of Development Survey 1937. Greater London (1938).

(with Sir Leslie Patrick Abercrombie) *A Plan for the City of Kingston upon Hull. Prepared for the City Council* (1945).

Sources:

Unpublished

Royal Institute of British Architects Library, Portland Place, London, papers of Sir Edwin Lutyens.

BCe.

MCe.

Published

Colin Amery and Margaret Richardson (eds), *Lutyens. The Work of the English Architect Sir Edwin Lutyens* (Arts Council of Great Britain, 1981).

DNB.

David Dunster (ed), *Edwin Lutyens* (Academy Editions, 1979).

Edwin Green, *Buildings for Bankers. Sir Edwin Lutyens and the Midland Bank 1921-1939* (Midland Bank, 1980).

Christopher Edward Clive Hussey, *The Life of Sir Edwin Lutyens* (Country Life, 1950).

Robert Grant Irving, *Indian Summer, Lutyens, Baker and Imperial Delhi* (Yale University Press, 1981).

Mary Lutyens, *Edwin Lutyens* (John Murray, 1980).

Daniell O'Neill, *Lutyens Country Houses* (Lund Humphries, 1980).

Margaret Richardson, *Catalogue of the Drawings Collection of the Royal Institute of British Architects. Edwin Lutyens* (Gregg International Publishers, 1973).

WWW.

Leonard Lyle, Lord Lyle of Westbourne, 1954 (courtesy of Tate & Lyle Ltd).

LYLE, Charles Ernest Leonard

1st Lord Lyle of Westbourne

(1882-1954)

Sugar refiner

Charles Ernest Leonard (known as Leonard) Lyle was born in Edmonton, Middlesex, on 22 July 1882, the son of Charles Lyle and his wife Margaret, daughter of James Brown of Dunedin. The Lyles were a family of shipowners based at Greenock. In 1865 Abram Lyle III, Leonard's grandfather, and four friends bought the Glebe Sugar Refining Co in Greenock. Leonard's father, Charles (1851-1929), began to work in the refinery in 1872. Some years later, the Lyles sold their interest in the Glebe and moved to London to build the Plaistow Sugar refinery. The refinery itself, built in 1881, was supervised by Charles Lyle (who was the most technically minded of the seven Lyle brothers). Most of the workers at the refinery were brought from Greenock with their families. In 1890 Abram Lyle & Sons, a private limited company was formed; its capital of £287,000 was divided equally between the six sons of Abram III.

Leonard Lyle was educated at Harrow and Trinity Hall, Cambridge. He joined Abram Lyle & Sons in 1903. On the retirement of his father in 1909 Leonard became a director of the company, which was still very much a family concern. All the directors were Lyles and other members of the family were also employed at the refinery and in recruiting workers in Greenock. Nothing is known of Leonard's particular role within the company.

Since 1880 the sugar refining business had been through very difficult times, mainly due to the competition of subsidised continental white beet sugar. Lyles were one of the few companies which managed to survive, thanks mainly to their technical knowledge and to the production of their famous 'Lyle's Golden Syrup' which began to be sold in cans in 1885.

By 1914, Abram Lyle & Sons was a well-run, but still only medium-sized family firm. During the war, like other refiners such as Tates, Lyles benefited from the decrease in competition, but Lyles did particularly well, because their Golden Syrup was not subject to price controls. In 1919 the company was converted into a public one, although the capital at first remained in the hands of the family (shares were offered to some non-family employees in 1920).

During the First World War, Leonard Lyle had left the company, serving as a captain in the Royal Army Service Corps and in the British Red Cross Society. In 1918 he was elected Coalition Unionist MP for the Stratford Division of West Ham, and served as Parliamentary Private Secretary to the Food Controller, Charles McCurdy, for a year from March 1920.

In 1921, Abram Lyle & Sons merged with the other great British refiner, Henry Tate & Sons. In 1918 the two Tate refineries had produced one-

Leonard Lyle laying the foundation stone at the Plaistow refinery in 1946 (courtesy of Tate & Lyle Ltd).

third of the sugar refined in Britain, and Lyle's Plaistow refinery about 13 per cent. Abram Lyle & Sons was sold to the new company, Tate & Lyle, for £2,862,000. The former shareholders of Lyles and Tates were attributed equal shares in the £1.1 million 6.5 per cent preference shares and £3,312,000 ordinary shares of the new company, and control was also equally divided. Leonard Lyle was made a director of the new company.

Lyle continued to serve in the Commons until his defeat in the election of November 1922. Elected Unionist MP for Epping in 1923, he resigned from the Commons in October 1924 to work full-time for Tate & Lyle. However, during his short political career he became a friend of Winston Churchill and of F E Smith, the First Earl of Birkenhead (who joined Tate & Lyle's board in 1928 when Leonard himself was elected chairman). Sir Leonard Lyle's political relations and his friendship with Churchill were very useful for Tate & Lyle and other sugar refiners who obtained a particularly favourable tariff in the 1928 budget. Knighted in 1923, Lyle was made a baronet in 1932.

Sir Leonard's tenure as chairman of Tate & Lyle (1928-38) was marked by the consolidation of the company as the main sugar refiner in Britain. In 1923 the three refineries of Tate & Lyle in London and Liverpool had produced about half of the total British output of refined sugar. In 1928 the company acquired 55 per cent of the £200,000 share capital of John Walker of Greenock, giving it a foothold in the third major centre of UK sugar refining (and, through Walkers, a half share in the old firm of Abram Lyle, the Glebe Sugar Refining Co). In 1929, the refinery of Fairrie Bros of Liverpool was acquired for about £500,000. The acquisition of another Liverpool refinery, that of Macfie & Sons, in 1938, gave Tate & Lyle 75 per cent of sugar refining capacity in the UK. During this period Tate & Lyle became involved in beet sugar production, which

The cartoon character Mr Cube in his fight against the nationalisation of sugar refining (courtesy of Tate & Lyle Ltd).

it had begun in 1925. In 1932 the 'Bury group' of factories controlled by Tate & Lyle represented 28 per cent of British raw beet sugar production. But in 1936, following recommendations from the Greene Committee, all beet sugar factories were amalgamated into the British Sugar Corporation, which exercised a monopoly. Ousted from sugar production in Britain, Tate & Lyle looked to alternative sources and, after some studies ordered by Sir Leonard, bought in 1938 cane estates and factories in the West Indies (Jamaica and Trinidad).

On retiring in 1938 Sir Leonard became president of the company, at that time a purely honorary position. But during the Second World War, as most of Tate & Lyle's directors were in the army or involved in other war work (Leonard's son Charles was in the Sugar Division of the Ministry of Food), he resumed some responsibilities in the company.

In 1940 Sir Leonard had returned to the House of Commons, this time as Conservative MP for Bournemouth. He did not seek re-election in July 1945 but left his seat to Churchill's close friend Brendan Bracken. This might be one of the reasons why Churchill gave Lyle an hereditary peerage in his resignation honours list. He took the title Lord Lyle of Westbourne.

Lord Lyle emerged as a familiar public figure in 1949. In that year the Labour Government included sugar refining among the activities it proposed to nationalise. In contact with his Tory friends (especially Churchill), Lord Lyle took the lead in the fight against nationalisation and for free enterprise. After the creation of the small cartoon character Mr Cube in 1949, Lyle was known as Lord Cube. Going from meeting to meeting, Lord Lyle led a very forceful campaign, pursued on his part with humour and spirit, engaging in numerous altercations with Herbert Morrison.

From 1950 onwards, Lord Lyle became a prominent figure in the free enterprise lobby: he was a director of Aims of Industry which actively campaigned on this issue.

Lyle took no part in businesses outside the sugar industry, except for a seat on the board of Lloyds Bank. He had a long-standing association with Queen Mary's Hospital for the East End, of which he was chairman, 1916-23, and later vice-president; and he was treasurer of Royal Wanstead School. He was chairman of East Dorset Conservative Association, 1932-40. In his youth he was a keen and useful tennis player and golfer. He represented England at tennis, and served as president and vice-president of the Lawn Tennis Association and was president of the Professional Golfers' Association.

Lyle married in 1904 Edith Louise (d 1942), daughter of John Levy of Rochester; they had a son and two daughters. Lord Lyle died at his home in Bournemouth on 6 March 1954, leaving £664,910 gross.

PHILIPPE CHALMIN

Writings:

Mr Cube's Fight Against Nationalisation (Hollis & Carter, 1954).

Sources:

Unpublished

BCe.

MCe.

PrC.

Information from Ann Alford, archivist of Tate & Lyle.

Published

Burke's Peerage and Baronetage.

Philippe Chalmin, *Tate and Lyle Géant du Sucre* (Paris: Economica, 1983).

Anthony Hugill, *Sugar and All That. A History of Tate & Lyle* (Gentry Books, 1978).

Oliver Lyle, *The Plaistow Story* (Tate & Lyle Ltd, 1960).

Times 8 Mar 1954.

WWMP.

WWW.

LYONS, Sir Joseph Nathaniel

(1847-1917)

Caterer and food manufacturer

Sir Joseph Lyons (from Mrs Stewart Menzies Modern Men of Mark *Herbert Jenkins, 1921).*

Joseph Nathaniel Lyons was born in Kennington, London, on 29 December 1847, the son of Nathaniel Lyons, an itinerant vendor of watches, rings and cheap jewellery, and his wife Hannah née Cohen. He attended the Borough Jewish School and began his working life as a water colour artist, exhibiting for a time at the Royal Institution. He was also an inventor of sorts, designing quick-selling gadgets, such as a stereoscope, which he hawked at various exhibitions in the 1880s.

Though not an entrepreneur in the classic mould, nor a particularly shrewd businessman, Joseph Lyons's natural, easy charm and flamboyant personality proved useful business assets and eventually brought him to the attention of Montague Gluckstein (qv), a distant relative. The Salmon and Gluckstein families were planning a refreshment stall at the Newcastle Jubilee Exhibition of 1887 but wished to distinguish it from their thriving tobacco enterprise. Montague Gluckstein had taken over the managerial side — indeed the catering project was his brain-child — but, in his own words, 'we wanted to find someone to act as ambassador to the new firm and negotiate with the exhibition authorities' {Beable (1926) 84}. Gluckstein travelled to Liverpool, where Lyons was running an exhibition stall, and, having written his terms down on an ordinary sheet of paper, recruited him as front-man for the proposed catering business.

Joseph Lyons became a shareholder and chairman of the company which bore his name, when it was formed in 1894 to operate restaurants and a chain of distinctive tea-shops offering a wide range of food at low prices and in pleasant surroundings. Under Lyons's chairmanship the growth of the company was spectacular. Although difficulties of supply and the rising cost of commodities caused some problems towards the end of the First World War, net profits were consistently high, rising from £57,776 in 1899 to £231,849 in 1907 and to £356,303 in 1914, whilst dividends during 1903-15 were never less than 30 per cent and in 1913-14 reached 42 per cent. At the time of Lyons's death authorised capital was £1,650,000. However, this was not entirely due to the company's colourful chairman. Power was concentrated in the hands of the board and decisions were never taken without lengthy consultation amongst the tightly-knit Gluckstein and Salmon family members, a policy that was to bring problems later in the firm's history. Although it would be wrong to underestimate Lyons's importance as the genial patron of the company's restaurants, or as a genuine entrepreneur in the exhibition business at an important stage in the firm's life, the real power lay with the Gluckstein brothers, especially Montague, in financing and planning the direction of J Lyons & Co Ltd.

Nevertheless, Joseph Lyons was an ideal figurehead for a catering business. Reputed to have been, perhaps, 'the greatest raconteur of his day' {*Jewish Chronicle* 29 June 1917}, he was at ease with both royalty and working people, and could often be found at the firm's Trocadero restaurant, where he held forth to journalists and interested regulars on the topics of the day. He continued to cultivate his artistic inclinations and at one point even took up writing detective stories. His generosity, though not well-publicised, found expression in his work for the Little Sisters of the Poor, in Hammersmith; the Music Hall Benevolent Fund; the Chelsea Hospital fête in 1908; and the Franco-British Bazaar in 1909. A DL for the County of London, he was greatly interested in the London Territorial Association, in the training plan of which he materially helped by introducing athletics. For these public services he received a knighthood in 1911.

Besides his chairmanship of J Lyons & Co Ltd, Lyons was also chairman of Strand Palace Hotel Ltd, of Hancocks Ltd (New Zealand), a vice-chairman of Trafford Park Ltd and director of Trafford Park Estates, Manchester Ltd.

He married Psyche, daughter of Isaac Cohen, manager of the Pavilion Theatre, Whitechapel Road. There were no children from the marriage. Sir Joseph Lyons died on 22 June 1917 and was buried at the Willesden cemetery of the United Synagogue. He left £58,967 gross.

DAVID J RICHARDSON

Writings:

Lyons Library [of Novels] (Cassell & Co, 1907).

(with Cecil Raleigh) *The Master Crime* (Lyons Library, 1907).

Sources:

Unpublished

BCe.

PrC.

David J Richardson, 'The History of the Catering Industry, with Special Reference to the Development of J Lyons & Co Ltd to 1939' (Kent PhD, 1970).

Published

Stephen Aris, *The Jews in Business* (Cape, 1970).

William H Beable, *Romance of Great Businesses* (2 vols, Heath Cranton Ltd, 1926) I.

Thomas C Bridges and Hubert H Tiltman, *Kings of Commerce* (G G Harrap & Co, 1928).

Paul H Emden, *Jews of Britain* (Sampson & Low, 1944).

Bernard Falk, *He Laughed in Fleet Street* (Hutchinson & Co, 1933).

Jewish Chronicle 29 June 1917.

Amy C Menzies, *Modern Men of Mark* (Herbert Jenkins Ltd, 1921).

Julian Salmon, 'Development and Organisation of J Lyons & Co Ltd' in Ronald S Edwards and Harry Townsend (eds), *Business Growth* (Macmillan, 1966).

Statist 89 (16 June 1917).

WWW.

LYONS, Sir William

(1901-)

Motor cycle, side-car and motorcar manufacturer

William Lyons was born at Blackpool on 4 September 1901, the second child of an Irish musician, William Lyons, who ran a music shop in the town, and his wife Minnie née Barcroft, a Lancashire girl. William, with his elder sister, Carol, was brought up in the family home in King Edward Avenue. He was educated at Arnold House School, Blackpool, until the age of seventeen, when he became a trainee with the firm founded by

William Lyons's agent's season ticket for 1919 Motor Exhibition (courtesy of Jaguar Cars).

Francis William Crossley (qv) in Manchester. By the end of the First World War he was selling cars for the Metropole Garage, Blackpool. A keen motor cyclist, in 1921 he bought a side-car for his Norton motor-cycle from a neighbour, William Walmsley (1893-1961), who had already produced several under the trademark 'Swallow', for local customers. Lyons saw the commercial advantages in making these distinctive side-cars in far greater numbers than the one a week produced by Walmsley and formed a partnership with Walmsley to do so. The two young men had £1,000 capital, guaranteed by their parents (Walmsley's father was a Stockport coal merchant) and the new company was floated on Lyons's twenty-first birthday in 1922. They had already found premises at 7-9 Bloomfield Road, Blackpool, above a printer's workshop and, with a new work force of eight men, began to produce ten side-cars a week. By the following year Swallow had their own stand at the Motor Cycle Show and four firms (Brough Superior, Coventry Eagle, Dot, Matador) displayed Swallow side-cars with their machines. The Swallow side-car differed considerably from its rivals; aluminium-finished and eight-sided, it was later produced in a pentagonal model. Lyons and Walmsley each took only £6 a week wages from the firm's profits although Walmsley was already married and Lyons was to marry in 1924 Greta Brown, daughter of a schoolmaster, Alfred J Brown.

In 1926 the firm moved to new premises in Cocker Street, Blackpool. There Lyons began to make Swallow bodies for the Austin Seven proprietary chassis, panelled in aluminium, to sell at £175. The firm changed its name in that year to indicate these new interests, becoming the Swallow Side-Car & Coachbuilding Co. The first Austin-Swallow, announced in the spring of 1927, sold very well and when production reached two cars a day and some 100 side-cars a week, larger premises were essential. Late in 1928 the firm moved to Coventry, to occupy a former munitions factory with a 13-acre site off Holbrooks Lane, and expanded their range to make bodies for Fiat, Standard and Swift. In the next year, 1929, Swallow Coachwork had a stand at the Motor Show at Olympia and two years later Lyons produced the first car to his own design, the SS1. Praised by the motoring press and selling at £325, its 16 hp engine came from the Standard Motor Co in Coventry. By 1933, Lyons was entering his cars in international trials, later an important feature of Jaguar's success, and different versions of the SS1 and SS2 were manufactured. Between 1931 and 1936 production consisted of 4,252 SS1s, 1,796 SS2s and 735 Swallow-bodied vehicles.

William Walmsley left the partnership following disagreements late in 1934. The firm went public as SS Cars Ltd in January 1935 and Lyons briefly sought external financial support from Motor Panels of Coventry. The authorised capital was increased from £10,000 to £250,000. Lyons became chairman and managing director of the new company and held 260,000 of the 480,000 issued 5s ordinary shares. A further change in Swallow was the use of the name Jaguar; in September 1935 the first Jaguar saloon was displayed prior to the Motor Show. The name Jaguar was chosen by Lyons from a list of animal names suggested to him by the Nelson Advertising Agency and had originally been used by Armstrong-Siddeley for a First World War aero engine. Lyons was joined by William Heynes, who left his draughtsman's job at the Humber Co to become Lyons's first chief engineer. When launching their new car Lyons invited people to guess its price (the 2.5 litre model actually sold for £385) and most estimates far exceeded the list price. In the years 1940-45 Jaguar Cars ceased car production, but the firm's war work included servicing Whitley bombers, making the centre sections for the Gloster Meteor aircraft and the production of side-cars for military use.

In 1945 the company changed its name to Jaguar Cars Ltd to lose the unfortunate wartime associations with the letters SS and in 1948 produced the first of its famous XK models. Lyons saw the importance of exports to the post-war economy and the firm instituted a sales drive in the USA in January 1947. He also began to produce his own engines. One of the firm's best-known models, the XK120, was launched at the London Motor Show in October 1948; available as a sports and saloon model, and selling at just below £1,000, it was instantly successful in terms of sales and racing. Production expanded and the firm moved in 1951-52 to new premises at Brown's Lane, Allesley, a village on the outskirts of Coventry, where it has remained. Jaguar successes at Le Mans in 1953 and 1955-57 helped secure essential export orders, so that customers ranged from Hollywood film stars to Indian princes. The versatility of the XK engine, however, also meant that it could be used in the Scorpion light tank, built by Alvis, and the Dennis D-series fire engine. In February 1957 a disastrous fire broke out at Allesley, damaging plant and a large number of cars, but production began again after only two days.

The 1960s were a decade of changes for Jaguar; Lyons set out to include smaller specialist firms within the company so that in 1960 he acquired the Daimler Co and the following year, Guy Motors. In 1963 he gained control of Coventry Climax Engines Ltd, founded by another entrepreneur, H Pelham Lee, and in 1964 the firm of Henry Meadows was taken over by Jaguar. The 1960s also saw the development of the XK's

Pre-war SS 2.5 (3.5) litre model (courtesy of Jaguar Cars).

successor, the famous E-type, which rapidly became a competition car though the company had ceased to sponsor its own works team some years earlier. However, by 1966 economic considerations appeared to favour even larger-scale enterprises; profits had stagnated at around £2 million a year in the 1960s, and the product range was ageing. The possibility of Jaguar's remaining a family firm had ended in 1955 when Lyons's only son, John Michael, was killed at the age of twenty-five while driving a Jaguar in France; both Lyons's daughters, Patricia and Mary, were interested in farming careers. Thus, in 1966, he agreed to merge Jaguar with the British Motor Corporation, then under the control of Sir George Harriman (qv). Lyons remained chairman of Jaguar Cars Ltd, and became a deputy chairman of BMC. Jaguar was to retain its independence and distinct identity, but this proved impossible in practice and Jaguar became inevitably involved in BMC's losses and decline. The original Jaguar standards of quality suffered and sales fell. Lyons opposed the Ryder Report recommendations for merging with Leyland and retired in 1972.

Lyons was knighted in 1957, for services to industry. Loughborough University awarded him an honorary D Tech and he also held a Royal Designer for Industry award and a fellowship of the Royal Society of Arts. He was president of the Fellowship of the Motor Industry (1957-59), of the Society of Motor Manufacturers and Traders (1950-51), of the Motor Industry Research Association (1954), and the Motor Trades Benevolent Fund (1954). He was made a freeman of the City of London in 1954 and received the Coventry Award of Merit in 1970; he became a patron of the College of Aeronautical and Auto Engineering in 1958.

As a designer of motor cars perhaps the most striking feature about William Lyons's career was that he received no kind of training at all. However, all those who worked with him emphasise that he had the ability to judge the lines of a car. He always insisted from the early days on very high standards of quality in materials and workmanship; he would make endless modifications, no matter how minor, until he was personally satisfied with a particular model. Early in his career he grasped the importance of advertising for sales. He always worked very long hours, expecting his men to do the same. Seven or ten days' holiday a year were all he allowed himself. His only recreation was golf and he had a one-hole golf course constructed on his farm. In 1937 he moved from 'Woodside', Gibbet Hill, Coventry, and bought a country house, Wappenbury Hall, near Leamington Spa, where he bred pedigree Jersey cattle and Suffolk sheep, although his activities have been reduced since a serious illness in 1979. His total involvement with Jaguar seemed to preclude an interest in cultural, community, religious or political activities; he apparently held no outside directorships.

Although he characteristically ran Jaguar as a one-man enterprise at the top, with no board meeting actually taking place until the BMC merger, he was able to select talented men to join the team and support him, such as Walter Hassan, Harry Munday, W M Heynes and F R W England. The firm took apprentices from an early period and strong family patterns among the employees can be discerned. His attitude to trades unions was that he was 'all for them' if their attitudes were 'positive' and 'businesslike' {oral, Andrew Whyte}. However, Lyons's style of management remained hierarchical so that, for example, a separate executives' dining room continued at Jaguar long after other firms had abandoned theirs. He was equally determined to give customers value for money and to prevent extravagance at the factory; he boasted that 'we were very strict with the overheads ... we never lost money' {*Sunday Times* Colour Supplement, 29 Aug 1982}. He was known to discriminate against the drivers of foreign cars and never welcomed familiarity from employees. He founded and developed a series of unique and stylish cars, with world-wide sales, and ran the firm as a personal enterprise. Possibly the tragedy of his son's death made him later consider as inevitable a merger with BMC and the resulting loss of direct control in his own company.

JOAN LANE

Writings:

The History of Jaguar and the Future of the Specialised Car in the British Motor Industry (Institute of the Motor Industry, 1969).

Sources:

Unpublished

Jaguar Cars, owners' registers, correspondence files, handbooks, brochures, photographs and reports (listed in Lane *Register* below).

Information from Andrew Whyte.

Published

Economist 28 Mar 1959, 12 Feb 1966.

Joan Lane, *A Register of Business Records of Coventry and Related Areas* (Coventry: Department of Politics and History, Lanchester Polytechnic, 1977).

Kenneth E Richardson, *Twentieth Century Coventry* (Coventry: City of Coventry, 1972).

Sunday Times Colour Supplement 1982.

VCH Warwickshire 8.

Andrew Whyte, *Jaguar: The History of a Great British Car* (Cambridge: Stephens, 1980).

WW 1982.

LYSAGHT, John

(1832-1895)

Galvanised sheet iron manufacturer

John Lysaght was born in March 1832, the youngest son of William Lysaght, a well-to-do farmer, of Hazelwood, Mallow, and his wife Frances, daughter of William Atkins of Fountainville, County Cork, in the South of Ireland. He spent his early years in the locality but was sent in his late teens to Birmingham and then Bristol, where his family already had both business and kinship connections, to further his education. In addition to training in the field of civil engineering, he established a friendship with Robert Clarke, who on the death of his father, inherited amongst other things an iron galvanising business at Temple Backs (close to where Temple Meads Station is today), Bristol. The young Clarke however, had neither the inclination nor the commercial aptitude to succeed his father, so in 1857, obviously flushed by his new found wealth, he made a gift of the works, which specialised in the 'zincing' of iron buckets, to John Lysaght. (The process of zincing iron or manufacturing galvanised iron was patented by John Crawford in 1837.)

When Lysaght commenced production, he employed only six men and a boy, whose wages ranged from 10d to 6s a day; the weekly wage bill for his first week's work, ending 4 July 1857, amounted to a mere £6 11s 3d. By 1860 Lysaght had already turned his attention to galvanising and corrugating sheet iron, a step which fully evidenced his enterprise and commercial confidence, as it was only in 1853 that steam power had been applied to corrugated iron manufacture, eventually transforming the industry. In addition, in his first year, Lysaght adopted the *ORB* trade mark, which became world famous by the end of the century. During the 1870s, Lysaght substantially expanded his range of galvanised products, particularly for the agricultural industry, to include fencing wire, cow cribs, manure pumps, corn and flour bins, turnip skips and beer cans (with a minimum capacity of over one gallon!). In the last entry in John Lysaght's first wages book, for the week ending 12 September 1864, 29 men and boys were employed and the weekly bill was £40 11s 5d.

The expansion of activity quickly necessitated more substantial premises however, and in 1869 production moved to St Vincent's, an extensive engineering works occupying four acres and bounded on one side by the Avon Canal and on the other by the Great Western Railway. The works had previously been occupied by Acraman, Morgan & Co who in 1837 had done much of the work for Brunel's *Great Western*, the first steamship to make regular Atlantic crossings. By 1878, 400 were employed and over 1,000 tons of galvanised products were leaving St Vincent's Ironworks monthly. Further expansion followed in 1876 when Lysaght ventured into the field of structural engineering, of which he had some knowledge, and acquired another canal-fronted premises at Netham, about two miles from St Vincent's. There he set up a constructional department equipped to manufacture a wide range of structural ironwork for public buildings, churches, railway stations, bridges, dock warehouses and the like. This branch quickly expanded and in particular the Netham works contributed largely to the growing export market.

From the start, Lysaght established strong links with the main suppliers of his basic raw material in the West Midlands, the puddled iron being transported to the Sharpness Docks at Gloucester, by canal, and then along the Severn and the Avon to the feeder canal at St Vincent's. As the scale of his enterprise grew, so also did it become increasingly necessary to achieve greater control over the supply of the iron, and consequently in 1876, the Swan Garden Ironworks, with eight rolling mills, at Wolverhampton was purchased from the firm of G B Thorneycroft for £23,000 to roll their own iron sheets. The Swan Garden Works had in fact been closed for a period before purchase, due to a prolonged trade recession, but Lysaght soon had it working close to its 25,000 tons annual capacity. So successful was this new arrangement that by 1885 Lysaght had acquired an additional four mills at the nearby Osier Bed Iron Works, and the total sheet rolling capacity had risen to 40,000 tons a year.

By the 1880s steel, with all its advantages, was beginning to replace iron in many fields, a transition which accelerated as the decade progressed. Lysaght fully kept up with the technological advances, by undertaking substantial capital re-equipping. The Brymbo Steel Works, near Wrexham, North Wales, with its basic open-hearth furnace erected by John Darby in 1883, became the major supplier of steel to Lysaght for the manufacture of his 'Best Tenax steel sheets (a splendid quality for working up)' {*The Lysaght Century*} which figures alongside the puddled iron sheets they were fast replacing in a Bristol price list of 1885. Three years earlier, two new double sheet mills had been laid down at Swan Garden and Lysaghts were fully prepared for the massive growth in demand for galvanised steel products, especially corrugated sheets, which the ensuing few decades were to see. John Lysaght had for a number of years advocated that the company should construct a new steel works, on a green field site. This it did in 1897 when the Orb Works was opened at Newport and became the company's sole producer of steel, two years after his death.

Lysaght had, almost from the start of his business, maintained a watchful eye on the potential of exports, and especially on the Australian market. In 1885 of the firm's total output of 40,000 tons, 90 per cent was exported, a proportion which was fairly stable throughout the 1880s and 1890s, with the bulk, around 70 per cent, being shipped to Australia. In 1880 Lysaght had set up, in conjunction with Australian interests, a central selling agency, the Victorian Galvanised Iron & Wire Co, while trade with New South Wales and Queensland continued to be handled under reciprocal agreements in Sydney and Brisbane. When confronted by the collusive actions of a shipping ring and high rates of exchange, Lysaght responded vigorously, making arrangements to circumvent these threats to profitability. John Lysaght's vision was fully evidenced after his death, when in 1899 these Australian 'agencies', after becoming fully owned branches of the Lysaght company, were combined as Lysaght's Galvanised Iron Pty Ltd, which in the twentieth century became one of Australia's major steel manufacturers.

John Lysaght was an astute businessman and a progressive employer whose courage was fully evidenced in 1878 when he purchased the Swan Garden Works at a time when, in his own words, he was 'only jogging on, trying to avoid as much loss as possible merely to keep the works going and my business together' {*ibid,* 14}. He was not a great advocate of committees, believing that the directness of the written word accomplished a more effective result, asserting that 'I have always been averse of meetings, because I cannot recollect any meeting that has been productive of the smallest good'. {*ibid,* 50} His forthright business manner is typified by his offer to Thorneycrofts in 1878: 'I will purchase the whole works as they stand, exclusive of finished or half-finished iron and pig iron, for the sum of £23,000 — possibly to others on the spot the Works are worth more, but to me they are not, because I should have to alter the entire plant in the course of a couple of years or so, to bring the Works into a form consistent with the latest improvements in the rolling of sheets — the impression I formed from the Works is that Thorneycroft could not make finished iron there at a profit except during extraordinary times' {*ibid,* 50}.

Although he encountered difficulties with the contract labour system which operated in the West Midlands, which he neither approved nor trusted, particularly becoming involved in numerous conflicts with the rollermen in Wolverhampton who were effectively 'contractors' for their own mills, Lysaght was a benevolent and loyal employer. At Bristol he was in a better position to mould his relationships with the men to his own humanitarian pattern and his employees were much the better for it. At St Vincent's Ironworks various amenities were introduced long before they were seen elsewhere. Thus by the 1880s, the workers at St Vincent's enjoyed a factory canteen with separate accommodation for males and females, a large meeting hall and recreation centre, a well-stocked library and a sick and medical club. In 1879 he negotiated with the rector of the local parish, Rev John Gladstone, for the adaptation of an unused church as a social centre. In a letter he fully describes his motives thus: 'I do not feel entitled to claim anything except that in giving, or assisting to give, an impetus towards the development of a movement by which the working man may learn to find some rational amusement, enjoyment and comfort outside the public house, I am taking a step in the right direction. I am happy to say that so far the men are taking advantage of the room etc and show every intention to profit by it' {*ibid*, 48}. In addition Lysaght gave full evidence of his altruistic spirit by ensuring employment opportunities for released prisoners from Bristol's Harefield Jail.

Although starting from small beginnings in 1857, John Lysaght had built up a substantial enterprise which was incorporated in 1880 with a registered capital of £162,000, to carry on 'the business of Ironmasters, Galvanisers, Constructional Engineers, Wire Netting and Hollow-ware Manufacturers'. By 1895 Lysaght employed 1,000 hands in Bristol and 1,500-2,000 at his two works in Wolverhampton.

Lysaght, a Conservative in his political sympathies, in 1883 gave a block of buildings in Baldwin Street, Bristol, to the local Conservative Party for its headquarters. Although not attracted to public life, he became a magistrate in Bristol and was appointed its High Sheriff in 1882. He had residences in Gloucestershire, Suffolk (Hengrave Hall) and a marine villa at Teignmouth, where he pursued his favourite pastime of yachting (being a member of the Royal Yacht Club).

Lysaght in 1858 married Ellen, daughter of Sidney Moss; she died in 1882. John Lysaght, suffering from a neck tumour, died aged sixty-three on 1 October 1895, leaving £424,214 gross.

He was succeeded as chairman of the company by his eldest surviving son, Frederick Percy, and as managing director by Sydney Royse Lysaght, his nephew, who had been company secretary since 1881. Sydney's brother, William Royse (qv), remained in control at Wolverhampton until he took over at Newport in 1901. Both were sons of his elder brother Thomas, a gifted architect, some of whose work can still be seen in the centre of Bristol.

COLIN BABER *and* TREVOR BOYNS

Sources:

Unpublished

MCe.

PrC.

Published

Bristol Mercury 2 Oct 1895.

Bristol Times and Mirror 2 Oct 1895.

Iron and Steel Trades Journal 5 Oct 1895.

The Lysaght Century 1857-1957 (Bristol: pp John Lysaght Ltd, 1957).

Midland Evening News 2 Oct 1895.

Western Daily Press 2 Oct 1895.

William Royse Lysaght (courtesy of Guest Keen & Nettlefolds).

LYSAGHT, William Royse

(1858-1945)

Steel manufacturer

William Royse Lysaght was born on 23 July 1858, the son of Thomas Royse Lysaght of Clifton and Mintinna, County Cork, Ireland, and his wife Emily Moss, daughter of Sidney Moss RN. The crucial family connection, however, was with his uncle, John Lysaght (qv), whose firm he ultimately joined, following the path of his elder brother Sidney Royse Lysaght (1856-1941). He was educated privately.

In the autumn of 1874 he entered the Gospel Oak Co's works at Tipton, Staffordshire, to learn the business of producing sheet iron. He was sent there because John Lysaght & Co had no rolling mills of their own and were, at this time, reliant upon outside suppliers of black sheet mostly from Staffordshire. If the business were to expand vertical integration seemed a priority. Accordingly, in 1878 John Lysaght purchased the Swan Garden Works at Wolverhampton and W R Lysaght was brought from Gospel Oak to run the newly-acquired plant. The Swan Garden Works had formerly belonged to Messrs Thorneycroft & Co (rollers of rails, plate and some sheet) so that many of the mills had to be replaced. Eventually, under W R Lysaght's management there were seven sheet mills operating — more than at any other works in the UK. Initially each mill had an output of about 30 tons per week. Under W R Lysaght technical improvements resulted: double and treble mills were put down and the diameter of the rolls increased to 24 inches. Overhead cranes were installed but output remained at around 45 tons per mill until the substitution of steel for wrought iron in the mid-1890s generated real gains in productivity. Then the abolition of 'pile' heating and bar rolling, the provision of bigger rolls, heavier trains and more powerful engines, together with the introduction of the eight-hour shift system in place of day rates, all added to the efficiency of the plant. Seven years after the purchase of the Swan Garden Works, John Lysaght acquired a further four rolling mills at the nearby Osier Bed Iron Works bought from Messrs

Sparrow, and management of this plant also fell to W R Lysaght. By 1885 the company's total sheet-rolling capacity had reached about 40,000 tons per annum. When John Lysaght died in October 1895, W R Lysaght was assisted at Wolverhampton by his younger cousin, Daniel Conner Lysaght (1869-1940), who had previously worked at Bristol. Thus began a close business relationship that was to dominate the company fortunes for the next forty years.

By the late 1890s when steel had superseded wrought iron, it was clear that Staffordshire was doomed as a sheet-producing region. New steelworks tended to be sited on the coast to receive imports of iron ore and because a high proportion of the finished product was exported. Bearing this in mind, John Lysaght, assisted by W R, set out to find a new location for the company's rolling mills. At first, in 1895, he considered moving to Barry Docks but the scheme collapsed and he finally decided to acquire 60 acres of farmland along the east bank of the River Usk on the southern outskirts of Newport. Although undeveloped, the area possessed excellent rail and port facilities and was close to the South Wales coalfield. There, with the help of the company's own Constructional Department at Netham, the Orb Iron Works were erected. In March 1898 D C Lysaght came from Wolverhampton with a staff of three to begin rolling operations with three mills. Soon these were run by nine sets of men on eight-hour shifts who had been induced to move from the remote Welsh village of Ynysmeudwy in the Tawe valley. The transfer proceeded smoothly with workers migrating from Staffordshire to Newport and in 1901 W R Lysaght himself left Wolverhampton to take charge at the Orb Works. The Osier Bed mills were sold but the larger Swan Garden Works was converted into a foundry which supplied Newport with chilled cast-iron mill rolls.

The Orb Works expanded at an impressive rate. By 1913 there were 42 hot mills and six engines. With a total workforce of 3,000, the sheet-rolling capacity rose to 200,000 tons per annum, of which 140,000 went to the St Vincent's Works for galvanising, carried in steam barges that sailed from the jetty at the Orb Works across the Bristol Channel.

Having re-located the company's rolling mills, it was felt that they should obtain closer control over their supplies of steel. The rising output of Newport together with the problem of ensuring consistent quality from a variety of producers led Lysaghts to consider further vertical integration. Accordingly W R Lysaght was deputed to find a site for a modern steelworks. His final choice was the Lincolnshire ironstone area at Scunthorpe, which offered plentiful deposits of open-face and cheaply-won iron ore in proximity to Yorkshire coal. They could also erect a jetty on the River Trent near Flixborough so that steel bar could be sent by boat directly to Newport. Construction of the Normanby Park Steelworks began in 1910 and was completed to the designs of John Darby (1856-1919) of Brymbo. It comprised three blast furnaces with 11 foot hearths, 152 coke ovens, four 45-ton open hearth furnaces, a 400-ton mixer and rolling mills with an annual output of 100,000 tons of sheet bar. The works were opened in 1912 and within six years the annual ingot output had risen to 131,000 tons.

W R Lysaght also played an important part in developing the company's activities in Australia. John Lysaght had operated various agencies there

The Orb Iron Works, Newport, photographed in the early years of the twentieth century when under the management of W R and D C Lysaght. The transport bridge over the River Usk stands in the distance (courtesy of Rheemco Ltd).

since the 1880s principally to sell corrugated iron, and in 1899 established Lysaghts Galvanised Iron Pty Ltd in Melbourne. Yet all manufacturing remained in Britain. The curtailment of supplies from Bristol caused by the outbreak of the First World War created pressures for a works to be laid down in Australia. Herbert Royse Lysaght (1862-1940), younger brother of S R and W R, had been placed in charge and supervised the project to construct rolling mills and galvanising plant at Newcastle, New South Wales. However, D C and W R Lysaghts' experience proved invaluable in setting up the works, and men from Bristol and Newport emigrated to form a nucleus of skilled staff. The first sheets were rolled in April 1921 and by the end of 1927 eight mills and five galvanising pots were installed and over 100,000 tons of sheets had been produced. A second plant, at Port Kembla, came into operation in 1936 but was subsequently re-built and opened three years later as the Springhill Works.

During the inter-war years, the Orb Works prospered because it was able to take advantage of expanding markets for electrical equipment and the demands of the motor car industry. Lysaghts supplied both Ford and Morris with sheet steel for body pressings. In addition, they rolled special sheet steel for transformers (where they became world leaders) together with vitreous-enamelling grades for use in the manufacture of gas and electric cookers, washing machines and refrigerators. The growing popularity of steel office furniture and partitioning created yet another field of demand for the Orb Works output. By 1928 the line of mills at Newport had risen to 48 and provision was made to roll sheets up to 72 inches in width; they were the largest of their kind in the world and had achieved an annual capacity of over 200,000 tons with a workforce of

3,500. W R and D C Lysaght were responsible for all these developments, the latter taking a special interest in electrical steels.

W R Lysaght was appointed a director of John Lysaght in 1892, while his elder brother, S R, became managing director with executive control at Bristol in 1895. Also in that year John Lysaght, the founder, was succeeded as chairman by his son, Frederick Percy Lysaght (1863-1905), who in 1905 was followed by Gerald S Lysaght (1869-1951). Concerned by the post-war depression, the latter, in turn, sold the company to Henry Seymour Berry (qv) in 1919 and in the following year John Lysaght Ltd amalgamated with GKN. The merger corresponded with W R Lysaght's appointment as joint managing director, a post he held until 1928 when, on the death of Berry, he became chairman. W R Lysaght retired at the end of 1939 when he took the specially created post of president, retaining this until his death in 1945. As a result of the union with GKN, he served as a director of that company from 1920 to 1945 and was appointed to directorships in several subsidiaries, including Joseph Sankey & Sons, Bayliss, Jones & Bayliss and John Garrington & Sons. In view of Lysaght's close connections in Australia with Broken Hill Pty (from whom they bought their steel bar), he also sat on their London board.

During the First World War W R Lysaght served as Spelter Adviser to the Ministry of Munitions. In November 1915 whilst estimating the demand for steel over the coming year, he discovered that a possible total output of 9,360,000 tons would fall short of an anticipated civil and military demand (12,051,000 tons) by over 2,500,000 tons of ingots. It was this survey that prompted moves which resulted in government control of steel-making and a policy of expansion through capital expenditure. For his work for the Ministry of Munitions, Lysaght received a CBE in 1918.

When at Wolverhampton he became a member of the Midland Wages Board, a commitment Lysaght retained for forty years. He vigorously opposed the contract system of operating piecework and used the occasion of the move to Newport to introduce shifts. In 1901 W R Lysaght was elected chairman of a local committee of the Wages Board for the Welsh Sheet Trade. In time this body became autonomous as the Sheet Trade Board, Lysaght serving as its chairman for nearly twenty-five years. He simplified negotiations with the unions by establishing a Sheet Makers' Conference in conjunction with Henry Summers, and encouraged the recognition of a single steel union at Newport. These two actions helped to ensure an excellent industrial relations record at the Orb Works. A member of the Iron and Steel Institute since 1888, W R Lysaght was elected to the Council in 1915, became a vice-president in 1924 and served as the president 1933-35.

Like his uncle, John, W R Lysaght never sought the limelight and took no great part in public life. Nevertheless, he did accept a number of outside positions becoming chairman of the Chamber of Commerce in Wolverhampton. He was a DL and JP for Monmouthshire and the county's High Sheriff in 1915. He was elected an underwriter at Lloyds in 1923. Besides being one of its founders, he sat as chairman of the Chepstow Racecourse Co, and was a prominent supporter and benefactor of the Newport Football Club. In recognition of his work at Newport Lysaght was made an honorary freeman of the County Borough in 1936.

It is surprising given his obvious talents as a manager that he did not assume the chairmanship of the company after the First World War, but assented to its take-over by the business empire of D A Thomas (qv) and Berry. He took a deep but paternalistic interest in the workforce and recalled, at a dinner to mark fifty years with the company in 1928, having run soup kitchens for his Wolverhampton workmen during spells of unemployment in the 1880s. He played the cornet in the company band and was responsible for the decision to loan the Newport workforce a total of over £50,000 when the coal strike brought the plant to a halt in 1926; when the dispute had been settled, the entire sum was swiftly repaid. As a tribute to his enduring concern, when a sports pavilion and recreation hall was completed near the Orb Works in December 1928, it was named the 'W R Lysaght Institute' in his honour. Part of his success in running the Newport mills can be attributed to his complementary relationship with D C Lysaght. The latter, akin to a chief of staff, intuitively perceived the issues at stake in technical innovation and in labour relations, where he had an Irish love of debate. W R Lysaght himself was deliberate in thought and sparing in the use of words.

In 1890 W R Lysaght married Effie Elizabeth Stavern, daughter of Rev J E Gladstone, of Wolverhampton. They had one son, Desmond Royse (1903-70), who entered the Orb Works and became a director, and two daughters. William Royse Lysaght died on 27 April 1945, aged eighty-six at his home in Castleford, Chepstow, Monmouthshire, leaving £277,368 gross.

EDGAR JONES

Writings:

Presidential address to the Iron and Steel Institute *Journal of the Iron and Steel Institute* 127 (1933).

Sources:

Unpublished

PrC.

Information from various GKN departments.

Interview with Mr E C Lysaght, December 1983.

Published

British Steelmaker Nov 1939, Feb 1940, June 1945.

James C Carr and Walter Taplin, *A History of the British Steel Industry* (Oxford: Blackwell, 1962).

Engineer 179 (4 May 1945).

Iron and Coal Trades Review 12 Jan 1940, 4 May 1945.

Journal of the Iron and Steel Institute 152 (1946).

The Lysaght Century 1857-1957 (Bristol: pp John Lysaght Ltd, 1957).

Lysaght Venture (Sydney: pp John Lysaght (Australia) Ltd, 1955).

Newport Encyclopaedia Coronation Year and Royal Visit Souvenir (Bristol, 1937).

The Western Daily Press 28 Apr 1945.

WWW.

LYTTELTON, Oliver

1st Viscount Chandos

(1893-1972)

Metal dealer and electrical manufacturer

Oliver Lyttelton was born in London on 15 March 1893, only surviving son of Alfred Lyttelton (1857-1913), by his second wife Edith Sophy (d 1948), daughter of Archibald Balfour. His father, who was seventh brother of the Eighth Viscount Cobham, was a barrister, and in 1893 Recorder of Hereford, who sat as a Conservative MP from 1895, in the Cabinet as Secretary for the Colonies in 1903-5, and afterwards on the board of the London & Westminster Bank and other companies. He was also a brilliant cricketer and distinguished sportsman, of intense personal charm, who was thought by most of his contemporaries to personify the best of Edwardian manliness and grace. Among Oliver Lyttelton's first cousins were the wives of A M Grenfell and W L Hichens (qqv).

Lyttelton was educated at a private day school in Baker Street, Marylebone, then at Eton in 1906-12, and Trinity College, Cambridge, reading classics and law and becoming a golf blue in 1914. Following the outbreak of war in August of that year, he left university without taking his degree and was commissioned into the 4th Battalion Bedfordshire Regiment. In December 1914 he became a subaltern in the Grenadier Guards. He was posted to France in January 1915, and fought in his first battle at Festubert in May 1915. From October 1915 to May 1917 Lyttelton was an adjutant, and singularly lucky to survive. Raymond Asquith wrote of him at this time, 'I like him but many of the junior officers think him too casual and conceited ... His chief defect ... is ... telling rather long and moderately good stories and laughing hysterically long before he comes to the point' {Joliffe (1980) 222}. Thrice mentioned in despatches, he was awarded the DSO in 1916 and Military Cross in 1918. In April of that year, when a brigade major, he was severely affected by mustard gas.

In 1919 he transferred to the Grenadiers' reserve of officers with the substantive rank of captain. He was at this time anxious to be able to marry a daughter of the Duke of Leeds, and in August 1919 joined the merchant bank of Brown, Shipley. This rich, solid partnership had originally been the British subsidiary of an American bank and retained close relations with Brown Bros of New York, Boston and Philadelphia. It specialised in foreign exchange (particularly dollars) and commercial credits. Lyttelton began at a salary of £180 a year (plus a Christmas bonus) as a clerk in the postal department, where his chief responsibility was to collect reports on the credit standing of the bank's customers and to answer general enquiries. The plan was to move Lyttelton from one department of the firm to another until he had mastered the workings of the business, and he was next transferred to the Foreign Exchange Department. Brown, Shipley was then the only bank in London which operated a common book in London, Boston, Philadelphia and New York so as to avoid paying commission on dollar/sterling transactions; they were therefore able to undercut other banks, and most dollar transactions in London were cleared through them. Lyttelton further widened his financial experience working in the Paying Cashier's Department and in the Securities Department. Although there was a flippant insouciance in some of Lyttelton's work at Brown, Shipley, he studied the theories and laws of banking, and after a year had a grounding in its practical basis. He supplemented his income by underwriting and speculation on a small scale, and by occasional successes on the turf.

In August 1920, however, Lyttelton was recruited by Sir Cecil Budd (qv) as a learner at the British Metal Corporation (BMC) with a salary of £600 a year. He was appointed general manager in January 1923. The origins of BMC lay in the serious dislocation of British strategic supplies during the First World War. The Merton family of Frankfurt, through their Metallgesellschaft and their Metallbank, had collected vast international non-ferrous metal interests before 1914: indeed it momentarily seemed after the outbreak of war that Metallgesellschaft might exert a stranglehold on crucial supplies to Britain. The Australian Prime Minister, W M Hughes, led denunciations of the Germans' control of the base-metal markets, and started a demagogic storm throughout the Empire. After a violent political campaign, the British Metal Corporation was established in 1918 to ensure that in future the British Empire was self-sufficient in non-ferrous metals. As Lyttelton recalled

> the British Metal Corporation was more than a mere money-making machine ... I count it is a piece of fortune that I should have been concerned with a company which had to be conducted with a dominant theme. It added point and spice to the more pedestrian task of making money for the shareholders and a livelihood for myself {Chandos (1962) 128}.

It was BMC's aim not only to ensure that strategically important minerals and metals were of British Empire origin, but also to direct them into Empire smelters and refineries and to keep control of the metal trade in reliable British hands, preferably those of BMC. It was evident that one company could not dominate imperial mining, smelting and refining in its entirety: the policy evolved by Budd and Lyttelton was to provide, instead, the finance, shipping and sales organisation, and to federate the major interests through a network of interlocking directorships and personal relations. Ironically, this in many ways paralleled the policies of Metallgesellschaft before 1914.

In 1917 a financier, Richard Tilden Smith (qv), formed the National Smelting Co, with British Government support, to increase zinc production. It erected factories at Avonmouth and Llansamlet near Swansea, and controlled 4 million shares in the Burma Corporation, which owned zinc, lead, silver and copper mines in the Shan states of Burma. In 1923-24, when Smith became financially encumbered, Lyttelton helped negotiate the purchase of his interests by BMC. This was a crucial step in BMC's growth, and Lyttelton was appointed a director in November 1924. He also joined the board of the Burma Corporation.

Much of the impetus for establishing BMC came from Australia, and after 1918 the Corporation was the sales agent of the vastly-productive Broken Hill Group of Australian mining companies. This led Lyttelton into close relations with C L Baillieu and W S Robinson (qqv), the latter in particular becoming a close friend and mentor. One of BMC's chief rivals was Henry Gardner, formerly London representative of the Mertons and father of Sir Charles Bruce Gardner (qv). Gardner held agencies for two important imperial companies, International Nickel and Consolidated Mining & Smelting of Canada; Lyttelton was able to gain his trust, arranging the merger of his interests with BMC's in the Amalgamated Metal Corporation in 1929. AMC was a holding company which held all the shares in both Gardners and BMC; with Lyttelton on the board it was the dominant British force in non-ferrous metals.

Just as Lyttelton negotiated a merger with BMC's main British rival, Henry Gardner, so he also undertook protracted discussions with their chief continental competitor, Metallgesellschaft. These talks were fraught with difficulties, but concluded with an exchange of shares, and an implicit understanding that AMC would direct their European purchases and sales through Metallgesellschaft, which would similarly use AMC in the British Empire. A comparable marketing treaty was reached by AMC with Société de Minerais in Brussels. Lyttelton became a director of Société de Minerais, Metallgesellschaft, and the latter's affiliated copper refinery, Norddeutsche Raffinerie. His other directorships at this time included the Imperial Smelting Corporation; the Scottish Stockholders Investment Trust; the Zinc Corporation, which was part of the Broken Hill group; and from May 1928 the Lake View Investment Trust, which controlled inter alia the Brixworth Ironstone Co. He was also chairman and managing director of the British Tin Investment Corporation formed in 1932 to acquire some of the assets of the British-American Tin Corporation. BMC also controlled a Swiss Company, Brametta, which held BMC's foreign investments, and owned the British Metal Stockholders Trust, the Manganese Bronze and Brass Co and half of the shares in Huntington Heberlein Ltd. Apart from these associations Lyttelton was chairman of Lightalloys Ltd of Kilburn. He was a member of the London committee of the English and Dutch Investment Trust and of the London advisory board of the Great Britain and Canada Investment Corporation. During the 1930s he sat on the Deportation of Aliens advisory committee of the Home Office. Together with industrialists like

Lionel Hichens he was on the council of the Industrial Reorganisation League founded by Harold Macmillan in 1933.

In the period after 1935, Lyttelton had many dealings with Whitehall officialdom, and concluded 'that the ignorance of Government Departments of the "market", or of the impact of quite simple transactions upon it, is only matched by their brazen commercial methods' {Chandos (1962) 150}. He sought in vain to persuade Whitehall to stockpile metals (especially copper) sensibly; forewarned in March 1939 that in the event of war he might be made Controller of Non-Ferrous Metals at the Ministry of Supply, he formed a plan for purchasing, licensing and allocating copper, tin, lead and zinc. In September 1939 he was confirmed as Controller and activated his plans, though not without pettifogging Treasury obstruction. Winston Churchill in June 1940 proposed to appoint Lyttelton as his personal liaison with munitions production, with a seat on the Supply Council, but was opposed by the socialist Minister of Supply, who feared it would undermine his power. Instead, in October 1940, Lyttelton was appointed President of the Board of Trade, becoming Conservative MP for Aldershot in the following month. In December his appointment as British Ambassador in Washington was mooted by Churchill, but in the event he remained at the Board of Trade until June 1941. During his nine months there, his main task was to reduce civilian demand on industrial output by rationing, price controls, materials allocation and the concentration of each industry into a few companies only.

In June 1941 Churchill sent Lyttelton to Cairo in the new post of Minister of State in the Middle East with a seat in the War Cabinet. The British had suffered many military reverses in that area, and Lyttelton was sent with wide powers. Starting with a staff of only four, he 'achieved a wonderful feat of improvisation' and by tact, dexterity and his own personality swiftly established his authority and placated local animosities {Birkenhead (1969) 195}. During his eight months in Cairo, he formed the Middle East War Council, imposed a more popularly-based Government on King Farouk and coped with a Persian currency crisis. He also reached agreement with General de Gaulle on the thorny question of the armistice with the Vichy French in Syria.

Lyttelton was appointed Minister of Production, with a seat in the War Cabinet, in February 1942, succeeding Lord Beaverbrook (qv), a man whom he disliked. He held this post until July 1945 (although considered for appointment as Viceroy of India in May 1943). From the outset Lyttelton sought to restore the link between strategy and production which had been severed when the service ministries' supply departments had been hived off to form the Ministry of Supply. Lyttelton was given extensive powers over raw materials, machine-tools and labour, and ran his department with the minimum of bureaucratic apparatus. The production problems which confronted him in 1942-45 were manifold, but Lyttelton met them with his customary self-confidence and decisiveness. Although witty and eloquent in private, he was handicapped by a poor parliamentary manner, and by his evident impatience with the periphrasis and circumlocution of second-rate political minds. On the disintegration of the coalition Government in May 1945, Lyttelton was again appointed

LYTTELTON Oliver

Office of the Minister of Production,
Great George Street,
S. W. 1.

23rd March, 1942.

Dear Sir Alexander

I am sorry that I have not sent
you an earlier reply to your letter of
the 10th March, in which you suggested
that the American Mission to India
should visit London on their way east.

I understand that the American
Mission will be flying direct to India
via Lagos, and in the present state of
air communications, a visit to the
United Kingdom would mean considerable
delay.   I think it is most important
that the Mission should reach India as
quickly as possible and that in the
circumstances, despite the advantages
to which you refer, it would be a mistake to divert the Mission via England.

Yours sincerely

Sir Alexander Roger, K.C.I.E.,
Surrey House,
Victoria Embankment,
W.C.2.

Letter from Oliver Lyttelton to Sir Alexander Roger, March 1942 (from the papers of Sir Alexander Roger).

President of the Board of Trade, also remaining Minister of Production, until the defeat of the Churchill Government in July. Lyttelton found electioneering 'most uncongenial' as he 'hate[d] the squabbling and vulgarity and slogans of a popular election' {Chandos (1962) 327}. Indeed he waited seven years after receiving a peerage in 1954 before speaking in the House of Lords.

While in Opposition, he remained MP for Aldershot, and throughout 1945-51 was one of the leading Conservative speakers on finance and trade in the House of Commons, chairing his party's Trade and Industry Committee and leading the fight against steel nationalisation. In late 1945 he became chairman of Associated Electrical Industries (AEI), which had been formed in 1929 out of the merger of Metropolitan-Vickers with

British Thomson-Houston, and which stood in urgent need of reorganisation.

> The central organisation was ... antiquated ... ; the constituent companies arranged their own finance; although their records and costings appeared to me to be a model, the information given to the Board was exiguous; the recruitment of staff, the secretarial and legal services, and control of finance fell far below the standards which I expected; above all, there was overlapping and competition between the constituent companies {Chandos (1962) 333}.

At his first board meeting Lyttelton asked each director privately to estimate AEI's reserves: the nearest was £14 million beneath the correct figure.

AEI's war production had been worth £215 million, and Lyttelton gave early attention to the transition to peace industries. The group's exports were worth nearly £14 million in 1947, and AEI made considerable investments in India, South Africa and Australia. Net profit for 1948 was over £2.5 million, while in 1949 the total value of orders on the books at one time exceeded £100 million. During 1946-49 some £16 million was invested in AEI, either by stock and loan issues, or by retention of profits. Nevertheless, Lyttelton failed to integrate the constituent companies of the group, and left behind organisational failings and a lavish style which were to prove disastrous.

Lyttelton was chairman of the Conservative Party's Finance Committee from 1950, and expected to become Chancellor of the Exchequer when Churchill formed his new administration in 1951. According to Lord Woolton (qv), however, Churchill 'dare not appoint Oliver Lyttelton [as Chancellor] because Oliver's reputation in the City was rather that of a gambler and market operator' {Seldon (1981) 154}; after contemplating Lyttelton's appointment as Minister of Materials and Rearmament, Churchill instead made him Secretary of State for the Colonies. He agreed to take this office (which necessitated his retirement from AEI) out of personal loyalty to Churchill, but only for a limited period, and thoughout his ensuing three years in the Cabinet, it was clear that 'Lyttelton derived enormous pleasure from life in the business world, and was anxious to return to it' {*ibid*, 349}. As an independent-minded politician, who was neither a timeserver nor a placeseeker, Lyttelton was trusted by Churchill, who like other colleagues savoured Lyttelton's ebullient and outspoken manner in Cabinet. At the Colonial Office Lyttelton was energetic, flexible and unexpectedly successful.

> Lyttelton had most of the outlook of the great Whigs. He was far too intelligent a man to believe that it was within the bounds of the politically possible to impede progress towards self-government. There was also a cynical streak in him which prevented him from agonizing too much at the imperfections of newly independent governments ... He got on famously with Orientals and Africans, provided they amused him and were congenial company ... he was astute in exploiting his charm for political purposes ... He could bully as well as flatter, and at times he rushed his fences {*Times* 22 Jan 1972}.

Lyttelton's most acute problems were in Malaya, the Central African Federation, Kenya, Nigeria, Malta, British Guiana and Uganda, and as was to be expected the success of his policies varied considerably between these places. He was also distinguished as the chief supporter of R A Butler's attempt to introduce a floating exchange rate in 1952.

He retired from politics in July 1954, when he was created Viscount Chandos, and resumed his chairmanship of AEI at a salary of £20,000 a year plus expenses. He raised £59 million from the public in 1955-58 to fund an enthusiastic expansion programme, which included heavy investment on research and development and the purchase of Siemens Brothers in 1955. Lyttelton's City contacts were ideal for raising money, but he had little technical understanding of electrical engineering, and by 1958 it was clear that his engineering advisers has been reckless and that the controls for sanctioning capital expenditure had been too lax. For example, a new factory at Larne cost £8 million, worked far beneath capacity and in 1957-69 averaged a loss of about £400,000 a year. From 1959 onwards the return on capital employed in AEI was increasingly worrying. At AEI Chandos was an autocrat, 'able to silence his co-directors by ridicule', who openly referred to his engineers as 'expendable' {Jones and Marriott (1970) 232, 234}. He asserted the role of AEI's central management, popularised the name of AEI instead of Metrovick, Ediswan and BTH, and developed the Hotpoint domestic appliance subsidiary. Hotpoint was despised by most AEI staff who had an exclusive preference for the prestige of heavy engineering projects, but this new subsidiary was an outstanding marketing success in 1956-59; subsequently it suffered serious reverses through over-capacity. AEI's venture into nuclear reactors at Aldermaston was equally discredited by 1962. Despite sweeping reorganisations by Chandos in 1954, 1960 and 1962, AEI's performance was a disappointment; his second chairmanship of AEI cannot be judged successful. During his nine years as chairman, its capital employed rose from £58 million to £150 million, while sales rose from £128 million to £213 million, but profits fell from £15.3 million to £6.6 million. Chandos retired from AEI aged seventy in 1963, and four years later AEI succumbed to a takeover by GEC. The relations between AEI's pure research department and applied research were poor, and the extreme extravagence of many engineering managers in the group was probably exacerbated by Chandos's policy of divisionalisation and 'loose patriarchal control' {ibid, 257}. Even his vigorous and often attractive personality could not master AEI's fatal heritage of organisational disorder and financial improvidence.

Chandos was a director of Imperial Chemical Industries in 1954-68 and of Alliance Assurance, 1954-69. Among other offices, he was president of the Advertising Association during 1945-69, of the English Opera Group in 1947-50 and of the Institute of Directors (1948-51 and 1954-63). The latter body was moribund when he took over, but under his aegis revived as a vigorous capitalists' ginger-group.

Arising out of his association with AEI, Chandos was president of the Electrical Research Association in 1955-56, of the British Electrical & Allied Manufacturers' Association during 1955-57, the British Electrical Development Association for 1955-58 and of the British Electrical Power Convention in 1959-60. During 1956-61 Chandos was president of Manchester College of Science and Technology. He was vice-president of the Locomotive & Allied Employers National Federation in 1958-63 and president of the Locomotive & Allied Manufacturers Association in 1960-63. Chandos was also president of the Market Research Association in 1960-64 and chairman of the committee of 1959-60 on the replacement of the 'Queen' liners. He chaired the Northern Ireland Development Council in 1955-65, was a Trustee of the National Gallery in 1958-65, president of Queen Elizabeth House, Oxford, in 1955-69, and a trustee of Churchill College, Cambridge, from 1958.

Dame Edith Lyttelton, Chandos' mother, had been active in the Vic-Wells, National and Stratford theatres, and he took special pleasure in serving as chairman of the National Theatre board in 1962-71 and as president from 1971. He was also a member of the South Bank Theatre board. An auditorium at the National Theatre is named Lyttelton after him. Though his greatest work for the National Theatre was in fund-raising, he attracted publicity by his opposition in 1967 to staging a play which traduced Winston Churchill.

A fellow Conservative politician, Hugh Fraser, described Oliver Chandos as 'enormous' and 'friendly':

> Few were more Rabelaisian yet none more fastidious. No one had more panache but few were more diffident. His acid sarcasm was a formidable instrument in negotiation. Yet he was without malice. The unkindest word he would say behind the back of his bitterest political opponent was to imitate — and brilliantly — his phrase or egregious absurdity. He was without rancour. Intrigue bored him. Once committed his loyalty was absolute ... he was the last in the classic tradition of the great British amateur. Scholar and wit, mentally and physically spacious, he was alarmed by ruthless personal ambition. Intellectually he was the last effective heir of country house politics and of the Gladstone family, the Balfours, and even the Souls { *Times* 28 Jan 1972}.

Oliver Chandos was a broad-minded, optimistic man, with an affable and booming manner, who brought zest to everything he did. He was a skilled raconteur, who was often the centre of gales of laughter, and larded his many successful negotiations (in both business and politics) with a well-judged mixture of raillery and flattery. He had a streak of cynicism, and some robust prejudices, but he was a man of wide outlook and experience, with a catholic mind. He was sworn of the Privy Council in 1940 and became a Knight of the Garter in 1970.

Lyttelton married in 1920 Lady Moira Godolphin Osborne (1892-1976), youngest daughter of the Tenth Duke of Leeds. They had three sons (of whom the second was killed in action in 1944) and a daughter. He died of kidney failure in London on 21 January 1972 leaving £78,637.

R P T DAVENPORT-HINES

Writings:

What Should We Do with the Peace? (Conservative and Unionist Party Organisation, 1943).

Memoirs (Bodley Head, 1962).

LYTTELTON Oliver

From Peace to War: A Study in Contrast 1857-1918 (Bodley Head, 1968).

letter on the Kabaka of Buganda *Times* 8 Jan 1970.

Sources:

Published

Lord Birkenhead, *Walter Monckton* (Weidenfeld & Nicolson, 1969).

John Hamill, *The Strange Career of Mr Hoover under Two Flags* (New York: William Faro, 1931).

Harold Hobson, 'Backstage Drama at the National Theatre' *Sunday Times* 18 Mar 1973.

John H Joliffe, *Raymond Asquith* (Collins, 1980).

Robert Jones and Oliver J D Marriott, *Anatomy of a Merger* (Cape, 1970).

Ernest Scott, *Australia during the War* (Sydney: Angus & Robertson, 1936).

Anthony Seldon, *Churchill's Indian Summer* (Hodder & Stoughton, 1981).

Times 22, 28 Jan 1972.

WWMP.

WWW.